8th International Conference on Reliability of Electrical Products and Electrical Contacts (ICREPEC 2022)

Xiamen, China
18-20 November 2022

Editors:

Jingqin Wang
Jingying Zhao

ISBN: 978-1-7138-7118-7

Printed from e-media with permission by:

Curran Associates, Inc.
57 Morehouse Lane
Red Hook, NY 12571

CURRAN ASSOCIATES INC. proceedings .com

Some format issues inherent in the e-media version may also appear in this print version.

International Academic Publishers Ltd.
137 Chaonei Dajie
Beijing 100010 China

Additional copies of this publication are available from:

Curran Associates, Inc.
57 Morehouse Lane
Red Hook, NY 12571 USA
Phone: 845-758-0400
Fax: 845-758-2633
Email: curran@proceedings.com
Web: www.proceedings.com

ICREPEC 8th 2022

PROCEEDINGS OF THE 8TH INTERNATIONAL CONFERENCE ON RELIABILITY OF ELECTRICAL PRODUCTS AND ELECTRICAL CONTACTS

NOVEMBER 18-20, 2022
HOWARD JOHNSON JIMEI LAKE PLAZA XIAMEN, XIAMEN, CHINA

Edited by
Jingqin Wang   Jingying Zhao

International Academic Publishers Ltd.

International Academic Publishers Ltd.

Edited by Jingqin Wang, Jingying Zhao
Proceedings of the 8th International Conference on Reliability of Electrical Products and Electrical Contacts

Proceedings of the 8th International Conference on Reliability of Electrical Products and Electrical Contacts

November 18-20, 2022
Howard Johnson Jimei Lake Plaza Xiamen, Xiamen, China

ICREPEC 8th 2022

Edited by

Jingqin Wang Jingying Zhao

Organized by

Electrical Products Reliability Professional Committee of Chinese Electrotechnical Society

Sponsored by

Xiamen Hongfa Electroacoustic Co., Ltd.

State Key Laboratory of Reliability and Intelligence of Electrical Equipment

Provincial and Ministerial Co-construction Collaborative Innovation Center on Reliability Technology of Electrical Products

Collaborative Innovation Center on Reliability Technology of Electrical Products of Hebei Province

Electrical Alloy Branch of China Electrical Equipment Industry Association

Suzhou Electrical Apparatus Science Academy Co., Ltd.

Institute of Reliability in Electrical Apparatus and Electronics of HIT

Anhui Xinrui Advanced Materials Co., Ltd.

Wenzhou Juxing Science and Technology Co., Ltd.

International Academic Publishers Ltd.

Preface

Welcome to the 8th International Conference on Reliability of Electrical Products and Electrical Contacts. It is a great pleasure and my distinct privilege as Chairman of the conference to welcome you to Xiamen, China. The 8th International Conference on Reliability of Electrical Products and Electrical Contacts will be held in Howard Johnson Jimei Lake Plaza Xiamen, Xiamen, China, from November 18 to 20, 2022. Besides the planned activities, the conference includes some technical visits. It is organized by Electrical Products Reliability Professional Committee of Chinese Electrotechnical Society, and sponsored by Xiamen Hongfa Electroacoustic Co., Ltd., State Key Laboratory of Reliability and Intelligence of Electrical Equipment, Provincial and Ministerial Co-construction Collaborative Innovation Center on Reliability Technology of Electrical Products, Collaborative Innovation Center on Reliability Technology of Electrical Products of Hebei Province, Electrical Alloy Branch of China Electrical Equipment Industry Association, Suzhou Electrical Apparatus Science Academy Co., Ltd., Institute of Reliability in Electrical Apparatus and Electronics of HIT, Anhui Xinrui Advanced Materials Co., Ltd., Wenzhou Juxing Science and Technology Co., Ltd..

Persons who attended the conference are engineers, scientists, managers of various companies and professors of the universities abroad and home.

The proceedings of the conference include more than 80 papers contributed by authors from different countries after peer reviewing. The papers presented authoritative comments on Reliability Design, Statistics of Reliability, Reliability Management, Reliability Manufacture, Failure Modes and Mechanism, Reliability Analysis, System and Software Reliability, Reliability Test Method and Test Device, Quality Management and Assurance, Reliability of Electrical Products and Equipment, Electrical Contact Phenomenon, Electrical Contact Failure and Testing, Environmental Effect on Electrical Contact, Contact Material, Contact Failure Simulation and Prediction, Safety Device and Other Related Topics.

In closing, please let me express my special thanks to the authors and presenters, our Conference Honorary Chair, Technical Program Committee, Organization Committee, International Advisory Committee, as well as the individuals, sponsors and organizations, who worked so hard to prepare the 8th International Conference on Reliability of Electrical Products and Electrical Contacts. As chairman of this conference, please allow me to express my gratitude for having had this unique opportunity to closely work with such a fine group of professional people. I am looking forward to continuing my support of the International Conference on Reliability of Electrical Products and Electrical Contacts.

Jiaomin Liu
Chairman

CONFERENCE ORGANIZATION

CONFERENCE CHAIRMAN

Jiaomin Liu

CONFERENCE HONORARY CHAIRMAN

Manjin Guo   Werner Johler (Switzerland)

TECHNICAL PROGRAM COMMITTEE

Chairman: Jingqin Wang

Vice Chairman: Jingwei Wu   Makoto Hasegawa   Jiaxin You   Le Xu

ORGANIZATION COMMITTEE

Chairman: Jingying Zhao

Vice Chairman: Jing Lin   Dcfcng Cui   Liang Shu   Jic Dcng

INTERNATIONAL COMMITTEE

Chairman: Feng Niu

Vice Chairman: Yao Wang   Jinchun Gao   Cen Chen   Ziran Wu

PROCEEDINGS EDITORAL BOARD

Chief Editors: Jingqin Wang   Jingying Zhao

Table of Contents

8th International Conference on Reliability of Electrical Products and Electrical Contacts, November 18-20, 2022 **(Invited Paper)**

Review of Recent Research on Electrical Products and Electrical Contacts

Chi H. Leung
Electric Contact Material Consultant
Export, Pennsylvania, USA
cleung1@yahoo.com

Abstract—**Since 2010, a lot of publications in areas of green energy such as photovoltaic, electrical vehicles, HVDC power distribution; and novel production methods such as additive manufacturing and 3D printing can be found. In this review, the published results relevant in the field of electrical products and electrical contacts are reviewed to get a better understanding of the technology trends, challenges and innovations to provide some directions for future work.**

Keywords-**photovoltaic, EV, hybrid switches, HVDC circuit breakers, additive manufacturing, 3D printing.**

I. INTRODUCTION

The paper is a digest of technical publications on electrical products and electrical contacts as they appear in US patents, IEEE Holm Conference, International Conference on Electrical Contacts, and materials science since 2000. The topics are focused mainly on: a) solid state vs electromechanical devices, b) renewable energy power switching and protection, c) new contact material, d) additive manufacturing of contact material.

I. SOLID STATE VS ELECTROMECHANICAL

Solid state vs electromechanical switches has been in discussion since late 1990's with advances in transistors, MOSFETs, IGBTs and thyristors etc. with speculations that this can eventually replace electrical contacts. A review of many electric contact applications by Schroder [1] in 2002 concluded that this will not happen because in power engineering the high power loss, and cost will be high. However the advances in new applications, reliability and intelligence products lead some additions of electronics into the products of switches, relays, contactors, circuit breakers that are of great interest to the technology trend.

A. Hybrid Switches

Hybrid switches have been proposed since 1980's to take advantage of the transistor junction to achieve arcless switching. A parallel path of transistor path and metallic contact path can by synchronized to drastically reduce arc erosion of the contact tips especially when thyristors were more available. This included a 5A 120VAC push button hybrid switch [2] to improve the electrical contact life (typically 25k cycles) to approach the mechanical life (typically 200k cycles). Another switch example [3] is for 270VDC at 100A nominal and 1500A interruption for aerospace where arc interruption in high altitude low pressure environment is also a factor in current limiting capabilities. The above mentioned parallel current paths, a metallic path to carry the steady state current to reduce heating, and an electron junction to suppress arc for transient switching durations, are simple approaches.

This hybrid concept was also investigated and demonstrated in a MEM relay that was made by micromachining technology and electrostatically actuated [4]. This was designed to replace a 14V automotive relays in low current applications. The minute contact gap of only around 3 μm and weak contact open force (<0.2mN) was assisted by a parallel electronic circuit to control arc erosion and contact welding. This parallel current path addition was integrated to the electrostatic actuation circuit to synchronize the opening and closing events, and resulted in significant increase in contact life and prevent welding.

This interest in MEM based switches for power applications was again examined by Keimel [5] showing many technical and cost issues that need to be resolved using MEMs in power applications. The use of MEM is quite successful in pin diodes secure communication systems designed to do frequency jumping and switching radio frequency low power portable devices where it can be challenging for electromechanical switches due to size, cost and speed considerations.

B. Intelligent Switches and Contactors

A way to use electronics in the design of contactors to prolong life and reliability is in the control of the contact opening and closing operations in an optimized way to minimize contact bounce and arcing. A hybrid contactor with synchronous switching thyristors and a pneumatic drive contactor was used to study the opening and closing velocity. Erosion and material transfer in such synchronous hybrid contactors were found to be 3 orders of magnitude, or 1000 times lower [6]. This is mainly to avoid high current arcing that created large amounts of contact material melting and erosion.

In integration of electronics to contactors, Zhou [7] reported on the prognostic and diagnostic technology for 24VDC actuated contactors and motor starters. A method predicted the erosion life and potential failures of a DC actuated 50A rated contactors by monitoring the DC coil current and contactor currents. Contact erosion increased over-travel and this is diagnosed in the closing time and coil current information.

A review of intelligent contactor design and its control technology was done by Zong in 2016 [8] who shared the experience in a wind turbine application in a AC690V contactors. The high reliability requirements of this contactor lead to a review of better technologies: a) no arc breaking control technologies, b) contact bounce elimination technologies; c) switching power technologies

C. *Automotive Electronics*

While most of the high DC voltage applications were previously in the aerospace or special DC machines, the transition of automotive power system was moving to higher voltages like from 14V to 42VDC to allow more power to be distributed with lower current. The challenges and chances for solid state relays and electromagnetic relays in 42V power net was discussed and concluded that SSR will gain ground in some higher than 14V applications [9]. Solid state relays have several milliohms of ON resistance and is still a challenge to packaging with good heatsinks and higher cost. SSR do get used in: a) high reliability, b) high switching speed and c) noiseless switching.

At higher DC voltages, the approaches to safe electromagnetic relay had been use of TEM (transverse magnetic field), arc chutes, double break designs or change the contact speeds. A paper on use of external magnetic fields in a DC42V relay to stretch the arc show the reduction of arc durations with the magnet [10]. An automotive relays with Ag/SnO_2 contact material can be successful when a 14V DC relay is modified to double break design [11]. Micro-arcing and arc erosion minimization using a 42V DC hybrid switching device was reported [12].

II. RENEWABLE ENERGY POWER, HVDC CIRCUIT PROTECTION:

DC switching has changed in the last 20 years and Jebramcik [13] studied the switching characteristics of arc chutes in DC contactors to help directions of designs. The challenges can be summarized as follows and some commercially available solutions are shown in Table 1.

a) 42V in automobiles low voltage circuits
b) 190/380V for buildings and appliances
c) 400V for data centers
d) 480/800V for high voltage drive train in electric vehicles
e) Up to 1500V in wind energy, photovoltaics, railways
f) 1000/30,000V power grids on cruise ships
g) Up to 800kV in multi terminal HVDC

A. *Automotive, Electric Vehicles*

In hybrid and electric vehicles, an example is a EVC250 contactor [14], rated for 450VDC, 250A nominal current and 6000A short circuit capabilities, and is available from aerospace design experiences. This is designed with arc suppressing magnets, double break, hermetically sealed, inert atmospheres, cooling by wall and optimized switching dynamics.

B. *Wind and Solar, generation and utilization*

Wind and solar power are more effectively generated and distributed in DC voltages. At the same time, the locations of such generators in large and remote areas make them vulnerable to lighting strike and wind damages to result in electrical surges. Solar power systems can be in 3 sizes [15] and all three systems require different levels of circuit breakers, switch disconnectors, surge protection devices, fuse and short circuit protection. Some 800VAC low voltage circuit breakers can be used with current derated for 1000VDC. Series connections of the poles to create double or triple break circuit breaker can also be successful.

a) Residential: with a safe and reliabile rooftop photovoltaic systems with a capacity of <20kW, low voltage.

b) Commercial/Industrial, with a capacity between 20 to 1000kW; low/medium voltage,

c) Utility scale, with performance of a small power plant and output of 600VDC to 1000VDC. The trend is to a 1500VDC, 3000A component requirement.

For residential applications, many low voltage AC switchgears can be used with series connected poles to lengthen and cool the arc. For commercial applications, Merkler et al [16] summarized a joint European Community R&D project "Direct current components+Grid" to setup a 380VDC 50A distribution system to promote the use of DC distribution and DC loads. A hybrid switch built with thyristors and galvanic isolator was tested in resistive and inductive loads at 400VDC at 30A nominal and 160A overload currents. Switching up to rated current is handled by the electronic side with long life span. Short circuit current switching and the nominal current flow were taken by the mechanical side. The use of electronic components to do the arc commutation seems a good solution.

C. *HVDC grid*

The architectures of AC and DC power distribution are as shown in fig. 1. For the protection of equipment in power surge situations, switches must be placed strategically. Hybrid HVDC breakers is a trending technology. A hybrid HVDC breaker was described by Callavik[17] for 320kV and transmission current of 2kA, and a breaking capacity of 9kA with 2ms delay time for opening the disconnector. StakPak IGBTs are rated for 4.5kV and the maximum rated fault current of 8.5kA is the limit for the existing generation of semiconductors (in 2021). Banks of IGBTs are interconnected to meet the voltage and current interruption requirements. The next generation of IGBT is up to 16kA.

A review of DC circuit breakers and their use in HVDC grids was made by Kostoulas [18]. Electromechanical HVDC circuit breakers are available up to 500kV, 5kA and a fault clearing time of the order of 100ms. This requires snubber circuits with active and passive components to create an inverse current to assist current interruption. Cost is high and speed is too slow to be effective. Solid state circuit breakers are faster and can work up to 150kV and their on-state losses are too high. Better hybrid approaches are still in developments.

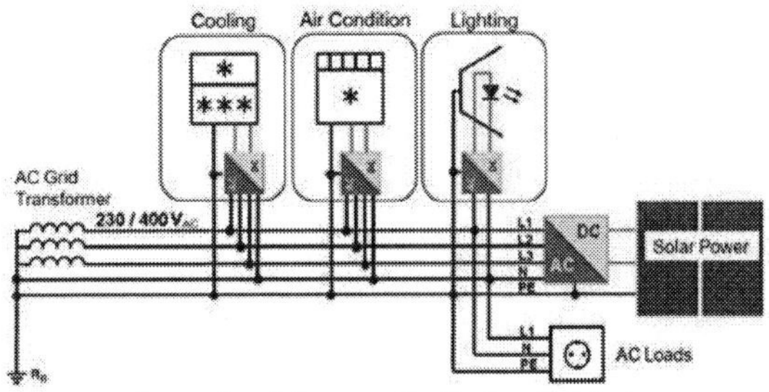

a. State of art AC power distribution Architecture

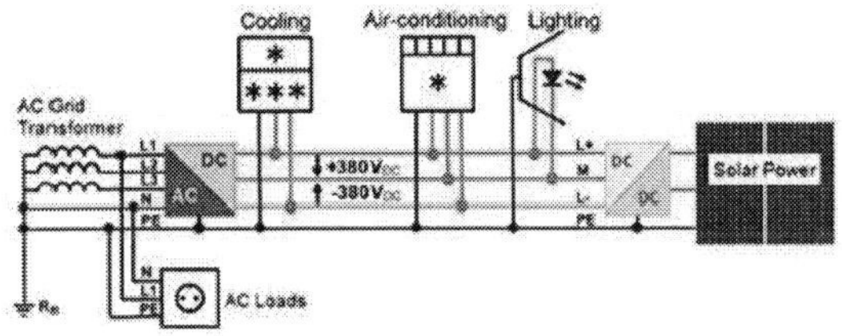

b. High efficiency DC power grid distribution architecture

Fig. 1 Power distribution architectures [17]

D. DC molded case circuit breaker

A new 10kA/600VDC hybrid DC molded case circuit breaker was presented by Zhou [19] using an existing low voltage AC MCCB switching mechanism and contact structure. The new hybrid design relied on the arc to absorb most of the inductance energy stored in a DC electrical system to limit the fault current to a lower acceptable level and then commutated to a smaller electronic package. The advantage is the use of traditional MCCB with thermal magnetic trip unit for all DC applications at a much reduced cost.

Mitsubishi [20] in US patent 10,910,817 in 2021 describes a low cost 300kV DC 10kA hybrid circuit breaker with forced commutating circuit of capacitor and inductor to force a reverse direction current through a vacuum circuit breaker when interruption is detected. A gas disconnector (tank filled with SF6, dry air, nitrogen, argon or CO2), a vacuum circuit breaker, a semiconductor switch made up the hybrid HVDC circuit breaker.

The design and selection of the electronic components in a hybrid switch or intelligent control can be a reliability factor in the HVDC circuit breaker and contactor. Many power cycling tests are used to evaluate discrete packaged thyristors and IGBTs used in solar inverters and low power controls. End of life failures are mainly due to lifted bond wire between the bond pad and chip. EOL cycles are devices depend on the current per bond [21].

III. Electrical Contact

Innovations in new electrical contact materials have been slow and most studies are on better material preparation techniques to reduce cost. In the circuit breaker contacts, AgW, AgWC, Ag/C, AgWC/C, CuW, CuCr remain the proven material. In the relays and contactors, the big push to replace Ag/CdO in the 1990's because of health concerns and implementations of ROHS resulted in a new class of contact material. SnO_2, In_2O_3 and ZnO have been commercially successful in many switches, relays and contactor applications. The innovations in the addition of minor amounts of additive oxides (WO2, Mo_2O_3, Bi_2O_2, CuO, Ag_2WO_4, LiO etc) and preparation methods (powder metallurgy, internal oxidation, chemical co-precipitation etc) have been successfully applied to commercial products. A review of Ag/SnO_2 contact material and arc erosion papers by Leung in 2008 [22] summarized the commercial successful products and applications. Behrens [23] in 2021 summarized the technical backgrounds, legal restrictions and substitutions in contact material.

A. Rare Earth Elements in Electric Contacts

With the ready availability of rare oxides in China, the work to find good uses of this in electrical contacts were started in the universities. Wang [24] at Hebei University in 2000 started long term research on rare earth oxides for use in relays and contactors. $Ag/12La_2O_3$ was selected because La_2O_3 has a high decomposition temperature (2350°C) compared with CdO (1000°C) and SnO_2 (1625°C). The chemical co-precipitation method successfully made a material of high mechanical properties. This was followed [25] with the chemical co-precipitation preparation of $88Ag/7SnO_2/3.5La_2O_3/1.5Bi_2O_3$ and some good electrical test results. This work was continued by Zhu and Wang[26] to a mixed oxide composition of. First, the powder metal composite process parameters of time, temperature and pressure were optimized to achieve high density material. Electrical tests in a 380V AC 40A contactor showed acceptable temperature rise and lower erosion than Ag/12CdO and $Ag/12SnO_2$ by 30%. This appeared a suitable substitute for Ag/CdO. The Wang group [27,28] continued investigating the addition of rare earth elements including La, Ce and Y to $AgSnO_2$. to improve electrical properties.

Zhejiang University [29,30] also has a research program to evaluate a class of compound oxides such as Zn_2SnO_4, $LaSrCuO_4$, Ti_2AlN, $La_2Sn_2O_7$ prepared by sol-gel method to improve the arc eroded contact surface resistance. This oxide synthesis is to advance the use of minor additive oxides in Ag/SnO_2 composites. In private communications with industry, the commercial interest of Ag/RE oxide contact material is still in academic study. However, it is important to say that these universities are educating engineers, developing materials, processes, and models that can only be supported long term in teaching institutes.

Some applications other than contacts may result and should continue to be supported by industry and government.

Sallais [31] compared the break arc duration of 15 combinations of Ag/RE oxide powder metal composites against the commonly available $AgSnO_2Bi_2O_3$ in 14V and 42VDC laboratory experiment test. Ag/ZrO_2 seems to have lower arc duration. Some RE oxides showed shorter arc duration than $AgSnO_2Bi_2O_3$ in resistive and inductive load up to 35A tests. However, erosion of all rare earth oxides and $AgSnO_2Bi_2O_3$ depend on load type and current. It suggested that much material improvements are necessary.

Shen [32] did work on internal oxidation of AgCd alloy with addition of rare earth elements (Sc, Y or Ce) at levels of .05, .10 to .50% to see the modification to the oxide distribution. This can be an area for further investigations in AgSnIn oxide contacts made by internal oxidation process.

B. *Graphene*

The graphene materials most commercially advanced are the small-area flakes and platelets. Graphene ink, made of 0.5 to 5μm size flakes of graphene dispersed in ethanol, was tested as a contact film [33]. The only benefit with a graphene film was in reduction of friction in reciprocating wear test.

For grapheme use in arcing contact material, Wang [34] prepared silver-graphene by chemical precipitation of silver on to graphene oxide particles; then through reduction to form silver-0.5% graphene powder. Followed by compaction, sinter and extrusion, a fully dense wire was prepared to make rivet contacts for evaluation. The control group of Ag/C was too brittle to be headed to a rivet contact. So it seems that the finely dispersed 0.5% grapheme did not degrade the wire ductility.

Commercially available Ag/C powder metal composites are widely used in residential and industrial circuit breakers with 2 to 5% graphite. Natural flake graphite powder of various particle sizes was mixed with silver powder. Manufacturing methods, such as press-sinter-repress or extrusion, can produce contacts with different erosion and weld resistance properties. Silver coated natural flake graphite powder, with up to 5wt.% graphite is made by chemical reduction of silver nitrate solution, precipitate coat the graphite particles. This type of powder is expensive and did not out perform traditional powder mixing.

This Ag/grapheme development was followed by Chen [35] who tested (Ag-graphene)/tungsten powder composites in a model switch test at 220VAC and 20A. The contact compositions compared were AgW50, (AgGr0.3)/W50 and (AgGr0.5)/W50. The arcing energy test with graphene was reduced by 30%, and contact erosion was reduced by 20%. This model switch test was extended to a commercial 3 pole 100A circuit breaker with some success. For such a 100A circuit breaker, an infiltration process is usually required to produce pore free AgW50 contact material. The real benefit of graphene in this material maybe due to the dispersion of the arc, reduction of arc time, and less thermal stress cracking in the microstructure. The chemical state of the grapheme powder after the sintering process at up to 900°C, and arc erosion process at up to 2000°C need to be examined in order to understand the benefits of graphene and reasons. It is not uncommon that a small amount of graphite or lampblack is added to tungsten powder in the manufacturing of AgW type of contact. This is to ensure that any oxide present in the tungsten powder will be reduced by the presence of C at high temperatures.

C. *High Speed Train Contact*

The rapid development of high speed rail in China has generated a lot of interest in the pantograph and catenary system for the transfer of power. Two contributions to the IEEE Holm conference were very informative. Wang [36] from Southwest Jiaotong University described the complex variables of lateral movement, vertical vibrations and flexible line contact at train speed that affected contact force and resistance. A test system tested a copper wire and a carbon brush combination. The best contact force and minimum contact resistance data was collected to support future development.

Similar works by the Liaoning Technical University measured the temperature rise of friction pairs under different contact current and flexible contact pressure conditions. The sliding speed is 380km/h and at current 300A to 1000A. The experiments with copper wire and copper carbon slide; and simulation models were impressive [37].

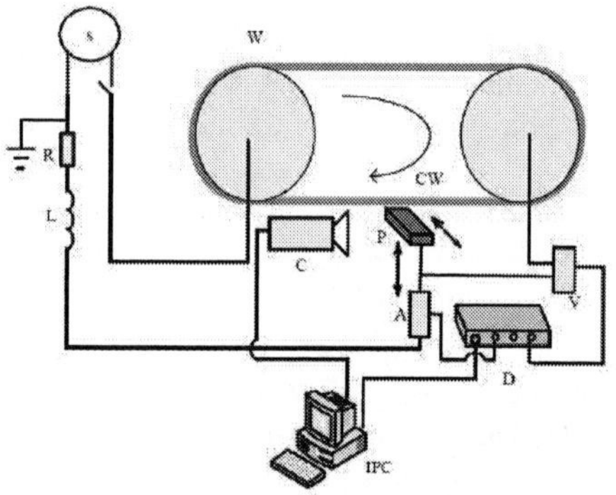

Fig. 2 Test apparatus of pantograph electrical contact, CW is contact wire, and P is pantograph. Wang [36]

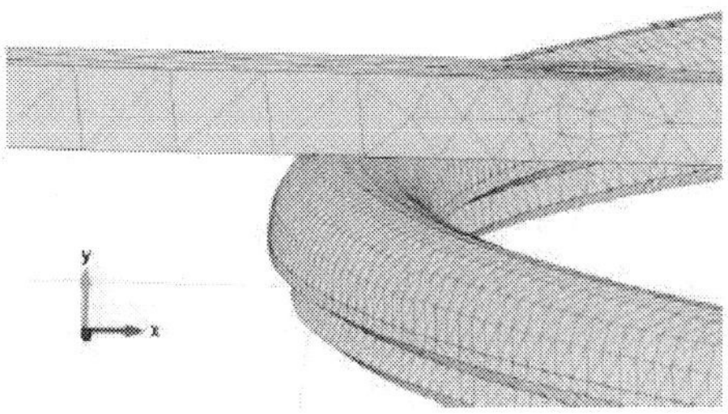

Fig. 3 3D simulation model of contact wire moving circularly in xz plane, and slide moves reciprocally in x-axis [37]

IV. Additive Manufacturing and 3D Printing

Additive manufacturing and 3D printing are developed to reduce tool cost and rapid prototype evaluations, Many articles have been written about AM and 3D printing, especially metallic material, so it will not be reviewed here. In the area of electrical contacts, some works have been reported.

Ngo [38] reviewed AM materials, methods, applications and challenges and found that the high cost, inferior mechanical properties and anisotropic behavior of 3D printed parts still limit the potential of large-scale printing. Also changes in the printing environment have an influence on the quality of finished parts. Drawbacks include mass production, inferior and anisotropic mechanical properties, limitation of materials and defects. Even in some highly promoted 3D printing of metal parts for aerospace, their applications are allowed only in non-mission critical parts.

In the area of electrical contacts (Ag/W, Ag/WC, Cu/W, Cu/Cr, Ag/SnO_2, Ag/C) additive manufacturing of metal matrix composites (MMC) would be a relevant area of interest. Yakout et al [39] reviewed Selective Laser Melting (SLM, a powder bed process), Fused Deposition Modeling (FDM, a wire fed process with a liquefier head), and Direct Energy Deposit (DED, a powder fed process), concluded the following challenges: a) maintaining the homogeneous distribution of components; b) feed stock of proper form (wire or powder) and uniform composition; c) tests to find the optimum process parameters of laser or plasma beam.

Copper-Tungsten powder metal composites with 50 to 90 wt% of tungsten have been commercially available for many years for use in electrical contacts. Metal Injection Molding, Press-Sinter and Press-Sinter-Infiltration can be used to prepare parts with >95% density, with a wide range of tungsten particle sizes designed for the functional performances.

Studies to make this material by cold spray process using copper electroplated tungsten powder were made and relatively unsuccessful because of porosities, loss of tungsten, and efficiency [40,41]. Another preparation was by hydrogen co-reduction of a mixture of copper tungstate, copper oxide and tungsten oxide mixtures to form a homogeneous mixture of Cu and W powder for cold spray [42,43]. Cold spray forming of CuW experiments were mostly tested for hard coating or thermal expansion applications.

The lifetime of cold-sprayed $AgSnO_2Bi_2O_3CuO$ contact for use as a contactor contact was reported by Rolland [44]. The idea was to cold sprayed multiple layers of material directly onto copper terminals to do quick tooling and prototype work. The spray formed contact material has about 18% porosities, erosion life of only 40% of the standard press-sinter-repress material, and also failed by coating de-bonding.

3D printing of functional electrical contacts was reported by Pawlikowski et al [45] where CiNiSi alloy powder was 3D printed by Selective Laser Melting to make battery terminal prototypes. The laser parameters were optimized to achieve 98.5% densities. Precipitation hardening heat treatment increased the terminal hardness to the specifications of the wrought C70250 material which is a more standard terminal material. Two main issues found were surface roughness and thin dimensions. The printed surfaces had to be grit-blasted to remove any partially adhered (sintered) powder and to provide some smoothening. The printed layer if <0.3mm will be difficult to maintain uniform thickness because of its roughness, and insufficient rigidity.

Duarte [46] reported a novel hot forging wire and arc additive manufacturing (HF-WAAM) design where an argon gas metal arc welding head melted a 1mm diameter AISI31L stainless steel wire onto a steel substrate. A vibrating actuator was integrated into the weld head and forged the just solidified deposit with a 55N hammer, to smooth and compress the porosities.

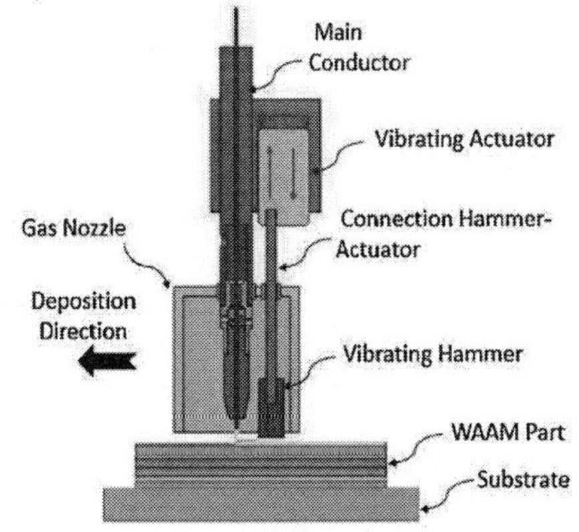

Fig 4 Hot forge wire and arc additive manufacturing drawing[46]

Functionally Graded Material (FGM): Arcing contacts are usually a homogeneous mixture of high conductivity material (Ag or Cu) and high melting hard material (W, WC, CdO, SnO_2). For example, the functional requirements of long erosion life and low weld force would be better with a low silver composition; and the low heat rise would be better with a high silver composition. In the normal function of a contact, the unpredictability occurrence of overload or short circuit currents would make a graded layer composition unreliable. There are designs with separate main contacts and arcing contacts seated side by side with different material compositions serving designed functions. Electrical contacts are typically produced in batches of many thousand pieces, so a low cost method is always preferred.

V. SUMMARY

Publications in the field of electrical products and electrical contacts show that challenges are there for new products to meet the growth of green power generation, electric vehicles, high speed train etc. Electronics are more integrated into contactors and circuit breakers both as a current path during arc commutation, or as smart control of the opening and closing dynamics to reduce arc durations.

In new contact material development, the discoveries such as use of rare earth oxide and grapheme are there but need to be further demonstrated in products. Power switching devices are safety related and the qualification tests are long and expensive so it is not uncommon that testing and production method optimizations will take years to complete. The hot topic of additive manufacturing is still in development stage for electric contact tip. Many 3D printing methods are there to be tried to prove the performance and cost effectiveness of the technology. Electric contacts can be considered as mission critical component in switching devices, so progress of adoption of new technology will be slow.

REFERENCES

[1] K. Schroder, "The Future Of Electrical Switching Contacts Under The Influence Of Electronics", ICEC 2002.

[2] S. Krstic, P. Theisen, "Push Button Hybrid Switch", IEEE Holm 1985

[3] P. Theisen,et al, "270VDC Hybrid Switch", Hom 1985.

[4] Han-Sheng Lee, et al, " Integrated Microrelays: Concept and Initial Results", Journal of microelectromechanical systemsm, v11, n2, april 2002.

[5] C. Keimel et al, "Microelectromechanical Systems Based Switches for Power Applications", IEEE transactions on industry applications, v48, n4, July-Aug 2013.

[6] G. Greitzke and M. Lindmayer, "Erosion and Material Transfer In Hybrid Contactors", ICEC 1986.

[7] Xin Zhou, et al, "Prognostic and Diagnostic Technology for Dc Actuated Contactors and Motor Starters", Holm 2006

[8] M. Zong, etal, "A Review of Intelligent Contactor Design and Its Control Technology", International Journal of Control and Automation, vol 9, no. 6, (2016).

[9] A. Korner, "Challenges and Chances for Solid State Relays and Electromagnetic Relays in Automobiles", ICEC2002.

[10] J. Sekikawa et al, "Characteristics of Break Arcs Driven by External magnetic Field in a DC42V resistive circuit", IEEE Holm 2008.

[11] O. Sakaguchi, et al "Performance Investigation of Contact Material in 42VDC Automotive Relay", ICEC 2002.

[12] J. Swingler, J. McBride, "Micro-arcing and Arc Erosion Minimization Using A 42v Dc Hybrid Switcing Devices", Holm 2004.

[13] J. Jebramcik and F. Berger, "Observations on Switching Characteristics of Arc Chutes in DC Contactors", ICEC 2014

[14] High Voltage Automotice Evc 250 Main Contactor, TE connectivity.

[15] ABB Publication, Solutions for Solar Energy, Low- and Medium-Voltage Components, Systems and Services, an ABB catalog 2022.

[16] P. Merkler et al, "Hybrid Switches in Protective Devices for Low Voltage DC Grids at Commercial Used Buildings", ICEC 2014.

[17] M. Callavik, etal "The Hybrid HVDC Breaker",ABB Grid Systems, Technical paper Nov 2012..

[18] Kostoulas, N.; Sitokonstantinou, V.; Idris, M.; Sterling, P.; Sayed, S.; Karaiskos, P.; DC Circuit Breakers and Their Use in HVDC Grids; Imperial College London: London, UK, 2011..

[19] X. Zhou, et al, "Hybrid DC Molded Case Circuit Breaker Technology", IEEE Holm 2021.

[20] US patent 10,910,817 DC circuit breaker, Mitsubishi Electric Corporatiom, Feb2, 2021.

[21] L. Borucki, "How Long will Your System Last, a Discrete IGBY Reliability Study", EE Power Technical Article, Dec 14, 2018.

[22] C. Leung and V. Behresn, "A Review of Ag-SnO_2 Contact Material and Arc Erosion", ICEC 2008

[23] V. Behrens, "Electrical Contacts and Hazardous Substances – Technical Backbrounds, Legal Restrictions and Substitutions", to be published IEEE Holm Conference 2022.

[24] J. Wang, et al,"Study on the Behavior of Silver Rare Earth Oxide Contact Material", IEEE Holm 2000.

[25] J. Wang, etal, "Study on a new Contact Material Ag/SnO_2-La_2O_3-Bi_2O_3", IEEE Holm 2001.

[26] Y. Zhu, J. Wang,"Preparation and Study on Performance for Silver Rare-Earth Alloy Electrical Contact Materials", IEEE Holm 2010

[27] Zhang et al, "Study on electrical {roperties of $AgSnO_2$ Contact Materials Doped with Rare-Earth La, Ce and Y", IEEE Transaction on CPMT, vol 9, issue 5, May 2019.

[28] K. Wang, etal, "Simulation and Experimental Research on Electrical Properties of $AgSnO_2$ Contact Materials Doped with Rare Earth Element Ce", IEEE Holm 2018

[29] Zhang Lingjie, etal,"Anti-arc Erosion Properties of Ag-La2SnO7/SnO2 Contacts", Rare metal Materials and Engineering, vol 45, issue 7, July 2016.

[30] Wu Xin-he, etal, "Advances in Eco-Friendly Oxide Reinforced Silver Based Electrcical Contact Materials", Precious Metals, vol 42, no.1, 2021

[31] D. Sallais, et al,"New Silver-Oxide Composites to Reduce Break Arc Duration and Its Subsequent Damages"' ICEC 2006.

[32] M. Shen, et al, "The Effect of Single Element Additions on the Microstructure and Properties of Ag-10CdO Electrical Contact Materials", Holm 1972.

[33] S. Noel, etal, "Graphene Films for Corrosion Protection of Gold Coated Cuprous Substratess in View Of An Application to Electrical Contacts", IEEE Holm 2012

[34] P. Wang etal, "In-Situ Synthesized Silver-Graphene Nanocomposite with Enhanced Electrical and Mechanical Properties", IEEE Holm 2017

[35] H. Chen, P, Wang, J. Hernandez, "Study of Silver-Graphene Tungsten Material for Low Voltage Electric Contact", IEEE Holm 2019

[36] Wang Wangang,et al,"Study on Charaxterization of Electrical Contact Between Pantograph and Catenary", IEEE Holm 2011

[37] Wang Zhiyong, et al," Temperature Characteristics of Sliding Friction Pair Undere High-Speed and Strong Current Conditions", IEEE Holm 2017

[38] T. Ngo, et al, "Additive manufacturing (3D printing): A review of Materials, Methods, Applications and Challenges", Composites Part B: Engineering, vol 1463, 15 June 2018

[39] M. Yakout, M. Elbestawi, "Additive Manufacturing of Composite Materials, an Overview". 6th International conference on Virtual Machining Process Technology (VMPT), Montreal, 2017.

[40] Hall, "Deposition Behavior in Cold Sprayed Cu-W Metal Matrix Composites", Sandia Lab, 2015

[41] N. Deng, et al, "Fabrication and Characterization of W-Cu Composite Coating with Different W Contents by Cold Spraying", Surface and Coatings Technology, v368, June 2019.

[42] pat5956560 Tungsten-Copper Composite Powder, Osram, 1999.

[43] Global Tungsten, copper coated tungsten powder, grade AM WCu for high velocity deposition (cold spray).

[44] G. Rolland, et al,"Lifetime of cold-sprayed electrical contacts", ICEC2012

[45] G. Pawlikowski, et al, "3D printing of Functional Electrical Contacts", IEEE Holm 2019

[46] V. Duarte, et al, "Hot Forging Wire and Arc Additive Manufacturing (HF-WAAM)", Additive Manufacturing, 35 (2020)

Table 1 - Switching capacity of commercially available switchgear with various arc extinction principles [13]

Arc extinction principle	U_N	I_N	Rated number of operations	Dimensions of switching device	Applications	Remarks
opening of contact	< 30V	< 150A	100.000	4 x 4 x 4cm	automobile, control circuits	also with $I_N \approx$ mA at higher voltages
hybrid switch	24V	10A	n/a	12 x 6 x 1,2cm	overload protection on distribution boards	semiconductor always in current path
gas filled (e.g. H_2) / arc lengthening / cooling by walls	400V 800V	300A 480A	1.000 10	10 x 7,5 x 6cm 7,5 x 6 x 6cm	battery switches	various gasses possible, resistive loads only (≤ DC-1)
use of splitter plates	750V	800A (50kA)	5.000	30 x 30 x 10cm	energy distribution	3 arcing chambers in series connection
use of splitter plates	1000V	2kA	50.000	44 x 40 x 25cm	wind energy, photovoltaics, railways	3 arcing chambers in series connection, DC-1
cooling by plates / ceramic walls	3kV	800A	2.000.000 mech.	35 x 30 x 16cm	traction in railways	2 arcing chambers in series connection, DC-1
cooling by plates / ceramic walls	3,6kV 1,8kV	4kA 8kA	80.000 mech.	100 x 70 x 50cm	traction / energy distribution in railways	–
hybrid switch	80kV	2kA (9kA)	n/a	large (HV isolation)	HVDC links	series connection according to system voltage
AC switch with additional commutation path	500kV	2,2kA	n/a	very large (HV isolation)	HVDC links	4 switches in series connection

8th International Conference on Reliability of Electrical Products and Electrical Contacts, November 18-20, 2022 **(Invited Paper)**

Investigations of Break Arc Characteristics of $AgSnO_2$ Contacts under Application of an External Magnetic Field in Inductive DC Load Conditions

Makoto Hasegawa, Shoya Sasaki, Shota Kosugi
Dept. of Opto-Electronic System Engineering
Chitose Institute of Science and Technology, Chitose, 066-8655, Japan
E-mail: hasegawa@photon.chitose.ac.jp Tel: +82-123-27-6059

Abstract—**Break operations of $AgSnO_2$ contact pairs were conducted in a DC inductive (L=5.7mH) load circuit with 14V-6A, 14V-11A, 20V-6A, 20A-9A and 20V-16A at different contact opening speeds from 1 to 200 mm/s and with/without external magnetic field application of about 150 mT in air, and break arc durations were measured and studied. Increases in contact opening speeds realized decreases total arc durations, but gaseous phase durations showed slight increases in the 14V circuit. Applied external magnetic field realized reductions mainly in gaseous phase durations, not in metallic phase durations. Such complicated influences should be well understood.**

Index Terms— **Arc duration, Magnetic field, Contact opening speed, $AgSnO_2$ contacts.**

I. INTRODUCTION

Components with electrical contacts are still being used in various applications, and performances of electrical contacts have great influences on reliabilities and lifetimes of the components. Therefore, understandings of electrical contact phenomena are still very important, although the related studies have been conducted for a long period of time.

The authors have studied break arc characteristics of Ag and Ag-based contacts such as $AgSnO_2$ in DC resistive or inductive load conditions with a 20V or smaller power supply voltage. Although such load conditions are common in various applications, sufficient results of studies have not been reported. Electrical contact phenomena in such load conditions may be slightly different from those in higher load conditions, and those studies are believed to be important.

In this paper, break operations of $AgSnO_2$ contact pairs were conducted in a DC inductive (L=5.7mH) load circuit with 14V-6A, 14V-11A, 20V-6A, 20A-9A and 20V-16A at different contact opening speeds from 1 to 200 mm/s and with/without external magnetic field application of about 150 mT in air, and break arc durations were measured. Influences of increases in contact opening speeds and application of an external magnetic field were studied.

II. EXPERIMENTAL PROCEDURES

Pairs of $AgSnO_2$ contacts (Ag88%-$SnO_2$12%, prepared by internal oxidation with no additives), as shown in Fig.1, were employed. Both stationary (right in Fig.1) and movable (left in Fig.1) electrodes were of solid rivet-type with a head thickness of about 1mm and a head diameter of about 3mm. The head of the stationary electrode was attached onto a metal plate (18mm x 6mm), while the head of the movable electrode was attached onto a spring plate (also 18mm x 6mm) made of phosphor bronze.

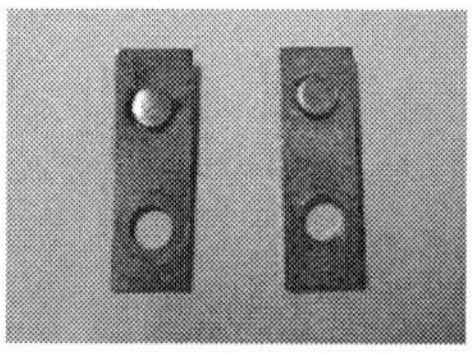

Fig. 1. Stationary (right) and movable (left) electrodes in this study.

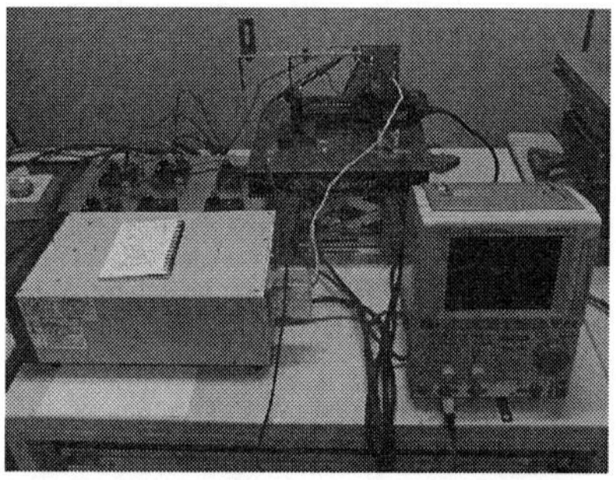

Fig. 2. The contact switching mechanism in this study.

The contact switching mechanism is shown in Fig.2, which was the same as employed in the authors' recent studies. The switching mechanism includes a motorized movable stage driven by an AC servo motor, and one electrode of a contact pair is fixed onto the movable stage as a movable electrode via a certain attachment jig. Switching operations of the contact pair can be realized via movements of the motorized stage by controlling the AC servo motor through instructions from a PC program. Upon contact opening, the movable electrode was moved from its closed position by 2 mm at a selected speed level.

The inductive load circuit in this study included an inductive component of about 5.7 mH. It was not intended to realize any specific applications, but rather, it was intended to mitigate influences of unregulated inductive components in the circuit (e.g., stray inductance components due to wirings) by employing such an intentional inductive component. No specific control for the load current flow was employed during the switching operations, and thus both break and make discharges occurred. Among them, only break arc discharges were investigated in this study.

For application of an external magnetic field, a piece of neodymium magnet (with 0.5 cm in height and 1.5 cm in diameter) was placed closed to the contact gap. With such a placement, the resultant magnetic flux density at the contact gap was measured to be about 150 mT, although it was not able to confirm whether the magnetic flux density was uniform in the contact gap.

TABLE I EXPERIMENTAL CONDITIONS

Contact material	Ag(88%)-SnO_2(12%)
Load circuit	DC inductive (L = 5.7 mH)
Load conditions	14V-6A, 14V-11A, 20V-6A, 20V-11A, and 20V-16A
Ambient environment	laboratory air (no control)
Contact opening speed	1, 2, 5, 10, 20, 50, 100, 200 mm/s
External magnetic field	0 mT and about 150 mT

Table I summarizes the experimental conditions employed in this study.

Before the test, the surfaces of both electrodes of a test contact pair were polished with #1000 sandpaper, and then wiped with methyl alcohol. Thereafter, the contact pair was mounted onto the switching mechanism with the movable electrode as an anode and the stationary electrode as a cathode. At the closed position, the movable anode electrode was slightly pushed backward by the mating stationary cathode electrode, thereby resulting in slight bending of the spring plate (an electrode assembly arm for the movable anode electrode) due to its elasticity. This may cause some wiping between the electrode surfaces, as is usual in commercial relays.

In each of the test conditions, about 25 to 30 voltage waveforms across the separating contacts upon contact opening (as well as flowing current waveforms) were recorded with a digital storage-scope (Yokogawa DL1620). Among them, the 10 waveforms were analyzed to determine respective arc durations, more specifically, the total break arc duration, the metallic phase duration, and the gaseous phase duration.

Such a measurement round was conducted several times for each of the operating conditions. Comparisons among the averages of different measurement rounds showed no significant differences, indicating good reproducibility of the measurements. Thus, the average values for the 10 waveforms obtained in a certain measurement round will be shown in the following figures.

III. Experimental Results

Fig.3 shows the relationships between the average total break arc durations and the contact opening speeds in the 14V load conditions with/without application of the external magnetic field of about 150mT.

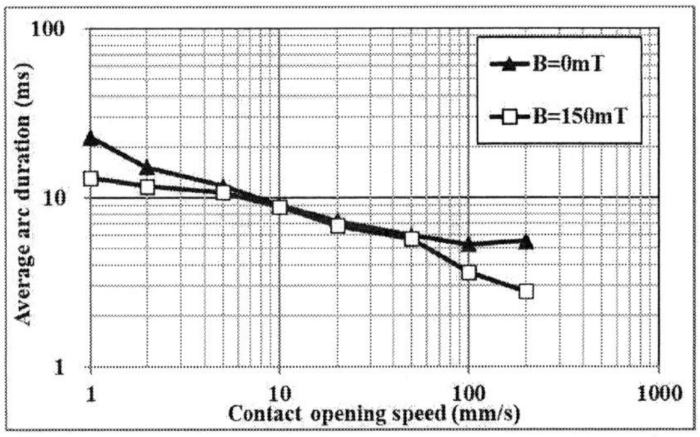

(a) 14V-6A

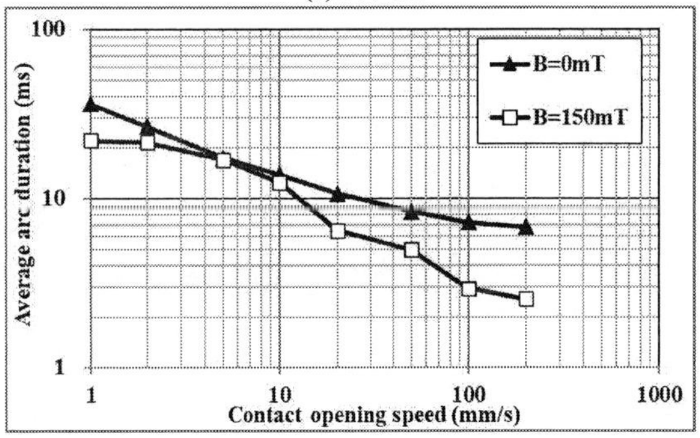

(b) 14V-11A

Fig. 3. The average total break arc duration characteristics at 14V.

The average total break arc durations show decreases with increases in the contact opening speeds both with/without application of the external magnetic field, but not in inversely proportional tendency. External magnetic field application realized significant decreases in the total break arc durations at the faster contact opening speed, but also slight decreases were found at the slower contact opening speeds.

The corresponding characteristics in the 20V load conditions are shown in Fig.4. The similar tendencies as in the 14V load conditions are also observed. In addition, reductions in the total break arc durations with the applied external magnetic field are found almost all the contact opening speed range.

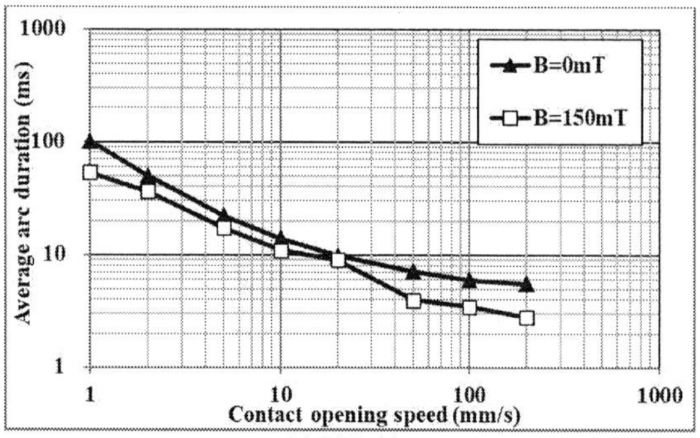

(a) 20V-6A

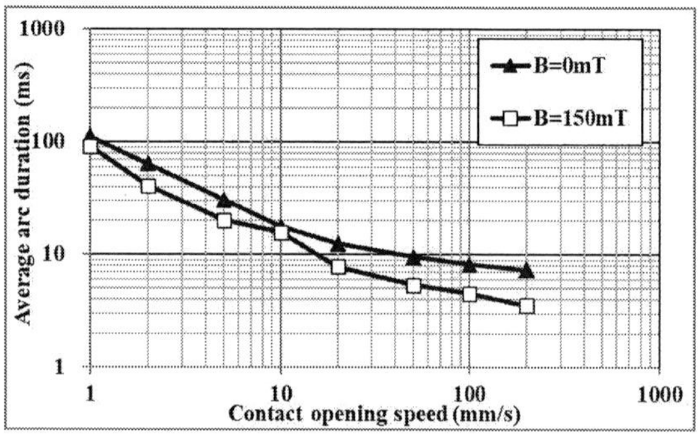

(b) 20V-11A

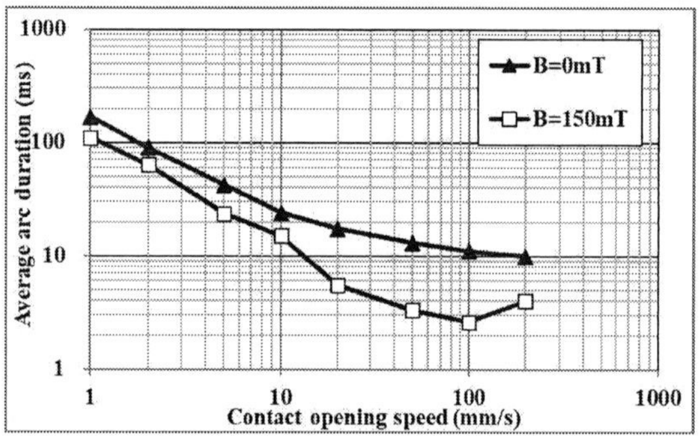

(c) 20V-16A

Fig. 4. The average total break arc duration characteristics at 20V.

Fig.5 shows the relationships between the average metallic phase durations and the contact opening speeds in the respective load conditions with/without application of the external magnetic field, while Fig.6 shows the relationships between the average gaseous phase durations and the contact opening speeds in the respective load conditions with/without application of the external magnetic field. It should be noted that due to the page space limitation, the results in the 20V-16A load condition are not shown here, but will be shown later.

The metallic phase durations show clear reduction tendencies, sometimes in inverse proportion to increases in the contact opening speeds. There are no shortening effects by applying the external magnetic field. Rather, slight increases in the metallic phase durations with the magnetic field application can be seen.

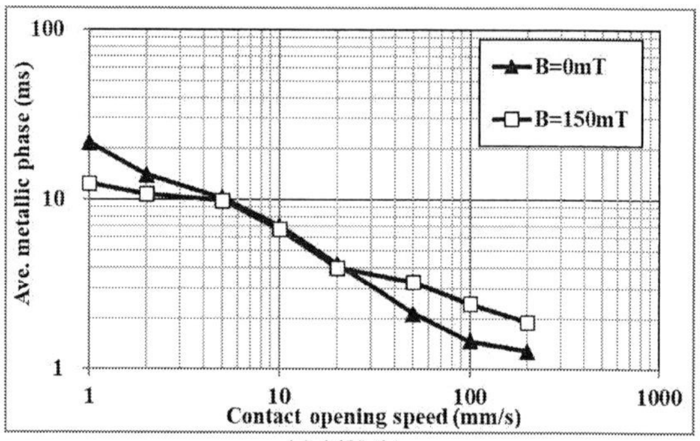

(a) 14V-6A

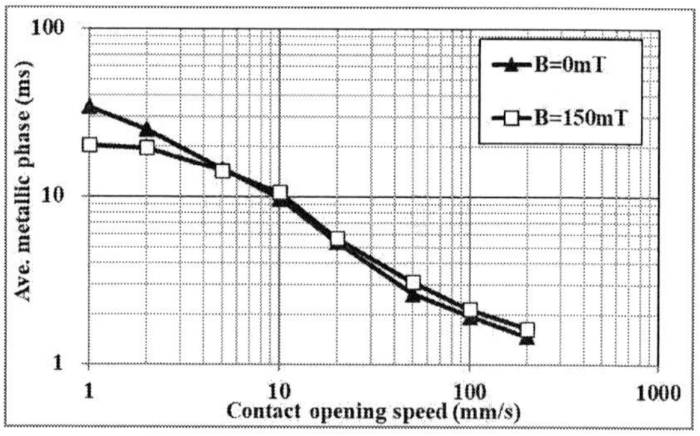

(b) 14V-11A

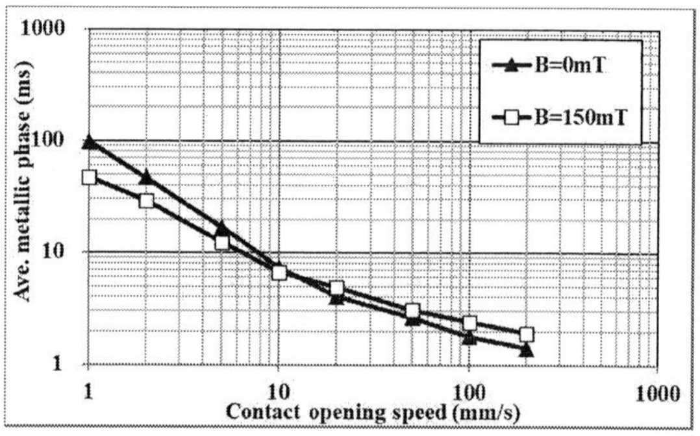

(c) 20V-6A

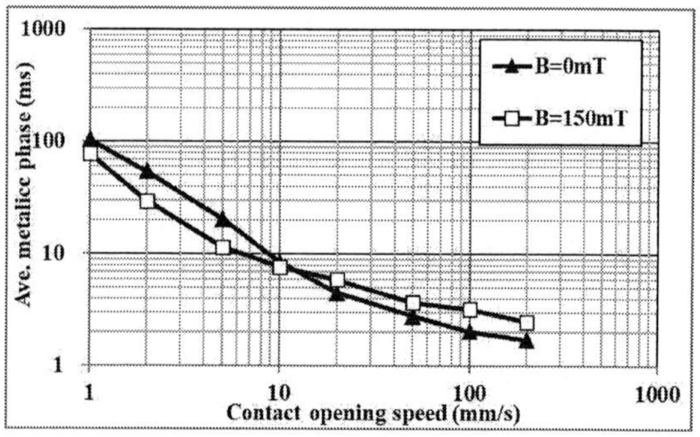

(d) 20V-11A

Fig. 5. The average metallic phase duration characteristics at the respective load conditions.

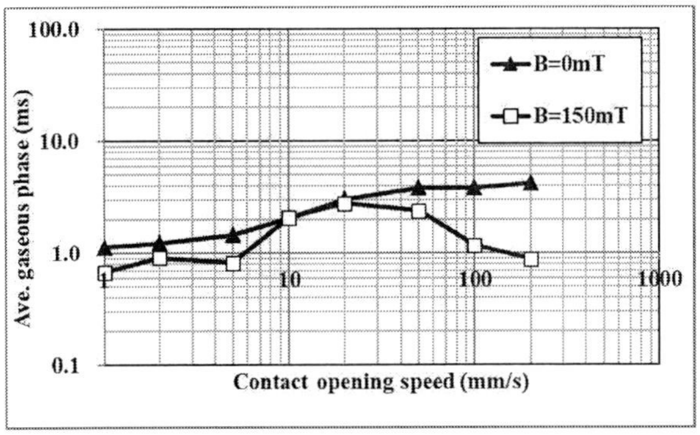

(a) 14V-6A

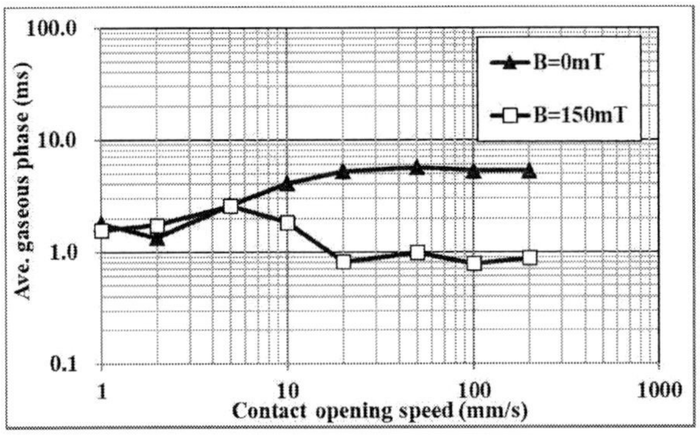

(b) 14V-11A

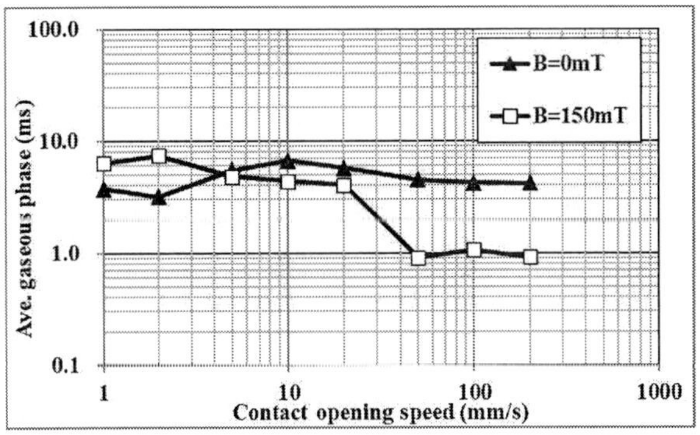

(c) 20V-6A

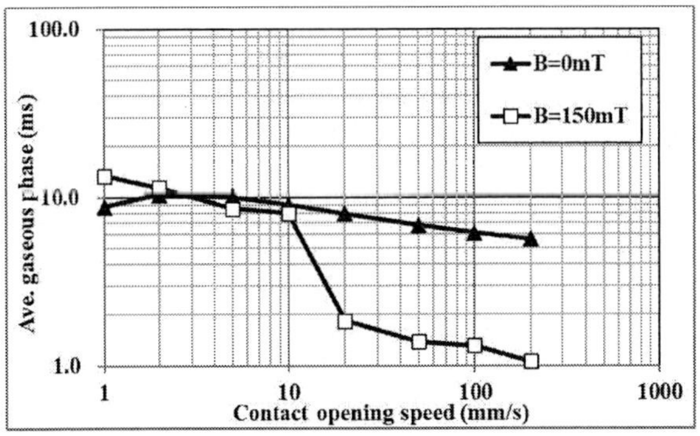

(d) 20V-11A

Fig. 6. The average gaseous phase duration characteristics at the respective load conditions.

In the gaseous phase duration characteristics, reduction effects due to application of the external magnetic field are clearly recognized at the faster contact opening speed levels in the 20V load conditions. Increases in the contact opening speeds do not exhibit such shortening effects for the gaseous phase durations, but in contrast, in the 14V load conditions, the increased contact opening speeds rather induced the slight increases in the gaseous phase durations.

Fig.7 shows the corresponding results in the 20V-16A load condition. The similar tendencies as described for the other load conditions are also recognizable.

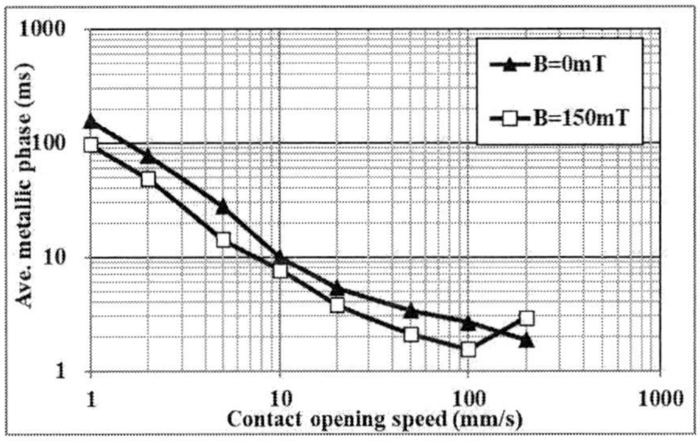

(a) average metallic phase duration characteristics at 20V-16A

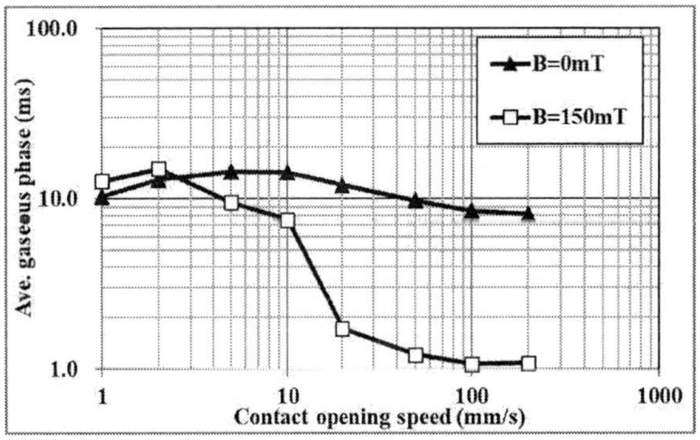

(b) average gaseous phase duration characteristics at 20V-16A

Fig. 7. The average metallic and gaseous phase duration characteristics in the 20V-16A load conditions.

IV. Discussions

A. Influences of increased contact opening speeds

Increases in contact opening speeds are often said to act as one of effective measures to reduce break arc durations [1-10]. The results as shown in Figs.3 and 4 indicate such shortening effects for the average total break arc durations. However, the often-said inversely proportional tendency cannot be found [11-14], and rather, in the faster opening speed range, the shortening effects seem to mitigate.

The average metallic phase duration characteristics show the inversely-proportion-like reduction tendencies with increases in the contact opening speeds in the slower speed range. However, in the faster speed range, such shortening effects seem to mitigate.

Speaking of the average gaseous phase duration characteristics, some increasing tendencies are even recognizable with increases in the contact opening speeds in the 14V load conditions. Any reasons for such results are not known, and there is the possibility of influences of inductive load conditions.

Thus, although increases in the contact opening speeds are certainly effective for reducing break arc durations, it is not the perfect solution that is applicable to all of load conditions.

B. Influences of application of external magnetic field

From the results in Figs.3 and 4, application of an external magnetic field is confirmed to be effective for shortening break arc durations especially at the larger load current levels. However, it should be noted that the applied external magnetic field has almost no effects for shortening the metallic phase durations, and mainly realizes reductions in the gaseous phase durations. This is caused by the well-known magnetic blown-out phenomena [15-16].

Based on the above-mentioned results, proper combination of the increased contact opening speeds and the applied external magnetic field will be effective for realizing reductions in the total break arc durations for a larger range of load conditions [17-19].

C. Peculiar break arc behaviors under the applied external magnetic field

In the 14V load conditions, slight decreases in the total break arc durations are recognizable at the slower contact opening speed levels such as 1 mm/s and 2 mm/s, as mentioned before with reference to Fig.3. Furthermore, in the 20V load conditions, such reduction tendencies are also recognizable at the slower contact opening speed levels, as shown in Fig.4. Interesting point is that any magnetic arc blown-out was not observed in such load conditions. In other words, in the operating conditions at the slower contact opening speeds and with the relatively smaller load conditions, certain reductions in the total break arc durations were recognized even without magnetic blown-out phenomena.

For the purpose of finding out any possible and reasonable explanations for such tendencies, the authors are currently trying to conduct observation of arc plasma movements in break arc discharges with a high-speed camera. Our preliminary results of investigations showed that when the magnetic blown-out was not observed, arc was found to move in the direction opposite to the Lorentz force direction after moving around over the electrode surface, and disappeared. With application of the magnetic field in the opposite direction was applied, the arc movement direction immediately before its extinction was also switched in the opposite direction [20-23].

Thus, some factors other than the Lorentz force level seem to have critical influences on the observed results.

V. CONCLUSIONS

Break operations of $AgSnO_2$ contact pairs were conducted in a DC inductive (L=5.7mH) load circuit with 14V-6A, 14V-11A, 20V-6A, 20A-9A and 20V-16A at different contact opening speeds from 1 to 200 mm/s and with/without external magnetic field application of about 150 mT in air, and break arc durations were measured and studied.

As the results, increases in contact opening speeds realized decreases total arc durations, but not in the inversely proportional tendency. In the faster opening speed range, the shortening effects seem to mitigate.

The average metallic phase duration characteristics show the inversely-proportion-like reduction tendencies with increases in the contact opening speeds only in the slower speed range. Moreover, increased contact opening speeds even induced slight increases in the gaseous phase duration in the 14V load conditions.

Application of an external magnetic field realized reductions mainly in gaseous phase durations, not in metallic phase durations. In the operating conditions at the slower contact opening speeds and with the relatively smaller load conditions, certain reductions in the total break arc durations were recognized without magnetic blown-out phenomena. In the non-magnetic-blown-out cases, some peculiar arc movements were observed. Mechanism for explaining such arc movements has not yet become clear, which will be investigated in the future.

ACKNOWLEDGMENT

The authors thank Tanaka Kikinzoku Kogyo Co., Ltd. for supplying contact samples used in this study. The authors also thank Photron Ltd., Japan, and Nobby Tech. Ltd., Japan, for their courtesy of respectively letting us use their high-speed camera.

REFERENCES

[1] T. Takagi, "Electrode temperature dependency of arc duration in contact break – Experiments on a few contact materials-", Proc. of 11st Intl. Conf. on Electric Contact Phenomena (ICEC1982), pp.251-255, June 1982.

[2] H. Ishida, H. Sugimoto, H. Sone and T. Takagi, "An experiment on the dependency of contact opening velocity on arc phenomena of slowly opening Ag and Pd contacts", Proc. of 17th Intl. Conf. on Electrical Contacts (ICEC1994), pp.45-50, July 1994.

[3] J.W.McBride and S.M.Sharkh, "The influence of contact opening velocity on arc characteristics", Proc. of 16th Intl. Conf. on Electrical Contacts (ICEC1992), pp.395-400, September 1992.

[4] Liang Huimin, Ma Guangcheng, Cai Ling, Xie Yong

and Xie Guoqiang, "Research on the relationship between contact breakaway initial speed and arc duration", Proc. 49th IEEE Holm Conf. on Electrical Contacts., pp.204-210, September 2003.

[5] G.Witter and Z.K.Chen, "A comparison for the effects of opening speed, contact gap and material type on electrical erosion for relays interrupting inductive automotive loads", Proc. 23rd Intl. Conf. on Electrical Contacts (ICEC2006), pp.17-21, June 2006.

[6] N. BenJemaa, L. Doublet, L. Morin, and D. Jeannot, "Break arc study for the new electrical level of 42 V in automotive applications", Proc. 47th IEEE Holm Conf. on Electrical Contacts, pp.50-55, September 2001.

[7] N. BenJemaa, "Contacts conduction and switching in DC levels", Proc. 48th IEEE Holm Conf. on Electrical Contacts, pp.1-15, October 2002.

[8] L. Doublet, N. BenJemaa, F. Hauner and D. Jeannot, "Electrical arc phenomena and its interaction on contact material at 42 volts DC for automotive applications", Proc. 50th IEEE Holm Conf. on Electrical Contacts, pp.8-14, Sepember 2004.

[9] D. Sallais, E. Carvou and N. BenJemaa, "Opening speed effect on arc duration and erosion and extinction gap for usual contact materials", Proc. 2nd Intl. Conf. on Reliability of Electrical Products and Electrical Contacts (ICREPEC2007), pp.73-77, March 2007.

[10] D. Sallais, N. BenJemaa, and E. Carvou, "Minimization of arc extinction gap in the opening speed range 1 cm/s - 1 m/s", Proc. 53rd IEEE Holm Conf. on Electrical Contacts, pp.239-243, September 2007.

[11] M. Hasegawa, "Break arc behaviors of Ag and $AgSnO_2$ contact pairs under different contact opening speeds in DC load circuits", Proc. 27th Intl. conf. on Electrical Contacts (ICEC2014), June 2014.

[12] M. Hasegawa, H. Sonobe and Y. Ohmae, "Influences of contact opening speeds in the range of 0.5 to 200mm/s on break arc behaviors of Ag and $AgSnO_2$ contacts in DC14V inductive load circuits of 1 to 5A", Proc. 60th IEEE Holm Conf. on Electrical Contacts, pp.14-18, October 2014.

[13] M. Hasegawa, "Influences of contact opening speeds on break arc behaviors of $AgSnO_2$ contact pairs in DC inductive load conditions", IEICE Trans. Electronics, Vol.E98-C, No.9, pp.923-927, September 2015.

[14] M. Hasegawa, H. Sonobe and N. Ohkawa, "Influences of contact opening speeds in the range of 0.5 to 200mm/s on break arc behaviors of $AgSnO_2$ contacts in DC conditions", Proc. 61st IEEE Holm Conf. on Electrical Contacts, pp.166-170, October 2015.

[15] A. Vassa, E. Carvou, S. Rivoirard, L. Doublet, C. Bourda, D. Jeannot, P. Ramoni, N. BenJemaa, and D. Givord, "Magnetic blowing of break arcs up to 360VDC", Proc. of 56th IEEE Holm Conf. on Electrical Contacts, pp.96-100, October 2010.

[16] A. Vassa, E. Carvou, S. Rivoirard, L. Doublet, C. Bourda, N. BenJemaa, and D. Givord, "DC-arc blowing under pulsed magnetic field", Proc. of 26th Intl. Conf. on Electrical Contacts, pp.23-29, May 2012.

[17] M. Hasegawa and S. Tokumitsu, "Break arc duration characteristics of $AgSnO_2$ contacts under magnetic field application with contact opening speeds in the range up to 200mm/s in DC load conditions", Proc. of 62nd IEEE Holm Conf. on Electrical Contacts, pp.119-124, October 2016.

[18] M. Hasegawa and S. Tokumitsu, "Influences of contact opening speeds up to 200mm/s and external magnetic field application on break arc duration characteristics of $AgSnO_2$ contacts in DC14V load conditions up to around 10A", IEEE Trans. on Components, Packaging and Manufacturing Technology, Vol.8, No.3, pp.375-382, March 2018.

[19] S. Tokumitsu and M. Hasegawa, "Effective shortening of break arc durations of Ag and several Ag-based contacts in DC load conditions with increased contact opening speeds and external magnetic field", Proc. 64th IEEE Holm Conf. on Electrical Contacts (together with 29th Intl. Conf. on Electrical Contacts), pp.87-94, October, 2018.

[20] S. Tokumitsu and M. Hasegawa, "Relationships between break arc behaviors of $AgSnO_2$ contacts and Lorentz force to be applied by an external magnetic force in a DC inductive load circuit up to 20V-17A", IEICE Trans. on Electronics, Vol.E102-C, No.9, pp.641-645, September 2019.

[21] S.Tokumitsu and M.Hasegawa, "Arc motion investigations of break arcs of $AgSnO_2$ contacts under applied external magnetic field in inductive DC load conditions", Proc. 65th IEEE Holm Conf. on Electrical Contacts, pp.95-100, September 2019.

[22] S. Tokumitsu and M. Hasegawa, "A study on break arc behaviors of $AgSnO_2$ contacts in an inductive load circuit up to DC20V-17A under application of external magnetic field", IEICE Trans. on Electronics (Japanese Edition), Vol.J102-C, No.10, pp.294-296, October 2019 (written in Japanese).

[23] M. Hasegawa and S. Tokumitsu, "Observations of peculiar break arc movements of $AgSnO_2$ contacts under applied external magnetic field in inductive DC load conditions up to 20V-17A", Proc. 66th IEEE Holm Conference on Electrical Contacts, pp.79-84, October 2021.

Makoto Hasegawa received his B.E., M.E. and Ph.D. degrees in electrical engineering from Keio University, Yokohama, Japan, in 1986, 1988 and 1991, respectively. After spending several years in industry, Dr. Hasegawa joined to Chitose Institute of Science and Technology, Hokkaido, Japan, at 2000, and he is now a Professor at the Department of Opto-Electronic

System Engineering of that institute. Prof. Hasegawa is currently involved in research on electrical contact phenomenon and related measuring techniques, optical sensing techniques, as well as science and engineering education researches. Prof. Hasegawa is a senior member of: the Institute of Electrical and Electronics Engineers (IEEE); and the Institute of Electronics, Information and Communication Engineers (IEICE). He is also a regular member of the International Society for Optics and Photonics (SPIE); the Institute of Electrical Engineers of Japan (IEEJ); the Japan Society of Applied Physics (JSAP); the Physics Education Society of Japan (PESJ); and Japan Association for College and University Education (JACUE).

Shoya Sasaki received his B.E. degree in opto-electronic system engineering from Chitose Institute of Science and Technology, Hokkaido, Japan at 2022. Mr. Sasaki was involved in the research of break arc characteristics and influences of increased contact opening speeds as well as external magnetic field application.

Shota Kosugi is now pursuing his B.E. degree in opto-electronic system engineering at Chitose Institute of Science and Technology, Hokkaido, Japan. Mr. Kosugi is now being involved in the research of break arc characteristics and influences of increased contact opening speeds as well as external magnetic field application.

Reliability-Oriented Control for Power Electronics Systems

Tiefu Zhao

University of North Carolina at Charlotte, USA

***Abstract*—The reliability of power electronics is critical for energy conversion systems to maintain safety, efficiency, and uptime. Power converter is regarded as one of the most fragile components in renewable energy systems, such as solar, wind, and ocean energy. Their failures can downgrade the system efficiency, cause catastrophic system breakdowns, and result in expensive economic losses. Among all the various failure causes investigated by researchers, thermal stress has been identified as one of the significant causes of power electronics modules. This thermal stress accelerates the degradation of semiconductor devices, downgrades the system quality and efficiency, and eventually causes catastrophic system breakdowns and extensive economic losses. Therefore, it is crucial to establish a fundamental control strategy with reliability targets at the power electronics control and operation level, thereby extending the component lifetime and improving the system reliability.**

The research team at the *University of North Carolina at Charlotte* has been working on the *reliability-oriented control strategy* for power converters. The team has introduced the reliability-related parameters previously not fully considered (such as energy mission profile, semiconductor temperature and stress, reliability and lifetime models, etc.) into the power converter control system, therefore offers a transformative way to significantly improve the system reliability. This talk will introduce the key technology milestones achieved and discuss the potential impact to extend the power electronic system lifetime, and improve the Operations & Maintenance (O&M) cost.

Speaker Bio:

Tiefu Zhao received the B.S. and M.S. degrees from Tsinghua University, Beijing, China, in 2003 and 2005, respectively, and the Ph.D. degree from North Carolina State University, Raleigh, in 2010, all in electrical engineering. From 2010 to 2016, he was with Eaton Corporation Research & Technology, Milwaukee, WI. He is currently an Associate Professor with the Department of Electrical and Computer Engineering and the Energy Production and Infrastructure Center (EPIC), University of North Carolina at Charlotte, Charlotte, NC, USA. His current research interests include solid state transformer, solid state circuit protection, wireless power transfer, wide bandgap device based power conversion, power electronics reliability and fault detection.

Dr. Zhao was the recipient of 2015 IAS Andrew W. Smith Outstanding Young Member Award and 2015 STEM Forward Young Engineer of the Year Award. His Ph.D. research on solid state transformer was named the world's top 10 emerging technologies by MIT technology review 2011. He received prize paper awards from the IEEE ECCE 2020 and ITEC 2021. He was an Associate Editor for the IEEE Journal of Emerging and Selected Topics in Power Electronics (JESTPE). He is the Founding Chair of the IEEE Charlotte section PELS/IAS/IES Chapter.

8th International Conference on Reliability of Electrical Products and Electrical Contacts, November 18-20, 2022 (**Invited Paper**)

Diagnosis of Inter-Turn Short Circuit Fault of AMB Based on Forgetting Factor Recursive Least Square Algorithm

Henghui Li[1], Lijian Wu[1], Zhenzhong Su[2], Junquan Chen[2], Zekai Lyu[1], Feng Niu[3]
[1]*College of Electrical Engineering, Zhejiang University, Hangzhou, China*
[2]*National Key Laboratory of Science and Technology on Vessel Integrated Power System, Naval University of Engineering, Wuhan, China*
[3]*State Key Laboratory of Reliability and Intelligence of Electrical Equipment, Hebei University of Technology, Tianjin, China*
E-mail: henghuili@zju.edu.cn

Abstract—**Fault diagnosis is one of the most important ways to improve the reliability of an active magnetic bearing (AMB) system. The inter-turn short circuit (ITSC) fault of an AMB may lead to catastrophic consequence such as rotor impact and winding open circuit. Hence, it is vital to diagnose the ITSC fault in real-time. To diagnosis the ITSC fault of AMB, a model of the AMB with ITSC fault is established in this paper. A method is proposed to extract the fault feature utilizing the forgetting factor recursive least square (FFRLS) algorithm. Furthermore, a compensation method based on look-up table is introduced to improve the robustness of the proposed method to the eccentricity of the rotor. The effectiveness of proposed method is verified by experiments.**

Index Terms— **Active magnetic bearing, Fault diagnosis, Inter-turn short circuit, Forgetting factor recursive least square algorithm.**

I. Introduction

The active magnetic bearings (AMB) have advantages over the mechanical bearing such as no lubrication, no mechanical contact, high operational speed, adjustable stiffness and damping, etc. Hence, they have been applied in many situations such as high speed and high energy density areas. However, the reliability of the AMB system is low compare to the mechanical bearing [1]. Failure of the AMB system can cause catastrophic consequences, which precludes the application of magnetic bearings in the industry [2]. Therefore, online fault detection is important to improve the reliability of the AMB system.

The fault of the magnetic bearing system can be generally classified as either internal or external. The internal fault consists of the power electronics or amplifier failure, the bearing magnetic coil failure, the computer software or hardware failure, etc. The external fault includes rotor impact, rotor mass loss, rotor deformation, rotor rub, sudden change in loading, etc. [3]. Many researches have been carried out to detect the fault of the magnetic bearing system. The continuous wavelet transform was applied to the analysis of rub-impact faults [4]. In [1], three types of real-time faults detection, correction, and identification algorithm were compared for vibration forces on the rotor of an AMB system, which focused on different kinds of analysis such as displacement analysis, current analysis, frequency fault detection, pattern recognition, etc. Reference [5] proposed a method which combined state observers and parameter estimation for a full fault diagnosis for the AMB system. A diagnosis algorithm is reported for the magnetic bearing based on a state-space model of the entire mechatronic system [6].

Although much attention has been devoted to general fault detection using either model-based methods or adaptive methods as well as fault-tolerant control methods, the investigation upon the specific inter-turn short circuit (ITSC) fault of magnetic bearing coils has not been much addressed. In the field of rotary motor, the detection of ITSC fault is also a hot topic. It is convenient to draw on the experience from the fault detection inside the area of the rotary motor. Motor current signature analysis (MCSA) has been profoundly researched because of the convenience of acquiring the current signal of stators [7]. Reference [8] used the amplitude of the sideband components of the stator current determine the severity of the ITSC fault. Besides MCSA, other methods have also been investigated. The instantaneous active and reactive power signature analysis was applied to the stator fault diagnosis of squirrel cage three-phase induction motors [9]. The ITSC fault of the rotary motor and the AMB system has certain similarities, therefore the diagnosis methods applied on the rotary motor can be the reference for the diagnosis of the ITSC fault of AMB.

The least mean square (LMS) algorithm can be used to estimate the parameters of a system, but it is not suitable for real-time implementation due to its shortcomings including slow convergence rate, insensitivity to the non-stationary signal, etc. [9]. Hence, the recursive form of the LMS algorithm, i.e. recursive least square (RLS) algorithm combined with the forgetting factor has been used on the parameter identification of the asynchronous motor and the synchronous motor to overcome the disadvantages of LMS algorithm [11]-[13].

This paper builds up the model of the AMB system with the ITSC fault and chooses the self-inductance as the fault signature according to the feature of the fault model. The LMS algorithm is adopted to estimate the self-inductance of the winding to diagnose the ITSC fault. The FFRLS algorithm is used for the online implementation of the LMS algorithm. A compensation method based on look-up table (LUT) is presented to improve the accuracy of the proposed method.

II. Fault Modeling of AMB with ITSC

In this paper, a type of AMB with 12-poles is considered as shown in Fig. 1. The poles of the AMB are divided into 4 groups, each consists of three adjacent poles marked in Fig. 1 with a dot-line frame, to generate force in different directions. The coils wound on a group of poles are connected in serial as a winding driven by one H-bridge power amplifier. It is worth noting that each coil in a group is wound in a certain direction as shown in Fig. 1. Hence, the magnetic coupling between different groups of poles can be neglected within the error tolerance.

Based on the structure of the winding and the magnetic circuit of a group of poles, the winding of the AMB can be modeled as a circuit composed of an inductor L and a resistor R. As shown in Fig. 2, ITSC fault causes the winding to split into a shorted part and a healthy part, each of which is represented by its self-inductance (L_1, L_2) and resistance (R_1, R_2), as well as the mutual inductance (M) between two parts. The shorted part of the winding is paralleled with R_f which represents the insulation situation between the shorted turns.

According to Kirchhoff laws, the circuit can be described with following equations

$$\begin{cases} U = L_1 \dfrac{dI_1}{dt} + M \dfrac{dI_2}{dt} + R_1 I_1 + R_f I_f \\ R_f I_f = L_2 \dfrac{dI_2}{dt} + M \dfrac{dI_1}{dt} + R_2 I_2 \\ I_1 = I_2 + I_f \end{cases} \tag{1}$$

where I_1, I_2 and I_f are the currents in the healthy part, the shorted part and R_f, respectively, and U is the input voltage on the winding. Take I_1 and I_2 as the state variables, the state-space model of the fault winding is given as

$$\begin{cases} \dfrac{d}{dt}\mathbf{X} = \mathbf{AX} + \mathbf{B}U \\ y = \mathbf{CX} \end{cases} \tag{2}$$

where

$\mathbf{X} = \begin{bmatrix} I_1 \\ I_2 \end{bmatrix}$, $\mathbf{A} = \begin{bmatrix} M & L_2 \\ L_1 + M & L_2 + M \end{bmatrix}^{-1} \begin{bmatrix} R_f & -R_f - R_2 \\ -R_1 & -R_2 \end{bmatrix}$, $\mathbf{B} = \begin{bmatrix} 0 \\ 1 \end{bmatrix}$,

$\mathbf{C} = \begin{bmatrix} 1 & 0 \end{bmatrix}$.

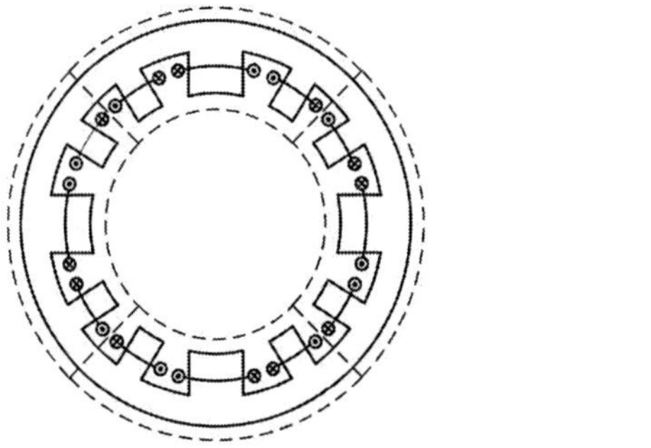

Fig. 1. Topology of the 12-poles AMB.

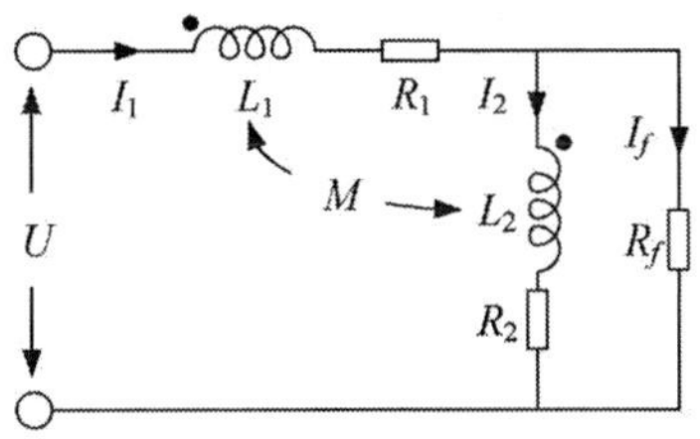

Fig. 2. Electrical circuit model of the winding of AMB with ITSC fault.

To simplify the state-space model and get a clear view of the fault model, the relationship between the value of the parameters of the fault circuit (L_1, L_2, M, R_1, R_2) and those of the normal circuit (L, R) is analyzed. According to the physical meaning of resistance and inductance, the parameter value of the fault circuit can be derived as

$$\begin{cases} R_1 = (1-\mu)R \\ R_2 = \mu R \\ L_1 = (1-\mu)^2 L' \\ L_2 = \mu^2 L' \\ M = k\mu(1-\mu)L' \end{cases} \tag{3}$$

where μ is the short circuit ratio, k is the coupling coefficient between healthy part and shorted part. It is obvious that L_1, L_2 and M should satisfy that

$$L = L_1 + L_2 + 2M \tag{4}$$

Hence, L' can be derived as

$$L' = \frac{L}{\mu^2 + (1-\mu)^2 + 2k\mu(1-\mu)} \tag{5}$$

Apply the Laplace Transform to the state-space model, the admittance transfer function of the winding with ITSC fault can be derived as

$$G(s) = \frac{I_1(s)}{U(s)} = \frac{\mu^2 L' s + \mu R + R_f}{a_2 s^2 + a_1 s + a_0} \quad (6)$$

where the coefficients of the denominator are defined as $a_2 = (1\text{-}k^2)(1\text{-}\mu)^2\mu^2 L'^2$, $a_1 = (1\text{-}\mu)\mu R L' + R_f L$, $a_0 = (1\text{-}\mu)\mu R_2 + R_f R$.

According to (6), the frequency response of the normal winding and the fault winding is shown in Fig. 3. It shows that when the ITSC fault occurs, the magnitude of the current increases in the fault winding excited by a certain frequency of voltage. This means the winding with the ITSC fault presents the characteristic of smaller self-inductance.

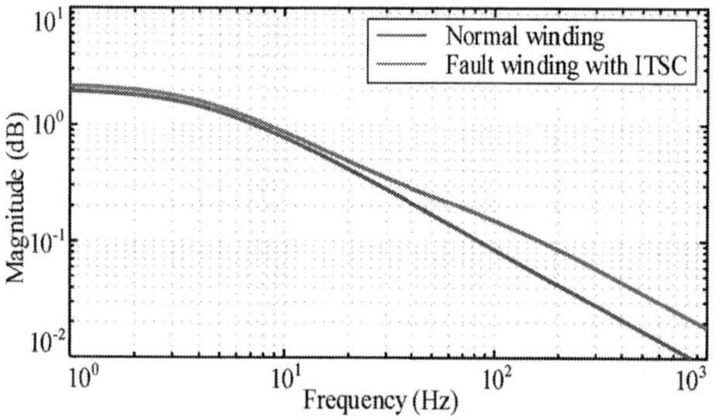

Fig. 3. Bode diagram of the admittance transfer function of the normal winding and the winding with ITSC fault.

III. Fault Diagnosis Based on LMS

A. Simplification and discretization of the fault model

As illustrated above, the equivalent self-inductance of the winding of an AMB decreases after the ITSC fault occurred. Hence, the self-inductance can be used as the characteristic quantity of the ITSC fault. To obtain the self-inductance of the winding of AMB, methods for system parameter identification, such as the LMS algorithm, are suitable to obtain the self-inductance. In this paper, the LMS algorithm is employed to estimate the self-inductance of the winding.

The discrete model of the AMB winding is needed for LMS algorithm. The fault winding of an AMB can be modeled as a second-order system with one input, the voltage of the winding, and one output, the current flowing into the winding. For simplification, the winding with ITSC is treated as a first-order system in this paper. Hence, the transfer function of the fault winding can be derived as

$$G(s) = \frac{I_1(s)}{U(s)} \approx \frac{1}{L_{eq} s + R_{eq}} \quad (7)$$

where L_{eq} and R_{eq} are the equivalent self-inductance and resistance. Then (7) can be discretized as

$$I(k) = (1 - \frac{R_{eq}}{L_{eq}} T_s) I(k-1) + \frac{T_s}{L_{eq}} U(k-1) \quad (8)$$

A. LMS algorithm

The discrete current equation of the winding can be written in the matrix form as

$$\mathbf{I}_k = \begin{bmatrix} \mathbf{I}_{k-1} & \mathbf{U}_{k-1} \end{bmatrix} \begin{bmatrix} \theta_1 \\ \theta_2 \end{bmatrix}^T = \mathbf{A}\boldsymbol{\theta} \quad (9)$$

where $\mathbf{I}_k = [I(k), I(k\text{-}1), \cdots, I(1)]^T$, $\mathbf{U}_k = [U(k), U(k\text{-}1), \cdots, U(1)]^T$, $\theta_1 = 1\text{-}R_{eq}T_s/L_{eq}$, $\theta_2 = T_s/L_{eq}$. According to the LMS algorithm, the parameters can be estimated with the following equation

$$\hat{\boldsymbol{\theta}} = (\mathbf{A}^T \mathbf{A})^{-1} \mathbf{A}^T \mathbf{I}_k \quad (10)$$

Then the self-inductance of the winding can be calculated by

$$\hat{L}_{eq} = \frac{T_s}{\hat{\theta}_2} \quad (11)$$

The ITSC fault can be recognized when the estimated parameter L_{eq} decreases lower than the presetting threshold which relates to the sensitivity of the fault diagnosis.

B. Implementation of LMS algorithm

The calculation of (10) is time consuming, which leads to difficulties in the real-time implementation of the diagnosis algorithm. To reduce the time consumption of the diagnosis algorithm, the RLS algorithm is adopted in this paper. The RLS algorithm is the recursive form of the LMS algorithm, saving the memory for storing the elements of matrix **A** and the time wasted on the repeated calculation of these elements. Furthermore, the forgetting factor is added to reduce the influence of the old data and increase the converging speed of the proposed diagnosis algorithm.

The matrix form of the FFRLS algorithm can be derived as

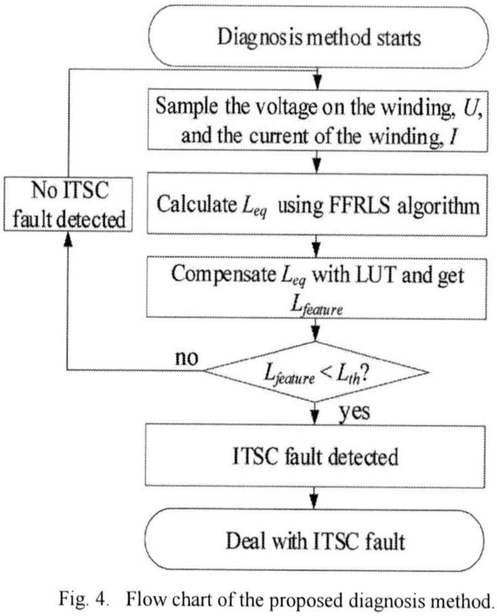

Fig. 4. Flow chart of the proposed diagnosis method.

$$\begin{cases} \mathbf{K}_{k+1} = \mathbf{P}_k \boldsymbol{\varphi}_{k+1} (\lambda + \boldsymbol{\varphi}_{k+1}^T \mathbf{P}_k \boldsymbol{\varphi}_{k+1})^{-1} \\ \mathbf{P}_{k+1} = \frac{1}{\lambda} (\mathbf{I} - \mathbf{K}_{k+1} \boldsymbol{\varphi}_{k+1}^T) \mathbf{P}_k \\ \hat{\boldsymbol{\theta}}_{k+1} = \hat{\boldsymbol{\theta}}_k + \mathbf{K}_{k+1} (y_{k+1} - \boldsymbol{\varphi}_{k+1}^T \hat{\boldsymbol{\theta}}_k) \end{cases} \tag{12}$$

where $\boldsymbol{\varphi}_k=[I(k\text{-}1), U(k\text{-}1)]$, $y_k=I(k)$, $\mathbf{K}_k$ is the gain matrix, $\mathbf{P}_k$ is the covariance matrix, λ is the forgetting factor. The estimated self-inductance of the winding can be calculated according to (11).

The input voltage on the winding can be obtained with voltage sensor directly, or with the corresponding PWM duty, i.e., the output of the current-loop PID controller. Since the voltage sensor is redundant for the voltage source power amplifier, the output of the current-loop PID controller is more suitable for the diagnosis of the ITSC fault. It is worth noting that if the output of the current-loop PID controller is used, the delay time from the end of the current control period to the update of the PWM register should be considered.

C. Compensation of the FFRLS result

The self-inductance of winding relates to the corresponding air gap length. The eccentricity of the rotor under the action of external force or the vibration of the rotor due to the unbalance force lead to the change of the winding self-inductance, and thereby reducing the accuracy of the proposed diagnosis method.

To improve the accuracy of the diagnosis method, an open-loop compensation method based on the LUT is introduced. The LUT contains some pairs of the self-inductance of winding and the corresponding air gap length, which can be acquired with the finite element method tool or experiments.

According to the displacement of rotor x_0, the self-inductance of the normal winding L_{nom} can be acquired with the stored LUT. Then the fault feature value $L_{feature}$ is obtained by dividing the FFRLS algorithm result L_{eq} with L_{nom}, which turns into a unitary value. Once $L_{feature}$ drops below the presetting threshold L_{th} which is much less than 1 p.u., then the ITSC fault of the winding is detected.

II. Experiment Results

The proposed diagnosis method is validated on the experimental rig shown in Fig. 5. Two 12-poles AMBs shown in Fig. 1 are used to levitate the rotor. The AMBs are driven by the voltage source power amplifier, which consists of 8 H-bridges. Each H-bridge is composed of 4 SiC MOSFETs. FPGA XC6SLX16 generates the driver signals of H-bridges. DSP TMS320F28346 is used to control the AMB system. The displacement of the rotor is measured by 4 eddy-current sensors. When the AMBs are not working, the rotor docks on the auxiliary bearings. The servo motor is adopted to drive the rotor. Parameters of the AMB system are listed in TABLE I.

The displacement of the rotor and the current in the test winding are both controlled with the PID controller. When the rotor is stably suspended at the equilibrium position and the rotating speed is 0 rpm, the output of the current-loop PID controller, the current in the corresponding winding, and the calculation result of the FFRLS algorithm are given in Fig. 6. Before the ITSC fault occurs, the estimated self-inductance of the winding is around 32 mH and is rippling due to sampling noise. When the ITSC fault occurs, the estimated self-inductance of the winding rapidly and significantly drops to around 25 mH.

Validation of the proposed algorithm is also accomplished when the rotor is suspended at the equilibrium position and rotating at 200 rpm, 500 rpm, and 1000 rpm. As shown in Fig. 7, the proposed algorithm is proved effective at different rotating speeds.

The influence of the forgetting factor ρ on the diagnosis process is also studied. As shown in Fig. 8, the increase of forgetting factor ρ results in a slower transition of estimated self-inductance from the normal value to the fault value when the ITSC fault occurs. At the same time, the ripple of the estimated self-inductance is reduced. Therefore the rapidness and the robustness of the proposed algorithm are determined by ρ when the sample rate of the system is fixed. By choosing an appropriate ρ, the compromise can be found between rapidness and robustness to get the best performance of the proposed algorithm.

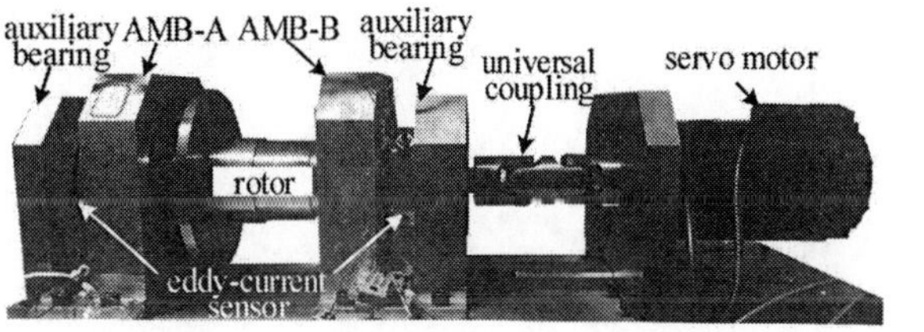

Fig. 5. Experiment rig.

TABLE I. Parameters of the Experiment Rig

Symbol	Description	Value
m	Mass of Rotor	4.13 kg
δ	Nominal air gap length	0.5 mm
δ_b	Protection air gap length	0.25mm
R	Resistance of Winding	0.5 Ω
J_r	Moment of inertia of the rotor around the radial direction	20284.29 kg·mm^2
J_z	Moment of inertia of the rotor around the radial direction	3585.67 kg·mm^2
l_a	Distance between the AMB-A and the center of mass of the rotor	79.00 mm
l_b	Distance between the AMB-B and the center of mass of the rotor	79.76 mm
k_s	Displacement Stiffness	0.49 N/μm
k_i	Current Stiffness	115.29 N/A

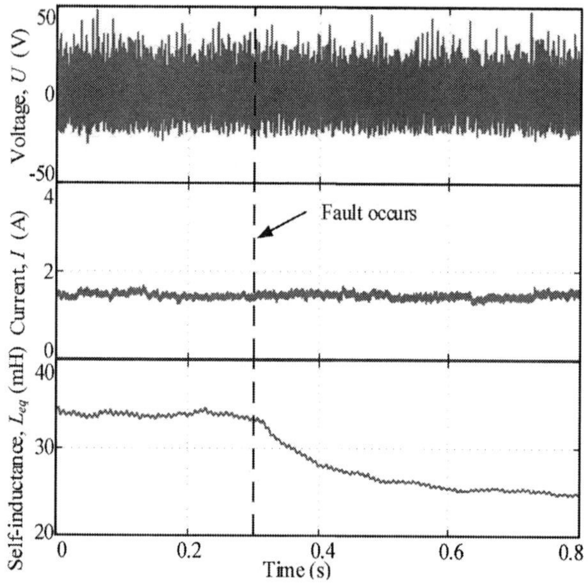

Fig. 6. Voltage, current and the estimated self-inductance of the test winding. (μ=10%, ρ=0.99995)

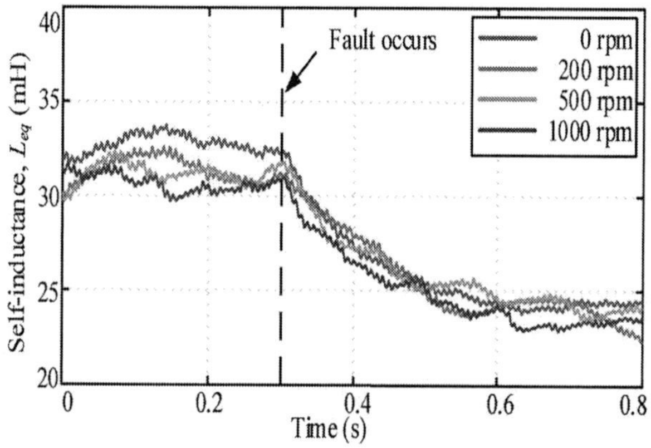

Fig. 7. Diagnosis results of the test winding at different rotating speed of rotor. (μ=10%, ρ=0.99995)

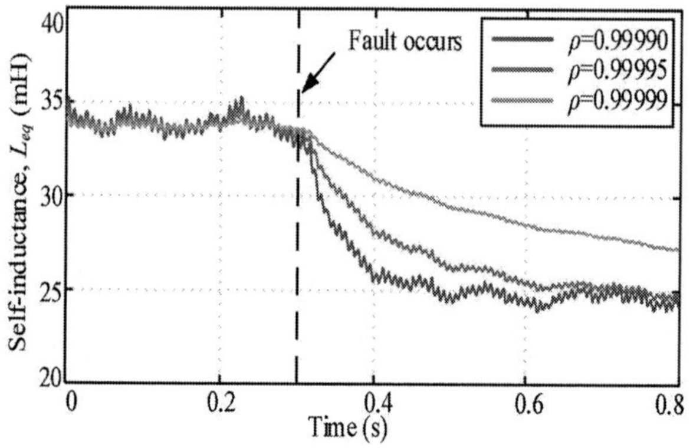

Fig. 8. Diagnosis results of the test winding with different forgetting factor ρ. (μ=10%)

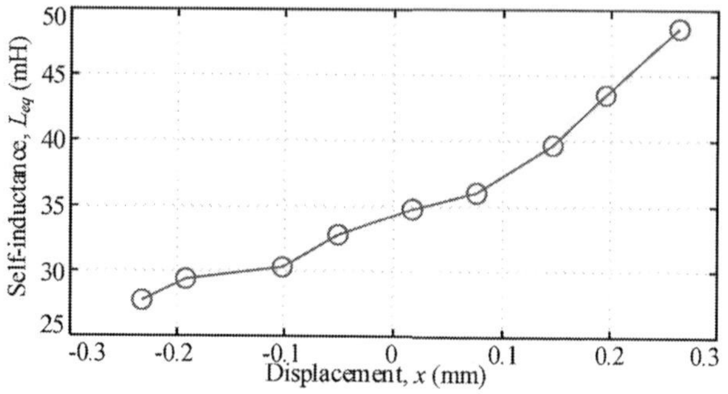

Fig. 9. Estimated self-inductance of the normal test winding at different rotor position. (μ=10%, ρ=0.99995)

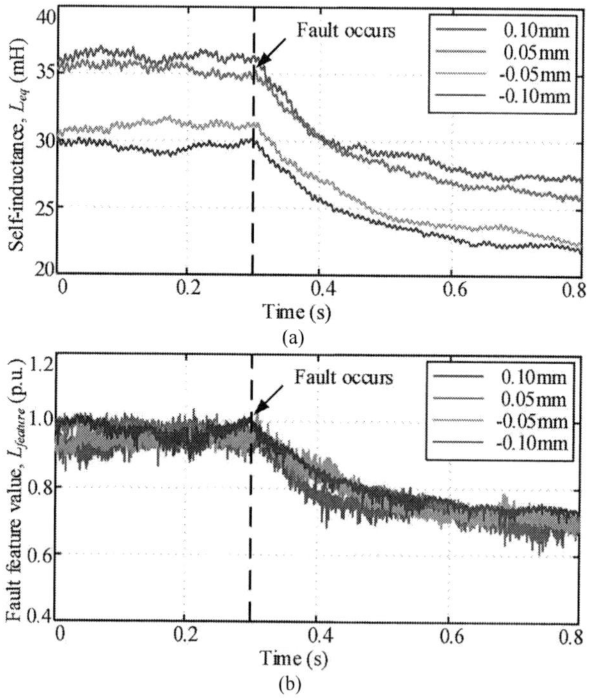

Fig. 10. Diagnosis results of the test winding at different rotor position. (a) estimated self-inductance L_{eq}, (b) compensated results $L_{feature}$. (μ=10%, ρ=0.99995)

To test the proposed method under situations where the rotor is levitated eccentrically, the self-inductance of the normal winding is estimated with the FFRLS algorithm when the rotor is suspended at different displacements. Fig. 9 illustrates the relationship between the estimated self-inductance of the normal test winding and the displacement of the rotor at the direction of the test winding.

An LUT is built up according to Fig. 9. Fig. 10 compares the original results and the results compensated with the LUT. Obviously, when the compensation is not employed, as shown in Fig. 10 (a), the displacement of the rotor makes it difficult to determine the threshold of the ITSC fault detection L_{th}. The compensated results $L_{feature}$, as shown in Fig. 10 (b), are much more robust compared to L_{eq}. Hence, the accuracy and robustness of the proposed method is improved by the compensation method based on the LUT.

III. Conclusion

In this paper, a diagnosis method based on the LMS algorithm is proposed for the ITSC fault of the AMB system. The ITSC fault of AMB's winding is modeled to obtain the characteristic of the ITSC fault. The self-inductance is selected as the signature of the ITSC fault, and the LMS algorithm is adopted to calculate this signature. Furthermore, the FFRLS algorithm, a recursive form of LMS algorithm with forgetting factor is applied to the online diagnosis of the ITSC fault. In addition, an open-loop LUT-based compensation method is introduced as well to reduce the influence of the fluctuation of the rotor and improve the accuracy of the proposed diagnosis method. Experiments under various situations are carried out to validate the proposed method. The experimental results confirm the accuracy and the robustness of the proposed method. The proposed scheme enables the handling of the ITSC fault such as ITSC fault-tolerant control and improves the reliability of the AMB system.

References

[1] R. Gouws and G. van Schoor, "A comparative study on fault detection and correction techniques on active magnetic bearing systems," *Proc. IEEE AFRICON*, 2007, pp. 1-10.

[2] M. Sahinkaya, M. Cole, and C. Burrows, "Fault detection and tolerance in synchronous vibration control of rotor-magnetic bearing systems," *Proc. Inst. Mech. Eng.*, Part C, 2001, 215(12): 1401-1416,.

[3] M. Cole, P.S. Keogh, M. Sahinkaya, and C. Burrows, "Towards fault-tolerant active control of rotor–magnetic bearing systems," *Control Eng. Pract.*, 2004, 12(4): 491-501,.

[4] Z. Peng, Y. He, Q. Lu, and F. Chu, "Feature extraction of the rub-impact rotor system by means of wavelet analysis," *J. Sound Vib.*, 2003,259(4):1000-1010,.

[5] N. Tsai, Y. King, and R. Lee, "Fault diagnosis for magnetic bearing systems," *Mech. Syst. Signal Pr.*, vol. 23, no. 4, pp. 1339-1351, 2009.

[6] M. Aenis, E. Knopf, and R. Nordmann, "Active magnetic bearings for the identification and fault diagnosis in turbomachinery," *Mechatronics*, 2002,12(8): 1011-1021.

[7] A. Gandhi, T. Corrigan, and L. Parsa, "Recent Advances in Modeling and Online Detection of Stator Interturn Faults in Electrical Motors," *IEEE Trans. Ind. Electron.*, 2011, 58(5):1564-1575

[8] J. Faiz, A. H. Exiri, and H. Nejadi-Koti, "Current-based inter-turn short circuit fault modeling in permanent magnet synchronous machine using magnetic equivalent circuit model," in *IEEE 10th International Conference on Compatibility, Power Electronics and Power Engineering (CPE-POWERENG)*, 2016, pp. 265-270.

[9] M. Drif and A. J. M. Cardoso, "Stator Fault Diagnostics in Squirrel Cage Three-Phase Induction Motor Drives Using the Instantaneous Active and Reactive Power Signature Analyses," *IEEE Trans. Ind. Informat*, 2014,10(2):1348-1360, May.

[10] L. Shan, H. Chen, J. Luan, and J. Li, "Application of adaptive forgetting factor RLS algorithm in target tracking," in *2017 Chinese Automation Congress (CAC)*, 2017, pp. 1838-1843.

[11] R. P. Vieira, R. Z. Azzolin, and H. A. Grundling, "Parameter identification of a single-phase induction motor using RLS algorithm," in *2009 Brazilian Power Electronics Conference (COBEP2009)*, 2009, pp. 517-523.

[12] H. Zhang, S. Gong, and Z. Dong, "On-line parameter identification of induction motor based On RLS algorithm," in *2013 International Conference on Electrical Machines and Systems (ICEMS)*, 2013, pp. 2132-2137.

[13] J. She, M. Xie, D. Li, M. Wu, Z. Liu, and W. Zhang, "A VFF-RLS Method of Inertia Identification for PMSM," in *2019 IEEE Conference on Control Technology and Applications (CCTA)*, 2019, pp. 942-943.

Research Progress of Fretting Wear under Electrical Contact Conditions

Minhao Zhu [1,2], Xinlong Liu [2], Jinfang Peng [1], Zhenbing Cai [1]
[1] Key Laboratory of Advanced Technology of Materials, Ministry of Education, Southwest Jiaotong University, Chengdu, 610031, China
[2] School of Mechatronics and Vehicle Engineering, East China Jiaotong University, Nanchang, 330013, China
E-mail: zhuminhao@swjtu.cn Tel: 13808007296

Abstract—**There are a large number of connecting interfaces between electric and electronic equipment and the key parts of the systems. The connectors are affected by external force, electricity, heat and other factors, the contact interfaces are prone to fretting wear, often cause electrical connection damage and failure. Therefore, it is very urgent and necessary to study the fretting wear mechanism and protection mechanism under the condition of electrical contact. Many researches have been carried out on fretting wear behavior, failure mechanism and influencing factors of electrical connectors at home and abroad, and important progress has been done. On the basis of summarizing the latest achievements of fretting wear theory, this paper reviews the research on fretting wear of electrical contact from the following aspects: 1) Fretting wear mechanism under electrical contact conditions; 2) Research on electrical contact materials; 3) The influence of environmental factors; 4) Theoretical calculation and finite element simulation of electrical contact; and the latest research progress of the author's team had been introduced. Finally, the development trends of fretting wear under electrical contact conditions are prospected.**

Index Terms— **Electrical contact, Fretting wear, Damage mechanism, Influence factors, Research status, Development trend.**

I. INTRODUCTION

Electrical contact refers to a state produced by the contact of 2 conductive materials due to electricity. It is an indispensable part of all electrical components and power electronic lines. Any electronic system must flow current from one conductor to another through the contact between the two conductors. The reliability of the interface between the current-carrying elements of an electrical/electronic device for the purpose of ensuring the continuity of the circuit is extremely important, and failure of the contact points may affect the reliable operation of the entire system. The stability and life of electrical contact and other reliability related research content are introduced. Therefore, electrical contact is an important interdisciplinary subject involving electricity, physics, chemistry, machinery, materials and tribology. Dr. Williamson, an international famous electrical contact scholar, has repeatedly stressed: "no reliable electronic connection, advanced electronics cannot be developed", , which shows the importance of electrical contact to the development of modern science[1].

Due to the fact that electronic equipment is difficult to avoid being subjected to various harsh environments in the process of use, such as external shock vibration, magnetostriction, pulse, etc., the relative movement with the very smaller relative displacement amplitude is unavoidable at the connection of electronic components, referred to as "fretting". This kind of fretting phenomenon brings extremely deadly harm to the electrical contact performance of electrical components. Wear and corrosion induced by fretting on the contact surface mostly exist at the same time. Fretting wear will cause the materials transfer and wear of conductive metal, and produce pollutants, which will cause the fluctuation and rapid rise of contact resistance, thus reducing the reliability of the connector (see Fig.1)[2-3]. Contact resistance is a basic, important parameter for electrical connections [4], which is closely related to the material, structure, manufacturing process and working environment. The results show that the coupling effect of fretting wear, oxidation and corrosion is the most important factor leading to the failure and degradation of electrical contact interface[5].

In view of this phenomenon, a lot of research has been carried out at home and abroad. With the development of industry, the understanding of electrical contact fretting damage is gradually deepened, which can be roughly divided into two stages. The first stage is the basic discipline establishment stage from the early 20th century to the 1950s. The phenomenon of "fretting corrosion" was first proposed by experts in the field of electrical contact in 1911[6]; In 1956, contact resistance was used to monitor fretting damage in steel samples [7]. But it was not until eight years later that Fairweather [8] elaborated that fretting was the main cause of instability and serious damage of electrical components.

However, the role of fretting was not widely regarded as an important influencing factor until 1974 that Bock and Whitley clarified its importance [9]. Since then, systematic research on electronic connector [10, 11] and automobile connector system [12, 13] has been studied. The second stage is from the 1960s to the present. In 1964, Fairweather found that fretting caused instability in telephone relays and switches [14]. However, fretting has not been paid enough attention as an important factor leading to electrical connection failure. With the development of science and technology and the need of engineering practice, people pay more and more attention to the harmful effect of electrical contact fretting damage. Since 1986, the National Natural Science Foundation of China (NSFC) has been supporting electrical contact research projects. Researchers have done a lot of work on influencing the fretting wear mechanism of electrical connectors, involving materials, coating types and thickness, contact force, displacement amplitude, frequency, temperature, relative humidity, lubrication, atmosphere, etc., and trying to continuously improve the service life of electrical contacts [15].

In this paper, based on the latest development of fretting wear theory, the main research progress of fretting wear under electrical contact conditions is reviewed.

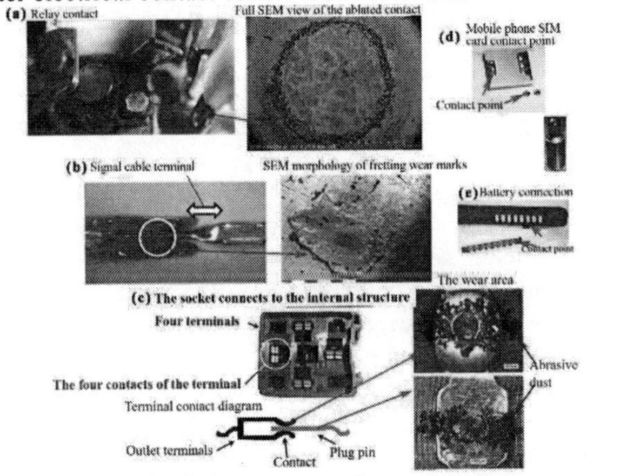

Fig. 1. Common electrical components and parts where fretting occurs

II. THE LATEST PROGRESS OF FRETTING WEAR THEOY

Literature [16, 17] is the most systematic summary in the research field of fretting wear in the past two decades. Fretting, different from that of another friction motion of sliding and rolling, is the relative movement between contact surface with very smaller displacement amplitude (usually in micron scale) which produced by mechanical vibration, electromagnetic vibration, fatigue load, and flow induced vibration and thermal cycle. And the contact surface usually is "static" in name. In general, fretting damage is divided into fretting wear, fretting fatigue and fretting corrosion. In the early stage, the boundary between fretting corrosion and fretting wear was blurred, or even mixed, but now there is a relatively clear definition, as shown in Fig.2. Fretting wear usually refers to the fretting caused by the external vibration of the contact pair due to the relative displacement of the contact surface, and the contact pair itself only bears local contact load or is subjected to fixed prestress (Fig. 2(a)). Fretting fatigue refers to the relative displacement of the contact surface caused by the deformation of the contact pair under the external alternating fatigue stress (Fig.2(b)). Fretting corrosion refers to the fretting damage occurring in electrolytes or other corrosive media (such as seawater, acid rain, corrosive atmosphere, etc.), in which corrosive action dominates (Fig.2(c)).

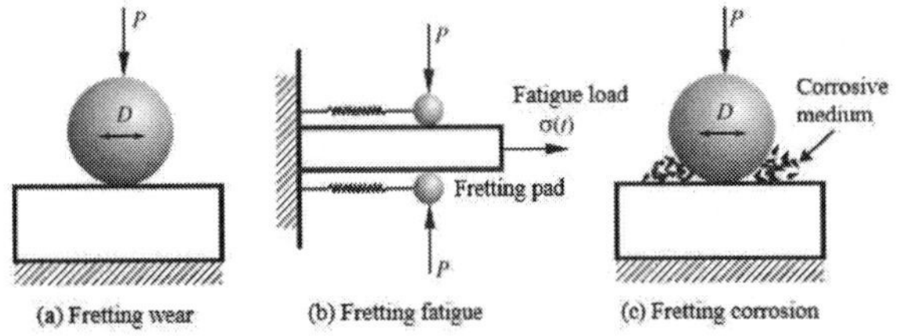

Fig. 2. Usual classification of fretting damage

Under the contact mode of ball/flat, fretting wear can be divided into four relative motion modes: tangential, radial, torsional and rotational fretting. Fretting damages in practical engineering is often a complex relative motion composed of several fretting modes. Fig.3 shows the classification of fretting wear in practical engineering. To study the complex fretting damages, the complex relative motion needs to be decoupled into single or composite fretting wear modes. At present, the research in the field of electrical contact mainly focuses on the tangential fretting wear mode, and the experimental simulation of complex relative motion has not been reported.

The main contents of fretting wear theory include:

(1) The running behavior and damage mechanisms of fretting wear are strongly affected by normal load, displacement amplitude, contact material properties, in addition, contact stiffness, frequency and service environment also have important effects.

(2) There are only three types of load-displacement curves in all fretting cycles (linear and elliptic curves correspond with partial slip; parallelogram curves correspond with gross slip).

(3) There are three regimes in the fretting running states: partial slip regime (PSR), slip regime (SR) and mixed fretting regime (MFR, which is the most dangerous regime for crack initiation and must have the relative motion state change during fretting). Generally, the all load-displacement curves in shape of parallelogram is defined as slip regime, and the all load-displacement curves in state of partial slip is defined as a partial slip regime (Fig.4). In the evolutionprocess of the fretting cycles, the transition

from partial slip to gross slip, from gross slip to partial slip, or even multiple inter-transformations will occur. This fretting running state is defined as the mixed fretting regime (Fig.4). The MFR usually corresponds to the occurrence of strong plastic deformation, work hardening and particle detachment at the contact interface. Crack initiation and propagation are the main characteristics of the MFR, and this regime often corresponds to the shortest service life.

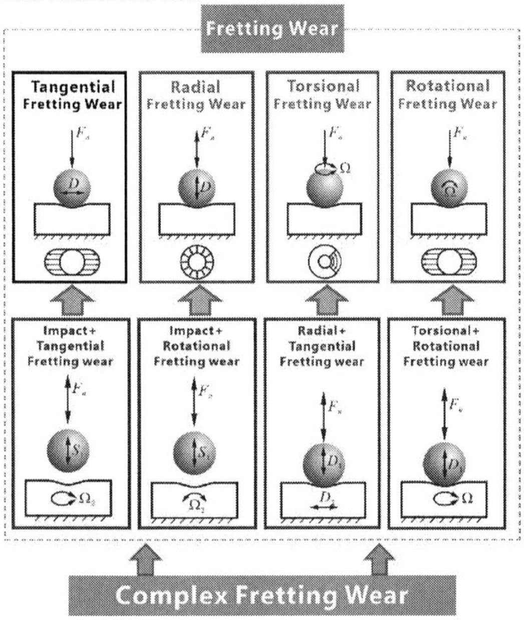

Fig. 3. Decoupling schematic of complex fretting wear

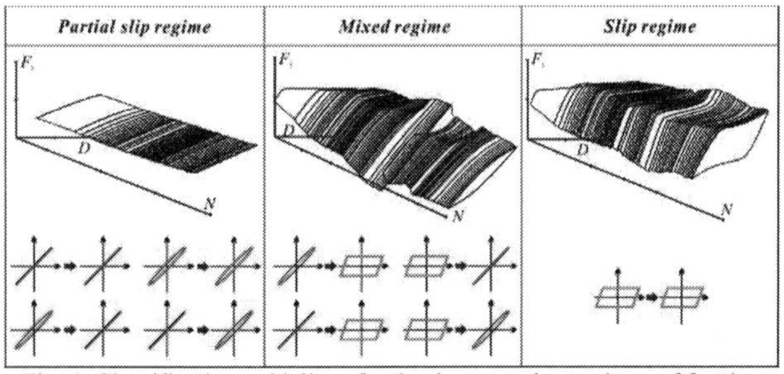

Fig. 4. Classification guidelines for the three running regimes of fretting wear

(4) Two types of fretting maps (running condition fretting map, RCFM and material response fretting maps (MRFM)) can be used to describe the fretting characteristics of the materials, so as to reveal the damage mechanism of the contact interface (Fig.5).

(5) During the process of fretting wear, the highest friction coefficient usually occurs in the MFR, which is related to the severe plastic deformation of the friction interface.

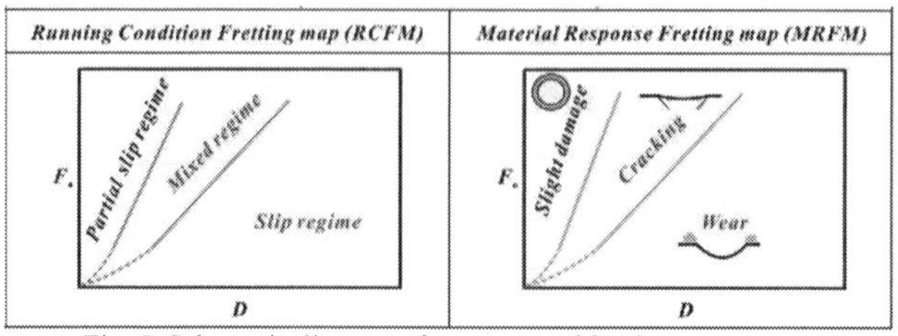

Fig. 5. Schematic diagram of two types of fretting maps

(6) The fretting wear mechanism involves all four basic wear mechanisms, and the final wear scars usually show abrasive wear, oxidation wear and fatigue wear (delamination) mechanisms, while the adhesive wear mainly appears in the early stage of the test.

(7) In the contact zone of fretting wear, there is usually a competitive relationship between local wear and fatigue. In the MFR, the crack growth rate is greater than the wear rate, and the damage is mainly cracking. In the SR, the wear rate is higher than the crack growth rate, and the micro-cracks are removed by wear, and the damage is manifested as a deep pit.

(8) The extent of fretting damage (such as oxidation, white layer, etc.) can be determined by the parameter T ($T = A \cdot \tau \cdot \delta \cdot \cos\theta$), that is, the damage is proportional to the shear stress and relative displacement of the contact interface, where A is the material and environment related constant, θ is the angle factor related to the composite fretting wear.

(9) Tribological oxidation plays an important role in the contact interface of fretting wear. Oxidative debris is not easy to discharge from the contact interface, which is beneficial to reduce the friction coefficient. The extent of tribological oxidation is closely related to the relative humidity in the environment. The higher the humidity is, the more serious the tribological oxidation occurs, because the friction hydration reaction occurs at the interface.

According to the above theoretical summary, the following protective strategies can be proposed for fretting wear:

(1)Eliminating slip regime and mixed fretting regime: According to the two types of fretting maps, the wear and crack formation mainly occur in the SR and MFR, while the damage in the PSR is slight. It can be considered to reduce the relative motion amplitude between the contact interfaces to make the fretting run in the partial slip state as far as possible. There are three specific methods: A) Increasing the normal load can transform the fretting running regime from the SR and MFR to the PSR, but this may cause a sharp increase in local stress and increase the risk of local fatigue damage; B) Reducing the tangential stiffness: in certain displacement amplitude, the increase of the flexibility of contact zone means that the enhancement of the elastic deformation ability of the contact zone. Thus, some or all of the fretting amplitude can be balanced by the elastic deformation of contact zone, resulting in the state of elastic coordination, namely running in the PSR (it is like wearing socks to keep your feet from getting worn out). C) Changing the structure design: can sometimes receive unexpected fretting damage protection effect, because the pressure distribution, topological contact mode or contact stiffness of the contact surface may be changed accordingly, thus changing the fretting running regimes.

(2) Increasing the strength of the contact surface: Through various surface engineering techniques, the surface strength of materials can be improved. A large number of studies have shown that most of the surface modification techniques are very effective for fretting protection in the PSR and MFR, which greatly improves the resistance to fretting fatigue cracking. The lifetime of the surface treatment layer is closely related to its thickness and contact condition. For example, when the maximum contact stress depth is similar to the thickness of the surface modified layer or coating, cracks are prone to form in the interface zone and lead to early failure.

(3) Reducing the coefficient of friction: The most common way is to take to reduce the friction coefficient through lubrication, however, for the semi-solid and liquid lubrication, due to the high contact pressures, it is difficult to form effective hydrodynamic lubrication film. On the contrary, in the MFR or the edge of PFR close to the MFR, due to the existence of microcracks, fluid lubricants may be squeezed into the crack tip, thus promoting the crack propagation. Therefore, the lubrication plays a harmful role at here. The preparation of solid lubrication coating with surface treatments can reduce the friction coefficient of the material surface and obtain a good anti-fretting wear effect.

(4) Selecting and matching of materials: Reasonable selection and matching of materials contact pairs play an important role in mitigating fretting damage. Under the condition that the structural strength can be satisfied, the material with better flexibility and large deformation can effectively absorb the relative slip, so as to reduce the surface damage. Selecting materials with high hardness and fatigue strength can effectively reduce fretting wear and inhibit the initiation and propagation of cracks. In addition, after reasonable selection of materials, the use of a small amount of third body generated in the initial stage of fretting for self-lubrication can also achieve the purpose of reducing the further damage of materials. Since one of the advantages of surface engineering is that a layer of special material can be constructed on the matrix material, surface engineering can be used to achieve reasonable material matching between contact pairs.

III. FRETTING WEAR MECHNISM AND CONTACT RESISTANCE UNDER ELECTRICAL CONTACT CONDITIONS

A. Influencing Factors of Fretting Wear Under Electrical Contact Conditions

A large number of studies have shown that the fretting behavior of contact interface is the most important cause of contact damage in electrical connections [18, 19].The transfer of interface materials, wear, oxidation corrosion, and debris accumulation induced by fretting will cause the change of friction coefficient and electrical contact resistance (ECR)[20]. Therefore, researchers have proposed a variety of models for the effect of fretting on ECR [21, 22]. The debris caused by fretting wear is entered into the contact interface, causing the change of ECR and reducing the conductive performance of the contact pair[23].

Noh et al. [24] studied the effect of the grain size of the third body on the electrical degradation and failure of the copper contact on the fretting interface, and the results show that the failure of the contact is caused by the formation of a dense oxide layer. Park[25] analyzed the evolution law of ECR rise caused by interface wear and oxidation under intermittent fretting wear and continuous wear conditions, and proved that fretting cycle and frequency have significant influence on fretting wear performance of connectors.

Ren et al. [26, 27] studied the fretting damage behavior of gold-plated copper alloy contacts in the temperature range of 25~125°C. The attenuation mechanism of fretting wear property of contacts under different current amplitudes was explored, and the typical characteristics of intermittent failure rate variation of interface during fretting cycles were analyzed. The results show that the main role of the gold plating layer is to soften and lubricate the contact surface. According to the variation of contact resistance, surface analysis technique and the principle of thermal balance, the performance attenuation mechanism of contact at different temperatures is proposed. Other studies have shown that the coupling effect of temperature and humidity has a more complex effect on the electrical contact performance of the connectors [28].

Damage under electrical contact conditions is related to vibration frequency, slip amplitude, contact load, current magnitude, temperature, wear time and other parameters[29-31]. According to the study of Hannel et al. [32], the debris is mainly produced in the slip regime, accompanied by oxidative wear, which leads to the increase of value of ECR. Therefore, the amplitude of transition displacement δ_t from partial slip regime to slip regime can be determined by the fretting wear experiments. When the amplitude of the fretting displacement of the electrical contact is greater than δ_t, the electrical contact performance is better, otherwise is poor. At the same time, the function relationship between the durability of electrical contact properties and the amplitude of fretting was proposed, and a functional model of long period stable running of ECR has obtained [33].

B. Study on Fretting Wear Mechanism of Electrical Contact

The fretting action is not easy to be detected in the early stage [34], Because electrical connector failure is usually associated with damage to the contact area caused by arcing and melting. The damage makes it very difficult to identify the wear products (debris and oxide accumulated on the contact surface). Fig.6 shows the typical fretting damage morphologies of electrical contact.

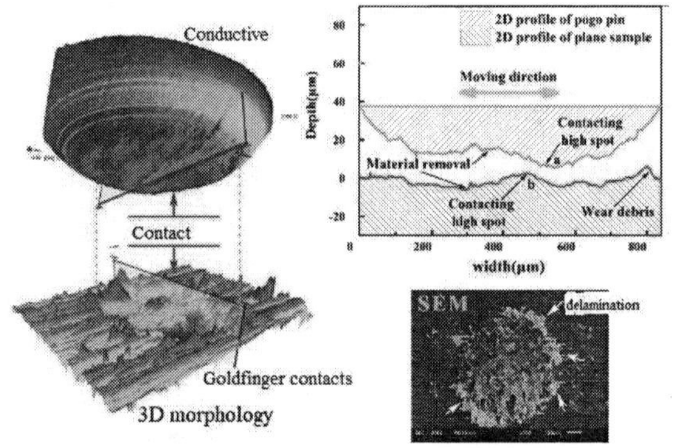

Fig.6. Fretting damage morphologies of electrical contacts

As shown in Fig.7, the author's team systematically studied the fretting wear behavior of pure copper in three different regimes under electrical contact conditions. The main results are as follows [17]:

(1) Effect of normal load (Fig.8)

When the normal load was 2N, the fretting run in the SR, and the friction coefficient presented the highest, which corresponded to the high and unstable ECR. With the increase of normal load, the fretting running regime changed to the direction of PSR, the friction coefficient decreased, and the ECR decreased significantly and stably.

(2) Effect of displacement amplitude (Fig.9)

When the normal load was constant, the displacement amplitude increased and the fretting running state changed from partial slip to gross slip. In the PSR (D=10 μm), the friction coefficient was low and stable, and the corresponding ECR was also stable. In the MFR (D=30 μm), the friction coefficient increased and kept at a high level, and the ECR also increased, showing a rapid rise in the late stage of the test. However, when the fretting entered into the SR (D=45 μm), the friction coefficient was at a high level. After the running-in stage, the contact resistance increased rapidly with the rapid increase of the friction coefficient and fluctuated greatly (which was closely related to the friction oxidation occurring at the same time), indicating that the contact interface was seriously damaged. This study shows that the critical value (threshold) δ_t for significant change in ECR was 20μm, that is, below 20μm, the ECR was in a low flat state.

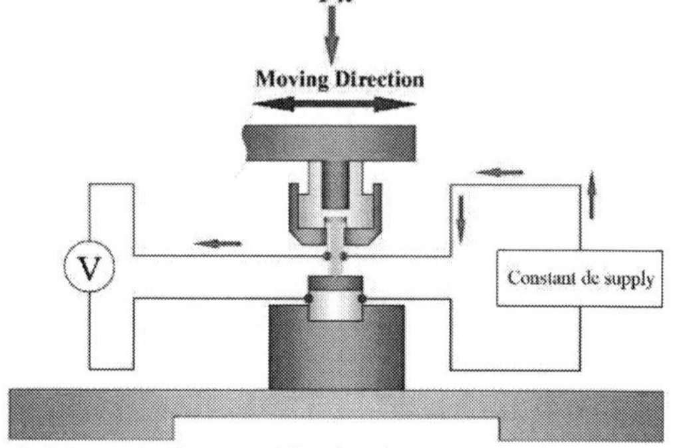

Fig. 7. Schematic diagram of the electric contact fretting wear test rig

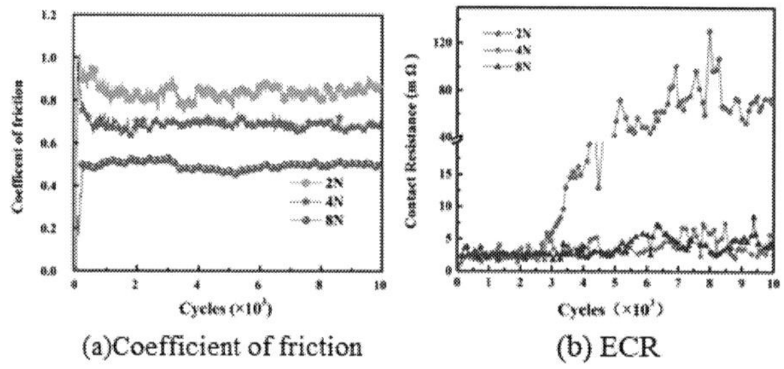

Fig. 8. Coefficient of friction and contact resistance under different normal loads: F_n=2, 4, 8N; D=40μm; I=0.02A; f=2Hz

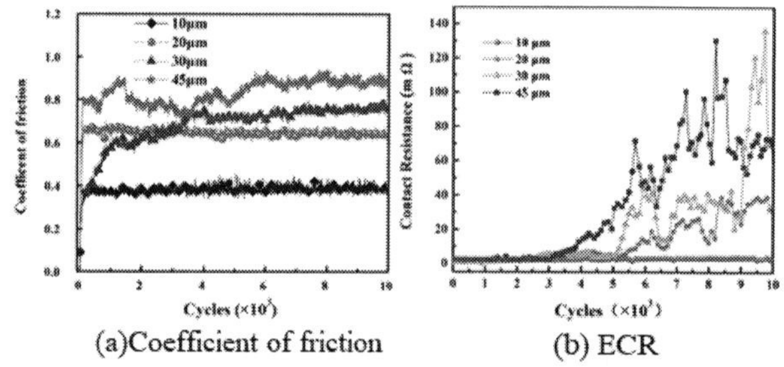

Fig. 9. Coefficient of friction and contact resistance under different displacement amplitudes: F_n=2N; D=10, 20, 30, 45μm; I=0.02A; f=2Hz

(3) Effect of fretting cycle (Fig.10)

The fretting damage increased with the increase of cycles. In the early stage of the test, there is a running-in stage, and the friction coefficient and ECR were both low due to the influence of surface pollution and adsorption films. At the N=10^3 cycles, the wear scars were elliptic, and the damage mechanism was mainly plastic deformation, abrasive wear and adhesive wear. At the N=5×10^3 cycles, the wear scars were irregular and round, and the phenomenon of delamination (fatigue wear mechanism) began to appear. At the N=10^4 cycles, the wear scars were approximately round deep pits, and the wear debris began to generate and accumulate in the contact zone, and the oxidative wear can continue.

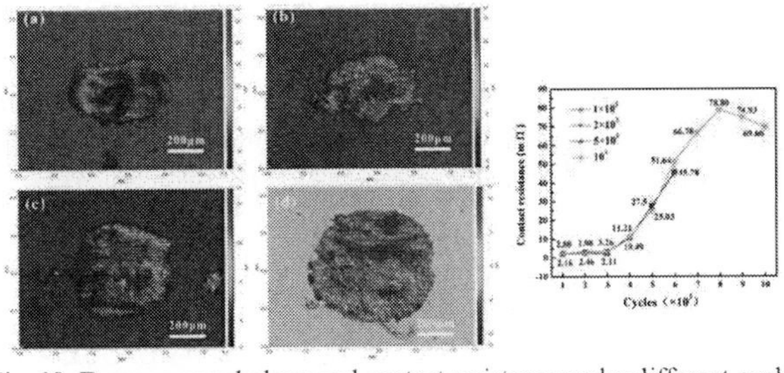

Fig. 10. Damage morphology and contact resistance under different cycle cycles (F_n=2N; D=45μm; I=0.02A; f=2Hz): a) $N_1=10^3$; b) $N_2=2\times10^3$; c) $N_3=5\times10^3$; d) $N_4=10^4$

(4) Effect of current intensity (Fig.11)

When the amplitude of the fretting displacement is less than the threshold δ_t, the ECR was less affected by the test parameters. However, when greater than δ_t, the fretting was in the gross slip state, which produced a large amount of debris, and easily acted tribological interaction with the moisture in the humid air, forming insulating oxidative products and leading to the rapid rise of ECR. As can be seen from Fig.11, the ECR decreased with the rise of current. When the current reached 1A, the ECR was basically in a low flat state and slightly increased in the later stage of the test. This is because of the high current, the oxide film formed in the contact zone is easy to be broken down or even melted by the current, resulting in a sharp decline in ECR. At the same time, under high current, the contact points are easy to heat, the material is easier to enter the plastic state, the damage presents adhesive wear, and the friction coefficient is therefore at a higher level.

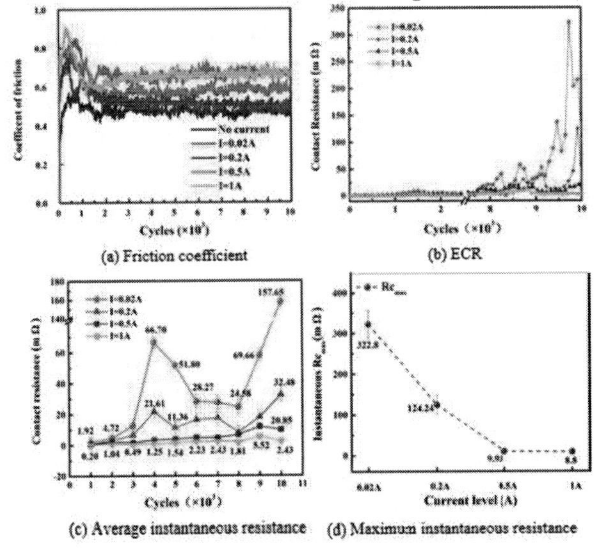

Fig.11. Coefficient of friction and contact resistance under different current intensities: F_n=2N; D=45μm; I=0, 0.02, 0.2, 0.5, 1A; f=2Hz

(5) Effect of surface roughness (Fig.12)

ECR, maximum instantaneous resistance $R_{c,max}$ and total average resistance $R_{c,average}$ are proportional to the roughness, that is, the rougher the contact surface, the worse its electrical contact performance. For the R_{a4}=0.116 μm, the average resistance showed a downward trend in the late fretting wear test, which may be the reason why the contact surface was gradually flattened and the contact area increased.

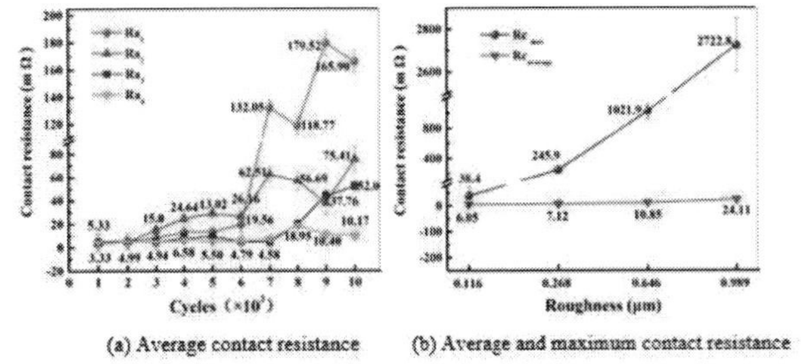

Fig.12. Contact resistance under different surface roughnesses (F_n=2N; D=45μm; I=0.02A; f=2Hz): Ra_1=0.989 μm, Ra_2=0.646 μm, Ra_3=0.268 μm, Ra_4=0.116 μm

C. Contact Resistance Theory

Electrical connectors must contact reliably. Generally, the occurrence of electrical contact failure is judged by whether the ECR is stable and maintained at a certain threshold [35]. The contact surface is uneven on the microscopic scale, and for all electrical contact materials, the actual contact area is only a small part of the theoretical contact area under a certain normal load (Fig.13)[36]. These areas of actual contact are called a-spots. The current must contract as it passes through these a-spots, causing changes in the ECR. The a-spot is the essential cause of the contraction resistance caused by the current passing through the actual contact area, and the ECR is an important parameter to evaluate the electrical contact performance. Lau *et al.* [37] introduced the "high-dimensional theory" of ECR to calculate the contact resistance of local shrinkage of finite length and finite transverse size in conductive current channels, and further extended and verified the classical theory of "a-spot" contact resistance of Holm and Timsit [38, 39]. If the current passing through the contact of the conductor increases or the ECR increases, the instantaneous temperature rise will inevitably occur in the contact area. When the temperature reaches the softening point and melting point of the contact conductor material, the a-spot and its nearby metals will soften and melt [40].

ECR is closely related to the surface state of the connector, such as surface roughness and oxide film thickness [41]. Narayanan *et al.* believed that the fretting damage was affected by the coupling effect of many factors, including frequency, amplitude, temperature, humidity, contact load, current, *etc.* ECR could maintain a certain stable period in the early stage, and fluctuated greatly in the later stage due to abrasive wear and oxidative wear [42]. Wan *et al.* [43] took copper plated contact as the object, obtained the degradation process of ECR during the whole life cycle, and determined the conditions and failure mechanism of intermittent failure caused by fretting frequency and displacement amplitude.

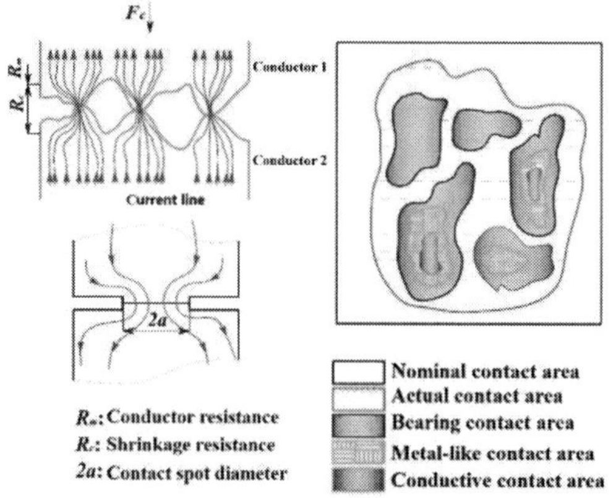

Fig.13. Schematic of current shrinkage and actual contact area

In summary, the research on fretting wear under electrical contact conditions mainly focuses on the fretting wear mechanism and ECR evolution law, and the key factors affecting the service life of the connector are identified with the goal of stable and durable running of ECR.

IV. Research on Electrical Contact Materials

With the continuous improvement of the performance requirements of electric contact materials, they are required to anti-fretting wear and oxidation resistance, corrosion resistance, arc erosion resistance and fusion welding resistance at the same time, so the research and development of new electrical contact materials has been the focus of research and development direction [44]. Various kinds of copper, silver, cobalt nickel alloy material and various excellent surface treatment and interface lubrication technologies were introduced, and many important research results were also obtained.

A. Electrical Contact Meterials

The results show that the alloys with higher hardness appear lower fretting wear, but the ECR is usually higher than that of other similar alloys [45]. Adding cobalt, nickel, tungsten, chromium, zirconium and other elements to the matrix material can greatly increase its hardness and reduce the resistivity, improve the wear and oxidation resistance of the alloy material, and prolong the service life [46]. Literature [47] summarizes the characteristics and existing problems of several common Cu-based, silver-based and gold-based electrical contact materials, and analyzes the current carrying tribological behavior, current carrying friction and wear mechanism, computational simulation research and existing problems of electric contact materials under different contact loads, currents and sliding speeds. In the future, it is suggested to develop excellent new electric contact materials and strengthen the research on the friction and wear behavior and failure mechanism of electric contact systems under multi-factor coupling. Some studies have verified that a lead-free solder has better wear and corrosion resistance as an electrical contact surface material through fretting wear tests [48]. By designing different Cu/C ratios, the authors obtained the optima l copper content of of electrical contact fretting wear performance [49].

B. Electrical Contact Surface Treatment Technologies

Surface treatment techniques can improve the electrical conductivity, wear and corrosion resistance of contacts. Generally, copper alloy is used as the substrate material for surface treatment, which mainly includes ion implantation, laser strengthening, deformation texture, electroplating, *etc*., and the coating materials include nickel, gold, silver or composite coatings [50].

On the one hand, the comprehensive service performance of electrical contact materials can be improved by surface treatment technologies, and on the other hand, the cost of precious metal materials can be saved.

Through electric contact fretting wear experiments at different stages and combined with the analysis of ECR, wear morphology and friction oxidation products, some studies have discussed the fretting failure mechanism of contacts, studied the influence of coating thickness and contact pressure on service life, and proposed the optimal material matching based on the analysis of life model [51]. Under fretting conditions, the electrical contact life of contact materials is related to contact pressure, coating thickness, corrosion time and so on [52]. Other studies show that the AgCu10 alloy after ion implantation greatly reduced the generation of wear particles, reduced the metal transfer during the wear process, reduced the oxidation pollution of wear particles, so as to improve the wear resistance and corrosion resistance of the alloy surface, and improve the electric contact fretting wear performance [53]. The service life of the electrical connector can also be extended by constructing the texture on the surface of the material, and it is closely related to the density, diameter and other geometric parameters of the texture [54]. When laser texture was prepared on tinned copper surface [55], the formation time of debris was related to ECR, and the results showed that laser interference pattern reduced the friction coefficient and ECR.

C. Interface Lubrication

Good interface lubrication has a significant effect on maintaining low contact resistance and friction coefficient. Therefore, some scholars have carried out research on the development of interface lubrication and self-lubricating materials.

Due to the low speed sliding characteristics of layered solid lubrication materials such as MoS_2 and WS_2, the feasibility and applicability of solid lubrication materials are mainly studied by analyzing the changes of ECR and friction coefficient [56]. Kang *et al.* [57] reported the mechanism of influence of lubrication on electrical contact fretting wear performance of tin-plating copper alloy, and found that the interface lubrication can effectively maintain low ECR at room temperature, while the influence of lubrication on contact resistance at high temperature was not obvious. Ag/C composite coating was prepared on the surface of copper base material, and polyaniline (PANI) was introduced as a conductive grease additive. The protective effect of boundary lubrication on the composite coating was studied [58]. Some studies have prepared GO films by electrophoretic deposition and investigated the electrical contact fretting performance under different surface roughness conditions. The results show that GO films can significantly reduce ECR, friction coefficient and wear volume [59].

Above results indicate that the introduction of interfacial lubrication technologies are also one of important research direction for improving the electric contact fretting wear performance.

V. STUDY ON THE INFLUENCE MECHANISM OF ENVIRONMENTAL FACTORS

A. Effect of dust/particles

It is found that the external environmental factors have a significant influence on the electrical contact fretting wear and failure of the connectors [60], including various dust, particulate matter and pollutants [61, 62] in the air, which are one of the important reasons for the increase of ECR and failure [63]. Based on this, fretting wear tests were carried out with mica, gypsum, fiber and square solution as the third body particles on the surface of the contact pairs. The results showed that the particles involved in the contact caused fluctuations in ECR, which caused abrasive wear, led to the detachment of the coatings, and accelerated the failure of electrical contact [64, 65]. The influencing factors of electrical connection reliability were analyzed from the aspects of contact surface pollutants, ECR and fretting effect of electrical connectors, and the relationship between relevant parameters in fretting and electrical contact reliability and the failure mechanism were revealed [66, 67]. According to the study of Zhou *et al.* [68], the surface exposed to air for a long time generated discrete corrosion products with island distribution, and the initial contact resistance was higher than the normal standard in the fretting process. When the island corrosion products were gradually worn away in the fretting process, the contact resistance also gradually decreased from runout to effective value. However, when wear debris is accumulated near the fretting scar, or when dust particles are embedded between the contact surfaces, or when the corrosion products in the contact zone are squeezed more compact due to fretting, the ECR increased, or even opened circuit, resulting in electrical contact failure. It is also found that the ECR of the contact surface with dust particles is much higher than that with soot. However, the introduction of soot and dust particles can alleviate the fretting wear of the samples [69].

The above studies show that environmental factors have a significant impact on the performance of electrical contact fretting wear. Tribological design can be carried out from the aspects of interface cleaning, protection, lubrication and oxidation resistance of materials to improve the electrical contact reliability of connectors.

B. Effect of temperature, humidity and oxygen content in the air

It is found that the temperature, humidity, oxygen content and other parameters in the air have significant effects on the electrical contact performance of the connectors. In this regard, Mengotti[70] studied the fretting corrosion of PCB board connectors, and analyzed the chemical composition and microstructure of the connection sites, as well as environmental factors such as humidity, temperature, temperature cycling and vibration.

The authors' team [71, 72] designed fretting wear tests of electrical contact materials under different temperature and humidity environment, and found that the contact interface intense oxidation wear caused a sharp rise in ECR. With the rise of temperatures, a large amount of oxide layer accumulated and separated the two contact surfaces, resulting in "broken circuit". The formation and accumulation of interfacial oxides are the main causes of electrical contact failure (Fig.14). However, relatively high humidity has a significant effect on maintaining a stable ECR. This is because the relatively high humidity environment has a certain lubrication effect on the contact interface, reducing the friction coefficient. At the same time, it plays a condensation effect on the debris between the interface, greatly reducing the probability of current contraction and thus reducing the ECR (Fig.15).

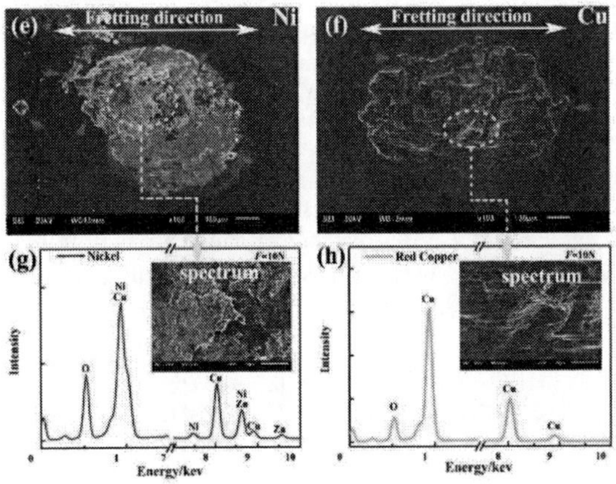

Fig.14 Morphologies of contact zones in high temperatures

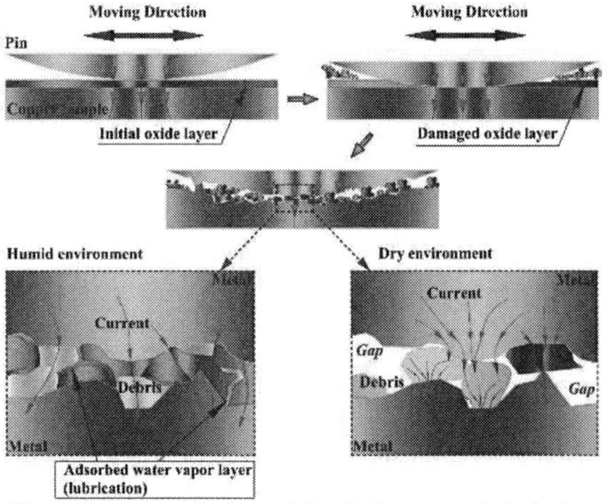

Fig.15 Damage mechanisms of electrical contact pairs in dry/wet environments

The fretting wear characteristics of copper/brass electrical contacts in different oxygen-containing environments were further investigated [73, 74], and it was found that the oxidation was the most severe in the environment of 30% O_2, and the wear mechanisms of copper under different oxygen environments were mainly manifested as oxidation, material transfer and delamination (Fig.16).

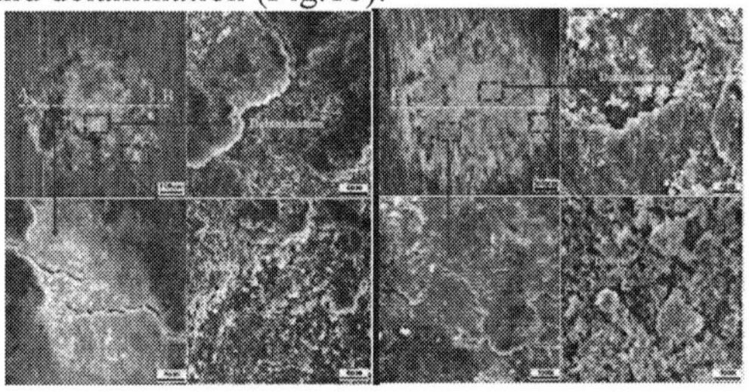
(a)10%O_2 (b)30% O_2

Fig.16 Damage morphologies contact zones under different oxygen levels

Fretting corrosion behavior in air and vacuum environment was studied by simulating vacuum environment [75]. The results showed that the electrical contact service life of tin coating contacts was prolonged with the increase of vacuum degree. It can be seen that the effect of oxidation corrosion on the failure behavior of electrical contact is very significant.

It can be seen that the oxygen content and humidity in the air can significantly affect the electrical contact fretting wear performance. It is of great significance to maintain good electrical contact by setting the appropriate environment oxygen content and humidity.

VI. THEORETICAL CALCULATION AND FINITE ELEMENT SIMULATION OF ELECTRICAL CONTACT

Theoretical calculation and numerical analysis are of great help to the analysis of fretting wear mechanism, ECR evolution law and life prediction, saving time and material cost.

Sawada *et al.* [76] analyzed the functional relationship between contact shape, load and ECR, as well as the relationship between shrinkage resistance and film resistance and ECR, and verified them through experiments. Mashimo *et al.* [77] raised the results of two-dimensional computational model simulation to three-dimensional space, and studied the ECR changes caused by particle generation, oxidation behavior in the contact zone and migration behavior between the connect interface. Some scholars also use the model based on equivalent resistance network to calculate the resistance distribution. In general, conjugate gradient method is used to solve the equation. The simulated resistance distribution is compared with the experimental results at last, which is in good agreement with the experimental results. This model can well describe the resistance variation trend and peak height caused by fretting corrosion. Masui *et al.*[78] simulated and calculated the electrostatic field distribution in the contact zone by establishing the electrostatic field analysis model of contact resistance, which was basically consistent with the fretting corrosion test results.

Fouvry *et al.*[79, 80] proposed a transfer function method for predicting the durability of electrical contact ECR, which aims to extrapolate the material study to practical connector applications. The "equivalent durability of contact resistance" parameter was introduced, and the fretting and vibration amplitudes were connected by the transfer function [81]. Combined with the fretting and connector vibration tests of Au-Co and Sn coating structures, it is shown that the basic fretting durability data can be used to approximate the vibration durability of connectors. The fretting damage degradation of electrical contact was simulated. The thermoelectric coupling effect was considered in the study, and the simulation model of ECR variation under different oxide components was established [82]. The finite element random distribution technique is used to simulate the distribution of copper oxide in different contact zones. Majid determined the elastic deformation effect under microscopic contact by superimposing the normal deformation caused by itself and adjacent contact points. The study shows that the elastic deformation effect under low contact pressure was an important factor[83]. Mohiuddi *et al.* [84] used the Holm-Kirschstein equation, Simmons equation and Kovacs equation to fit the experimental data of the conductivity of carbon nanotube enhanced PEEK, and determined the contact resistance and thickness of the tunnel effect layer.

The above numerical analysis method and the finite element simulation has achieved certain results. However, due to the variety and complexity of connector types and structures, the use environment varies greatly. Therefore, the current finite element simulation is only for the operation conditions and application environment of specific connectors, combined with fretting experiments to carry out some failure analysis, and put forward the design improvement strategy. However, the mechanisms of electrical contact fretting wear under multi-factor coupling cannot be simulated. Thus, how to improve the applicability and accuracy of finite element simulation model is one of the important development directions in the future.

VII. SUMMARY

Many achievements have been made in the research of electrical contact fretting wear, but limited by the test conditions, many studies are not deep and systematic enough. From the perspective of future development, there are the following development trends:

(1)Research on the basic theory of fretting wear: Significant progress has been made in the theory of fretting wear. In the field of electrical contact, it is necessary to develop standardized test rig and methods to make the research of different scholars comparable. In addition, the theory of fretting wear maps are extended to the field of electric contact fretting wear.

(2)New electrical contact materials: Emphasis should be placed on introducing new technologies and new materials to improve the technological level, especially adding different alloying elements or reinforcing materials to improve the comprehensive performance of electrical contact materials, and developing advanced material preparation and processing technologies to improve the machining performance of electrical contact materials and reduce costs.

(3)Surface treatment technology: The effectiveness of surface engineering technologies have been fully recognized, and the next step should be strengthened to introduce new surface treatment technologies and means to improve the anti-fretting wear and anti-fretting corrosion properties of electrical contact materials.

(4) Numerical simulation and life prediction: Materials Genome Initiative (MGI) project has been widely recognized, and it is necessary to strengthen high-throughput experiments and high-throughput simulation calculations under electrical contact conditions, and establish a service performance database in the field of electrical contact. The finite element numerical simulation has made great progress, so it is necessary to strengthen the application in the field of electrical contact, and strengthen the service life model building and life prediction research of electrical connectors, so as to serve the needs of the industry.

REFERENCES

[1] J.G.Zhang, Vigorously developing electrical contact science -- an important interdisciplinary science [J]. China Mechanical Engineering,1999(09):14-16+3.

[2] Ren Wanbin, Jiao Yubin, Zhai Guofu. Review on Fretting Wear of Electrical Connectors [J]. Journal of M echanical and Electrical Components, 2010, 30(1):11.

[3] Park Y W, Narayanan T, Kang Y L. Fretting corrosion of tin-plated contacts [J]. Tribology International, 2008, 41(7): 616-628.

[4] Xu Jun, Li Kun. Research on Contact Resistance of Electrical Contact [J]. Electrical Materials, 2011(1): 10-14.

[5] Du Yong-guo, ZHANG Wei-jun, HU Jun-Sui. Electrical Contact and Electrical Contact Materials (I) [J]. Electrical Materials, 2005(02): 44-46.

[6] Eden E M, Rose W N, Cunningham F L. The endurance of metals [C]. Proceedings of the Institution of Mechanical Engineers, 1911, 4: 839-974.

[7] Fenner A J. Fretting, corrosion and its influence on fatigue failure [C]. Inter. Conf. Fatigue of Metals, Inst. Mech. Eng., London, 1956. 1956: 11-17.

[8] Fairweather A. Development of resistance and microphone noise at a disturbed contact [C]. Proc. 2nd Int. Symp. on Electrical Contact Phenomena, Graz, Technische Hochschule, Graz, May 1964. 1964: 316-319.

[9] Bock E M, Whitley J H. Fretting corrosion in electric contacts [C]. Electric Contacts-1974, 1974: 128.

[10] Lee A, Mamrick M. Fretting corrosion of tin-plated copper alloy[C]. IEEE Transactions on Components, Hybrids, and Manufacturing Technology, 1987, 10(1): 63-67.

[11] Schneegans O. Fretting degradation of tin-plated contacts studied by means of a new electrical cartography technique based on atomic force microscopy [C]. Proc. International Conf on Electrical Contact Phenomena, 1998. 1998: 187- 193.

[12] Klungtvedt K, Braunovic M. Effect of intergranular cohesion on the intermittency of automotive headlamp switch contacts [C]. Electrical Contacts, 2001. Proceedings of the Forty-Seventh IEEE Holm Conference on. IEEE, 2001: 56-72.

[13] Mottine J, B. Reagor. Investigation of fretting corrosion at dissimilar metal interfaces in socketed IC device applications [C]. IEEE transactions on components, hybrids, and manufacturing technology, 1984, 7(1): 61-68.

[14] Fairweather A, Lazenby F, Marr D. Development of resistance at a disturbed contact: with special reference to silver, copper and nickel-silver [J]. Proceedings of the Institution of Electrical Engineers, 1976, 123 (5) : 465-471.

[15] Yu Da-zhao, Liu Qi, Feng Li-Jun, Cheng Xian-bin. A review of fretting corrosion damage behavior and mechanism of electrical connectors [J]. Surface technology,2021,50(12):233-245.

[16] Zhu Minhao, CAI Zhenbing, Zhou Zhongrong. Fretting Wear Theory [M]. Beijing: Science Press, 2021

[17] Zhu Minhao, CAI Zhenbing, Zhou Zhongrong. Fretting Wear under Special Conditions [M]. Beijing: Science Press, 2022

[18] Tristani L, Zindine E M, Boyer L, et al. Mechanical

modeling of fretting cycles in electrical contacts [J]. Wear, 2001, 249 (1) : 12-19.
[19] Malucci R D. Fretting corrosion degradation, threshold behavior and contact instability [electrical contacts] [C]. Electrical Contacts, 2003. Proceedings of the Forty-Ninth IEEE Holm Conference on. IEEE, 2003: 2-15.
[20] Antler M . Survey of Contact Fretting in Electrical Connectors [J]. IEEE Transactions on Components Hybrids & Manufacturing Technology, 1985, 8(1):87-104.
[21] Bryant M D. Assessment of fretting failure models of electrical connectors [C]. Electrical Contacts, 1994. Proceedings of the Fortieth IEEE Holm Conference on Electrical Contacts. IEEE, 1994: 167-175.
[22] Boyer L, Tristani L. A model for the contact resistance evolution during a fretting test [C]. Proc. Int. Conf. Electrical Contacts. 2000: 457-463.
[23] Saka N, Ming J L, Suh N P. The-role of tribology -in electrical-contact-phenomena [J]. Wear, 1984, 100(1-3): 77-105.
[24] Noh H J, Kim J W, Lee S M, et al. Effect of grain size on the electrical failure of copper contacts in fretting motion [J]. Tribology International, 2017, 111: 39-45.
[25] Park Y W. Effect of intermittent fretting on corrosion behavior in electrical contact[J]. Wear, 2010, 268: 353-360.
[26] Ren W, Wang P, Fu Y, et al. Effects of temperature on fretting corrosion behaviors of gold-plated copper alloy electrical contacts [J]. Tribology International, 2015, 83: 1- 11.
[27] Ren W , Wang P , Song J , et al. Effects of current load on wear and fretting corrosion of gold-plated electrical contacts [J]. Tribology International, 2014, 70:75-82.
[28]Kong Z, Huang R, Xu L. Investigation of electrical properties and morphology of several contact materials after cyclic damp-heat and sliding [C]. 26th International Conference on Electrical Contacts (ICEC 2012).
[29] M, Antler. Electrical effects of fretting connector contact materials: A review- Science Direct [J]. Wear, 1985, 106(1-3): 5-33.
[30] Fu R, Choe S Y B, Jackson R L, et al. Vibration-Induced Changes in the Contact Resistance of High Power Electrical Connectors for Hybrid Vehicles [J]. IEEE Transactions on Components, Packaging, and Manufacturing Technology, 2012, 2(2): 185-193.
[31] Han D W, Kim H K. Effect of normal forces on fretting corrosion of tin-coated electrical contacts[J]. Microelectronics Reliability, 2017, 79: 321-327.
[32] Hannel S, Fouvry S, Kapsa P, et al. The fretting sliding transition as a criterion for electrical contact performance[J]. Wear, 2001, 249(9):761-770.
[33] Laporte J, Fouvry S, Alquier O. Prediction of electrical contact resistance failure of Ag/Ag plated contact subjected to complex fretting-reciprocating sliding [J]. Wear, 2017, 376-377: 656-669.
[34] E. Carvou, N. B. Jemaa. Time and level analysis of contact voltage intermittences induced by fretting in power connector. Electrical contacts-2007, the 53rd ieee holm conference on. IEEE, 2007: 211-215.
[35] Fouvry S, Jedrzejczyk P, Chalandon P, et al. From fretting to connector vibration tests: a "transfer function" approach to predict electrical contact resistance endurance [C]// the International Conference on Electrical Contacts. VDE, 2014.
[36] Kraytsberg A, Auinat M, Ein-Eli Y. Reduced contact resistance of PEM fuel cell's bipolar plates via surface texturing [J]. Journal of Power Sources, 2007, 164(2): 697- 703.
[37] Lau Y Y, Tang W. A higher dimensional theory of electrical contact resistance [J]. Journal of Applied Physics, 2009, 105 (12) : 124902.
[38] Holm, R. Electric contacts: Theory and application /-4th ed [M]. Springer, 1979.
[39] Timsit R S, IEEE Trans. Compon. Packag. Technol. 22, 85\u00011999.
[40] Taheri P, Hsieh S, Bahrami M. Investigating electrical contact resistance losses in lithium-ion battery assemblies for hybrid and electric vehicles [J]. Journal of Power Sources, 2011, 196(15): 6525-6533.
[41] Crinon E, Evans J T. The effect of surface roughness, oxide film thickness and interfacial sliding on the electrical contact resistance of aluminium [J]. Materials Science &Engineering A, 1998, 242(1-2): 121-128.
[42] Narayanan T, Park Y W, Kang Y L. Fretting-corrosion mappingof tin-plated copper alloy contacts [J]. Wear, 2007, 262 (1-2) : 228-233.
[43] Ren Wanbin, Wang Peng, Ma Xiaoming, Xue Shengjun, Cui Li, Zhai Guofu. Intermittent Failure of Contact Induced by fretting. Tribology, 2013, 33(04): 382-387.
[44] CAI Jiangnan, Yang Fanger, Qiu Kaifeng, Chen Lesheng, Zheng Xiaohua. A novel electrical contact material Ag/La_(1-X)Sr_xCoO_3 [J]. Electronic Components and Materials, 2014, 33(07): 1-3.
[45] Beloufa A. Conduction degradation by fretting corrosion phenomena for contact samples made of high-copper alloys [J]. Tribology International, 2010, 43(11): 2110-2119.
[46] Lin X Y, Xu L J, Shao Y C, et al. Research on Fretting Resistance and Fretting Wear Property of Ni-Au Contact Pair [C]. 2011 IEEE 57th Holm Conference on Electrical Contacts (Holm), 2011: 1-6
[47] Xie Bohua, Ju Pengfei, Geely, et al. Advances in tribology of electrical contact Materials. Tribology, 2019, 39(5):13.
[48] Ji W, Pecht M G. Contact resistance and fretting corrosion of lead-free alloy coated electrical contacts [J]. IEEE Transactions on Components & Packaging Technologies, 2006, 29(2): 402-410.

[49] Liu X L, Cai Z B, XA Qian. Fretting wear behavior of brass/copper-graphite composites as a contactor material under electrical contact[J]. International Journal of Mechanical Sciences, 2020, 184: 105703.
[50] Zheng Ji, Zhu Jia, Ouyang Jinlin. Study on Cu-based Electrical Contact Composites [J]. Tribology, 1995(01): 19- 28.
[51] Ito T, Sawada S, Hattori Y, et al. Microscopy Study of Fretting Corrosion Caused by the Tin Plating Thickness[C]// Electrical Contacts, 2008. Proceedings of the 54th IEEE Holm Conference on. IEEE, 2008.
[52] Laporte J, Perrinet O, Fouvry S. Prediction of the electrical contact resistance endurance of silver-plated coatings subject to fretting wear, using a friction energy density approach [J]. Wear, 2015, 330-331:170-181.
[53] Wang Ermin, Wang Xiaozhen, He An-Li, ZHANG Tong-He, Liang Hong. Study on Improvement of fretting Wear of Electrical Contact by ion Implantation [J]. Journal of Aeronautical Materials, 2000(03): 49-55.
[54] Esteves M, Ramalho A, Ramos F. Electrical performance of textured stainless steel under fretting [J]. Tribology International, 2017, 110: 41-51.
[55] Souza, N, Muecklich, et al. Wear debris and electrical resistance in textured Sn-coated Cu contacts subjected to fretting[J]. Wear An International Journal on the Science & Technology of Friction Lubrication & Wear, 2015.
[56] Y.Watanabe. High-speed Sliding Characteristics of Cu-Sn- based Composite Materials containing lamellar Solid Lubricants by contact resistance studies. Wear, 2008, 264(7): 624-631.
[57] Narayanan T, Park Y W, Kang Y L. Fretting corrosion of lubricated tin plated copper alloy contacts: Effect of temperature [J]. Tribology International, 2008, 41(2): 87-102.
[58] Chen J, Xia Y, Hu Y, et al. Tribological performance and conductive capacity of Ag coating under boundary lubrication [J]. Tribology International, 2017, 110: 161-172.
[59] Gong Congyu, Liu Shanbang, Cao Zhongqing, Nie Yuchen, CAI Zhenbing. Microelectrodynamic contact properties of graphene oxide films prepared by electrophoretic deposition [J]. Surface Technology, 2021, 50(08): 227-236.
[60] Zhou Y, Yang L, Hao W, et al. Electrical Contact Behavior of Several Typical Materials in Dust at Static and Dynamic Conditions[C]. Electrical Contacts (HOLM), 2010 Proceedings of the 56th IEEE Holm Conference on. IEEE, 2010.
[61] Wang H. Experimental study on the influence of hard particles and organic pollutants on the reliability of electrical contacts [D]. Beijing University of Posts and Telecommunications,2010.
[62] Lv Y. Study on the influence of environmental pollutants on the reliability of electrical contact and electronic equipment protection [D]. Beijing University of Posts and Telecommunications,2016.
[63] Zhou Yilin, Zhang Jigao. Study on Natural Corrosion and Electrical Contact Characteristics of Contact Gold Plated Materials [J]. Electronic Components and Materials, 2001(04): 11-13+48.
[64] Ma Aili, Zhou Yilin. Influence of Mechanical Properties of Mica Particles on Reliability of Electrical Contacts [J]. Mechanical and Electrical Components, 2009, 29(04):14-19.
[65] Liu Hongda. Influence of Several Typical Components in Dust on Electrical Contact Reliability [D]. Beijing University of Posts and Telecommunications,2011.
[66] He Zhanping. Research on Influence and Method of Fretting Factors in Electrical Contact Fault [D]. Beijing University of Posts and Telecommunications.
[67] Feng Cuifeng. Contaminant characteristics and formation mechanism of electrical contact fault surface of failed mobile phone [D]. Beijing University of Posts and Telecommunications,2010.
[68] Zhou Yilin, Zhang Jigao. Microelectrodynamic Characteristics of Corrosion Materials on the Surface of Common Contact Materials [J]. Electronic Components and Materials, 2002(04):9-11.
[69]Wang Peng-guan, CAO Zhong-qing, Chen Hai-chao, PENG Jin-fang, CAI Zhen-bing. Influence of Soot and Dust Particles on Fretting Wear Properties of Red Copper in Electric Contact. Materials for Mechanical Engineering, 2019, 43(12): 12-18.
[70] Mengotti E, Duarte L I, Pippola J, et al. Fretting corrosion: Analysis of the failure mechanism for low voltage drives applications. Microelectronics Reliability, 2014, 54(9): 2109-2114.
[71] Liu Xinlong, CAI Zhenbing, Liu Shanbang, Peng Jinfang, Zhu Minhao. Effect of Temperature on Electrocontact fretting properties of Nickel and Copper. The Chinese Journal of Nonferrous Metals, 2018, 28(5): 944-954.
[72] Xin-Long Liu, Zhen-Bin Cai, Min-Hao Zhu, Et al. Effect of elevated temperature on fretting wear under electric contact[J]. Wear, 2017, S 376 -- 377:643-655.
[73] Xin-Long Liu, Zhen-Bin Cai; Shan-Bang Liu; Xiao-Jun Xu; Min-Hao Zhu. Effect of different atmospheres on the electrical contact performance of electronic components under fretting wear., Journal of Physics D: Applied Physics, 2018, 51: 155302
[74] He Li-Ping, PENG Jin-fang, CAI Zhen-bing, ZHU Min-hao. Tribology, 2022, 42(4): 680-689.
[75] Song J. Fretting corrosion behavior of electrical contacts with tin coating in atmosphere and vacuum [J]. Wear, 2019, 426:1439.
[76] Sawada S, Shimizu K, Shimada S, et al. Prediction of electrical contact resistance of tin-plated and silver-plated terminals [J]. SEI Technical Review, 37 (71) : 2010-43.
[77] Mashimo K, Ishimaru Y. Computational modeling and

analysis of a contact pair for the prediction of fretting dependent electrical contact resistance [C]. Electrical Contacts (Holm), 2011 IEEE 57th Holm Conference on. IEEE, 2011: 1-6.
[78] Masui S, Sawada S, Tamai T, et al. Measurement of contact resistance distribution in fretting corrosion track for the tin plated contacts [J]. IEICE Technical Report, 2011, 110:1- 6.
[79] Fouvry S, Jedrzejczyk P, Chalandon P, et al. From fretting to connector vibration tests: a" transfer function" approach to predict electrical contact resistance endurance [C]. ICEC 2014; The 27th International Conference on Electrical Contacts; Proceedings of. VDE, 2014: 1-6.
[80] Fouvry S, Laporte J, Perrinet O, et al. Fretting wear of low current electrical contacts: Quantification of electrical endurance [C]. Electrical Contacts, 2017 IEEE Holm Conference on. IEEE, 2017: 1-11.
[81] Fouvry S, Jedrzejczyk P, Chalandon P. Introduction of an exponential formulation to quantify the electrical endurance of micro-contacts enduring fretting wear: Application to Sn, Ag and Au coatings [J]. Wear, 2011, 271(9-10): 1524-1534.
[82]Lee K Y, Jeong D K, Kim J H. Simulational study of electrical contact degradation under fretting corrosion [J]. Tribology international, 2011, 44 (12) : 1651-1658.
[83] Bahrami M, Yovanovich M M, Culham J R. Thermal contact resistance at low contact pressure: Effect of elastic deformation [J]. International Journal of Heat and Mass Transfer, 2005, 48(16): 3284-3293.
[84] Mohiuddin M, Hoa S V. Estimation of contact resistance and its effect on electrical conductivity of CNT/PEEK composites [J]. Composites Science and Technology, 2013, 79: 42-48.

Dr. Min-hao ZHU became a professor of Southwest Jiaotong University in 2001, and became a Chief Professor of Southwest Jiaotong University in 2015. He has become a Yangtze River Scholar Professor of Ministry of Education of China in 2014, has acquired a National Natural Science Fund for Distinguished Young Scholars of NSFC in 2010.
Over the past two decades, he has mainly studied on fretting wear, fretting fatigue, tribology of railway and surface engineering. His doctoral dissertation was won a prize of the Author of National Excellent Doctoral Dissertation of China in 2005. He won a SNECMA AWARD in 2003 (SNECMA is a French company, and a famous aerospace engine manufacturing company in the word). He as the second honorees received an award of the Second Prize of National Natural Science of China in 2006, which was on study of fretting wear. He has issued 3 books, more than 400 papers and was licensed 40 patents of China.

8th International Conference on Reliability of Electrical Products and Electrical Contacts, November 18-20, 2022 **(Invited Paper)**

A Wiener-based Degradation Model Considering Four-Source Uncertainties and Nonlinearity

Bokai Zheng, Xuerong Ye*, Guofu Zhai

Harbin Institute of Technology, Harbin, 150000, China
*E-mail: xuelai1981@163.com Tel: 13946177562

***Abstract*—Uncertainty and nonlinearity are two nonnegligible features in product degradation processes. However, most Wiener-based degradation models only involve part of them, which undermines the goodness of fit and the accuracy of reliability assessment. To confront this problem, this paper proposes a Wiener-based degradation model jointly considering four-source uncertainties (including the initial performance characteristic (IPC) variability, unit-to-unit variability, temporal uncertainty, and measurement errors) and nonlinearity. The analytical forms of the failure time distribution and reliability function of the proposed model are derived. Then, statistical inference is developed based on the maximum likelihood estimation (MLE) method. Furthermore, we demonstrate the effectiveness and superiority of the proposed model via a simulation study.**

***Index Terms*— Degradation data analysis, Wiener process, four-source uncertainties, nonlinearity.**

I. INTRODUCTION

Since some high-reliable products are exposed to harsh environments (such as high voltage, high temperature, and salt atmosphere) for a long time during their operations, some of their performance characteristics may gradually deteriorate. A soft failure occurs when one of the performance characteristics exceeds the preset failure threshold. Degradation data analysis that establishes a degradation model based on observed degradation data to describe the product degradation paths is widely applied to assess the reliability of high-reliable products due to its high time efficiency and appreciable estimation accuracy [1, 2].

Thanks to the ability to model the nonmonotonic degradation processes with stochastic dynamics [3, 4], the Wiener process stands out among a large number of degradation models and becomes a preferred option for degradation data analysis. The basic Wiener process is expressed as:

$$X(t) = X_0 + \beta t + \sigma_B B(t), \tag{1}$$

where $X(t)$ is the performance characteristic value at time t; X_0 is the IPC; β denotes the degradation rate; σ_B represents the diffusion parameter; $B(\cdot)$ refers to the Brown motion.

Affected by factors such as the dispersion of processing technology and the precision of test equipment, uncertainty is a critical feature that exists in product degradation processes [5]. In general, in addition to the temporal uncertainty that has involved in the Wiener process ($\sigma_B B(t)$ captures the temporal uncertainty in Eq. (1)), there are other three-source uncertainties (including initial performance characteristic (IPC) variability, unit-to-unit variability, and measurement errors) responsible for the uncertainty of degradation processes [6, 7], and many studies have been devoted to introducing these three-source uncertainties into the basic Wiener process to extend its applicability. Both the IPC variability and unit-to-unit variability originate from the heterogeneity among products and are generally modelled by randomizing the IPC X_0 and degradation rate β in the Wiener process, respectively. For example, Hao et al. [7] assumed that the IPC followed a normal distribution to capture the IPC variability. Li et al. [8] described the unit-to-unit variability by normalizing the degradation rate. Measurement errors are caused by the precision of test equipment, which is usually described by a normal distribution with zero mean and assumed to be independent at different measurements [8]. In addition to the uncertainty, nonlinearity is another considerable feature commonly appearing in product degradation processes. Accordingly, many studies optimize the basic Wiener process by introducing nonlinearity. An effective method proposed by Whitmore [9] replaces t in Eq. (1) with a time transform function $\Lambda(t)$, which is also applied in the work of Pan et al. [10].

From the above analysis, the four-source uncertainties, including IPC variability, unit-to-unit variability, temporal uncertainty, measurement errors, and nonlinearity are critical features that need to be considered simultaneously in Winner-based degradation modelling. However, most degradation models cover part of the above features, which motivates our study.

This paper develops a new Wiener process that takes the four-source variability, including IPC variability, unit-to-unit variability, temporal uncertainty, and measurement errors, and nonlinearity into account. Meanwhile, the reliability function is derived, and the parameter estimation method based on maximum likelihood estimation (MLE) is provided.

The remaining of this paper is arranged as follows. Section II introduces the proposed degradation model and deduces its corresponding failure time distribution and reliability function. Section III develops statistical inference. Section IV applies a simulation study to demonstrate the effectiveness and superiority of the proposed model.

II. Degradation Modelling and Reliability Function Derivation

The proposed model involves four-source variability (including IPC variability, unit-to-unit variability, temporal uncertainty, and measurement errors) and nonlinearity is expressed as:

$$X(t) = X_0 + \beta\Lambda(t) + \sigma_B B(\Lambda(t)) + \varepsilon, \tag{2}$$

where $X_0 \sim N(\mu_0, \sigma_0^2)$ to capture the IPC variability; $\beta \sim N(\mu_\beta, \sigma_\beta^2)$ to describe the unit-to-unit variability; $\sigma_B B(\Lambda(t))$ is applied to denote the temporal uncertainty; ε stands for measurement errors. It is assumed to follow $N(0, \sigma_\varepsilon^2)$ and be independent at different measurements. For simplicity, the proposed model in Eq. (2) is denoted as M0.

Let D_f represent the failure threshold. The lifetime T is defined as the first time that the real performance characteristic exceeds D_f, i.e.,

$$T = \inf\{t \mid X_0 + \beta\Lambda(t) + \sigma_B B(\Lambda(t)) \geq D_f\}. \tag{3}$$

According to the study of Pan et al. [10], the conditional probability density function (PDF) of the lifetime with fixed X_0 and β can be expressed as

$$f_T(t \mid X_0, \beta) = \frac{D_f - X_0}{\sqrt{2\pi\sigma_B^2 \Lambda^3(t)}} \exp\left(\frac{-(D_f - X_0 - \beta\Lambda(t))^2}{2\sigma_B^2 \Lambda(t)}\right) \frac{d\Lambda(t)}{dt}. \tag{4}$$

Based on the law of probability, we can integrate X_0 and β out of Eq. (4):

$$f_T(t) = \int_{-\infty}^{+\infty} \left(\left(\int_{-\infty}^{+\infty} \left(f_T(t \mid X_0, \beta) f_{X_0}(X_0) \right) dX_0 \right) f_\beta(\beta) \right) d\beta, \tag{5}$$

where $f_{X_0}(X_0)$ and $f_\beta(\beta)$ are the PDF of X_0 and β, respectively.

The integral result is:

$$f_T(t) = \left(\frac{\mu_\beta \sigma_0^2 + (\sigma_\beta^2 \Lambda(t) + \sigma_B^2)(D_f - \mu_0)}{S} \right) \times \exp\left(\frac{-(D_f - \mu_0 - \mu_\beta \Lambda(t))^2}{2S} \right) \frac{1}{\sqrt{2\pi S}} \frac{d\Lambda(t)}{dt}, \tag{6}$$

where $S = \sigma_0^2 + \sigma_\beta^2 \Lambda^2(t) + \sigma_B^2 \Lambda(t)$.

The cumulative distribution function (CDF) of lifetime is:

$$F_T(t) = \int_0^t f_T(u)\, du, \tag{7}$$

which can be calculated by the numerical integration method.

The reliability function can be calculated as:

$$R(t) = 1 - F_T(t). \tag{8}$$

III. Statistical Inference

Assume that N samples are observed in a degradation test. All samples share the same test schedule and are tested k times. X_{ij} is used to denote the observed degradation data at the jth measurement of the ith sample, where $i = 1, 2, \ldots, N$ and $j = 1, 2, \ldots, k$. The jth measurement is performed at time t_j, and $\Lambda(t_j)$ is simplified as Λ_j. Let $\mathbf{X}_i$ and $\mathbf{\Lambda}$ represent $(X_{i1}, X_{i2}, \ldots, X_{ik})'$ and $(\Lambda_1, \Lambda_2, \ldots, \Lambda_k)'$, respectively. According to Eq. (2), $\mathbf{X}_i$ follows a multivariate normal distribution, and its mean vector $\boldsymbol{\mu}$ and covariance matrix are $\boldsymbol{\Sigma}$ are:

$$\begin{cases} \boldsymbol{\mu} = \mu_0 \mathbf{e}_{k,1} + \mu_\beta \mathbf{\Lambda} \\ \boldsymbol{\Sigma} = \sigma_0^2 \mathbf{e}_{k,k} + \sigma_\beta^2 \mathbf{\Lambda}\mathbf{\Lambda}' + \sigma_B^2 \mathbf{\Omega} + \sigma_\varepsilon^2 \mathbf{I}_k \end{cases}, \tag{9}$$

where $\mathbf{e}_{k,1}$ and $\mathbf{e}_{k,k}$ are a k-dimensional column vector and square matrix with all-ones elements, respectively; $\mathbf{I}_k$ is a k-dimensional identity matrix;

$$\mathbf{\Omega} = \begin{bmatrix} \Lambda_1 & \Lambda_1 & \cdots & \Lambda_1 \\ \Lambda_1 & \Lambda_2 & \cdots & \Lambda_2 \\ \vdots & \vdots & \ddots & \vdots \\ \Lambda_1 & \Lambda_2 & \cdots & \Lambda_k \end{bmatrix}.$$

Let $\mathbf{b}$ refer to the unknown parameter set in $\Lambda(t)$. Then, the unknown parameters in Eq. (2) can be summarized as $\boldsymbol{\theta} = (\mu_0, \sigma_0^2, \mu_\beta, \sigma_\beta^2, \sigma_B^2, \sigma_\varepsilon^2, \mathbf{b})$. Based on Eq. (9), the log-likelihood function for $\boldsymbol{\theta}$ can be expressed as:

$$l(\boldsymbol{\theta}) = -\frac{kN}{2}\ln(2\pi) - \frac{N}{2}\ln(|\boldsymbol{\Sigma}|) - \frac{1}{2}\sum_{i=1}^{N}\left((\mathbf{X}_i - \boldsymbol{\mu})' \boldsymbol{\Sigma}^{-1} (\mathbf{X}_i - \boldsymbol{\mu}) \right). \tag{10}$$

Maximizing $l(\boldsymbol{\theta})$ is equivalent to minimizing $-l(\boldsymbol{\theta})$, which is nonlinear programming and can be solved by the interior-point method [11].

IV. Simulation Study

This section compares the proposed model with its four limiting cases via a simulation study to demonstrate the effectiveness and superiority of the proposed model. Since all Wiener processes contain temporal uncertainty, the four limiting cases ignore IPC variability, unit-to-unit variability, measurement errors, and nonlinearity, respectively. The first limiting case denoted by M1 fails to capture the IPC variability, and its expression is shown as:

$$\mathrm{M1}: X(t)=\beta\Lambda(t)+\sigma_B B(\Lambda(t))+\varepsilon. \quad (11)$$

The second liming model denoted by M2 does not consider the unit-to-unit variability, whose expression is:

$$\mathrm{M2}: X(t)=X_0+\beta_f\Lambda(t)+\sigma_B B(\Lambda(t))+\varepsilon, \quad (12)$$

where β_f is a constant denoting the degradation rate. The third limiting model is represented by M3 and ignores measurement errors, which can be expressed as:

TABLE I
PARAMETER ESTIMATION AND AIC RESULTS FOR CANDIDATE MODELS

Model	μ_0	σ_0	μ_β	σ_β	σ_B	σ_ε	b	AIC
M0	1.5098	0.2944	0.1985	2.9506×10^{-2}	2.0051×10^{-2}	1.9931×10^{-2}	0.5006	-2.2354×10^{5}
M1	-	-	0.1988	2.9520×10^{-2}	2.1264×10^{-2}	1.9833×10^{-2}	0.5002	-
M2	1.5097	0.2950	0.1995	-	3.5113×10^{-2}	1.8469×10^{-2}	0.4993	-2.1905×10^{5}
M3	1.5100	0.2952	0.1600	3.2778×10^{-5}	7.7675×10^{-2}	-	0.5559	-2.0253×10^{5}
M4	1.5127	0.2952	2.8363×10^{-2}	3.9468×10^{-6}	4.0162×10^{-2}	5.1356×10^{-3}	-	-1.7404×10^{5}

$$\mathrm{M3}: X(t)=X_0+\beta\Lambda(t)+\sigma_B B(\Lambda(t)). \quad (13)$$

As shown in Eq. (14), the last liming model represented by M4 does not consider nonlinearity and let $\Lambda(t) = t$.

$$\mathrm{M4}: X(t)=X_0+\beta t+\sigma_B B(t)+\varepsilon \quad (14)$$

Based on M0 (the proposed model), the degradation data $\mathbf{W}$ of 1000 samples are generated, where $\Lambda(t)$ is assumed to be a power-law function, i.e., $\Lambda(t) = t^b$; all samples are inspected at $t = (0, 1, \ldots, 49)$ with the test step $\Delta t = 1$; the unknown parameters in M0 are fixed with $\mu_0 = 1.5$, $\sigma_0 = 0.3$, $\mu_\beta = 0.2$, $\sigma_\beta = 0.03$, $\sigma_B = 0.02$, $\sigma_\varepsilon = 0.02$, and $b = 0.5$.

We apply M0 to M4 to fit $\mathbf{W}$, respectively, and the parameter estimation results of all candidates are displayed in TABLE I. To compare the goodness of fit, we calculate the Akaike information criterions (AICs) of M0, M2, M3, and M4 (Before using M2, the degradation data should be processed to satisfy $X_0 = 0$, which leads to the difference between the degradation data fitted by M1 and M0, M2, M3, and M4. Therefore, the AIC of M2 cannot participate in the comparison.) are calculated and posted in TABLE I. TABLE I shows that the parameter estimators of M0 are close to the corresponding true values, which verifies the effectiveness of the MLE-based parameter estimation method introduced in Section III. In addition, compared with M2, M3, and M4, M0 with the minimum AIC implies that degradation models without unit-to-unit variability, measurement errors, and nonlinearity will significantly undermine the goodness of fit, and it is necessary to involve these features in degradation models.

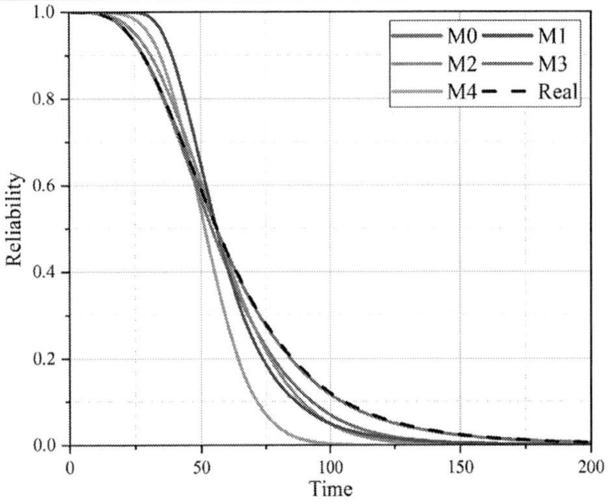

Fig. 1. Reliability functions of all candidate models and real reliability function.

Furthermore, we obtain the reliability function of M0 based on Eqs. (6) to (8), which is plotted in Fig. 1. For comparison, we also calculate the reliability functions corresponding to other candidates and the real reliability function and plot them in Fig. 1. As shown in Fig. 1, the reliability function corresponding to M0 nearly coincides with the real case. While the reliability functions associated with M1 to M4 are all distinct from the real reliability function. The above phenomenons indicate that degradation models considering IPC variability, unit-to-unit variability, measurement errors, and nonlinearity can greatly improve the accuracy of the reliability estimation, which confirms the necessity of containing the four features in degradation modelling.

V. CONCLUSION

For the uncertainties and nonlinearity in product degradation processes, this paper proposes a Winner-based degradation model that considers four-source uncertainties (including IPC variability, unit-to-unit variability, temporal uncertainty, and measurement errors) and nonlinearity. The derivation of the failure time distribution and reliability function of the proposed model in analytical forms are provided. A MLE-based method is developed to estimate unknown parameters in the proposed model. Through a simulation study, we compare the proposed model with its four limiting cases. The results show that the proposed model can provide the most accurate data fitting and reliability estimation, which verifies the effectiveness and superiority of the proposed model and the necessity of containing IPC variability, unit-to-unit variability, temporal uncertainty, measurement errors, and nonlinearity in degradation modelling.

References

[1] J. X. Li, Z. H. Wang, Y. B. Zhang, C. R. Liu, and H. M. Fu, "A nonlinear Wiener process degradation model with autoregressive errors," *Rel. Eng. Syst. Saf.*, 2018, 173: 48-57

[2] Z. S. Ye and M. Xie, "Stochastic modelling and analysis of degradation for highly reliable products," *Appl. Stoch. Models Bus. Ind.*, 2015, 31(1): 16-32

[3] G. Z. Pan, X. B. Li, Y. Q. Li, D. Li, and C. H. Wang, "Statistical analysis method for accelerated life testing with incomplete data and competing failure modes," *Microelectron. Rel.*, 2021, 126

[4] Z. X. Zhang, X. S. Si, C. H. Hu, and Y. G. Lei, "Degradation data analysis and remaining useful life estimation: A review on Wiener-process-based methods," *Eur. J. Oper. Res., 2018,* 271(3): 775-796

[5] B. K. Zheng, C. Chen, W. Zhang, R. Fu, Y. F. Hu, Y. G. Lin, C. Q. Wang, G F. Zhai, "Reliability estimation of complex systems based on a Wiener process with random effects and D-vine copulas," *Microelectron. Rel.*, 2022.

[6] Z. X. Zhang, X. S. Si, C. H. Hu, Q. Zhang, T. M. Li, and C. Q. Xu, "Planning Repeated Degradation Testing for Products With Three-Source Variability," *IEEE Trans. Rel.*, 2016, 65(2): 640-647

[7] S. H. Hao, J. Yang, and C. Berenguer, "Nonlinear step-stress accelerated degradation modelling considering three sources of variability," *Rel. Eng. Syst. Saf.*, 2018, 172: 207-215

[8] J. X. Li, Z. H. Wang, Y. B. Zhang, H. M. Fu, C. R. Liu, and S. Krishnaswamy, "Degradation data analysis based on a generalized Wiener process subject to measurement error," *Mech. Syst. Signal Process*, 2017, 94: 57-72

[9] G. Whitmore, "Estimating degradation by a Wiener diffusion process subject to measurement error," *LDA*, 1995, 1(3): 307-319,

[10] D. H. Pan, Y. T. Wei, H. Z. Fang, and W. Z. Yang, "A reliability estimation approach via Wiener degradation model with measurement errors," *Appl. Math. Comput.*, 2018, 320: 131-141,.

[11] S. Mehrotra, "On the implementation of a primal-dual interior point method," *SIAM J. Optim.*, 1992, 2(4): 575-601,

8th International Conference on Reliability of Electrical Products and Electrical Contacts, November 18-20, 2022 **(Invited Paper)**

Review of Encapsulation Insulation Reliability and Failure Mechanism for High Voltage Power Electronics Modules

Boya Zhang, Xingwen Li, Kaixuan Li
State Key Laboratory of Electrical Insulation and Power Equipment
Xi'an Jiaotong University, Xi'an, 710049, China
E-mail: zhangby@xjtu.edu.cn Tel: 029-82663623

Abstract—**Power electronics modules have been widely used in flexible HVDC power transmission, new energy power generation, high-speed trains, electric vehicles, etc. And they have been developing towards higher voltage level, higher power density, faster switching speed and higher working temperature. Therefore, the problem of encapsulation insulation reliability becomes more and more prominent. In this paper, the insulation structure, materials and requirements of the encapsulation system in currently widely used bond-wired high voltage Si-based IGBT modules are analyzed. The dielectric and aging characteristics of the encapsulation insulation materials are summarized. Then, the partial discharge characteristics of the encapsulation structure and the failure mechanism of interfacial insulation as well as its influencing factors are analyzed. On this basis, methods to improve the reliability of encapsulation insulation are summarized. Finally, towards the development trend of SiC-based semiconductor devices in the future, the main difficulties and challenges in the encapsulation insulation of the new generation high-voltage power electronics modules are pointed out and related problems are prospected.**

Index Terms— **insulation degradation, electrical tree, silicone gel, high temperature, high frequency, high slew rate**

I. INTRODUCTION

The trend towards more and all electric apparatuses and more electrification will lead to a higher electrical demand. Increases in electrical power demand can be provided by either higher voltages or higher currents. Owing to weight and voltage drop, an increase in current is not preferred; thus, higher voltages are being considered. Another trend is to reduce the size and weight of apparatuses. These two trends result in the high-voltage, high-power-density concept.

It is expected that by 2030, 80% of all electric power will flow through power electronics systems [1]. In regards to the high-voltage, high-power-density concept, WBG power modules made from materials such as SiC and GaN, which can tolerate higher voltages and currents than Si-based modules, are considered to be the most promising solution to reducing the size and weight of power conversion systems.

For WBG devices, in addition to the trend towards higher breakdown voltage capability, known as the blocking voltage, volume reduction and, thus, power density increases have also been targeted. For example, while the blocking voltage for commercial Si insulated gate bipolar transistors (IGBT) is 6.5 kV, the highest blocking voltage for SiC IGBTs is 15 kV for 80 A and 24 kV for 30 A [2]. Compared to the 6.5 kV Si-based solutions, the 15 kV SiC-based power module has one-third the volume, which translates into higher electric stress within the module. This leads to extremely high electric stress, E, within the module, leading to unacceptable partial discharge (PD) levels and, in turn, insulation degradation and, eventually, breakdown of the module.

One of the merits of WBG devices is that their slew rates and switching frequencies are much higher than Si-based devices. However, frequency and slew rate are two of the most critical factors of a voltage pulse, influencing the level of degradation of the insulation systems exposed to such pulse [3],[4]. For solid dielectrics, it was experimentally shown that the shorter the rise time, the larger the PD magnitude; thus, the shorter the lifetime [5],[6]. Furthermore, lifetime decreases with increasing frequency [7],[8]. This will be a problem for the silicone gel and ceramic dielectrics because these insulators will experience high slew rates (dv/dt) (ranging from tens to hundreds of kV/μs) and repetitive (frequencies ranging from hundreds of kHz to MHz) voltage pulses.

WBG power devices also exhibit reduced conduction and switching losses and are able to operate at higher temperatures-up to 500°C has been targeted. This adds thermal stress on top of the two stresses mentioned above (i.e., high electric field and high slew rate, high frequency square wave voltages) [9],[10]. It is expected that these three stresses will lead to accelerated aging and degradation of the insulation materials used in next-generation WBG power modules.

This manuscript critically reviews recent efforts and presents technical gaps and challenges for developing insulation materials and systems for next-generation WBG-based devices for power electronics modules. A thorough and in-depth review of PD measurements, failure analyses, and control in high-power Si-IGBT modules has been done.

II. DIELECTRIC PROPERTIES OF ENCAPSULATION MATERIAL

Two common insulation materials used in power electronic modules are ceramic substrates and silicone gel. As the main insulation system, ceramic substrates ensure electrical insulation between active components and the baseplate, which is generally grounded. Silicone gel is used for encapsulation to prevent in situ electrical discharges in air and to protect substrates, semiconductors, and connections against humidity, dirt, and vibration.

Various in-depth studies have been conducted on the physical and chemical properties of silicone gel in the past decades. The studies include the analysis of morphology, synthesis mechanism, viscosity, adhesion as well as the dielectric, breakdown strength, and thermal properties of silicone gels. The volume resistivity and dielectric strength of silicone gel under various curing conditions were studied in [11]. The conductivity of silicone gel under DC stress at different temperatures was analyzed in [12]. The dielectric breakdown behavior in silicone gel was studied in [13,],[14], considering the influence of temperature, humidity, and material processing. Dielectric losses and breakdown fields of silicone gel under a wide temperature range were measured in [15], and the breakdown strength of silicone gel in needle-plane geometry under AC, DC, and impulse voltages was studied in [16].

Recently, we also performed characterizations on the dielectric properties silicone gel. In terms of temperature dependence of silicone gel, an improved Cole-Cole model was used to simulate the dielectric response process of the silicone gel, which has been showed in Fig.1. where the influence of temperature on the dielectric characteristic parameters was identified. In particular, the dielectric loss density under PWM voltage was calculated, and the temperature rise of the encapsulation structure caused by the dielectric loss was observed. It was found that the high-frequency dielectric constant at 200°C decreases by 24% compared to room temperature; when the temperature is raised to 180°C, the volume resistivity drops by three orders of magnitude, and the breakdown strength of silicone gel is reduced by 50% compared with room temperature. The dielectric loss under PWM voltage increases by four orders of magnitude as the temperature increases up to 200°C. In terms of humidity response of silicone gels, the moisture absorption, chemical, and electrical properties of silicone gel under 85°C&85%RH with long aging time is characterized. The results showed that the wettest position locates at the mid-depth in silicone gels after desorption, which can be called as "depth effect". Besides, the mass loss during the aging is also observed and the competition of absorption and dissolution is analyzed. Moreover, it is found that the moisture intrusion on electrical performance degradation is delayed.

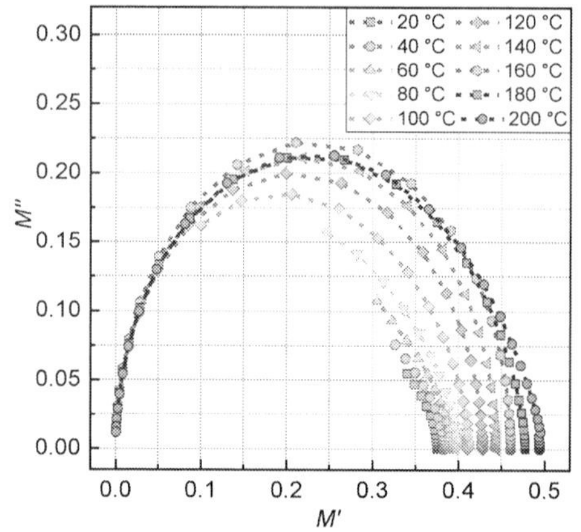

Fig. 1. Cole-Cole diagram of the silicone gel at different temperatures.

III. ELECTRICAL DEGRADATION OF ENCAPSULATION MATERIAL

In the following sections, the detection methods of partial discharge (PD) for high dv/dt are evaluated. The general features of electrical treeing degradation resulting from PD activities in silicone gel are reviewed and future research needs are highlighted.

A. Detection Methods of Partial Discharge for High dv/dt

The current standard commonly used for IGBT working at 1.5 kV or more is IEC 61287-1 [17]. The applied voltage is an AC root mean square voltage (50 or 60 Hz) equal to 1.5Um/ 2 or higher, where Um is the maximum blocking voltage of the module. The voltage is ramped up to 1.5Um/ 2 in 10 s, and is maintained for t1 = 1min as shown in Fig. 2. During this time t1, some PDs may be observed. After t1, the voltage is decreased to 1.1Um/ 2 in 10s. The voltage 1.1Um/ 2 is applied for t2 = 30s. During the last 5s of t2 , the level of PD is measured. A typical value to pass the test for a component and a subassembly is 10 and 50 pC, respectively. However, IGBT modules are subjected to PWM stress type and the PD behavior under 50 or 60Hz AC sinusoidal voltage

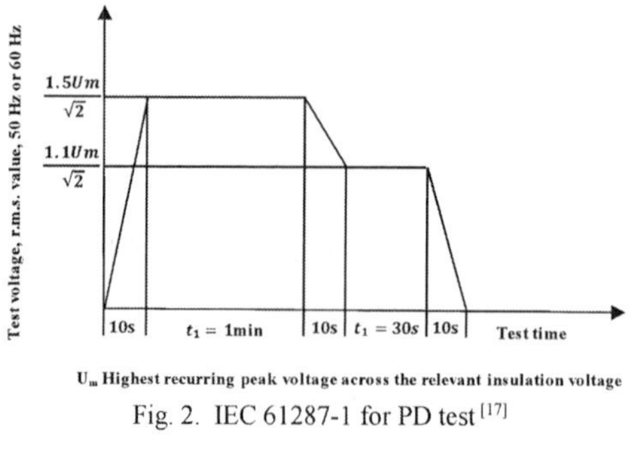

Fig. 2. IEC 61287-1 for PD test [17]

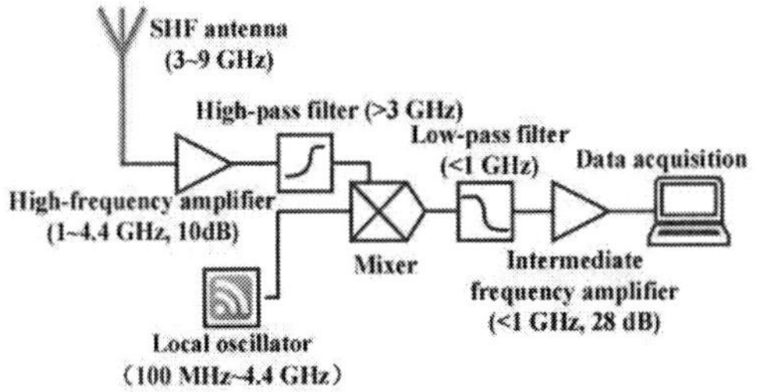

Fig. 3. Schematic of the SHF PD detection system [18]

is different from fast rise bipolar high frequency square wave voltages. Thus, it calls a need for new standards to consider an actual test voltage for power electronic modules.

Some solutions have been proposed recently. A Super-High-Frequency (SHF)-down-mixing PD detection system was proposed [18]. The PD detection system is composed of an SHF sensor, a high-frequency amplifier, a high-pass filter, a mixer, an intermediate frequency amplifier, and a low-pass filter, as shown in Fig. 3. PD signals are picked up by the antenna, and the signal is amplified and filtered to eliminate interference. The cut-off frequency of the high-pass filter should be higher than 3 GHz, the stop-band should contain the most frequency components of the interference signal. The filtered SHF signal is input to the mixer, and the local oscillator generates a sinusoidal signal with a frequency around 3 GHz. Through the low-pass filter and the intermediate frequency amplifier, the difference-frequency signal whose frequency is much lower than 3 GHz is output to an oscilloscope. Sadly, the accuracy of this system is only 20pC.

The high dv/dt partial discharge detection system based on photomultiplier tube (PMT) and high frequency current transformer (HFCT) is also verified [19]. The PD test circuit is shown in Fig. 4. A faraday cage, a line filter, an isolation transformer, and several common mode chokes were used to limit the EMI noise caused by switching events. A photomultiplier tube PMT was implemented to trigger PD detection due to its good ant interference ability. A 95 MHz bandwidth 50 Ω shunt resistor and a 200 MHz bandwidth HFCT were selected for PD current measurement. The resolution of the measurement system is 1 pC. This system requires a strict darkroom environment.

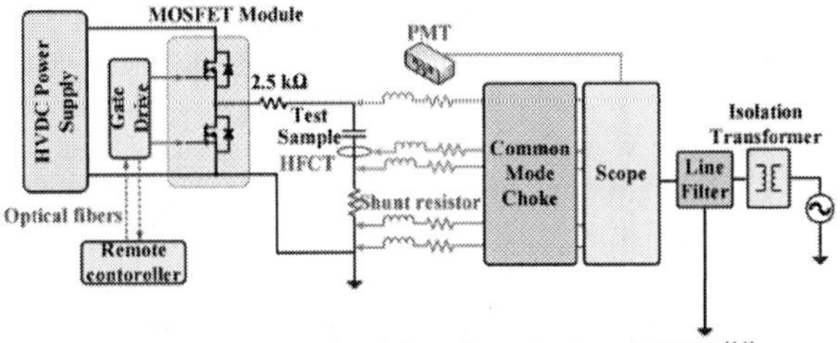

Fig. 4. PD test setup circuit based oon PMT and HFCT [19].

B. *Morphologies of Electrical Treeing in Silicone Gel*

Due to the flexible polymer network chains, silicone gel possesses a unique two-phase liquid-solid nature, which makes the tree morphologies in silicone gel very different from solid materials. It was shown that under AC voltage, there is a filamentary branched component of trees in silicone gel that is retained after electrical field is removed, like in solids, as well as bubble-like cavities that expand, become isolated, collapse during growth, like in liquid [20],[21].

This phenomenon was analyzed in detail in a fascinating experiment performed on a range of samples made by varying the ratio of two liquid components (A and B) used for cross-linking a commercial silicone gel [22]. As shown in Fig.5a, the regions at < 40%A and > 95%A correspond to a liquid phase. Maximum hardening appears at 66-70%A. In between the liquid and the elastomer phases are gel-like products (i.e., around 50%A and 85%A). The electrical treeing behaviors of different compositions are shown in Fig.5b. In the liquid region, only streamers are grown, while in the elastomer region, only branched tree structures that are similar in form to those found in other solid dielectrics are observed (Fig.5b-III). This kind of tree suffers from irreversible chemical changes such as chain scissions and further carbonization, so the structure is retained after removal of the applied voltage.

Gel samples exhibit treeing behavior that includes features typical of both liquids and solids, and show different self-healing mechanisms depending on the degree of curing. Near the gel-liquid boundary with 45%A (Fig.5b-I), a complete and fast self-healing behavior on the order of microseconds to tenths of a second was observed. This behavior during voltage application can be regarded as the first self-healing stage.

At the manufacturer's recommended composition, i.e., gel sample with 50%A (Fig.5b-II), the growth of electrical trees involved the formation of near-spherical cavities on the tips of the filaments. These cavities in gels are, in fact, slow streamers with shorter and wider dimensions compared to those found in liquids [23]-[25]. They expand, collapse, and disappear, as do such cavities in liquid breakdown structures [24], [26], [27], on a timescale of a few seconds through the same mechanism as the first self-healing stage. However, the repetition of discharges makes the cavities stable. These new quasi-permanent cavities add to the fractal trees that are the backbone of the degradation structure. Unlike more rigid dielectrics, such as epoxy resin and polyethylene, the flexible elastic nature of the gel allows the structure to contract and gradually fade once the voltage is removed [20]; this is known as the second stage of self-healing.

It should be noted that silicone gel is not a liquid so its self-healing capability is not unlimited. Some filamentary structures can be retained if the gel suffers from repetitive discharges. This can be regarded as a form of irreversible degradation such as observed in [28], [29].

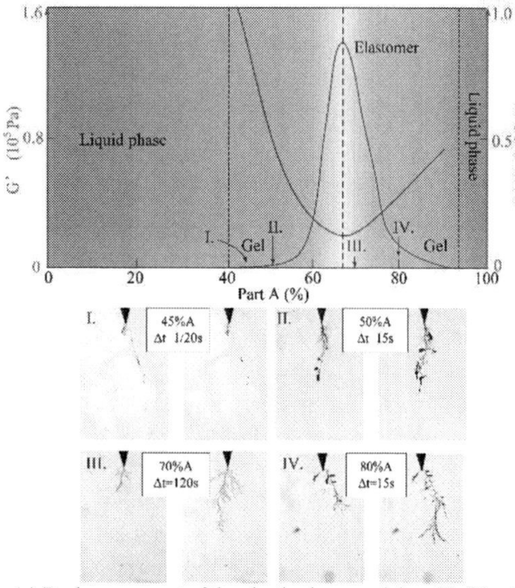

Fig. 5. (a) Real component of the elastic shear modulus, G', (blue line) and loss tangent, tanδ, (red line, tanδ=G''/G' where G'' is the imaginary component of the elastic shear modulus) after completion of the curing process at 65°C as a function of the concentration of A; (b) Comparison of electrical treeing morphologies of cured samples with different ratios of components [22].

The dynamics of the electrical treeing in silicone gels was further explored by measuring the dynamic change of potential distributions during surface discharge at the gel-substrate interface using the Pockels technique [30], [31] where the measured potential directly revealed the amount of accumulated charge on the cavity surface.

IV. MITIGATION METHODS

Four solutions have been proposed for electric field reduction and PD control within envisioned high voltage, compact packaging design of power modules: 1) geometrical techniques [32]-[36], 2) applying nonlinear field-dependent conductivity (FDC) materials as coatings on high field regions [37] or field-dependent permittivity (FDP) fillers in silicone gel [38], 3) using high-temperature (up to 350°C) insulating liquids as a potential replacement for silicone gels [39]-[41], and 4) combined geometrical techniques and applying nonlinear field-dependent conductivity layers [42]-[48].

A ferroelectric filler, barium titanate, was added in the base silicone gel to form an FDP stress-relieving dielectric material [38]. However, this technique has two limits. First, the mentioned stress-relieving merit disappears above a specific temperature known as the Curie point. For pure barium titanate, this temperature is ~130°C [38]. Another issue is that an increase in the rate of the filler increases viscosity dramatically. The viscosity of the filled gel with 15% barium titanate by volume increases by five times [38]. A rate of more than 15% by volume of barium titanate likely cannot be used due to the viscosity issue. It is crystal clear that this method has a critical thermal limitation for use in WBG-based power modules where the temperatures go beyond 200°C.

Although the dielectric strength of a high temperature non-polar dibenzyltoluene (DBT) liquid, JARYTHERM® DBT [49], proposed in [39]-[41] as an encapsulant in high-temperature power electronics modules is higher than other dielectric liquids, its dielectric strength at 350°C decreases to about 58% of its initial value at 20°C. However, PD measurements in [41] shows promising results for these high temperature liquids as an alternative for silicone gel. To the best of our knowledge, there are only three papers [39]-[41] proposing DBT as an alternative for silicone gel for high-temperature WBG power modules. It indicates that this topic is very immature. In our view, the high temperature issue, especially beyond 200°C, will be much more challenging than the high electric field stress issue for next-generation WBG power modules.

The geometrical techniques for electric field reduction within power modules include 1) metal layer offset [32], [33], 2) protruding substrate [32], [34], 3) stacked substrate [35], and 4) 3D module layers [36]. In this regard, the 3D module layer method leads to an increase of 20% in stray inductance [36].

Studies in [42]-[48] prove that geometrical techniques including 1) metal layer offset, 2) protruding substrate, and 3) stacked substrate design, either individually or combined, cannot solve the high electric field issue in high voltage high-density WBG power modules. The use of a combination of the aforementioned geometrical methods and applying a nonlinear FDC layer were examined in [42]-[48]. The combination used for blocking voltages up to 30 kV addressed the issue well. Moreover, an electric field criterion based on precise dimensions of a power module and its PD measurement was introduced in [47]. References [47], [48] can be used as a guideline to design the insulation system for next-generation compact WBG power modules, meeting both the one-minute insulation and PD tests based on IEC 61287-1, which is the only existing standard for insulation performance of power electronics modules. It was shown that the proposed method brought E down to the criterion values well, and that an electric field reduction of 66% and 91% in AlN substrate and silicone gel, respectively could be achieved through the proposed method compared with using the protruding substrate design alone [48].

Another technical gap and challenge is to develop advanced processing techniques to deposit thin layers of nonlinear FDC material with thicknesses ranging from a few ten to a few hundred μm. In this regard, an innovative method to tailor functionally graded materials by local handling of high permittivity ceramic particles of $SrTiO3$ into epoxy resin using electrophoresis was reported in [49]. As shown in Fig. 6, by applying a DC electric field onto the liquid composite compound, i.e., liquid epoxy resin with a hardener and $SrTiO3$ particles, before curing it in order to freeze the particles exactly where they have accumulated, the desired particle concentration gradient near the high voltage electrode was achieved. The thickness and distribution of the particles can be adjusted by controlling the electrophoretic force. As a result, the permittivity of the accumulated layer can be increased in value ranging between 22 and 24 in the frequency range under test.

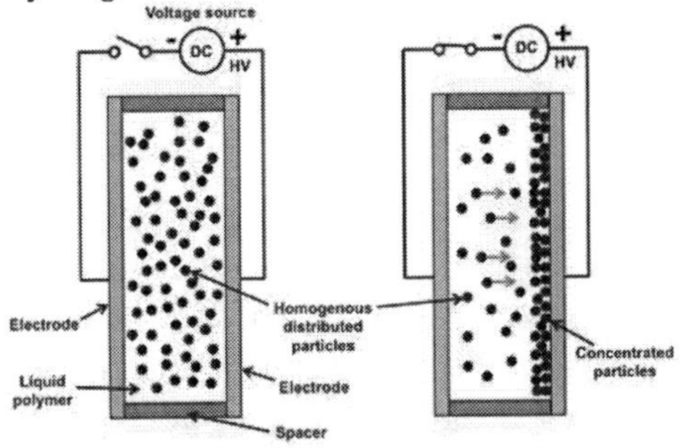

Fig. 6. Electrophoresis process principle under DC voltage for structuring FGM polymer/ceramic composites [49].

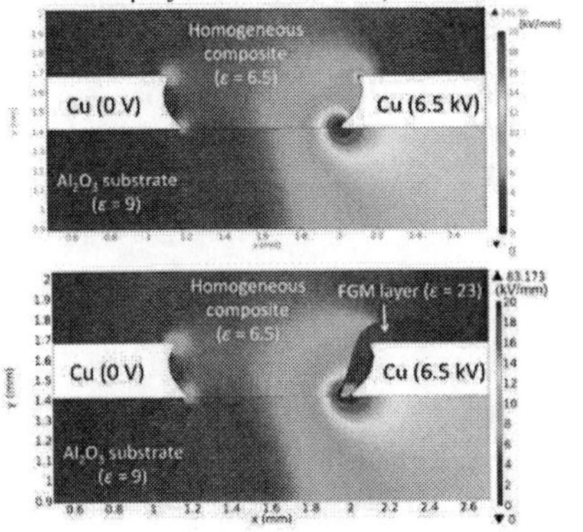

Fig. 7. Electrostatic field simulations of the DBC structure with and without an FGM layer [49].

This strategy was successfully applied to metalized DBC substrates used in power electronics modules. By applying DC voltage on the metalized Cu electrode during the curing process, an accumulated layer consisting of SrTiO3 particles was formed. This high permittivity layer covers the Cu electrode, especially around the two sharp tips where the field enhancement is the highest. The efficiency of the method is shown by performing a field simulation in Fig.7.

The field enhancement at the triple point is significantly reduced to only 1/3 of the original design. The breakdown tests also highlighted a 70% improvement in breakdown voltage compared to neat epoxy encapsulation. Such a field grading material (FGM) method, patented in France [50], can self-adaptively tailor the insulating materials and selectively heal the defects that occur during the system packaging assembly.

A field grading substrate was also proposed recently in [51], where the idea is to modify the part of the substrate ceramic at the triple point with higher conductivity. Fig.8 shows the impact of this field grading method on the electric field distribution by modifying the AlN conductivity by a factor of 1×10^6. The maximum electric field value is significantly reduced and occurs at region B, which is away from the triple point area.

In the geometric technique proposed in [52], [53], a gap between the top Cu electrodes was created to form a mesa structure, leading to significant electric field reduction as shown in Fig.9. This mesa structure was fabricated as shown in Fig.10 by an ultrasonic machining technique. Even though the machining introduces some protuberances on the upper corner of the Cu electrode, a 30% increase in the PD inception voltage (PDIV) was observed in the mesa structure compared to the conventional one.

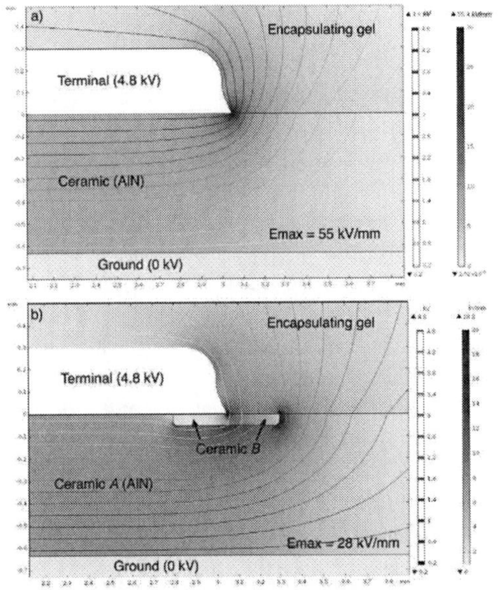

Fig. 8. Field simulations of the (a) conventional DBC structure and (b) substrate with a higher conductivity in region B [51].

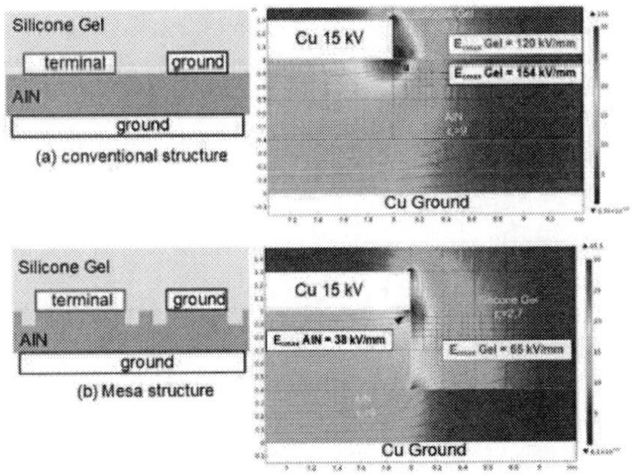

Fig. 9. The geometry of (a) conventional structure and (b) mesa structure and the corresponding electric field distribution [52].

Further, considering the electric field alone is not enough, failure mitigation at high temperature has also attracted attention in the latest researches. A feasible nonlinear composite material (NCM) as coating to optimize the electric field distribution in IGBT modules, considering electrical stress and thermal stress was proposed in [54]. An inorganic material, a low-melting-point (Tmelt< 500℃) lead glass was evaluated, as a potential high-temperature encapsulant for SiC power modules in [9].

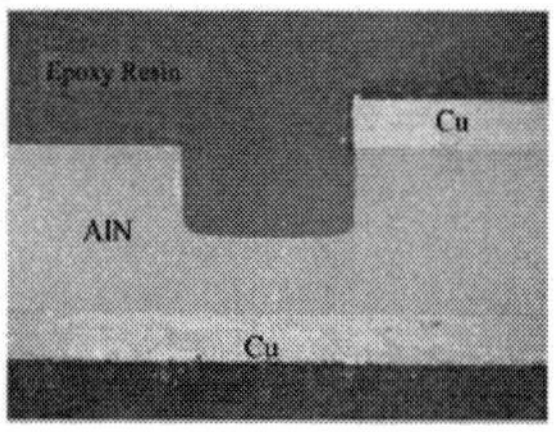

Fig. 10. A cross-sectional view of the mesa structure built by ultrasonic machining [52].

V. CONCLUSIONS AND PERSPECTIVES

This paper presents a critical review of recent efforts to address the expected accelerated aging and degradation of insulation materials used within envisioned high voltage, high-density WBG power modules. Technical gaps and future research needs in two main areas were highlighted and discussed: 1) elucidating the mechanisms and phenomena behind prebreakdown in insulation materials employed within the mentioned power modules through both experimental investigation and modeling, and 2) developing mitigation methods. Combined geometrical techniques with nonlinear FDC materials applied to high electric field regions and using high temperature liquid dielectrics instead of silicone gel were highlighted as promising methods to address the high electric stress and high temperature issues, respectively. The existing standard, IEC 61287-1, for PD testing of power modules that use a 50/60 Hz sinusoidal voltage cannot simulate the real-world situation for insulation materials for future WBG power modules under high slew rates (ranging from tens to hundreds of kV/μs) and repetitive (frequencies ranging from hundreds of kHz to MHz) voltage pulses. Due to targeting the operation of these WBG power modules up to 500°C, thermal stress will play a critical role in insulation degradation and is needed to be considered both when developing a new standard for insulation testing of WBG power modules and when developing mitigation methods.

REFERENCES

[1] U.S. Department of Energy, Electricity Delivery and Energy Reliability, "Power electronics research and development, program plan," 2011.

[2] B. Passmore and C. O'Neal, "High-voltage SiC power modules for 10–25 kV applications," Power Electron. Europe Mag., 2016, (1): 22–24,.

[3] T. J. A. Hammarstrom, "Partial discharge characteristics at ultrashort voltage risetimes," *IEEE Trans. Dielect. Electr. Insul.*, 2018, 25(6)

[4] M. Ghassemi, "Accelerated insulation aging due to fast, repetitivevoltages: A review identifying challenges and future research needs," *IEEE Trans. Dielect. Electr. Insul.*, 2019, 26(5)

[5] P. Wang, G. C. Montanari, and A. Cavallini, "Partial discharge phenomenology and induced aging behavior in rotating machines controlled by power electronics," IEEE Trans. Ind. Electron., 2014, 61(12):7105–7112

[6] A. A. Abdelmalik, A. Nysveen, and L. Lundgaard, "Influence of fast rise voltage and pressure on partial discharges in liquid embedded power electronics," IEEE Trans. Dielect. Electr. Insul., 2015, 22(5): 2770–2779.

[7] B. Zhang, M. Ghassemi, Y. Zhang, "Insulation Materials and Systems for Power Electronics Modules: A Review Identifying Challenges and Future Research Needs," IEEE Trans. Dielect. Electr. Insul., 2021, 28(1): 290-302

[8] Y. Zhang et al "Electrical trees and their growth in silicone rubber at various frequencies," Energies, 2018, 11(2): 327–338

[9] L. Liu, D. Nam, B. Guo, J. Ewanchuk, R. Burgos and G. -Q. Lu, "Glass for Encapsulating High-Temperature Power Modules," in IEEE Journal of Emerging and Selected Topics in Power Electronics, 2021, 9(3): 3725-3734

[10] Y. Lin et al., "Temperature- and Degradation- Dependent Maximum Electric Field Stress in Wire-bonding Power Modules under PWM Waves," in IEEE Journal of Emerging and Selected Topics in Power Electronics, 2022

[11] Nung-Pyo Hong, Byung-Ki Song, Soo-Won Lee, Won-Chul Kim, Pil-Gyu Im, and Jin-Woong Hong, "The electrical properties of silicone gel due to curing condition," in *Proc. IEEE Int. Conf. Conduct. Breakdown Solid Dielectr. (ICSD'98)*, Vasteras, Sweden, 1998: 218-220.

[12] F. Breit, D. Malec, and T. Lebey, "Investigations on DC conductivity and space charge in silicone gel," in *Proc. IEEE Conf. Electr. Insul. Dielectr. Phenom. (CEIDP)*, Cancun, Mexico, 2002: 48-51.

[13] G. Finis, A. Claudi, and G. Malin, "Dielectric breakdown strength of silicone gel under various environmental conditions," in *Proc. IEEE* Russ. *Power Tech, (PowerTech)*, St. Petersburg, Russia, 2005:1-6

[14] G. Finis, A. Claudi, and G. Malin, "On the dielectric breakdown behavior of silicone gel under various stress conditions," *IEEE Trans. Dielectr. Electr. Insul.*, 2007,14(2): 487- 494

[15] M. T. Do, J. -L. Auge, and O. Lesaint, "Dielectric losses and breakdown in silicone gel," in *Proc. IEEE Conf. Electr. Insul. Dielectr. Phenom. (CEIDP)*, Kansas City, USA, 2006:541-544.

[16] M. T. Do, J. -L. Auge, and O. Lesaint, "Breakdown field in silicone gel under needle-plane geometry," in *Proc. Int. Symp. Elect. Insulating Mater. (ISEIM)*, Yokkaichi, Japan, 2008. 222- 225.

[17] IEC 61287-1: Railway applications – power converters installed on board rolling stock – part 1: characteristics and test methods, 2014.

[18] Y. Wang, D. Ying, Z. Yuan, H. Peng, J. Wu, Y. Yi et al, "Space-charge accumulation and its impact on high-voltage power module partial discharge under DC and PWM waves: testing and modeling," IEEE Trans. Power Electron., 2021, 36(10): 11097–11108

[19] H. You, Z. Wei, B. Hu, Z. Zhao, R. Na, and J. Wang, "Partial discharge behaviors in power modules under square pulses with ultrafast dv/dt," IEEE Trans. Power Electron., 2021, 36(3): 2611–2620

[20] S. J. Dodd, L. Salvatierra, L. A. Dissado, and E. Mola, "Electrical trees in silicone gel: a combination of liquid and solid behaviour patterns," Annu. Rep. Conf. Electr. Insul. Dielectr. Phenom. (CEIDP), 2013: 1018–1021.

[21] P. Mancinelli, A. Cavallini, S. J. Dodd, N. M. Chalashkanov, and L. A. Dissado, "Analysis of electrical tree inception in silicone gels," IEEE Trans. Dielectr. Electr. Insul., 2017, 24(6): 3974–3984,.

[22] P. Gournay and O. Lesaint, "On the gaseous nature of positive filamentary streamers in hydrocarbon liquids. II: Propagation, growth and collapse of gaseous filaments in pentane," J. Phys. D: Appl. Phys., 1994, 27:2117–2127

[23] P. Gournay and O. Lesaint, "On the gaseous nature of positive filamentary streamers in hydrocarbon liquids. II: Propagation, growth and collapse of gaseous filaments in pentane," J. Phys. D: Appl. Phys.,1994, 27, pp. 2117–2127, 1994.

[24] A. Beroual, M. Zhan, A. Badeut, K. Kist, A. J. Schwabe, H. Yamashita, K. Yamazawa, M. Danikas, W. G. Chadband, and Y. Torshin, "Propagation and structure of streamers in liquid dielectrics," IEEE Electr. Insul. Mag., 1998, 14(2):16–17

[25] H. Akiyama, "Streamer discharges in liquids and their applications," IEEE Trans. Dielectr. Electr. Insul., 2000, 7(5): 646–652

[26] P. K. Watson, W. G. Chadband, M. Sadeghzadeh-Araghi, "The role of electrostatic and hydrodynamic forces in the negative point breakdown in liquid dielectrics," IEEE Trans. Dielectr. Electr. Insul., 1991, 26: 543–559

[27] T. Aka-Ngnui and A. Beroual, "Bubble dynamics and transition into streamers in liquid dielectrics under a high divergent electric field," J. Phys. D: Appl. Phys., 2001, 34: 1408–1412,.

[28] T. M. Do, O. Lesaint, and J. L. Augé, "Streamers and partial discharge mechanisms in silicone gel under impulse and AC voltages," IEEE Trans. Dielectr. Electr. Insul., 2008: 15(6) : 1526–1534,.

[29] T. M. Do, J. L. Augé, and O. Lesaint, "A study of parameters influencing streamer inception in silicone gel," IEEE Trans. Dielectr. Electr. Insul., 2009, 16(3): 893–899.

[30] M. Sato, A. Kumada, K. Hidaka, K. Yamashiro, Y. Hayase, and T. Takano, "On the nature of surface discharges in silicone-gel: Pre-breakdown discharges in cavities," Annu. Rep. Conf. Electr. Insul. Dielectr. Phenom. (CEIDP), 2014: 19–22.

[31] M. Sato, A. Kumada, K. Hidaka, K. Yamashiro, Y. Hayase, and T. Takano, "Dynamic potential distributions of surface discharge in silicone gel," IEEE Trans. Dielectr. Electr. Insul., 2015, 22(3): 1733–1738,

[32] M. Ghassemi, "Geometrical techniques for electric field control in (Ultra) wide bandgap power electronics modules," IEEE Electr. Insul. Conf. (EIC), 2018: 589–592.

[33] C. F. Bayer, E. Baer, U. Waltrich, D. Malipaard, and A. Schletz, "Simulation of the electric field strength in the vicinity of metallization edges on dielectric substrates," IEEE Trans. Dielectrics Electr. Insul., 2015, 22(1): 257–265.

[34] H. Reynes, C. Buttay, and H. Morel, "Protruding ceramic substrates for high voltage packaging of wide bandgap semiconductors," IEEE Workshop Wide Bandgap Power Devices Appl. (WiPDA), 2017: 404–410.

[35] O. Hohlfelder, R. Bayerer, T. Hunger, and H. Hartung, "Stacked substrates for high voltage applications," Int. Conf. Integr. Power Electron. Syst. (CIPS), 2012: 1–4.

[36] D. Frey, J. L. Schanen, J. L. Auge, and O. Lesaint, "Electric field investigation in high voltage power modules using finite element simulations and partial discharge measurements," IEEE Conf. Ind. Appl. Soc. Annu. Meeting (IAS), 2003: 1000–1005.

[37] L. Donzel and J. Schuderer, "Nonlinear resistive electric field control for power electronic modules," IEEE Trans. Dielectr. Electr. Insul., 2012. 19(3): 955–959, 2012.

[38] N. Wang, I. Cotton, J. Robertson, S. Follmann, K. Evans, and D. Newcombe, "Partial discharge control in a power electronic module using high permittivity non-linear dielectrics," IEEE Trans. Dielectr. Electr. Insul., 2010, 17(4): 1319–1326, 2010.

[39] D. J. Muslim, O. Lesaint, R. Hanna, J. L. Reboud, and N. I. Sinisuka, "Electrical characterization of dibenzyltoluene liquid at high temperature s up to 350°C," Annu. Rep. Conf. Electr. Insul. Dielectr. Phenom. (CEIDP), 2018: 58–61.

[40] J. Muslim, O. Lesaint, R. Hanna, and N. I. Sinisuka, "Streamer generation and propagation in Dibenzyltoluene and Ester liquids under high temperature," IEEE Int. Conf. Dielectr. Liquids (ICDL), 2019, pp. 1–4.

[41] J. Muslim, O. Lesaint, R. Hanna, and N. I. Sinisuka, "Partial discharge measurements on Dibenzyltoluene for high temperature encapsulant application up to 350°C," IEEE Int. Conf. Dielectr. Liquids (ICDL), 2019, pp. 1–4.

[42] M. M. Tousi and M. Ghassemi, "Electric field control by nonlinear field dependent conductivity dielectrics characterization for high voltage power module packaging," IEEE Int. Workshop Integr. Power Packag. (IWIPP), 2019, pp. 54–58.

[43] M. M. Tousi and M. Ghassemi, "Nonlinear field dependent conductivity materials for electric field control within next-generation wide bandgap power electronics modules," IEEE Electr. Insul. Conf. (EIC), 2019, pp. 63–66.

[44] M. M. Tousi and M. Ghassemi, "Nonlinear resistive electric field grading in high-voltage, high-power wide bandgap power module packaging," IEEE Energy Convers. Congr. Expo. (ECCE), 2019, pp. 7124–7129.

[45] M. M. Tousi and M. Ghassemi, "Electrical insulation packaging for a 20-kV high density wide bandgap power module," IEEE Energy Convers. Congr. Expo. (ECCE), 2019: 4162–4166.

[46] M. M. Tousi and M. Ghassemi, "The effect of type of voltage (sinusoidal and square waveform) and the frequency on the performance of nonlinear field-dependent conductivity coatings for electric field control in power electronic modules," Annu. Rep. Conf. Electr. Insul. Dielectr. Phenom. (CEIDP), 2019: 601–604.

[47] M. M. Tousi and M. Ghassemi, "Combined geometrical techniques and applying nonlinear field dependent conductivity layers to address the high electric field stress issue in high voltage high-density wide bandgap power modules," IEEE Trans. Dielectr. Electr. Insul., 2020, 27(1): 305–313,.

[48] M. M. Tousi and M. Ghassemi, "Nonlinear field dependent conductivity for electric field grading in wide bandgap power electronic modules," IEEE J. Emerg. Sel. Topics Power Electron., 2020, 8(1): 343–350

[49] S. Diaham, Z. Valdez Nava, L. Lévêque, T. T. Le, L. Laudebat, and T. Lebey, "An original in-situ way to build field grading materials (FGM) with permittivity gradient using electrophoresis," IEEE Int. Conf. Dielectr. (ICD), 2018, pp. 1–4.

[50] S. Diaham, Z. Valdez Nava, L. Lévèque, G. Belijar, L. Laudebat and T. Lebey, "Procédé de traitement d'un matériau électriquement isolant lui conférant des propriétés de gradation de champ électrique auto-adaptatives pour composants électriques," Int. Patent application, 2016.

[51] Z. Valdez-Nava, D. Kenfaui, M. -L. Locatelli, L. Laudebat, and S. Guillemet, "Ceramic substrates for high voltage power electronics: past, present and future," IEEE Int. Workshop Integr. Power Packag. (IWIPP), 2019, 91–96.

[52] H. Hourdequin, L. Laudebat, M.-L. Locatelli, Z. Valdez-Nava, and P. Bidan, "Metallized ceramic substrate with mesa structure for voltage ramp-up of power modules," Eur. Phys. J. Appl. Phys., 2019, 87: 20903

[53] H. Hourdequin, L. Laudebat, M.-L. Locatelli, and P. Bidan, "Design of packaging structures for high voltage power electronics devices: electric field stress on insulation," IEEE Int. Conf. Dielectr. (ICD), 2016: 999–1002.

[54] K. Li, B. Zhang, X. Li, F. Yan, and L. Wang. "Electric field mitigation in high-voltage high-power IGBT modules using nonlinear conductivity composites," IEEE Trans. Compon. Packaging Technol., 2021, 11(11: 1844–1855

Boya Zhang (Member, IEEE) was born in Xi'an, China in 1990. He received the B.S. and Ph.D degree in electrical engineering from Tsinghua University, Beijing, China, in 2013 and 2018, respectively. He was a visiting scholar at Institute of Materials Science, University of Connecticut, USA, from 2016 to 2017. He is currently an associate professor with Xi'an Jiaotong University, China. His research interests include power equipment, insulation technologies, and gas discharge plasma

8th International Conference on Reliability of Electrical Products and Electrical Contacts, November 18-20, 2022 **(Invited Paper)**

Online Assessment of Ground-Wall Insulation Condition in Inverter-Fed Motors Using Time and Frequency Domain Characteristics of Leakage Current

Feng Niu[1], Chaofan Zhang[1], Jian Zhang[2], Shaopo Huang[3], Youtong Fang[2]

[1)] Key Laboratory of Electromagnetic Field and Electrical Apparatus Reliability of Hebei Province, Hebei University of Technology, Tianjin, 300401

[2)] College of Electrical Engineering, Zhejiang University, Hangzhou, 310027

[3)] College of Information Engineering, Beijing Institute of Petrochemical Technology, Beijing, 102617

Email: niufeng@hebut.edu.cn TEL:13502041597

***Abstract*—With the development of pulse width modulation (PWM) technique, inverter-fed motors have been widely used in areas such as industrial production and electric vehicles. While improving the control performance, the pulsed voltages with high frequency, generated by inverter, also accelerate the degradation of motor insulation. To guarantee the reliability of motor system, it is critical to monitor the insulation condition of inverter-fed motors in real time. The ground-wall (GW) insulation model is established to analyze the relationship between GW insulation and leakage current. And an online monitoring scheme of GW insulation condition is proposed based on the time and frequency domain characteristics of leakage current. The common-mode and differential-mode harmonics are combined to identify the degradation degree and position, and the initial oscillation amplitude is used to identify the degradation phase. The experiments are carried out on a vector-controlled permanent magnet synchronous motor. The results show that the proposed method can detect incipient degradation and locate degradation position with high accuracy.**

***Index Terms*— Condition assessment, ground-wall (GW) insulation, inverter-fed motors (IFMs), leakage current.**

I. Introduction

Inverter-fed motors (IFMs) have been widely used in many fields, e.g. high-speed railway, wind power generation and industrial machinery, where high reliability is essential for system operation. As one of the most severe failures of motors, stator insulation failure accounts for 30%-40% of total failures [1]. Therefore, it is critical to assess the insulation condition of IFMs in real-time.

Many offline testing methods have been proposed to detect the insulation degradation of motors, such as insulation resistance test and polarization index test, DC and AC high potential test, dissipation factor (DF) test, and offline partial discharge (PD) test [2]. However, these offline methods are time-consuming and the tested motors must be removed from service. Therefore, online insulation condition assessment has drawn great attention for its instantaneity and efficiency.

Online PD monitoring is one of the most common techniques to monitor insulation condition of motors. However, this technique is susceptible to noise and requires the installation of specialized PD current sensor [3]. Recently, the online monitoring methods of motor insulation based on phase current and leakage current have drawn great attention of researchers. In [4], the root mean square deviation (RMSD) of transient phase current is utilized for insulation condition monitoring of stator winding. To further investigate the effect of dv/dt on the value of RMSD, the transient phase currents under different MOSFET switching speeds are analyzed in [5]. In [6], a high frequency model of line-end coil is established to analyze the transient phase current in frequency domain. Using the amplitude-frequency features of transient phase current, the insulation degradation near terminal end can be detected. Overall, the existing transient current monitoring methods need to monitor the current signatures up to MHz, which is a significant challenge for the sensor system.

The leakage current based method is another promising solution which has been studied by many researchers [7]-[12]. In [7]-[8], the measurement method of differential-mode (DM) leakage current is proposed to monitor the leakage current in each phase, and the equivalent insulation resistance and capacitance are obtained to assess the condition of GW insulation. However, the DM leakage current measurement needs three high-sensitivity current transformers which are high-cost, and it cannot monitor three-lead motors because the neutral point is not accessible. In [9]-[10], the equivalent capacitance of overall GW insulation is derived from the common-mode (CM) leakage current and voltage. This method can monitor the insulation condition of three-lead IFMs, but does not consider the effect of degradation position. In [11], the time domain characteristics of leakage current are used to identify the degradation degree and position of GW insulation. However, the degradation degree and position cannot be assessed individually in this method. In [12], the CM impedance spectrum is used to distinguish the insulation degradation at different positions. However, this method needs to monitor the CM leakage current in high-frequency range, and hence, the high-bandwidth sensor and high sampling rate are required.

The main contribution of this paper lies in two aspects. Firstly, the relationship between the time and frequency domain characteristics of leakage current and GW insulation degradation is clearly clarified using the stator winding insulation model established in low frequency range. Secondly, an online monitoring method is proposed to identify the degree, position and phase of GW insulation degradation based on the time and frequency domain characteristics of leakage current.

II. Relationship between Leakage Current and GW Insulation in IFMs

A. Equivalent Circuit Model of Stator Winding with GW Insulation Degradation.

To analyze the relationship between leakage current and GW insulation, an electrical model of stator winding insulation is established in low frequency range (around 0 Hz to 100 kHz). The GW insulation can be modeled as an equivalent capacitance and resistance, in parallel, which represent the capacitive coupling and dielectric losses, respectively [7]-[8]. The equivalent circuit model of stator winding with insulation degradation in phase C is shown in Fig. 1, where $U_{a,b,c}$ denote the three-phase PWM voltages, R_s and L_s denote the stator resistance and inductance, respectively, R_g and C_g denote the GW insulation resistance and capacitance, respectively. Point N is the neutral end, point D is the position of GW insulation degradation, and x is the ratio of the turn numbers from the terminal end to point D to the whole phase winding.

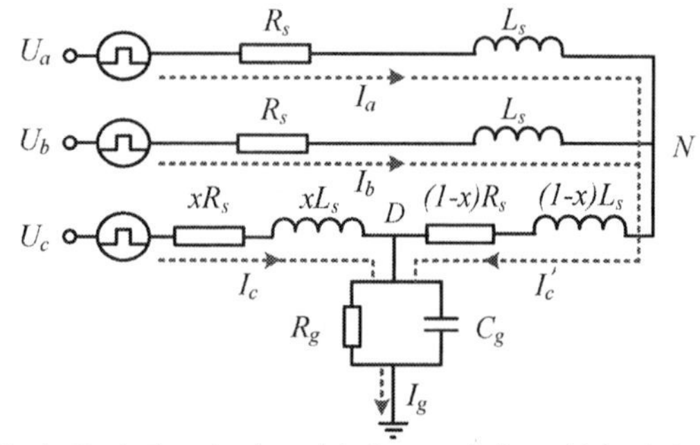

Fig. 1. Equivalent circuit model of stator winding with insulation degradation in phase C.

The three-phase PWM voltages can be replaced with an equivalent voltage source and the branches can be equal to a RLC series circuit shown as Fig. 2, where k, Z, and U_g represent the stator impedance coefficient, equivalent circuit impedance, and equivalent GW voltage source, respectively. The circuit parameters are represented as

$$k = \frac{x(3-2x)}{3} \quad (1)$$

$$Z = k(R_s + j\omega L_s) + \frac{1}{j\omega C_g} \quad (2)$$

$$\tilde{U}_g = \frac{(3-2x)\tilde{U}_c + x(\tilde{U}_a + \tilde{U}_b)}{3} \quad (3)$$

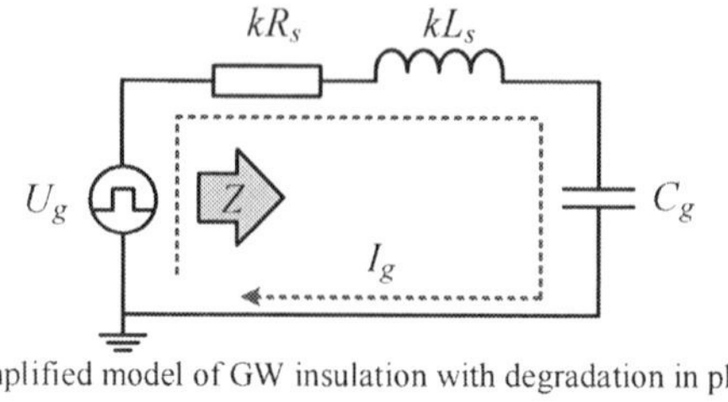

Fig. 2. Simplified model of GW insulation with degradation in phase C.

B. Voltage Distribution in Stator Winding.

The Double Fourier Integral (DFI) analysis is adopted to identify the voltage harmonics under sinusoidal PWM technique, and the Fourier representation of voltage of phase A is shown as

$$\begin{aligned} U_a(t) = {} & \frac{E_d}{2} + \frac{\alpha E_d}{2}\sin(\omega_0 t) \\ & + \frac{2E_d}{m\pi}\left\{ \sum_{m=1}^{\infty} J_0\left(\frac{\alpha m\pi}{2}\right)\sin\frac{m\pi}{2}\cos(m\omega_c t) \right. \\ & \left. + \sum_{m=1}^{\infty}\sum_{n=-\infty, n\neq 0}^{\infty} J_n\left(\frac{\alpha m\pi}{2}\right)\sin\left[\frac{(m-n)\pi}{2}\right]\cos(m\omega_c t + n\omega_0 t) \right\} \end{aligned} \quad (4)$$

where E_d is the DC bus voltage, ω_0 is the fundamental angular frequency, ω_c is the carrier angular frequency (the switching angular frequency of inverter), α is the modulation index, and $J_k(x)$ denotes the kth-order Bessel function.

The PWM voltage could be divided into CM voltage and DM voltage. The CM voltage at each phase has the same amplitude and phase angle at each CM frequency, and it only contributes to leakage current. By contrast, the DM voltage at each phase has the same amplitude and differs by 120-degree in phase angle at the same DM frequency, and it contributes to not only leakage current but also load current.

The CM voltage can be calculated as the average value of three-phase voltages. Based on (3), the equivalent GW voltage source U_g at CM frequency is derived as

$$\begin{aligned} \tilde{U}_{g,CM} &= (1-x)\tilde{U}_{c,CM} + \frac{x(\tilde{U}_{a,CM} + \tilde{U}_{b,CM} + \tilde{U}_{c,CM})}{3} \\ &= \tilde{U}_{c,CM} \end{aligned} \quad (5)$$

The equivalent GW voltage source U_g at DM frequency is derived from (3) and (5) as

$$\tilde{U}_{g,DM} = (1-x)\tilde{U}_{c,DM} \quad (6)$$

It can be seen from (5) and (6) that the $U_{g,CM}$ is equal to the CM voltage in phase C and is not affected by degradation position x, but the $U_{g,DM}$ decreases linearly with the increasing of degradation position x.

The CM frequency and DM frequency can be derived from fundamental frequency f_0 and switching frequency f_c

as (7) and (8), respectively.

$$f_1 = (2m-1)f_c \pm 2nf_0 \tag{7}$$

$$f_2 = 2mf_c \pm (2n+1)f_0 \tag{8}$$

where $m = 1, 2, 3, \ldots, n = 0, 1, 2, \ldots$. When n is a multiple of 3, f_1 denotes CM frequency, otherwise, f_1 denotes DM frequency. When $2n + 1$ is a multiple of 3, f_2 denotes CM frequency, otherwise, f_2 denotes DM frequency.

C. Mathematical Model of Leakage Current in Time and Frequency Domain.

According to Fig. 3, the mathematical representation of leakage current in frequency domain is expressed as

$$\tilde{I}_g = \frac{\tilde{U}_g}{Z} = \frac{j\omega C_g[(3-2x)\tilde{U}_c + x(\tilde{U}_a + \tilde{U}_b)]}{3 - 3k\omega^2 C_g L_s + j\omega 3kC_g R_s} \tag{9}$$

where $\omega = 2\pi f$. When f is the CM frequency, I_g represents CM leakage current, otherwise, I_g represents DM leakage current.

The leakage current is mainly contributed by the high dv/dt occurring at the rising and falling edges of PWM voltage. Therefore, the equivalent GW voltage source U_g can be equal to a series of square-wave pulses, and the leakage current in time domain can be regarded as the step response of RLC circuit as

$$i_g(t) = \frac{E}{k\sqrt{\frac{L_s}{kC_g} - \frac{R_s^2}{4}}} e^{-\frac{R_s}{2L_s}t} \sin\left(\sqrt{\frac{1}{kL_sC_g} - \frac{R_s^2}{4L_s^2}}t\right) \tag{10}$$

where $E = +E_d$ for the rising edge, $E = -E_d$ for the falling edge.

As shown in (9) and (10), both the time domain and frequency domain characteristics of leakage current are related to the degradation position x and insulation capacitance C_g. Therefore, it is possible to assess the GW insulation degradation degree and location using the characteristics of leakage current in time and frequency domain.

III. PROPOSED ONLINE MONITORING METHOD OF GW INSULATION CONDITION FOR IFMS

According to the above analysis, a new online monitoring method is proposed to assess the GW insulation condition of IFMs. Based on the characteristics of leakage current in time and frequency domain, the insulation degradation degree, position, and phase can be assessed separately.

A. Assessment of Degradation Degree

The degradation degree of GW insulation is identified by the CM leakage current $I_{g,CM}$. According to (5) and (9), the CM leakage current $I_{g,CM}$ is derived as

$$\tilde{I}_{g,CM} = \frac{-3\omega C_g(\sqrt{3}+j)\frac{E_d}{m\pi}J_0(\frac{\alpha n\pi}{2})}{3 + x(3-2x)\omega C_g(-\omega L_s + jR_s)} \tag{11}$$

where $\omega = 2m\pi f_c$, $m = 1,3,5, \ldots$.

During the operation of IFMs, the DC bus voltage E_d and the modulation index α are usually constant, and the stator resistance R_s and stator inductance L_s can be obtained by online parameter identification methods. According to (11), the CM leakage current $I_{g,CM}$ from 4000 Hz to 44000 Hz under different insulation capacitances and degradation positions are shown in Fig. 3. It can be seen from Fig. 3(a) that the $I_{g,CM}$ increases linearly with the increasing of C_g from 0 to 1 nF, and it reaches to the highest value at 4000 Hz switching frequency and tends to decrease as CM frequency increases. In addition, the $I_{g,CM}$ remains nearly constant when the degradation position x changes as shown in Fig .3(b). Therefore, the $I_{g,CM}$ is highly sensitive to C_g but is almost not affected by the degradation position. Using the amplitude of CM leakage current, the degree of GW insulation degradation can be identified.

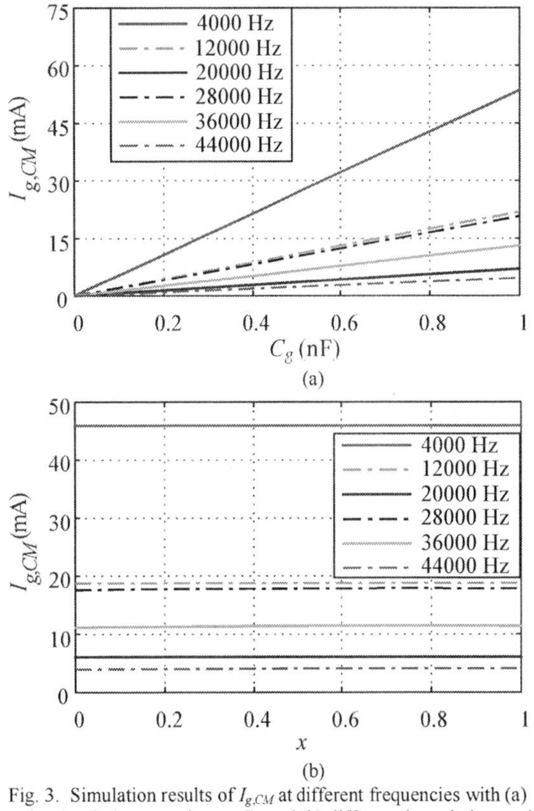

Fig. 3. Simulation results of $I_{g,CM}$ at different frequencies with (a) increasing insulation capacitance C_g, and (b) different degradation position x.

B. Assessment of Degradation Position

The degradation position of GW insulation is identified by combining the DM and CM leakage current.

The DM leakage current is derived from (6) and (9) as

$$\tilde{I}_{g,DM} = \frac{(3x-3)\omega C_g(\sqrt{3}+j)\frac{E_d}{m\pi}J_k(\frac{\alpha n\pi}{2})}{3+x(3-2x)\omega C_g(-\omega L_s + jR_s)} \tag{12}$$

where $\omega = 2m\pi f_c + 2\pi f_0$, and $m = 2,4,6, \ldots$.

According to (12), the DM leakage current $I_{g,DM}$ from 8050 Hz to 48050 Hz under different insulation capacitances and degradation positions are shown in Fig. 4. It can be seen from Fig. 4(a) that the $I_{g,DM}$ increases as C_g increases from 0 to 1 nF, and the $I_{g,DM}$ at 8050 Hz is larger than those at other frequencies. Fig. 4(b) shows that the $I_{g,DM}$ decreases linearly with the increasing x and is almost zero near the neutral end. It is shown that the $I_{g,DM}$ is not only affected by C_g, but also by x. Therefore, the degradation position x can be identified by $I_{g,DM}$.

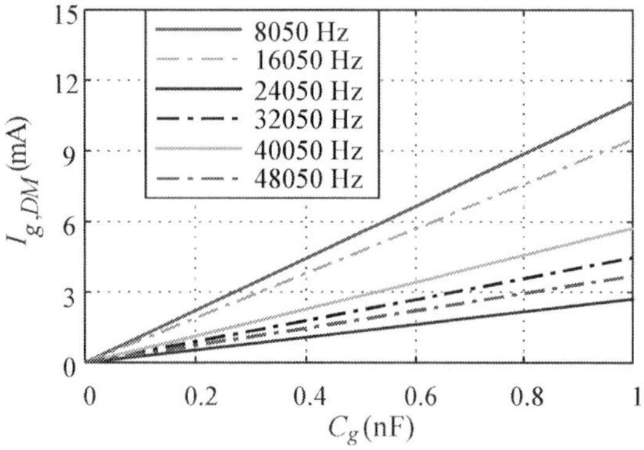

(a)

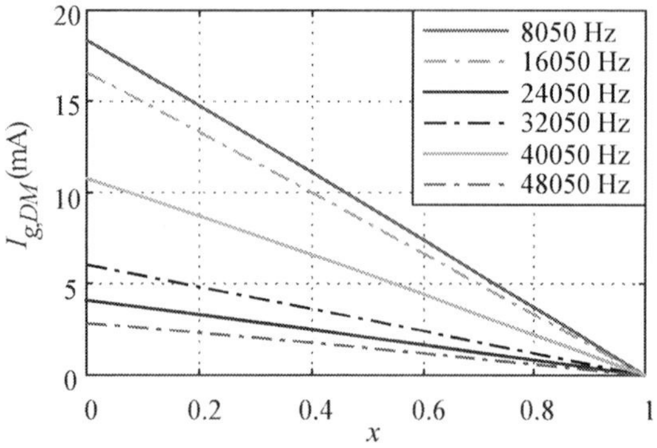

(b)

Fig. 4. Simulation results of $I_{g,DM}$ at different frequencies with (a) increasing insulation capacitance C_g, and (b) different degradation position x.

C. Assessment of Degradation Phase

The degradation phase of GW insulation is identified by the initial oscillation amplitude of leakage current, which is derived from (10) as

$$A_{mp} = \frac{E}{k\sqrt{\frac{L_s}{kC_g} - \frac{R_s^2}{4}}} \tag{13}$$

where $E = +E_d$ for the rising edge, $E = -E_d$ for the falling edge. It can be seen from (13) that the A_{mp} changes with the variation of C_g and k when E_d, R_s and L_s are fixed, and hence, the A_{mp} is affected by the GW insulation impedance.

The RLC circuit shown in Fig. 2 is simulated using MATLAB/Simulink. The C_g is set as 220 pF, and the degradation position is in phase C ($x = 0.5$). It can be seen from Fig. 5 that the leakage current is excited by the rising edge of PWM voltage and decays to zero after several oscillation periods. The A_{mp} excited by the PWM voltages of phase A and phase B are both 58 mA because the insulation conditions of these two phases are same. The A_{mp} excited by PWM voltage of phase C is 150 mA, which is larger than that of the above two cases. Therefore, the degradation phase can be identified by comparing the A_{mp} of leakage currents excited by the corresponding three step phase voltages.

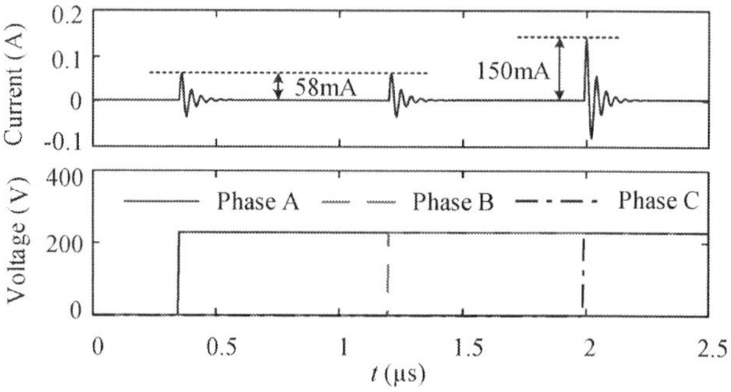

Fig. 5. Simulation of transient leakage currents excited by the corresponding three step phase voltages. The degradation is introduced in phase C with $x = 0.5$.

IV. Experimental Verification

The schematic diagram of insulation monitoring is shown in Fig. 6. The under-test motor is a 3kW inverter-fed permanent magnetic synchronous motor (PMSM). The FFT are adopted to analyze the CM leakage current and DM leakage current. The values of $I_{g,CM}$, $I_{g,DM}$, and A_{mp} under healthy condition are stored in a lookup table as the references, and their increments under degradation cases are obtained to assess the GW insulation condition.

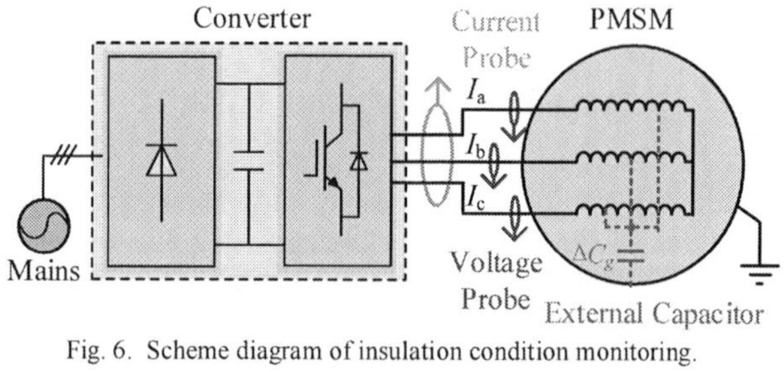

Fig. 6. Scheme diagram of insulation condition monitoring.

A Validation of Degradation Degree Assessment

The external capacitor ΔC_g, ranging from 0.1 to 1 nF, is connected between the tap of phase C and ground to simulate the GW insulation degradation. The CM leakage current increment under various capacitances of ΔC_g and degradation positions are obtained and shown in Fig. 7. It is shown that the $\Delta I_{g,CM}$ increases with the increasing ΔC_g, and the slopes of $\Delta I_{g,CM}$ are nearly the same at different x. Hence, the $\Delta I_{g,CM}$ is not affected by x and can be used to assess the degradation degree of GW insulation.

B. Validation of Degradation Position Assessment

The effect of x and ΔC_g on the $\Delta I_{g,DM}$ is shown in Fig. 8, which shows that the $\Delta I_{g,DM}$ increases with the increasing ΔC_g when the x is fixed, but its slope decreases from the maximum value to near zero with the increasing of x.

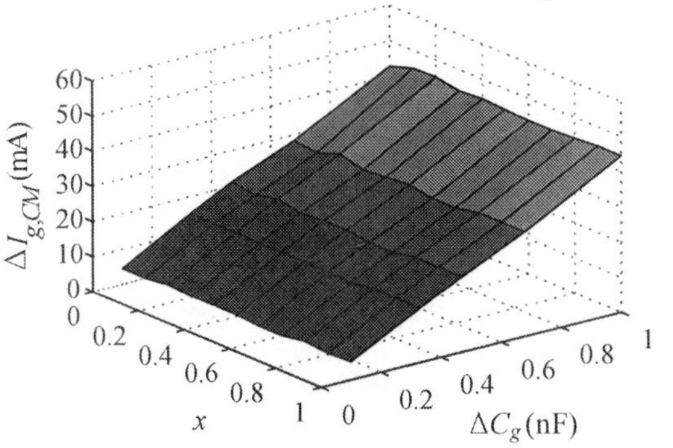

Fig. 7. Experimental results of $\Delta I_{g,CM}$ (4000 Hz) with different external capacitor ΔC_g and degradation position x.

Therefore, the $\Delta I_{g,DM}$ contains the information of both degradation degree and position. In this paper, the degradation position is identified by the ratio of the change in $I_{g,DM}$ to the change in $I_{g,CM}$ as shown in (14), where the variables with superscript * represent the measured results under degradation cases.

$$K = \frac{I^*_{g,DM} - I_{g,DM}}{I^*_{g,CM} - I_{g,CM}} \tag{14}$$

The slope K under different ΔC_g and x, derived from the $\Delta I_{g,CM}$ at 4000 Hz and $\Delta I_{g,DM}$ at 8050 Hz, is shown in Fig. 9. It is shown that the K remains nearly unchanged with ΔC_g at any x, but it decreases with the increasing x. Therefore, the value of K is only affected by x, i.e., it can be used to identify the degradation position.

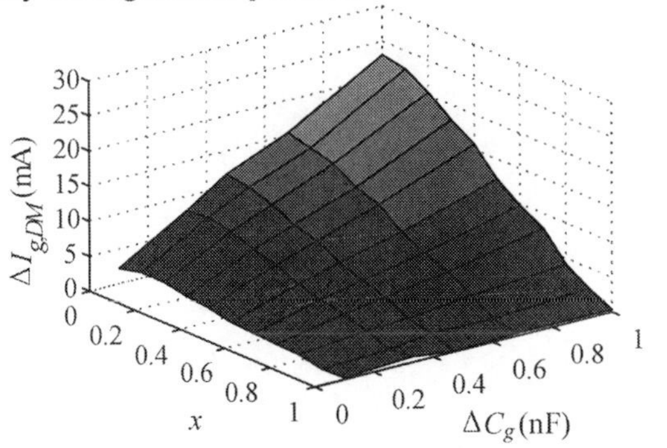

Fig. 8. Experimental results of $\Delta I_{g,DM}$ (8050 Hz) with different external capacitor ΔC_g and degradation position x.

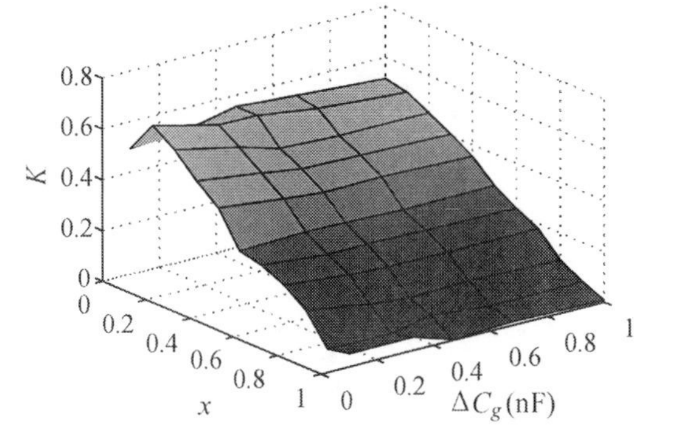

Fig. 9. Experimental results of K with different external capacitor ΔC_g and degradation position x.

C. Validation of Degradation Phase Assessment

The increment of initial oscillation amplitude, with respect to the values in healthy condition, ΔA_{mp}, is used to identify the degradation phase. The ΔA_{mp} under different ΔC_g with fixed degradation position at $x = 0.5$ is shown in Fig. 10, where the $\Delta A_{mp\text{-}A,B,C}$ represent the ΔA_{mp} of leakage currents excited by the corresponding phase voltages. It can be seen that the $\Delta A_{mp\text{-}C}$ gradually increases with the increasing of ΔC_g, and the values of $\Delta A_{mp\text{-}A}$ and $\Delta A_{mp\text{-}B}$ are small and are not affected by ΔC_g. Therefore, the degradation phase can be identified by the difference between $\Delta A_{mp\text{-}A,B,C}$.

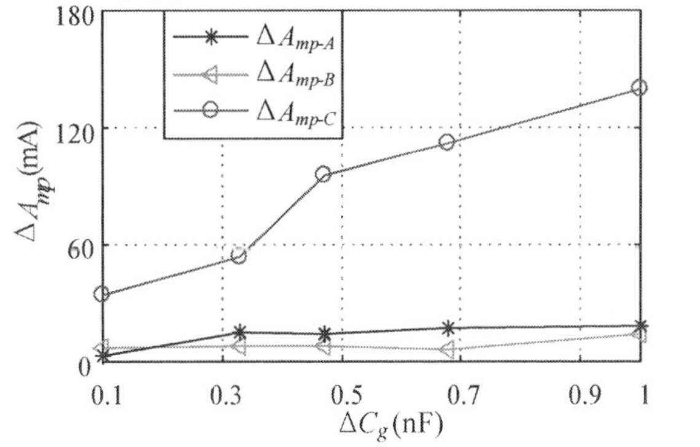

Fig. 10. Experimental results of $\Delta A_{mp\text{-}A,B,C}$ with increasing external capacitor ΔC_g.

V. Conclusion

Accurate online GW insulation condition assessment is critical for the reliable operation of IFMs. In this paper, a new monitoring method of GW insulation condition is proposed based on the time and frequency domain characteristics of leakage current. The theoretical analysis and experimental results show that both the CM and DM harmonics of leakage current are affected by degradation degree in low frequency range, whereas the DM harmonics are also affected by degradation position. Furthermore, the initial oscillation amplitude of leakage current is highly related to the GW insulation condition of each phase. Compared with previous methods, the proposed method can identify the degradation degree and position of GW insulation separately, and its requirement of monitoring bandwidth is lower. It can also identify the degradation phase of GW insulation, which is beneficial for the precise maintenance of motor insulation system.

REFERENCES

[1] P. Zhang, Y. Du, T. G. Habetler and B. Lu, "A survey of condition monitoring and protection methods for medium-voltage induction motors," *IEEE Transactions on Industry Applications*, 2011, 47(1): 34-46.

[2] G. C. Stone *et al*., *Electrical Insulation for Rotating Machines: Design, Evaluation, Aging, Testing, and Repair*, 2nd ed, Hoboken NJ, USA: IEEE Press, 2014.

[3] G. C. Stone, H. G. Sedding, and C. Chan, "Experience with online partial discharge measurement in high-voltage inverter-fed motors," *IEEE Transactions on Industry Applications*, 2018, 54(1):866-872

[4] C. Zoeller, M. A. Vogelsberger, R. Fasching, W. Grubelnik, and T. M. Wolbank, "Evaluation and current-response-based identification of insulation degradation for high utilized electrical machines in railway application," *IEEE Transactions on Industry Applications*, 2017, 53(3): 2679-2689.

[5] C. Zoeller, M. A. Vogelsberger, T. M. Wolbank, and H. Ertl, "Impact of SiC semiconductors switching transition speed on insulation health state monitoring of traction machines," *IET Power Electronics*, 2016, 9(15): 2769-2775

[6] H. Li, Y. Gu, D. Xiang, P. Zhang, P. Yue and Y. Cui, "Online condition monitoring of line-end coils insulation for inverter-fed machine by switching oscillation mode decomposition," *IEEE Transactions on Industrial Electronics*, 2022, 69(11): 11697-11708

[7] S. B. Lee, J. Yang, K. Younsi, and R. M. Bharadwaj, "An online groundwall and phase-to-phase insulation quality assessment technique for AC machine stator windings," *IEEE Transactions on Industry Applications*, 2006, 42(4)

[8] D. Zheng and P. Zhang, "An online groundwall and phase-to-phase stator insulation monitoring method for inverter-fed machine," *IEEE Transactions on Industrial Electronics*, 2021, 68(6): 5303-5313

[9] P. Zhang, K. Younsi, and P. Neti, "A novel online stator ground-wall insulation monitoring scheme for inverter-fed AC motors," *IEEE* Transactions on Industry Applications, 2015, 51, no. (3): 2201-2207

[10] I. Tsyokhla, A. Griffo, and J. Wang, "Online condition monitoring for diagnosis and prognosis of insulation degradation of inverter-fed machines," *IEEE Transactions on Industrial Electronics*, 2019, 66(10): 8126-8135

[11] F. Niu *et al*., "An online groundwall insulation monitoring method based on transient characteristics of leakage current for inverter-fed motors," *IEEE Transactions on Power Electronics*, 2022, 37(8): 9745-9753

[12] D. Zheng, G. Lu and P. Zhang, "An improved online stator insulation monitoring method based on common-mode impedance spectrum considering the effect of ageing position," *IEEE Transactions on Industry Applications*, 2022, 58(3): 3558-3566

8th International Conference on Reliability of Electrical Products and Electrical Contacts, November 18-20, 2022**(Invited Paper)**

The Interfacial Adhesion of Contacting Pairs with Different Surface Morphologies and Roughness Gradients Deposited by Magnetron Sputtering

Xue Zhou, Guofu Zhai

Harbin Institute of technology, Harbin, 150000, China

E-mail: zhouxue@hit.edu.cn Tel: 18503695609

***Abstract*—Micro-Electromechanical-Relay (MER) has widely achieved application in the field of engineering thanks to the excellent features and ever-growing interest in microelectronic products. However, the interfacial adhesion between gold-plated contact pairs in MER usually bring about operating failure of normally closed contacts limiting the reliability level of MER. The coating quality determining interfacial adhesion of millinewton-scale metals of contact pair is considered as a critical factor to fabricate smaller, more reliable and efficient MER. The fabrication of high reliability MER requires an optimized design based on the understanding of the interfacial adhesion properties of the constituent coating homogeneous structure. In this study, the gold coating deposited on the surface of contact pairs are introduced by magnetron sputtering, and as-obtained contact pairs are assembled to achieve various contact combinations and, to some extent, simulate real contact conditions. The interfacial adhesion involving the contact pairs with different surface morphologies and roughness gradients and associated adhesion type is built with the help of mechanical adhesion theory to explain the nature of interfacial adhesion.**

***Index Terms*— Magnetron sputtering, Cold adhesion, Roughness.**

I. Introduction

Micro-Electromechanical-Relay has been extensively applicated in electric vehicle, communication equipment, household appliances and weapon systems because of its extraordinary features including, but not limited to, high off-isolation, low insertion loss and low power consumption [1]. It is well-known that the achieving signal transitions is mainly determined to the contact pairs integrated on the MER, the failure of contact pairs could cause the notable decrease of the reliability of relay. In this case, silver-based alloy has been a preferred contact material in electronic applications for long time owing to their excellent thermal/electrical stability [2]. However, Ag-based alloy has a serious propensity to form oxide film on the contacts surface, which affects the increase in contact resistance and degrades contact reliability of relay.

To address this issue, a frequently used solution is to introduce various coating as interlayer spacers to prevent the oxidation of Ag-based alloy substrate as much as possible, among all the coating materials, the gold is one of the most potential coating materials and has been successfully applicated in the various occasions due to its better surface properties like low resistivity, excellent anti-corrosion, and low propensity to form alien-film on the contacts surface. Based on this strategy, a thin overlay of gold coating is deposited onto the surface of contacts of separable micro-electrical equipment used in high reliability or aggressive environments industrial applications. Even though gold coating indeed partially mitigate the problem of the oxidation of contact pairs, the interfacial adhesion between gold-plated contact pairs is more severe than those of Ag-based alloy without gold coating by virtue of the high adhesion of gold coating, leading to the properties of MER are not as good as expected, largely limited the contact reliability, in order to eliminate these opposing problems, many of the researchers and research institutions has been to investigate the parameters relating to the performance indicators of gold-plated contact pairs including, but not limited to, coating material and quality [1], and to analyze the principle of the interfacial adhesion trying to solve this issue [3]. According to research, interfacial adhesion are strongly related to the mechanical properties of coating and operating environment [4]. The surface properties of coating play a critical role in optimizing the interfacial adhesion between contact pairs, in comparison with gold coating fabricated by the traditional electroplating, the magnetron sputtering may be an better alternative project thanks to its high deposition rates and low contamination of deposits, which can generate an uniform coating with better control of composition, good crystallinity and fewer defects, and endowing the plated-parts excellent mechanical (such as high wear resistance and hardness) and anti-corrosion properties, which brings a probability of preparation of the high-quality coating. To the best of our knowledge, the systematic studies on the relationship between the surface morphology and roughness of coating prepared by magnetron sputtering and the interfacial adhesion between contact pairs have not been reported.

In this paper, the effect of substrate with different surface morphologies on the migration of sputtered particles during magnetron sputtering is systematically studied, and the as-obtained contact pairs are assembled to achieve various contact combinations involving the different surface morphologies and roughness gradients, to some extent, simulate real contact conditions.

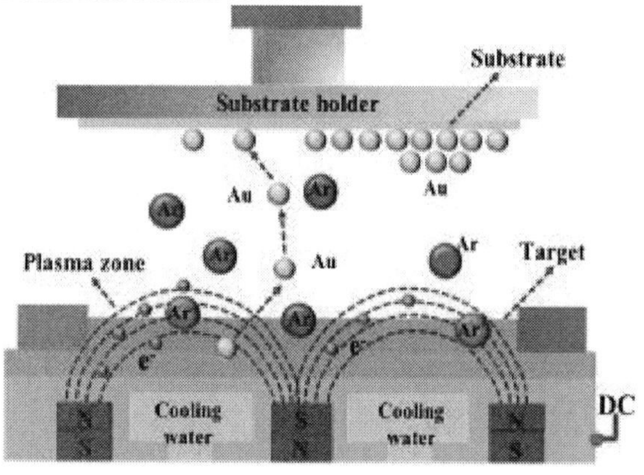

Fig.1 The transported ions during the sputtering process.

II. Experiment

The prepared gold coating with a thickness of 0.5μm on the surface of contact pairs by adopting a direct current magnetron sputtering system is as follows. First, the contact pairs composed of Ag-based alloy (spring and static contact) are cleaned ultrasonically in acetone and alcohol solvents in turn for 10min to remove surface impureness and grease, and then high-purity argon is used as the sputtering gas, the base pressure and sputtering one is set to $3x10^{-4}$Pa and 1.5Pa, and the sputtering power, bias pressure, time and substrate temperature is 200W, -100V, 8min, 50°C, respectively, during which the gold target is bombarded by energetic ions, generating a glow discharge plasma, the gold particles originated from the bombardment process are deposited on the surface of contact pairs and form a densely coating with a thickness of 0.5μm, as shown in Fig.1

III. Results And Discussion

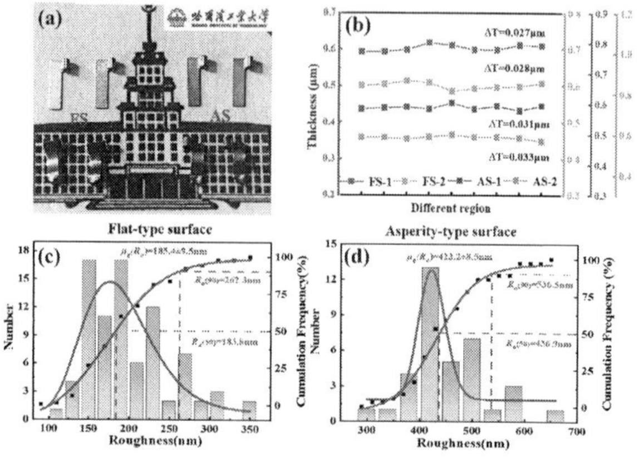

Fig. 2. (a) The digital photos of contact pairs; (b) The thickness of gold coating for four-types spring contact in different region; (c, d) The roughness distribution for surface morphologies of spring contact.

The surface morphological and roughness features in the contacting region of 150 randomly sampled sputtering specimen contact pairs (Fig. 2a) are characterized using a confocal microscope, where the roughness ranges are 150~200nm, 250~350nm and 400~550nm, including flat-type and asperity-type surface morphologies and denoting as FS-1, FS-1, AS-1 and AS-2, respectively. In order to improve accurate for evaluating surface state, each roughness result obtained for a typical spring is the mean value of all measurements obtained by randomly selecting four regions in contacting locations and conducting measurements four times on the corresponding surface. The recorded roughness results uniformly show a Gaussian-like distribution (Fig. 2c and d), which average roughness of two-types morphologies springs is 185.4±9.5nm and 423.2±8.5nm, respectively. The thickness uniformity of prepared gold coating for contact pairs is evaluated by measuring ten data points in the contacting region with a coating thickness gauge, which demonstrates good consistency (Fig. 2b). In comparison, AS-1 (0.031μm), AS-2 spring (0.033μm) and micro-corrugated contact AS-2 spring (0.029μm) exhibits a wider range than those of FS-1 (0.027μm) and FS-2 (0.028μm), which could be attributed to the surface state of the spring and the crystallinity of the deposited gold grains.

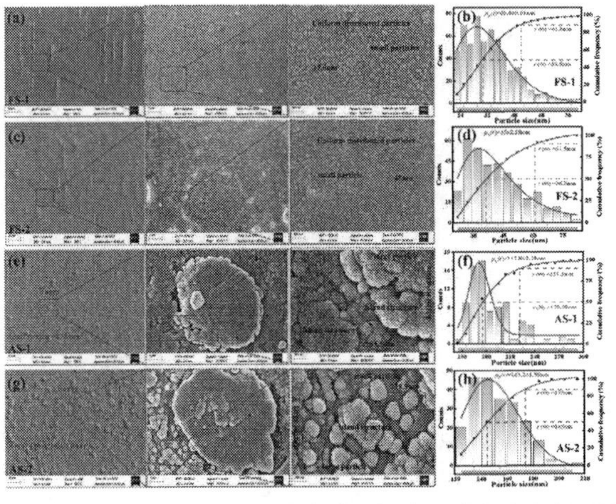
Fig. 3. The comparison of surface morphologies of springs of (a) FS-1; (b) FS-2; (c) AS-1and (d) AS-2.

Scanning electron microscope (SEM) images of contact pair surface morphology further show that the AS springs and micro-corrugated contacts have a rougher surface than the FS one, as presented in Fig. 3, the surface of the FS springs and micro-corrugated contacts is uniformly deposited by nano-scale gold grains presenting dense structures without the distinct coating defects (such as pores and cracks), which attribute to the gold grains sputtered onto flat-morphological substrate could be coalesced into the ordered and smooth continuous coating, and calculating mean size of gold grains are about 40.59 nm and 37 nm with the most common diameter being 30nm. In contrast, the raw substrate of AS springs with bumps after sputtering appears the progressive accumulation and coalescence of gold grains to form bright clusters that are denoted as island structures of increasing size and accompanied by the generation of nodules and voids in their surroundings. More importantly, the Au grains can easily agglomerate and obtain a larger island structure at high areal density of the bumps than those deposited with low areal density, and thus, more micron-sized nodules and voids are generated and mean size of irregular islands increased from 117.8 nm to 149.2 nm and 140.5 nm with varying of the areal density of bumps from 473/nm^2 to 3027/nm^2, which lead to the surface of AS spring is rougher compared to the raw AS by comparing the linear scanning results of gold-plated springs and raw springs. Because all of the sputtering parameters for springs are identical, the formation of gold islands can be attributed to the effect of bumps on grain movement during the sputtering process. Generally, these bumps block the orderly migration of gold grains when grains arrived at the substrate, and result in crystallizing into loosely packed clusters, and thus concluded that the agglomeration of gold particles is correlation with the number of bumps.

The mechanical properties of coatings are measured using a nano-indenter with a constant indentation depth of 60nm, the typical load-depth curves of loading-unloading process of FS-1, FS-2, AS-1 and AS-2 are depicted on Fig.1m-p. As shown by the load curves, the indentation depth increases with the increase of load, the tip nose of unloading curve is due to the inability to completely release internal stress during fast unloading. The nano-hardness (H) and elastic module (E) of specimens are shown in table 1, respectively. Obviously, the hardness of AS coatings is higher than that of FS coatings. The difference in the hardness may be caused by the development of microstructure, which ascribed to the surface bumps of AS springs provides a large number of heterogeneous nucleation sites to stack more grains, resulting in the enhancement of surface hardness. When the number of bumps further increases leads to the notable coarsening of the crystals, and in turn AS-1 (1.185Gpa) is stronger hardness than AS-2 (1.085 Gpa). Furthermore, the ratio of H/E could represent elastic-plastic property of coating materials, the H/E of AS springs (0.012 and 0.017) is much higher than those of FS (0.007 and 0.009), indicating its best resistance to deformation.

To investigate the interfacial adhesion properties of various contacting combinations (group 1 (FS-1 spring and contact), group 2 (FS-2 spring and contact), group 3 (AS-1 spring and contact) and group 4 (AS-2 spring and contact)), and 20 specimens in each group are taken to measure adhesion force. The typical force-displacement curves for the adhesion between contact pairs (Fig.4 a-d) in every contacting combination revealed that the adhesion force between contact pairs decreased as the roughness gradients increased. The adhesion force of FS (FS-1 and FS-2) and AS springs (AS-1 and AS-2) decreases from 27 mN to17.2 mN, 43.5mN to 22.2mN, respectively) when the surface roughness of the springs increases. All measured adhesion forces are summarized in Fig. 4, most of the adhesion force generated in these measurements fluctuate within less than of 10% of the average value, revealing the change of adhesion force each contacting combination remain almost stable. It is discovered that the contacting combination of FS-2 spring and micro-corrugated contact are of a rather low the mean adhesion force (13.6 mN) compared with FS-1 (18.5 mN), this is far lower than those of many previously reported adhesion failure cases in MER, whereas the combinations of AS springs and micro-corrugated contacts have inferior anti-adhesion performance, and their (AS-1 and AS-2) mean adhesion force reaches up to 28 mN and 25 mN, respectively. The significant change of adhesion force confirmed the effect of surface morphologies and roughness gradients of springs, and the interfacial adhesion of contacting combination of AS springs and micro-corrugated contacts is distinct due to the intrinsically high surface energy of atoms on an asperity surface.

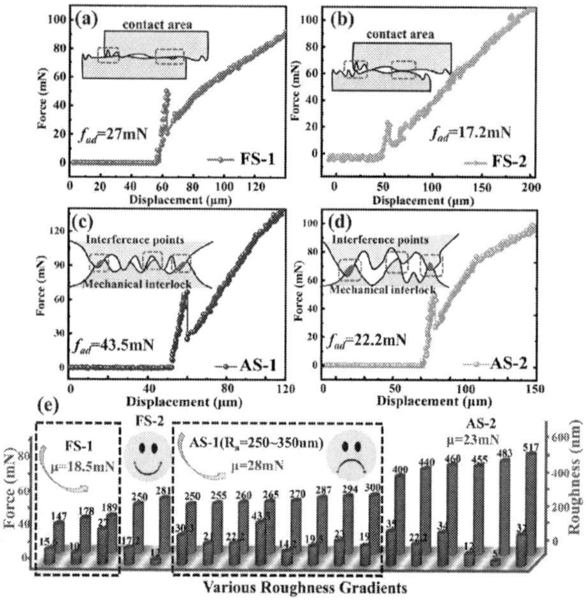

Fig. 4. The typical force-displacement curves of springs occurring cold adhesion at various roughness gradients; (a) FS-1, (b) FS-2; (c) AS-1, (d) AS-2; (e) The relationship between the adhesion force, the roughness and the surface morphology of springs.

In order to demonstrate the feasibility of magnetron sputtering applied in the relay with aspect to the coating of contact pairs compared to the coating fabricated by the traditional electroplating technique. The gold coating is deposited onto the Ag-based alloy substrate using magnetron sputtering, the as-obtained contact pairs are assembled to achieve various contact combinations and, to some extent, simulate real contact conditions. The screening experiments including mechanical vibration particle impact noise detection, and Low and middle level operation under the low and high temperature for 80 randomly sampled relays assembled from the contact pair fabricated by the electroplating and magnetron sputtering respectively are performed to evaluate the adaptability and reliability of the mechanical environment. The measurement results show the failure rate of cold adhesion between contact pairs prepared by the electroplating method reaches up to 15% and 7% respectively after two screening experiments. It should be noted that some Chinese relay manufacturers have reported that the failure rate of batches relays resulted by the cold adhesion reaches up to 15~25% over the whole failures model after the screening experiment, while the failure rate of contact pairs fabricated by magnetron sputtering is only 6.25% and 4%. Additionally, the failure rate of voltage difference of closed and breaking process after treating high temperature of 185℃ of gold-plated contact pair fabricated by magnetron sputtering in micro-relay also shows immense reliability, as shown in table I and II. This is far lower than that of many previously reported adhesion failure cases in micro-relay compared to the coating fabricated by the tradition electroplating technique.

TABLE I
THE COMPARISON OF FAILURE RATE OF COLD ADHESION IN EACH EXPERIMENTAL PHASE AFTER THE CONTACT PAIRS PREPARED BY ELECTROPLATING (ED) AND MAGNETRON SPUTTERING (MS) TECHNIQUES ARE INSTALLED ON THE RELAY

Experiment	First		Second	
	MS	ED	MS	ED
Random vibration	3	1	/	1
Sinusoidal vibration	/	/	/	1
Particle impact noise detection	/	/	/	1
Low-level operation under the high temperature	1	3	/	2
Low-level operation under the low temperature	/	/	2	/
Middle-level operation under the high temperature	/	4	/	/
Middle-level operation under the low temperature	/	1	/	/
The failure rate of cold adhesion	6.25%	15%	4%	7%

TABLE II
THE RATIO OF RELAYS WHOSE VOLTAGE DIFFERENCE IS HIGHER THAN 0.4V BEFORE AND AFTER BEING BAKED IN VACUUM AT 185℃.

Experiment	First		Second	
	MS	ED	MS	ED
Vacuum bake at 185℃	27.5%	45%	8%	18%

IV. CONCLUSION

The magnetron sputtering is considerable potential technique for depositing gold coating onto alloy-based alloy substrate compared to the traditional electroplating. The coating prepared by magnetron sputtering enable endowing plated-parts various excellent physical and mechanical properties (such as good porosity, crystallinity and fewer defects), which brings a probability of preparation of the high-quality coating compared to the traditional electroplating technique. In addition, the contamination and treatment of heavy-metal and wastewater during electroplating process usually significantly increase the cost. and it demonstrates that these contact theories in this paper for different roughness gradients and surface morphologies have great potential for use in MER engineering.

References

[1] W. Ren, C. Zhang, Q. Du, D. Du, H. Wang, Experimental investigation of cold adhesion failure physical mechanism of gold-plated contact within the Micro-Electromechanical Relay, *Eng. Fail. Anal.*, 121, 105151, 2021.

[2] Z. J. Lin, S. Y. Fan, M. M. Liu, S. H. Liu, J. G. Li, J. P. Li and X. D. Sun, Excellent anti-arc erosion performance

and corresponding mechanisms of a nickel-belt-reinforced silver-based electrical contact material, *Journal of Alloy and compounds*, 788, 163-171, 2019.

[3] M. Ciavarella, J. Joe, A. Papangelo, J.R. Barber, The role of adhesion in contact mechanics, *J. R. Soc. Interface*, 16, 20180738, 2019.

[4] G. Gregori, D.R. Clarke, The interrelation between adhesion, contact creep, and roughness on the life of gold contacts in radio-frequency microswitches, *J. Appl. Phys.*, 100, 094904, 2006.

Xue Zhou received the Ph.D. degree from Harbin Institute of Technology, Harbin, China, in 2010. He is currently a Professor with Harbin Institute of Technology, Harbin, China. His research interests include arc with electrical contact and intellectual electric apparatus.

8th International Conference on Reliability of
Electrical Products and Electrical Contacts,
November 18-20, 2022

Research and Improvement Suggestions on the Corrosion Phenomenon of Iron Parts in the Internal Micro-environment of Relay

Qingxing Su, Changliu Jiang, Lei Yi, Ningyi Lu

Xiamen Hongfa Electroacoustic CO., LTD, Xiamen, 361021, China
E-mail: suqingxing1120@126.com Tel: 15860766487

***Abstract*—With the higher reliability of relay products, more attention has been paid to the influence of varied micro-environment caused by the production of arc during the operation. In this paper, the corrosion phenomenon of iron parts of relays after electrical life test has been analyzed. It is confirmed that the formation of acidic substances is the primary cause of the corrosion of iron parts. Here the acidic substances are the reaction production of water vapor (H_2O) and compounds of nitrogen and oxygen (NxOy) produced in air under the action of arc. According to the corrosion mechanism, the various internal micro-environment of relays during the electrical life test has been simulated, and a rapid method for the evaluation of the corrosion resistance of the iron parts has been carried out.**

***Index Terms*— Relay, Micro-environment, Magnetic circuit iron, Corrosion mechanism**

I. INTRODUCTION

Metal corrosion refers to the deterioration caused by chemical changes in the environment. According to the reaction mechanism, metal corrosion can be classified as chemical corrosion and electrochemical corrosion. Chemical corrosion is based on chemical reaction in dry atmosphere or non-electrolyte environment. Electrochemical corrosion is based on the formation of two electrodes of metal and electrolyte to form corrosive primary battery. Metal corrosion can be classified as localized corrosion and total corrosion according to its morphology. Localized corrosion forms of spot corrosion, galvanic corrosion, crevice corrosion, abrasion corrosion, etc. The mechanisms of different corrosion forms are different[1]. The causes of metal corrosion include environmental factors (external factors) and material factors (internal factors).

Xiaofeng Zhu[2] analyzed that the main reason for the corrosion of relay components in the switch box is the high temperature and high humidity. The most important factor affecting the corrosion of metal is humidity. Chongfeng Liang[3] analyzed the harm of humidity to electrical equipment and the corrosion mechanism in humid environment. Kai Liu[4] analyzed the harm of condensation in terminal box to power equipment corrosion, and studied the condensation mechanism.

(a) Not corroded iron of Relay A1 (b) Corroded iron of Relay A2

(c) Corroded iron of Relay B (d) Corroded iron of Relay C

Fig. 1. Different relay corrosion after electrical life test

The corrosion of the iron parts in relay to a certain extent will bring harm to the relay as Fig.1. It will affect the appearance of the relay, resulting in the reduction of the over travel (OT) and the excessive actuation voltage. With the higher reliability of relay products, people pay more and more attention to the influence of varied micro-environment caused by the production of arc during the operation. However, the mechanism analysis and application research of iron corrosion in relay based on the change of micro-environment are few. Therefore all important parameters have to be taken into consideration to get a full and complete understanding of the problem.

In this paper, through the systematic analysis of the corrosion form and composition of iron parts in relay after the electrical life test, we confirmed that the formation of acidic substances is the primary cause of the corrosion of iron parts. The acidic substances are the reaction production of water vapor (H_2O) and NxOy produced by N_2 and O_2 in a relay under the arc action. According to the corrosion mechanism, the various internal micro-environment of relays during the electrical life test has been simulated, and the fast evaluation method of the corrosion resistance of the iron parts is explored.

II. Test Method

After electrical life test of the relay samples from different quality of iron parts, the corrosion type, products and content were analyzed by SEM-EDS, FT-IR, ICP-OES, IC and other instruments. In order to further accelerate the corrosion resistance of different iron parts, the fast evaluation method of corrosion resistance of relay iron parts is discussed by using the combined testing environment of different temperatures and humidity.

A. Analysis of the components of corrosion products

1) SEM-EDS analysis of corrosion on relay iron surface

As shown in Fig.2, SEM-EDS detected higher content of N and O and lower content of Ni in the serious corrosion area (position 1) than that in the slight corrosion area (position 2). In the area of position 3, it is mainly Ni, while N is not founded and the content of O and Fe is a little.

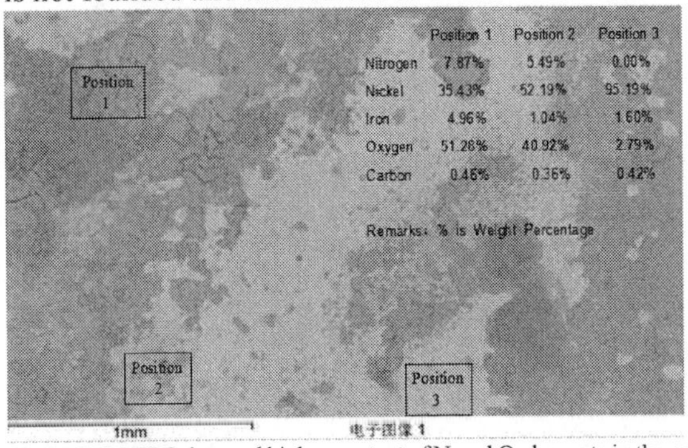

Fig.2. SEM-EDS detected higher content of N and O elements in the corrosion area than in the normal area.

2) FT-IR analysis of corrosion on relay iron surface

Four relays named A, B, C and D were tested 100,000 operations under the same electrical life condition (NO contacts, 250Va.c., 16A , cosΦ=0.75, 1s ON: 9s OFF). As shown in Fig.3, there were obvious peaks near the infrared spectrum 1350 cm^{-1} on the surface of armature of A, B and C. It was inferred that these relays contained nitrate. However, no obvious corrosion was found on the armature surface of relay D, and no obvious peak was found near the infrared spectrum 1350 cm^{-1}. It was inferred that the armature surface contains very small amount of nitrate if not absent. The results of the infrared spectrum 1350 cm^{-1} at the corrosion site of relay iron parts are consistent with the results of SEM-EDS which has the higher content of N and O.

3) ICP-OES analysis of corrosion on relay iron surface

Put relay E (Fig.4. a) and F (Fig.4. b) armature after electrical life test (NO contacts, 250Va.c., 16A , cosΦ=0.75, 1s ON: 9s OFF) into a clean beaker. Add ultra pure water to a certain scale. Vibrate and clean the corrosion products of armature surface by ultrasonic cleaning equipment. Transfer the corrosion solution to the volumetric flask and filter it. Analyze the content of Ni, Cu and Fe in the filtered corrosion solution by ICP-OES. There are more content of Ni, Cu and Fe in serious corrosion of Relay F armature than that in slight corrosion of Relay E as shown in Fig.4.

The matrix materials of armature of relay E and F is Fe. The inner layer coating is Cu with the thickness of 1~3 μm. The outer layer coating is Ni with the thickness of 3~7 μm.

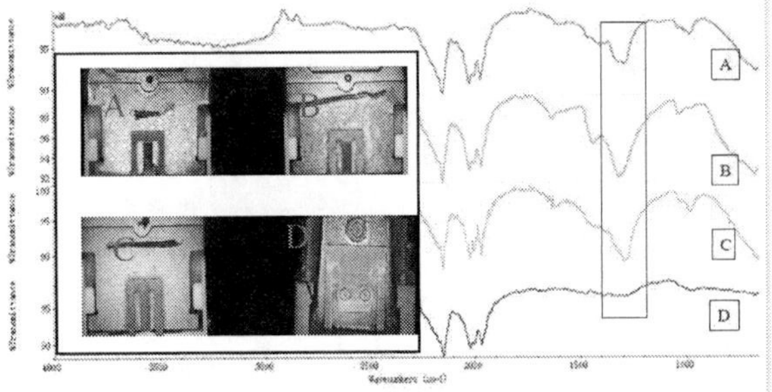

Fig.3. There are obvious peaks near 1350cm^{-1} in the corrosion site where may contains nitrate by FT-IR.

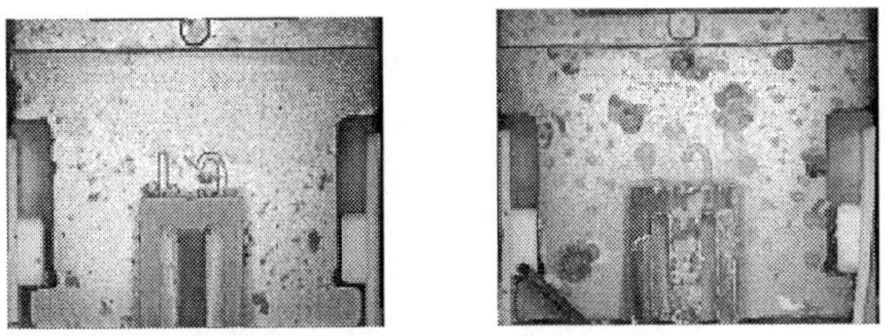

(a) Relay E	(b) Relay F
Electric life 100,000 times	Electric life 100,000 times
Slight corrosion	Serious corrosion
Ni: 0.36 mg/l	Ni:2.28 mg/l
Cu:0.12 mg/l	Cu:0.36 mg/l
Fe: N.D.	Fe:0.06 mg/l

Fig.4. Analysis concentration of Ni, Cu and Fe in the solution of armature surface corrosion by ICP-OES.

4) IC analysis of anionic concentration in the solution of iron corrosion products

Higher concentration of NO_x^- (NO_3^- and NO_2^-) was detected in relay F than relay E as shown in Fig.5. While NO_3^- and NO_2^- were not detected in the corrosion solution of relay G without electrical life test. After 100,000 operations under the same electrical life test of relay H from competitor, there is no obvious corrosion on the surface of iron parts, but 1.45mg/l NO_x^- was detected in the iron corrosion solution. It was shown that the production of nitrogen oxides (NO_x) is related to the electrical life test. The armature of relay H from competitor is plated with Ni with the thickness of 3~7 μm. The obvious difference between competitor iron and the iron in E、F or G is that the former has very few Si (<50 μg/g), but the latter has excessive Si (1000~2000 μg/g). The excessive

Si may aggravate the grain boundary corrosion of iron parts.

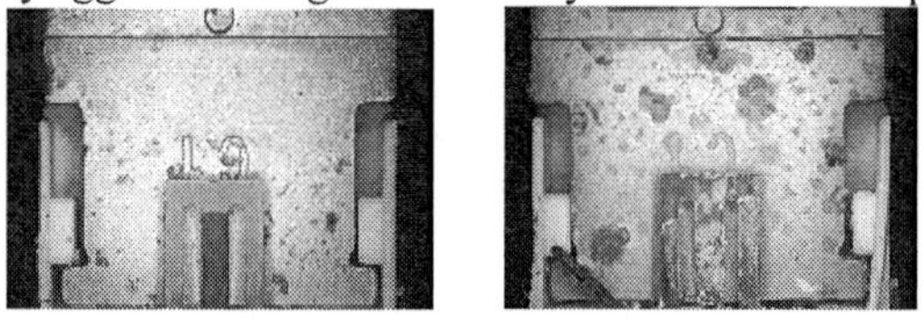

(a) Relay E
Electric life 100,000 times
$C(NO_x^-) = 2.42$ mg/l

(b) Relay F
Electric life 100,000 times
$C(NO_x^-) = 13.31$ mg/l

(c) Relay G
Electric life 0 times
$C(NO_x^-)$ = N.D.

(d) Relay H
Electric life 100,000 times
$C(NO_x^-) = 1.45$ mg/l

Fig.5. IC analyses anionic concentration (NO_3^- and NO_2^-) in solution of iron corrosion products from different relays

B. Electrical life test of different temperatures and humidity

The same batch of relays were put into three different temperatures and humidity for electrical life test to 100,000 times. The results show that the corrosion degree of iron parts is the most serious in high humidity as Fig.6c.

(a) 25°C 40% humidity (b) 55°C 20% humidity (c) 55°C 80% humidity

Fig.6. Life test in different temperatures and humidity

III. Results and Discussion

A. Discussion on the form of corrosion products of iron

1) Iron corrosion is divided into five categories according to the severity

Observe the relay after electrical life test according to the corrosion degree of iron surface from light to heavy (Fig.7). Corrosion can be divided into five categories according to severity: no corrosion (Fig.7.a)→ beginning corrosion (Fig.7.b) → light corrosion (Fig.7.c) → medium corrosion (Fig.7.d) → heavy corrosion (Fig.7.e).

2) Classification of iron corrosion according to micro mechanism

The metal corrosion can be divided into spot corrosion, fretting wear corrosion, galvanic corrosion, crevice corrosion and other types. Spot corrosion focuses on a small area of metal surface and penetrates into the metal interior[1]. Spot corrosion usually starts from a defective part of the metal material, then the loss of metallic luster → localized spot corrosion → spot corrosion gradually spread → comprehensive corrosion. Fig.8a shows the spot corrosion morphology. Fretting wear corrosion is the result of the synergistic effect of fretting wear and corrosion as Fig.8b. Fretting refers to the relative movement with periodic small amplitude, then micro-pores or spots appear on the surface of metal coating. In addition, the corrosion of corrosive substances makes the fretting wear position susceptible to produce more corrosion. Galvanic corrosion is also known as contact corrosion or dissimilar metal corrosion. When two different metals or alloys are in contact, the corrosion rate of the metal with a negative potential in the solution increases (armature plated with Ni, anode), while the metal with a positive potential is protected as cathode in compression spring (Fig.8c). Crevice corrosion is a form of localized corrosion, which occur at the joint of metal and metal or metal and nonmetal (Fig.8d).

(a) No corrosion (b) Beginning corrosion (c) Light corrosion

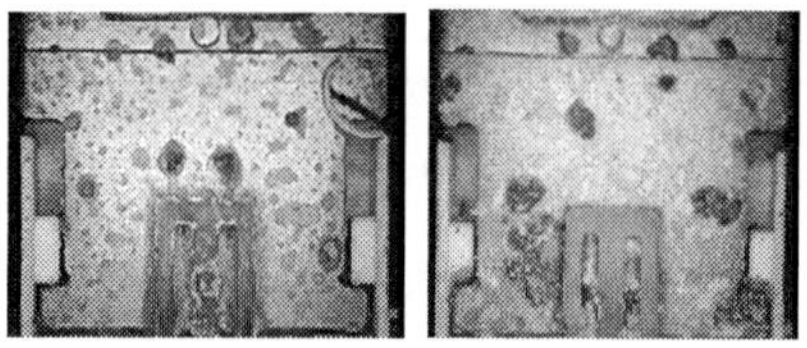

(d) Medium corrosion (e) Heavy corrosion

Fig.7. The photograph of the corrosion according to severity

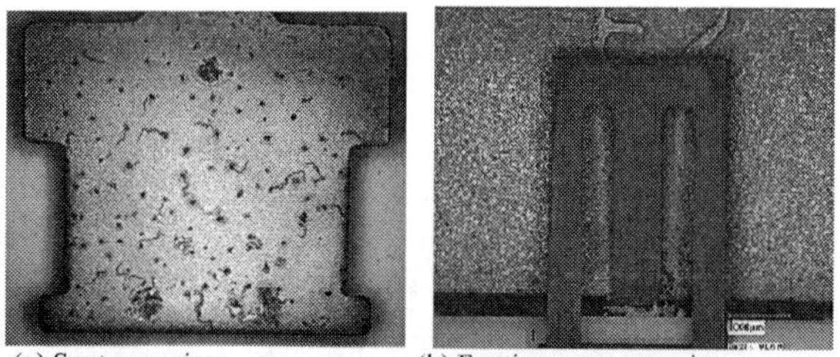

(a) Spot corrosion (b) Fretting wear corrosion

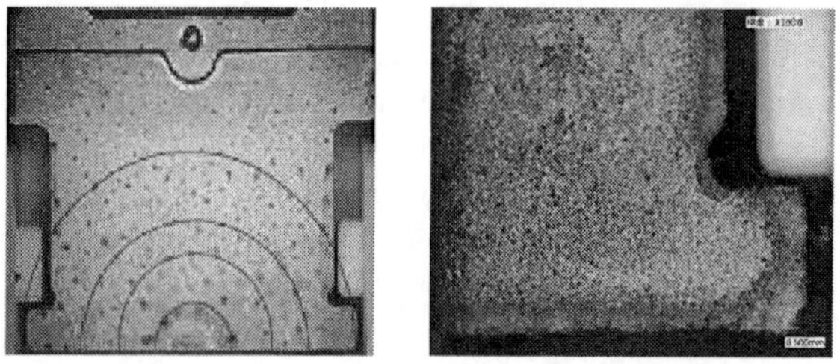

(c) Galvanic corrosion (d) Crevice corrosion

Fig.8. Morphology of different corrosion mechanism

3) Spot corrosion is the main form of localized corrosion of relay iron parts

44 relays out of 50 with the corrosion form were spot corrosion. It is indicated that spot corrosion is the main form of localized iron corrosion. The Ni plating layer under the armature corrosion position of the relay with spot corrosion became thinner (Fig.9b), and Fe matrix was corroded (Fig.9c). The corrosion extends along the metal grain boundary to the depth of the iron base.

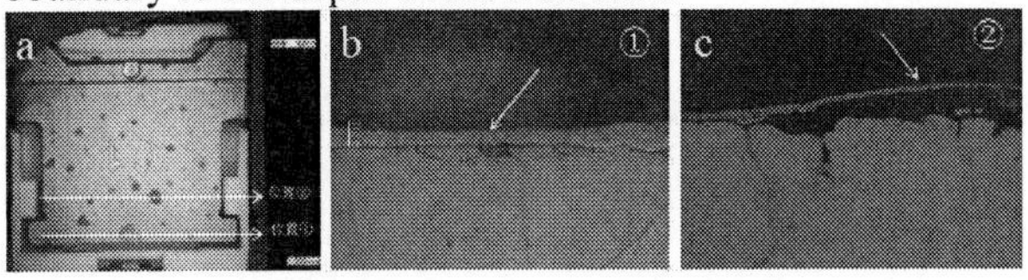

(a) Corrosion morphology of the armature surface of Relay I after electrical life test (NO contacts, 250 Va.c., 16 A , cosΦ = 0.75, 1s ON: 9s OFF).

(b) The Ni coating at position ① became thin.

(c) The Ni coating at position ② became thin and bulged.

Fig.9. The Ni plating layer under the corrosion position of relay armature with spot corrosion becomes thin

4) Discussion the production condition of spot corrosion of relay iron parts

When the iron coating is damaged due to defect (Fig.10), spot corrosion will occur on the metal with cathode coating on the surface, such as Ni coating of iron parts. Then the iron matrix under the damaged area and the undamaged area of iron coating will form a activation-deactivation corrosion cell. The deactivation surface (iron coating) is a cathode, and the area is much larger than the activation area. The corrosion develops to the deep iron matrix and forms small holes.

Spot corrosion also occurs in the medium with special ions, such as uneven adsorption of NO_3^- and NO_2^- compounds on the surface of iron parts[1].

Spot corrosion also occurs above a critical potential, which is called spot corrosion potential. When the iron parts are in corrosion solution and the corrosion potential exceeds the spot corrosion potential, uniform spot corrosion will occur.

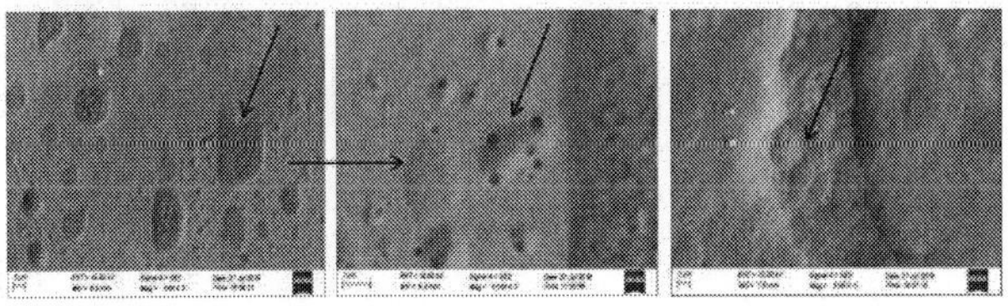

(a) Corrosion on iron surface (b) Surface holes of iron parts (c) Surface pits of iron parts

Fig.10. There are some defects on the surface of iron plating

B. Discussion on the composition of corrosion products of iron parts

1) The mechanism of HNOx produced by lightning

HNO_x is one of the main sources of acid rain[5]. A large number of authors have done a lot of analysis and research on the mechanism of HNO_x produced by lightning[6]. The main chemical reaction theories are as below[7]:

$e + N_2 \rightarrow N + N$,

$e + O_2 \rightarrow O + O$,

$N + O_2 \rightarrow NO + O$,

$O + N_2 \rightarrow NO + N$,

$NO + NO + O_2 \rightarrow 2NO_2$,

$NO + NO + O_2 \rightarrow NO_2 + N + O_2$,

$NO_x + H_2O \rightarrow HNO_x$

2) Discussion on the mechanism of HNOx produced in relay

For the relay, the arc is similar to the lightning in the atmospheric environment. But the relay cavity is relatively small, so the concentration of NOx and HNOx generated inside relay may be relatively large.

The results of SEM-EDS, FT-IR, ICP-OES and IC analysis of the corrosive products further confirmed that: under the action of relay arc, the N_2 and O_2 of internal relay will produce NOx, and generate HNOx with internal environment moisture. The main corrosion type of relay iron parts after the electrical life is the electrochemical corrosion reaction between the Ni coating and HNOx.

The causes of iron corrosion have external environmental factors and internal material factors. The following is a brief discussion.

C. Discussion on the environmental factors affecting corrosion of iron

1) The relationship between corrosion rate of iron and the thickness of water film on the surface

Water can react with NO_x to produce HNO_x, but also provide a medium for iron corrosion.When the relay works and the surrounding humidity is high, the water film is easy to form on the surface of the iron parts, because the temperature difference inside the relay will change. The relationship between the corrosion rate of iron parts and the thickness of water film formed on the surface is shown in Fig.11[8]

In zone I, there are several molecular layers of adsorbed water film on the metal surface, the thickness of which is less than 0.01μm. No continuous electrolyte is formed, and the corrosion rate of metal is very low.

In zone II, when the humidity exceeds the critical value, the thickness of the water film on the metal surface is between 0.01 μm and 1um. Due to the rapid diffusion of oxygen, the corrosion rate of the metal is multiplied.

In zone III, with the further increase of water film thickness, a visible liquid film will be formed. At this time, due to the barrier of the liquid film, the diffusion of oxygen becomes difficult, so the corrosion rate of the metal is correspondingly reduced.

In zone IV, when the thickness of water film increases

gradually to form water drop, the thickness of water film is more than 1 mm. The corrosion rate is similar to that of metal immersed in liquid.

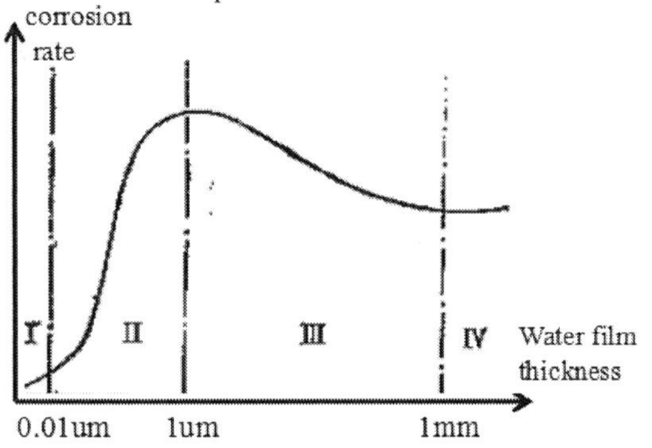

Fig.11. Relationship between thickness of water layer on metal surface and corrosion rate[8]

When the thickness of water film on the surface of the iron parts is in the area II and III, the iron are prone to corrosion. At this time, the corrosion speed is related to the thickness of the water film.Therefore, the analysis of relay iron environment can further promote understanding corrosion of relay iron parts.

2) Discussion on the mechanism of increasing iron corrosion in high humidity environment

When water molecules are adsorbed on the surface of the iron parts, they can react with water chemically. At this time, the condensation of water on the surface of iron is called chemical condensation. When the relative humidity is between 70% and 80%, HNO_x will agglomerate on the surface of iron and react with Ni coating. The formation of electrolyte nickel nitrate aggravates the corrosion of iron parts.

When the relative humidity of metal storage environment is lower than its critical value, the temperature has little effect on the corrosion rate. However high the temperature is, because the environment is dry, the metal is not easy to corrode. When the relative humidity reaches the critical value of metal corrosion, the influence of temperature plays a significant role. At this time, when the temperature increases by 10 °C, the corrosion rate increases by about two times[3].

The main effect of temperature is that cause condensation on the metal surface and accelerate the corrosion, when the temperature is greatly reduced. Large temperature difference between day-night and in-outdoor temperature will make the condensation happen. If the condensation happens periodically, iron parts will corrode seriously, when not coated properly.

D. Discussion on material factors affecting corrosion of relay iron

1) Discussion on spot corrosion resistance of iron coating

Spot corrosion occurs above a critical potential, when the iron parts are in the corrosion solution. The corrosion potential exceeds the spot potential, uniform spot corrosion will occur. When two different metals contact, the corrosion rate of the metal with negative potential increases, while the metal with positive potential is protected.

For the common coating of relay iron parts, the potential of Cu electrode is +0.337, Sn is +0.007, Ni is -0.25, Fe is -0.44. Cu is relatively the most positive, and the corrosion resistance is the strongest, followed by Sn, Ni, and finally Fe. Therefore, generally, the outer layer of Cu plated iron parts has strong corrosion resistance.

2) Discussion on the influence of defects of iron coating on corrosion

There are quality defects on the surface and inside the coating of some iron parts (Fig.12). These defects will weaken the protection ability of the coating and cannot effectively prevent the oxygen and water in the air from being immersed. For example, the high humidity environment discussed in the previous will accelerate the corrosion of iron parts.

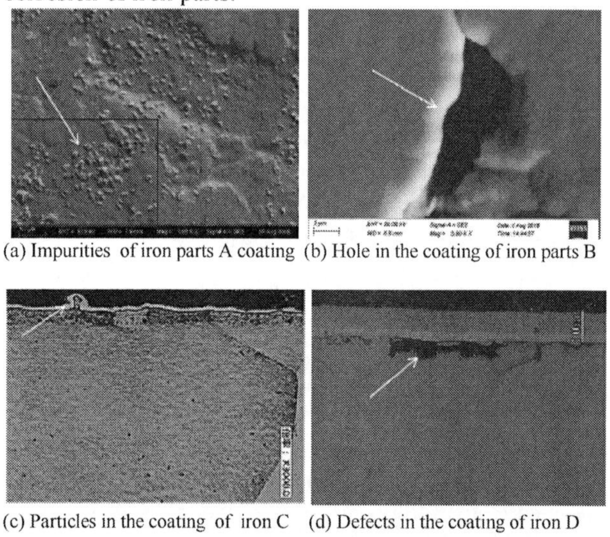

(a) Impurities of iron parts A coating (b) Hole in the coating of iron parts B

(c) Particles in the coating of iron C (d) Defects in the coating of iron D

Fig.12. Defects in the coating quality of iron parts

In addition, the nitric acid compound produced during the operation of the relay will agglomerate on the surface of the iron parts, and the corrosion will occur first at the defective part of the coating.

E. Discussion on evaluation method of coating quality of iron parts

The internal micro-environment of relay is complex, so a constant test environment is needed to evaluate the corrosion resistance of iron coating.

Salt spray test method (Fig.13a), in which the mechanism of Cl^- corrosion of iron parts is completely different from that of HNO_x corrosion. The speed of nitric acid liquid corrosion of iron parts is fast (Fig.13b), but the method belongs to comprehensive corrosion, and there is no small difference in corrosion. The speed of HNO_3 vapour is fast (Fig.13c), but the temperature and humidity are uncontrollable, and the edge of iron parts surface is prone to condense. Gas corrosion test box method is fast, the temperature, humidity and the concentration of NO_x can be effectively controlled, so the surface of iron parts is uniformly corroded as shown in Fig.13 d.

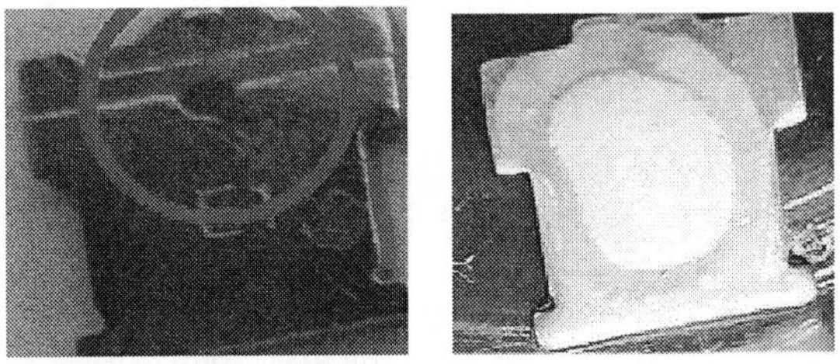

(a) Sat spray test (b) HNO_3 liquid corrosion

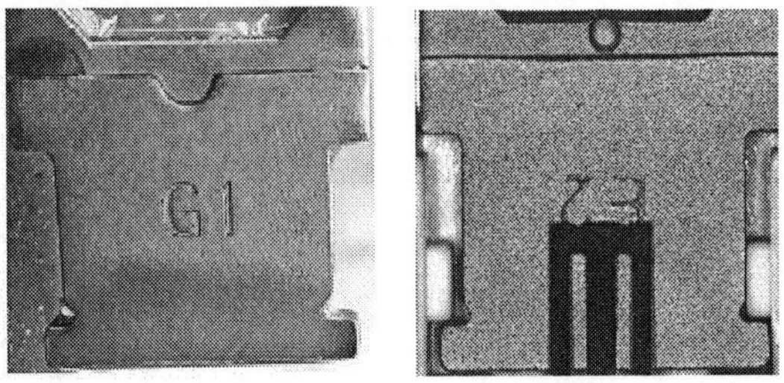

(c) HNO_3 vapour corrosion (d) Gas corrosion test

Fig.13. Comparison of evaluation methods for coating quality of relay iron parts

IV. Conclusion

(1) The observation of corrosion form shows that spot corrosion is the most important form of iron corrosion, and spot corrosion often occurs on the surface or internal defects of the iron coating.

(2) The analysis of corrosion products shows that the corrosion of relay iron parts after electrical life test is mainly the electrochemical corrosion of Ni coating and HNOx electrolytic medium. N_2 and O_2 in the relay generate NOx under the action of arc, and generate HNOx in combination with water vapor.

(3) The combination test of different temperature and humidity shows that high humidity environment is the most important environmental factor affecting the corrosion of iron parts inside the relay.

(4) The method of gas corrosion test chamber to evaluate the quality of iron coating is effective.

V. Improvement suggestions

Improve the coating quality of iron parts, such as cleaning the iron-based surface before plating to avoid surface impurity adhesion, coating holes and other defects.

References

[1] Dejun Yang , Zhuoshen Shen. Metal corrosion [M]. Beijing: Metallurgical Industry Press, 1999.

[2] Xiaofeng Zhu, Weihua Tang, Hanlin Liu. Study on corrosion mechanism of siemens series knife switch relay and moisture-proof treatment of mechanism box [J], science and Technology Plaza, 2015, 10 (13): 50-59.

[3] Chongfeng Liang, Wei Wang, Tao Yang. Discussion on key problems of moisture-proof electrical equipment [J]. Clean and air conditioning technology, 2012, 12 (4): 8-12.

[4] Kai Liu, Gongze Zhang.Discussion on formation mechanism and prevention measures of condensation in terminal box of substation [J]. Journal of Jiangxi Electric Power Vocational and technical college, 2014, 27 (3): 2014.

[5] Junjun Zhou, Xiushu Ying. The mechanism of NO_x produced by lightning and the estimation of NO_x produced by lightning in inland China [J]. Plateau Meteorology, 2002, 21 (5), 501-506.

[6] Ping Yuan, Xueyan Zhao. Theoretical study on NO production by lightning [J]. Journal of Northwest Normal University, 2009, 45 (3), 33-36.

[7] Feifei Wang, Shuran Li, et al. NO_x produced by arc discharge and its oxidation to ammonium sulfite [J]. Journal of environmental engineering, 2015, 9 (1), 281-285.

[8] Yingjun Pan, Heng Zhang, Jing Liu. Materials environment [M]. Metallurgical Industry Press, 2004.

Remaining Useful Life Prediction of Insulation Materials by Fusing Field Degradation Data and Accelerated Degradation Data

Jiajin Wang, Qin Zhang, Jinhao Shen, Jian Zhang, Youtong Fang

College of Electrical Engineering
Zhejiang University, Hangzhou, 310027, China
E-mail: jiajin@zju.edu.cn Tel: 18178905302

Abstract—**Fusing field degradation data and accelerated degradation data can effectively improve the accuracy of reliability assessment and life prediction, which is of great significance for prognostics and health management of equipment. In this paper, polyimide film, the mainstream material for the main insulation of electric motors, is studied. Thermal stress is one of the most important factors leading to its gradual deterioration and eventual failure. Therefore, an accelerated degradation test is designed for the insulation material, which is periodically aged under stress levels higher than the normal operating temperature, and sufficient degradation data are obtained in a relatively short period of time. The degradation process of the insulating material is described by the Wiener process, and the Arrhenius equation is selected as the acceleration equation based on the degradation mechanism. Assuming that the random parameters of the Wiener process obey the conjugate prior distribution, the accelerated degradation data are used as prior information to solve the prior estimation of the hyperparameters by the Expectation-Maximization algorithm. The field degradation data are fused and the model parameters are updated in real time based on Bayesian theory to predict the remaining useful life prediction of insulation materials. The method provides a strong basis for the transition from planned maintenance to condition-based maintenance of electric motors.**

Index Terms—**Accelerated degradation test, Bayesian theory, Remaining useful life, Wiener process**

I. Introduction

Traditional reliability technology aims to obtain failure data, which has the shortcomings of long test cycle and low efficiency, and it is difficult to obtain enough failure data for long-life and high-reliability products. With the rapid development of signal processing and sensing technologies, the condition monitoring data of equipment, i.e., performance degradation data, can directly provide information related to health status and can predict the degradation trend of performance characteristics and remaining useful life in the time domain to evaluate the reliability of equipment, thus significantly improving the operational efficiency of equipment [1]. Therefore, reliability assessment techniques based on degradation data provide an effective way to solve modern reliability engineering problems.

The degradation rate of highly reliable products under normal stress is slow, and it is difficult to collect enough useful performance degradation data in a short time, so it has become a major difficulty to accurately predict their remaining useful life. Accelerated degradation test can obtain more useful degradation data in a shorter period of time and effectively improve the test efficiency and prediction accuracy. Therefore, the accelerated degradation test technique is gradually gaining attention in the field of reliability, and the theory of life prediction based on accelerated degradation data is developing rapidly. Since the degradation process of products is stochastic in nature, stochastic processes are well suited for modeling the performance degradation process of products. Currently, the most widely used stochastic process models are the Wiener process [2] and the Gamma process [3]. The Gamma process is only suitable for modeling strictly monotonic performance degradation processes, while the Wiener process is a stochastic process with smooth properties that can model both strictly monotonic and non-monotonic performance degradation processes. The Wiener process has good computational properties and is usually preferred as a model for performance degradation [4].

Currently, Bayesian theory is an effective method to fuse multiple sources of information. For predicting the individual remaining life of a product, most of the existing literature takes the performance degradation data of the product under normal stress as the prior information. Gebraeel et al. fused the overall degradation data, the individual field degradation data and the actual working condition information to estimate the posterior expectation of the model parameters based on Bayesian theory to achieve the life prediction of bearings under variable load conditions [5]. Liao et al. used EM algorithm for parameter estimation of the offline degradation model with historical data, and the online phase updates the model parameters according to the Bayesian method to introduce an expression for life prediction based on the first arrival time at the failure threshold [6]. Wen et al. divided the life prediction into an offline phase and an online phase for parameter estimation and parameter update, respectively, and calculated the remaining life using Monte Carlo simulation [7]. Huang et al. proposed an adaptive tilting Wiener model to simulate the degradation drift of industrial devices and updated the drift parameters based on an improved Kalman filtering method [8]. Yan et al. established a general prediction framework by jointly using online change point detection, parameter estimation, and remaining life prediction [9]. In order to improve the accuracy of reliability assessment, how to effectively fuse more and more realistic degradation data for statistical analysis has become a hot research direction.

The main insulation of motor stator will undergo complex physical and chemical changes, such as volatilization, cracking, and puckering, due to the heat of increasing temperature, leading to the deterioration and aging of the main insulation material, resulting in the deterioration of motor operating performance. The higher the temperature, the faster the insulation aging, the shorter the life. Therefore, life prediction of motor insulation materials can improve the reliability of motor operation and reduce the economic loss caused by equipment failure. In this paper, accelerated degradation tests are performed on polyimide films under stresses well above normal temperatures, and the values of the parameters characterizing the degradation of insulation properties are measured at the end of each aging cycle as degradation data. A performance degradation model based on Wiener process and Arrhenius is established, and the accelerated degradation data is used as the prior information to update the model parameters based on Bayesian theory and fusion of field information to predict the remaining useful life.

II. Accelerated Degradation Model Based on Wiener Process

The degradation process of insulating materials has a certain stochastic nature, which is suitable for modeling its degradation by using the Wiener process. The degradation processes under different thermal stresses obey the same stochastic process, while the model parameters have different values. Combined with the Arrhenius equation, the model parameters under normal thermal stress can be extrapolated. After setting the failure threshold, the distribution function of product failure time can be determined from the degradation model according to the concept of first reach time, and then the life prediction of the product can be realized.

A. Performance Degradation Modeling

The accelerated degradation data are modeled assuming that the degradation process of the properties of the insulation material obeys the Wiener process. The Wiener process degradation model is expressed as

$$Y(t) = \mu t + \sigma B(t) \tag{1}$$

Where μ is the drift parameter, σ is the diffusion coefficient, $B(t)$ is the standard Brownian motion, and the initial amount of degradation is 0. From the nature of the Wiener process, it is known that the degradation increment $\Delta Y(t) = Y(t+\Delta t) - Y(t)$ obeys a normal distribution $\Delta Y(t) \sim N(\mu\Delta t, \sigma^2\Delta t)$. The independent increments are cumulated and derived as $Y(t) \sim N(\mu t, \sigma^2 t)$, and the probability density function (PDF) of $Y(t)$ can be obtained as

$$f(y) = \frac{1}{\sqrt{2\pi\sigma^2 t}} \exp\left[-\frac{(y-\mu t)^2}{2\sigma^2 t}\right] \tag{2}$$

The failure threshold of the performance parameter is set to D. Based on the first pass time theory, the product life ξ can be defined as the time when $Y(t)$ first passes at D, $\xi = \inf\{t \mid Y(t) \geq D\}$. The cumulative distribution function (CDF) of the product lifetime obeys the following inverse Gaussian distribution.

$$F(t) = \Phi\left(\frac{\mu t - D}{\sigma\sqrt{t}}\right) + \exp\left(\frac{2\mu D}{\sigma^2}\right)\Phi\left(-\frac{\mu t + D}{\sigma\sqrt{t}}\right) \tag{3}$$

Where $\Phi(\cdot)$ is the standard normal CDF. The PDF is

$$f(t) = \frac{D}{\sqrt{2\pi\sigma^2 t^3}} \exp\left[-\frac{(D-\mu t)^2}{2\sigma^2 t}\right] \tag{4}$$

The average life of the product is $\bar{\xi} = D/\mu$.

When the amount of degradation $Y(t) < D$ of the individual product, set $D' = D - Y(t)$, the PDF of the remaining useful life (RUL) can be written as

$$f_{\text{RUL}}(t;\mu,\sigma,D') = \frac{D'}{\sqrt{2\pi\sigma^2 t^3}} \exp\left[-\frac{(D'-\mu t)^2}{2\sigma^2 t}\right] \tag{5}$$

Taking the expected value of RUL as the predicted value, $\widehat{\text{RUL}}$ can be calculated by the following equation.

$$\widehat{\text{RUL}} = E(\text{RUL}) = \int_0^\infty t \cdot f_{\text{RUL}} dt = D'/\mu \tag{6}$$

B. Accelerated Degradation Modeling

Let $F_k(t_k)$, $F_h(t_h)$ be the CDF of the product at any two stress levels S_k, S_h, respectively, and when $F_k(t_k) = F_h(t_h)$, the acceleration factor $A_{k,h}$ for S_k equivalent to S_h can be defined as

$$A_{k,h} = t_h / t_k \tag{7}$$

The principle of invariance of the acceleration factor means that $A_{k,h}$ are constants determined only by the stress levels S_k, S_h. The following relations between μ and σ of the Wiener process are derived.

$$A_{k,h} = \mu_k / \mu_h = \sigma_k^2 / \sigma_h^2 \tag{8}$$

The Arrhenius equation is widely used to describe the effect of temperature on the rate of product degradation. Assuming that the temperature T is the accelerating stress, the variation law between the parameters of the degradation model and the level of the accelerating stress can be described by the Arrhenius model. The drift parameter under the k-th accelerating temperature stress T_k is expressed as

$$\mu_k = \exp(\gamma_1 - \gamma_2 / T_k) \tag{9}$$

The diffusion parameter under T_k is expressed as

$$\sigma_k = \exp(\gamma_3 - \gamma_4 / T_k) \tag{10}$$

Where γ_2, γ_2, γ_3, γ_4 are undetermined coefficients. To satisfy the principle of constant acceleration factor, then $\gamma_4 = 0.5\gamma_2$, the accelerated degradation model is established as

$$Y(t) \sim N\left(\exp(\gamma_1 - \gamma_2 / T)t, \exp(2\gamma_3 - \gamma_2 / T)t\right) \tag{11}$$

C. Model Parameter Estimation

According to the independent incremental property of the Wiener accelerated degradation model, the following likelihood function is established at each accelerated stress T_k ($k = 1,2,\ldots,M$).

$$L(\mu_k, \sigma_k) = \prod_{j=1}^{N_k} \prod_{i=1}^{H_{jk}} \frac{1}{\sqrt{2\pi\sigma_k^2 \Delta t_{ijk}}} \exp\left[-\frac{\left(\Delta y_{ijk} - \mu_k \Delta t_{ijk}\right)^2}{2\sigma_k^2 \Delta t_{ijk}}\right] \tag{12}$$

Firstly, the likelihood function is taken as logarithm, and the partial derivatives of each parameter are obtained from the log-likelihood function, and then the great likelihood estimates of the parameters when each partial derivative is 0 are solved. The vector of parameter estimates is obtained as $\hat{\mu} = (\hat{\mu}_1, \hat{\mu}_2, \ldots, \hat{\mu}_M)$, $\hat{\sigma} = (\hat{\sigma}_1, \hat{\sigma}_2, \ldots, \hat{\sigma}_M)$. It is obtained that

$$\begin{aligned} \ln \hat{\mu}_k &= \gamma_1 - \gamma_2 / T_k \\ \ln \hat{\sigma}_k &= \gamma_3 - 0.5\gamma_2 / T_k \end{aligned} \tag{13}$$

The following matrix equation is established

$$\begin{bmatrix} \ln \hat{\mu}_1 \\ \vdots \\ \ln \hat{\mu}_M \\ \ln \hat{\sigma}_1 \\ \vdots \\ \ln \hat{\sigma}_M \end{bmatrix} = \begin{bmatrix} 1 & -1/T_1 & 0 \\ \vdots & \vdots & \vdots \\ 1 & -1/T_M & 0 \\ 0 & -0.5/T_1 & 1 \\ \vdots & \vdots & \vdots \\ 0 & -0.5/T_M & 1 \end{bmatrix} \begin{bmatrix} \gamma_1 \\ \gamma_2 \\ \gamma_3 \end{bmatrix} \tag{14}$$

Solve the matrix equation to obtain the least squares estimate $\hat{\gamma}_1^*, \hat{\gamma}_2^*, \hat{\gamma}_3^*$.

III. Bayesian Update of Model Parameters under Conjugate Prior Distribution

To describe the heterogeneity among different individuals, the parameters μ, σ of degradation process can be set as random parameters obeying a certain distribution. For the Wiener process, assume that μ, ω ($\omega = 1/\sigma^2$) obey the following conjugate prior distribution.

$$\begin{cases} \omega = 1/\sigma^2 \sim Ga(a,b) \\ \mu \mid \omega \sim N(c, d/\omega) \end{cases} \tag{15}$$

Where Ga(·) denotes the Gamma distribution, $N(\cdot)$ denotes the Normal distribution, and a, b, c, d are hyperparameters.

A. Conversion of Prior Data

The accelerated degradation data is converted according to the measurement time, and the conversion relationship is as follows

$$\begin{aligned} t_{ij(k0)} &= t_{ijk} \cdot A_{k,0} \\ x_{ij(k0)} &= x_{ijk} \end{aligned} \tag{16}$$

Simply, denoted $t_{ij(k0)}$ by t_{iz}, denoted $x_{ij(k0)}$ by x_{iz}, where $i = 1,2,\ldots,n_z$, $z = 1,2,\ldots,N$, n_z is the number of measurements of the z-th product, N is the total number of products, $N = \sum_{k=1}^{n} n_k$.

B. Prior Estimates of Hyperparameters Based on EM

Use all (x_{iz}, t_{iz}) to build a full likelihood function with parameters μ_z, ω_z and hyperparameters a, b, c, d as follows

$$\begin{aligned} &L(\mu_z, \omega_z, a, b, c, d) \\ &= \prod_{i=1}^{n_z} \prod_{z=1}^{N} \frac{\omega_z^{0.5}}{\sqrt{2\pi\Delta t_{iz}}} \exp\left(\frac{-\omega_z \left(\Delta x_{iz} - \mu_z \Delta t_{iz}\right)^2}{2\Delta t_{iz}}\right) \\ &\prod_{z=1}^{N} \frac{\omega_z^{0.5}}{\sqrt{2\pi d}} \exp\left(\frac{-\omega_z (\mu_z - c)^2}{2d}\right) \frac{b^a}{\Gamma(a)} \omega_z^{a-1} \exp(-b\omega_z) \end{aligned} \tag{17}$$

The analytic equation of $\hat{a}, \hat{b}, \hat{c}, \hat{d}$ can be obtained from (17), where $\hat{a}$ can be obtained from the following equation.

$$\psi(\hat{a}) - \ln \hat{a} = \frac{1}{N} \sum_{z=1}^{N} \ln \omega_z + \ln N - \ln \sum_{z=1}^{N} \omega_z \tag{18}$$

where, $\psi(\cdot)$ is the digamma distribution function. The analytic equations of $\hat{b}, \hat{c}, \hat{d}$ are

$$\hat{b} = N \cdot \hat{a} \Big/ \sum_{z=1}^{N} \omega_z \tag{19}$$

$$\hat{c} = \sum_{z=1}^{N} \omega_z \mu_z \Big/ \sum_{z=1}^{N} \omega_z \tag{20}$$

$$\hat{d} = \frac{1}{N} \sum_{z=1}^{N} \left(\omega_z \mu_z^2 - 2\hat{c}\omega_z \mu_z + \hat{c}^2 \omega_z\right) \tag{21}$$

Since the parameters μ_z, ω_z are implicit data and $\hat{a}, \hat{b}, \hat{c}, \hat{d}$ cannot be solved directly, the EM algorithm is used to iteratively solve the problem. In the E-step, it is necessary to find the expected value of the term $\omega_z, \ln\omega_z, \omega_z\mu_z, \omega_z\mu_z^2$ containing the implicit data. Assuming that $\hat{a}_k, \hat{b}_k, \hat{c}_k, \hat{d}_k$ is the estimated value obtained after k iterations, the expected value of the implied data term in the k+1-th iteration is

$$E(\omega_z) = \frac{\left(\hat{a}_k + \frac{n_z}{2}\right)}{\left(\hat{b}_k + \frac{\hat{c}_k^2}{2\hat{d}_k} - \frac{\left(\hat{d}_k \sum_{i=1}^{n_z-1} \Delta x_{iz} + \hat{c}_k\right)^2}{2\left(\hat{d}_k^2 \sum_{i=1}^{n_z-1} \Delta t_{iz} + \hat{d}_k\right)} + \sum_{i=1}^{n_z-1} \frac{\Delta x_{iz}^2}{2\Delta t_{iz}}\right)} \tag{22}$$

$$E(\ln\omega_z) = \psi\left(\hat{a}_k + \frac{n_z}{2}\right) - \ln\left(\hat{b}_k + \frac{\hat{c}_k^2}{2\hat{d}_k} - \frac{\left(\hat{d}_k \sum_{i=1}^{n_z-1} \Delta x_{iz} + \hat{c}_k\right)^2}{2\left(\hat{d}_k^2 \sum_{i=1}^{n_z-1} \Delta t_{iz} + \hat{d}_k\right)} + \sum_{i=1}^{n_z-1} \frac{\Delta x_{iz}^2}{2\Delta t_{iz}}\right) \tag{23}$$

$$E(\omega_z\mu_z) = E(\omega_z E(\mu_z \mid \omega_z)) = E(\omega_z)\frac{\hat{d}_k \sum_{i=1}^{n_z-1} \Delta x_{iz} + \hat{c}_k}{\hat{d}_k \sum_{i=1}^{n_z-1} \Delta t_{iz} + 1} \tag{24}$$

$$E(\omega_z\mu_z^2) = E(\omega_z E(\mu_z^2 \mid \omega_z)) = E(\omega_z)\left(\frac{\hat{d}_k \sum_{i=1}^{n_z-1} \Delta x_{iz} + \hat{c}_k}{\hat{d}_k \sum_{i=1}^{n_z-1} \Delta t_{iz} + 1}\right)^2 + \frac{\hat{d}_k}{\hat{d}_k \sum_{i=1}^{n_z-1} \Delta t_{iz} + 1} \tag{25}$$

After several recursive iterations until all four hyperparameter values converge to a given accuracy, the resulting hyperparameter value is the final estimate. The accuracy threshold is set as the relative error of the hyperparameter estimates of two adjacent iterations, none of whose values is greater than 10^{-6}.

C. Posterior Expectation of Parameters Based on Bayesian

Since the conjugate prior distribution of the stochastic parameter has the same form as its posterior distribution, the posterior estimate of the hyperparameter can be derived from the Bayesian formula

$$f(\mu,\omega \mid \Delta X) = \frac{L(\Delta X \mid \mu,\omega)\cdot f(\mu,\omega)}{\int_0^{+\infty}\int_{-\infty}^{+\infty} L(\Delta X \mid \mu,\omega)\cdot f(\mu,\omega)\mathrm{d}\mu\mathrm{d}\omega} \tag{26}$$

where $L(\Delta X \mid \mu,\omega)$ is the likelihood function, $f(\mu,\omega)$ is the joint prior density function, and $f(\mu,\omega \mid \Delta X)$ is the joint posterior density function. Combining

$$f(\mu,\omega) = \frac{\omega^{1/2}}{\sqrt{2\pi\hat{d}}}\exp\left(\frac{-\omega(\mu-\hat{c})^2}{2\hat{d}}\right)\frac{\hat{b}^{\hat{a}}}{\Gamma(\hat{a})}\omega^{\hat{a}-1}\exp(-\hat{b}\omega) \tag{27}$$

$$L(\Delta X \mid \mu,\omega) = \prod_{j=1}^{m-1}\frac{\omega^{1/2}}{\sqrt{2\pi\Delta t_j}}\exp\left(\frac{-\omega(\Delta X_j - \mu\Delta t_j)^2}{2\Delta t_j}\right) \tag{28}$$

into (26), then

$$\begin{aligned} & f(\mu,\omega \mid \Delta X) \\ & \propto L(\Delta X \mid \mu,\omega)\cdot f(\mu,\omega) \\ & \propto \omega^{\frac{(m-1)}{2}+\hat{a}-1}\exp\left[-\omega\left(\hat{b} + \frac{\hat{c}^2}{2\hat{d}} - \frac{\left(\hat{d}\sum_{j=1}^{m-1}\Delta X_j + \hat{c}\right)^2}{2\left(\hat{d}^2\sum_{j=1}^{m-1}\Delta t_j + \hat{d}\right)} + \sum_{j=1}^{m-1}\frac{\Delta X_j^2}{2\Delta t_j}\right)\right] \\ & \quad \cdot\omega^{1/2}\exp\left[-\frac{\omega}{2}\frac{\left(\mu - \frac{\hat{d}\sum_{j=1}^{m-1}\Delta X_j + \hat{c}}{\hat{d}\sum_{j=1}^{m-1}\Delta t_j + 1}\right)^2}{\frac{\hat{d}}{\hat{d}\sum_{j=1}^{m-1}\Delta t_j + 1}}\right] \end{aligned} \tag{29}$$

The posterior estimates of the hyperparameters are

$$\begin{aligned} \hat{a} \mid \Delta X &= \frac{m-1}{2} + \hat{a} \\ \hat{b} \mid \Delta X &= \hat{b} + \frac{\hat{c}^2}{2\hat{d}} - \frac{\left(\hat{d}\sum_{j=1}^{m-1}\Delta X_j + \hat{c}\right)^2}{2\left(\hat{d}^2\sum_{j=1}^{m-1}\Delta t_j + \hat{d}\right)} + \sum_{j=1}^{m-1}\frac{\Delta X_j^2}{2\Delta t_j} \\ \hat{c} \mid \Delta X &= \frac{\hat{d}\sum_{j=1}^{m-1}\Delta X_j + \hat{c}}{\hat{d}\sum_{j=1}^{m-1}\Delta t_j + 1} \\ \hat{d} \mid \Delta X &= \frac{\hat{d}}{\hat{d}\sum_{j=1}^{m-1}\Delta t_j + 1} \end{aligned} \tag{30}$$

The posterior expectation $E(\mu \mid \Delta X)$, $E(\omega \mid \Delta X)$ of the random parameter μ, ω can be further derived by substituting (5) and (6) to obtain the posterior PDF and posterior prediction $\widehat{\mathrm{RUL}}$.

IV. Tests and Results

According to IEC 60505:2011, in order to produce rapid aging, at least three higher temperatures should be selected for the test. Accelerated aging tests were performed on the motor insulation material polyimide films at accelerated temperature stresses $T_1 = 563.15$ K, $T_2 = 573.15$ K, and $T_3 = 583.15$ K, respectively. The accelerated degradation data measured at T_1, T_2, and T_3 temperatures were used as the a prior information for the life prediction model to construct the overall life prediction model of the product. To verify the validity and accuracy of the RUL prediction model proposed in this paper, the degradation data at $T_0 = 543.15$ K were used as the field monitoring data, and the model parameters were updated by Bayesian method to predict the RUL at T_0.

A. Accelerated Heat Aging Test Setup

Taking 0.25mm, 6050 type polyimide film as the test sample, 21 samples were selected and divided into 3 groups on average. Before the accelerated aging test, each sample was pretreated, and the characterization parameters of its insulation properties before aging were measured, and the value was taken as the initial value. Under each group of accelerated temperature stress, 7 samples were simultaneously put into an oven for thermal aging to avoid random errors caused by test operations. The aging cycle settings at three different temperatures are shown in TABLE I. At the end of each aging cycle, the samples are subjected to an insulation diagnostic test. In this test, the Megger IDX300 insulation diagnostic system is directly used to test the insulation performance.

B. Data of Accelerated Aging Test

The dielectric loss angle tangent value tanδ was selected as an index to characterize the performance degradation, and the failure threshold of tanδ was set to $D = 0.005$ according to IEC 60674-2. The accelerated aging data are shown in Fig. 1. The higher the temperature, the faster the rate of performance degradation.

TABLE I
AGING CYCLES AT DIFFERENT TEMPERATURE STRESSES

Temperature	Aging Time (h)						
$T_1 = 563.15$ K	20	40	60	100	140	180	200
$T_2 = 573.15$ K	20	40	60	100	140		
$T_3 = 583.15$ K	20	40	60	100			

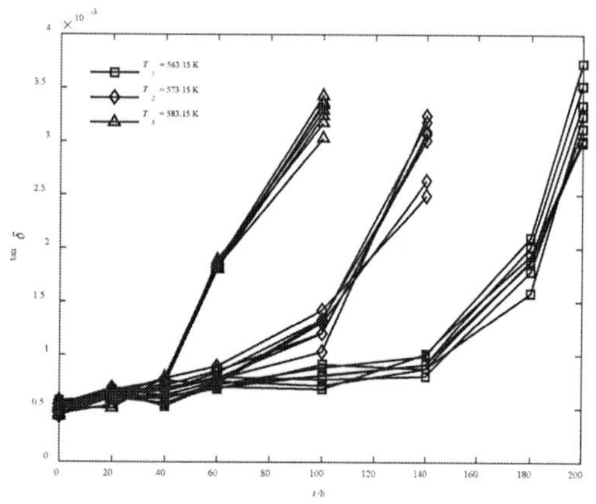

Fig. 1. Accelerated degradation data

TABLE II
ESTIMATES OF MODEL PARAMETERS UNDER DIFFERENT TEMPERATURE STRESSES

Temperature	Model Parameters	
	μ	σ
$T_1 = 563.15$ K	1.3907×10^{-5}	8.4095×10^{-5}
$T_2 = 573.15$ K	1.7581×10^{-5}	8.9632×10^{-5}
$T_3 = 583.15$ K	2.7697×10^{-5}	9.4980×10^{-5}
$T_0 = 543.15$ K	7.3612×10^{-6}	5.5801×10^{-5}

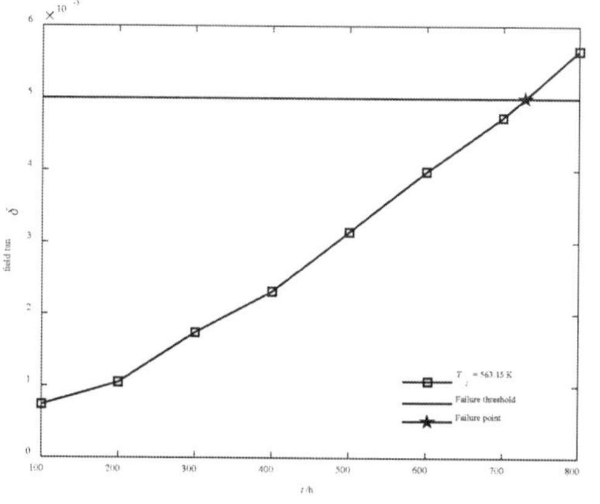

Fig. 2. Field degradation data

C. Life Prediction Results and Analysis

The accelerated aging data were modeled and the model parameters were estimated according to Section II, and the results are shown in TABLE II. It is reasonable that the higher the temperature, the larger the drift parameter and the diffusion parameter of the degradation model.

Based on Section III, the accelerated degradation data under temperature stresses T_1, T_2, and T_3 are converted to T_0 according to the acceleration factor as the prior data. The prior estimates of the hyperparameters in the degradation model were obtained according to the EM algorithm as $(\hat{a}_1, \hat{b}_1, \hat{c}_1, \hat{d}_1) = (26.1664, 1.1505\text{e-}7, 7.3553\text{e-}6, 8.5225\text{e-}5)$.

The degradation data under temperature stress T_0 are shown in Fig. 2. As can be seen from Fig. 2, the sample degradation trajectory passes the failure threshold after the 7-th measurement data. The actual lifetime of this sample is about $L = 729$ h.

Let RUL_1 be the predicted remaining useful life of an individual obtained using accelerated degradation data only, and RUL_2 be the predicted remaining useful life of an individual obtained by fusing accelerated degradation data and field degradation data. The RUL_1, RUL_2 and actual RUL for the field measurement moment $t = 100$ h and six measurement moments thereafter are shown in TABLE III. The change curves of RUL_1, RUL_2, actual RUL and the PDF curve of RUL_2 are shown in Fig. 3.

TABLE IIII
THE RUL ESTIMATION RESULTS OF THE INDIVIDUAL

Parameters (h)	Measure Time (h)						
	100	200	300	400	500	600	700
RUL_1	579	479	379	279	179	79	
RUL_2	582	542	447	370	255	140	37
Actual RUL	629	529	429	329	229	129	29

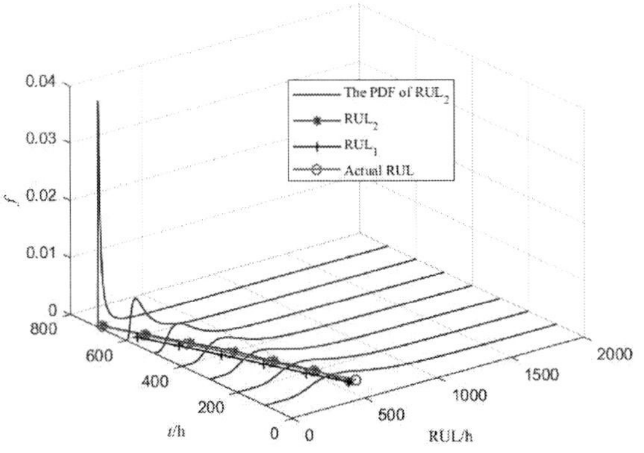

Fig. 3. The change curves of RUL_1, RUL_2, actual RUL and the PDF curve of RUL_2

V. CONCLUSION

In this paper, a conjugate prior distribution degradation model based on the Wiener process is proposed to predict the remaining useful life of a product by fusing field degradation data and accelerated degradation data through Bayesian theory. The method first builds a performance degradation model in the offline stage using accelerated degradation data and determines the prior estimates of the model parameters by the EM algorithm. Then, the posterior expectations of the model parameters are updated using Bayesian theory by fusing the field degradation data to calculate the remaining useful life of the product and its probability density function. The study of polyimide films demonstrates that the remaining useful life prediction method fusing field degradation data and accelerated degradation data has higher prediction accuracy.

ACKNOWLEDGMENT

This work was supported in part by the National Natural Science Foundation of China under Grant 51977192 and in part by Project supported by the Ningbo science and technology innovation 2025 major project (20211ZDYF020218).

From TABLE III and Fig. 3, it can be seen that RUL_2 at each measurement moment is significantly closer to the actual RUL than RUL_1, proving that fusing accelerated degradation data and field degradation data effectively improves the prediction accuracy of RUL compared to using accelerated degradation data only. The accuracy of the prediction is also improving with the increase of field degradation data, and the width of the PDF curve of RUL_2 keeps getting narrower with time also indicates that the prediction accuracy is improving.

REFERENCES

[1] J. Guo, Z. Li, and M. Li, "A review on prognostics methods for engineering systems," *IEEE Transactions on Reliability*, 2019, 69(3): 1110–1129,.

[2] X. Zhao, B. Liu, and Y. Liu, "Reliability modeling and analysis of load-sharing systems with continuously degrading components," IEEE Transactions on Reliability, 2018, 67(3): 1096–1110

[3] J. M. van Noortwijk, "A survey of the application of gamma processes in maintenance," *Reliability Engineering & System Safety*, 2009, 94(1): 2–21,.

[4] M. A. Freitas, M. L. G. de Toledo, E. A. Colosimo, and M. C. Pires, "Using degradation data to assess reliability: a case study on train wheel degradation," *Quality and Reliability Engineering International*, 2009, 25(5): 607–629,.

[5] N. Gebraeel and J. Pan, "Prognostic degradation models for computing and updating residual life distributions in a time-varying environment," *IEEE Transactions on Reliability*, 2008, 57(4): 539–550,.

[6] G. Liao, H. Yin, M. Chen, and Z. Lin, "Remaining useful life prediction for multi-phase deteriorating process based on wiener process," *Reliability Engineering & System Safety*, 2021, 207: 107361,.

[7] Y. Wen, J. Wu, D. Das, and T.-L. B. Tseng, "Degradation modeling and rul prediction using wiener process subject to multiple change points and unit heterogeneity," *Reliability Engineering & System Safety*, 2018, 176: 113–124,.

[8] Z. Huang, Z. Xu, X. Ke, W. Wang, and Y. Sun, "Remaining useful life prediction for an adaptive skew-wiener process model," *Mechanical Systems and Signal Processing*, 2017, 87: 294–306,.

[9] B. Yan, X. Ma, G. Huang, and Y. Zhao, "Two-stage physics-based wiener process models for online rul prediction in field vibration data," *Mechanical Systems and Signal Processing*, 2021, 152: 107378,.

8th International Conference on Reliability of
Electrical Products and Electrical Contacts,
November 18-20, 2022

Influence of Static Arc and Moving Arc on Erosion Characteristics of High Power DC Relay Contacts

Guobin Hou, Dandan Zhang, Zhenbiao Li

Huazhong University of Science and Technology, Wuhan, 430074, China
E-mail: 253618338@qq.com Tel: 18049073605

Abstract—**Contact erosion under the action of arc is the key to restrict the development of DC relays. Based on this, this paper studies the influence of static arc and moving arc on contact erosion characteristics in high-power DC relay. Firstly, the erosion characteristics of contacts under the action of static arc without magnetic blowing and magnetic blowing moving arc are respectively carried out through simulation. The temperature field distribution of the contact and the phase transition process of the molten pool are obtained. The evolution characteristics of the size of the molten crater, the width and depth of the molten pool in the two cases are compared. The vaporization erosion and splash erosion in the two cases are compared and calculated. The results show that the erosion caused by the static arc will continue to increase and is uncontrollable. The total erosion amount is 1.84 times that of the magnetic blowing moving arc, and the magnetic blowing moving arc has less influence on the electrical contact performance of the contacts. After that, the arc erosion experiment is carried out, the accuracy of the simulation of the magnetic blowing arc erosion is verified. And the difference of contact erosion characteristics under the action of static arc and magnetic blowing arc is clarified. The simulation method established in this paper has practical significance for the optimal design of relay products.**

Index Terms— **DC relay, static arc, magnetic blowing moving arc, erosion, molten pool.**

I. INTRODUCTION

DC electromagnetic relays are widely used in various important fields, and are one of the indispensable basic components in national high-precision technology and national industrial equipment [1]. Relay contacts are important components for relays to achieve on-off functions, and there are strict standards and requirements for the contact system in terms of corrosion resistance, welding resistance, and contact resistance [2],[3]. Contact erosion caused by the arc generated in the relay breaking process is ubiquitous, and the accumulation of contact erosion for a long time will cause the function of the relay system to degrade. For high-power HVDC relays, since there is no arc extinguishing chamber, contact gap stretching and magnetic blowing are used to extinguish the arc. Therefore, exploring the erosion characteristics of contacts under the action of high-power magnetic blowing moving DC arc has important significance for studying how to improve the erosion resistance of contact materials.

At present, scholars at home and abroad have made some research and discussion on the erosion of relay contacts under the action of arcs. The change process of arc erosion that cannot be observed in experiments can be obtained by modeling and simulation methods, but most of the current researches are carried out experimentally, while simulation research is relatively less. Thus, the mechanism of arc erosion and the effect of static arc without magnetic blowing and magnetic blowing moving arc on contact erosion cannot be clearly clarified.

Yukio Nakagawa made the contact equivalent as a stack of multiple sheets, and calculated the mass of the electrode melted and evaporated through the temperature distribution, so as to analyze the amount of erosion [4]. However, the model is relatively simplified and not accurate enough. Wang et al. established a simplified model of the force of the molten pool, and theoretically and qualitatively analyzed the process of molten pool erosion [5]. Chabrerie established a three-dimensional model of the contact and obtained the total melting amount of the contact [6]. However, the above scholars only theoretically and qualitatively analyzed the process of contact erosion under the action of static arc, and failed to accurately obtain the temperature distribution of the contact, the evolution process of the molten pool and the calculation of the erosion amount. In addition, no attention was paid to the influence of magnetic blowing moving arc on erosion.

Professor Li's team established a molten pool flow model by studying the characteristics of splash erosion, calculated the distribution of the molten pool flow field and thermal field, and proposed two splash erosion models based on energy fluctuation and probability statistics, respectively [7]-[10]. This paper will further consider the vaporization erosion, and the erosion of the magnetic blowing moving arc under the condition of high power, and improve the erosion model.

In summary, there are few studies on the contact erosion characteristics of high-power DC relays under the action of arc. Both vaporization erosion and splash erosion are not considered in previous studies. Especially the erosion characteristics of contacts under the action of magnetic blowing moving arc are still unclear. And there is a lack of comparative research on the effects of moving arc and static arc on contact erosion, which is not conducive to clarifying the arc erosion mechanism. Based on this, the contact erosion models under the action of a static arc without magnetic blowing and a moving arc with magnetic blowing are established in this paper. The temperature field distribution and phase transition process of the contacts are analyzed. And the evolution of the melt pool and the difference in the amount of erosion are compared between the two cases. The accuracy of the calculation model is verified by conducting arc erosion experiments. The work of this paper helps to provide a reference for improving the arc erosion resistance of relays.

II. Simulation Model

The contact will undergo the transformation of solid phase, liquid phase and gas phase under the heating effect of the arc, so the model needs to consider the physical process of heat transfer and phase transformation.

A. Geometric Model

The electrical contact of the relay is a cylinder with a diameter of 10mm and a height of 3mm, and the contact material is CuCr40 (the mass fraction of Cr is 40%). The geometric model of the arc acting on the contact surface is shown in Fig. 1. In this paper, the simulation calculation of the contact erosion under the action of the static arc without magnetic blowing and the magnetic blowing moving arc is carried out respectively. For the static arc without magnetic blowing, the arc has a motion velocity of 0, erosion occurs only in the center of the contact. For the magnetic blowing motion arc, the arc moves at a velocity v until it reaches the edge of the contact. According to the arc experiment conducted by our research team, the average arc breaking time of CuCr40 contact is 15.38 ms under the condition of 270 V/100 A, and the arc movement time on the contact surface is 3 ms [11].

B. Government Equations and Boundary Conditions

1) Heat conduction

Under the heating action of the arc, the temperature distribution of the contact satisfies the following formula:

$$\rho C_p \frac{\partial T}{\partial t} + \rho C_p \boldsymbol{u} \cdot \nabla T - \nabla \cdot (k \nabla T) = 0 \quad (1)$$

where ρ is the density; C_p is the heat capacity; T is the temperature; t is the time; $\boldsymbol{u}$ is the molten pool velocity vector; k is the thermal conductivity.

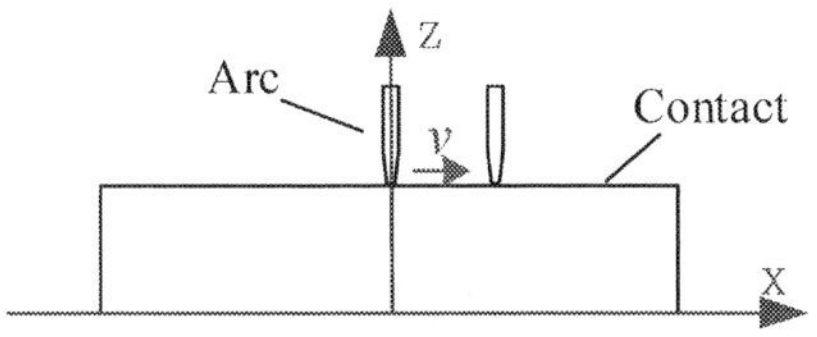

Fig. 1. Geometric model.

2) Phase transition

For the material property changes involved in the phase transition process, the sensible heat capacity method is adopted for equivalent treatment. The solid phase and the liquid phase are state 1 and state 2 respectively, then the material density ρ, heat capacity C_p, and thermal conductivity k can be expressed as:

$$\begin{aligned} &\rho = \theta_1 \rho_1 + \theta_2 \rho_2 \\ &C_P = \frac{1}{\rho}(\theta_1 \rho_1 C_{P,1} + \theta_2 \rho_2 C_{P,2}) + L_{1\to 2} \frac{\partial \alpha_m}{\partial T} \\ &\alpha_m = \frac{1}{2} \frac{\theta_2 \rho_2 - \theta_1 \rho_1}{\theta_1 \rho_1 + \theta_2 \rho_2} \\ &k = \theta_1 k_1 + \theta_2 k_2 \\ &\theta_1 + \theta_2 = 1 \end{aligned} \quad (2)$$

where α_m is the mass fraction; $L_{1\text{-}2}$ is the latent heat of fusion; θ_1 is the solid phase ratio; θ_2 is the liquid phase ratio. For composite contacts, the calculation is performed using the linear superposition principle based on the mass fraction in combination with the handbook of engineering materials [12].

3) Boundary conditions

The upper surface of the contact is the arc action surface, so the heat flux density $q(x,y,t)$ of the moving arc from outside to inside is applied on the contact surface, and it and it moves along the positive x-axis. The heat flux density obeys the Gaussian distribution, and the expression is as follows:

$$q(x,y,t) = q_{\max} \cdot \exp(-\frac{(x - v \cdot t)^2 + y^2}{2\sigma^2}) \quad (3)$$

where q_{max} is the peak heat flux density at the center of the arc root; σ is the standard deviation of the Gaussian distribution; v is the motion speed of the magnetic blowing arc, which moves in the positive direction of the x-axis. For the static arc without magnetic blowing, v=0.

About 97% of the arc energy is transmitted from the arc root to the contact. According to the 3σ principle of normal distribution, it can be obtained: $3\sigma = r_0$, r_0 is the radius of the arc root [13]. The research of Robertson shows that under the condition of high current, the arc root area and arc current satisfy $\pi r_0^2 = 1.67\times10^{-9} I_{arc}$ [14]. According to the arc model of Borkowski [13], the peak heat flux can be calculated by $q_{max} = P/2\pi\sigma^2$, where P is the power of the arc acting on the contact.

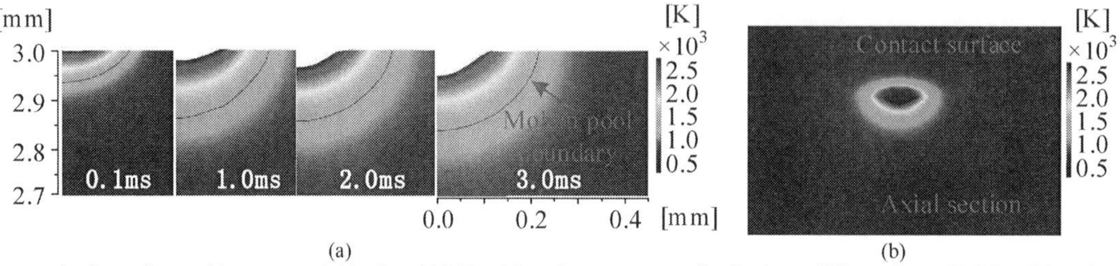

Fig. 2. Contact erosion by static arc without magnetic blowing. (a) 2-D axial section temperature distribution at different times. (b) 3-D axial section temperature distribution at t=3 ms

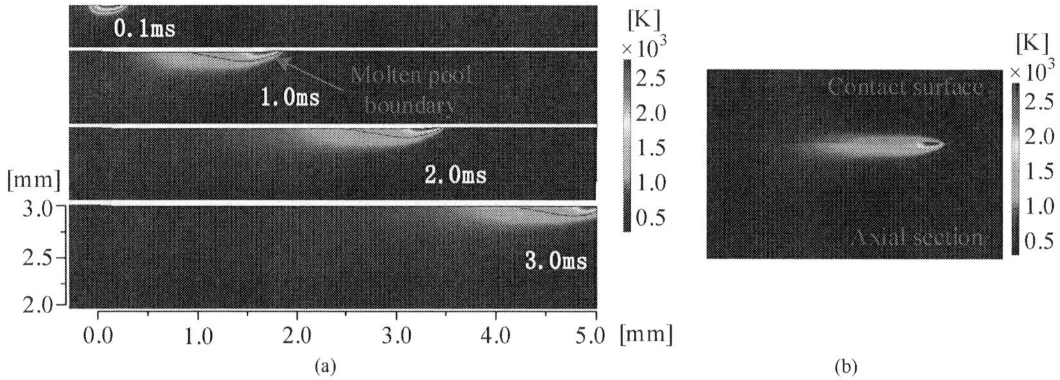

Fig. 3. Contact erosion by magnetic blowing moving arc. (a) 2-D axial section temperature distribution at different times. (b) 3-D axial section temperature distribution at t=2 ms

The side and bottom surfaces of the contact are natural convection heat transfer, which is simulated by the convection heat transfer coefficient, and it can be set to 10 W/(m^2*K) [15]. The external ambient temperature is 293.15K.

After the contact surface is heated by the arc, the temperature will gradually increase and reach the boiling point, and then it will be converted into a gaseous state after absorbing the latent heat of vaporization, resulting in vaporization erosion. In this paper, the effect of vaporization erosion rate on the loss of contact material is considered by calculating the heat absorbed by the contact surface after the contact surface reaches the boiling point.

III. Simulation Results and Discussion

A. Erosion Results of Static Arc without Magnetic Blowing

Fig. 2(a). shows the evolution of the contact molten pool under the action of a static arc without magnetic blowing at different times. It can be seen that as the ablation time increases, the liquid molten pool area becomes larger and larger. And after the temperature of the center of the molten pool reaches the boiling point, vaporization corrosion occurs, and more and more contact materials are lost by vaporization erosion. At any time, the width of the molten pool is greater than the depth, which is related to the arc heat flux density acting on the contact surface and the heat source shows a Gaussian distribution. Fig. 2(b). shows the erosion of the contacts after 3 ms of static arc without magnetic blowing. It can be seen that if the arc is stationary, a clear crater will be formed in the center of the contact. For the splash erosion of the molten pool, the calculations will be made below. When t=3 ms, the depth of the molten crater caused by vaporization erosion is 0.05 mm and the width is 0.22 mm, forming a serious contact defect. The arcing time on the contact surface used in this calculation adopts the action time of the magnetic blowing moving arc, which is 3 ms. But in fact, the arcing time of the static arc without magnetic blowing will be longer. Therefore, for high-power relays, the erosion caused by the static arc without magnetic blowing will be very serious, which will greatly reduce the electrical contact reliability of the contacts.

B. Erosion Results of Magnetic Blowing Moving Arc

Fig. 3. shows the erosion results of the magnetic blowing moving arc, showing the temperature distribution of the 2-D axial section and the 3-D axial section, respectively. It can be seen that, compared with the static arc without magnetic blowing, the crater of the contact produced by the vaporization erosion is not obvious under the action of the magnetic blowing moving arc. However, there is still a small amount of contact material that is heated to the boiling point causing material loss. At any time, the width of the molten pool is greater than the depth. In addition, due to the influence of the moving arc, the heated area behind the arc cools slowly, so that when the arc moves to the edge of the contact, the contact behind the arc is not completely cooled, forming a "smearing phenomenon". If re-ignition occurs in the back-arc area at this time, it will cause secondary erosion to the area where the contact has been ablated. And since the contacts are still at a high temperature, the effect of secondary erosion will be even worse. On the whole, compared with the static arc without magnetic blowing, the vaporization erosion of the contact caused by the magnetic blowing moving arc is greatly reduced, and the impact on the material loss is small. Therefore, for high-power relays, the use of magnetic blowing to extinguish the arc has a positive effect on reducing the deterioration of the electrical contact performance of the arc to the contacts.

C. Comparison of Erosion Results of Static Arc without Magnetic Blowing and Magnetic Blowing Moving Arc

Fig. 4. shows the comparison curve of the molten pool width under the action of the static arc without magnetic blowing and the magnetic blowing moving arc. It can be seen that under the action of the static arc without magnetic blowing, the width increase of the molten pool of the contact slows down and becomes stable after 0.5 ms. For the magnetic blowing arc, the width of the molten pool tends to stabilize after 0.9 ms, and the width of the molten pool suddenly drops at 3.0 ms, because the center of the arc root has moved to the edge of the contact. Due to the lateral movement of the magnetic blowing arc on the contact surface, the width of the molten pool is larger than that of the static arc. Under the action of the magnetic blowing moving arc, the maximum value of the molten pool width appears at 2.9 ms, which is 0.98 mm; for the static arc, it appears at 3.0 ms, which is 0.42 mm. Finally, the molten pool widths under both moving arc and stationary arc tend to be stable, indicating that for a heat source with a Gaussian distribution, the molten pool width of the contacts is controllable.

Fig. 5. shows the comparison curve of the molten pool depth under the action of the static arc without magnetic blowing and the magnetic blowing moving arc. It can be seen that the depth of the molten pool of the contact will continue to increase when there is no magnetic blowing static arc. The growth rate is faster before 0.5 ms, and after 0.5 ms, the growth rate decreases but still increases. For the magnetic blowing moving arc, the molten pool depth tends to be stable after 0.4 ms, indicating that the magnetic blowing moving arc has little effect on the molten pool depth and reduces the axial erosion of the contacts. On the whole, the molten pool depth caused by the static arc is greater than that of the moving arc. Under the action of the static arc, the maximum value of the molten pool width appears at 3.0 ms, which is 0.16 mm; for the static arc, it appears at 2.9 ms, which is 0.10 mm. The results show that for the moving arc heat source with Gaussian distribution, the melt pool depth tends to be stable. However, the depth of the molten pool caused by the static arc heat source is uncontrollable, which has a serious impact on the electrical contact performance of the contacts.

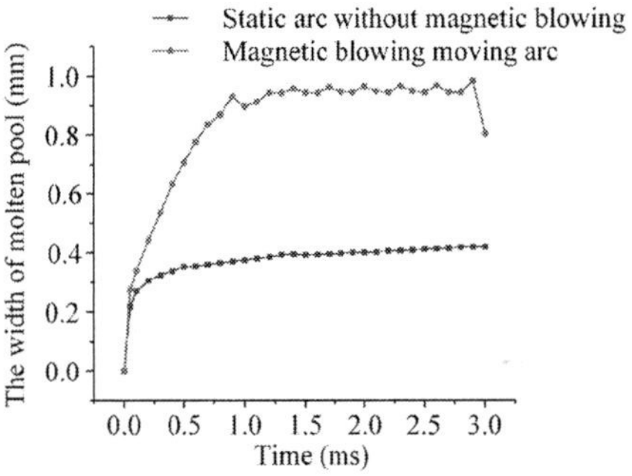

Fig. 4. Comparison of the width of the contact molten pool under the action of static arc and moving arc.

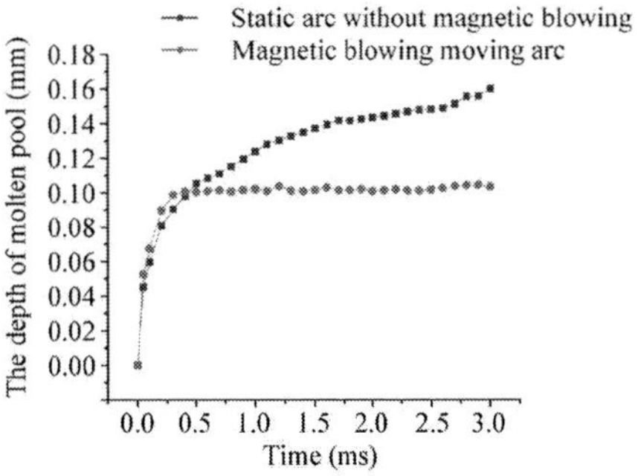

Fig. 5. Comparison of the depth of the contact molten pool under the action of static arc and moving arc.

In addition to the vaporization erosion analyzed above, splash erosion can also occur in the liquid molten pool resulting in material loss. Moreover, under the condition of high voltage and high current, the erosion of the electrical contacts of the relay is mainly dominated by splash erosion [16]. On the basis of the probabilistic and statistical model proposed by Wu [7]-[9], the mass loss caused by the vaporization erosion is accumulated, and the vaporization and splash erosion amounts are calculated for the static arc without magnetic blowing and the magnetic blowing moving arc in this paper, the results are shown in Table 1. It can be seen that the vaporization erosion and splash erosion under the action of the static arc are both greater than those of the moving arc, and the total erosion is 1.84 times that of the moving arc. It shows that the static arc without magnetic blowing can have a serious impact on the material loss of the contacts.

TABLE I

COMPARISON OF THE EROSION AMOUNT (ug)

Simulation Conditions	Evaporation Erosion	Splash Erosion	Total Erosion
Static arc	10.73	81.03	91.76
Moving arc	6.48	43.51	49.99

IV. Comparison of Erosion Experiment and Simulation Results

A. Platform and Conditions of Experiment

The breaking experiments of CuCr40 contacts were carried out under the condition of voltage 270V and current 100A. The contact is rivet type (Φ10mm×3mm), the moving contact is the anode, and the static contact is the cathode. The breaking speed is 90 mm/s, and the transverse magnetic field is 80 mT. Three pairs of contacts were used to carry out the breaking experiment, and the number of times of opening and closing and the amount of erosion after the experiment were recorded.

B. Experimental Results and Comparison with Simulation

The erosion results of three pairs of CuCr40 contacts show that the average erosion amount of anode is -72.960 μg/time, the average erosion amount of cathode is 8.375 μg/time, and the average erosion amount of contacts is -64.585 μg/time. Negative numbers represent contact weight loss, and positive numbers represent contact weight gain.

Comparing the erosion test results with the simulation results in Table 1, the erosion amount under the action of the magnetic blowing moving arc is 22.60% lower than the experimental result, while the erosion amount under the action of the static arc without magnetic blowing is 42.08% higher than the experimental result. It is reasonable that the simulation result of the magnetic blowing arc is lower, because the ablation of the arc on the side of the contact is ignored in the simulation. The static arc is high, indicating that the contact erosion of the static arc will be very serious under high power conditions compared with the moving arc.

V. CONCLUSION

By establishing the contact erosion model under the action of arc, the erosion characteristics of the contact under the action of static arc without magnetic blowing and magnetic blowing moving arc are respectively studied. And carried out arc erosion experiments. Concluded as follow.

1) Under the action of the static arc, the material in the central arc root area of the contact is heated and vaporized, resulting in mass loss, the formation of molten craters, and the serious contact defects.

2) Under the action of the magnetic blowing motion arc, only a very small amount of contact material is eroded by vaporization. The heated area behind the arc is not completely cooled, resulting in "smearing phenomenon". If re-breakdown occurs in the back-arc region, it will cause more severe erosion. Compared with the static arc, the magnetic blowing moving arc has less influence on the material loss of the contacts.

3) The width of the molten pool under the action of the static arc and the moving arc is greater than the depth of the molten pool. The width of the molten pool under the action of the static arc is smaller than that of the moving arc, but the depth of the molten pool is larger and uncontrollable. Under the action of static arc, the erosion amount of vaporization and splash are larger than that of moving arc, and the total erosion amount is 1.84 times that of moving arc.

4) By comparing the erosion experimental results and the simulation results, the rationality of the magnetic blowing moving arc erosion model and the severity of the contact erosion caused by the static arc are verified, and the difference of erosion between the static arc and the moving arc is clarified. The simulation model established in this paper can provide a theoretical reference for the optimization of the contact erosion resistance.

References

[1] G. Zhai, K. Bo, X. Zhou, and Y. Zhang, "Investigation on Breaking Arc in DC High-Power Relays: A Review," *Diangong Jishu Xuebao/Transactions of China Electrotechnical Society*, 2017, 32(22):251-263.

[2] T. Atsumi, J. Sekikawa, and T. Kubono, "Characteristics of Break Arcs Driven by Transverse Magnetic Field in a DC High-Voltage Resistive Circuit," *Ieice Trans Electron*, 2010, 93(9):1393-1398.

[3] H. Ono, J. Sekikawa, and T. Kubono, "Arc Duration of Break Arcs Magnetically Blown-Out in a DC 450V Resistive Circuit," *Ieice Trans Electron*, 2012, 95(9):1515-1521.

[4] Y. Nakagawa and Y. Yoshioka, "Theoretical Calculation of the Process of Contact Arc Erosion Using a One-Dimensional Contact Model," *IEEE Transactions on Components Hybrids & Manufacturing Technology*, 1978, 1(1):99-102.

[5] K. Wang and Q. Wang, "Erosion of silver-base material contacts by breaking arcs," *IEEE transactions on components, hybrids, and manufacturing technology*, 1991, 14(2): 293-297.

[6] J.P. Chabrerie and J. Devautour, "A numerical model for thermal processes in an electrode submitted to an arc in air and its experimental verification," *IEEE Transactions on Components Hybrids & Manufacturing Technology,* 16.4(1993):449-455.

[7] X. Wu and Z Li, "Model on sputter erosion of electrical contact material," *IEEE Holm Conference on Electrical Contacts*, IEEE, 2002.

[8] X. Wu, M. Di, Z. Li, and C Liu. "The composition change of contact material surface," *Electrical Contacts, 2003. Proceedings of the Forty-Ninth IEEE Holm Conference*, IEEE, 2003.

[9] X. Wu, Z. Li, M. Di, X. Song, and X. Wang, "Investigation on the Characteristics of Sputter Erosion and Particle Movement in Molten Pool of Electrical Contacts," *Proceedings of the 1st International Conference on Reliability of Electrical Products and*

Electrical Contacts, Huazhong University of Science & Technology, 430074, China, 2004.

[10] X. Wu, Z. Li, M. Di, Z. Wei, and X. Song, "Simulation of particle flow in molten pool of electric contact of power switch," *International Universities Power Engineering Conference*, IEEE, 2004.

[11] Y. Liao, et al. "Experimental study on contact materials CuW, CuCr and their different matings under DC270V/100A," *Advanced Technology of Electrical Engineering and Energy*, 2018.

[12] E.A. Brandes and G.B. Brook. *Smithells metals reference book*. Elsevier, 2013.

[13] P. Borkowski and E. Walczuk, "Thermal models of short arc between high current contacts," *IEEE Holm Conference on Electrical Contacts*, IEEE, 2016.

[14] S. Robertson, "A finite element analysis of the thermal behavior of contacts," *IEEE Transactions on Components, Hybrids, and Manufacturing Technology*, 1982, 5(1): 3-10.

[15] V. R. Voller and C. Prakash, "A fixed grid numerical modelling methodology for convection-diffusion mushy region phase-change problems," *International Journal of Heat & Mass Transfer*, 1987, 30(8):1709-1719.

[16] J. Swingler and J. McBride, "Modeling of energy transport in arcing electrical contacts to determine mass loss," *IEEE Transactions on Components, Packaging, and Manufacturing Technology. Part A*, 1998, 21(1): 54-60.

Design and Signal Integrity Analysis of the Wafer of A High-Speed Backplane Connector

Xueyan Lin, Yongsheng Zhou, Xin An

Beijing University of Posts and Telecommunications, Beijing, 100876, China
E-mail: xylin@bupt.edu.cn Tel: 13611123628

***Abstract*—In this paper, a high-speed backplane connector wafer is designed by using the three-dimensional electromagnetic simulation software CST Microwave Studio, which has good signal integrity in the frequency range of 0-28GHz. This paper mainly analyzes the effect of the following factors, the corner design of the transmission line from the horizontal section to the vertical section, the unequal length of the transmission line in the differential pair, the excessive crosstalk between the transmission lines, and the unequal potential of the grounding terminal. The following design criteria are obtained in this paper: Adopting the 135° corner to realize the transition from the horizontal section to the vertical section can reduce the influence of the corner structure on the signal; The trapezoidal structure is added outside the transmission line with short length, and the influence of different transmission line lengths on signal transmission quality can be reduced by skin effect; Increasing the thickness of the ground terminal can increase the shielding between the signal terminals and reduce the crosstalk; Connecting the grounding terminal with the metal shielding layer with the grounding pin can reduce the influence of the electromagnetic field generated by the signal on the grounding terminal and improve the signal transmission performance.**

***Index Terms*— High-speed backplane connector, CST simulation, Signal integrity, Design criteria**

I. INTRODUCTION

With the development of electronic technology and communication technology, the transmission rate of signals is gradually increasing. At present, the general connector rate in the market is between 10Gbps and 40Gbps. The transmission rate of the new generation of high-speed backplane connectors will reach 56Gbps (for non-return to zero code NRZ). Even up to 112Gbps (for 4-pulse amplitude modulation signal PAM4) [1]. In the design process of an electronic system, the size of the system is getting smaller and smaller, the components and wires on the printed circuit board become more and more dense, the frequency of the signal becomes higher and higher, and the rising edge becomes steeper and steeper. These put forward higher requirements for the electronic system. If the design is improper, a series of signal integrity problems such as reflection and crosstalk will occur [2]-[3]. As the core of the electronic equipment interconnection system, the signal integrity of electrical connectors determines the transmission quality of the signal in the system [4]-[5]. Therefore, it is particularly important to study the signal integrity of electrical connectors in the design of the electronic equipment.

Tanking the wafer of a high-speed backplane connector as the research object, this paper uses the three-dimensional electromagnetic simulation software CST microwave studio to design the terminal layer, the conductive adhesive layer, the plastic layer and the metal shielding layer of the wafer, and proposes solutions to the problems of the corner design from the horizontal section to the vertical section of the terminal layer, the unequal length of the transmission lines in the differential pair, the excessive crosstalk between the transmission lines and the unequal potential of the ground terminals. Therefore, the connector wafer can meet the requirements of the signal integrity indexes such as impedance, loss and crosstalk in the frequency of 0-28GHz.

II. DESIGN OF THE WAFER OF THE HIGH-SPEED BACKPLANE CONNECTOR

A. Structural design of the wafer

The high-speed backplane connector is divided into two parts: a plug and a socket. The socket is composed of a shield, signal pins and a base, and the plug is composed of a fixed bracket, wafers and a base. The wafers are divided into two types: wafer A and wafer B, their structure composition is the same, but the arrangement is staggered. The backplane connectors are stacked to realize product expansion [6].

As shown in Fig. 2, the wafer is composed of four parts: the terminal layer, the plastic layer, the conductive adhesive layer and the metal shielding layer. The terminal layer is composed of signal terminals and grounding terminals, which mainly plays the role of signal transmission and grounding; The plastic layer is wrapped on the terminal layer by injection molding, which mainly plays the role of fix and support, and also can adjust the impedance; The conductive adhesive and the metal shielding layer play the role of protection and electromagnetic shielding [6].

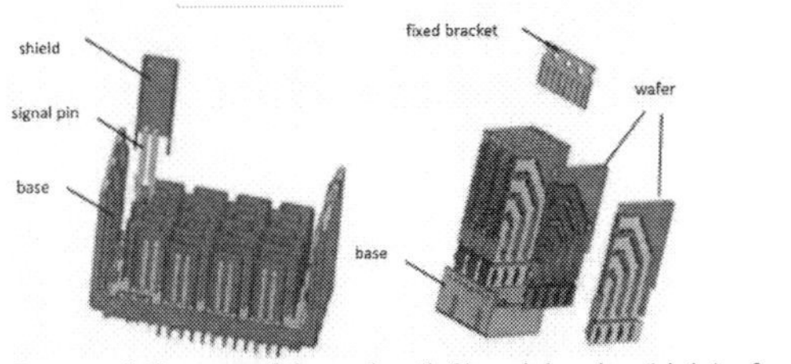

Fig. 1. Structural diagram of the socket (left) and the plug (right) of a high-speed backplane connector

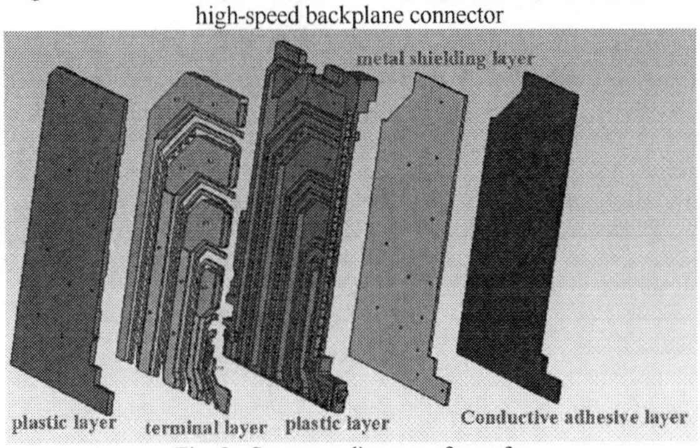

Fig. 2. Structure diagram of a wafer

The adjacent wafers in the backplane connector are electromagnetically separated by the metal shielding layer, and their terminal layers are distributed in a staggered manner. Therefore, the mutual influence between wafers is very small, and only the internal structure of a single wafer needs to be designed.

B. Design requirements for signal integrity parameters

The signal integrity parameters of the high-speed backplane connector mainly include impedance matching, insertion loss, return loss, near end crosstalk and far end crosstalk. Their design requirements are as follows, where "insertion loss > -2.5dB@28GHz " indicates that the insertion loss at 28ghz frequency is greater than - 2.5dB.

(1) Impedance matching: 90±5Ω

(2) Insertion loss: >-2.5dB@28GHz

(3) Return loss: <-15dB@28GHz

(4) Near end crosstalk: <-40dB@28GHz

(5) Far end crosstalk: <-40dB@28GHz

C. Design of terminal layer

As shown in the left figure of Fig. 3, there are 16 fixed fish-eye terminals at the right horizontal end and 13 fixed pins at the lower vertical end of each wafer, which are respectively connected with other communication systems to transmit high-speed differential signals. Among these 16 terminals, 8 signal terminals (numbers 1-8) constitute 4 differential pairs, and the other 8 are ground terminals. The signal enters from the fish-eye terminal at the horizontal end of the differential pair, passes through the differential pair of the terminal layer to be designed, and is transmitted to the pin at the vertical end and sent out.

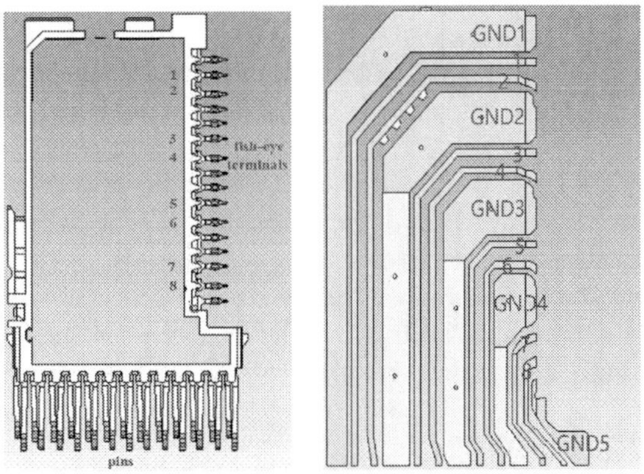

Fig. 3. Structure design of the wafer
(left: the external frame; right: structure of the terminal layer)

The right diagram of Fig. 3 is the designed terminal layer, which is composed of 8 signal terminals and 5 grounding terminals, and every 2 signal terminals form a differential pair. There are 4 differential pairs in the terminal layer, and the adjacent differential pairs are separated by wide grounding terminals to reduce the signal crosstalk between them. There are ground pins on the ground terminal to connect with the metal shield layer to ensure that the potential of all ground terminals is equal. The small dots in the right diagram of Fig. 3 are the ground pins. In the design process of the terminal layer, it is necessary to comprehensively consider the structural size and signal integrity requirements of the transmission line, especially the following four points:

1) Corner design

In the transmission process, the signal needs to be transferred from the horizontal section to the vertical section, so the terminal needs to be bent in the design. 135 ° corner shall be designed at the turning to meet better signal transmission performance [7], and 135 ° corner design shall be adopted for the first 6 signal terminals. Because the design space of signal terminals 7 and 8 is limited, the minimum value of impedance will be less than 85Ω if they are designed at 135 ° corners, which does not meet the design requirements. Therefore, the signal terminals 7 and 8 are changed from the horizontal section to the vertical section in a gradual manner.

2) Equal length design of the difference pairs

In order to ensure the same transmission delay of the signal in the differential pair, it is required that the lengths of the two signal lines in the differential pair should be the same as far as possible, and the length difference between the lines is generally required to be less than 20% of the spatial extension of the rising edge of the signal [8]-[9]. In this design, the rise time t_r of the signal is 31ps, and the propagation speed v of the signal on the differential transmission line is calculated as 1.82×10^{11} mm/s according to (1), where c is the light speed of 3×10^{11} mm/s, ε_r is the dielectric constant of the dielectric layer, and the dielectric constant of the plastic layer is 2.7. The length of the signal rising edge space extending by 20% is calculated 1.14mm according to (2). In the differential pair 1, the signal terminal 1 is 1.44mm longer than the signal terminal 2, which exceeds 20% of the spatial extension of the rising edge of the signal. Therefore, a trapezoid is added to the outside of the signal terminal 2, and the current skin effect in high frequency is used to increase the actual transmission distance of the signal and reduce the length difference within the differential pair. The length difference between the signal terminals in the other three differential pairs is less than 20% of the spatial extension of the rising edge of the signal, so it is unnecessary to add a "trapezoid" structure.

$$v = \frac{c}{\sqrt{\varepsilon_r}} = \frac{3\times10^{11} mm/s}{\sqrt{2.7}} = 1.82\times10^{11} mm/s \quad (1)$$

$$l = 0.2\times v\times t_r = 1.14mm \quad (2)$$

3) Crosstalk design

Crosstalk refers to the coupling between two signal terminals. It is a noise signal caused by mutual inductance and mutual capacitance between signal terminals. To reduce crosstalk, it is necessary to strengthen the shielding effect between signal terminals [10]. If the wiring space allows, the grounding signal line can be inserted between the signal lines with serious crosstalk for isolation, so as to reduce crosstalk [3]. In this design, a wide grounding terminal is designed between every two differential pairs to enhance signal shielding. Because the spacing between adjacent differential pairs in the vertical section is smaller than that between the horizontal section, it is necessary to thicken the grounding terminal of the vertical section to achieve better shielding effect. The thickness of the horizontal section (green part) of GND2, GND3, GND4 terminals in Fig. 3 is 0.77mm, and the thickness of the vertical section (yellow part) is 0.97mm.

4) Grounding design

The ground terminal is connected to the outer surface of the coaxial port to ensure that they have the same potential. In the case of high frequency, the grounding terminal is required to isolate the electric field and magnetic field generated by the signal terminal. Different grounding terminals receive different electric and magnetic fields because of different distances from the signal terminals on both sides and different signal terminal structures. Therefore, the grounding terminals are connected to the metal shielding layer through grounding pins to ensure that there is a consistent potential between the grounding terminals, to reduce the impact of the electromagnetic field generated by the signal on the connector, and to improve the signal transmission performance.

In this design, the terminal layer is made of copper with conductivity of 2.3×10^7 S/m, thermal conductivity 171.626 W/K/m and density 8.82×10^3 Kg/m^3。

D. Plastic layer design

In this design, with the terminal layer as the center and the outer frame as the boundary, the plastic layer that can embed the terminal layer is designed, as shown in Fig. 4. On the one hand, the plastic layer plays a role of fixing and supporting, and on the other hand, it can also change the impedance by adjusting the material. The material of the plastic layer is aniline group, the dielectric constant is 2.7, and the dissipation factor is 0.005.

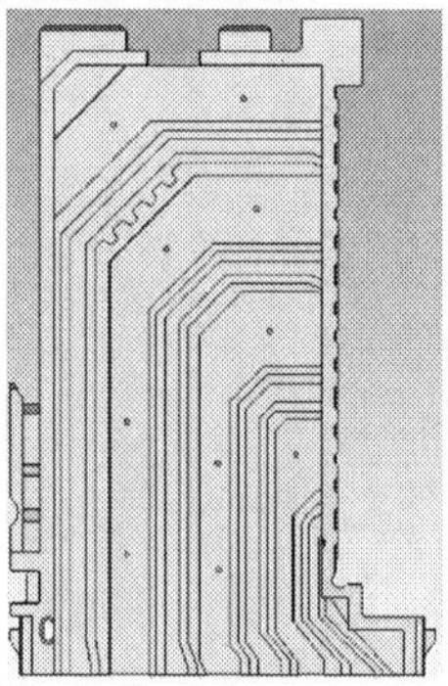

Fig. 4. Plastic layer structure

E. Shielding layer design

The shielding layer of the backplane connector includes a metal shielding layer and a conductive adhesive layer, and the structure is shown in Fig.5. The metal shielding layer is fixed on the outside of the plastic layer to support, protect and shield electromagnetic interference. The material is the same copper as the terminal layer. The conductive adhesive layer is fixed on the outside of the metal shielding layer, and Polyone PA66 material is used. The dielectric constant is 3.6, the dissipation factor is 0.03 when the working frequency is greater than 1MHz, and the density is 1.14×10^3kg/m^3

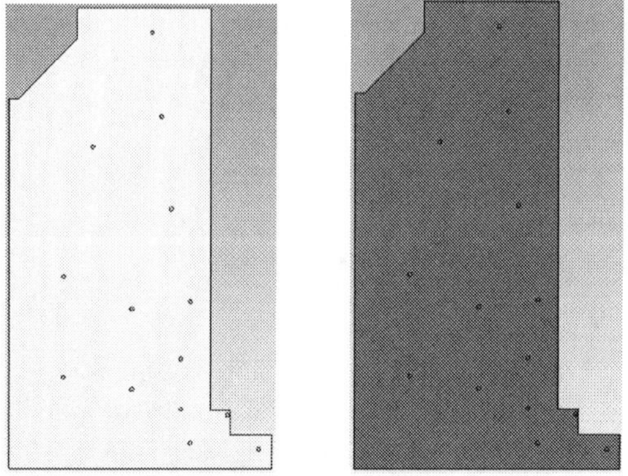

Fig. 5. Structural diagram of metal shielding layer (left) and conductive adhesive layer (right)

F. Overall structure design of the wafer

According to the design in section C to section E, the

structural design of a wafer of the high-speed backplane connector is completed. The explosion diagram is shown in Fig.2. The five layers are stacked together to obtain the wafer structure shown in the left diagram of Fig. 7.

III. SIGNAL INTEGRITY SIMULATION ANALYSIS

A. CST simulation scheme

This design uses CST simulation software to simulate the signal integrity of the wafer model, and the flow chart is shown in Fig.6. First, create a new project document and set the basic parameters such as unit (such as length in mm), frequency range (0-28GHz), boundary condition (ideal electrical boundary) and background material (normal air). Then, import the created wafer model, check whether there is interference in the model, and set the materials of each part of the wafer. Next, the solver (set as the time domain solver), the port (set as the coaxial differential port) and the excitation mode (Gaussian signal) are set. After the above settings are completed, the simulation solution calculation can be carried out to obtain the S parameters and TDR impedance of each port, and analyze the simulation results.

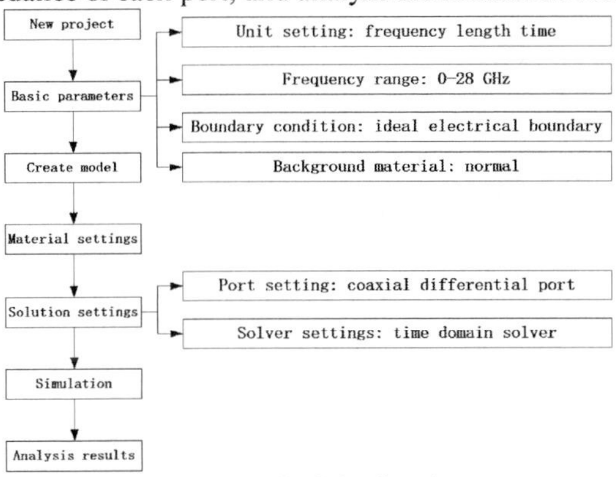

Fig. 6. CST simulation flow chart

B. Coaxial port design

After the model is established, the most critical step is to add the excitation source to the model. In this design, a coaxial port is added to outside of the differential pairs, the inner circle of the coaxial port contacts the signal terminal to input the signal, while the outer frame contacts the ground terminal to maintain zero potential.

The characteristic impedance calculation formula of the coaxial port is shown in (3), wherein ε_r is the relative dielectric constant of the dielectric layer, D is the outer diameter of the coaxial port, and d is the inner diameter of the coaxial port. In this design, the differential characteristic impedance of the differential pair is 90Ω, so the single end characteristic impedance Z_0 of the coaxial port is 45Ω. The inner circle diameter of the coaxial port is slightly larger than the width of the signal terminal, taking 0.35mm. Substituting Z_0= 45Ω, ε_r =1 (dielectric constant of air) and d= 0.35mm into (3), D=0.74mm is obtained. The port distribution settings and the main view of the ports of the wafer model are shown in Fig. 7.

$$Z_0 = \frac{60}{\sqrt{\varepsilon_r}} \times \ln \frac{D}{d} \tag{3}$$

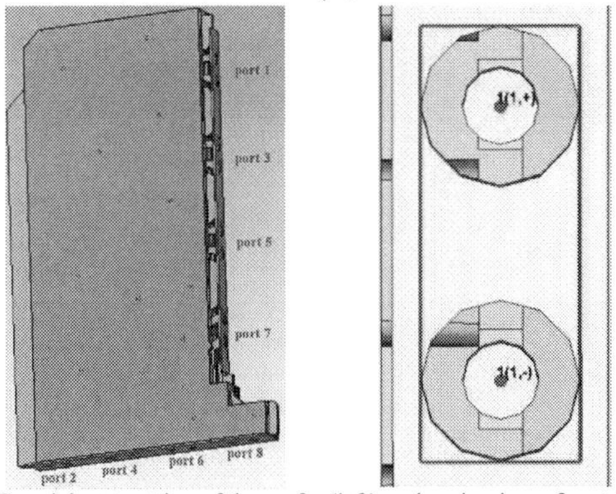

Fig. 7. Coaxial port setting of the wafer (left) and main view of port 1 (right)

C. Simulation results and analysis

After the coaxial port is set, the wafer model is simulated, and the return loss, insertion loss, near end crosstalk, far end crosstalk and TDR impedance are shown in Fig. 8 to Fig. 12 respectively.

The return loss results are shown in Fig.8. S11, S33, S55 and S77 are the return loss of differential ports 1 and 2, differential ports 3 and 4, differential ports 5 and 6, and differential ports 7 and 8 respectively. The maximum value of the return loss of the four groups is kept below -15dB, of which S11 achieves the maximum value of -15.74dB at 25.2GHz, S33 achieves the maximum value of -15.63dB at 16.9GHz, S55 achieves the maximum value of -18.50dB at 27.8GHz, and S77 achieves the maximum value of -17.24dB at 26.5GHz. All of them meet the design requirement.

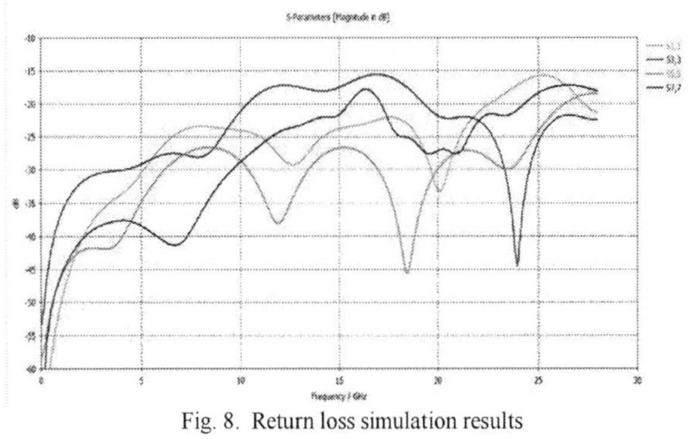

Fig. 8. Return loss simulation results

The insertion loss results are shown in Fig. 9. S21, S43, S65 and S87 are the insertion loss of differential ports 1 and 2, differential ports 3 and 4, differential ports 5 and 6, and differential ports 7 and 8 respectively. The minimum value of the insertion loss of the four groups is kept above -2.5dB, among which S21 reaches the minimum value of -2.05dB at 25.0GHz, S43 reaches the minimum value of -2.36dB at 28.0GHz, S65 reaches the minimum value of -2.48dB at 28.0GHz, and S87 reaches the minimum value of -2.00dB at 26.15GHz. All of them meet the design requirement.

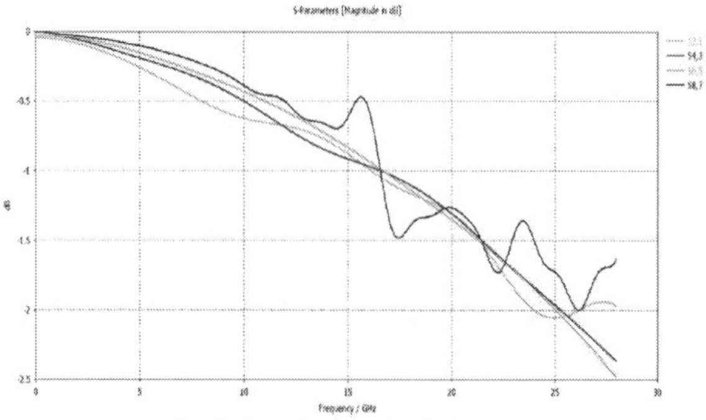

Fig. 9. Insertion loss simulation results

Results of the near end crosstalk are shown in Fig. 10. S31, S53 and S75 are near end crosstalk between differential ports 1 and 3, differential ports 3 and 5, and differential ports 5 and 7 respectively. The maximum value of the near end crosstalk of the three groups is kept below -40dB, of which S31 achieves the maximum value of -45.68dB at 25.4GHz, S53 achieves the maximum value of -42.49dB at 25.3GHz, and S75 achieves the maximum value of -44.91dB at 24.8GHz. All of them meet the design requirement.

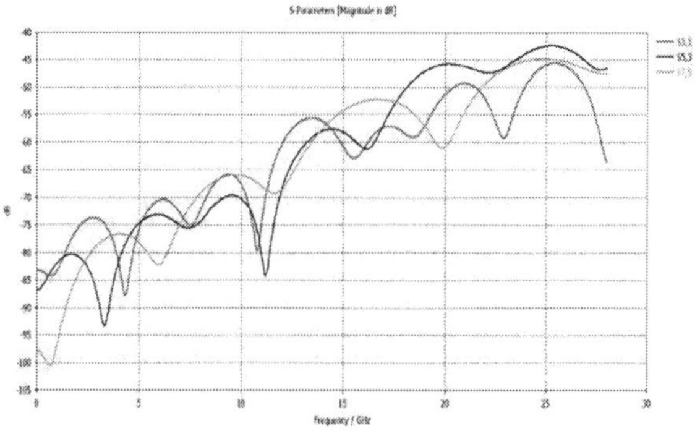

Fig. 10. Near end crosstalk simulation results

Results of the far end crosstalk are shown in Fig. 11. S41, S63 and S85 are the far end crosstalk between differential ports 1 and 4, differential ports 3 and 6, and differential ports 5 and 8 respectively. The maximum value of the far end crosstalk of the three groups is kept below -40dB, of which S41 achieved the maximum value of -46.63dB at 25.9GHz, S63 achieved the maximum value of -41.34dB at 28.0GHz, and S85 achieved the maximum value of -41.09dB at 28.0GHz. All of them meet the design requirement.

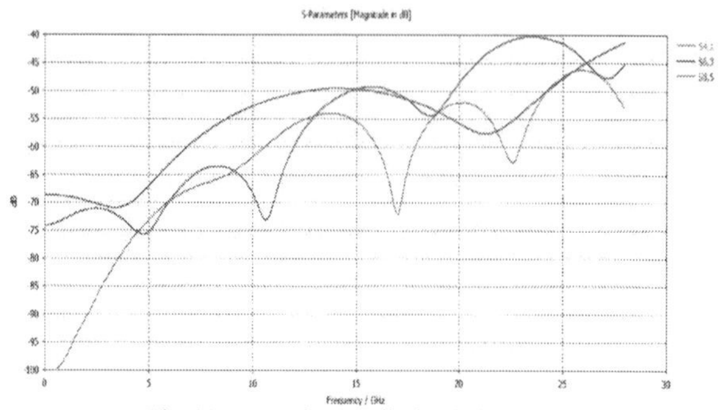

Fig. 11. Far end crosstalk simulation results

The simulation results of TDR impedance are shown in Fig. 12. TDR[1], TDR[3], TDR[5] and TDR[7] are the TDR impedance of differential pairs 1 and 2, 3 and 4, 5 and 6, 7 and 8 respectively. The impedance of the four groups are all within the range of 90± 5Ω, of which the range of TDR[1] is 86.9Ω-92.3Ω, the range of TDR[3] is 86.2Ω-93.0Ω, the range of TDR[5] is 89.8Ω-92.9Ω, and the range of TDR[7] is 89.5Ω-92.9Ω. All of them meet the design requirement.

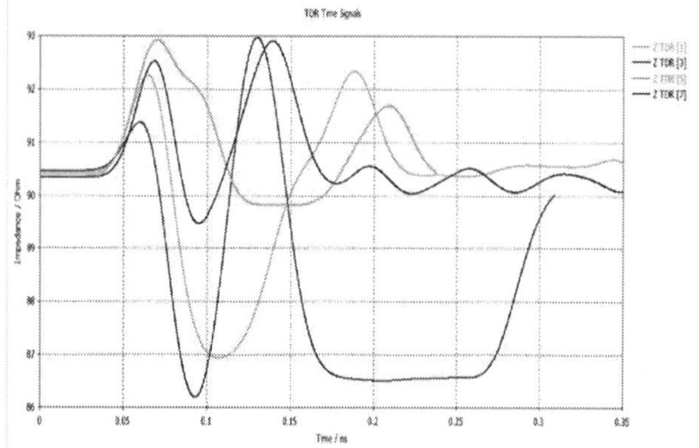

Fig. 12. TDR impedance simulation results

IV. CONCLUSION

When designing high-speed connectors, in order to meet the requirements of signal integrity, including impedance matching, reducing signal loss, reflection and crosstalk, it is necessary to consider the comprehensive influence of the structure, size, arrangement and placement, materials and other factors of the connector components.

The wafer of the high-speed backplane connector designed in this paper is composed of a terminal layer, a plastic layer, a metal shielding layer and a conductive adhesive layer. The design methods and key points of the terminal layer are as follows:

1) For the first 6 signal terminals, a 135 ° corner is used to realize the transition of the signal line from the horizontal section to the vertical section, while for the last 2 signal terminals with limited space, the transition from the horizontal section to the vertical section is used in a gradual manner, so as to reduce the influence of the terminal structure change on the signal transmission and meet the better signal transmission performance.

2) Since the length difference between the signal terminals 1 and 2 in the differential pair 1 exceeds 20% of the spatial extension of the signal rising edge, a trapezoidal structure is added at the corner of the signal terminal 2 to reduce the length difference between the two terminals in the differential pair, which is less than 20% of the spatial extension of the signal rising edge.

3) By increasing the thickness of the ground terminals, the shielding effect between the differential signal terminals is strengthened and their crosstalk is reduced.

4) Some grounding pins are designed on the grounding terminals and connected with the metal shield layer to ensure that the grounding terminals and the metal shield layer have the same zero potential to ensure the high-speed signal transmission performance.

The transmission performance of the wafer model of the high-speed backplane connector is simulated and analyzed by CST software. The signal integrity parameters such as return loss, insertion loss, near end crosstalk, far end crosstalk and TDR impedance meet the design requirements. Therefore, the design of the wafer model of the high-speed backplane connector is successful.

However, the insertion loss of the signal terminals 7 and 8 decreases oscillating with the frequency and needs to be optimized. The signal integrity parameters of the high-speed backplane connector wafer also need to be tested to verify.

ACKNOWLEDGMENT

The authors of this paper are very grateful to Amphenol (Changzhou) upscale connector Co., Ltd. for the project cooperation support.

REFERENCES

[1] Y. Q. Cao, Y. Wang, Q. Q. Chen, Q. F. Mu, "The Structure Design and Analysis of 56G High-speed Backplane Connector," *Electromechanical Components*, 2021,41(06): 6-10.

[2] G. Gao, B. Yang, X. D. Duan, Y. Li, "Research on the influence of vias on signal transmission in multi-layer PCB," *2017 13th IEEE International Conference on Electronic Measurement & Instruments (ICEMI)*, 2017: 406-409.

[3] J. Liu, M. Zhang, G. Hu, "Analysis of Power Supply And Signal Integrity of High Speed PCB Board," *2019 IEEE 8th Joint International Information Technology and Artificial Intelligence Conference (ITAIC)*, 2019: 412-416.

[4] W.J. Yu, Z. Zeng, B. Peng, et al, "Multi-Objective Optimum Design of High-Speed Backplane Connector Using Particle Swarm Optimization," *IEEE Access*, 2018:1.

[5] R. Ji , J. C. Gao, G. T. Flowers G, et al, "The Effect of Electrical Connector Degradation on High-Frequency Signal Transmission,"*IEEE Transactions on Components, Packaging, and Manufacturing Technology*, 2017, pp. 1-10.

[6] B. Xu, "The design and application of the high-speed backplane connector,"*Nanjing University of Posts and Telecommunications*, 2017.

[7] K. W. Wang, J. H. Wang, "Study on the transmission and reflection properties of the microstrip line bend," *Journal of Microwaves*, 2006, 22(3):4.

[8] J. N. Chang, X. Z. Ren, " Structural design and analysis of high-speed backplane connector," *Practical Electronics*, 2020(10), pp. 75-76.

[9] Z. Yang, Y. K. Gao, S. L. Li, C. C. Sun, Y. F. Zhao, "Research on Signal Integrity in High-Speed Interconnection Channel Based on SIwave," *2021 IEEE 3rd International Conference on Circuits and Systems (ICCS)*. 2021: 78-82.

[10] X. P. Liu, J. Zuo, H. Chen, et al, "Analysis of signal crosstalk optimization of connector," *Electromechanical Components*, 2022, 42(2):5.

Xueyan Lin, female, was born in May 1971. In June 1992, she graduated from the Department of mechanical and electronic engineering of Xi'an University of Electronic Science and technology and received a bachelor's degree in electronic equipment structure. In March 1995, she graduated from the department of mechanical and electronic engineering of Beijing University of Posts and telecommunications and got the master's degree of engineering in mechanical design. In July 2009, she received the Ph.D. degree of engineering in circuit and system of Beijing University of Posts and telecommunications.

Xueyan Lin is now an associate professor and master supervisor of the school of artificial intelligence, Beijing University of Posts and telecommunications. She is engaged in the research of electrical connection and connector failure mechanism, reliability detection technology, signal integrity analysis and design, control system design and other fields.

Simulation of Electrodynamic Stability Based on Electromagnetic-Structure Coupling

Fangang Hong

XiaMen HongFa Electroacoustic Co., Ltd., Fujian, Xiamen, 361021
Email:1002708@hongfa.cn TEL:15606016981

Abstract—**The stability of relay against short-circuit electrodynamic force is an important index to evaluate its reliability. Through the simulation analysis of short-circuit electrodynamic force, it can provide important reference significance for the structural design of prototype in the early stage of product. This paper takes the structure of a certain type of relay as the research object, the micro-conductive bridge is used to simulate the contact between contacts, and the electromagnetic field calculation model of conductive circuit is established. Meanwhile, the calculation model of electromagnetic suction and structural reaction force is established. Based on the application of multi-physical field simulation, the electrodynamic stability of the relay is analyzed through the coupling simulation of electromagnetic field and structural field.**

Index Terms—**Relay, Electrodynamic force, Holm force Electromagnetic suction force, Structural reaction force.**

I. INTRODUCTION

In recent years, with the rapid development of new infrastructure, power relay has been widely used in 5G base station, new energy vehicle charging pile and other fields. These fields have strict requirements on whether the relay can work reliably under various extreme conditions. Among them, whether the relay can work reliably under short circuit is a very important standard, and electrodynamic stability is a key indicator to evaluate whether it can work normally under short circuit. Therefore, in the early stage of development, it is of great significance to analyze the electrodynamic stability and optimize the structure of the relay through numerical simulation technology.

The key point of the analysis of the electrodynamic stability of the relay under short circuit is the study of the electrodynamic force of the contact system. The Holm force and the electrodynamic force between the conductor circuits constitute the electrodynamic force of the contact system. With the rapid development of computer technology and finite element analysis, simulation technology has become an important means to study the electrodynamic force of low-voltage electrical contact system. Three finite element modeling methods for simulating current contraction between contacts are introduced, and the advantages and disadvantages of the three models are compared in [3]. The authors used 3-D finite element analysis, introduced the conductive bridge model as the contact point, simulated the current contraction between the contacts, calculated the electrodynamic force acting on the contacts, and verified the feasibility of this method in [4-6]. Based on the electro-magnetic coupling analysis, the Holm force between the contacts and the Loren force on the movable conductive rod are calculated and analyzed in [7-9].

In this paper, based on the multi physical field simulation technology of electromagnetic-structure coupling, the micro conductive bridge is used to simulate the contact between contacts, and the electromagnetic field calculation model of the conductive circuit is established. At the same time, the calculation model of the structural reaction force of the contact system and the suction force of the magnetic circuit system is established. Through the coupling calculation of the electrodynamic force, the structural reaction force and the electromagnetic suction force, the electrodynamic stability of the relay is evaluated.

II. RESEARCH OBJECT

The research object of this paper is a high-power power relay, and the relevant model structure is selected. As shown in Fig. 1, in which the static conductive sheet, the static conductive lead-out sheet and the dynamic and static contact are symmetrical structures.

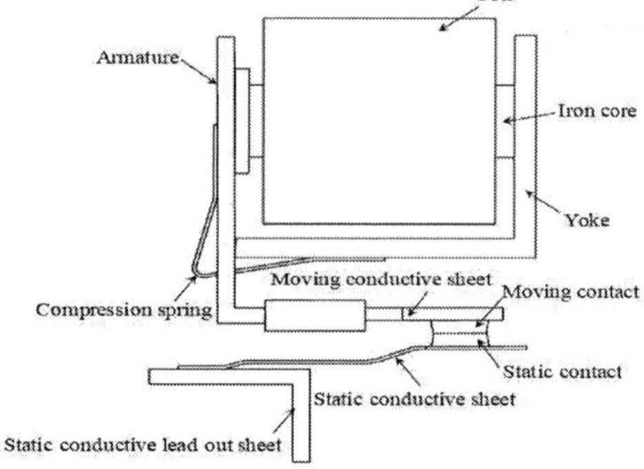

Fig. 1. Relay correlation model.

III. CALCULATION MODEL OF ELECTRIC FORCE OF CONTACT SYSTEM

The electrodynamic forces of the relay contact system are mainly composed of two parts. One part is the electrodynamic force between conductors generated by the magnetic field generated by the contact circuit current acting on the conductor; the other part is that the current flows through the contact point of the contact, and the current line shrinks, the magnetic field generated by the shrinking current acts on the shrinking current, resulting in an electrodynamic repulsion force between the contacts, which is called Holm force. Both of them are essentially Lorentz magnetic forces. Under the normal rated current, the electrodynamic force of the contact system is not large, but in the case of short circuit, the impact current is dozens of times of the rated current, and the Lorentz magnetic force is proportional to the square of the current. Therefore, the electrodynamic force of the contact system is very large at this time, which will affect the normal contact of the contacts.

A. Calculation Model of Holm Force Between Contacts

The cylinder conductive bridge model is used to simulate the contraction phenomenon of the contact current line of the moving and static contacts. The material properties are consistent with the surface material of the contact. The height is generally taken from several micrometers to several tens of micrometers, and this paper takes 10 micrometers.

Holm force F_H can be represented by (1).

$$F_H = \frac{\mu_0 i^2}{4\pi} \ln \frac{R}{r} \tag{1}$$

Where r is the equivalent radius of the conductive spot, R is the equivalent radius of the contact, and μ_0 is the vacuum permeability.

The equivalent radius of the conductive spot can be expressed by (2).

$$r = \sqrt{\frac{F_k}{\pi \xi H}} \tag{2}$$

Where ξ is the contact surface condition, between 0.3 and 0.6, generally 0.45 is preferred; F_k is the pre-compression force between contacts; H is Brinell hardness of the contact material.

B. Computational Model of Lorentz Force in Contact Circuit

The Lorentz force of the contact circuit is closely related to the structure and shape of the contact circuit. Due to the diversity and irregularity of the contact circuit structure, the conductor arms cannot be approximately parallel. Suppose the current density in the conductor is $\vec{J}$, the magnetic induction intensity is $\vec{B}$, the conductor volume is V, and the electrodynamic force received by the conductor is

$$F_L = \int_V F_i dv = \int_V (\vec{J}_i \times \vec{B}_i) dv \tag{3}$$

Without considering the influence of eddy current on electrodynamic force, the equation of constant field is used to calculate the current density distribution and magnetic induction intensity, and the current density satisfies (4) and (5).

$$\vec{J} = \nabla \times \vec{D} \tag{4}$$

$$\nabla \times \left(\frac{1}{\sigma} \nabla \times \vec{D}\right) = 0 \tag{5}$$

The boundary condition is

$$\oint_s \vec{D} \cdot dl = I \tag{6}$$

Where σ is the conductivity, $\vec{D}$ is the vector potential, and I is the current flowing through the conductor.

After the distribution of the current density is obtained, the distribution of the magnetic induction intensity can be obtained in the entire magnetic field region according to the relationship between the electromagnetic induction intensity and the current density.

C. Calculation of Short-Circuit Impulse Current

When a short circuit occurs in a single-phase AC circuit, in addition to the sinusoidal periodic component, the short-circuit current in the transition process also contains a non-periodic component, which is expressed by (7).

$$i = I_m[\sin(\omega t + \psi - \varphi) - \sin(\psi - \varphi) e^{-\frac{R}{L}t}] \tag{7}$$

When $\psi - \varphi = -\pi/2$, the short-circuit current is the largest at this time.

$$i = I_m[-\cos \omega t + e^{-t/\tau}] \tag{8}$$

The short-term withstand current of the relay is 1.5KA, the power factor is 0.95, and τ is obtained according to the power factor, when t is 0.01, the short-circuit current reaches its peak value, and its maximum peak value is 2.12KA.

IV. ELECTRODYNAMIC SIMULATION OF CONTACT SYSTEM

Based on the electromagnetic-structural coupling simulation, the electrodynamic force of the contact system is analyzed, and the simulation flow is shown in Fig. 2.

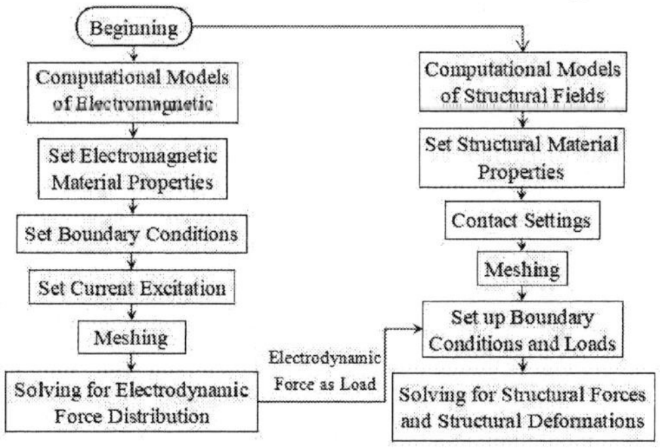

Fig. 2. Simulation Flow

Through the electromagnetic field simulation, the conductive loop is energized for 2.12KA, and the electrodynamic force distribution of the conductive loop is calculated. Fig. 3 and Fig. 4 are the Lorentz force density distribution of the contact loop and the Holm force density distribution between the contacts.

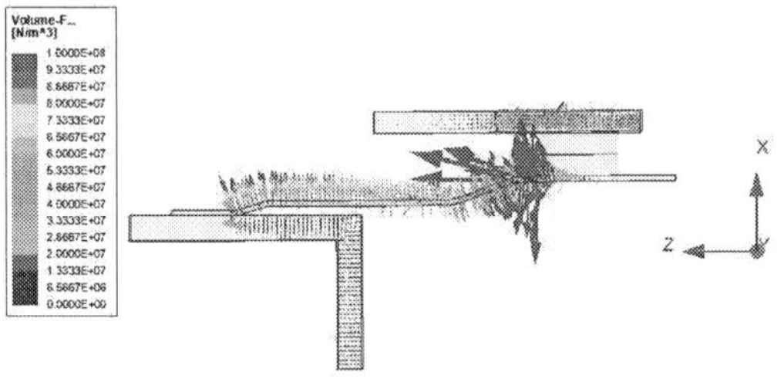

Fig. 3. Lorentz force distribution in contact loop

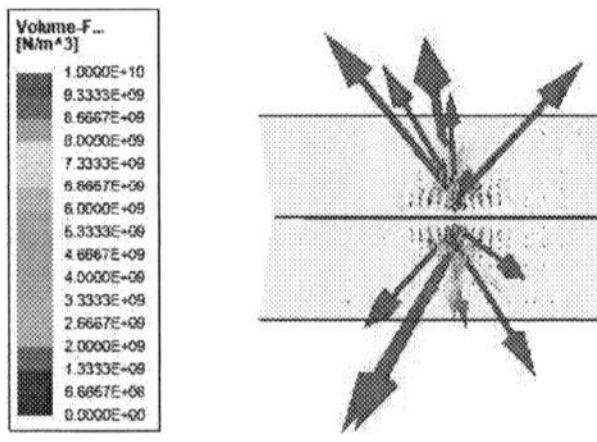

Fig. 4. Holm force distribution between contacts

According to the distribution of the electrodynamic force density of the whole contact circuit, it is found that in addition to the large electrodynamic repulsion force at the contact position, the static conductive lead out piece, the static conductive piece and the dynamic conductive piece are also subject to certain electrodynamic force. Through the post-processing calculation of the software, the electrodynamic force value and direction of each part can be obtained, as shown in Table I. The vector of the electrodynamic force is taken as the reference coordinate in Fig. 3.

TABLE I
CALCULATION RESULT OF ELECTRODYNAMIC FORCE

Part	Electrodynamic Force/N
Static conductive sheet I	(1.92,0.42,0.42)
Static conductive sheet II	(1.92,-0.42,0.42)
Static conductive lead out sheet I	(-1.5,0.38,0.19)
Static conductive lead out sheet II	(-1.5,-0.38,0.19)
Static contact I	(-1.78,0.14,0.03)
Static contact II	(-1.78,-0.14,0.03)
Moving conductive sheet	(0.89,0,0.39)
Moving contact I	(1.91,0.12,-0.02)
Moving contact II	(1.91,-0.12,-0.02)

After calculating the electrodynamic force of each part through the electromagnetic field, the electrodynamic force is coupled into the structural field, and the contact and constraint are set in the structural field. Finally, through the coupling simulation of the two, the force situation at key positions is analyzed, as shown in Fig. 5.

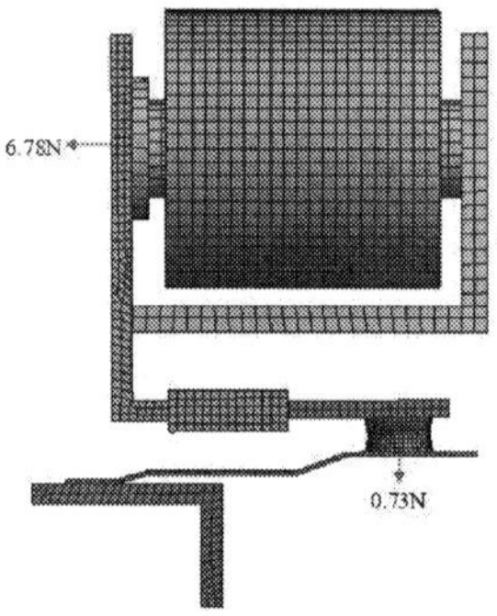

Fig. 5. Stress at key positions of the structure

The force on the static contact and the armature is mainly analyzed. Each static contact is subjected to a force in the negative direction of the x-axis, and the armature is subjected to a force in the positive direction of the z-axis at the center point of the iron core. Both forces cause the contacts to open. Therefore, in order to ensure that the contacts are still reliably closed under short-circuit conditions, the closing pressure of each static contact must be greater than 0.73N, and the suction force of the armature must be greater than the reaction force it receives.

V. ANALYSIS OF ELECTRODYNAMIC STABILITY

The structure of the relay under short circuit is mainly affected by the combined effect of three forces: electrodynamic force, reaction force and electromagnetic suction force, as shown in Fig. 6.

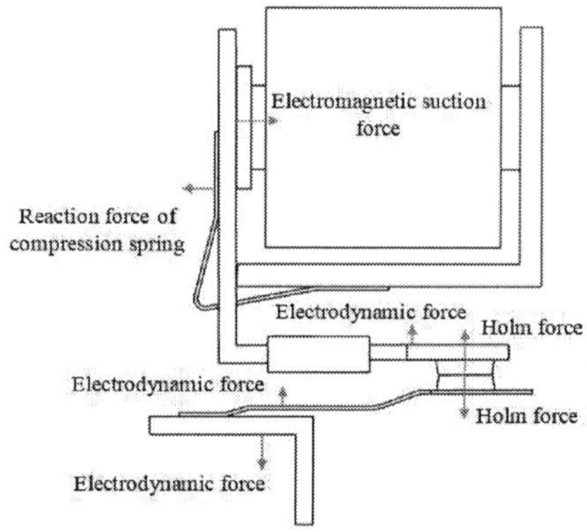

Fig. 6. Force condition of relay under short circuit

In order to ensure that the dynamic and static contacts do not open during a short circuit. on the one hand, it is necessary to ensure that the static contacts do not lean back, that is, the resultant force of the closing force and the electrodynamic force on the static contacts must point to the moving contacts, and on the other hand, it is necessary to ensure that the armature always maintains in the closed state, the electromagnetic suction force on the armature must be greater than the reaction force it receives.

As analyzed in Section IV, the closing pressure of each static contact must be greater than 0.73N to ensure that the static contact does not open. The closing pressure is controlled by adjusting the bending angle of the static conductive sheet. The closing pressure is controlled to be 1.2N with a certain margin relative to the electrodynamic force. The electrodynamic force of the conductive loop is coupled to the structure field where the static contact has a closing pressure and the armature is subjected to the reaction force of the compression spring, and finally the reaction force of the armature is calculated.

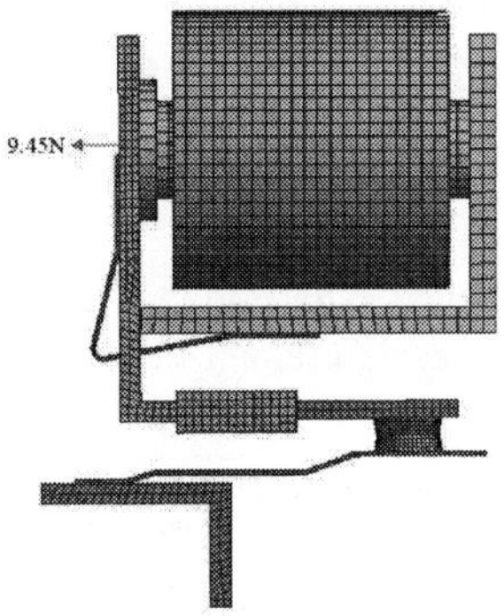

Fig. 7. Reaction force on armature

As shown in Fig. 7, the reaction force received by the armature at the center point of the iron core is 9.45N. From this, it can be obtained that the electromagnetic suction force received by the armature at this position must be greater than 9.45N to ensure that it does not open during a short circuit. The electromagnetic suction force when the armature is closed is calculated by the electromagnetic field. The voltage rises from 0 to 100%, and the voltage rises by 10% each time. The calculation results are shown in Fig. 8.

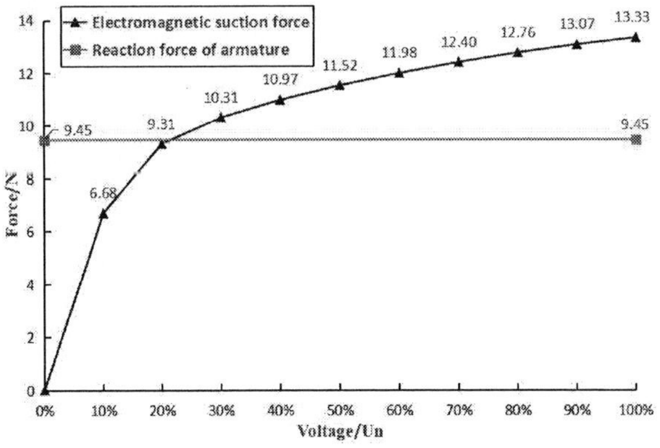

Fig. 8. Electromagnetic attraction of relays at different voltages

It can be seen from the data in Fig. 8 that the electromagnetic suction force of the armature under the excitation of 30% Un is 10.31N, which is greater than the armature reaction force of 9.45N, and has a certain margin, which can be stably maintained under short circuit, so the pressure of the static contact is controlled at 1.2 N, as long as the holding voltage of the armature is not less than 30%Un, the contacts can still be in stable contact during short circuit. On this basis, the pressure can be regulated according to the actual holding voltage requirements of the product and combined with the force of the static contact.

The above is a numerical simulation method that first determines the electrodynamic force of each part through the simulation of electrodynamic force, then couples the electrodynamic force with the structural reaction force, and cooperate with electromagnetic suction force to analyze the reliability of the contact system under short-circuit.

VI. ANALYSIS AND VERIFICATION OF SHORT-TERM TOLERANCE TEST

The short-time withstand capability test of the relay is a necessary step to verify the accuracy of its electrodynamic stability simulation analysis. The relay studied in this paper is subjected to short-circuit current test in accordance with the IEC62752.2006, and its ability to pass the test under the same short-circuit impulse current and different pressures is analyzed.

Select 12 samples and divide them into 4 groups with 3 samples in each group. The corresponding pressure of each group is different. Adjust the pressure according to the above simulation results. The grouping is as shown in Table II.

TABLE II
GROUPING OF TEST SAMPLES

Group	Pressure/N
1	0.4-0.6
2	0.6-0.75
3	0.75-0.9
4	0.9-1.2

The load condition is 277V.a.c., 50Hz, the power factor is 0.95, and the effective value of the short-circuit current is 1500A. The test process is as follows:

1) Apply excitation to the relay to close the contacts and keep the voltage drop at 35%Un;
2) Apply a short-circuit impulse current to the load circuit

of relay, and observe whether the contacts are opened during the period;

3) Disconnect the load and after the relay cools, observe whether the relay is bonded or welded.

Contact impassability, bonding or fusion welding are taken as the failure criteria, and the test results are shown in Table III.

TABLE III
RESULTS OF SHORT CIRCUIT CURRENT TESTS UNDER DIFFERENT PRESSURES

Group	Number of Contacts Disconnected / Piece	Number of Contacts Bonding or Welding / Piece
1	3/3	0/3
2	2/3	1/3
3	0/3	1/3
4	0/3	0/3

According to the test results in Table III, it can be seen that the closing pressure is between 0.4-0.6N, and the failure mode of the samples is that the contacts are disconnected, indicating that the closing pressure of the contacts is completely smaller than the electrodynamic force, resulting in being opened. when the closing pressure is between 0.6-0.75N, the failure mode of two samples is disconnection, and the failure mode of a sample is bonding or welding failure, indicating that the contact closing pressure is still less than the electrodynamic force, but it is close to the electrodynamic force. When the closing pressure is between 0.75-0.9N, only one sample is failure of bonding or welding, indicating that the contact closing pressure is greater than or equal to the electrodynamic force. When the closing pressure is between 0.9-1.2N, the test results of the samples are all OK, indicating that the contact closing pressure is completely greater than the electrodynamic force, and there is a certain margin.

The test results show that the actual electrodynamic force of the contact is at the lower limit of 0.75-0.9N, while the simulation results show that the electrodynamic force of the contact is 0.73N, which is relatively close to each other. At the same time, when the coil voltage is 35%Un, the test of the samples in the closing pressure range of 0.9-1.2N can be passed, indicating that the above simulation analysis of electrodynamic stability has good reliability.

VII. CONCLUSION

Electrodynamic stability is an important indicator for evaluating the short-term withstand capability of relays. This paper expounds a simulation research method for electrodynamic stability based on electromagnetic-structural field coupling. The simulation of the electrodynamic force is carried out through the electromagnetic field, and it is coupled into the structural field to analyze the structural force. Combined with the electromagnetic suction force, the electrodynamic stability is evaluated, and the accuracy is verified through the actual test.

Electrodynamic force is difficult to measure in actual tests, and it is difficult to analyze the force of relay under short-circuit condition. When the short-time withstand capacity fails, a large number of tests are often required to repeatedly verify. The simulation analysis of electrodynamic stability can analyze the force of relay under short-circuit condition, providing a reliable reference for design.

When designing the anti-short-circuit structure in the early stage of product design, the simulation analysis of electrodynamic stability can provide an effective theoretical analysis for the optimization of the anti-short-circuit structure, and cooperate with the actual test, which greatly improves the research efficiency.

REFERENCES

[1] R.Holm. Electric Contacts[M]. New York: Springer-Verlag, 1967.

[2] Greenwood JA. Constriction Resistance and the Real Area of Contact[J]. British Journal of Applied Physics, 1966, 17(12): 1621-1632.

[3] Deng Xiaofeng, Qu Jianyu, Hou Guobin, et al. Overview of research about short-time withstand performance for air circuit breaker[J]. Electrical & Energy Management Technology, 2017(12): 1-7.

[4] Li Xingwen, Chen Degui, Liu Hongwu, et al. 3-D finite element analysis of electro-dynamic repulsion forces acting on contacts[J]. High Volt Appar, 2004, 40(1): 53-55.

[5] Niu Chunping, Dong Delong, Sun Hao, etc. Finite element analysis of short-time withstand current of air circuit breaker[J]. Electric Power Automation Equipment, 2014, 34(2): 85-90.

[6] Liu Zhiwei, Li Xingwen, Qu Jianyu. 3-D finite-element analysis on short-time withstand performance for bridge-type contacts of air circuit breaker[J]. Electrical & Energy Management Technology, 2016(16): 1-6.

[7] Li Xingwen, Chen Degui, Xiang Honggang, et al. 3-D finite element nonlinear analysis and experimental study of electro-dynamic repulsion force in molded case circuit breakers[J]. Proceedings of the CSEE, 2004, 24(2):

150-155.
[8] Zheng Nan, Su Xiuping, Qiao Yanhua, et al. Study on electrodynamic repulsion force simulated analysis of circuit breaker contact structure[J]. Electrical & Energy Management Technology, 2016, 1(8): 32-35.
[9] Qiao Yanhua, Su Xiuping, Dong Tianying. Simulation and optimization on electrodynamic repulsion force of contact system in circuit breaker with oil dashpot[J]. Electrical & Energy Management Technology, 2017(16): 1-5, 21.
[10]Zhang Kai. Study on electro-dynamic force of apparatus contacts based on Finite element analysis of ansys[D]. Hebei University of Technology, 2006: 10-35.

Experimental Investigation of the Electrical Contact Resistance Characteristics for $AgSnO_2$ Contacts

Chao Zhang[1,2], Zhihao Gu[1], Wanbin Ren[1], Jian Liu[2]
1. School of Electrical Engineering and Automation, Harbin Institute of Technology, Harbin, 150001, China
2. School of Instrumentation Science and Engineering, Harbin Institute of Technology, Harbin, 150001, China
E-mail: zhangchao100@hit.edu.cn

Abstract—**The electrical contact resistance characteristics are important to evaluate the electrical contact performance of electrode materials. Higher contact resistance not only increases power consumption and temperature rise, but also causes undesirable interconnectivity between electrode materials, which further influences the electrical lifespan and reliability of switching devices. In this paper, the relationship between contact resistance and load force, is analyzed for $AgSnO_2$ contacts, and compared with the calculation results for smooth surfaces. Then, the experimental results of $AgSnO_2$ contacts with bright surface and matt surface are discussed, and the influences of the number and size of contact *a*-spots on the relationship between contact resistance and load force are investigated explicitly. It is found that besides the surface roughness of electrode material, the denser asperities with smaller curvature radii for matt surfaces could efficiently reduce the contact resistance.**

Index Terms—**contact resistance, load force, $AgSnO_2$ contacts, contact *a*-spot, surface roughness**

I. INTRODUCTION

Electrode materials are widespread used in many electrical and electronic components, such as electromechanical devices, connectors, micro-electromechanical systems and switch gears to conduct load currents [1-3]. All surfaces of electrode materials are microscopically rough even for the macroscopically polished surface. The electrical contact resistance across an interface is an important quantity and closely related to the physical properties of the electrode materials, contact structure, surface state, load force and load current. The low and stable contact resistance could decrease the temperature rise and power consumption, and further improve the electrical lifespan and reliability of switching devices.

The theory of contact resistance has long remained an academic hot issue. In the 1940s, Holm [4] firstly presented the theoretical calculation method for the constriction resistance of a single circular *a*-spot based on the electrical resistivity of electrode materials and the contact radius of the contact *a*-spot. In combination with the Hertz contact and Tabor theory, it is found that the constriction resistance is proportional to the contact load force with -1/3 and -1/2 exponential powers for the elastic and plastic deformation. Aiming to calculate the total conductance of rough surfaces, Greenwood and Williamson [5] further proposed the contact mechanics model by assuming the asperity heights following the Gaussian distribution. Liu et al. [6] calculated the electrical contact characteristics between a hemi-sphere and rough Au/CNT surfaces with parameter S_q ranging from 0.1-1 μm, and found that the contact resistance would increase with surface roughness.

In addition, much interests are attracted to investigate the relationship between electrical contact resistance and contact load force considering the surface topography of electrode materials by the experimental method. Hernot *et al.* [7] reported that the discrepancy between the theoretical and experimental results of contact resistance for bulk metal (Ag, Au, Pd, Ni), especially for low contact force, is induced by ignoring the surface roughness of the electrode materials. Kwon *et al.* [8] showed that the relationship between contact resistance and load force for the gold thin film contacts with S_q (root mean square) of 0.0036 μm and 0.0069 μm could be divided into three regions, and the power exponent of load force transit from -0.45 in the stable contact regime to -0.08 in the saturated regime.

In the view of practical manufacture method, the surface topography of electrode materials has significant influences on the electrical contact resistance characteristics. There has also been a considerable research effort to restrain the contact resistance to the utmost extent [9-11].

The purpose of this paper is to investigate the role of surface topography of electrode materials on the contact resistance with the help of the relationship between electrical contact resistance and load force. Thus, the experimental results of $AgSnO_2$ electrodes with bright and matt features are compared, and influences of the number and size of contact *a*-spots on the contact resistance are interpreted explicitly.

II. Experimental Details

A. Test rig

In general, the designed test rig allows studying the measurement of contact resistance between two electrode materials under the selectable load force and load current. It was designed to fulfill these three goals, i.e.:

- Variable load forces to achieve pure elastic or elastic–plastic contact mode.
- Different electrical current levels to discriminate the roles of electrical loads and mechanical loads in contact resistance.
- Highly efficient test for batches of rivet contacts: 10 s for single contact pair and 2 min for maximum 12 contact pairs automatically.

A schematic diagram of the test rig is shown in Fig.1. The mechanical platform includes the three-dimension motion module, electrode clamping module and flexible loading module. The electrode holder is fixed on the base, and there are twelve workstations in one row. Fig. 2 schematically shows the four-wire measurement setup, including the probe holder structure and the electrode clamping structure of one measurement workstation. The probe holder is attached to a "bow" type Beryllium bronze belt (stiffness is about 0.4 N/mm) to achieve the flexible contact with low load force. A force transducer is connected vertically with it for the measurement of load force. The required open circuit voltage and the load current for measurement contact resistance are provided by the measurement unit. The measurement resolution of contact resistance is 0.01 mΩ by using the four-wire method. The measurement unit is interfaced to a personal computer using a USB cable. The data acquisition and logging process are controlled through a PC with the help of LabVIEW software specifically programmed for this purpose.

B. Sample description and experimental method

The selected electrode material is $AgSnO_2(12)$, and the applied additive is In_2O_3. The geometry of the movable sample and static sample are shown in Fig.3. And two representative $AgSnO_2(12)$ electrodes with different surface topographies are selected to investigate the electrical contact characteristics. The surface topographies of the bright electrode and matt electrode with a scanning area of 1280×1280 μm^2 are shown in Fig.4(a)-(d). The measured parameter S_q (root mean square height), which represents the height fluctuation of each point in the concerned region relative to the mean height, is 27.87 μm and 28.64 μm for bright electrode and matt electrode, respectively. The measured hardness of the $AgSnO_2(12)$ material is 73.7HV(0.1N) and the electrical resistivity is 2.35×10^{-8} Ω·m. The details of the experimental conditions are listed in Table I.

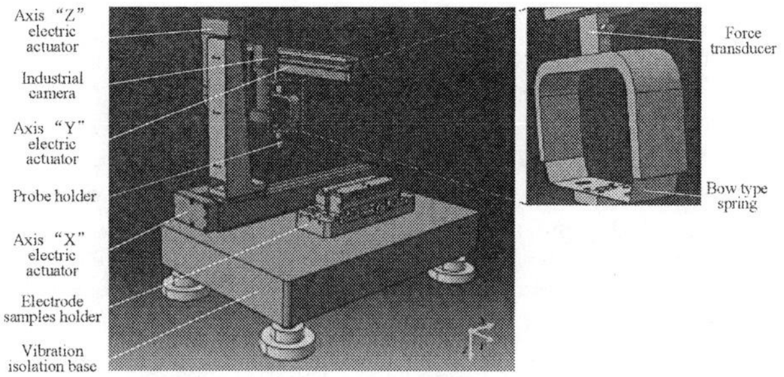

Fig. 1 3D model of the mechanical structure.

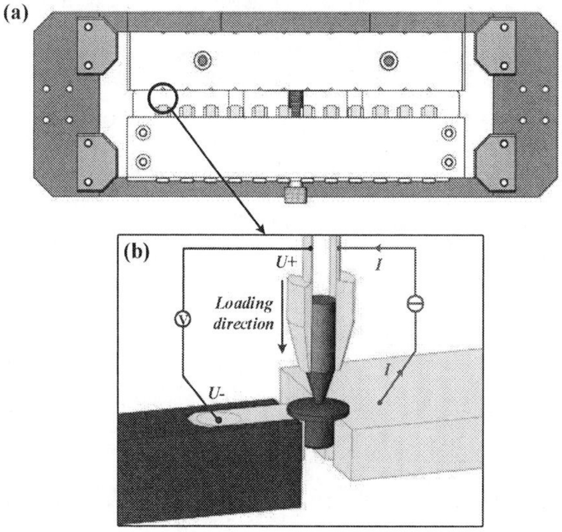

Fig. 2 The schematic diagram of the clamping electrode sample. (a) The top view of the samples holder. (b) The four-wire configuration of one measurement workstation.

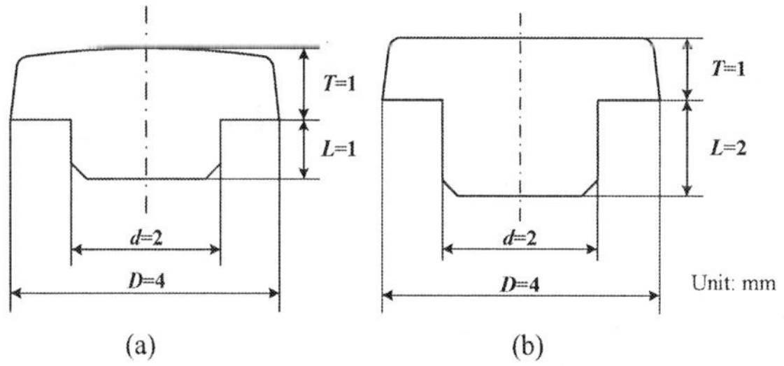

(a) (b)

Fig. 3 The sizes of electrode. (a) Movable sample. (b) Static sample.

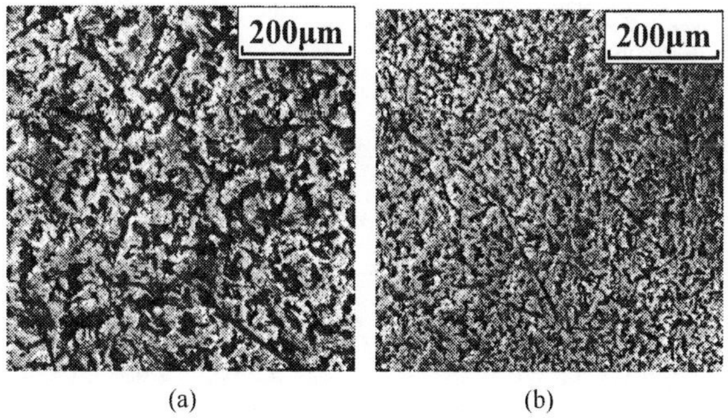

(a) (b)

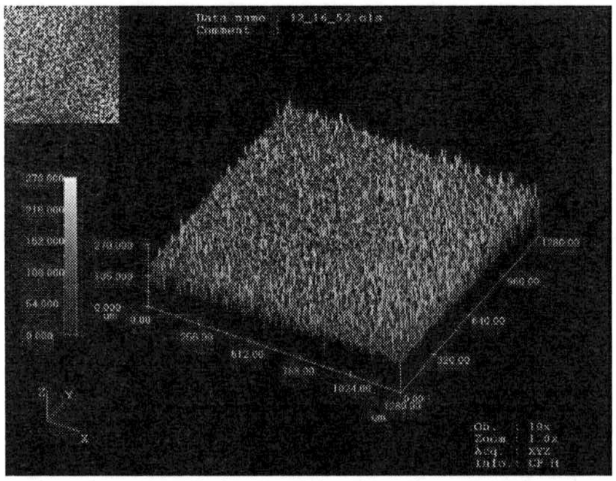

(c)

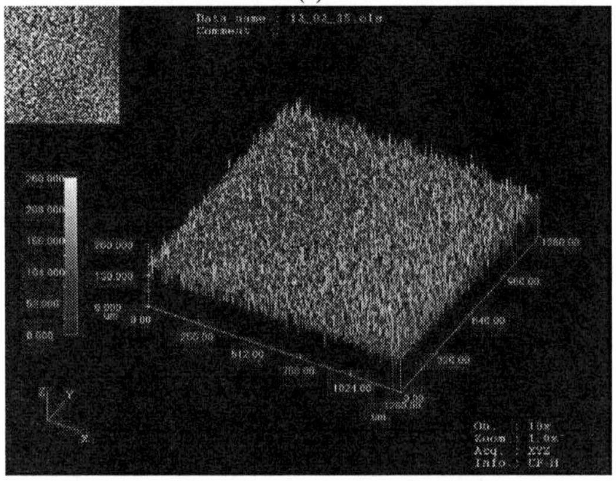

(d)

Fig. 4 The laser confocal pictures for the bright and matt electrodes. (a) The surface topography of the bright electrode. (b) The surface topography of the matt electrode. (c) The surface wireframe of the bright electrode. (d) The surface wireframe of the matt electrode.

TABLE I
EXPERIMENTAL CONDITIONS

Initial load force	0.05N
Increment step of load force	0.05N
Final load force	5N
Load voltage	6V
Load current	10mA
Environment	Temperature 19°C-22°C Humidity 57% RH

III. Results and Discussion

A. *Description of the typical R_c-F curve*

The variation in the average value and error band of the measured contact resistance of the $AgSnO_2(12)$ electrode material with bright feature as a function of load force for electrical current of 10mA is plotted in Fig.5. And the contact resistance curve is calculated statistically by 20 groups of electrode samples. The average value of contact resistance decreases nonlinearly from 2.61 mΩ to 0.19 mΩ with the load force increasing from 0.05 N to 5 N. The contact resistance could be divided into two different stages and fitted by the power law $R_c \sim F_c^{-m}$ in the logarithmic coordinates. The fitting results show that the index m is 0.45 when the load force is lower than 0.6 N. After that, the index m increases to 0.83, which means a faster variation rate for contact resistance. Thus, the load force of 0.6 N between two stages is further defined as the transition force F_t. Additionally, the error band of experimental results indicates that the contact resistance is scattered even for the same batch electrode contacts. The fluctuation value of contact resistance decreases from 0.283 mΩ to 0.018 mΩ with the load force increasing from 0.05 N to 5 N, which indicates that larger load force is beneficial for the stability of contact resistance. The bandwidth value of the contact resistance error band of 0.566 mΩ accounts for 22.98% of the average value of 2.46 mΩ for the load force of 0.05 N. And the percentage increases to 23.53% when the load force reaches up to 5 N.

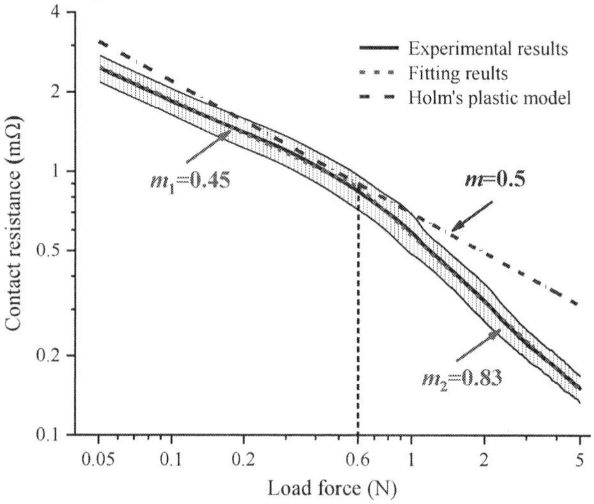

Fig. 5 The variation in contact resistance as a function of the load force for $AgSnO_2(12)$ contacts with bright surface.

Holm's solution for contact resistance of materials with smooth surfaces under the plastic deformation situation is also plotted in Fig.5 for comparison. It is noted that the theoretical value of contact resistance decreases with the exponential power of -0.5 invariably as the contact load force increasing from 0.05 N to 5 N. When the load force is lower than the transition force F_t = 0.6 N, the contact resistance calculation results of $AgSnO_2(12)$ electrode material are always higher than the experimental results, and the maximum deviation reaches up to 0.65 mΩ when the load force is 0.05 N. After that, the deviation between calculation and experimental results of contact resistance decreases to 0.047 mΩ with the load force of 0.45 N. The fitting index m of experimental results gradually approaches the theoretical value of 0.5. This could be attributed to the fact that the contact material deforms elastically under the lower load force. When the load force is larger than the transition force of F_t = 0.6 N, the calculation results of contact resistance are always higher than the experimental results. The deviation increases slightly and tends to be 0.16 mΩ when the load force reaches up to 5 N. The comparison results indicate that the decrement trend of experimental results with such two indexes is different from the contact resistance calculation results obtained by the traditional Holm theory.

B. Effects of contact a-spots on contact resistance

The variation in the average value and error band of the measured contact resistance for $AgSnO_2$(12) electrode with bright and matt features for comparison as a function of load force for electrical current of 10mA is plotted in Fig.6. Each curve of contact resistance is calculated statistically by 20 groups of electrode samples with bright surface or matt surface. As shown, the average value of contact resistance for the matt electrode material is always lower than that of the bright one. The contact resistance average value and standard deviation of samples with bright surface and matt surface are 0.192±0.098 mΩ and 0.162±0.008 mΩ for load force of 5 N, respectively. And the contact resistance of the matt electrode decreases 18.52% compared with that of the bright electrode, which indicates that the electrode surface with matt features could effectively produce the low and stable contact resistance under the condition of setting load force.

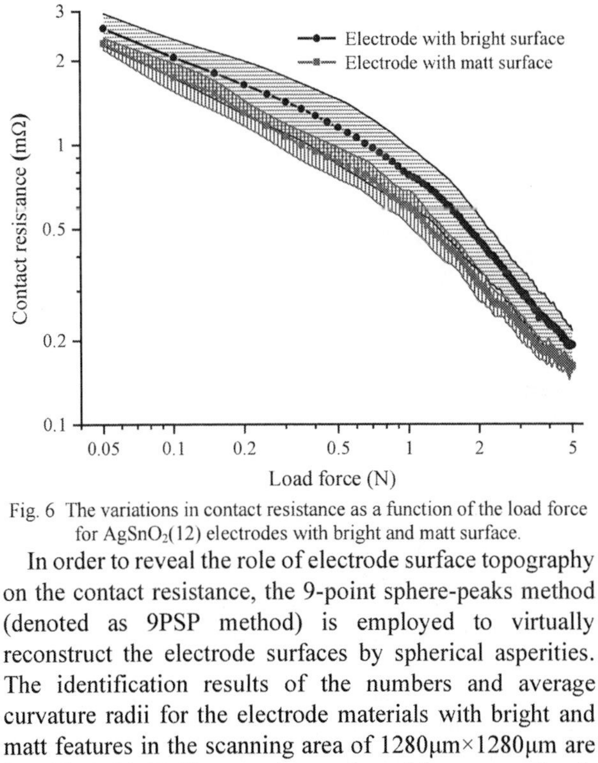

Fig. 6 The variations in contact resistance as a function of the load force for $AgSnO_2$(12) electrodes with bright and matt surface.

In order to reveal the role of electrode surface topography on the contact resistance, the 9-point sphere-peaks method (denoted as 9PSP method) is employed to virtually reconstruct the electrode surfaces by spherical asperities. The identification results of the numbers and average curvature radii for the electrode materials with bright and matt features in the scanning area of 1280μm×1280μm are listed in Table II. The asperity number of the matt surface is 5867, which is more 56.3% than the numbers of 3754 for the bright surface. And the average radii of the electrode with matt surface is also smaller. The relative positions and height distributions of the identified 3D asperity-peaks for the electrode with bright surface and matt surface are shown in Fig.7. It is noted that the asperities of the matt surface are denser than that of the bright surface. And it is inferred that there are more contact *a*-spots for the matt electrode in the actual contact process.

TABLE II
THE STATISTICAL PARAMETERS OF ASPERITIES FOR ELECTRODES WITH BRIGHT SURFACE AND MATT SURFACE

	The number of asperities ($1280\times1280\mu m^2$)	The average curvature radius of asperities (μm)
The bright surface	3754	7.07
The matt surface	5867	6.04

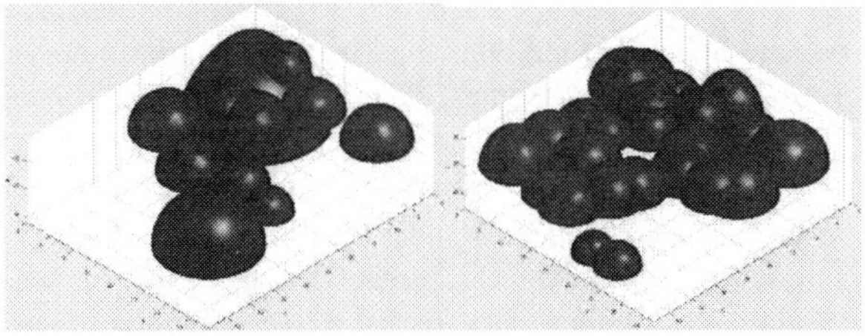

(a) (b)

Fig. 7 Three-dimensional distributions of the asperities identified by the 9PSP method. (a) The bright surface. (b) The matt surface.

For one single circular *a*-spot, the produced contact resistance could be calculated by the contact area S as

$$R_c = \frac{\rho\sqrt{\pi}}{2\sqrt{S}} \quad (1)$$

Then, it is assumed that the total area of N contact *a*-spots is S. Thus, the parallel contact resistance of N contact *a*-spots could be written as

$$R_c^{'} = \frac{\rho\sqrt{\pi}}{2\sum_{i=1}^{N}\sqrt{S_i}} \quad (2)$$

where ρ is the electrical resistivity of the electrode material. The normalized contact resistance R_c^* calculated by the contact area of S and S_i is as follows

$$R_c^* = \frac{R_c^{'}}{R_c} = \frac{\sqrt{S}}{\sum_{i=1}^{N}\sqrt{S_i}} \quad (3)$$

Thus, the normalized contact resistance could be further expressed by the load force F_i for each contact *a*-spot as

$$R_c^* = \frac{\sqrt{F}}{\sum_{i=1}^{N}\sqrt{F_i}} \quad (4)$$

As shown, the normalized contact resistance depends closely on the contact area or load force of each contact *a*-spot for the same total contact area or load force. For the case of N=2, there are two contact *a*-spots and the contact area are S_1 and S_2, respectively. It is assumed that the initial contact areas of two contact *a*-spots are S_1=0.01S and S_2=S-S_1=0.99S. Then, the contact area S_1 increases in steps of 0.01S until S_1 reaches up to 0.5S. Thus, the variations in the minimum, average and maximum normalized contact resistance R_c^* calculated by (3) as a function of the number of contact *a*-spots are plotted in Fig.8. And the variations in the normalized contact resistance R_c^* for the same area of each *a*-spot calculated by (4) as a function of the normalized load force F^* with varied number of contact *a*-spots are also plotted in Fig.9.

When the area of one contact *a*-spot approaches S for N contact *a*-spots, the contact resistance is mainly determined by this contact *a*-spot and reaches the maximum value. Meanwhile, it is found that the average and minimum value of the normalized contact resistance decreases nonlinearly with the number of contact *a*-spots increasing. When the number of contact *a*-spots is smaller than 5, the average value of the normalized contact resistance decreases sharply (shown in Fig.8). And the contact resistance always has an obvious decrement with the number of contact *a*-spots increasing one by one (shown in Fig.9). After that, the variation rate of the normalized contact resistance becomes slower for the same load force. In addition, the total contact resistance reaches the minimum value and always decreases rapidly with an exponential power of -0.5 as the number of contact *a*-spots increasing when the area of each *a*-spot is equal. This means that the contact resistance is determined by the number of contact *a*-spots for the fixed contact area when the number of contact *a*-spots is relative smaller. And the contact resistance could further decrease to the minimum value when the contact reigon is distributed averagely to each contact *a*-spot.

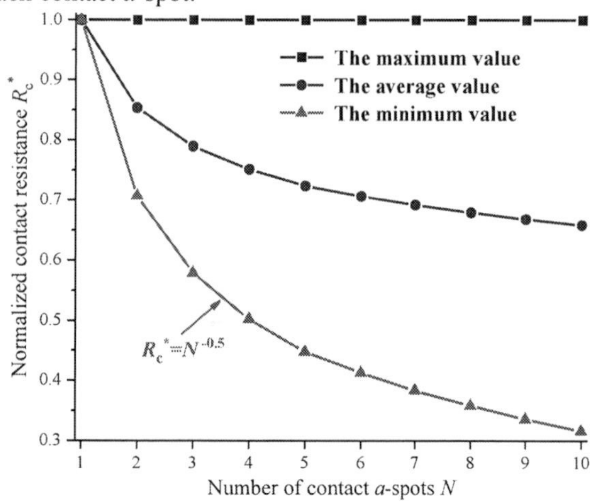

Fig. 8 The variations in the minimum, average and maximum normalized contact resistance as a function of the number of contact *a*-spots

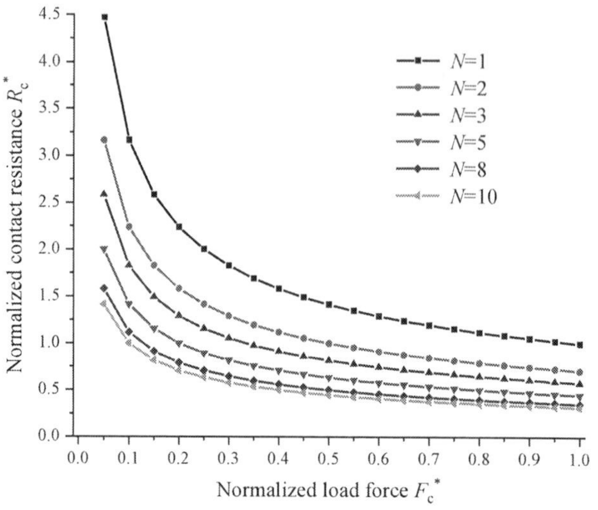

Fig. 9 The variations in the normalized contact resistance as a function of the normalized load force with varied number of contact *a*-spots

In combination with the contact resistance calculation results (shown in Fig.8), the average value of contact resistance is determined by the number of contact *a*-spots. According to the comparative analysis of the surface topography for the electrode materials, the matt surface has more asperities under the given contact region. And the contact interface of the mated electrode materials with matt feature could produce more contact *a*-spots under the applied load force. Thus, the average value of contact resistance for the electrode material with matt surface is always lower than that for the bright surface when the contact load force increases from 0.05 N to 5 N.

When the load force is larger than 2.1 N, the maximum value of the contact resistance for bathes of the electrode contacts with matt surface is lower than the minimum value of contact resistance for the bright surface. It is inferred that the number of the existed contact *a*-spot is sufficient enough that the newly produced contact *a*-spots have little influence on the contact resistance fluctuation. Thus, the fluctuation ranges of the contact resistance for two kinds of electrode surface both becomes narrower, and the increased number of *a*-spots mainly causes the decrement of the contact resistance. And the electrode material with matt surface, which has a statistical feature with more *a*-spots and relatively uniformly smaller contact radii, could produce a lower and more stable contact resistance compared with the bright surface with increment of the contact load force.

The above analysis indicates that the number of the contact *a*-spots is the critical factor for the contact resistance average value for batches of the electrode contacts, and more contact *a*-spots could produce a lower contact resistance. In addition, the uniform size of the contact *a*-spots could restrain the fluctuation and improving the stability of the contact resistance.

IV. CONCLUSION

This paper manly investigates influences of surface topography for $AgSnO_2$ contacts on the relationship between contact resistance and load force by the experimental method. Experimental results indicate that the contact resistance of $AgSnO_2$ contacts with matt surface is always lower than the bright surface, and the error band of the contact resistance is narrower. The detailed analysis reveals that the number of the contact *a*-spots is the critical factor for the contact resistance average value for batches of the electrode contacts, and more contact *a*-spots could produce a lower contact resistance for the given load force. In addition, the uniform size of the contact *a*-spots and the lager load force is beneficial for restraining the fluctuation and improving the stability of the contact resistance.

ACKNOWLEDGMENT

The authors express their gratitude for the kind support provided by The National Natural Science Foundation of China (Contract Number 51377029 and 51777039).

REFERENCES

[1] Z. K. Chen and G. J. Witter, "Electrical contacts for automotive applications: A review," IEICE Trans. Electron., vol. E87C, 2004, (8): 1248-1254

[2] A. Basu, G. G. Adams and N. E. McGruer, "A review of micro-contact physics, materials, and failure mechanisms in direct-contact RF MEMS switches," J. Micromech. Microeng, 2016, 26(10)

[3] P. G. Slade, Electrical Contacts: Principles and Applications, USA , 2014: 4-11.

[4] R. Holm. Electric Contacts: Theory and Application, USA: Springer-Verlag, 1967: 14-16.

[5] Greenwood, J.A., Williamson, J.B.P.: Contact of nominally flat surfaces. Proc. R. Soc. London A 295, 1966: 300–319.

[6] Liu H, McBride J W. A Finite-Element-Based Contact Resistance Model for Rough Surfaces: Applied to a Bilayered Au/MWCNT Composite[J]. IEEE Transactions on Components, Packaging, and Manufacturing Technology, 2018, 8(6): 919-926.

[7] X. Hernot, A. Senouci, A. E. Manfalouti, N. B. Jemaa and R. E.Abdi. "Contact Resistance Law for Elasto-Plastic Domains in the Force Range (1mN-10N)," IEICE Transactions on Electronics, 2003, E86-C(6): 874-879.

[8] H. Kwon, S. S. Jang, Y. H. Park, T. S. Kim, Y. D. Kim, H. J. Nam and Y. C. Joo. "Investigation of the Electrical Contact Behaviors in Au-to-Au Thin-film Contacts for RF MEMS Switches," Journal of Micromech. Microeng, 2008, 18(10): 105010.

[9] Z. A. Tong, J. W. Wen, K. Li. Vacuum arc characteristics of a new type of curved-surface contact for high-frequency forced interruption in aero applications[J]. Vacuum, 2021(196): 110754.

[10] F. Pennec, D. Peyrou, D. Leray, et al. Impact of the Surface Roughness Description on the Electrical Contact Resistance of Ohmic Switches Under Low Actuation Forces [J]. IEEE Transactions on Components Packaging and Manufacturing Technology, 2012, 2(1): 85-94.

[11] S. Fernandez, R. Pena, M. T. Rodrigo, at al. Optimization of surface morphology and electrical properties of Ti/Al/Ti-W/Au ohmic contacts to n-GaN by two-step annealing method [J]. Semiconductor Science and Technology, 2008, 23(4): 045021.

8th International Conference on Reliability of Electrical Products and Electrical Contacts, November 18-20, 2022

Impact of Vias in Interconnect Channels on High-speed Signal Transmission

Chaoyi Wang[1], Jinchun Gao[1], Kaixuan Song[1], Yuqi Zhou[1], Zhijiao Chen[1], Xiaolong Xu[2], Jun Xie[2]

[1]School of Electronic Engineering, Beijing University of Posts and Telecommunications, Beijing, 100876, China

[2] The 54th Research Institute of China Electronics Technology Group Corporation, Shijiazhuang, Hebei, 050081, China

E-mail: gjc@bupt.edu.cn

Abstract—**With the continuous advancement of high density, high speed and miniaturization trend of integrated circuits, the multilayer high-speed printed circuit board (PCB) and high density interconnect (HDI) technology are increasingly widely applied. As a key structure of multilayer circuit boards, vias are one of the main research objects in high-speed electronic interconnects. In this paper, based on the actual structure and material, a 3D electromagnetic field model of the interconnect transmission channel was developed, which consists of connectors, microstrip lines, anti-pads and vias. The transmission performance of the interconnect channel is improved through the optimizations and analyses in vias and anti-pads, which is verified using the experimental tests. In order to analyze the high-speed signal transmission capability of the interconnect channel, an equivalent circuit model of the high-speed interconnect system was proposed, where 31-order pseudo random binary sequence (PRBS) data was used as the signal source at the rate of 18 Gbps. It can be found that an excellent eye opening could be obtained in this system, and the bit error rate (BER) is lower than 10^{-12}, which indicate that high-speed data could be transmitted without significant distortion in the optimized interconnect channel.**

Index Terms—**High-speed signal, vias, anti-pad, eye diagram, high-speed interconnect.**

I. Introduction

Fifth-generation (5G) communication technology has been widely used in the daily life of human society in recent years, while the continuous advancements of miniaturization, high frequency, high speed and high reliability in electronic products have been developed. With regard to that high frequency and high-speed signals have been commonly applied in communication systems, signal transmission would be affected by small structures of radio frequency (RF) circuits. Mandic *et al.* [1] developed the comparatively accurate equivalent circuit models of three SubMiniature version A (SMA) connectors based on measurements, including the through-hole (TH) SMA connector. Song *et al.* [2]-[3] presented three compensation schemes for the size of solder joint, the structure of dielectric between solder joint and non-solder joint, and the structure of anti-pads in ground (GND) plane. For the third scheme, a cascade circuit model with the π type and T type circuits was proposed to quantitatively analyze the electromagnetic characteristic of the soldering transition area with anti-pads. Ben *et al.* [4] improved the signal integrity of the transition from SMA connectors to the PCB through anti-pad, back-drilling, GND vias, and diving board.

With the urgent requirement of ultrarapid data transmission rate in 5G era, and the rapid development of integrated circuits, at present, the multilayer high-speed PCB and HDI technology are extensively investigated. As one of the key structures in multilayer PCB, interconnect vias are the bridges to connect those circuits in different layers, which are worth further study. Kung *et al.* [5] proposed a build-up (BU) spiral including an appropriate number of GND vias with optimized positions, for further enhancing the impedance matching of the signal via in the six-layer package routings. Ravelo *et al.* [6] analyzed theoretically and designed a low-pass (LP) negative group delay (NGD) circuit, in accordance with the via GND structure. Li *et al.* [7] simulated and analyzed the impact of GND vias around the signal via on high-speed signal transmission, the diameter, number and position of ground vias included. Jaze *et al.* [8] studied the common mode noise caused by nearby ground vias when differential signals were transmitted between different PCB layers on signal vias. Ahmad *et al.* [9] investigated the effect of reducing the number of GND vias on high-speed data transmission, focusing on DDR3 and GDDR3/5 memory technology.

There may be many impedance discontinuities in the use of multilayer PCB nowadays. In this current work, problems of impedance mismatch caused by the signal via and the transition between connectors and PCB are simultaneously studied. The impedance of soldering transition between RF connectors and microstrip components is compensated by optimizing the structure of anti-pads in GND planes. According to the designs for the structure of interconnect via and GND vias in the presented PCB, the performance of the transmission channel is enhanced. In addition, the impact of the proposed channel with vias on high-speed signal transmission is investigated, and it can be indicated that this channel could transmit high-speed data well through the experimental measurements and simulations.

II. Modeling Simulation and Analysis

A. 3D Electromagnetic Field Model

With regard to the reality and simulation accuracy, based on actual sizes in this paper, channel models are developed with the ratio of one to one, including high-frequency test fixtures of SMA RF connectors. The 3D electromagnetic field model consists of SMA connectors, microstrip lines, vias, pads and anti-pads, as illustrated in Fig. 1. Inner conductors of those two SMA connectors are soldered to microstrip lines, and for a unified reference ground, through eight GND vias, the outer conductor of each SMA connector is connected with GND 1 and GND 2, which are two-layer ground planes in the middle of PCB.

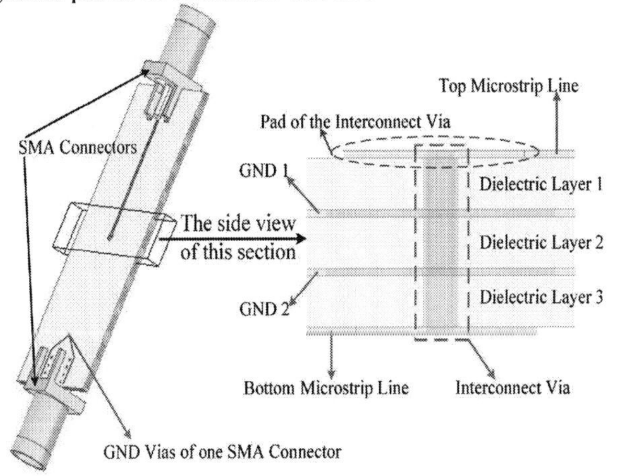

Fig. 1. 3D electromagnetic field structure in the initial model of the interconnect channel

A single interconnect via may result in serious impedance mismatch using high-speed multilayer PCB. As the side view shown in Fig. 1, the structure of PCB in presented transmission channels is four-layer, in which the microstrip signal lines are distributed on the top and bottom layers, and signals could be transmitted among different layers by the interconnect via. The empirical formula for calculating parallel parasitic capacitance of vias is shown below:

$$C = \frac{1.41\varepsilon_r T D_1}{D_2 - D_1} \tag{1}$$

where D_1 is the diameter of the via pad, D_2 is the diameter of the via anti-pad, T is the thickness of PCB, and ε_r is the relative permittivity of the circuit board. The series parasitic inductance of vias could be estimated as follows:

$$L = 5.08h\left[\ln\left(\frac{4h}{d}\right)+1\right] \tag{2}$$

where h and d respectively denote the length and diameter of the via. With constant other conditions, the characteristic impedance of vias could be increased by reducing diameters of via pads, increasing the size of via anti-pads, and reducing the via aperture, considering equation (1) and (2). Accordingly, the impedance of the interconnect via in the initial model is finally designed approaching 50 Ω through optimizations of those three diameters above. The medium in dielectric layer 1, 2 and 3 is all Rogers 4350B which has a relative permittivity of 3.48. Microstrip lines and ground plane GND 1 and GND 2 are made of copper with a thickness of 0.035 mm, and the width of microstrip lines is 0.54 mm.

PCB usually should be connected to other devices by means of connectors in practical application, where impedance discontinuities could be found in the soldering transition between SMA connectors and PCB. It is demonstrated that the impedance of the soldering transition between RF connectors and microstrip line components is capacitive. As a result, anti-pads could be added in ground planes to reduce the face area of the signal line and GND at the solder joint, for impedance compensation [2]-[3]. Accordingly, on the basis of the initial model shown in Fig. 1, four rectangular anti-pads in the middle two layers of PCB are constructed on both ends of ground plane GND 1 and GND 2 as illustrated in Fig. 2, and the model 2 is then obtained. Only the structure of the two-layer GND planes in model 2 is further designed in comparison to the initial model. Optimizing the length and width of anti-pads, the problem of impedance mismatch caused by solder joints of SMA connectors is further improved.

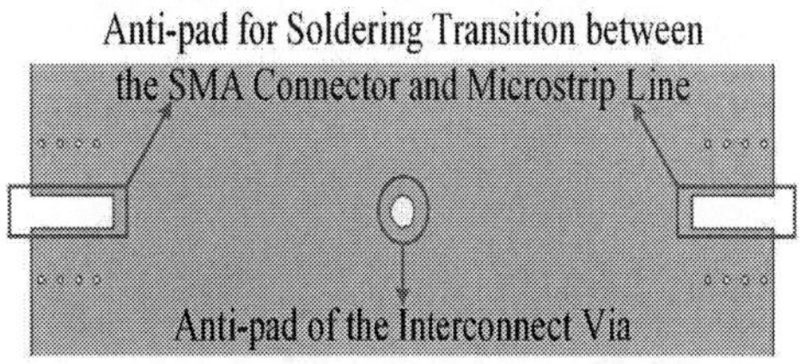

Fig. 2. Schematic top view of ground plane GND 1 and GND 2 in model 2

Due to the more complex structure of multilayer PCB with an interconnect via, the overall transmission performance of the channel should be further enhanced. The structure of model 2 is hence treated as a primitive channel form, and six GND vias are firstly added around the interconnect via according to the experience of industries, while the position and structure of these GND vias are optimized, for obtaining model 3 shown in Fig. 3 (a). Based on those above, a set of metal GND vias array is then designed on both sides of microstrip lines in this current study, and model 4 is attained, which is illustrated as Fig. 3 (b).

Initial model, model 2, model 3 and model 4 are

respectively identified by S1, S2, S3 and S4, for a better understanding of the modeling simulation. The simulated frequency range is from 0 to 18 GHz, this is because that the maximum frequency using SMA connectors is typically 18 GHz in reality. Inspection of the entire frequency band in Fig. 4 shows that model 4 achieves the best return loss, which is less than -14.77 dB. As shown in Fig. 5, the maximum values of the S_{21} parameter for these models from initial model to model 4 are respectively -11.71 dB, -7.66 dB, -2.87 dB, and -1.05 dB. In addition, all curves of the S_{21} parameter have varying fluctuations to a certain extent, except model 4 which curve is comparatively steady.

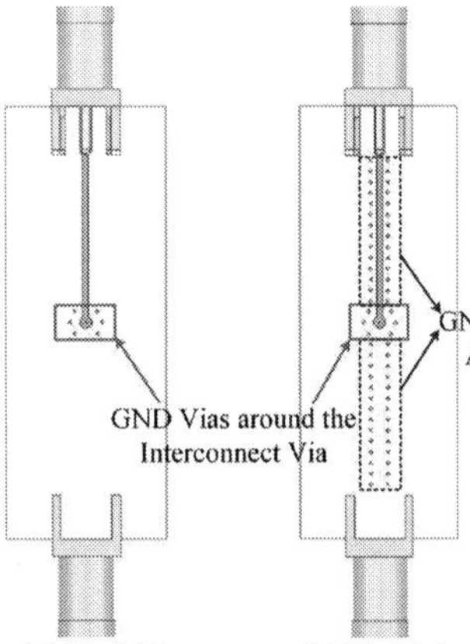

Fig. 3. Structure diagram of channel models in top view

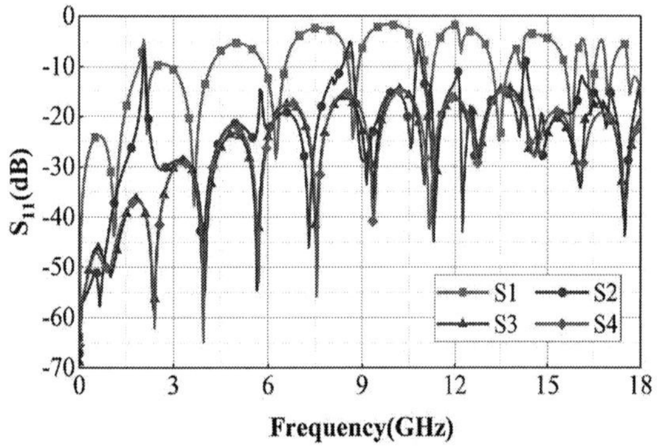

Fig. 4. S_{11} parameters of each channel model in simulation

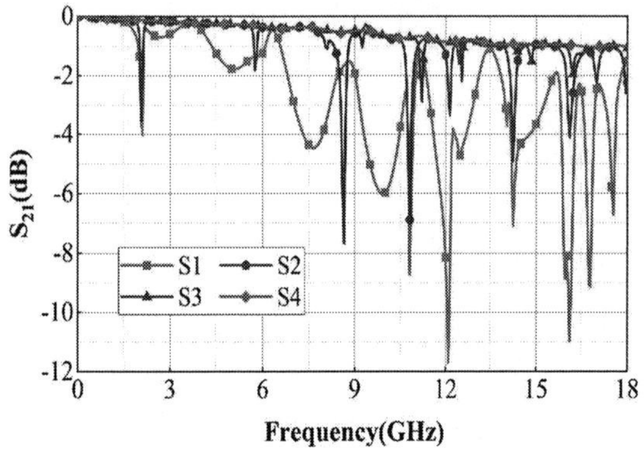

Fig. 5. S_{21} parameters of each channel model in simulation

The results in Fig. 6 provide insight into the effect of channel modeling 4 on group delay. It can be seen that only channel 4 approximately obtains both smooth and flat group delay with a 17 ps fluctuation in all, while curves of group delay in other models have sharp jitters. However, differences of curves between model 3 and 4 could be neglected, for the case of group delay in the low frequency band. As a result, the high frequency transmission performance of these four models is gradually enhanced in accordance with the model sequence. It could also be inferred that model 4 attains almost linear phase response so that data can be transmitted without significant phase distortion, which is crucial to interconnect channels transmitting high-speed signals, for inspection of Fig. 6. The transmission performance of model 4 is accordingly improved comprehensively.

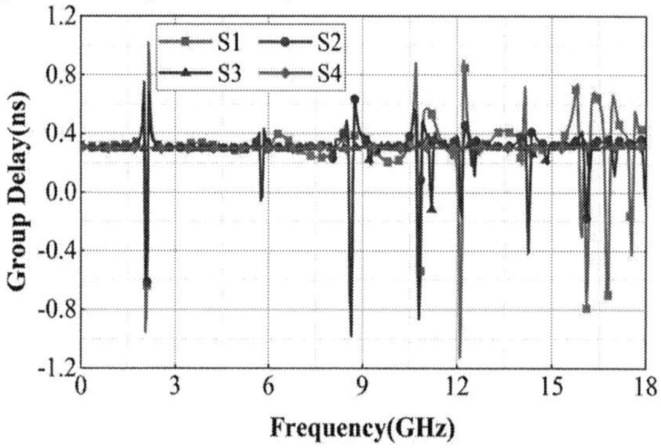

Fig. 6. Group delay of each channel model in simulation

B. *High-speed Signal*

A rather flat group delay is usually required of channels for transmitting high-speed data. This is because high-speed signals are broadband with abundant spectral components. It is widely acknowledged that the signal main lobe could be only considered in high-speed interconnects. For instance, with regard to an ideal single-polarity PRBS signal $f(t)$ with 1-volt amplitude, when the first bit of the signal sequence is set as "1" and Gibbs phenomenon is neglected, $f(t)$ could be described as follows based on Fourier Transform [10]:

$$f(t) \approx A_0 + \sum_{n=1}^{2^m-1} A_n \cos\left(n\Omega t + \varphi_n\right) \ , \ n \in N^* \tag{3}$$

where m is the order of PRBS signal, A_0 indicates the DC component, and Ω is the angular frequency of the fundamental wave. The $n\Omega$ refers to other harmonics, A_n and φ_n respectively denotes the amplitude and phase of the corresponding frequency component. These above parameters can be calculated by:

$$
\begin{cases}
A_0 = \dfrac{2^{m-1}}{2^m - 1} \\[2ex]
A_n = \left| \dfrac{2\sin(\frac{n\pi}{2^m - 1})}{n\pi} \displaystyle\sum_k e^{-j\frac{2n\pi(k+\frac{1}{2})}{2^m - 1}} \right| \\[2ex]
\Omega = \dfrac{2\pi}{\left(2^m - 1\right)T_b} \\[2ex]
\angle\varphi_n = \dfrac{\displaystyle\sum_k e^{-j\frac{2n\pi(k+\frac{1}{2})}{2^m-1}}}{\left|\displaystyle\sum_k e^{-j\frac{2n\pi(k+\frac{1}{2})}{2^m-1}}\right|}
\end{cases}
, \quad k \in \left[1-2^{m-1}\ ,\ 2^{m-1}-2\right] \,\&\, k \in Z, \quad n \in N^* \tag{4}
$$

where T_b is the symbol length (s), and there are 2^{m-1} values of k which are exactly determined by the bit sequence of the PRBS signal. For a 4-order PRBS signal with the periodic sequence of "101011001000111" at the bit rate of 1.5 Gbps, it is obtained that k can take eight values of -7, -3, -2, -1, 0, 2, 4 and 5 according to equation (3) and (4). And A_n is calculated as 8/15, 0.2647, 0.2589, 0.2495, 0.2366, 0.2205, 0.2018, 0.1809, 0.1583, 0.1345, 0.1103, 0.0861, 0.0624, 0.0398, 0.0189 and 0 when n ranges from 0 to 15. A_0 denotes DC and A_{15} is 0, as a result, the corresponding φ_n could be neglected, and the remaining values of φ_n are -20.5°, 63.5°, 72°, -128.5°, 60°, -36°, -27.5°, -152.5°, -144°, 120°, -51.5°, 108°, 116.5° and -159.5° in sequence. It could be found that the time domain signal waveform based on equation (3) is in positive agreement with that of actual PRBS, according to the comparison in Fig. 7. With regard to fluctuations of the curve derived from equation (3), this is mainly caused by the lower order of PRBS4 in this example, which is not sufficient for expressing actual signals. Equation (3) will be closer to the signal in real life with a higher accuracy for a higher value of m. All in all, the flat group delay is paramount important for high-speed signal transmission as above.

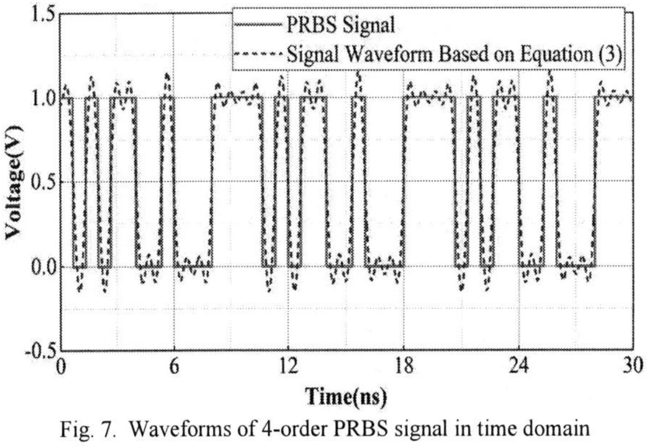

Fig. 7. Waveforms of 4-order PRBS signal in time domain

Equivalent circuit models of interconnect systems were developed to transmit 18 Gbps baseband signals, where a 31-order single-polarity PRBS signal was generated by the signal source with the amplitude of 1 V, for the presented four channel models in this paper.

With regard to the outputs of different channel models, inspection of Fig. 8 shows that every simulated eye diagram distinctly provides a varying eye opening. Comparison of (a), (b), (c) and (d) in Fig. 8 provides insight into that the eye diagram performance of model 4 is significantly excellent, while the initial model is the worst. As illustrated in Fig. 9, high-speed signals could be transmitted through these four models with the error-free operation (BER<10^{-12}) in different ranges. It could be found that the BER is less than 10^{-12} within almost an entire unit interval (UI), observing the timing bathtub of model 4 in Fig. 9 (a). As voltage bathtub curves shown in Fig. 9 (b), it could be indicated that high-speed data is transmitted in model 4 with negligible deterioration, where the eye height of the output is close to 1 V which is almost equal to the amplitude of the system input signal. The above analysis demonstrates that the designed channel model 4 exhibits an outstanding capability on high-speed transmission, where an excellent eye opening and the error-free operation are all obtained with 2^{31}-1 pattern of PRBS signal.

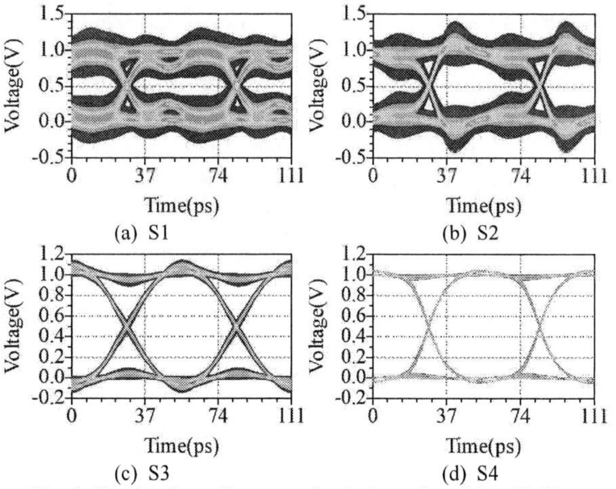

Fig. 8. Simulated eye diagrams of each channel model at 18 Gbps

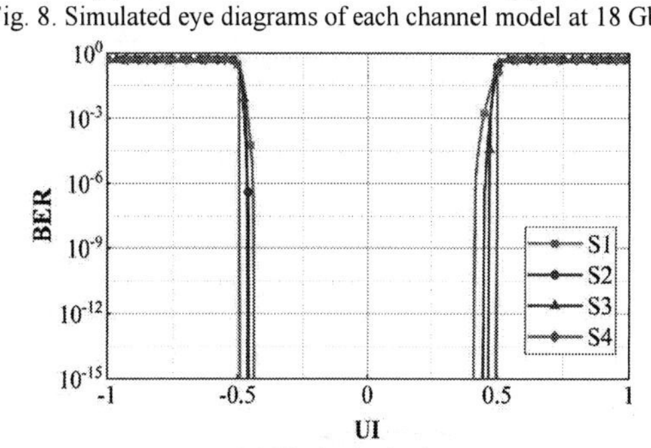

(a) Timing bathtub

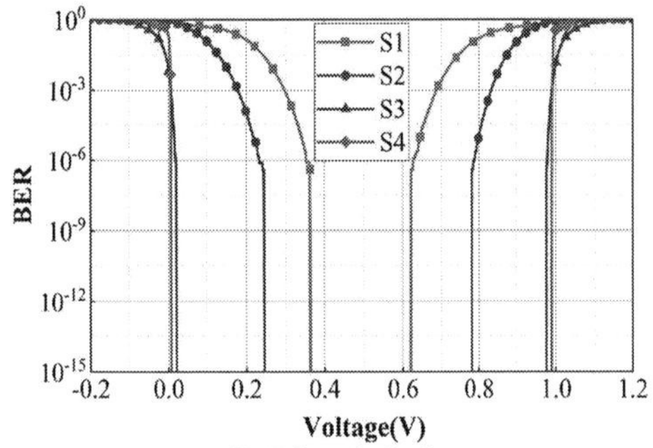

(b) Voltage bathtub

Fig. 9. Simulated BER bathtub curves

III. Experimental Measurement and Discussion

In order to verify the impact of vias in interconnect channels on high-speed signal transmission, samples of those four models are fabricated. The channel samples were tested using a vector network analyzer (VNA), which was calibrated by SOLT in the frequency range from 10 MHz to 18 GHz. Symbol M1, M2, M3 and M4 are used to respectively indicate initial channel, channel 2, channel 3 and channel 4, providing a better evaluating and comparison between simulations and experiments. As shown in Fig. 10, model 4 achieves the best return loss, which is less than -10 dB except for a small band close to the maximum frequency of SMA connectors. Inspection of the entire frequency band in Fig. 11 shows that only the maximum values of the S_{21} parameter in channel 4 is approximately higher than -3 dB.

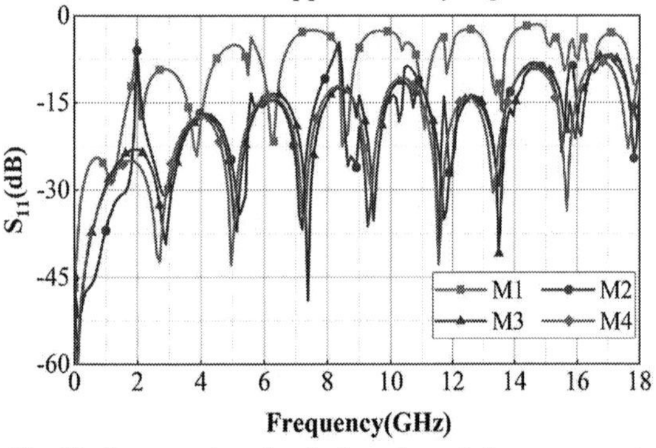

Fig. 10. S_{11} parameters of each channel sample in measurements

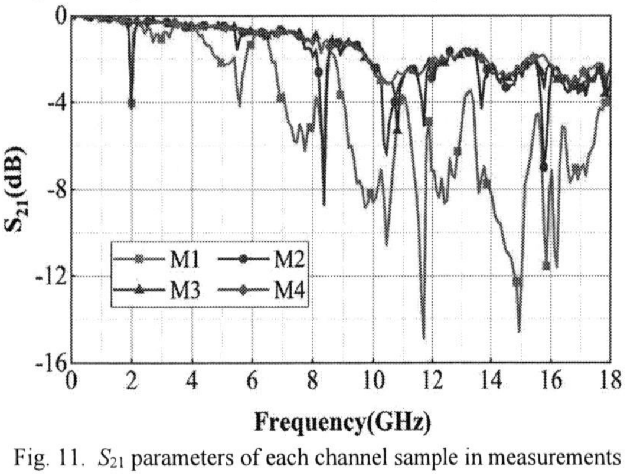

Fig. 11. S_{21} parameters of each channel sample in measurements

Although experimental measurements are all inferior to simulations, S parameters performed in VNA shows similar trends as simulations, for comparing Fig. 10 and Fig. 4, Fig. 11 and Fig. 5 respectively. These differences are attributable to minor variations between the model and the actual physical samples. And inevitable errors exist in experimental tests, fabrications of channel samples, manual assembling of PCB and SMA connectors. In addition, both the conductor and dielectric layers in the model are treated as lossless, which mainly result in an increase for the measurement values of S parameters compared with simulations, especially near the maximum frequency limited by the SMA connector.

For a better evaluating of these samples on high-speed data transmission, a 31-order PRBS signal at 18 Gbps is simulated and analyzed transmitting through the presented four channels, based on measured S parameters. The amplitude of the input signal is 1 V, eye diagrams of each channel are shown in Fig. 12, and the corresponding BER bathtub curves are illustrated in Fig. 13. Inspection of Fig. 12 and Fig. 13 shows that the eye diagram of the initial channel is almost closed with the worst high-speed transmission capability, while channel 4 has the best performance, which are completely in accordance with the simulations. However, it can be found that the high-speed transmission performance of channel 3 is only slightly lower than that of channel 4. This is mainly because that the S_{21} measurements for channel 3 and channel 4 are in good agreement at the low frequency band approximatively from 0 to 11 GHz. It is indicated that the amplitude of the PRBS signal is mainly related to low frequency components from equation (3) and (4). In addition, measurements are lower than simulations. Those above all determine that the varying in eye diagram parameters between sample 3 and 4 could be neglected.

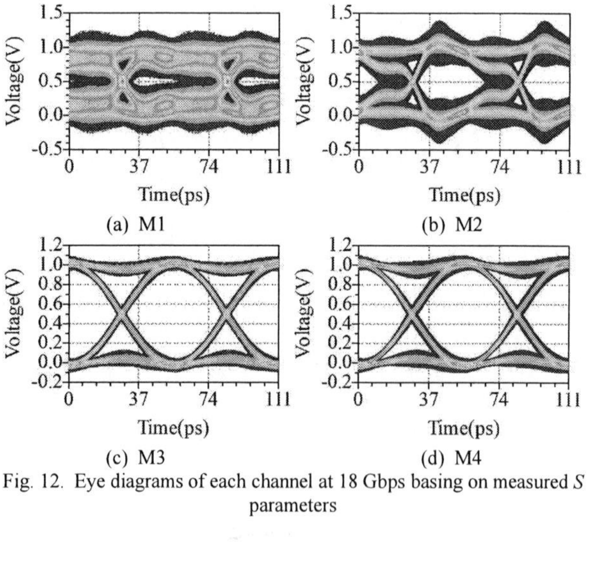

(a) M1 (b) M2

(c) M3 (d) M4

Fig. 12. Eye diagrams of each channel at 18 Gbps basing on measured S parameters

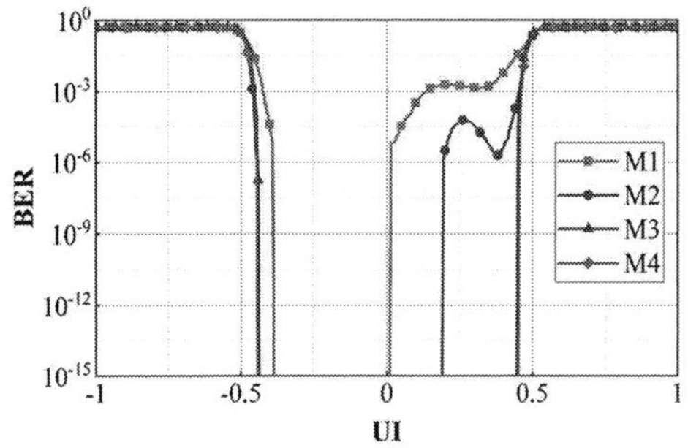

(a) Timing bathtub

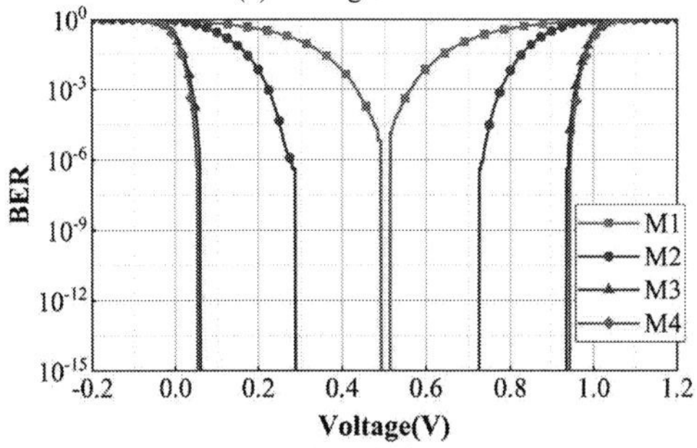

(b) Voltage bathtub

Fig. 13. BER bathtub curves basing on measured *S* parameters

In order to distinctly demonstrate that the proposed design in this paper could improve the performance of the interconnect channel with a signal via on high-speed signal transmission, Table I provides the specific parameters of those eye diagrams based on simulated or measured data, according to Fig. 8, Fig. 9, Fig. 12 and Fig. 13. As shown in Table I, the transmission performance of the designed channel 4 is significantly enhanced, compared with that of the initial channel. Simulations and experiments indicate that optimizing the structure of GND planes and vias can effectively compensate the impedance mismatch in multilayer PCB. The high-speed and high-frequency performance of the interconnect via could then be improved.

TABLE I PARAMETERS OF EACH EYE DIAGRAM

	S1	M1	S2	M2	S3	M3	S4	M4
Eye Height (mV)	209	21	535	437	951	890	983	906
Eye Width (ps)	46	22	50	35	51	50	55	51

IV. CONCLUSION

The impact of vias in interconnect channels on high-speed signal transmission is investigated in this current work. The electromagnetic model and the equivalent circuit were developed to analyze the effect of vias in interconnect channels from the perspective of frequency domain and time domain. A series of experiments was also conducted to validate the models and test the model results.

In the analysis of the high-speed signal transmission channels with an interconnection via, anti-pads and vias were designed and optimized. With regard to those four proposed channel models from initial channel to channel 4, it is important to note that the overall transmission performances of these channels are progressively improved through methods of optimizing sizes for the signal via with pads and anti-pads, designing structures of rectangular anti-pads in GND 1 and GND 2, adding GND vias in the vicinity of the interconnect via and constructing the GND vias array beside microstrip lines, respectively.

The trends of measurement curves are in favorable agreement with those of simulations, and it could be found that the designed channel 4 has achieved the best performance on high frequency transmission compared with other channels. For transmitting PRBS signal with 2^{31}-1 pattern at 18 Gbps, excellent eye opening and error-free operation are obtained according to the output of channel 4, which indicate that high-speed data could be transmitted well in the optimized channel of this study.

ACKNOWLEDGMENT

This work was supported by the National Natural Science Foundation of China (No. 51877010).

REFERENCES

[1] T. Mandic, M. Magerl and A. Baric, "Sequential Buildup of Broadband Equivalent Circuit Model for Low-Cost SMA Connectors," in IEEE Transactions on Electromagnetic Compatibility, 2019, 61(1): 242-250

[2] K. Song, J. Gao, Z. Wang, B. Ali, H. M. Bilal, and G. Xie, "A Method of Improving Signal Integrity of Solder Joints," The 7th International Conference on Reliability of Electrical Products and Electrical Contacts, 2019, 244-247.

[3] K. Song, J. Gao, Z. Wang, G. Xie, X. Li, and G. Shi, "Study of the Impedance Compensation of the Welding Transition Section of the RF Connector and Micro Strip Line," Acta Electronica Sinica. 2019, 47(11): 2241-2247

[4] R. Ben, S. Hu, X. Li and Z. Fu, "Signal intergrity analysis for SMA via on the PCB," IEEE 9th International Conference on Communication Software and Networks, 2017, 865-869

[5] M. -L. Kung, L. -Y. Lin, K. -H. Lin, H. -H. Cheng, Y. -H. Tien and Y. -C. Ding, "Build-Up Spiral and GND Vias for Improving Signal Integrity of Signal Core Vias," in IEEE Transactions on Components, Packaging and Manufacturing Technology, 2021, 11(11):2031-2034

[6] B. Ravelo, F. Wan, S. Lalléchère, W. Rahajandraibe, P. Thakur and A. Thakur, "Innovative Theory of Low-Pass NGD via-Hole-Ground Circuit," IEEE Access, 2020, 8:130172-130182,.

[7] C. Li and X. Kuang, "Effects of ground vias on high-speed signal transmission in high-speed PCB design," 11th International Conference on Electronic Packaging Technology & High Density Packaging, 2010: 88-91

[8] A. Jaze, B. Arhambaul and S. Conno, "Mode conversion due to asymmetric GND via configuration," 2012 IEEE International Symposium on Electromagnetic Compatibility, 2012, 363-368.
[9] H. Ahmad and A. Badesha, "Impact of GND-PTH stitches in DDR3/GDDR3/GDDR5 Memory controller packages," 2011 8th Workshop on Electromagnetic Compatibility of Integrated Circuits, 2011： 99-104.
[10] D. Wu, Analysis of Signals and Linear Systems (4th Edition). Higher Education Press, Beijing. 2005

Integrated Intelligent Closed-loop Control and Simulation of Electromagnetic Contactor

Xingxin Zheng[1], Longfei Tang[1,2,3]*

[1]College of Electrical Engineering and Automation, Fuzhou University, Fuzhou, 350108, China
[2]Fujian Key Laboratory of New Energy Generation and Power Conversion, Fuzhou, 350108, China
[3]Fujian Province University Engineering Research Center of Smart Distribution Grid Equipment, Fuzhou, 350108, China
Email:tlftel@fzu.edu.cn TEL:13950364569

Abstract—**In this paper, the switching power supply chip is cleverly applied to the integrated control of electromagnetic contactors, so that the intelligent control module has the advantages of high integration, reliable circuit, small size, and low cost. The integrated drive circuit switch works in a dynamic self-powered mode, which overcomes the defect that the traditional contactor drive scheme requires an auxiliary power supply and reduces the hardware volume and cost. The current sensing is integrated inside the chip, no external current detection circuit is needed, which further simplifies the hardware control scheme. Using Multisim and LabVIEW software co-simulation, the integrated control circuit transient simulation model and the magnetic circuit dynamic model of the electromagnetic contactor are established respectively. With the current closed-loop control strategy in LabVIEW, an intelligent co-simulation system integrating the contactor body, hardware control circuit and software control strategy is formed. The feasibility of the integrated control scheme is verified by experiments. The control scheme uses few active devices, high integration, greatly reduces hardware power consumption and volume, and improves the operational reliability and life of the electromagnetic contactor.**

Index Terms— **electromagnetic contactor, integrated control, dynamic self-powered, co-simulation.**

I. INTRODUCTION

Electromagnetic contactor is a widely used low-voltage control electrical appliance. With the improvement of the modernization level of industrial production, the requirements for its life and reliability are getting higher and higher [1]. Due to the large number of electronic components in the control module, the reliability and life are affected, and the use is also limited to a certain extent [2-3]. In recent years, scholars at home and abroad have done a lot of research work in the field of contactor intelligent control. Xu, Zhang. [4] and Xu, Zhang. [5] proposed a contactor DC excitation control scheme, which changed the excitation mode of the contactor from AC to DC. Tang and Xu. [6] designed the PWM current closed-loop control technology of contactor, which enabled the contactor to flexibly adjust the excitation current in a wide voltage range. Xu and Zhang. [7] used an intelligent control system to dynamically control the whole process of contactor pulling, holding and breaking. Reference [8-9] studied the dynamic clamping process of contactor in detail and realized the closed-loop control of contactor displacement by estimating the real-time displacement of the moving core, to reduce the contact spring in the clamping process. Tang and Xu. [10] proposed a slope closed-loop control scheme for AC contactors, using the slope outer loop to control the current inner loop to reduce the contact bounce during the starting process. Tang, Han, and Xu. [11] used the neural network model to estimate the contact just-closing speed, and a fuzzy logic controller with the feedback of the contact just-closing speed was designed. By controlling the excitation time of the contactor current loop, the contact just-closing speed approached the given small reference value successively, which in turn suppresses contact bounce. Tang and Xu. [12] applies the integrated control chip in the field of power supply transformation to the intelligent control of electromagnetic switches and shows that the integrated control of electromagnetic switches can be realized by using the existing integrated control chip after reasonable design of peripheral circuit, but it is limited to the control capacity of the integrated chip. It can only be used for the integrated closed-loop control of small capacity electromagnetic switches such as AC solenoid valves with small excitation energy.

In this paper, the integrated switching power supply chip is introduced into the intelligent control of the electromagnetic contactor, and the driving switch adopts the

This work was supported by the Natural Science Foundation of Fujian Province under Grant 2021J01634.

dynamic self-power supply mode to simplify the hardware circuit. The integrated chip can output current information without external current sensor, reducing hardware cost. The dsPIC33F digital controller is used as the control core, and the three-state current closed-loop control strategy is adopted, which considers the steady state energy saving maintenance of the electromagnetic contactor and the rapid dynamic regulation of the coil current. The feasibility of the integrated intelligent closed-loop control strategy is verified by Multisim and Labview co-simulation and experiment respectively. Through the research on the contactor integrated control scheme, the quality and reliability of the electromagnetic contactor can be effectively improved, and the cost of the intelligent control module can be reduced at the same time.

II. Integrated Intelligent Control Principle

A. Electromagnetic Contactor Model

The structure of the electromagnetic contactor is shown in Fig. 1. It adopts the design principle of exciting high current to start and small current to maintain. When the current flows through the coil, electromagnetic suction is generated, and the switch contacts are pulled in through the pull-in of the dynamic and static iron cores, thereby completing the on-off of the contactor. The contactor mainly includes moving iron core, static iron core, moving contact, static contact, contact spring, reaction spring, coil and other parts.

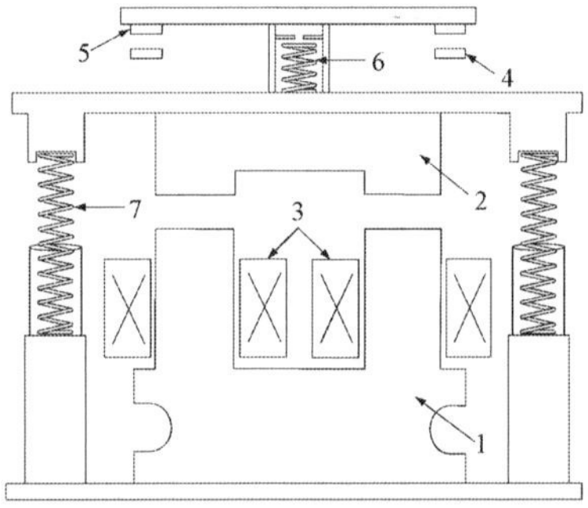

1. Static iron core 2. Moving iron core 3. Coil 4. Static contact 5. Moving contact 6. Contact spring 7. Reaction spring.

Fig. 1. Schematic diagram of electromagnetic contactor structure.

The electromagnetic mechanism satisfies the voltage balance equation and D'Alembert's mechanical motion equation during the motion, as shown in formula (1):

$$\begin{cases} \dfrac{d\psi}{dt} = -e = u_{\text{coil}} - i_{\text{coil}} R_{\text{coil}} \\ \dfrac{dv}{dt} = \dfrac{F_x - F_f}{m} \\ \dfrac{dx}{dt} = v \\ \psi\big|_{t=0} = 0, v\big|_{t=0} = 0, x\big|_{t=0} = 0 \end{cases} \tag{1}$$

Where u_{coil} is the coil voltage, i_{coil} is the coil current, R_{coil} is the coil resistance, is the magnetic flux linkage, e is the coil induced electromotive force, F_x is the electromagnetic attraction force, F_f is the spring reaction force, m is the equivalent mass of the movable part, x is the displacement of the movable iron core, and v is the speed of the movable iron core.

B. Integrated Hardware Circuit

The integrated hardware drive circuit of the electromagnetic contactor is shown in Fig. 2: B_1 is a rectifier bridge, and C_1 is a filter capacitor, which rectifies the AC input voltage into a relatively stable DC voltage for the electromagnetic contactor coil excitation.

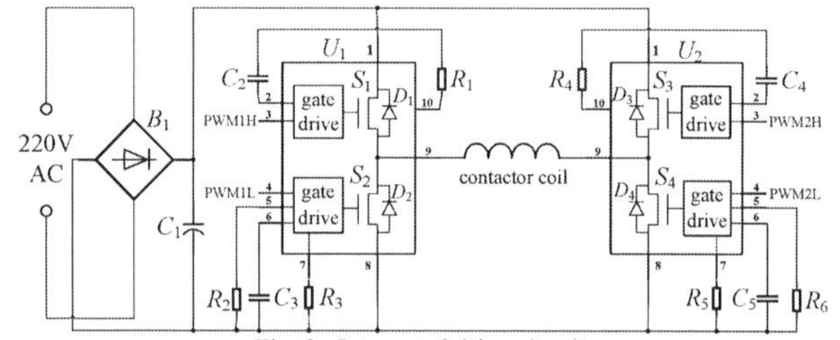

Fig. 2. Integrated drive circuit.

U_1 and U_2 are integrated half-bridge chips with two power FREDFET switches and the two integrated chips form a full-bridge drive circuit. 1-10 are the external pins of the integrated chips U_1 and U_2 respectively, and various functions of the chip are realized through the corresponding configuration. C_2, C_4, C_3, and C_5 are the gate bypass capacitors of the upper and lower switches of U_1 and U_2, respectively. The internal integrated switches S_1, S_2, S_3, and S_4 all use dynamic self-power supply. The specific working principle is as follows: the internal current source directly draws the current from the input voltage bus and charges the external gate bypass capacitor of the switch through the internal voltage regulator. When the switch is turned on, the energy stored in the capacitor is used to work. The integrated chip outputs the current information of the lower switch source and drain through the SenseFET current detection method. R_2 and R_6 are small signal resistors, which convert the current signal into a voltage signal for sampling by the microcontroller ADC. R_1, R_4 and R_3, R_6 are current-limiting resistors, which provide adjustable self-locking current-limiting thresholds for the upper and lower switches of U_1 and U_2, respectively. Pins 3 and 4 are respectively the upper and lower switches logic level control input terminals, and the coil excitation current can be flexibly adjusted through the PWM signal.

C. Intelligent Closed-loop Control Strategy

The electromagnetic contactor adopts the mode of exciting high current to start, and small current to maintain, without reverse current, so only control the state of S_1 and S_4 switches during the control process, and S_2 and S_4 can be turned off. Three circuit states are defined according to the polarity of the voltage applied across the coil: When S_1 and S_4 are turned on at the same time, the forward excitation voltage is applied to both ends of the contactor coil, and the circuit state is defined as state +1; When S_1 is turned off and S_4 is turned on, the coil current flows through S_4 and diode D_2, and the voltage across the coil is approximately 0V, and the circuit state is defined as state 0 at this time; When S_1 and S_4 are turned off at the same time, the coil current continues to flow through D_2 and D_3, and the negative voltage is applied to both ends of the coil. At this time, the circuit state is defined as state -1.

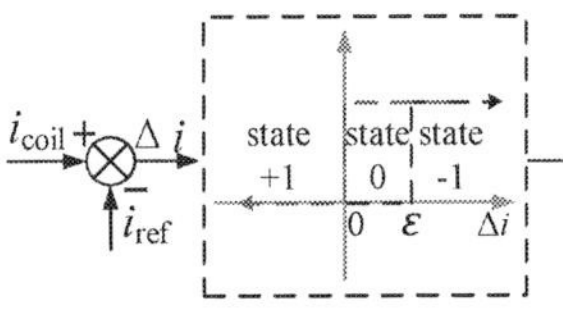

Voltage status	S_1, S_4 switch status	Current change
state +1	(on, on)	↑↑
state 0	(off, on)	↓
state -1	(off, off)	↓↓

↑↑means fast rise, ↓↓means rapid decline, ↓means slow decline.
Fig. 3. Three-state current closed-loop control principle.

The principle of three-state current closed-loop control is shown in Fig. 3: The three-state current closed-loop control is constructed using the hysteresis control method, and ε is the hysteresis width. The coil current i_{coil} output by the chip's current output pin is compared with the set current reference value i_{ref} to obtain the current error Δi, that is, $\Delta i = i_{coil} - i_{ref}$. When $\Delta i<0$, the state +1 circuit is used, and the coil current rises rapidly; when $0<\Delta i<\varepsilon$, the state 0 circuit is used, and the coil current decreases slowly; when $\Delta i>\varepsilon$, the state -1 circuit is used, and the coil current rapidly decreases. According to the current error Δi and the hysteresis width ε, the circuit state is automatically selected, the coil current is flexibly controlled, and the performance of the electromagnetic contactor is optimized.

D. *Software Programming*

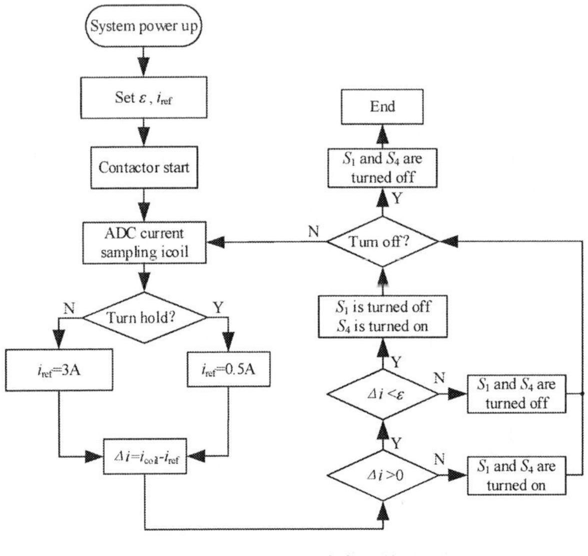

Fig. 4. System work flow chart.

The dsPIC33FJ16GS502 digital signal controller is selected as the embedded system control core. The software system mainly includes PWM module, ADC sampling module, timer module and so on.

The working flow chart of the system is shown in Fig. 4: Initially set the hysteresis width ε, the starting current reference value is set to 3A, and the holding current reference value is 0.5A. During the starting process, the coil current is dynamically maintained at 3A by three-state current closed-loop control. After the timer is timed for 100ms, the current reference value is set at 0.5A. The coil current is maintained near the reference value by automatically adjusting the switching state. In the breaking stage, the switch will all be closed, and the coil electricity will flow rapidly through the diode to 0, so as to complete the switching operation.

III. Co-Simulation Analysis of Electro-Magnetic Contactor

A. *Co-simulation Modeling*

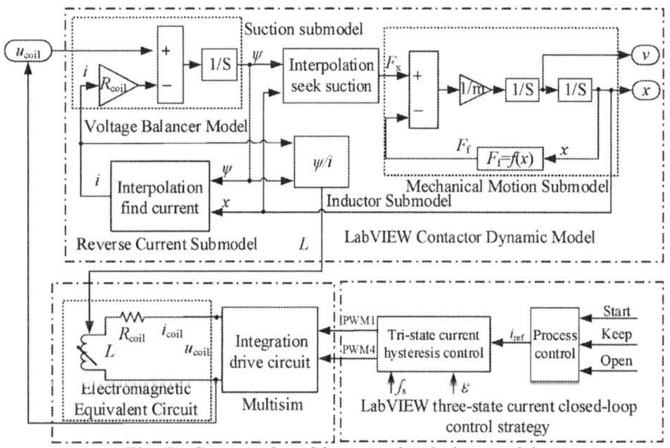

Fig. 5. Current closed-loop co-simulation model.

LabVIEW and Multisim are used to build the co-simulation model shown in Fig. 5, which is divided into three parts: the dynamic model of the contactor, the electromagnetic equivalent circuit, and the integrated drive circuit.

The dynamic model of electromagnetic contactor was built in LabVIEW, including voltage balance sub-model, inductance sub-model, mechanical motion sub-model, suction sub-model and inverse current sub-model obtained by two-dimensional interpolation. The equivalent inductance of the contactor is calculated in each simulation step, and the inductance value of the electromagnetic equivalent circuit in Multisim is changed through the data transmission node to simulate the nonlinear change of the magnetic circuit inductance during the action of the electromagnetic contactor.

The equivalent circuit of electromagnetic contactor is constructed in Multisim, and the three-state current closed-loop control strategy is constructed in LabVIEW. The coil current in Multisim is input into LabVIEW as a feedback amount through the bidirectional data transmission node, and the three-state current closed-loop control strategy is constructed in LabVIEW. The starting current reference value is set as 3A, the holding current reference value as 0.5A, and the error between coil current and reference value Δi and hysteresis width ε are calculated. The switch state is selected automatically and the coil current is controlled flexibly. The feasibility of the integrated control scheme is preliminarily verified by simulation.

B. Simulation Waveforms Analysis

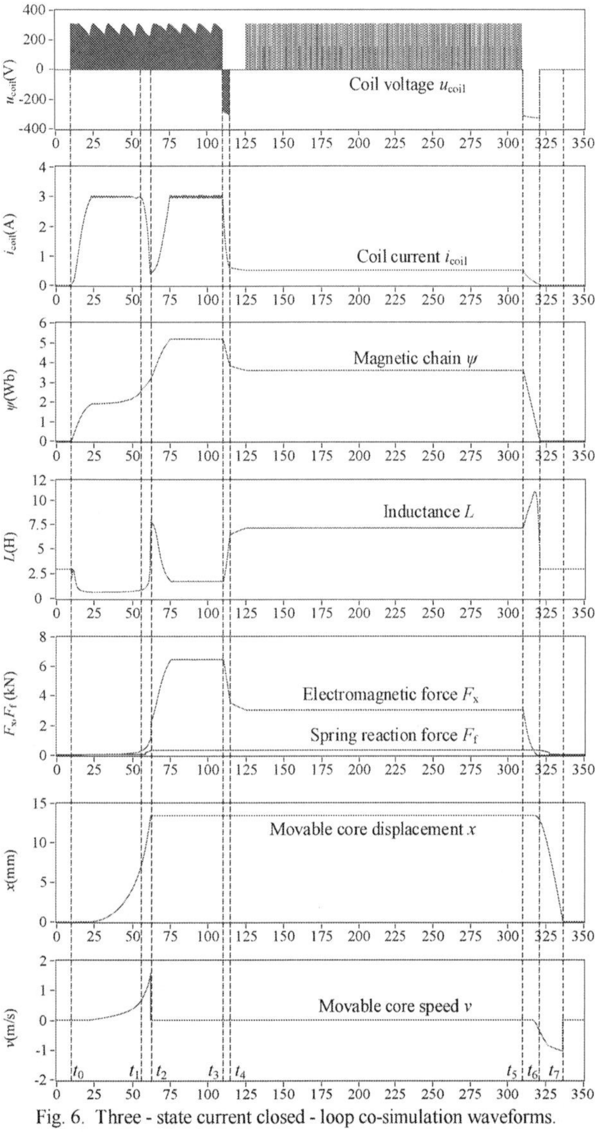

Fig. 6. Three - state current closed - loop co-simulation waveforms.

Co-simulation is used to simulate the three-state current closed-loop dynamic process of the electromagnetic contactor. In order to take into account the dynamic self-power supply of the integrated drive switch and the current detection function, the PWM drive signal duty cycle adjustment range is 0%~80%, and the frequency is 20kHz. The starting current reference value is set to 3A, and the starting time lasts 100ms. Then enter the hold phase, the hold current reference value is set to 0.5A, and the three-state current closed-loop control strategy is used to automatically adjust the coil current to keep the current dynamically around the reference value. The simulation waveform is shown in Fig. 6.

At t_0, the electromagnetic contactor starts to start, and the reference value of the starting current is 3A. At this time, the coil current is less than the reference value, the switches S_1 and S_4 are turned on, the state +1 circuit is selected, and the forward voltage is applied to both ends of the coil, so that the coil current quickly reaches the reference value, and the circuit state is automatically adjusted to keep the coil current dynamically constant. At t_1, due to the action of the contactor moving back EMF, the coil current is forced to start to drop, and at t_2 the moving and static iron cores of the contactor are completely pulled in. Then, according to the current error Δi and the hysteresis width ε, the appropriate circuit state is automatically selected to keep the current dynamic at 3A, and the start-up process ends at t_3. At this time, it starts to enter the hold phase, the hold current reference value is set to 0.5A, the state -1 circuit is selected, and the negative voltage is applied to both ends of the coil, so that the coil current drops rapidly, and the coil current drops to the hold reference value 0.5A at t_4. , and then automatically switch through the hysteresis controller to keep the coil current stable near the reference value. At t_5, the contactor enters the opening stage, switches S_1 and S_4 are all closed, and the state -1 circuit is selected, the coil current drops rapidly, and the current drops to 0 at t_6. As the coil current decreases, the dynamic and static iron cores begin to separate, and the dynamic and static iron cores are completely separated at t_7, and the opening process ends.

IV. EXPERIMENTAL VERIFICATION

A. Hardware Control System

The experimental site is shown in Fig. 7: Taking CJ20-630A electromagnetic contactor as the control object, an integrated hardware control system is built, including 220V AC input power supply, integrated hardware control circuit, etc.

The rectifier filter circuit converts the AC input voltage into a relatively stable DC voltage for the excitation of the contactor coil. The electromagnetic contactor drive circuit is formed by two integrated half-bridge chips, which are used to flexibly control the current of the contactor coil. With dsPIC33FJ16GS502 as the control system MCU, the current i_{sense} output by the IPH pin of the chip is read through the ADC sampling module and converted into the coil current i_{coil}, the three-state current hysteresis controller automatically selects the appropriate circuit state, and flexibly adjusts the contactor coil current size, to optimize the dynamic process of the electromagnetic contactor. The displacement and speed of the movable iron core during the working process of the contactor are detected by the laser displacement sensor, and the oscilloscope is used to display various dynamic parameters during the operation of the contactor.

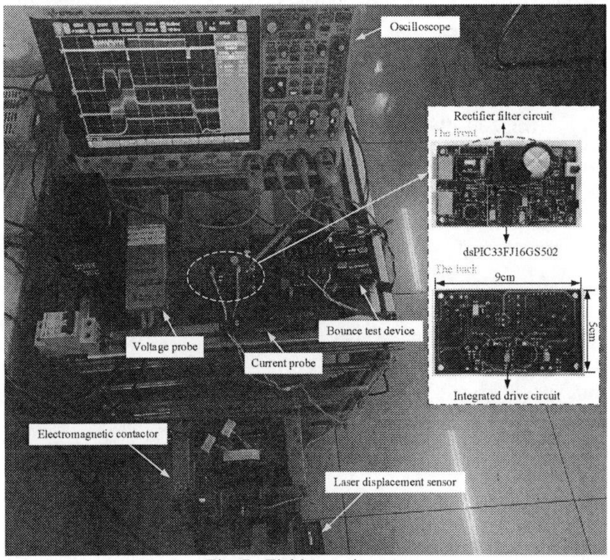

Fig. 7. Field experiment.

B. *Closed-loop Control Experimental Verification*

The three-state current closed-loop experimental waveforms obtained by the above integrated hardware control system are shown in Fig. 8. The starting current reference value is set to 3A, the starting time lasts 100ms, and the holding current reference value is 0.5A, and the duration is 200ms. The PWM frequency is 20kHz, and the duty cycle adjustment range is 0%~80%.

t_0-t_3 period: starting stage, the contactor starts to start at time t_0. At this time, the coil current is less than the starting current reference value, and the state +1 circuit is selected to rapidly increase the coil current to the reference value. At t_1, due to the action of the moving back EMF, the coil current is forced to start to drop, and the moving and static iron cores are completely pulled in at t_2. The state +1 circuit is selected to make the current rise to the vicinity of the reference value, and then the current hysteresis controller automatically selects the appropriate circuit state to dynamically maintain the coil current around 3A.

t_3-t_5 period: holding period, the holding phase starts at t_3, the current reference value is set to 0.5A, and the state -1 circuit is selected, the coil current drops rapidly, and at t_4, it drops to the vicinity of the reference value, and then transitions to the stable holding phase, The hysteresis controller automatically adjusts the circuit state to keep the current dynamic at 0.5A.

t_5-t_7 period: the opening stage, all switches are turned off at t_5, the state -1 circuit is selected, the negative voltage is applied to both ends of the coil, the coil current drops rapidly, and drops to 0 at t_6. At t_7, the dynamic and static iron cores are completely separated, and the opening process ends.

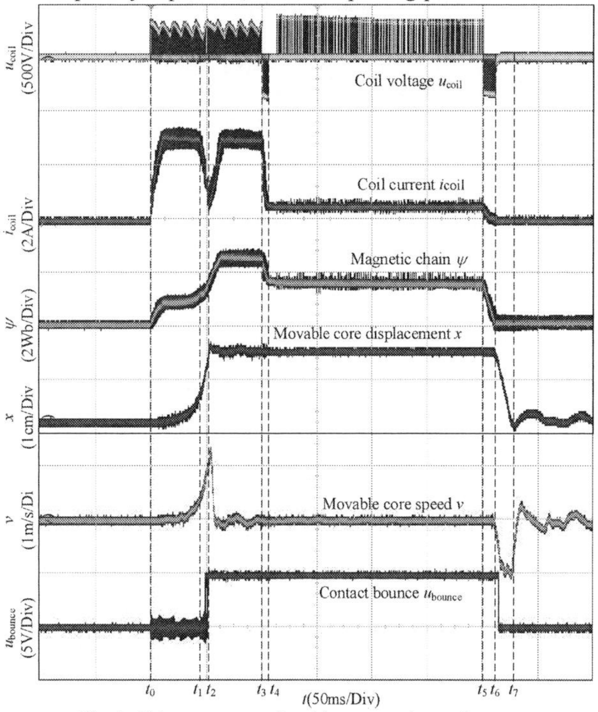

Fig. 8. Tri-state current closed-loop control waveforms.

V. Conclusion

1) The integrated switching power supply chip is applied to the integrated control of the electromagnetic contactor. The switch works in the dynamic self-supply mode, which overcomes the defect that the traditional control scheme needs auxiliary power supply. The chip integrates SenseFET current sensing, eliminating the need for external current detection and amplification, simplifying the hardware control scheme.

2) Three-state current closed-loop control strategy is adopted to improve the dynamic response speed of coil current. Current is used as feedback control quantity, which has the characteristics of natural current limiting and avoids coil heating and short circuit. The breaking process controls the electromagnetic system to rapidly demagnetize and improve the breaking speed of the contactor.

3) Using Multisim and LabVIEW software co-simulation, the transient simulation model of integrated control circuit and the dynamic model of magnetic circuit of electromagnetic contactor are established respectively. Combined with the current closed-loop control strategy in LabVIEW, an intelligent co-simulation system integrating contactor body, hardware control circuit and software control strategy is formed.

References

[1] Sevov, D. Allcock, R. Luna, and J. Bowen, "Motor reacceleration to improve process uptime," IEEE Transactions on Industry Applications, 2016, 52(1): 684-691

[2] Wu Jingxuan, Xu Zhihong. Model-free adaptive control strategy for electromagnetic contactor suction process [J]. Proceedings of the CSEE, 2020, 40(05): 1663-1673.

[3] Zhuang Jierong, Xu Zhihong. Research on multi variable feedback suction control strategy for electromagnetic contactor [J]. Proceedings of the CSEE, 2019, 39(05): 1516-1526.

[4] Xu Zhihong, Zhang Peiming. Research on dynamic closing course of intelligent AC contactor[J]. Proceedings of the CSEE, 2007, 27(18): 108-113.

[5] Xu Z H, Zhang P M. Intelligent control technology of AC contactor[C] Proceedings of the 2005 IEEE/PES Transmission and Distribution Conference and Exhibition: Asia and Pacific . Dalian , China : IEEE, 2005: 1-5.

[6] Tang Longfei, Xu Zhihong. Design of control module for closed-loop chopper starting ac contactor [J]. Proceedings of the CSEE, 2013,33 (18): 132-139.

[7] Xu Zhihong, Zhang Peiming. Study on Dynamic Clamping Process of Intelligent AC Contactor [J]. Proceedings of the CSEE, 2007,27 (18): 108-113.

[8] Moraes P M d S D, Perin A J. An electronic control unit for reducing contact bounce in electromagnetic contactors[J]. IEEE Transactions on Industrial Electronics, 2008, 55(2): 861-870.

[9] Espinosa A G, Ruiz J R R, Morera X A. A sensorless method for controlling the closure of a contactor[J]. IEEE Transactions on Magnetics, 2007, 43(10): 3896-3903.

[10] Tang Longfei, Xu Zhihong. Closed-loop control technology of ac contactor slope [J]. Proceedings of the CSEE, 2017,37 (3): 956-964.

[11] L.Tang, Z. Han, and Z. Xu, "A Sequential Adaptive Control Strategy for the Contact Colliding Speed of Contactors Based on Fuzzy Control," IEEE Transactions on Industrial Electronics, 2021, 68(7) : 6064-6074.

[12] Tang Longfei, Xu Zhihong. Design of intelligent control module for ac solenoid valve [J]. Transactions of the China electrotechnical society, 2014, 29(5): 246-253, 260.

Xingxin Zheng is currently pursuing the M.S. degree in electric engineering from the College of Electrical Engineering and Automation, Fuzhou University, China. His research interests include electric apparatus and its intelligent technology. 200127175@fzu.edu.cn.

Longfei Tang (Senior Member, IEEE) received his B.Sc. degree in electrical engineering and automation from Fuzhou University in 2009 and his Ph.D. degree in electric machines and electric apparatus from Fuzhou University in 2015. Now he is a professor at Fuzhou University, China. His research interests include electric apparatus and its intelligent technology. Corresponding author: tlftel@fzu.edu.cn.

8th International Conference on Reliability of
Electrical Products and Electrical Contacts,
November 18-20, 2022

Simplified Calculation Model for Contact Resistance of Fractal Rough Surfaces

Changgeng Zhang, Baichuan Yu, Yongjian Li, Qingxin Yang

State Key Laboratory of Reliability and Intelligence of Electrical Equipment
Hebei University of Technology, Tianjin, 300401, China
E-mail: changgeng.zhang@hebut.edu.cn Tel: 13821932497

***Abstract*—Contact resistance is an important indicator to evaluate the stability and reliability of electrical connections. For the problems that contact analysis of fractal theory is more complicated and contact network is difficult to construct, a simplified calculation model of contact resistance of rough surface containing fractal characteristics and contact deformation process is proposed. The fractal theory and Monte Carlo random theory are used to generate the rough electrical contact surface, explore the contact deformation mechanism of micro-convex body at different scales, obtain the quantitative relationship between real contact area and contact load, and then construct a contact resistance network calculation model containing contaminated film layer, and quantitatively analyze the change law and influencing factors. The results show that the fractal dimension *D* mainly affects the complexity of the surface contour, and the characteristic parameter *G* affects the height of the contour; there exists an optimal value of 1.5 for the fractal dimension *D*, when the real contact area of the surface is the largest; the contact resistance size is affected by various factors, and the contaminated film layer is the most important factor, and it is important to research on the contaminated film layer for the contact reliability. The model provides a theoretical basis for further research on heat transfer, frictional wear and radiation on rough surfaces.**

***Index Terms*—fractal, rough surface, contact characteristics, contact resistance**

I. INTRODUCTION

Fixed electrical contacts are commonly used in the connection of various types of electrical equipment, and the Electrical Contact Resistance (ECR), an integral part of the electrical connection, is an important indicator to evaluate the stability and safety reliability of the electrical connection. In a real contact environment, the contact surface is not completely smooth, but contains surface roughness, processing texture and corrugation and other geometric features. That is, strictly speaking, any electrical contact surface is a rough surface at the microscopic scale. When two rough surfaces are in contact, the actual contact area is much smaller than the macroscopic apparent contact area, and the electric current occurs at a number of discrete contact points with violent current contraction, and the shape and distribution of micro-contact points and the local contraction of the conductive channel have an impact on the current distribution. How to carve the rough surface and predict the number and area of discrete contact points is crucial to the calculation of ECR.

Surface morphology has undergone a research process from simple to complex, from statistical stochastic to fractal from the initial Greenwood-Williamson model, to the subsequent random theory of rough surfaces, elliptical contact statistical model, the rough surfaces constructed based on statistical characteristic parameters have never been able to overcome the dependence on the detection accuracy of measuring instruments[1]. An essential characteristic parameters *D* and *G* characterizing the surface morphology were proposed by Majumdar et al[2] for the subsequent morphological studies, where the fractal dimension *D* and the characteristic scale *G*. Subsequent research scholars studied rough surfaces with isotropic and anisotropic characteristics based on fractal theory and concluded that only specially treated surfaces are isotropic, such as shot peening, while ground and flat honed surfaces are more directional[3].

Rough surfaces are usually constructed to study the contact properties and transport properties of the contact surfaces. When contact occurs between two rough planes, the actual contact occurs between a portion of asperity bodies. These asperity bodies are deformed by forces and form several discrete contact surfaces on the contact surface.The earliest statistical model of microscopic contact mechanics was proposed by Greenwood and Willianson[4]. This model assumed that the curvature of the asperity bodies on the rough surface was the same and the height satisfied Gaussian distribution, and only elastic deformation of the asperity bodies occurred during the contact, from which the relationship between the actual contact area and the contact pressure was deduced. Subsequent scholars have further extended the application of the G-W model to contact stiffness[5-6], sliding contact[7], and contact damping[8-9]. Although the subsequent methods consider the elastic-plastic deformation and multiscale of asperity bodies, the dependence of their surface morphology parameters on the resolution and sampling length of the measurement instruments is never resolved. Therefore, the analytical results of the contact models established based on statistical models are not unique. Another approach is the contact model constructed by fractal geometry theory for rough surfaces and then established. Majumdar established an early contact model for rough surfaces based on the W-M function, namely the M-B fractal contact model[2]. This model uses scale independent parameters such as D and G to achieve the characterization of two-dimensional rough cross sections and obtains the relationship between the actual contact area of the rough surface and the contact load by combining the Hertz contact theory and the area distribution law of the ocean islands.

Nevertheless, the M-B model makes many ideal assumptions that the elastic-plastic deformation of the asperity body is an abrupt process and there is no transition state; the asperity body base is rigid and does not deform; and the adjacent asperity bodies are independent of each other, etc. The M-B contact model has been revised and supplemented by subsequent researchers. To represent the process of mutual coupling between asperity bodies in which several contact patches merge into a larger contact region with increasing compression, Persson proposed a multiscale contact model[10]. The model assumes that the contact pressure diffuses over the contact pressure space with increasing resolution, and the process can be described by a diffusion equation that characterizes the actual contact area versus contact pressure. For the transition mechanism of asperity contact from elastic to fully plastic deformation, a series of contact models have been proposed to obtain the relationship between the actual contact area and the average contact pressure during elastic-plastic contact of asperity bodies[11-13]. Although the contact models constructed in the above literature are experimentally verified to have certain accuracy, it is difficult to construct a suitable contact resistance network for the solution of ECR because the rough plane structure is too complex and the coupling between asperity bodies in the contact state is too strong. To obtain the contact resistance network, the key contact characteristics of the rough surface must be retained as much as possible, while the contact plane is simplified.

In this paper, based on the rough surface contact model, the contact resistance calculation model is established based on the surface profile and material properties of the contact material. The fractal theory is used to determine the morphological characteristics of the asperity set, and then the Monte Carlo method is used to construct the rough surface. The contact characteristics of the sinusoidal asperity body are equated when the asperity set is in contact, and then the quantitative relationship between the real contact area and the contact load is obtained, and its correctness is verified by the comparative analysis with the experimental data. Based on this, a computational model of contact resistance network containing contaminated film layer is constructed.

A. Rough surface morphology structure

For the purpose of analysis, the contact between two rough surfaces is usually simplified to the contact between an isotropic equivalent rough surface and a rigid ideal surface, and the equivalent rough surface has the morphological characteristics and material properties of the two rough surfaces. From the two-dimensional Weierstrass-Mandelbrot (W-M) function, it is known that the cosine wave-like micro-convex body is the most basic unit constituting the rough surface. If the coupling effect between adjacent asperity and the strain-hardening effect of the material during the contact is neglected, and assuming that the profile of the asperity along the cross section perpendicular to the normal height is circular, the profile of the asperity before deformation can be described as

$$z(x) = G^{D-1} l^{2-D} \cos\frac{\pi x}{l}, -\frac{l}{2} < x < \frac{l}{2} \tag{1}$$

where $z(x)$ denotes the asperity profile height curve; D is the fractal dimension ($1<D<2$); G is the characteristic scale parameter reflecting the profile curve; l is the asperity base diameter; δ is the asperity height under the base diameter of l, satisfying $\delta=G^{D-1}l^{2-D}$.

Asperities of different scales with basal diameter l satisfy the island area distribution law above sea level and the Monte Carlo random size distribution law[14]

$$N(L \geq l) = (\frac{l_{\max}}{l})^D \tag{2}$$

The base diameter l_i and the corresponding height δ_i of the asperity body at different scales can be expressed by the following equation

$$l_i = \frac{l_{\min}}{(1-R_i)^{1/D}} = (\frac{l_{\min}}{l_{\max}})\frac{l_{\max}}{(1-R_i)^{1/D}} \tag{3}$$

$$\delta_i = G^{D-1}[(\frac{l_{\min}}{l_{\max}})\frac{l_{\max}}{(1-R_i)^{1/D}}]^{2-D} \tag{4}$$

where l_{max} and l_{min} correspond to the maximum and minimum asperity base diameters, respectively, R_i is the random number, i =1, 2, 3, ... N, and N is the total number of random numbers generated, satisfying $N=[(l_{max}/l_{min})^D]$. The asperity corresponding to l_{max} is called the level 1 asperity, the asperity corresponding to l_{min} is called the level N asperity, and the rest of the asperities are arranged sequentially according to the size of the base diameter. l_i with upper and lower limits of l_{max} and l_{min} respectively, the random range of R_i

$$0 \le R_i \le 1 - \left(\frac{l_{\min}}{l_{\max}}\right)^D \tag{5}$$

The structure formed by the forward stacking of asperities of different scales with cosine functions of contours is called an asperity set, where the asperity corresponding to l_{max} is used as the base of the asperity set, the asperity of level 2 is stacked on top of the asperity of level 1, and so on, and a total of N asperity sets of different levels can be generated. Figure 1 shows the asperity set of N stacked structures obtained by the number of layers, where h_n is the height obtained by forward stacking of n levels of asperities of different scales, which can be expressed as

$$h_n = G^{(D-1)} l_{\max}^{(2-D)} + \sum_{m=1}^{n-1} \delta_i \tag{6}$$

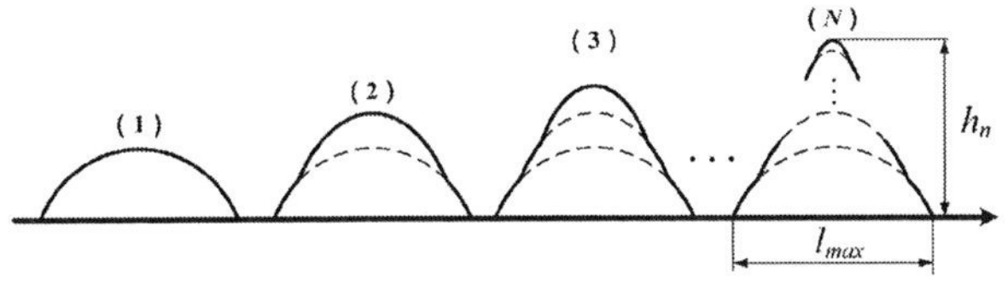

Fig. 1. Set of asperity bodies with different scale stacking structures

Most of the rough surface contour heights satisfy Gaussian distribution, and the number of generated asperity heights is corrected by dividing the sequentially arranged asperity heights into 11 intervals with equal spacing, and each interval is replicated with a number of randomly selected heights, and the replication multiplier satisfies Gaussian distribution. The number of replicated asperity bodies N replaces the initial number of asperity bodies N. The distribution of the height intervals of the asperity bodies before and after the correction is shown in Fig. 2.

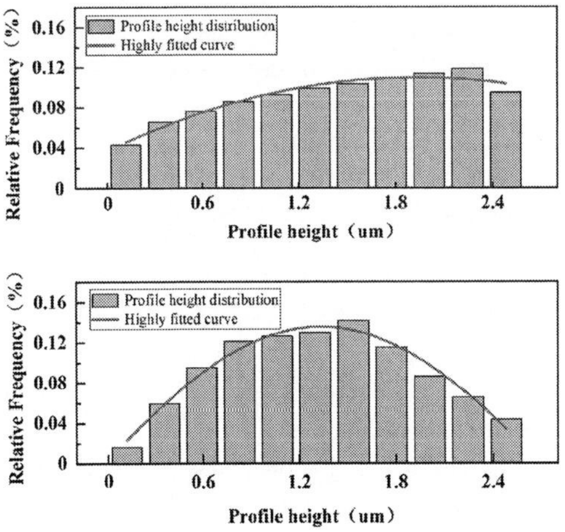

Fig. 2. Height interval distribution of asperity set before and after correction

The equivalent rough surface consists of several sets of asperities with different stacked layers in the plane according to the Monte Carlo random distribution law. In this model, the macroscopic contact plane is a square plane with side length L. The set of asperities is randomly distributed on the plane and does not intersect with the plane boundary. The coordinates ($x(i)$, $y(i)$) of the circle center of the base of the asperity set can be expressed as

$$\begin{cases} x(i) = 0.5 l_{\max} + (L - l_{\max}) R_{a1} \\ y(i) = 0.5 l_{\max} + (L - l_{\max}) R_{a2} \end{cases} \tag{7}$$

where R_{a1} and R_{a2} are two random numbers between 0 and 1 such that the coordinates ($x(i)$, $y(i)$) satisfy $0.5l_{max} \leqslant x(i), y(i) \leqslant L-0.5l_{max}$ and are randomly distributed.

From the assumptions of Eq. (7), it is clear that the sets of asperity bodies are independent of each other, and if adjacent sets of asperity bodies overlap, the position coordinates are regenerated until there is no intersection between each set of asperity bodies in the full plane, and the specific judgment criteria can be realized by comparing the sum of the distance from the center of the circle of adjacent sets of asperity bodies and the base radius.

$$\sqrt{(x(i)-x(j))^2 + (y(i)-y(j))^2} \ge l_{\max} \quad 0<i, j \text{ and } i \ne j \tag{8}$$

The morphological characteristics of the micro-convex body set are determined by the two-dimensional W-M function, and then the rough surface is constructed by the Monte Carlo method to programmatically simulate the three-dimensional rough surface morphology under different fractal parameters, as shown in Fig. 3. Both the fractal dimension D and the characteristic scale parameter G are negatively correlated with the height of the rough surface profile, and G, as the base of δ_i, has a much greater effect on the height of the asperity body than D as a power, which leads to the conclusion that the variation of the characteristic scale parameter G reflects more the height of the entire rough surface profile and determines the overall surface flatness and roughness. According to Eq. $N=[(l_{max}/l_{min})^D]$, the fractal dimension D is positively correlated with the number of asperity sets. As the number of fractal dimensions increases, the number of asperity sets increases, the distance between them decreases, and the asperity sets appear to squeeze and fuse with each other, and the 3D contours become more and more dense and complex. In Figs. 3(d)-(e), D is kept constant, G power exponentially decreases, and the height of the surface profile significantly decreases, but the effect on the morphology and complexity is smaller. Thus the variation of the characteristic scale parameter G reflects more the height of the whole rough surface profile and determines the overall surface flatness and roughness.

B. Contact properties solving

The contact properties of the asperity set on a rough surface directly affect the mechanical properties on the whole surface, and the relationship between the total contact load and the true contact area between rough surfaces is promoted by studying the contact properties of a single asperity set. The asperity set is a multilayer stacked structure, and its overall profile can be approximated as a sinusoidal asperity structure with the same height and base length as the asperity set, as shown in Fig. 4, then the study of contact properties of the asperity set can be equated to the study of sinusoidal asperity.

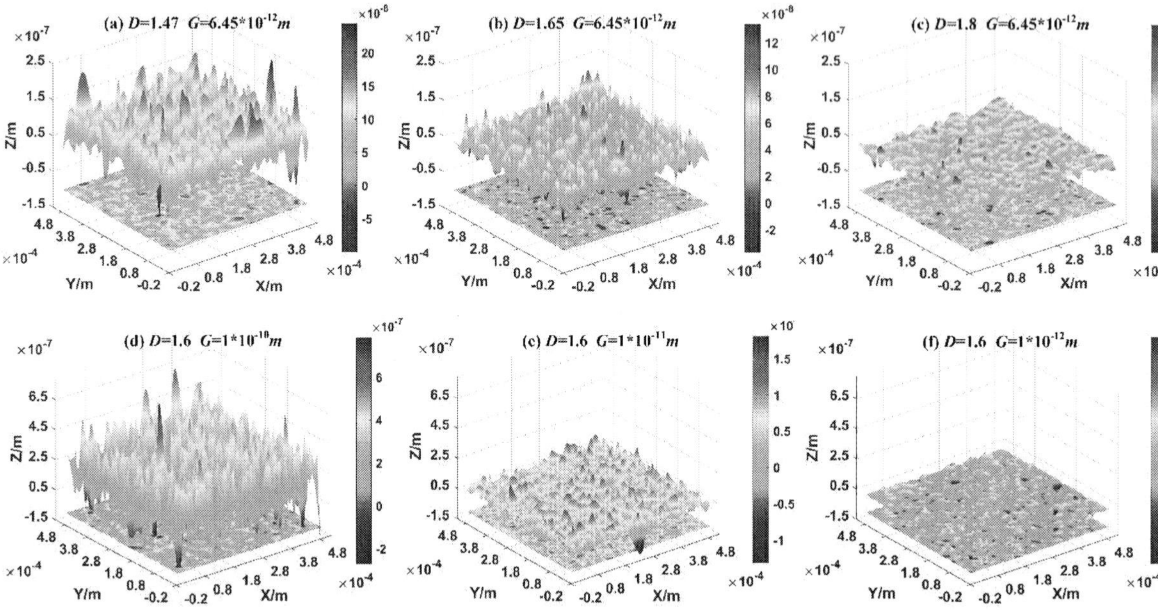

Fig. 3. 3D rough surface under different D and G

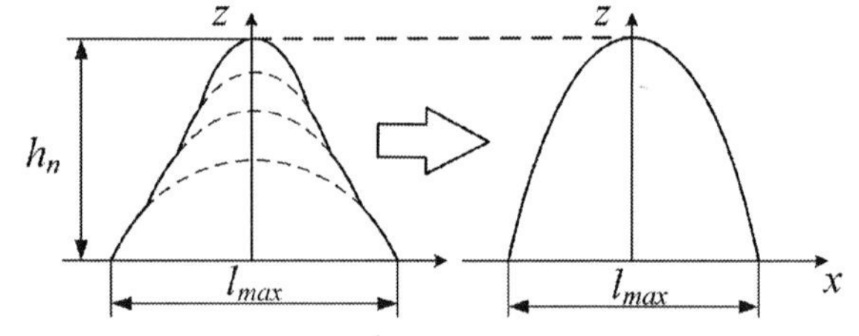

Fig. 4. Equivalent schematic diagram of the asperity set

Jackson analyzed the complete contact process of a three-dimensional sinusoidal contact body based on finite elements and obtained a fitting equation for the contact area versus contact load[15]

$$A=\begin{cases} A_{JGH1}\left(1-\left[\dfrac{\bar{p}}{p^*}\right]^{1.51}\right)+A_{JGH2}\left[\dfrac{\bar{p}}{p^*}\right]^{1.04} & \dfrac{\bar{p}}{p^*}<0.8 \\ A_{JGH2} & \dfrac{\bar{p}}{p^*}\geq 0.8 \end{cases} \tag{9}$$

Where: A is the actual contact area of a single asperity; $\bar{p}$ is the average contact pressure of a sinusoidal asperity satisfying $\bar{p}=F/l_{max}^2$, F is the contact load of this sinusoidal asperity; p^* is the average contact pressure of a asperity under complete deformation of force and amplitude height of 0 satisfying $p^*=\sqrt{2}\pi E^* h_n / l_{\max}$, where E^* is the equivalent sinusoidal asperity Young's modulus, which can be obtained from the Poisson's ratio and elastic modulus υ_1, υ_2 and E_1, E_2 of the two original contact surfaces by the formula $E^*=E_1E_2/(E_2(1-\upsilon_1^2)+(E_2(1-\upsilon_2^2))$. A_{JGH1} and A_{JGH2} are the first contact area and the second contact area of Jackson's sinusoidal asperity body contact model, satisfying

$$\begin{cases} A_{JGH1}=2\pi(l_{\max})^2\left[\dfrac{3}{8\pi}\dfrac{\bar{p}}{p^*}\right]^{2/3} \\ A_{JGH2}=(l_{\max})^2\left(1-\dfrac{3}{2\pi}\left[1-\dfrac{\bar{p}}{p^*}\right]\right) \end{cases} \tag{10}$$

Fig. 5 represents a single sinusoidal asperity body in contact with a rigid plane, the dashed part is the original contour of the asperity body, the solid part is the deformed contour of the asperity body, and the contact area is an ideal circle. r_i is the radius of the asperity contact spot, d is the distance of the rigid plane from the base plane of the asperity body, and the real contact area of the asperity body $A_i=\pi r_i^2$.

For a sinusoidal asperity body contact structure, the contact spot radius r_i can be obtained from the following equation[16]

$$r_i=\left(\sqrt{\frac{h_i}{d}-0.75}-0.5\right)\frac{l_{\max}}{2} \qquad 0\leq d\leq \frac{1}{3}h_i \tag{11}$$

By specifying the distance d between the rigid plane and the base plane, the radius r_i and area A_i of the contact spot of the sinusoidal asperity in the plane can be found, and then the contact load F_i can be obtained from Eq. (9). Extending to the whole contact plane, all sinusoidal asperity in the plane with height greater than d are in contact with the rigid plane, and the contact area and contact load can be obtained from Eqs. (9) and (11). The true contact area A_r and the total contact load F of the plane are the sum of the true contact area and the contact load of the discrete contacting asperities, respectively, denoted as

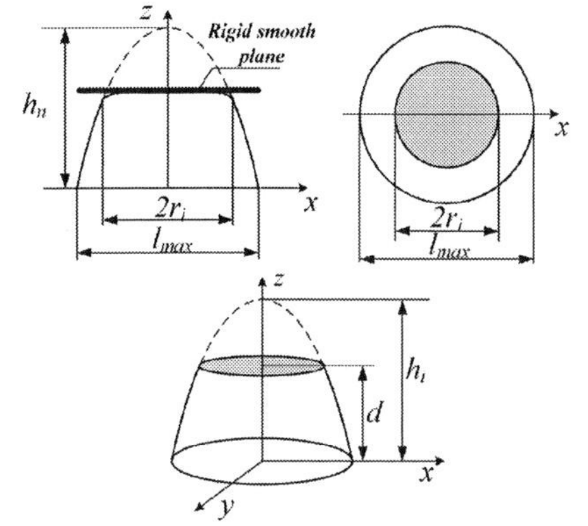

Fig. 5. Single sinusoidal asperity body contact model

$$\begin{cases} A_r = \sum_{i=1}^{n'} \pi r_i^2 \\ F = \sum_{i=1}^{n'} F_i \end{cases} \tag{12}$$

where: n' is the number of contacting asperities.

C. Contact resistance model

According to the classical shrinkage resistance theory[17], the shrinkage resistance R_c of a sinusoidal asperity body with base diameter l_{max} and contact spot radius r_i can be approximated as

$$R_c = \left[\frac{\rho}{2r_i}\right]\left[\overline{R_{co}} + s_F\left(\frac{d}{r_i}\right)\right] \tag{13}$$

where

$$s_F = \frac{4}{\pi}\left(\frac{2r_i}{l_{\max}}\right)\left[1 - \frac{2r_i}{l_{\max}}\right] \tag{14}$$

$$\overline{R_{co}} = 1 - 1.41581\left(\frac{2r_i}{l_{\max}}\right) + 0.063\left(\frac{2r_i}{l_{\max}}\right)^2 + 0.15261\left(\frac{2r_i}{l_{\max}}\right)^3 + 0.19998\left(\frac{2r_i}{l_{\max}}\right)^4 \tag{15}$$

where ρ is the equivalent rough surface substrate material resistivity, $\rho = \rho_1 + \rho_2$, ρ_1 and ρ_2 are the two original contact material resistivity; s_F is the contractional slope; $\overline{R_{co}}$ is the classical contraction resistance fitting formula.

When the electrical contact surface is exposed to high humidity and severe pollution for a long time, the asperity will be covered with a contaminated film layer such as sulfide film, oxide film and other surface films. The presence of the contaminated film layer will further affect the current density distribution in the contraction region, generating another additional resistance, called the film resistance R_f

$$R_f = \rho_f \frac{d_c}{\pi r_i^2} \tag{16}$$

Where: ρ_f is the resistivity of the contaminated film layer; d_c is the thickness of the contaminated film layer. The contraction resistance and oxide film resistance on the asperity are connected in series on the circuit, while the asperities of different scales are connected in parallel on the plane, and the equivalent circuit model of contact resistance can be established as shown in Fig. 6, which has a total contraction resistance R

$$R = \frac{1}{\sum_{i=1}^{n'} \frac{1}{R_i}} \tag{17}$$

where R_i is the contact resistance of sinusoidal asperities of different scales, satisfying $R_i = R_{ci} + R_{fi}$.

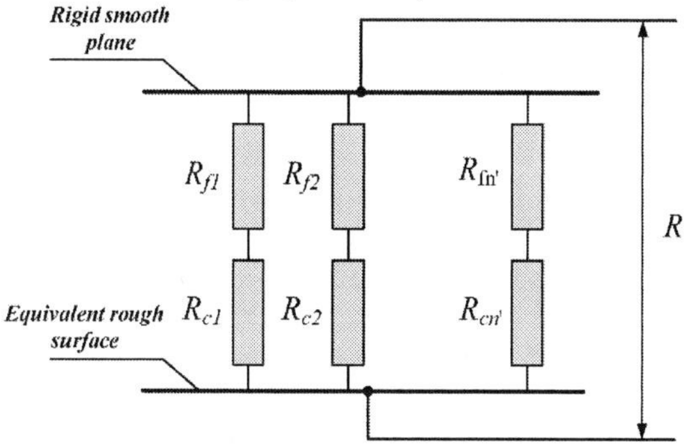

Fig. 6. Contact resistance equivalent circuit model

D. Results and Analysis

Based on the mathematical model constructed above, the relationship between total contact load and true contact area and contact resistance for equivalent rough and rigid smooth surfaces is investigated, and the calculated parameters are shown in Table 1. To facilitate the analysis, A_r, F and R are normalized into dimensionless quantitates, $A_r^* = A_r/L^2$, $F^* = F/(E^*L^2)$, $R^* = RL^2/(\rho + \rho_f)$.

TABLE I

CONTACT RESISTANCE MODEL CALCULATION PARAMETERS

Paramaters	Range of Values
D	1.3~1.7
G/m	10^{-8}~10^{-15}
l_{max}/m	3×10^{-7}
l_{min}/m	5×10^{-9}
L/m	5×10^{-4}
E^*/Pa	5.064×10^{10}
$\rho/(\Omega m)$	4.317×10^{-8}
$\rho_f/(\Omega m)$	10^{-4}~10^{3}
d_c/um	0.1~25

Fig. 7 shows the variation of A_r^* versus F^* for $G=10^{-11}$m. From the figure, it can be seen that at the fractal dimension D less than 1.5, the increase of D helps to increase the contact rate and improve the contact properties of the material surface. In this range as D increases, the rough surface fineness increases, the number of asperities in contact with the rigid plane keeps increasing, and the contact area keeps increasing. When D is greater than 1.5, the size of larger contacts decreases, while the increase in the number of small asperities on the rough surface is much faster than the decrease in the size of large asperities, and the proportion of large asperity contacts increases rather than decreases.

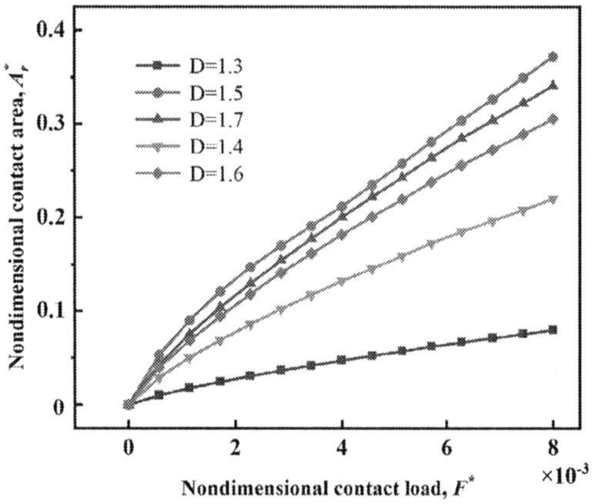

Fig. 7. Variation of A_r^* versus F^* for G=10^{-11}m

Fig. 8 shows the variation of A_r^* versus F^* for D=1.53. From the figure, it can be seen that A_r^* increases linearly with the increase of F^* when the fractal dimension D is a constant value. It can also be seen that the larger the characteristic scale G is under the same load, the smaller the actual contact area is. The reason for this phenomenon is that the size of G determines the flatness and roughness of the overall surface, and the larger G is, the larger the difference in asperity amplitude is, and under the same contact load, the presence of higher asperities causes a large number of low asperities not to make contact, resulting in a smaller overall contact area. Therefore, improving the machining accuracy and reducing the roughness of the contact part surface are beneficial to improve the contact performance.

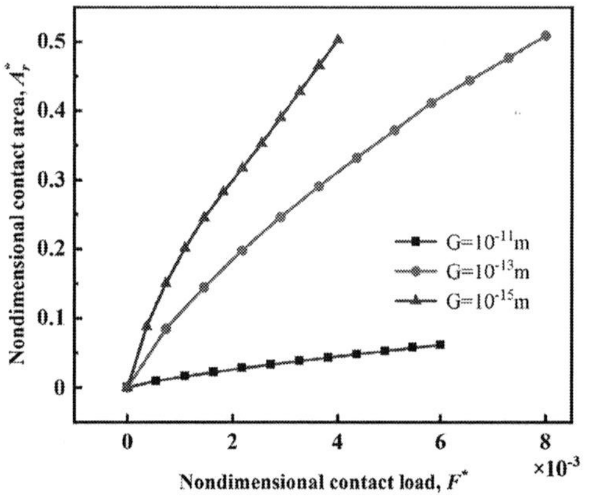

Fig. 8. Variation of A_r^* versus F^* for D=1.53

To verify the correctness of the contact models in this paper, the contact pressure and contact area data obtained from the model calculations were compared with the G-W model, M-B model, and Bhushan experimental data, as shown in Fig. 9. The surface morphology and material parameters are set as D=1.53, G=4×10^{-13}m, A_a=10^{-8}m^2, E^*=1.80Gpa. The predicted curves of the three contact models and the measured curves have the same trend, and the predicted data of the model in this paper and the experimental data basically match, which can prove the correctness of the model. Under the light load of $F^* \leq 2\times10^{-3}$, the M-B model agrees well with the experimental data, and with the increase of load, the M-B model deviates from the experimental data to a certain extent. The reason is that on real contact, the protrusions on two rough surfaces may disappear or merge into larger contact patches, and the process involves coupling before the contact area, and the contact model with the asperities as the smallest unit is difficult to effectively characterize the contact morphology under heavy load. the G-W model mainly focuses on elastic contact, ignores local plastic deformation, and underestimates the real contact area. Similar to the M-B model, the model in this paper ignores the interaction between contacting asperities, which is reflected in the calculation results with high accuracy for $F^* \leqslant 4\times10^{-3}$ medium and light loads, but its simplified contact analysis helps to extend to different applications.

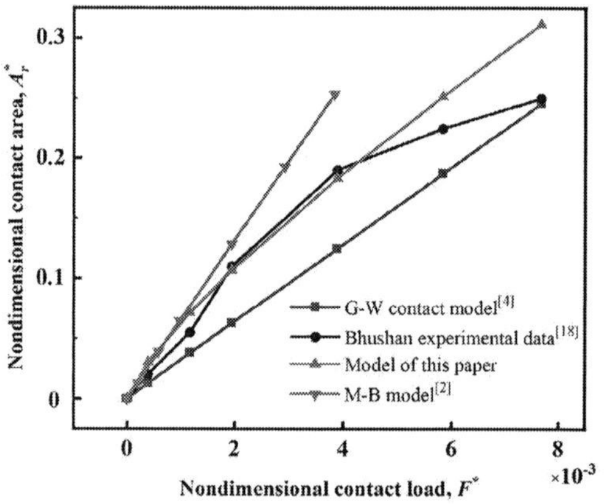

Fig. 9. Comparison of model theoretical values and experimental data

Fig. 10 shows the variation relationship between F^* and R^* under different fractal parameters under clean and rough surface. From Fig. 10(a), it can be seen that the contact resistance tends to decrease with the increase of contact load, and the contact resistance is minimized when D=1.5, which basically satisfies the law that the smaller the actual contact area is, the larger the contact resistance is in combination with Fig. 7. From Fig. 10(b), it can be seen that the influence of the characteristic scale parameter G on the contact resistance is much larger than that of the fractal dimension D. The smaller G is, the smaller the contact resistance is while the rate of decline increases, which is because G is positively correlated with the maximum height difference of the profile, and the height difference decreases will significantly increase the number of contact asperities, and the parallel branch increases, which reduces the current resistance at the contact interface.

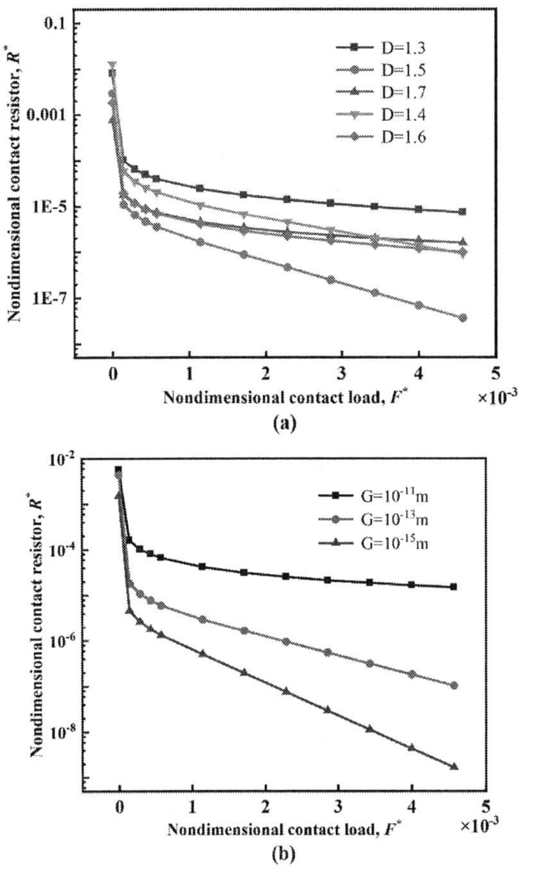

Fig. 10. Variation of A_r^* versus F^* for d_c=0um

Fig. 11 shows the variation of contact resistance R with the resistivity ρ_f of the contaminated film layer for surface parameters D=1.53, G=10^{-9}m, and dimensionless contact pressure F^*=1.29. When the electrical contact surface is completely clean and ideal pure metal contact occurs, the contact resistance caused by the current line contraction is R=8.05×10^{-4}Ω. When the contaminated film meets d_c=1um and ρ_f=10^{-4}Ωm, the contact resistance R=29.1×10^{-4}Ω, which is of the same order of magnitude as the metal contact resistance and the value is low enough for good contact performance. With the increase of film resistivity and thickness, the effect of shrinkage resistance is masked by the film resistance.

III. Conclusion

In this paper, based on fractal theory and Monte Carlo stochastic method, a computational model reflecting the contact characteristics and contact resistance between solid rough contact interfaces is proposed. The rough surfaces of electrical contacts are constructed and simulated, and the effects of different fractal parameters on the rough surface morphology are compared and analyzed. By studying the contact characteristics of sinusoidal asperities that retain the base diameter and height of the stacked structure asperities, a functional relationship between the real contact area of the rough surface and the load is derived, and a contact resistance network model is constructed accordingly, and the following conclusions are obtained.

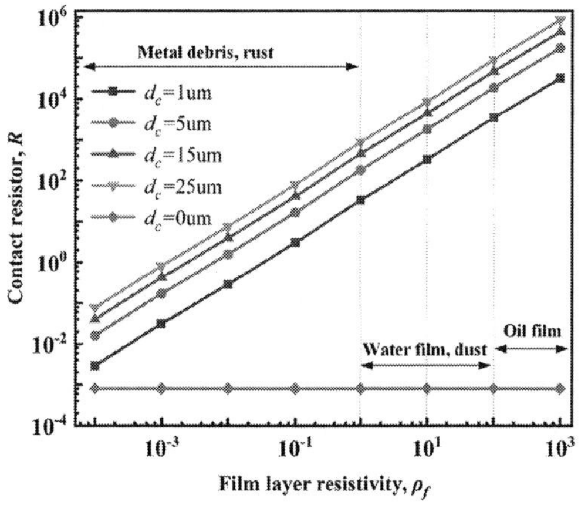

Fig. 11. Variation of ρ_f versus R

(1) The rough plane constructed by fractal theory and Monte Carlo stochastic method satisfies: the larger the fractal dimension D, the finer the rough surface; the larger the characteristic parameter G, the larger the height difference of the surface profile. This conclusion has the same characteristic law with the rough surface constructed by the traditional W-M function.

(2) When the fractal dimension D=1.5, the real contact area of the rough surface under the same contact pressure is the largest and the contact resistance is the smallest, which has the best contact characteristics; the contact load has an approximately linear relationship with the real contact area; the comparative analysis with the experimental data shows that the contact model established in this paper has good accuracy under light load conditions, but under heavy load conditions, due to the failure to consider the multi-scale coupling of asperities and contact spot There is a certain deviation under heavy load conditions because the multi-scale coupling of asperities and contact spots are not considered.

(3) The contaminated film layer on the contact surface is the most important factor affecting the contact resistance. The contact resistance under the contaminated film thickness d_c ≤1um and resistivity ρ_f ≤10^{-4}Ωm is of the same order of magnitude as the contact resistance on the clean surface.

Since the contact resistance plays a key role in the thermal performance and expected service life of electrical contacts, the model can provide a useful reference for reliability verification and optimal design of electrical equipment with multiple contacts, while the analysis of surface configuration and contact characteristics involved in this paper can be applied to other transport properties of rough surfaces, such as frictional wear, heat transfer, etc.

ACKNOWLEDGMENT

This work was supported by the National Natural Science Foundation of China under a major project priority NO. 92066206.

REFERENCES

[1] D. J. Whitehouse, "The properties of random surfaces of significance in their contact" , *A. Mathematical and Physical Sciences*. 1970，316(1524): 97-121.

[2] A. Majumdar, "Fractal model of elastic-plastic contact between rough surfaces" , *Journal of Tribology-Transactions of the Asme*. 1991, 113(1): 1-11.

[3] T. R. Thomas, "Fractal characterization of the anisotropy of rough surfaces" in *Wear*. 1990, 232(1): 41-50.

[4] J. A. Greenwood, "Contact of nominally flat surfaces" , *Proceedings of the royal society of London. Series A. Mathematical and physical sciences*. 1966, 295(1442): 300-319.

[5] X. Zhang, "The model of normal contact stiffness of joint interfaces incorporating elastoplastic deformation mechanism" , *Journal of Vibration Engineering*. 2015, 28(1): 91-99.

[6] Q. Chen, "Research on fractal model of normal contact stiffness between two spheroidal joint surfaces considering friction factor" , *Tribology International*. 2016, 97: 253-264.

[7] Z. Song, "Contact mechanics analysis of oscillatory sliding of a rigid fractal surface against an elastic–plastic half-space" in *Philosophical Magazine*. 2014, 94(28): 3215-3233.

[8] W. Fu, "Theoretical model for the contact stiffness and damping of mechanical joint surface", *Journal of Mechanical Engineering*.2017, 53(9): 73-82.

[9] X. Zhang, "Fractal model of tangential contact damping of plane joint interfaces with simulation", *Journal of Xi'an Jiaotong University*. 2011, 45(5):74-213.

[10] B. N. J Persson, "Elastic contact between randomly rough surfaces: comparison of theory with numerical results" , *Physical review B*. 2002, 65(18): 184106.

[11] Y. Zhao, "An asperity microcontact model incorporating the transition from elastic deformation to fully plastic flow" , *Journal of Tribology*. 2000, 122(1): 86-93.

[12] L. Kogut, "Elastic-plastic contact analysis of a sphere and a rigid flat", *Journal of Applied Mechanics*. 2002, 65(5): 657-662.

[13] R. L. Jackson, "A finite element study of elasto-plastic hemispherical contact against a rigid flat" in *Journal of Tribology*. 2005, 127(2): 343-354.

[14] M. Zhou, "A Monte Carlo method for simulating fractal surfaces" , *Physica A: Statistical Mechanics and its Applications*. 2007, 386(1): 176-186.

[15] V. Krithivasan, "An analysis of three-dimensional elasto-plastic sinusoidal contact" in *Tribology Letters*. 2007, 27(1): 31-43.

[16] M. Zhou, "Fractal model for thermal contact conductance" , *J. Heat Transfer*. 2008, 130(10):101301.

[17] Y. Y. Lau, "A higher dimensional theory of electrical contact resistance", *Journal of Applied Physics*. 2009, 105(12): 124902.

[18] B. Bushan, "The real area of contact in polymeric magnetic media—II: Experimental data and analysis" , *ASLE transactions*. 1985, 28(2):181-197.

Changgeng Zhang (M'2016) Changgeng Zhang was born in Heilongjiang, China, in 1985. He received the B.E. degree from Tianjin Polytechnic University, Tianjin, China, in 2009, the M.S. degree from Nankai University, Tianjin, China, in 2012, and the Ph.D. degree from the Hebei University of Technology (HEBUT), Tianjin, China, in 2017. From December 2018 to December 2019, he was a Visiting Scholar with the Ohio State University, Ohio, USA. He is currently an Associate Professor of electrical engineering in the School of Electrical Engineering, HEBUT. His research interests include magnetic properties measurement, finite element analysis, and modeling of magnetic materials.

Research on Spatial Positioning and Posture Recognition for Miniature Circuit Breaker Components Based on 3D Model Point Cloud Registration

Juntao Yan[1], Xiaofeng Xu[3], Ziran Wu[1, 2], Guichu Wu[3], Yaowei Wu[2], Weifei Qian[1], Haibo Xu[2]
[1] Technology Institute of Wenzhou University in Yueqing, Wenzhou, 325699, China
[2] Engineering Research Center of Low-Voltage Apparatus Technology of Zhejiang Province, Wenzhou University, Wenzhou, 325035, China
[3] Zhejiang Juchuang Smartech Co., Ltd., Wenzhou, 325036, China
E-mail: naturex@wzu.edu.cn, Tel: 18857745619

***Abstract*—The paper proposes a stereo-vision-based cross-source point cloud registration method that matches 3D models of components to the scene point clouds for spatial position and posture recognition in the flexible automatic assembly of miniature circuit breakers (MCBs). The 3D model of each component is converted to a model surface point cloud as a matching template by voxel down-sampling, and the scene point cloud is filtered, clustered, and segmented into candidate matching regions. A combination of rough matching and fine registration is applied to improve the matching precision. Point cloud features are extracted by Intrinsic Shape Signatures (ISS), described by Fast Point Feature Histogram (FPFH), and roughly matched by Sample Consensus Initial Alignment (SAC-IA). To improve the search efficiency, the fine registration employs Iterative Closest Point (ICP) with a K-dimensional Tree (KD-tree) and Random Sample Consensus (RANSAC) to improve the performance of ICP. The experimental result shows that the proposed method achieves a maximum matching angle error within ±0.5° and a maximum matching position error within ±0.2 mm. The precision meets the requirements of the flexible assembly of MCB components.**

***Index Terms*— 3D stereo vision; point cloud registration; posture recognition; flexible assembly**

I. INTRODUCTION

With the development of manufacture industry in China, the requirement for automatic flexible assembly increases quickly [1], [2]. At present, the 2D machine vision based on RGB cameras is the common choice in the automatic assembly area [3], [4]. However, since the 2D vision has no depth information, there are usually challenges in component recognition of complex scene including staking, height difference, blurred edge features, etc. [5], [6], which caused low precision, robustness and efficiency. The 3D vision can solve the issues that of high difficulties in the 2D vision [7]. However, 3D vision processing is majorly applied in assembly processes of relatively large-sized components, represented by automotive assembly [8], the applications for mini-sized components are not as popular because of the requirement of the point cloud and the processing algorithm. Therefore, there is a wide development space of the mini-sized components recognition research with 3D vision [9], [10]. There are multiple researchers contributing to this area. Birdal et al. [11] proposed a recognition method that cut the scene point cloud and matched by point-to-point features. However, it was unable to apply the occluded scene and could hardly get the precious recognition results. Wu et al. [12] proposed a 3D scene rebuild method based on fast point feature histogram and iterative closest point. Liu et al. [13] proposed a method that acquired the edge description symbol of point-to-point features to match with each other, but this method just selected a part of geometry features of the point cloud, which could guarantee the recognition robustness. The methods above come up with recognition matching to object of a single type component scene, there are some limitations in terms of matching precision and stability.

Different from the existing vision matching methods, this paper proposed a 3D vision recognition method which gets accurate position and posture of the inner components for miniature circuit breakers [14], shown by Fig. 1.

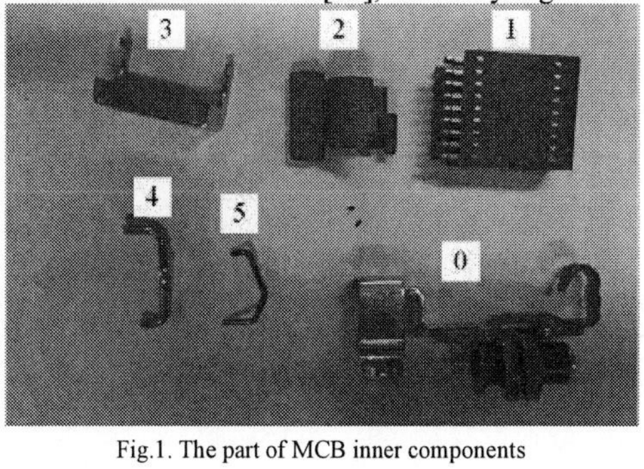

Fig.1. The part of MCB inner components

The components are mini-sized, multiplex-shaped and complex-structured, with blurred surfaces and edges. It is a big challenge of fast flexible assembly since it is very difficult to achieve position and posture accurately by efficient 2D vision processing. Therefore, a 3D-vision-based method is proposed for spatial positioning and posture recognition of MCBs components based on an improved matching process that applies the point clouds of the design models of the components. Compared with traditional point cloud approaches, the information and features of the surface point clouds sampled from the design models are completer and more sufficient, which is beneficial to improve the precision of point cloud registration. At the same time, the sampled design model has all surface information of the components, i.e., the type, position and posture of a component can be accurately matched in a scene with multiple components which are randomly placed and postured. The rough matching method is proposed under the consideration of balancing the efficiency and accuracy. A hybrid approach of multiple operators including Intrinsic Shape Signatures (ISS) [15], Fast Point Feature Histogram (FPFH) [16] and Sample Consensus Initial Alignment (SAC-IA) [16], [17] is applied. After the rough matching, a fine registration is used. To improve the search efficiency, the fine registration employs Iterative Closest Point (ICP) [15], [18] with a K-dimensional Tree (KD-tree) [19] which obtains a set of point pairs of minimum Euclidian distances between the source and target point clouds. Meanwhile, Random Sample Consensus (RANSAC) [20] is employed to remove incorrect matching point pairs to further improve the performance of the ICP algorithm. The proposed method can effectively resolve the local optimal problem that occurs in the classic ICP algorithm. Finally, the result is visualized by moving a design model to the registered position and posture.

II. Requirement and Scheme

A. Requirement Analysis

Considering the minimal diameter of an MCB component is approximately 1 mm, the precision of the point cloud camera must be higher than 0.1 mm.= In addition, in order to scan all components in the camera's field of view, the dimensions of the view field must be greater than 90 mm × 70 mm. Therefore, a Phoxi 3D Scanner XS point cloud camera with a precision of 0.055 mm using structured light is selected to meet the requirements. The main parameters of the camera are shown in Table I.

TABLE I

THE MAIN PARAMETERS OF THE POINT CLOUD CAMERA

Parameter	Value
Brand	Photoneo
Model Specifications	PhoXi 3D Scanner XS
Point to point distance (sweet spot)	0.055mm
Scanning range	161-205mm
Optimal scanning distance (sweet spot)	181mm
Scanning area (sweet spot)	118*78mm

B. Hardware Design

The hardware diagram of the 3D visual recognition system is shown in Fig.2. The system consists of four parts: a 3D point cloud camera, a component tray, MCB components, and a host PC. The 3D point cloud camera collects point clouds of the components on the tray, and sends the data to host PC. The host PC computes the registration between the 3D design models component point cloud via a series of point cloud processing algorithms proposed in this paper. of the devices of the 3D visual recognition system is shown in Fig. 3.

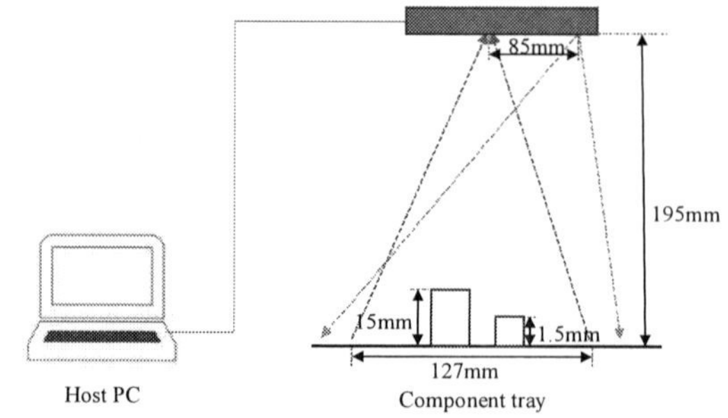

Fig.2. Hardware design of 3D visual recognition system

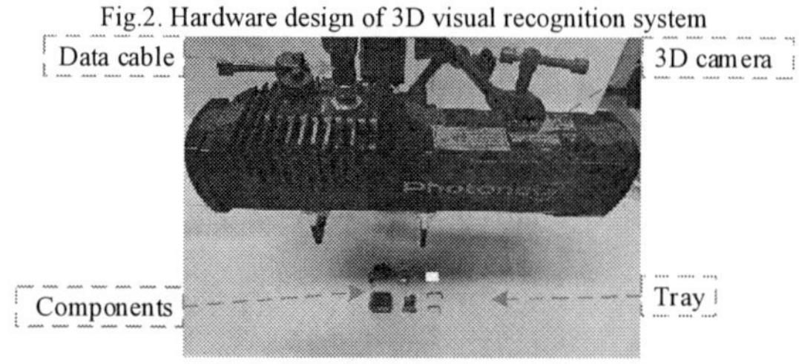

Fig.3. 3D visual recognition system

III. Recognition Process

The process of the 3D visual recognition is illustrated in Fig.4. The process is divided into four stages: preprocessing, rough matching, fine registration, and visualization.

A. Surface Point Clouds of Design Models

The preprocessing includes 3D design model sampling and scene point cloud acquisition, filtering, clustering, and segmentation. Since 3D models have richer feature information than model point cloud, in order to achieve the matching between point cloud pairs, the design models are down-sampled before matching. We convert design models into model surface point clouds (MSPCs) by a sampling interval of the camera precision (0.055 mm). Compared with traditional point cloud approaches, The MSPC that sampled from a design model contains more complete information and more sufficient features, which is beneficial to improve the accuracy of point cloud matching. At the same time, the sampled design model has all surface information of a component, therefore, the type, position and posture can be accurately matched in a scene with multiple randomly-postured components. Fig. 5 and Fig. 6 show the surface point cloud model obtained from the 3D design model.

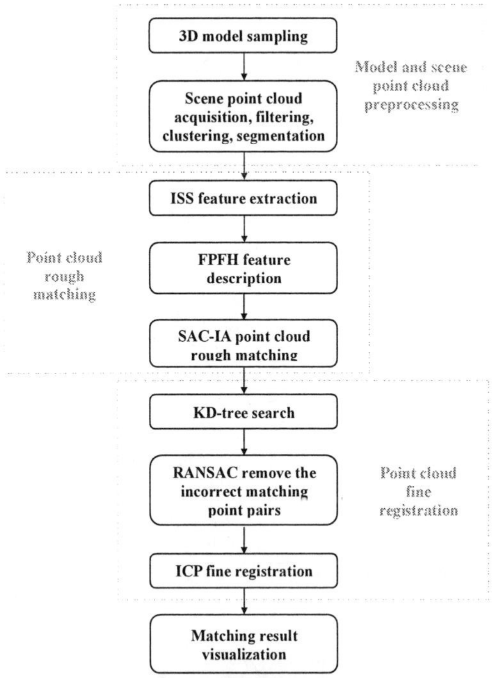

Fig. 4. The modular flow diagram of 3D visual recognition

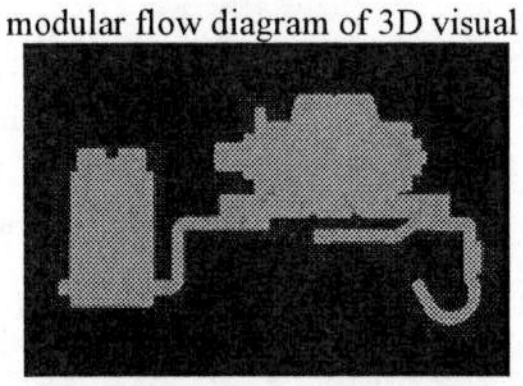

Fig. 5. 3D design model of the magnetic system component

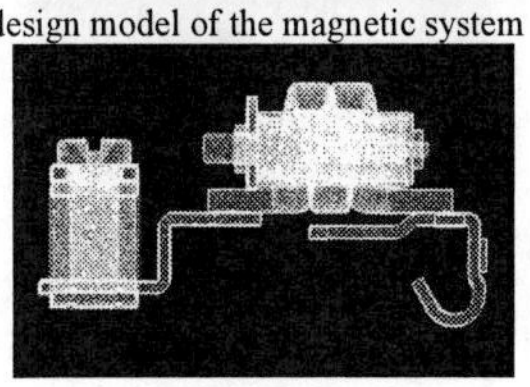

Fig.6.Sampled surface point cloud of the magnetic system component

B. Preprocessing of Scene Point Clouds

A scene point cloud is the point cloud of the area to be matched. It is obtained by the 3D point cloud camera. The preprocessing of the scene point cloud can avoid global matching and improve the matching efficiency. Before matching, the scene point cloud is filtered, clustered, and segmented to obtain candidate matching regions. In the subsequent matching process, only the candidate matching regions are matched. Hence, the matching efficiency is greatly improved. The origin scene point cloud in Fig. 7.

The original scene point cloud is down-sampled by voxel filtering, which simplifies the point cloud without loss of shape features. In the original scene point cloud (OSPC) acquired by the camera, a large part of the point cloud is the background of the tray, which is not useful and leads to mismatches, as well as increases the calculation. SAC segmentation [16] combined with parameter tuning is used to remove the background plane of the point cloud. The point cloud after removing the background plane is shown in Fig.8.

Fig. 7. The original scene point cloud

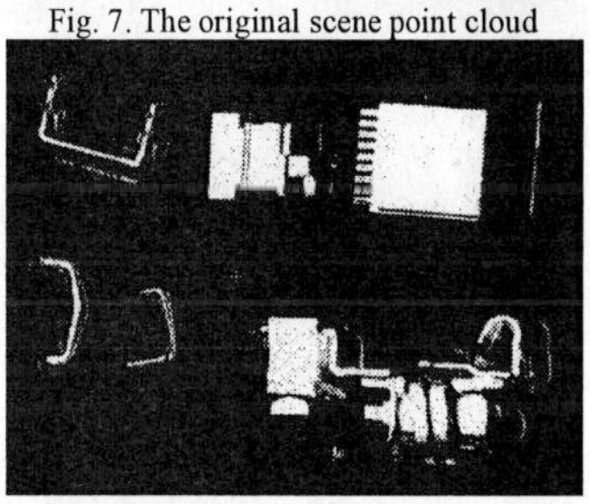

Fig. 8. Point cloud after removing background plane

The scene point cloud is clustered and segmented by the Euclidean distance. The upper and lower thresholds of the number of points in a point cloud cluster are determined according to the distribution of the number of points of the component. The point cloud clusters that are too large or too small, or too far from the center of clusters, are further filtered out. Finally, point cloud clusters meeting the requirements are kept. The segmented and filtered point cloud subsets (termed "candidate point clouds", CPC) are rendered in different colors to distinguish different point cloud regions, as shown in Fig. 9. The colored regions are selected as the candidates for rough matching and fine registration of the following stages.

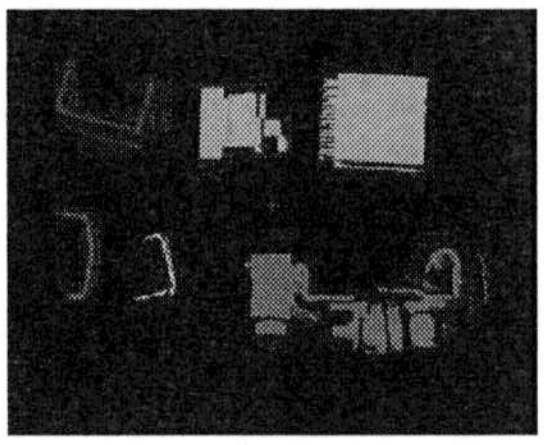

Fig. 9. Color rendering of cluster segmentation results

C. *Point Cloud Rough Matching*

Before applying the surface point cloud of a component to the processed scene point cloud for rough matching, the candidate regions with point counts close to the surface point cloud are selected, while the regions with significant point counts are skipped, to further improve the efficiency. The point cloud rough matching employs ISS [15] to extract point cloud features, and the FPFH operator [16] is used to describe the features. SAC-IA [17] is employed to roughly match the surface point cloud to the segmented point cloud. The procedure of the rough matching by SAC-IA are as following steps:

(1) select sampling points according to conditions: Select n sampling points from the candidate point cloud, and meanwhile, to ensure the discrimination of the FPFH features of each sampling point, the distance between each sampling point should be greater than the set threshold.

(2) search the corresponding point pair set: According to the FPFH features of the sampled points, nearest neighbor searching is used in the model surface point cloud to find the point pairs with the smallest difference between the FPFH features of the MSPC and the CPC, and RANSAC [20] is used to remove incorrectly matched point pairs to obtain optimized point pairs with similar feature set.

(3) obtain the optimal transformation parameters: First, the MSPC is transformed according to the matched point pair set obtained in Step 2, and then the matching effect is evaluated by the sum function of the distances between the transformed MSPC and the CPC. The Huber function is used to compute the sum function of the distance error.

$$Huber = \sum_{i=1}^{n} H(l_i) \tag{1}$$

$$H(l_i) = \begin{cases} \frac{1}{2} l_i^2, & \| l_i \| < m_l \\ \frac{1}{2} m_l (2 \| l_i \| - m_l), & \| l_i \| > m_l \end{cases} \tag{2}$$

where m_l is the preset threshold, l_i is the distance error of the *i-th* corresponding point pair after transform. The optimal transform is thus achieved for rough matching by finding the minimum error computed by equation (2).

As shown in Fig. 10, the original scene point cloud obtained by the 3D point cloud camera is color-rendered according to the depth information, which is used as a comparison before matching.

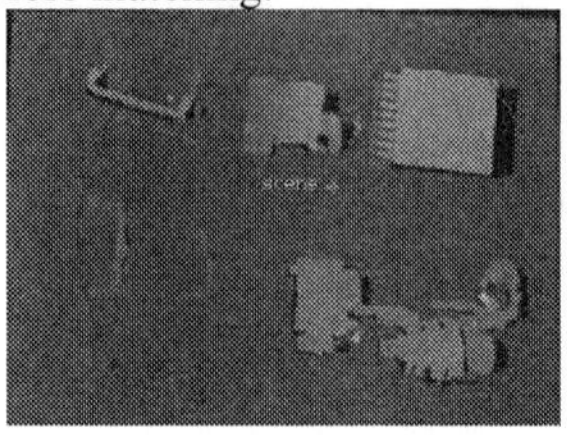

Fig. 10. Original scene point cloud rendering

Fig. 11 shows the match result obtained by the rough matching of the magnetic system component. It is illustrated that the rough matching process achieves the approximate position and direction, but the error can still be observed.

Fig. 11. Rough matching rendering

D. *Point Cloud Fine Registration*

The point cloud fine registration employs ICP [15] with a KD-tree [19] which obtains a set of point pairs of minimum Euclidian distances between the source and target point cloud. Meanwhile, RANSAC is employed to remove the incorrect matching point pairs to further improve the performance of ICP. The proposed method can effectively resolve the local optimal problem that occurs in the classic ICP algorithm. Since the precision of classic ICP is influenced by the initial position, the rough matching result is applied as the initial position of the fine registration to improve the effect of the iterative optimization of ICP.

Assuming the point set of the CPC is $S=\{s_1, s_2, s_3, \dots s_m\}$, where m is the point count of the CPC, and the transformed MSPC is $G=\{g_1, g_2, g_3, \dots g_n\}$, where n is the point count of the MSPC. The threshold of the mean squared error for each iteration is denoted by E. The threshold of the mean square error difference between two adjacent iterations is represented by e. The maximum number of optimization iterations is k_{max}. The iterative optimization process of the fine registration is described as following steps:

(1) obtain the optimized set of corresponding point pairs: Each g_i in G is searched within S to obtain a preliminary corresponding point pair set by finding the minimum Euclidean distance via the KD-tree search algorithm, and then the RANSAC algorithm is used to remove point pairs with large matching errors. Hence, the

optimized corresponding point pair set $\{(s_i, g_i) \mid i<n\}$ is obtained.

(2) get the transform parameters R and T according to the point pair set obtained in Step (1): the transform parameters R and T is achieved by finding the minimum value of the target function $f(R, T)$ as the optimization objective, obtain. The target function $f(R, T)$ is as follows:

$$f(R,T) = \frac{1}{n}\sum_{i=1}^{n} \| g_i - (Rs_i + T) \|^2 \quad (3)$$

(3) update the MSPC by the transform parameters R and T obtained in Step (2): The MSPC update formula is as follows, where k is the number of iterations, S_k is the point cloud before the update, and S_{k+1} is the point cloud after this update.

$$S_{k+1} = R\,S_k + T \quad (4)$$

(4) calculate iteratively and judge the threshold: The mean square error d_k and d_{k+1} after this iteration is calculated by the equation (5) and (6), and then a judgement whether any of the threshold conditions ($d_k<E$, $d_{k+1}-d_k<e$, $k>=k_{max}$) are met is performed. If any of the conditions are met, the iteration stops; otherwise, go back to Step (1).

$$d_k = \frac{1}{n}\sum_{i=1}^{n} \| g_i^k - s_i^k \| \quad (5)$$

$$d_{k+1} = \frac{1}{n}\sum_{i=1}^{n} \| g_i^{k+1} - s_i^{k+1} \| \quad (6)$$

(5) perform point cloud registration after iterative optimization: The result of the last iteration is used as the optimal matching, and the optimal transform parameters R and T is obtained. The MSPC is transformed by the parameters and registered to the CPC. Thus, the final registration is accomplished, as shown in Fig. 12, which is updated from the rough matching result shown in Fig. 11. It can be observed that the matching precision between the MSPC and the SPC, including both the position and the rotation, is significantly improved.

Fig. 12. Fine registration result rendering

E. *Visual Rendering of Registration Results*

As shown in Fig. 13, to verify the effectiveness of the matching method, six different components are tested, and the fine registration results are obtained in different scenes. Then, the 3D design model of the component is transformed by the rotation and translation matrices obtained by the point cloud fine registration, and the transformed model is fitted and rendered, so as to visually display the matching result. Meanwhile, the spatial position and rotation angle information of the component are displayed.

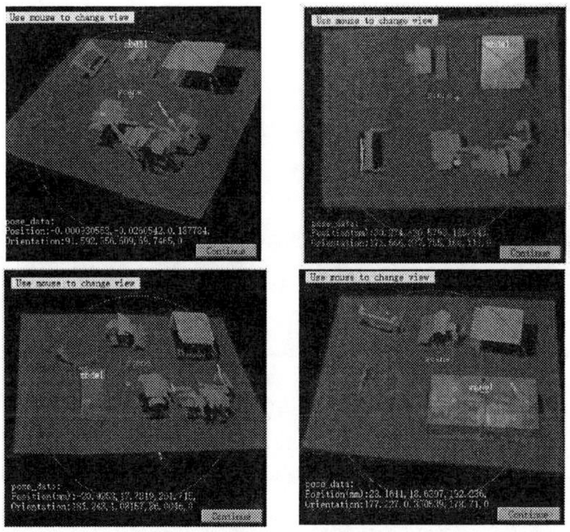

Fig.13. Visual rendering of various component recognition results

IV. Experiment and Analysis

As shown in Table II, to verify the effectiveness of the method proposed in this paper, the evaluation of NDT, classic ICP and our method are presented comparing matching errors. Selecting the magnetic system component as the example, the matching process is executed 10 times for each method. The comparison shows that NDT and classic ICP get higher matching errors than that of our method.

TABLE II
Matching Error Comparison Table of Different Methods

Method	Average value of position error(mm)	Average value of angle error(°)
NDT	2.16	3.28
Classic ICP	0.82	1.16
Our method	0.15	0.41

As shown in Table III, position and posture results of the matching for different components are presented. The type, position and rotation of each component is computed, and they are compared with the ground truth. The component labels correspond to the labels in Fig. 1. The ground-truth position (x, y, z) and rotation (α, β, γ) of a component are measured by an industrial robot, which uses its gripper to calibrate the appropriate gripping position and angle of the component. The camera scans the point cloud after the robot moves out of the field, and thus the matching results and the errors can be computed. Table III shows that the accuracy of type recognition reaches 100%, the maximum error of the rotation angle is (0.42, 0.41, 0.43)°, and the maximum position error is (0.17, 0.16, 0.15) mm. Multiple repetitive tests show the matching error is within ± 0.2 mm and ± 0.5°, which proves the high precision of the proposed method.

V. CONCLUSIONS

In this paper, a position and posture recognition method of MCB components by matching 3D design models to scene point clouds is proposed. The method combines point cloud rough matching with fine registration to reach high matching efficiency and accuracy. RANSAC is employed to remove the incorrect matching point pairs to further improve the performance of the ICP algorithm, which effectively resolve the local optimal problem of the classic ICP algorithm. The experimental result shows that the proposed method achieves a maximum matching angle error within ±0.5° and a maximum matching positioning error within ±0.2 mm. The precision meets the requirements of the flexible assembly for MCB components.

VI. ACKNOWLEDGEMENT

This work was supported in part by the Wenzhou Municipal Science and Technology Bureau under Grant ZG2020049, and in part by the Department of Education of Zhejiang Province under Grant Y202044245.

TABLE III

TYPE POSITION AND POSTURE OF COMPONENT RECOGNITION COMPARISON TABLE

Component label	rotation angle (α, β, γ) (°)			Gripping point coordinates (x, y, z) (mm)		
	The mean of the absolute value of the error: 0.337, 0.305, 0.272			The mean of the absolute value of the error: 0.117 ,0.133, 0.117		
	Standard deviation of the absolute value of the error: 0.076 ,0.099, 0.101			Standard deviation of the absolute value of the error: 0.034 ,0.028 ,0.020		
	Ground truth	Result	Error	Ground truth	Result	Error
0	0.00, 0.00, 40.00	0.41, 0.39, 40.43	0.41, 0.39, 0.43	-15.00, 18.00, 192.30	-15.13, 18.14, 192.20	-0.13, 0.14, -0.10
1	90.00, 0.00, 10.00	90.42, 0.26, 9.76	0.42, 0.26, -0.24	20.50, 30.00, 186.00	20.42, 30.16, 186.11	-0.08, 0.16, 0.11
2	60.00, 300.00, 70.00	59.72, 300.41, 69.65	-0.28, 0.41, -0.35	-10.00, -2.00, 187.50	-9.87, -2.15, 187.65	0.13, -0.15, 0.15
3	90.00, 45.00, 25.00	89.63, 45.34, 25.26	-0.37, 0.34, 0.26	-25.50, -5.00, 187.60	-25.39, -5.08, 187.49	0.11, -0.08, -0.11
4	20.00, 60.00, 5.00	20.31, 60.29, 5.19	0.31, 0.29, 0.19	30.00, -8.00, 191.70	30.08, -8.13, 191.60	0.08, -0.13, -0.10
5	22.00, 60.00, 7.00	22.23, 59.86, 7.16	0.23, -0.14, 0.16	15.00, -6.00, 193.50	15.17, -5.86, 193.63	0.17, 0.14, 0.13

REFERENCES

[1] Q. Zhou, R. Chen, H. Bin, C. Liu, J. Yu, and X. Yu, "An Automatic Surface Defect Inspection System for Automobiles Using Machine Vision Methods," *Sensors*, vol. 19, p. 644, Feb. 2019.

[2] R.-G. Zhou and D.-Q. Liu, "Quantum Image Edge Extraction Based on Improved Sobel Operator," *International Journal of Theoretical Physics*, vol. 58, pp. 1–17, Jun. 2019

[3] Kyle Krajewski, "Torque Control for Automated Assembly," *Assembly*, vol. 62, no. 10, pp. 56–58, 2019.

[4] V. G. Teodor, V. Păunoiu, F. Susac, and N. Baroiu, "Optimization of the measurement path for the car body parts inspection," *Measurement*, vol. 146, pp. 15–23, Nov. 2019.

[5] G. Xiao, Y. Li, Q. Xia, X. Cheng, and W. Chen, "Research on the on-line dimensional accuracy measurement method of conical spun workpieces based on machine vision technology," *Measurement*, vol. 148, p. 106881, Dec. 2019.

[6] John Sprovieri, "Automated Assembly System Roundup," *Assembly*, vol. 62, no. 11, pp. 66–69, 2019.

[7] C. Li, C. Yang, Z. Ju, and A. S. K. Annamalai, "An enhanced teaching interface for a robot using DMP and GMR," *Int J Intell Robot Appl*, vol. 2, no. 1, pp. 110–121, Mar. 2018.

[8] Z. Xiao, J. Gao, D. Wu, L. Zhang, and X. Chen, "A fast 3D object recognition algorithm using plane-constrained point pair features," *Multimed Tools Appl*, vol. 79, no. 39, pp. 29305–29325, Oct. 2020.

[9] Igor Jovančević *et al.*, "3D Point Cloud Analysis for Detection and Characterization of Defects on Airplane Exterior Surface," *Journal of Nondestructive Evaluation*, vol. 36, no. 4, 2017.

[10] G. Billings and M. Johnson-Roberson, "SilhoNet: An RGB Method for 6D Object Pose Estimation," *IEEE Robotics and Automation Letters*, vol. 4, no. 4, pp. 3727–3734, 2019.

[11] T. Birdal and S. Ilic, "Point Pair Features Based Object Detection and Pose Estimation Revisited," in *2015 International Conference on 3D Vision*, 2015, pp. 527–535.

[12] P. Wu, W. Li, and M. Yan, "3D scene reconstruction based on improved ICP algorithm," *Microprocessors and Microsystems*, vol. 75, p. 103064, Jun. 2020.

[13] D. Liu, S. Arai, J. Miao, J. Kinugawa, Z. Wang, and K. Kosuge, "Point Pair Feature-Based Pose Estimation with Multiple Edge Appearance Models (PPF-MEAM) for Robotic Bin Picking," *Sensors*, vol. 18, no. 8, Art. no. 8, Aug. 2018.

[14] Kui Li, Jianguo Lu, Yi Wu, Zhijun Qin, and Dongmei Yao, "Research on the overload protection reliability of moulded case circuit-breakers and its test device," *Journal of Zhejiang University(Science A:An International Applied Physics & Engineering Journal)*, no. 03, pp. 453–458, 2007.

[15] N. Senin, B. M. Colosimo, and M. Pacella, "Point set augmentation through fitting for enhanced ICP registration of point clouds in multisensor coordinate metrology," *Robotics and Computer-Integrated Manufacturing*, vol. 29, no. 1, pp. 39–52, Feb. 2013.

[16] R. B. Rusu, N. Blodow, and M. Beetz, "Fast Point Feature Histograms (FPFH) for 3D registration," in *2009 IEEE International Conference on Robotics and Automation*, 2009, pp. 3212–3217.

[17] R. B. Rusu, N. Blodow, Z. C. Marton, and M. Beetz, "Aligning point cloud views using persistent feature histograms," in *2008 IEEE/RSJ International Conference on Intelligent Robots and Systems*, Sep. 2008, pp. 3384–3391.

[18] P. J. Besl, "A method for registration of 3d shapes," *IEEE Transactions on Pattern Analysis and Machine Intelligence*, vol. 14, no. 2, pp. 239–256, 1992.

[19] N. Kalpitha, S. Murali, "Object Classification using SVM and KD-Tree," *International Journal of Recent Technology and Engineering*, vol. 8, no. 6, 2020.

[20] M. A. Fischler and R. C. Bolles, "Random Sample Consensus: A Paradigm for Model Fitting with Applications to Image Analysis and Automated Cartography," *Readings in Computer Vision*, M. A. Fischler and O. Firschein, Eds. San Francisco (CA): Morgan Kaufmann, 1987: 726–740.

Simulation and Research on Dynamic Characteristics of Temperature Rise and Heat Trip of Miniature Circuit Breaker

Haisheng Niu[1], Zhihong Xu[1,2,3]
[1]College of Electrical Engineering and Automation, Fuzhou University, Fuzhou, 350108, China
[2]Fujian Key Laboratory of New Energy Generation and Power Conversion, Fuzhou, 350108, China
[3]Fujian Province University Engineering Research Center of Smart Distribution Grid Equipment, Fuzhou, 350108, China
E-mail: 641936593@qq.com Tel: 13178116282

Abstract—**Miniature circuit breakers belong to long-term access to the electrical circuit, and its steady-state operation is directly related to its performance. Too high temperature rise will reduce its service life and reliability, resulting in security risks. Taking the miniature circuit breaker as the research object, this paper establishes the three-dimensional simulation model of its temperature field, and simulates the temperature rise characteristics. According to the structural characteristics of miniature circuit breaker, the heat exchange way is changed, and the wiring terminal is exposed to the external air for convection heat dissipation. The effectiveness is verified by the temperature rise results obtained from the experiment. On this basis, the electro-thermo-structural coupling simulation of bimetallic strip thermal release is carried out. The simplified two-layer model of bimetal and the three-layer model based on multi-layer theory are constructed and compared. It is concluded that the three-layer model can better reflect the thermal deformation characteristics of bimetallic strip. In order to improve the reliability of circuit breaker overload protection, building a parametric virtual prototyping design platform for miniature circuit breaker. Based on the platform, parametric analysis of the width, thickness and effective heating length of the bimetallic strip is carried out to determine the key structural parameters affecting the tripping characteristics.**

Index Terms—**Bimetallic strip, parametric analysis, temperature rise characteristics, thermal overload releaser, virtual prototyping design platform**

I. INTRODUCTION

Miniature circuit breakers are widely used in power distribution systems to protect against overload and overcurrent. In overload protection, the bimetallic strip is generally used. The working principle is that metals with different expansion coefficients are welded together and then bend to the side with a lower expansion coefficient when heated, which drives the mini-circuit breaker operating mechanism to complete tripping and realize overload protection. Therefore, the tripping characteristics of the thermal release directly affect the protection ability of the circuit breaker. In order to improve the stability of overload protection, it is not only necessary to improve the accuracy of the thermal tripping model, but also to change the traditional development method which only uses experiments.

The simulation of circuit breaker temperature rise needs to simplify the complex internal structure. In reference [1], the simplified interior is filled with air, convection is ignored and the equivalent thermal conductivity is calculated as the thermal conductivity of the internal air. In literature [2], two composite heat dissipation coefficients composed of convective heat dissipation coefficient and radiation heat dissipation coefficient are calculated. The composite heat dissipation coefficient in large space is used to simulate the natural convective heat dissipation of external air and shell, and the composite heat dissipation coefficient in restricted space is loaded onto the surface of the inner part of the circuit breaker. The conductive loop that is not in contact with the shell is covered by air, which neglects the convective heat dissipation between the terminal and the air.

At present, among the two types of protection of mini-circuit breakers, there are many researches on overcurrent protection, which focus on multi-body dynamics simulation of magnetic trip. There is a complete simulation process and secondary development of this. However, there are relatively few studies on the simulation of overload protection. Literature [3] studies the general design method of thermal bimetal sheet of mini-circuit breaker and the regulation method of technical parameters. Combined with experiments and simulations, literature [4] introduces the influence of temperature variation of thermal bimetallic elements on thermal deformation displacement and thrust, and analyzes the influence of other factors such as temperature range and welding quality on delay tripping characteristics. Literature [5] establishes a detailed and complete model including the middle layer according to the structure of the bimetallic strip, simulates the temperature change and deformation process at different times, and obtains the thermal trip time.

In order to improve the stability of overload protection of miniature circuit breaker, this paper introduces the theory of multi-layer calculation in modeling, constructs a more accurate 3D simulation model of thermal release, and makes a comparative analysis with the commonly used double-layer model. In the aspect of simulation, a virtual prototyping design platform for temperature field of miniature circuit breaker is developed by using advanced programming language, and the structural parameters are analyzed.

II. Miniature Circuit Breaker Virtual Prototype Model

A. Construction of Miniature Circuit Breaker

The structure of miniature circuit breaker is shown in Fig.1. The rated working current is 63A and it is mainly composed of magnetic trip, operating mechanism, arc extinguishing system, conductive loop and thermal overload releaser. During normal operation, the operating mechanism is artificially pushed to complete the closing and locking state, and the thermal release device of the conductive loop system monitoring the current.

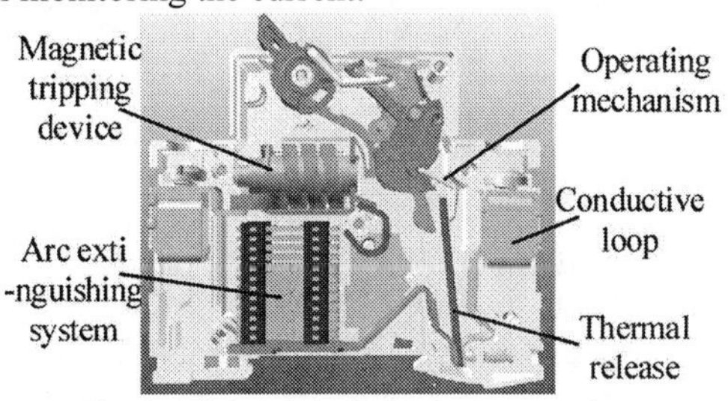

Fig. 1. Miniature circuit breaker construction.

B. Temperature Field Calculation Model of Miniature Circuit Breaker

The Miniature circuit breaker generates joule heat from the conducting loop at the rated current. Heat dissipation can be accomplished through contact with the internal air and the outer shell, convection heat dissipation between the outer shell and the outer shell, and convection heat dissipation between the terminal and the outer air. When the heat exchange between the system and the environment ends, the thermal equilibrium state is reached. The differential equation of steady state thermal analysis is:

$$\lambda(\partial^2 T \partial x^{-2} + \partial^2 T \partial y^{-2} + \partial^2 T \partial z^{-2}) = -q_v \quad (1)$$

For transient thermal analysis, the differential equation is:

$$\rho c \partial T \partial t^{-1} = \lambda\left(\partial^2 T \partial x^{-2} + \partial^2 T \partial y^{-2} + \partial^2 T \partial z^{-2}\right) + q_v \quad (2)$$

In the above formula, ρ is density, c is specific heat, T is temperature, λ is thermal conductivity, q_v is heat of formation per unit volume, T is time, x, y, z are coordinate components.

The heat source for the normal operation of the miniature circuit breaker is the conductive loop system, which is wrapped in the internal air of the appliance and a small amount is in direct contact with the shell. The main heat dissipation way is heat exchange of conductive loop and internal air, heat conduction of internal air and shell contact, thermal convection of shell and external air. It can be seen from the structural characteristics of the research object that the circuit breaker isolates the terminal from the internal air by using the baffle of the shell itself, and most areas of the terminal is exposed to the external air. The material of the conductive loop system parts has high thermal conductivity, and the heat transmitted between parts of conductive circuit cannot be simply treated as heat conduction through contact with the internal air, which is a relatively inefficient way of heat dissipation. Therefore, the heat dissipation route is changed to expose the wiring terminals and dissipate heat by natural convection with the external air. The heat dissipation coefficient adopts the large-space composite heat dissipation coefficient that changes with the temperature [2]. The whole heat dissipation path is shown in Fig.2, CV stands for thermal convection and CD stands for heat conduction.

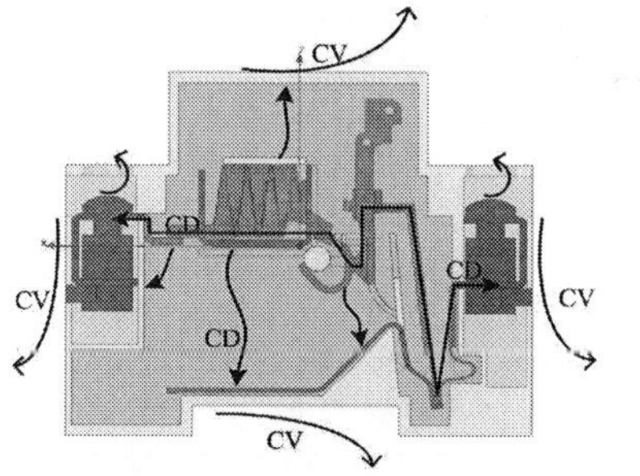

Fig. 2. Heat dissipation path of miniature circuit breaker.

C. Simulation model of Thermal Overload Releaser

In the multi-field coupling simulation of the bimetallic strip, in addition to the active layer and passive layer, there is also a third metallic layer to improve both electrical and thermal conductivity. Generally, it is necessary to simplify the model and adopt a double-layer structure, and the theoretical deflection is obtained by VillarCeau formula [6]. It can be seen that when $E_1=E_2$ and $t_1=t_2$, K can achieve the maximum deflection, that is, the structural parameters of the passive layer and the active layer are consistent. The elastic modulus of the passive layer and the active layer of the bimetallic strip is different, so the thickness values t_1 and t_2 are different according to the formula. The bilayer simplified simulation model takes the same thickness value, the resistivity and elastic modulus are also the same, and the thermal expansion coefficient needs to be modified according to the temperature flexivity.

$$K = 1.5(\alpha_2 - \alpha_1)\Delta T(t_1 + t_2)^{-1}$$
$$\left(1 + 0.25\left(E_1 t_1^2 - E_2 t_2^2\right)^2 E_1^{-1} t_1^{-1} E_2^{-1} t_2^{-1}(t_1 + t_2)^{-1}\right) \quad (3)$$

Where α_1 and α_2 are the expansion coefficients. E_1 and E_2 are the elastic modulus . ΔT is the temperature rise. t_1 and t_2 are the thickness.

A common bimetallic strip contains only active and passive layers. A resistive thermal bimetallic strip having the property of controlling the tripping characteristic by varying the magnitude of the current, generally consisting of three or more layers of material. In order to increase the application range and resistance margin of the bimetallic strip, an intermediate layer is added. *Cu* and *Ni* with low resistivity and moderate thermal expansion coefficient are selected. According to the temperature flexivity, resistivity and material parameters of each layer of the bimetallic strip, the theoretical thickness ratio of the three-layer bimetallic strip can be obtained from the following formula:

$$\begin{cases} S_1 + S_2 + S_3 = 1 \\ \rho_1\rho_2\rho_3\left(S_1\rho_2\rho_3 + S_2\rho_1\rho_3 + S_3\rho_1\rho_2\right)^{-1} = \rho_b \\ M\left(M_1 + M_2 + M_3\right)\left(n_1 + n_2 + n_3 + N_1 + N_2 + N_3\right)^{-1} = F_b \end{cases} \quad (4)$$

Where, $S_i(i=1,2,3)$ is the thickness ratio of each layer. $E_i(i=1,2,3)$ is the elastic modulus of each layer. $\rho_i(i=1,2,3)$ is the resistivity of each layer. ρ_b is the comprehensive resistivity. F_b is the temperature flexivity.

When calculating the thickness ratio of each layer, there will be more than one solution, so it is necessary to screen the results. In the three-layer theoretical calculation, only the temperature flexivity and comprehensive resistivity of the bimetallic strip are used, and the comprehensive elastic modulus is not used. Therefore, the comprehensive elastic modulus of the bimetallic strip model obtained by theory is calculated and compared with the nameplate value. There are two ways to calculate the comprehensive elastic modulus (5) and (6):

$$E_b = \sum_{i=1}^{3} E_i S_i \quad (5)$$

$$(1-\mu_b)\delta^{-1}\sum_{i=1}^{3} E_i S_i \delta (1-\mu_i)^{-1} = E_b \quad (6)$$

$$\mu_b = \left(\sum_{i=1}^{3} E_i S_i \mu_i \left(1-\mu_i^2\right)^{-1}\right) / \left(\sum_{i=1}^{3} E_i S_i (1-\mu_i)^{-1}\right) \quad (7)$$

Where, $u_i(i=1,2,3)$ is the poisson's ratio of each layer. u_b is the comprehensive poisson's ratio. and δ is the thickness.

Equation 5 calculates the radial equivalent elastic modulus of bimetallic strip directly according to the proportion of each layer. Equation 6 ignores the effect of each layer, assumes that the material is homogeneous, introduces the influence of poisson's ratio, and the result is better than equation 6.

The bimetallic strip used in this paper belongs to a series of high sensitive resistors. The active and passive layers are Mn72Ni10Cu18 and Ni36 respectively, and the middle layer is Cu. The calculation results of thickness ratio are as follows:

Table 1 the ratio of each layer and error value

passive layer	middle layer	active layer	error value
0.2335	0.3503	0.4162	8.72 %

III. SIMULATION RESULT AND EXPERIMENTAL VERIFICATION

A. Simulation Result of Temperature Rise

Fig.3 shows the temperature rise distribution diagram inside the miniature circuit breaker. It can be seen that the temperature at the contact, braided wire, and bimetal solder joint are high. There is a difference in the temperature rise of the terminals. The contact position of moving contact and static contact appears at the highest temperature point. The main reason is that there is conductive spot between them, which simulate contact resistance, and due to small cutting area and length, its heat dissipation ability is weak.

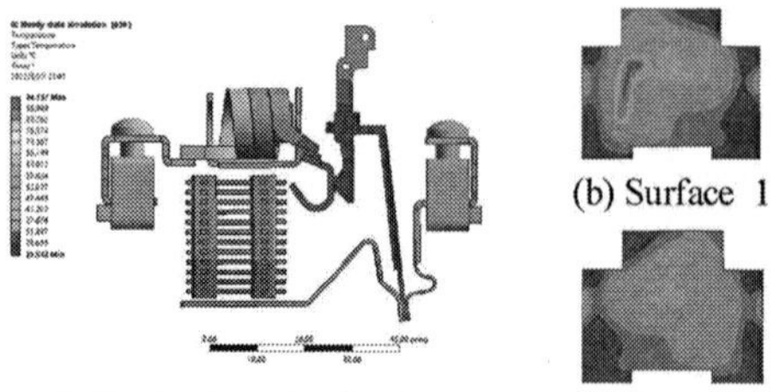

(a) Internal conductive loop (b) Surface 1 (c) Surface 2

Fig. 3. Simulation result of temperature rise.

Fig. 3 (b) and (c) show the temperature distribution of the shell. In Figure (b), the higher temperature is the contact position between braided wire and shell. In Figure (c), the highest temperature is located in the center due to the contact between the static contact and the shell.

B. Simulation Results of Thermal Trip and Comparison of Two Simulation Models

This section compares the equivalent simplified two-layer model with the three-layer model established by theoretical calculation. The simulation power supply adopts 1.13In. The material settings of each layer are the resistivity, elastic modulus, density of the bimetallic strip, and their expansion coefficients are modified by the flexivity. The materials of each layer of the three-layer model are set according to the properties of the layer itself.

Electric field simulation results of the two simulation models are shown in Fig. 4. The current starts from the welding spot and passes through the bimetal strip to the connecting plate. The difference between the two models lies in the current path in the bimetal strip. In the three-layer model, because the conductivity of copper is much higher than that of the other two layers, most of the current passes through the middle layer, while in the two-layer model, the current flow of each layer is approximately equal.

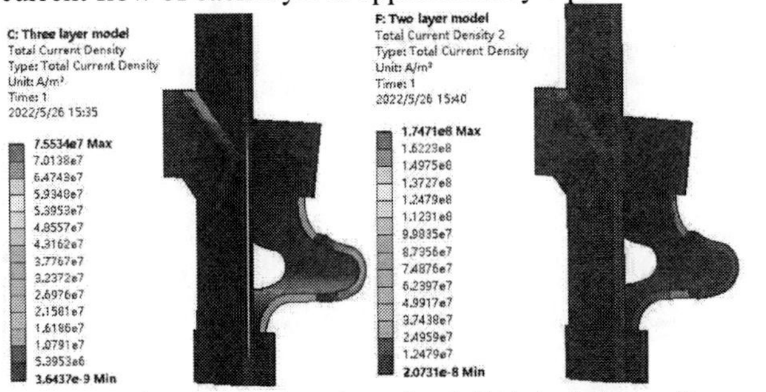

Fig. 4. Three-layer and two-layer electric field simulation results.

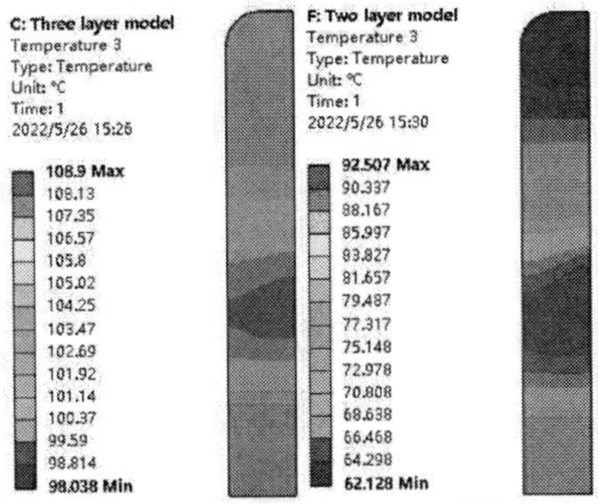

Fig. 5. Three-layer and two-layer temperature field simulation results.

Fig. 5 Simulation results of temperature. For the temperature distribution of the two-layer model, the high temperature area is mainly concentrated near the welding spot, and the difference between the lowest temperature end and the highest temperature spot is large. For the temperature distribution of the three-layer model, the high temperature zone is concentrated at the welding spot, and the highest temperature difference is within 10 K. Cu intermediate layer has higher thermal conductivity, which makes heat conduction higher, so the temperature distribution of the three-layer model is more uniform than that of the simplified two-layer model. At the same time, due to the difference of electric field joule heat, the maximum temperature difference between the two models is 12 K. It can be seen that the copper layer can not only improve the resistance characteristics of the bimetallic strip, but also improve the temperature distribution, which is beneficial to deformation.

Fig. 6 shows the simulation results of the structural field. The deformation of the three-layer model is larger than that of the two-layer model, which is close to 0.2mm.

From the above comparison, it can be seen that the three-layer simulation model, compared with the two-layer model, can better simulate the distribution characteristics of each field of the bimetallic strip. However, the proportion of each layer calculated by multi-layer theory is different from that of the actual product [6], which is caused by problems such as material characteristics and technology. The correction coefficient is given in reference [7], which is comprehensively determined by the three factors of temperature, composite speed and material deformation characteristics during bimetallic strip composite, ranging from 1.0 to 1.8. At the same time, when calculating the proportion of each layer, it can be seen that the theoretical results are greatly affected by the resistivity, thermal expansion coefficient, elastic modulus and other parameters of each layer material. Slight fluctuations, resulting in significant changes in results. Therefore, there are still some problems to be solved when multi-layer model is applied to simulation.

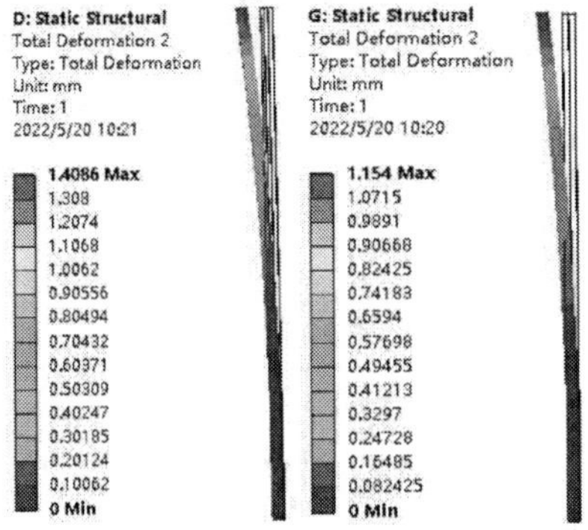

Fig. 6. Three-layer and two-layer structural field simulation results.

C. *Experimental Verification*

In order to verify the simulation model, a miniature circuit breaker temperature rise experiment system is built. The temperature is measured by a JK-32C multi-channel thermometer with an external K-type thermocouple. The rated current, 1.13In in cold state and 1.45In in hot state are measured respectively. The experimental site is shown in Fig. 7. The measuring points of thermocouple include moving contact, static contact, incoming terminal, terminal, free end and welding point of bimetallic strip. The temperature rise of the shell end cover and base is extracted by shooting with a thermal imager.

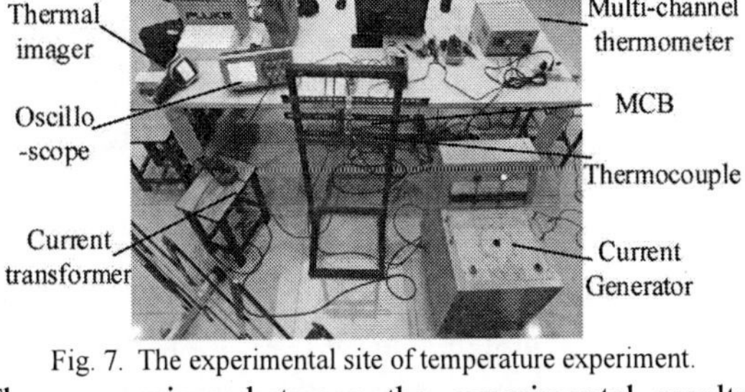

Fig. 7. The experimental site of temperature experiment.

The comparison between the experimental results of temperature rise and the simulation is shown in Fig. 8, including the stable temperature rise of rated current at each measurement point and the transient temperature rise of 1.45In in the hot state of the bimetallic strip. It can be seen that the error of the simulation results is within the permissible range.

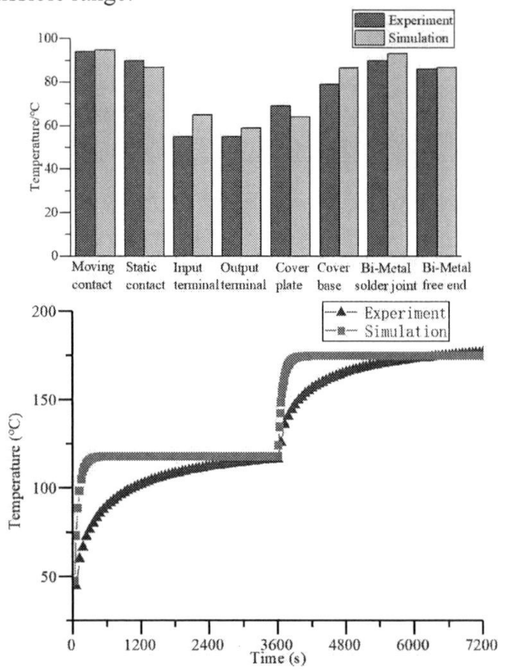

Fig. 8. Comparison between simulation and experiment.

IV. INFLUENCE ANALYSIS OF STRUCTURAL PARAMETERS OF BIMETALLIC STRIP

In order to design and analyze miniature circuit breaker quickly and efficiently, this paper uses C# programming language to establish a virtual prototyping design platform. The effective heating length, the width and the thickness of the bimetal strip are simulated, and determine the value range of optimization variables.

A. Virtual Prototyping Design Platform.

The interface of temperature field simulation platform is shown in Fig. 9, which consists of four modules: structure parameter setting, material setting, simulation setting and result display. According to the tree structure input simulation parameters, and then call the software to calculate, and finally display the post-processing results. The main function of the simulation setting module is to select different loads, including 1.13In, 1.45In in hot state and 2.25In, and configure different simulation time accordingly.

The simulation design framework is shown in Fig.10. The C# program obtains structural parameters, materials, simulation settings and other parameters. Then, it writes them into the Python script driving the Workbench home page. This script file is executed while the software is running on the interface to realize the interaction with ANSYS Workbench. Python scripts include calls to JScript required by Mechanical and DM modules to realize meshing, load setting, result output and other functions.

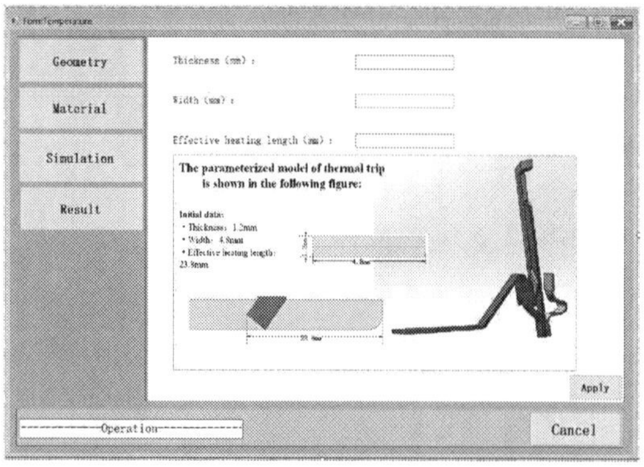

Fig. 9. Virtual prototyping design platform.

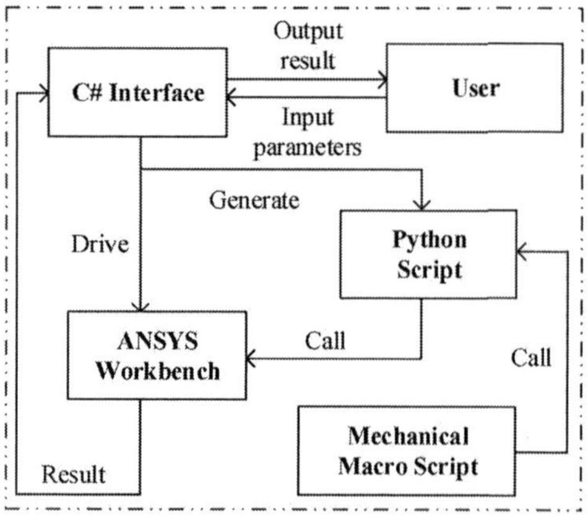

Fig. 10. Simulation design framework.

B. Parameter Analysis of Bimetal Strip Structure

By changing the structure size of the bimetal strip, the thermal tripping characteristics can be adjusted to improve the stability of overload protection. The width of the bimetal strip varies from 3mm to 4.8mm, the thickness from 2mm to 5mm, and the effective heating length is 5mm to 33mm. The offset required for tripping of the object in this paper is 1.5mm, and the tripping force is 0.588~0.784 N.

Fig. 11 shows the influence of bimetallic strip thickness on tripping parameters. With the increase of thickness, the conductive cross-sectional area increases, the resistance decreases, and the joule heat generated decreases, resulting in a downward trend of temperature rise and deformation, and an increase in thrust. Therefore, according to tripping requirements, the thickness size is selected as 0.8~1.2mm, which can ensure no tripping at 1.13In and tripping at 1.45In.

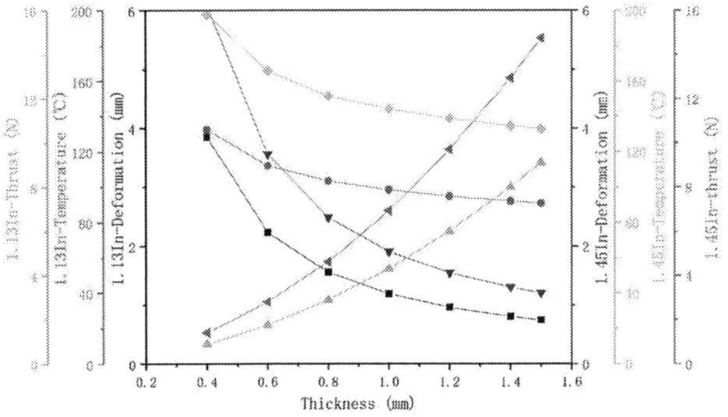

Fig. 11. Influence curve of different thickness.

Fig. 12 shows the influence of the width of the bimetallic strip on the tripping parameters. The influence of the width on temperature rise and deformation is negatively correlated. With the increase of the width, the thrust gradually increases. Width variation is independent of deflection, but is proportional to thrust, and temperature is proportional to thrust, so overall thrust shows an increasing trend. The selection of the width size needs to take into account the size of the shell, ranging from 5 to 10mm.

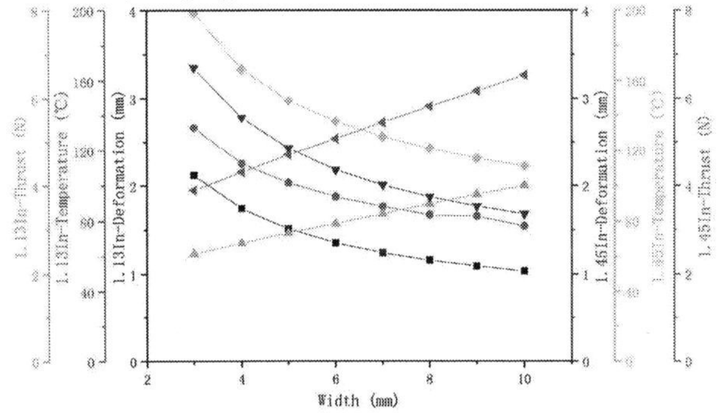

Fig. 12. Influence curve of different width.

In the case of different effective heating length, the curves of temperature rise, deformation and thrust are shown in Fig. 13. With the increase of effective heating length, the three factors increase gradually, and the change is close to linear. The selection of effective heating length is 6~10mm.

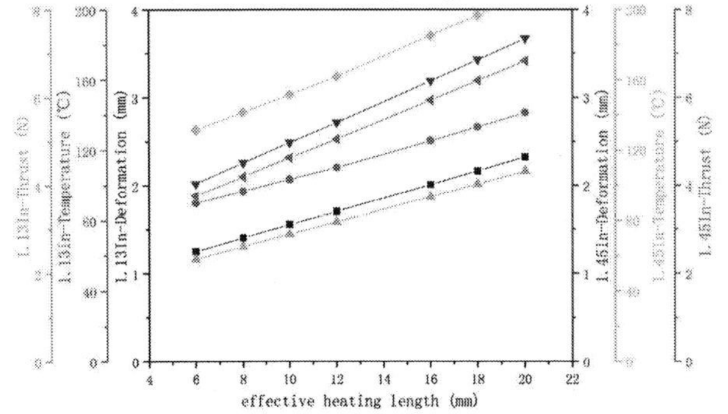

Fig. 13. Influence curve of different effective heating length.

V. Conclusion

Focusing on the overload protection of miniature circuit breaker, this paper establishes the temperature field simulation model and multi - field coupling simulation model of electrical - thermal - structure coupling of thermal overload releaser. The accuracy of the model is verified by experiments. The following conclusions are obtained:

1) The heat dissipation path of the miniature circuit breaker is improved. According to its structure, the terminals wrapped by the internal air are exposed and convective heat dissipation is conducted with the external air, so as to better restore the temperature rise distribution of the miniature circuit breaker to achieve thermal balance.

2) From the aspects of electric field, temperature field and structure field, the simplified two-layer model and the three-layer model obtained by multi-layer theoretical calculation are compared and analyzed. The simulation model based on the three-layer bimetallic strip thermal overload releaser can simulate the working characteristics more realistically, but there are still some problems such as thickness ratio that needs to be corrected.

3) Based on the thermal release simulation model, a virtual prototyping design platform is established to analyze the influence of structural parameters of bimetallic strip thickness, width and effective heating length on temperature rise, deformation and thrust, and determine the selection range of three key parameters affecting overload protection.

References

[1] Frei P U, Weichert H O. Advanced thermal simulation of a circuit breaker[C]// Proceedings of the 50th IEEE Holm Conference on Electrical Contacts and the 22nd International Conference on Electrical Contacts Electrical Contacts, 2004. IEEE, 2004.

[2] Li Feng. Simulation research on temperature field of miniature circuit breaker[D]. Hebei University of Technology,2016

[3] XU Wenliang, He Weilong. Thermal overload protection for low voltage apparatus and simulation of thermal bimetal[J], Electrical & Energy Management Technology, 2021(6):6

[4] Zhu Cong, Xu Tingwei, Luo Xinyu, Zhu Min. Optimal design MCCB bimetallic strip based on Workbench[J]. Marine Electric & Electronic Technology, 2021, 41(5):5.

[5] HU Jinli. Simulation and experimental study on thermal trip of MCB[J]. Electrical & Energy Management Technology,2021.

[6] Zhu Daming, Pan Hao, Wang Hao. Determination the thickness ratio of thermal bimetallic components[J]. Electrical Engineering Materials, 1999, 000(002):33-35.

[7] Xu Zhuohui. Resistance series thermal bimetallic material design and manufacturing[J]. Low Voltage Apparatus, 1998(6):3.

First Author, Haisheng Niu is currently pursuing the M.S. degree in the College of Electrical Engineering and Automation, Fuzhou University, Fuzhou, China. His current research interests include electrical appliances and simulation technology.

Corresponding Author, Xu Zhihong (1963-), professor and doctoral supervisor, with research interests in electrical appliances and intelligent technology, 641936593@qq.com.

8th International Conference on Reliability of
Electrical Products and Electrical Contacts,
November 18-20, 2022

Application of DOE in Accelerated Life Testing (ALT)

Guangzhi Zhang, Asia Wang

Shanghai Liangxin Electrical Co., Ltd., Shanghai, 201315, China
E-mail: zhangguangzhi@sh-liangxin.com Tel: 18621550069

***Abstract*—With the continuous development of Chinese Electric power system, the life requirements of Low-Voltage Electrical Apparatus are becoming higher and higher, and the time cycle of product life verification is becoming longer and longer. The traditional life verification method has been unable to meet the needs, so it is necessary to introduce the Accelerated Life Testing technology to shorten the test cycles. Firstly, this paper introduced the method and advantages of Accelerated Life Testing (ALT). The problem often encountered in the formulation of ALT scheme is put forward, that is, how to obtain the effective combination of acceleration factors under the existing conditions. At present, the method of changing one factor at a time (OFAT) can be used to find the effective factors, but the number of testing is too many. Then, the method of Design for Six Sigma and one of its tools-Design of Experiment (DOE) is introduced. By using OFAT and DOE to analyze the same case, it is found that DOE method can greatly improve the selection efficiency of acceleration factor combination, and the validity of the test scheme generated by DOE is verified by software. Then the test scheme generated by DOE was tested in real project, and the results were compared with the original data, which further verified that the accelerated life testing method can effectively improve the efficiency of product life testing.**

***Index Terms*— DOE (Design of Experiments), ALT (Accelerated Life Test), Electrical Life Testing.**

I. INTRODUCTION

In the process of new product developing, we generally define the objectives of the product at the concept stage, including the life timing. In the detailed design stage, we will tear down the objective into various design elements. In the verification stage, we will test samples to verify whether the designed objectives are met or not. Most of functional objectives can be tested in a short time, but the verification of life timing needs to be through a long time of testing, and the product development cycle does not allow too long testing time, so it needs accelerated life testing (ALT).

II. ACCELERATED LIFE TESTING (ALT)

The normal life testing is verified the time that the sample can be worked or stored under normal service stress. ALT (Accelerated Life Test) refers to the method of using stress greater than normal to make the sample fail in a short time, so as to predict the reliability under normal working or storage conditions. ALT is mature testing method based on statistical theory. On the basis of reasonable engineering statistical assumptions, it is a test method to use the statistical model related to the physical failure law to convert the reliability information obtained in the accelerated environment beyond the normal stress level, and obtain the reproducible numerical estimation of the reliability characteristics of the sample under normal service conditions. China has specially launched the national standard GB/T 34986-2017 Product Acceleration Test Method for Accelerated Life Testing. The premise of accelerated life testing is to ensure that the failure mechanism of product is not changed.

ALT [1,2] can greatly save product developing and testing time and costs, and improve product development progress. However, a series of problems will be encountered when designing the accelerated life test plan, such as: what are the effective accelerated stress factors? How to arrange these acceleration factors? Which values are appropriate? How to prepare the test plan? How to arrange the number of samples? Is it fixed number truncation or fixed time truncation? These problems will be confused by each engineer. In the early stage, almost everyone's test plan is to change the value of one accelerated stress, while the other stresses remain fixed. After understood the distribution of this accelerated stress; Then adjust the value of the second accelerated stress, and keep other stresses unchanged. After finding out the distribution of the second accelerated stress, study the third......, This method needs to find out the most influential accelerated stress factors by comparison after all the accelerated stress factors are found out, and then carry out the combined test to finally get the optimal accelerated test scheme. Although this method has greatly saved the time of life test, it can be operated in this way before learning Six Sigma Design.

III. DESIGN OF EXPERIMENTS

Six Sigma Design has brought us a very useful tool for accelerating life test --- design of experiments(DOE) [3] . DOE was first proposed by British Ronald Fisher in the 1920s, and achieved fruitful results in the practice of agricultural production. The proposal of DOE greatly improved the R & D efficiency of scientists in their research fields. In the 1930s and 1940s, it was gradually promoted and applied in industrial production in Britain and America, and was introduced into China in the early 1960s, and was strongly promoted and applied. DOE refers to a series of systematic tests, in which the input factors are changed pertinently, so as to determine the reasons for significant changes of output response. Through the definition of DOE, we can find that the purpose of accelerated life test is consistent with DOE.

Originally, the method we used to accelerate the life test research is to change one parameter at a time - OFAT (one factor at a time), as shown in Figure 1; DOE is a method to change several parameters at the same time, as shown in Figure 2; OFAT is feasible when accelerated stress A and accelerated stress B simultaneously affect the dependent response - life test time t, and A and B both do not affected each other; However, OFAT is not enough if A and B have superimposed effect, and hybrid test is also required.

DOE is much more efficient than OFAT method. It can consider the effects of multiple accelerated stresses at one time (parallel analysis); At the same time, consider the interaction between different stress factors; Obtain as much information as possible through the least number of tests; It can better find the optimal accelerated test scheme in the accelerated life test.

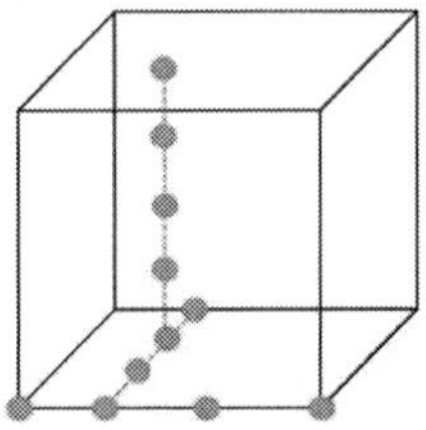

Figure 1 OFAT

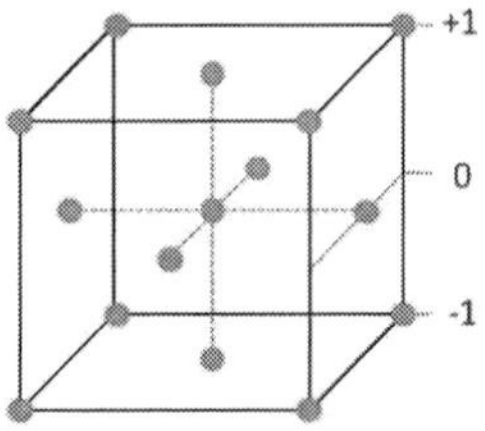

Figure 2 DOE

IV. APPLICATION OF DOE IN ALT

Let's take an example to see how to use DOE to establish a test scheme for accelerated life testing;

The design life of one type relay is 15 million cycles, the operating frequency is 3600 cycles per hour; To verify the electrical life testing[4], if normal stress test is adopted, the required test time is as follows:

$$15000000 \div 3600 \approx 4167 \text{ hours} \approx 174 \text{ days} \quad (1)$$

This test time is almost half a year, which is unbearable for engineers. They hope to use accelerated life test method. Based on previous research, we found that the following stress factors have a great impact on electrical life:

Stress 1 is temperature stress, and the stress factor follows the Arrhenius relationship model. The applied stress is 300K, and the test stress range is 300K~360K.

Stress 2 is voltage stress, and the stress factor follows the power function relationship model. The applied stress is 4V, and the test stress range is 4V~10V;

The total number of samples is 150pcs;

Firstly, we use the method of OFAT to generate the test scheme. Since the accelerated life test generally does not have a linear distribution, we adopt a three-level scheme:

Stress factor 1: Level 1 is 300K; Level 2 is 330k; Level 3 is 360K;

Stress factor 2: Level 1 is 4V; Level 2 is 7V; Level 3 is 10V;

The design scheme input into Minitab is shown in Table 1 below. It can be seen that through OFAT, we need to test at least 9 times to get the corresponding value of acceleration coefficient:

Table 1 OFAT test plan

Test sequence	Temperature	Voltage
1	1	1
2	1	2
3	1	3
4	2	1
5	2	2
6	2	3
7	3	1
8	3	2
9	3	3

Then, we use DOE method to generate the test plan. Since the normal use stress is when the two stress factor levels are 1, it is not considered in the accelerated life test plan. After DOE partial factor evaluation, we get the following plan as our DOE accelerated life test plan, and the corresponding sample allocation is carried out, as shown in Table 2:

Table 2 DOE test plan

Test sequence	Temperature	Voltage	samples
1	2	1	54
2	3	3	54
3	1	2	42

We also validated the relevant accelerated test plan through Weibull++ . Under this program, the ratio of the expected bilateral upper limit to the expected lower limit of

Plan	test cycles (Million)	The number of failed units after the test cycle is reached
1	11	1
	11.2	5
	11.4	14
	11.6	18
	11.8	11
	>12	5
2	3	3
	3.2	6
	3.4	12
	3.6	20
	3.8	10
	>4	3
3	8	2
	8.2	4
	8.4	11
	8.6	16
	8.8	6
	>9	3

B1 life is 1.6412 at the 95% confidence level, which proves that the program is effective, as shown in Figure 3.

We bring the test plan into the laboratory for validating. After testing, we get the following results, as shown in Table 3.

Through data analysis, we can get the life distribution diagram, which is equivalent to the conventional test conditions under the accelerated test condition, as shown in Figure 4.

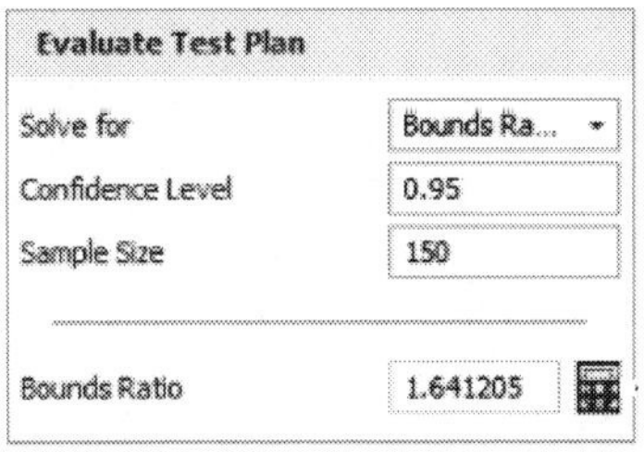

Figure 3 Test plan effectiveness evaluation chart

Table 3 Accelerated electrical life test results

Through calculation, we get that the acceleration coefficient under accelerated test is 4.42, in other words, the test cycles of the samples under accelerated stress reaches $1500 \div 4.42 \approx 3.4$ million times, that is, about 3.4 million times under accelerated test is equivalent to 15million times under normal working stress, and the required test time is about:

$$3400000 \div 3600 = 945 \text{ hours} \approx 40 \text{ days} \quad (2)$$

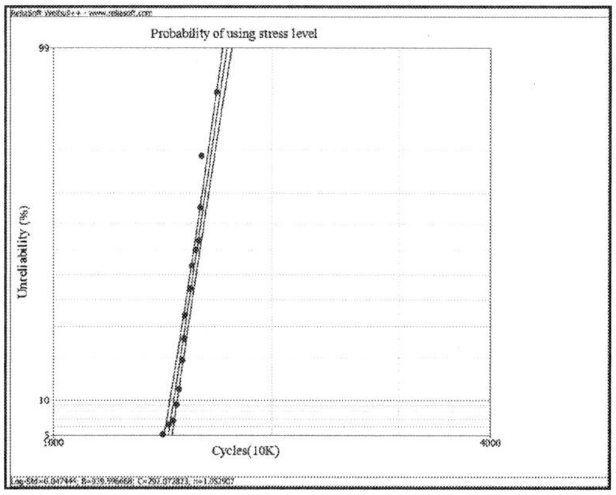

Figure 4 Stress reliability distribution diagram

With this scheme, the test cycle is 40 days, compared with 174 days in the original scheme, which is 77% shorter than the original scheme.

V. Conclusion

Through analysis, we found that using DOE only needs 3 times testing , while using OFAT method, because we have 2 factors and 3 levels, a total of $3^2 = 9$ times testing are required. Using DOE method significantly reduces the number of tests. At the same time, using DOE method can effectively improve the efficiency of accelerated life test program and shorten our test time and cost, On the other hand, the use of DOE in accelerated life testing is also of great help to expand the scope of application of DOE.

References

[1] GB/T 34986-2017 Accelerated test method for products

[2] E. A.Elsayed, Zhou Yang. Reliability Engineering (Second Edition) Beijing: Electronic Industry Press, 2016

[3] Zhen He. Six Sigma Management (Third Edition) Beijing: China Renmin University Press, 2014

[4] GB/T 15510-2008 General rules for reliability test of electromagnetic relays for control

8th International Conference on Reliability of
Electrical Products and Electrical Contacts,
November 18-20, 2022

Electromagnetic Phase Line Transfer Switch Based on Synchronous Transfer Control Strategy

Xingjie Chen[1], Zhihong Xu[1,2,3]

[1]College of Electrical Engineering and Automation, Fuzhou University, Fuzhou, 350108, China
[2]Fujian Key Laboratory of New Energy Generation and Power Conversion, Fuzhou, 350108, China
[3]Fujian Province University Engineering Research Center of Smart Distribution Grid Equipment, Fuzhou, 350108, China
E-mail: 641936593@qq.com Tel: 13178116282

***Abstract*—A large number of single-phase loads in low-voltage distribution network and the popularity of distributed generation system make a large number of three-phase load unbalance problems appear in distribution network. The three-phase current and voltage unbalance caused by three-phase load unbalance will increase the line loss of distribution network and affect the operation state of power equipment. Aiming at the problems of large loss, high cost, limited capacity and lack of physical fracture in the phase line transfer switch based on solid-state switch and hybrid switch, an electromagnetic phase line transfer switch based on synchronous transfer control strategy is designed in this paper. The switch redistributes the phase sequence of the load in the distribution network through the synchronous phase line transfer strategy, so that the three-phase load unbalance can reach the threshold again without affecting the working state of the load. Different from the power electronic device that uses the compensation method to solve the three-phase unbalance problem, the switch solves the three-phase unbalance problem by adjusting the three-phase load. It does not need to provide reactive power compensation for the distribution network, reduce the system loss and cost, and will not have an electrical impact on the distribution network.**

***Index Terms*— Three phase unbalance, electromagnetic switch, synchronous switch technology, phase line transfer**

I. Introduction

Although the low-voltage distribution network is planned in the state of three-phase load balance, in practice, due to the randomness of users' electricity consumption, the disorder of distribution network expansion and the imperfection of supervision [1], there are three-phase parameter asymmetry, load unbalance and other [2] problems. The unbalance of three-phase load will further cause the output of distribution transformer to become smaller and the loss to increase. The loss of the line increases. The electric equipment cannot work normally. At present, in view of the three-phase unbalance in the low-voltage distribution network, domestic and foreign experts want to get a feasible scheme to deal with the three-phase unbalance in the distribution network while ensuring that the three-phase unbalance meets the requirements, reducing the loss of the distribution network and improving the power quality of the distribution network [3].

The first is the compensation method, which suppresses the unbalance in the distribution network and improves the power quality through the reactive power compensation of the device without adjusting the load phase. Literature [4] through an unbalance treatment device that improves the circuit topology. Although the three-phase current unbalance of the transformer is reduced to a certain extent, the cost of this treatment device makes it uneconomical to install it in some stations. Moreover, due to the limitation of the capacity of power electronic devices in the device, it is difficult to obtain ideal treatment effect in some stations with serious unbalance or large capacity.

The second is the load redistribution method, which redistributes the load phase sequence through the phase line transfer switch to achieve the purpose of restraining the three-phase unbalance. Literature [5] uses solid-state switch as phase line transfer switch. Although the solid-state switch can achieve fast operation, but its on-state loss is large, serious heating, and there is no physical fracture. Literature [6-7] uses three groups of electromagnetic switches and power electronic switches in parallel to form a phase line transfer switch. Although it has the characteristics of fast switching and low loss in long-term operation, such hybrid switch will still be limited by the capacity of power electronic devices when increasing its capacity. Moreover, due to the large number of components, the production cost and operating cost are increased. In the process of phase line transfer by power electronic switch, there is also the problem of lack of physical fracture.

In order to solve the above problems, Based on the single-pole electromagnetic switch, this paper develops an electromagnetic phase line transfer switch based on the synchronous transfer control strategy. As shown in Figure 1, the switch is mainly composed of two parts: phase line transfer controller and electromagnetic switch body. Its on-state loss is small, simple structure, low cost, and easy to improve the working capacity of the switch, there is a physical fracture in the phase line transfer process, can effectively avoid safety hazards. In view of the defect of large dispersion of closing and opening time of electromagnetic switch, the suppression measures are formulated to make the electromagnetic switch suitable for phase line transfer. The synchronous transfer control strategy is designed to realize "current zero crossing opening and voltage zero crossing closing", and meet the technical requirements of duration of phase line transfer less than 50ms and interruption interval of current during phase transfer less than 10ms proposed in T/CEC 207-2019 Technical specification for low voltage automatic load balancing device of transfer-phase switching.

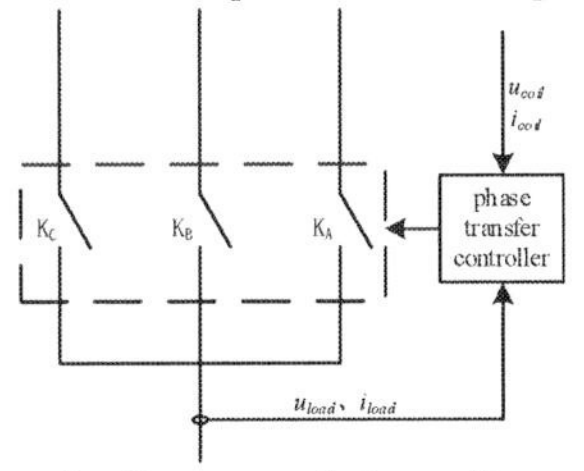

Fig. 1. Schematic diagram of phase line transfer switch

II. Suppression of Dispersion of Operation Time

Because of the mechanical mechanism and control mode of electromagnetic switch itself, the closing and opening time of electromagnetic switch is dispersed. This will seriously affect the working condition of phase line transfer switch, so that the switch cannot meet the time requirements of load transfer process, and even produce electrical impact on the distribution network.

A. Suppression of Dispersion of Closing Time

The closing time of electromagnetic switch is divided into closing actuation time and closing movement time as shown in Figure 2. Therefore, the dispersion of closing time can be divided into the dispersion of closing actuation time and the dispersion of closing movement time. Where, T_{xd} is the closing time, T_{xcd} is the closing actuation time, and T_{xrd} is the closing movement time.

Assume that the power supply voltage is:

$$u_{ac} = U_m \sin \omega t \tag{1}$$

u_{ac} is the power supply voltage of the control loop, U_m is the peak of the supply voltage, ω is the frequency of the supply voltage.

The coil voltage closing at $t = \varphi / \omega$ is:

$$u_{coil} = U_m \sin(\omega t + \varphi) \tag{2}$$

u_{coil} is the coil voltage, φ is the phase of the power supply voltage at the moment when the control circuit switch is closed.

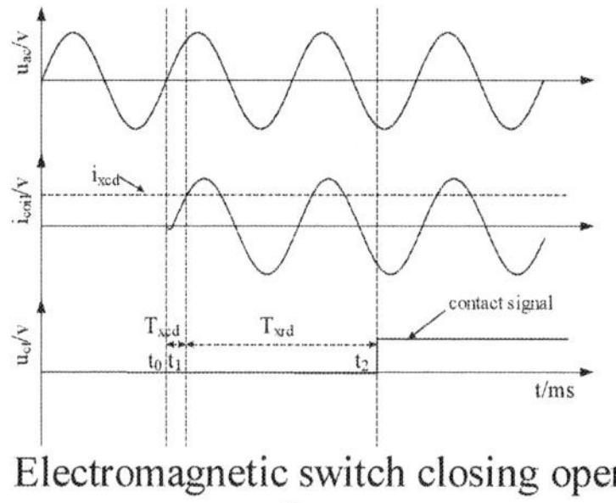

Fig. 2. Electromagnetic switch closing operation waveform

The voltage balance equation of the control circuit during operation is as follows:

$$u_{coil} = i_{coil} R_{coil} + L_{coil} \frac{d\psi}{dt} \tag{3}$$

R_{coil} is the coil current, ψ is the flux linkage of the coil.

Substitute $\psi = L_{coil} i_{coil}$ into (3) to obtain:

$$u_{coil} = i_{coil} R_{coil} + L_{coil} \frac{di_{coil}}{dt} + i_{coil} \frac{dL_{coil}}{dt} \tag{4}$$

When the moving core is in the touch stage, because the air gap between the moving and static cores is large, it can be considered that L_{coil} is a constant value at this time, so (4) can be changed to:

$$u_{coil} = i_{coil} R_{coil} + L_{coil} \frac{di_{coil}}{dt} \tag{5}$$

Substitute (2) into (5) to obtain:

$$i_{coil} = I_m \sin(\omega t + \varphi - \beta) - I_m \sin(\varphi - \beta) e^{-\frac{t}{T}} \tag{6}$$

I_m is the coil current peak, β is the control loop impedance Angle.

According to equation (6), it can be concluded that the randomness of control loop φ will affect i_{coil}, so that the change of i_{coil} appears randomness, thus resulting in the dispersion of T_{xcd}. In addition, the randomness of the change of i_{coil} makes the change of i_{coil} inconsistent in the suction movement stage, which further causes the dispersion of T_{xrd}. If i_{coil} changes in the same way, the dispersion of T_{xrd} will be mainly affected by the mechanical structure and working environment of the electromagnetic switch.

To sum up, the dispersion of T_{xcd} and T_{xrd} can be inhibited by suppressing the influence of randomness of control loop φ on i_{coil}. Therefore, the corresponding phasing program and control circuit can be used to make the control loop keep φ consistent every time it closes, and then keep the change of i_{coil} consistent, so as to achieve the purpose of restraining the dispersion of T_{xd}.

Although the phase selection control can restrain the dispersion of T_{xd}, the fixed phase angle closing will increase the complexity of control and also make the phase line transfer time longer, so it is not the best choice in phase line transfer control. Therefore, the control loop circuit topology as shown in Figure 3 is designed to change the AC control of the electromagnetic switch to DC control, and by connecting the capacitor C_0 behind the rectifier bridge, the pulsation of the DC voltage is reduced, so that the change of i_{coil} under any closing phase angle is consistent, and the dispersion of T_{xcd} is effectively reduced. The control mode of electromagnetic switch is current closed-loop control mode. In Figure 3: D_1, D_2, D_3, D_4 are rectifier bridges; S_1 is power electronic switch tube; D_0 is freewheeling diode; C_0 is a capacitor of 470uf/450v.

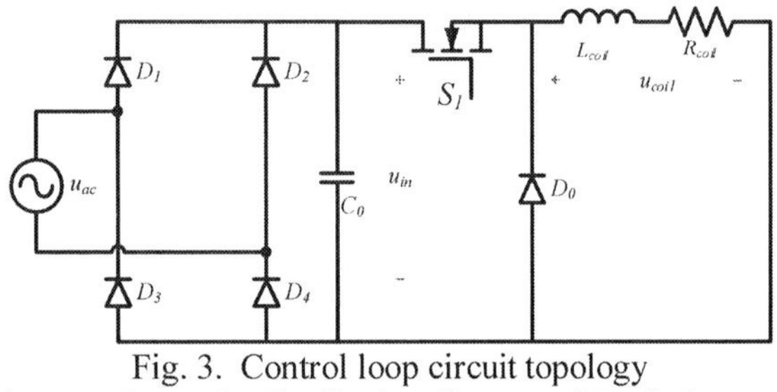

Fig. 3. Control loop circuit topology

Figure 4 shows the distribution diagram of T_{xcd} before and after the suppression measures are applied for 50 consecutive operations of prototype A and B under the random closing phase angle in the current closed-loop control mode. By comparing the T_{xcd} distribution and standard deviation of different prototypes before and after suppression, it can be concluded that the suppression measures effectively suppress the dispersion of T_{xcd}. The contact rated current of prototype A and B is 80A and 630A, respectively, and the contact rated voltage is 400V.

Figure 5 shows the distribution diagram of T_{xrd} before and after the suppression measures are applied for prototype A and B under the same experimental conditions. By comparing the distribution of T_{xrd} and standard deviation before and after the suppression of different prototypes, it can be concluded that the suppression measures can also effectively suppress the dispersion of T_{xrd}.

B. Suppression of Dispersion of opening time

The opening time of the electromagnetic switch is divided into opening actuation time and opening movement time, as shown in Figure 6. Therefore, the dispersion of opening time can be divided into the dispersion of opening actuation time and the dispersion of opening movement time. Figure 6 shows the coil current waveform in the opening process under the current closed-loop control mode. At t_0, the electromagnetic switch performs opening, the moving core still remains stationary, and i_{coil} is maintained by the magnetic field energy stored in the coil, and i_{coil} will continue to decrease due to damping until it is less than the minimum value of the holding current, and the moving and static core begin to separate. At t_1, the moving core starts to move, and at this time it is in the stage of opening movement, and the i_{coil} rises in the reverse direction due to the change of the magnetic circuit. At t_2, the displacement of the moving core reaches overtravel, and the moving and static contacts begin to separate. At t3, the moving core returns to the initial position, and the i_{coil} decreases under the action of damping until it becomes zero. Where, T_{fd} is the opening time, T_{fcd} is the opening actuation time, T_{frd} is the opening movement time, and i_{xcmin} is the minimum value of the holding current.

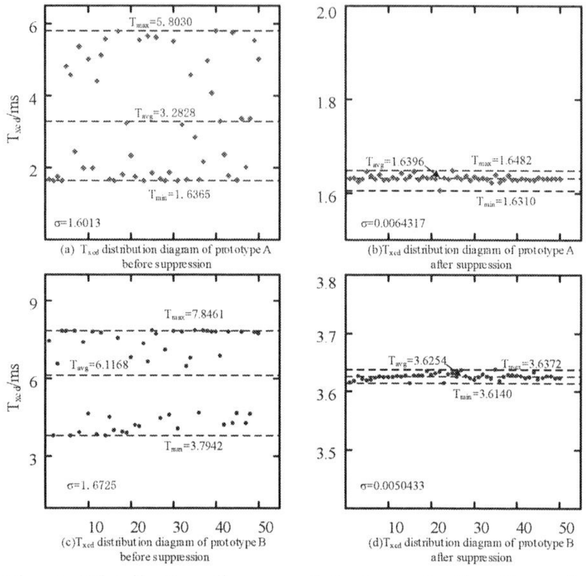

Fig. 4. Distribution diagram of closing actuation time of prototype A and B

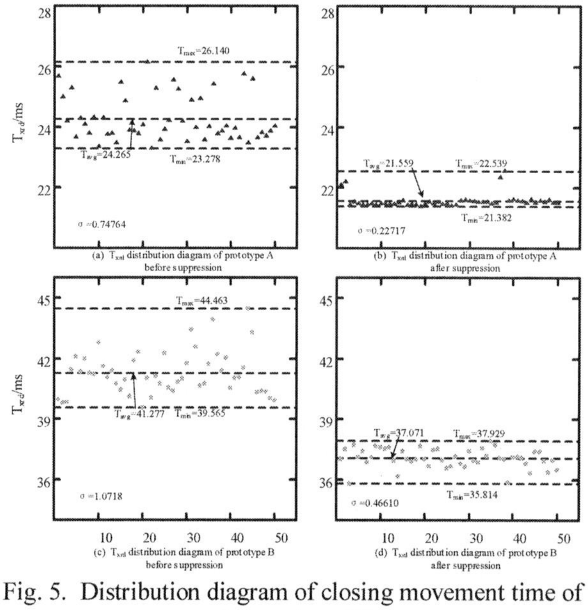

Fig. 5. Distribution diagram of closing movement time of prototype A and B

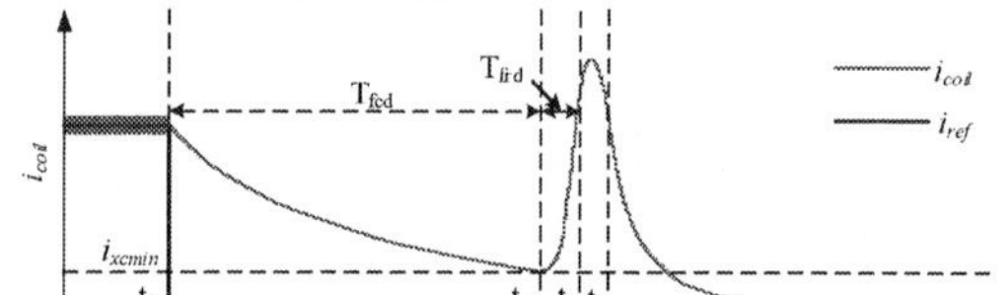

Fig. 6. Electromagnetic switch opening operation waveform

Under the complex electromagnetic coupling mentioned above, the reasons for the dispersion of T_{fcd} and T_{frd} are also complicated. In view of this phenomenon, the change of i_{coil} was suppressed to make i_{coil} decline as quickly and stably as possible in the whole process of opening, thus achieving the purpose of restraining T_{fd} dispersion.

In the holding stage, the coil can be switched at switching frequency under two working states of excitation and continuous current, so that the i_{coil} remains dynamically stable. Assume that L_{coil} is constant and u_{coil} is constant.

When S_1 is turned on, it can be obtained from equation (5):

$$\Delta i_{coil}^{+} = \frac{U_{coil}}{R_{coil}}(1 - e^{-t\frac{R_{coil}}{L_{coil}}}) \tag{7}$$

When S_1 is turned off, it can be obtained from equation (5):

$$\Delta i_{coil}^{-} = \frac{U_{coil}}{R_{coil}} e^{-t\frac{R_{coil}}{L_{coil}}} \tag{8}$$

When i_{coil} is continuous, it can be obtained from equation (7) (8) that the turn on and turn off time of S_1 within a switching cycle will determine the ripple size of i_{coil}.

When the current is continuous, the BUCK circuit satisfies the following equation:

$$U_{coil} = DU_{in} \tag{9}$$

Substitute $i_{rxc}R_{coil}=U_{coil}$ into equation (9) to get:

$$D = \frac{i_{rxc}R_{coil}}{U_{in}} \tag{10}$$

i_{rxc} is the reference value of holding current, D is the duty cycle of holding.

According to equation (10), the appropriate D can reduce the i_{coil} ripple, so as to achieve the purpose of reducing the dispersion of i_{coil} size when the coil is out of power, and then suppress the dispersion of T_{fcd}.

In order to further reduce the dispersion of T_{fd} and make i_{coil} drop rapidly, a reverse voltage branch is added, which is mainly composed of switch tube S_2 and TVS diodes in parallel, as shown in Figure 7. When the electromagnetic switch enters the opening process, S_2 is controlled to close, TVS works, and a reverse voltage U_{TVS} is applied at both ends of the coil to make i_{coil} drop rapidly. In order to weaken the influence of the change of i_{coil} on T_{fd}, and then inhibit the dispersion of T_{fcd} and T_{frd}. Among them, the control circuit has three working modes (1) excitation, (2) continuous current and (3) demagnetization, as shown in Figure 7.

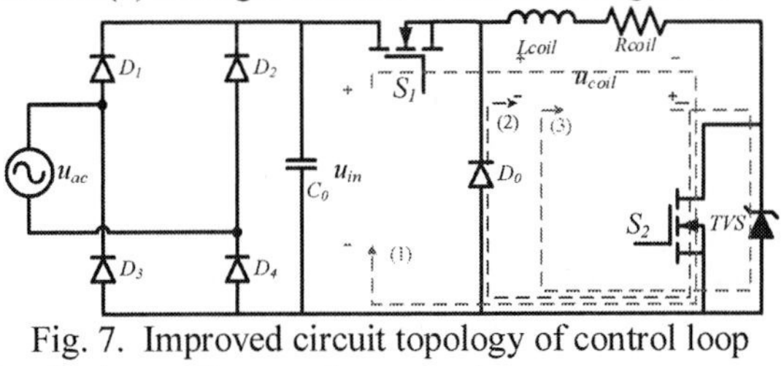

Fig. 7. Improved circuit topology of control loop

Fig. 8 shows the maximum, minimum, average, and standard deviation of T_{fcd} and T_{frd} of prototype A and B under different conditions for 50 consecutive operations. By comparing 8(a) and (b), it can be concluded that the standard deviation and average value of T_{fcd} can be effectively reduced by selecting a more appropriate D or increasing U_{TVS} for different prototypes, proving that suppression measures can effectively reduce the dispersion of T_{fcd}. By comparing 8(c) and (d), it can be concluded that applying U_{TVS} makes i_{coil} decline rapidly and stably, making the phenomenon of i_{coil} reverse rise disappear [14]. The moving and static iron cores separate after the i_{coil} decreases to zero, eliminating the influence of the i_{coil} reverse rise phenomenon on the opening process, and effectively restraining the dispersion of T_{frd}. The i_{rxc} of prototype A and B were 0.03A and 0.5A respectively. F_0:D=100%,U_{TVS}=0V;F_1:D=0.6%/4.5%,U_{TVS}=0V;F_2:D=100%,U_{TVS}=220V;F_3:D=0.6%/4.5%,U_{TVS}=220V.

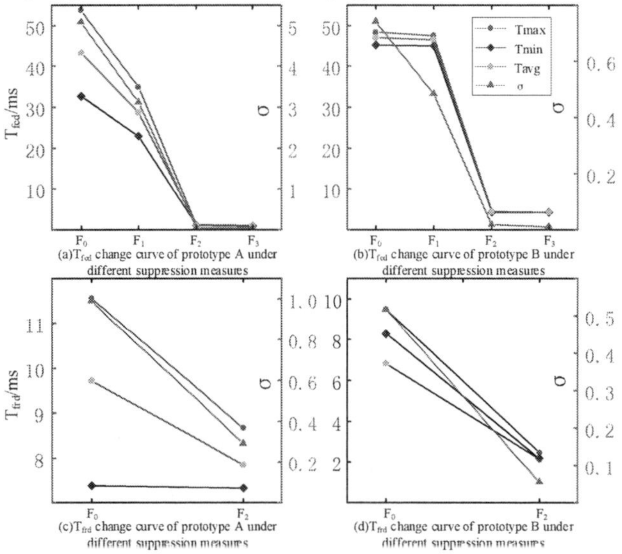

Fig.8. Change curve of T_{fcd} and T_{frd} under different suppression measures of prototype A and B

III. SYNCHRONOUS TRANSFER CONTROL OF PHASE LINE TRANSFER SWITCH

In order to suppress the impact of load transfer on distribution network and the ablation of contact caused by arc during contact opening, synchronous switching technology is applied to phase line transfer control to close the contact at a specific moment and opening the contact when the load current zero crossing.

Taking the transfer of pure resistive load from phase B to phase C as an example, the action sequence of synchronous transfer control strategy is designed as shown in Figure 9. The phase-line transfer command is received at t_0 and the load current zero is detected at t_1. The phase line transfer process enters the preparation stage. On the one hand, after T_1 delay, the coil of phase B electromagnetic switch is powered off at t_4, and after T_2 delay, the phase B electromagnetic switch will remove the load from the distribution network at the time of load current zero point t_5.

On the other hand, due to the slow operation speed of the electromagnetic switch, when controlling the opening of the current phase electromagnetic switch, it is necessary to control the closing of the cut-in phase electromagnetic switch at the same time. Therefore, after the time t_1, the zero point of the C-phase voltage is detected at the same time, and the zero point of the C-phase voltage is detected at the time of t_2. After T_3 delay, the phase C electromagnetic switch is powered on at t_3, and then after T_4 delay, the load is connected to the distribution network again through phase C at t_6 of phase C voltage zero point. Among them, T_1 is the current phase opening compensation delay, T_2 is the opening time, T_3 is the cut-in phase closing compensation delay, T_4 is the closing time, T_5 is the load power-off time, and T_x is the opening compensation delay, 10n is the integer half-wave time required for the current phase electromagnetic switch delay.

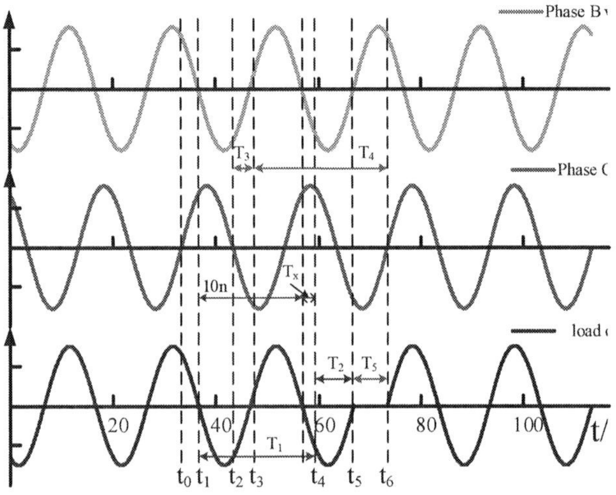

Figure. 9. Waveform diagram of load transfer from phase B to phase C

In the process of realizing the above action sequence, due to the slow operation speed of cut-in phase electromagnetic switch, and the load power-off time in the process of phase line transfer needs to be less than 10ms, it needs to be reasonably configured between each delay. the most critical is the solution of n transition half waves that need to be delayed for the current phase electromagnetic switch. The specific solution process is as follows.

$$T_1 = 10n + T_x \tag{11}$$

$$T_1 + T_2 = T_3 + T_4 = 10k(k = 1,2,3...) \tag{12}$$

Substituting equation (11) into equation (12), it can be concluded that n satisfies the following equation:

$$n = \frac{T_3 + T_4 - T_2 - T_x}{10} \tag{13}$$

Figure 10 is the control flow chart of phase line transfer. The phase line transfer controller judges whether to switch the load at the node controlled by the phase line transfer switch according to the command sent by the phase selection controller. If it is necessary to switch, enter the transfer control program for transfer, exit the transfer control program after completing the load transfer, and enter the stable holding stage.

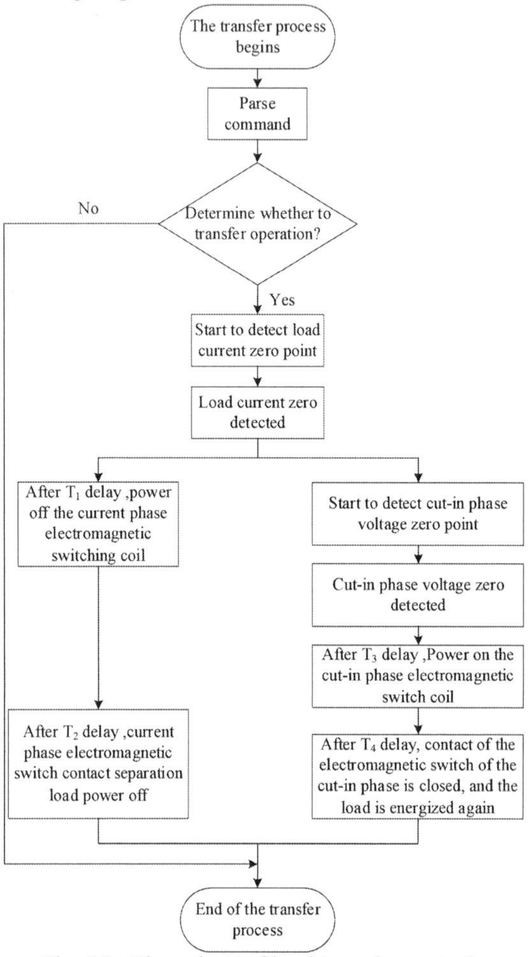

Fig. 10. Flow chart of load transfer control

IV. Experimental Verification

With NI CompactRIO controller as the control core and electromagnetic phase line transfer switch as the test object, the synchronous transfer control strategy is written into an embedded program to control the transfer process of phase line transfer switch. Main experimental equipment: programmable AC power supply, phase line transfer switch, NI CompactRIO controller, host computer, etc.

Figure 11 is the waveform diagram of the two-phase transfer experiment of the phase line transfer switch on the pure resistive load initially connected to phase B. Figure 11(a) shows the experimental waveform of phase B transfer to phase C. After receiving the transfer command at t_0, the transfer is carried out according to the action sequence of synchronous phase line transfer control strategy, realizing "current zero crossing opening and voltage zero crossing closing". The load power-off time t_5=6.96ms is less than 10ms, and the whole switching time t_0-t_6 is less than 50ms. Figure 11 (b) is the experimental waveform diagram of switching from phase B to phase C and then from phase C to phase B. Receive the transfer command at t_0, repeat the above operations, and realize "current zero crossing opening and voltage zero crossing closing". The load power-off time t_5=3.48ms is less than 10ms, and the whole switching time t_0-t_6 is less than 50ms. From the experimental results, it can be concluded that the designed phase line transfer switch can meet the needs of phase line transfer.

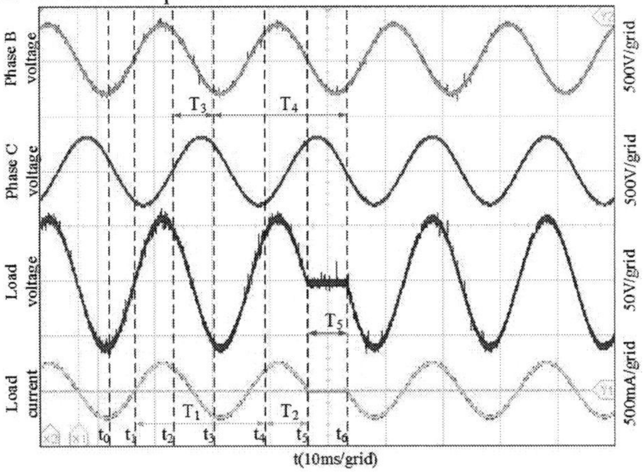

(a) Waveform diagram of phase B transfer to phase C

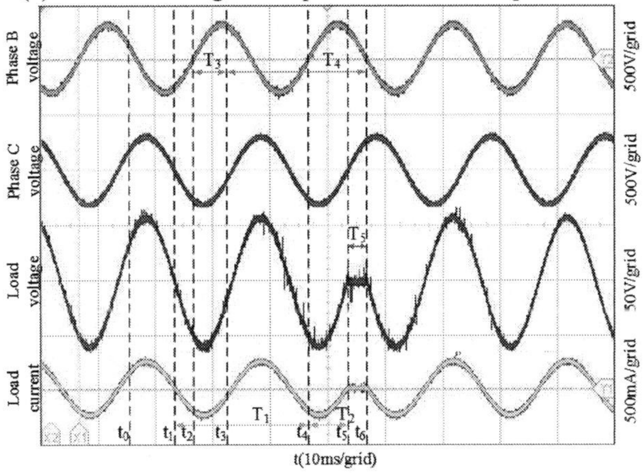

(b) Waveform diagram of phase C transfer to phase B

Fig. 11. Experimental waveform of transfer process

V. CONCLUSION

In this paper, an electromagnetic phase line transfer switch is developed to control the three-phase load unbalance in distribution network. Based on the study of the cause of the dispersion of the closing and opening time of the electromagnetic switch, the suppression measures are put forward, and the corresponding control circuit and control program are designed accordingly, so that the electromagnetic switch can be used for precise control in the process of phase line transfer. Based on the synchronous transfer control strategy, the embedded control program is developed, and the experiment verifies that the phase line transfer switch can realize "current zero crossing opening and voltage zero crossing closing", the load power off time is less than 10ms, and the whole switching time is less than 50ms. Moreover, the electromagnetic phase line transfer switch has the advantages of simple and flexible structure, low cost and easy to improve the contact capacity, which provides ideas for the research and development of phase line transfer switch.

REFERENCES

[1] Shen Kai. Research on Load Compensation Strategy of Three-phase Unbalance in Distribution Network Based on APF [D]. ShenYang Institute of Engineering, 2016.

[2] Zhang Yongjun, Liu Siliang, Jiang Jinqun, Yi Yingqi, Li Qinhao. Research Review on Low- voltage Intelligent Distribution Network Technology [J]. Guangdong Electric Power, 2019, 32(01):1-12.

[3] Liu Yan. Research on The Method of Reducing the Three-phase Unbalance Rate of Low-voltage Distribution Network [J]. Science and Technology, 2016, 26(36):78+150.

[4] Ji Qiuhua, Wei Zheng, Wang Tong, Chen Chao. Research on the Control Strategy for Three-phase Unbalanced Load in Distribution Area [J]. Power Electronics, 2020, 54(02):32-34+46.

[5] Huang Shengli, Li Hongtao. Research on Three phase Unbalanced Loads Based on Solid-state Intelligent Switching-Phase Switch [J]. Electrical & Energy Management Technology, 2016(05):13-17+81.

[6] Zhang Jianbin, Xu Zhihong. Design of Intelligent Commutation Switch Based on Parallel-Series Connection [J]. Electrical & Energy Management Technology, 2021(05):30-36.

[7] Zhang Erchao. Research on the Control of Three Phase Unbalance Based on Intelligent Switching-Phase Switch [D]. University of Electronic Science and Technology of China, 2018.

[8] Tang Longfei, Xu Zhihong. Design of an AC Contactor Control Module Started by Closed Loop Chopping [J]. Proceedings of the CSEE, 2013, 33(18):132-139+5.

[9] Zhang Changkun, Xu Zhihong. Sensorless Online Opening Time Estimation of Contactors [J]. Proceedings of the CSEE, 2022, 42(10):3805-3815.

First Author, Xingjie Chen is currently pursuing the M.S. degree in the College of Electrical Engineering and Automation, Fuzhou University, Fuzhou, China. His current research interests include electrical appliances and intelligent technology.

Corresponding Author, Zhihong Xu (1963-) , professor and doctoral supervisor, with research interests in electrical appliances and intelligent technology, 641936593@qq.com.

8th International Conference on Reliability of
Electrical Products and Electrical Contacts,
November 18-20, 2022

Reliability Analysis and Optimization Design of Reconfigurable Hybrid Topology Constant Current / Constant Voltage IPT System

Bo Wen[1],Yonggang Li[1],Yulong Cui[2]

[1)] North China Electric Power University (Baoding), Hebei, 071000
[2)] Beijing University of Chemical Technology, Beijing,100029
Email: wbwyyxno1@163.com TEL:18594085031

***Abstract*—The hybrid charging method of constant current (CC)/constant voltage(CV) is of great significance to improve the life and reliability of the battery. To achieve CC/CV charging and switch between CC topology and CV topology, reconfigurable hybrid topologies are frequently used in researches on inductive power transfer(IPT) systems.In this paper, the output characteristics of typical topologies of IPT system are analyzed and summarized, and the principle of several typical reconfigurable hybrid topologies is analyzed; Based on IEC 61709 the reliability of circuit components of wireless charging systems with different reconfigurable hybrid topologies is analyzed, and the reliability of different reconfigurable hybrid topologies is compared; A reconfigurable hybrid topology based on the primary inverter design is proposed to improve the reliability. The output characteristic analysis and soft switch design are carried out to further improve the system operation reliability. It is proved that the proposed design has certain advantages over the traditional reconfigurable topology inductive power transmission system in reliability.**

***Index Terms*—constant current(CC), constant voltage(CV), inductuive power transfer(IPT),IEC61709, reliability**

I. INTRODUCTION

With the depletion of fossil energy and the increasingly prominent environmental problems, the research and application of new energy vehicles have received extensive attention. Compared with the traditional plug-in charging method, wireless charging technology has many advantages such as non-contact, safety, convenience and efficiency, which can effectively promote the intelligent and user-friendly charging process of new energy vehicles.

The constant current/constant voltage charging mode is one of the main charging modes of new energy vehicles because of its advantages of fast charging and extending battery life. There are three main ways to realize the constant current/constant voltage charging mode of the wireless charging system: adding DC- DC conversion circuit, frequency conversion control, reconfigurable hybrid topology. Among them, the method of reconfigurable hybrid topology is simpler in design and easier to realize the advantages of zero phase (ZPA) in the whole charging process. Many constant current/constant voltage wireless charging systems use this implementation in the design and research. , the main disadvantage of the reconfigurable hybrid topology is that it needs to add additional capacitors, inductance components and switching switches, which will increase the complexity of the system and increase the possibility of system failure. Several typical reconfigurable hybrid topology schemes are analyzed and studied, and a more reliable reconfigurable hybrid topology is proposed.

II. INTRODUCTION OF CONSTANT CURRENT/CONSTANT VOLTAGE WIRELESS CHARGING

Since the equivalent impedance of the lithium battery in the car is constantly changing during the charging process, the constant current/constant voltage means that the output current or voltage of the charging system does not change with the change of the load impedance. The constant current and constant voltage charging modes have their own advantages and disadvantages. , the constant current mode charges quickly, but may cause overcharge to damage the battery life, the constant voltage mode is safer, but the charging speed is relatively slow [1], so the first constant current and then constant voltage charging mode can take into account the advantages of both charging methods It has received extensive attention, and the typical constant current/constant voltage charging curve is shown in Figure 1.

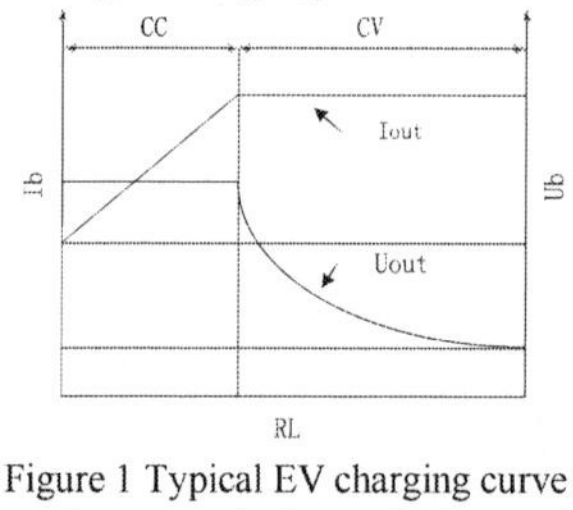

Figure 1 Typical EV charging curve

The output characteristics of the wireless charging system are mainly determined by the compensation topology. Different compensation topologies have different output characteristics. The existing compensation topologies for each output characteristic are shown in Table 1. The compensation topology with the same resonance condition and similar structure is selected by designing additional A reconfigurable hybrid topology can be formed by switching the output mode of the switching element. The switching action structure of the reconfigurable hybrid topology mainly includes three situations: primary side switching, secondary side switching, and simultaneous switching of primary and secondary sides [3]. Figure 234 below shows three typical examples. (The other parts of the conventional wireless charging system are similar, so this paper mainly analyzes the part from the primary side compensation network to the secondary side rectifier)

Table 1 Various topology output types

CC	CV
S-S	S-P
P-P	P-S
LCL-LCL	LCL-S
LCC-LCC	LCC-S
LCC-P	S-LCC

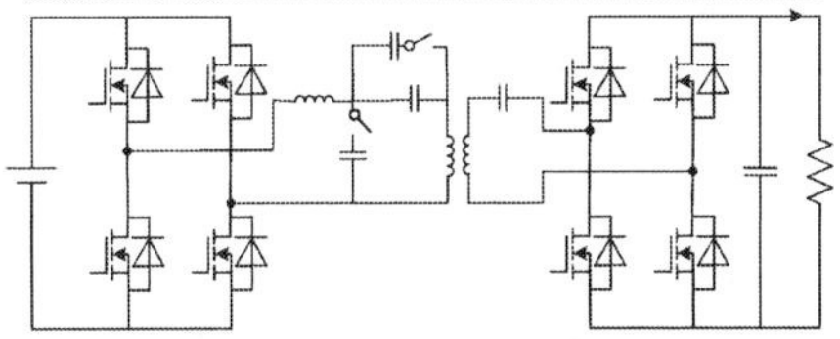

Figure 2 Primary switched topology

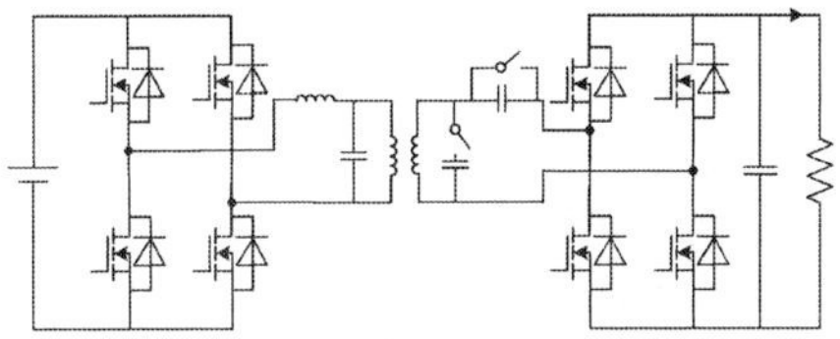

Figure 3 Secondary-side switched topology

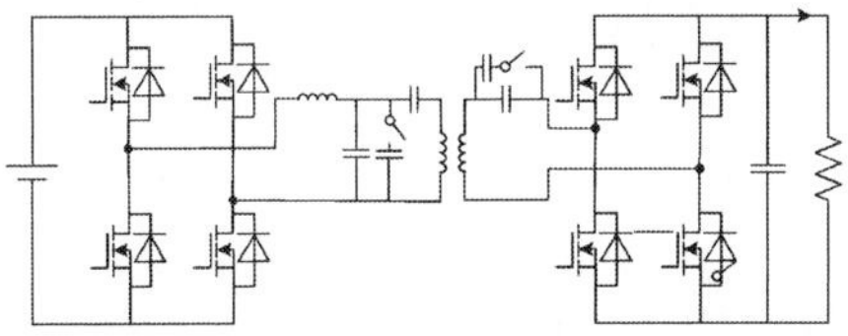

Figure 4 Simultaneous switching topology of primary and secondary sides

The AC switch used is composed of two mosfets as shown in Figure 5. It can be seen that the hybrid switching topology generally requires more than two AC switches, as well as additional capacitive and inductive components.

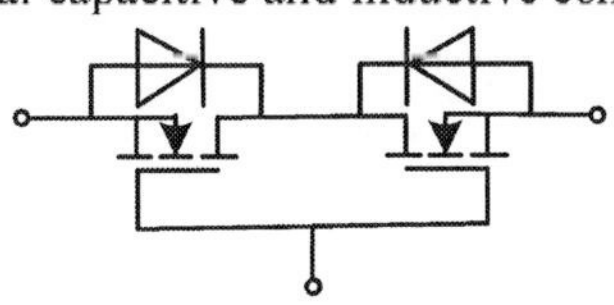

Figure 5 AC switch

III. RELIABILITY CALCULATION

Reliability can be defined as the ability of a product to perform a specified function under specified conditions and within a specified time. In order to facilitate the quantitative analysis of reliability, this paper refers to the reliability prediction method defined by the IEC61709 standard, which is widely used in the world.

Standards usually define the failure rate as a composite value that includes all failure modes. And the failure rate of an electrical device can be considered as the sum of the failure rates of all modes, as follows:

$$\lambda_{component} = \sum_{i=1}^{n} \left(\lambda_{mode}\right)_i \quad (1)$$

where $\left(\lambda_{mode}\right)_i$ is the component failure rate for failure mode i and n is the number of failure modes.

Since the equipment cannot be guaranteed to operate under the reference conditions in practical applications, different usage conditions and application environments will affect the failure rate of the equipment. Therefore, a stress factor model is introduced to quantify the influence of different operating conditions, so as to obtain a more reasonable failure rate. The calculation formula of the failure rate in actual conditions is as follows:

$$\lambda = \lambda_{ref} \times \pi_U \times \pi_I \times \pi_T \times \pi_E \times \pi_S \times \pi_{ES} \quad (2)$$

λ_{ref} is the reference failure rate;

π_U is the voltage-dependent factor;

π_I is the current-dependent factor;

π_T is a temperature dependent factor;

π_E is the environmental application factor;

π_S is the switching rate related factor;

π_{ES} is the electrical stress-dependent factor;

The reliability of the three typical hybrid switching topologies shown in the figure is evaluated according to the IEC61709 standard. For the convenience of comparison, it is assumed that the three topologies operate at a power level of 3.3kW, the input voltage of the inverter is 220V, and the working states of various components are basically the same.

A. mosfet failure rate

The IEC61709 standard stipulates that the formula for the failure rate of the mosfet under specific conditions is:

$$\lambda = \lambda_{ref} \times \pi_T \quad (3)$$

$$\pi_T = exp\left[\frac{E_{a1}}{k_0}\left(\frac{1}{T_{ref}} - \frac{1}{T_{op}}\right)\right] \quad (4)$$

The above equation is derived from the Arrhenius equation, which describes the temperature dependence of the failure rate.

E_{a1} is the activation energy [eV]; k_0 =8.616 × 10^−5 eV/K ; T_0=313K ; T_{ref} for the reference temperature [°K];T_{op} for operating temperature [°K];

It can be seen that the main factor affecting the failure rate of the mosfet is the operating temperature. Since the

IEC61709 standard does not provide the failure rate value under the reference conditions, the reference failure rate is set as 0.0715 (10^-6/h) [2] with reference to the domestic standard. The reference temperature of the available high-frequency mosfet is 125°C, and the value of the temperature correlation factor according to the IEC61709 standard is:

Table 2 Temperature related factors π_T

θ_{op}	30	35	40	45
π_T	0.019	0.023	0.028	0.035

The operating room temperature is taken as 25°C, referring to the APTM50HM75STG mosfet array data, the operating temperature is taken as 30.23°C through simulation calculation. $\lambda=\lambda_{ref}\times\pi_T=1.3585\times10^{-9}$

The above formula shows that the actual failure rate of mosfet is 1.3585×10-9/h

B. Failure rate of capacitor and inductor work

The IEC61709 standard stipulates that the formula for the failure rate of capacitors under specific conditions is:

$$\lambda=\lambda_{ref}\times\pi_T\times\pi_U \tag{5}$$

$$\pi_U=exp\left\{C_3\left[\left(\frac{U_{op}}{U_{rat}}\right)^{C_2}-\left(\frac{U_{ref}}{U_{rat}}\right)^{C2}\right]\right\} \tag{6}$$

Among them: U_{op} is the working current; U_{ref} is the reference current; U_{rat} is the rated current; C_2 and C_3 are constants, the size can refer to the corresponding table.

Table 3 Voltage dependent factors π_U

U_{op}/U_{rat}	0.1	0.2	0.3	0.4	0.5
π_U	0.26	0.36	0.50	0.71	1

Capacitive elements in the system are usually selected with a rated voltage that is more than 200% of the rated voltage of the system to ensure sufficient operating margin and ensure more stable operation of the system. Therefore, it is desirable to select 1 according to the table. By referring to iec6179 to find table 47, =1.8 can be obtained by calculation:

$$\lambda=\lambda_{ref}\times\pi_T\times\pi_U=4.554\times10^{-8}\ /\mathrm{h}$$

The failure rate model under the specific conditions of the inductor is:

$$\lambda=\lambda_{ref}\times\pi_T \tag{7}$$

The failure rate of the inductive components found in the IEC6179 standard is 2.435×10-8/h

C. overall failure rate

According to the results of Equation 1 and Section 3.2, the overall reference failure rate of the reconfigurable hybrid topology can be calculated as shown in the following table.

Table 4 Failure rate of each structure

structure type	failure rate(/h)
Primary switching	2.2281e-07
Secondary switching	1.7727e-07
switch on both sides	2.6835e-07

It can be seen from the above calculation that the increase of inductance and capacitance components has a great impact on the failure rate of the system. The failure rate of the secondary switching structure is relatively low, but the switching structure is located on the secondary side, that is, the vehicle side, and the space on the vehicle side is relatively small compared to the primary side. And the poor working environment will bring more unstable factors.

IV. TOPOLOGY OPTIMIZATION

According to the above analysis, it can be seen that to improve the hybrid switching topology, the switching structure should be placed on the primary side as much as possible, and the number of components should be minimized. This paper proposes a new hybrid switching topology based on LCC-P and S-P topology, as shown in the figure

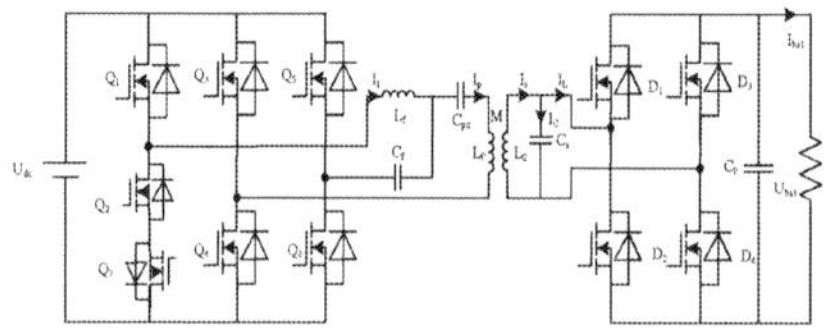

Figure 6 Hybrid topology

The switching of output characteristics is realized by changing the operating mode of the inverter. The specific working method is shown in the figure.

In CC mode, Q1, Q4, Q6 are turned on/off at the same time, Q2, Q3, Q5, Q7 are turned on/off at the same time, the system in Figure 7 is in the LCC-P compensation topology, with constant current output.

In CV mode, Q1, Q2, and Q7 are always in the off state, and Q3, Q4, Q5, and Q6 form a full-bridge inverter. The system in Figure 8 is in SS compensation topology, with constant voltage output.

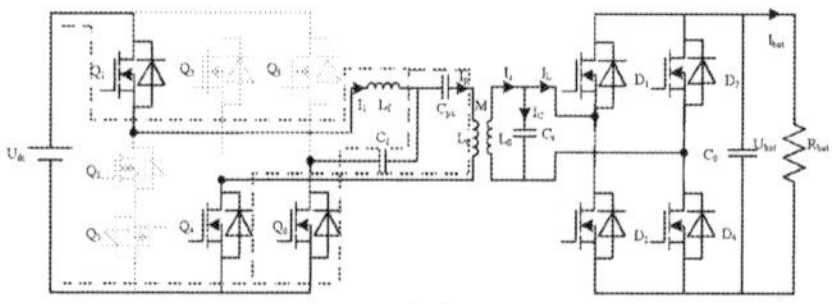

(a)

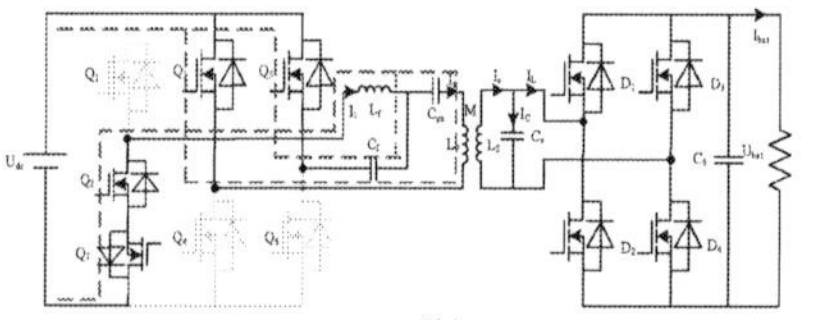

(b)

Figure 7 Operation in constant current mode.

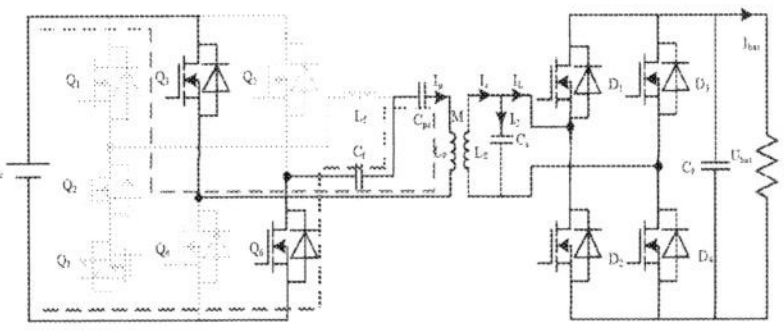

(a)

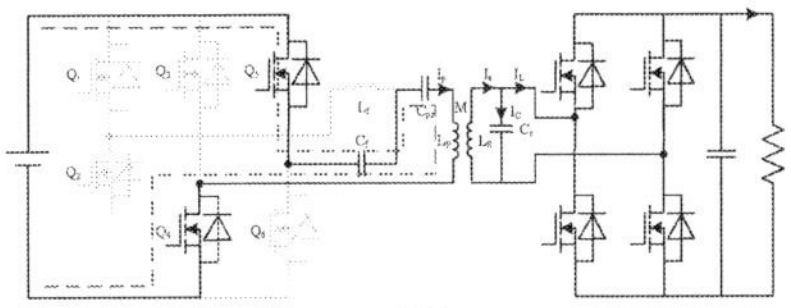

(b)

Figure 8 Operation in constant voltage mode

According to Equation 1, the failure rate is 1.7591e-07/h. It can be seen that the failure rate of the switching structure proposed in this paper is lower than the three switching structures mentioned above, Fig. 9 shows that the system can achieve constant current/constant voltage output through simulation.

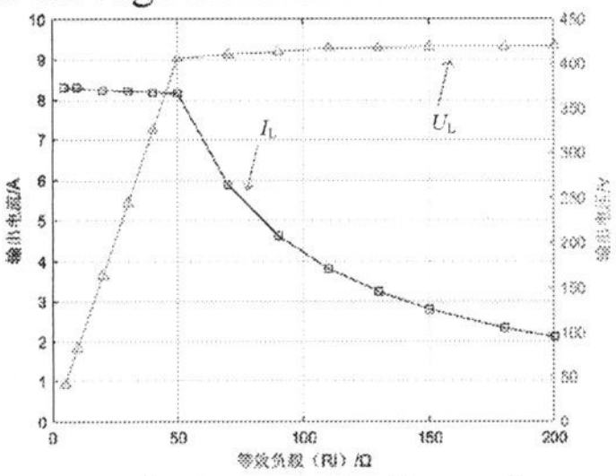

Fig. 9 simulation curve of system output voltage and current changing with load resistance

V. Analysis of New Topology Soft Switching Mode

The principle of the switching topology proposed in this paper is to switch the output characteristics from constant current to constant voltage output by switching from LCC-P to S-P topology. When the operating frequency of the system satisfies Equation 8, both output modes can be realized. Purely resistive.

$$\omega = \frac{1}{\sqrt{L_f C_f}} = \frac{1}{\sqrt{L_s C_s}} = \frac{1}{\sqrt{L_p \left(C_f // C_{pz}\right)\left(1-k^2\right)}} \quad (8)$$

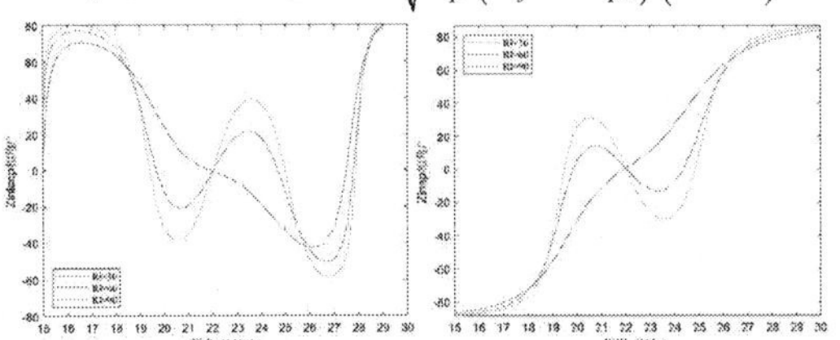

(a) LCC mode (b) SP mode

Fig. 10 Characteristics of system impedance angle with frequency

Taking the operating frequency of 22kHz as an example, the system impedance angle changes with frequency as shown in the figure. It can be seen that the two topologies are purely resistive at the same frequency.

For high-power wireless charging systems, the high power density of switching devices in the inverter will cause power loss and reduce system reliability. In order to reduce the switching loss of MOSFET-based inverters and improve system reliability, compared with the ZPA state, The realization of ZVS working state is more important. Theoretically, the perfect zero-voltage switching state should be that the system is in a fully compensated state, and the phase angle is zero, so that the inverter voltage source switch switches at the current zero-crossing point, but in fact, due to the influence of the dead time of the driving signal, when the system It is difficult to realize zero-voltage switching when operating in the ZPA state, so in order to achieve zero-voltage switching, the total impedance of the system should be inductive [4].

This can be achieved by adjusting the compensation capacitor parameters while keeping the system operating at the same frequency. The two sets of topologies are fixed and other parameters remain unchanged, and the compensation element parameters are adjusted within 20% to obtain the variation characteristics of the input impedance angle with the parameters as shown in Figure 11. It can be seen from Figure 11 that the adjustment of Cpz, Cf, and Cs parameters will have opposite effects on the phase angle of the two sets of topologies. The topology is inductive at the same time. The primary side compensation inductance Lf is only connected to the system in the LCC-P mode. Adjusting its parameters can independently change the impedance angle of the LCC-P mode. At the same time, the impact of the impedance angle in the reasonable adjustment of the capacitor parameters is opposite to that of Lf. One makes it possible to realize that both sets of topologies are inductive.

During the constant current/constant voltage charging process of electric vehicles, the equivalent load of the system will continue to rise. When the compensation component parameters are adjusted and do not meet the aforementioned resonance conditions, the impedance angles of the LCC-P and S-P topologies will change differently as the load rises. , the change trend is shown in Figure 12. When the compensation parameter is greater than the resonance value, the impedance angle of the LCC-P topology increases with the increase of the load, and the impedance angle of the S-P topology decreases with the increase of the load. When the compensation parameter is less than At the resonance value, the impedance angle of the LCC-P topology decreases with the increase of the load, and the impedance angle of the S-P topology increases with the increase of the load.

It can be seen from Figure 11 that increasing Lf and Cf at the same time can make the input impedances of the two topologies become inductive together. At this time, the impedance angle of the LCC-P topology increases with the increase of the load, and the impedance angle of the S-P topology decreases with the increase of the load. Trend, according to the charging principle of constant current/constant voltage, LCC-P as a constant current output topology starts to work when the charging load is the lowest, until it reaches the maximum current and the load impedance rises to a certain value, and switches to the S-P topology and enters the constant voltage mode. Continues until the end of charging, and the load impedance rises to the maximum value when the charging current stops.

To sum up, the adjustment of the compensation parameters only needs to ensure that the input impedance angle of the LCC-P topology meets the ZVS condition of Equation 9 when the load is the smallest, and that the input impedance angle of the S-P topology meets the ZVS condition of Equation 9 when the load is the largest. The whole process of ensuring the system operation can realize ZVS.

$$i_{t0} + i_{td} \geq \frac{4C_{oss}U_{dc}}{t_d}, (i_{td} \geq 0) \quad (9)$$

where: C_{oss} is the junction capacitance of the switch; i_{t0} is the output current of the inverter at the moment when the switch tube is turned off, the turn-off current; i_{td} end current for dead time; t_d is the dead time.

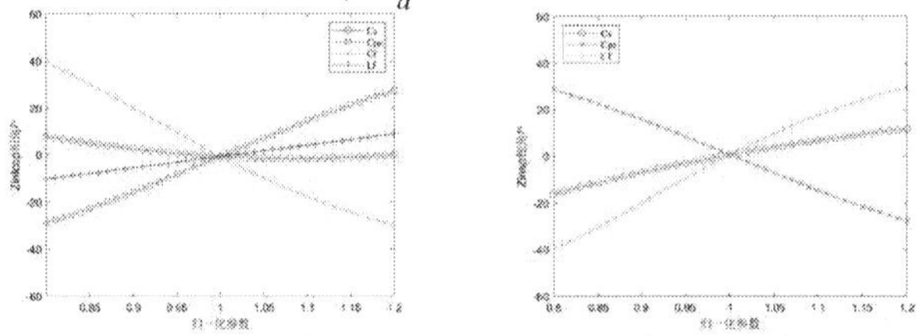

(a) LCCP mode (b) SP mode

Fig. 11 Input impedance angle when the parameters of the resonant element are adjusted

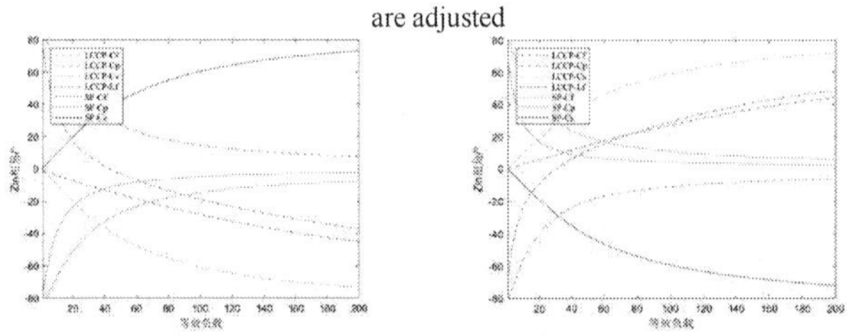

(a) parameter 0.8 times (b) parameter 1.2 times

Figure 12 Change of input impedance angle with load after adjustment of resonant element parameters

VI. Conclusion

This paper analyzes the reliability of the constant current / constant voltage wireless charging system with the hybrid switching topology structure, proposes the hybrid switching topology optimization design with higher reliability by summarizing and analyzing, analyzes the change law of the proposed topology impedance angle, and designs the soft switch operation mode to further improve the reliability. The research results provide a reference for the design and application of the magnetic coupling resonant wireless charging system.

References

[1] Mai Ruikun, Chen Yang, Liu Yeran. Research on IPT constant current and constant voltage battery charging based on variable compensation parameters [J]. Chinese Journal of Electrical Engineering 2016, 36(21):6.

[2] Cui Yulong, Wang Huiming, Li Liu. Research on the reliability of magnetically coupled resonant wireless charging device for electric vehicles [C]// The 5th International Conference on Reliability and Electrical Contact of Electrical Products. 2014.

[3] Chen Y , Zhang H , Park S J , et al. A Switching Hybrid LCC-S Compensation Topology for Constant Current/Voltage EV Wireless Charging[J]. IEEE Access, 2019, PP(99):1-1.

[4] Wang Fusheng, Guo Juanjuan, Wang Wenyang, et al. Parameter optimization design method for soft switching of electric vehicle wireless charging system [J]. Chinese Journal of Electrical Engineering, 2019(S01):10.

8th International Conference on Reliability of
Electrical Products and Electrical Contacts,
November 18-20, 2022

Research on Potential Fault State Probability Model of Multi State Electronic Equipment

Jingde Huang[1,2], Long Ling[1], Zijie Chen[1], Peihao Han[1]

[1)] Zhuhai College of Science and Technology, Zhuhai, China, 519041
[2)] Guangdong Intelligent Vision Precision Detection Engineering Technology Research Center, Zhuhai, 519041
Email: jdh925@sina.com TEL:13387852971

Abstract—**Potential fault is an objective existence in equipment operation. Aiming at the problem that it is difficult to diagnose the hidden fault state of multi-state electronic equipment, firstly, a Bayesian network model considering failure correlation is established to describe the correlation between system states and the properties of multi-state working mode of electronic equipment with mathematical relationship; Secondly, based on the analysis of the three-states of electronic equipment 'safety state-potential fault-fault state', the three-states probability model based on Improved Bayesian model is established, and a set of state recognition model suitable for potential fault diagnosis of multi state electronic equipment unit structure is formed ; Finally, the effectiveness of the model is verified by a typical electronic system. The experimental results show that the theoretical method and model can better identify the potential fault state of electronic equipment, and provide a scientific theoretical basis for preventive diagnosis and maintenance.**

Index Terms— **Electronic Equipment, Multi State System, Potential Fault, Failure Correlation, State Probability Model.**

I. INTRODUCTION

The existence of latent faults of electronic equipment seriously threatens its performance. Effective evaluation of potential failure is an important way to improve the integrity of equipment. Generally, the degradation failure mode of electronic equipment has two characteristics: first, the failure of the unit is not due to the qualitative change of its physical properties, but the gradual decline of its functional parameters, so there is no clear boundary between normal and failure; Second, the failure of the unit is gradual in time. This kind of failure can be collectively referred to as variable failure or gradual failure. Multi state reliability theory is an effective method to deal with this kind of problem.

The existing equipment multi state reliability theoretical models are mostly applied to the mechanical field, and the established models are sometimes not very applicable to electronic equipment[1-3]. At the same time, most of the existing multi state reliability models are based on independent assumptions, and do not comprehensively consider the correlation between states. Therefore, the established models will inevitably produce certain errors in practical application. Aiming at the problem of implicit fault diagnosis of polymorphic electronic equipment, this paper establishes a fault diagnosis model for polymorphic systems on the basis of considering failure correlation.

II. IMPROVED BAYESIAN NETWORK BASED ON FAILURE CORRELATION

A. Failure correlation model based on correlation factor

The set of related components problem is usually a quadruple, where

(1) $\psi - [P_R, P_M, P_F]^T$ is the reliability vector of the relevant component group, P_R is the safety state probability of the relevant component group, P_M is the intermediary state probability of the relevant component group, and P_F is the failure state probability of the relevant component group;

(2) G is the reliability structure of related components of related component groups. For typical systems, it represents the series parallel relationship of related components of related component groups;

(3) $\Psi = \begin{bmatrix} P_{R1} & P_{R2} & \cdots & P_{Rk} \\ P_{M1} & P_{M2} & \cdots & P_{Mk} \\ P_{F1} & P_{F2} & \cdots & P_{Fk} \end{bmatrix}$ is the reliability matrix of related component groups. P_{Rj} is the safety state probability of the j element in the relevant element group, P_{Mj} is the intermediary state probability of the j element in the relevant element group, and P_{Fj} is the failure state probability of the j element in the relevant element group;

(4) $\lambda \in [0,1]$ is the correlation factor of the relevant component group. For a group of related components, the

correlation factor is a constant.

A: $(G, \Psi, \lambda) \mapsto \psi$ is the deterministic mapping from (G, Ψ, λ) to ψ, that is, the determined (G, Ψ, λ) can uniquely determine the reliability vector ψ of the relevant component group.

For deterministic Ψ and λ, the following functional relationship can be obtained:

$$\psi = G(\Psi, \lambda) \tag{1}$$

B. Improved Bayesian network model

In engineering practice, for the equipment in normal working condition, the on-site data we detect are no failure information. Considering the three-level working state of "safety intermediary failure" of the equipment, the potential failure is an objective existence in the operation of the equipment, and the "no failure" of the equipment at this time is not absolutely "safe". Therefore, how to evaluate the intermediate (potential failure) probability of modules or components under the condition of no failure of electronic equipment system is the primary problem to be solved[4-7].

Traditional Bayesian networks are based on two states and independence. With the deepening of research, although the Bayesian based multi state reliability model has been established, the model thus established is still based on the assumption of independent conditions, and it is unable to effectively analyze the failure related conditions of multi state electronic equipment[8-11]. Therefore, it is necessary to establish a Bayesian network model based on correlation factors. In order to express the correlation between system states and the nature of multi state working mode of electronic equipment, the conditional probability table in the traditional Bayesian network model is replaced by the correlation vector table (DVT). As shown in Figure 1:

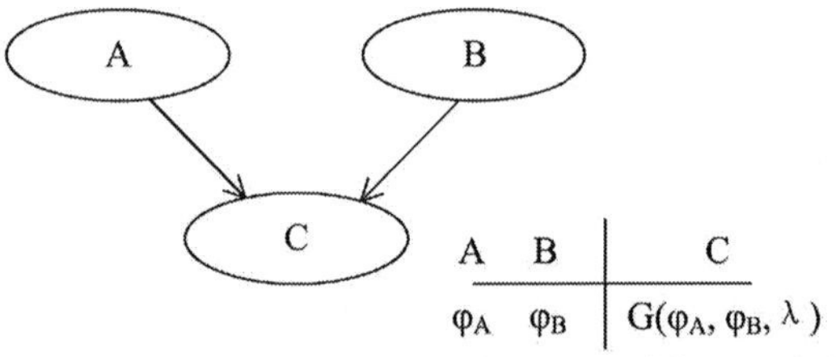

Fig. 1. Improved Bayesian network model based on failure correlation.

In Figure 1, the correlation vector table describes the relationship between the state vector of C, the state vector of a and B, and the correlation factor λ.

For the above figure, it can be obtained from the Bayesian formula that the conditional probability that A is in the intermediary under the condition that C has no failure can be expressed as:

$$P(A^M \mid C^{\bar{F}}) = \frac{P(C^{\bar{F}} \mid A^M)P(A^M)}{P(C^{\bar{F}})} \tag{2}$$

III. State Probability Model Based on Improved Bayesian Network

In order to facilitate the establishment of the system reliability evaluation model, the following assumptions are made for the system:

(1) The system and components have three states: Safety (R), intermediary (M) and failure (F);

(2) Failure correlation between system and component states, and the relevant strength of relevant component groups is determined by the correlation factor λ.

Based on the improved Bayesian network, this paper focuses on the state probability model of typical systems.

A. Image Morphological Analysis

Under the condition of state independence, the state of the series system is the lowest state of the constituent elements, that is, as long as one element fails, the system will fail; The system is safe only when all components are safe. The state of the system is the same as the worst state of its components.

(1) Two element series system

Figure 2 shows the reliability block diagram of a series system composed of two three state elements, and the reliability vectors of the units are $[P_{R1}, P_{M1}, P_{F1}]$ and $[P_{R2}, P_{M2}, P_{F2}]$ respectively.

Fig. 2. A series system composed of two three state elements.

According to the above figure, a Bayesian network model of a series system composed of two three state elements can be established, as shown in Figure 1.

First, the three-level working mode of "safety intermediary failure" is transformed into the two-level working mode of "safety non safety", and the solution is

$$P_R = T_\lambda(P_{R1}, P_{R2}) = \frac{P_{R1}P_{R2}}{\lambda + (1-\lambda)(P_{R1} + P_{R2} - P_{R1}P_{R2})} \tag{3}$$

Secondly, the "safety intermediary failure" three-level working mode of each unit is transformed into the "non failure failure" two-level working mode, and the solution is obtained

$$P_F = S_\lambda(P_{F1}, P_{F2}) = \frac{(P_{F1} + P_{F2}) + (\lambda - 2)P_{F1}P_{F2}}{1 + (\lambda - 1)P_{F1}P_{F2}} \tag{4}$$

Finally, according to the relationship between intermediate probability, safety probability and failure probability, the solution can be obtained

$$P_M = 1 - P_R - P_F \tag{5}$$

(2) Multi element series system

Assuming that the series structure of the system is shown in Figure 3, which is composed of n elements, and the three states of the system and elements are described as: 1 (safety), 0.5 (potential failure), 0 (failure), the state function of the system can be expressed as

$$\phi(X) = \min\{x_i\} \quad (i = 1, 2, \cdots, n) \tag{6}$$

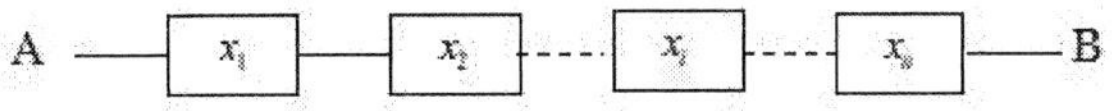

Fig. 3. Series system composed of multiple elements.

Suppose that the state probabilities of the i unit in safety, potential failure and failure are $P(x_i=1)$, $P(x_i=0.5)$ and $P(x_i=0)$ respectively, then the state probabilities of the system are:

$$\begin{cases} P(X=1)=\prod_{i=1}^{n} P(x_i=1) \\ P(X=0.5)=\prod_{i=1}^{n}[P(x_i=1)+P(X=0.5)]-\prod_{i=1}^{n} P(x_i=1) \\ P(X=0)=1-\prod_{i=1}^{n}[P(x_i=1)+P(X=0.5)] \end{cases} \quad (7)$$

B. Parallel system composed of three state elements

(1) Two element parallel system

Figure 4 shows the reliability block diagram of the parallel system composed of two three state elements, and the reliability vectors of the units are $[P_{R1}, P_{M1}, P_{F1}]$ and $[P_{R2}, P_{M2}, P_{F2}]$ respectively.

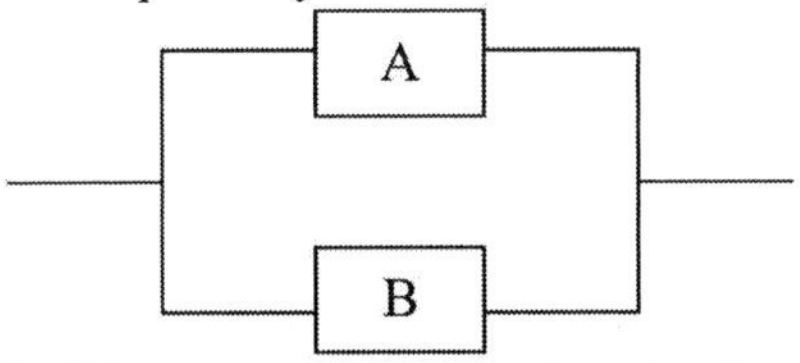

Fig. 4. Parallel system composed of two three state elements.

According to figure 4, the Bayesian network model of the system can also be established, as shown in Figure 1.

First, the three-level working mode of "safety intermediary failure" is transformed into the two-level working mode of "safety non safety", and the solution is

$$P_R = S_\lambda(P_{R1}, P_{R2}) = \frac{(P_{R1}+P_{R2})+(\lambda-2)P_{R1}P_{R2}}{1+(\lambda-1)P_{R1}P_{R2}} \quad (8)$$

Secondly, the "safety intermediary failure" three-level working mode of each unit is transformed into the "non failure failure" two-level working mode, and the solution is obtained

$$P_F = T_\lambda(P_{F1}, P_{F2}) = \frac{P_{F1}P_{F2}}{\lambda+(1-\lambda)(P_{F1}+P_{F2}-P_{F1}P_{F2})} \quad (9)$$

Finally, according to the relationship between intermediate probability, safety probability and failure probability, the solution can be obtained

$$P_M = 1-P_R-P_F \quad (10)$$

(2) Multi element parallel system

Assuming that the parallel structure of the system is shown in Figure 5, which is composed of n elements, and the three states of the system and elements are described as: 1 (safety), 0.5 (potential failure), 0 (failure), the state function of the system is expressed as:

$$\phi(X)=\max\{x_i\} \quad (i=1,2,\cdots,n) \quad (11)$$

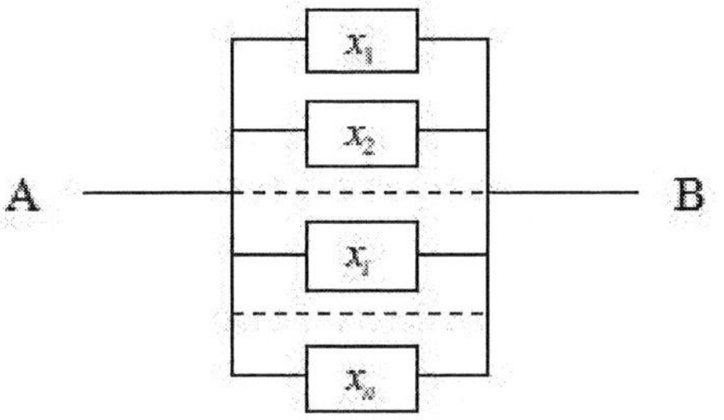

Fig. 5. Parallel system composed of multiple elements.

Suppose that the state probabilities of the i unit in safety, potential failure and failure are $P(x_i=1)$, $P(x_i=0.5)$ and $P(x_i=0)$ respectively, then the state probabilities of the system are:

$$\begin{cases} P(X=1)=1-\prod_{i=1}^{n}[P(x_i=0.5)+P(x_i=0)] \\ P(X=0.5)=\prod_{i=1}^{n}[P(x_i=0.5)+P(x_i=0)]-\prod_{i=1}^{n} P(x_i=0) \\ P(X=0)=\prod_{i=1}^{n} P(x_i=0) \end{cases} \quad (12)$$

C. Unit structure with potential failure

In the system or module, in order to effectively determine the key links of the unit structure, we take n_i-1 test item for reliability evaluation, set the unit reliability index obtained without considering the j test item as $R_{Li,j}\ (j=1,2,\cdots,n_i)$, and rearrange $R_{Li,j}$ from small to large to get:

$$R_{Li,1}^* \le R_{Li,2}^* \le \cdots \le R_{Li,j}^* \le \cdots \le R_{Li,n_i}^* \quad (13)$$

and

$$R_{Li} \le R_{Li,1}^* \le R_{Li,2}^* \le \cdots \le R_{Li,j}^* \le \cdots \le R_{Li,n_i}^* \quad (14)$$

It can be seen from the above formula that the test item corresponding to reliability index R_{Li,n_i}^* has the greatest impact on the evaluation of unit reliability index. Therefore, it can be considered that the test item corresponding to reliability index R_{Li,n_i}^* is the key tracking item of the unit.

To sum up, for the system or module, if the unit has a three-level working mode of "safety intermediary failure", it can be considered that the unit reliability obtained by considering all detection items is the unit safety state probability, and the failure probability obtained without considering key tracking items is the unit failure state probability, The difference between the reliability obtained when the key tracking items are not considered and the reliability obtained when all testing items are considered is the probability of potential failure of the unit, that is:

$$\begin{cases} P(x_i = 1) = R_{Li} \\ P(x_i = 0.5) = R_{Li,n_i}{}^{*} - R_{Li} \\ P(x_i = 0) = 1 - R_{Li,n_i}{}^{*} \end{cases} \quad (15)$$

IV. EXPERIMENTAL VERIFICATION

Taking a laser ranging system as an example, the system is composed of power supply (D), control circuit (K), photoelectric converter (G), shaping amplifier (X), rotor (Z), amplifier (F), trigger circuit (C), counter (J) and other modules. Among them, photoelectric converter and shaping amplifier are mutual compensation and backup; The rotor, amplifier and trigger circuit form a compensation backup system. The Bayesian network model of the system is shown in Figure 6.

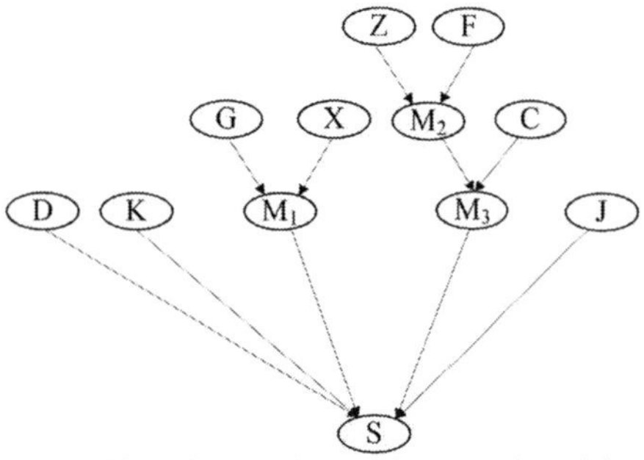

Fig. 6. Systematic Bayesian network model.

The control circuit, photoelectric converter and shaping amplifier in the system have three states, namely: 1 (safety), 0.5 (potential failure) and 0 (failure); Other units have two states, namely: 1 (safety) and 0 (fault).

Test the test items of each unit of the system, and substitute the test data into equation (15) to obtain the occurrence probability of the state of each unit of the system, as shown in Table 1:

TABLE I

PROBABILITY OF STATE OCCURRENCE OF EACH UNIT OF THE SYSTEM

state	D	K	G	X	Z	F	C	J
1	0.997	0.79	0.804	0.833	0.993	0.99	0.994	0.995
0.5	0	0.18	0.192	0.165	0	0	0	0
0	0.003	0.03	0.004	0.002	0.007	0.01	0.006	0.005

The system state probability can be obtained by substituting the data in Table 1 into equations (7) and (12), as shown in Table 2:

TABLE 2

SYSTEM STATE PROBABILITY

State probability	S
1	0.7580
0.5	0.2042
0	0.0379

The conditional probability of each element in each state when system S is in potential failure (0.5 state) is calculated by Bayes formula in formula (1), as shown in Table 3:

TABLE 3

STATE CONDITIONAL PROBABILITY OF EACH COMPONENT OF THE SYSTEM

conditional probability	D	K	G	X	Z	F	C	J
1	1	0.1256	0.7030	0.7284	0.9930	0.9901	0.9941	1
0.5	0	0.8744	0.2909	0.2684	0	0	0	0
0	0	0	0.0060	0.0032	0.0070	0.0099	0.0059	0

It can be seen from table 3 that when considering the potential failure state of the laser ranging system, the conditional probability that the control circuit (K) is in potential failure is the highest, so it is necessary to strengthen the detection of the camera controller in engineering practice.

V CONCLUSION

In view of the limitations of traditional Bayesian network in dealing with the reliability of multi state related systems, considering the trend of system degradation, this paper introduces the failure related factors into Bayesian network, establishes a multi state Bayesian network model based on the related factors, and proposes a multi state electronic equipment state probability model with potential failure units, which truly reflects the working reality of the system, It realizes the effective evaluation of the state probability of multi state electronic equipment. It provides a new technical way to improve the efficiency of fault diagnosis of equipment potential failure model and carry out the research of potential fault diagnosis technology, and also provides a theoretical basis for condition based maintenance support of complex equipment..

ACKNOWLEDGMENT

This paper is supported by Key Special Foundation of universities in Guangdong Province (2020zdzx2032) and national entrepreneurship practice Foundation (S202113684014S、S202113684015S).

REFERENCES

[1] Z D, Zhao J M, LI H P, et al. A Fault Diagnosis Method of a Plunger Pump Based on SA-EMD-PNN[J]. Journal of Vibration and Shock, 2019, 38 (8):145—152.

[2] Zou M, Xue L, Gai H J, et al. Identification of the shear parameters for lunar regolith based on a GA-BP neural network. Journal of Terramechanics, 2020, 89:21-29.

[3] Xie Li-yang, Zhou Jin-yu, Hao Chang-zhong. System-level load-strength interference based reliability modeling ofk-out-of-nsystem. Reliability Engineering and System Safety, 2004, 84: 311-317

[4] Xie Z H, Zhang Y, Jin C. Predition of coal spontaneous combustion in goaf based on the BP neural network. Procedia Engineering. 2012, (43): 88-92.

[5] Li Q, Xu Z Y. Parameter Identification Method Research

Based on the BP Neural Network and Space Search. Applied Mechanics and Materials, 2014, 2987:1165-1169.
[6] Wu Y, Zeng Z X. A rapid detection method of earthquake infrasonic wave based on decision-making tree and the BP neural network. International Journal of Information and Communication Technology, 2019, 14(3):295-307.
[7] Xie L Y, Zhou J Y, Hao C Z. System-level load-strength interference based reliability modeling of k-out-of-n system]. Reliability Engineering and System Safety, 2004, 84:311-317.
[8] Xie L Y, Zhou J Y, Wang Y Y. System reliability evaluation-an extended load-strength interference analysis approach, The 11th International Conference on Industrial Engineering And Engineering Management, Shenyang China, 2005,4: 883-887.
[9]Xiao R G, Li K, Sun L Y, et al. The Prediction of liquid holdup in horizontal pipe with BP neural network. Energy Science & Engineering, 2020, 8(6):2159-2168.
[10]Liu J, Ashraf M A. Face recognition method based on GA-BP neural network algorithm. Open Physics, 2018, 16(1). 1056-1065.
[11]Levitin G. Incorporating common-cause failures into no repairable multi-state series-parallel system analysis. IEEE Transactions on Reliability, 2001, 50(4). 380-388.

Jingde Huang, who is mainly engaged in the field of machine vision technology, doctor and professor.

Optimization Research on Electrodynamic Repulsion of DC Contactor

Lin Xia, Changchun Chi, Chen Chen

Shanghai Dianji University, Shanghai, 201306
Email: 401166927@qq.com TEL: 18101961157

***Abstract*—Short-circuit faults in the circuit can make the electric repulsion between DC contactor contacts increase sharply, resulting in contact bouncing or even contact melting, thus affecting the safety and reliability of the circuit. The NDZ3T DC contactor using in the electric vehicle charging pile is taken as the object of the study. A cylindrical model is used to simulate the conductive bridge, and ANSYS is used to calculate the electric repulsion between the contacts. The electric repulsion is improved by using DT4, a magnetic separation block that can weaken the magnetic field. Two types of U-shaped spacers with openings facing upward and downward were designed, and the effects of different thicknesses of the spacers on the electric repulsion were investigated. The structure of the contact was modified and its effect on the electric repulsion was studied. A comparison shows that a U-shaped spacer with a downward opening has a stronger ability to weaken the electric repulsion than a U-shaped spacer with an upward opening. Although the hollow contact plate cannot affect the electric repulsion, on this basis, adding a U-shaped magnetic isolation block with the opening downward will have a higher electric repulsion than the original structure of adding the U-shaped magnetic isolation block with the opening downward. The repulsion force decreases about 4N. The results of the study have significant implications for reducing electric repulsion, improving the short-time tolerance of the circuit, and enhancing circuit safety.**

I. Introduction

To accelerate the green and low-carbon transformation of energy, the number of new energy vehicles in China continues to rise and charging infrastructure is becoming more popular [1,2]. The safety and reliability of DC contactors, which are widely used in electric vehicle charging stations and charging piles, are becoming the subject of research. The electric repulsion of DC contactors consists of the electrodynamic force between conductors and the Holm force between contacts. The strong inrush current generated by a short circuit during charging will cause the electric repulsion to increase sharply and the static and dynamic contacts to separate, while the high temperature arc between the contacts will cause the contact surfaces to melt and weld, or even explode the DC contactor. Contact abnormal opening and damage will affect the normal work of other electrical components, which will become one of the hidden dangers in the development of new energy vehicles.

Domestic scholars have done a lot of research on the optimization of electric repulsion of electrical appliances. Early literature [3] used finite element software to establish a conductive bridge model to calculate the electric repulsion between contacts and validate it successfully. After that, studies on the electric repulsion of circuit breakers, relays, contactors and other electrical appliances were carried out one after another [4-9]. The electric repulsion can be weakened by modifying the contact structure, and in reference [10], the electric repulsion was significantly optimized by adding tubular electric pure iron to the contacts. The literature [11] proposed to optimize the electric repulsion of DC contactors using square electric pure iron, but the effect of other shapes of DT4 on the electric repulsion was not discussed.

Electric pure iron in a magnetic field can reduce the magnetic field strength in a conductor, which in turn reduces the electric repulsion. In this paper, we compare the effect of U-shaped pure electrical iron on the electric repulsion and design a new conductive structure to study the effect of this structure on the electric repulsion, and finally combine the pure electrical iron with the new conductive structure to achieve the optimization of the electric repulsion.

II. Mathematical Model of DC Contactor Electric Repulsion

A. Holm force between contacts

When two smooth and flat conductive metals are laminated together due to external pressure, the area where contact really occurs is actually very small, only a few thousandths of the macroscopic overlapping contact area, which is also the area of current conduction, called this tiny contact area for the conductive spot. When the current passes through the conductive spot, the magnetic field generated by the contracted current line will make the static and dynamic contacts produce the opposite direction of the Holm force. Considering the conductive spot as a circular area, the Holm force F_H for a pair of static and dynamic contacts is calculated as follows.

$$F_H = \frac{\mu_0}{4\pi} I^2 ln\frac{R}{r} \quad (1)$$

Where: μ_0 is the air permeability , $\mu_0 = 4\pi \times 10^{-7} H/m$; I is the current flowing through the contact; R is the radius of the static contact; r is the radius of the conductive spot, and its calculation formula is as follows.

$$r = \sqrt{\frac{F_k}{\pi \xi H}} \quad (2)$$

Where: F_k is the pre-compression force between the contacts; H is the Brinell hardness of the contact material; ξ is the roughness of the contact surface, usually taken $\xi = 0.45$, $r = 0.26mm$ is obtained by the formula .

B. Electrodynamic force between loop conductors

The Beal-Shavall's law is a common formula for calculating the electrodynamic force of an appliance, and its expression is [12].

$$F_L = \frac{\mu_0}{4\pi} I^2 K_h \quad (3)$$

where: K_h is the loop factor, only with the shape of the circuit of the current-carrying conductor, distribution position, length, the medium between the conductors, K_h of the simple conductor circuit is easier to derive.

The circuit conductors of the contact mechanism are considered as two conductors parallel to each other and perpendicular to the structure of the other conductor, as shown in Figure 1. Based on the given current direction and magnetic field direction, the left-hand rule is applied to determine the direction of the electrodynamic force of the conductor circuit.

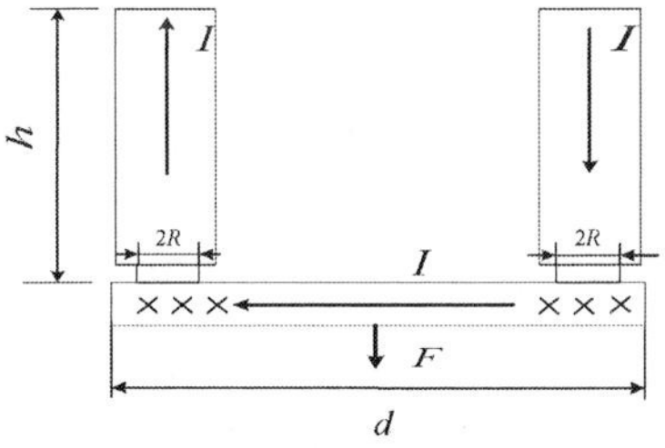

Fig. 1. DC contactor contact structure.

For two perpendicular linear finite length conductors, the loop factor K_h is expressed as follows.

$$K_h = ln\frac{(h+\sqrt{h^2+R^2})d}{R(h+\sqrt{h^2+d^2})} \quad (4)$$

Where: h is the vertical conductor to get height; d is the length of the horizontal conductor, take $h = 115mm$, $d = 25.5mm$. Since K_h is simplified as

$$K_h = ln\frac{2hd}{R(h+\sqrt{h^2+d^2})} \quad (5)$$

The contact structure exists with two sets of two mutually perpendicular conductors, the conductor with current flowing vertically downward with the horizontal conductor and the horizontal conductor with current flowing vertically upward. Therefore, the expression for the electrodynamic force received by the horizontal conductor is followed as:

$$F_L = 2 \times \frac{\mu_0}{4\pi} I^2 K_h \quad (6)$$

The electric repulsion force on the contact structure consists of the Holm force between the contacts and the electrodynamic force between the conductor loops, which is expressed as:

$$F_C = 2F_H + F_L \quad (7)$$

C. Introduction to the working principle of electrotechnical pure iron

When the DT4 is in the magnetic field $\boldsymbol{H}_0$, a corresponding additional magnetic field $\boldsymbol{H}'$ is generated, which is expressed as follows.

$$\boldsymbol{H}' = \chi_m \boldsymbol{H}_0 = (\mu_{rDT4} - 1)\boldsymbol{H}_0 \quad (8)$$

where: χ_m is the magnetization; μ_{rDT4} is the relative magnetic permeability of DT4.

The direction of the additional magnetic field is opposite to the direction of the external magnetic field, thus weakening the magnetic field near the electrotechnical outgoing iron. The magnetic field $\boldsymbol{H}$ around an electric pure iron is

$$\boldsymbol{H} - \boldsymbol{H}_0 - \boldsymbol{H}' \quad (9)$$

At this point the magnetic induction $\boldsymbol{B}$ is expressed as follows:

$$\boldsymbol{B} = \mu_0 \mu_r \boldsymbol{H} \quad (10)$$

where: μ_r is the relative magnetic permeability of the conducting medium.

The use of electric pure iron weakens the magnetic field strength of the contact structure, thereby reducing the electric repulsive force on the conductor circuit. The effect of electro-pure iron on the electric repulsion is determined by varying the thickness and shape of the electro-pure iron for different parameters.

III. FINITE ELEMENT MODELING OF THE CONTACT CONDUCTIVE CIRCUIT

The conductor circuit of the contact was modeled using ANSYS software, as shown in Figure 2.

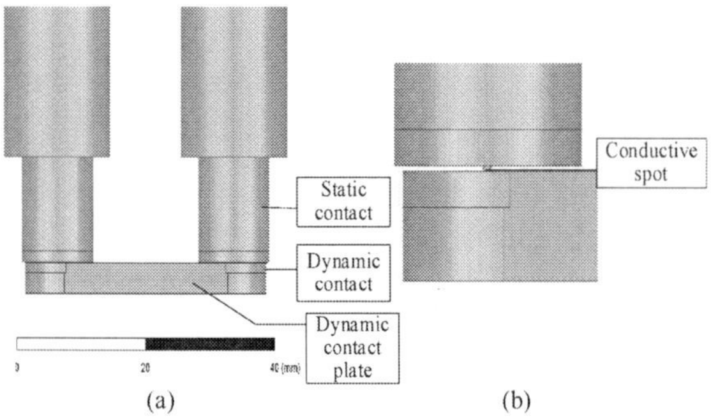

Fig. 2. DC contactor current-carrying conductor model.

Figure 2(a) shows the overall structure of the conductive circuit of the DC contactor, while Figure 2(b) shows an enlarged view of the connection between the movable and static contacts. In this paper, it is assumed that there is only one conductive spot between the static and dynamic contacts, and the conductive spot is simulated by a cylindrical conductor. The height of the conductive spot is taken as 0.15 mm [13]. The material of the dynamic contact, static contact, dynamic contact plate, and conductive spot is copper. the flow of the electric repulsion analysis of the conductive circuit of the DC contactor conductor in ANSYS is shown in Figure 3.

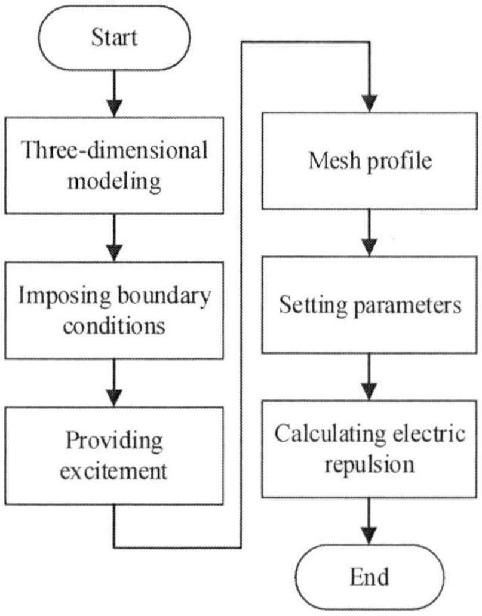

Fig. 3. ANSYS electric repulsion analysis flow chart.

IV. Results and Analysis of the Experiment

A. Mathematical Model Validation of the Contact System

The theoretical and simulated values of the conductor loop electrodynamic repulsion and Holm force are compared as shown in TABLE I and TABLE II, respectively.

From Table 1, the theoretical and simulated values of the conductor loop electrodynamic forces are similar for different short-circuit currents, and the error is always maintained at 2.1%. From Table 2, the difference between the theoretical and simulated values of the Holm force becomes obvious when the current gradually becomes larger, and the error remains at 27.8%, which is probably because the theoretical calculation of the Holm force still has some influencing factors that are not taken into account. The theoretical calculation cannot accurately reflect the complex current and magnetic field of the three-dimensional structure, while the finite element simulation has a better simulation of the current and magnetic field of the three-dimensional structure, and the results will be more accurate.

TABLE I
Comparison Of Theoretical And Simulated Values Of Electric Repulsion Of Conductor Loops

Current /kA	Conductor circuit electrodynamics /N		Error /%
	Theoretical value	Simulation value	
1	0.30	0.31	2.1%
2	1.22	1.24	2.1%
3	2.74	2.80	2.1%
4	4.87	4.97	2.1%
5	7.61	7.77	2.1%
6	10.96	11.19	2.1%
7	14.91	15.23	2.1%
8	19.48	19.90	2.1%

TABLE II
Comparison Of Theoretical And Simulated Values Of Homer Force

Current /kA	Holm force /N		Error /%
	Theoretical value	Simulation value	
1	0.61	0.78	27.8%
2	2.44	3.12	27.8%
3	5.49	7.02	27.8%
4	9.77	12.49	27.8%
5	15.26	19.51	27.8%
6	21.97	28.09	27.8%
7	29.91	38.24	27.8%
8	39.06	49.94	27.8%

B. Effect of U-shaped electric pure iron on electric repulsion

The maximum short time withstand current of DC contactor on the market is 8kA, so the maximum short circuit current of this paper is 8kA. The U-shaped electric pure iron is designed on the surface of the laminated contact plate, with the opening facing up and the opening facing down, as shown in Figure 4.

Varying the thickness H of the electric pure iron in the range of 1 mm to 5 mm, when the current is 8 kA, the magnitude of the electric repulsion is shown in TABLE III.

As can be seen from TABLE III, the electric repulsion force increases instead of decreases as the thickness increases when the electric pure iron with the opening upward is placed on the dynamic contact plate, and decreases as the thickness increases when the electric pure iron with the opening downward is placed on the dynamic contact plate. As the DC contactor used in this paper, after the overtravel, the final pressure of the dynamic contact plate by the reaction spring is 29N, and the direction is vertical upward, so when using the U-shaped electric pure iron with the thickness of 5mm and the opening downward, the electric repulsion can be offset, so that the dynamic and static contacts are no longer repelled.

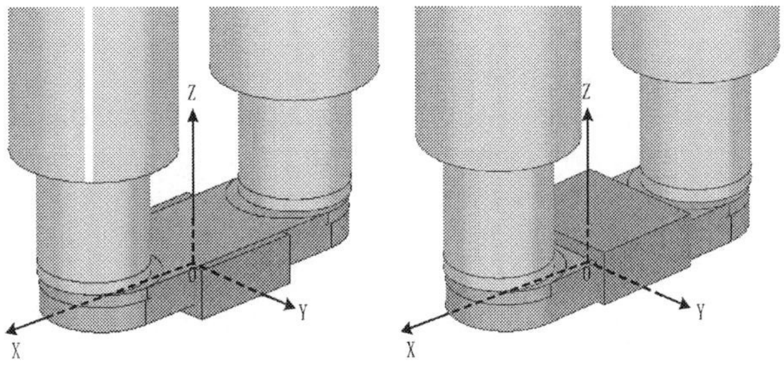

Fig. 4. schematic diagram of the placement of electric pure iron.

TABLE III
ELECTRIC REPULSION AT DIFFERENT THICKNESSES AND POSITIONS OF ELECTRIC PURE IRON

U-shaped DT4 Placement	Electric repulsion /N				
	1mm DT4	2mm DT4	3mm DT4	4mm DT4	5mm DT4
opening facing up	85.47	93.81	98.93	102.96	104.31
opening facing down	54.05	43.59	35.75	29.41	24.15

C. contactor contact system optimization

The dynamic contact plate is modified as shown in Figure 5, so that the current passing through the dynamic contact plate is divided into two, and the size of this hollowed rectangular body is set to 12×3×3.05mm, and the magnitude of the electric repulsion of the DC contactor is calculated at a current of 1~8kA.

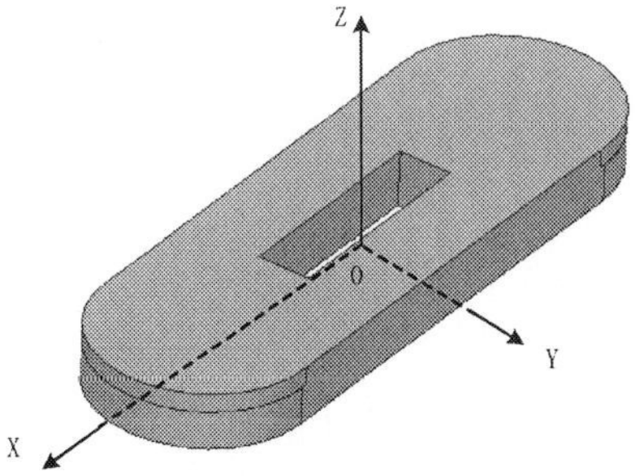

Figure 5

Fig. 5. schematic diagram of dynamic contact plate modification.

The calculated results were compared with the electric repulsion when the dynamic contact plate was not modified, and the results are shown in TABLE IV.

From TABLE IV, it can be seen that the hollowing out of the contact plate does not directly affect the magnitude of the DC contactor electric repulsion. Then add the U-shaped electric pure iron with the opening facing down on the modified contact plate, set the short-circuit current to 8kA, change the thickness of the electric pure iron to 1~5mm, and compare the calculated results with the original contact plate with the U-shaped opening facing down on the electric pure iron, as shown in TABLE V.

As can be seen from TABLE V, when the dynamic contact plate is hollowed out, and then add different thicknesses of U-shaped electric pure iron with the opening facing down, the electric repulsion will be further reduced, the reduced value is around 4N.

TABLE IV
COMPARISON OF ELECTRIC REPULSION BETWEEN ORIGINAL AND HOLLOWED DYNAMIC CONTACT PLATES

Current /kA	Electric repulsion /N	
	The original dynamic contact plate	Hollowed dynamic contact plate
1	1.09	1.07
2	4.36	4.27
3	9.82	9.61
4	17.46	17.08
5	27.28	26.68
6	39.28	38.42
7	53.47	52.30
8	69.84	68.31

TABLE V
ELECTRIC REPULSION OF DIFFERENT THICKNESSES OF ELECTRIC PURE IRON UNDER THE HOLLOWED DYNAMIC CONTACT PLATE

Thickness of U-shaped DT4 /mm	Electric repulsion /N		Differential value /N
	The original dynamic contact plate	Hollowed dynamic contact plate	
1	54.05	49.89	4.15
2	43.59	39.41	4.18
3	35.75	31.38	4.37
4	29.41	25.04	4.36
5	24.15	20.34	3.81

V. CONCLUSION

In this paper, we modeled the contact system of DC contactor of electric vehicle charging pile and calculated its electric repulsion, and optimized the electric repulsion by using electric pure iron, and the following results were obtained.

(1) The weakening of the electric repulsion by the U-shaped electric pure iron with downward opening is better than that by the U-shaped electric pure iron with upward opening, and the electric repulsion becomes smaller as the thickness of the electric pure iron increases.

(2) Hollowing out the dynamic contact plate does not have a direct effect on the electric repulsion force, but when a downward-opening U-shaped pure electric iron is added to the moving contact plate, the electric repulsion force obtained is about 4 N smaller than that obtained when a

downward-opening U-shaped pure electric iron is added under the original moving contact plate.

By studying the shape and thickness of the pure electrical iron, the short-time current withstand capability of the DC contactor is improved, and the safety and reliability of the DC contactor under short-circuit circuit is enhanced.

References

[1] Y. H. Wang, L. W. Yang, W. Jiang, C. Z. Liu , Y. Wang. "Review on Equipment and Control Strategies of DC Power Grid." *Power System Technology*, 2018,42(1): 12-24

[2] Q. Q. Chen," The development of electric vehicles and the integration of four networks and four streams. " *Science & Technology Review* ,2021, 39(17)

[3] X. W. Li, D. G. Chen, H.W. Wu, Z. P. Li and H. G. Gang, " 3-D Finite Element Analysis of Electro-dynamic Repulsion Forces Acting on Contacts. " , *High Voltage Apparatus* , 2004,1:53-55

[4] W. Wang, L. X. Shao, X. M. Zeng and S. H. Fang,"Characteristic analysis and test verification of high power permanent magnet DC contactor." *Electrical & Energy Management Technology* , 2019, 7: 1-5+29,.

[5] F. Y. Guo, Y. H. Zhang, Z. Y. Wang, L. Li and X. L. Wang, "Experimental analysis of the welding phenomenon of AC relay." *Journal of Liaoning Technical University (Natural Science)* , 2020, 39(3): 259-264

[6] G. Z. Zhang, J. C. Yi, P. Zhao, W. L. Wang, "Simulating Calculation of Short-Circuit Dynamic Stability for Air Circuit Breaker." *Electrical & Energy Management Technology* , 2020, 4: 54-61.

[7] G. F. Yu, Z. L. Yuan and X. Zheng," Analysis of Electric-Dynamic Repulsion Force Between Contacts of High Voltage DC Relay " *Electrical & Energy Management Technology* , 2020, 09: 13-17

[8] A. K. Zhou, "Analysis of Electro-Dynamic Force of Bridge Shaped Contact in Medium Voltage Vacuum Circuit Breaker." *Electrical & Energy Management Technology* , 2019, 13: 5-37+45

[9] G. H. She and ZHANG Pengyu, "Simulation Analysis and Research on Short-Term." *Electrical & Energy Management Technology* , 2019, 7: 34-39

[10] H. J. Dong, et al, "Electro-Dynamic Repulsion Force Calculation and Structure Optimization of The Contacts in 12kV Vacuum Interrupter ."*High Voltage Engineering*, 2022

[11] J. S. Chen and C. C. CHI," Simulation and optimization of electric repulsion force in contact system of DC contactor. " *Journal of Shanghai Dianji University* , 2021, 24(1):13-18

[12] H. Yu, H. Liang, K. Bo, X. Ye ,et al, "Virtual Prototype and Optimal Design of Short Circuit Current Capability of Magnetic Latching Relay", 2018 IEEE Holm Conference on Electrical Contacts, 2018: 124-129.

[13] A. Popescu, E. Lazarescu, F. M. Frigura-Iliasa, L. Dolga, H. E. Filipescu and A. Andreea, "Analytical Model for the Electrodynamical Forces inside Electrical Contacts of Commutation Devices", 20th International Scientific Conference on Electric Power Engineering (EPE), 2019: 1-4.

8th International Conference on Reliability of Electrical Products and Electrical Contacts, November 18-20, 2022

Investigation on the Performance Degradation Characteristics of the Sliding Electrical Contact of the Brush and Slip Ring

Bin Liang[1], Hansheng Zhang[2], Jiayi Qian[2], Yilin Zhou[2]

[1] Automation School, Beijing University of Posts and Telecommunications, Beijing, 100876, China

[2] School of Artificial Intelligence, Beijing University of Posts and Telecommunications, Beijing, 100876, China

E-mail: ylzhou@bupt.edu.cn Tel: 18910480362

Abstract—**As a sliding electrical connection part in a radar equipment, brush and slip ring contacts ensure a stable and reliable connection of electric energy and signals between rotating part and fixed part. A manufactory extended the pre-running-in period of the brush and the slip ring from 2 hours to 60 hours to increase the contact area between the flat surface of the blocky brush and the curved surface of the slip ring. However, an ablation on the contact zone occurred within one year after being put into use. In this paper, the relationship between the pre-running in process of the brush and slip ring and both the wear mechanism of the contact surface and the degradation characteristics of the electrical contact performance was studied by simulating the actual pre-running in process. Based on the analysis of wear debris oxidation and accumulation caused by the excessive pre-running in of the brush, the original reasons for the performance degradation of the sliding electrical contact of the brush and slip ring and the ablative failure of the contact interface were analyzed.**

Index Terms— **brush and slip ring, sliding electrical contact, wear mechanism**

I. INTRODUCTION

As a key electrical connection component in a radar equipment, the brush and slip ring ensures stable and reliable connection of electric energy and signals between the rotating part and the fixed part of the radar [0]. The brush and slip ring contact is also a key component of various other precision instruments such as turntables, centrifuges, and inertial navigation equipment [2].

In practical applications, the blocky brushes are usually carried out the pre-running in process before the brush and slip ring is put into use. The purpose is to make the end face of the blocky brush and the contact interface of the slip ring have the same curvature so as to increase the mechanical contact area between the brush and the slip ring. After a manufactory extended the pre-running in time of the brushes from 2 hours to 60 hours, the ablation failure of the contact area occurred within one year after the brush and the slip ring was put into use, as shown in Fig. 1.

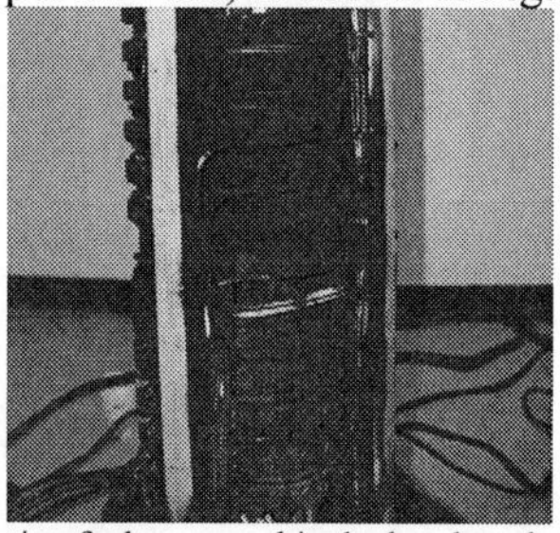

Fig. 1. Severe ablation fault occurred in the brush and slip ring system during use.

Preliminary judgment based on relevant data and fault phenomena shows that the wear of the brushes during the running-in process aggravates the accumulation of wear debris inside the slip ring structure, which reduces the insulation resistance between adjacent slip rings and between the slip ring and the outer casing, but also reduces the creepage distance, and ablation is caused by short-circuit discharge under high-voltage conditions [3]-[4]. However, after cleaning the wear debris [4], the brush and slip ring still suffers from ablation in a short period of using time. It can be seen cleaning the wear debris cannot fundamentally solve the ablation problem, and there may be other failure mechanisms that cause high temperature ablation of the slip ring.

When studying the burning problem of a certain type of slip ring, Songbai Xiang et al. found that the friction and vibration between the brush and slip rings would cause serious wear of the brush, the edge of the brush would peel off, and the contact resistance would increase due to the decrease of the contact area [4]. In addition, the rise of ambient temperature leads to the stress relaxation of the loading spring of the brush, which will reduce the contact force and further increase the contact resistance. The slip ring forms parallel contact pairs with multiple brushes, and the contact resistance of each pair under different contact forces are inconsistent, resulting in uneven shunting [5]. The temperature of different brushes is polarized [6], and contacts with low contact resistance will be distributed with greater current, resulting in joule heat increase and thermal failure.

Although the blocky brush made of silver-copper-carbon material can have high weldability resistance and low and stable contact resistance, it has large wear, high erosion rate and poor arc extinguishing performance. P. C. Wingert et al. [7] carefully observed the metal morphology of the silver-carbon cathode contact after the static gap discharge test and found that the material damage caused by the cathodic arc effect was almost uniformly distributed directly on the surface of the anode contact. There was a silver-plated metal particle with a mound-like structure around the anode contact surface, and a silver-plated metal with a mesh-like wall around the cathode contact surface, wherein the cylindrical metal particles were mainly solidified from the inner metal layer of the electrical contact. Gray and Grpharney [8] explained some types of arc morphologies in some studies, arguing that the columnar root structure of the arc tended to be stable on a graphitic silver-like particle with molten silver around it, and due to the increase in the internal pressure generated by the arc cylinder caused it to bulge around. When the arc root was extinguished or transferred to other parts, the heat was also removed from the contact, and the originally molten metal turned into a solid state. Naoki Fukuda [9] studied the relationship between the change of Ag content on the voltage drop and wear of the brush and slip ring, and the results showed that the contact voltage drop and wear were optimal when brushes with 60-80% silver content were used.

The thermal failure of electrical contacts is possibly related to the insulation discharge between different levels of slip rings, the welding of the contact area between the brushes and the slip rings, and the arc generated between the brushes and the bus rings. The slip ring is an electromechanical integrated feeder component. The stable electrical contact between the brushes and the slip ring is the core element of its normal operation. The size and the change rate of the contact resistance [10] are the main indicators to evaluate the quality of the slip ring. Excessive contact resistance will increase the temperature rise of the contact part, which will accelerate the oxidation of the contact interface surface, thereby decreasing the effective electrical contact area.

According to the above research results, the ablation fault of the brush and slip ring after the extended pre-running in process needs to be further studied based on wear detection and electrical contact degradation mechanism. In this paper, through the running in wear experiment design of the brush and slip ring, the relationship between the running in process of the brush and the wear of the brush contact surface, as well as the degradation of the electrical contact performance is explored, and the original reasons for the ablation fault of the contact interface of the brush and slip ring are analyzed.

II. Ablation Failure Analysis of Brush and Slip Rings

The contact resistance of several groups of brush and slip ring contact pairs with ablation faults was measured and the degradation range of contact resistance was counted. Then through the observation of the contact interface between the brush and the slip ring, the ablation degree and characteristics were classified from the weak to the heavy state, and the possible causes of ablation failure were preliminarily analyzed combined with the actual working conditions.

A. Contact Resistance of the Ablated Brush and Slip Ring Contacts

In the brush and slip ring system, every four brushes are assembled in one brush holder, and form four parallel contact pairs with one slip ring. The assembly structure is shown in Fig. 2. The material parameters of brushes and slip rings are shown in Table I.

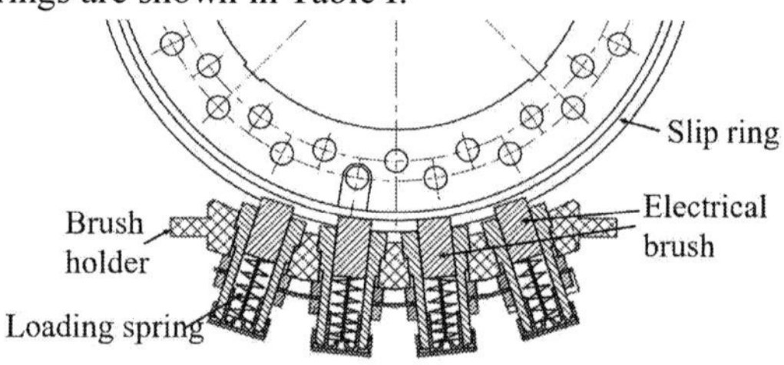

Fig. 2. Assembly structure of four brushes and one slip ring.

TABLE I
MATERIAL PARAMETERS OF BRUSH AND SLIP RING

	Material	Composition
Brush	Silver carbon alloy JF390-1	77%Ag, 14%Cu, 6%Graphite, 3%C fiber
Brush Lisp Ring	Silver copper nickel alloy AgCuNi20-2	78% Ag, 20%Cu, 2%Ni

For the brush and slip ring system with ablation in Fig. 1, the four-point method [11] was used to test the contact resistance of 24 ablated brush and slip ring contact pairs for 5 times, and the average value was obtained. The current was set to 100mA, and the open circuit voltage was set to 2V. The standard contact resistance of a single pair of brush and slip rings should not exceed 12mΩ, and in the failed brush and slip ring, 75% of the contact resistance exceeded the standard value, which would cause a larger temperature rise at the contact interface.

B. Ablation Failure Phenomenon of the Brush and Slip Ring

In the faulty brush and slip ring equipment, the ablated brushes were disassembled, and their ablation degree and morphological characteristics were observed, as shown in Fig. 3. It can be observed that the brush contact surface is cut off after welding, the metal of the slip ring was ablated in a large area, and the brush holder was partially melted.

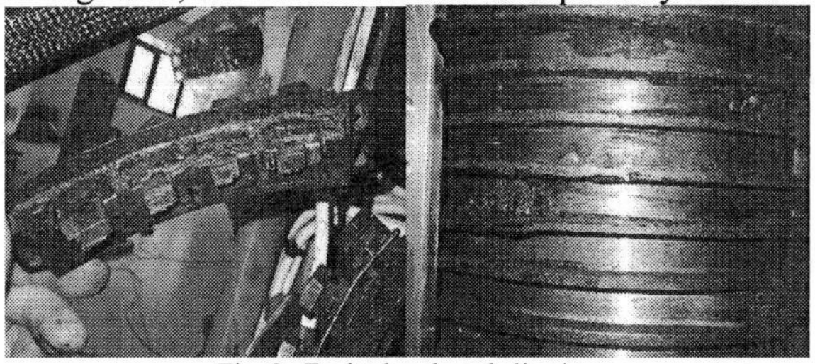

Fig. 3. Faulty brush and slip ring

C. Analysis on Ablation Fault Causes of Brush and Slip Ring

The actual working conditions of the brush and slip ring were as follows: in the case of non-energization, the brush slid relative to the slip ring from the non-working position and stopped when it reached the working position. At this time, there was a millisecond-level short-term impulse current (I_i=1500A) when the power supply array was powered on, and then the contact interface of the brush and slip ring turned to pass the workload (I_0=60A). After the work was over, the working load current was turned off, the brush slid in the opposite direction, and returned to the non-working position. During this process, no current passed through the contact interface, but there was a voltage.

The fault analysis was carried out combined with the actual working condition and ablation phenomenon of brush and slip ring system. Firstly, there were three possible sources of heat. They were Joule heat, the discharge heating on the insulation material due to wear debris of brushes and the arc ablation. Among them, wear debris reduced the insulation between electrodes and lead to surface discharge heating, which required a large amount of wear debris and could be distributed across adjacent electrodes in a high-strength electric field. The resulting ablation should be concentrated on the insulating material between the two electrodes, which was inconsistent with the brush and slip ring metal ablation phenomenon. The condition of arc ablation was that the electrical contacts between the brush and the slip ring must be destroyed before the arc was formed, and a very high electric field strength was formed between the contact interface between the brush and the slip ring. If one of the 4 parallel contacts was still conducting electricity, no arcing can form, so this was not the initial cause of ablation.

The third possibility was that Joule heat was formed under high current conditions, and it was difficult to dissipate heat from the contact interface, resulting in a local temperature rise of the brush and slip ring system. Combined with the phenomena that melting of the brush and slip ring was around the contact area, the brushes were partially cut off and the brush holder was retracted, it showed that the contact area of brush and slip ring should be the main heat source. The local temperature rise in the contact interface of the brush and slip ring caused the softening and welding of the interface material and the bonding between the brush and brush holder. In the sliding process of brush and slip ring reset, the tangential force cut off the contact bonding interface, making the interface lose its original surface roughness and increased the wear and contact resistance of the material. The sliding of the rough interface might also cause the brush to bounce during the sliding process, and the spring applying normal force would relax stress due to temperature rise, resulting in insufficient contact force. If the high temperature made the brush holder material softened, resulting in greater friction, bonding, the brush cannot pop out to guaranty the contact force, so that the contact resistance further increased. The brush holder and the slip ring separator were organic materials with low thermal decomposition temperature and easy released of organic pollutants, which further aggravated the increase of the contact resistance. Therefore, it was inferred that the initial failure reason should be the thermal failure caused by the welding of the interface material due to the rise of the interface temperature of the electrical contacts.

III. Experimental Design of Brush and Slip Ring Wear

Based on the primary fault analysis of the ablative brush and slip ring system, it was speculated that extending the pre-running in time would lead to a series of phenomena, such as intensified contact wear, increased contact resistance, contact welding, elastic force degradation of loading spring, and caused the brush to retract into the brush holder and failed to reset, which would lead to the final ablative fault. In this section, the pre-running in process of the brush and slip ring was simulated by experiments, and the relationship between the wear mechanism of the brush and the degradation characteristics of the electrical contact performance in the running-in simulation experiment was explored, and the possibility of the welding on the contact interface of the brush and slip ring was analyzed.

A. Samples of Brush and Slip Ring and Experimental Equipment

Select 4 groups of new brush and bus ring samples, each group of 2 brushes, marked as No.1 and No.2 respectively. The brush samples and corresponding markings were shown in Table II.

TABLE II
Brush Samples and Corresponding Labels

Groups	NO.1		NO.2		NO.3		NO.4	
Label	1-1	1-2	2-1	2-2	3-1	3-2	4-1	4-2

T

he brush pre-running in simulation experiment was carried out by using the brush and slip ring running-in equipment shown in Fig. 4.

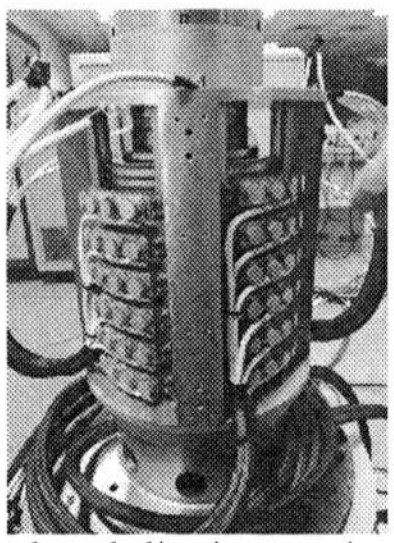

Fig. 4. The brush and slip ring running-in equipment.

B. Simulating Experimental Method for Wear of Brush and Slip Ring

In the brush and slip ring running in equipment, the No.1 and No.2 brushes in the first group were respectively assembled in the brush holders of two adjacent slip rings, and then the contact pairs were connected in series. The slip ring was stationary, the brushes were rotated clockwise for 58 hours at a speed of 5s/r, and then reversed counterclockwise for 2 hours.

In each experiment, the brush samples from the same group were used for the running in wear experiment for 60 hours. The equipment rotation was paused at the end of 1h, 2h, 3h, 5h, 7h, 10h, 13h, 17h, 22h, 27h, 32h, 40h, 50h, 56h, 58h and 60h of the running in time, and the No.1 brush was taken out to measure the wear extent. No. 2 brush was assembled from the beginning of the experiment until the end of 60 hours before being removed for measurement.

C. Detection Scheme for Brush Wear

The wear effect of running in process on brush contact interface was analyzed through the measurement and observation of the brush quality changes, the wear depth and the roughness of every zones of contact surface, the wear area after different running in time, as well as through the contact surface morphology and composition detection.

D. On-line Monitoring Method of Sliding Contact Resistance

Altai USB2861 data acquisition card and Puyuan DP832A constant current source were used to measure the sliding contact resistance of two contact pairs in series [12]. The data acquisition card recorded the sliding contact resistance 85 times during a relative rotation of the brush and slip ring (5 seconds).

IV. Analysis of Characteristic for Sliding Contact Resistance of Brush and Slip Ring

During the running in process, because the contact surfaces of the brushes and the slip ring were relatively motion, the contact resistance varied with the periodic sliding. According to the sliding contact resistance data of brush 1-1 in the running in process, the average sliding contact resistance within every hour (720 cycles, 5s per cycle) was counted, and the curve of the average sliding contact resistance of a single contact in the brush and slip ring with the running in time was drawn, as shown in Fig. 5.

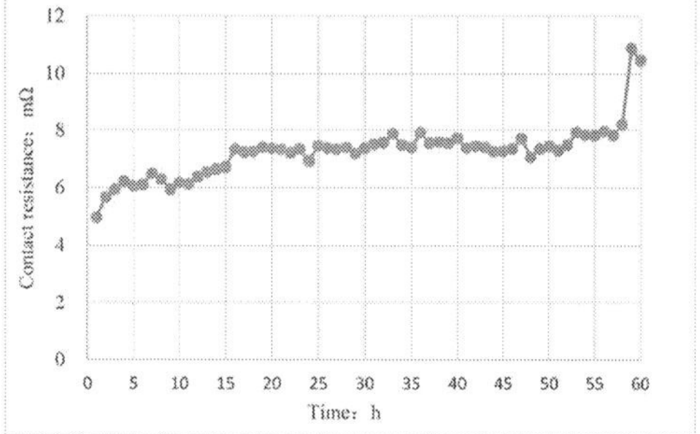

Fig. 5. Average sliding contact resistance of brush and slip ring

During the 1st, 5th, 10th, 25th, 40th, 58th and 60th hours of the running in wear experiment, the sliding resistance data of a single contact pair for each cycle (85 sampling points) were taken, and the contact resistance was a logarithmic coordinate, as shown in Fig. 6.

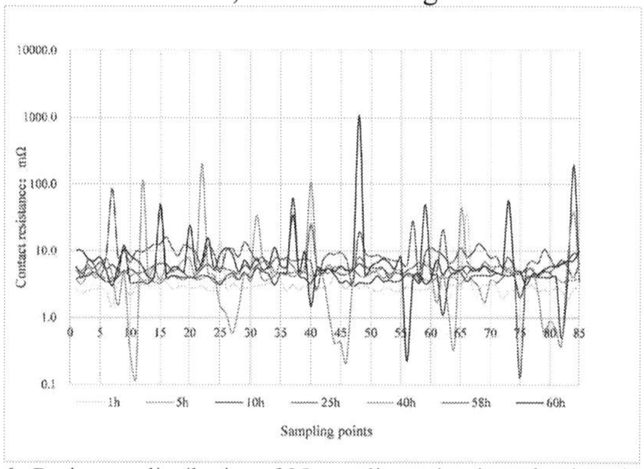

Fig. 6. Resistance distribution of 85 sampling points in each selected cycle

According to Fig. 5 and Fig. 6, in the first 15 hours of running in wear experiment, the average sliding contact resistance gradually increased from 5mΩ to 7.3 mΩ. After 15 hours, the growth of sliding resistance began to slow down, the average value of contact resistance tended to be stable and did not exceed 8mΩ, and the sliding contact resistance showed unstable fluctuations. During the 15-40 hours of running in, the average value of sliding resistance increased slowly, and the fluctuation of sampling value within the sliding resistance period was aggravated, and the high value points above 500mΩ frequently appeared. After 58 hours of running, the average sliding contact resistance increased significantly, reaching 10.9mΩ, which was twice the initial value, because the brush was reversed for 2 hours.

V. Analysis of Sliding Wear Characteristics

In this section, according to the wear characteristics of brush weight loss, surface wear depth and roughness, wear area, wear surface morphology and composition, and combined with the variation characteristics of sliding contact resistance, the wear degree and mechanism of brush contact surface in running in simulation experiment were studied.

A. *Weight Loss of Brush*

The weight loss of the four groups of brush samples in Table 1 at different stages during the running in process was calculated, and their average and standard deviation were shown in Fig. 7.

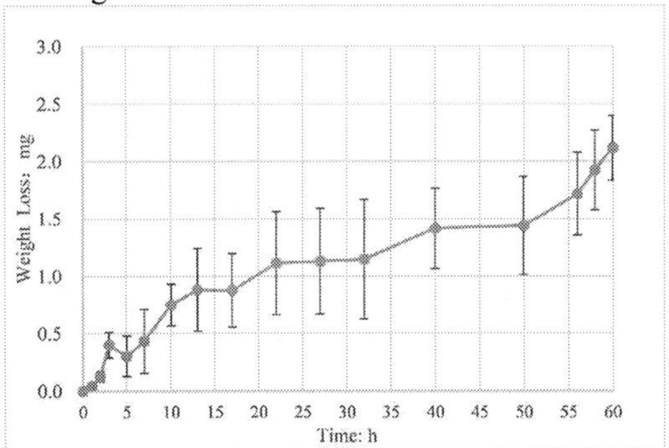

Fig. 7. Weight loss of brushes in running-in wear experiment

The average weight loss of the four brush samples was 2.12mg (±0.28mg) after 60 hours of wear in the running-in equipment. In the first 10 hours of running-in, the weight loss curve gradually increased, indicating that the brush contact interface was in the stage of severe wear. After 15 hours, the curve gradually became gentle, and the brush began to enter the stable wear stage. After 58 hours of running, the weight loss curve increased significantly due to the 2-hour reversal of the equipment.

B. *Wear Depth and Roughness of Brush Contact Surface*

As shown in Fig. 8, the brush contact interface was divided into 9 zones. Zone 1-3 was the proximal end of contact, that was the end where the brush enters the contact area; zone 4-6 was the middle end; and zone 7-9 was the distal end of contact, that was the end where the brush detached from the contact area. During the process of the running in experiment, the relative rotation of the brush and slip ring was paused in different stages, and the brushes were removed from the running in equipment. The wear depth of the center points of the nine zones in this stage was recorded by a micrometer and a clamping device, and the average roughness of the nine zones in this stage was detected by a three-dimensional profiler.

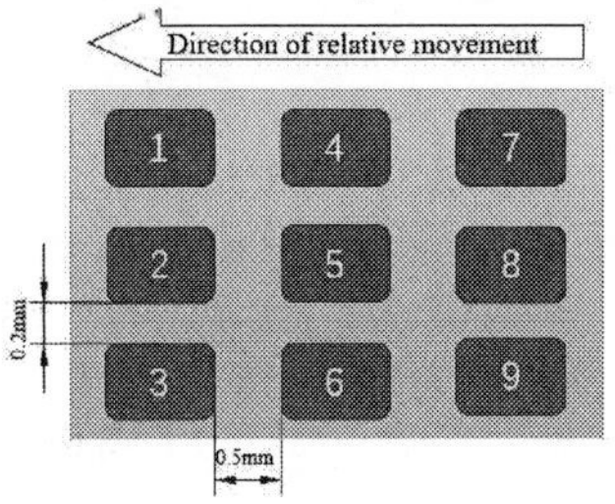

Fig. 8. The 9-point method division of the brush surface

The average values of wear depth and roughness in zones 1-3, 4-6 and 7-9 of the four groups of brush samples were calculated. The relationship between wear depth and running in time was shown in Fig. 9. The relationship between roughness and running in time was shown in Fig. 10.

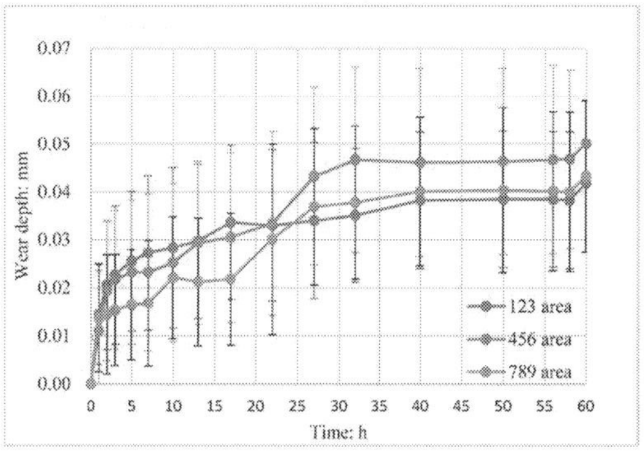

Fig. 9. Changes of wear depth of brush contact interface

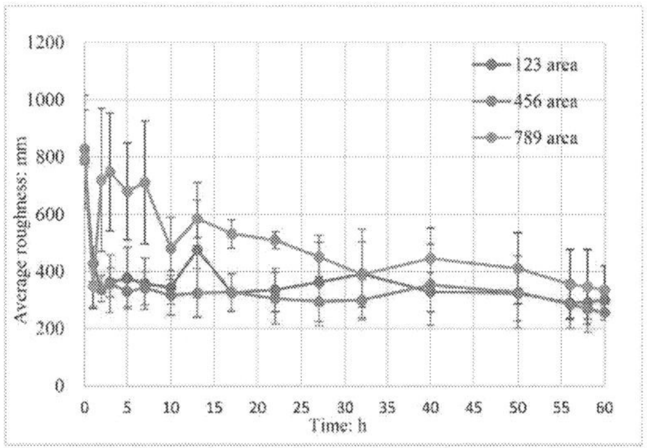

Fig. 10. Changes of roughness of brush contact interface

According to Fig. 9-10, within the first 15 hours of running in test, zone 1-3 of the brush contact interface first began to enter the state of severe wear, while zone 456 and zone 7-9 wore slowly. After 15 hours of running in time, the severe wear of the contact interface began to spread to the central zone 4-6, and the wear of the front end 1-3 zone slowed, while the wear depth of the central zone increased rapidly, and the remote zone 7-9 also began to enter the state of severe wear with time. After 40 hours of brush running in, the contact interface was almost completely covered by the wear area, and the wear area of the brush contact interface tended to be stable and increased slowly. During the last 2 hours of running-in, the wear depth of the brush contact interface increased slightly due to the reversal. The roughness of zone 1-3 and zone 4-6 decreased rapidly in the first 2 hours, and then remained basically unchanged. The roughness of zone 7-9 decreased gradually in 60 hours.

C. *Wear Area of Brush Contact Surface*

The photo of the contact interface of the brush was binarized using ImageJ image processing software. During the running in process, the proportion of black pixels in the binarized image can more intuitively reflect the change of the running in wear area of the brush contact interface compared with the increment of the initial state.

After binarizing the contact interface of the four groups of brush samples, the increment of black pixels at each stage compared with the initial state was counted, and the average and standard deviation were shown in Fig. 11.

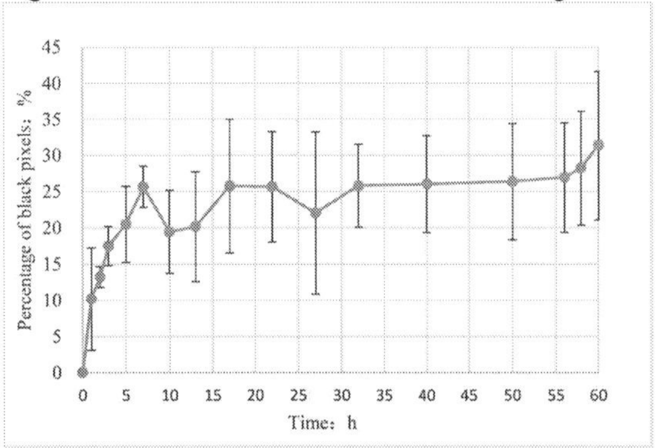

Fig. 11. Increment of running in wear area of brush contact surface

It can be seen from Fig. 11 that in the first 7 hours of wear, the wear area of the brush contact interface increased significantly. After 10 hours, the increase of black pixels in the binarized image was slow, and reached a plateau after 15 hours, after which no large fluctuations occurred. The wear area increased in the last 2 hours due to reverse rotation.

D. Brush Contact Surface Morphology and Compositions

Taking the brush 4-1 of the fourth group as an example, the contact interface of the brush without running in wear, after 22 hours, after 40 hours, and after 60 hours of running in wear was magnified by 1000 times respectively using a scanning electron microscope. The surface morphology was shown in Fig. 12(a) ~ (d).

a. without running-in b. after 22 hours

c. after 40 hours d. after 60 hours

Fig. 12. Surface morphology of brushes in different running-in wear stages

Fig. 12a showed the original morphology feature of a new brush sample. The lateral grooves and the dispersion of the mixture were formed on the surface after different time of wear, that is, the phenomenon of adhesive wear occurred. The difference was that after 22 hours of wear, the width of the grooves on the surface varied greatly, and two grooves were significantly wider than the other grooves, indicating that at this stage, the large particles were generated to scratch the contact surface severely. The mechanism was mainly abrasive wear. After 40 hours of wear, the difference in gully width decreased, and after 60 hours of wear, the width of each gully became closer, and the grooves on the surface were evenly distributed, which showed that from 20 hours to 60 hours, with the increase of wear time, the surface wear condition tended to be stable, and the surface was rarely damaged by large abrasive particles. The wear mechanism at this stage was mainly adhesive wear.

In addition to the different characteristics of the gully, the distribution of the mixture formed by the surface wear debris and metal oxides on the worn surface was also different after different wear times. With the increase of wear time, the surface mixture changed from a sparse and scattered distribution to a random scattered distribution and finally to a concentrated distribution of flakes, which indicated that with the increase of wear time, various components were mixed and dispersed on the wear surface, and the mixture had a tendency of concentrated distribution.

The element composition detection was carried out on the similar characteristic areas of the brush wear surface after different wear times. According to the atomic percentage distribution of carbon (C), oxygen (O), and metal elements (Ag and Cu) in the composition detection results of each stage, it was found that in the early stage of wear, due to the large contact roughness, there were more microscopic uneven contact points in the contact surface to cause friction and wear, which gradually destroyed the interface and formed larger abrasive particles to damage the surface, and the surface was more likely to form oxides. In the later stage of wear, with the continuous progress of sliding and the destruction of oxides, larger abrasive particles no longer existed in the contact surface, and the surface wear tended to be stable. The degree of oxidation in the worn area was significantly higher than that in the unworn area, and the oxide content indicated that the wear process was more prone to the formation of oxides. The unworn brush surface also had some oxides due to the influence of oxygen in the environment, and during the wear process, the oxides increased rapidly to gradually stabilize, so the contact resistance of the brush and slip ring contact pairs also increased firstly and then tended to be stable with the content of oxide.

VI. Discussion

In this paper, by simulating the brush pre-running in process, the relationship between the running in process of the brush and slip ring and the wear mechanism of the brush contact interface and the degradation characteristics of the electrical contact performance was explored, and the possibility of welding of the brush and slip ring contact interface was studied, as well as the initial reason for the ablation fault was analyzed.

According to the results of the brush weight loss, the wear depth, the surface roughness change and wear area change of the brush contact interface during the wear process, the wear rate was not constant with the running in process. Within the first 15 hours of the running in, the zone 1-3 of the brush contact interface first began to enter a state of severe wear, and other areas wore more slowly. At this stage, the generation of wear debris on the brush contact interface and the damage of the contact interface led to the average value of sliding resistance gradually increased. Within 15-40 hours of running in, the area with severe wear began to spread to the middle and the distal zones of the contact interface, until the contact interface was almost completely covered by the worn area, and the contact interface oxide gradually formed. The larger particles of the brush material mixed with oxide damaged the contact interface, so the contact resistance fluctuated erratically, and the average value of sliding contact resistance increased slowly. After 40 hours wear of the brush and slip ring, the contact interface was almost completely covered by the wear area, and the sliding contact resistance did not increase. The sliding contact resistance fluctuated and frequently appeared high values above 500mΩ. After 58 hours, the brushes were reversed and ran in for 2 hours, and the wear of the original distal zone 7-9 of the contact interface was aggravated, and the sliding contact resistance increased slightly again.

Due to the high contact resistance caused by sliding, the brush and slip ring may be welded under the condition of high impact current, which becomes the initial reason for the final ablation failure.

VII. Conclusion

In this paper, both the contact resistance measurement and the surface morphology and element component detection were carried out for brush and slip ring in a radar system with ablation failure after an extended pre-running in time. It was inferred that the initial failure was caused by welding of interface materials due to the interface temperature rise of electrical contact. Then, a simulation experiment was designed to explore the relationship between the pre-running in process of the brush and slip ring and the wear mechanism of the brush contact surface and the degradation characteristics of the electrical contact performance, and to analyze the possibility of welding on the contact interface of the brush and slip ring.

The research showed that after extending the pre-running in period of the brush and slip ring from 2 hours to 60 hours, the contact interface turned into severe wear, leading to the wear debris accumulation, the abrasive particle oxidation and other phenomena. The sliding electrical contact performance of the brush and slip ring degraded, and the sliding resistance elevated and fluctuated. In the subsequent actual use process, the contact interface is prone to abnormal temperature rise under the impact of large current, resulting in welding of the contact material, aggravating the wear of the contact interface, and further degrading the electrical contact performance. Therefore, the degradation of electrical contact performance caused by the extended pre-running in period is an initial reason for the ablation fault of brush and slip ring system.

References

[1] L. H. Ping, P. Q. Huang, R. K. Zhang, et al., "Radar structure and technology" *Beijing Electronic Industry Press*, Beijing, (1994).

[2] W. Zhang, "Analysis of Contact Problems in Slip-Ring" in *Fire Control Radar Technology*, 38. 03. (2009): 78-82.

[3] Y. G. Zhu, "Burning Analysis and Treatment of Slide Ring and Carbon Brush of Tubular Unit" in *Electric Power System Equipment*, 03. (2019): 179-180.

[4] S. B. Siang, J. B. Hu, "Analysis of the Burning Problem of a Slip Ring" in *Electronic Product Reliability and Environmental Testing*, 36. 02. (2018): 41-45.

[5] Y. A. Wang, "Cause Analysis and Treatment of Generator Carbon Brush Heating" in *Sciences & Wealth*, 36. (2017): 63.

[6] S. C. Huang, C. Li, "Analysis of Abnormally High Temperature of Carbon Brushes and Temporary Solutions" in *Electrotechnics Electric*, 08. (2019): 72-73.

[7] L. C. Cheng, P. C. Wingert. "Effect of Graphite Particle Size and Treatment on The Performance of Silver Graphite Contact Materials" in *Electrical Engineering Materials*, 02. (1994): 1-7.

[8] E. Gray, J. Pharney. "Electrode Erosion by Particle Ejection in Low-current Arcs" in *Journal of Applied Physics*, 45. (02): 667–671.

[9] Naoki Fukuda, Koichiro Sawa. "Contact Voltage Drop and Brush Wear Characteristics for Various Silver

Content of the Silver Graphite Brush in Slip Ring System" [C]. 2018 IEEE Holm Conference on Electrical Contacts, Albuquerque, NM, USA, (2018)521-525.

[10] C. F. Dai, "Contact Resistance in a Low-Frequency Slip Ring" in *Electro-Mechanical Engineering*, 01. (1995): 44-52.

[11] Saberi Saeid et al. A New Development of Four-Point Method to Measure the Electrical Resistivity in Situ During Plastic Deformation. in *Measurement*, 2021, 180.

[12] F. C. Gu et al. "Development of a High-Speed Data Acquisition Card for Partial Discharge Measurement". in *IEEE Access*, 2019, 07: 140312-140318.

8th International Conference on Reliability of Electrical Products and Electrical Contacts, November 18-20, 2022

Calculation Method of DC Contactor Temperature Field and Arc Heating in Life Test

Ruyao Li, Wenying Yang, Huimin Liang

Harbin Institute of Technology, Harbin, 150001, China

E-mail: liruyao1992@foxmail.com Tel: 15114583654

Abstract—**When the DC contactor operates, arc with high instantaneous power will be generated, which will increase the temperature of the arc extinguishing chamber. When the operating frequency of the contactor is low, the effect of the arc on the overall temperature rise of the contactor is not obvious and is often ignored. However, under the working conditions of frequent actions such as life experiments, the arc will cause the contactor to heat up significantly, which will affect the key parameters of predicting life and working reliability. Aiming at the calculation problem of temperature rise caused by arc in the contactor life test, this paper combines the arc simulation model based on magnetohydrodynamics (MHD) and the dynamic characteristic model of the contactor, and proposes a method including electromagnetism-thermal-motion-fluid Multiphysics coupled arc heating and contactor temperature rise calculation method. In the model, the arcing when the contactor is opened and the bouncing arcing when it is closed are considered, and the influence of temperature on the permanent magnetic field and thus on the arcing time and arcing energy is considered. Through the comparison of simulation and experimental data, the feasibility of the method proposed in this paper is proved, which can provide a reference for the thermal design, life and reliability prediction of contactor products.**

***Index Terms*—Contactor, thermal Calculation, arc, MHD**

I. INTRODUCTION

With the use and development of new energy sources, DC contactors are more widely used in electric vehicles, charging piles and other occasions where large currents need to be connected. Its usage and technical indicators are also gradually increasing. The DC contactor will generate arcs during the opening and closing bounces, and with the generation of large energy, the temperature of the arc extinguishing chamber will increase. Especially in the life test and accelerated life test of continuous operation, when the contactor operates frequently, the arc generates more energy, which makes the temperature rise of the contactor obvious. In addition to being destructive to components, life experiments with large loads have high requirements and losses on experimental equipment, resulting in a lot of time and manpower and material consumption in the research and development process. With the introduction of the concept of digital twin, the production of components such as contactors is more and more closely related to the digital model. Simulation is the core technology to ensure the correspondence between the digital twin and the component entity, and the accuracy needs to be improved as much as possible. Temperature is a core parameter in multifield simulations. It affects the coil resistance and permanent magnet performance, which in turn affects the working characteristics of the contactor such as the electromotive force of the electromagnetic coil and the arc blowing speed when breaking. At the same time, the temperature affects the arc energy and thus affects the temperature rise, forming the coupling between electricity, magnetism, heat, force and fluid.

Life testing is often used to check whether components are qualified or not, and to estimate the remaining life of equipment. Liu et al. established a degradation model of electromagnetic contactors for high-speed trains based on the overtravel time [1]. Sun et al. studied the relationship between the arc energy and other factors and the electrical life of the AC contactor, and then used the back-propagation neural network to train the prediction model [2]. Yu et al. established a life prediction model for high-voltage DC power relays based on gray theory with the characteristic parameters of operating voltage and operating time [3]. In the above study, the working characteristic parameters were measured under the working condition of frequent contactor action, but the parameters such as action time were mostly related to temperature. And the arc power is also related to the temperature to form a coupling relationship, which leads to the mutual influence of the working parameters and the temperature. The effect of arc-induced temperature rise on these parameters has not been considered in related studies.

To obtain the arc energy calculation method of the arc, first obtain the arc characteristics. For the macroscopic arc characteristics, the MHD model is often used. Li et al.

established a simplified two-dimensional dynamic arc model based on the MHD model, and analyzed the arc laws under different breaking speeds and load characteristics [4]. Based on MHD, Cao et al. established the air arc model of the metal shunt plate arc extinguisher of the DC contactor [5,6]. Niu et al. applied the MHD model to establish a three-dimensional arc simulation model to analyze the arc motion during the current interruption of an air circuit breaker [7]. Rong et al. studied the internal fault arc phenomenon in a closed container, and simulated the arc process ignited by alternating current between two rod-shaped electrodes in the air [8]. Zhong et al. established a calculation model of arc net emissivity for thermal radiation, which is the main energy transfer process of high-temperature arc plasma [9]. In the direction of arc modeling and simulation, Shu et al. proposed a model for calculating the arc temperature during air gap discharge based on the energy balance equation [10], but this method is suitable for strong discharge occasions with large air gaps, not suitable for small air gaps. Khakpour et al. established an arc model based on physical parameters, and analyzed the influence of arc temperature changes on the electrical characteristics of free-burning arcs, including voltage and power [11]. Obraztsov et al. established a two-dimensional axisymmetric model to simulate the combustion of an AC arc in air between two electrodes, and analyzed the velocity distribution, temperature on the axis, and voltage drop across the arc [12]. The research on arc heating usually focuses on arc welding, train pantograph and catenary [13], and the research on arc in the contactor arc extinguishing chamber is usually arc extinguishing and ablation. Instead, studies on the effects of temperature rise generally focus more on the erosive properties of the arc. There is a lack of research on arc heating in contactor components, and further research is needed on the effect of temperature on magnetic blowing and the heating of bouncing arcs.

The arc itself involves the coupling of electromagnetic, temperature, and fluid, and the interaction with the dynamic process of the contactor, which requires multi-physics coupling calculation and solution. In this paper, the calculation of the arc energy between the contacts of the contactor is used as the key technology of the heating calculation of the dynamic process of the contactor. And take into account the arc energy generated during the closed bounce, which is often ignored in previous studies. The process analysis of the arc energy transfer to the inside of the contactor is given, and the temperature distribution of the DC contactor under frequent operation is obtained by combining the three-dimensional temperature rise model of the arc extinguishing chamber.

II. Arc Power Calculation Model

The structure of the DC contactor used in this paper is shown in Figure 1. As one of the energy sources of temperature rise, the arc is generated between the moving and static contacts, including the arcing during opening and the arcing during the closing bounce.

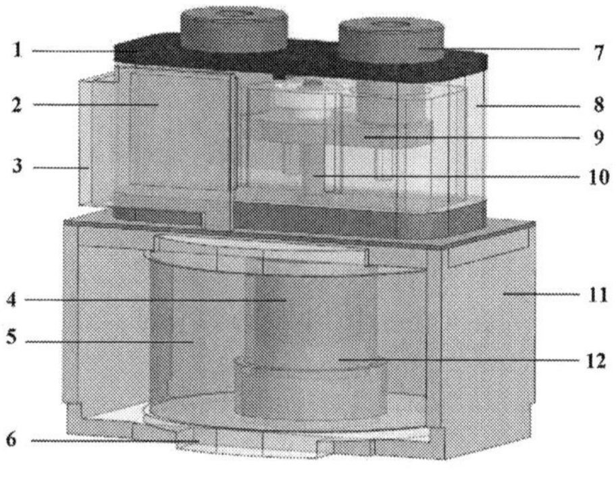

Fig. 1. Schematic diagram of DC contactor structure.
1-insulating rubber; 2-permanent magnet; 3-magnet frame; 4-iron core; 5-coil; 6-coil frame; 7-static contact; 8-ceramic interrupter; 9-moving contact; 10-connecting rod; 11-yoke; 12-armature

A. Arc MHD Model

The arc energy in the breaking process is the main source of arc heating in DC contactors. An arc is formed during the separation of the main circuit contacts, and the arc moves to the edge of the contact under the action of the magnetic field and air flow and is elongated until it is blown away. In this paper, the magnetohydrodynamic theory is used to construct a blowing arc model, in which the air and arc parts follow the mass continuity and are described by the mass continuity equation

$$\frac{\partial \rho}{\partial t} + \nabla \cdot (\rho V) = 0 \tag{1}$$

where ρ is the fluid density, V is the fluid velocity vector, and t is the computation time. The Stokes momentum conservation equation is used to solve for the velocity vector.

$$\frac{\partial \rho v_i}{\partial t} + \nabla \cdot (\rho v_i V) = \nabla \cdot (\eta \nabla v_i) - \frac{\partial P}{\partial x_i} + (\boldsymbol{J} \times \boldsymbol{B})_i \tag{2}$$

where v_i is the ith component of the velocity vector, η is the dynamic viscosity of the arc, P is the internal pressure of the arc, $\boldsymbol{J}$ is the current density vector, and $\boldsymbol{B}$ is the applied magnetic flux density vector. The heat balance between the energy produced and the energy dissipated in the cell is described by the energy conservation equation for the local temperature of entropy.

$$\frac{\partial (\rho H)}{\partial t} + \nabla \cdot (\rho H V) = \nabla \cdot (\frac{\lambda}{c_p} \nabla H) + \sigma E^2 \tag{3}$$

Where H is the enthalpy, λ is the thermal conductivity, c_p is the constant pressure specific heat, σ is the electrical conductivity, and E is the electric field strength. The magnetic vector potential calculation method is used to solve the electromagnetic field in the region.

$$\boldsymbol{B} = \nabla \times \boldsymbol{A} \tag{4}$$

$$\boldsymbol{E} = -\nabla \Phi \tag{5}$$

$$\boldsymbol{J} = \sigma E \tag{6}$$

$$\nabla \cdot (\nabla A) = -\mu J \quad (7)$$

$$\nabla \cdot (\sigma \nabla \Phi) = 0 \quad (8)$$

Where A is the magnetic potential vector, Φ is the electric potential, and μ is the magnetic permeability.

The arc blowing process includes the coupling effect of electromagnetic thermodynamic fluid, and the solution is too complicated. The following assumptions are adopted in this paper. (1) The arc plasma is a thermal plasma, which is approximated by local thermodynamic equilibrium. (2) The ignition process is not included in the model, and the arc part is initialized at the initial temperature of 10000K locally between the contacts. (3) Ablation and metal evaporation from contacts are not considered.

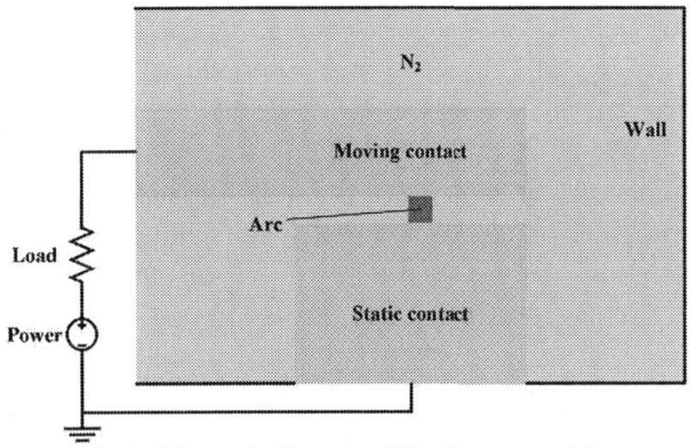

Fig. 2. Schematic diagram of blowing arc model.

Figure 2 shows the arc blowing model in the sealed arc extinguishing chamber. Because the arc extinguishing chamber is a symmetrical structure, in order to reduce the difficulty of simulation and reduce the calculation time, a half-element finite element model containing only one set of contacts is established. The material of the moving and static contacts is oxygen-free copper, the static contact is grounded, and the moving contact is connected to the load end in the circuit. The gas in the arc-extinguishing chamber is nitrogen, and the pressure is one atmosphere. The parameters of its conductivity, thermal conductivity, and dynamic viscosity are referred to in the literature [14, 15], as well as the Gas Discharge Plasma Basic Database (GPLAS) published by the School of Electrical Engineering, Xi'an Jiaotong University. An inward 100mT magnetic field perpendicular to the plane is applied to the model. The model adopts a moving deformation mesh, the initial contact distance is 0.2mm, and the separation speed is 1.5m/s. When the quality of the mesh is reduced to a preset threshold due to deformation, the back Euler method is used to re-mesh.

When the contactor load is 600V100A, the load in the corresponding model is 300V voltage and 100A current. The simulation results are shown in Figure 3. It can be seen from the simulation cloud diagram that the arc is elongated as the contact distance increases during the breaking process of the contactor. At the same time, the arc moves to the edge of the contact under the action of the magnetic field, until the contact gap is blown out and the energy is dissipated until it is extinguished.

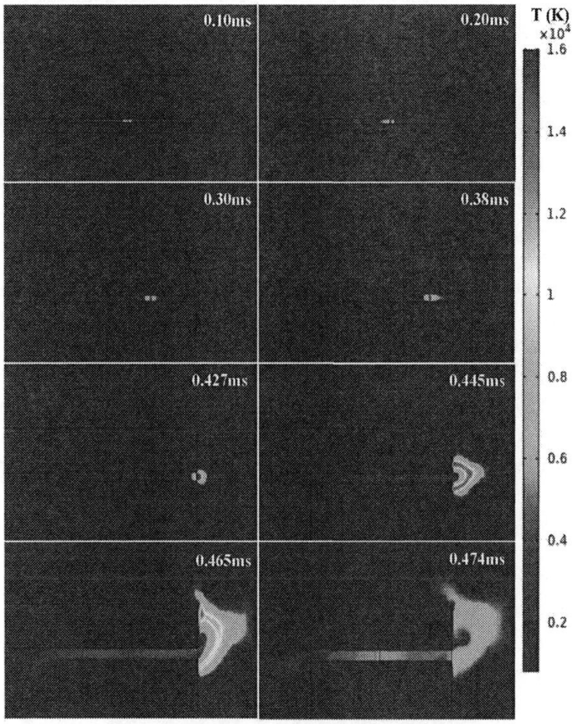

Fig. 3. Temperature field during arc blowing.

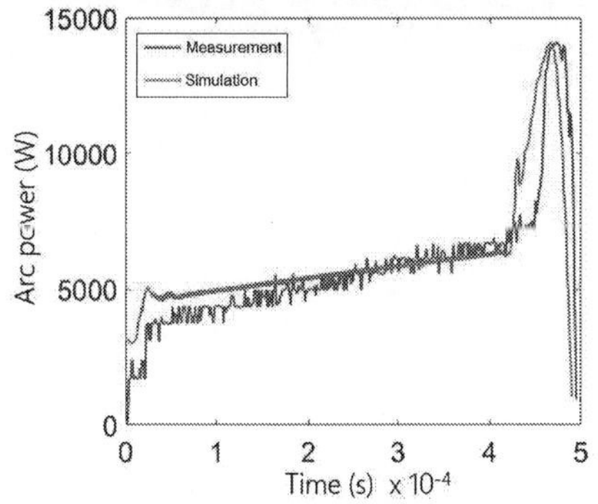

Fig. 4. Arc power curve.

The arc power curve obtained by the product of voltage and current measured by simulation and experiment under load conditions of 600V and 100A is shown in Figure 4. The voltage and current curves obtained from the simulation are in good agreement with the measured data. Integrating the arc power curve can obtain the arc energy generated during a breaking process. The energy of the primary arc is 2.863J by integrating the measured power curve, and the energy of the primary arc is 2.673J obtained by integrating the power curve obtained by the simulation. The error between the simulation and the measurement of the primary arc energy is 6.64%. Therefore, the simulation method can be used to predict the arcing energy of the DC contactor.

B. Influence of permanent magnet temperature on arc characteristics

The arc-blowing magnetic field is provided for the arc-extinguishing chamber with four permanent magnets opposed to each other, made of neodymium iron boron (NdFeB). NdFeB has the largest magnetic energy product among commonly used magnets, so it is often used in electrical equipment to provide a magnetic field, but it is significantly affected by temperature. Depending on the grade of NdFeB material, the Curie temperature Tc is between 320°C and 460°C. But before reaching the Curie temperature of complete demagnetization, the magnetic properties of NdFeB have already begun to decay with the increase of temperature. The maximum working temperature Tw of different grades of NdFeB is between 80°C and 150°C. After the maximum working temperature is exceeded, the magnetic properties begin to decay rapidly. And when the temperature is cooled, its magnetic properties cannot be fully recovered, and there will be a large permanent loss.

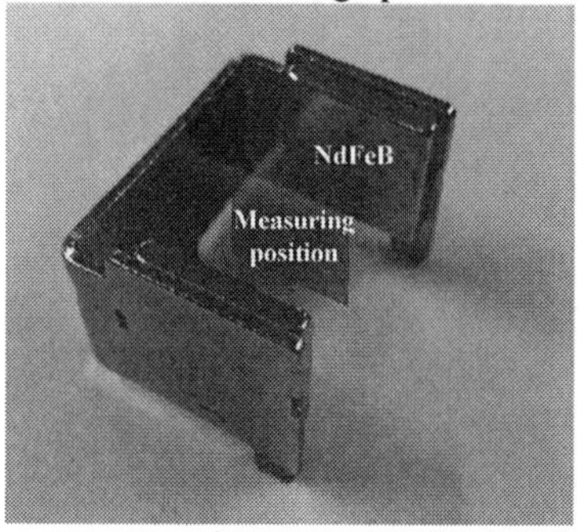

Fig. 5. Permanent magnet for experiment and measuring position.

Figure 5 shows the NdFeB permanent magnet in the DC contactor used in this paper, which is heated in a constant temperature box. After the temperature is stable, measure the middle position of the two opposite permanent magnets in the figure, that is, the maximum magnetic induction intensity at the arc blowing position.

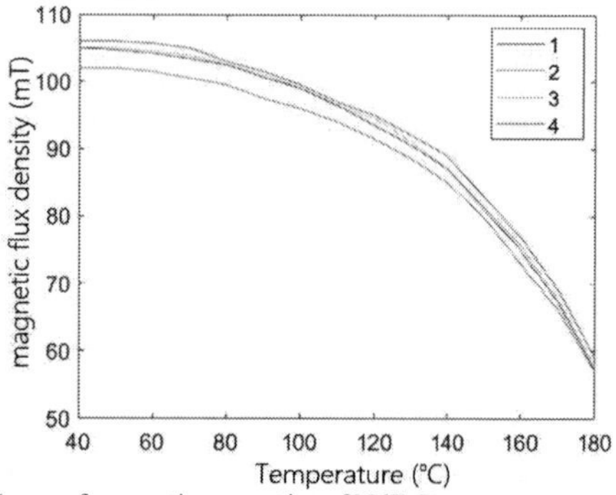

Fig. 6. Curve of magnetic properties of NdFeB permanent magnet with temperature.

Four groups of permanent magnets were measured, and the changes in their magnetic properties from 40 °C to 180 °C are shown in Figure 6. NdFeB permanent magnets are less affected by temperature within 60°C, and the magnetic induction intensity at the measurement position remains above 100mT. Then, with the increase of temperature, the magnetic properties drop rapidly, and the magnetic induction intensity at the measurement position drops below 60mT. When cooled from 180°C to room temperature, the magnetic induction intensity at the measurement position recovered to about 75mT, which suffered a large loss of magnetic properties. However, the temperature rise of high-power contactors is usually high, and the influence of temperature on the arc blowing permanent magnet needs to be considered.

The experimental statistics of the arc energy under different applied magnetic induction intensity are carried out. The permanent magnet used in the contactor is heated to reduce its magnetic performance, prepare 6 groups of contactors of 50mT-100mT, conduct the breaking experiment and calculate the single arc energy, the load is unified as a resistive load of 600V100A, each group Measure 500 times. At the same time, the simulation method is used to compare the obtained data under the same conditions. The comparison between the boxplot of the arc energy experimental data and the simulation curve is shown in Figure 7. The statistical data obtained from the experimental measurement are consistent with the trend of the simulation results. The stronger the arc blowing magnetic field, the faster the arc extinguishing speed and the lower the arc energy.

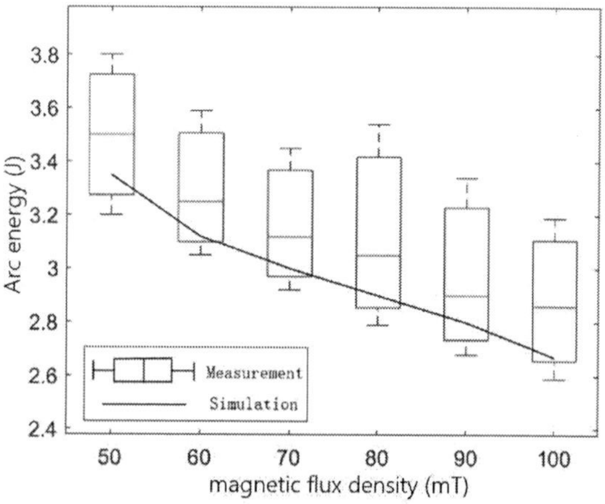

Fig. 7. Comparison of arc energy data under different magnetic induction intensity.

C. Contact bounce curve calculation

The moving process of the moving contact is the cooperation process of the magnetic circuit part, that is, the electromagnetic system, the reaction force system and the moving part. The solution of the action process of the magnetic circuit part is based on Maxwell's equations combined with the following voltage balance equations and motion equations.

$$U = IR + \mathrm{d}\psi / \mathrm{d}t \quad (9)$$

$$F_e = M\mathrm{d}v / \mathrm{d}t + F_x \quad (10)$$

$$v = \mathrm{d}x / \mathrm{d}t \tag{11}$$

Where U is the coil voltage, I is the coil current, and R is the coil resistance. Ψ is the flux linkage, and t is the time. M is the total mass of the armature, connecting rod, moving contact and other moving parts. F_e is the electromagnetic force, and F_x is the total reaction force provided by the reaction force system (return spring and overtravel spring). v is the moving speed of the armature, and x is the displacement of the armature. The mechanical model of the reaction force system and contact bounce is shown in Figure 8. In this model, the armature and the connecting rod are regarded as a whole. The equation of motion of the armature is

$$F_1 = M_1 a_1 + k_1 x + k_2 (x - y) + c_1 v \tag{12}$$

$$F_2 = M_2 a_2 + k_2 (x - y) + c_2 v_2 \tag{13}$$

Where F_1 is the resultant force of the armature and the connecting rod, and F_2 is the resultant force of the moving contact. M_1 is the mass of the armature and connecting rod, and M_2 is the mass of the moving contact. a_1 and a_2 are the accelerations of the armature and the moving contact, respectively. k_1 is the elastic coefficient of the return spring, and k_2 is the elastic coefficient of the overtravel spring. y is the displacement of the moving contact, c_1 is the damping coefficient of the return spring, and c_2 is the damping coefficient of the overtravel spring. v_2 is the moving speed of the moving contact. At the same time, F_1 and F_2 are

$$F_1 = F_d + F_c + F_f + F_e \tag{14}$$

$$F_2 = F_d + F_c + F_p \tag{15}$$

Among them, F_d is the force between the moving contact and the connecting rod block, F_f is the pre-pressure of the return spring, and F_c is the pre-pressure of the overtravel spring. F_p is the collision force between the moving contact and the static contact, and its expression is

$$F_p = k_p \delta_p^n + c_p \delta_p^n v_p \tag{16}$$

Where k_p is the contact stiffness of the dynamic and static contacts, and δ_p is the penetration displacement when the dynamic and static contacts collide. n is the collision force index between the moving contact and the static contact, and c_p is the collision damping coefficient of the moving and static contacts. v_p is the penetration velocity at the time of collision.

The finite element method is used to calculate the electromagnetic force, and the multi-body dynamics software is used for co-simulation. The calculated bouncing displacement curve, the measured contact bouncing curve and the bouncing arc voltage are shown in Figure 9. The arc waveform during bouncing also corresponds to the time of three bouncings. After that, because the gap generated by the bouncing is too small, it is difficult to generate continuous arcing, and it is difficult to sample and capture. However, the arcing time during the bounce can be set accordingly to the time of the first three bounces. The bouncing waveform obtained by simulation is accurate.

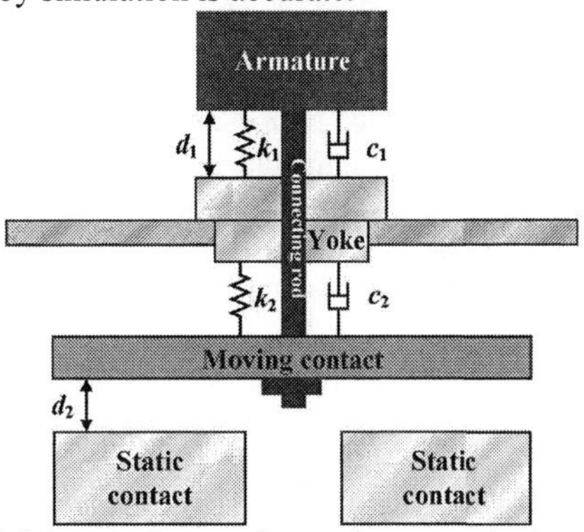

Fig. 8. Schematic diagram of contact bounce mechanics model.

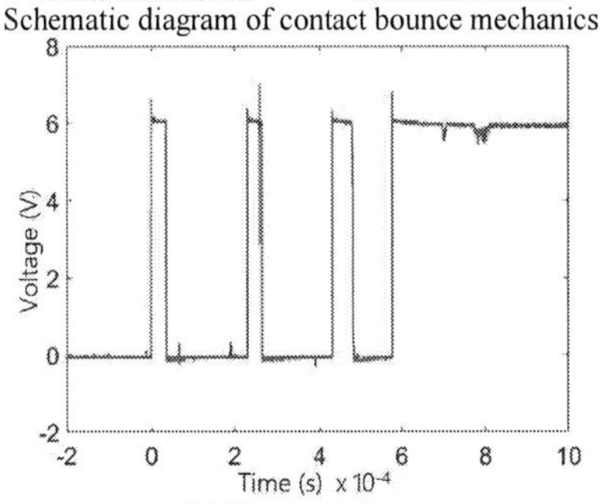

(a)_Bounce voltage

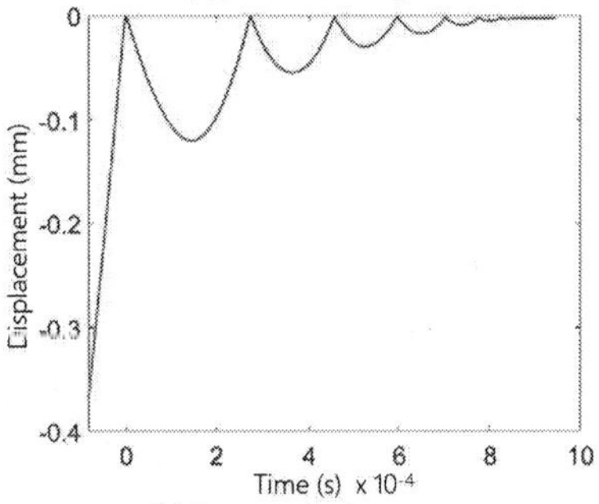

(b)_Bounce displacement

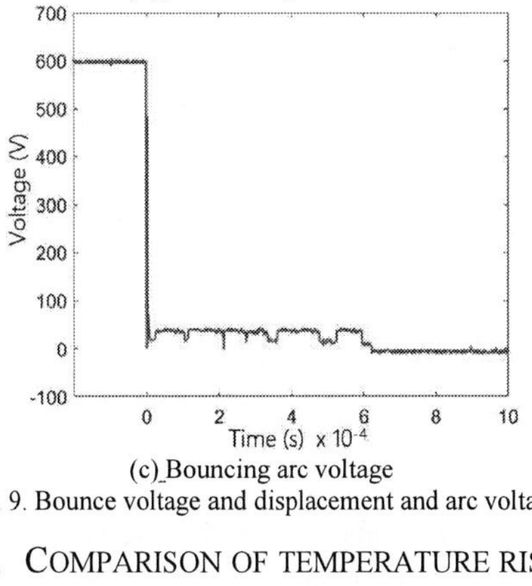

(c)_Bouncing arc voltage

Fig. 9. Bounce voltage and displacement and arc voltage

III. Comparison of Temperature Rise Measurement and Simulation Results of Contactor Life Test

Based on the above modeling content, in the life

experiment when the ambient temperature is 298.15K, the load voltage is 600V, the current is 100A, and the operating frequency is 1s on and 1s off, the temperature measurement and simulation results of the contactor are shown in Figure 10. The temperature of the sampling point is measured by a thermocouple, and the simulated temperature is consistent with the measurement result. The steady-state temperature rise is 45.4K from the measurement of the contact lead terminal position, and the simulated steady-state temperature rise is 48.9K, with an error of 7.71%. The measured temperature rise of the permanent magnet position is 37.6K, the simulated temperature rise is 35.9K, and the error is -4.52%. The measured temperature rise of the outer layer of the coil is 41.8K, the simulated temperature rise is 42.9K, and the error is 2.63%. The overall error is within acceptable limits.

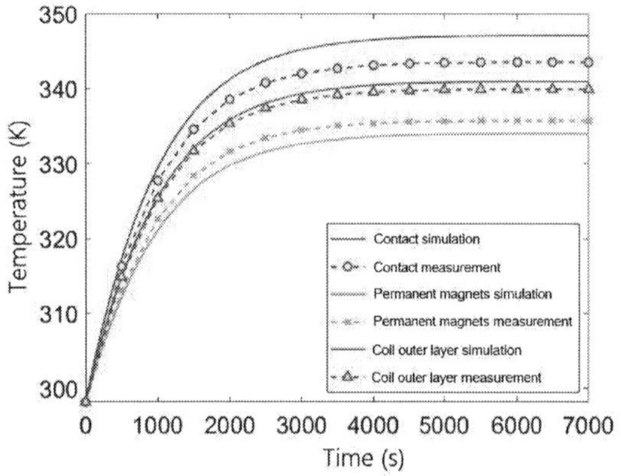

Fig. 10. Contactor temperature in life test

IV. Conclusion

This paper proposes an arc power calculation method for DC contactors that can couple the effects of temperature field, electromagnetic field and mechanical force multi-physics field. The influence of contactor breaking arc and bouncing arc on the contactor temperature rise is considered. Through the comparison with the experimental results and data analysis, the following conclusions are drawn. 1) The MHD model is suitable for simulating DC contactor arc breaking and arc energy calculation, and the simulated voltage curve is consistent with the actual measurement. The error between simulation and measurement of primary arc energy is 6.64%, and the calculated results are close to the experimental results. 2) The increase in temperature will reduce the magnetic properties of the permanent magnet, which will in turn affect the arc energy by affecting the arc blowing speed. 3) In the life test considering the breaking arc and the bouncing arc, the error between the steady-state simulation results of the DC contactor temperature rise model and the actual measurement is within 7.71%. The research in this paper can provide a reference for future contactor thermal design, life and reliability prediction and digital twin modeling.

References

[1] J Liu, A Chen, Y Yan . et al., "Reliability Evaluation Method of Electromagnetic Contactor Used in High-Speed Train," *TRANS OF CHINA ELECTR SOCIETY*, 2018, 33(2): 461-471

[2] Sun Y, Zhang Y, Xu C, et al., "A novel life prediction method for railway safety relays using degradation parameters," *IEEE INTEL TRANSP SY*, 2018, 10(3): 48-56

[3] Yu G, Chiu Y, Zheng X, et al., "Contact pressure of high-voltage DC power relay change and life prediction and structure optimization," *ADV MECH ENG*, 2021,13(2): 1-15

[4] Li J, Chen Y, Cao Y, "Study on the influence of breaking parameters and load characteristics on arc energy", *4th ICEPE-ST*, 2017, 1: 573-576.

[5] Cao Y, Liu K, Li J, et al, "Research on the influence factors of arc characteristics in the arc extinguish chamber in DC contactor breaking process" , *4th ICEPE-ST*, 2017, 1:338-341

[6] J Li, K Liu, Y Cao, et al., "Arc Root Development and Its Influence on Arc Reigniting During the Breaking Process of the DC Contactor," *Proceedings of the CSEE*, 2019, 39(4): 1241-1250

[7] Niu C, Ding J, Yang F, et al., "The influence of contact space on arc commutation process in air circuit breaker," *Plasma Science & Technology*, 2016, 18(5): 460-464

[8] Rong M, Li M, Wu Y, et al., "3-D MHD modeling of internal fault arc in a closed container," *IEEE T Power Deliver*, 2017, 32(3):1220-1227

[9] L Zhong, X Wang, M Rong, "Calculation of Net Emission Coefficients of SF_6-Cu Arc in High- Voltage Circuit Breakers," *Trans Of China Electr Society*, 2018, 33(23): 5600-5606

[10] Shu L, Yang Z, Jiang X, et al., "Study on arc temperature calculation model for air gap discharge," *Int T Electr Energy*, 2014, 24(12):1664-1670

[11] Khakpour A, Uhrlandt D, Methling R, et al., "Impact of temperature changing on voltage and power of an electric arc," *Electr Pow Syst Res*, 2017, 143(1):73-83

[12] Obraztsov N V, Frolov V Y, Popov V E, et al., "Time dependent 2-dimensional model of an alternating current arc," in *International Conference on PhysicA*, 2018, 1: 1-6

[13] Ma S, Gao H, and Zheng S, "Spectroscopic measurement of temperatures in pulsed TIG welding arcs," *J Phys D Appl Phys*, 2011, 44(40):1-12

[14] Bo K, Zhou X, Zhai G, "Investigation on Arc Dwell and Restriking Characteristics in DC High-Power Relay," *IEEE T PLASMA SCI*, 2017, 45(6): 1032-1042

[15] Bo K, Zhou X, Zhai G, "Simulation of arc dwelling behavior during bridge type contact opening process for high-power relay," *IEEE T COMP PACK MAN*, 2018,8(6): 975- 981

8th International Conference on Reliability of
Electrical Products and Electrical Contacts,
November 18-20, 2022

Fault Feature Detection and Simulation of Electronic Products Based on Visual Image Analysis

Zhangyu Huang

Department of Electronic, Electrical and Systems Engineering
University of Birmingham, Birmingham, B152TT, United Kingdom

E-mail: zxh118@student.bham.ac.uk Tel: 17640316855

***Abstract*—The randomness of electronic fault, instability of state and uncertainty of duration are the key factors leading to the changeful abnormal state and occasional fault of electronic unit, which are difficult to detect and diagnose. However, when the fault occurs or disappears, the visual image of unit structure will inevitably produce micro distortion. Based on the analysis of visual image effect, this paper proposed a visual image signal processing method, established an analytical model based on KNN and realised the solution process, and accurately located the defect feature area. The example verifies the evolution process of the visual image signal of the unit structure of electronic products, reveals the mapping relationship between the grey change of the unit structure image and the edge feature when the electronic fault starts and disappears, which provides theoretical and technical support for improving the reliability level of equipment and ensuring the safety production efficiency.**

***Index Terms*— Visual image; Morphological analysis; Edge feature extraction; Detection and simulation; Electronic fault.**

I. INTRODUCTION

Electronic fault has obvious latent, intermittent, and transient characteristics, which restricts the production quality level, safety, reliability and supportability of complex equipment. From the perspective of the expansion trend of electronic faults, even under transient operation conditions, electronic faults do not belong to the typical steady-state fault category, and the duration is random and may be very short. At present, countries all over the world cannot identify such faults from the characteristics of stable operation [1-2]. Considering that the symptom information of electronic fault initiation and expansion in the project has been reflected in its internal unit structure in advance, and the stress change when the electronic fault occurs and disappears induces the distorted image of the electronic unit structure [3-4], therefore, the defect characteristics of electronic products are identified from the image information change when the electronic fault occurs and disappears, and the defect area of electronic products is located based on the visual image effect, It is helpful to explore the harm degree, development law and damage mechanism of electronic fault, and can effectively break through the technical bottleneck of difficult electronic fault detection and easy missed diagnosis and misdiagnosis. It also has positive theoretical significance and application value for accurately evaluating the overall reliability level of equipment and ensuring safe operation.

II. VISUAL IMAGE EFFECT ANALYSIS METHOD

A. *Visual Image Acquisition*

Due to the instability of electronic fault signal, its attenuation speed increases with the deepening of detection level, and is affected by external interference signals, which makes the existing detection technology difficult to meet the accuracy requirements of deep-seated electronic fault detection, and greatly increases the difficulty of electronic product fault detection. Considering that the change of the qualitative change state of the unit structure of electronic products is related to its geometric parameters, material, excitation current frequency and other technical parameters, the change of fractal dimension caused by the transient distortion of the strain image of the unit structure when the early fault occurs and disappears can be expressed as the unexpected change of a single parameter or the abnormal change of the feature vector composed of multiple parameters, The signal processing and analysis of the unit structure visual image can provide an effective technical means for accurately extracting the original information of the defect characteristics of hidden electronic products.

1) We reasonably determine the technical parameters of the optical camera, focus on tracking the data jump in the detection signal according to the signal shape and characteristics of electronic units with transient faults with different frequencies, and find the defect feature information hidden in noise and other interference signals through independent variable analysis algorithm.

2) Taking the collected signal as the input sample, we conduct multivariate principal component analysis on the

signal characteristics in time domain and frequency domain, obtain the eigenvalue and eigenvector, and select the dimension after dimensionality reduction to generate sensitive features. This sensitive eigenvector maintains the original information in the eigenvector before dimensionality reduction.

3) The sensitive features are taken as the input samples in the recognition process, and the feature separation of periodic pulse signals with transient faults is completed by feature extraction algorithm.

B. Defect Characteristic Analysis Process

1) Visual image information allosteric analysis process

After obtaining the strain image at the time of fault initiation or disappearance based on machine vision detection technology, the unstructured data model with spatial correlation is established by combining the qualitative change state of unit structure and the distortion effect of strain image. Based on the spatial correlation between pixels, the KNN model and algorithm for strain image information migration are analysed, the fractal dimension of the image when the strain image is distorted is tracked, and the sensitive features are separated by jump shape, This sensitive feature vector maintains the original information in the edge feature vector [5-6].

On the basis of the above work, the unstructured data based on visual information optimizes the sensitive feature vector, takes it as the feature parameter to describe the distortion effect of strain image, introduces the step competition strategy, encourages the weak and suppresses the strong in the internal competition, realizes the compensation of the edge signal structure of strain image, and establishes the modal data set of visual image deformation information and sensitive feature vector.

2) Edge feature recognition and quantitative evaluation process

Based on the modal data set with defect features and the KNN analytical model of visual information migration, a quantitative evaluation platform is constructed to analyse the relationship between the number of parameters in the process of visual information migration and the data scale. The fractal dimension containing hidden defect feature signals is constructed by using the image grey fractal theory, and the key parameters such as information entropy and spectral entropy in the model are analysed from two aspects of time and frequency, A mapping set reflecting the abnormal symptoms of unit structure and sensitive feature vectors is formed, which is recorded as the domain of $S=\{X,Y\}=\{(x_i,y_i)\mid x_i\in R^n, y_i\in R, i=1,2,\cdots,\mathrm{N}\}$ and S as the early failure feature set, and the data set is grouped according to the time series order.

III. Visual Image Signal Processing Method

A. Image Morphological Analysis

mage segmentation mainly divides the image into disjoint connected regions. Each region meets the specific regional consistency, and different regions have some differences. Accurate image segmentation is a process of labelling each pixel in the image. This process makes the pixels with the same label have some common visual characteristics, and the result is to obtain the set of sub regions on the image, or a collection of contour lines extracted from the image. Each pixel in a sub region is similar under the measurement of certain characteristics or the calculated characteristics, such as colour, brightness, and texture, while the adjacent regions are very different under the measurement of certain characteristics.

Considering the existence of edge burrs and connecting fracture areas in the strain image, it is necessary to fill such small fracture areas or blank points without changing the overall area of the area to make the above areas smoother. According to the principle of image morphological analysis, firstly, the expansion operation is carried out on the target area to obtain the maximum value of the overlapping part of area $f(x,y)$ and area b of the original image, which is recorded as

$$[f\oplus b](x,y)=\max_{(s,t)\in b}\{f(x-s,y-t)\} \tag{1}$$

Secondly, the corrosion operation is carried out on the target area to obtain the minimum value of the overlapping part of area $f(x,y)$ and area b of the original image, which is recorded as

$$[f\Theta b](x,y)=\min_{(s,t)\in b}\{f(x+s,y+t)\} \tag{2}$$

f the closing operation $f(x,y)$ of the original image is recorded as $f\bullet b$, the smoothing function of the edge burr and the connecting fracture area is

$$f\bullet b=(f\oplus b)\Theta b \tag{3}$$

B. Image Segmentation Method Based on KNN

Classifier based image segmentation is a supervised classifier application. Like many classification algorithms, it includes two stages: classifier learning and classification. The representative areas in each class of the image are input into the classifier as training data for learning, and then the trained classifier is used to classify the whole image pixels, and then the image segmentation is completed according to the pixel categories. KNN stores the characteristics and categories of all given training data, and classifies each new sample based on K-nearest neighbour in the training data. The classification principle of KNN is shown in Figure 1.

As shown in Figure 1, in the 2D feature space, each training sample is composed of two eigenvalues and a class label. Each class is represented by three training samples, in which class A is represented by three samples A_1, A_2 and A_3; Class B is represented by three samples B_1, B_2 and B_3; The category of new sample N is determined by KNN classification. Assuming that a new sample N is classified with training data, the k nearest neighbour of N depends on the training data.

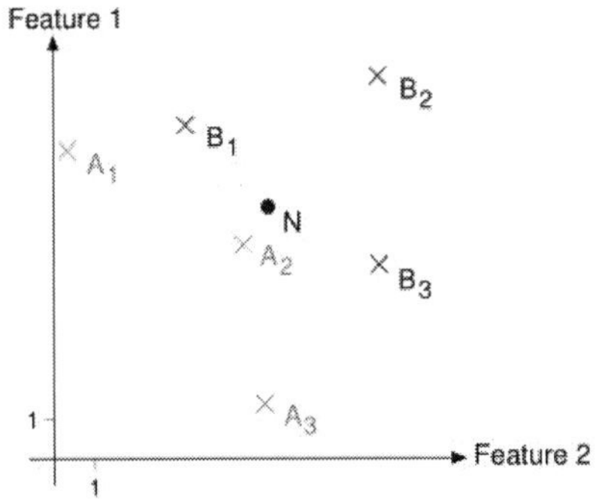

Fig. 1. KNN classification schematic diagram.

For example, when $K = 1$, only the nearest neighbour of n is determined, and its class label can be directly assigned to the new sample. Since the training sample A_2 here is closest to N, the new sample n is classified as class A. Assuming that K is set to a value greater than 1, the category of new sample n must be determined from the category of k nearest neighbour samples in its training data. For example, when $K = 3$, it is necessary to determine the three nearest neighbours of N, and the weighted method can be used to consider the distance from n to K nearest neighbour. The biggest advantage of KNN is that it directly leads to the training steps. Therefore, KNN classifier is suitable for testing various structures of training data; At the same time, new feasible training data can be added to the classifier at any time. Its disadvantage is that KNN classifier contains complete training data and needs to consume a lot of memory.

C. Analysis of KNN Classifier Algorithm

For the image segmentation algorithm based on KNN classifier, before the algorithm is executed, the parameters of the classifier segmentation algorithm must meet two requirements: one is to reasonably determine the quantitative value of KNN feature dimension, and the other is to reject the class threshold. During classification, the sample is classified to a threshold size that is not the current existing class. The algorithm analysis steps are as follows:

Step 1: create KNN classifier model_ class_ knn()

Step 2: add training samples to KNN classifier add_ samples_ image_ class_ knn ()

Step 3: train KNN classifier_ class_ knn ()

Step 4: classify the image by KNN segmentation_ image_ class_ knn ()

①create_ class_ knn (: : NumDim : KNNHandle)

//Function: create a k-nearest neighbor (k-NN) data structure.

//Feature number of parameters: dim

Output - handle knnhandle of KNN classifier

②add_ samples_ image_ class_ knn (Image, ClassRegions : : KNNHandle :)

//Function: add the training samples from the image to the k nearest neighbor (KNN) specified by knhandle.

//Parameter: input - input image

——Regions of the trained category

——Handle to KNN classifier

③train_ class_ knn (: : KNNHandle, GenParamName, GenParamValue :)

//Function: create search tree for k-NN classifier.

//Parameter: input - handle knnhandle of KNN classifier

——The name of the general parameter genparamname that can be adjusted when the KNN classifier is created

——The value genparamvalue of the general parameter that can be adjusted when the KNN classifier is created

④classify_ image_ class_ knn (Image : ClassRegions, Distancelmage : KNNHandle, RejectionThreshold :)

//Function: use a k-nearest neighbor classifier (KNN) knhandle to perform a pixel classification on the multi-channel image.

//Parameter: input - input image

——Handle to KNN classifier

——Rejectionthreshold of rejected classification

Output - divided category classregions

——Distance of nearest neighbor of pixel distanceimage

IV. EXPERIMENTAL VERIFICATION AND SIMULATION

The original image of an electronic unit is shown in Figure 2.

Fig. 2. Original image of electronic product.

Considering that the grey value distribution of the image reflects the filtering effect, in order to verify the effectiveness of the model, focus on tracking the image edge signal for smoothing and structural compensation, and obtain the smooth image and grey profile of obvious difference edge burr and connecting fracture area, as shown in Figure 3.

It can be seen from the above figure that the gray distribution information and change trend of the output image are obviously different, and the edge feature area of the image with defects has superior convergence, which can effectively segment the image defect features and extract the fault mode.

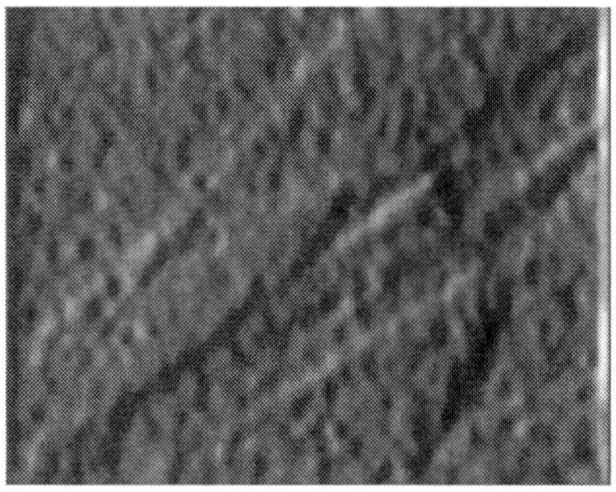

(a) Smoothing coefficient 2.025

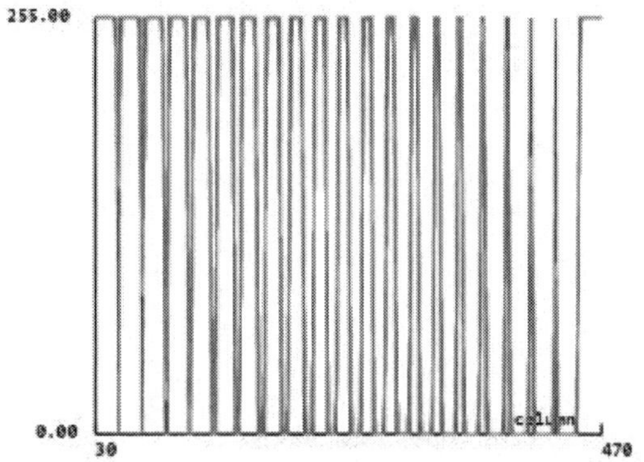

(b) Gray image of characteristic area

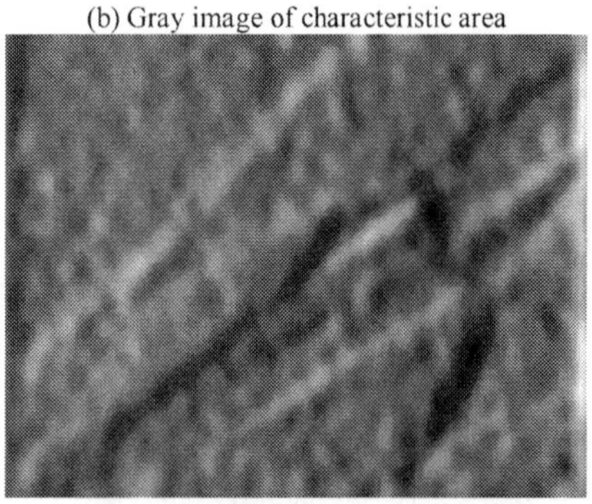

(c) Smoothing coefficient 2.550

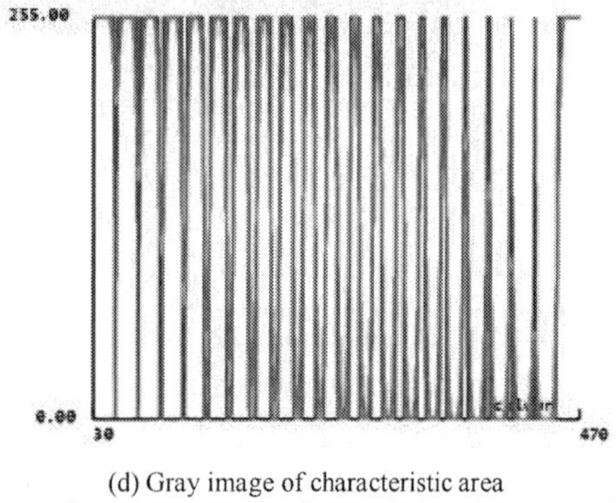

(d) Gray image of characteristic area

Fig.3 Image edge structure and its characteristic region gray scale image.

V. CONCLUSION

Based on visual image analysis, a set of defect feature detection method for electronic products is proposed, and the visual image acquisition, smoothing and segmentation method containing defect signal is established, which is conducive to the quantitative analysis and accurate positioning of early faults of electronic products and makes up for the shortcomings of electronic fault detection methods. The conclusions are as follows:

1) The visual image effect analysis method is studied, and the image morphological analysis model and defect feature segmentation method are established, which effectively improves the edge structure signal processing efficiency and reduces the missed diagnosis rate of defects.

2) The relationship between the characteristic signal of defect edge and the grey convergence region is proved through example analysis, which effectively solves the problem of defect location and lays a technical foundation for extracting fault mode.

REFERENCES

[1]Aleksendric D, Bellini C, Carlone P, et al. Neural-fuzzy optimization of thick composites curing process. Materials and Manufacturing Processes. 2019, 33(3): 262-273

[2]Siavash S, Ali T, et al. Leakage fault detection in Electro-Hydraulic Servo Systems using a nonlinear representation learning approach. ISA Transactions. 2018, 73:154-164

[3]Wang X, Hill Tl, et al. Model updating strategy for structures with localised nonlinearities using frequency response measurements. Mechanical Systems and Signal Processing. 2018, 100: 940-961

[4]Sergio Rt, Felipe At, ,et al. Osteopathic manual therapy in heart failure patients: A randomized clinical trial. Journal of Bodywork & Movement Therapies. 2018, 22(2):293-299

[5] Dragan A, Costanzo B, Pierpaolo C, et al. Neural-fuzzy optimization of thick composites curing process. Materials and Manufacturing Processes, 2019 33(3): 262-273

[6] Spreco A, Eriksson O, Dahlstrom Ö, Timpka T. Influenza detection and prediction algorithms: comparative accuracy trial in Östergötland county, Sweden. Epidemiology and infection, 2017, 145(10): 2166-2175

Zhangyu Huang, who is mainly engaged in research in the field of electronic engineering, obtained the second-class first degree of honorary electronic engineering from Central Lancashire University in 2021, then studied at the University of Birmingham and obtained the master's degree of electronic and communication engineering in 2022.

8th International Conference on Reliability of
Electrical Products and Electrical Contacts,
November 18-20, 2022

Application of Co-simulation Design and 3D Printing Rapid Prototyping in Electromagnetic Switch

Jingfeng Dong[1], Jierong Zhuang[1,2,3], Zhihong Xu[1,2,3]

[1]College of Electrical Engineering and Automation, Fuzhou University, Fuzhou 350116
[2]Fujian Province University Engineering Research Center of Smart Distribution Grid Equipment, Fuzhou University, Fuzhou 350116
[3]Fujian Key Laboratory of New Energy Generation and Power Conversion, Fuzhou University, Fuzhou 350116
Email: jierong@foxmail.com TEL: 13489958049

Abstract—**Electromagnetic mechanism is an important factor affecting the performance of electromagnetic switches. Its design is faced with the problems of long development cycle and high verification cost. Therefore, this paper takes a contactor as an example to explore the application of co-simulation technology and 3D printing technology in the design of electromagnetic mechanism. Firstly, the co-simulation model of the contactor is established. At the same time, the parameters of the switch body are measured and the excitation ampere turns are calculated according to the reaction force characteristics. The electromagnetic field and mechanical field co-simulation technology is used to simulate the dynamic characteristics of the electromagnetic switch such as collision bounce, and the design scheme is preliminarily verified. Finally, 3D printing technology is used to print the coil skeleton, complete coil winding and intelligent control, and verify the rationality and accuracy of the coil design. In this paper, co-simulation technology and 3D printing technology are used to quickly verify the design scheme, which can effectively shorten the design time and reduce the verification cost. It has certain reference significance for the research and development and optimization design of electromagnetic switch products.**

Index Terms— **Electromagnetic switch, coil design, co-simulation, 3D printing**

I. INTRODUCTION

Electromagnetic switch is one of the important basic components in the electrical industry. It is widely used in automatic control and power systems, and plays the role of power transmission and distribution, protection and control of electrical equipment [1]-[2]. With the increasing complexity and control requirements of power systems, its performance requirements are also increased [3]. As the action execution part of the electromagnetic switch, the electromagnetic mechanism controls the connection and disconnection of the main circuit through the attraction force generated when the excitation coil is energized and the spring reaction force [4], and its performance directly determines the performance of the entire electromagnetic switch. Therefore, the research and development and optimization design of the electromagnetic mechanism are of great importance to the electromagnetic switch.

The research and development design of electromagnetic mechanism combines multi-disciplinary theories such as machinery and electromagnetism [5]. In the research and development process, it's necessary to carry out the calculation and research of electromechanical coupling. However, the current electromechanical coupling calculation methods mostly adopt single electromagnetic field simulation to obtain two-dimensional interpolation tables of electromagnetic switch displacement, current and suction, and then substitute the interpolated electromagnetic suction into the mechanical equation of motion for solving [6]. This method cannot truly reflect the impact of collision bounce of moving parts of electromagnetic switches on electromagnetic parameters [7], and collision bounce is one of the main factors affecting the mechanical and electrical life of electromagnetic switches. At the same time, the research and development design of electromagnetic mechanism often needs to verify its rationality and accuracy through physical manufacturing and experiment. This traditional research and development design mode not only has a long development cycle, but also has a high manufacturing cost.

Benefiting from the rapid development of multi-body dynamics and 3D printing technology, new ideas are provided for solving the above problems. In this paper, take a type of contactor as an example, using multi-field co-simulation technology and 3D printing technology to quickly verify the coil design, which effectively avoids the shortcomings of traditional design methods such as long development cycle and high cost. It has certain reference and reference significance for the development and optimization of the design.

II. Multiphysics Co-Simulation

This paper takes a small AC contactor as the research object, and its structure is shown in Fig.1. Its electromagnetic mechanism mainly includes excitation coil, core spring, movable and static iron core and the air gap between them.

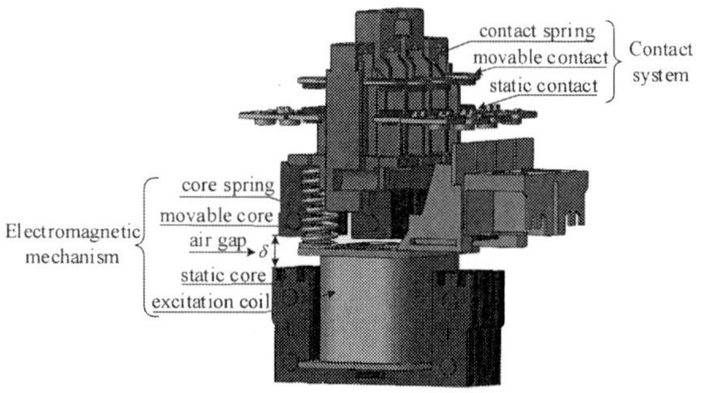

Fig. 1. Schematic diagram of the structure of the contactor

A. Multiphysics co-simulation model establishment

Considering that the single electromagnetic field finite element simulation software cannot simulate the bouncing behavior of the moving parts of the electromagnetic switch in the real situation in the process of suction, and suppressing the bouncing is one of the main goals of the optimal design of the electromagnetic mechanism. Therefore, a multi-field co-simulation model of electromagnetic switch is built in this paper, and its design process is shown in Fig.2.

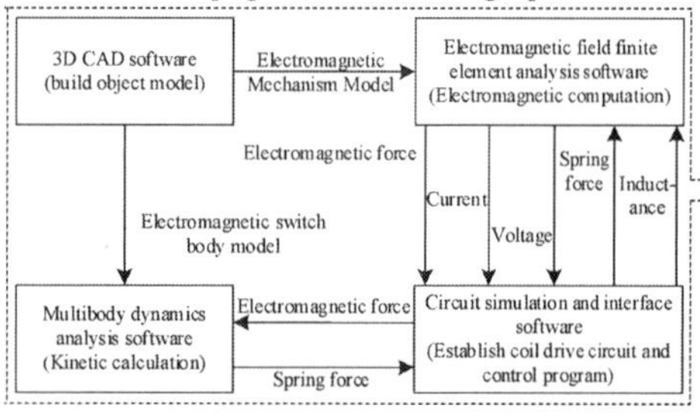

Fig. 2. Electromagnetic field-mechanical field co-simulation design process

The design flow of multi-field co-simulation model of electromagnetic switch is firstly to establish the ontology model and electromagnetic mechanism model of the research object in 3D CAD modeling software. Secondly, the model of electromagnetic mechanism was imported into the finite element software of electromagnetic field to realize the real-time calculation of electromagnetic parameters. Then, the ontology model of the research object was imported into the multi-body dynamics software and the corresponding constraints were added. Finally, the coil drive circuit and control program are built in the circuit simulation and interface software, and the data exchange between two software is realized simultaneously.

B. Coil Design

By measuring the contactor's opening distance of movable and static cores, the opening distance of movable and static contact, the core force spring and the contact spring stiffness coefficient and the initial compression amount, the spring force characteristics of the contactor are finally obtained as shown in Fig.3.

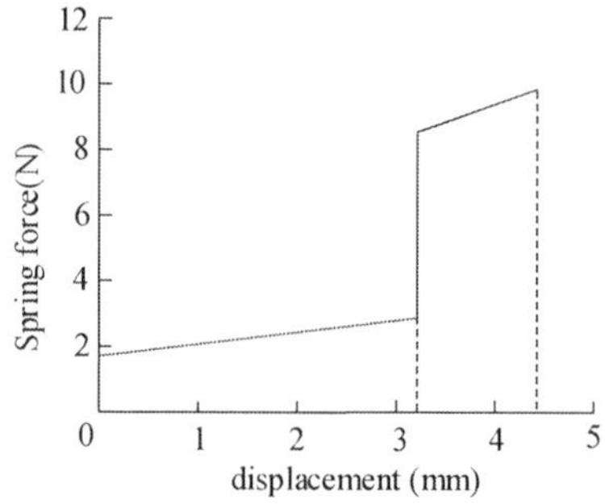

Fig. 3. Contactor reaction force characteristics

The core used in the contactor is a double E-type core, and the formula for calculating the electromagnetic attraction force under the condition of constant magnetic potential is:

$$F_m = \frac{1}{4}(IN)^2 \mu_0 \frac{A}{\delta^2} \tag{2}$$

Among them: F_m is the electromagnetic attraction force; IN is the ampere-turn; μ_0 is the vacuum permeability; A is the area of the cross section of the magnetic pole; δ is the air gap between the movable and static cores.

From this, the ampere-turn calculation formula can be obtained as follows:

$$IN = \sqrt{\frac{4F\delta}{\mu A}} \tag{3}$$

When the contactor is in the off position, take δ =4.3mm, $F_m \approx$2N, A=147.20mm^2, then the excitation ampere-turn IN is:

$$IN = \sqrt{\frac{4\times 2\times 4.3^2}{4\pi\times 10^{-7}\times 147.20}} \approx 895 \tag{4}$$

When the contactor is in the pull-in position, the dynamic and static iron cores are not absolutely pulled in, but there is a tiny air gap. According to the manufacturing process of the industry, the air gap is about 0.01~0.1mm. Take δ =0.1mm, $F_m \approx$ 9.76N, A=147.20mm^2, then the excitation ampere-turn IN in the holding stage is:

$$IN = \sqrt{\frac{4\times 9.76\times 0.1}{4\pi\times 10\times 147.20}} \approx 46 \tag{5}$$

According to the engineering design experience, when the holding reference current is set to 3 times the critical holding current, it can ensure the reliable holding of the contacts and avoid additional losses [8]. Therefore, if it can meet the requirements of disconnection δ = 4.3mm, IN = 895, and suction δ = 0.1mm, IN = 138, the contactor can work reliably. Take I=0.3A in the pull-in position, then N=

460 turns. If N=460 turns are taken, then I=895/460=1.95A in the disconnected position. Take I=2A to select the coil wire, and select the current density as J=15A/mm^2, then the area of the wire corresponding to the 2A current is about 0.13mm^2, and the diameter of the wire is 0.4mm.

In the manufacturing process of the wire, the insulation layer of the wire will inevitably occupy part of the area, so this must be taken into account in the coil design. According to the standard IEC 60317, the filling factor of enameled wire with a diameter of 0.4mm is 0.842. When the number of coil turns is 460 turns, the coil window area is:

$$S = \frac{460 \times 0.1257}{0.842} \approx 68.68 \text{ mm}^2 \tag{6}$$

After measuring the size of the static iron core, it can be known that the area of the window between the column and the side column of the static iron core is 8.90× 18.96mm^2. After reserving the thickness of the coil bobbin, the coil window is designed to be a rectangle of 4× 17.20mm^2, as shown in Fig.4.

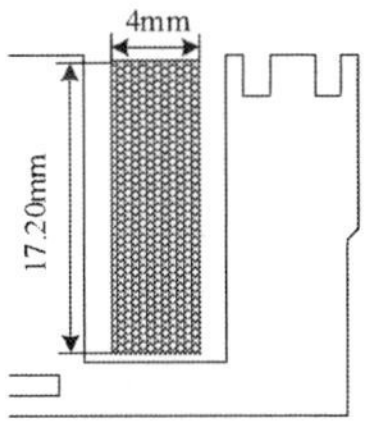

Fig. 4. Parameter design of the coil

C. Co-simulation verification

In order to preliminarily verify the accuracy and rationality of the coil design, the dynamic characteristics of the contactor are simulated by using the electromagnetic field-mechanical field co-simulation model. The control strategy adopts current closed-loop control. The reference values of starting current and holding current are set to 2A and 0.3A respectively. The simulation waveforms of coil voltage, current and displacement of movable core are shown in Fig.5.

The starting process of the contactor in Fig.5 can be divided into the following stages. After time t_0, the contactor starts t_0 start, at this time, the coil current is less than the reference value of the pull-in current, the main control switch is turned on, and the coil current follows an exponential law It rises rapidly until it reaches the reference value at t_1. At this stage, the electromagnetic force rises rapidly with the increase of the current. During the period from t_1 to t_2, the coil current is stable near the reference value. Affected by the electromagnetic force, the movable core begins to overcome the spring force. In the period of t_2~t_3, with the increase of the movable core speed, the counter electromotive force continues to increase, forcing the coil current to drop, until the movable and static cores snap together, and the counter electromotive force disappears. During this period, the coil current is always less than the reference value, The main control switch tube is turned on, and when the counter electromotive force disappears, the coil current rises to the reference value exponentially again; in the period of t_3~t_4, the coil current is maintained near the reference value under the current closed-loop control, until t_4 time, the contactor start completed, turn to hold. After this time, the coil voltage is close to 0, and the current slowly drops to the holding reference value until time t_5. It can be seen from the figure that the set current reference value can make the contactor work reliably, which preliminarily verifies the correctness and rationality of the coil design. At the same time, the bouncing behavior of the core during the working process of the electromagnetic switch is successfully simulated, and subsequent research on bouncing suppression can be carried out on this co-simulation system, including changing the control strategy, core and spring parameters, etc.

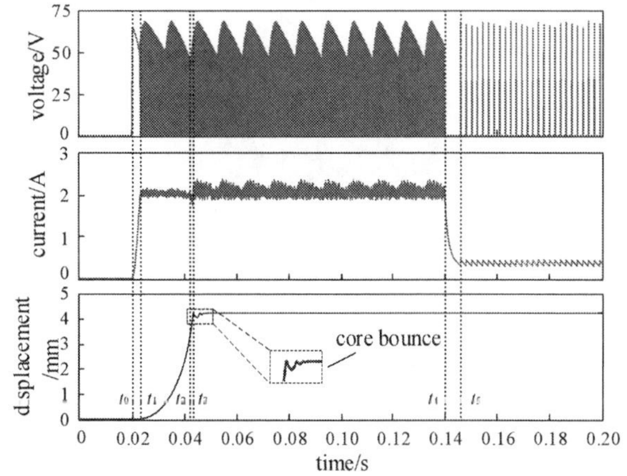

Fig. 5. Contactor current closed-loop simulation waveform

III. 3D PRINTING TECHNOLOGY AND EXPERIMENT

A. 3D printing rapid prototyping technology

The reason for the long development cycle and high development cost of electromagnetic switch products is that in the traditional research and development method, the key dimensions of the product need to be continuously debugged and multiple times of mold opening verification. Through the introduction of 3D printing rapid prototyping technology, the design scheme can be quickly transformed into real objects and verified, which can effectively shorten the development cycle and reduce production costs. When using 3D printing technology to design a product model, it is generally necessary to first model the design in the 3D CAD modeling software, and then import the model into the slicing software in STL format, and set a reasonable printing material, speed, and filling degree. After waiting for the parameters, print it, and finally polish and polish the printed physical product.

In this paper, the coil bobbin of the research object is redesigned to make it more suitable for the designed coil window. The printed coil bobbin is shown in Fig.6.

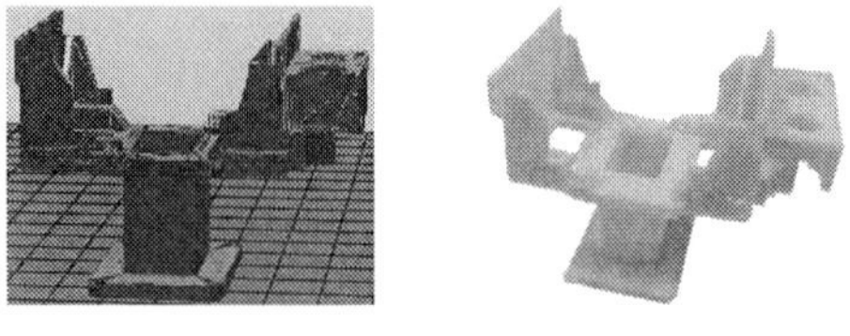

(a) Design of coil bobbin (b) Actual coil bobbin

Fig. 6. 3D printing of the coil bobbin

B. Experimental verification

In order to further verify the accuracy and rationality of the coil design, the skeleton shown in Fig.6 is used to wind the coil, and the wound coil is loaded into the contactor shown in Fig.1 for power-on experiments. The control strategy and current reference value are the same as the above simulation, and the PWM control frequency is set to 10kHz. The experimental waveforms of the coil voltage, current, and displacement of the movable core are shown in Fig.7.

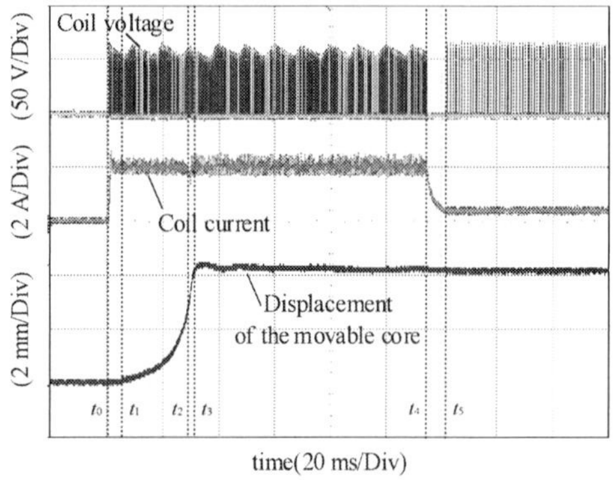

Fig. 7. Contactor current closed-loop experimental waveform

At time t_0, the contactor starts, and the current quickly rises to the suction reference value. At time t_1, the movable core begins to move, and with the increase of the moving speed of the core, the counter electromotive force increases continuously. At time t_2, the current appears to force down, and at time t_3, the current rises again to the reference value, until time t_4, the contactor starting process ends. After time t_4, the coil voltage is close to 0, and the current begins to decrease slowly until time t_5, when the current decreases to the holding reference value. As can be seen from the forced decline of coil current and the core displacement curve in Fig.7, the redesigned coil can ensure the reliable operation of the contactor.

IV. CONCLUSION

In this paper, multi-field co-simulation of electromagnetic switch was established, and 3D printing rapid prototyping technology was introduced. Taking coil design as an example, the design of electromagnetic mechanism was verified by combination of virtual and real, which effectively shortened the research and development time and reduced the verification cost, and provided a new research and design idea for the design developers of electromagnetic mechanism.

ACKNOWLEDGMENT

The authors are thankful for the support of the Natural Science Foundation of Fujian Province of China (No. 2020J05134) and the Key Laboratory of Special Machine and High Voltage Apparatus (Shenyang University of Technology), Ministry of Education (No. KFKT202002) to carry out this study.

REFERENCES

[1] P Zhang, "Research on technology of intelligent low voltage electrical apparatus", *Electrical & Energy Management Technology*, 2019, （15） :10-20.

[2] J Wang, G Zhang, Z Song, Y Geng, "Internet of Things, Big Data, Smart Appliances: the Future of Power Equipment Development", *High Voltage Appliances,* 2018, (19): 1-9

[3] L Tang, W Chen, Z Xu, "A Direct Electromagnetic Force Closed-loop Control Strategy for a Contactor", *IEEE Transactions on Industrial Electronics*. 2022

[4] J Wu, Z Xu, "A model-free adaptive control strategy for actuation of electromagnetic contactors" , *Proceedings of the CSEE*, 2020, 40(5):1663-1672

[5] C Fang, X Chang, "Simulation research on high-speed mechanical switchgear with gas damper based on multi-physics coupling method", *High Voltage Apparatus*, 2019, 55(8): 48-57.

[6] Z Xu, L Tang, "Co-simulation and digital control technology of the intelligent AC contactor", *Proceedings of the CSEE*, 2015, 35(11): 2870-2878.

[7] L Guo, B Liang, S Zhang, L Shu, Z Wu, "Coupling Dynamics Simulation and Experimental Research of Intelligent AC Contactor Considering Freewheeling", *Electrical & Energy Management Technology*, 2018, (12):19-24+29

[8] J Zhuang, Z Xu, "The multivariate feedback control strategy for electromagnetic contactor holding", *Proceedings of the CSEE*, 2019, 39(5): 1516-1526

Jingfeng Dong is currently pursuing the M.S. degree in electric engineering from the College of Electrical Engineering and Automation, Fuzhou University, China. His research interests include electric apparatus and its intelligent technology.

Jierong Zhuang, male, born in 1989, Ph.D., associate professor. He is mainly engaged in the electrical apparatus and intelligent technologies. Corresponding author: jierong@foxmail.com.

Zhihong Xu, female, born in 1963, Ph.D., professor, doctoral tutor. She is mainly engaged in the electrical apparatus and intelligent technologies.

Research on the Identification Method of Household Appliances Based on Optimized Convolutional Neural Network

Yunxiang Jia[1], Changchun Chi[1], Haifeng Mao[2]

[1]School of Electrical Engineering, Shanghai Dianji University, Shanghai, 201306, China
[2]Suzhou Future Electric Co., Ltd, Suzhou, 215100, China
E-mail: 2879836132@qq.com Tel: 17802531591

***Abstract*—Aiming at how to ensure the safe use of household appliances by residents, non-intrusive load monitoring technology is adopted, and load identification is the main problem of non-intrusive load monitoring technology. The method of optimized convolutional neural network can well overcome the problem of load identification. Based on two-dimensional V-I trajectory load characteristics and the convolutional neural network identification algorithm, studying the load identification method, and analyze the feature recognition process of self-learning extraction of V-I trajectory graph by convolutional neural network. And particle swarm optimization algorithm is adopted to optimize the configuration of convolutional neural network hyperparameters to solve the problem of classification performance uncertainty caused by the traditional manual operation to configure network parameters, so that the classification performance of convolutional neural network tends to be optimal and load identification accuracy is improved. Studies have shown that the optimized convolutional neural network shows good recognition performance and can accurately identify the type of electrical appliances, so as to enhance the reliability of load monitoring technology, provide a safe environment for electrical appliances, and ensure the safety of residents' lives and property.**

***Index Terms*— Non-intrusive load monitoring, load identification, particle swarm optimization algorithm, optimized convolutional neural network.**

I. INTRODUCTION

With the gradual acceleration of the pace of economic development, the quality of life and consumption level of the people keep improving, many kinds of new household appliances are widely used[1], bringing many conveniences to people's daily life. But it comes with some security risks, such as long-term high-load operation, improper use of electrical appliances to generate high temperature, complex internal components or short-circuit combustion of unqualified quality, which may cause dangerous accidents such as fire or even explosion[4]. Therefore, the non-intrusive load monitoring method is used to monitor the use of electrical appliances, and load identification is its important difficulties. With the intelligent development of electrical appliances, the load characteristics are becoming more complex, and it is more difficult to mine and extract load characteristics, resulting in a decrease in the recognition accuracy, affecting the overall load monitoring accuracy, and it is difficult to maintain a safe electricity environment to protect residents' lives and property[5].

The non-intrusive load identification method is to install intelligence at the power supply entrance to identify and monitor the internal electrical appliances of the residents[7], and to extract the characteristics of the electrical appliances to identify them, many in-depth studies have been done on non-invasive load identification technology at home and abroad. Based on the most traditional active power feature in the steady-state feature, the literature[8] extracts its sequence eigenvalues and contour singular values, and uses a multi-feature sequence fusion algorithm to identify larger power loads; the literature[9] establishes linear and nonlinear load model databases based on steady-state voltage and current features to identify the newly added load through model matching; the literature[10] color-codes the V-I trajectory, and uses sampling transfer learning to identify the load to prevent the uniqueness of the newly added load trajectory. In recent years, with the continuous development of self-learning artificial intelligence technology, the self-learning extraction feature recognition technology for the voltage-current trajectory has emerged[11], and the feature information is trained to construct a classification model, and the effect has been affirmed by people.

The convolutional neural network classification model can extract and recognize the load characteristics by self-learning, but the classification performance of classification model obtained by manual operation is uncertain and difficult to deal with the increasingly complex load identification work. Therefore, the particle swarm optimization algorithm is used to optimize the convolutional neural network hyperparameters[15]. The optimized convolutional neural network classification model has better self-learning feature extraction ability and higher accuracy in identifying electrical appliances, which has far-reaching significance for the development of non-intrusive load monitoring.

II. Load Identification Process Based On Convolutional Neural Network

A. V-I trajectory load characteristics

The load characteristics of the electrical V-I trajectory are based on the differences in the internal structure and devices of electrical appliance, and convert the voltage and current data of the electrical appliance during stable operation into two-dimensional trajectory images, so as to intuitively shows the differences of track shapes of different electrical appliances. So according to the load characteristics, to identify the image to identify the electrical type.

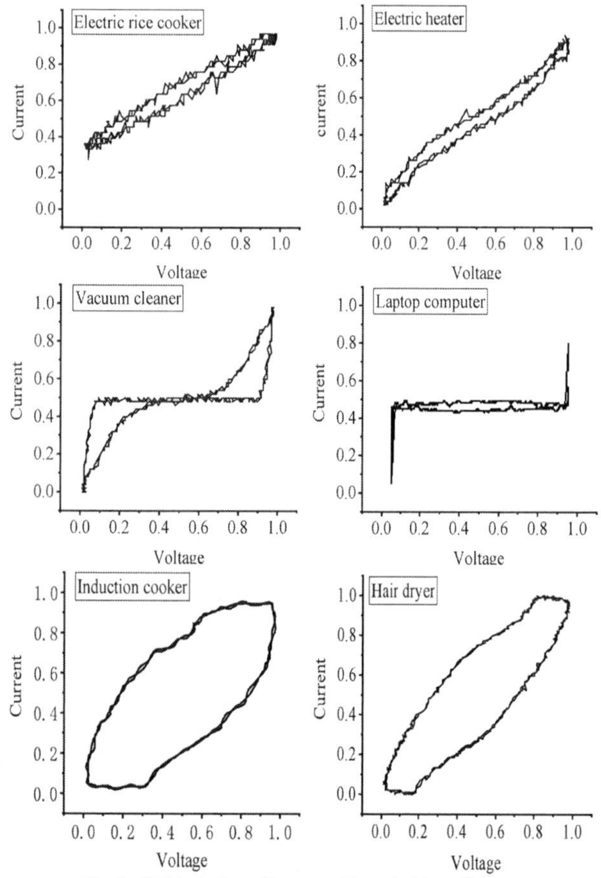

Fig. 1. V-I trajectory diagram of household appliances.

B. Convolutional Neural Network Self-learning Feature Extraction

Convolutional neural network is a multi-layer perceptron designed for two-dimensional image recognition, Convolutional layer weight sharing, pooling layer downsampling and neuron local connection are its main features. When it is applied to identify and classify the V-I trajectory map, it shows the advantages of zooming, panning, and maintaining the invariance of the trajectory feature map. The convolutional neural network is mainly composed of feature extraction layers combined with convolutional layers and pooling layers, and classification layers combined with fully connected layers and a softmax layer.

1) The convolutional layer is the core layer of the convolutional neural network, It uses discrete convolution to learn and extract features from the V-I trajectory map of household appliances. The convolution kernel, as a shared discrete two-dimensional filter, performing an inner product operation on the pixels in the local area of the two-dimensional V-I trajectory map, filtering out useless information to generate a filter map, and using offsets to form many feature maps of the same size.

$$X_j^l = f(\sum_{i \in M_j} X_j^{l-1} * K_j^l + b_j^l) \quad (1)$$

In the formula: X_j^{l-1} and X_j^l are the input and output of the trajectory feature map; f is a nonlinear function; M_j is the local area trajectory map set; $*$ is the convolution symbol; K_j^l is the convolution kernel; b_j^l is the bias.

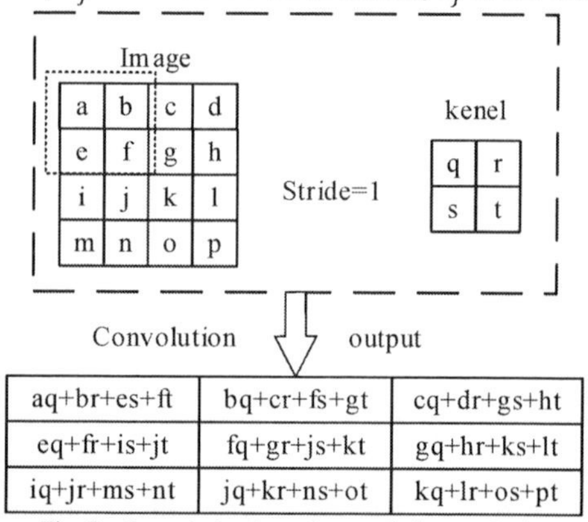

Fig. 2. Convolution kernel convolution method.

2) The pooling layer mainly compresses the size of the feature map space and performs down-sampling to reduce network parameters. The pixel values in the trajectory map area are extracted by maximum or average pooling, and the feature information of the trajectory map can be kept unchanged, thus reducing the amount of calculation and improving the network training speed, The pooling process is as follows:

$$X_j^l = f(\beta_j^l pooling(X_j^{l-1}) + b_j^l) \quad (2)$$

In the formula: β_j^l and b_j^l are bias parameters; *pool* is the pooling downsampling function.

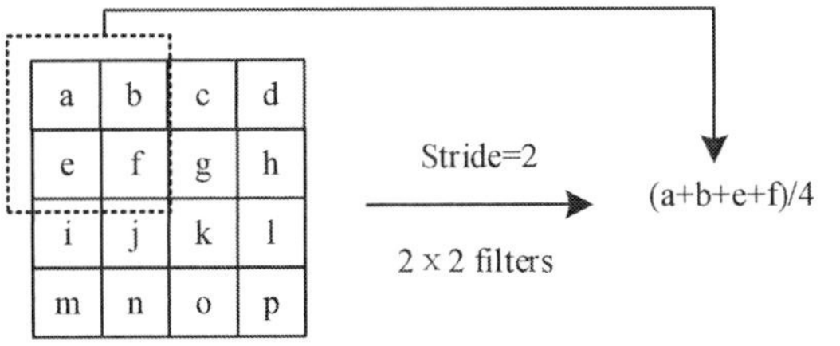

Fig. 3. Average pooling.

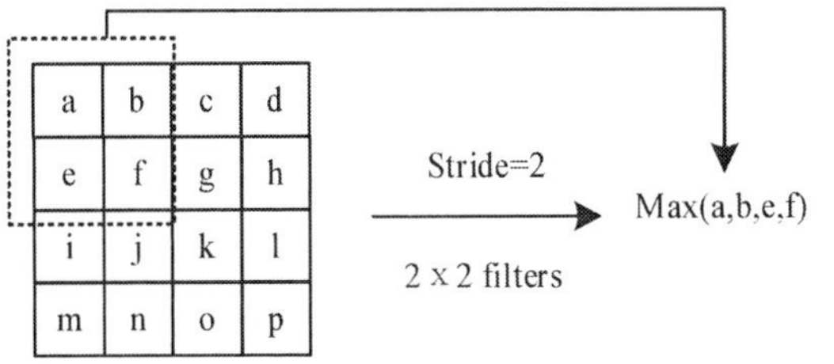

Fig. 4. Max pooling.

3) The fully connected layer is used to integrate the discriminative local feature information in the extracted trajectory feature map, and the DropOut layer is often placed in front of it to prevent overfitting. After the initial data features of the V-I trajectory map are mapped to the latent feature space, the integrated and summarized features are mapped to the sample label space through the full connection layer, and finally the recognition and classification results are output in the form of electrical classification probability by softmax classifier.

$$S_j = \frac{e^{a_j}}{\sum_{k=1}^{c} e^{a_k}} \tag{3}$$

In the formula: c is the total number of trajectory maps; a_j is the eigenvalue of the category j of the electrical appliance type.

III. Optimized Convolutional Neural Network

A. Particle Swarm Optimization Algorithm

Particle swarm optimization algorithm is based on the heuristic search foraging principle of birds. According to the initial food range information stored by the particle itself and the group, the bird is regarded as a particle, and the initial velocity vector $V_i(0)$ and the initial position $X_i(0)$ are determined. Then, in the process of particle search optimization, by the particle search ability of the weight coefficient ω and the learning factor c is used to adjust the change speed of the particle approaching the extreme value, Particles cooperate and share information with each other, and constantly update the partial extreme value $p_{best}(i)$ and the global extreme value $g_{best}(i)$ in the particle population N, until the velocity vector and position information of the optimal particle solution are finally obtained.

$$V_i(0) = V_{max} - r(V_{max} - V_{min}) \tag{4}$$

$$X_i(0) = 0.1RS + G \tag{5}$$

$$V_i' = \omega V_i + c_1 r_1 (p_{best}(i) - X_i) + c_2 r_2 (g_{best}(i) - X_i) \tag{6}$$

$$X_i' = X_i + V_i' \tag{7}$$

In the formula: V_{max} and V_{min} are the upper and lower limits of initialization speed; RS is a random value (-1,1); G is the empirical value; V_i, X_i and V_i', X_i' are the information before and after the speed and position adjustment; c_1 and c_2 are learning factors of local extreme value and global extreme value; r, r_1, r_2 are extreme value influence degree disturbance factors;

In the process of optimizing and confirming the optimal speed and position information, it is necessary to calculate the fitness value of all particles, and screen out the particle population with better speed vector and position according to their pros and cons.

$$Fitness = \frac{1}{N} \sum_{i=1}^{N} \sum_{j=1}^{M} (W_{j,i}^{d} - W_{j,i})^2 \tag{8}$$

Where M is the number of outputs after updating, $W_{j,i}^d$ and $W_{j,i}$ are expected output and actual output state values. When the error between the two state values tends to be smaller than the final expected error value, the optimization process ends.

B. Optimize Convolutional Neural Network

Convolutional neural network classification models with different hyperparameter configurations have uneven classification effects, and the uncertainty of manual operation will make the classification performance locally optimal. Therefore, particle swarm optimization algorithm is used to optimize its network structure and search for the optimal hyperparameters, so that the classification performance of the load classification model tends to be optimal.

Firstly, according to the value range of hyperparameters, the particle swarm optimization algorithm is used for optimization, and the hyperparameters are regarded as particles to carry out the optimization process. According to the fitness value of the hyperparameters, the optimized hyperparameters are continuously brought in, and select the hyperparameter groups that can optimize the classification performance. Thus, the optimized convolutional neural network load classification model is finally obtained, its classification performance will be tested, and the classification results are evaluated.

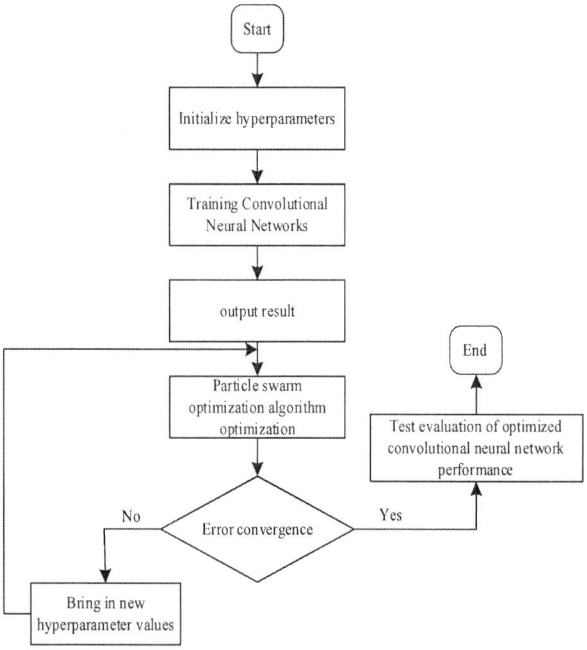

Fig. 5. Optimizing Convolutional Neural Network Flowchart.

In order to better optimize the convolutional neural network and avoid the over-fitting problem caused by repeated network training, the volatility rate is used to evaluate the stability of the classification performance of the optimized convolutional neural network load classification model. When the volatility tends to be stable, and the difference of load classification performance decreases, the optimization work of hyperparameters by the particle swarm optimization algorithm ends, and finally the optimized convolutional neural network load classification model with stable classification performance can be obtained.

$$CV = \frac{N \times \sum_i^N accuracy^k[i]}{\sqrt{\sum_i^N (accuracy^k[k] - \frac{\sum_i^N accuracy^k[i]}{N})^2}} \quad (9)$$

Among them, $accuracy^k[k]$ is the classification accuracy of the ith particle at the training stage K.

IV. Load Classification Test Result

Build a convolutional neural network load classification model through matlab, optimize its hyperparameter configuration with particle swarm optimization algorithm, select the main hyperparameters that affect the classification performance, and determine its value range, among which hyperparameters such as convolution kernel and learning rate are related to classification performance, and the selected hyperparameters are listed in Table 1. In the process of hyperparameter optimization, in order to better find the optimal hyperparameter values, the local and global learning factors in the particle swarm optimization algorithm are set as 1.49445, the inertia weight is set as 0.8, to train the network and update the hyperparameters.

In the process of the particle swarm optimization algorithm finding the optimal value of the convolutional neural network hyperparameter, the inertia weight can accelerate the convergence speed of the particle swarm optimization algorithm, so that it has a good search ability to quickly find the local and global hyperparameter extreme value. The learning factor can control the change acceleration relationship between local and global extrema, and find closer to better hyperparameters faster. In this process, the fitness value of hyperparameters gradually converges until it tends to be stable, and the search for optimal hyperparameters is over.

TABLE I
HYPERPARAMETERS AND THEIR VALUE RANGES

Hyperparameter	Ranges
number of convolution kernels	2~32
size of convolution kernels	3x3,5x5,7x7,9x9
pooling type	Max、Average
Dropout layer probability	0,0.05,0.1,0.15,0.2,0.25,0.3
CNN learning rate	0.01~1

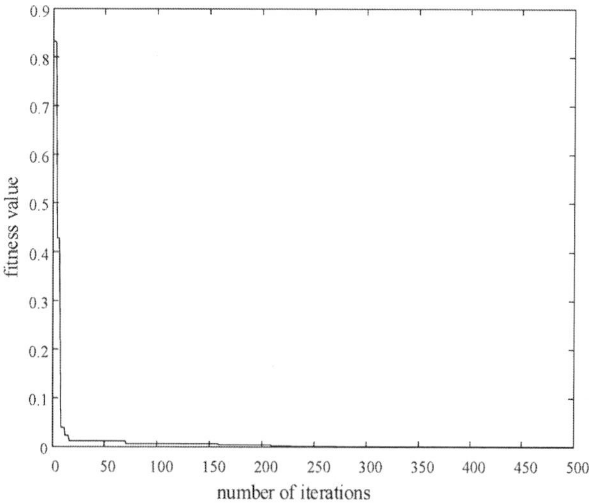

Fig. 6. Fitness value change curve.

After the particle swarm optimization algorithm searches for the optimal value of the hyperparameters of the convolutional neural network, the specific hyperparameter optimization results are shown in the following table, among which the differences in the selection of hyperparameters for different convolutional layers are obvious.

TABLE II
HYPERPARAMETER OPTIMIZATION RESULTS

Network layer	Hyperparameter	Result
Convolution layer 1	number of convolution kernels	21
	size of convolution kernels	7x7
Pooling layer 1	pooling type	Max-pooling
Convolution layer 2	number of convolution kernels	28
	size of convolution kernels	5x5
Pooling layer 2	pooling type	Max-pooling
Convolution layer 3	number of convolution kernels	25
	size of convolution kernels	3x3
Pooling layer 3	pooling type	Max-pooling
	Dropout layer probability	0.15
	CNN learning rate	0.43

After the multi-round training optimization, the learning factors and inertia weights are self-learning to find the optimal value of hyperparameters, from local optimal to global optimal. With the deepening of training, the volatility gradually decreases and tends to be flat, and the overall classification performance of the optimized convolutional neural network is stable, and performance testing and evaluation can be carried out.

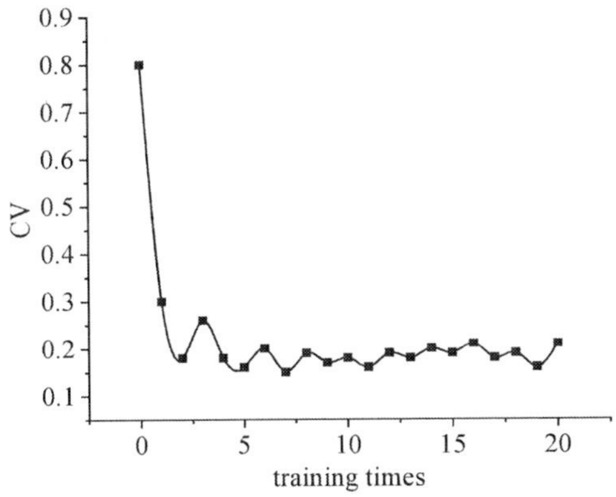

FIG. 7. FITNESS VALUE CHANGE CURVE.

After inputting the test set, finally the softmax classifier is used to output a feature vector whose sum is one, in which each value is the probability of predicting the type of electrical appliances, and the maximum probability is taken as the recognition accuracy rate. According to the analysis of the test results, the classification accuracy has been greatly improved, and the overall electrical appliance recognition accuracy has been further improved.

TABLE III
IDENTIFICATION ACCURACY OF HOUSEHOID APPLIANCES

Electrical appliances	Before optimization	After optimization
Electric rice cooker	97.24%	98.67%
Electric heater	97.83%	98.78%
Vacuum cleaner	93.74%	95.23%
Laptop computer	93.57%	95.04%
Induction cooker	93.27%	94.12%
Hair dryer	95.93%	97.86%

V. CONCOLUSION

In this paper, a kind of load identification method based on optimized convolutional neural network is studied under the non-intrusive load monitoring mode for residential electricity consumption. Based on the two-dimensional V-I trajectory map of load characteristics, the method optimizing the configuration of convolutional neural network hyperparameters through particle swarm optimization algorithm, and improves the recognition and classification performance of self-learning feature extraction of the classification model, thereby improving the recognition accuracy. Aiming at the basic research of load identification under non-intrusive load monitoring, the optimized convolutional neural network has good classification accuracy, can quickly and accurately identify the type of electrical appliances to ensure the safety of residents' lives and property, which has far-reaching significance for the reliability research of load monitoring technology.

REFERENCES

[1] Jing Tu, Ming Zhou, Gengyin Li, etc. Distributed optimization strategy of potential game for electricity sales companies for residents' demand response [J]. Chinese Journal of Electrical Engineering, 2020, 40(02): 400-411.

[2] Jing Luo, Weiqing Sun. Research on the trade model of wind energy consumption considering demand response [J]. Zhejiang Electric Power, 2020, 39(12): 50-57.

[3] Yibo Fang, Xiaodong Yuan, Juntao Fei, etc. Identification of energy storage capacity in distribution network based on demand-side response [J]. Electric Power Engineering Technology, 2019, 38(06): 61-68.

[4] Qiangqiang Zhao, Changchun Chi. Feature Extraction of Series Arc Fault Based on Variational Mode Decomposition [J]. Journal of Shanghai Institute of Electrical Engineering, 2021, 24(06):332-338.

[5] Yixin Yu, Yanli Liu. Challenging Problems of Smart Grid [J].Automation of Electric Power Systems, 2015, 39(02):1-5.
[6] Li Zhang, Tao Zhang, Hongwei Zhang, etc. A Load Identification Method Based on Multi-parameter Hidden Markov Model [J]. Power System Protection and Control, 2019, 47(20):81-90.
[7] Hart G. W. Nonintrusive appliance load monitoring [J]. Proceedings of the IEEE, 1992, 80(12):1870-1891.
[8] Dongsheng Yang, Liang Kong, Bo Hu, etc. Load identification method based on multi-feature sequence fusion [J].Automation of Electric Power Systems, 2017, 41(22):66-73.
[9] Bing Qi, Liya Liu, Lu Han, etc. Appliance Load Identification Algorithm Based on System Model [J]. Electrical Measurement and Instrumentation, 2018, 55(07):23-30.
[10] Chi Liu, Xue Wang, Wei You. Non-Intrusive Load Monitoring by Voltage-Current Trajectory Enabled Transfer Learning [J]. IEEE Trans. Smart Grid, 2019, 10(5): 5609-5619.
[11] Hong Chen, Zhibin Yu. Recognition of Household Appliances Based on Deep Transfer Learning [J]. Sensors and Microsystems, 2020, 39(06): 48-50+54.
[12] Du, Liang, He, Dawei, Harley, Ronald G., Habetler, ThomasG. Electric Load Classification by Binary Voltage-Current Trajectory Mapping [J]. IEEE transactions on smart grid, 2016, 7(1): 358-365.
[13] GAO J K, KARA E C, GIRI S, et al. A feasibility study ofautomated plug-load identification from high-frequency measurements[C]// 2015 IEEE Global Conference on Signaland Information Processing (GlobalSIP), December 14-16, 2015, Orlando, USA.
[14] Ying Wang, Wei Yang, Xianyong Xiao, etc. Non-intrusive Residential Load Monitoring Method Based on U-I Trajectory Curve Refinement Recognition [J]. Power Grid Technology, 2021, 45(10):4104-4113.
[15] Bin Wang, Danni Wang, Qiaoyong Jiang, etc. Research on Competitive Particle Swarm Optimization Algorithm Based on Multi-objective [J/OL]. Journal of Xi'an University of Technology: 1-10[2022-03-23].
[16] Bowen Yang, Weiyi Qian. Adaptive Particle Swarm Optimization Algorithm with Multiple Inertia Weights [J]. Journal of Bohai University (Natural Science Edition), 2021, 42(01):41-48+90.

8th International Conference on Reliability of
Electrical Products and Electrical Contacts,
November 18-20, 2022

Effect of Industrial Pure Iron Substrate on Corrosion of Electroplated Copper Coating

Shengmao Wu[1,2], Xianhua Chen[2]

[1]Xiamen Hongfa Electroacoustic Co., Ltd., Xiamen, 361000, China
[2]Xiamen Jinyue Electric Co., Ltd., Xiamen, 361021, China
E-mail:1002608@hongfa.cn TEL:17306027854

***Abstract*—The changes of appearance and material properties of industrial pure iron relay stamping parts after annealed treatment and electroplating were analyzed by field emission scanning electron microscopy (SEM) and electrochemical test. The influencing factors of oxidation/corrosion and blackening defect existed on the surface of the electroplated parts were investigated. It was found that the blackening defect existed on the surface of the electroplated copper layer, and the composition of corrosion products was similar to that of the electroplating solution. By comparing the electrochemical properties of different substrates, it is shown that serious grain boundary corrosion exists in the acid pickling process of DT4E. By characterizing the microstructure and elemental composition of the materials after annealed treatment, it was found that the segregation and agglomeration of Si in the surface grain boundaries. Therefore, corrosion failure cause analysis of copper coating on relay parts was intergranular corrosion of substrate during annealed treatment and acid pickling process.**

***Index Terms*— Copper plating, intergranular corrosion industrial pure iron,**

I. Introduction

Due to its good physical and mechanical properties, such as excellent impact toughness, plasticity, high magnetic susceptibility and low coercivity, industrial pure iron has been widely used in the fields of electronics, aerospace, energy development and national defense security, such as electrical components, magnetic materials, amorphous products, relays, etc.[1]

Industrial pure iron is an ultra-low carbon steel, which can be divided into different grades according to different magnetic properties. Among them, DT4 grade is one of the most important materials for the magnetic circuit structure of electromagnetic relay, and is used to punch into armature, yoke or other parts. As the magnetic properties and corrosion resistance of parts can affect the performance and quality of relay, annealed treatment is usually carried out on the pure iron parts to reduce their coercive force. Also, electroplating treatment such as copper plating and nickel plating is used to improve the corrosion resistance performance.

After complex manufacturing process, industrial pure iron parts may have various defects, such as burr and imprint during stamping process, high coercivity after annealing, oxidation/corrosion of electroplating parts[2] etc. For electroplating parts, there is a kind of oxidation corrosion "blackening defect" in the surface defects of electroplating copper coating, that is, electroplating copper parts after the standard quality inspection and warehousing, after 3~5 days of storage or circulation, the surface of parts produces serious oxidation corrosion black spots. The defect greatly reduces the protective performance of the parts and brings serious hidden danger to the finished relay. In order to identify corrosion failure cause of copper coating on relay parts, the important influence factors was studied by means of scanning electron microscopy, in-situ morphology analysis and electrochemical analysis. It was found that the acid pickling of substrate was the immediate cause of blackening defect, and the segregation and agglomeration of Si in the surface grain boundaries had occurred during annealed treatment. On this basis, the generating mechanism of blackening defect on the coating of pure iron substrate was discussed.

II. Materials and Methods

The materials used in the experiment were DT4E pure iron belt of a domestic factory, CM1 pure iron belt of CSC from Taiwan, and REF60 iron belt of ThyssenKrupp from Germany. The composition is shown in Table I. The sample preparation process was as follows: stamping processing → cleaning → annealed treatment → degreasing → acid pickling → water washing → soaking in sodium hydroxide solution → water washing → copper plating → water washing → acid neutralization → water washing → passivation treatment→ three-level pure water washing → drying.

TABLE I

COMPOSITION OF PURE IRON BELT

Mark	C (%)	Si (%)	Mn (%)	P (%)	S (%)	Al (%)
DT4E	0.002	0.083	0.24	0.013	0.001	<0.001
CM1	0.002	0.003	0.18	0.019	0.003	0.003
REF60	0.004	0.004	0.21	0.012	0.006	0.051

The appearance of the samples was recorded by digital camera. The micromorphology was analyzed by ZEISS field emission scanning electron microscope and element composition was identified by energy dispersive X-ray spectroscopy (EDS). The metallographic section was analyzed by Buehler cutting and polishing machine, and observed by KEYENCE high magnification microscope.

The electrochemical test samples were DT4E and REF60 pure iron, and the materials were encapsulated to prepare electrodes. The test methods include open circuit potential, constant current corrosion, etc. Three-electrode system was used for electrochemical test, saturated calomel electrode was used for reference electrode, 1M hydrochloric acid solution and 0.5M oxalic acid solution are used as electrolyte respectively. The test was performed on a CHI660E electrochemical workstation.

The annealed treatment test samples, DT4E and CM1 substrate, were annealed in a crawler tunnel furnace protected by ammonia decomposition gas.

III. Results and discussion

The appearance of DT4E sample after copper plating is shown in Fig. 1. There are blackening corrosion defect on the surface, which is same to the situation in the manufacturing process of relay parts. No blackening defect existed on the surface of CM1 and REF60 samples.

Fig. 1. Blackening defect existed on the surface of the electroplated copper layer when using DT4E

A. Micromorphology and elemental composition analysis

The micromorphology of the blackening defect are shown in Fig. 2. The EDS quantitative analysis results (Table II) show that the oxidation blackening part contains not only Cu, but also O, Na, K and other elements. The high proportion about O indicates that copper was oxidized. Generally, Na and K do not exist on the surface of the plated copper coating. One possibility was that they may come from the complexing agent NaCN as conductive salt and KOH in cyanide copper plating solution. In order to further confirm the source of elements, in-situ morphology analysis was used.

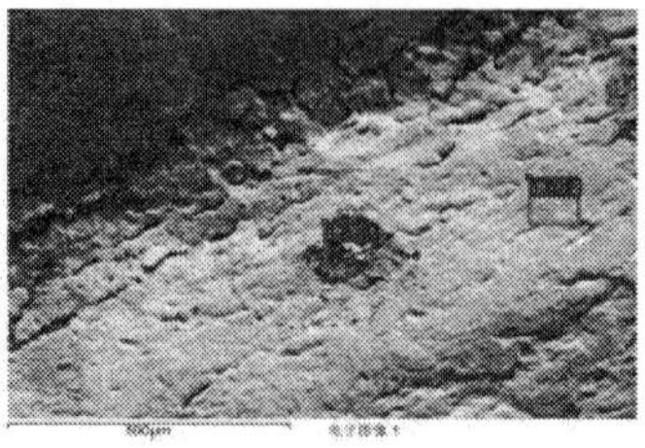

Fig. 2. The SEM images of Blackening defect

TABLE II

THE RESULTS OF EDS SPECTRUM ANALYSIS OF BLACKENING DEFECT

Element	C	O	Na	Si	K	Fe	Cu	Total
Wt% 1#	1.91	39.38	29.03	0.15	1.11	0.74	27.68	100.00
Wt% 2#	0.96	0.65	0	0	0	1.73	96.66	100.00

B. In situ morphology analysis

Figure 3a) shows the morphology of the blackening defect. In order to determine whether is normal under the plating layer, the part was deplated by the deplating reagent which did not corrode iron. The morphology of the corresponding position after deplating is shown in Figure 3b) and the height distribution figure 3c). As a result, there were cracks in the substrate at the oxidation area.

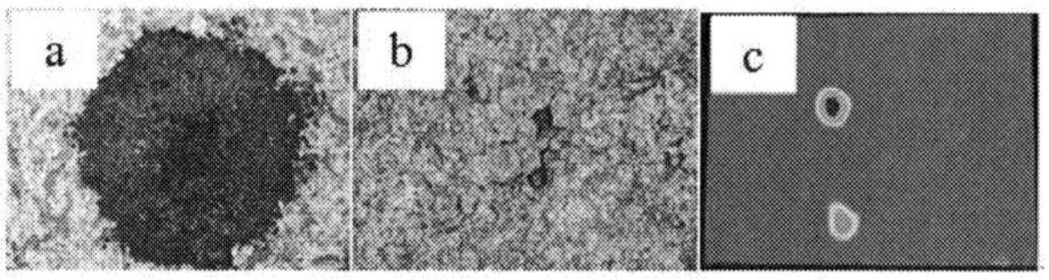

Fig. 3. The morphology analysis of blackening sample after deplating using DT4E substrate

C. Electrochemical analysis of electrical pure iron

All the cracks under the blackening defect were corroded along the grain boundary, as shown in Fig. 4, which means intergranular corrosion existed on the pure iron parts during acid pickling process. Therefore, electrochemical methods were used to study the intergranular corrosion of the substrate in acidic solution.

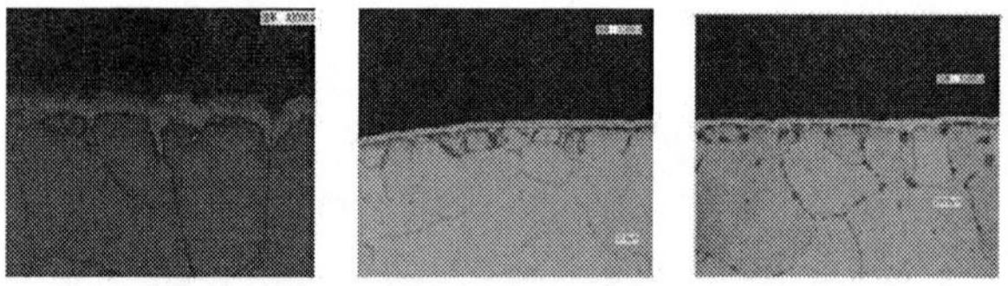

Fig. 4. Cross-section characterization of blackening defect

In order to simulate the intergranular corrosion of the substrate during the acid pickling process, DT4E and REF60 pure iron samples after annealed were tested in oxalic acid and hydrochloric acid solution, which were marked as D1 (corrosion DT4E sample), D2 (non corrosion DT4E sample) and R (REF60 sample).

In oxalic acid solution, the galvanostatic corrosion tests of the original surface and polished surface were carried out, and the surface of the sample after the corrosion test was observed by metallographic microscope. It is found that the original surface of sample D1 was network corrosion, the surface of sample D2 was spot corrosion, and the surface of sample R was no obvious corrosion, which indicates that the intergranular corrosion resistance of DT4E sample is worse than that of REF60. The result of constant-current corrosion test in hydrochloric acid solution was shown in Fig. 5. It shows the corrosion process of REF60 material in hydrochloric acid environment existed passivation phenomenon, but DT4E pure iron is not. In summary, the surface intergranular corrosion resistance of DT4E is worse than that of REF60 substrate.

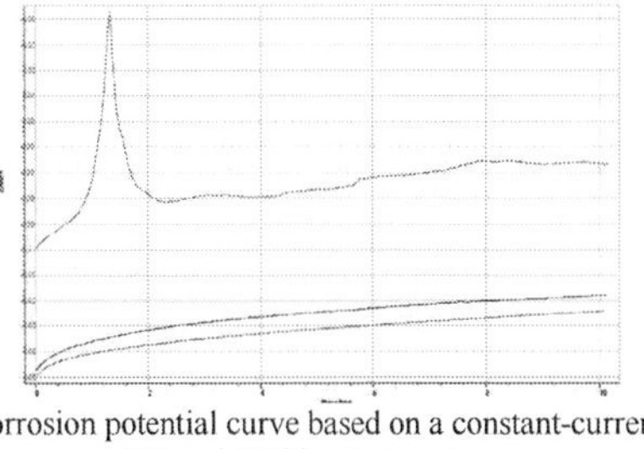

Fig. 5. The corrosion potential curve based on a constant-current method (D1:red,D2:blue,R:green)

D. *Annealed treatment*

Through three stages of heating, heat preservation and cooling, the grains in the material gradually grow after annealed. The whole process needs to be carried out in a protective atmosphere such as ammonia decomposition gas to prevent oxidation on the surface [3]. By comparing the differences between DT4E and CM1 pure iron samples before and after annealed, it was found that the element segregation phenomenon appears at the surface grain boundary of DT4E sample after annealed, as shown in Fig. 6c), and CM1 sample was unchanged Fig. 6d).

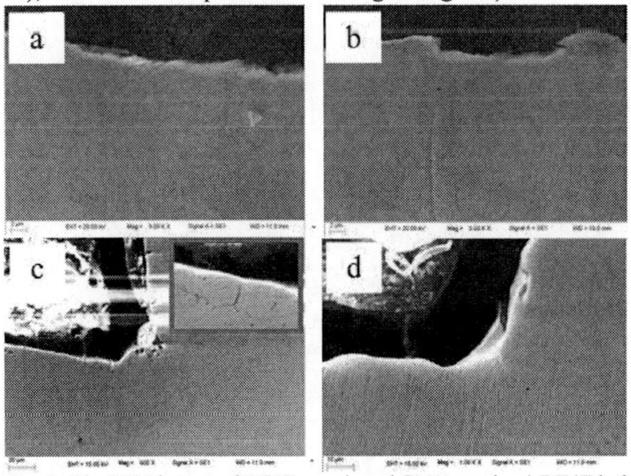

Fig. 6. The SEM images of DT4E sample and CM1 sample. a) DT4E before annealed, b) CM1 sample before annealed,c) DT4E after annealed, d) CM1 sample after annealed.

Fig. 7 shows the surface of DT4E sample after annealed treatment. It can be seen that the white dot like arising particles on the surface of DT4E sample are obvious. These white arising particles contain obvious elements of Si and Mn (as shown in Table III), which were oxidized and enriched on the surface. Some "pits" were also observed on the surface of the parts after annealed, and there were clear regular blocky substances inside. It was found that the main component of these regular shapes is silicon oxide, which is formed by the enrichment of silicon oxide at the grain boundary and the shedding of the grain in the shallow surface layer. The result also could be consistent with the grain boundary enrichment observed in the cross section of the parts after annealed treatment.

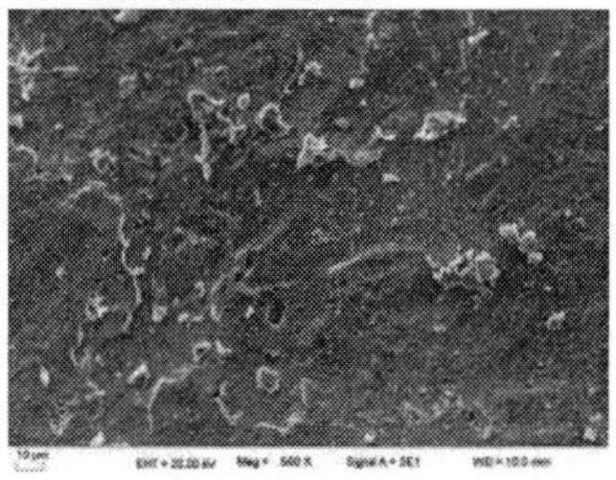

Fig. 7. The SEM images of DT4E sample after annealed treatment

TABLE III

THE RESULTS OF EDX SPECTRUM ANALYSIS

Element	C	Si	Mn	Fe	O	Total
Wt%	4.54	30.51	1.21	12.84	50.89	100

E. *Discuss*

By comparing the performance characterization results of DT4E, CM1 and REF60 industrial pure iron belt, it was found that after annealed treatment, segregation and agglomeration of Si occurs in DT4E samples, mainly in the surface grain boundary attachments, which directly causes the weakening of some grain boundaries of the pure iron surface, Thus, the weakened grain boundaries in the process of electroplating and acid pickling lead to form the cracks.

It can be seen from the material composition table that the silicon element of DT4E is much higher than that of CM1 and REF60 pure iron materials. Although the literature shows that the addition of silicon element to the electrical pure iron can change the magnetic properties [4] and mechanical properties [5] of the material, because silicon is very easy to react with oxygen to form silicon dioxide. But the equilibrium oxygen partial pressure of silicon is in the order of 10^{-30}, and the selective oxidation will occur if the purity of the protective atmosphere is slightly insufficient, which has a serious impact on the surface grain boundary of the material.

IV. CONCLUSION

(1) Corrosion failure cause analysis of copper plating on relay parts: the electrical pure iron substrate is selectively oxidized during the annealed process, and silicon element will be enriched and segregated at the surface grain boundary, resulting in weakening of the grain boundary. The weakened grain boundary in the acid pickling process is easy to form cracks. During copper plating, the plating solution

remains at the crack, where the plating layer cannot be densely deposited in. So blackening corrosion defect will appear on the surface at a later date.

(2) The electrochemical method was used to compare the grain boundary corrosion resistance of different substrates. The corrosion resistance of different manufacturers is quite different. It is suggested to add corrosion inhibitor in order to avoid hyperactive corrosion the substrate during acid pickling.

(3) The proportion of element components of the industrial pure iron is very important. Especially for the content of Si, it is easy to cause segregation and agglomeration in the surface grain boundaries under the condition of insufficient atmosphere protection. It is suggested to consider appropriate adjustment of the component distribution ratio in the smelting process.

ACKNOWLEDGMENT

The author thanks Dr. Yuan-yuan Yan for providing information about material.

REFERENCES

[1] Y. H. Niu, H. J. Wang "Research progress and production status of pure iron" in Electrical Steel, 2022, 3: 29-33.

[2] X. H. Chen, "The recrystallization and magnetic properties of Armco iron" in Acta Metallurgica Sinica, 1958, 3: 227-230.

[3] L. C. Tai, "Effect of silicon on the properties of iron-based magnetic powder cores" in Powder Metallurgy Industry, 2016, 26(6): 20-23.

[4] L. H. Xu, H. P. Zhao et al "Effect of silicon on the properties of iron-based magnetic powder cores" in Powder Metallurgy Industry, 2016, 26(6): 20-23.

[5] M. Z. Zhou, B. Y. Wen et al "Effect of Mg/Si ratio on natural aging and precipitation strengthening of 6000 series aluminum alloys" in Transactions of Materials and Heat Treatment, 2015, 36(4): 68-72

Three-Dimensional Simulation of Electromagnetic System of AC Contactor and Research on Characteristics of Shading Coil

Jun Feng[1], Zhihong Xu[1,2,3]

[1]College of Electrical Engineering and Automation, Fuzhou University, Fuzhou, 350116, China
[2]Fujian Key Laboratory of New Energy Power Generation and Power Conversion, Fuzhou, 350116, China
[3]Fujian Province University Engineering Research Center of Smart Distribution Grid Equipment, Fuzhou, 350116, China
Email: 641936593@qq.com Tel: 13178116282

Abstract*—AC contactor is a switching device used for frequently switching on and off AC circuits, and the dynamic characteristics of its electromagnetic system are related to the safety and reliability of the entire electrical main circuits. In this paper, a certain type of three-phase AC contactor double E-type electromagnetic system was taken as the research object, and the three-dimensional simulation model of the double E-type electromagnetic system was established by Ansys Maxwell, and the dynamic characteristics of the electromagnetic system such as current, displacement, velocity and suction force during the pull-in and holding process of AC contactors were analyzed by the simulation, and the correctness and feasibility of the established simulation model were verified by experiments. On this basis, The influence of the eddy current in the shading coil, the structure of the shading coil and the installation position of the shading coil on the dynamic characteristics of the electromagnetic system were analyzed emphatically. The simulation results show that the eddy current in the shading coil mainly affects the dynamic characteristics of the electromagnetic system in the holding process, the structure of the shading coil has a great impact on the pull-in process, and the installation position of the shading coil affects the whole dynamic process of the electromagnetic system. The above research results can provide some theoretical basis and reference value for the further optimization design of the electromagnetic system of the AC contactor.

***Index Terms*—Ac contactor, Dynamic characteristics, Electromagnetic system, Shading coil, Three-dimensional simulation.**

I. INTRODUCTION

AC contactor is an automatically controlled switching appliance, which is often used to frequently switch on and off AC main circuits and large-capacity control circuits [1]. Due to the application characteristics of "frequent operation" of the contactor, it is required that the contactor must have good dynamic characteristics [2]. Nowadays, the field of contactors has ushered in new development opportunities, and there are new and higher requirements for various performance and service life of contactors [3]-[4]. It is of fundamental and strategic importance to study and analyze the dynamic characteristics of AC contactors during the pull-in and holding process [5].

The static characteristics of the AC contactor are the characteristics of the electromagnetic system when the magnetic potential and the air gap value change infinitely slow. Because of the nonlinearity of magnetic circuit calculation and the interaction of variables during the motion of the electromagnetic mechanism, the dynamic characteristics of the electromagnetic system are more complex than the static characteristics. The dynamic characteristics of the electromagnetic mechanism include current characteristics, time characteristics, velocity characteristics and displacement characteristics.

At present, with the maturity and development of finite element simulation and analysis software technology, the "field" method is mainly used for the simulation calculation of the dynamic process of the electromagnetic mechanism of the AC contactor, that is, the Ansys Maxwell finite element simulation software is used to calculate the dynamic process of the electromagnetic mechanism of the contactor. References [6]-[7] established a finite element simulation model of the electromagnetic system of the AC contactor based on Maxwell, and studied and analyzed the influence of the structure and application scene of the electromagnetic system on the dynamic characteristics; References [8]-[9] uses Maxwell 3D finite element simulation software to simulate and analyze the influence of dynamic and static iron core structures, as well as the characteristics of current, time and final velocity; Reference [10] based on ANSOFT finite element software, simulates and calculates the action values of AC contactor when it is pull-in and released, and verifies that the action values meets the standard requirements of low-voltage switching appliance.

In this paper, the electromagnetic system of three-phase AC contactor was taken as the research object, and the electromagnetic system simulation model was established in Ansys Maxwell. Simulates and calculates the dynamic characteristics of the electromagnetic system, and uses experiments to verify the correctness and feasibility of the simulation model established by Ansys Maxwell. In addition, the effects of eddy currents in the shading coil, the structure and installation position of the shading coil on the dynamic characteristics of the electromagnetic system are analyzed.

II. Theoretical Basis of Three-Dimensional Simulation Calculation of Electromagnetic Mechanism

A. Theoretical Basis of Motion of Electromagnetic Mechanism

The dynamic process of the electromagnetic mechanism of the AC contactor includes the changes of electric, magnetic, thermal and mechanical parameters. Since the dynamic process of the electromagnetic mechanism has a very short time, and the electromagnetic mechanism has thermal inertia, the change of heat is very small and can be ignored [11]. Therefore, the differential equations of the pull-in process and the breaking process of the electromagnetic mechanism are shown in equations (1) and equations (2).

$$\begin{cases} \dfrac{\mathrm{d}\Psi}{\mathrm{d}t} = U - iR \\ \dfrac{\mathrm{d}v}{\mathrm{d}t} = \dfrac{\left[F_x - F_f\left(x, \dfrac{\mathrm{d}x}{\mathrm{d}t}\right)\right]}{m} \\ \dfrac{\mathrm{d}x}{\mathrm{d}t} = v \\ \Psi\big|_{t=0} = \Psi_0 = 0,\ v\big|_{t=0} = v_0 = 0,\ x\big|_{t=0} = x_0 = 0 \end{cases} \tag{1}$$

$$\begin{cases} \dfrac{\mathrm{d}\Psi}{\mathrm{d}t} = U - iR \\ \dfrac{\mathrm{d}v}{\mathrm{d}t} = \dfrac{\left[F_f\left(x, \dfrac{\mathrm{d}x}{\mathrm{d}t}\right) - F_x\right]}{m} \\ \dfrac{\mathrm{d}x}{\mathrm{d}t} = v \\ \Psi\big|_{t=0} = \Psi_0 = \Psi_s,\ v\big|_{t=0} = v_0 = 0,\ x\big|_{t=0} = x_0 = 0 \end{cases} \tag{2}$$

In the above two equations, U is the coil voltage; R is the coil resistance; i is the coil current; Ψ is the total magnetic chain of the electromagnetic mechanism; m is the mass of the moving parts; x is the displacement of the moving iron core; t is the time; F_x is the suction force; F_f is the reaction force.

B. Theoretical Basis of Finite Element Simulation

Maxwell's equations are the theoretical basis for solving electromagnetic fields. The equations include Maxwell's Ampere's law, Faraday's law of electromagnetic induction, Gauss's law of magnetic flux, and Gauss's law of electric flux. The differential form of the equations is shown in equation (3).

$$\begin{cases} \nabla \times \vec{H} = \vec{J} + \dfrac{\partial \vec{D}}{\partial t} \\ \nabla \times \vec{E} = -\dfrac{\partial \vec{B}}{\partial t} \\ \nabla \cdot \vec{B} = 0 \\ \nabla \cdot \vec{D} = \rho \end{cases} \tag{3}$$

In the equations, $\vec{H}$ is the magnetic field strength, the unit is $\mathrm{A/m}$; $\vec{J}$ is the current density, the unit is $\mathrm{A/m^2}$; $\vec{D}$ is the electric flux density, the unit is $\mathrm{C/m^2}$; $\vec{E}$ is the electric field strength, the unit is $\mathrm{V/m}$; $\vec{B}$ is the magnetic induction strength, also known as the magnetic flux density, the unit is T; ρ is the charge density.

Where ∇ is the Hamiltonian. $\nabla = \dfrac{\partial}{\partial x}\vec{i} + \dfrac{\partial}{\partial y}\vec{j} + \dfrac{\partial}{\partial z}\vec{k}$.

The constitutive relation is shown in equation (4).

$$\begin{cases} \vec{D} = \varepsilon \vec{E} \\ \vec{B} = \mu \vec{H} \\ \vec{J} = \sigma \vec{E} \end{cases} \tag{4}$$

In the equations, ε is the permittivity, the unit is $\mathrm{F/m}$; μ is the magnetic permeability, the unit is $\mathrm{H/m}$; σ is the electrical conductivity, the unit is $\mathrm{S/m}$.

Since the dynamic process of the electromagnetic mechanism sought in this paper is a low-frequency transient magnetic field, Maxwell's equations can be written in the form of equation (5) [12].

$$\begin{cases} \nabla \times \dfrac{1}{\sigma} \nabla \times \vec{H} + \dfrac{\partial \vec{B}}{\partial t} = 0 \\ \nabla \cdot \vec{B} = 0 \end{cases} \tag{5}$$

In this paper, when dealing with the mechanical transient process, the displacement is calculated discretely, as shown in equation. (6) [12].

$$\left\{\frac{\mathrm{d}x}{\mathrm{d}t}\right\}^{t+\Delta t} = \frac{\{x^{t+\Delta t}\} - \{x^t\}}{\Delta t} \tag{6}$$

Where x is the displacement of the moving iron core.

III. ESTABLISHMENT OF THREE-DIMENSIONAL FINITE ELEMENT SIMULATION MODEL OF ELECTROMAGNETIC SYSTEM

The electromagnetic mechanism of the three-phase AC contactor studied in this paper is a double E-type iron core, the rated voltage of the coil is 110V (AC, 50Hz), the coil resistance is 39.48Ω, and the number of turns is 1350.

By modeling in SolidWorks and then importing it into Ansys Maxwell finite element software, a three-dimensional simulation model of the electromagnetic system of a three-phase AC contactor was established. The simulation model includes moving iron core, static iron core, coil, and shading coil. And the motion domain of the moving iron core and the solution domain of the simulation model. The establishing simulation model is shown in Fig. 1.

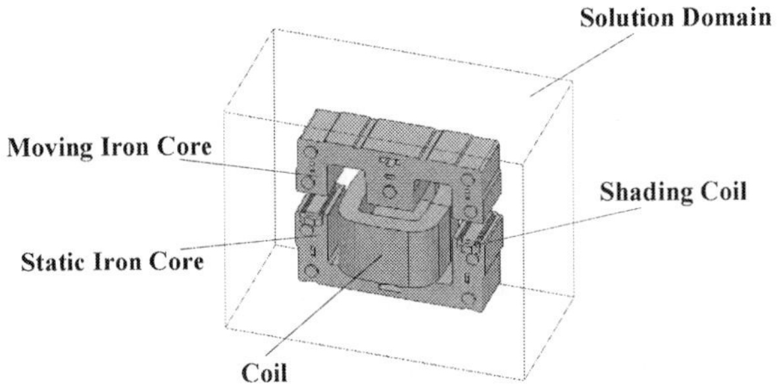

Fig. 1. Three-dimensional simulation model of electromagnetic system.

The reaction force characteristic of the three-phase AC contactor is composed of a set of reaction force springs and three sets of main contact springs. The reaction force spring is tower-shaped, and the three groups of main contact springs are all column-shaped. For the reaction spring and the main contact spring, 12 groups of discrete points of $F-x$ were measured with a digital force gauge. Then MATLAB is used to fit the curves, and the values of the 12 sets of spring stiffness coefficients of the reaction spring k_r and the main contact spring k_m are obtained respectively, after the maximum value and the minimum value are removed, and then calculate the average value. The expression of the force characteristic function as shown in equation (7).

$$F(x)=\begin{cases}261.51x+5.81 & (0\le x\le 4.5)\\ 3143.88x+8.679335 & (4.5\le x\le 6.95)\end{cases} \qquad (7)$$

IV. SIMULATION RESULTS AND EXPERIMENTAL VERIFICATION

A. Current characteristics

The current waveforms of the coils under different phase angles of 0° , 30° , 60° , 90° , 120° and 150° , obtained by the simulation of the closing phase angle of the electromagnetic mechanism are shown in Fig. 2.

The coil current waveform shows that when the closing phase angles are 0° , 30° and 60° , the pull-in time is shorter, and when the closing phase angles are 90° , 120° and 150° , the pull-in time is longer. When the closing phase angle is in the interval $0°\sim 60°$, the current value is larger, and the magnetic flux can be quickly established, and F_{XL} is larger, so that $F_{XL} > F_{FL}$, the moving iron core can be quickly touched, move forward quickly, and quickly reach the position where the moving and static iron cores are completely closed. When the closing phase angle is in the interval $90°\sim 150°$, the current value is smaller, the magnetic flux is smaller, and F_{XL} is smaller, so that $F_{XL} < F_{FL}$, the moving iron core cannot be touched, and it needs to wait until the next waveform arrives, when $F_{XL} > F_{FL}$ to be touched, and this process needs to consume a certain amount of time, so the total pull-in time is longer. When the moving and static iron cores are completely closed and enter the holding stage, the coil current waveforms at each closing phase angle are approximately triangle waves.

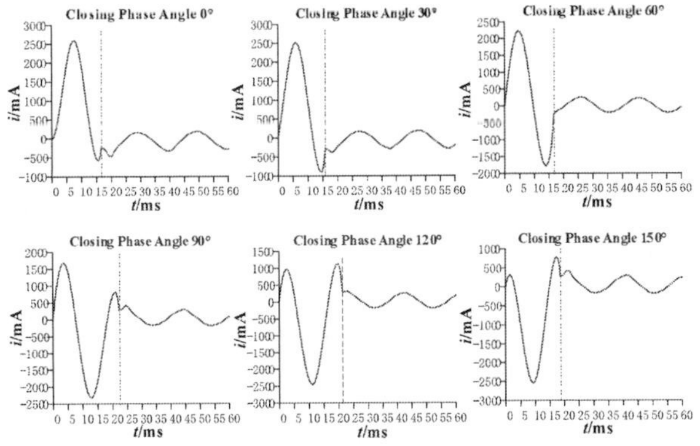

Fig. 2. Coil current waveform under different closing phase angles.

B. Displacement characteristics

The displacement waveforms of the moving iron core under different phase angles of 0° , 30° , 60° , 90° , 120° and 150° , obtained by the simulation of the closing phase angle of the electromagnetic mechanism are shown in Fig. 3.

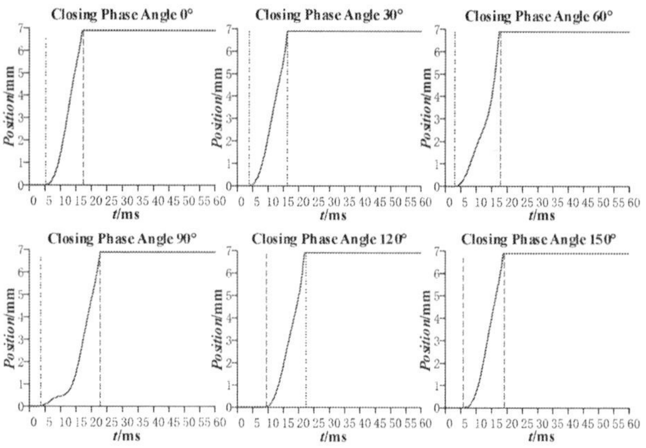

Fig. 3. Displacement waveform of moving iron core under different closing phase angles.

The displacement waveform of the moving iron core shows that the starting point of the displacement curve is not at the moment of 0ms , and the starting point and the end point of the displacement curve under each closing phase angle are different. When there is a current in the coil, the establishment of the magnetic flux requires a process, and when the current increases to a certain value, it can be ensured that $F_{XL} > F_{FL}$, at this time, the moving iron core can be touched, the moving iron core starts to move, and the moving iron core has displacement, and this moment is the starting point of the displacement curve. According to the analysis in A, under different closing phase angles, the pull-in time of the electromagnetic mechanism is different, that is, under the same displacement, the moving time of the moving iron core is different, which is consistent with the time used for the complete closing of the moving core in Fig. 2.

C. *Velocity characteristics*

The velocity waveforms of the motion of the moving iron core under different phase angles of 0° , 30° , 60° , 90° , 120° and 150° , obtained by the simulation of the closing phase angle of the electromagnetic mechanism are shown in Fig. 4.

Since the velocity waveforms at each closing phase angle are similar, for the convenience of analysis, two representative closing phase angles, 0° and 90° , are selected to analyze their velocity characteristics. Take the waveform when the closing phase angle is 0° as an example. In the OA section, the current is smaller, the current is still in the rising period, F_{XL} is smaller, $F_{XL} < F_{FL}$, the moving iron core is not touched, so the velocity of the moving iron core is 0; In the AB section, the moving iron core accelerates forward, and the velocity becomes larger and larger; In the BC section, due to the fluctuation of the current leads to the fluctuation of the electromagnetic attraction force, the air gap is still larger at this time, and the shading coil has not yet played a role, which makes the phenomenon of temporarily appear, so the moving iron core at this time must be do a deceleration movement for a period of time, due to inertia, although the moving iron core is doing a deceleration movement, it is still moving forward; In the CD section, the air gap is smaller at this time, the effect of the shading coil is embodied, and the fluctuation of the current is added, so that the phenomenon of $F_{XL} > F_{FL}$ occurs again, and the moving iron core accelerated forward movement, and pulls in at point D ; In the DE section, after the moving iron core is pulled in, the velocity quickly decreases to 0.

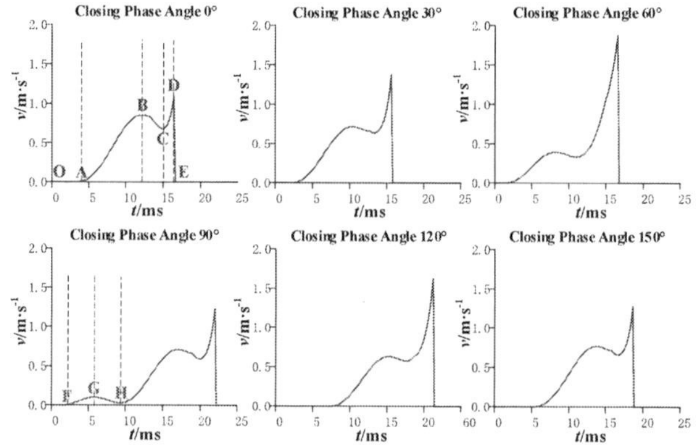

Fig. 4. Velocity waveform of moving iron core under different closing phase angles.

The velocity waveform with the closing phase angle 90° is quite special. The moving iron core in the GH section is decelerating movement because of the current fluctuation. The current value at this time decreases, so that $F_{XL} < F_{FL}$, it needs to wait until the next waveform arrives, and the current value increases. When it is large, $F_{XL} > F_{FL}$ will appear again, and the moving iron core will accelerate movement again.

D. *Magnetic flux distribution characteristics during the pull-in process*

Taking the closing phase angle of 0° as an example, considering the closing phase angle, the pull-in time of the moving iron core is within 20ms , Magnetic flux distribution of moving and static iron cores at times 0ms , 4ms , 8ms , 12ms , 16ms and 20ms during the pull-in process is analyzed. The magnetic flux distribution diagram at the above times is shown in Fig. 5.

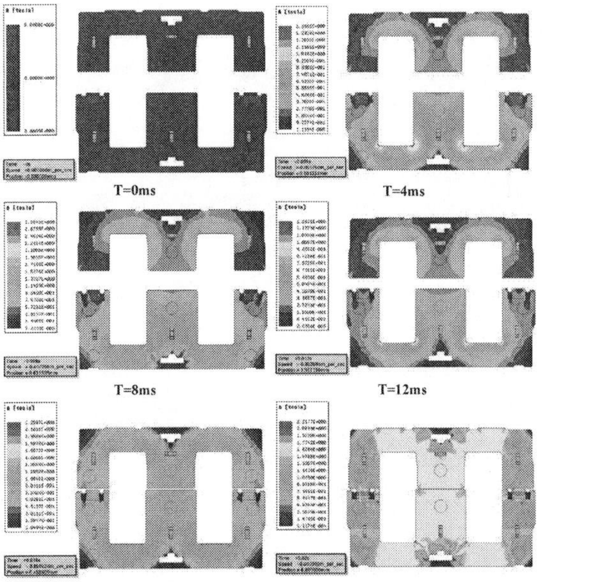

Fig. 5. The magnetic flux distribution diagram of the moving and static iron cores at different times during the pull-in process.

During the pull-in process, the change relationship of the magnetic flux at different times is shown in equation (8):

$$\begin{cases} U = iR + \dfrac{\mathrm{d}\Psi}{\mathrm{d}t} \\ \Psi = N\Phi \\ \Phi = \dfrac{NI}{R_\mathrm{m} + R_\delta} \end{cases} \quad (8)$$

When $\mathrm{T} = 0\mathrm{ms}$, the coil current is 0, and the magnetic flux has not yet been established, so the magnetic flux of the moving and static iron cores is 0. When $\mathrm{T} = 4\mathrm{ms}$, the current has passed through the coil, the magnetic flux has been established, and the moving iron core has moved for a period of displacement, but at this time, the air gap between the moving and static iron cores is larger, and the air reluctance is larger, and most of the magnetic potential is concentrated on the air gap reluctance, so the magnetic flux in the moving and static iron cores is smaller. When $\mathrm{T} = 8\mathrm{ms}$, although the moving iron core moves for another period of displacement, the air gap is still larger at this time, and most of the magnetic potential is still concentrated on the air gap reluctance. In the above process, due to the larger air gap, there is more magnetic flux leakage, and the magnetic flux distribution on the moving and static iron cores is not uniform. The coil is on the static iron core, the static iron core distributes more magnetic flux, and the moving iron core distributes less magnetic flux. It can be seen from the magnetic flux distribution diagrams of $\mathrm{T} = 12\mathrm{ms}$, $\mathrm{T} = 16\mathrm{ms}$ and $\mathrm{T} = 20\mathrm{ms}$ that as the moving iron core continues to move forward, the air gap decreases, the magnetic flux leakage decreases, the air gap reluctance decreases, and the magnetic potential concentrated on the air gap reluctance decreases. The magnetic potential distributed on the moving and static iron cores increases, the magnetic flux passing through the moving and static iron cores increases gradually, and the distribution of the magnetic fluxes of the moving and static iron cores tends to be uniform.

E. Experimental verification

The experimental devices mainly include a three-phase AC contactor, an optional closing device, a laser displacement sensor and an oscilloscope. The comparison between the current waveform measured by the experiment and the current waveform obtained by the simulation is shown in Fig. 6. It can be seen intuitively that the fitting degree of the two is very high.

In order to quantitatively calculate the error between the simulation and the experiment, the pull-in time of the simulated and experimental of moving iron cores and the peak current of the simulated and experimental of coils during the pull-in process were compared and analyzed. The comparison results of the pull-in time and the coil peak current are shown in Table 1 and Table 2. The comparison results show that the error between the simulation and the experiment is less than 10%, and the experiment verifies the correctness and feasibility of the model built by the simulation.

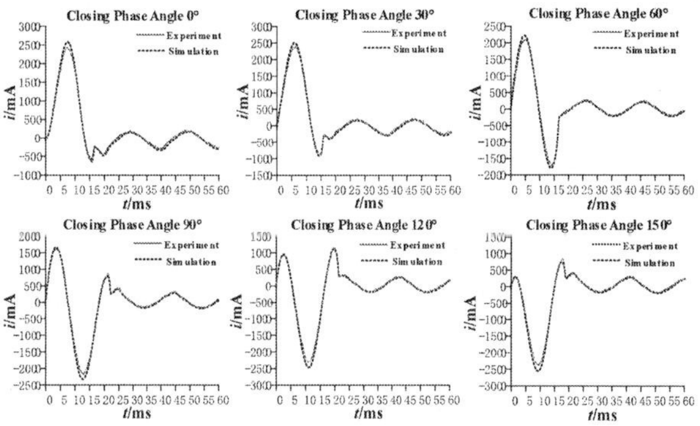

Fig. 6. Comparison of current waveform simulation and experiment.

TABLE I
COMPARISON BETWEEN SIMULATION AND EXPERIMENTAL MOVING IRON CORE PULL-IN TIME

θ / t/ms	0°	30°	60°	90°	120°	150°
$t_{\mathrm{simulation}}$	16.6	15.8	16.8	22.2	21.4	18.8
$t_{\mathrm{experiment}}$	16.8	16.2	17	22.3	21.6	18.9
η_{error}(%)	1.2	2.53	1.19	0.45	0.93	0.53

TABLE II
COMPARISON BETWEEN SIMULATION AND EXPERIMENTAL COIL PEAK CURRENTS

i/A \ θ	0°	30°	60°	90°	120°	150°
$I_{P\text{simulation}}$	2.587	2.512	2.223	-2.316	-2.453	-2.542
$I_{P\text{experiment}}$	2.438	2.406	2.094	-2.188	-2.313	-2.375
η_{error} (%)	5.76	4.22	5.8	5.53	5.71	6.57

V. INFLUENCE OF SHADING COIL ON DYNAMIC CHARACTERISTICS OF ELECTROMAGNETIC SYSTEM

A. Eddy currents in shading coil

The eddy currents in the shading coil have an important influence on the holding process of the electromagnetic mechanism. Taking the closing phase angle 0° as an example, the simulation comparison diagram with and without eddy currents in the shading coil is shown in Fig. 7.

The presence or absence of eddy currents in the shading coil have a smaller influence on the pull-in process of the AC contactor, and the larger influence is in the holding process. During the holding process, the coil current will be distorted when the eddy currents in the shading coil are not considered. This is because, in the holding process, when there is no eddy currents in the shading coil, the moving iron core will oscillate. At this time, the air gap will increase, the air gap reluctance will increase, and the coil current will also increase, when reflected in the coil current waveform, the coil current waveform will be distorted, as shown in the current waveform in Fig. 7. In the holding process, the coil current will protrude a small "sharp corner" on the basis of the approximate triangle wave. It can be seen from the displacement waveform that when there is no eddy current in the shading coil, the moving iron core will oscillate, and when it is reflected on the displacement waveform, the moving iron core will have a reverse displacement. On the velocity waveform, during the holding process, the moving iron core stops moving, and the velocity is zero. When the eddy current in the shading coil is not considered, the moving iron core oscillates, so the velocity waveform will show that the moving iron core moves in the opposite direction. At the same time, the comparative analysis with and without eddy current in the shading coil proves the importance of the eddy current in the shading coil during the holding process of the moving iron core, and shows that the shading coil is an indispensable part of the electromagnetic mechanism of the AC contactor.

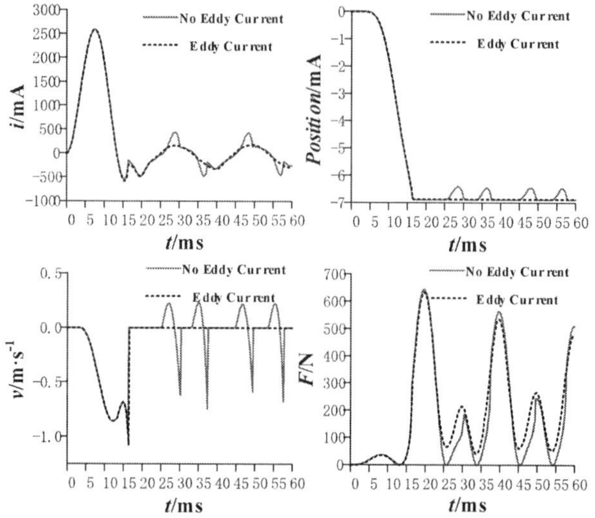

Fig. 7. Comparison of simulation with and without considering eddy currents in the shading coil.

B. The structure and installation position of the shading coil

Taking the closing phase angle 0° as an example, in order not to affect the actual structure of the moving and static iron cores, under the condition that the lateral width W and thickness H of the shading coil remain unchanged, the longitudinal length ΔL of the shading coil is increased. The relationship between the change amount ΔL of the longitudinal length of the shading coil and the average electromagnetic attraction force, and the influence of the shading coil at different positions in the vertical direction on the electromagnetic attraction force is studied and analyzed, as shown in Fig. 8.

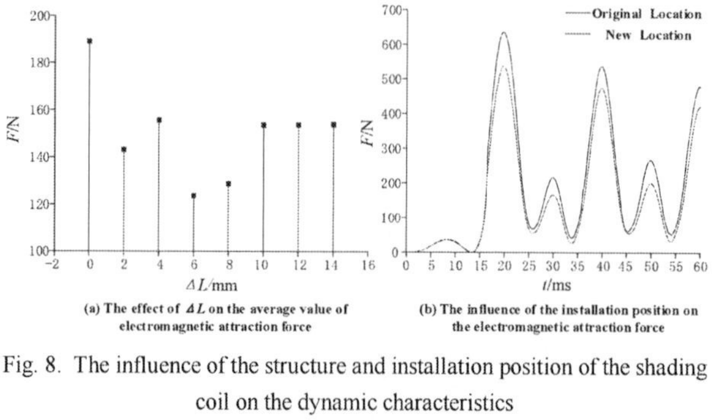

Fig. 8. The influence of the structure and installation position of the shading coil on the dynamic characteristics

VI. CONCLUSION

In this paper, the dynamic characteristics of the three-phase AC contactor double E-type electromagnetic system are simulated and analyzed, and the correctness and feasibility of the established simulation model are verified by experiments. The effects of the eddy currents in the shading coil, the structure and installation position of the shading coil on the dynamic characteristics of the electromagnetic system are analyzed.

1) The eddy current in the shading coil will affect the dynamic characteristics of the electromagnetic system in the holding process. In the actual design of the electromagnetic system, the eddy current in the shading coil should be appropriately increased so that no bounce occurs in the holding process.

2) The longitudinal length of the shading coil is not too long, and the installation position is not too high. Increasing the longitudinal length of the shading coil will reduce the electromagnetic attraction force, increase the resistance, increase the loss, increase the temperature rise, and affect the heat dissipation.

ACKNOWLEDGMENT

This work was supported in part by the University-Industry Cooperation Project of Fujian Provincial Science and Technology Department under Grant 2021Y4002 and in part by the Fujian Province Science and Technology Innovation Leading Talent Funding Project under Grant 00387024.

REFERENCES

[1] XU Zhihong. Electrical Theoretical Basis[M]. Beijing: China Machine Press, 2014.

[2] LIN Zhijia. Research and Application of Contactor Drive Optimization Technology[D]. China University of Mining and Technology, 2019.

[3] KONG Xiaoli. Analysis of Low-pressure Control and Protection Intelligent Technology[J]. Hei Longjiang Science, 2020,11(22):106-107.

[4] GUAN Ruiliang. Open a New Era of Smart Appliances[J]. Electrical Application, 2019,38(04):7-9.

[5] TIAN Haibo. Study on Structure and Robustness of AC Contactor Electromagnetic System[D]. Hebei University of Technology, 2019.

[6] HUANG Rencan. Option of AC Contactor's Electronic-magnetic System Based on Maxwell[J]. Electric Switchgear, 2018,56(05):48-52.

[7] CUI Jingrui. Research on Dynamic Characteristics and Failure Mechanism Analysis of The AC Contactors Under the Vibration Condition[D]. Hebei University of Technology, 2020.

[8] YUAN Xuebin, OUYANG Zhenguo, CAO Yong. Analysis of AC Contactor's Dynamic Characteristics Based on Maxwell[J]. Electrical & Energy Management Technology, 2017(22):17-21.

[9] LI Xue, FU Liang, XU Xiaowei. Simulation and Experimental Verification of the Influence of Static and Dynamic Iron Core Structure of AC Contactor on Electromagnetic Properties[J]. Electrical & Energy Management Technology, 2018(12):55-60.

[10] SU Xiuping, TIAN Haibo, FU Zhe, CHENG Haofeng. Simulation Calculation of Action Values of AC Contactor [J]. Mechanical Design and Manufacturing, 2020(12):19-23.

[11] FEI Hongjun. Dynamic Analysis and Calculation of Electromagnetic Mechanism[M]. Fujian Province, Department of Electrical Engineering, Fuzhou University, 2002-01-01.

[12] LI Rui, XU Zhihong. 3D Simulation Design of AC Electromagnetic Mechanism Based on Maxwell[J]. Electrical & Energy Management Technology, 2016(08):1-7+15.

Jun Feng (1994-) is currently working toward the M.S. degree from the College of Electrical Engineering and Automation, Fuzhou University, Fuzhou, China.

His research interests include electrical apparatuses and intelligent technologies.

Zhihong Xu (1963-) received the B.Sc. and M.Eng. degrees in electrical engineering, and the Ph.D. degree in electric machines and eletric apparatus from Fuzhou University, Fuzhou, China, in 1983, 1998, and 2006, respectively.

She is currently the Dean with the Electrical Engineering School, Fuzhou University. Her research interests include electrical apparatuses and intelligent technologies.

Knowledge-Enhanced Traction Online Household Abnormal Load Detection and Power Consumption Prediction

Yanmei Jiang [1,2], Mingsheng Liu[1]

[1)] State Key Laboratory of Reliability and Intelligence of Electrical Equipment, Hebei University of Technology, Tianjin, 300401

[2)] Department of Rail Transportation, Hebei Jiaotong Vocational and Technical College, Shijiazhuang, 050035

Email: weiyi_jim@163.com TEL:15690313289; liums601001@sina.com TEL:18632110656

Abstract—**For the outliers of household electricity sampling data and the low prediction accuracy of load power consumption, this paper presents a load abnormal detection and power consumption prediction model based on the multi-stage data and behavior feature fusion representation learning, MDB-FFP. Considering the sparsity of the abnormal load data, the model is combined with the external factors (such as climate and holidays) and the multi-stage data (days, week and month). The model utilizes the Holt-Winters algorithm to decompose the load sampling data by the time series and to achieve the fine-grained detection of load outliers of the power consumption; the knowledge graph of the daily electricity consumption is constructed based on the external factors, and combined with the maximizes the information of local adjacent nodes of Graph Attention Network (GAT) to realize the load spatio-temporal features representation learning; using the RNN-LSTM architecture to achieve the load lifelong learning. The extensive experimental results show that MDB-FFP model significantly improves the accuracy of load prediction model, and the model has the good performance advantages.**

***Keywords*- Abnormal load detection, Power consumption forecast , Holt-Winters, GAT , RNN-LSTM**

I. INTRODUCTION

Non-intrusive load monitoring system (NILM) is the core of the smart grid IoT system, and NILM plays an important role in the intelligent management of the power system of the "Load-User" sides[1,2]. Improving the performance of the NILM system and reducing the error rate of the load prediction model has become the focus of research in this field. The load forecasting methods based on the mathematical optimization model have the problems: low prediction accuracy, poor model reliability, and a high error rate of the load identification. To solve the above problems, numerous studies have done a lot of work[3]. [4] propose a multi-layer forecasting model to improve the accuracy of the ultra-short-term load forecasting, and in the model, the data features of multi-source data fusion are constructed. [5] uses the Bayesian algorithm to optimize the single load forecasting model, and it can effectively improve the performance of the load combination prediction model. [6] A cloud prediction model based on the Markov chain is proposed, which uses the validity concept to predict the combined loads and to improve the reliability of the model.

The load forecasting method based on the data drive is also gradually playing advantage in non-invasive load identification. In [7], the author uses an improved convolutional neural network (CNN) to improve the accuracy of the load prediction; this model utilizes the bidirectional gating cycle module in CNN to extract the time characteristics of load data, and then the feedback networks can improve the stability of the model through parameter optimization. In [8], the author pays more attention to the external related factors such as weather and humidity in the historical load sampling data, and uses a variational mode decomposition technique to decompose the data in fine granularity; the method mainly improves the learning ability of the load feature representation and uses a recurrent neural network model based on long and short memory period (RNN-LSTM) as a predictor to achieve accurate load prediction. In [9], the coupling characteristics between the multi-source load data and the external load influencing factors is employed as the input vector of the load forecasting model, and to improve its accuracy and performance of load forecasting model. [10] constructs the RNN-LSTM model to realize the classification and prediction of the characteristics of fixed and fluctuating loads; the method considers the behavior characteristics of the daily consumption, and the simulation results show that the method is effective for the accuracy of the load forecasting. In [11], an improved deep residual

S&T Program of Hebei through grant (20310101D)

network model is designed to reduce the error rate of the load prediction results and improve the generalization ability of the model, the experimental results show that the two-stage integration strategy can improve the stability of the model.

However, at present, the designed way based on mathematical optimization and the single data-driven prediction way still has some limitations: the ability of the load characteristic representation is limited, which affects the prediction accuracy ; the prediction accuracy is improved by enlarging the size of the network pattern, but there is local optimization and the computational burden is increased ; the existing the sparsity of load data. To effectively solve the above problems, this paper proposes a method for household load anomaly detection and power consumption prediction based on multi-stage data and behavioral feature fusion representation learning (MDB-FFP). This model not only focuses on the time dependence of load but also considers the influence of the related factors such as climate and holidays on the historical load data. To solve the problem of outliers in load sampling data, the Holt-Winters algorithm is used to decompose the load sampling data and to realize the fine-grained detection of the outliers and eliminate outliers; constructing the behavior-based knowledge graph of daily electricity load, and using the graph attention neural network (GAT) to maximize the information of local neighboring nodes and to enhance the representation learning ability of the load spatio-temporal sampling data; accomplish the RNN-LSTM model architecture to realize load lifelong learning and prediction.

II. LOAD ANOMALY DETECTION BASED ON HOLT-WINTERS

In the actual sampling process, the data sampling error is caused by the unavoidable equipment operation error and the unstable load signal, which reduces the utilization of load data. In this paper, the addition model in the Holt-Winters algorithm is used to decompose the load sampling data series. By fine-grained analysis of the data seasonality, trend, and residual factor, the monitoring and preprocessing of abnormal load data are realized. The addition model of the Holt-Winter algorithm is mainly used in the linear time trend and relatively stable seasonal change. Suppose that the time series y, the time series value is y_t at the time t, the mathematical expression of the algorithm is as follows:

$$y^{*}_{i+t} = a_i + b_i t + c_{i+t} \qquad (1)$$

where, y_i is the smoothed sequence y^* i, a is the intercept, b is trend, c is the seasonal factor of the additive model, i=1,2,3,…,I, t>0, is the number of the backward smoothing periods. In this paper, y_i represents the actual measured value of load sampled data at time i, y^* i represents the load prediction value after smoothing.

In the additive decomposition equation of the Holt-Winter algorithm, a, b, c represents the trend, the seasonal seasonality, and the residual value of the time series respectively. The time series $y_i=a_i+b_i+c_i$, s is the length of the season, and the smoothing coefficients are α and β, respectively. The decomposition factor is expressed as follows:

$$\begin{cases} a_i = \alpha * (y_i - c_{i-s}) + (1-\alpha) * a_{i-1}, 0 < \alpha < 1 \\ b_i = \gamma * (y_i - a_i) + (1-\gamma) * b_{i-s}, 0 < \gamma < 1 \\ c_i = y_i - a_i - b_i \end{cases} \qquad (2)$$

where, the time series residuals are c_i, and it represents the value after removing the trend and season factors from the original time series. The predicted value can be obtained by the following mathematical formula:

$$y_{I+t} = a_I + b_I t + c_{I+t-s} \qquad (3)$$

In the paper, the exponential smoothing algorithm of Holt-winter is used to preprocess the abnormal data and the missing data in the load time series. The detailed design of the method is that: the load time series sampling data are decomposed into a trend, the season, and the residual factors; the trend and the seasonal variation of the load data are estimated by using the exponential smoothing method, and the final data value is predicted. In Figure 1, the load measurement value Figrue 1(a) and the preprocessed value Figure 1(b) are compared. The results show that the Holt-winter method can improve the validity of load data.

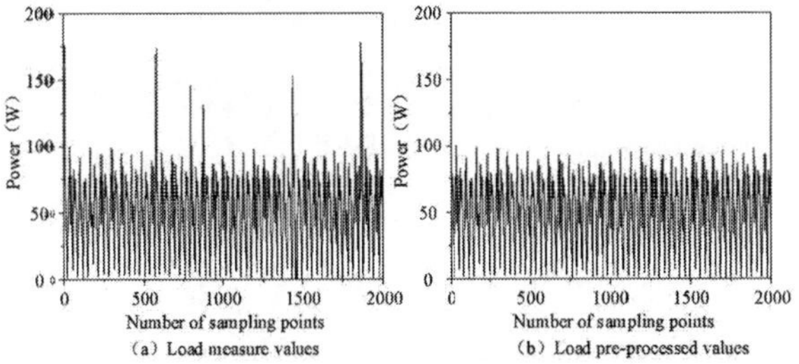

Figure 1 Comparison of the load measurement and pretreatment values

III. LOAD FEATURE LEARNING GAT-BASED

The CNN model, the wavelet analysis (WA), and the clustering algorithm (CA) have been widely used in the representation learning of load abstract features. However, these methods still have low discrimination and poor interpretability of load features. This paper presents a graph attention neural network based on the maximizing information of the local neighboring nodes (Local node maximization graph attention network, LNM-GAT) to realize the representation learning of the load characteristics. The structure schematic of the

LNM-GAT model is shown in Figure 2.

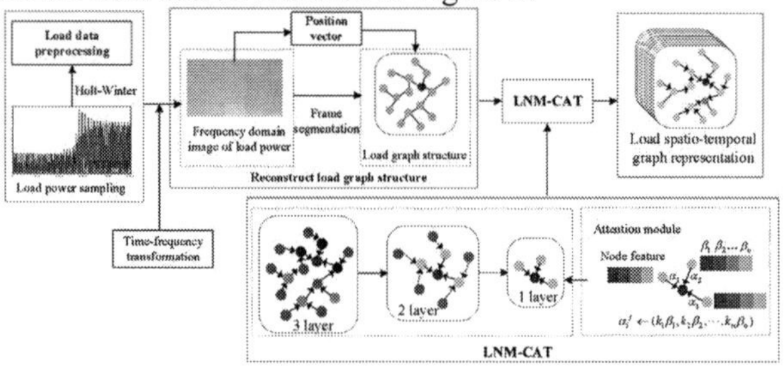

Figure 2 Schematic diagram of LNM-GAT model

From Figure 2, the design principles of the NM-GAT model include the load data acquisition and preprocessing, the load graph-structure reconstruction, the learning of the load spatio-temporal representation graph, and the LNM-GAT model. In the load data acquisition and data processing, the Holt-Winter algorithm is used to denoise the raw load data and complete the data; the image mapping of the load data is realized by the time-frequency conversion technology, and the load map structure is constructed by the frame image segmentation technology and the location vector of the single frame image position is saved; the spatio-temporal representation graph of the load is constructed.

The attention module is added to the graph neural network, and to realize that the more important nodes get the higher weight value in the process of neighborhood aggregation. Figure 3 shows the structural design of the attention mechanism.

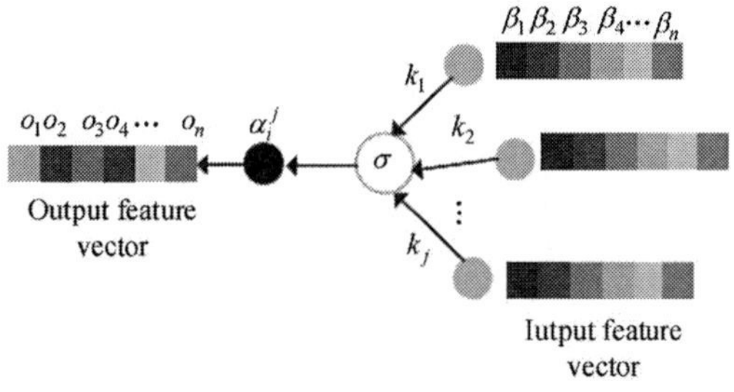

Figure 3 Structural design diagram of the attention mechanism

Where, the input eigenvector is $(\beta_1, \beta_2, \beta_3, \cdots, \beta_n)$, $n \in N$, the output feature vector is $(o_1, o_2, o_3, \cdots, o_n)$, $n \in N$; $(k_1, k_2, k_3, \cdots, k_j)$ represents the weight sequence of adjacent nodes, the activation function σ is *sigmod*。 The expression of the output vector is as follows:

$$o_m = \text{sigmod}\left(\sum_{n \in N_m} c_{nm} k_j \beta_n\right) \tag{3}$$

N_m represents all adjacent regions of the node m, β_n is the feature input vector of the node n, k_j is the weight matrix. The expression of the attention coefficient c_{nm} is:

$$c_{nm} = soft\max_m\left(\lambda_{nm}\right) = \frac{\exp(\lambda_{nm})}{\sum_{p \in N_m} \exp(\lambda_{np})} \tag{4}$$

λ_{np} represents the influence of the node p on the node n.

IV. LOAD FORECASTING MODEL MDB-FFP AND LIFELONG LEARNING

A. Load Forecasting Model MDB-FFP

In this paper, a time prediction model based on multi-stage data and behavioral feature fusion representation learning is proposed for improving the accuracy and performance of the load forecasting model. The mathematical expression of this model is defined as:

$$F(t) = xd\mathrm{L}(F(\mathrm{D}(t)),t) + xw\mathrm{L}(F(\mathrm{W}(t)),t) + xm\mathrm{L}(F(\mathrm{M}(t)),t) + \kappa c \tag{5}$$

Where, D represents the daily periodic load, W represents the weekly periodic load, and M represents the monthly periodic load; xd, xw, and xm are the weight coefficients of daily, weekly and monthly cycle loads, respectively; L represents the LSTM prediction model, and κc represents the external factors (temperature, humidity, and holidays, etc.). The design architecture of the MDB-FFP model is shown in Figure 4:

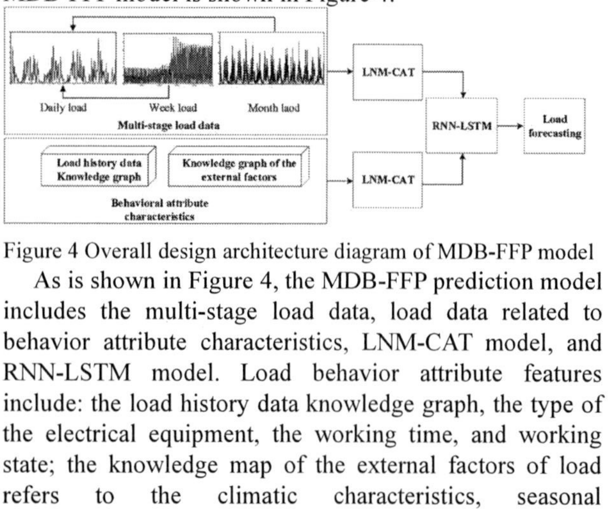

Figure 4 Overall design architecture diagram of MDB-FFP model

As is shown in Figure 4, the MDB-FFP prediction model includes the multi-stage load data, load data related to behavior attribute characteristics, LNM-CAT model, and RNN-LSTM model. Load behavior attribute features include: the load history data knowledge graph, the type of the electrical equipment, the working time, and working state; the knowledge map of the external factors of load refers to the climatic characteristics, seasonal characteristics, and the major holiday data related to load measurement data. The LNM-CAT model is used to learn the graph structure representation of the load sampled data and the load behavior characteristics, which is used as the input vector of the RNN-LSTM model. RNN-LSTM model deals with the time-dependent prediction through the gate structure, and the main gate structure: input gate, output gate, and forget gate.

The input gate structure determines which data can be input into the model. Its mathematical expression is as follows:

$$\begin{cases} F\_in(t) = \sigma(W_{fin} \cdot [h(t-1), x(t)] + b_{in}) \\ F\_C'(t) = \tanh(W_{fc} \cdot [h(t-1), x(t)] + b_c) \end{cases} \tag{6}$$

where， σ denotes the activation function Sigmoid, $h(t\text{-}1)$ denotes the hidden layer state of the model at the previous time $t\text{-}1$, $x(t)$ denotes the input sequence at the current time

t, $F\_C'(t)$ denotes the update of state at time t; b_{in} denotes the input gate offset, W_{fin} denotes the weight vector.

Output gate: according to RNN-LSTM, the output gate is used to determine the output of the data, and it is defined as:

$$\begin{cases} F\_out(t) = \sigma\left(W_{fout} \cdot [h(t-1), x(t)] + b_{out}\right) \\ h(t) = F\_out * \tanh(F\_C(t)) \end{cases} \quad (7)$$

where, σ denotes the activation function, $h(t)$ denotes the update state of the model hidden layer at time t, b_{out} represents the output gate offset, W_{fout} represents the weight vector.

Forget gate mainly determines which data are deleted and retains valid values as the input of the model. Its expression is as follows:

$$F\_f(t) = \sigma\left(W_{ff} \cdot [h(t-1), x(t)] + b_{ff}\right) \quad (8)$$

where, σ denotes the activation function, b_{ff} represents the offset of the forget door, W_{ff} represents the weight vector.

B. Load Lifelong Learning

This paper constructs a lifelong learning and prediction mechanism of the load based on multi-task for the generalization of load prediction model, as shown in Figure 5.

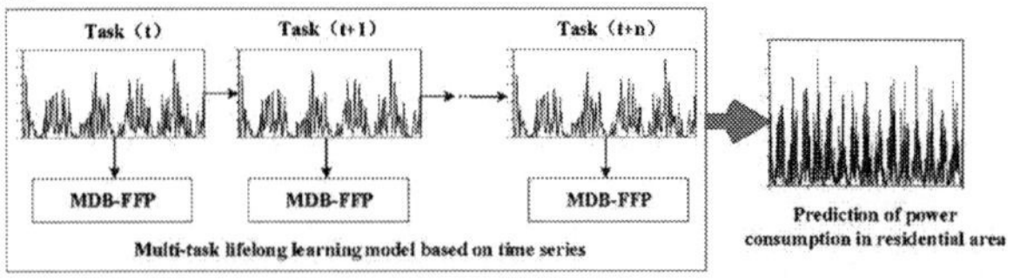

Figure 5 Lifelong learning prediction mechanism

From Figure 5, the lifelong learning mechanism based on the load prediction model is the multi-task learning based on time series, and using MDB-FFP model to realize the learning of the load forecasting task. This mechanism is extended from the prediction of the individual user's household power consumption to the prediction of the load energy consumption in the whole area.

V. EXPERIMENT SETTINGS

A. Experimental Data

The experimental data of this paper are collected from 50 households in a residential area in a city of Hebei Province from January 2014 to July 2018. The load data set is divided into three parts: 60% of the training datasets (TRD), 20% of the testing datasets (TSD), and 20% of the verifying datasets (VED). To ensure the validity of the experimental data, this paper uses the time series Holt-Winter exponential smoothing method to denoise and preprocess the load sampled data.

B. Experimental Criteria

The experiment selects the average precision (AP) and the root mean square error (RMSE) as the measure of the performance of experimental models. The calculation formula of AP is as follows:

$$AP_f = \frac{\sum Precision_f}{M_f} = \frac{\sum\left(\frac{TP_f}{TO_f}\right)}{M_f} \quad (9)$$

where, the number of correct loads predicted is TP_f, target number of loads TO_f, M_f is the total load. The calculation formula of RMSE is as follows:

$$RMSE_f = \sqrt{\sum_{t=0}^{t=T}\left(PF_p - PF_r\right)^2 / M} \quad (10)$$

where, PF_{fP} is the predicted load value, PF_{fr} is the measurement of load.

C. Experimental Results and Discussion

In this paper, the classical model of the load forecasting relevance vector machine (RVM), Hidden Markov Model (HMM), and CNN-LSTM are selected as the baseline model for the comparative test of the prediction performance. To ensure the validity of the experimental data, cross-validation is carried out six times for each dataset in the experiment.

The training dataset TRD and the testing dataset TSD are used to train and test the RVM, HMM, CNN-LSTM, and MDB-FFP models respectively, the AP of each model on the different dataset are shown in Figure 6.

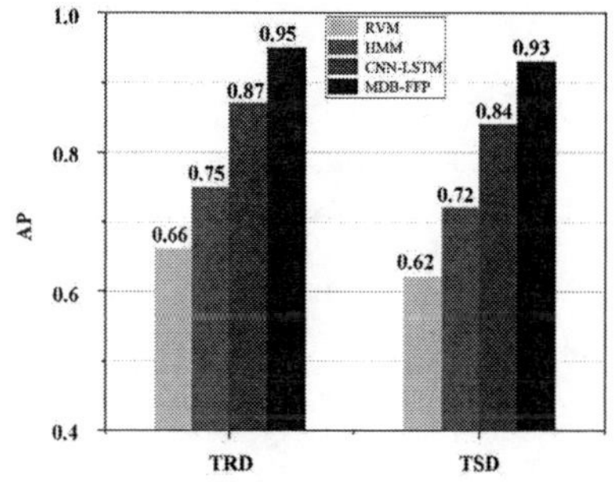

Figure 5 AP of five forecasting models in the training process and test process

From Figure 6, the AP values of the MDB-FFP model on two datasets are the highest, 0.95 and 0.93; the second best is the CNN-LSTM model, 0.87 and 0.84; the AP of HMM model is 0.75 and 0.72; RVM model is 0.66 and 0.62. The HMM model does not significantly improve the accuracy of load combination prediction; the advantage of CNN in the CNN-LSTM model lies in the extraction of load characteristics. However, for historical load data considering external influencing factors, the prediction accuracy of this model is not high. In the MDB-FFP model, the graph attention mechanism is used to enhance the representation and learning ability of abstract load features. Meanwhile, the use of graph structure can realize the interpretability of load features and improve the accuracy of load prediction. To verify the performance of the model, the validation dataset VED is employed, the AP and RMSE of the five models are shown in Table 1:

Tab.1 The validation results of training model

model	AP	RMSE
RVM	0.64	0.32
HMM	0.72	0.25
CNN-LSTM	0.85	0.11
MDB-FFP	**0.93**	**0.05**

From Tab. 1, the performance indicators of the four prediction models on the validation dataset VED show that the AP of the MDB-FFP model is the highest at 0.93, which is 0.8 higher than the CNN-LSTM model. The AP of the RVM model is the lowest, which is only 0.64. The performance index RMSE of the MDB-FFP is only 0.05, and the prediction effect is better than the other three types of models.

The experiment randomly selects the load power data of a household from January 2016 to May 2016 for prediction, the prediction results are shown in Figure 7. The RMSE value of the MDB-FFP model is the lowest in the five consecutive months of load forecasting, which indicates that the performance of the model is good.

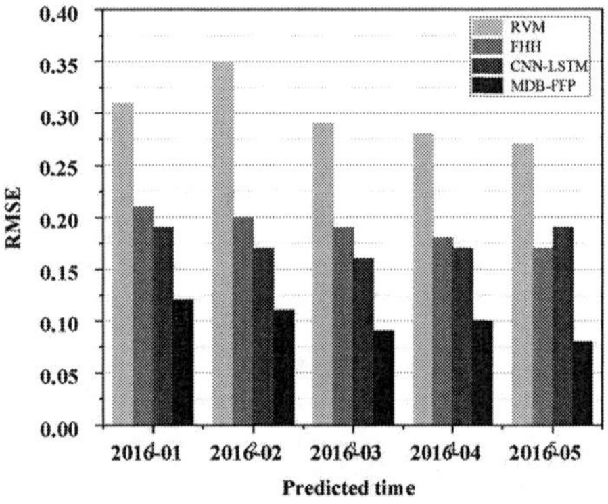

Figure 7 Results of five forecasting models

VI. CONCLUSION

This paper proposes MDB-FFP model to improve the accuracy and stability of the load forecasting model. The model uses the Holt-Winters algorithm to improve the effectiveness of load sampling data; GAT is used to maximize the information of local neighboring nodes to improve the learning ability of load features; the RNN-LSTM model was built to realize lifelong learning and prediction of load.

REFERENCES

[1] Lei Yiqin, Sun Zhaolong, Ye Zhiwei, etc. Research on non-intrusive Monitoring Method of power system load. *Transactions of China Electrotechnical Society*, ,2021, 36(11): 2288-2297

[2] Chen Kexu, Ma Jian, Liu Jiahan, "Research on non-intrusive Monitoring Method of power system load," *Transactions of China Electrotechnical Society*, 2019, 34(19): 4135-4142

[3] Xu Qingshan, Lou Oudie, Zhen Aixia, "Noninvasive load decomposition method based on nearest neighbor propagation clustering and genetic optimization," *Transactions of China Electrotechnical Society*, 2018, 33(16): 4135-4142

[4] Fan Shixiong, Liu Xinwei, Yu Yijun, "Super-short-term bus load forecasting method based on multi-source data and model fusion," *Power System Technology*, 2021, 45(01): 243-250

[5] Zi Yanling, "Research on power load combination Prediction based on Feature extraction and Bayesian optimization," Hunan Normal University, 2021.

[6] Yin Xinglu, Xiao Xianyong, Sun Xiaolu, "Bus load prediction model screening and variable weighet combination prediction based on prediction validity and Markov - cloud model," *Electric power automation equipment*, 2015, 35(03): 114-119

[7] Zou Zhi, Wu Tiezhou, Zhang Xiaoxing, etc. "Short-term load forecasting based on Bayesian optimized CNN-Bigr U hybrid neural network," *Electric power automation equipment*, 2022, 35(03)

[8] Li Shanshou, Ma Xiaodie, Pan Luqian, etc. "Research on short-term load forecasting model based on VMD and LSTM-CNN," *Electric power automation equipment*, 2022.

[9] Lv Zhonglin, Gu Jie, Meng Lu. "Short-term load forecasting of integrated energy system based on coupling feature and multi-task learning," *Electric power automation equipment*, 46(11), 2022.

[10] Liu, Y.L. Wang, J.Y., "Long Short-Term Memory Based Refined Load Prediction Utilizing Non-Intrusive Load Monitoring," *IEEE Power and Energy Society General Meeting PESGM*, Washington, 2021.

[11] Chen K.J., Chen, K.L., and Wang, Q. "Short-Term Load Forecasting With Deep Residual Networks," *IEEE Transactions On Smart Grid*, 2019, 10: 3943-3952

[12] Kim Tae-Young and Cho Sung-Bae, "Particle Swarm Optimization-based CNN-LSTM Networks for Forecasting Energy Consumption," IEEE Congress on Evolutionary Computation (CEC), 2019: 1510-1516, New Zealand

Study on Contact Reliability of Railway Signal Relay

Zhengyuan Zhao, Mingjun Xie, Zhijun Han, Xueqiang Li, Yan Liu, Zhepei Zhang

Xi'an Railway Signal Co., Ltd. Shenyang 710100,China
E-mail: 863901620@126.com Tel: 86-29-82362834 Fax: 86-29-82362834

***Abstract*—Relay contact due to the pull rod, contact strip, armature, the influence of the intrinsic factors such as the magnetic circuit, every contact between the contact position is different, at the same time due to the contact pressure between contact, contact scanning cheng, contact clearance, clearance of contact bounce, the influence of the parameters, such as, and contact surface morphology characteristics, composition, its height information, roughness and fractal dimension is different, And the load conditions, atmospheric environment, vibration magnetic field and other factors borne by the contact on site will affect the contact reliability of relay. At the same time, there are many influence factors involved in the production process of relay, the method of analyzing data is relatively lacking, and the application of foreword technology is relatively few, so the reliability research of relay needs to be further discussed.**

***Keyword*—Contact spot, Contact pressure drop, Big data.**

I. INTRODUCTION

The core of relay contact reliability is "contact", for example, the contact forms of contact include point contact, line contact and surface contact; The number of contact spots of the contact; The contact area is large or small; The contact area has different shapes; The contact position is high and low, with deviation and positive; There are mechanical wear and electrical wear in the contact process; There are rolling and sliding during contact..

Due to the influence of inherent factors such as pull rod, contact piece, armature, magnetic circuit, etc., the contact position between contacts will be different each time. Meanwhile, due to the influence of parameters such as contact pressure, contact sweep, contact clearance, contact bounce, support piece clearance, etc., as well as the difference of contact surface topography, composition, height information, roughness, fractal dimension, etc., and the load conditions Atmospheric environment, vibration magnetic field and other factors will affect the contact reliability of relay contact.

The research of relay contact reliability needs to understand the carrier fundamentally and carry out scientific research by combining relevant analysis methods.

II. DESCRIPTION OF RELIABILITY STUDY CARRIER

The railway signal safety relay is a DC 24V series heavy elastic DC electromagnetic relay. Its typical structure is a non-polar relay. The representative of the non-polar relay is XXXX relay. All other types of relays are derived from the non-polar relay.

XXXX relay is composed of contact system and DC electromagnetic system. The contact system is located above the electromagnetic system, as shown in Fig. 1:

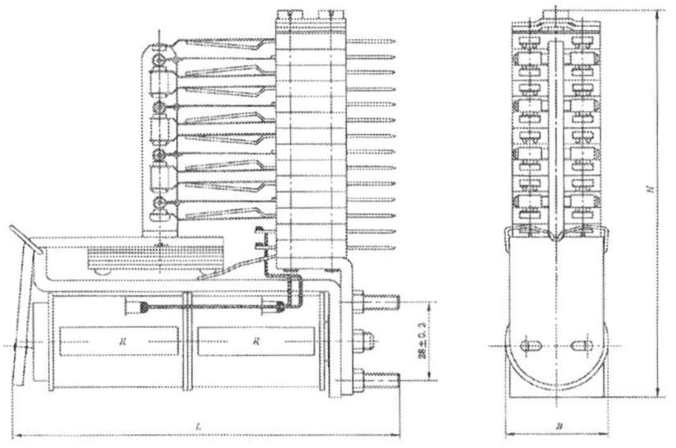

Fig. 1 internal structure of relay

The contact system includes movable part (pull rod, contact piece and contact) and fixed part (supporting piece, insulator and fastening device of fixed contact piece); The electromagnetic system is composed of four parts: iron core, L-type yoke, angle type armature and coil. In fact, there are various contradictions in XXXX relay, which affect the reliability of relay. For example, between contact clearance and contact travel; Between contact pressure and working value; Between the moving contact and the stationary contact; Between the coil and the magnetic circuit; But the main contradiction that plays a leading role is the contradiction between the electromagnetic system and the contact system. Their opposition and unity constitute the special essence of the relay. The electromagnetic system is the main aspect of the relay contradiction, because the electromagnetic system is always in the active (traction) state while the contact system is in the passive (resistance) state during the working process of the relay, so the quality of the magnetic circuit characteristics plays a leading role in the relay. However, since the magnetic circuit system is very complex in testing, testing and calculation under actual conditions, and almost all the performance parameters of the relay tested on the site or in the laboratory are concentrated in the contact system, such as contact pressure, contact gap, contact resistance, contact bounce, etc. At the same time, the contact system is an important part of the relay. For any relay, the normal working state of the relay is directly reflected by the relay contact system. At the same time, it is found that 70% ~ 80% of the faults occur in the contact system through the statistics of the field fault relay data for many years. Therefore, it is necessary to have a comprehensive understanding of the contact system when designing, improving, testing and analyzing the reliability of the relay.

The work of the contact system is divided into three situations: closed state, pull in process and open process. The contact closing state is divided into the front contact closing and the rear contact closing. The contact in the closed state shall mainly meet the reliable electrical contact and transmit the on-site signal in real time without interruption. This working state is the core and the key. In fact, the other two processes serve it. The two processes of making and breaking are related to the magnetic circuit system, and the magnetic circuit system of the pole less relay is a branchless magnetic circuit. After DC voltage is applied to the relay coil, the current I in the coil magnetizes the core and generates working magnetic flux in the core. It enters the armature through the main working air gap at the pole shoe of the core, enters the yoke through the second working air gap, and then returns to the core to form a closed circuit. At the working air gap, due to the action of the working magnetic flux, electromagnetic attraction is generated between the iron core and the armature. When the electromagnetic attraction is enough to overcome the resistance of the mechanical load, the armature and the iron core are attracted, which is the attraction process of the relay; When the coil is powered off, the electromagnetic attraction between the iron core and the armature decreases to gradually disappear, the resistance of the mechanical load is greater than the electromagnetic attraction, and the armature and the iron core are separated, which is the breaking process of the relay.

The contact system for the pull in process goes through six stages:

1) The rear contact is in the working position;

2) The contact moment between the rear contact point and the support plate;

3) The moment when the moving contact and the rear contact are separated;

4) Contact moment between moving contact and fron contact;

5) The moment when the front contact leaves the support plate;

6) The front contact is in working state.

The contact system for the disconnection process goes through six stages:

1) The front contact is in the working position;

2) The contact moment between the front contact and the support plate;

3) The moment when the moving contact and the rear contact are separated;

4) Contact moment between moving contact and front contact;

5) The moment when the front contact leaves the support plate;

6) The front contact is in working state.

Combined with the six stages experienced by the relay in and out process, a large amount of data is collected from them, including electrical parameters, mechanical parameters, time parameters, motion parameters and micro parameters, and the reliability of these data is analyzed comprehensively.

III. Research Method of Contact Reliability

In order to ensure product quality, meet customer needs and impr、ions of developing and producing products. For the relay, the design, process, production and other processes have been very mature after decades of training, but the relay involves many influence factors in the production process, the method of analyzing data is relatively lacking, and the application of foreword technology is relatively small. Therefore, the reliability of relay is studied from the following three aspects.

1) 5M1E analysis method

5M1E analysis method specifically refers to man / man: the operator's understanding of quality, technical proficiency, physical condition, etc; Machine: accuracy and maintenance of machine equipment and fixtures; Material: composition, physical and chemical properties of materials; Method: it includes processing technology, tooling selection, operating procedures, etc; Measurement: whether the measurement method is standard and correct; Environment: temperature, humidity, lighting and cleaning conditions of the working place. Process is the basic link of product formation, and process quality is the basis of ensuring product quality. Process quality has an important impact on product quality, production cost and production efficiency. Process standardization plays a key role in ensuring process quality. Process standardization plays a prominent role in process quality improvement. Process quality is affected by six factors of 5M1E, i.e. human, machine, material, method, environment and measurement. Process standardization is to seek the standardization of 5M1E. In fact, we need to establish 5M1E standardization not only in the product process, but also in the product design, product test, product certification, etc. only by establishing standardization and starting from the most basic can we ensure the reliability of the product.

2) PDCA cycle method

In addition to using 5M1E analysis method to analyze the reliability, it can also be combined with PDCA cycle method to conduct in-depth reliability analysis and research. PDCA cycle is standardization - Execution - recheck - reorganization. There is another saying, that is, make a standard first, do it, find problems after completion, check - improve - do it again - standardize again. These two cycles are actually the same. Just as we have drawings and process documents for relay production, we produce them according to the drawings, and check the parts after production. If we find problems, we may improve the process methods, or improve the tooling and mold, and then check the parts after improvement. If the parts meet the requirements, we will standardize the drawings or process documents. In fact, as long as we follow this procedure and do every step in a down-to-earth manner, High quality and reliable products can be produced. Every time we turn the PDCA cycle in production and operation, the unqualified products will be reduced and the product quality will be higher and higher. This cycle needs each of our employees to run, personal PDCA cycle, so that individuals can make continuous progress; The PDCA cycle of the Department will also enable the Department to make continuous progress, step by step.

The soul of PDCA cycle is integrated into the production and operation of relays. I think there are two points: first, small-scale changes must be made, and each change must be carefully summarized and recorded; The second is to continue to cycle. The premise is that each small loop is changed and cycled on the basis of verification and confirmation. Reliability work is not only a scientific method but also a process of constant self affirmation. With a good process, there will surely be good results, high reliability parts and components, and high reliability, high stability and high quality products.

3) Big data analysis

Big data is a general term that describes a series of technologies from data generation, transmission, storage, analysis to display. Therefore, big data is not only reflected in quantity, but also in application analysis. Big data has five characteristics, which are huge data volume, low value density, various data types, fast processing speed, accuracy and reliability. Data analysis is the core step of reliability analysis big data processing process. Through data extraction and integration, raw data for big data processing can be obtained from heterogeneous data sources. Users can analyze and process these data according to their own needs, such as data mining, machine learning, data statistics, etc. data analysis can be used for product performance analysis, decision support, prediction systems, etc. Through data analysis, we can grasp the information in the data. According to the different purposes of big data analysis and processing, big data analysis can be divided into descriptive analysis, diagnostic analysis, predictive analysis and normative analysis.

From the initial design to the production of the prototype, from the first article identification to the small batch trial production, from the type test to the batch production, from the product inspection to the packaging protection, from the delivery of the finished products to the field application, the relay has done a lot of tests and tests to fully verify and confirm each link. Each link will generate a large amount of test data. From the perspective of LCC management, only when the characteristics of the whole life cycle from "life" to "death" of the relay are clearly understood can we create excellent products and create a world-class high reliable railway signal relay.

Relay performance parameters often focus on mechanical parameters and electrical parameters. Other parameters such as time parameters, magnetic parameters, three-dimensional parameters, composition parameters and motion parameters are less concerned, mainly because there are no particularly good test means or methods. For relay products, it is a control device whose output will jump when its input (electric, magnetic, force and heat) reaches the set value. Therefore, to comprehensively analyze the relay performance, all parameters of the relay should be collected and analyzed. See Figure 2 for specific big data analysis methods.

From the above figure, we can see that if we want to obtain various results displayed on the visual layer, we need a large amount of data to be layered, partitioned and staged. These large amounts of data can not be analyzed by traditional methods. Therefore, following the trend of the times, we introduce the concept of big data into our relay reliability analysis. After several years of efforts, we have gained some experience in data collection layer, data purification layer, information storage layer and data processing layer. We believe that with the continuous progress of data processing, we will eventually reach the data visualization layer.

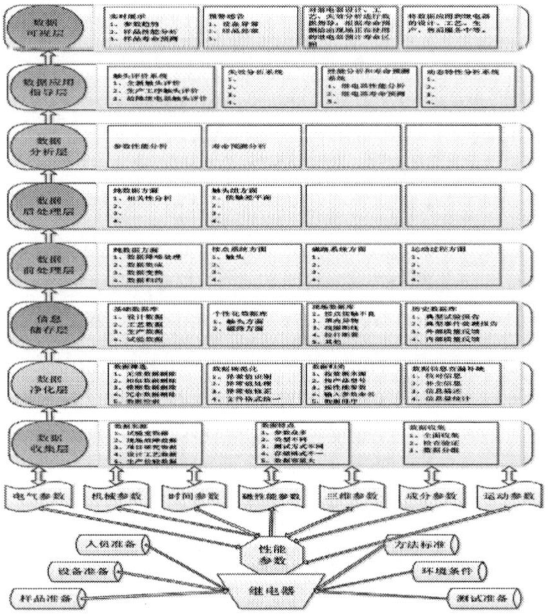

Fig. 2 thinking map of relay reliability big data analysis

IV. SPECIFIC EXAMPLE ANALYSIS

At this stage, there are 38 kinds of parameters for relay testing. However, when so many parameters are put together, which is the most important and which is the least important. For the relay, there are neither the most important nor the least important, but there will be relatively strong correlation parameters, such as the pull in value and pull in time, contact voltage drop and contact resistance from the perspective of relay mechanism. Therefore, correlation analysis and processing shall be carried out for the values of various parameters of the relay, Find out the representative parameters for analysis, so as to analyze the performance status of the relay and determine the reliability of relay operation in the later stage.

In order to make the judgment conclusion more convincing, the concept of correlation coefficient is introduced. Correlation coefficient is to examine the degree of correlation between two variables. Although the covariance can reflect the correlation degree of two random variables, the magnitude of the covariance difference cannot well measure the correlation degree of two random variables. In order to better measure the degree of association between the two variables, Pearson correlation coefficient was used.

Pearson correlation coefficient is obtained by dividing the covariance by the standard deviation of two variables, namely:

$$P = \frac{\text{cov}(x,y)}{} = \frac{E[(x-x_i)(y-y_i)]}{}$$

As for the correlation between the parameters, we find that there is an interaction and interaction relationship between the two data by drawing a scatter diagram, and even the similarity between some variables is very high. At this time, it is necessary to replace the data group with strong correlation with a group of representative and independent data. We use Pearson correlation coefficient to calculate. Generally, the correlation strength of variables is judged by the following value ranges, as shown in Table 1:

Table 1 value range of correlation coefficient (taking absolute value)

0.8-1.0	extremely strong correlation
0.6-0.8	strong correlation
0.4-0.6	moderate correlation
0.2-0.4	weak correlation
0.0-0.2	extremely weak correlation or correlation

The Pearson correlation coefficient is calculated between two variables based on the data after the abnormal value is processed. The thermodynamic diagram of the correlation coefficient between variables is shown in Fig. 6. The data with the correlation coefficient (taking the absolute value) between 0.8 and 1.0 is assumed to be extremely strong correlation, only one representative group is retained, and the rest related to it are deleted.

The correlation between the two parameters can be judged by the correlation coefficient between the parameters. For the parameters with strong correlation, a group of parameters can be selected and retained, and the remaining parameters can be removed. The parameter retention method: select the correlation coefficient with other parameters and small parameters.

The absolute value sum of the correlation coefficients of all parameters and their order are shown in the following table. By observing the thermodynamic diagram of correlation coefficient among variables, delete the variables with strong correlation. For the variables with strong correlation, the retention method is: for the two variables with strong correlation and weak correlation with other variables, calculate the sum of the absolute values of their correlation coefficients with other variables, and retain the variables with small correlation; For the variables with more than 2 strong correlations, the absolute value of correlation coefficient with other variables and the maximum and minimum variables shall be removed first, and the remaining variables shall be the ones with the minimum.

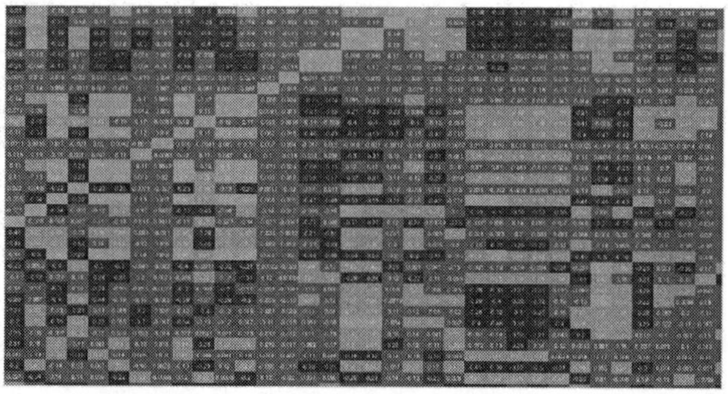

Fig. 3 thermodynamic diagram of correlation coefficient

According to the correlation coefficient before the parameters obtained from the correlation coefficient thermal map, the parameter pairs with strong correlation are calculated as follows: working value - reverse working value, front coil resistance - rear coil resistance, contact resistance of dynamic closing 2 - contact resistance of dynamic closing 3, contact resistance of dynamic breaking 3, contact 1 / 3 pull in time of contact 2 / 4 dynamic breaking overtravel time, contact resistance of dynamic closing 8 - contact pressure of dynamic breaking 1, Contact 1 dynamic closing overtravel time - contact 3 dynamic closing overtravel time, contact 12 release free movement time - contact 34 release free movement time, contact 1 breaking voltage - contact 2 / 3 / 4 breaking voltage, ablation area (moving contact) - contact pressure of dynamic closing 1, final displacement during the closing process - Maximum displacement during the release process.

According to the sum of the absolute values of the correlation coefficients of the parameters, the remaining parameters of the above-mentioned parameter pairs with strong correlation are determined as follows (selected and smaller parameters): working value, front ring resistance, contact resistance of dynamic closing 3, contact contact resistance of contact 1, contact resistance of dynamic closing 8, contact 1 dynamic closing overtravel time, contact 34 release free movement time, contact 4 breaking voltage, contact pressure of dynamic closing 1, and final displacement during the closing process. And the remaining parameters whose correlation coefficient with other parameters does not exceed 0.8. See Table 2 for details.

The above is a brief description of the correlation analysis method and an example demonstration. In fact, there are many correlation analysis methods, such as AHP analytic hierarchy process. In actual application, we need to use the most suitable method for analysis.

Table 2 value range of correlation coefficient (taking absolute value)

参数	相关系数绝对值和	排序	参数	相关系数绝对值和	排序
释放值 V	2.22E+01	26	触头 34 吸合自由运动时间	5.55E+01	50
工作值 V	2.96E+01	4	触头 12 释放自由运动时间	6.89E+01	2
反向工作值 V	3.09E+01	1	触头 34 释放自由运动时间	6.99E+01	3
前圈（R20）	2.39E+01	28	触头 1 接触压降	5.53E+01	59
后圈（R20）	2.53E+01	27	触头 2 接触压降	6.21E+01	37
动合 1 接点电阻	2.88E+01	18	触头 3 接触压降	6.07E+01	47
动合 2 接点电阻	2.99E+01	19	触头 4 接触压降	5.52E+01	74
动合 3 接点电阻	2.57E+01	42	触头 1 断开电压	7.16E+01	11
动合 4 接点电阻	2.02E+01	70	触头 2 断开电压	7.43E+01	7
动合 5 接点电阻	2.62E+01	44	触头 3 断开电压	7.35E+01	12
动合 6 接点电阻	2.29E+01	62	触头 4 断开电压	7.37E+01	17
动合 7 接点电阻	3.00E+01	40	材料转移（动触头）	7.45E+01	14
动合 8 接点电阻	2.48E+01	66	材料转移（静触头）	7.14E+01	31
动断 1 接点电阻	2.70E+01	58	烧蚀区域（动触头）	7.45E+01	25
动断 2 接点电阻	2.95E+01	53	烧蚀区域（静触头）	7.57E+01	22
动断 3 接点电阻	3.74E+01	24	动合 1 接点压力	7.12E+01	46
动断 4 接点电阻	3.20E+01	51	动合 2 接点压力	6.73E+01	71
动断 5 接点电阻	3.99E+01	23	动合 3 接点压力	7.44E+01	43
动断 6 接点电阻	3.49E+01	48	动合 4 接点压力	7.03E+01	61
动断 7 接点电阻	3.46E+01	54	动合 5 接点压力	7.02E+01	68
动断 8 接点电阻	4.08E+01	30	动合 6 接点压力	7.17E+01	64
吸合电压	4.91E+01	5	动合 7 接点压力	7.27E+01	63
释放电压	3.75E+01	52	动合 8 接点压力	7.30E+01	72
线圈触动时间	3.76E+01	56	动断 1 接点压力	7.88E+01	49
线圈稳流值	3.64E+01	69	动断 2 接点压力	8.30E+01	32
线圈稳压值	4.55E+01	29	动断 3 接点压力	8.31E+01	39
触头 1 吸合时间	5.66E+01	21	动断 4 接点压力	8.53E+01	33
触头 2 释放时间	3.96E+01	67	动断 5 接点压力	9.25E+01	9
触头 2 动断超程时间	5.18E+01	20	动断 6 接点压力	9.13E+01	16
触头 1 动合超程时间	4.89E+01	36	动断 7 接点压力	9.34E+01	13
触头 2 燃弧时间	4.09E+01	73	动断 8 接点压力	9.36E+01	15
触头 1 弹跳时间	3.39E+01	77	绝对间隙 mm(整机)	8.43E+01	55
触头 3 吸合时间	5.92E+01	8	接点齐度（动合）	8.35E+01	65
触头 4 释放时间	5.17E+01	41	接点齐度（动断）	8.60E+01	57
触头 4 动断超程时间	5.34E+01	6	吸合过程中最大位移量	8.52E+01	60
触头 3 动合超程时间	5.50E+01	35	吸合过程中最终位移量	9.19E+01	38
触头 4 燃弧时间	4.28E+01	75	释放过程中最大位移量	9.53E+01	33
触头 3 弹跳时间	4.02E+01	76	释放过程中最终位移量	1.02E+02	9
触头 12 吸合自由运动时间	5.56E+01	45			

V. CONCLUDING REMARKS

The reliability research of railway signal relay should be analyzed in combination with actual products, actual working conditions, actual test data and appropriate methods, so as to scientifically and reasonably evaluate the reliability of relay.

REFERENCES

[1] GB / T 7417-2010, Railway signal AX series relay [S]

[2] GB / T 6902-2010, Railway signal relay test method [S]

[3] Hu Yaohua. Signal relay and maintenance (on the book) [M]. Beijing: China Railway Publishing House, 1998: 9.

[4] Liu Wei.Zhou dasan Development of AN Series Relays [J]. Railway Signalling & Communication, 2003, 39(2)

Digital Twin Model Design of Three-phase Inverter for Reliability Prediction

Cen Chen [1], Chengzhi Sun[1], Wei Zheng[1,2], Yuchen Zhang[2], Yi Xu[1], Xuerong Ye[1], Guofu Zhai[1]

[1)] Department of Electric Engineering and Automation, Harbin Institute of Technology, Harbin, 150001

[2)] Beijing Aerospace Automatic Control Research Institute, Beijing, 100089

Email: 21S006057@stu.hit.edu.cn TEL: 18800418894

Abstract—**Three-phase inverter is widely used in DC-AC power supply, motor drive, photovoltaic inverter, etc., whose reliability and stability are fundamental of efficient operation of various electrical systems. Digital twin technology can realize the life cycle performance analysis of the product by ingeniously combining data derived from multi-source and multi-level. Aiming at the reliability prediction, Saber, ANSYS and other software are used as carriers, and a 270V DC three-phase inverter is carried out to study the method of establishing the digital prototype model by integrating circuit models, behavior models and physical models. On this basis, taking DC/DC modules, diodes, MOSFETs, operational amplifiers, drivers as examples, the equivalent injection method of physics of failure models integrating performance degradation and functional failure is studied. Finally, a test method for products is researched to verify the validity and accuracy of the three-phase inverter digital twin model.**

Index Terms— **Three phase inverter, digital prototype model, failure physical model, test method**

I. INTRODUCTION

With the development of electric propulsion technology, three-phase inverters are widely used for AC loads, such as conventional three-phase balanced electric or heating loads [1], and single-phase loads such as DC motors. As the core device of DC-AC power conversion, it is responsible for the stable power supply function of equipment, and its reliability is the key to the normal operation of electrical equipment [2].

In the actual use of three-phase inverter, the performance parameters of electronic components are degraded due to external high temperature and vibration. When the degradation goes to a certain extent, the parameter drift will exceed the regulation tolerance of the three-phase inverter control system, which will make the three-phase output unstable and reduce the efficiency, and lead to a potential threat to its reliability. Further, if the electronic components, especially the key components, continue to degrade to the failure threshold, or even arise open and short circuits, the system may have catastrophic failures such as continuous breakdown and burning of components, which will have a substantial and serious impact on the reliability of the three-phase inverter. Therefore, the digital twin model, the digital prototype of the three-phase inverter are of importance to the accurate simulation of the working life and state of the three-phase inverter, and also ensure the healthy operation of the three-phase inverter and improve the reliability of the equipment.

Accurate reliability prediction of electronic components is the basis of accurate reliability prediction of three-phase inverter. The relevant failure statistics show that [3, 4], power semiconductor devices and capacitors are the weak links in the life of three-phase inverters and the focus of reliability prediction. At present, the reliability prediction methods of components can be divided into two categories: one is to predict the reliability of components based on the historical failure rate data in the reliability prediction manual or industry standards, using empirical formulas including quality grade, service conditions and other factors, which is called the manual based reliability prediction method; The other is to establish the relationship between product life, manufacturing process and service conditions according to the physical or chemical change process of device failure, which is called reliability prediction method based on failure physics.

Three phase inverters need to work normally in a variety of temperature environments, and most of the materials in electronic components have temperature characteristics [5, 6]. At present, the research on three-phase inverter is mainly based on fixed temperature and fixed working condition [7]. In this case, if the MOSFET and capacitor in the have continuous temperature characteristics, the change of parameters will affect the static and dynamic characteristics of the system. Therefore, it is necessary to incorporate temperature into the reliability prediction of three-phase inverter, and it can be used as the basis for life prediction.

To sum up, this paper builds a digital twin model of three-phase inverter, including electrical model and thermal model, by using the device temperature characteristic model considering wide temperature conditions. The test method of products is studied to verify the accuracy of the digital twin model. This provides a model basis for the reliability prediction of three-phase inverter.

II. Digital Twin Model Design of Three-Phase Inverter

A. Circuit modeling of three-phase inverter based on Saber

Each MOSFET in the three-phase inverter is driven by a single driving chip and forms a switching network. Finally, a PWM equal amplitude amplified voltage square wave with an amplitude of ± VCC is output at the port of the switching network. In practical conditions, the load of the three-phase inverter is often the motor, so the square wave is filtered by the support capacitor and then connected to the resistive-inductive load. Therefore, the output phase current is a sine wave or a high-frequency sawtooth wave with a sine wave envelope. Use current sampling to measure the phase current signal and send it back to the control board. In the control board part, the sine wave with a given target amplitude is compared with the preset triangular wave carrier signal to form the SPWM wave of the next cycle, and this process is repeated until the effective value of the output current reaches the predetermined value.

The main performance indexes of the three-phase inverter used in this paper are as follows in Table 1:

TABLE I
MAIN PERFORMANCE INDEXES OF THREE-PHASE INVERTER

Parameter	Value
Input voltage	270V
Control frequency	1.65kHz
Output voltage	±270V
Peak-peak value of Output Current	±24A
Output current frequency	50Hz

This paper uses the above-mentioned indicators to verify the accuracy of the three-phase inverter simulation model.

When establishing the circuit simulation model of the three-phase inverter, to ensure the simulation accuracy, this paper takes the SiC MOSFET used as an example to carry out simulation modeling. Its equivalent circuit is shown in Fig. 1, where C_{GD} is the gate drain capacitance, C_{DS} is the drain source capacitance, C_{GS} is the gate source capacitance, D is the body diode, and R_* is the series resistance of each electrode.

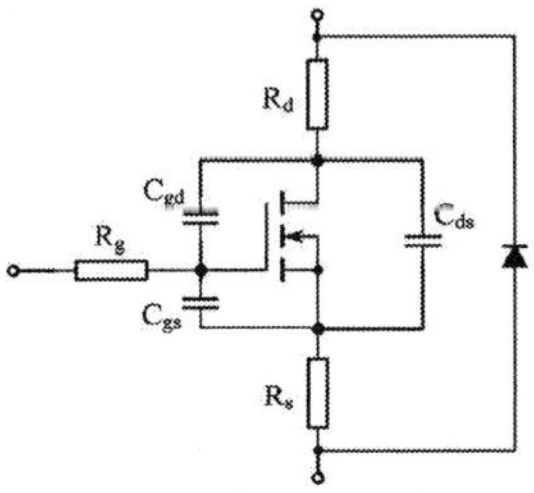

Fig. 1 Typical MOSFET equivalent model

Use *Model Architect* to model the SiC MOSFET component, as shown in Fig. 2. Use modeling tools to trace, take points and fit according to the component manual.

After the device modeling is completed, the circuit

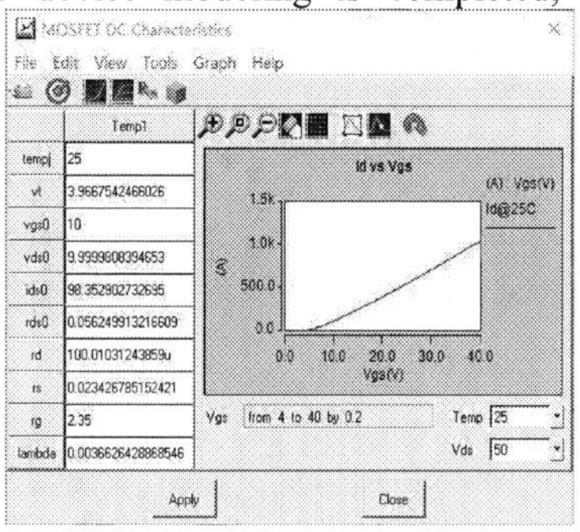

Fig.2 MOSFET modeling process using model architect

simulation model of the three-phase inverter is built in Saber, as shown in Fig. 3. The simulation results and the voltage across the sampling resistor are shown in Fig. 4. It can be seen from the figure that the output frequency of the three-phase inverter is 49.97Hz, the peak to peak value of

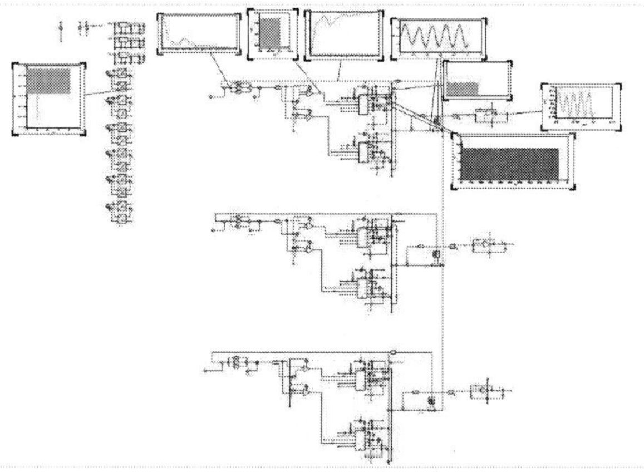

Fig. 3 Circuit model of three-phase inverter

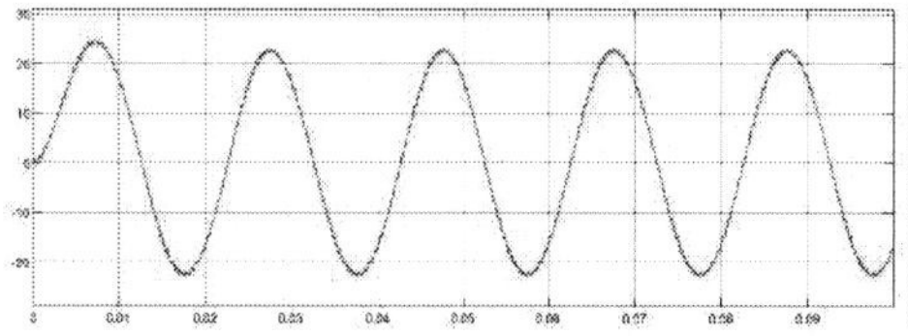

Fig. 4 simulation output of three-phase inverter circuit

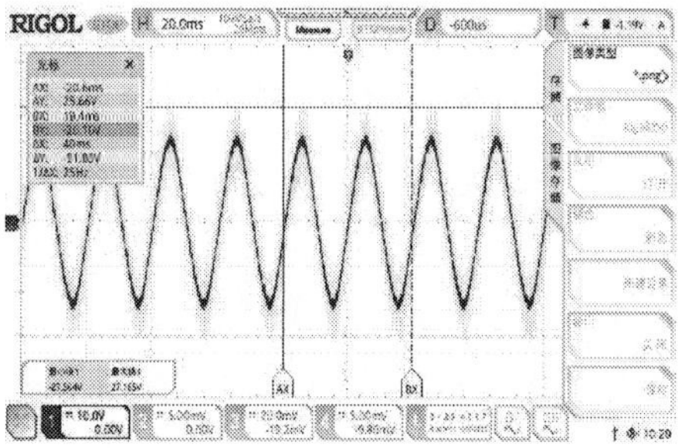

Fig. 5 output measurement waveform

the output current is 23.9A, and the effective value is 13.8A.

Draw the PCB of the three-phase inverter and build the physical circuit of the three-phase inverter. The waveforms at both ends of the measured resistance are shown in Fig. 5. The measured output frequency of the three-phase inverter is 51.536Hz, the output peak to peak value is 23.55A, and the effective value is 13.6A. The deviation from the simulation is 3.04% for the output frequency, 1.48% for the output peak to peak value, and 1.45% for the output effective value. It can be seen that the accuracy of the circuit simulation model of the three-phase inverter can support the modeling of the digital prototype within the allowable error of 5%.

B. Thermal modeling of three-phase inverter based on ANSYS Workbench

In this paper, the steady-state thermal module in ANSYS Workbench is used for thermal simulation. Combined with the results of circuit simulation and sensitivity analysis, the heating power of key components is determined; The parameters such as heating power (or voltage and current) determined in the circuit are injected into the thermal model to achieve the simulation results of the steady-state heat of the circuit under ideal conditions.

The main steps of temperature field analysis are as follows: (1) Establishment of the geometric model of three-phase inverter; (2) Material setting and environment setting of circuit components; (3) Set the heat source; (4) Set the solution and determine the boundary conditions; (5) Mesh; (6) Solve.

Fig. 6 Simulation results of three-phase inverter

After the geometric modeling is completed, the unimportant components can be simplified, such as chip resistance and capacitance. After that, the three-phase inverter model needs to be divided into networks, and finally the solution method can be set automatically. See Fig. 6 for the simulation results. It can be seen that the MOSFET itself generates heat seriously, and will affect the surrounding capacitance and resistance temperature. Test verification is carried out by thermocouple temperature measurement, as shown in Fig. 7. The simulation results of multiple temperature points are cole and compared with the measured results. The simulation accuracy is also about 5%. It can be considered that within this tolerance range, the accuracy of the thermal simulation model of the three-phase inverter can also support the modeling of the digital prototype.

Fig. 7 Temperature measurement of three-phase inverter

III. Equivalent Injection Method of Failure Physical Model Based on Insight

A. Physical model analysis of device failure of three-phase inverter

In this section, the MOSFET, as the core device of the three-phase inverter, is taken as an example to introduce the failure physical model of its typical parameters.

The degradation of MOSFET can be reflected by parameters such as threshold voltage and gate leakage current. Among them, the measurement of the gate leakage current is to characterize the health state of the MOSFET gate oxide through the above parameters. Mieko Matsumura proposed a two-component model of threshold voltage [8]:

$$\Delta V_{th-st} = A + B \cdot t^{n} \quad (1)$$

Wei [9] further refined the degradation characterization model of the above formula at the high-level stress stage:

$$\Delta V_{th-st} = A + E \cdot V_{GS}^{n'} \cdot \exp\left(\frac{-E_a}{kT}\right) \cdot t^{n} \quad (2)$$

Where E_a is the activation energy; n is a constant, which represents the long-range degradation rate of the gate oxygen interface under the applied gate bias stress; E, n' is a constant.

The characterization effect of gate leakage current on MOSFET failure is reflected in [10]:

$$\lambda(t,T_j) = \left[\beta / \left(C \times e^{E_a/(k_b \times T_j)}\right)\right] \cdot \left[t / \left(C \times e^{E_a/(k_b \times T_j)}\right)\right]^{\beta-1} \quad (3)$$

λ Is the instantaneous failure rate, t is the time, E_a is the activation energy, and k_b is the Boltzmann constant, β, C is a constant. The above model considers time, temperature and other factors. Based on the above model, the threshold voltage, instantaneous failure rate and other parameters of the MOSFET at a given stress and time are obtained, and the failure rate estimation under the current state is given.

Similarly, there are similar failure physical models for other components and their parameters in the circuit, as shown in Table 2.

TABLE 2
FAILURE PHYSICAL MODELS OF PARAMETERS IN THE CIRCUIT

Para.	Failure physical model
Resistance	$\ln\frac{\Delta R}{R}=\left(B\cdot\ln(t)+C\right)\cdot\frac{1}{T}+D\cdot\ln(t)+F$
Cap. ESR	$C_{ESR}=A\cdot\exp\left(-E/kT\right)$
Capacitance	$C=A_1+A_2\exp(-E/kT)\cdot t$

B. *Parameter injection method based on batch script*

Isight is a simulation analysis process automation and multidisciplinary & multi-objective optimization tool, which provides a visual and flexible simulation process building platform. In this paper, Isight is used to complete a batch of Saber simulations. The interface of Isight is shown in Fig. 8. For Saber's batch simulation, its visual program design is relatively simple: first, establish a data interface, that is, Data Exchanger, and then enter batch simulation.

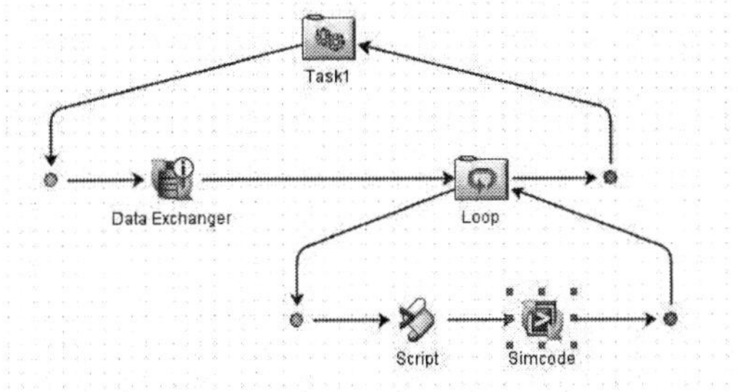

Fig. 8 Isight interface

The batch simulation is realized by a loop, which contains the content of batch script data writing and the file of circuit simulation.

The file containing device parameters in saber simulation circuit is .sin file, as shown in Fig. 9. The name, label, port netlist and parameter value of the device are indicated in the document.

The method of parameter injection based on batch script is as follows: Based on the established failure physical model of each component in the three-phase inverter, combined with the inverter's service time and the electrothermal stress results obtained from the previous round of electrical simulation and thermal simulation, the parameters of each component at a certain time point are obtained. Save these data in TXT files. Read and import them into the .sin file of Saber through Isight, and then conduct multiple rounds of simulation using the specified parameters at the specified time which imported.

IV. RESEARCH ON PRODUCT TESTING METHOD OF THREE-PHASE INVERTER

Establishing accurate temperature characteristics of key components is the premise to obtain the working state of inverter, and to accurately evaluate the reliability of three-phase inverter through electrothermal coupling simulation. The temperature characteristic test scheme of components is formulated as follows:

Instruments and equipment: LCR meter TH2829A, thermostat and power supply. The test process is as follow:

S1: Set the starting temperature as 20°C. As the maximum temperature resistance of MOSFET junction is 125°C, to avoid MOSFET failure in high-temperature test which causes the distortion of the temperature curve, this paper sets the end temperature as 110°C, sets the step value as 5°C, and there are 19 sampling points.

S2: A special temperature characteristic test board is designed for each type of device to facilitate device fixation. Place the test board in the thermostat, and the port of the device is led out with a shield wire of equal length. Before the shield wire is led out, the resistance value of the equal-length shield wire shall be tested first. Here, the slight resistance change of some shield line segments extending into the temperature box is ignored.

S3: Start heating, keep the temperature of the test point for about 10 minutes, and start reading.

S4: Raise the temperature to the next temperature point, and repeat S3 until the measurement is completed.

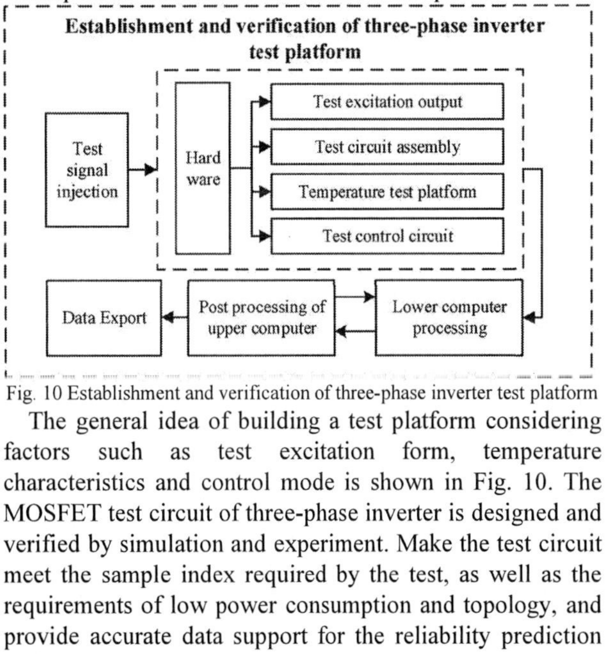

Fig. 10 Establishment and verification of three-phase inverter test platform

The general idea of building a test platform considering factors such as test excitation form, temperature characteristics and control mode is shown in Fig. 10. The MOSFET test circuit of three-phase inverter is designed and verified by simulation and experiment. Make the test circuit meet the sample index required by the test, as well as the requirements of low power consumption and topology, and provide accurate data support for the reliability prediction of three-phase inverter.

V. CONCLUSION

With the aim of reliability prediction, a digital twin model of three-phase inverter is built in this paper. To realize this, the paper builds the circuit model based on the circuit topology of the three-phase inverter, and its geometric model and thermal model. The paper realizes the electrothermal coupling simulation, and builds the digital twin model based on it for experimental verification. Then, the equivalent injection method of failure physical model based on Isight is studied, and based on temperature characteristics and parameter disturbance, the temperature characteristic test scheme of components is designed, and the test method of three-phase inverter products is studied to verify the validity and accuracy of the digital twin model of three-phase inverter.

REFERENCES

[1] Liu Ping, Liu Meiqi, Miao Yiru, Liu Tao, Li Sha nhu, Huang Shoudao. Characteristic analysis and c ontrol of three-phase four wire inverter based on LCC [J/OL]. Power automation equipment, 2022, 1-15

[2] Chen Jie, Xi Lijun, Zhu Wu, et al Research on c ontrol strategy of three-phase four wire Metro Aux iliary Inverter [J] Journal of railways, 2012, 32 (4): 34-38.

[3] Yang S, Bryant A, Mawby P, et al. An Industry-Based Survey of Reliability in Power Electronic C onverters[J]. IEEE Transactions on Industry Appli cations, 2011, 47(3): 1441-1451.

[4] Niu Hao, Reliability evaluation and optimization d esign of switching power supply considering worki ng profile [D]. Harbin Institute of technology, 202 1.

[5] Sun Bo, Robustness parameter design of switching power supply considering temperature effect [D]. Harbin Institute of technology, 2017

[6] Li Jianwen, Zhu Yongtao. Investigation on thermal variation characteristics of domestic fixed resistors [J]. Journal of Northwestern University (NATUR AL SCIENCE EDITION), 2013,43 (02): 198-202.

[7] Sun Quan, Peng Fei, Li Hongsheng, Yu Xianghai, sun Guodong. Inverter fault diagnosis method bas ed on cgan-cnn under sample imbalance [J/OL]. J ournal of power supply: 2022, 1-14

[8] Matsumura M, Kobayashi K, Mori Y, et al. Two-component model for long-term prediction of thres hold voltage shifts in SiC MOSFETs under negati ve bias stress [J]. Jpn. J. Appl. Phys., 2015,54,04 DP12.

[9] Wei Jiaxing, Research on reliability mechanism an d model of silicon carbide based power MOSFET [D]. Southeast University, 2019.

[10] Z. Ni, X. Lyu, O. P. Yadav, B. N. Singh, S. Zhe ng and D. Cao, "Overview of Real-Time Lifetime Prediction and Extension for SiC Power Converte rs," in IEEE Transactions on Power Electronics, 2 020, 35(8): 7765-7794

Research on Contactor Hardware-in-loop Simulation Technology

Yongren Yan[1], Longfei Tang[1,2,3]*

[1]College of Electrical Engineering and Automation, Fuzhou University, Fuzhou, 350108, China
[2]Fujian Key Laboratory of New Energy Generation and Power Conversion, Fuzhou, 350108, China
[3]Fujian Province University Engineering Research Center of Smart Distribution Grid Equipment, Fuzhou, 350108, China
E-mail: tlftel@fzu.edu.cn Tel:13950364569

***Abstract*—Hardware-in-loop simulation system can verify the effectiveness and reliability of the control system more conveniently and truly. In this paper, a contactor hardware-in-loop simulation model construction method is proposed and configured on field programmable gate array (FPGA) platform to achieve hardware-in-loop simulation. The model uses the data obtained by static measurement method and bilinear interpolation method to map the nonlinear relationship between current, electromagnetic force and flux linkage and displacement. The continuous process of voltage balance and mechanical motion is discretized to realize integral calculation. Combined with FPGA platform parallelization and pipeline arithmetic processing, the contactor state can be solved at high speed. Experiments were carried out on the hardware-in-loop model and the actual contactor under current closed-loop control, and the accuracy of the contactor hardware-in-loop model was verified. The designed hardware-in-the-loop model can interconnect with the actual hardware control system and provide a platform for system reliability verification. It can also simulate the failure of contactor and conduct fault experiments when the actual conditions are not available or relatively dangerous.**

***Index Terms*— bilinear interpolation, contactor hardware-in-loop model, FPGA**

I. INTRODUCTION

Contactor is the most common control electrical appliances, widely used in the national life and industrial production, occupies an important position. In recent years, with the development of electrical intelligence, especially under the background of "double carbon" target proposed in our country, various intelligent control schemes of the contactor have also been gradually developed, promoting the contactor towards low energy consumption and low noise development[1-3].

Hardware-in-loop simulation is a technology that can verify control scheme at low cost. It combines the physical hardware of the control system with the real-time simulation of the controlled object, which can reflect the performance of the control system more realistically, verify the rationality of the system scheme, and greatly shorten the development cycle of the control system. Now it has been widely used in control fields such as vehicles, motors, power electronics and power systems[4-5]. In literature [6], a mixed analytical model of phase inductance of switched reluctance motor was proposed. The phase inductance was solved piecewise based on whether the stator and rotor teeth overlap, and the continuous function of phase inductance with respect to current and rotor position was constructed by using Bezier approximation method. Finally, the hardware-in-the-loop simulation was realized on FPGA platform. The accuracy of the model is proved. Based on RT-LAB controller hardware-in-the-loop simulation technology, literature [7] proposed a multi-controller hardware-in-the-loop photovoltaic DC microgrid simulation platform development scheme. Through the platform model and the physical interface circuit, the relevant tests of the microgrid system are carried out. The test results fully reflect the real operation characteristics of the system under test.

The application of hardware-in-loop simulation system in electrical switching field is not much. At present, the control system of contactors and other switching appliances is mainly developed based on pure digital co-simulation system, which provides a reference and idea for the construction of hardware-in-loop simulation system. In literature [8], SPICE circuit simulation and contactor dynamic simulation were completely integrated, and a point-by-point closed-loop simulation system integrating intelligent control module and contactor body was realized by using the dynamic process mathematical model of contactor.

Literature [9] puts forward a method of constructing a contactor simulation model. This paper uses neural network method to fit the nonlinear relationship among electromagnetic force, flux, current and displacement of contactor, and verifies the rationality of the simulation model through experiments. However, the accuracy of the

This work was supported by the Natural Science Foundation of Fujian Province under Grant 2021J01634.

nonlinear model constructed by neural network cannot be guaranteed, and there may be errors in the trend of displacements and motion back potentials, and there is insufficient stability, output characteristics are related to the number of neurons and training data sets, and it is difficult to select and change.

In order to realize the construction of contactors hardware-in-loop simulation system, this paper firstly uses the characteristics of FPGA parallel operation, combined with the mathematical model of contactors, divides the contactors into several sub-modules: mechanical movement, voltage balance, current reverse calculation, force reverse calculation, and builds a simulation model of parallel operation and data interaction of each module in FPGA. For the shortage of using neural network to build current reverse and suction reverse model, using the bilinear interpolation method to fit the three-dimensional surface of displacement-flux-force more reliably and directly and displacement-flux-current, so as to solve the internal differential equation of the contactor, and improve the reliability and accuracy of the model. An experimental system with NI sb-RIO as the controller and NI Compact-RIO as the model running platform is set up. The correctness of the hardware-in-loop simulation system is verified. The contactor hardware-in-loop simulation system constructed in this paper can reflect the dynamic characteristics of the contactor in the actual situation more truly and simulate the interaction between the control system and the switching appliance. It provides an idea for the construction of hardware-in-loop simulation model of electromagnetic switches and facilitates the development of complex intelligent control scheme of contractors and the verification of fault-tolerant control under extreme conditions.

II. Mathematical Model of Contactor

In the process of contactor movement, the electrical parameters and mechanical parameters are coupled with each other, and due to the existence of magnetic circuit saturation phenomenon, the variation of electromagnetic parameters of contactor presents nonlinear characteristics. The dynamic process of contactor motion satisfies the voltage balance equation on the circuit, D 'Alembert mechanical motion equation on the motion, and Maxwell equation on the magnetic field. The contactor's mathematical model can be established from these aspects to describe the dynamic process of contactor's motion.

A. Voltage balance equation

The contactor follows the voltage balance equation during its movement:

$$u_{\text{coil}} = i_{\text{coil}} R_{\text{coil}} - E = i_{\text{coil}} R_{\text{coil}} + \frac{d\psi}{dt} \tag{1}$$

Where i_{coil} is the coil current, R_{coil} is the coil resistance, and $d\Psi/dt$ is the induced electromotive force caused by flux changes during the moving core movement

B. Mechanical equation of motion

The contactor satisfies the D 'Alembert mechanical equation of motion during its movement:

$$F_x - F_f = m\frac{d^2x}{dt^2} \tag{2}$$

Where F_x is force; F_f is the reaction force; m is the equivalent mass of the movable part; x is the moving core displacement.

The electromagnetic force of the contactor and the spring reaction force act together to make the moving core move. The reaction force F_f comes from two main springs and three contact springs, which can be expressed as:

$$F_f = \begin{cases} 2(k_1x + F_a), & (0 \le x \le x_a) \\ 3\left[k_2(x - x_a) + F_b\right] + 2(k_1x + F_a), & (x_a < x \le x_b) \end{cases} \tag{3}$$

Where k_1 is the stiffness coefficient of the main spring; k_2 is the stiffness coefficient of the contact spring; F_a is main spring initial pressure; F_b is the initial pressure of the contact spring; x_a is the opening distance of moving contact and static contact; x_b is the open distance between moving core and static core.

C. The relation between electric - magnetic - force

In addition to the voltage balance equation and the mechanical motion equation mentioned above, there are also two binary functional expressions which cannot be described by the equation

$$i = f_1(\Psi, \delta) \tag{4}$$

$$F_x = f_2(i, \delta) \tag{5}$$

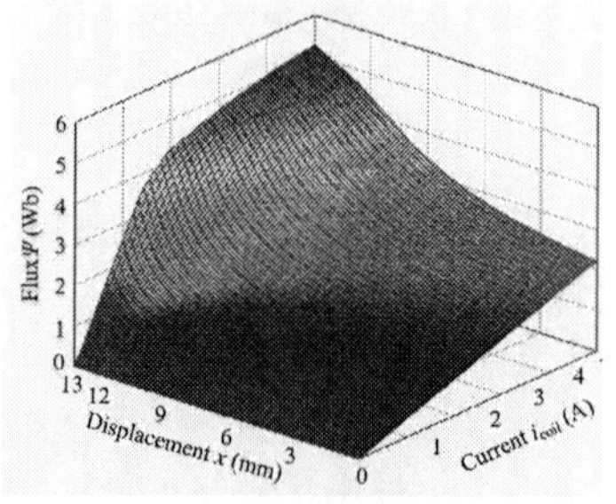

Fig. 1. Correspondence between flux displacement and current

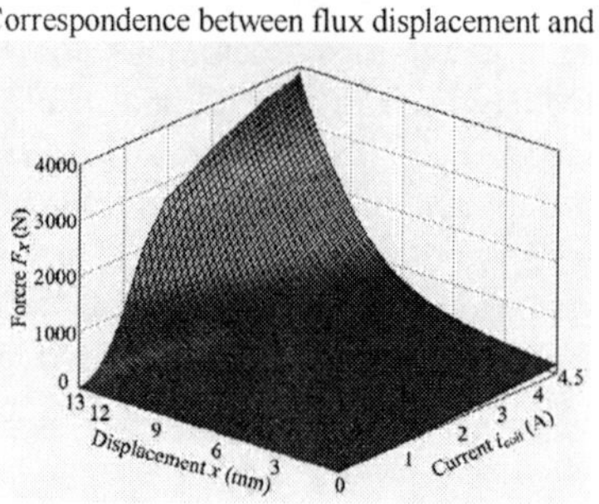

Fig. 2. The relationship between force, displacement and current

In other words, without considering the influence of eddy current and hysteresis loss, current and force are binary functions of flux and air gap. This mapping relationship is related to the structural materials and other parameters of the electromagnetic mechanism, and is also the core of the characteristics of the reaction contactors. Literature [10] also describes the one-to-one correspondence between flux, displacements and current and force, displacements and current. The mapped three-dimensional surface is shown as figure 1 and figure 2.

The static measurement method of contactor provides a method for the measurement of the nonlinear relationship of the actual contactor. The data table of the corresponding relationship between the two groups of hardware-in-loop simulation model is obtained by this method, and the specific data measurement principle is shown in the reference [11].

III. THE CONSTRUCTION OF HARDWARE-IN-LOOP MODEL BASED ON FPGA

The core of hardware-in-the-loop simulation system is to accurately simulate the dynamic changes of parameters in real time under the input and output these parameters signals for observation and construction of closed-loop control strategy. The running speed of simulation model also affects the authenticity and accuracy of simulation model. Programmable logic controller (FPGA) has the characteristics of fast computing speed and parallel running of cyclic programs, so it is very suitable for constructing hardware-in-the-loop simulation system. Therefore, the NI Compact-RIO system is selected as the platform for constructing contactor hardware in loop simulation system. It not only has the FPGA module that can use LabVIEW graphical programming, but also is equipped with multiple analog output module resources to facilitate the simulation output of each parameter of the model.

A. Voltage balancing module

According to the voltage balance equation:

$$u_{\text{coil}} = i_{\text{coil}} R_{\text{coil}} + \frac{d\psi}{dt} \qquad (6)$$

The coil resistance is regarded as a fixed value, and the instantaneous voltage value is equal to the sum of the coil resistance voltage drop and flux change rate. In the hardware in the loop system discrete time steps should be adopted to replace the contactors continuous system, and the sampling and simulation body calculation should be completed in each step. Voltage sampling is passed in the voltage balance module. In combination with formula (7), the flux variation in this time step can be calculated as follows:

$$\Delta\varphi = (u_{\text{coil}} - i_{\text{coil}} R_{\text{coil}}) \times \Delta t \qquad (7)$$

The current value is obtained from the reverse current module at the last moment. In this way, once the initial value of the flux is given at the beginning moment, the system's flux value can be calculated in real time by the accumulation of each step length. The module program is shown in the figure 3.

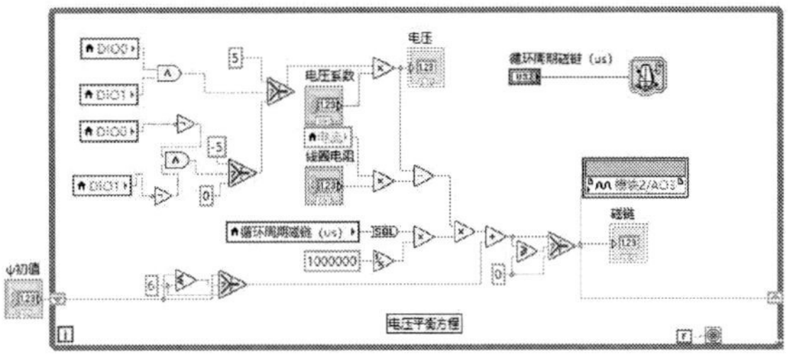

Fig. 3. Voltage balance module program

B. General Current reverse and suction reverse modules

In the construction of contactor body model, the part reflecting the coupling relationship of electric, magnetic and force inside the contactor is the key part. Due to the flux – displacement-current and displacement-current-force have a one-to-one correspondence relationship, through the method of simulation calculation of static measurement method or can get different current and flux linkage. Due to the one-to-one correspondence in flux – displacement-current and displacement-current-force, the force and flux corresponding to different currents and displacements can be obtained by static measurement or simulation calculation. The flux can be calculated by the voltage balance module. The displacement can be calculated according to the D 'Alembert mechanical equation of motion. In this way, the inverse problem of current and suction is transformed into the problem of solving the current and further finding the force based on the known relation surface, flux and displacement parameters.

In this paper, bilinear interpolation method, which is commonly used in computer image processing, is used to construct the relation surface by using the flux-displacement-current and force-displacement-current one-to-one correspondence data obtained by static measurement. Since the measured data is a discrete data table, the simulation in any state also needs to take the current and suction as the solution object and use the other two inputs to interpolate in FPGA.

One-dimensional linear interpolation is a simple and easy interpolation method. Its interpolation function is a polynomial of degree one. Let $y=f(x)$ has the values y_0 and y_1 at two points x_0 and x_1, respectively. For any value of x in the interval $[x_0,x_1]$:

$$i(\psi, x_a) = \frac{\psi - \psi_{b+1}}{\psi_b - \psi_{b+1}} \cdot i(\psi_b, x_a) + \frac{\psi - \psi_b}{\psi_{b+1} - \psi_b} \cdot i(\psi_{b+1}, x_a) \qquad (8)$$

$$i(\psi, x_{a+1}) = \frac{\psi - \psi_{b+1}}{\psi_b - \psi_{b+1}} \cdot i(\psi_b, x_{a+1}) + \frac{\psi - \psi_b}{\psi_{b+1} - \psi_b} \cdot i(\psi_{b+1}, x_{a+1}) \qquad (9)$$

Based on these two values of one-dimensional linear interpolation to solve the current value at this time:

$$i(\psi,x)=\frac{x-x_{a+1}}{x_a-x_{a+1}}\cdot i(\psi,x_{a+1})+\frac{x-x_a}{x_{a+1}-x_a}\cdot i(\psi,x_a) \quad (10)$$

According to the above principles, the inverse current module program is written as shown in figure 4.

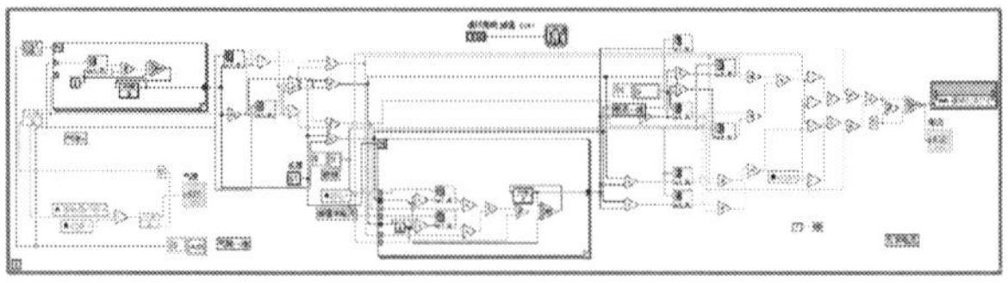

Fig. 4. Reverse current module program

So far, the current is solved by a two-dimensional linear interpolation method. The interpolation solution of force is similar to this process and will not be repeated. The difference is that the input of force reverse module is the solved current and air gap. The program of force reverse module is shown in figure 5.

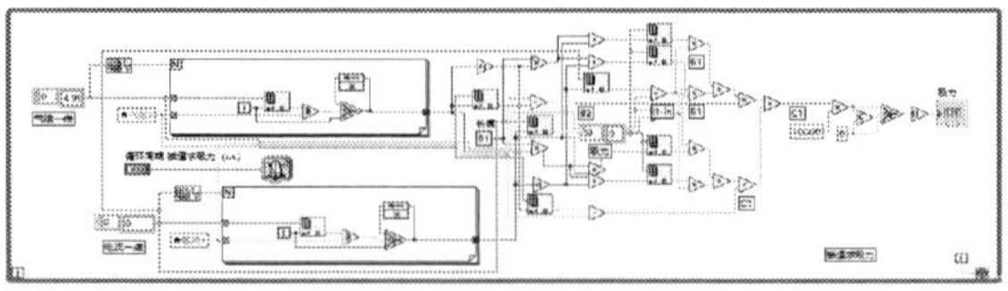

Fig. 5. Reverse force module program

C. Mechanical motion simulation module

The function of the mechanical motion module is to calculate the displacement change and velocity change in a time step according to the D 'Alembert mechanical motion equation and reflect the real motion state of the contactor through cumulative simulation and integral calculation.

$$\Delta V=\frac{F_x-f}{m}\cdot\Delta t \quad (11)$$

$$\Delta x=v\cdot\Delta t \quad (12)$$

When the contactor stroke and 0 value position are reached, the boundary is set to simulate the speed mutation under the effect of collision and limit. The specific program is shown in figure 6.

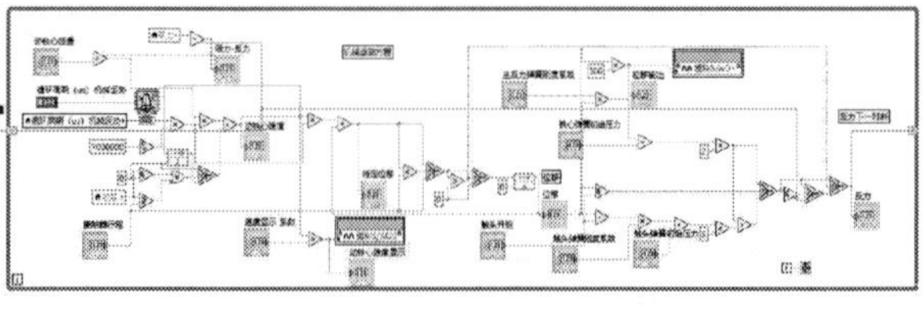

Fig. 6. Mechanical motion module program

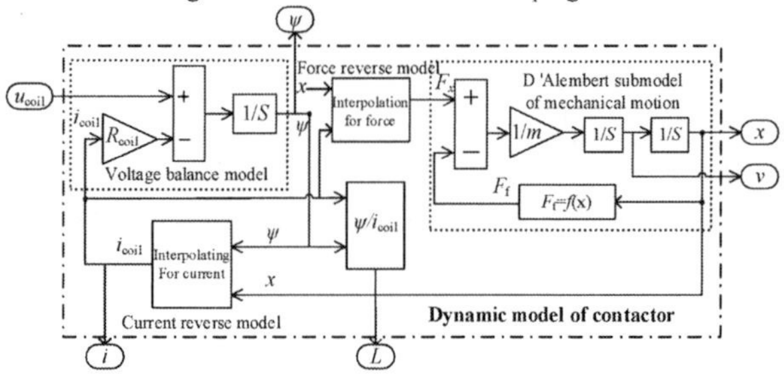

Fig. 7. Hardware in loop simulation model structure

These modules run in parallel, and their data interact with each other. Together, they constitute the hardware-in-loop simulation model of the contactor. The block diagram is shown in figure 7.

IV. Experimental verification based on NI Compact RIO

The experimental platform uses the NI sb-RIO system as the controller to output PWM driving signal. When the PWM signal is connected to the actual driving circuit, it can form the contactor physical control experimental platform together with the sensor and the host computer. At the same time, when the PWM signal is output to the hardware-in-loop simulation model running in Compact RIO system through DIO module. The parameters of the analog contactor are transferred to the NI sb-RIO controller through AO module to form a closed-loop control system of the hardware-in-loop simulation model. The two systems can run simultaneously to facilitate comparative experiments. The hardware connection diagram is shown in figure 8.

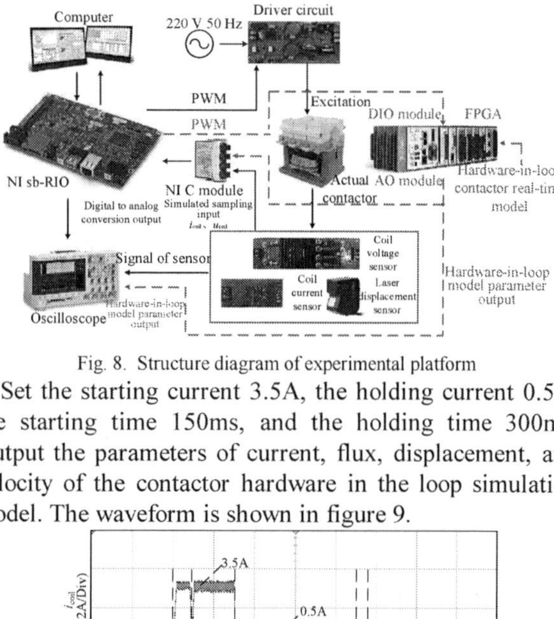

Fig. 8. Structure diagram of experimental platform

Set the starting current 3.5A, the holding current 0.5A, the starting time 150ms, and the holding time 300ms. Output the parameters of current, flux, displacement, and velocity of the contactor hardware in the loop simulation model. The waveform is shown in figure 9.

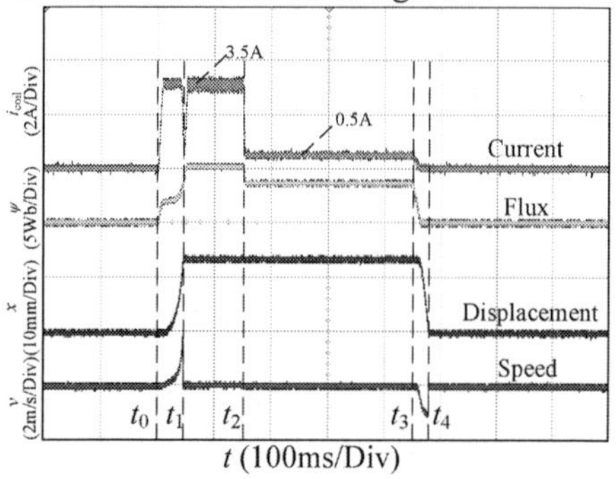

Fig. 9. Waveform of hardware in loop model

The closing process begins at time t_0, the coil begins to excite, and the coil current rises. At time t_1, the core collision completes the closing process, and the back electromotive force causes the current to drop to the minimum value and the velocity to reach the maximum value. From t_1 to t_2, the current continues to rise as the reference value of the closing current. It enters the holding state at time t_2, and the current drops rapidly to the reference value of the holding current. The breaking process begins at time t_3, and the current drops to 0. The moving core is separated from the static core after holding for a while until t_4 completes the breaking process.

To verify the accuracy of the hardware in the loop simulation model, the NI sb-RIO controller is used to control the actual contactor in the current closed-loop control mode and send the driving signal to the hardware-in-loop simulation model running in the NI Compact RIO. The closing current is 3.6A, the holding current is 0.5A, the closing time is 150ms, and the holding time is 300ms. The laser displacement sensor is used to measure the actual contactor displacement, and the two are compared. The waveform is shown in figure 10.

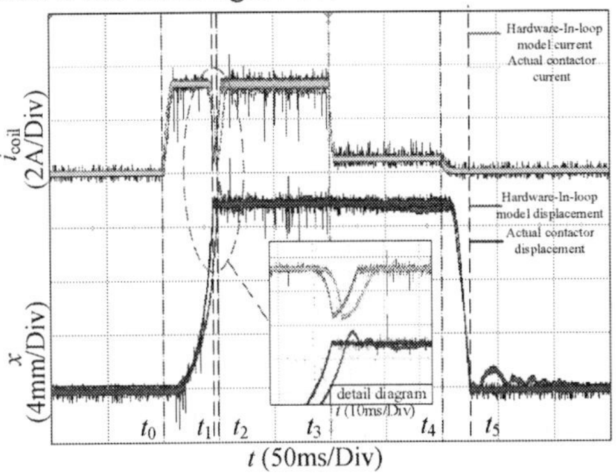

Fig. 10. Current and displacement contrast waveform

It can be seen that the current waveform and displacement waveform output by the model basically coincide with the waveform of the actual contactor, which verifies the rationality and accuracy of the hardware-in-loop simulation model. It can be seen from figure 10 that the hardware-in-loop model reaches the maximum displacement of the moving core at time t_1 while the actual contactor reaches this position at time t_2. The displacement of hardware- in-loop model will reach the closed position before the actual contactor. This is due to the hardware model does not calculate friction and other reasons. But the position of its back electromotive force is strictly corresponding to the displacement, that is, when the displacement reaches the stroke, the back electromotive force also reaches the maximum. It is proved that the hardware in-loop model can accurately reflect the contactor parameter variation law.

REFERENCES

[1] Z. Zheng, W. Ren and T. Wang, "Experimental Investigation of the Breaking Arc Behavior and Interruption Mechanisms for AC Contactors," in IEEE Transactions on Plasma Science, vol. 2021,49(1): 389-395

[2] S. Zheng, F. Niu, K. Li, S. Huang, Z. Liu and Y. Wu, "Analysis of Electrical Life Distribution Characteristics of AC Contactor Based on Performance Degradation," IEEE Transactions on Components, Packaging and Manufacturing Technology, 2018, 8(9):1604-1613

[3] X. Wang, H. Lin, S. L. Ho, S. Fang, P. Jin, "Analysis of Dynamic Characteristics of Permanent Magnet Contactor With Sensorless Displacement Profile Control," IEEE Transactions on Magnetics, 2010, 46,(6):1633-1636

[4] Z. R. Ivanović, E. M. Adžić, M. S. Vekić, S. U. Grabić, N. L. Čelanović and V. A. Katić, "HIL Evaluation of Power Flow Control Strategies for Energy Storage Connected to Smart Grid Under Unbalanced Conditions," IEEE Transactions on Power Electronics, 2012, 27(11): 4699-4710

[5] Wang Zhifu, Sun Qingle, Li Haolong, Wang Xu, Guo Yifeng, Liang Changchun, Wang Rui. Review of Hardware in Loop Simulation Technology for New Energy Vehicle Driving Motor [J]. Electric Transmission, 2022,52(01):3-12.

[6] Zheng Tong, XU Fengqiu, Chen Meng, XU Xianze. A hardware-in-loop simulation model for switched reluctance motor [J]. Journal of huazhong university of science and technology (natural science edition), 2019, 47(09):72-77.

[7] Shen Hua, Chen Geliang, Lin Lin, Zhang Xiaolin. Development of optical storage DC microgrid Controller Hardware in Loop Simulation platform [J]. Electrical Appliances & Energy Efficiency Management Technology, 2020, (05):62-66.

[8] Xu Zhihong, Tang Longfei. Integration simulation and digital control technology of intelligent ac contactor [J]. Proceedings of the CSEE, 2015, 35(11):2870-2878.

[9] Tang L, Han Z, Xu Z. Neural network-based co-simulation technology for intelligent contactors[J]. IEEE Transactions on Magnetics, 2020, 56(2): 1-8.

[10] Qin TaoTao, Dong Enyuan, Chen Yushuo, et al. Vacuum circuit breaker tracking control [J]. Proceedings of the CSEE, 2014, 34 (33): 5983-5990.

[11] Tang Longfei, Chen Hao, Ke Changhui. Research on Measurement Method of Contactor Static Characteristics [J]. Proceedings of the CSEE :1-10

Yongren Yan is currently pursuing the M.S. degree in electric engineering from the College of Electrical Engineering and Automation, Fuzhou University, China. His research interests include electric apparatus and its intelligent technology. 2673495545@qq.com.

Longfei Tang (Senior Member, IEEE) received his B.Sc. degree in electrical engineering and automation from Fuzhou University in 2009 and his Ph.D. degree in electric machines and electric apparatus from Fuzhou University in 2015. Now he is a professor at Fuzhou University, China. His research interests include electric apparatus and its intelligent technology. Corresponding author: tlftel@fzu.edu.cn.

8th International Conference on Reliability of Electrical Products and Electrical Contacts, November 18-20, 2022

FFT Mediator Loss Angle Measurement Algorithm Based on New Combined Window Phase Difference Correction

Ning Li, Changchun Chi, Zhentao Guo

College of Electrical Engineering, Shanghai Dianji University, Shanghai, 201306
E-mail: 2193587525@qq.com TEL:15565601658

Abstract—**Insulating property of high-voltage electrical appliance has an important indicator. It is the dielectric loss angle. That can be used to assess and forecast the working life of the electrical equipment. For measuring the insulating medium's dielectric loss angel accurately and improving the stability and accuracy of harmonic detection algorithm, a new type of cosine combination window is built. On account of the theory of measurement of dielectric loss angle, the paper infers a phase difference correction measurement algorithm basing on Nuttall-Blackman-Harris window to measure dielectric loss angle. The algorithm has easier calculated amount. The paper sets up measurement model through MATLAB/Simulink. When fundamental frequency, harmonic injection and signal-to-noise ratio make a difference, the paper proceeds simulation analysis basing the algorithm of paper and other algorithms. By comparing measuring and detection precision. The algorithm increases the reliability of detecting insulating property of high-voltage electrical apparatus. It is important to realize the goal that electrical equipment has steady operation and electric system works with high quality.**

Index Terms—**mediator angle, convolutional combined window function, phase difference correction, MATLAB/Simulink.**

I. INTRODUCTION

Nowadays, the increasing demand for electricity in various fields also makes the installed capacity of the power network increase accordingly, and the accidents caused by the damage to the insulation performance of electrical equipment in China every year occur frequently, so if the power system can work safely and stably, and can also transmit high-quality electrical energy, then it is necessary to control the insulation performance of electrical equipment stably and accurately. The dielectric loss angle is an important indicator of the insulation ability of electrical equipment, so the insulation performance[1] of electrical equipment can be grasped by measuring the dielectric loss angle.

At present, the measurement of the mediator angle generally has two kinds of hardware method and software method, the hardware method is usually affected by environmental factors so that the measured data error is large, so the software measurement method is usually used, and the harmonic analysis method[2] in the software measurement method is widely used because of its high stability and accuracy. Synchronous sampling of the signal can accurately measure the size of the dielectric loss angle, but the sampling is usually non-synchronous sampling, and the harmonic analysis method of the power grid signal is deviated due to the spectral leakage and fence[6] effect during the non-periodic sampling, which affects the measurement result of the final dielectric loss angle. In order to make the measurement of the mediator angle more accurate, the commonly used method is to add windowing to the grid signal, in this regard, many scholars have analyzed different window functions, in reference[9], the authors combine the Hanning window and Nuttall window to obtain a combination window function with good sidelobe performance, reference[10] for a single window function for self-convolution, although the sidelobe performance has been strengthened, but the convolution operation increases the amount of calculation.

In this paper, a new Nuttall-Blackman-Harris cosine combined window is constructed by using the good sidelobe performance[14] of Blackman-Harris window and Nuttall window. The algorithm and other algorithms are simulated under different experimental environments, and the reliability of the mediator loss angle measurement algorithm is verified by analyzing the simulation results.

II. THE PRINCIPLE OF MEASURING THE MEDIATOR LOSS ANGLE

In actual use, the use of electrical equipment will always be accompanied by dielectric loss, and the capacitors in the equipment will have both capacitive reactance and impedance. Figure 1 below is the equivalent circuit model of the capacitive device and the vector diagram of the inflow current and voltage.

$u(t)$ is total voltage, $i(t)$ is total current, I_C and I_R are the current value of the capacitor and resistance, θ is power factor angle, and δ is dielectric loss angle.

From Figure 1 (b), we can see that the value of the insulation medium loss factor and the dielectric loss angle are mutually redundant, and knowing the value of the dielectric loss angle δ can immediately obtain the insulation dielectric loss factor, and the insulation performance of the electrical equipment can be estimated.

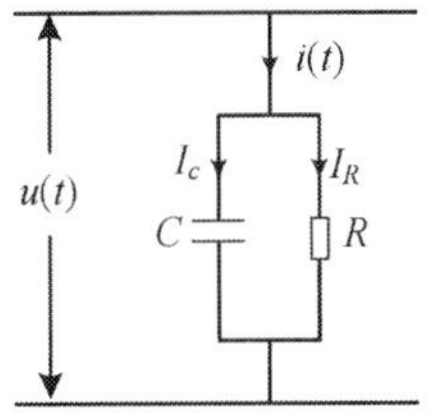

(a) Equivalent circuit diagram

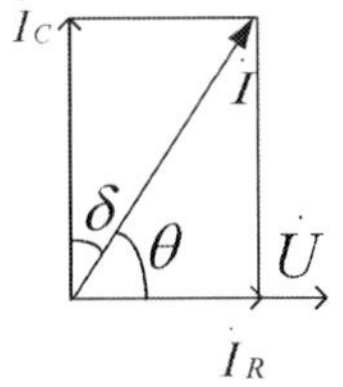

(b) Vector graph

Fig.1 Equivalent circuit and vector diagram of a capacitive device

In Figure 1(a), The total voltage and total current in the circuit are:

$$u(t) = U_m \sin(\omega t + \theta_u) \tag{1}$$

$$i(t) = I_m \sin(\omega t + \theta_i) \tag{2}$$

Loss power of insulating media in an AC environment writing:

$$P = u(t) I_R = \omega C U^2 \tan\delta \tag{3}$$

In the formula, the dielectric loss factor can be expressed as:

$$\tan\delta = \frac{I_R}{I_C} = \frac{1}{\omega C R} \tag{4}$$

w, C, *u* are constants, and the combined formula (3) and formula (4) obtain the loss power *P*:

$$P = K \tan\delta \tag{5}$$

In Equation (5), K is constant.

Equation (5) shows that the dielectric loss power is proportional to the dielectric loss angle, so the insulation damage of the electrical equipment can be obtained directly by measuring the dielectric loss angle. The mediator angle expression is:

$$\delta = \frac{\pi}{2} - \theta = \frac{\pi}{2} - (\theta_i - \theta_u) \tag{6}$$

From equation (6), it can be seen that the magnitude of the dielectric loss angle is equal to the difference between the primary phase angle of the fundamental voltage and the current.

III. The New Nuttall-Blackman-Harris Cosine Combinatorial Window Function

A. Blackman-Harris window function

The Blackman-Harris (BH) window spectrum is simple, its sidelobe characteristics are better than other classical window functions, and the time domain expression is:

$$\omega_{BH}(n) = 0.35875 - 0.48829\cos(\frac{2\pi}{N}n) + 0.14128(\frac{4\pi}{N}n) - 0.01168\cos(\frac{6\pi}{N}n) \tag{7}$$

In the formula, n=0, 1, ..., N-1. TableIis a comparison of the sidelobe performance of several common cosine window functions:

TABLE I
SIDELOBE CHARACTERISTICS OF CLASSICAL WINDOW FUNCTIONS

Window function	Sidelobe peak level /dB	Sidelobe decay rate /(dB/oct)
Hanning	-31.47	18
Hamming	-43.19	6
Blackman	-58.11	18
Blackman-Harris	-92.00	6
Rife-Vincent	-61.00	18

As can be seen from the table, in the classical window function, the largest absolute value of the sidelobe peak level is the Blackman-Harris window, and it is significantly higher than several other window functions, although the progressive decay rate is low, but the gap between several window functions is not very large, on the whole, the Blackman-Harris window sidelobe performance is the best.

B. Nuttall window function

A Nuttall window is a common cosine combinatorial window whose time domain expression is:

$$\omega_N(n) = \sum_{m=0}^{M-1} (-1)^m b_m \cos(\frac{2\pi}{N} nm) \tag{8}$$

In the formula, M represents the number of terms of the window function, n=0, 1, ..., N-1, and N is the length of the window function. Table II are several common Nuttall window function side-flap performances:

TABLE II
SEVERAL COMMON SIDE LOBE PROPERTIES OF NUTTALL WINDOWS

Nuttall window type	Sidelobe peak level /dB	Sidelobe decay rate /(dB/oct)
3 minimal side lobes	-71.49	6
4 minimal side lobes	-98.20	6
4 items 1st order	-93.30	18
4 items 3 order	-82.60	30

From Table 2, it can be seen that the absolute value of the

peak level of the 4 common Nuttall window flaps is not much different, all of which are around -85dB, but the side lobe attenuation rate is quite different, and the sidelobe decay rate of the 4 3rd-order Nuttall windows is about 2 times that of the 4 1st-order Nuttall windows, 5 times that of the 3 smallest sidelobe Nuttall windows and 4 smallest sidelobe Nuttall windows, and in general, the sidelobe performance of the 4 3rd-order Nuttall windows is the best.

C. *Construction of Nuttall-Blackman-Harris windows*

From the above analysis, it can be known that the Blackman-Harris window and the 4th-order 3-term Nuttall window have better sidelobe characteristics than other window functions, combined with the sidelobe performance characteristics of these two windows, the Blackman-Harris window and Nuttall window are combined to construct a new window function of Nuttall-Blackman-Harris (NBH). If the Weight of the Nuttall Window function is β and the Weight of the Blackman-Harris Window is λ, the time domain expression of the New Window function is:

$$\omega_{NBH}(n) = \beta\omega_N(n) + \lambda\omega_{BH}(n) \quad (9)$$

Bringing equations (7) and (8) into equation (9), the time domain expression for the new window function is:

$$\omega_{NBH}(n) = \beta[0.3587 - 0.48829\cos(\frac{4\pi}{N}n) - 0.01168\cos(\frac{6\pi}{N}n)] + \gamma[\sum_{m=0}^{M-1}(-1)^m b_m \cos(\frac{2\pi}{N}nm)] \quad (10)$$

Equation (10) in the sum of β, γ two is 1, the use of MATLAB to find the optimal solution of β and λ in equation (10), after analysis and calculation, it is obtained that when $\beta = \lambda = 0.5$, the sidelobe performance of the cosine combination window is the best, and its time domain expression is:

$$\omega_{NBH}(n) = \sum_{m=0}^{3}(-1)^m b_m \cos(2\pi mn/N) \quad (11)$$

In the formula, b_0=0.3488495, b_1=0.485134, b_2=0.1511505, b_3=0.014866. The conditions $b_0+b_1+b_2+b_3=1$, $b_0-b_1+b_2-b_3=0$ are met, so the new combination window can be named Nuttall-Blackman-Harris cosine combinatorial window. Its amplitude-frequency response curve is shown in Fig.2.

As can be seen from Fig.2, the new combined window function shows good sidelobe characteristics, the peak level of the sidelobe is -104dB, the sidelobe attenuation rate is 48dB/oct, and the sidelobe performance is greatly improved compared with the Blackman-Harris window and the 4th order 3 Nuttall window, so the ability to suppress spectral leakage and fence effect is also stronger, making the calculation accuracy of δ higher.

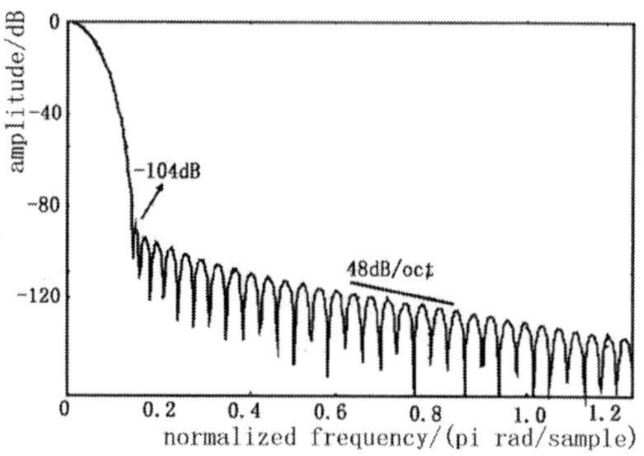

Fig.2 Nuttall-Blackman-Harris cosine combined window frequency response

IV. Method For Measuring Dielectric Loss Angle Based on Phase Difference Correction of New Combined Window

In the study of window functions, many scholars improve the performance of the side lobe by convoluting the window function itself, although the side lobe performance is improved, but the convolution of the window function will increase the amount of computation. In this paper, the spectral line interpolation algorithm is not used, and the mediator loss angle is measured by the more convenient phase difference correction method.

Let a harmonic component in the grid signal be:

$$x(t) = A_m \sin(2\pi f_m t + \varphi_m) \quad (12)$$

In the formula, m is the number of fundamental or harmonics, f_m is fundamental or m-order harmonic frequency, A_m is fundamental or m-order harmonic frequency, θ_m is fundamental or m-order harmonic phase.

Add Nuttall-Blackman-Harris window processing to this signal, with a window length of N, through the Fourier transform is:

$$F(x(t)w(t)) = A_m W(f - f_m)e^{-j[\pi N(f-f_m)-\theta_m]} \quad (13)$$

Sampling the signal $x(t)$ with the sampling frequency f_s results in a sampling discrete sequence of samples:

$$x(n) = A_m \sin(2\pi f_m n / f_s + \varphi_m) \quad (14)$$

The discrete sequence is intercepted to obtain two N-point-long fragments, where the number of points translated between the two fragments is L, and equation (13) is substituted to formula (14), and after the Fourier transform, the discrete spectral fragments can be obtained:

$$X(k_m) = A_m W(\Delta k_m)e^{j\theta_m} \quad (15)$$

In the formula, the difference between the actual frequency of the m_{th}-order harmonic and the frequency of the corresponding spectral line in the spectrum is expressed in

Δk_m,

$$\Delta k_m = k_m - mk_0 \tag{16}$$

In equation (16), k_m is the m_{th} spectral line, k_0 is the spectral line corresponding to the fundamental wave in the spectral line, $k_m=(f_m N)/f_s$. When sampling periodically, $k_1= k_0= f_0$, However, in the actual measurement, it is a non-periodic sampling, so $\Delta k_m \neq 0$, At this point, the frequency corresponding to the m_{th}-order harmonic should be $f_m=mf_0$, The frequency of the k_m root line is $f'_m=(f_s * k_m)/N$, So the frequency error is:

$$\Delta f_m = f_m - f_m' = \Delta k_m f_s / N \tag{17}$$

Suppose the frequency of the k_m-line is f_m, According to Equation (10), the phase angle of the k_m spectral line can be expressed as:

$$\phi_m = \theta_m + \pi \Delta k_m \tag{18}$$

If the discrete spectral fragment of the second fragment is $X'(k_m)$ and the length between the two fragments is L, the phase angle of the k_m spectral line is for the spectrum of the second band:

$$\phi'_m = \phi_m - 2\pi f_m L / f_s N \tag{19}$$

Therefore, the phase difference between two fragments can be expressed as:

$$\Delta\phi = -2\pi f_m L / f_s N \tag{20}$$

By equation (17) and formula (20) can be derived frequency correction amount is:

$$\Delta k_m = -f'_m N / f_s - \Delta\phi N^2 / 2\pi L \tag{21}$$

According to equation (21), the corrected k-order harmonic phase can be obtained:

$$\varphi_m = \arg[X(k_m)] - \arg[W(\frac{2\pi \Delta k_m}{N})] \tag{22}$$

Based on the measurement principle of the dielectric loss angle, the voltage and current initial phases φ_u and φ_i of the fundamental signal can be obtained by equation (22), the value of m is 1, and the value of the voltage current obtained can be substituted to equation (6) to find the value of the dielectric loss angle δ.

V. Simulation Analysis

This article uses the voltage model and simulation circuit of the reference[15], and the dielectric loss angle simulation model is shown in Fig.3, and the voltage signal containing the harmonic current is set to:

$$u(t) = 220[\sin(2\pi f_0 + \pi / 3) + 1.008\% * \sin(2\pi * 3 f_0 + \pi / 4) + 0.611\% * \sin(2\pi * 5 f_0 t + \pi / 6)] \tag{23}$$

In the formula, capacitance value C is 519.02pF, R is 22.67kΩ, f_0 is 50Hz. The true value of the mediator angle δ is 0.004209, In order to verify the reliability of the proposed algorithm, the mediator angle is measured under different conditions, and the relative error of the mediator loss angle measurement of the proposed algorithm and other classical algorithms is compared and analyzed.

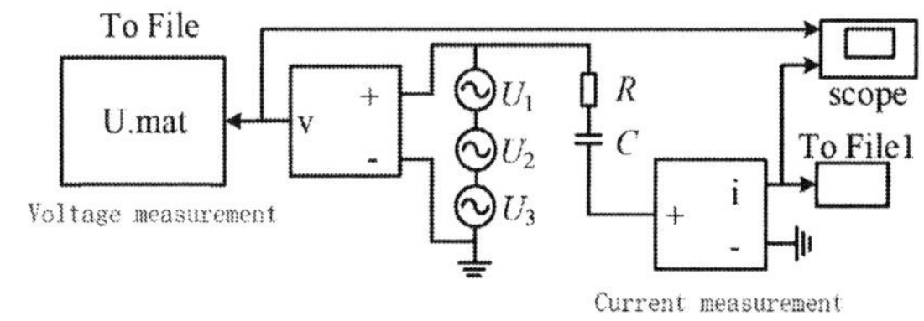

Fig.3 Simulation model of the mediator angle

A. The effect on measurements when the fundamental frequency fluctuates

When the power system is working, the power frequency will fluctuate in a small range, take the fundamental frequency at 49.5-50.5Hz for analysis, and measure the dielectric loss angle based on the 4th order 3 Nuttall window, Blackman-Harris window and Nuttall-Blackman-Harris window phase difference correction algorithm, set the sampling frequency to 3000Hz, the number of sampling points is 512, and the measurement error is shown in Fig.4.

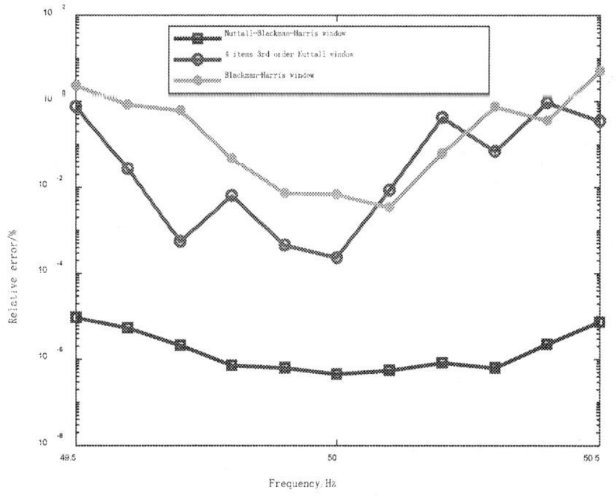

Fig.4 The influence of frequency fluctuations on the measurement results

As can be seen from Fig.2, the new combined window function shows good sidelobe characteristics, the peak level of the sidelobe is -104dB, the sidelobe attenuation rate is 48dB/oct, and the sidelobe performance is greatly improved compared with the Blackman-Harris window and the 4th order 3 Nuttall window, so the ability to suppress spectral leakage and fence effect is also stronger, making the calculation accuracy of δ higher.

B. Harmonic injections vary in time on the effects of measurements

The grid signal will inevitably be accompanied by the generation of harmonics, and in these harmonics, the proportion of the 3rd harmonic is the largest, and the interference is also the largest, so let's analyze the impact of the different proportions of the 3rd harmonic on the measurement, of which the harmonic proportion is increased from 0 to 8%, the fundamental frequency is 50Hz, and the signal is analyzed with phase difference correction based on the 4th order 3-term Nuttall window, Blackman-Harris window and Nuttall-Blackman-Harris window. The relative error of the resulting mediator angle measurement is shown in Fig.5.

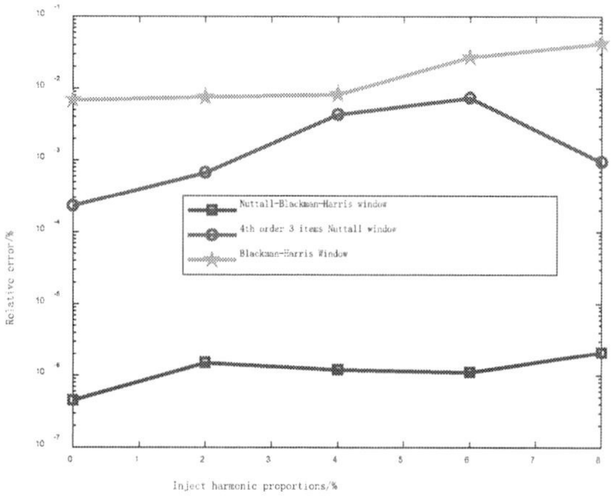

Fig.5 The effect of harmonic injection on the measurement result

It can be seen from the simulation diagram that the measurement errors of the three algorithms are small under the same conditions, but the relative error of the dielectric loss angle measurement of the algorithm in this paper is 3 to 4 orders of magnitude more accurate than that of the 4-term 3rd-order Nuttall window, and 4 to 5 orders of magnitude more accurate than the Blackman-Harris window.

C. The effect of white noise generation on the measurement

There is white noise in the working environment of the power grid, and the generation of white noise is accidental, which will have an impact on the measurement of the dielectric loss angle, and the white noise is added to the signal, the size is 10, 30, 50, 70, 90dB, based on the algorithm proposed in this paper, the dielectric loss angle is measured. Considering the characteristics of white noise, take 100 measurement results and find the average value, and compare the maximum measurement error with the simulation results as shown in Fig.6.

According to Fig.6, it can be seen that the signal-to-noise ratio will lead to a smaller and smaller measurement error of the mediator loss angle, when the signal-to-noise ratio is not higher than 30dB, the relative error of the measurement is larger, when the signal-to-noise ratio is greater than 50dB, the measurement accuracy is in the order of 10^{-9}, the measurement is more accurate, and it can also be seen in the figure that taking the average value when measuring can improve the measurement accuracy very well.

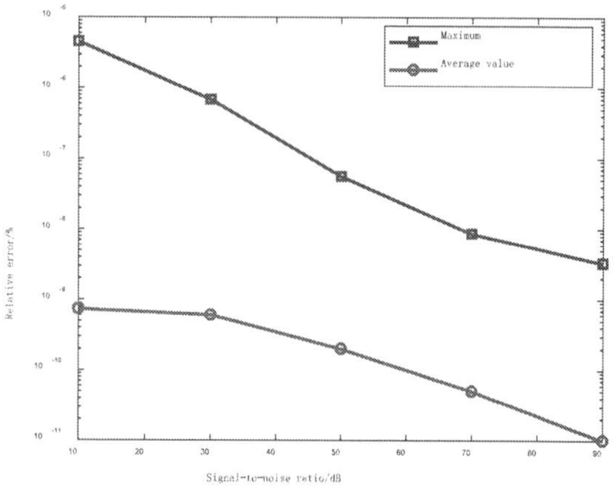

Fig.6 The effect of the signal-to-noise ratio on the measurement

VI. CONCLUSION

The spectral characteristics of Blackman-Harris window and Nuttall window are studied, and a new cosine combined window is constructed, and a new dielectric loss angle measurement algorithm based on the phase difference correction algorithm of the new combined window is derived by using the phase difference correction algorithm. Through simulation experiments, the relative error of the dielectric loss angle is measured under the conditions of fundamental frequency change, injection of different proportional harmonics and signal-to-noise ratio, respectively, and the results show that the stability of the medial loss angle measurement algorithm in this paper is better and the measurement accuracy is high. In this paper, the mediator loss angle algorithm is more accurate and reliable, which provides a good research direction for the detection of insulation performance of electrical equipment.

REFERENCES

[1] Li, J. and Yang., Z. H., "Research on the measurement of the dielectric loss angle of capacitive equipment based on windowed interpolation harmonic analysis method" *Yunnan Electric Power Technology*, vol. 48, no. 02, pp. 38-41, 2020.

[2] Chen, H. Y., Wu, W. X. and Zheng, W. D., "A review of harmonic detection methods for power systems" *Electrical technology*, 2019, 20(09):1-6.

[3] Guo, Z. T., Chi, C. C. and Wu, Y., "FFT harmonic detection algorithm based on Blackman self-multiplication-convolutional window," *Electrical measurement and instrumentation*, 2019, 56(13):16-32.

[4] Yi, F., Liang, J. and Xu, W., "Analysis of field partial discharge anomalies of 500 kV transformers," *Shandong Electric Power Technology*, 2020, 47(08):10-13.

[5] Wang, G. Li, J. F. and Chen, X. D., "An improved interpolation harmonic analysis algorithm based on frequency compensation," *Power system protection and control*, 2018, 46(24): 1-7.

[6] Wang, Y. Tan, J. W. Rui, S. X. and so on, "Study on harmonic characteristics and inhibition of grid-connected wind power generation with high permeability," *Grids and clean energy*, 2018, 34(09): 59-66

[7] Zhang, J. M. Liu, K. P. and Wang, L., "A fast algorithm for harmonic analysis based on quadral line interpolation FFT," *Power system protection and control*, 2017, 45(01): 139-145.

[8] Kuwalek Piotr. The problem of "spectrum leakage" in the measurementof harmonics[J]. *ITM Web of Conferences*, 2019, 28(8):365-368.

[9] Li, Y. Wang, H. Y. and Wang W. Q., "Hybrid convolutional window harmonic analysis method based on Hanning and Nuttall," *Journal of Solar Energy*, 2018, 39(12): 3363-3370.

[10] Xie, Y. Q. Wang, G. and Zeng, D. H., "A cross-band harmonic detection DFT algorithm based on a first-order self-convolutional Kaiser window," *Guangdong Electric Power*, 2021, 34(06): 79-88,.

[11] Wang, Z. and Chen, Z., "Based on the improved Hanning window function, the high-precision and concise algorithm for harmonic detection between power systems is improved," *Journal of Inner Mongolia Normal University*, 2021, 50(06): 559-564.

[12] Liu, T. Zhuang, S. Y. Chen, X. W. and so on., "A new energy metering algorithm based on the three-peak interpolation of the fourth-order Hanning self-multiplicing window FFT," *Electrical measurement and instrumentation*, 2017, 54(21): 1-6.

[13] Zhang, J. and Zheng, J. F. Sparse Representation Based Dielectric Loss Angle Measurement[J]. *The Open Electrical ; Electronic Engineering Journal*, 2015, 9(1).

[14] Ben, S. J. Ge, N. C. and Shen, X. W., "High-precision power harmonic detection based on phase difference correction method," *Electrical measurement and instrumentation*, 2007, (02): 13-15.

[15] Zhang, Q. Wang, H. Y. Wang, W. Q. and so on., "A dielectric loss angle measurement method based on the interpolation of the three spectral lines of mixed convolutional windows," *Power capacitors with reactive power compensation*, 2020, 41(06):125-131

Design of CPS Rotary Electromagnetic Operating Mechanism

Wenwei Yang[1], Longfei Tang[1,2,3]*

[1]College of Electrical Engineering and Automation, Fuzhou University, Fuzhou 350108, China
[2]Fujian Key Laboratory of New Energy Generation and Power Conversion, Fuzhou 350108, China
[3]Fujian Province University Engineering Research Center of Smart Distribution Grid Equipment, Fuzhou, 350108, China
E-mail:tlftel@fzu.edu.cn Tel:13950364569

Abstract—**In this paper, a rotating electromagnetic operating mechanism for control and protection switches (CPS) is designed based on the principle of magnetic circuit "reluctance minimization". The forward and reverse rotation of the moving core of the operating mechanism is used to realize the opening and closing operation of the contact system. The operating mechanism can adjust the excitation state of the opening and closing coil in a closed loop during the operation, and then adjust the opening and closing speed. When switching on or off the normal load current, it can reduce the contact bounce in the closing process, reduce the mechanical impact in the opening process, and has a higher electrical and mechanical life; When breaking the overload and short circuit current, the reverse electromagnetic force can be applied quickly to cut off the fault current together with the counterforce of the spring. It has both control and protection functions and is designed as a double breakpoint structure. When holding, only the spring is used to provide holding force to maintain the closing state, and there is no need to install locking device. The overall parts are few, the structure is simple, and there is no holding power consumption. A finite element simulation model was established in COMSOL for calculation, and MATLAB and Simulink were used to co-simulate the dynamic process of the mechanism under current closed-loop control. The simulation results show that the model is feasible.**

Index Terms— **rotary electromagnetic mechanism, double breakpoint, control and protection switch, Finite element simulation**

I. INTRODUCTION

Compared with the early traditional electromagnetic operating mechanism, the CPS operating mechanism can better improve the continuous operation performance and work reliability of the control and protection system and can complete the task of line control and fault cutting [1-3]. There are many reports on the design of new operating mechanisms. In reference [4], based on the coaxial double circular coil model with parallel arrangement, the basic analytical formula for calculating electromagnetic thrust is derived. A new electromagnetic thrust mechanism and its dynamic analysis method are given. The repulsive mechanism and permanent magnet mechanism were compared and analyzed experimentally in literature [5], and the differences in performance parameters of the two mechanisms were obtained. The results show that the repulsive mechanism has its own advantages in starting time, initial acceleration and overall average velocity, and the experimental results can provide certain guidance for the design of high-voltage switch operating mechanism. Literature [6] proposes a new type of magnetic mechanism, which adopts the principle that the charged coil is forced in the magnetic field generated by the permanent magnet to carry out the long stroke drive and adopts the auxiliary permanent magnet to hold.

The rapid development of operating mechanism has higher and higher requirements on simulation technology [7]. In literature [8], Maxwell software was used to establish a static simulation model of permanent magnet operating mechanism to explore the optimal structure, parameters and energy efficiency of contactor. Literature [9] puts forward a coupling simulation method that can complete the integration solution of electromagnetic variables and mechanical variables.

In this paper, a new type of rotating CPS electromagnetic operating mechanism is proposed, and its working principles in control and protection states are analyzed in detail. Then, the finite element modeling analysis of this mechanism is carried out, and the performance of the mechanism under current closed-loop control is simulated by COMSOL and Simulink co-simulation, and the feasibility of the design is verified.

II. THE WORK PRINCIPLE

The designed rotating electromagnetic mechanism model

This work was supported by the Natural Science Foundation of Fujian Province under Grant 2021J01634.

is similar to the structural principle of switched reluctance motor. The principle of rotating CPS operating mechanism is as follows: The structural diagram of the mechanism is shown in figure 1. In the picture, the contact is in the open state and the spring is not in the central axis position, so it can provide a tangential spring tension. The spring tension F_l can be decomposed into two forces, a radial force F_n and a tangential force $F_t=F_l*\sin\theta$. When the moving iron core rotates counterclockwise, F_t will drive it to rotate. However, influenced by the limit of the guide rail, the dynamic and static contact can be reliably maintained in the open state.

When the moving contacts and static contacts are in the closing state, the closing coil is energized at this time. When the current flows through the closing coil, the moving core teeth and the static core teeth corresponding to the closing coil are not aligned, which will lead to serious distortion of the magnetic field, resulting in an electromagnetic torque force showing reluctance property, whose direction is the direction that the moving core teeth corresponding to the closing coil are aligned with the static core teeth.

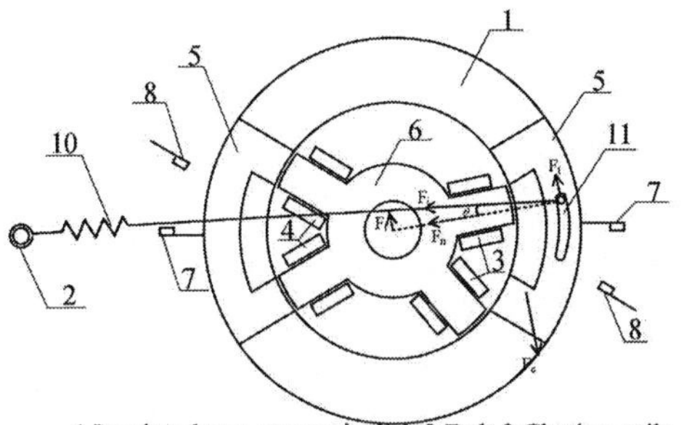

1.Insulated non-magnetic disk 2.Bolt 3.Closing coils 4. Breaking coil 5.Dynamic core 6.Static iron core 7.Moving contact 8.Fixed contact 10.Tension spring 11.Guide rail

Fig. 1. Schematic diagram of the structure of the electromagnetic operating mechanism

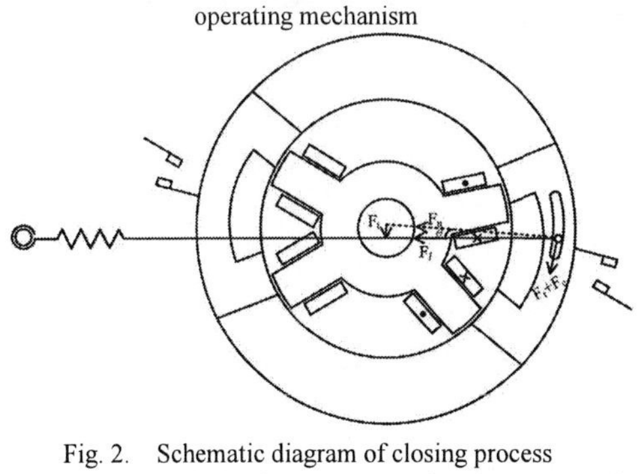

Fig. 2. Schematic diagram of closing process

When the tangential electromagnetic force F_c rises to greater than the holding force F_t, the moving core is activated and moves clockwise to the central axis of the static core tooth. In the process of rotation, when the spring does not cross the central axis, θ Angle will be smaller and smaller, tangential force F_t is smaller and smaller, that is, the rotation process by the resistance is decreasing, the moving core is accelerating; When tension spring over the Angle of rotation axis Angle of θ began to increase, tangential force F_t began to increase. At this time, F_t and F_c are in the same direction, and they work together to rotate the moving core until it coincides with the central axis of the static core, reaching the position of "tooth relative to tooth". At this time, the contact is just closed reliably, and the movement stroke is just reached the maximum value defined by the arc guide of the frame, and the whole closing process is completed.

As shown in figure 3, When the closing moving core moves to the position aligned with the static core teeth, the closing process is completed. After that, the closing coil is powered off. The mechanism relies on the spring tension to overcome the contact spring reaction force and keep the contact stably closed. Combined with the closed-loop control scheme, the excitation state of the closing coil can be flexibly adjusted in the closing process, or the opening coil can be flexibly guided to generate electromagnetic force in the opposite direction, so as to control the synthetic vector electromagnetic force of the mechanism, so as to accurately control the closing speed and improve the closing performance of the switch.

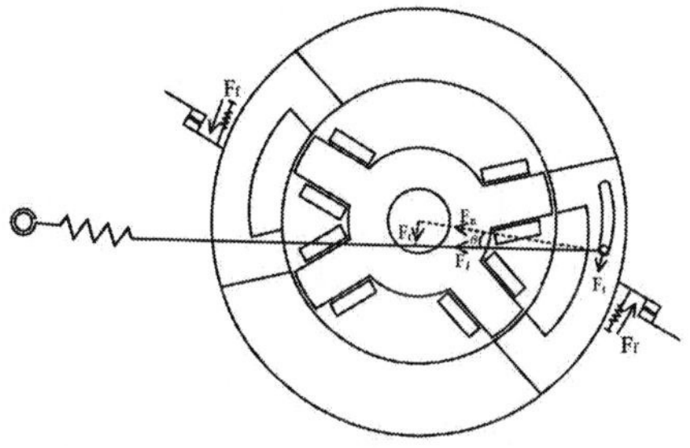

Fig. 3. Schematic diagram of closing state

If you want to break fault current: just energize the breaking coil, make the operating mechanism move quickly so as to cut off the fault current as soon as possible. The specific process is similar to that when only the closing coil is energized in the closing process, which will not be repeated here. To perform normal breaking operations, you can flexibly adjust coil excitation state through the closed loop control scheme, or flexible conduction closing coil to generate the opposite direction of the electromagnetic force, and control the vector electromagnetic force, thus to accurate control of brake speed, reduce the break force, improve the mechanical life of operating mechanism.

III. FINITE ELEMENT MODEL ESTABLISHMENT

A. model building

In order to verify the feasibility of the rotating CPS operating mechanism, COMSOL was used to carry out the finite element simulation calculation of electro-magnetic-force coupling.

According to experience and rough estimation, the structure parameters of the operating mechanism are set, the moving core radius is set as 100mm, the static core radius is set as 65mm. In order to give consideration to the solution accuracy and computational efficiency, the chamfering and rounding of the structure are ignored, and the magnetic field distribution of the vertical and Z-axis sections is considered to be the same, so the model is simplified into two dimensions to achieve the purpose of simplifying the calculation. The overall structure of the operating mechanism is preliminarily conceived, and the model of CPS operating mechanism is established in COMSOL geometry to form the assembly drawing. In order to improve the convergence and accuracy of model calculation, the model is divided into triangular mesh by pre-processing, and the mesh of narrow air gap between stator and stator cores is encrypted.

According to the above, a two-dimensional finite element simulation model of the operating mechanism is established. The figure before and after the specific mesh generation is shown in figure 4.

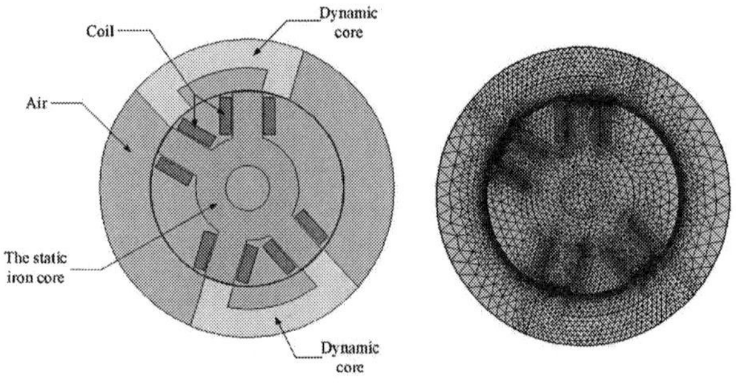

Fig. 4. Simulation model of the mechanism before and after mesh generation

The material parameters of each part of the operating mechanism are set in the software. The electromagnetic characteristics and mechanical output characteristics of the operating mechanism are related to its structure and material parameters. The relevant parameters adopted in this paper are given as shown in Table 1.

TABLE 1
STRUCTURE AND MATERIAL PARAMETERS OF EACH PART OF THE OPERATING MECHANISM

The number of turns of the split coil	1000
Resistance of split-gate coil (Ω)	23.5
Moving core stroke (°)	17
Moment of inertia (J)	0.01
Core material	DW360-50

The rotating electromagnetic mechanism moves under the action of torque. According to the basic principle of mechanics, the mechanical equation of the moving core at any position within the limit range can be obtained:

$$J\frac{d\omega}{dt} = T_{\mathrm{j}} - T_{\mathrm{L}} - F\omega \quad (1)$$

Where, J is the moment of inertia of the moving core, ω is the rotor angular velocity, T_{j} is the electromagnetic torque, T_{L} is the load torque, and F is the damping coefficient.

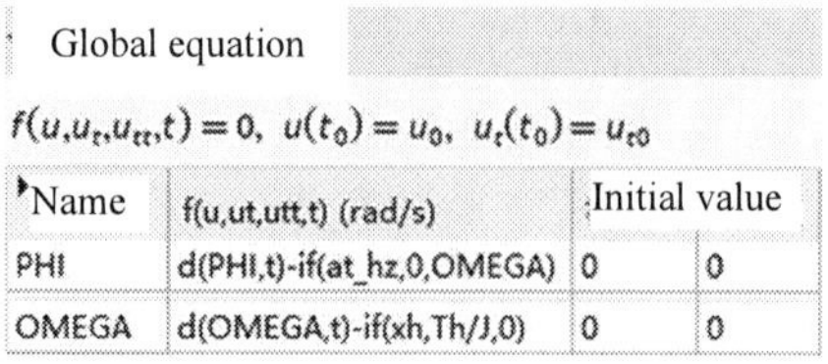

Fig. 5. Setup of equation of motion

The calculation of load torque is determined by the working state of the spring. The specific calculation method is as follows:

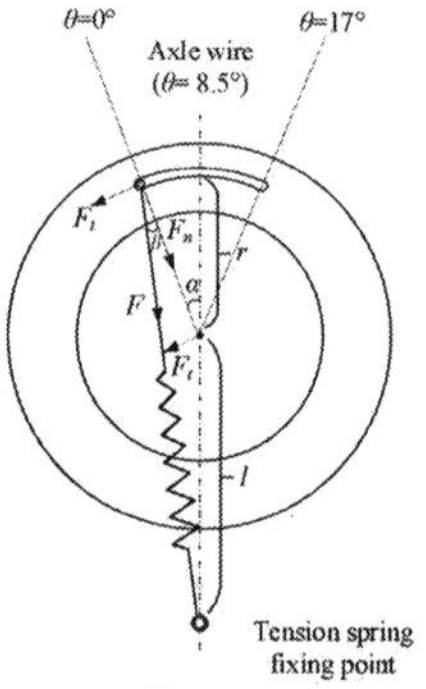

Fig. 6. Torque diagram of tension spring

As shown in figure 6, one end of the spring is fixed on the guide rail to rotate with the core, and the other end is fixed on a fixed point to keep it stationary. The full rotation Angle is set as 17°. When the rotation Angle of the moving core is 8.5°, the tension spring coincides with the central axis and does not produce tangential torque. When the rotation Angle of the moving core is not 8.5°, the spring deviated α° from the central axis, and the tension force F of the spring will be decomposed into the tangential force Ft. At this time, the torque Tt of the spring can be expressed as:

$$T_t = F_t \cdot r \cdot \sin\beta = \frac{rk\left(\sqrt{(r\cos\alpha + l)^2 + (r\sin\alpha)^2} - l_0\right) l \sin\alpha}{\sqrt{(r\cos\alpha + l)^2 + (r\sin\alpha)^2}} \quad (2)$$

Where: r is the distance from the center of the rotating shaft to the guide rail; L is the distance from the center of the rotating shaft to the fixed point of the tension spring; k is the stiffness coefficient of tension spring; L_0 is the initial length of the tension spring.

According to equation (2), set the counter torque of the mechanism to simulate the spring operation. At this point, the model is completed, and steady state and transient calculations are carried out based on the above model construction.

B. Simulation results and analysis

By steady-state solution of the model, the magnetic field strength, flux density and other electromagnetic parameters of the moving core at different positions can be obtained. figure 7 and figure 8 show the distribution of magnetic dense cloud and magnetic force lines when the moving core is in the breaking position, the middle position and the closing position (the rotation angles of the moving core are 0°, 8.5° and 17°, respectively) when the closing coil and the breaking coil are energized alone.

It can be seen from the figure that when the relative positions of static and static cores are different, the influence of the variation of air-gap reluctance on the magnetic field distribution inside the operating mechanism is as follows: when the moving core teeth are not aligned with the static core teeth, the air-gap reluctance is large, the magnetic force lines are dispersed and seriously distorted, and a considerable part of the magnetic force lines flow from the yoke of the static and static core, resulting in more magnetic leakage and smaller average magnetic induction intensity of the core. As rotation, moving core relative tooth movement core area is increasing, the air gap magnetic resistance decreasing, When the moving core and the static core corresponding to the energized coil are exactly aligned with the teeth, the air-gap reluctance reaches the minimum, and most of the magnetic force lines flow along the dynamic and static core, forming a closed loop. In this case, the magnetic leakage is small, the average magnetic induction intensity of the core is the maximum.

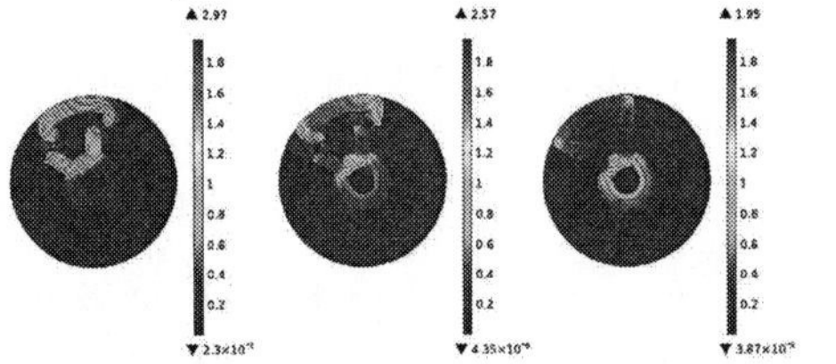

Fig. 7. Distribution of magnetic field lines in the breaking state

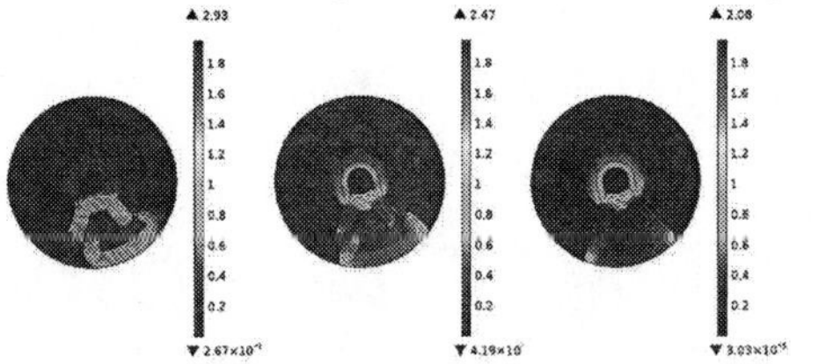

Fig. 8. Distribution of magnetic field lines in closing state

The two-dimensional diagrams of axial torque, reaction force, angular displacement, coil current and time of the mechanism are also obtained through simulation, as shown in figure 9 and figure 10.

When the current of the switching coil is fixed as 5A, the angular displacement of the moving core gradually increases with time from time t_0, and it moves to the central axis position at time t_1 and completes the distance at time t_2. The axial torque basically decreases with the increase of the core angular displacement. The reaction torque decreases with the increase of the angular displacement of the core. At time t_1, the reaction torque decreases to 0 at the position of the central axis. After crossing the central axis, the reaction torque reverses, and its value increases with the increase of the angular displacement of the moving core, until the limit reaction torque is fixed at time t_2, and the switching state is maintained.

Similar to the opening process, when the closing coil current is fixed as 5A, the moving core starts to move at time t_0 and completes closing at time t_2.

IV. Co-simulation Setup

Based on the finite element model, a co-simulation model was established by using COMSOL Controls toolbox and MATLAB Simulink simulation module to simulate the dynamic characteristics of the mechanism under the control strategy. The data exchange process between them is shown in figure 11.

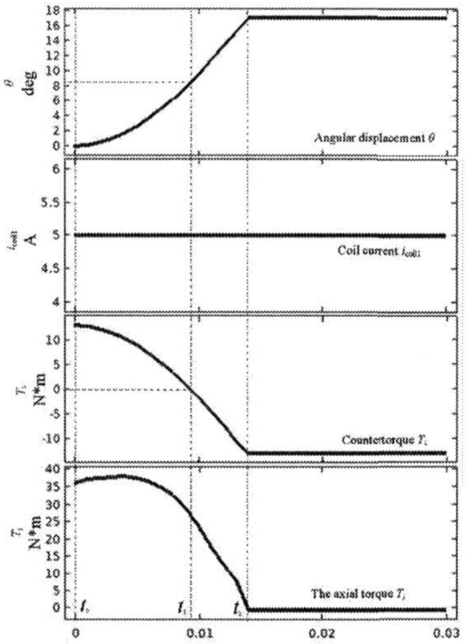

Fig. 9. Curve of each parameter of the sluicing process

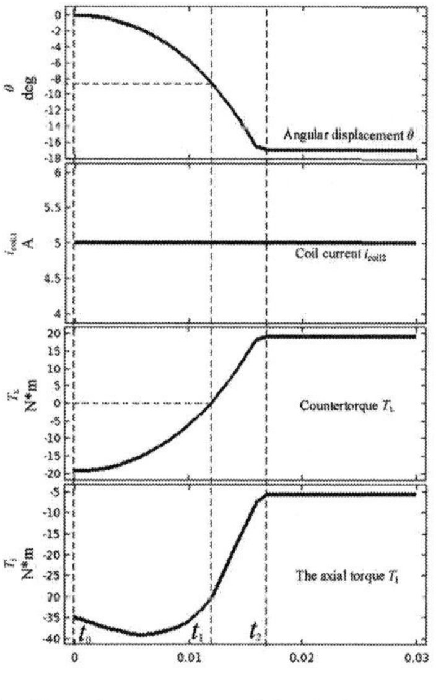

Fig. 10. The parameters of the closing process

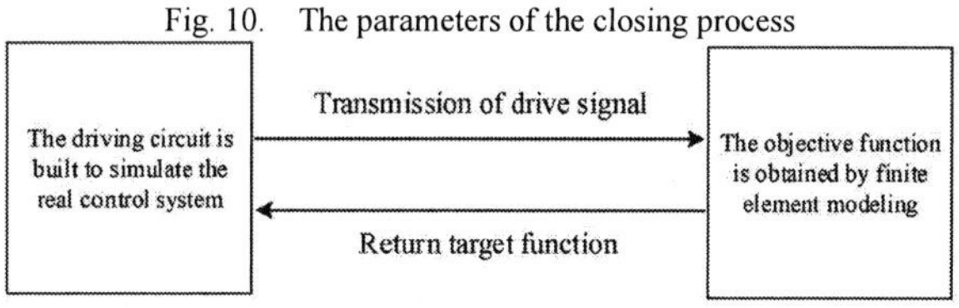

Fig. 11. Schematic diagram of co-simulation

The co-simulation model was built in Simulink, and the co-simulation was performed through LiveLink for Simulink. The COMSOL model was integrated into the Simulink block diagram to establish the mechanism ontology. The co-simulation model is shown in figure 12.

The overall principle is as follows: the 220V AC power supply is rectified by the rectifier bridge composed of D_1, D_2, D_3 and D_4, and then transformed into a relatively stable DC voltage U_C by C_1 filtering. The switches S_1 and S_4 and diodes D_5 and D_6 form an asymmetric half-bridge circuit. The closing or breaking coil is equivalent to a resistor in series with the real-time updated inductor. The measured coil voltage is input to the COMSOL model, and the calculated inductor is real-time interactive to the variable inductor in Simulink, and output torque, current and other parameters for easy observation. The current is output to the control module as a feedback parameter, and after comparing with the reference value, the module outputs PWM control switch state. In this way, the overall co-simulation model is built.

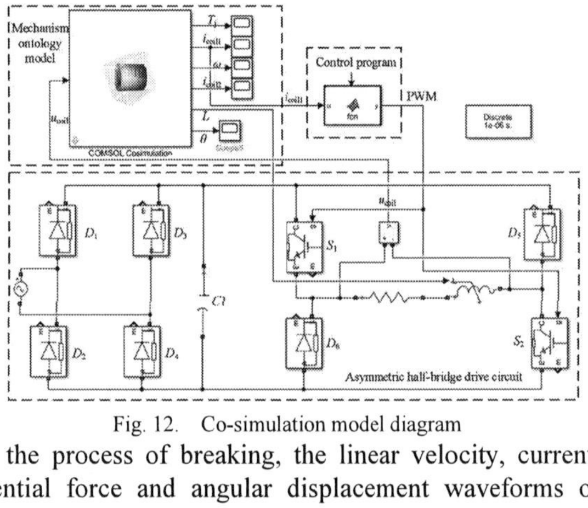

Fig. 12. Co-simulation model diagram

In the process of breaking, the linear velocity, current, tangential force and angular displacement waveforms of moving core of the mechanism under current closed-loop are shown in figure 11.

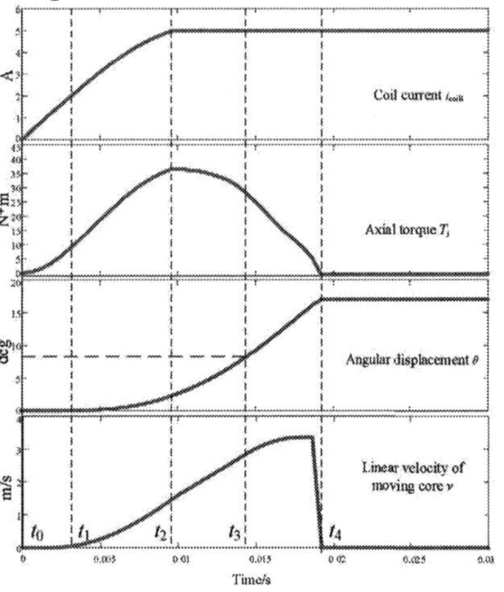

Fig. 13. Parameter curve under current closed-loop

CPS operating mechanism under 5A current closed-loop control parameter graph as shown in figure 13, current start to rise at time t_0; at time t_1, electromagnetic torque is greater than the spring torque agencies began to action; at t_2 , current value after reaching 5A reference value to maintain the value until t_3 moment leaped over central axis, moving core spring torque reverse; at t_4 moment, moving core reach the limit position, The closing process is complete. With the increase of the angle of the moving core, the torque increases first and then decreases. The final velocity of the moving core is 3.4m/s, and the opening process is the same as the closing process. The above simulation analysis results show that the electromagnetic torque of CPS operating mechanism meets the design index, which preliminarily verifies the rationality of the design scheme of CPS operating mechanism

V. Prototype Making and Experiment

A. structure design

The assembly of CPS operating mechanism and the installation of contact are designed according to the proposed principle. The structure diagram of moving parts is shown in figure 14(a), and the explosion diagram of moving parts is shown in figure 14(b). In order to reduce eddy current loss and hysteresis loss, the core material is laminated with silicon steel sheets. The moving core is composed of two symmetrical arc-shaped cores, which move with the non-magnetically conductive and insulated disk, and are fixed between them by bolts. The rotating double-break contact system formed by the core can be directly controlled by the electromagnetic mechanism. A coil group is wound around the static core to provide the electromagnetic force.

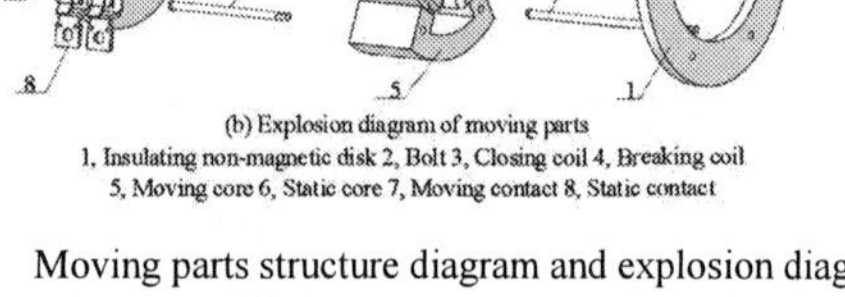

Fig. 14. Moving parts structure diagram and explosion diagram

B. experimental verification

The above simulation has verified the feasibility of the mechanism theory proposed in this paper. The machine is processed according to the engineering drawings drawn and assembled into the initial experimental prototype, as shown in figure 15.

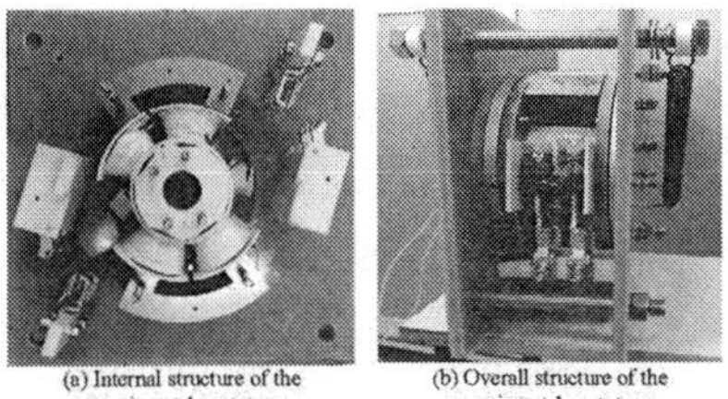

(a) Internal structure of the experimental prototype (b) Overall structure of the experimental prototype

Fig. 15. Structure diagram of experimental prototype

The experimental prototype was connected to the rapid control prototype system[10], and the current closed-loop control operation was carried out in NI cRIO to control the closing, holding and breaking of the experimental prototype in the whole process. The experimental waveform is shown in figure 16.

Starting at time t_0, coil voltage is capacitor voltage $+U_c$, current rises, the moving core starts to act when torque is greater than the reaction torque; The current value of closing coil at t_1 time reaches the reference value 5A; Then the coil voltage is switched between $+U_c$ and $-U_c$ to maintain the current value. At time t_2, the moving core moves to the limit position to complete the closing process. At t_3, the coil voltage is $-U_c$, and the current drops from 5A to 0. The opening process starts from t_4, the process is similar to closing, and ends at t_7.

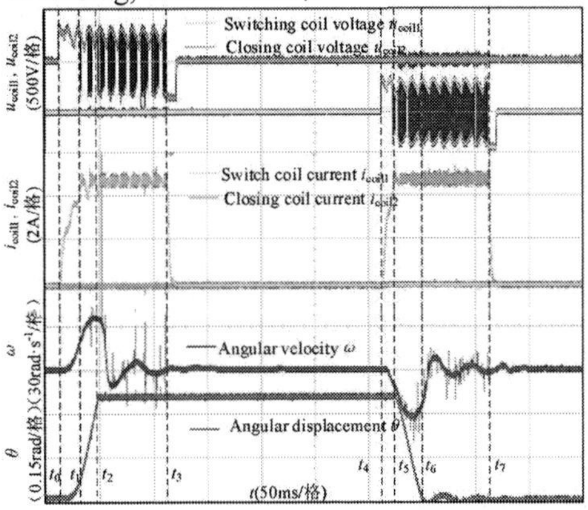

Fig. 16. Waveform of current closed-loop experiment

In the process of closing and breaking, there are some errors between the final velocity and angular displacement curves of the moving core measured by experiment and the simulation results. The reasons are summarized as follows: errors will be introduced in the process of installing tension springs, resulting in differences between simulated and actual mechanical loads; The simulation neglects the influence of friction force and damping coefficient in real motion. However, the trend of the simulated current and the angular displacement waveform of the moving core are basically consistent with the experimental waveform, which verifies the correctness of the simulation model and the practical feasibility of the experimental prototype.

VI. Conclusion

In this paper, a new type of rotating electromagnetic CPS operating mechanism is designed, which has few parts, using spring to provide holding force, simple structure, and has the ability of normal control and quick breaking of fault current. The feasibility of the scheme was verified by the simulation calculation of the designed operating mechanism and the co-simulation model of the operating mechanism was built. The dynamic characteristics of the mechanism under the current closed-loop control were obtained, which provided a platform for the design of the control system. It is of great significance to the design of CPS operating mechanism and the development of energy-saving and miniaturization.

References

[1] Takeda M , Yamamoto H , Hosokawa Y , et al. A low loss solid-state transfer switch using hybrid switch devices[C]// International Power Electronics & Motion Control Conference. IEEE, 2000.

[2] Y. Liu, H. Yuan, D. Chen and H. Yuan, "Experiment and Simulation Research on the Influence of Different Main Contact System on the Interruption Performance of Control and Protective Switch," IEEE Transactions on Power Delivery, 2010，25（3）：1556-1563

[3] M. Izadi, A. Safdarian, M. Moeini-Aghtaie and M. Lehtonen, "Optimal Placement of Protective and Controlling Devices in Electric Power Distribution Systems: A MIP Model," IEEE Access, 2019，7：122827-122837

[4] Li Qingmin, Liu Weidong, Qian Jiali. An Analysis Method of Electromagnetic Thrust Mechanism [J]. Transactions of China Electrotechnical Society, 2004, (02) : 20-24+40.

[5] Dong Enyuan, Li Bo, Zou Jiyan. Comparison and Analysis of Experimental Performance of Ultra-High Speed repulsive Mechanism and permanent magnet Mechanism [J]. High Voltage Apparatus,2007(02):125-126.

[6] Dong Enyuan, Liu Gang, Zou Qitao, Du Guangbo. New magnetic mechanism for long stroke circuit breaker operation [J]. High voltage technology, 2010,36(03):816-820.

[7] G. Bizjak, P. Zunko and D. Povh, "Circuit breaker model for digital simulation based on Mayr's and Cassie's differential arc equations," in IEEE Transactions on Power Delivery, 1995，10(3）:1310-1315

[8] Shu Liang, Xu Chengwen, Wu Guichu, Zhu Xiangou, Zhao Sheng. Research on coupling modeling method for numerical calculation of motion characteristics of electromagnetic operating mechanism [J]. Proceedings of the CSEE, 2015, 35(17):4524-4530.

[9] Wang Kedian, Xu Haibo. Simulation Technology of Virtual Prototype and Its Application in Operating Mechanism of Vacuum Circuit Breaker [J]. High Voltage Electrical Apparatus, 2003(06):1-3.

[10] Zhuang Jierong, Xu Zhihong. Design of contactor

demagnetization control module with energy storage and release mode [J]. Proceedings of the CSEE, 2018, 38(21): 6470-6480+6509.

Wenwei Yang is currently pursuing the M.S. degree in electric engineering from the College of Electrical Engineering and Automation, Fuzhou University, China. His research interests include electric apparatus and its intelligent technology. 1724194053@qq.com.

Longfei Tang (Senior Member, IEEE) received his B.Sc. degree in electrical engineering and automation from Fuzhou University in 2009 and his Ph.D. degree in electric machines and electric apparatus from Fuzhou University in 2015. Now he is a professor at Fuzhou University, China. His research interests include electric apparatus and its intelligent technology. Corresponding author: tlftel@fzu.edu.cn.

Effect of In_2O_3 and SnO_2 on Electrical Contact Properties of AgCuO Materials

Xiaolong Zhou[1], Defeng Cui[2], Yidi Hu[3], Wensong Ten[1], Li Chen[1], Xiaolong Li[1], Zhiguo Li[1]

[1)] Faculty of Materials Science and Engineering, Kunming University of Science and Technology, Kunming, 650093

[2)] Guilin Electric Appliance Research Institute Co. LTD, Guilin, 54104

[3)] College of Optoelectronic Manufacturing, Zhejiang Polytechnic of Industry and Trade, Wenzhou, 325026

Email:kmzxlong@163.com TEL:15087063410

Abstract—**The electrical contact properties of $AgCuOIn_2O_3$, $AgCuOSnO_2$ and $AgCuOIn_2O_3SnO_2$ about multi-component MeO reinforced silver based electrical contact materials are explored. The fusion welding force, contact resistance, material transfer characteristics and mass loss of the three kinds of electrical contact materials are analyzed under the conditions of 18V, 25A and 10000 tests. The results show that $AgCuO(10)In_2O_3(2)SnO_2(1)$ has the best comprehensive performance. In this paper, the $AgCuO(10)In_2O_3(3.5)$ electric contact materials are artificially induced to form fusion welding, and the redistribution law of CuO and In_2O_3 in the Ag molten pool is analyzed. The results show that the CuO density is low and easy to float, and the gas generated by its decomposition causes the material splashing, leading to the largest mass loss of $AgCuOIn_2O_3$. After fusion welding, large MeO particles are not easy to flow with the flow of the melt, which drives the fluidity of the surrounding Ag melt to decrease, resulting in MeO poor zone.**

Keywords—**AgMeO, Electrical Contact Materials, Electrical Contact Properties, Multi-component MeO**

I. INTRODUCTION

Silver metal oxide (AgMeO) is an important electrical contact material. It has the advantages of resistance to fusion welding, resistance to arc burning, and excellent switching operation characteristics. It has become a widely used electrical contact material in low-voltage electrical appliances [1-6]. The application and research in recent years show that single MeO reinforced AgMeO electrical contact material can not completely replace the toxic AgCdO electrical contact material and can not fully meet the market demand. AgMeO electrical contact materials reinforced by multi-element MeO can improve the comprehensive properties of AgMeO, which is the main trend of AgMeO electrical contact materials research at present. The most representative product is $AgSnO_2In_2O_3$ electrical contact materials. By tracking the data of the industry association in the past five years, it is found that the market share of $AgSnO_2In_2O_3$ electrical contact materials in China is increasing year by year [7-8]. The research on multi-element MeO reinforced silver based electrical contact materials formed by adding other MeO to $AgSnO_2$ is also increasing year by year, such as adding $Bi_2Sn_2O_7$ to $AgSnO_2$ to study its interface wettability and physical properties [9]; Bi_2O_3, TiO_2 and CeO_2 were added to $AgSnO_2$ to study its physical properties and electrical contact properties [10]; (CuO, Fe_2O_3) was added to $AgSnO_2$ to study its physical properties [11]. We studied the microstructure and electrical contact properties of $AgSnO_2NiO$ and other multi-element MeO reinforced silver based electrical contact materials [12].

This paper mainly analyzes the electrical contact properties of $AgCuOIn_2O_3$, $AgCuOSnO_2$ and $AgCuOIn_2O_3SnO_2$ synthesized by in-situ reactive, so as to have a deep understanding of the electrical contact properties of multi-element MeO reinforced silver based electrical contact materials.

II. EXPERIMENTAL CONDITIONS

In this paper, $AgCuO(10)In_2O_3(2)$, $AgCuO(10)SnO_2(2)$ and $AgCuO(10)In_2O_3(2)SnO_2(1)$ synthesized by in-situ reaction were used as the research objects. The electrical contact properties of the three materials were analyzed under the conditions of 18V voltage, 25A current and 1mm contact distance.

III. RESULT ANALYSIS

The welding force, contact resistance and mass loss after 10000 times of $AgCuO(10)In_2O_3(2)$, $AgCuO(10)SnO_2(2)$ and $AgCuO(10)In_2O_3(2)$ $SnO_2(1)$ were analyzed.

A. *Welding force analysis*

The magnitude of welding force reflects the index of anti-welding performance of electrical contact materials. The relationship curve between welding force and test times of three kinds of electrical contact materials is shown in Figure 1. It can be seen from Figure 1 that the fusion welding force of AgCuO(10)In_2O_3(2) is mainly in the range of 3.1-9.9cN, and the number of abrupt fusion welding forces is small; The fusion welding force of AgCuO(10)SnO_2(2) is mainly in the range of 5.1-11.4cN, and the number of mutation fusion welding forces is more. The fusion welding force of AgCuO (10) In_2O_3 (2) SnO_2 (1) is mainly in the range of 4.9-11.4cN, and the number of mutation fusion welding forces is similar to that of AgCuO (10) SnO_2 (2).

B. Contact resistance analysis

The smaller the contact resistance, the better the stability, which is the guarantee of the working reliability of the contact element. The relationship between contact resistance and test times of three kinds of electrical contact materials is shown in Figure 2. The interval value, interval difference and average value of contact resistance of three materials are obtained from Figure 2, as shown in Table 1.

Table 1 shows that the contact resistance of AgCuO(10)SnO_2(2) is higher than that of AgCuO(10)In_2O_3(2) at the same MeO content, and the contact resistance increases with the increase of MeO content, which conforms to the general rule. According to the interval value and difference of the three materials, the change range of contact resistance of AgCuO containing SnO_2 is smaller than that of AgCuO containing In_2O_3, and the change range of contact resistance of AgCuO containing SnO_2 and In_2O_3 is in the middle.

C. Quality loss analysis

Figure 3 shows the mass loss of three electrical contact materials after 10000 contact tests at 18V and 25A.

It can be seen from Figure 3 that the transfer mass of AgCuO anode and cathode materials containing SnO_2 is the largest, and it is mainly transferred from the anode to the cathode; The results show that the transfer mass of AgCuO anode and cathode materials containing In_2O_3 is the second, and mainly from the cathode to the anode; The transfer mass of AgCuO anode and cathode materials containing SnO_2 and In_2O_3 is the smallest. According to the total mass loss after 10000 contact tests, the total mass of AgCuO containing SnO_2 and In_2O_3 has no loss, which is related to the transfer of SnO_2 containing AgCuO materials from anode to cathode and In_2O_3 containing AgCuO materials from cathode to anode.

IV. DISCUSSION

A. Influence of wetting angle on electrical contact performance

AgMeO arc erosion behavior is directly related to the size of the molten pool and the distribution of MeO in the molten pool during the arc process. The size of the molten pool is related to the arc energy and the arc extinguishing characteristics of MeO; The distribution of MeO in the molten pool is closely related to the interface wettability of silver liquid, the viscosity of Ag-MeO system, and the fluidity of MeO. According to Young's equation [13], the relationship between wetting angle and interfacial tension is:

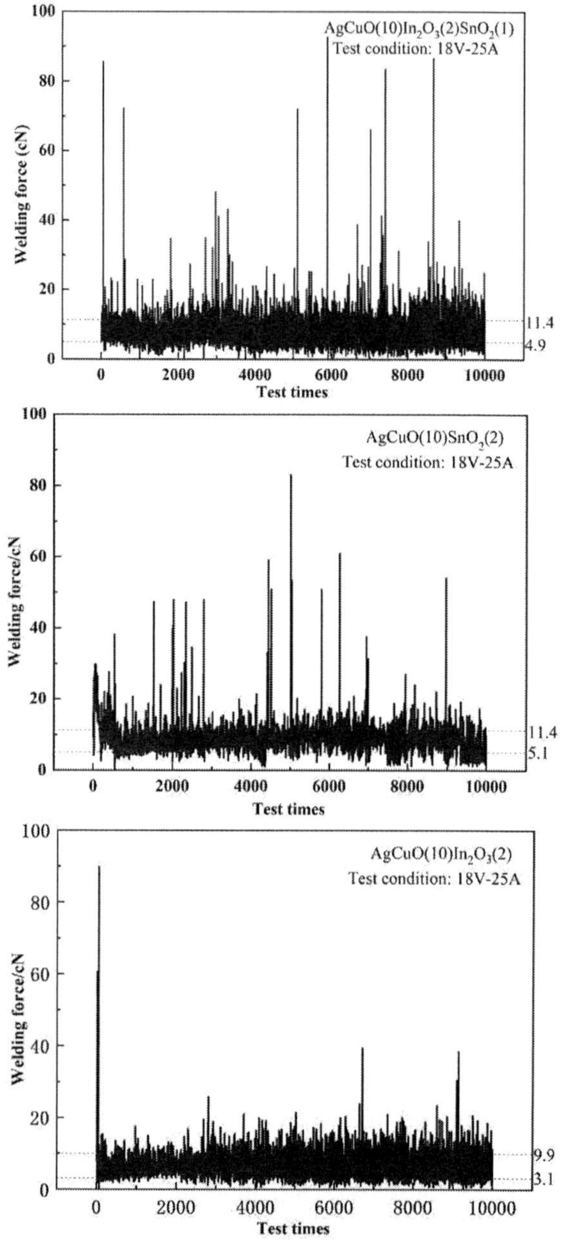

Fig. 1. Relation curve between fusion welding force and test times of three kinds of electrical contact materials

Table 1 Interval value, difference value and average value of contact resistance of three materials (mΩ)

Electrical contact materials	Interval value	Difference	average value
AgCuO(10)In_2O_3(2)	0.13-4.06	3.93	2.07
AgCuO(10)SnO_2(2)	1.15-3.09	1.94	2.12
AgCuO(10)In_2O_3(2)SnO_2(1)	2.24-4.39	2.15	3.32

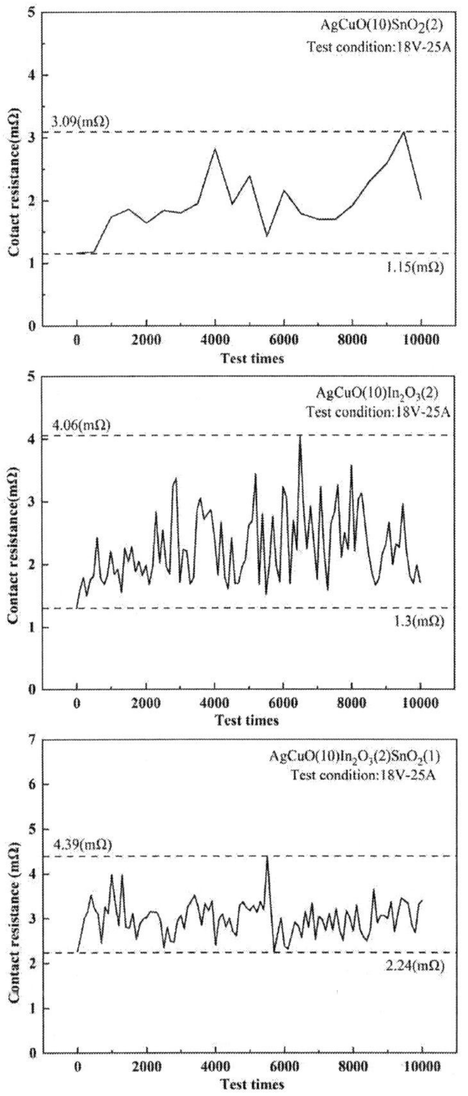

Fig. 2. Relation curve between contact resistance and test times of three kinds of electrical contact materials

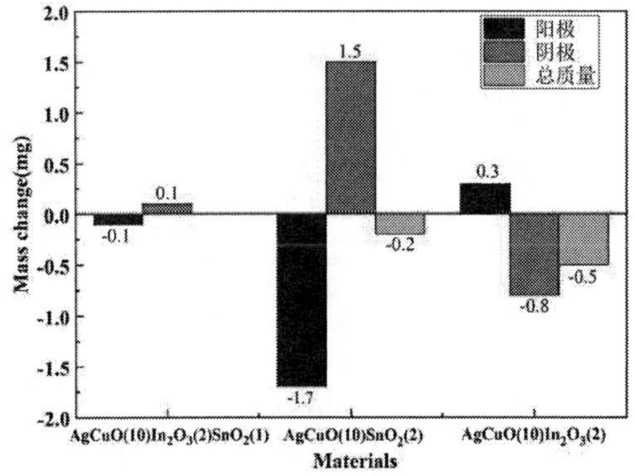

Fig. 3. Mass loss diagram of three electrical contact materials

$$\cos\theta = \frac{\sigma_{SG} - \sigma_{LS}}{\sigma_{GL}}$$

θ is the wetting angle, σ_{ij} is the interface energy between two phases. Obviously, the wetting angle is determined by σ_{SG}, σ_{Ls} and σ_{GL} jointly decides: (1) when $\theta = 0°$, the liquid phase can completely wet the solid surface; (2) When $0° < \theta \leqslant 90°$, the liquid phase can wet the solid surface, and the interface bonding strength is high; When $90° < \theta \leqslant 180°$, the liquid phase cannot wet the solid surface, the interface bonding is weak, and it is easy to generate droplet splashing. Wetting angle θ of MeO and liquid Ag is shown in Table 2 (except In_2O_3).

Table 2 Wetting angle θ of MeO and liquid Ag

Oxide	CdO	In_2O_3	CuO	Cu_2O	SnO_2
Wetting angle	82	-	54	22	90

According to table 2, the wetting angle of MeO is basically $0° < \theta \leqslant 90°$, but the order of wetting angle from small to large is Cu_2O < CuO < CDO < SnO_2, indicating that $AgSnO_2$ is the electrical contact material with the weakest bonding strength between MeO and Ag, which is the main reason for the poor processing performance of $AgSnO_2$. Fig. 4 is the metallographic diagram of the longitudinal section after arc erosion of AgCuO (10) In_2O_3 (3.5). It can be seen from Figure 4 that the microstructure of $AgCuOIn_2O_3$ is the microstructure of wire in the area not eroded by the arc. Both large CuO particles and small In_2O_3 particles are linear along the plastic processing direction. In the area eroded by the arc, the distribution of MeO is no longer linear along the plastic processing direction, the number of CuO per unit area of large particles is significantly reduced, and there are MeO poor areas (such as area a in Figure 4), In_2O_3 rich areas (such as area B in Figure 4) and holes (such as area C in Figure 4). The main reason is that CuO particles will decompose under the action of arc to form fine Cu_2O particles and oxygen. When the molten pool solidifies, the fine Cu_2O is oxidized to fine CuO, resulting in the reduction of large particle CuO per unit area; The decomposed oxygen causes uneven distribution of oxygen partial pressure in the molten pool, and the excess oxygen has no time to overflow during solidification, resulting in holes. In addition, the decomposition of CuO changed the wettability and interfacial adhesion between MeO and Ag matrix, resulting in the redistribution of MeO in the molten pool, forming a MeO poor zone and an In_2O_3 rich zone.

In order to further understand the change of molten pool density after arc erosion, we conducted hardness tests on the arc erosion and non-erosion areas of $AgCuOIn_2O_3$, as shown in Figure 5. The hardness values tested are shown in Table 3.

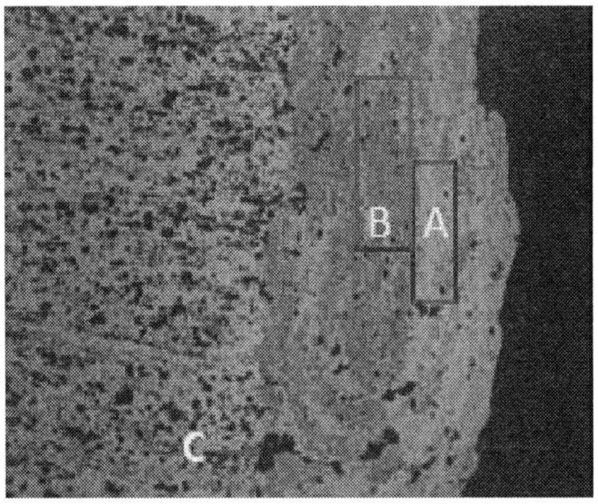

Fig. 4. Metallographic diagram of longitudinal section after arc erosion of AgCuO (10) In_2O_3 (3.5)

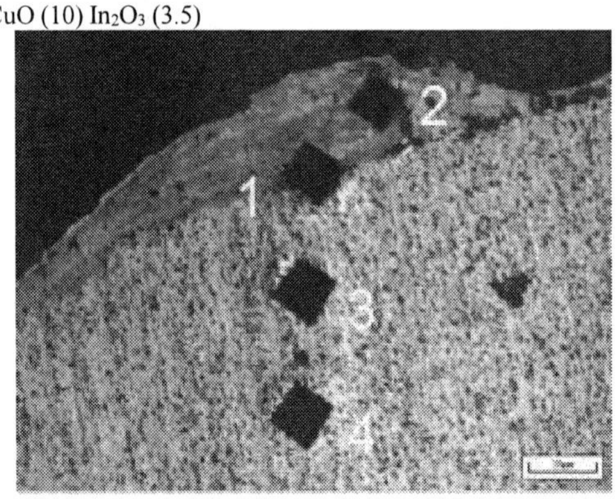

Fig. 5. Metallographic diagram of AgCuO (10) In_2O_3 (3.5) longitudinal section hardness test points

Table 3 Microhardness value on longitudinal section after arc erosion of $AgCuOIn_2O_3$

Serial number	1	2	3	4
HV	302.3	298.1	345.7	345.8

Table 4 Physical performance parameters of MeO

Oxide	CDO	CuO	In_2O_3	SnO_2
Density g/cm3	8.15	6.31	7.18	6.95
Decomposition temperature/℃	1360	1359	700	2373

According to Fig. 5 and table 4, the hardness of the arc erosion zone is the highest, which is the second child of the hardness of the erosion and non-erosion zones, and the hardness of the arc erosion zone is the lowest (position 2). The main reason is that there are pores in the solidification zone of the molten pool (as indicated by C in Fig. 4), which leads to the reduction of density and hardness in this zone.

B. effect of MeO properties on electrical contact performance

For AgMeO electrical contact materials, MeO particles are dispersed in molten silver, which not only has internal friction resistance in liquid, but also has friction between liquid and solid particles. Compared with pure liquid metal system, its viscosity increases significantly, and its flowability becomes worse.

The stability of MeO in high temperature environment is related to the viscosity coefficient and material loss of the whole multivariate system. In molten liquid silver, if the second phase particles do not decompose, they can play a good role in preventing the material from splashing under the action of arc.

Physical performance parameters of MeO tested are shown in Table 3.

It can be seen from table 4 that CuO and CDO are the closest at decomposition temperature, which is the theoretical basis for the arc extinguishing characteristics of AgCuO [14]. The density of CuO and SnO_2 is low, and they are easy to float in the arc molten pool. However, considering the good wettability of CuO and Ag, it can limit the floating of CuO in the molten pool. The wettability of SnO_2 and Ag is poor, and it is easier to float in the molten pool. This is the reason for the high contact resistance of $AgSnO_2$ electrical contact material and the large temperature rise during electrical contact. In addition, although the floating of CuO in the molten pool is limited due to its wettability, the limiting effect is limited after all, and the distribution of CuO on the surface of the molten pool is not low. In addition, the decomposition of CuO under the action of arc will inevitably lead to material splashing, which is the main reason for the mass loss of AgCuO (10) In_2O_3 (2) electrical contact material in the three kinds of electrical contact materials.

C. Redistribution of multiple MeO in molten pool

In order to analyze the influence of the interaction between electricity and magnetism on the redistribution of MeO in the molten pool of $AgCuOIn_2O_3$ electrical contact material during arc erosion, artificially form the contact fusion welding, and analyze the metallography of the longitudinal section of the cathode and anode of the fusion welding point, as shown in Figure 6. It can be seen from Figure 6 that under the condition of arc erosion, the number and size of MeO in the area of fusion welding of $AgCuOIn_2O_3$ electrical contact material are significantly less than that in the area without arc erosion (as shown in area B in Figure 6 (a)), and it is found that CuO is agglomerated and accompanied by large pores (as shown in area a in Figure 6 (a)), which further explains that in the process of arc erosion, On the one hand, the decomposition of CuO particles makes it difficult for the generated oxygen to quickly overflow and generate pores. On the other hand, it shows that the molten $AgCuOIn_2O_3$ electrical contact material formed during fusion welding causes MeO flow due to the stirring force and melt convection effect caused by the arc (as shown in area C in Figure 6 (b)). In addition, from Figure 6 (a), we can also observe that there are CuO particles faintly in the large pores (as indicated by the arrow f in Figure 6 (a)), which is mainly due to the fact that during the convection process of the molten state of $AgCuOIn_2O_3$ electrical contact material, the large particles of CuO are easy to be blocked in some places, forming the agglomeration of CuO. These agglomerated particles are further affected by the arc, The overall temperature of the electrical contact increases, resulting in the decomposition of CuO to form Cu_2O and oxygen, which is wrapped in the melt and cannot overflow, resulting in large bubbles in the melt here. When the melt solidifies, the large bubbles are compressed by the surrounding condensed solids, resulting in a certain oxygen partial pressure in the bubbles, which will re oxidize the Cu_2O existing in the bubbles to form CuO particles, Due to sufficient oxygen and copper, relatively large CuO particles are formed (the CuO particles indicated by arrow F in Figure 6 (a) are significantly larger than those in the area not eroded by the arc); In fact, CuO particles that are much larger than those in the area without arc erosion can also be seen in area D in Figure 6 (b), which is also caused by the above reasons; Moreover, it is also found from Figure 6 that the location where such large bubbles appear is most likely to be concentrated at the junction of the arc erosion zone and the non-erosion zone (as indicated by the arrow f in Figure 6 (a) and as shown by the region g in Figure 6 (b)). This is mainly because at the non-junction, the oxygen decomposed by CuO is easy to overflow from the melt during the convection process of the melt, and there are sufficient CuO particles at the junction, It is easy to decompose under the action of electric arc, resulting in the formation of bubbles. Due to the poor fluidity of the melt, the oxygen decomposed by CuO is not easy to overflow from the melt. It can also be seen from area a in Figure 6 (a) that bubbles and large particles of CuO will converge to the boundary of the molten pool due to the fluid flow in the molten pool. At this time, when the arc acts repeatedly, a large number of CuO will decompose and lead to sputtering, which will promote the Cu_2O spatter formed by the decomposition of CuO in the convergence area, which is also the reason for the largest mass loss of $AgCuO(10)In_2O_3(2)$ among the three electrical contact materials.

According to figure 6 (b), the morphology of MeO arranged along the flow direction of the melt can be observed, as shown in area C in Figure 6 (b). In this area, it is also found that MeO arranged along the flow direction of the melt is mainly fine MeO particles, indicating that fine MeO can be more dispersed in AgMeO melt during arc erosion, This is beneficial to increase the viscosity of the molten pool formed by arc erosion. The increase of viscosity can reduce the spatter of materials in the process of arc erosion, reduce material loss and improve the service life of materials. As shown in Figure 6 (b), in region E, the larger particles of MeO and the silver matrix form a relatively MeO poor region (there are more white Ag rich regions in region E in Figure 6 (b)), which indicates that large particles of MeO are not easy to flow with the flow of molten body in the arc eroded molten pool, The fluidity of the Ag melt around it is reduced (especially the MeO with good wettability with the matrix silver, which can be explained from the fact that the MeO particles in area E in Figure 6 (b) are basically CuO with larger particles), resulting in a MeO poor area.

It can also be seen from Fig. 6 that most of the agglomeration areas of CuO particles are basically distributed at the boundary of the melt (or the surface of the melt) after fusion welding, as shown in area a in Fig. 6 (a) and area D in Fig. 6 (b), which indicates that the MeO of large particles may play an important role in the fusion welding resistance of AgMeO. When there are only fine particles of MeO in AgMeO, it is easy to form convection in the molten pool, It affects the distribution of MeO particles, increases the viscosity of the molten pool, increases the contact force in the contact process, and thus affects the fusion welding resistance of AgMeO.

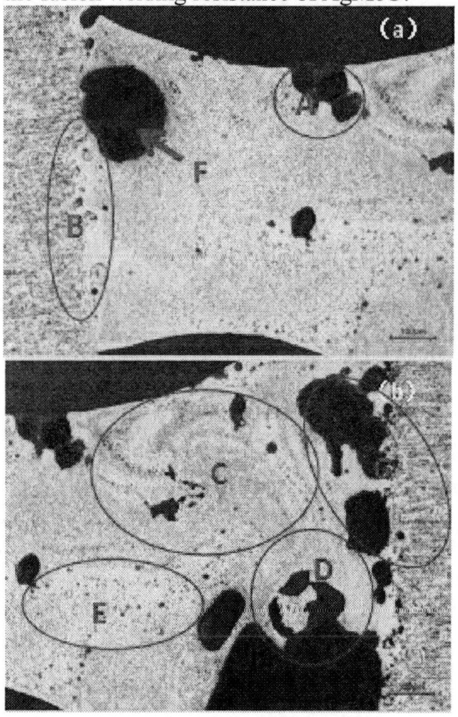

Fig. 6. Metallographic diagram of arc erosion of $AgCuOIn_2O_3$ electrical contact material
(a)Anodic part (b) Cathodic part

V. CONLUSION

In this paper, the electrical contact properties of three kinds of multi-element MeO reinforced silver based electrical contact materials at 18V and 5A were studied

1) The welding force of $AgCuO(10)In_2O_3(2)$ is mainly in the range of 3.1-9.9cN, and the number of abrupt welding forces is less; The fusion welding force of $AgCuO(10)SnO_2(2)$ is mainly in the range of 5.1-11.4cN, and the number of mutation fusion welding forces is more. The fusion welding force of $AgCuO(10)In_2O_3(2)SnO_2(1)$ is mainly in the range of 4.9-11.4cN, and the number of mutation fusion welding forces is similar to that of $AgCuO(10)SnO_2(2)$.

2) At the same MeO content, the contact resistance of $AgCuO(10)SnO_2(2)$ is higher than that of $AgCuO(10)In_2O_3(2)$, and the change range of contact resistance of $AgCuO(10)In_2O_3(2)SnO_2(1)$ is between the two.

3) The transfer mass of AgCuO anode and cathode materials containing SnO_2 is the largest, and it is mainly transferred from anode to cathode; The results show that the transfer mass of AgCuO anode and cathode materials containing In_2O_3 is the second, and mainly from the cathode to the anode; The transfer mass of AgCuO anode and cathode materials containing SnO_2 and In_2O_3 is the smallest, and the mass loss is close to zero.

4) For the $AgCuOIn_2O_3$ electrical contact material, the low density of CuO is easy to float up, and the gas generated by its decomposition increases the spatter of the material, which makes the $AgCuOIn_2O_3$ mass loss of the material the largest; In addition, the existence of large CuO particles reduces the fluidity of the molten pool, resulting in a MeO poor zone.

Acknowledgment

We gratefully thank for the Key Project of Natural Science Foundation of Yunnan Province, China (Grant NO. 2017FA027); Yunnan Province Major Science and Technology Special Plan(NO. 2102AB080008) and National Natural Science Foundation of China (NO.51967008)

REFERENCES

[1] Hangyu Li, Xianhui Wang, Zhudong Hu, et al.. Effect of Ni Addition on The Arc-erosion Behavior of Ag-4wt.%SnO_2 Electrical Contact Material. Journal of Alloys and Compounds, 2020, 829: 154487.

[2] Chengfa Mu1,Tao Shen, Hui Yang,et al.. Investigation of the Microstructure and Electrical Performance of $Ag/SnO_2In_2O_3$ Contacts with Nickel Addition Fabricated by Internal Oxidation .Journal of Electronic Materials, 2022

[3] Hangyu Li, Xianhui Wang, Zhudong Hu, Yanfeng Liu. Investigation of Arc Erosion Mechanism for Tin Dioxide-Reinforced Silver-Based Electrical Contact Material Under Direct Current. Journal of Electronic Materials, 2020, 49(8): 4730-4740

[4] Xu Tao , Chen Xu , Liu Xinyu, et al.Two-Step Sintering Process of AgSnO2 Electric Contact Materials. Rare Metal Materials And Engineering, 2016, 45 (1) : 232-236

[5] WANG Haitao, WEN Panlong, LIANG Lei, et al. Effect of wettability on properties of AgSnO2TiO2 contact material. Electronic Components And Materials, 2016, 35(7): 80-83

[6] SUN Shaoxia , DU Jing, WEI Mingxia, et al. Study on Surface Arc Erosion of AgSnO2 Electrical Contact Materials Prepared by Mechanical Mixing and Coating Method. Precious Metals, 2016, 37 (11): 7-13

[7] Dong Sha.Electrical contact materials industry status and development trend forecast[C]. China Electrical Appliances Industry Association Electrical Alloy Branch Annual Meeting 2018. Foshan Guangdong, 2018

[8] Dong Sha.The latest version of the EU RoHS Directive explained[C]. China Electrical Appliances Industry Association Electrical Alloy Branch Annual Meeting 2019.Jiujang Jiangxi, 2019

[9] Zheng Xiaohua,Wang Chun,Shen Tao,et al. Effect of Bi2Sn2O7 Doping on Interfacial Wettability and Physical Properties of Ag/SnO2 Materials. Rare Metal Materials And Engineering, 2022， 51(2):552-558

[10] Wang Haitao, Wang Lianzheng, Wang Zixiang. Physical and Electrical Contact Properties of Ag-SnO_2 Contact Materials Doped with Different Particle Size Additives. Rare Metal Materials and Engineering. 2019, 48(2):458-462

[11] Zheng Xiaohua , Wu Junchen , Wang Guicong, et al.Physical Properties of Ag/SnO2 Electrical Contacts Materials with Co-doping of CuO and Fe2O3. Rare Metal Materials And Engineering, 2020,49(7):2594-2500

[12] Zhou Xiaolong,Xiong Aihu,Liu Manmen,et al. Electrical Contact Properties of AgSnO2NiO Electrical Contact Material. Rare Metal Materials And Engineering, 2019,48(9):2885-2892

[13] M. Isaiev, S. Burian, L. Bulavin, W. Chaze, M. Gradeck, G. Castanet, S. Merabia, P. Keblinski, K. Termentzidis. Gibbs adsorption impact on a nanodroplet shape: modification of young-laplace equation. The Journal of Physical Chemistry B, 2018, 122(12): 3176–3183

[14] TAO Qi-ying,ZHOU Xiao-long,ZHOU Yun-hong,et al.Electrical contact properties of AgCuO electrical contact materials.The Chinese Journal of Nonferrous Metals, 2015,25（5）:1244-1249

8th International Conference on Reliability of
Electrical Products and Electrical Contacts,
November 18-20, 2022

Investigation of Nuisance Tripping of Residual Current Devices in Low-voltage Power System

Runan Song, Penghe Zhang, Yang Xue, Yining Yang

China Electric Power Research Institute, Beijing, 100192
E-mail: songrunan@epri.sgcc.com.cn Tel: 18526444196

Abstract—**Leakage circuit breakers are widely used in low-voltage distribution systems to prevent personal shock and electrical fire accidents. With the increasing of power electronic equipment, the residual current waveforms in the system are gradually complicated, and the operation characteristics of circuit breakers are required to be higher. In this paper, the frequency conversion speed regulating system is taken as the research object, and the approximate model of complex leakage signal is established to analyze the action characteristics of circuit breaker. The dynamic simulation model of residual current transformer is established by MATLAB/Simulink. It is found that the action characteristics of circuit breaker mainly depend on the leakage fault identification mechanism of detection circuit. By analyzing the working characteristics of ASICS commonly used in residual current devices, it is proposed that the leakage detection method which meets the requirements of B-type leakage action characteristics should be adopted for fault identification.**

Index Terms—**Leakage circuit breaker, compound residual current, variable-frequency speed control system, residual current transformer**

I. Introduction

With the development of smart grid, the nonlinear load using power electronic technology is increasing. According to statistics, the proportion of nonlinear loads in the power grid is over 20% at present, and there are a large number of harmonic components, such as harmonics, interharmonics and subharmonics, in the voltage and current of these nonlinear loads[1-4]. As the residual current generated by nonlinear load becomes complex, the residual current waveform is no longer a pure sine wave, but a complex waveform containing a variety of AC and DC components, or even a smooth DC waveform[5-8]. Nowadays all kinds of power electronic devices have become the largest harmonic source, mainly including all kinds of rectifier devices and frequency control devices. The power electronic equipment with rectifying device mainly produces pulsating DC residual current and smooth DC residual current; In addition to the pulsatile DC and smooth DC residual current, the frequency control device also produces compound residual current related to the motor rotation frequency and PWM carrier frequency, whose frequency range can reach 0~1000Hz, or even higher[9].

When grounding faults occur in the distribution network containing rectifier and switching elements, residual currents with different waveforms will be generated[10]. As in the three-phase grid voltage through the rectifier bridge, bridge inverter control motor system, the leakage failure occurring at different positions of the leakage current waveform are different: the three-phase grid voltage input port leakage fault occurs, because here is symmetrical three-phase sine voltage, therefore when leakage fault waveform shows the characteristics of standard sinusoidal current; When the fault occurs between the rectifier bridge and the inverter bridge, the fault current is mainly pulsating DC current waveform. When leakage fault occurs at the outlet side of the inverter, due to the use of IGBT and other power switching devices, high frequency components including the frequency of switching devices and their frequency doubling components appear in the leakage current, whose frequency can reach tens of kHz.

With the increase of leakage current waveform types, scholars at home and abroad have conducted a lot of research on residual current protection device detection and protection methods of different leakage current waveforms: S. Czapp et al.[11] studied the low-frequency trip characteristics of the residual current device, and the analysis results showed that when the frequency of the residual current was significantly lower than 50Hz, many commonly used residual current devices could not detect the residual current. T. Kudo et al. [12] proposed an AC-DC ground drain current sensor using fluxgate sensor. The fluxgate current sensor with self-excitation system can be used to detect small AC/DC current of 10mA, which provides high sensitivity for wide range current sensing. K. Li et al.[13-14] designed a current sensor consisting only of a magnetic core and winding, which could measure nonlinear currents with arbitrary waveforms and linear currents from DC to thousands of Hertz, and proposed a new fault leakage current detection method with protected dead zone elimination. This method can not only measure the root mean square value of leakage current, but also measure the variation of leakage current.

In summary, scholars at home and abroad have conducted a lot of research on sensor design and detection methods for different leakage current waveforms. At present, the AC type residual current leakage circuit breaker is often used in the distribution network for leakage protection. With the increase of the complexity of the leakage current waveform characteristics when the distribution network is faulty, the AC type residual current leakage circuit breaker often appears the phenomenon of refusal or misoperation.[15] The research of scholars lacks a detailed analysis of the reasons for the refusal or misoperation of AC type residual current leakage circuit breaker. Therefore, through the analysis of leakage characteristics of frequency conversion speed regulation system, this paper proposes to establish an approximate equivalent model of complex leakage signal with compound residual current. By analyzing the action characteristics of compound residual current with different frequency components, it is found that the leakage fault identification mechanism of detection circuit is the main reason that affects the action characteristics of AC leakage circuit breaker.

Under the condition of increasing nonlinear load, the AC type leakage circuit breaker which is widely used in China is prone to leakage rejection. Therefore, it is necessary to study the influence of nonlinear residual current on the operation characteristics of AC type leakage circuit breaker, analyze its failure mechanism and propose solutions.

II. SIMULATION ANALYSIS OF RESIDUAL CURRENT TRANSFORMER

Because the magnetization curve of the actual core is nonlinear, it is difficult to accurately analyze the analytical expression of RCT under the action of pulsating DC residual current. However, Matlab/Similink can be used to establish RCT simulation model for dynamic simulation of the working state of the core. Firstly, according to the measured magnetization curve of the core, the inverse tangent function is used to describe the magnetization characteristics of the core (ignoring hysteresis and eddy current loss), and the magnetization curve equation of the core is obtained as follows:

$$B = 0.31 * \arctan(0.86 * H) \tag{1}$$

RCT dynamic simulation model is established according to the magnetic potential balance relationship of the core, as sh own in Fig. 1. The simulation model mainly includes Residu al Current Module, RCT Module and sampling resistance (). RCT module is the core part of the simulation model. Its inp ut signal is the excitation magnetic potential, and its output s ignal is the inductance voltage of the transformer. The residu al current module can generate various pulsating DC signals, which are used to simulate and analyze the RCT module. Th e pulsating DC signal, induced voltage signal, core magnetic induction intensity B, magnetic field intensity H and perme ability μ were observed simultaneously by oscilloscope.

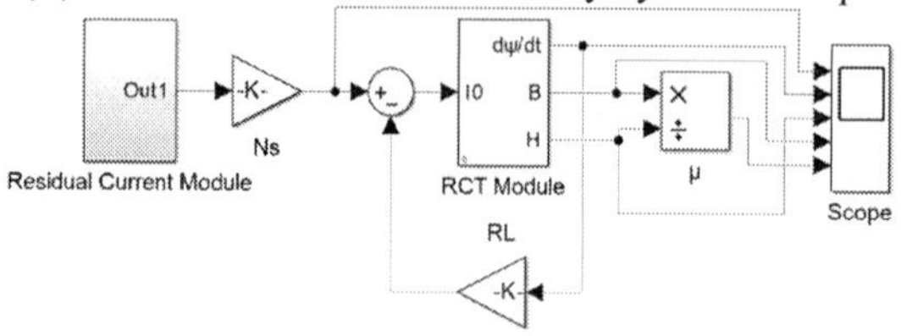

Fig. 1. RCT simulation model.

III. INFLUENCE OF COMPOUND RESIDUAL CURRENT ON OPERATION CHARACTERISTICS OF AC TYPE LEAKAGE CIRCUIT BREAKER

A. Analysis of leakage characteristics of frequency conversion speed regulating system

Frequency conversion speed control system is a combinatio n of motor technology, power electronics technology, micro electronics technology and control technology as one of the advanced automation system, with high efficiency, energy s aving, smooth start, wide speed range and many other advan tages, widely used in various industrial fields. Frequency co nversion speed regulation system is generally composed of f requency converter, control circuit and AC motor, etc. Its ty pical structure is shown in Fig. 2. Frequency converter is the core part of frequency conversion speed regulation system, usually using AC-DC-AC variable current control mode to work, first of all, the input power frequency alternating curre nt through the rectifier circuit into DC, and then through the inverter circuit into frequency modulation voltage alternatin g current drive motor.

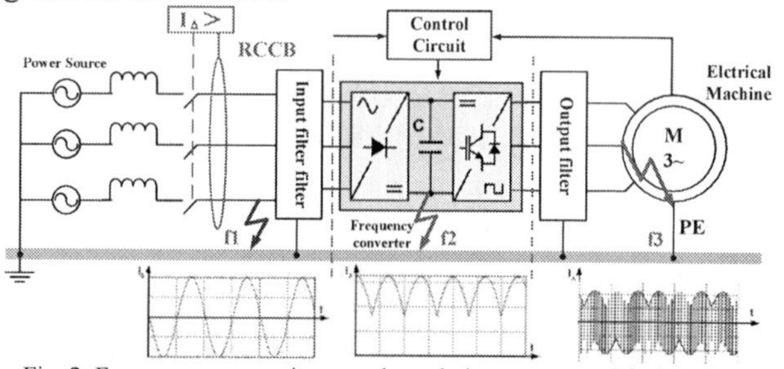

Fig. 2. Frequency conversion speed regulating system and fault leakage current at different positions.

The leakage circuit breaker is usually installed at the power input end of the frequency conversion speed regulation system. Leakage faults may occur at three positions in the frequency conversion speed regulation system, which are located at the power input side of the frequency converter (f1), the internal rectifier link of the frequency converter (f2) and the inverter output side of the frequency converter (f3). Due to the different system voltage waveforms at different positions, the corresponding leakage current waveforms are also different, as shown in Fig. 2. When the leakage fault occurs on the input side of the frequency converter, the leakage current is the power frequency sinusoidal signal.

When leakage fault occurs in the rectifier link of frequency converter due to insulation damage, the leakage current is pulsating DC or smooth DC signal. When leakage fault occurs on the inverter output side, the leakage current is a composite current signal containing the motor rotation frequency and the PWM carrier frequency of the inverter. Considering the influence of high-frequency leakage current caused by common mode filter capacitor and cable distributed capacitor in frequency conversion speed regulation system, the actual fault leakage current waveform is more complex and contains inherent leakage signal with large amplitude.

The influence of compound residual current on the operation characteristics of AC type leakage circuit breaker can be studied by discussing the operation characteristics of AC type leakage circuit breaker when fault leakage occurs at F3 position. Figure 3 shows the leakage current waveform when resistive leakage fault occurs at position F3 of the frequency conversion and speed regulation system in the laboratory. It can be seen that the envelope of the current waveform is related to the rotation frequency of the motor, while the details of the current waveform are related to the carrier frequency of the converter. According to spectrum analysis of current waveform, fault leakage current mainly includes motor rotation frequency component, carrier frequency component and each harmonic of carrier frequency, as shown in Fig. 4.

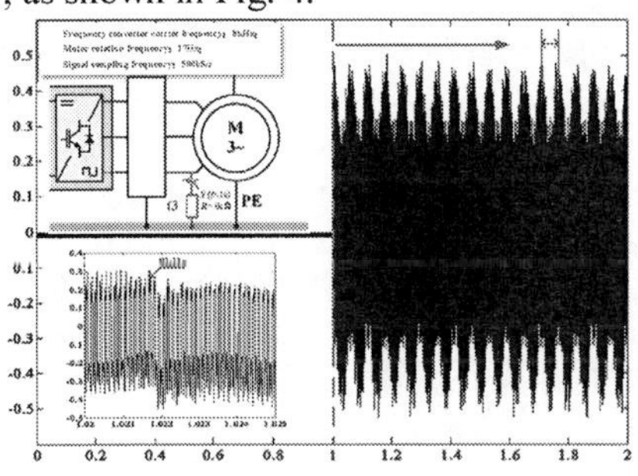

Fig. 3 f3 Location fault leakage current measured waveform

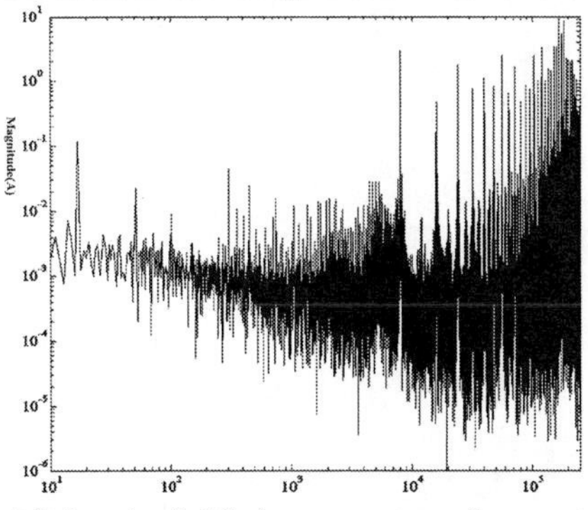

Fig. 4 f3 Location fault leakage current waveform spectrum

Obviously, it is difficult to establish an accurate mathematical model to describe the leakage current of variable frequency speed regulating system. Without considering the common mode filter capacitors and cable caused by distributed capacitance, etc under the condition of high frequency leakage current, you can pick and choose the leakage current of power frequency components, motor rotation frequency and carrier frequency component as its characteristic, according to certain relations to establish this kind of complex leakage signal approximation model, namely compound residual current, so that the motion characteristics of residual current circuit breaker for quantitative evaluation.

B. Analysis of composite residual current characteristics of different frequency components

IEC62423-2009（GB22794）has made detailed provisions on the composite residual current, which is composed of the rated leakage frequency component, 1kHz frequency component and 10Hz frequency component of a certain amplitude. The relationship between each frequency component and rated residual action current is shown in TABLE I. The values of 10Hz and 1kHz represent the motor rotation frequency and frequency converter carrier frequency under the most severe conditions, respectively, and the ratio of different frequency signals in the test remains unchanged.

TABLE I
COMPONENT VALUES AND ACTION LIMITS OF DIFFERENT FREQUENCIES IN THE TEST CURRENT

The values of the components at different frequencies (RMS)			Compound initial current value (RMS)
$I_{Rated\ frequency\ time}$	I_{1kHz}	$I_{F_{electromotor}}$ (10Hz)	I_Δ
0.138 $I_{\Delta n}$	0.138 $I_{\Delta n}$	0.035 $I_{\Delta n}$	0.2 I_Δ
Lower limit of action	0.5 $I_{\Delta n}$	Upper limit of action	1.4 I_Δ

The proportional relation between RMS of different frequency components and RMS of compound residual current is

$$\frac{I_F}{I_C}=\frac{I_F}{\sqrt{I_{10Hz}^2+I_{50Hz}^2+I_{1kHz}^2}} \tag{2}$$

Where, I_F is the effective values of the three frequency components in TABLE I, namely, I_{10Hz}、I_{50Hz} and I_{1kHz} ; I_C is the effective value of the composite residual current, and its initial value is $0.2I_{\Delta n}$.

According to Equation (2.4), I_{10Hz} is 18% of I_C, I_{50Hz} and I_{1kHz} each is 69% of I_C, the sum of I_{50Hz} and I_{1kHz} is 98% of I_C.

Composite residual current signals with different frequency components were used as typical test signals, and the rated residual operating current of the samples was 30mA. According to IEC62423-2009, the leakage action value of five AC type leakage circuit breakers (numbered RCD1-RCD5) from different manufacturers is tested according to the F type leakage circuit breaker test method. The test results are shown in Figure 5. It can be seen that only the action characteristics of RCD5 meet the requirements, and its leakage action value is 33mA. The leakage action value of other samples exceeded 100mA, and the leakage action current of RCD4 even reached 150mA.

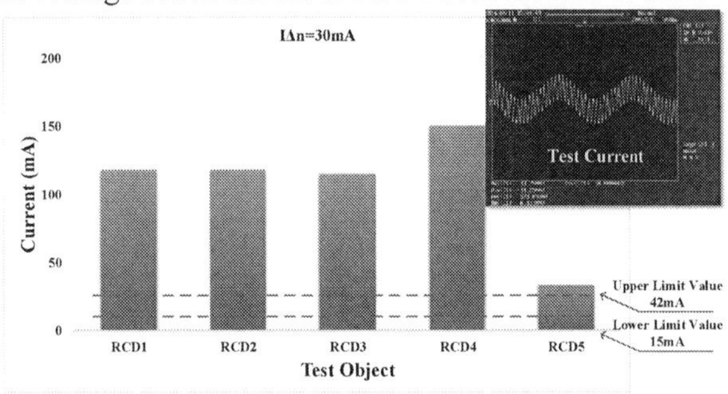

Fig. 5 RCD1~RCD5 action value under compound residual current

The electromagnetic residual current transformer is not sensitive to low-frequency signals, and its lower cut-off frequency is usually about 20Hz. Therefore, the residual current transformer cannot detect the 10Hz component of the composite residual current. However, its 10Hz component accounts for a relatively small proportion, which generally does not affect the normal operation of the residual current transformer, neither saturates the residual current transformer, nor causes large measurement errors.

Since the action value of RCD4 is the largest under the composite residual current, the residual current transformer of RCD4 is selected for detailed analysis. The combined residual current of 50mA and 100mA is used to test the residual current transformer, and the sampling resistance is 100ω. The test results are shown in Fig. 6. It can be seen that in the case of two different composite residual currents, the 10Hz component of the output signal of the residual current transformer is almost zero, and the amplitudes of the 50Hz and 1kHz components are basically the same and very close to the theoretical value (the error is within 5%).

The RMS of the compound residual current in the two cases are 50.5mA and 101mA respectively (the error is within 5%), which is consistent with the theoretical analysis. The results show that the residual current transformer can accurately measure the 50Hz and 1kHz components of the composite residual current. Therefore, the leakage action characteristics of AC leakage circuit breaker under compound residual current mainly depend on the leakage fault identification mechanism of the detection circuit.

IV. Leakage Detection and Analysis Based on ASIC

Common AC leakage circuit breaker detection circuit is divided into discrete component circuit and leakage protection chip circuit two. According to circuit analysis, RCD1~RCD4 uses leakage protection chip (VG54123) circuit, RCD5 uses discrete component circuit.

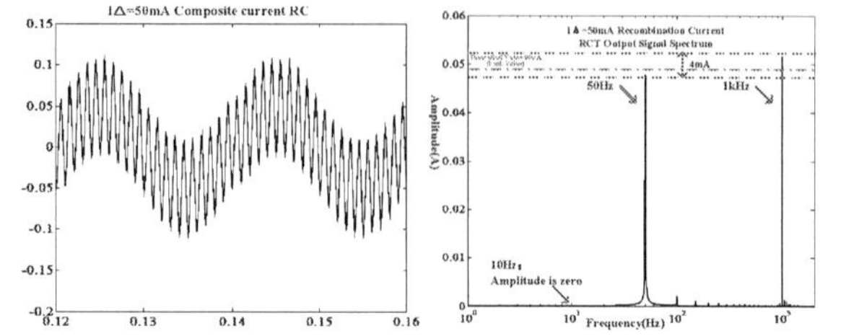

Fig. (a) 50mA Compound residual current

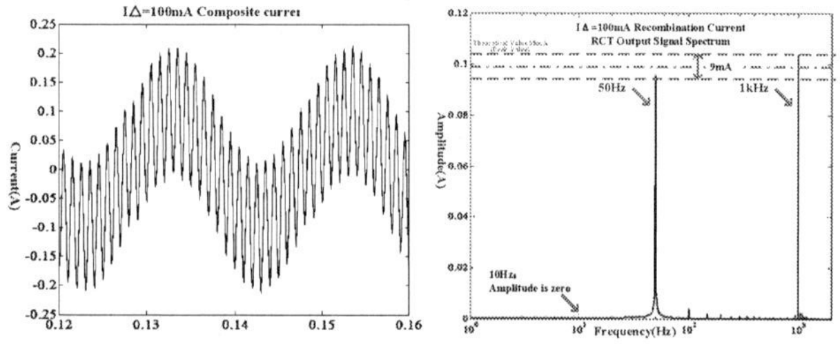

Fig. (b) 100mA Compound residual current

Fig. 6 RCT output characteristics under compound residual current

Discrete component circuit realizes leakage fault identification by comparing the forward half wave signal of leakage current with a set threshold. This paper mainly studies the special chip for leakage protection. Taking M54123 as an example, the principle of leakage protection circuit based on M54123 is shown in Fig 7. The output voltage VT of the secondary circuit of the transformer is input to the input terminal of the integrated circuit (ports 1 and 2), this voltage is compared with the internal reference voltage VREF of the M54123 chip. When VT > VREF, the output potential of the differential amplifier (port 7) becomes high potential immediately. After C4 integration, the trigger driver is opened to make the SCR on and drive the trip. In the leakage signal input link, capacitors C1, C2 and resistors R2 form a high-frequency filtering circuit to prevent high-frequency interference. The circuit has a certain attenuation effect on the 1kHz component of the composite current, the internal schematic diagram of the chip is shown in Fig 8.

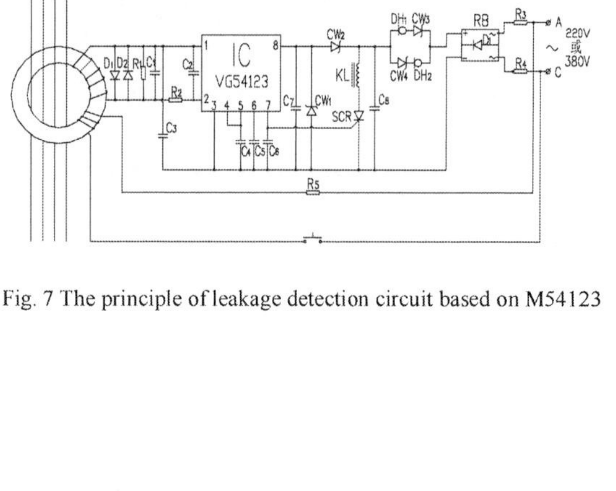

Fig. 7 The principle of leakage detection circuit based on M54123

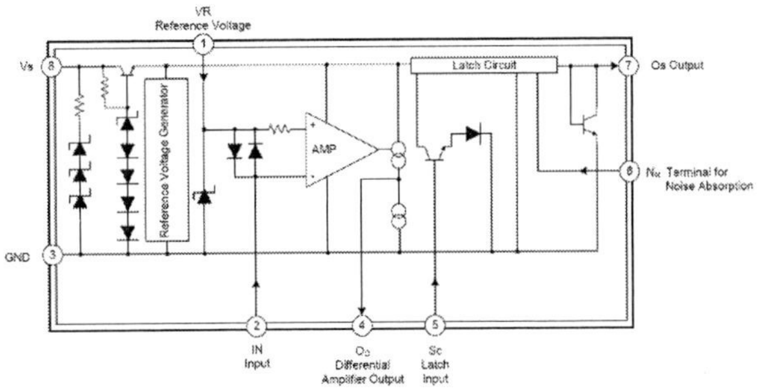

Fig. 8 Schematic diagram of internal circuit of M54123 chip

The leakage fault identification method of the leakage detection circuit based on M54123 is similar to the leakage fault identification method of the discrete component circuit, which is to judge the leakage fault by comparing the leakage current with the set threshold. The difference is that the discrete component circuit does not consider the duration of the leakage current exceeding the threshold value, the leakage current once exceeds the threshold value immediately action, so its anti-interference ability is relatively poor; The leakage detection circuit based on M54123 has a short delay. The time constant τ of the chip and the integrating capacitor C4 is usually about 5ms, which means that the circuit will filter out pulses of short duration.

The RCT output signal under 100mA composite current is analyzed by the leakage comparison threshold of 35mA (corresponding to the effective value of sinusoidal current is 25mA), and the working process of M54123 leakage detection circuit is simulated, as shown in Fig. 9. It can be seen from Fig. 9 that, under the comparison threshold of 35mA, the pulse width of the comparison output is less than 1ms, and the widest pulse is about 0.5ms. Obviously, these pulses will be identified as interference signals by the detection circuit and will not trigger the leakage action. This is the main reason why the M54123 leakage detection circuit can not act correctly on the compound residual current.

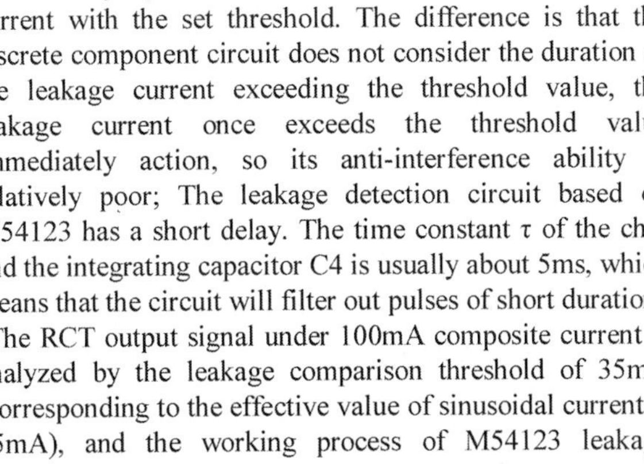

Fig. 9 The threshold value comparison

To sum up, the leakage circuit breaker based on discrete components can operate correctly on the compound residual current, but the discrete component circuit has the problems of large action current dispersion, poor anti-interference ability, and more misactions, and is gradually replaced by leakage protection special chip. The special chip for leakage protection cannot meet the requirement of compound residual current protection in principle. Considering that the leakage current of frequency conversion speed regulation system includes sinusoidal AC, smooth DC and compound current and other waveform signals, it is better to use the leakage detection method to meet the requirements of B-type leakage action characteristics for fault identification.

ACKNOWLEDGMENT

This work is supported by General Science and Technology Project of State Grid Corporation of China-Research on key technologies of customer-side IOT sensing and state monitoring assessment of electricity safety.

REFERENCES

[1] M. J. Maza-Ortega, E. Acha, S. García, and A. Gómez-Expósito, "Overview of power electronics technology and applications in power generation transmission and distribution," J. Mod. Power Syst. Clean Energy, 2017, 5(4): 499–514

[2] G. Lou, Q. Yang, W. Gu, X. Quan, J. M. Guerrero and S. Li, "Analysis and Design of Hybrid Harmonic Suppression Scheme for VSG Considering Nonlinear Loads and Distorted Grid," in IEEE Transactions on Energy Conversion, 2021, 36(4): 3096-3107

[3] Y. Sun, X. Xie, L. Zhang and S. Li, "A Voltage Adaptive Dynamic Harmonic Model of Nonlinear Home Appliances," in IEEE Transactions on Industrial Electronics, 2020,67(5): 3607-3617

[4] E. Oggier, F. Botterón, J. Ochoa Sosa, G. G. Oggier and G. O. García, "Digital Control of a Three-Phase Four-Leg Inverter to Feeds Non-Linear Loads", IEEE Latin America Transactions, 2021, 19(5): 780-789

[5] J. Geng, Y. Liu and L. Jia, "Research of Residual Current Transformer Fault Self-Diagnosis Based on Fractal Theory," 2018 2nd IEEE Conference on Energy Internet and Energy System Integration (EI2), 2018: 1-9.

[6] T. Kudo, S. Kuribara, and Y. Takahashi, "Wide-range AC/DC earth leakage current sensor using fluxgate with self-excitation system," SENSORS, 2011 IEEE, Limerick, Ireland, 2011: 512-515.

[7] Lee, T.M. The effects of harmonics on the operational characteristics of residual-current circuit breakers[C]. Proceedings of EMPD '95, 1995, 2: 548-553.

[8] Xiang Luo; Du, Y.; Wang, X.H.; Chen, M.L.; Tripping characteristics of residual current devices under non-sinusoidal currents[J]. IEEE T IND APPL., 2011, 47(3). 1515-1521

[9] Czapp, Stanislaw. The impact of higher-order harmonics on tripping of residual current devices[C]. 13th International Power Electronics and Motion Control

Conference. Sep.1-3, 2008.Poznan, Poland: 2059-2065.
[10] Czapp, Stanislaw. The effect of earth fault current harmonics on tripping of residual current devices[C]. Proceedings of the International School on Nonsinusoidal Currents and Compensation. June 10-13, Lagow, Poland: 1-6.
[11] S. Czapp, K. Dobrzynski, J. Klucznik and Z. Lubosny, "Low-frequency tripping characteristics of residual current devices," 2017 IEEE International Conference on Environment and Electrical Engineering and 2017 IEEE Industrial and Commercial Power Systems Europe (EEEIC / I&CPS Europe), 2017:1-4.
[12] T. Kudo, S. Kuribara and Y. Takahashi, "Wide-range ac / dc earth leakage current sensor using fluxgate with self-excitation system," SENSORS, 2011 IEEE, 2011: 512-515.
[13] K. Li, F. Niu, Y. Wu, Y. Wang, Y. H. Dai, L. L. Wang, and E. P. Li, "Nonlinear current detection based on magnetic modulation technology," IEEE Trans. Magn., 2015, 51(11): 1-4
[14] K. Li, J. Y. Lin, F. Niu, Y. Wang, Q. Li, Z. T. Guo, and Y. Wu, "A novel fault leakage current detection method with protection dead-zone elimination," IEEE Instrum Meas Mag, 2021,70: 1-9,.
[15] Y. Han. A Novel Multi-Functional Leakage Current Protector IC Design[J]. Chinese Journal Of Semiconductors, 2005(08):1537-1542.

Runan Song received the M.E. degree in electrical and automation from the School of Electrical and Electronics Engineering, Tianjin University, Tianjin, China, in 2020. She is currently an Assistant Engineer with China Electric Power Research Institute. Her research interests include electricity theft detection and measurement instrumentation.

Penghe Zhang received the Ph.D. degree in high voltage and insulation technology from the School of Electrical and Electronic Engineering, Huazhong University of Science and Technology, Wuhan, China, in 2012. She is currently a Professor-Level Senior Engineer with the China Electric Power Research Institute. Her research interests include measurement instrumentation fault diagnosis and electricity theft detection.

Yang Xue received the M.E. degree in in high voltage and insulation from the School of Electrical and Electronics Engineering, North China Electric Power University, Beijing, China, in 2011. He is currently a Senior Engineer with China Electric Power Research Institute. His research interests include measurement instrumentation fault diagnosis and electricity theft detection.

Yining Yang received the B.E. and M.E. degrees in electrical and automation from the School of Electrical and Electronics Engineering, North China Electric Power University, Beijing, China, in 2016 and 2019, respectively. She is currently an Assistant Engineer with China Electric Power Research Institute. Her research interests include electricity theft detection and measurement instrumentation.

8th International Conference on Reliability of Electrical Products and Electrical Contacts, November 18-20, 2022

Convective Heat Transfer Coefficient Calculation and Thermal Performance Simulation of Rectangular Connectors

Xueyan Lin, Yuanpei Zhang

Beijing University of Posts and Telecommunications, Beijing, 100876, China
Email: xylin@bupt.edu.cn Tel:13611123628

Abstract— **According to the dimensional method and the iterative method, this paper calculates the convection heat transfer coefficient of the rectangular connector, compiles the MATLAB program and designs the MATLAB GUI interface for the calculation of the convection heat transfer coefficient. The convection heat transfer coefficient under this condition can be obtained by inputting the current, the number, size and material parameters of the contact pairs, the size of the connector shell and the external ambient temperature on the GUI interface. It provides a fast and accurate convection heat transfer coefficient value for the ANSYS simulation analysis of the thermal performance of rectangular connectors. In this paper, the ANSYS software is used to simulate the thermal performance of rectangular connectors, and the effects of convection heat transfer coefficient, emissivity, connector shell size, current and other parameters on the thermal performance of the connector are analyzed.**

Index Terms—**Rectangular connector, Convective heat transfer coefficient, MATLAB GUI, Thermal simulation.**

I. INTRODUCTION

When the current passes through the contact of the electrical connector, the Joule heat generated by the body resistance of the contact and the contact resistance between the pin and the hole is the main source of the temperature rise of the electrical connector. Inside the connector, heat is transferred to the shell through the heat conduction of the contact and insulator. Outside the connector, heat is dissipated to the atmospheric environment by convection and radiation. When the connector works, if the heat generation and heat dissipation reach the thermal balance, the temperature rise of the connector (the difference between the connector temperature and the ambient temperature) will reach a stable value. If the heat generated is greater than the heat dissipation, the heat balance is destroyed, which will greatly increase the temperature rise of the connector, and even exceed 50°C. High temperature reduces the elasticity of the socket, softens the insulating material or accelerates the process of physical and chemical changes, resulting in poor contact of the contact pair, reduced insulation performance, and even electrical breakdown or short circuit. Therefore, if the temperature rise of the connector is not considered or cannot be accurately predicted, it may lead to serious consequences, especially when the connector is used in harsh environments.

The basic properties of connectors include mechanical properties, electrical properties and environmental properties. The thermal performance of the connector is a common environmental performance. In order to avoid the adverse consequences of excessive high temperature rise and to improve the reliability of the connector design, the temperature rise of the connector must be accurately evaluated to ensure that the connector will not produce thermal performance failure. In the simulation analysis and design of the thermal performance of the connector with ANSYS, a key problem is to obtain the convection heat transfer coefficient. The commonly used method is to use the empirical value of the convection heat transfer coefficient. For example, when the connector works in the atmospheric environment at room temperature, the natural convection heat transfer coefficient of the air is 5 ~ 25 W/(m^2·°C) [1], while the natural convection heat transfer coefficient in the indoor windless environment is about 4 ~ 5 W/(m^2·°C) [2]. In fact, there are many factors affecting the convective heat transfer coefficient of the connector, such as the physical properties of the fluid, the flow rate of the fluid, the shape of the connector, the placement form of the connector, etc. the convective heat transfer coefficient obtained according to the experience is bound to cause great errors in the simulation analysis of the thermal performance. Based on the theory of heat transfer, the convection heat transfer coefficient of the object can be accurately obtained by dimensional analysis and iterative calculation. Wu Shanshan[3] designed a MATLAB program and obtained that the natural convection heat transfer coefficient of air of a certain electric vehicle connector is 12.8 W/(m^2·°C) when the ambient temperature is 25 °C and the rated current is 250A. Cheng Yu and Zhang Juwei [4] used the

ANSYS software to conduct structural thermal analysis, and obtained that the natural convection heat transfer coefficient of the air outside the pipe is between 1~10 W/(m^2·°C), which decreases with the increase of temperature. Chen Meng et al. [5] used the experimental correlation of natural convection heat transfer and the structural steady-state thermal analysis of ANSYS software to carry out iterative calculation through APDL language programming, and also obtained that the natural convection heat transfer coefficient of air is between 1~10 W/(m^2·°C), and the natural convection heat transfer coefficient of water is generally between 200~1000 W/(m^2·°C). The authors [6] obtained that the natural convection heat transfer coefficient of the circular connector with the shell diameter of 20mm, the length of 60mm, the contact conductor radius of 5mm, the material of Cu and horizontal placement in the air at a temperature of 25 °C with a current of 250A is 8.27 W/(m^2·°C).

In this paper, the convection heat transfer coefficient of rectangular connector is calculated according to the dimensional method and iterative method. The software MATLAB is used to compile the program for calculating the convection heat transfer coefficient, and the MATLAB GUI is used to design the interface for calculating the convection heat transfer coefficient of the rectangular connector. The convection heat transfer coefficient under this condition can be obtained by inputting the current, the number, material parameters and dimensions of contacts, the shell size and the external environmental temperature on the GUI interface. This provides a fast and accurate convection heat transfer coefficient value for the ANSYS simulation analysis of the thermal performance of rectangular connectors. In this paper, ANSYS software is used to simulate the thermal performance of the rectangular connector, and the effects of convection heat transfer coefficient, emissivity, connector shell size, current and other parameters on the thermal performance of the connector are analyzed.

II. CALCULATION OF CONVECTIVE HEAT TRANSFER COEFFICIENT BY ITERATIVE METHOD

A. Thermal circuit diagram of the rectangular connector

The shape of the rectangular connector is shown in Figure 1. The length L, width W and height h of the shell are 72mm, 34mm and 15mm respectively, and the material is zinc alloy. There are 8 contacts with a diameter of 0.98mm and made of gold plating on copper substrate inside the connector; An insulator made of PC is filled between the contact and the shell.

Fig.1. The outline drawing of the rectangular connector

The thermal circuit diagram of the rectangular connector is shown in Figure 2. When the current I flows through the contact with resistance R, Joule heat I^{2}R is generated, which increases the conductor temperature to T_c. This heat is transferred to the outer surface of the shell by means of insulator heat conduction with thermal resistance of $R_{\lambda 1}$ and shell heat conduction with thermal resistance of $R_{\lambda 2}$, so that the temperature rises to T_w. Then the heat is transferred to the external environment with temperature T_0 through natural convection heat transfer with thermal resistance R_c and radiation heat transfer with thermal resistance R_r.

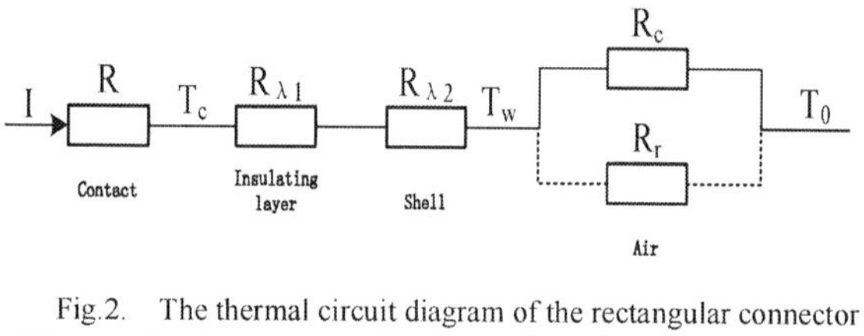

Fig.2. The thermal circuit diagram of the rectangular connector

The radiant heat transfer capacity of the connector is usually far less than the convective heat transfer capacity, so the radiant heat transfer of the connector shell can be ignored. At this time, the heat balance equation is shown in (1):

$$\frac{T_c - T_w}{R_{\lambda 1} + R_{\lambda 2}} = h_c A_c (T_w - T_0) = \mathrm{I}^2 R \qquad (1)$$

In Eq. (1), A_c is the convection heat transfer area of the rectangular connector shell, in which the area of the front and rear vertical plates is *Lh*, the area of the hot face upward plate is *Lw*, and the area of the hot face downward plate is *Lw*, while the left and right vertical plates are energized, so the convection heat transfer is ignored.

B. Calculation of convection heat transfer coefficient of the rectangular connector

The convective heat transfer coefficient h_c is calculated by (2):

$$h_c = \frac{C(Gr \times \mathrm{Pr})_m^n \lambda_f}{\mathrm{D}} = C\frac{\lambda_f}{D}[\frac{\alpha_v g D^3 (T_w - T_0)}{\mu^2} \times \mathrm{Pr}]_{\mathrm{m}}^n \qquad (2)$$

In Eq. (2), h_c is the convective heat transfer coefficient (W/(m^2·K)); λ_f is the thermal conductivity of air (W/(m·K)); D is the characteristic dimension (m) of the rectangular connector, in which the characteristic dimension of the plate with the hot face upward or downward is calculated by (3), and the characteristic dimension of the vertical plate is the height; α_v is the thermal expansion coefficient of air, $\alpha_v=1/T$; g is gravitational acceleration (m/s^2); μ is the kinematic viscosity of air(m^2/s); Pr is the Prandtl number of air; Gr is the Grashov number of air; T_w is the connector shell temperature(°C); T_0 is the the ambient temperature (°C); The lower corner mark m represents the qualitative temperature T, $T=(T_w+T_0)/2$; Coefficient C and superscript n are taken according to the product of Gr and Pr values, as shown in TABLE I.

$$D=\frac{L\times w}{2\times(L+w)} \quad (3)$$

TABLE I
C AND N VALUES OF RECTANGULAR CONNECTORS

	Gr×Pr	flow pattern	C	n
The vertical plates	10^4-10^9	laminar flow	0.59	1/4
	10^9-10^{12}	turbulent flow	0.13	1/3
the hot face upward plate	10^4-10^8	laminar flow	0.54	1/4
	10^8-10^{11}	turbulent flow	0.14	1/3
the hot face downward plate	10^4-10^9	laminar flow	0.27	1/4

There are two parameters to be solved in (2): the convection heat transfer coefficient h_c and the shell temperature T_w, so it can only be calculated by iterative method. It is necessary to set a initial temperature rise $dt=T_w-T_0$, and then calculate the h_c value from the iterative flow chart shown in Fig.3, until the deviation between the temperature rise calculation result and the initial setting value is small enough (set to <0.1), and the iterative calculation is completed.

C. Critical feature size of the rectangular connector

In order to enable the rectangular connector to conduct convective heat transfer, that is, to calculate the convective heat transfer coefficient of the rectangular connector, Gr×Pr value is required to be greater than 10^4.

Under the initial assumed temperature rise *dt*, *hc* is calculated from (2):

$$h_c=C\frac{\lambda_f}{D}[\frac{\alpha_v gD^3dt}{\mu^2}\times\Pr]_m^n \quad (4)$$

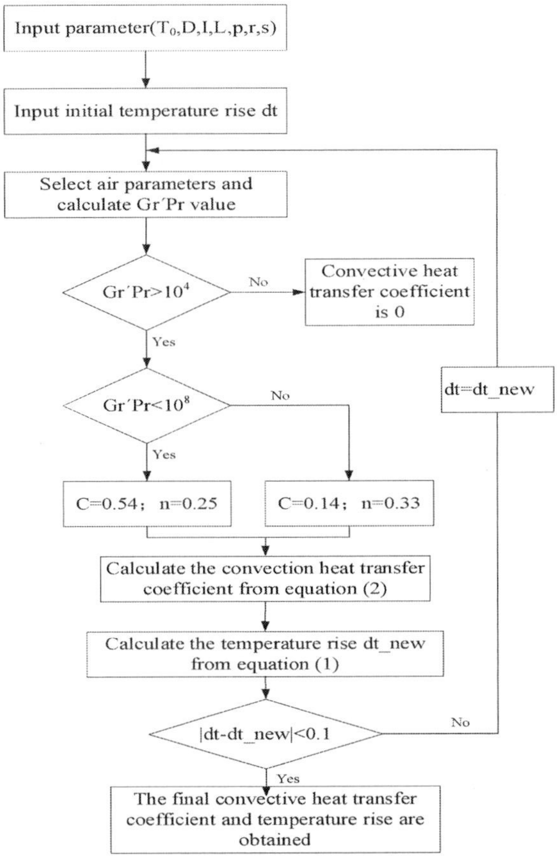

Fig.3. The iterative calculation flow chart of the convection heat transfer coefficient of the rectangular connector

The new temperature rise "dt_ new" is obtained, after (4) is substituted into (1):

$$dt\_new=\frac{I^2R}{h_cA_c}=\frac{\mu^{2n}I^2R}{C\lambda_f\alpha_v^n g^n D^{3n-1}dt^n \Pr^n A_c} \quad (5)$$

The iterative calculation is completed only when $|dt\_new-dt|<0.1$, so at this time, it can be considered that $dt\_new=dt$, and then (6) can be obtained:

$$dt\_new=\sqrt[n+1]{\frac{\mu^{2n}I^2R}{C\lambda_f\alpha_v^n g^n D^{3n-1}\Pr^n A_c}} \quad (6)$$

In order to make *hc*>0, it can be seen from TABLE I that Gr×Pr>10^4, that is:

$$\frac{\alpha_v gD^3dt\_new}{\mu^2}\times\Pr>10^4 \quad (7)$$

Therefore, the minimum value of the feature size shown by (8) is obtained:

$$D>10^{(n+1)}\sqrt[4]{\frac{\mu^2C\lambda_f A_c}{\alpha_v gI^2R\Pr}} \quad (8)$$

III. MATLAB PROGRAMMING AND GUI INTERFACE DESIGNING

In order to simplify the complicated iterative calculation of the convection heat transfer coefficient of the rectangular connectors, this paper develops the MATLAB program and designs the MATLAB GUI interface.

A. Writing the MATLAB functions

In this paper, the following three functions are created to calculate the convection heat transfer coefficient *hc* of the rectangular connector vertical plate, the hot face up plate and the hot face down plate respectively.

[hc]=vertical_slab (T0,I,p,r,s,L,w,h) ;

[hc]= up_slab(T0,I,p,r,s,L,w,h) ;

[hc]= down_slab(T0,I,p,r,s,L,w,h);

The input parameters of these three functions include ambient temperature T_0, current I, contact resistivity ρ, contact radius r, contacts number s, connector shell length L, width w and height h.

B. The MATLAB GUI interface design

Using the MATLAB app function, the Matlab GUI interface for calculating the convection heat transfer coefficient and temperature rise of the rectangular connector is designed, as shown in Fig.4. Input the values of ambient temperature, current, resistivity, contact radius, contact pairs, connector length, connector width, connector height and other parameters in the input parameter box on the left, and then click the "calculate" button to output the convection heat transfer coefficients of the "top", "bottom" and "side" of the rectangular connector in the output parameter box on the right side of the interface.

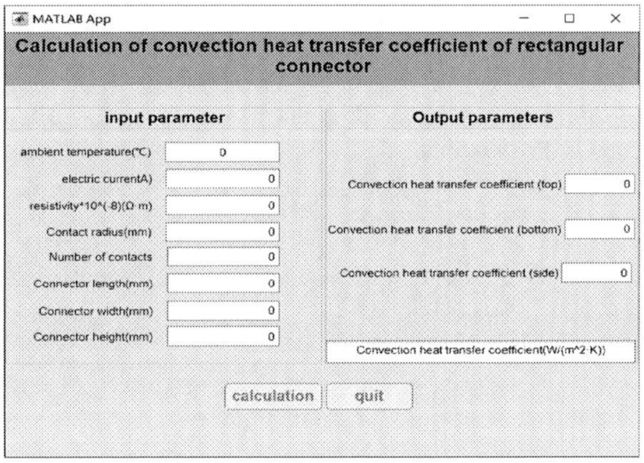

Fig.4. The GUI interface of the convection heat transfer coefficient of the rectangular connector

Input the shell length *L*=72mm, width *w*=34mm and height *h*=15mm of the rectangular connector shown in Fig.1 into the input parameter window of Fig.4. Because it does not meet the requirements of Gr×Pr>10^4, the convection heat transfer coefficient of the output parameter window is zero, which indicates that the heat transferred to the outer shell of the rectangular connector cannot be dissipated into the atmospheric environment through the natural convection heat transfer of air.

C. Effect of rectangular connector placement on convective heat transfer coefficient

Rectangular connectors can be placed in the following three ways in actual use: flat (length L, width W, height h), vertical 1 (length L, width h, height w), vertical 2 (length W, width h, height L). Matlab GUI calculates the convection heat transfer coefficient in these three cases, and the results are shown in TABLE II.

TABLE II

CONVECTIVE HEAT TRANSFER COEFFICIENT OF THE RECTANGULAR CONNECTOR IN THREE PLACEMENT MODES

（L=72mm, w=34mm, h=15mm）

hc (W/(m^2·K))	Flat (length L, width W, height h)	Vertical 1 (length L, width h, height w)	Vertical 2 (length W, width h, height L)
The vertical plates	0	0	0 0
The hot face upward plate	0	0	Not applicable
The hot face downward plate	0	0	Not applicable

It can be seen from table 2 that the convection heat transfer coefficients of the three placement ways of the connector are all zero, which indicates that the shell size of the connector is too small to dissipate heat by convection. The shell size must be appropriately increased to improve the heat dissipation capacity of the connector and reduce the temperature rise.

IV. SIMULATION ANALYSIS OF THERMAL PERFORMANCE OF RECTANGULAR CONNECTORS

A. Steady state thermal simulation process

The steady-state thermal simulation of rectangular connectors by ANSYS uses the electric and steady state thermal simulation modules, as shown in Fig. 5.

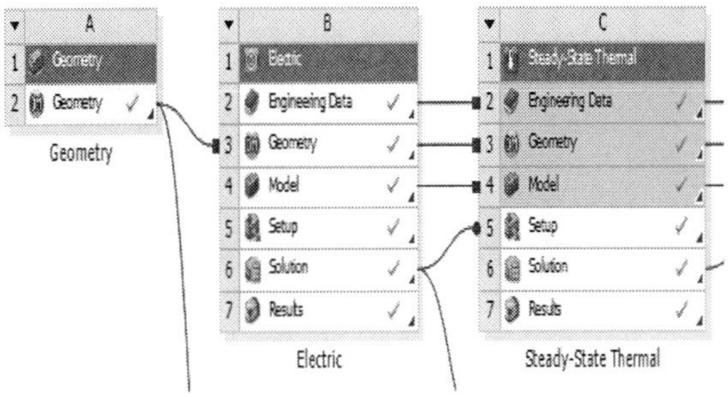

Fig.5. ANSYS steady state thermal simulation process

B. Set material parameters

The material parameters used in the steady-state thermal simulation of the rectangular connector shown in Fig.1 are thermal conductivity and resistivity, as shown in TABLE III.

TABLE III

MATERIAL PARAMETERS OF THE RECTANGULAR CONNECTOR

Name	Material	Thermal conductivityW /(m·K)	Resistivity Ω·m
Contacts	Beryllium bronze	160	8.2×10^{-8}
Insulator (dielectric layer)	PC	0.2	/
Shell	Zn alloy	218	/

C. Set boundary conditions

1) Boundary conditions of the electric module

Set the current of 5A at one end of the contact and the voltage of 0V at the other end to indicate the current flow direction. The current of each contact is 0.625A.

2) Boundary conditions of the steady state thermal module

Set the ambient temperature to 25°C. The connector is energized to generate heat, and the output of the electric module is used as the thermal load input of the current module simulation. The convection heat transfer coefficient calculated by the MATLAB GUI is applied to each outer surface of the rectangular connector shell.

In ANSYS thermal simulation, if the input convection heat transfer coefficient is zero, the thermal simulation cannot be completed. It is necessary to set a small convection heat transfer coefficient, which is first set to 0.1 W/(m^2·K).

D. Simulation results

When the radiation heat transfer of the rectangular connector shell is not considered, that is, when the radiation rate is 0, the steady-state thermal simulation results are shown in Fig. 6 to Fig. 9 respectively.

Fig.6. The temperature distribution cloud diagram of the rectangular connector shell

Fig.7. The temperature distribution cloud diagram of the rectangular connector contact

Fig.8. The temperature distribution cloud diagram of the dielectric layer of the rectangular connector

Fig.9. The temperature distribution cloud diagram of the rectangular connector section

The average temperature of the shell is 32.03 °C, and the average temperature of the contact is 32.54 °C. The internal temperature rise which is equal to the contact temperature minus the shell temperature, is 0.51 °C, and the external temperature rise which is equal to the shell temperature minus the ambient temperature (25 °C) is 7.03 °C.

V. ANALYSIS OF INFLUENCING FACTORS

A. The convective heat transfer coefficient and the emissivity

When the steady-state thermal performance of the rectangular connector shown in Fig.1 is simulated, the convection heat transfer coefficient *hc* (W/(m^2·K)) is set to 0.01, 0.05 and 0.1 respectively, and the emissivity ε is set to 0, 0.2 and 0.5 respectively. The steady-state thermal simulation results of the rectangular connector under the nine heat dissipation boundary conditions are listed in TABLE IV.

TABLE IV
THE TEMPERATURE SIMULATION RESULTS UNDER 9 HEAT DISSIPATION BOUNDARY CONDITIONS

Temperature (°C)	*hc*=0.01 W/(m^2·K)		
	ε=0	ε=0.2	ε=0.5
Contact area	96.43	26.07	25.72
Shell	95.92	25.57	25.22
Internal temperature rise	0.51	0.50	0.50
External temperature rise	70.92	0.57	0.22
Temperature (°C)	*hc*=0.05 W/(m^2·K)		
	ε=0	ε=0.2	ε=0.5
Contact area	39.68	26.05	25.72
Shell	39.17	25.55	25.21
Internal temperature rise	0.51	0.50	0.51
External temperature rise	14.17	0.55	0.21
Temperature (°C)	*hc*=0.1 W/(m^2·K)		
	ε=0	ε=0.2	ε=0.5
Contact area	32.54	26.03	25.72
Shell	32.03	25.53	25.21
Internal temperature rise	0.51	0.50	0.51
External temperature rise	7.03	0.53	0.21

When a current of 5A is applied to the contact of the rectangular connector, the temperature difference between the components of the rectangular connector is about 0.5 °C when the thermal balance is reached.

The external temperature rise of the connector is closely related to the emissivity. When the emissivity is 0, that is, the connector shell cannot radiate heat, the lowest external temperature rise is 7°C and occurs when the convection heat transfer coefficient is 0.1 W/(m^2·K); The highest external temperature rise is 71°C, which occurs when the convection heat transfer coefficient is 0.01 W/(m^2·K). This is not consistent with the actual situation, because the temperature rise of the rectangular connector meets the requirements when the rated current of 5A is applied. If the emissivity is set, that is, the connector shell radiates heat through radiation, the maximum external temperature rise is 0.53 °C ~ 0.57 °C when the emissivity is 0.2, and the minimum external temperature rise is 0.21 °C ~ 0.22 °C when the emissivity is 0.5, which is consistent with the actual working condition of the rectangular connector.

B. The shell size and the current

In order to make the convection heat transfer mode of the connector work, or to calculate the convection heat transfer coefficient of the rectangular connector, it is necessary to increase the contact size, the housing size and the current value of the rectangular connector.

After the shell length of 120mm, the width of 60mm, the height of 20mm, the ambient temperature of 25°C, the current of 250A, the resistivity of 1.77 × 10^{-8} Ω·m, the contact radius of 0.9mm and the contact pairs of 8 pairs are input in the input parameter window of Fig. 4, it can be calculated that the convective heat transfer coefficient of the horizontal plate (hot surface facing upward) of the rectangular connector is 8.44 W/(m^2·K), the convective heat transfer coefficient of the horizontal plate (hot surface facing downward) is 4.8 W/(m^2·K) and the convective heat transfer coefficient of the vertical plate is 11.11 W/(m^2·K).

When radiation heat transfer is not considered, the steady-state thermal simulation result of ANSYS is that the average temperature of the shell is 32.70°C, the average temperature of the contact is 33.12°C, the internal temperature rise is 0.42°C, and the external temperature rise is 7.7°C. The temperature rise is similar to that of small rectangular connector when small current is applied, which indicates that convection heat transfer plays an important role in reducing the temperature rise.

VI. CONCLUSIONS

In this paper, the convection heat transfer coefficient of the rectangular connector is calculated according to the dimension method and the iteration method, the MATLAB program for calculating the convection heat transfer coefficient is compiled, and the MATLAB GUI interface is designed. The convection heat transfer coefficient can be obtained by inputting the current, the number, size and material parameters of the contact, the size of the connector shell and the external environment temperature on the GUI interface. This provides an accurate value of the convection heat transfer coefficient for ANSYS simulation analysis of thermal performance of the rectangular connector. If the convective heat transfer coefficient is obtained 0, it indicates that the connector cannot radiate heat to the atmosphere through convective heat transfer.

In this paper, the convective heat transfer coefficients

of a rectangular connector in three placement modes are calculated. The results are all 0, indicating that the shell size of the connector is too small to dissipate heat through convection. If the convection heat transfer coefficient is set to 0 in ANSYS, the thermal simulation cannot be completed, and a smaller convection heat transfer coefficient needs to be set, such as 0.1 $W/(m^2{\cdot}K)$. In order to reduce the error of thermal simulation analysis results, it is suggested to input the radiation rate of the shell.

In this paper, the thermal performance of the rectangular connector is simulated by ANSYS software, and the influence of convection heat transfer coefficient, radiation rate, connector shell size, current and other parameters on the thermal performance of the connector is analyzed. In order to reduce the temperature rise of the connector, the convective heat dissipation capacity of the connector should be given full play, and it is suggested to appropriately increase the contact size and shell size of the rectangular connector. When the size of the rectangular connector is increased by less than 2 times, but the current carrying capacity is increased by 50 times, the external temperature rise is less than 8°C. The advantage of this design is to increase the current carrying capacity and maintain the lower temperature rise, but the disadvantage is that it cannot meet the needs of miniaturization of the connector.

REFERENCES

[1] L.Y. Yao, "Study on the key influencing factors of power connector design", *Beijing University of Posts and Telecommunications*, 2018.

[2] N. Yang, "Simulation study on temperature rise of power connector", *Electromechanical components*, 2017, 37(05): 32-35.

[3] S.S. Wu, "Study on thermal performance of charging connector for electric vehicle", *Beijing University of Posts and Telecommunications*, 2020.

[4] Y. Cheng, J.W. Zhang, "Determination of natural convection heat transfer coefficient outside pipeline based on ANSYS", *Contemporary chemical industry*, 2015, 44(11): 2720-2722.

[5] M. Chen, "Research on calculation method of natural convection heat transfer coefficient based on ANSYS", *Modern computer (Professional Edition)*, 2016(11): 24-26.

[6] X.Y. Lin, Y.P. Zhang, "Convective heat transfer coefficient of the circular connector", *Electromechanical components*, 2022, 42(3): 19-23.

Xueyan Lin, female, was born in May 1971. In June 1992, she graduated from the Department of mechanical and electronic engineering of Xi'an University of Electronic Science and technology and received a bachelor's degree in electronic equipment structure. In March 1995, she graduated from the department of mechanical and electronic engineering of Beijing University of Posts and telecommunications and got the master's degree of engineering in mechanical design. In July 2009, she received the Ph.D. degree of engineering in circuit and system of Beijing University of Posts and telecommunications.

Xueyan Lin is now an associate professor and master supervisor of the school of artificial intelligence, Beijing University of Posts and telecommunications. She is engaged in the research of electrical connection and connector failure mechanism, reliability detection technology, signal integrity analysis and design, control system design and other fields.

A Displacement Estimation Method for Bi-stable Mechanism with Permanent Magnet Based on NN

Yaole Huang[1], Longfei Tang[1,2,3]*
[1]College of Electrical Engineering and Automation, Fuzhou University, Fuzhou, 350108, China
[2]Fujian Key Laboratory of New Energy Generation and Power Conversion, Fuzhou, 350108, China
[3] Fujian Province University Engineering Research Center of Smart Distribution Grid Equipment, Fuzhou, 350108, China
Email: tlftel@fzu.edu.cn Tel:13950364569

***Abstract*—In this paper, a displacement estimation method for bistable permanent magnet(PM) mechanism of circuit breaker(CB) is proposed, which realizes the breaking and making displacement estimation of actuator through neural network(NN). First, the static characteristic parameters are calculated by finite element simulation according to the corresponding relationship between the displacement, current and flux linkage of the bistable PM mechanism, and we constructed a static data table base on this. Then, we build a NN using parametric linear neuron (PReLU) which rely on static data, and imported with current and flux linkage as input and displacement as expectation. After offline training, we transplant the NN into the co-simulation of the actuator to test the fitting accuracy of the NN. Finally, the NN is compiled into embedded hardware, and the estimation accuracy of the NN is verified in real time through hardware experiments.**

***Keywords*—bi-stable PM mechanism, displacement estimation, neural network**

I. Introduction

The circuit breaker(CB) is an important protective appliance in the power grid, and the reliability and stability of its work depend on the operating mechanism that controls the CB. The bistable permanent magnet(PM) mechanism is one of the actuators for operating the CB. Its electromagnetic start-up and PM holding working mode is conducive to reducing power consumption and intelligent control. In [1], weakening control method is used to improve the action speed of the bistable PM mechanism. Sensorless displacement estimation methods have been extensively studied in the contactor and monostable PM actuators. In [2], fuzzy control is used to estimate the speed of the moving core through the coil voltage and current, and then realizes the sensorless displacement estimation of the contactor; In [3], to correct the displacement of the vacuum CB in real time, fuzzy control is used; In [4], fuzzy control is also used to realize sensorless displacement estimation and fault diagnosis of contactors. With the rapid development of artificial intelligence, neural network(NN) are increasingly used in the control field of actuators [5]. Benefiting from the powerful fitting ability of the neural network, the simulation[6], control[7] and displacement estimation[8-9] of actuators can be realized more accurately. In this paper, we calculate the static characteristic data of the bistable PM mechanism through finite element simulation, build a NN to fit the static data set, and realize the fitting of the electromagnetic coupling relationship under different displacements of the bistable PM mechanism. The NN is compiled into the embedded hardware to realize the displacement estimation of the moving core [10].

This work was supported by the Natural Science Foundation of Fujian Province under Grant 2021J01634.

II. Analysis of Action Process

The breaking and making operation of the bistable PM mechanism is controlled by two coils sharing a magnetic circuit, and the electromagnetic coupling relationship during the operation is very complicated. The magnetic circuit of the actuator is simplified as shown in Figure 1, which includes the ampere turns i_2N_2, i_1N_1 of the breaking and making coil, the equivalent reluctance R_2, R_1 of the breaking and making magnetic circuit, as well as the PM potential and PM resistance F_{pm}, R_{pm}.

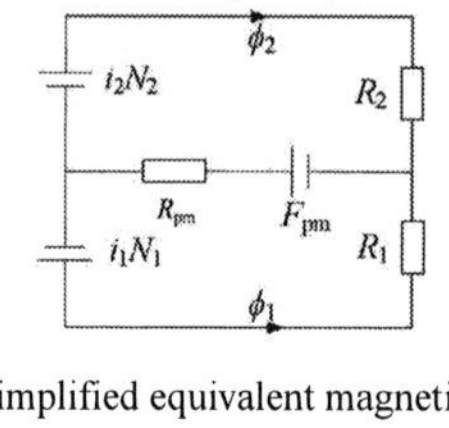

Fig.1. simplified equivalent magnetic circuit

According to Kirchhoff's law of magnetic circuit, there is the following expression:

$$\begin{cases} \psi_1 = N_1\phi_1 = \dfrac{1}{\Delta}[i_1N_1(R_2+R_{pm}) - i_2N_2R_{pm} + F_{pm}R_2] \\ \psi_2 = N_2\phi_2 = \dfrac{1}{\Delta}[i_2N_2(R_1+R_{pm}) - i_1N_1R_{pm} + F_{pm}R_1] \\ \Delta = R_1R_2 + R_1R_{pm} + R_2R_{pm} \end{cases} \tag{1}$$

Among them, ψ_1 and ψ_2 are the making flux linkage and the breaking flux linkage. For the specific derivation process, please refer to the literature [11]. In the analysis, the core reluctance and leakage reluctance are ignored, only R_1, R_2 are considered to be related to the making air gap δ, and there is a relationship::

$$\begin{cases} R_1 = \dfrac{\delta}{\mu_0 S} \\ R_2 = \dfrac{l-\delta}{\mu_0 S} \end{cases} \tag{2}$$

S is the cross-sectional area of the moving core, μ_0 is the air permeability, and $l-\delta$ is the breaking air gap. When the displacement of the moving iron core is fixed, the two air gaps are also fixed, so R_1, R_2, F_{pm}, R_{pm} can be considered as constants.

$$\begin{cases} \dfrac{\partial\psi_1}{\partial i_1} = \dfrac{N_1(R_2+R_{pm})}{\Delta} \\ \dfrac{\partial\psi_2}{\partial i_1} = -\dfrac{N_1R_{pm}}{\Delta} \\ \dfrac{\partial\psi_1}{\partial i_2} = -\dfrac{N_2R_{pm}}{\Delta} \\ \dfrac{\partial\psi_2}{\partial i_2} = \dfrac{N_2(R_1+R_{pm})}{\Delta} \end{cases} \tag{3}$$

According to $\partial\psi_1/\partial i_1>0$ and $\partial\psi_2/\partial i_1<0$ of formula (3), when the displacement of the moving iron core and the opening current are fixed, the closing current is positively correlated with the making flux linkage, and is negative correlated with the breaking flux linkage; when $\partial\psi1/\partial i2<0$ and $\partial\psi2/\partial i2>0$, the relationship between the breaking current and the flux linkage is opposite to the above.

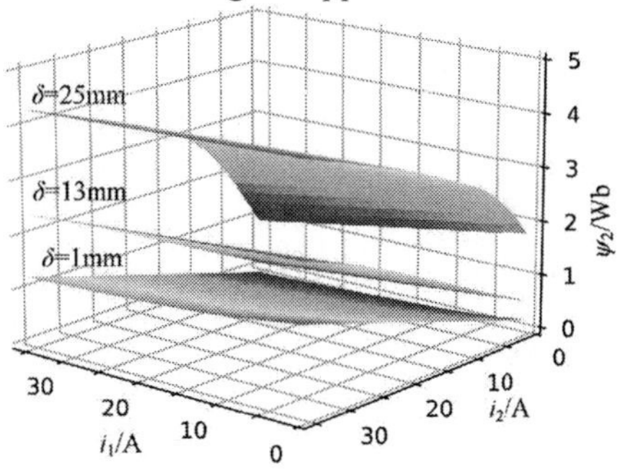

Fig.2. breaking flux linkage under different displacements

The flux linkage of the breaking coil under different displacements is shown in Fig.2. Due to the structural symmetry of the bistable PM mechanism, the finite element simulation of the making flux linkage is consistent with the above results, and under normal operating current, the flux linkage surfaces at different displacements do not intersect. It can be seen that when the currents of the two coils are fixed, the two flux linkages are in one-to-one correspondence with the displacement of the moving core. According to the above analysis, it can be known that in each state of the action of the actuator, the displacement of the moving core and the current of the breaking and making coil are monotonically corresponding to the flux linkage of the breaking and making coil. According to this relationship, the (i_1, i_2, ψ_1, ψ_2)→δ model is constructed by inversion, which provides a theoretical basis for realizing the sensorless displacement estimator of the bistable PM mechanism.

III. CONSTRUCT THE NN MODEL

In order to estimate the displacement of the bistable PM mechanism, a mathematical model based on the static data table is built. In this paper, the BP-like NN is used to estimate the displacement of the moving core. After filtering and preprocessing static data, it will be input to the NN for training.

A. Data Preprocessing

Because the amplitudes of each feature parameter of the static data table are inconsistent, it should to be preprocessed before the NN training starts. The feature parameters are dimensionless by normalization, so that all the data samples have equal weights in the NN. Normalize the data to the [-1, 1] interval, the formula is as follows:

$$x_i^* = 2\cdot\frac{x_i - x_{min}}{x_{max} - x_{min}} - 1 \tag{4}$$

The static data table is divided into two parts: the making process and the breaking process, and the characteristic parameters are screened from the data table with the current during the action of the actuators as the boundary. Therefore, we choose the displacement of the moving core, the current of the breaking and making coils, and the flux linkage as the characteristic parameters, and develope the displacement estimation method of the bistable PM mechanism[12].

B. Building and Training Process of Model

BP NN is composed of input layer, hidden layer and output layer, including two processes of forward and backward propagation. In the first process, the input data is calculated form input layer , hidden layer to output layer, and output the result; Backpropagation uses an iterative algorithm such as gradient descent to reversely update the weights and biases of each layer by calculating the deviation of the result from the expectation. After the static data table is preprocessed, its dimension and total amount are still relatively large. To obtain higher accuracy, we use 3 hidden layers. At the same time, parametric linear neuron (PReLU) is used as the neuron to solve the problem of gradient explosion and dissipation in the training process. The network structure is shown in Fig. 3.

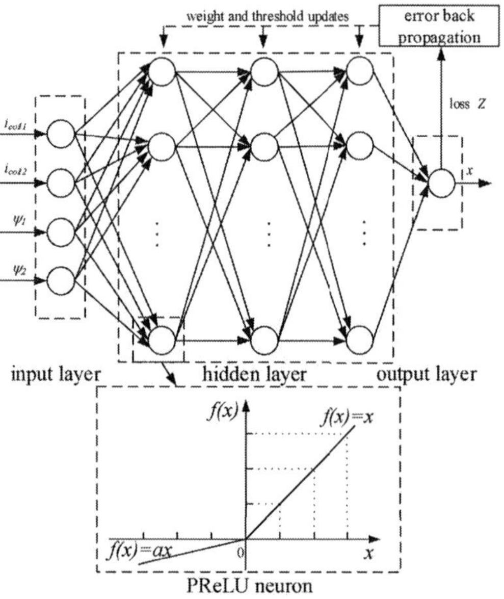

Fig. 3. neural network structure

The function of PReLU is as follows:

$$f(x) = max(0, x) + min(ax, 0) \tag{5}$$

Compared with traditional nonlinear neurons, PReLU whose function is piecewise linear does not contain the natural constant *e*, and its training cycle is shorter and runs faster in embedded. For the linear neuron ReLU used in CNN, the function slope *a* of PReLU in the negative semi-axis is not 0, which can be updated through training. This move avoids zero gradients that can occur during ReLU training and improves accuracy without introducing parameters that increase the risk of overfitting[13].

The first 90% of the preprocessed static data is used as the training set for NN training, and the last 10% is used as the validation set to test the model accuracy. In the training phase, in order to update the weights efficiently and reduce oscillation, the adam optimizer is used to adjust the learning rate and gradient calculation method. We use the mean absolute value of error (MAE) between the calculated result and the sample expectation as the loss function.

After multiple rounds of training, the NN may only learn the data relationship of the sample points, which will lead to overfitting and reduce generalization. We use the Earlystoping setting to monitor the loss function to terminate the training. When there is no significant improvement in the loss function, this setting will terminate the current round of training. Each time the NN completes an iteration, the training set is reordered and training continues.

IV. CO-SIMULATION MODEL VALIDATION

When the offline training is completed, the NN is transplanted into LabVIEW to build a forward network model in order to verify its accuracy. Considering that the flux linkage of the coils cannot be measured directly during the action of the actuators, an integral flux linkage observer is designed based on the magnetic circuit voltage balance equation. Its formula is as follows:

$$\psi=\int\left(u_{\text{coil}}-i_{\text{coil}}R_{\text{coil}}\right)dt \tag{6}$$

The flux linkage observer and the NN displacement estimator are combined and transplanted to the current closed-loop co-simulation of the bistable PM mechanism to verify the accuracy of the NN.

Fig. 4 and Fig. 5 are the changes of each parameter in the process of making and breaking in the co-simulation. Taking the making process as example, the IGBT is turned on when the capacitor is charged until t_0, and the making coil current increases, which increases the making coil flux, and gradually cancels the PM field in the breaking coil, so that breaking coil flux decreases. The induced voltage of the breaking coil increases due to mutual inductance.

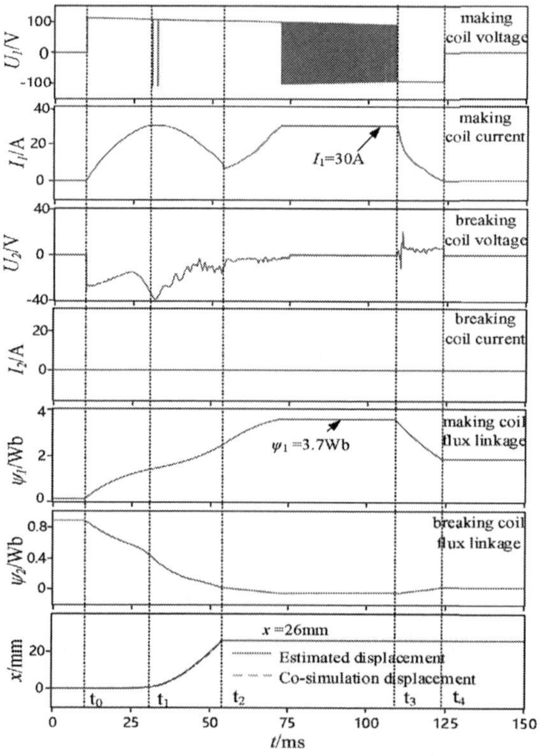

Fig.4. waveform of each parameter in the making process in Co-simulation

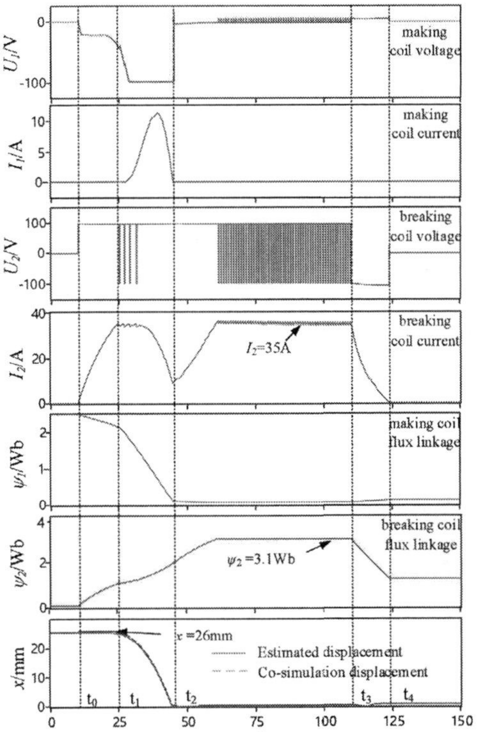

Fig.5. waveform of each parameter in the breaking process in Co-simulation

At the time of t_1~t_2, the moving core starts to move because of the greater electromagnetic force than the reaction force, and the back EMF of its movement causes the making coil current to drop; The air gap of the breaking coil increases, and its PM flux linkage decreases. At time t_2, the moving core reaches the making position, the back EMF returns to 0, and the making coil current gradually rises. At t_3, the IGBT is turned off, and the actuators is transferred to PM holding. Until time t_4, the voltage and current of the making coil drop to 0, and the making coil flux is equal to the PM holding flux, and the action ends. The process of breaking and making is similar, but the moving core moves faster, and the induced voltage generated on the making coil will be higher than the capacitor voltage, leading to the reverse diode of the IGBT conduct. The NN displacement estimator calculates the displacement at this moment, which shows that the NN has a well accuracy.

V. HARDWARE EXPERIMENTAL VERIFICATION

The hardware drive of the bistable PM mechanism is composed of the embedded :NI sbRIO-9629 (sb board) , with the drive circuit, voltage sensor and current sensor, as shown in Fig 6. The sb board controls the action of the actuators through the drive circuit, and simultaneously collects the voltage and current data from sensors to realize the closed-loop control of the actuators.

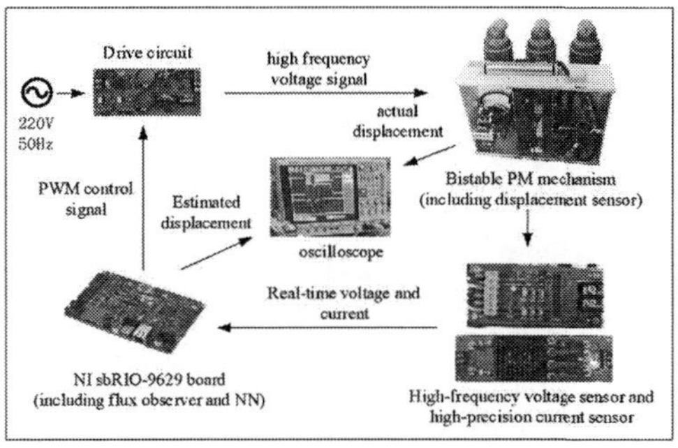

Fig.6. bistable PM mechanism control and testing system

Write the NN into the FPGA-based sb board. In order to verify the accuracy of the NN, the bistable PM mechanism is controlled to make and break, and the displacement estimation accuracy is judged by comparing the curves output by the displacement sensor and the NN, as shown in Fig. 7 and Fig.8.

It can be seen that the electromechanical parameters in the process of t_0~t_4 in Fig.7 and Fig.8 are basically consistent with the waveforms in the co-simulation. Considering the influence of signal interference and circuit stray inductance and capacitance, the current closed-loop and integral flux linkage observers work normally. It can be seen that the NN can effectively estimate the displacement of the moving core of the bistable PM mechanism, but there are still some deviation in the results. They are from: modeling of finite element simulation, neural network, integration of flux linkage observer, and the influence of mechanism's reaction spring.

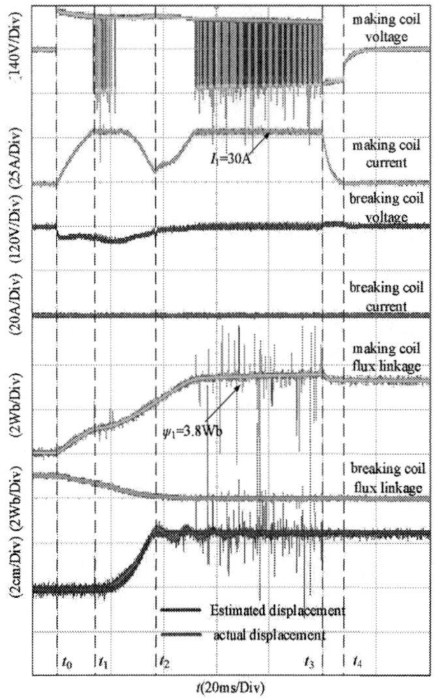

Fig.7. experimental waveform of making process

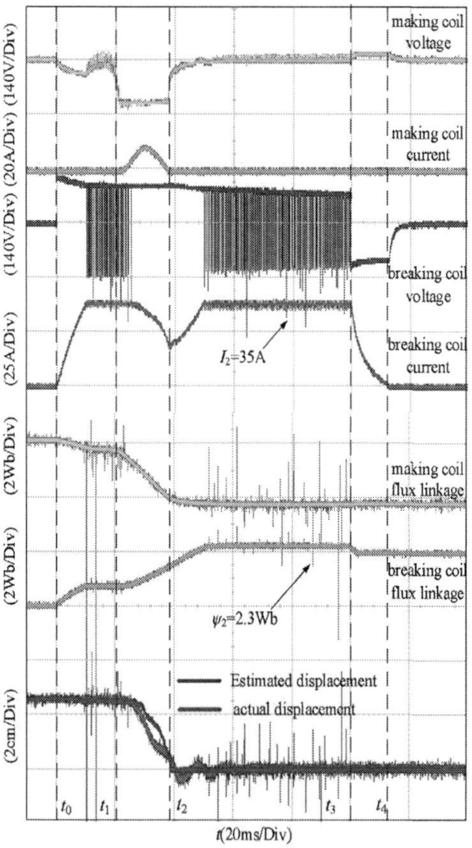

Fig.8. experimental waveform of breaking process

VI. CONCLUSION

In this paper, by constructing a NN based on the static data table of the bistable PM mechanism, the displacement of the moving core during the two process is effectively estimated. We have the following conclusions:

1) There is a one-to-one correspondence between the making and breaking coil currents i_1, i_2, displacement x and flux linkage ψ_1, ψ_2 of the bistable PM mechanism;

2) The NN can fit the electromagnetic coupling relationship of the bistable PM mechanism through the static data table calculated by finite element simulation, and realize effective estimation sensorless.

Since there is still a deviation between the output of the NN and the displacement sensor, how to reduce it will be the work after the end of this research. At the same time, using the NN to fit parameters such as suction is also the direction after this research.

REFERENCES

[1] Li Bin, Guo Fengyi, Wang Zhiyong, Tao Hongwei, Xu Lianzhou, Zhang Fenglong.Bi-State PMA Optimization Design and Intelligent Controller[J]. Transactions of China Electrotechnical Society,2013,28(10):83-89. (in Chinese)

[2] Espinosa A G , Ruiz J , Morera X A . A Sensorless Method for Controlling the Closure of a Contactor[J]. IEEE Transactions on Magnetics, 2007, 43(10):3896-3903.

[3] Dong E , Qin T , Wang Y , et al. Experimental Research on Speed Control of Vacuum Breaker[J]. IEEE Transactions on Power Delivery, 2013, 28(4):2594-2601.

[4] Espinosa A G , Ruiz J , Cusido J , et al. Sensorless Control and Fault Diagnosis of Electromechanical Contactors[J]. IEEE Transactions on Industrial Electronics, 2008, 55(10):3742-3750.

[5] Li K , Li X , Zheng S , et al. Residual Electrical Life Prediction for AC Contactor Based on BP Neural Network[J]. Transactions of China Electrotechnical Society, 2017. (in Chinese)

[6] T. Longfei, H. Zhiping and X. Zhihong.Neural Network-Based Co-Simulation Technology for Intelligent Contactors[J]. IEEE Transactions on Magnetics, 2020, PP(99):1-1.

[7] Wang Xianbing , Lin Heyun , Fang Shuhua , Ren Qiwen , Jin Ping. Analysis of Flux-weakening Control and Dynamic Characteristic for Making Process of Sensorless Intelligent Permanent Magnet Contactor[J]. Proceedings of the CSEE,2011, 31(18):7. (in Chinese)

[8] Tang Longfei , Chen Hao , Xu Zhihong , Zhang Yong. A Sensorless Breaking and Closing Displacement Tracking Control Strategy of Contactors [J]. Proceedings of the CSEE:1-12. (in Chinese)

[9] Tang Longfei , Chen Hao , Ke Changhui. A Method for Measuring the Static Characteristics of Contactors [J]. Proceedings of the CSEE:1-10. (in Chinese)

[10] W. Yang, J. Guo, Y. Liu and G. Zhai, Multi-Objective Optimization of Contactor's Characteristics Based on RBF Neural Networks and Hybrid Method[J]. IEEE Transactions on Magnetics, 2019:1-4.

[11] Shuhua Fang, Qingdong Liu, Heyun Lin, S. L. Ho. A Novel Flux Weakening Control Strategy for Permanent Magnet Actuator of Vacuum Circuit Breaker[J]. IEEE Transactions on Industrial Electronics, 2016, 63(4):1-1.

[12]Liu Shuxin , Gao Shizhen , Liu Yang , Li Jing , Cao Yundong. Residual Life Prediction of AC Contactor Based on LSTM [J]. High Voltage Engineering:1-11. (in Chinese)

[13]K. He, X. Zhang, S. Ren and J. Sun, Delving Deep into Rectifiers: Surpassing Human-Level Performance on ImageNet Classification[C]// CVPR. IEEE Computer Society, 2015.

Yaole Huang is currently pursuing the M.S. degree in electric engineering from the College of Electrical Engineering and Automation,

Fuzhou University, China. His research interests include electric apparatus and its intelligent technology. 1813306140@qq.com.

Longfei Tang (Senior Member, IEEE) received his B.Sc. degree in electrical engineering and automation from Fuzhou University in 2009 and his Ph.D. degree in electric machines and electric apparatus from Fuzhou University in 2015. Now he is a professor at Fuzhou University, China. His research interests include electric apparatus and its intelligent technology. Corresponding author: tlftel@fzu.edu.cn.

Electrical Properties of Graphene-doped Silver-nickel Contact Material

Dekao Hu, Jingqin Wang, Yancai Zhu

State Key Laboratory of Reliability and Intelligence of Electrical Equipment, Hebei University of Technology, Tianjin, 300401, China
E-mail: 202031404013@hebut.edu.cn Tel: 13682162057

***Abstract*—Silver-nickel composite contact materials have good electrical conductivity, processing performance and other advantages that are widely used in low-voltage switches, electrical appliances, instruments, and meters, and their performance will affect the safety, service life, and reliability of the use of electrical appliances. Adding a small number of additives can effectively improve the comprehensive performance of Ag/Ni contact materials. Graphene has a good effect on strengthening the metal matrix material because of its physical properties such as better electrical conductivity and mechanical properties. In this paper, a small amount of graphene filter cake powder with different mass fractions was added to Ag/Ni composites by powder metallurgy method, and the samples were subjected to electrical contact tests to measure their properties such as fusion welding force and arc ignition energy after ball milling and mixing, pressing, initial firing, re-pressing, and re-firing processes. The results show that the doping of trace graphene has a certain improvement effect on Ag/Ni contact materials in terms of fusion welding resistance and arc extinguishing ability. The trace addition of graphene enhances the electrical properties of Ag/Ni contacts and promotes their application in electrical contact materials.**

***Index Terms*—Ag/Ni, contact materials, electrical properties, graphene**

I. Introduction

Silver-based contact materials have been widely used in low-voltage electrical appliances because of their good overall performance. In 2003, the European Union issued two important documents, the Directive on End-of-life Electrical and Electronic Equipment and the Directive on the Restriction of the Use of Certain Hazardous Substances in Electrical and Electronic Equipment, which clearly require the non-hazardous use of electronic and electrical devices and prohibit the continued application of AgCdO electrical contact materials [1]. Therefore, the research on the performance improvement of cadmium-free silver-based contact materials has important theoretical and application values. Silver-nickel composite contact materials are widely used in low-voltage switches, electrical appliances, and precision contacts because of their good electrical conductivity and easy processing, and their performance affects the safety, reliability, and lifetime of electrical appliances. Silver-nickel contact material can replace the toxic AgCdO contact material under certain circumstances to reduce its environmental hazards.

The silver-nickel contact material may melt and weld under high current conditions and reduce the service life of the contact. When melt welding occurs in the contact material, the contact point will stick together and material transfer will occur, reducing the operational reliability of the appliance. With the increase in current level requirements, there are more stringent requirements for Ag/Ni contact material resistance to melt welding and arc erosion [2]. Several studies have shown that doping additive modification of Ag/Ni contact materials can enhance their properties, such as metal, and metal oxides, and thus improve the material's resistance to arc erosion and melt welding [3]-[4].

Graphene is a two-dimensional honeycomb monolayer sheet carbon material composed of carbon atoms hybridized with sp2, which has been widely studied for its high carrier mobility, high mechanical strength, good thermal conductivity, high electrical conductivity, and large specific surface area [5]- [8]. Graphene has unique two-dimensional material properties and a zero-band gap, semi-metallic energy band structure [9]-[10], which is valuable for applications in semiconductors, nanomaterials, and energy storage [11]-[13]. Graphene was used as an additive to enhance the overall electrical conductivity or mechanical properties of the composites by enhancing the metal matrix such as copper-based, aluminum-based, and silver-based [14]-[16]. Liu et al. employed graphene as an additive for copper-based composites with electrical contacts. Chemical silver plating coating of graphene with copper powder was investigated. The Gr/Cu composites were prepared using ball milling and cold pressing sintering processes. Physicochemical properties such as hardness, relative density, and electrical conductivity were tested. The results showed that the relative density, hardness and electrical conductivity of the materials obtained with the optimum process parameters were 90.0%, 53.4 HB and 76.2 IACS%, respectively, for an optimum addition of graphene of 0.2 wt% [17]. In this paper, graphene was used as an additive to improve the electrical properties of silver-nickel contacts.

II. Experimental Method

A. Experimental procedures and tests

Silver powder, nickel powder, graphene filter cake and ethanol (99.99% purity) were used as raw materials by powder metallurgy method. The graphene filter cake is a graphene wet cake prepared by ultrasonic physical method, the number of graphene layers is 1-10, the graphene content is 20±1wt%, the rest of the content is deionized water and a small amount of dispersant, its specific surface area is 194.5 m2/g, it has good electrical conductivity and good dispersion in water or ethanol.

Four samples were prepared by weighing four 10g powders in the mass ratio of silver, nickel and graphene filter cake of 84.80:15:0.20、84.90:15:0.10、 84.95:15:0.05 and 85:15:0 and adding 50 ml of ethanol into the ball mill jar. The powders were ball-milled in a high-energy ball mill at 600 r/min for 2 h and then dried in a vacuum drying oven at 80 °C for 1 h. The powders were pressed and shaped by ordinary molding method at 560 Mpa into a circular cake block material with a radius of 10 mm and a thickness of about 2.8 mm; sintered in an argon atmosphere tube furnace at 750 °C for 3 h, and then repressurized at 950 MPa. Finally, the samples were cut into contact materials of 3.2 mm in diameter, and electrical contact experiments were conducted using the JF04D electrical contact material test system of Kunming Precious Metals Research Institute, with the contact pressure set at 86 cN, the test voltage at 24 V Dc and 15 A Dc. The number of measurements was 100,000 times to measure the arc ignition energy and fusion welding force.

III. Electrical Properties of Contact Materials

A. Physical Properties

Test the electrical conductivity of the sample using a metal conductivity tester. Use a Vickers hardness tester to measure the sample its hardness. The Vickers hardness tester uses a positive quadrilateral cone indenter that is pressed into the surface of the contact material under the test force, and after holding for a specified time, the force is removed and the length of the diagonal of the indentation on the surface of the sample is measured to obtain the Vickers hardness. The measurement results are shown in Table 1.

The results show that the addition of a small amount of graphene can improve the overall performance of the material, and the conductivity shows a trend of decreasing with the increase of graphene addition. The silver-nickel contacts showed the best conductivity performance with a doping content of about 0.1 wt%, which resulted in 43.8 IACS%, an increase of about 6% compared to the contacts without graphene addition. Overall, the conductivity was slightly improved, but the effect was not significant.

TABLE 1 HARDNESS AND ELECTICAL CONDUCTIVITY OF GRAPHENE-DOPED Ag/Ni CONTACTS

Sample	Sample content	conductivity/(IACS%)	hardness/Hv
A	AgNi15-0.20 g Gr	39.6	99.28
B	AgNi15-0.10 g Gr	41.4	110.09
C	AgNi15-0.05 g Gr	43.8	115.29
D	AgNi15	41.1	107.98

The hardness of the samples showed a gradual decrease with increasing graphene content. At 0.1 wt% doping content,the silver-nickel graphene material showed a maximum hardness of 115.29 Hv, which became larger and improved by about 6.3% compared to the silver-nickel material without graphene addition. The silver-nickel contact material with high hardness is more durable and does not deform more in working conditions. The enhanced wear resistance of the hard contact material reduces the fusion welding area and reduces the fusion welding phenomenon of the contact. conclusion section is required. Although a conclusion may review the main points of the paper, do not replicate the abstract as the conclusion. A conclusion might elaborate on the importance of the work or suggest applications and extensions.

B. Arc energy of Ag/Ni contacts

In the working condition of the contacts, the arc discharge phenomenon will occur between the contacts. The instantaneous spark arc generated by the current has a high temperature, the arc formed will release energy, the electric contact material under the action of the arc force will occur material evaporation, spattering and other arc erosion phenomenon, this phenomenon makes the contact surface material melting, spattering. Usually, the arc energy is often used to characterize the damage caused by the arc on the contact surface, the smaller the arc energy, the smaller the ablation of the arc on the contact. The results of measuring the arc energy of the contacts of the four samples are shown in Figure 1, and the mean and variance of the four samples are statistically analyzed in Table 2.

Among the four sets of results, the arc energy of graphene-doped samples B and C were lower than that of undoped sample D. The arc energy curve of the undoped contact (sample D) gradually increased at the beginning of a

TABLE 2 AVERAGE BURNING ARC ENERGY AND DISTRIBUTION VARIANCE

Samples	Sample content	Average arc energy/(mJ)	Variance
A	AgNi15-0.20 g Gr	257.79	693.52
B	AgNi15-0.10 g Gr	175.00	136.51
C	AgNi15-0.05 g Gr	192.08	436.14
D	AgNi15	225.77	720.86

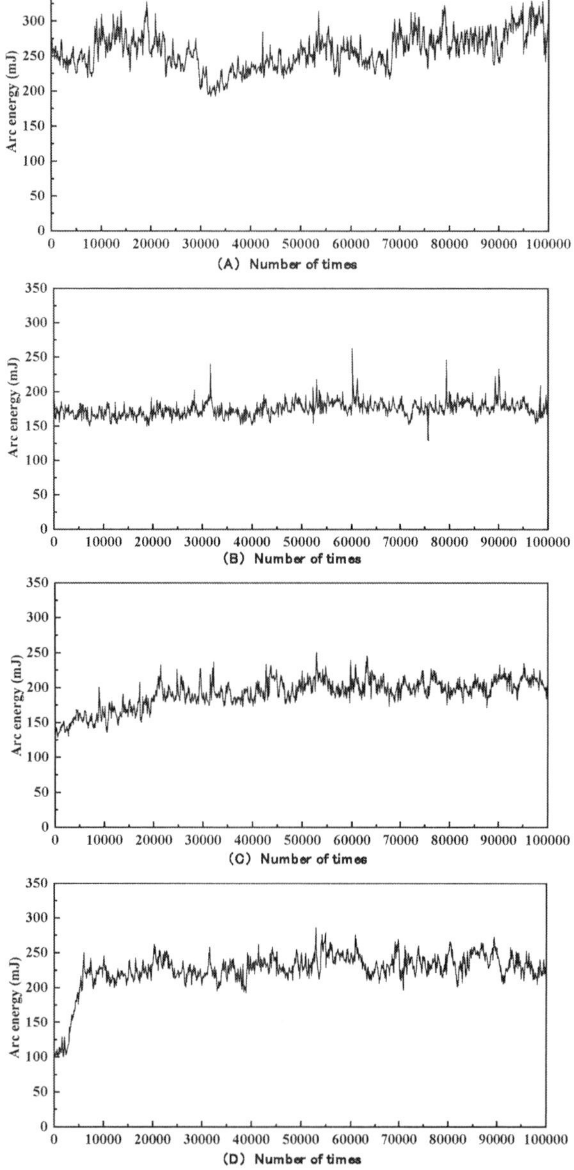

Figure 1 arc ignition energy of Ag/Ni contact

period of time and changed less up to a certain level, remaining at about 230 mJ, but the arc energy was higher, with an average arc energy of about 225.77 mJ. At a graphene doping of about 0.2 Compared with sample D without graphene doping, the average arc ignition energy decreased by about 22.48%. The results indicate that graphene doped with about 0.2 wt% of had the lowest arc-burning energy and produced less arc energy, which could reduce the fusion and ablation of the contact by the arc.

C. Contact angle measurement

The wetting angle is the main parameter characterizing the molecular interactions between liquids and solids. Contact material in the process of repeated contact, high-temperature state produces a certain melting precipitation effect. A small

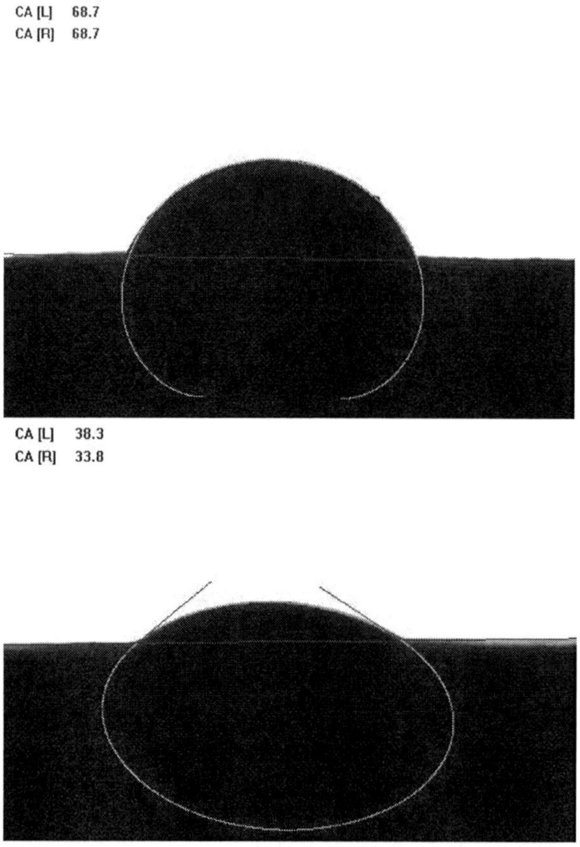

Figure 2 Contact angle of contact materials: (A) Silver-Nickel ;(B) Silver-Graphene-Nickel

amount of Ni element will be dissolved in the silver matrix melt pool, and when the temperature decreases, the arc is extinguished and Ni will precipitate again. Under the repeated action of the arc, Ni particles are continuously dissolved and precipitated in the silver solution, which will enhance the bonding strength of silver and nickel. When the measured contact angle is smaller, the higher the bonding stability of Ag and Ni at high temperature, the better the bonding of Ag and Ni, and the less likely to produce material spattering and reduce material burnout.

The nickel powder in the form of a round cake is pressed into a block material with a diameter of 10 mm and a height of 1 mm. Two different powders (pure silver powder and silver-graphene composite powder) were weighed and deposited on the substrate, both weighing 0.3 g. The silver-graphene powder contained 1 wt% graphene and was heated to 1000 °C for 30 min under evacuated conditions to fully melt the silver powder and silver-graphene composite powder on the nickel block substrate. After waiting for the sample to cool, the contact angle change after the addition of graphene was measured using a contact angle measuring instrument HD camera fit.

As shown in Figure 2, figure (A) is the contact angle of

silver and nickel without the addition of graphene, the average is 68.7°, and figure (B) is the contact angle of silver-graphene composite powder with nickel, the average is 36.05°. The contact angle changed from high to low after the addition of trace amounts of graphene, which shows that The wettability between Ag and Ni was improved using graphene. This facilitates the bonding of silver and nickel, which helps to lessen material loss brought on by arcing action.

D. Welding force of Ag/Ni contacts

The melt welding force is usually used to evaluate the melt welding resistance of the contact material, the melt welding force refers to the minimum disconnecting force required to break the melt welding contact. The smaller the welding force, the less likely the contact is to melt weld in the operating condition. The melting force for different mass fractions of doped graphene is shown in Figure 3. The statistical analysis of the mean and variance of the results is shown in Table 3.

The silver-nickel material without graphene doping (sample D) has the largest variance distribution of the melt soldering force distribution among the four groups of samples, indicating that the force swings more generally and is less stable under working conditions. After 51550, the welding force remained at about 74 cN, which indicates that the undoped Ag/Ni contacts are less stable due to possible adhesion or material transfer during contact. The variance distribution of the melting force indicates the stability of the contact under working conditions, and the larger the variance, the higher and lower the melting force and the less stability. At a graphene doping level of roughly 0.4 wt%, the contact (sample A) exhibited the lowest melt force, with an average value of about 43.89 cN. When compared to the contact without graphene doping, the welding forces of sample A decreased on average by about 37.48%. The variance is also smaller and more even in distribution, relatively stable in working conditions, and less prone to phenomena such as adhesion.

Samples	Sample content	Welding force/(cN)	Variance
A	AgNi15-0.20 g Gr	43.89	13.65
B	AgNi15-0.10 g Gr	74.31	51.80
C	AgNi15-0.05 g Gr	66.21	30.74
D	AgNi15	70.21	54.06

TABLE 3 WELDING FORCE OF Ag/Ni CONTACT

IV. CONCLUSION

In this paper, graphene filter cake powder was used as a non-toxic and environmentally friendly additive to prepare silver-nickel-graphene composites by powder metallurgy method. Four samples were prepared by weighing 10g of powder in the mass ratio of silver, nickel and graphene filter cake of 84.80:15:0.20, 84.90:15:0.10, 84.95:15:0.05, and 85:15:0. After we performed the pressing, sintering, repressing and refired processes on the samples, we compared the effects of adding different mass ratios of graphene on the performance of electrical properties of the contact materials. The conclusions are as follows.

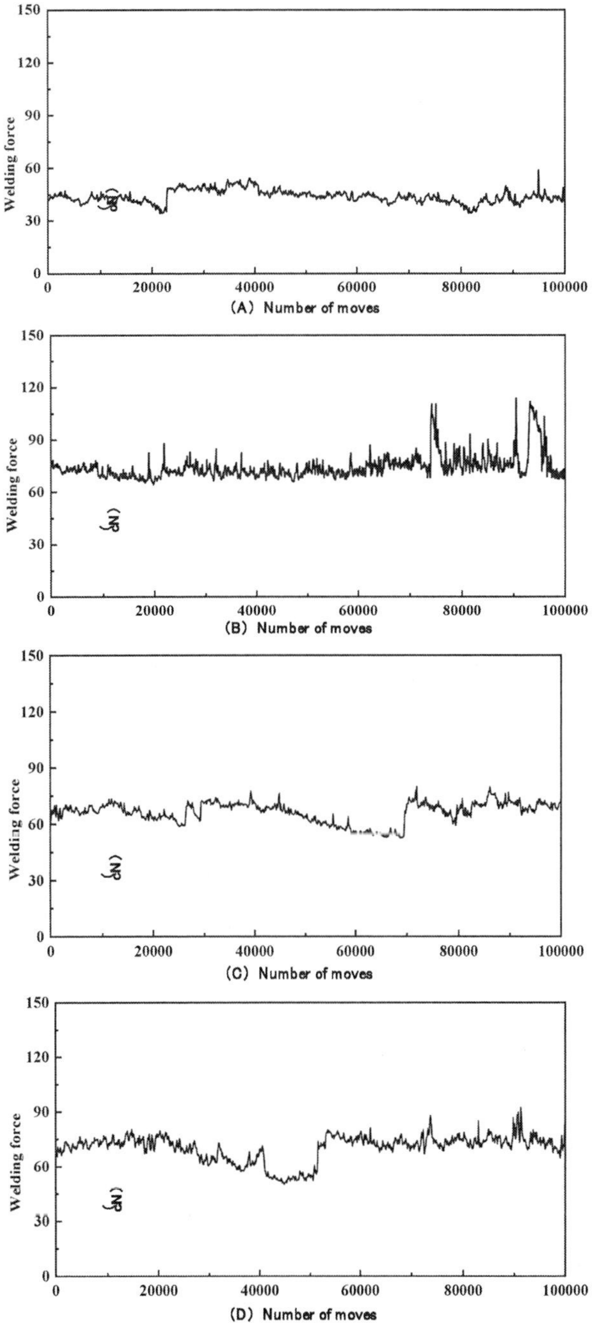

Figure 3 Fusing force of Ag/Ni contact material

(1) There was a slight increase in electrical conductivity after adding trace amounts of graphene. The electrical conductivity was 43.8 IACS% when graphene was added at

about 0.1%wt. The hardness of the samples also tended to increase with the decrease of the content, and the best result was achieved with the addition of 0.5%wt, which increased 6.3% compared to the contact material without graphene.

(2) Graphene doping amount of about 0.2 wt%, the lowest energy generated by the arc. The average arc energy was about 175.00 mJ. Compared with the contact material without graphene doping, the average arc energy decreased by about 22.48%, which could reduce the damage to the contact by the arc.

(3) The addition of trace amounts of graphene can make the contact angle of the two metals, silver and nickel, smaller and increase the wettability. When the contacts are repeatedly contacted, the viscosity of the resulting melt pool increases, which will reduce the loss of material.

(4) The addition of trace graphene reduces the fusion welding force and reduces the image of fusion welding and adhesion occurring in the contacts. When the amount of graphene added is about 0.4%wt, the melt soldering force is reduced by about 37.48% and the contacts have the best anti-melt soldering effect.

ACKNOWLEDGMENT

This research was funding by the National Natural Science Foundation of China (Grant No. 51777057) and The Central Leading Local Science and Technology Development Funds Project (Grant No. 216Z1011G)

REFERENCES

[1] Wang J, Chang Y, Zhu Y, Zhang G, Huang G. Study on Simulation and Experiment of Y-Mo Co-Doped AgSnO2 Contact Materials. Crystals. 2021,11(7):724.

[2] Zheng Xinjian and Wang Qiping, "The types and the formation mechanisms of AgNi contact morphology due to breaking arc erosion, Proceedings of IEEE Holm Conference on Electrical Contacts, 1993: 97-102.

[3] Lin Z, Fan S, Liu M, Liu S, Li J-G, Li J, et al. Excellent anti-arc erosion performance and corresponding mechanisms of a nickel-belt-reinforced silver-based electrical contact material. Journal of Alloys and Compounds. 2019: 163-171.

[4] C. H. Leung and A. Lee, "Electric contact materials and their erosion in automotive DC relays," Electrical Contacts - 1991 Proceedings of the Thirty-Seventh IEEE HOLM Conference on Electrical Contacts, 1991: 114-121.

[5] Blake, P., E. W. Hill, A. H. Castro Neto, K. S. Novoselov, D. Jiang, R. Yang, T. J. Booth, and A. K. Geim. "Making graphene visible. Applied physics, 2007,（6）.

[6] Bolotin KI, Ghahari F, Shulman MD, Stormer HL, Kim P. Observation of the fractional quantum Hall effect in graphene. Nature. 2009，462(7270):196-9.

[7] Novoselov K S, Geim A K, Morozov S V, et al. Two-Dimensional Gas of Massless Dirac Fermions in Graphene[J]. Nature, 2005.

[8] Lee C, Wei X, Kysar JW, Hone J. Measurement of the elastic properties and intrinsic strength of monolayer graphene. science. 2008，321(5887):385-388.

[9] Sprinkle M, Siegel D, Hu Y, Hicks J, Tejeda A, Taleb-Ibrahimi A, Le Fèvre P, Bertran F, Vizzini S, Enriquez H, Chiang S. First direct observation of a nearly ideal graphene band structure. Physical Review Letters. 2009,103(22).

[10] Gui G, Li J, Zhong J. Band structure engineering of graphene by strain: First-principles calculations. Physical Review B. 2008;78(7).

[11] Neto AC, Guinea F, Peres NM, Novoselov KS, Geim AK. The electronic properties of graphene. Reviews of modern physics. 2009，81(1).

[12] Stankovich S, Dikin DA, Dommett GH, Kohlhaas KM, Zimney EJ, Stach EA, Piner RD, Nguyen ST, Ruoff RS. Graphene-based composite materials. nature. 2006, 442(7100): 282-286.

[13] Zhu J, Yang D, Yin Z, Yan Q, Zhang H. Graphene and graphene-based materials for energy storage applications. Small. 2014，10(17): 3480-98.

[14] Bartolucci SF, Paras J, Rafiee MA, Rafiee J, Lee S, Kapoor D, Koratkar N. Graphene–aluminum nanocomposites. Materials Science and Engineering: A. 2011, 528(27):7933-7.

[15] Mu C, Xiong D, Li Y, et al. Ultrahigh Electrical Conductivity of Graphene Embedded in Metals[J]. Advanced Functional Materials, 2019, 29(17).

[16] Gao R, Hu N, Yang Z, Zhu Q, Chai J, Su Y, Zhang L, Zhang Y. like graphene-Ag composite films with enhanced mechanical and electrical properties. Nanoscale research letters. 2013, 8(1):1-8.

[17] Liu H, Teng X, Wu W, Wu X, Leng J, Geng H. Effect of graphene addition on properties of Cu-based composites for electrical contacts. Materials Research Express. 2017, 4(6).

Dekao Hu, (1994-), M.S. student. His research interests are in electrical contact materials.

Jingqin wang,（1964-）, doctor of engineering, professor, doctoral supervisor, and professor of the Hebei University of Technology, China. director of Hebei Electrical Product Reliability Technology Collaborative Innovation Center. The research direction is electrical reliability theory and its application, electrical contact theory and its application.

Research on the Influence of Intelligent Composite Technology on the Performance of Relay Contact

Wenhua Li[1], Zhong Wang[1], Hejun Zhu[2], Bo Jiang[1], Jiacong Wang[1]

[1)] State Key Laboratory of Reliability and Intelligence of Electrical Equipment, Hebei University of Technology, Tianjin, 300401, China

[2)] Shenyang Railway Signal Co., Ltd, Shenyang, 110025, China

Email: liwenhua@hebut.edu.cn TEL:13312176902

Abstract—**Intelligent composite technology is a method to realize non arc breaking of relay. Its principle is that the composite branch and relay cooperate in the process of relay breaking, and provide free wheeling circuit for contact current at the moment of contact breaking to achieve the purpose of eliminating arc. This paper takes the electrical contact characteristics of composite relay as the research object, and evaluates the performance of composite technology from two aspects: contact action characteristics measurement and contact performance data analysis. In this paper, the working principle of the intelligent composite technology used to realize the non arc breaking of the traditional relay is first described, and the suppression effect of the composite relay on the arc when the contact is disconnected is compared through experiments. After that, for each group of relays operating 100000 times under the condition of DC 220V / 2.5A, the 3D topography of the contact surface was measured by the analysis equipment and the surface composition was analyzed by EDS, and the composite relay was superior to the traditional relay according to the contact resistance, contact surface topography, composition and other parameters. Finally, based on the experimental results, the current breaking time ratio and contact erosion height ratio are extracted to evaluate the arc extinguishing performance of the composite technology.**

Index Terms— **direct current, signal relay, Composite design, electric arc.**

I. Introduction

The signal relay studied in this paper is an electromagnetic relay which works in the signal control part of the railway system. Its reliability and safety are the necessary conditions to ensure the normal operation and safe and reliable operation of the railway control signal equipment. The mechanical contact system is the part with the shortest electrical life in the electromagnetic relay. The contact in the working process is affected by mechanical wear, environmental corrosion, arc erosion and contact bounce, and its failure efficiency is higher than that of other parts. There is bright arc in the breaking process of the relay contact of this model. Under the condition of sufficient working voltage, spark discharge will occur when the contact is disconnected, and molten pool and crack will occur on the surface of the contact. Therefore, arc erosion has the greatest impact on the electrical contact material, which is the most important factor affecting the electrical life and reliability of the contact material [1]. Under the influence of contact material degradation and arc erosion, the breaking life of relay under DC working environment is only several thousand times. Breaking the arc will cause the contact resistance of the contact to increase and the surface of the contact surface to produce ablation pits, and the breaking arc of the contact is considered to be the main cause of ablation. For intrinsically safe inductive circuits, the unnatural discharge time is related to the arc discharge energy of the two parts of the circuit. The experimental results show that the influence of the arc energy composition of the power supply is greater [2]. At the same time, the ablation of relay contacts working in the DC circuit will be more serious because the DC arc is not easy to extinguish and the arc releases a large amount of heat during combustion [3].

The high falsification, short service life and high failure rate caused by arc erosion of signal relay restrict the safe operation of railway system. In order to improve its electrical life, reduce the failure rate and solve the arc ablation problem of the relay, scholars at home and abroad have put forward various solutions to the arc extinguishing of the relay contact. In this paper, intelligent composite technology is adopted to eliminate the breaking arc of relay contact. The working principle of this composite design is: in the process of relay disconnection, an IGBT composite branch is connected in parallel with the relay to make the IGBT of the composite branch conductive at the same time when the relay disconnection coil is powered on. The logic circuit intelligently judges that the IGBT is turned off after the commutation is completed, and provides a commutation circuit for the contact current to achieve the purpose of eliminating the arc.

II. INTELLIGENT COMPOSITE TECHNOLOGY

Contact material erosion is a comprehensive reflection of mechanical wear, arc erosion, environmental erosion and contact bounce. Arc erosion and contact bounce are widely recognized by scholars as the main causes of contact failure [4]. The decline of the electrical contact performance of the contact is manifested by the increase of the contact resistance and the bad appearance of the contact surface. This contact characteristic will reduce the electrical life of the relay, and eventually lead to the paralysis of the relay and even the whole system.

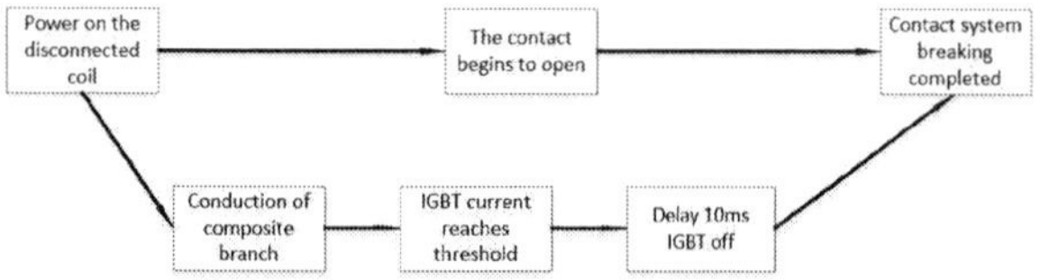

Fig. 1 Flow chart of opening action of composite relay

The composite technology includes signal detection part, control circuit part and converter circuit part. As shown in Fig. 1, the working principle is that the composite branch operates in parallel on the mechanical contact of the relay. When the closing coil of the relay is powered on, the composite branch detects that the signal starts to work, instantaneously controls the IGBT to conduct, and provides a commutation path for the mechanical contact to be disconnected. When the detection circuit measures that the current flowing through the composite branch is greater than 2.5A, it provides the signal to the control circuit, which drives the IGBT to open after a delay of 10ms, and completes the current exchange process of the mechanical contact of the relay. After the circuit completes the commutation, the common mode inductance in the composite branch stores part of the energy, which is released through the R-C loop of the composite branch.

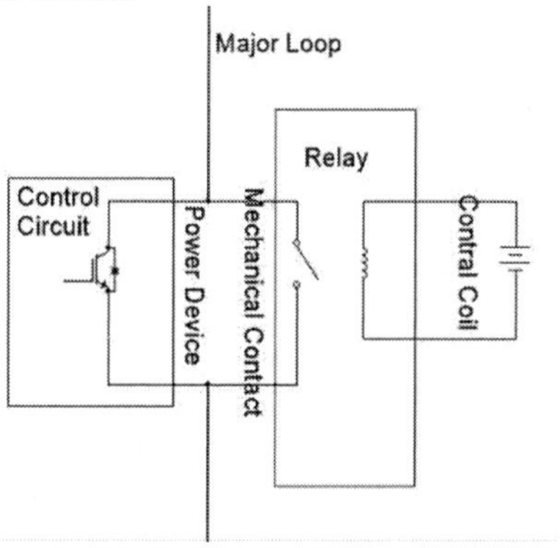

Fig. 2 Structure diagram of composite relay

The composite branch operates in parallel at both ends of the relay contact, and its structure diagram is shown in Fig. 2. The left side is the main circuit composed of the power device IGBT of the composite branch, and the right side is the contact of the relay and its control circuit. The IGBT of the composite branch is connected in parallel at both ends of the contact as a free wheeling circuit for the current when the contact is disconnected.

III. ANALYSIS OF ACTION CHARACTERISTICS OF COMPOSITE RELAY

The application of intelligent composite technology has changed the working process when the relay is disconnected. The arc generated by the relay contact during the breaking process is composed of the power supply and the inductance. After applying the composite technology, there is a commutation circuit in the mechanical contact breaking process, which reduces the breaking time of the contact current. At the same time, the energy of the inductance in the circuit will not be released during the contact breaking, which greatly reduces the arc energy during the contact breaking. According to the analysis of the principle of arc ablation, the main influencing factors of arc ablation are arc voltage, current and contact current breaking time.

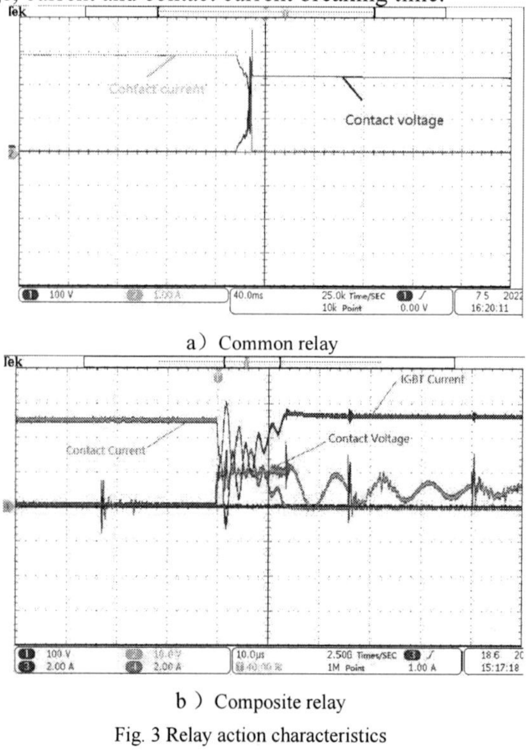

Fig. 3 Relay action characteristics

As shown in Fig. 3. a, the breaking time of mechanical contact current of normal relay without composite technology is 16ms, and the arc voltage of contact breaking rises slowly in the first half, changes sharply in the second half, and there is a step mutation in the second half; After applying the composite technology, the action characteristics are as shown in Fig. 3. b. The breaking time of the mechanical contact current of the composite relay becomes 12us. There is a current commutation circuit in the breaking process of the contact. The breaking voltage of the mechanical contact is about 10V, which is stable as the voltage drop of the conductive tube of the power device after a period of time. The current of the mechanical contact fluctuates during the breaking process, and finally transits smoothly to the final state.

Since the initial and final states of contact voltage and current are consistent between them. In order to evaluate the performance of the composite design technology, the contact current breaking time is selected as the evaluation of the arc erosion of the two groups of relays, and the effect of the composite technology is evaluated by the current breaking time ratio between the two.

$$\alpha = \frac{Current\ breaking\ time\ of\ composite\ relay}{Current\ breaking\ time\ of\ common\ relay} \quad (1)$$

After taking the average value through multiple measurements, the contact current breaking time of the relay under normal operation is 16ms; After the composite technology is applied, the contact current breaking time under the working condition of the relay is 12us. Bring the data into Formula 1 to get $\alpha = 0.00075$。 The arc root movement after arc burning can be divided into two stages. In the first stage, there is no obvious large-scale movement within the random movement time of the arc, which is the main period causing ablation on the contact surface [5]. After applying the composite technology, the breaking time of the contact current becomes about 1 / 1300 of the original. Therefore, the arc energy generated when the relay contact is disconnected becomes smaller and the random movement time of the arc becomes shorter, thus greatly reducing the impact of arc erosion on the contact.

IV. EXPERIMENTAL RESULT

In order to analyze the contact ablation after the relay test under the action of composite technology, three groups of comparative experiments were set up. Different ablation causes were taken as variables to analyze the impact of composite technology on the relay by comparing the experimental results. The experimental principle is shown in Fig. 4. In order to eliminate the influence of other erosion causes on the relay contact during operation, the following experiments are designed. The experimental conditions of the relay are DC 220V and the load circuit is inductive. After the contacts under different conditions are broken 100000 times, the influence of the composite technology on the contact surface morphology, material and electrical contact performance is analyzed. The experimental relay is divided into three groups. Relay 1 operates without load to verify the mechanical wear of the contact; Relay 2 applies composite technology to operate under load; Relay 3 operates normally with load as a comparison item.

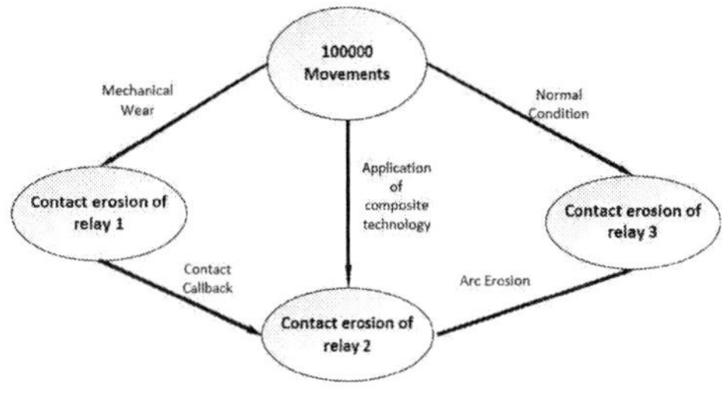

Fig. 4 Experimental schematic diagram

As the main index to measure the electrical contact performance of the contact, the contact resistance is the most intuitive response to the effect of the composite technology on the contact.

Table 1 contact resistance (mΩ)

	Relay 1	Relay 2	Relay 3
contact resistance	5.25	10.18	69.47

By analyzing the data of the contact resistance values of each group of relays in Table 1, it can be concluded that the contact resistance of relay group 2 changes less than that of control group 1. The failure contact resistance of this type of relay equipment manual is 50m Ω. Under the application of composite technology, the contact resistance of the contact is still within the allowable range of safe operation. Compared with the contact resistance of relay group 3 under normal working conditions, it can be seen that the contact erosion of relay group 2 with composite technology has been significantly improved. Under the action of breaking arc, the electrode material of relay contact will melt, vaporize or even sputter and melt,vaporize or even sputter molten metal droplets, causing erosion and transfer to the material. After arc erosion, the contact material mainly changes in contact quality, contact material composition, surface morphology and contact resistance [6]. The breaking arc of the relay is the main factor affecting its contact performance. The breaking arc causes the most serious ablation of the contact due to its long time, large energy and the influence of contact material decomposition, oxidation and other factors. According to the experimental data, the contact resistance of the composite relay after the experiment is only 1 / 7 of the contact resistance of the normal relay. Therefore, the composite technology has greatly improved the reliability of the relay contact system.

Contact resistance is an intuitive reflection of contact performance, but the contact surface morphology is the most direct reflection of contact surface erosion. Fig. 5 is obtained by scanning the relay contact surface after the test with the contact three-dimensional topography measuring device.

The surface of relay operated under normal working environment is severely ablated. As shown in Fig. 5. a, the ablation area and depth of arc ablation are large, and obvious pits are generated on the surface of stationary contact, resulting in a large loss of contact materials. The mechanism of arc erosion is extremely complex. At present, the mainstream idea is to vividly reflect the process of arc erosion mechanism through the physical model of micro particle movement. At present, it is believed that arc erosion is caused by surface erosion caused by arc discharge when the contact is in the working state for a long time [7]; After the application of the composite technology, the contact surface topography is shown in Fig. 5. b. the relay contact surface topography becomes better, and the area of the contact surface ablation pit becomes smaller. After the application of the composite technology, the area of the contact surface ablation area is significantly reduced.

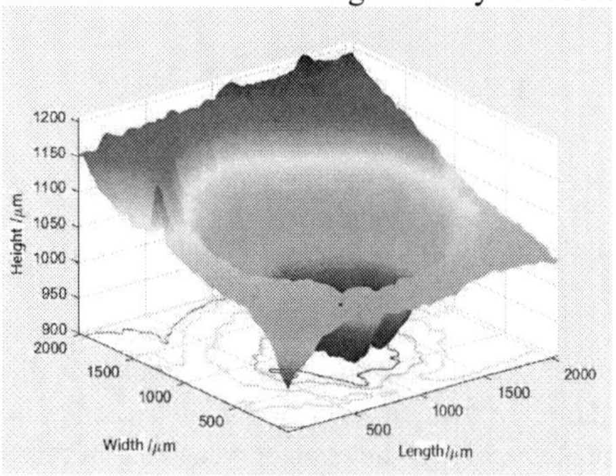

a) Common relay

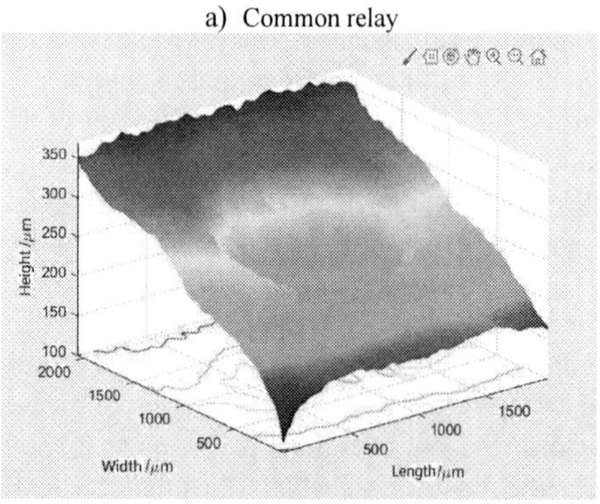

b) Composite relay

Fig. 5 Three dimensional topography of contact

The edge of the scanning area far from the striking point is selected as the reference point, and the height of the three-dimensional topography of the contact is taken as the reaction of the contact erosion.

$$\gamma = \frac{\textit{Contact erosion height of composite relay}}{\textit{Contact erosion height of common relay}} \quad (2)$$

After applying the composite technology to the relay, the test results show that the electrical contact performance of the contact has been greatly improved, and the ablation pit on the contact surface has been greatly reduced from the area to the depth. After the experiment, the ablation pit depth of the relay operating normally is about 1200um, and the ablation pit depth of the composite relay is about 350um. Bring the height difference of the three-dimensional shape of the contact into formula 2, and calculate $\lambda = 0.29$。 According to the experimental data, the contact erosion height of the composite relay after the experiment is only 3 / 10 of that of the normal operating relay. Combined with the analysis of the relay's operating characteristics, it can be seen that the composite technology has significantly improved the area and depth of the contact surface ablation area by eliminating the breaking arc when the contact is disconnected.

There are two factors affecting contact resistance, one is the contact surface topography, and the other is the contact surface material. The relay contact material in the experiment is silver cadmium oxide alloy.

Table 2 Proportion of elements on contact surface

	Relay 1		Relay 2		Relay 3	
	Ag	Cd	Ag	Cd	Ag	Cd
Element proportion	62.42	9.69	48.97	30.14	32.63	19.37

The melting points of the two metals in the material are above 1000 degrees. The energy spectrum analysis of the relay contact under different experimental conditions after the test is carried out with an energy spectrometer to obtain Table 2. According to the data in Table 2, the reference object of the experiment is relay group 1 where the contact is mechanically impacted. The proportion of contact elements in relay group 2 where the composite technology is applied changes obviously, the proportion of element Ag decreases, and the proportion of element Cd increases. This indicates that other influencing factors of contact erosion cause the change of element content on the contact surface and affect the small increase of contact resistance. In relay group 3 under normal working environment, under the influence of arc ablation and other factors, the proportion of Ag element is slightly lower than that of relay group 2, and the proportion of Cd element is significantly lower. At the same time, the contact EDS shows that there is more o element in the contact surface and the content is higher. For AgCdO contact materials, a layer of silver is generally plated on the contact surface. The decomposition temperature of CDO in AgCdO is low, and at 1360 ℃, CdO decomposes into Cd and oxygen. Therefore, the AgCdO contact forms a low-density layer of CdO or a metal oxide layer on the surface after multiple arc actions [8]. The complex physical and chemical reactions during contact breaking accelerate the decomposition and oxidation of the metal on the contact surface. These metal compounds formed after decomposition and oxidation are agglomerated into blocks and attached to the contact surface. If the contact between the moving and stationary contacts occurs at the convex position formed by these metals, the contact area will be reduced, the shrinkage resistance will be increased, and even the contact failure will be caused [9]. The experimental results show that under the action of contact breaking arc, the contact material of normal relay is seriously oxidized, while the composite technology suppresses the arc during contact breaking, so that the oxidation phenomenon of contact material does not occur.

V. CONCLUSION

Aiming at the problems such as short electrical life of relay contact under working conditions and serious erosion of contact by DC arc, this paper designs a composite device running in parallel at both ends of relay contact with intelligent composite technology as the core, which eliminates the breaking arc of contact, and analyzes the contact resistance, surface 3D morphology and surface composition of contact after 100000 tests through setting comparative experiments, The improvement effect of intelligent composite technology on relay contact erosion is obtained. The main conclusions are as follows:

(1) The initial and final state of the contact of the composite relay will not change when the contact is broken, but the composite technology reduces the current breaking time of the mechanical contact from 16ms to 12us through the commutation branch, and the current breaking time ratio α 1 / 1300 to eliminate the ablation of the relay contact by the breaking DC arc.

(2) After the relay is applied with composite technology, the inhibition effect of arc erosion is very obvious. On the one hand, the erosion area of the contact is obviously smaller; On the other hand, the erosion height parameter of the contact λ 3 / 10 of the original; At the same time, the composite technology can inhibit the oxidation of metal materials caused by the relay breaking arc.

(3) Combined with the working principle of the composite technology to analyze the contact erosion phenomenon after the test, the composite technology only eliminates the influence of the relay breaking arc. Although it has no effect on other arc erosion factors, it has met the needs of users. Combined with the service life of relay and the reliability brought by continuous optimization design, the influence of influencing factors on contact erosion can be ignored.

REFERENCES

[1] Yu Jie, Chen Jingchao, Zhou Xiaolong. AgSnO_ 2. Molecular dynamics simulation of arc erosion characteristics of contact materials [J]. Materials engineering, 2010 (03): 8-12.

[2] Meng Qinghai, Wen Jing. Energy analysis of unnatural arc discharge in intrinsically safe inductive circuit [J]. Electrical explosion protection, 2020 (03): 1-5

[3] Liqiao,Jiao, Hang,Yang, Yun. Current sharing compensation control method for interleaved current source isolated bidirectional DC/DC converters[J]. Journal of Power Electronics, 2021.

[4] Shuxuan Song,Weifeng Zhang. Study on Parallel Current Sharing Technology of Power Module, DC Charging Pile for Electric Vehicle[P]. 2020.

[5] Cao Qichun, Liu Xiangjun. Simulation analysis and Experimental Research on arc motion of high voltage DC relay [J]. Journal of electrical technology, 2019, 34 (22): 4699-4707.

[6] Zhai Guofu, Bo Kai, Zhou Xue, Zhang Yong. Summary of arc research on DC high power relay [J]. Journal of electrotechnics, 2017,32 (22): 251-263

[7] Li Zhen, Wang Zhaobin, Chen Kangning. Comparison of preparation processes of silver tin oxide contacts and summary of arc erosion characteristics [J]. Electrical materials, 2021 (04): 3-9

[8] Zhao Xinghai, Liu Wei Research on contact failure mechanism of railway signal relay [C]. The Fifth International Conference on reliability and electrical contact of electrical products, 2014:396-399

[9] Ling Guoping, Xue Tian, Ni Mengliang, Liu Yuanting. Study on Arc Erosion Products of silver metal oxide contact materials [J]. Precious metals, 2008 (03): 1-5.

A Control Strategy Verification System for Bistable Permanent Magnet Circuit Breaker

Shixu Luan[1], Longfei Tang[1,2,3]*

[1] College of Electrical Engineering and Automation, Fuzhou University, Fuzhou, 350108, China
[2] Fujian Key Laboratory of New Energy Generation and Power Conversion, Fuzhou, 350108, China
[3] Fujian Province University Engineering Research Center of Smart Distribution Grid Equipment, Fuzhou, 350108, China
E-mail: tlftel@fzu.edu.cn Tel: 13950364569

***Abstract*—The bistable permanent magnet circuit breaker(PMCB) not only has the advantages of strong controllability of electromagnetic actuator, but also has the characteristics of locking in the opening or closing position. In view of the above characteristics, this paper introduces a control strategy verification system with NI sbRIO-9629 as the core controller, which consists of co-simulation system and hardware control system. Firstly, the action and excitation characteristics of bistable PMCB are analyzed. The motion model, parameter solving model and simulation control model of bistable permanent magnet actuator(PMA) are built in LabVIEW. The opening and closing coil driving circuit is built in Multisim. The data interaction between LabVIEW and Multisim is used to realize the point-by-point closed-loop co-simulation. Then, this paper designs flexible and reliable three-state coil driving circuit and power supply module, signal detection module and other hardware parts. And sbRIO-9629 is used to process the signal and control the driving circuit. Finally, the single-coil current closed-loop control method is co-simulated and verified by experiments. Thus, a whole set of interlocking research system of bistable PMA from co-simulation methods to graphical programming and to control strategy verification is constructed, which greatly reduces the period of strategy development and experimental verification for researchers.**

***Index Terms*— bistable permanent magnet circuit breaker, control strategy verification system, co-simulation, current closed-loop.**

I. INTRODUCTION

Under the background of "carbon peaking and carbon neutrality goals ", people put forward higher requirements for the continuity, safety and automation level of power supply, and the corresponding requirements for switch performance in the distribution network also increase accordingly. As one of the main switching elements in the distribution network, the circuit breaker's intelligence level and reliability directly affect the stability and automation of the entire distribution system [1]. At present, in the low-voltage distribution network, the frame circuit breaker actuator mostly adopts a mature spring mechanism, which has stable operating characteristics and is not affected by the power supply voltage [2]. But there are also obvious shortcomings: the breaking and closing performance is largely dependent on the mechanical energy release of the spring, which is difficult to control flexibly; the actuator has many parts and complex transmission, which increases the risk of mechanical failure. The PMA designed by combining the electromagnetic mechanism and the permanent magnet not only has the advantages of strong controllability of electromagnetic actuator, but also can realize the permanent-magnet lock at the breaking and closing positions. This feature greatly reduces the number of components and greatly improves the reliability and mechanical life of the mechanism [3]. Therefore, in theory, replacing the spring mechanism with a permanent magnet mechanism can significantly improve the performance of the switch.

Reference [4] designed a drive circuit for the actuator of a bistable PMCB, and used a hysteresis method to control the excitation current closed-loop, which reduced the action dispersion of the circuit breaker during wide-voltage operation. Reference [5] proposed a hybrid PWM control method to improve the control accuracy of coil current on the basis of hysteresis. Reference [6]–[7] uses the bistable PMCB for synchronous breaking and closing control under current closed-loop control, and uses neural network to predict the contact action time and compensate for the change of action time caused by external factors. The core of the above methods is to ensure the consistency of the action of the

This work was supported by the Natural Science Foundation of Fujian Province under Grant 2021J01634.

actuator by controlling the coil current to track the reference current. In [8], a displacement sensor is installed in the PMCB, and the actuator is tracked with a closed-loop strategy to achieve accurate control of the action process. Reference [9] designed a bistable PMCB drive circuit with auxiliary capacitors, under closed-loop control, the breaking and closing coils are simultaneously applied with currents in opposite directions to weaken the permanent magnet holding force, thereby improving the speed of action response. Most of the above methods perform strategy optimization or circuit improvement on the basis of coil current closed-loop control, so as to improve the operating characteristics of the circuit breaker. However, to build a control system of a bistable permanent magnet switch for a specific strategy not only lacks versatility, but also has a long period of hardware design and strategy verification.

This paper designs a bistable permanent magnet switch control strategy verification system based on NI sbRIO-9629 single-board controller. The whole system integrates co-simulation, data acquisition and intelligent control, which can easily and quickly embed the control strategy of the bistable permanent magnet switch into the hardware system for verification. The co-simulation system can flexibly respond to the requirements of various hardware control circuits, not only can write simulation programs efficiently and quickly, but also can build an intuitive operation interface. Flexible and reliable hardware control system and data acquisition system can be equipped with a variety of control strategies for experimental verification. The general-purpose programming environment and graphical programming language allow developers to quickly adjust and optimize strategies. This integrated simulation and verification system provides a good platform for the research on intelligent control of bistable permanent magnet switches, reducing the cost and shortening the cycle on research and development.

II. Closed-Loop Control Strategy

A. Structure and Motion Characteristics of Bistable PMCB

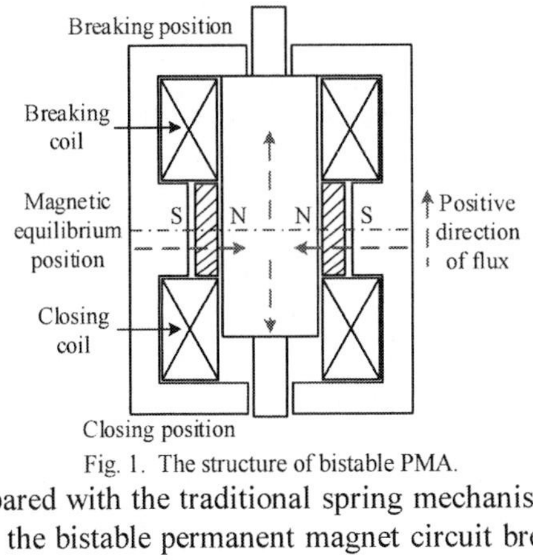

Fig. 1. The structure of bistable PMA.

Compared with the traditional spring mechanism circuit breaker, the bistable permanent magnet circuit breaker has the advantages of simple structure, long life and high reliability. Its cross-sectional view is shown in Fig 1. When the circuit breaker does not need to act, the coil does not need to be energized, and only the magnetic energy of the permanent magnet part can realize the permanent magnet lock at the breaking and closing positions of the movable iron core. When breaking or closing operation is required, the breaking coil or closing coil can be energized, and the movable iron core can complete the breaking and closing operations under the combined magnetic field force generated by the electromagnetic force of the coil and the permanent magnet force of the permanent magnet.

In order to realize the intelligent control of the bistable PMA, it is necessary to study its motion process [10]. The bistable PMCB often uses energy storage capacitors to power the coils. Combining with D'Alembert's equation of motion, it can be seen that the bistable PMA always satisfies the following differential equations during the movement process, as shown in (1):

$$\begin{cases} U_C = iR + \mathrm{d}\psi / \mathrm{d}t \\ i = -C(\mathrm{d}U_C / \mathrm{d}t) \\ \mathrm{d}^2 x / \mathrm{d}t^2 = (F_x - F_f) / m \end{cases} \tag{1}$$

Where: U_C is the initial voltage of the energy storage capacitor. i is the opening and closing coil current. R is the coil resistance. ψ is the flux linkage of the electromagnetic system. C is the capacitance of the energy storage capacitor. x is the displacement of the movable iron core. F_x is the electromagnetic attraction force of the movable iron core. F_f is the reaction force of the movable iron core. By analyzing the motion characteristics of the bistable PMA, it can be seen that in its intelligent control, the breaking and closing coil currents are the parameters that directly affect the excitation state of the circuit breaker [11].

B. Single-coil Current Closed-loop Control Strategy

Ignoring magnetic flux leakage, when there is no permanent magnetic field in the bistable actuator, the breaking and closing coils share the same magnetic circuit, so when the breaking coil is energized, an induced electromotive force is bound to be generated in the closing coil. If the circuit in which the closing coil is located can provide a current path for the induced potential, thereby generating an induced current, the electromagnetic force induced on the closing coil will affect the response speed of the actuator [9]. Similarly, the mutual inductance effect on the breaking coil during the closing operation is also the same.

In order to realize the good compatibility of various control strategies with bistable PMCB, it is necessary to design a set of coil drive circuits that can flexibly control both the breaking and closing coils. Therefore, this system adopts a dual-coil three-state drive circuit, as shown in Fig. 2. In order to avoid the influence of the mutual inductance between the above-mentioned double coils, this paper designs to connect the breaking and closing coil drive circuit and the rectifier filter circuit through a mechanical switch with physical contacts, and flexibly choose which coil is connected to the control loop.

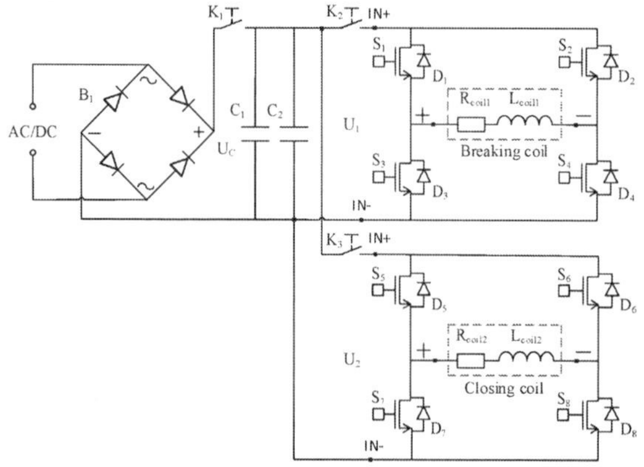

Fig. 2. The drive circuit topology of bistable PMA.

In the figure, B_1 is a rectifier module; C_1 and C_2 are large-capacity energy storage capacitors; K_1, K_2 and K_3 are mechanical switches; S_1, S_2, S_3, S_4, S_5, S_6, S_7 and S_8 are IGBT switches; R_{coil1}, L_{coil1} and R_{coil2}, L_{coil2} are the equivalent resistance and variable inductance of the breaking and closing coils, respectively.

The principle of current closed-loop control in the breaking process: Switches K_1 and K_2 are closed, and K_3 is opened, so that the breaking coil is connected to the power supply circuit separately. The input AC and DC power is rectified by the rectifier module to obtain relatively flat DC power, and then charges the energy storage capacitors C_1 and C_2. Then, the voltage across the coil is changed by controlling the on-off of the switch S_1, S_2, S_3, and S_4. After excitation, the FPGA detects the current of the breaking coil through the current sensor to obtain i_{coil1}, and then compares it with the reference current i_{ref1}. If $\Delta i_1<0$, the excitation state is selected as +1, S_1 and S_3 are turned on at the same time, the breaking coil is in the forward excitation state, and the coil current rises rapidly. If $\Delta i_1>\varepsilon_1$, the excitation state is selected as -1, and S_1 and S_3 are turned off at the same time. Due to the existence of the coil inductance, the current cannot immediately drop to zero. At this time, the coil current feeds back energy to the energy storage capacitor along the paths D_3, R_{coil1}, L_{coil1}, and D_2, the coil is in a negative pressure state, and the coil current drops rapidly. Finally, the fast tracking of the breaking coil current to the preset reference current is realized. The closed-loop control process is shown in Fig. 3, where the hysteresis frequency f_{s1} is set to 20kHz.

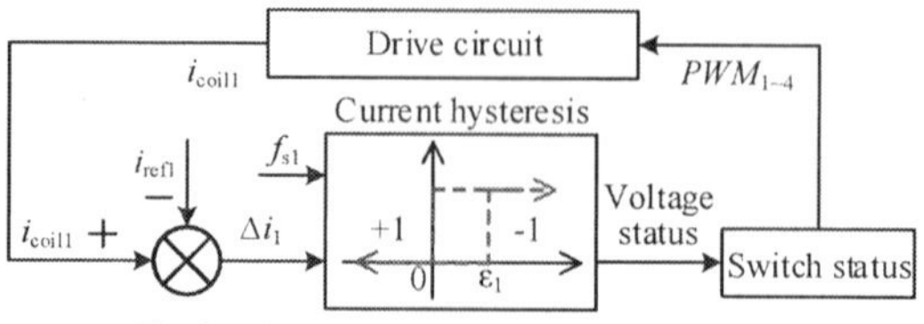

Fig. 3. Single-coil current closed-loop process.

III. CO-SIMULATION

A. Co-simulation Principle

NI LabVIEW uses dataflow and graphical programming language (G language) for programming. As a general programming environment, it provides a wealth of controls and can easily create a user interface. It is widely used in the field of test and measurement, industrial control and electromechanical equipment simulation.

The mechanical motion sub-model, voltage balance sub-model, reverse current sub-model, suction solution sub-model and parameter solution sub-model of the bistable PMA are built in LabVIEW, as shown in Fig. 4. Meanwhile, the drive circuit of the breaking and closing coils is designed in Multisim.

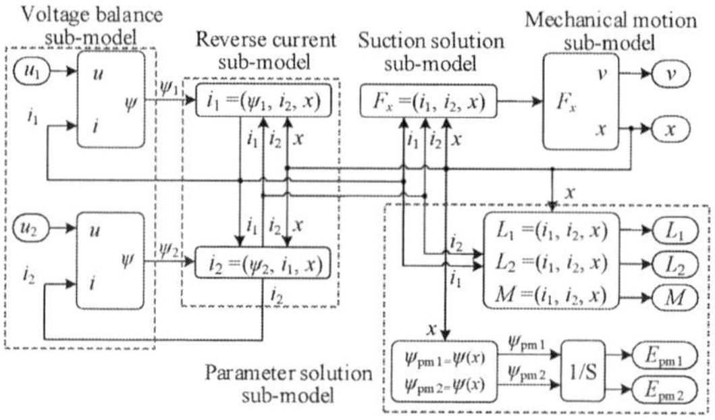

Fig. 4. Co-simulation principle.

Then, using the integrated co-simulation principle as shown in Fig. 5, a two-way data transmission channel is established between Multisim and LabVIEW. So that two independent simulation software can exchange data at each time step and use the exchanged data for the next simulation step. In this process, LabVIEW transmits the PWM drive signal and variable inductance parameters of the three-state drive circuit to Multisim. Multisim transmits the coil voltage and current value to LabVIEW as the excitation and feedback control quantities of the dynamic model of the circuit breaker.

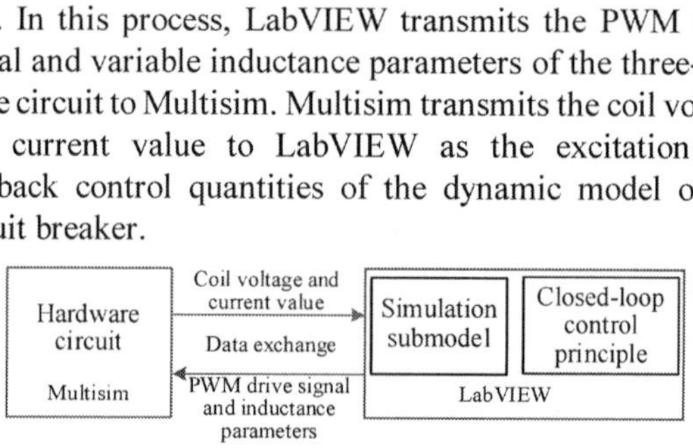

Fig. 5. Integrated co-simulation principle.

B. Co-simulation Verification

In the co-simulation, the voltage of the energy storage capacitor is DC100V, the total operation time is set to 100ms, the PWM control frequency is set to 20kHz, the breaking and closing coil resistances are set to 1.3Ω and 0.8Ω respectively, and the closed-loop reference value of the breaking coil current is set to 35A.

Fig. 6 shows the voltage and current of the breaking coil and the displacement of movable iron core during the breaking process obtained by the co-simulation of LabVIEW and Multisim. The breaking process of the circuit breaker starts at time t_0, the system starts to excite from the discharge of the energy storage capacitor, and the current of the breaking coil reaches the reference value at time t_1, and the dynamic balance is maintained around 35A under the current closed-loop control. At this time, the flux linkage at the breaking position and the electromagnetic attraction force on the movable iron core continue to increase until the electromagnetic attraction force is greater than the combined force of the reaction force and the permanent magnetic force, and the movable iron core begins to move to the breaking position. During the movement of the movable iron core, the current of the breaking coil is forced to drop due to the influence of the opposite potential [12]. At t_2, the movable iron core reaches to the breaking position, and is stably maintained at the breaking position by the combined action of the electromagnetic attraction force of the breaking coil and the permanent magnetic force. After that, the breaking coil continues to be excited during the period of t_2~t_3, and the current rises to 35A again and maintains dynamically around this value. After t_3, the excitation of the breaking coil by the energy storage capacitor is stopped, and the current is freewheeling along the body diode in the drive circuit. Until t_4, the loop current decays to zero, the coil voltage returns to zero, and the movable iron core can be reliably locked in the breaking steady position only by the permanent magnetic force.

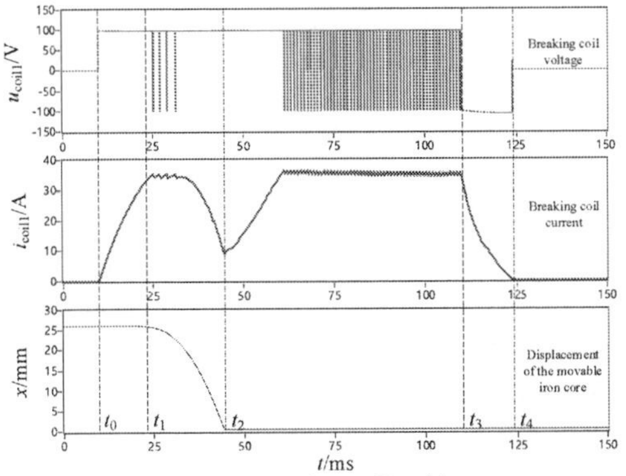

Fig. 6. Simulation waveform of breaking process.

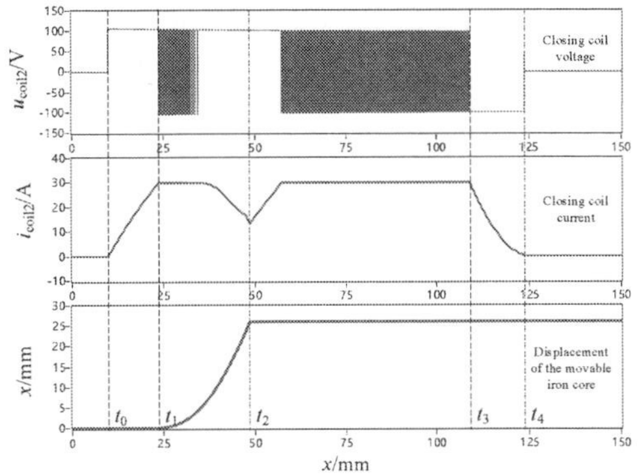

Fig. 7. Simulation waveform of closing process.

The structure of the bistable PMCB is not completely symmetrical. Factors such as the number of coil turns, coil resistance, and the reaction force of the actuator are not exactly the same, so that the excitation characteristics and motion characteristics of the circuit breaker during the breaking and closing process are not completely consistent. The closing process curve is shown in Fig. 7. During the closing operation, the reference value of the coil current is set to 30A, and other parameters are the same as the breaking process settings. During the breaking and closing operations, the movable iron core is equivalent to completing a reciprocating motion, that is, the process of crossing from one steady position to another steady position.

IV. Experimental Verification

A. The Structure of the Hardware System

Fig. 8 is the overall structure diagram of the hardware part of the bistable PMCB control strategy verification system designed and built for this design.

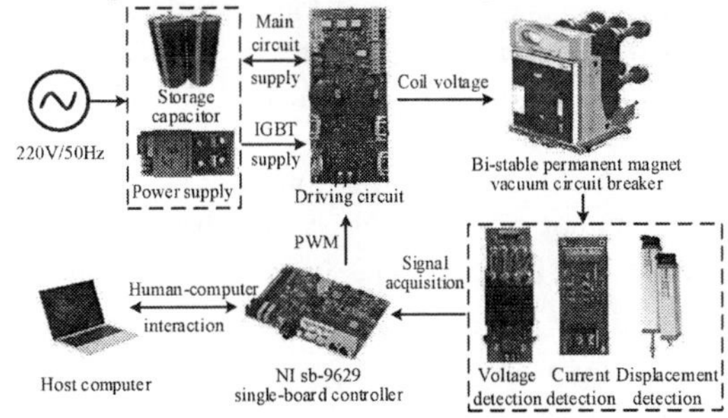

Fig. 8. Hardware overall structure diagram.

The host computer of this system uses NI LabVIEW 2020 as the software control platform, and uses the NI sbRIO-9629 single-board controller as the core control module. The high-frequency voltage and current signal sampling module is designed using LEM's high-frequency voltage and current sensors for the collection of feedback signals, and the power supply module is used as the power of the signal sampling module. Taking the short-term discharge of the energy storage capacitor as the excitation source, a three-state drive circuit that is flexible and controllable for both coils is designed, and finally a complete set of efficient, reliable and flexible intelligent control system for bistable PMCB is formed.

B. Core Controller

The research object of this design is a bistable PMCB. To perform digital closed-loop control of the breaking and closing coils respectively under the three-state drive circuit, it needs to occupy a lot of digital I/O and analog I/O. So the core controller of this design uses sbRIO-9629 produced by NI. This is an embedded CompactRIO single-board controller that integrates a real-time processor, a reconfigurable FPGA, and ample digital I/O. In addition, the controller also has 4 16-bit analog inputs with a maximum total sampling rate of 233KS/s, 4 16-bit analog outputs with a maximum total refresh rate of 298KS/s, and 4 DIO ports with 5v withstand voltage. Its built-in RMC connector can connect two C series I/O modules or an expansion board with 96 2.5 V/3.3 V single-ended digital I/O ports. Using the sbRIO-9629 single board and the in-line RMC expansion I/O can greatly meet the design requirements for hardware resources, and at the same time, it also has the advantages of small size, convenient connection, and convenient development and design.

C. Software Design

FPGA adopts the concept of programmable gate array, which has the characteristics of static repeatable programming and dynamic system reconfiguration, so that the function of hardware can be modified by programming like software. It allows engineers to freely design the control system through graphical programming or hardware description language, and can design and modify it at any time without changing the hardware circuit, which greatly shortens the design time, reduces the PCB area, and improves system reliability. In addition, FPGA can realize parallel operations between tasks, and can perform multiple logics such as addition and multiplication at the same time, and the computing power is more powerful.

Taking the breaking operation as an example, the software design process is shown in Fig. 9. Configure the underlying frequency, frequency division coefficient, duty cycle coefficient, PID and other parameters of the PWM digital module to generate a PWM_DO output as a PWM signal. Then use the PWM periodic signal PWM_Clock to trigger the analog acquisition module to perform single-cycle sampling of coil voltage and current. The sampling point is set at 1/4 of the PWM single cycle to avoid collecting the peak value of current and voltage, so as to reduce the influence of the sampling process on the closed-loop control [13]. The control method adopts the hysteresis current closed-loop form in Section 2.2, which is simple, stable, and easy to verify. Finally, the generated PWM signal is output through RMC/DIO1_4 to isolate and drive the IGBT in the three-state circuit.

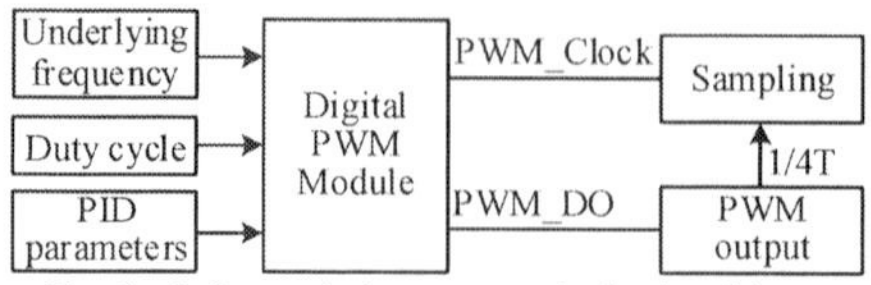

Fig. 9. Software design process during breaking.

Fig. 10 shows the upper computer control panel of the single-coil current closed-loop FPGA program of the system. The written FPGA program can generate corresponding input and output interfaces, buttons, indicator lights and other controls on the front panel. These interfaces are convenient for users to debug and modify the internal parameters of the program online.

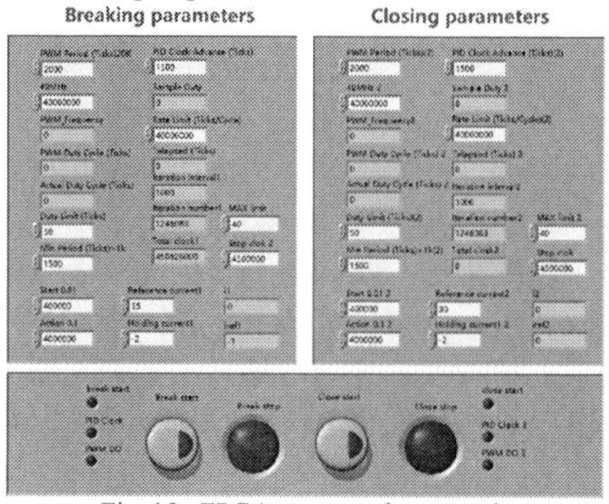

Fig. 10. FPGA program front panel.

D. Waveform Analysis

Write the FPGA bottom-level program into sb-9629 and embed it into the hardware control system for quick experimental verification. Fig. 11 is the coil voltage, current, displacement, and contact bounce experimental waveforms obtained when the bistable PMCB breaking coil closed-loop 35A, and Figure 12 is the experimental waveform when the closing coil closed-loop 30A.

Comparing the co-simulation waveform diagram and the experimental waveform diagram of the circuit breaker operation process, it can be seen that the co-simulation system has a good consistency with the hardware control system, and can be used to quickly verify the feasibility of the control strategy. Under the current closed-loop control, the bistable PMCB can accurately control the coil current in a wide voltage range, reduce the influence of the working voltage on the action characteristics, and improve the action consistency of the breaking and closing process.

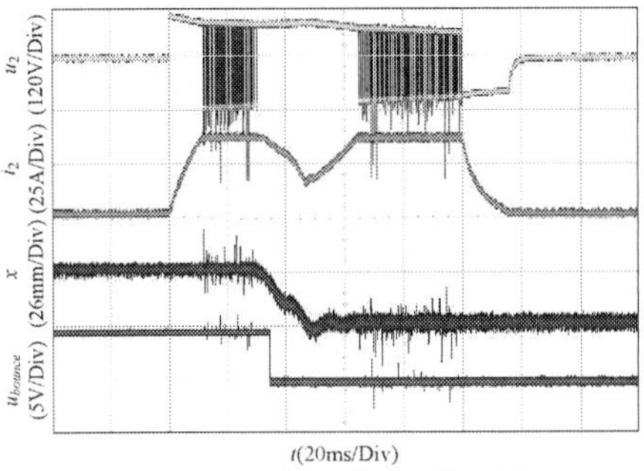

Fig. 11. The experimental waveform of breaking process.

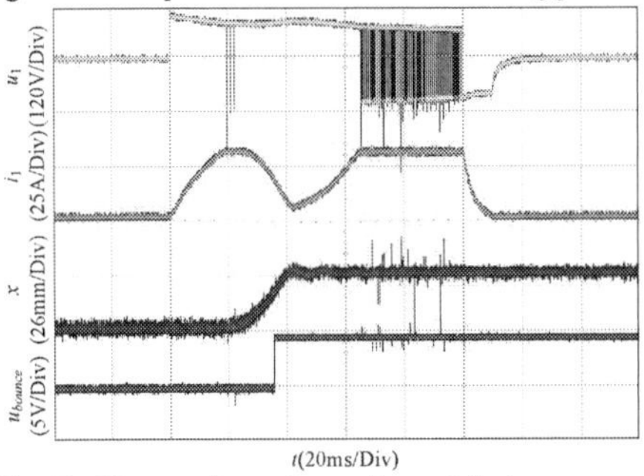

Fig. 12. The experimental waveform of closing process.

V. Conclusion

In this paper, a bistable PMCB control strategy verification system based on NI sbRIO-9629 has been developed. The whole system integrates co-simulation, data acquisition and processing, and intelligent control. The following conclusions are drawn through co-simulation and experiments.

1) The co-simulation system can carry out a reasonable simulation verification of the control strategy to ensure the feasibility and security of the strategy implementation; The hardware control system can easily embed the control strategy for verification, which improves the flexibility of development and shortens the development cycle;
2) Under the current closed-loop control, the bistable PMCB has a wide voltage operation capability, which improves the consistency of the operating characteristics and the controllability and reliability of the breaking and closing process of the bistable PMCB.
3) The whole system has strong versatility, and can easily combine the control parameters such as flux linkage and displacement on the basis of current closed-loop to simulate and experimentally verify various high-performance closed-loop feedback control systems.

References

[1] L. Shu, C Xu, G. Wu, X. Zhu and S. Zhao, "Coupled Modeling and Numerical Calculations of the Dynamic Characteristics of Magnetic Actuator" , *Proceedings of the CSEE*, 2015, 35: 4524–4530.

[2] J. Jiang, H. Lin and S. Fang, "Optimization Design of a Permanent Magnet Actuator for 126-kV Vacuum Circuit Breaker", IEEE Transactions on Applied Superconductivity, 2018, 28: 1-5.

[3] Kyung Il Woo and Byung Il Kwon, "Characteristic analysis and modification of PM-type magnetic circuit breaker", IEEE Transactions on Magnetics, 2004, 40: 691-694.

[4] J. Lu, Y. Wang, J. Xie and Y. Liu, "Control Method for Permanent Magnetic Vacuum Circuit Breaker Based on Coil Current" in *High Voltage Engineering*, 2013, 39: 860–868.

[5] J. Lu, J. Liu, Y. Han, Z. Ye and Q. Yu, "Control Method for Improving Reliability of Closing and Opening Permanent Magnetic Vacuum Circuit Breaker", *High Voltage Engineering*, 2016, 42: 3989–3995.

[6] Q. Zhang and H. Yuan, "Design and Realization of Synchronous Opening and Closing Control System of Vacuum Circuit Breaker with Permanent Magnet Mechanism" in *Electric Power Automation Equipment*, 2010, 30: 98–103.

[7] J. Ma and B. Xiao, "Prediction of synchronous closing time based on permanent magnetic actuator" , *Journal of HEFEI University of Technology*, 2015, 8: 600–604.

[8] T. Qin, E. Dong, Y. Chen, X. Duan and J. Zou, "Path Tracking Control of Vacuum Circuit Breaker", *Proceedings of the CSEE*, 2014, 34: 5983–5990.

[9] S. Fang, Q. Liu, H. Lin and S. L. Ho, "A Novel Flux-Weakening Control Strategy for Permanent-Magnet Actuator of Vacuum Circuit Breaker" in IEEE Transactions on Industrial Electronics, 2016, 63: 2275-2283.

[10] X. Cheng, X. Yuan, G. Ge and J. Zhu, "Permanent Magnet Mechanism Control System with High Operation Stability of Vacuum Switch", *Transactions of China Electrotechnical Society*, 2021, 36: 4617–4626.

[11] L. Tang, H. Qu and Z. Xu, "Research on Double Closed-Loop Control Strategy of Contactors Based on Flux Linkage Observers" , IEEE Transactions on Industrial Electronics, 2022, 69: 2769-2779.

[12] L. Tang, W. Chen and Z. Xu, "The Self-Correcting Control Strategy of a Single Flux Linkage Closed Loop for a Contactor" in IEEE Transactions on Industrial Electronics, 2022, 69: 11521-11530.

[13] L. Tang and Z. Xu, "A Slope Closed-loop Control Technology of AC Contactors" in *Proceedings of the CSEE*, 2017, 37: 956–965.

Shixu Luan is currently pursuing the M.S. degree in electric engineering from the College of Electrical Engineering and Automation, Fuzhou University, China. His research interests include electric apparatus and its intelligent technology. 200120009@fzu.edu.cn.

Longfei Tang (Senior Member, IEEE) received his B.Sc. degree in electrical engineering and automation from Fuzhou University in 2009 and his Ph.D. degree in electric machines and electric apparatus from Fuzhou University in 2015. Now he is a professor at Fuzhou University, China. His research interests include electric apparatus and its intelligent technology. Corresponding author: tlftel@fzu.edu.cn.

Study on $AgSnO_2$ Material for Magnetic Latching Relay

Yangfang Chen, Xiaofang Yan, Xiaoping Bai, Jie Li, YiBo You

Zhejiang Fuda Alloy Material Technology Co., Ltd., Wenzhou, Zhejiang, China, 325000
E-mail: cyf@china-fuda.com Tel: 15968767475

Abstract—**Magnetic latching relay was widely used in smart meters, synchronous switches, smart homes, automation equipment and other fields, which played an important role in automatic connection and disconnection of circuits. The difference was that the normally closed or normally open state of the magnetic latching relay completely depended on the function of the permanent magnetic steel, and the switching state was triggered by the pulse ele-ctric signal of a certain width. When the relay was under the condition of large current, the current impact on the contact was enhanced significantly, resulting in early bonding of the contact, which affected the service life of the relay. This paper mainly studied the electrical parameters such as arc energy, arc time, welding force and contact burning mechanism of different silver tin oxide electrical contact materials. It would provide a reference for the development of electrical contact materials.**

Keywords— **Magnetic latching relay; $AgSnO_2$; electrical contact materials;**

I. Introduction

Magnetic latching relays were mainly used in the control of smart meters, IC card meters, prepaid meters, synchronous switches, composite switches, solar street light control, smart home, automation equipment and other systems. When the magnetic latching relay works under high current conditions, the arc energy caused by the current was very large, which could easily lead to the bonding of the relay contacts in the early stage of operation, and the dynamic and static points could not be broken normally, which would cause the relay to produce bonding failure, which was easy to cause other serious consequences. Therefore, it was very important to study the early bonding problem of electrical contact materials.

Many researchers have also conducted research on contact materials for magnetic latching relays. Literature 1 [1] pointed out that adding WO_3 and CuO additives to $AgSnO_2$ materials could improve the creep resistance of the materials. CuO could reduce the overall creep amount and steady-state creep rate by 55% when the stress was 50MPa. and 40%, and at the same time could improve the interface strength of AgSnO2 material, could effectively improve the generation and propagation of cracks. Reference 2 [2] pointed out that, on the basis of the $AgSnO_2$ material composite system, the morphology and structure of SnO_2 were controlled and the space skeleton model was designed to solve the dispersion problem of SnO_2 in the Ag matrix. The close combination of Ag and SnO_2 uses the space skeleton restraint to limit the floating of SnO_2 under long-term arc erosion, avoiding the performance degradation caused by the enrichment of SnO_2 on the surface of the contact material. Reference 3[3] studied the welding phenomenon of the contacts of the magnetic latching relay during service. During the operation of the relay, the continuous closing and breaking of the contacts will make the working condition of the contact surface worse, resulting in more bounce of the contacts in the subsequent closing process. Multiple bounces would significantly increase the arcing time and arc energy. The surface of the moving and static contacts would produce molten pools of various shapes and sizes under the action of the high temperature of the arc. When the contact was closed again, if it contacts the position of the molten pool, it was easy to have static fusion welding in the contact process, resulting in bonding, that was, relay failure.

In the actual use of magnetic latching relays, welding problems caused by contact bonding often occur. In this paper, the simulated electrical performance parameters between ordinary silver tin oxide materials and materials prepared by special processes are studied, including parameters such as arcing time, arcing energy, welding force, and contact surface morphology characteristics after the test. It was expected to provide a useful reference for the research and design of electrical contact materials used in magnetic latching relays.

II. Other Introductions

1.Test method and process

The pre-oxidation method was one of the most commonly used methods for preparing silver tin oxide electrical contact materials. The materials prepared by this method have good burnout resistance and breaking properties, and have been widely used in the field of magnetic latching relays.

After the improvement, the hardness of the material was increased by about 10HV, the tensile strength was increased by about 15MPa, the elongation was reduced by 9%, and the resistivity was 0.04μΩ.cm higher than that of the traditional material.

TABLE I

COMPARISON ON COMPOSITION OF THE MATERIALS

Category	Content(wt.%)			Remarks
	Ag	SnO_2	Additives	
Common materials	88	Remain	1	
Improved material	88	Remain	2	

The process of material preparation in this paper was as follows: The raw material was smelted, then water atomized to make powder, and then dried, pre-oxidized, isostatically pressed, formed into a blank before extrusion, and then extruded and drawn to obtain the required wire φ1.9 [soft]. The pre-oxidation process flow was: smelting → water atomization pulverizing → powder oxidation → isostatic pressing → extrusion → finished product drawing.

The microscopic structure of $AgSnO_2$ was examined and analyzed with SEM and the density was tested with water displacement method and hardness was tested with MICROH ARD-NESS MHV2000 hardness tester and the tensile strength and the elongation were tested with LJ-1000 material testing machine and the resistivity was tested with TH2512B intelligent DC resistance tester.

Meanwhile, the electrical properties were tested with electrical life simulation tester of contact material which was developed with a China's university. The simulation electrical properties tester of new model was showed in the following figure: mainly including XYZ three axes displacement sliders, driving system composed of direct acting electromagnet and push rod, electromagnetic stroke positioning linkage and relay seat. The system could adjust the working point of the push rod by adjusting displacement sliders of Z axis and Y axis, and could adjust displacement slider of X axis of electromagnetic stroke positioning linkage to control the limiting stopper so as to adjust the idle stroke and excess of stroke of the push rod. The adjusting precision of the position is 10μm. The device can easily replace the contact spring system of different relays for simulation test, and can simultaneously measure the contact voltage, current and welding force.

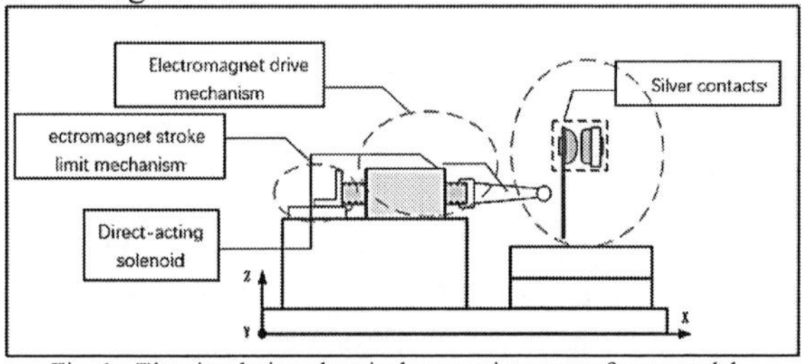

Fig. 1. The simulation electrical properties tester of new model

All above testing data including contact voltage, contact current and dynamic force are acquired by the commercial DAQ system (PCI1706, Advantech, Taiwan), which has a measurement resolution of 16 bits and a sampling frequency of 250kHz. The instrument is interfaced to a personal computer using serial port RS232. Data acquisition and logging process are controlled by a PC with the help of LabVIEW software specifically programmed for this purpose.

TABLE II

SIMULATED ELECTRICAL PERFORMANCE TEST CONDITIONS

Category	AC voltage	AC current	On off frequency	Load category	Remarks
Simulated electrical performance test	250VAC	25A	1s,on 1s,off	Resistive load	
Relay test		100A	5s,on 9s,off		

2.Test Results and Discussions

First, the mechanical and physical properties of the conventional material and the improved material were compared. The specific data were shown in Table 3. It could be seen that the hardness and tensile strength of the improved material were improved, but the elongation was lower than that of the traditional material.

After the improvement, the hardness of the material was increased by about 10HV, the tensile strength was increased by about 15MPa, the elongation was reduced by 9%, and the resistivity was 0.04μΩ.cm higher than that of the traditional material.

TABLE III

COMPARISON ON MECHANICAL AND PHYSICAL PRO-PERTIES

Category	Tensile stength (MPa)	Elongatong (%)	Elctrical resistivity (μΩ.cm)	Density (g/cm^3)	Hardness value (HV0.3)		
Common materials	300	19	2.2	9.77	85.6	86.7	86.2
Improved material	315	10	2.24	9.77	95.2	98.4	97.3

Fig 2 shows a comparison of the microstructures of conventional and special materials. It could be seen that the oxide particle size of the traditional material was relatively coarse, and most of the particles were above 1 μm, while the oxide particle size of the improved material in this study was relatively fine, and most of the particles were below 1 μm in size. According to the existing research on materials science, adding a second phase component to the metal could strengthen the metal. In this study, the oxide particle size of the conventional material was larger, while the particle size of the modified material was smaller, and most of the particle size was below 1 μm. According to the principle of dispersion strengthen-ing, the fine particles would increase the hardness, tensile strength and other properties of materials. Therefore, the hardness and tensile strength of the materials prepared in this study were higher than those of conventional materials, but their elongation was lower than conventional materials.

The electrical properties of the two materials were

compared in Tables 4 and 5. It could be seen that the 95% confidence interval of Weibull curve, the electric life of simulated electrical life of conventional materials and special materials were 56,003and 118,161 times respectively. The average electrical life of the improved material was about 62,158 times higher than that of conventional material. It could be seen from Table 5 that the relay test results of the traditional material and the improved material were 3664 times and 11,204 times respectively. The electrical life of the improved material was about 7540 times higher than that of conventional material. It could be seen from the above data that the simulated electrical performance of the improved material and the actual electrical life of the relay were better than that of those of the traditional material. The two materials showed the same electrical life law on the simulated test machine as the actual relay test. Therefore, the differences between the two materials could be studied in detail with data from simulated electrical performance tests.

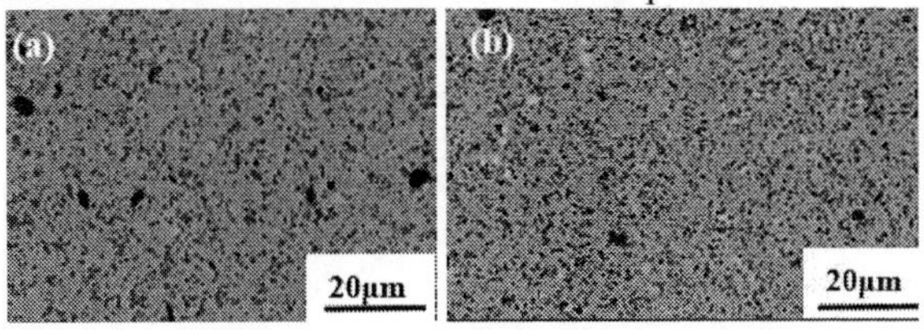

Fig. 2. Comparison on microstructure between conventional materials and special materials (SEM)

a) Common materials 2000x;b) Improved material 2000x

TABLE IV

COMPARISON ON SIMULATED ELECTRICAL LIFE RESULTS

Category	Simulated electric life (Operations)					
	Data 1	Data 2	Data 3	Data 4	Data 5	ρ0.95
Common materials	54698	52368	49586	55412	48769	56003
Improved material	99858	117846	102569	102546	112305	118161

TABLE V

COMPARISON ON ELECTRICAL LIFE RESULTS OF RELAY

Category	Electrical life results of relay (Operations)					
	Data 1	Data 2	Data 3	Data 4	Data 5	ρ0.95
Common materials	2356	3541	2569	3358	3205	3664
Improved material	10254	11025	10896	11125	10457	11204

In order to further understand the reasons for the difference in electrical performance between conventional and improved materials in simulated electrical properties and relay tests, and to gain a more complete understanding of the characteristics of arcing, In this paper, traditional materials and improved materials with simulated electrical lifetimes of 55,412 and 102,546 times were selected, and the arc energy, arc time, welding force, and burn-out contact morphology were compared and studied.

Fig 3 shows the comparison of the arc energy, arc time and welding force of the traditional material and the improved material in the simulated electrical performance test. It could be seen from the figure that under the same current level, the arc energy of the improved material was 3050.59mJ within the 95% confidence interval, and the arc energy of the traditional material was 2950mJ.The arcing time of the improved material was 8.801ms within the 95% confidence interval, and the traditional material was 8.764ms.The difference was very obvious in the welding force within the 95% confidence interval. The welding force of the improved material was 0.015N, and the traditional material was 0.124N. This is due to the higher hardness of the improved material, which effectively improves the welding performance of the contacts when they were in contact.

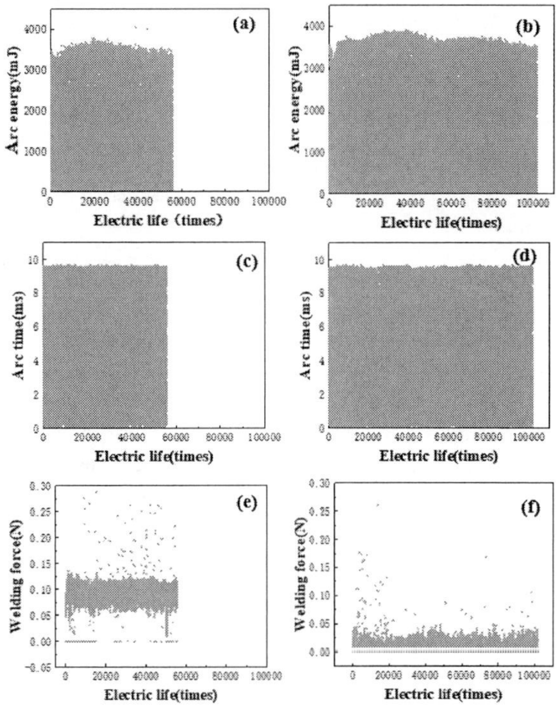

Fig. 3. Comparison on arc energy and arc time、 welding force between common materials and improved materials in electrical performance simulated test.

(a) arc energy of common materials;

(b) arc energy of improved materials;

(c) arc time of common materials;

(d) arc time of improved materials;

(e)welding force of common materials;

(d) welding force of improved materials.

Fig 4 shows the surface morphology of the contact after arc burn in the simulated electrical performance test. As could be seen from Figure 4, the contact surface prepared by the traditional material has very serious ablation marks. At the same time, a large area of collapse occurs at the edge of the contact, which affects the electrical life of the contact.

In conclusion, the electrical life of the improved material was better than that of the traditional material. Due to its low hardness, the contacts made of traditional materials have worse wear resistance than that of the improved materials during the service process with the repeated action of a large current, so a large area of potholes appear in the middle of the working surface. The material at the contact part has been consumed, and a large number of collapses have occurred at the edge, which affects the overall structure of the rivet contact, reduces the breaking ability of the contact, and causes the final bond failure.

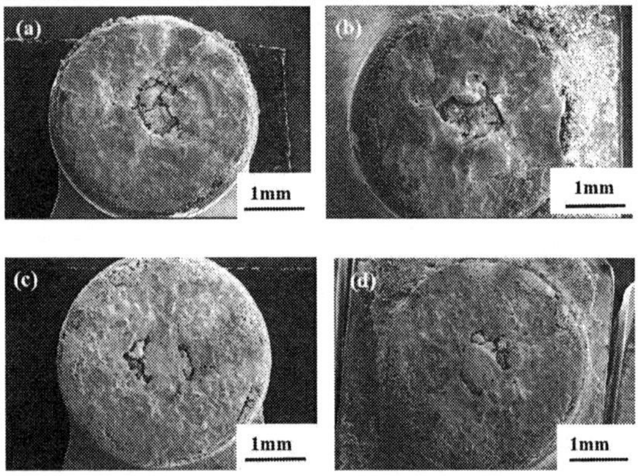

Fig. 4. Comparison on contact surface macro morph-ology after arc burning during electrical performance simulated test.
(a) moving contact of common material, 55412 failure;
(b) static contact of common l material, 55412 failure;
(c) moving contact of improved material, 102546 failure;
(d) static contact of improved material, 102546 failure;

According to the above test results, in the magnetic latching relay, improving the electrical wear resistance of the contact material was one of the main research directions to improve the electrical life of the material. At the same time, considering different types of load conditions and different relay structures, it was necessary to further study and adjust the ratio of additives to improve the breaking performance and anti-welding ability of the material.

III. Conclusion

Based on the results and discussions presented above, the conclusions were obtained as below:

(1) Compared with the traditional material, the improved material has higher hardness, higher tensile strength, lower elongation and higher resistivity.

(2) The 95% confidence interval of the Weibull curve shows that the simulated electrical lifetimes of the traditional material and the improved material were 56003 times and 118161 times, respectively.

(3) The failure of traditional materials was due to the poor electrical wear resistance caused by the lower hardness of the contacts, and a large area of ablation pits appear in the middle of the working surface under the repeated action of high current. Part of the contact material had been consumed, and a large number of collapses had occurred at the edge of the contact, which affected the overall structure of the rivet contact and reduced the breaking ability of the contact. However, due to its better electrical wear resistance, the improved material could reach a higher lifetime before failure occurs.

(4) The higher hardness of the improved material could improve the electrical wear resistance of the contact and reduce the material loss on the contact surface under high current. At the same time, the presence of high additive content improved the anti-fusion welding ability of the material effectively. Therefore, it exhibited more excellent electrical performance under the condition of simulated electrical life.

References

[1] Tianyang Yang.,Yuanyuan Ma.,Longxiao Zhang.,Wenjie Feng.,Jinggui Li.,Qianxue Fang.:Effect of oxide additives on creep resistance of Ag-SnO2 electrical contact materials: Rare Metal Materials and Engineering. 2021(4):2-3.

[2] Longjin Wang.,Chong Fu.,Jing Ning.,Xu Li.,Qingxin Li.,Yang Lu.:Research progress and development trend of Ag SnO2 electrical contact materials.Precious Metals2021(3):1-3

[3] Xiaoping B., Guowei L., Wei W., Mingjiang Z., Wanhuan L., Libing Z., Yaping Z.: ICEC. 2012:368-374.

[4] John J.Sher, Charles J. Luebke, Kevin L. Parker: ICEC. 2012:1-2.

[5] Liqiang L., Xiaofang Y., Wei W., Jifeng X., Ning Z.: The Investigation on the Production Process of AgSnO2 Contact Materials by AgSn Powder Pre-oxidation. ICEC. 2012:362-363.

[6] Jie L., Xiaofang Y., Xiaoping B., Liqiang L., Suhua L., Wei W.: Effect of different In contents on hardness and microstructure of AgSnIn alloy during internal oxidation. The Institute of Electronics, Information and Communication Engineers Technical Report, 2013[C], 113(298): 96-98.

[7] Jie L., Wei W., Xiaoping B, Xiaofang Y., Heng W., Liqiang L.: Study on the effect of different indium content on arc erosion performance of AgSnO2 contacts under simulated automobile relay conditions. Electrical appliances and energy efficiency management technology. 2016(3): 22-26.

[8] Fuqi D., Ji Z., Zhihao R., Jian L.: Study on the arc erosion performance of AGW and AgSnO2 contact materials under the condition of simulated automobile relay. Electrical materials. 2009, 1: 6-9.

[9] Schimmel G., Kempf B., Rettenmayr M.: Exudation of Ag and Cu In Internal oxidized Ag-Sn-In-(Cu) Alloys. Material Letters. 2009:1521-1524.

[10] Zhenbiao L.: IEEE Holm'96 and ICEC'96 electrical contact conference and contact materials. Electrical materials. 1997(1):10-11.

[11] Verma A., Anantharaman T.: Internal oxidation of rapidly solidified silver-tin-indium alloy powders. Journal of Materials Science. 1992(27): 5623-5628.

Low-voltage Series Arc Fault Detection Based on Autoregressive Model

Luyao Zhao[1], Changchun Chi[1], Haifeng Mao[2]

[1]School of Electrical Engineering, Shanghai Dianji University, Shanghai, 201306, China
[2]Suzhou Future Electrical Co., LTD., Suzhou, 215000, China
E-mail: o1x737@163.com Tel: 19983686023

***Abstract*—According to the difference of the frequency of the current before and after the arc fault, the spectral characteristics are different, a method of the arc fault detection based on the prediction error ratio of the autoregressive model (AR) is proposed. The current signals before and after the fault of the low-voltage load circuit are built into the AR model, and then the model parameters are extracted by the modified covariance method. Finally, the classification of the low-voltage load in the normal circuit and the faulty circuit is realized based on the prediction error ratio. Finally, use the extracted feature quantities to establish threshold comparison arc fault discrimination algorithms for low-voltage loads commonly used in households such as hair dryers and notebook computers, and perform reliability verification. The results show that the AR model prediction error ratio of the current signal can effectively characterize the arc fault feature quantity without misjudgment of startup. The method in this paper can effectively identify arc faults without misjudgment, and provide references and ideas for the reliability research of arc fault protection circuit breakers.**

***Index Terms*— arc fault, prediction error, AR model, reliability research.**

I. INTRODUCTION

In the power supply and distribution system, faults such as loose conductor connection between electrical connectors or damaged insulation in the line will lead to arcs at the fault point, and because such arcs are connected in series between the load and the line when they occur, also known as Series arc fault. When a series arc fault occurs in the line, the change of the current amplitude is small, which cannot be detected by ordinary circuit breakers, and the series arc can exist in the line for a long time. The sparks generated by the series arc fault can cause combustibles to burn and even explode in severe cases. In 2020, the number of electrical fires in the country will be about 87,000, accounting for about one-third of the number of fires in the country [1]. Therefore, in order to improve the reliability of arc fault protectors, reduce electrical fires, and ensure the safe life and production of personnel, arc fault detection is an urgent problem to be solved.

The arcing process of arc fault is accompanied by complex physical and chemical reactions, including photoelectric mixing, radiation and temperature field interaction. References [2-5] realize arc fault detection based on pink noise, arc light, arc radiation, and radio frequency signals, respectively, but the above detection methods need to install sensors, so they are only suitable for switch cabinets and power distribution cabinets. The current mainstream detection method is the line current signal. When an arc fault occurs, the current waveform will be severely distorted and high-order harmonics will be generated. Therefore, based on the original current time-domain characteristics such as the number of high-frequency pulses[6], the difference between adjacent cycle current waveforms[7], current The features such as the rate of rise and the flat shoulder area[8] and the proportional coefficient of zero rest time[9] are used to diagnose faults. Secondly, there are also features used to detect arc faults in the frequency domain. For example, the literature [10-12] uses wavelet and Fourier transform to analyze the current, and extracts the contribution rate of the characteristics of each frequency band to the signal as a feature, so as to realize the fault. detection. Finally, due to the existence of arcs, energy aliasing will occur, and the eigenvalues can also be characterized by energy signal features such as energy entropy [13]. The user terminal is a multi-load mixed party, and the feature changes before and after the fault are aliased, which needs to be classified and diagnosed by an artificial intelligence algorithm. Intelligent algorithms widely used in the field of arc fault detection include support vector machines[14, 15], machine learning[16], BP neural network and particle swarm algorithm[17, 18], decision trees[19, 20], etc. These smart algorithms have a detection rate of over 97%. The above detection has excellent performance in the fault diagnosis rate, but in actual working conditions, it faces the problems of complex algorithm process, insufficient fault judgment time, and the need to install sensors at the fault point in advance. The detection method is not universal. Therefore, finding an arc fault detection method that is simple in feature extraction and adaptable to working conditions is the focus of this paper.

The spectral characteristics are different due to the difference in frequency of the current before and after the arc fault occurs. According to this feature, this paper establishes an AR model based on the random signal of the current, and uses the modified covariance method to estimate the model parameters, which can effectively characterize the spectral characteristics and energy changes of the current signal. The arc fault feature is represented by the AR model prediction error ratio of the current signal before and after the arc fault, so as to achieve the purpose of detecting the arc fault.

II. Application Analysis of AR Parameter Model in Arc Fault Identification

According to the linear model of discrete random signal, a discrete random signal x(n) can be regarded as the output of a white noise u(n) through a filter [21], and the parameter model is shown in Figure 1.

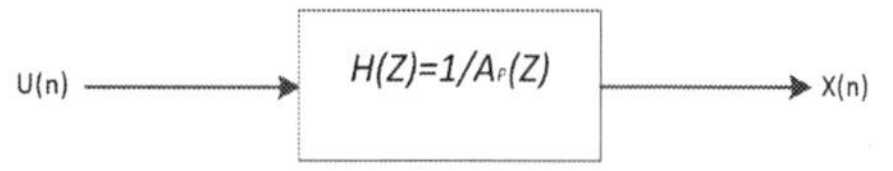

Fig 1 P-order parametric model of x(n)

The random signal x(n) in Figure 1 is generated by the linear combination of multiple past values x(n-k) and the current excitation value u(n):

$$x(n) = u(n) - \sum_{k=1}^{p} a_k x(n-k) \tag{1}$$

The system function of this model is:

$$H(Z) = \frac{1}{A(Z)} = \frac{1}{1 + \sum_{k=1}^{p} a_k Z^{-K}} \tag{2}$$

In the formula, P is the system order, a_k is the filter coefficient, there are no zeros in the system function, only poles, so the AR model is also called all-pole modeling, represented by $AR_{(p)}$.

AR parameter model estimation is to determine the model order *P*, filter coefficients a_k and prediction error $e_{(n)}$. The AR model parameter estimation can be solved by the covariance method, the modified covariance method, the autocorrelation method and the Burg algorithm. Here, the modified covariance method is adopted. The purpose of estimating AR parameters is achieved by making the average ρ^ of the forward and backward prediction error power of the random signal to be minimal. In addition, the quality of the power spectrum is greatly affected by the order *P*. If the value of *P* is small, it will be too smooth and the accuracy will be insufficient. If *P* is too large, false peaks may be generated, resulting in spectral line separation. In this paper, the order p=5 of the AR model is given by the final prediction error criterion (FPE, final predidyion error) combined with the analysis of experimental data. Because the slope of the power spectrum can be represented by the complex poles of the autoregressive model, when the mode of the complex poles approaches the unit circle, the peak value of the corresponding signal power spectrum increases, and when the mode of the complex poles is far away from the unit circle, the corresponding signal power spectrum becomes flatter. Figure 2 is the current signal of the primary arc fault, which is the current signal in the normal working state before 0.08 seconds. After 0.08 seconds is the current signal after arc fault. It can be seen from Fig 2a) that after the arc fault occurs, the current waveform is distorted, the burrs increase, and the peak value becomes larger. Because the prediction error of the AR parameter model is equal to the energy of the white noise [22], before and after the arc fault occurs, the energy of the white noise changes, and the power spectral density also changes, so the prediction error can represent the power spectrum difference of the same signal wave in different periods. As shown in Fig 2b), the power spectral density distribution of the current signal can be clearly seen from the time-frequency distribution diagram of the current signal. With the occurrence of arc faults, the power spectral density of the current signal shows an increasing trend. The power spectrum of the current signal in the normal working state is relatively flat, so it can be obtained that the prediction error of the current signal AR model under the normal working state is smaller than the prediction error of the current signal AR model when an arc fault occurs, and the ratio of the two is larger. In this paper, the prediction error ratio of the current signal AR model is used as the eigenvalue to detect the series arc fault.

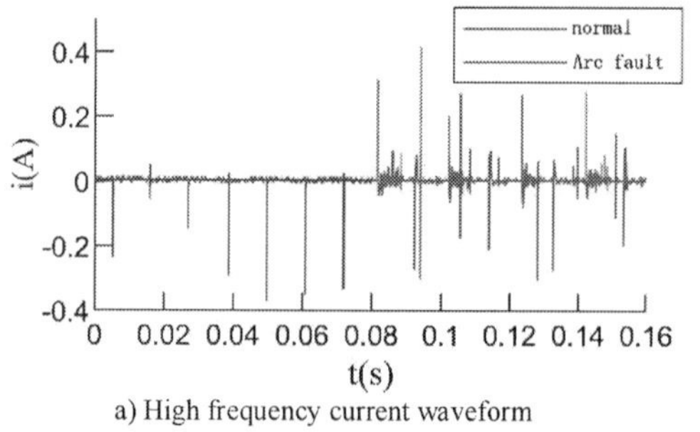

a) High frequency current waveform

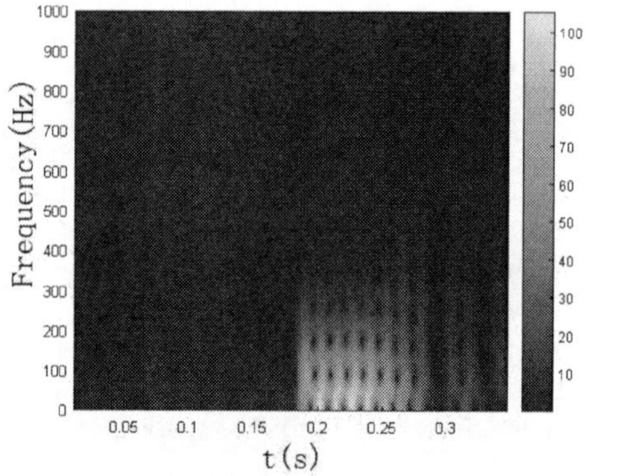

b) Time-frequency distribution of current signal

Fig. 2. High-frequency current waveform and time-frequency distribution

III. EXPERIMENTS AND DATA PROCESSING METHODS

A. Experimental platform construction

Considering that it is difficult to obtain the current data when an arc fault occurs in the actual line, a low-voltage series arc fault experimental platform is built to simulate the arc fault. The experimental platform includes power supply, oscilloscope, arc fault occurrence platform, data acquisition device. The power supply is an isolated voltage-regulated power supply produced by Zhejiang Photovoltaic Electric Company, which can output 0-300v AC and DC voltage. The experiment used 220v AC voltage unchanged. The experiment uses a Tektronix TBS2104 oscilloscope with a sampling frequency of 62.5 kHz and a cut-off frequency of 1 kHz. The arc generator is shown in Fig 3a). The arc generator is composed of an electrode regulator, a fixed carbon electrode, a movable copper electrode, and a number of isolation switches. The schematic diagram of the experiment is shown in Fig 3b). The circuit simulates the circuit when an arc fault occurs in the line, and connects the arc generator in series to the circuit. The loads in the experiment are selected from the typical linear and nonlinear loads commonly seen in households. Linear loads include hair dryers of different powers, and non-linear loads include laptops, vacuum cleaner, switching power supplies, etc.

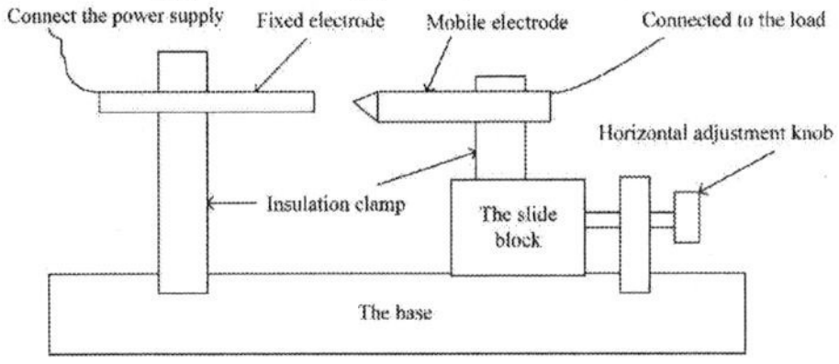

a) Schematic diagram of series arc fault generator

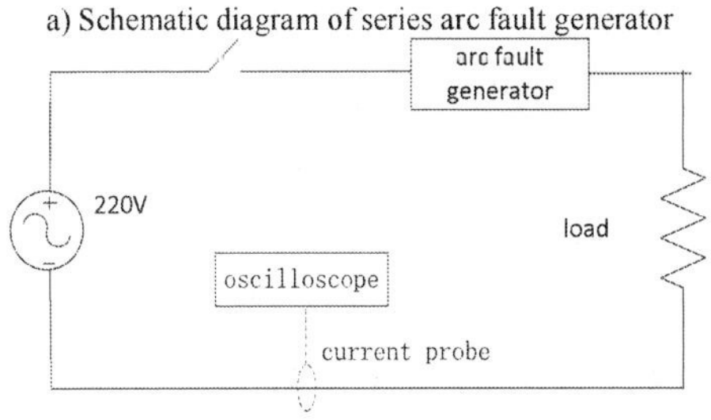

b) Experimental schematic

Fig. 3. Arc fault generator and experimental schematic

B. Modeling of current signal parameters

According to the principle of all-pole modeling of the signal, the current signal x(n) can be expressed by equation (1) as a linear combination of multiple past values x(n-k) and the current excitation value u(n), Set x(n) to have P signals before time n, namely x(n-p), x(n-p+1), ..., x(n-1), and predict x(n) according to the P data:

$$\hat{x}(n) = -\sum_{k=1}^{p} a_k x(n-k) \tag{3}$$

where $\hat{x}(n)$ is the predicted value, and the prediction error is:

$$e(n) = x(n) - \hat{x}(n) \tag{4}$$

The filter coefficients are obtained by the modified variance method. For the observed data $x(0)$, $x(1)$,...,$x(N-1)$, the forward prediction error power and the backward prediction error power are obtained by forward prediction and backward prediction respectively:

$$\hat{\rho}^f = \frac{1}{N-P} \sum_{n=p}^{N-1} [x(n) + \sum_{k=1}^{p} a(k)x(n-k)]^2 \tag{5}$$

and

$$\hat{\rho}^b = \frac{1}{N-P} \sum_{n=0}^{N-1-p} [x(n) + \sum_{k=1}^{p} a(k)x(n+k)]^2 \tag{6}$$

Then the average value of forward prediction error power and backward prediction error power is

$$\hat{\rho} = \frac{1}{2}(\hat{\rho}^f + \hat{\rho}^b) \tag{7}$$

Here, $\hat{\rho}$ is set to be very small to estimate the AR parameters. After completing the modeling of the signal parameters, the analysis of the signal becomes the analysis of the model function.

C. Extraction of eigenvalues and fault judgment

When the low-voltage load is working normally, the high-frequency component of the current in the loop is less, and the power spectrum is relatively stable. An arc fault occurs in the line, the current waveform is distorted, the periodic characteristic changes from a stable state to an unstable state, the power spectral density increases, and the energy increases. Therefore, it can be concluded that the AR model prediction errors of the current before and after the load circuit fault are different. Intercept the current waveform data for analysis. The specific method is as follows:

1)Select the data segment, and select two segments of data with typical power density characteristics from the current signal when the load is working normally and when the circuit has an arc fault, and denote them as x(t), y(t) respectively.

2)The current data x(t) and y(t) are normalized respectively, and then a P-order AR full-pole model is established. Combined with the analysis of experimental data, the model order here is P=5. Under the condition that the order is determined, the AR model prediction error e_x and e_y can be calculated to calculate the prediction error ratio, $re = e_y/e_x$, Here the prediction error ratio is used as the eigenvalue of the signal classification.

3)Compare the characteristic value re with the threshold value $r_{e\text{-}th}$, if the characteristic value re exceeds the corresponding threshold value $r_{e\text{-}th}$, the fault characteristic accumulator C_n performs the accumulation operation, and the accumulator increases by 1.

4)At the same time, in order to prevent the influence of the interference signal, a decrement operation is also designed. If the characteristic value re is less than the threshold value $r_{e\text{-}th}$, the accumulator C_n is reduced by 1 until it is zero. This can prevent the disturbance of a certain cycle current from causing misjudgment by the arc fault detection system and eliminate the disturbance. At the same time, the stronger the arc fault characteristic quantity, the faster the action protection time.

5)The fault characteristic accumulator Cn is compared with the threshold value accumulator $C_{n\text{-}th}$. If Cn exceeds the threshold value, the fault flag is set to 1, indicating that an arc fault occurs on the line. Otherwise, enter the next current cycle sampling.

Reliability verification, for arc fault identification, after the eigenvalues are given, it is necessary to verify whether the eigenvalues can effectively distinguish the normal current and the arc fault current through a large number of experiments. Fig 4 shows the low-voltage series arc fault detection process [21].

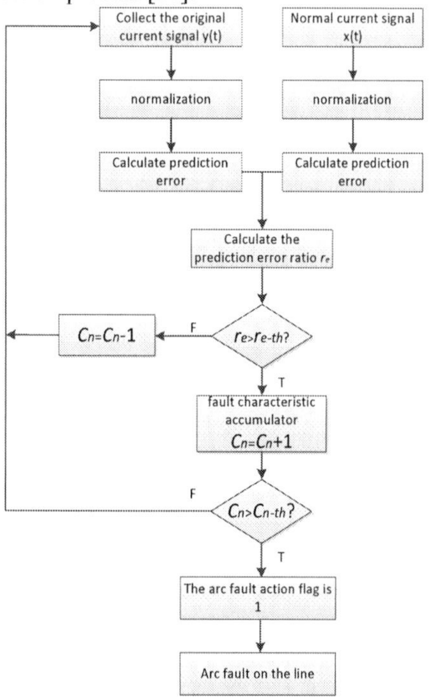

Fig.4. Arc fault detection process

IV. SERIES ARC FAULT IDENTIFICATION

In the series arc fault experiment, the type of the series connected load in the circuit has a great influence on the current waveform, and the degree of waveform distortion is different when the arc fault occurs for different types of loads. In order to ensure the universality of the experiment, the loads selected here are the shielded loads specified in GB/T 31143-2014 [23]and the common low-voltage loads in some households.

TABLE I
EXPERIMENTAL LOAD TYPES

load type	load
Linear load	Hair dryer 800W power level Hair dryer 1600W power level Electric kettle
nonlinear load	laptop Hand drill Vacuum cleaner

In the experiment, the current signals were collected for linear and nonlinear loads in normal loop and when arc appeared. It should be noted here that the arc fault generator is composed of a fixed electrode and a moving electrode. When the load is connected to the circuit in series during the experiment, the lateral adjustment knob needs to be manually twisted to control the distance between the two electrodes until a stable arc. Due to the manual operation, the distance between each electrode cannot be strictly controlled, so each load is measured 5 times, and the error between the measured values is analyzed to ensure the accuracy of the experimental data. After the measurement, it is known that the error of the results obtained in each experiment is small, and the influence of the distance between the two electrodes on the experimental results can be ignored.

A. Series arc fault detection

As shown in Fig 5a) and 5b) below are the current waveforms of the linear load under arc and no arc conditions. The normal working current waveform of the linear load is a sine wave as a whole. When an arc fault occurs, the waveform is distorted, the current zero-crossing point waveform rise rate increases, and the time domain characteristics are obvious. Fig 5c) and 5d) are the non-linear load current waveforms measured under normal working and fault conditions respectively after the electric drill is connected in series to the loop. As can be seen from the figure, due to the special working principle of the electric drill, it contains a large flat shoulder current during normal operation, and the time domain characteristics of the current waveform and the waveform of the linear load are not obvious, and it is difficult to tell whether an arc fault occurs or not only in the time domain.

Fig 6 shows the AR model prediction error ratio plane measured by 100 random samples of various loads. Based on the linear discrimination, the classification decision boundary, that is, the prediction error ratio threshold, can be given. Combined with the experimental results, the load prediction error ratio threshold based on the AR parameter model is 1.25. If the prediction error ratio is greater than 1.25, the arc fault accumulator will increase by 1. If the accumulator value is greater than the set threshold, it is considered that the circuit has an arc fault. The loop works normally if the prediction error ratio is less than 1.25. This parameter requires a lot of experiments and actual data verification. If the number of experimental samples is large enough, the classification threshold can be adjusted to improve the accuracy.

The test results of all load experiments are shown in Table 3 below. It can be seen that the AR model does not misjudge the experimental load, and the action time meets the standard time, which verifies the feasibility of the model to detect arc faults.

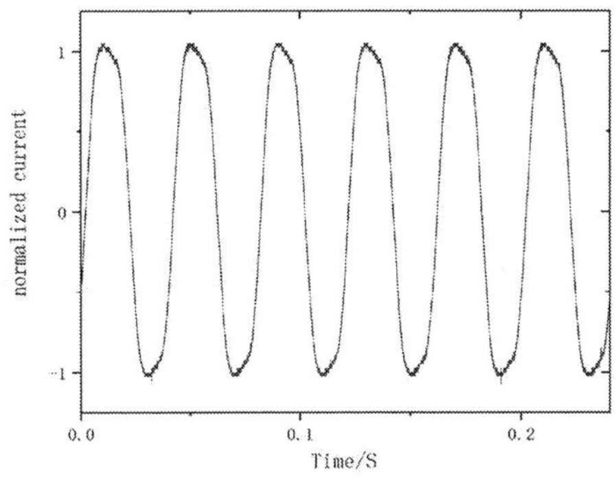

a) Linear load normal operating current

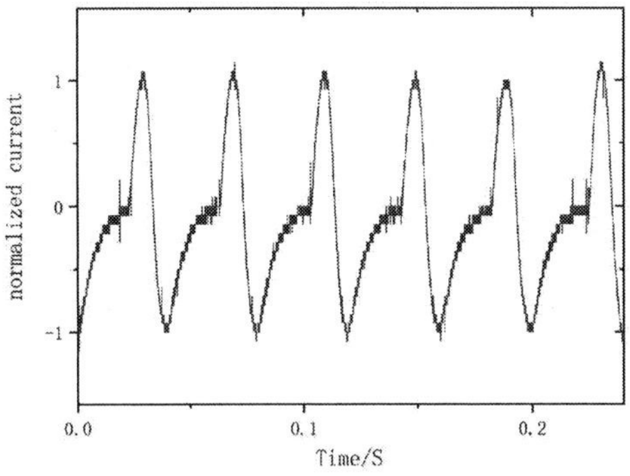

b) Linear load fault working current

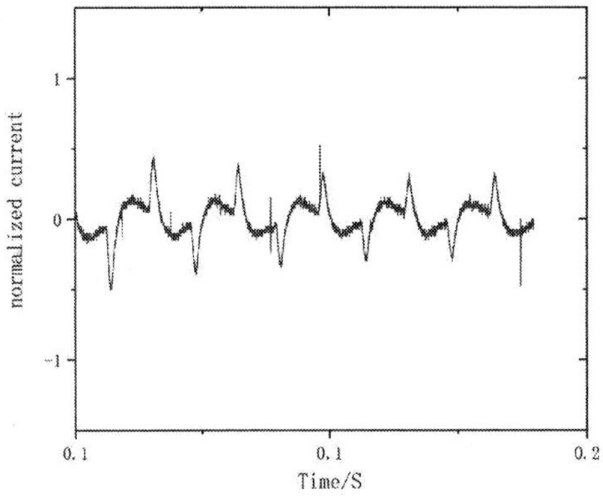

c) Non-linear load normal working current

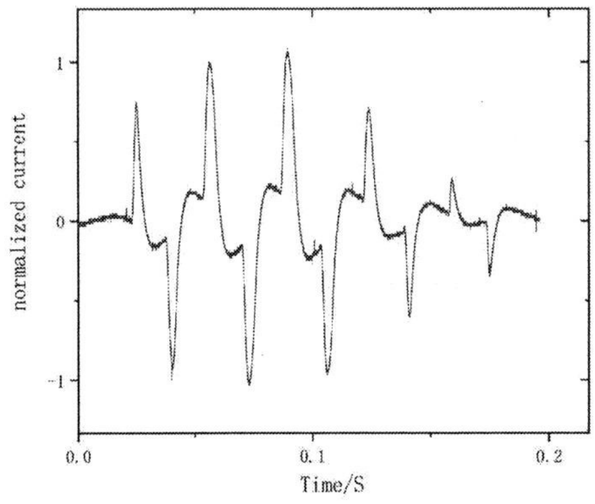

d) Non-linear load arc fault current

Fig.5. Linear and nonlinear load current waveforms

TABLE II
MODEL PARAMETERS

state	load type	prediction error
Normal	Hair dryer 800W power level	6.624*10-4
	Hair dryer 1600W power level	7.902*10-4
	Electric kettle	6.321*10-4
	laptop	7.392*10-4
	Hand drill	1.157*10-3
	Vacuum cleaner	1.029*10-3
Fault	Hair dryer 800W power level	2.191*10-3
	Hair dryer 1600W power level	1.909*10-3
	Electric kettle	3.899*10-3
	laptop	9.527*10-4
	Hand drill	1.979*10-3
	Vacuum cleaner	1.674*10-3

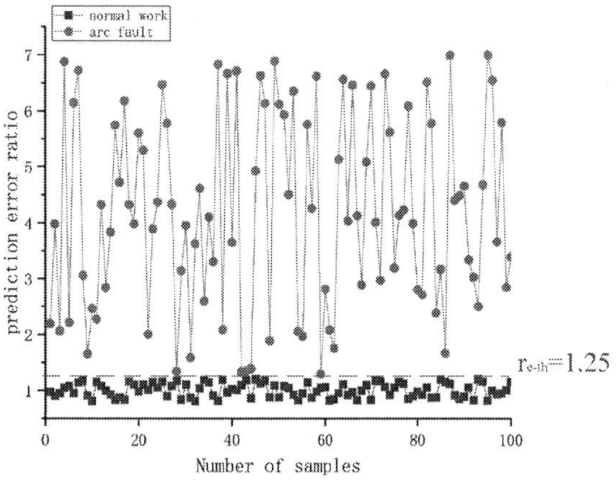

Fig.6. Prediction error ratio of linear load normal operation and arc fault

TABLE III
STATISTICAL RESULTS OF ARC FAULT DETECTION

Load type	Detection time	Startup misjudgment
Hair dryer 800W power level	0.17s~0.21s	F
Hair dryer 1600W power level	0.16s~0.20s	F
Electric kettle	0.16s~0.19s	F
laptop	0.20s~0.22s	F
Hand drill	0.15s~0.18s	F
Vacuum cleaner	0.19s~0.22s	F

V. CONCLUSION

Aiming at the problem of improving the reliability of the action of the Arc Fault Circuit interrupters. In this paper, an arc fault judgment method based on digital signal modeling is studied. The results are as follows:

1)The characteristics of arc fault current are analyzed from the perspective of energy domain. Before and after the occurrence of arc fault, the energy of white noise changes, and the power spectral density also changes. According to this feature, it is found that power spectral density estimation can represent arc fault parameters.

2)Establish an AR model based on the current signals before and after the load arc fault, obtain the prediction error of the model parameters, and use the prediction error ratio to characterize the arc current feature.

3)Use the extracted feature quantities to establish a threshold comparison algorithm for arc fault discrimination, and conduct reliability verification. The experimental results show that under the premise of a small number of samples, the prediction error ratio can effectively distinguish the arc fault of a single load. If the experimental sample If the number is large enough, the classification threshold can be adjusted and the accuracy can be improved.

REFERENCES

[1] National fire and police response in 2020[OL]. URL: [2021-03-07]. https: //www. 119.gov.cn /article / 41kpo4CAQyv.

[2] J. C. Kim, B. Lehman and R. Ball, "A Series DC Arc Fault Detection Algorithm Based on PV Operating Characteristics and Detailed Extraction of Pink Noise Behavior," 2021 IEEE Applied Power Electronics Conference and Exposition (APEC), 2021: 989-994

[3] Q.F Y, W.H L, Y. Y, "Multi-branch series arc fault det ection method based on deep short-term memory networ k," Journal of Computer Applications, 2021,41(S1):321-326.

[4] S. Zhao, Y. Wang, F. Niu, et al, "A Series DC Arc Fault Detection Method Based on Steady Pattern of High-Frequency Electromagnetic Radiation," in IEEE Transactions on Plasma Science, 2019, 47(9): 4370-4377

[5] X. Q, J. S, L. X, et al. "Electromagnetic radiation characteristics of series DC arc fault and its determining factors". IEEE Transactions on Plasma Science, 2018, 46(11): 4028 - 4036.

[6] B. G, J. R, G. X. "Novel series arc fault detector using high-frequency coupling analysis and multi-indicator algorithm". IEEE Access, 2019, 7: 92161 - 92170.

[7] P. S, R.G D, R.L Y, "Detection Method of Arc Fault in Series with Wavelet Entropy," Proceedings of the CSEE, 2010(S1): 232-236.

[8] G.W L, H. B M, D. N Z, "Series Arc Fault Detection Technology Based on Multi-feature Fusion Neural Network, High Voltage Engineering," 2021,47(02): 463-471

[9] H.J Z, H. Y Q, K.L, "A series fault arc detection method based on the fusion of correlation theory and zero current feature," Chinese Journal of Scientific Instrument, 2020, 41(04):218-228

[10]X. M L, Y. Z Y. D C, "Series arc fault diagnosis of AC system based on multi-feature fusion," Power System Technology, 2014, 38(03):795-801

[11]R.H C, Y W, C. Y W, el at, "Series Arc Fault Identification Method in Aviation Lines Based on Multi-Information Fusion," Transactions of China Electrotechnical Society , 2019, 34(S1):118-125.

[12]Y. M, S.L C, Z.H W, el at, "A DC Arc Fault Detection Method Based on Catboost Algorithm for Different Electrode Materials," Journal of Xi'an Jiaotong University.2022: 1-11

[13]W. Z, H.W C, J.J L, el at, "Research on fault arc detection algorithm based on wavelet packet de-noise and EMD decomposition," Electrical Measurement & Instrumentation, 2019, 56(06):117-121.

[14]Z.H X, "Detection of Low-voltage Arc Fault Based on Support Vector Machine," Proceedings of the CSU-EPSA, 2012, 2(3):128-131.

[15]R.H C, S.M W, "Aeronautical series fault arc detection based on multi-dimensional feature quantities," Science Technology and Engineering, 2017, 17(13):38-43.

[16]Y. W, J. C, S.L L, et al, "Series fault arc detection based on Stacking model fusion," Application of Electronic Technique, 2021, 47(11):53-57

[17]Y. Z, Y.L L, et al, "Series fault arc identification method based on BP neural network optimized by PSO," Transducer and Microsystem Technologies, 2016, 35(07): 22-25.

[18]Qu Na, Chen Jiatong, Zuo Jiankai, et al. "PSO-SOM Neural Network Algorithm for Series Arc Fault Detection." Advances in Mathematical Physics, 2020

[19]XIAO Q, GUO M, CHEN D. "High-impedance fault detection method based on one-dimensional Variational Prototyping-Encoder for distribution networks ." IEEE Systems Journal, 2021: 1 - 11.

[20]Y. Y, L.J H, P. L, et al, "Arc fault detection based on multi-dimension feature extraction," Journal of Electronic Measurement and Instrumentation,2021,35(10):107-115

[21]Y.J, X.Z G, L.L N, "Series Arc Fault Identification in Low Voltage System Based on Autoregressive Parameter Model ," Transactions of China Electrotechnical Society, 2011, 26(08): 213-219

[22]B.H W, "Modern digital signal processing," Beijing: Xidian University Press, 2011

[23]GB/T 31143—2014. General requirements for arc fault detection devices, Beijing: China Standard Press, 2015.

Research on Quality Inspection Method of Cylinder Connector Based on Machine Vision

Jingde Huang[1,2], Junxin Yu[1], Peihao Han[1], Zijie Chen[1]

1) Zhuhai College of Science and Technology, Zhuhai, 519041

2) Guangdong Intelligent Vision Precision Detection Engineering Technology Research Center, Zhuhai, 519041

Email: jdh925@sina.com TEL:13387852971

***Abstract*—In order to realize the rapid identification, positioning and measurement of cylinder connectors in industrial production, a inspection method of cylinder connectors based on machine vision is proposed. Firstly, aiming at the visual image with insufficient field definition, an image sharpening model is established to enhance the edge or contour of the image; Secondly, based on the transformation and correction of visual image, the feature extraction model of image is established and the detection algorithm is optimized; Finally, the positioning, size and machining accuracy of typical connectors are simulated. By comparing and analyzing the influence of different models on the detection efficiency and detection effect under specific conditions, it shows that the machine vision technology improves the industrial production efficiency and detection stability.**

***Index Terms*— Machine Vision, Visual Image, Quality Inspection, Image Sharpening, Edge Extraction.**

I. INTRODUCTION

In industrial production, the traditional manual detection method has low detection accuracy, slow speed, poor stability and high cost, which cannot meet the high-speed and accurate detection requirements of industrial automation production[1-3]. At present, when using machine vision detection methods, we face the following key problems: first, in the process of imaging and image transmission, due to low lens resolution, poor focusing of imaging system or image compression, the image target contour will become blurred and the details will be unclear. Even if the visual image is smoothed by algorithm, the image definition will be reduced; Second, due to the influence of many factors, the visual image characteristics in engineering practice deviate from the actual value. Therefore, it is necessary to adjust and restore the visual image, establish a scientific mathematical model to quantitatively describe the image position, size and shape, and perform geometric correction on the visual image; Third, in engineering practice, due to the influence of noise, uneven illumination or other factors, the obtained edge points are often intermittent. To solve the above problems, this paper proposes a method of quality inspection of cylinder connections based on machine vision.

II. SHARPENING MODEL OF VISUAL IMAGE

In the process of imaging and image transmission, due to low lens resolution, poor focusing of imaging system or image compression, the image target contour will become blurred and the details will not be clear; After the image is smoothed by algorithm, the sharpness of the image will also be reduced, and image sharpening is needed to enhance the edge or contour of the image.

A. Gradient sharpening

The adjacent mean value and weighted average method can make the image smooth, and then the corresponding difference method is used to sharpen the image. Differential algorithm is to enhance the high-frequency components by calculating the rate of change of the signal, so that the outline of the image is clearer. Because the blur of the image is essentially caused by average or integral calculation of the image, in order to make the edge extending in any direction clear from the blurred edge, differential operation can be carried out on the image to obtain an image with clearer characteristics [4-6].

In image processing, first-order differentiation is realized by gradient algorithm. For function image $f(x,y)$, its gradient at point (x,y) is a vector, which is mathematically defined as a vector

$$\nabla f(x,y)=\begin{bmatrix} G_x \\ G_y \end{bmatrix}=\begin{bmatrix} \partial f/\partial x \\ \partial f/\partial y \end{bmatrix} \tag{1}$$

Its direction represents the direction of the maximum rate of change of function $f(x,y)$, and its size is the amplitude of the gradient

$$|\nabla f(x,y)| = \sqrt{(\frac{\partial f}{\partial x})^2 + (\frac{\partial f}{\partial y})^2} \tag{2}$$

From the above formula, we can get that the value of gradient is the increase of unit distance of $f(x,y)$ in the direction of its maximum rate of change. After approximating the differential with difference, the above formula can be written as:

$$G[f(x,y)] = \sqrt{[f(i,j) - f(i,j+1)]^2 + [f(i,j) - f(i+1,j)]^2} \tag{3}$$

In order to improve the operation speed and facilitate programming, when the calculation accuracy is not high, the absolute difference algorithm can be used to approximate as:

$$G[f(x,y)] = |[f(i,j) - f(i,j+1)]| + |[f(i,j) - f(i+1,j)]| \tag{4}$$

This algorithm can also be called horizontal and vertical difference method, which is a classical gradient algorithm. Another gradient algorithm is the cross checking calculation, which is called Robert gradient method, which is expressed as:

$$G[f(x,y)] = \sqrt{[f(i,j) - f(i+1,j+1)]^2 + [f(i+1,j) - f(i,j)]^2} \tag{5}$$

This method can also be approximated by the absolute difference algorithm as:

$$G[f(x,y)] = |[f(i,j) - f(i+1,j+1)]| + |[f(i+1,j) - f(i,j+1)]| \tag{6}$$

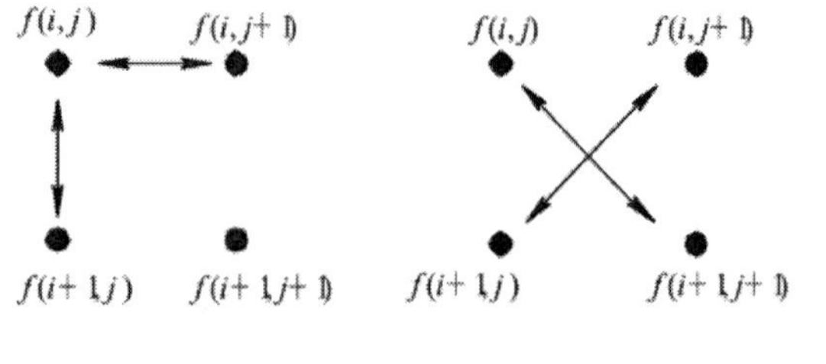

a.Horizontal and vertical difference method b.Cross difference method

Fig. 1. Schematic diagram of difference method.

B. Sobel sharpening

When sharpening images with gradient differentiation, noise, fringes and other interference information will be enhanced. Sobel operator can solve this problem to a certain extent. Sobel sharpening is a first-order differential sharpening and a kind of gradient sharpening. This sharpening mainly obtains the derivative image of the image, so as to sharpen the image at the edge of the image. Sobel sharpening has a better effect on image blur caused by average or integral operation[7-8].

Sobel sharpening is to obtain the image edge through Sobel filtering, locate the edge of the image through the edge image, obtain the non main edge of the image with the edge as the boundary, and eliminate the non main edge at the same time, so as to achieve the effect of sharpening the image. Sobel sharpening effect is shown in Figure 2.

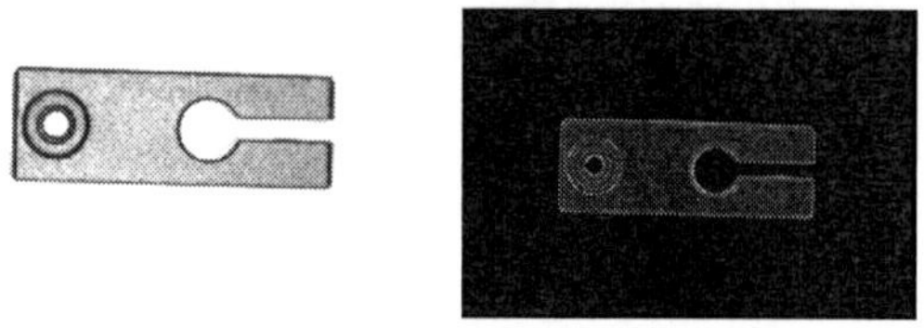

a.Grayscale b.Laplacian sharpening

Fig. 2. Sobel sharpening effect picture.

C. Laplace sharpening

The principle of Laplace sharpening image is related to the mutation degree of the surrounding pixels of an image pixel to this pixel. It is based on the change degree of image pixels, that is, the second-order differential. The first-order differential of a function describes the direction in which the function image changes, while the second-order differential describes the speed of image change, that is, whether it changes sharply or gently. The expression of Laplace sharpening is.

$$\nabla^2 f(x,y) = \frac{\partial^2(x,y)}{\partial x^2} + \frac{\partial^2(x,y)}{\partial y^2} \tag{7}$$

The second-order differential can reflect the transition degree of image pigments, and the transition from black to white is relatively sharp. When the gray value of the pixel in the center of the neighborhood is lower than the average value of the gray values of other pixels in its neighborhood, the gray value of the pixel needs to be reduced, otherwise it needs to be increased, so as to realize the sharpening of the image. The effect of Laplace sharpening is shown in Figure 3.

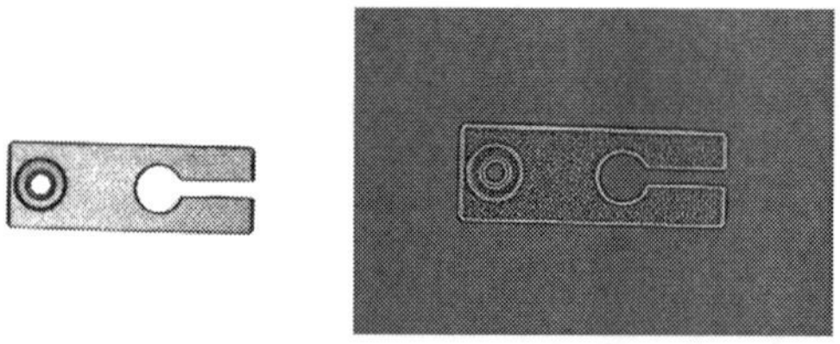

a.Grayscale b.Sobel sharpening

Fig. 3.Laplace sharpening effect picture.

III. Transformation and Correction of Visual Image

Due to the influence of many factors, the actual picture obtained in the application may be different from the imagination, so it needs to be adjusted and restored[9-10]. Image transformation and correction refers to using mathematical modeling methods to describe the known conditions of image position, size, shape and so on, using these conditions to determine the model parameters, and geometric correction of the image according to the model.

A. Similarity transformation

Similarity transformation: transform from one plane / solid figure to another, keep the shape unchanged (size, direction and position are variable) in the process of change, and any similarity transformation can be decomposed into a combination of equal scale scaling, translation and rotation. Its mathematical expression is as follows:

$$p_t = T \cdot R \cdot S \cdot p_0 = \begin{bmatrix} 1 & 0 & x_t \\ 0 & 1 & y_t \\ 0 & 0 & 1 \end{bmatrix} \begin{bmatrix} \cos\gamma & -\sin\gamma & 0 \\ \sin\gamma & \cos\gamma & 0 \\ 0 & 0 & 1 \end{bmatrix} \begin{bmatrix} S & 0 & 0 \\ 0 & S & 0 \\ 0 & 0 & 1 \end{bmatrix} \cdot p_0 \qquad (8)$$

B. Affine transformation

Affine transformation: the transformation from one plane / solid figure to another plane / solid figure, and the transformation that keeps the straight line and parallel line unchanged in the process of transformation is called affine transformation. Any affine transformation can be decomposed into a combination of scaling, translation, rotation and shear. The mathematical expression of affine transformation is as follows:

$$\text{Pan: } p_t = T \cdot p_0 = \begin{bmatrix} 1 & 0 & x_t \\ 0 & 1 & y_t \\ 0 & 0 & 1 \end{bmatrix} \cdot p_0 \qquad (9)$$

$$\text{Rotation: } p_t = R \cdot p_0 = \begin{bmatrix} \cos\gamma & -\sin\gamma & 0 \\ \sin\gamma & \cos\gamma & 0 \\ 0 & 0 & 1 \end{bmatrix} \cdot p_0 \qquad (10)$$

$$\text{Zoom: } p_t = S \cdot p_0 = \begin{bmatrix} S & 0 & 0 \\ 0 & S & 0 \\ 0 & 0 & 1 \end{bmatrix} \cdot p_0 \qquad (11)$$

C. Projection transformation

Projection transformation: the transformation from a three-dimensional image of an object to a two-dimensional image is called projection transformation. Its expression is

$$\begin{bmatrix} u' \\ v' \\ w' \end{bmatrix} = \begin{bmatrix} a_{11} & a_{12} & a_{13} \\ a_{21} & a_{22} & a_{23} \\ a_{31} & a_{32} & a_{33} \end{bmatrix} \begin{bmatrix} x \\ y \\ 1 \end{bmatrix} \qquad (12)$$

During projection transformation, straight lines will be mapped into straight lines. Any 2D projection transformation can be represented by 3x3 reversible matrix, and any 3D projection transformation can be represented by 4x4 reversible matrix.

Affine transformation can be regarded as a special form of projection transformation. As long as a_{31}, a_{32} and a_{33} of the projection transformation matrix are taken as 0. Therefore, projection transformation can realize translation, scaling, shear and affine transformation.

IV. EDGE EXTRACTION MODEL BASED ON HOUGH TRANSFORM

In practical applications, due to the influence of noise, uneven illumination or other factors, the edge points are often intermittent. The usual edge extraction algorithm combines pixels into meaningful boundaries through connection processing, and the line segments in the image can be found and connected through Hough transform.

Hough transform is a method of parameter estimation by voting. It transforms the detection problem into parameter space through the line point dual relationship between image space and Hough parameter space.

The polar coordinate expression of the linear equation is:

$$\rho = x\cos\theta + y\sin\theta \qquad (13)$$

A. Hough transform line detection algorithm

(1) Quantify the parameter space, establish a two-dimensional cumulative array, and initialize it to 0;

(2) The coordinates of each feature point in the image space are substituted into the linear polar coordinate equation;

(3) According to r and θ adding 1 to the corresponding array element;

(4) After all target points are processed, find out the maximum element value in the cumulative array, which is the linear model parameter (r^*, θ^*).

B. Hough transform circle detection algorithm

(1) According to the accuracy requirements, the parameter spaces a and b are quantized to establish a two-dimensional cumulative array $A(a,b)$ and initialize it to zero.

(2) Calculate the tangent value of the gradient angle of the edge contour image;

(3) Scan the image from left to right, from top to bottom. If the current point (x, y) is determined to be the edge point, find out the tangent value of its corresponding gradient angle, and then according to the formula

$$b = a\tan\theta_i - x_i\tan\theta_i + y_i \qquad (14)$$

Calculate the value of b corresponding to each a.

(4) Substitute the values of a and b into the following formula

$$A(a,b) = A(a,b) + 1 \qquad (15)$$

(5) Complete all points according to steps (3) and (4);

(6) Find out the coordinate position corresponding to the maximum value in the cumulative array, and the result is the coordinate of the center of the circle;

(7) By substituting the coordinates of the center of the circle into the equation of the circle in the image space, the distance from all edge points to the coordinates of the center of the circle can be calculated, in which the parameter value with the highest frequency can be found, and the obtained parameter is the radius parameter of the circle.

$$(x_i - a)^2 + (y_i - b)^2 = r^2 \qquad (16)$$

V. Experimental Simulation and Verification

In Halcon software, pretreatment is carried out for a certain type of connector, and then add is used respectively_ metrology_ object_ line_ Measure operator and add_ metrology_ object_ circle_ Measure operator to fit lines and circles. In the fitting process, the line fitting operator gives the coordinate values of the starting and ending points of the target line (the circle fitting operator gives the coordinates of the center of the target circle and the radius of the fitting circle), the half length of the edge in the vertical and tangent directions, the Sigma value of the Gaussian function and the threshold value of the edge gradient. After fitting the target line and circle, you can use distance_ PL operator to measure the distance from the line to the center of the circle. The fitting results of each part are shown in Figure 4.

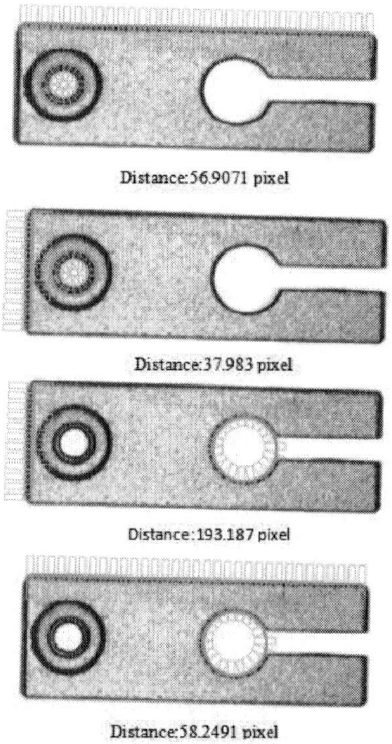

Fig. 4.Effect drawing of distance detection from circle center to straight line.

It can be seen from Figure 4 that after finding the target with template matching, add can be used_ metrology_ object_ line_ Measure and other operators to achieve the fitting of lines, circles, rectangles and other targets. After fitting the determined targets, you can use distance_ pl、angle_ Ll and other operators calculate the distance from point to line or the angle between two lines, which is helpful to achieve accurate positioning.

VI. Conclusion

In order to recognize, locate and measure the connecting block of the cylinder support in industrial production, this paper proposes a detection method of the connecting block of the cylinder support based on machine vision. Firstly, the target object and the background are separated by preprocessing the image; Secondly, reasonably extract the target area, create a template and set template parameters; Finally, according to the Hough transform, the matching target object is fitted with the edge line segment and hole position of the object, so as to realize the rapid detection of the target. The simulation results show that using machine vision technology can greatly improve the accuracy and speed of connector detection in industrial production process.

Acknowledgment

This paper is supported by Key Special Foundation of universities in Guangdong Province (2020zdzx2032) and national entrepreneurship practice Foundation (S202113684014S、S202113684015S).

References

[1] Li Hui, Sheng Ruqian, Zhou Haomin Parameter detection of spur gear based on Halcon Journal of Hunan Institute of Technology (NATURAL SCIENCE EDITION), 2022,35 (01): 41-43.

[2] Sun Yu, Xu Gang Research on workpiece recognition and location based on Halcon Journal of Xinyu University, 2018,23 (06): 39-44.

[3] Li Qingjun, Meng Qinghao, Shen Yan, Su Bo Research and application of image smoothing technology Scientific and technological innovation and application, 2022,12 (02): 165-167.

[4] Li Xiaodong The design of machine vision based automatic inspection system Electronic technology, 2021,50 (12): 18-19.

[5] Fu Binbin The application and development trend of industrial machine vision China industry and informatization, 2021 (11): 18-24.

[6] Deng Rongqi, Zhu Cuixia The application of machine vision technology in machine manufacturing and automation Electronic technology and software engineering, 2021 (18): 108-109.

[7] Yang Guihua, Liu Zhiyi, Wang Xiaowen Research on multi-target workpiece classification, recognition and location based on machine vision Machine tools and hydraulics, 2021,49 (11): 82-86+126.

[8] Zhang Yan, Cui Xiaomeng Image enhancement based on gray transformation Packaging engineering, 2010,31 (19): 95-98.

[9] Han Yali Research on image precision measurement algorithm Zhengzhou University, 2010.

[10] Xu Fei Research on vision guided positioning technology in robot assembly Yanshan University, 2015.

Jingde Huang, who is mainly engaged in the field of machine vision technology, doctor and professor.

The Difference and Connection between Fault Tree Analysis (FTA) and Causal Chain Analysis (CCA)

Asia Wang

Shanghai Liangxin Electrical Co., Ltd., Shanghai, 201315, China
E-mail: wangdongya@sh-liangxin.com Tel: 15902152420

Abstract—**Fault analysis is one of the main development directions of reliability work. Normally fault analysis tools mainly include fish-bone diagram analysis method, 5WHY method, FMEA, Cause and Effect Matrix, etc; However, the structure of low-voltage electrical system is becoming more and more complex, and simple fault analysis tools can not systematically analyze the logical relationship between various faults. This paper first introduces several failure and risk analysis tools commonly used in the process of reliability design, such as FMEA, FMECA, FTA, etc; Then it introduces the Causal Chain Analysis(CCA) used in innovation problem solving theory (TRIZ); These two tools can systematically analyze the causal chain of faults. By using CCA and FTA tools to analyze the same actual case, the FTA and CCA tool are deeply compared, the differences and connections between the two tools are pointed out; At the same time, by comparing the establishment process and analysis process of each tool, their advantages and disadvantages and priority range are given, which provides a reference for the majority of R&D to choose a suitable fault analysis tool in reliability analysis.**

Index Terms— **Breaker, DFR (Design For Reliability), FTA (Fault Tree Analysis), TRIZ (Innovative Problem Solving Theory), CCA (Causal Chain Analysis).**

I. INTRODUCTION

With the continuous growth of enterprise innovation ability, they are not only satisfied with designing and producing a qualified product, but also strive to design and produce products with high quality, high reliability and high value. In this process, the theory of reliability design and innovative problem solving is gradually accepted by some enterprises, and many advanced R&D tools are constantly used. Among these tools, the tools for failure cause analysis are used most frequently. There are many tools that can do the failure cause analysis, such as fish-bone diagram analysis, FMEA, causal matrix, Fault Tree Analysis commonly used in reliability design (DFR) and Causal Chain Analysis commonly used in innovative problem solving theory (TRIZ). Among them, Fault Tree Analysis tools and Causal Chain Analysis tools are paid more and more attention because of their strong systematization and logicality. However, in the process of using, engineers are often confused about when to use which tool, and there is an urgent need to understand its similarities and differences and scope of application. This paper will make a detailed comparison between the two tools.

II. DESIGNING FOR RELIABILITY

According to GB3187-1994 Terminology of Reliability and Maintainability, Reliability is defined as the ability of a product to complete specified functions under specified conditions and within specified time. Generalized Design for Reliability[1,2] includes:

(1) Reliability design: including determining reliability index, tearing down reliability index, predicting reliability, and designing specified reliability index into assembly & parts;

(2) Reliability Testing & Analysis: mainly refers to evaluate reliability and failure analysis, including necessary reliability test and fault analysis;

(3) Reliability manufacturing: mainly refers to the reliable and stable production of designed parts and assembly.

In the process of reliability design, we normally use failure and risk analysis tools, such as FMEA, FMECA, FTA, etc.

FMEA (failure mode and effect analysis) [3] is the abbreviation of potential failure mode and effect analysis. It is a tool for risk analysis in product design stage and process design stage. It mainly finds out all potential failure modes, failure consequences and failure causes, so as to take necessary measures in advance to improve the quality and reliability of products.

FMECA (Failure Mode Effects & criticality analysis)[4] is the abbreviation of failure mode, failure consequence and criticality analysis. FMECA is the extension of FMEA, which uses criticality to quantify the analysis.

FTA is the abbreviation of Fault Tree Analysis, also known as Failure Tree Analysis[5,6], as shown in Figure 1. It is one of the tools for system reliability and safety analysis.

Fault Tree Analysis includes qualitative analysis and quantitative analysis. The main purpose of qualitative analysis is to find out the causes and combinations of the failure events related to the system, that is, to find out the minimum cut set of all the top events in the fault tree; The main purpose of quantitative analysis is to calculate the probability of top event and other quantitative indicators when the probability of all bottom events is given. FTA can analyze the influence of the combination of various fault factors on the system. FMECA is the foundation of FTA.

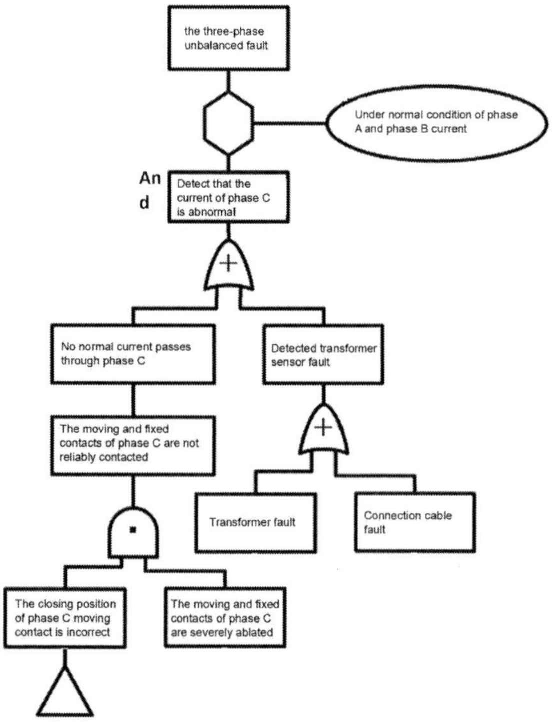

Figure 1 Fault Tree Analysis

III. INNOVATIVE PROBLEM SOLVING THEORY

TRIZ theory[7] was summarized by G.S. Altshuller, an inventor and educator of the former Soviet Union, through the analysis of a large number of patents and innovation cases. TRIZ is mainly used to solve problems in the process of invention. After more than 60 years of application and development, TRIZ theory has been gradually spread all over the world. The TRIZ theory itself is also constantly enriched and expanded, and gradually developed into a modern TRIZ theory on the basis of the classical TRIZ theory. Compared with classic TRIZ, modern TRIZ has a great expansion in many aspects, such as problem-solving ideas, tool content, application purposes and so on. At present, more and more engineers apply TRIZ to solve specific technical problems in the process of production and R&D, and a large number of patents have been produced.

Causal Chain Analysis(CCA) is a tool to analyze problems in modern TRIZ theory. CCA is an analysis method to identify and analyze the key causes of engineering systems, as shown in Figure 2.

It is completed through the analysis of defect transmission causes by establishing a causal chain. It is a tool to connect the initial defects with the key causes. CCA plays a very important role in the process of using modern TRIZ to solve problems.

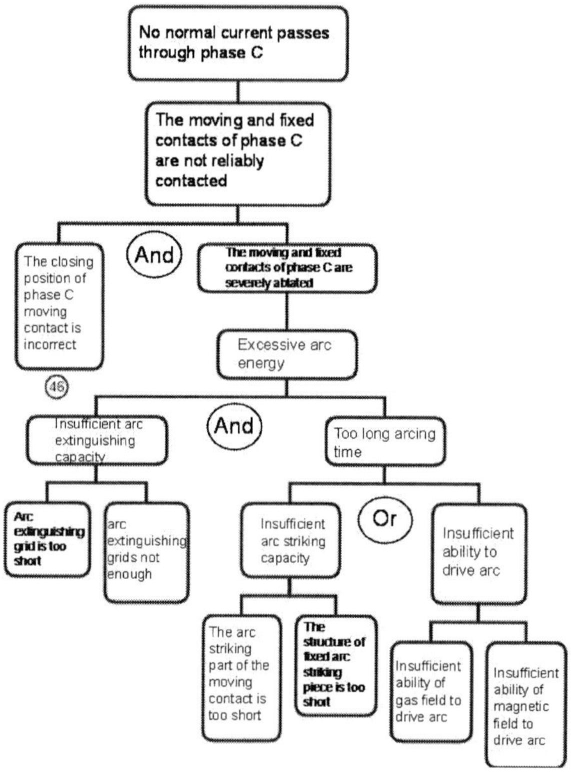

Figure 2 causal chain analysis

IV. THE DIFFERENCE AND CONNECTION BETWEEN FTA AND CCA

1) Differences and connections of analysis objects:

The object of FTA is all kinds of events, including fault events and success events; In FTA, all kinds of fault states or abnormal conditions are called fault events, and all kinds of intact states or normal conditions are called successful events.

The object of CCA is various defects, which are the objective facts that hinder the achievement of the project purpose.

2) Differences and relations between symbols of analysis objects:

There are 8 types of event symbols in FTA[8].

There are only two types of event symbols (defect symbols) in the CCA. See Table 1 for details.

3) The difference and connection of operation symbols:

There are 7 types of symbols and 2 types of transfer symbols in FTA.

There are only three types of operation symbols in CCA, as shown in Table 2.

Table 1 Comparison of analysis event symbols

Event symbols of FTA		Event symbols of CCA	
Symbol name	Definitions	Symbol name	Definitions
bottom event	The bottom event is the cause event that only causes other events in FTA	initial defect	Initial defect are adverse events to project goals
basic event	A basic event is an event at the base of the analysis for which no explanation is required	defect	A defect other than Initial defect
Undiscovered event	an event whose cause should be further ascertained, but whose cause is not necessary or cannot be ascertained at the present time		
result event	an event caused by another event or combination of events in a FTA		
top event	the result event concerned in FTA		
intermediate event	a result event that lies between a bottom event and a top event		
special event	events which need special symbols to indicate their particularity or attract attention in FTA		
switch event	a special event that must or must not happen under normal working conditions		
conditional event	special events that describe the specific constraints on which logic gates operate		

4) The difference and connection between the top event and the initial defect:

The top event is the top of FTA. It is the result event of the joint action of all events. It is the output event of the operation symbols in the fault tree, not the input event. Top events can be direct events or indirect events. Generally, events that need to be eliminated are specified for customers and projects; There can be several top events in a project.

The initial defect is the starting point of CCA, which determines the direction of causal chain. Generally, the obvious defects or the defects encountered at the beginning of the project are not regarded as the initial defects, because once we define the initial defects at a relatively low level, we will lose a lot of opportunities. There may be more than one initial defects in a project.

5) How to identify top events and initial defects:

(1) Top event [9] is an event that the system does not expect to occur, or a fault event designated for logical analysis.

These events are at the top of the fault tree. Common top events are: leakage, control failure, insulation failure, vehicle out of control, lightning strike, etc.

Table 2 Comparison of analysis and operation symbols

Operative Symbol of FTA		Operative Symbol of CCA	
Symbol name	Definitions	Symbol name	Definitions
And Gate	And gate indicates that an output event occurs only when all input events occur	And	And refers to a defect that must have several reasons to affect the higher level
Or Gate	Or gate indicates that an output event occurs when at least one input event occurs	Or	Or refers to the fact that each cause can independently affect the next level of defect
Inverse Gate	Inverse gate indicates that the output event is the opposite of the input event	+	+ means that the cause at the bottom contributes proportionately to the defect at the top
Determine Gate	Determine gate indicates that an output event occurs only when r or more of n input events occur		
Order And Gate	Order and gate indicates that output events occur only when input events occur in a specified order		
Exclusive Gate	Exclusive gate indicates that an output event occurs only when a single input event occurs		
Forbidden Gate	Forbidden gate indicates that only when a conditional event occurs, the producer of the input event causes the output event to occur		
Turn to symbol, Turn back symbol	The same transfer symbol is used to indicate the location of a subtree		
Similar Turn to, Similar Turn back	The similar transition symbol is used to indicate the location of the similar subtree		

(2) The initial defect[10] is the opposite of the project goal. In many cases, the initial defects of the project are not clear. The identification of the initial defects can be achieved by using the method of step-by-step backward deduction: starting from a relatively obvious defect in the project, as the initial defect, push backward to what consequences this defect can lead to, rather than deduce the cause of the defect forward. We will record this consequence and then deduce backward, Until we found that several undetermined initial defects derived continuously have little relevance to this

project. In this way, we have a series of undetermined initial defects, as shown in Figure 3; Next, we need to find one of these undetermined initial defects as the initial defect. After determining the initial defect, we can reverse the initial defect to see whether the reversed initial defect can be used as the purpose of the project. The principle is to find the initial defects from the super system first or from the last process.

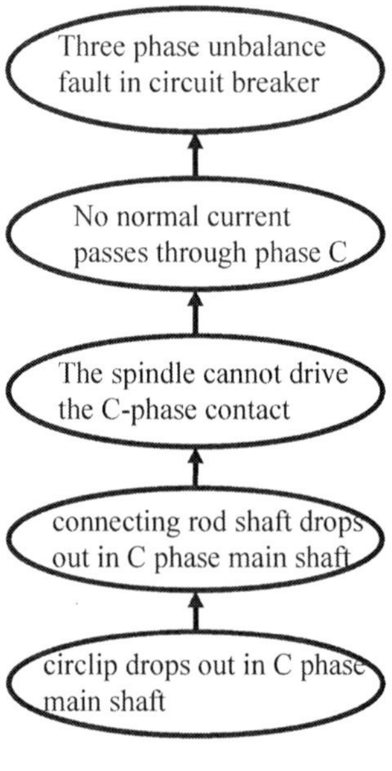

Figure 3 identifying initial defects

6) The difference and connection the end condition between FTA and CCA:

(1) The end condition of FTA is:

- All input events cannot be decomposed to find the next level of events.
- It is unnecessary to decompose until the fault mechanism or probability distribution of the event (bottom event) is known.

(2) The end condition of CCA is:

- When you can't continue to find the next reason.
- When natural phenomena are reached.
- When the limit of physics, chemistry, biology or geometry is reached.
- When reaching the limit of system / regulation / industry standard / right / cost / human, etc.
- According to the situation of the project, if further excavation is irrelevant to the project.

7) The difference and connection between FTA and CCA process:

Fault tree analysis and causal chain analysis are MECE principles (Mutually Exclusive and Collectively Exhaustive), that is, no overlap and no omission.

(1) FTA process [11]:

The qualitative analysis of fault tree is mainly to find out all the minimum cut sets that lead to top events in the fault tree. A cut set is a set of several bottom events that cause the top event of a fault tree to occur. If any bottom event in the cut set does not occur, the top event does not occur, and such a cut set is the minimum cut set. Generally, all minimum cut sets are obtained by the downward method or the upward method.

By analyzing the minimum cut set and importance obtained from the fault tree, the weak links in the design are determined, so as to take targeted measures to improve the reliability and safety of products.

(2) CCA process:

Starting from the initial defect, analyze its influencing factors, get the intermediate defect, and then continue to excavate the influencing factors of the next level until the end defect.

Find out the key defects, which refer to the defects found through CCA, which have not been tried before and need to be solved in the future. The key problem is to find the key defects in the defects of "and" operation symbol connection, or to find the defects with a high proportion in the defects of "+" operation symbol connection as the key defects.

Turn key defects into key problems, look for possible solutions from various reasons, and excavate possible contradictions from various reasons at the same time. So as to form a table of key defects; See Table 3. By trying to solve each of the key defects, we can find a variety of solutions to solve the initial defects.

Table 3 key defects

Serial Number	Critical Defect	key Question	Possible Solutions	Contradiction Described
1	Too much movement of connecting rod shaft	How to make the connecting rod shaft not move after loading and easy to disassemble;	Two half shafts with lugs are assembled with each other, clamped upside-down, and the circlip spring is cancelled;	
2	Circlip falled off	How to make the spring has enough force and does not fall off;		The size of the spring should be large enough to ensure sufficient force; The size of the spring should be small enough to ensure non-interference
3	The position and size of the arm are incorrect	How to ensure the size and position of the spindle arm	Check with gages before assembly	
4	Insufficient space for base to yield	How to ensure sufficient space for base relinquishment		The space of the base should be large to ensure no interference; The space of the base should be small to ensure enough air pressure blowing arc ability and strength;

V. EXAMPLE ANALYSIS

Now, an example is given to illustrate the advantages and disadvantages of these two analysis methods by using FTA and CCA respectively.

During the use of a certain type of ACB at the client, there was no normal current in phase C, resulting in three-phase imbalance fault. After analysis by technicians, it was found that the contact rod shaft of phase C fell off, as shown in Figure 4. Next, we will analyze the cause of the fault through FTA and CCA.

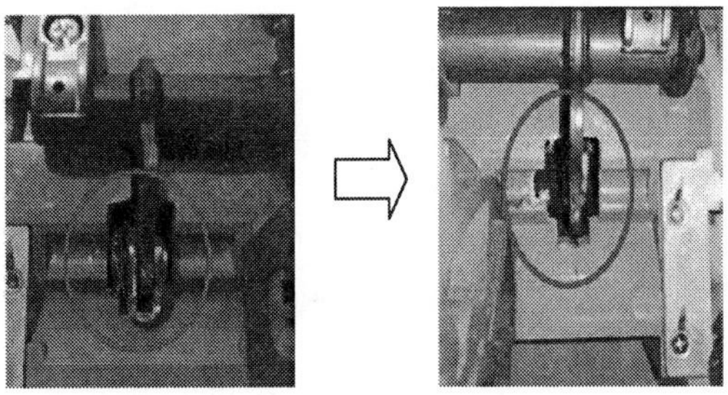

normal product failure product

Figure 4 failure status

1) First of all, conduct CCA. The first step is to identify the initial defects, and deduce the consequences from the obvious defects of the project. We found a total of five undetermined initial defects, as shown in Figure 3. Combined with the resources and time of the project team, the project team finally determined that there is no normal current in phase C as the initial defect of the project.

Find the initial defect, and we try to reverse the initial defect. The result of the reversal is that the c-phase current is normal - this is the purpose of the project. The initial defect selection is correct.

Next, the CCA of the initial defects is carried out, as shown in Figure 2. The reason why the connecting rod shaft falls off is included in the chain with the incorrect closing position of the moving contact in the figure, as shown in Figure 5.

Through the analysis of the cause and effect chain of the connecting rod shaft, we found the key defects; See Table 3. Through the key defects and contradiction pairs, find a series of methods to solve the key defects according to the way of TRIZ to solve the problem, so as to solve the project purpose.

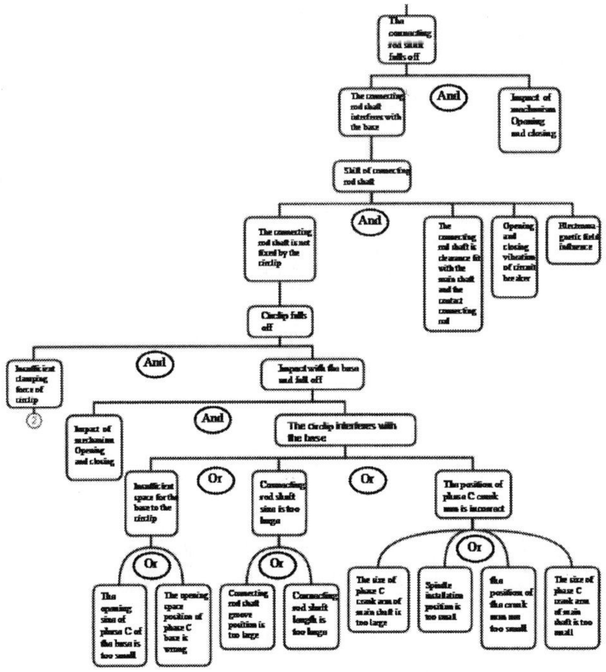

Fig. 5 CCA of connecting rod shaft falling off

2) Next, carry out FTA, which generally starts from determining the top event. In this example, the top event is the three-phase unbalanced fault of the circuit breaker. Next, the fault tree analysis of the top event is carried out, as shown in Figure 1.

The causes of three-phase unbalance fault of circuit breaker are huge, including 249 bottom events, 121 intermediate events and 122 operation symbols, basically including all the causes of three-phase unbalance fault of circuit breaker. Figure 6 shows some contents of the falling off fault of the connecting rod shaft. Through FTA, we can find all the influencing events that affect the three-phase imbalance fault, find the minimum cut level, and then take measures for all the events in the minimum cut level, which can effectively improve the reliability of products.

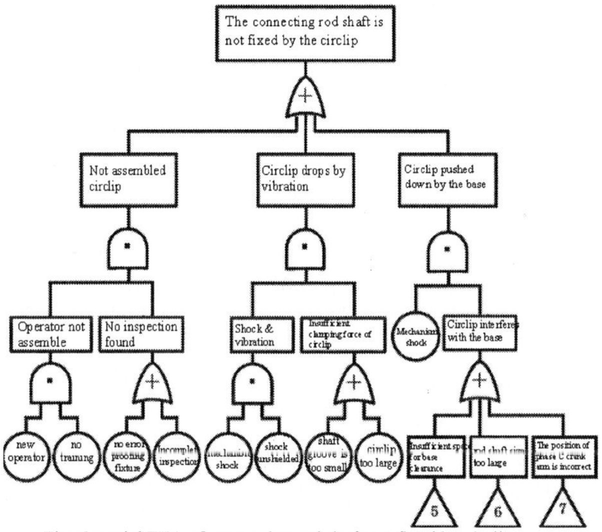

Fig. 6 partial FTA of connecting rod shaft not fixed by circlip

VI. CONCLUSION

1) Through the comparison of the above cases, we can find the following similarities:

(1) CCA and FTA are not only to solve the problem, but to find the best solution by giving a variety of ways to solve the problem, so as to systematically improve the reliability of products;

(2) As long as we find an opportunity to solve the problem, the commonly used cause analysis tools such as 8D and fish-bone diagram will end the analysis. It is often not the best way, and it may also bring other problems that have not been found. CCA and FTA can find a variety of solutions at the same time, which can select the best from the best. At the same time, other secondary problems are also systematically considered.

(3) CCA and FTA both rely on the professional ability and

experience of analysts. They both need the support of FMEA or FMECA documents and the participation of teams.

2) At the same time, CCA and FTA are also different:

(1) CCA is more convenient and concise in the process of problem and defect analysis; One of the disadvantages of FTA is tedious. From the determination of the top event to the qualitative analysis of the built fault tree, all possible combinations need to be tested in the fault tree in turn. The combination that can make the top event appear is the cut set, which requires a lot of work.

(2) The starting point of CCA is to find out the key defects. The key defects are generally not terminal defects. In most cases, they are composed of intermediate defects, and the scope of solution is the content of the key defects table; The starting point of FTA is to find out the minimum cut set including the bottom event, and the scope of solution is all events in the minimum cut set including the bottom event.

(3) CCA generally finds the key defects, then solves the key defects, realizes the goal of the project, and improves the reliability; FTA finds the weak links in the design by looking for the minimum cut set, and then takes measures to improve the reliability and safety of the system. Their purposes are not exactly the same.

(4) CCA can only be used for qualitative analysis, while FTA can be used for quantitative analysis, using approximate method to estimate the upper and lower limits of system failure rate; Then the importance of each event in the cut set is obtained.

Therefore, CCA and FTA are both tools for analyzing failure or fault problems. For the analysis of a single problem, CCA is more convenient, and for the analysis of system problems, FTA is more systematic.

References

[1] Zhizhong Mou, Design For Reliability, Beijing: China Machine Press, 1993

[2] E. A. Elsayed, Zhou Yang, Reliability Engineering (Second Edition), Beijing: Electronic Industry Press, 2016

[3] GB/T 7826-2012 System Reliability Analysis Technology - Failure Mode and Effect Analysis (FMEA) Procedure

[4] GJB/Z 1391-2006 Guide for Failure Mode Impact and Hazard Analysis

[5] Bangchun Wen, Mechanical Design Manual - Fatigue Strength and Reliability Design (Fifth Edition), Beijing: China Machine Press, 2014

[6] Dinghua Shi, Songrui Wang, Fault Tree Analysis Technology Method and Theory, Beijing: Beijing Normal University Press, 1993

[7] Yongwei Sun, TRIZ - the Golden Key to Opening The Door of Innovation I, Beijing: Science Press, 2015

[8] GB4888-2009 Fault Tree Terms and Symbols

[9] GB7829-87 Fault Tree Analysis Program

[10] Yongwei Sun, TRIZ - the Golden Key to Opening The Door of Innovation II, Beijing: Science Press, 2020

[11] GJB/Z 768A-1998 Fault Tree Analysis Guide

Research on Indirect Measurement and Calculation Method of Contact Pressure Based on Machine Vision Technology

Wenhua Li[1], Xinglin Yang[1], Wei Li[2], Cheng Xu[1], Wenze Zhao[1], Weiming Wang[1]

[1] State Key Laboratory of Reliability and Intelligence of Electrical Equipment, Hebei University of Technology, Tianjin, 300401

[2] Shenyang Railway Signal Co.,Ltd., Shenyang,110025

E-mail: liwenhua@hebut.edu.cn Tel:13312176902

***Abstract*—Machine vision technology is a new method to obtain relay parameters, which greatly improves the efficiency and precision of industrial production. Having established a mathematical model of the supporting structure of the fixed contact reed, this paper analyzes the structural factors that affect the contact pressure measurement and obtains the relationship between the deflection of the reed structure and the pressure on the mechanics of materials. Machine vision technology is used to process the moving image of the target and extract its features, and the moving track of the stationary contact is accurately detected. By studying the relationship between the stationary contact displacement and pressure, the calculated results of the contact pressure is proposed. After the correlation analysis of the factors that affects the contact pressure value is finished, the structure model of neural network is built and the final pressure value is calculated. It is the first time to analyze and measure the contact pressure by combining mechanics and machine vision technology. Comparing with the conventional manual force measurement method, the result of experiment shows that the proposed method improves the precision accuracy of measurement and the stability vastly , and exploring the structural factors that affect the pressure measurement can provide a theoretical reference for the contact reliability and service life of the product at the initial stage of design.**

***Keywords*—Machine vision; Contact pressure; neural network; mathematical model.**

I. Introduction

Under the specified conditions, when the relay is in the released or working state, after the moving contact and the stationary contact are in stable contact, there will be a pressure to ensure the electrical contact between the moving contact and the stationary contact is good. This pressure is called contact pressure[1].

The contact pressure acts on the surface of the contact to improve the anti-vibration ability of the reed, ensure that the contact resistance of the contact is small and tends to be stable, and ensure that the relay works reliably under specified conditions. Contact pressure is a very important parameter for relay contacts. When designing the product at first, it needs many tests before it can be selected properly. If the contact pressure of the contact is chosen to be very small, it will be detrimental to the contact resistance, and the good electrical contact between the moving and static contacts cannot be guaranteed, so the reliability requirements of the relay cannot be met. If the contact pressure of the contact is selected to be large, it is necessary to increase the operation power of the relay, and increase the mechanical friction and wear of the contact, which is detrimental to the working life of the relay contact [2-3].

At present, the measurement of contact pressure is mainly static, and it mainly depends on manual measurement. When the relay is in a stable state, the tester gradually increases the pressure of the end point of the dynamometer at the contact point by using the cooperation of the dynamometer and the socket, and reads at the moment when the dynamic and static contacts are disconnected. This indicator is the contact pressure value at this point. However, it should be noted that the focus of the dynamometer should be on the reed close to the front end of the contact, and the measuring rod of the dynamometer should be parallel to the plane of the reed. Because it is manual measurement, it is easy to cause poor stability and low reliability of reading due to subjective factors, observation angle and other reasons, thus affecting the accuracy of measurement results. Therefore, how to measure the contact pressure accurately and efficiently is a problem worth studying [4].

In recent years, the development of machine vision technology is faster and faster. With its advantages of fast processing speed, high precision and non-contact, machine vision technology has a place in all industries. Image acquisition, image processing and analysis are also a new method to obtain instrument parameters [5].

Firstly, this paper analyzes the stress of the support structure of the static contact, builds a mathematical model, and puts forward a contact pressure measurement method combining machine vision technology with BP neural network algorithm. This method can quickly, efficiently and accurately calculate the contact pressure values of multiple static contacts.

II. STRESS ANALYSIS OF THE STRUCTURE AND ESTABLISHMENT OF MATHEMATICAL MODEL.

A. Stress Analysis of Static Contact Support Structure

Firstly, in order to facilitate the analysis and calculation of the reed support structure, the following assumptions are put forward:

1)The maximum deformation of the supporting structure of the reed is within the elastic limit, satisfying Hooke's law.

2) The cross-section, length and thickness of the reed are always the same, ignoring the influence caused by the fatigue damage of structural materials;

3) The quality of the reed and the static contact itself is ignored, that is, the influence of the dead weight of the reed and the static contact on its elasticity is not considered;

4) Because the length of the reed is much larger than the width and height of its cross section, the reed can be simplified as a rod when studying the action of external force[6].

Based on the above assumption, and the distribution range of the force on the stationary contact is far less than the length of the reed, we treat the force on the stationary contact as a concentrated force. The concentrated force acting on the relay stationary contact reed is perpendicular to the axis of the reed, which makes the original straight axis become a curve after deformation, that is, the supporting structure of the reed bends. Combined with the knowledge of material mechanics, the supporting structure of reed is treated as a cantilever beam. Fig. 1 shows the position of the stress endpoint P (static contact) of the reed before and after stress. P is the position of the static contact before stress, and P′ is the position of the static contact after stress.

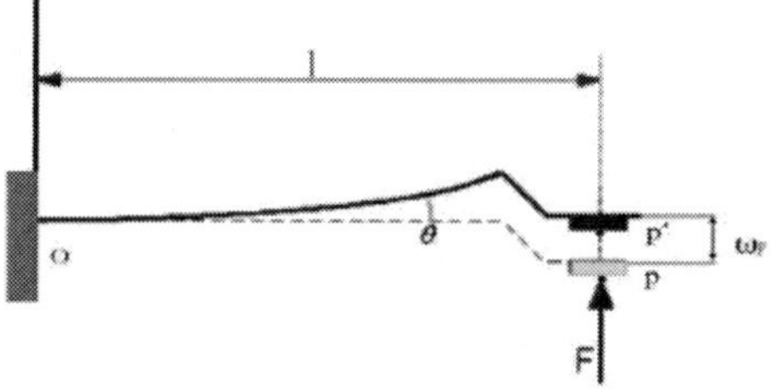

Fig. 1. Stress diagram of reed support structure

In the process of the static contact supporting structure's stress deformation, ignoring the influence of its own weight, the static contact will be pushed upward by the moving contact. This thrust is the armature pull-in movement, which drives the relay connecting rod and the moving contact to move upward, and pushes the static contact to move upward. The static contact supporting structure is made of elastic material, which will deform after being stressed, resulting in downward elastic force. Finally, when the armature is fully pulled in, the elastic force is equal to the thrust, and the moving and static contacts are in a balanced state.

In engineering, the contact pressure refers to the pressure between the static contact and the dynamic contact when the static contact is in a stable state, so we only need to consider the force acting on the static contact when the static contact is in a stable state.

B. Establishment of Mathematical Model

E is the elastic modulus of the reed; L is the total length from the stationary contact of the reed to the bottom of the reed; I is the moment of inertia of the cross-sectional area of the reed to the neutral axis of the cross-section; M is the reed width; N is the thickness of the reed; The unit f is n, the unit e is Mpa, and the others are mm ..

Formula (2.1) is a differential equation of deflection curve, which is applicable to the bending deformation of the reed support structure in this paper [7]. The formula (2.2) is the calculation formula of the moment of inertia of the support structure.

$$\frac{\frac{d^2\omega}{dx^2}}{\left[1+\left(\frac{d\omega}{dx}\right)^2\right]^{\frac{3}{2}}}=\frac{M}{EI} \tag{2.1}$$

$$I=\frac{mn^3}{12} \tag{2.2}$$

Usually, the span of the static contact is much smaller than the deflection. Deflection is the linear displacement of the static contact P perpendicular to the beam axis when the system is in equilibrium with the static contact P in free state, which is the length of the longitudinal displacement L, and the span is the lateral displacement of the static contact P. The deflection curve = f (x) is a very flat curve with a small turning angle.

$$\theta\approx\tan\theta=\frac{d\omega}{dx}=f'(x) \tag{2.3}$$

Because dΩ/dx is very small, its flat result is even smaller, so equation (2.1) can be simplified as an approximate differential equation:

$$\frac{d^2\omega}{dx^2}=\frac{M}{EI} \tag{2.4}$$

Assuming that the direction of the reed support structure is the X-axis direction, the bending of its arbitrary cross section is:

$$M=-F(l-x) \tag{2.5}$$

From formulas (2.3) and (2.4), the differential equation of the deflection curve is obtained:

$$EI\omega''=-F(l-x) \tag{2.6}$$

For this integral:

$$EI\omega'=\frac{F}{6}x^2-\frac{Fl}{2}x+A \tag{2.7}$$

$$EI\omega=\frac{F}{6}x^3-\frac{Fl}{2}x^2+Ax+B \tag{2.8}$$

At the fixed end o, the rotation angle and deflection should be equal to zero, and x=0 should be brought into the formulas (2.7) and (2.8):

$$A= EI\theta_0 =0 \tag{2.9}$$

$$B= EI\omega_0 =0 \tag{2.10}$$

Substitute the obtained integral constants A and B for Equation (2.7) and Equation (2.8), and get the equation of rotation angle and deflection curve as follows:

$$EI\omega' = \frac{F}{6}x^2 - \frac{Fl}{2}x \tag{2.11}$$

$$EI\omega = \frac{F}{6}x^3 - \frac{Fl}{2}x^2 \tag{2.12}$$

The abscissa x=1 of the stress point p is substituted into the above formula to obtain:

$$\theta_P = \frac{Fl^2}{2EI} \tag{2.13}$$

$$\omega_P = \frac{Fl^3}{3EI} \tag{2.14}$$

Equation (2.14) is the formula for calculating the deflection of the static contact, in which the parameter f is the concentrated force exerted on the static contact, i.e. the contact pressure, E is the elastic modulus of the relay reed of 110GPa, l is the distance between the stressed point and the fixed end point of 40mm, I is the moment of inertia of the cross section, n is the thickness of the reed of 7mm, and m is the width of the reed of 0.4mm. The formula for calculating contact pressure can be obtained from the above formula:

$$F= \frac{3E}{l^3} \cdot \frac{mn^3}{12} \cdot \omega_P \tag{2.15}$$

C. *Structural Factors Affecting Contact Pressure measurement*

Actually, the reed support structure is not a straight cantilever structure, and there is a corner behind the stress point P, which makes the established mathematical model affected by the shape parameters [8];

In addition, when designing the relay, the silver contacts on the slender slot port will vibrate when they are in contact, which will affect the performance parameters such as contact resistance and contact jumping. Therefore, in order to reduce the vibration when the moving and static contacts are in contact, an initial pressure is applied between the supporting plate and the reed, as shown in Fig. 2, so as to ensure that the contact can eliminate the vibration and shorten the complete closing time of the contact. However, this initial pressure will make the static contact support structure deform to a certain extent, making the measured deformation smaller than the actual deformation, thus affecting the measurement results.

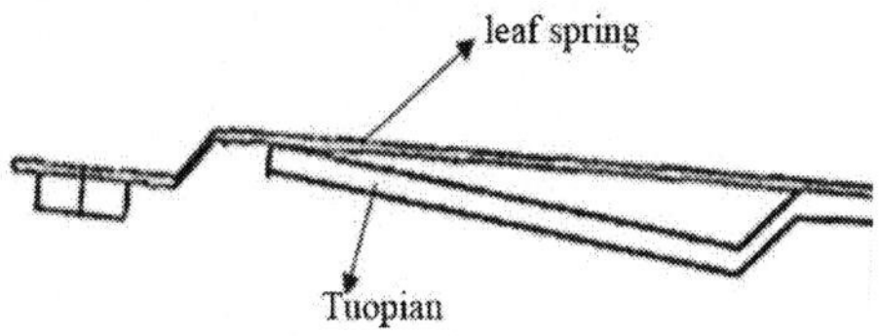

Fig. 2. Structure diagram of reed and supporting piece

In order to solve this problem, we need to revise the data obtained by the calculation formula to reduce the experimental error.

III. MEASUREMENT PROCESS OF CONTACT PRESSURE

In this paper, the computer is used instead of the W3ZRRoperator to measure the contact pressure, which makes up for the deficiency of human eyes in space and function [9]. From the previous analysis, we can know that we can get the pressure value of the static contact by derivation only by measuring the deflection of the static contact. Fig. 3 is a flow chart of measuring contact pressure by machine vision technology. Firstly, a series of images of the moving process of several pairs of static contacts of the relay are taken by image acquisition equipment such as high-speed cameras, then the images are preprocessed, then the static contacts are identified and tracked, and the time-displacement images of the static contacts are obtained and drawn. Finally, the contact pressure of the relay is obtained according to the deflection value of the static contacts.

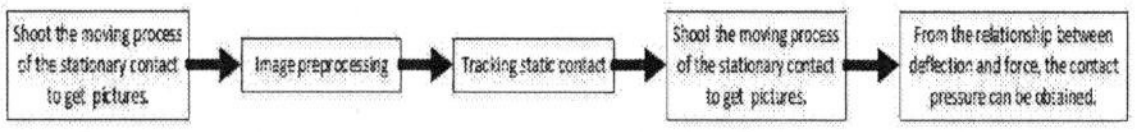

Fig. 3. Schematic diagram of contact pressure measurement process

However, in the process of photographing the relay, the quality of the picture will be affected by some problems, such as illumination intensity, inaccurate focus and noise interference, which will affect the recognition and tracking of the target in the image, resulting in a big error in the final result. Therefore, it is very important to adopt efficient and appropriate image processing, recognition and tracking algorithms.

IV. PROCESSING TECHNOLOGY OF TARGET IMAGE

A. *Image Preprocessing*

In addition to the target to be recognized, the image also has other parts, such as support rods, moving contacts, markers, etc., which will interfere with the recognition of the target. Therefore, it is necessary to preprocess the image to improve the recognition accuracy and speed up the operation.

1) Grayscale and binarization of images

In the process of image processing and motion tracking, the gray image is usually used as the input image, which can greatly improve the calculation speed. Let the pixel value of each pixel in the image be R=G=B, and the values of r, g, and b are weighted according to a certain weight to finally be the gray value of the pixel. After this operation is performed on all pixels, the image becomes a gray image [10]. The image in this paper is converted according to formula (3.1):

$$Gary=0.31R+0.113G+0.567B \tag{4.1}$$

Where R, G and B respectively represent their corresponding color channels, and the value range of each color channel is 0-255. Then obtain the histogram of the gray image of the front of the relay, as shown in Fig. 4.

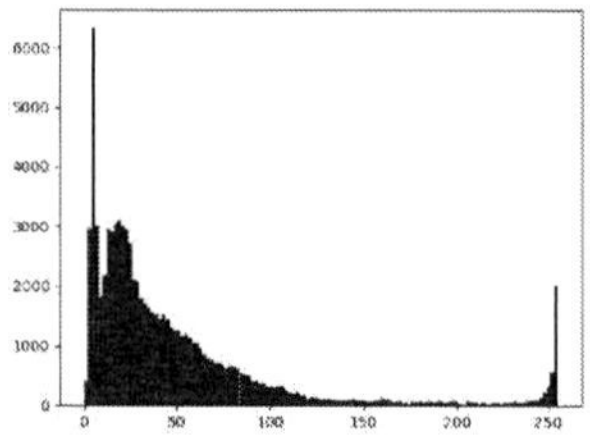

Fig. 4. Gray image histogram

According to the distribution of the histogram, choose the appropriate threshold T as the threshold value [11], and use formula (4.2) to convert the image into a binary image.

$$f(x,y) = \begin{cases} 1, & T \geq 0 \\ 0, & T < 0 \end{cases} \qquad (4.2)$$

The original image and binarized image of the relay are shown in Fig. 5:

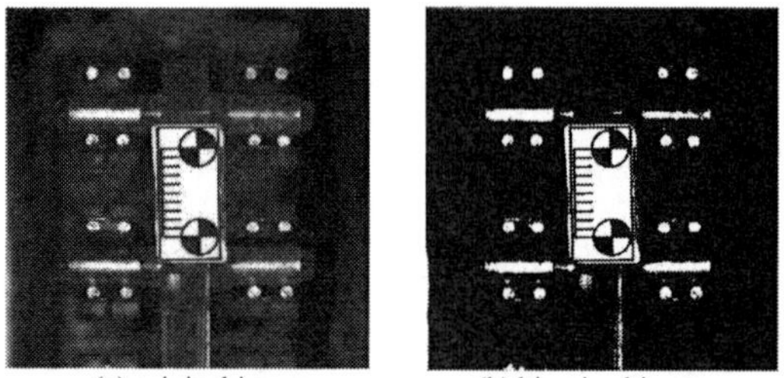
(a) original image (b) binarized image
Fig. 5. Original image and its binarized image

2) Image filtering

Because the lighting environment, circuits and electronic components will make the image produce noise, these noise drops will lower the quality of the image, which will bring adverse effects on the image processing and recognition and tracking, so it is necessary to denoise the image. Gaussian filter is selected to filter and denoise the image, and its template coefficient decreases with the increase of the distance from the center of the template [12], namely:

$$f(x,y) = \frac{1}{(\sqrt{2\pi}\sigma)^2} * e^{\frac{-((x-\bar{x})^2+(y-\bar{y})^2)^2}{2\sigma^2}} \qquad (4.3)$$

Gaussian filtering can blur the image to a lesser extent, which can better keep the overall details of the image, as shown in Fig. 6:

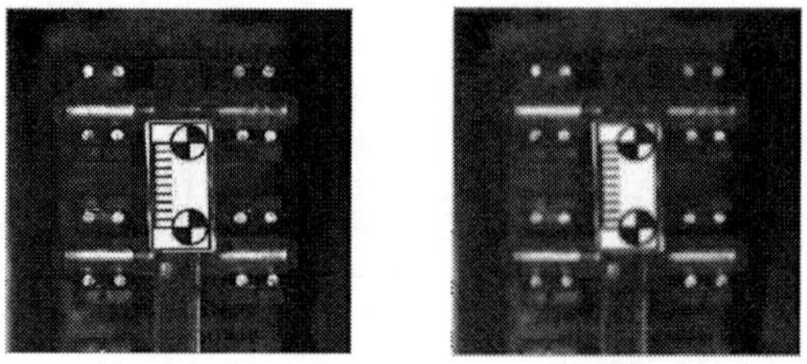
(a) original image (b) filtered image
Fig. 6. Original image and its filtered image

B. Image Target Location Algorithm

When measuring the deflection of the static contact, the template matching positioning algorithm is adopted. In machine vision, template matching has become the most widely used image location algorithm because of its simple principle, easy realization and high accuracy. The input image of the template is a grayscale image, which is a positioning strategy based on grayscale matching, and an image registration algorithm that calculates the grayscale difference of corresponding pixels between two consecutive images[13]. Its principle is: first create the template, then select the appropriate template matching algorithm, set the similarity threshold, and obtain the matching result.

The establishment process of template is very important. A good template can make the target recognition more accurate and improve the accuracy. In this paper, the establishment of the upper contact template is taken as an example. First, the input first frame image is masked to intercept the target area of the upper contact, and then the grayscale processing and binarization processing are carried out respectively. The Soble operator edge detection algorithm is used to obtain the edge information of the upper contact. Finally, the minimum circumscribed rectangle of the closed-loop edge is drawn to complete the template establishment. The process is shown in Fig. 7:

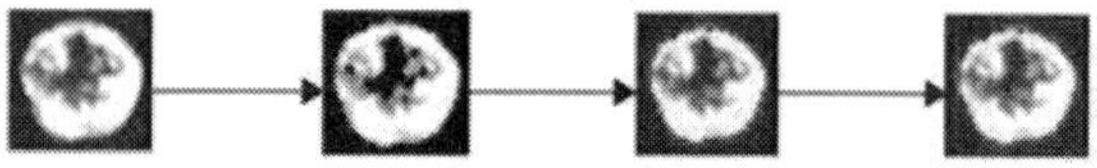
Fig. 7 Establishment of static contact template

After the template is created, it is necessary to select the template matching algorithm. In this paper, TM_CCORR NORMED matching algorithm is adopted, and the calculation formula is as follows:

$$R(x,y) = \frac{\sum_{x',y'} T(x',y') I(x+x',y+y')}{\sqrt{\sum_{x',y'} T(x',y')^2 \sum_{x',y'} I(x+x',y+y')^2}} \qquad (4.4)$$

The effect diagram after template matching tracking is shown in Fig. 8:

Fig. 8. Target tracking renderings

The blue area is the result of tracking and identifying the static contact. It can be found that the tracking result is ideal and can be matched to the correct position.

C. Normalization of Pixel Value And Actual Distance Value

In this paper, a logo combining BMW logo and scale is proposed. The centers of the two BMW logos are 1cm, as shown in Fig. 9

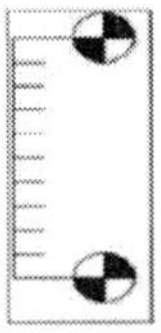

Fig. 9. BMW ruler

Two BMWs are marked as circles, which can be quickly and accurately identified during image processing. Stick it on the connecting rod of the relay, and during image recognition, two BMW signs will be recognized, so as to obtain the pixel coordinate values (x1, y1) and (x2, y2) of the centers of the two BMW signs. The relationship between the actual value and the pixel value can be obtained by formula (4.5).

$$1\text{cm} = (\sqrt{(x1-x2)^2+(y1-y2)^2})\ \text{px} \qquad (4.5)$$

V. BP NEURAL NETWORK

Fig. 10 shows the structural framework of BP neural network, including input layer, hidden layer and input layer. BP neural network has the characteristics of self-adaptation and self-adjustment. By processing the data, the weights and thresholds of neurons in each layer can be determined, so that association can be made and the data can be predicted.

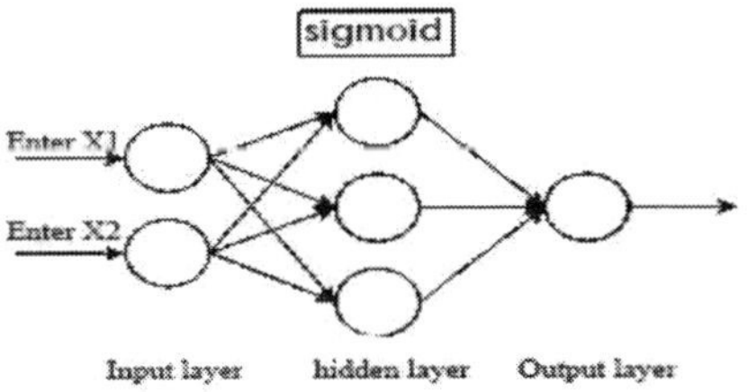

Fig. 10. BP neural network structure framework

Equation (5.1) is the s-type transfer function sigmoid used in the hidden layer, and the linear transfer function purelin is used in the output layer, which has a good fitting effect when processing data.

$$sigmod(x) = \frac{1}{1+exp\,(-x)} \qquad (5.1)$$

BP neural network algorithm is an iterative algorithm, and its basic idea is:

1. Data is transmitted from the input layer to the hidden layer node, and after being processed by the hidden layer node layer by layer, an output is generated and transmitted to the output layer;

2. Define a loss function, assuming that the predicted target of the sample is Yp, the real target is Y, and the function is:

$$loss = 1/N \sum (Yp - Y)^2 \qquad (5.2)$$

The parameter N is any value, usually a positive integer, which is convenient for calculation. If that output error propagate in the forward direction at the output layer doe not reach the ideal value, the error signal is returned along the original connection path;

3. By modifying the weights and offsets of neurons in each layer, the error function value is minimized; Repeat the above process and train the model until the desired output is obtained. In this paper, the gradient descent method is used to update and solve its weight and offset.

A. Gradient Descent Method Updates Weight And Bias

Gradient descent method is an optimization algorithm that makes the loss function smaller and smaller. Iterative solution is carried out step by step along the direction of the gradient vector of the function to obtain the minimized loss function and model parameters. Fig. 11 is the flow chart of the basic idea of gradient descent method.

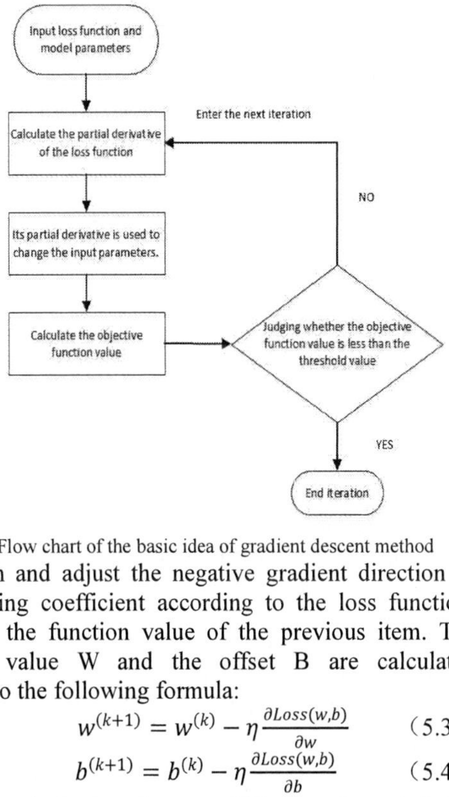

Fig. 11. Flow chart of the basic idea of gradient descent method

Search and adjust the negative gradient direction of the weighting coefficient according to the loss function, and attach the function value of the previous item. The weighting value W and the offset B are calculated according to the following formula:

$$w^{(k+1)} = w^{(k)} - \eta \frac{\partial Loss(w,b)}{\partial w} \qquad (5.3)$$

$$b^{(k+1)} = b^{(k)} - \eta \frac{\partial Loss(w,b)}{\partial b} \qquad (5.4)$$

Where η is the learning rate, if the learning rate is too low, the cost function will converge very slowly and the running time will be prolonged; If the learning rate is too high, the loss function may not decrease at every variable, resulting in inability to converge. In this paper, η=0.001.

B. Learning Steps of BP Neural Network

The learning steps of BP neural network are as follows:

1, performing initialization, randomly assigning the weight w and the offset b to any number within (-1,1), and determining the loss function, learning rate and training times;

2. Randomly select the input sample and the corresponding expected output;

3. According to the error between the expected output and the actual value of BP neural network, calculate the partial derivative of the error function to the weight W and the offset B;

4. According to the partial derivative, update the weight and offset according to formulas (5.3) and (5.4);

5. Repeat the above steps for each sample until the iteration stops when the error of the network output is less than the set threshold.

VI. EXPERIMENTAL RESULTS AND ANALYSIS

The machine vision technology is used to identify and track the relay stationary contacts, and the computer is used to obtain the coordinate position parameters of the center points of several pairs of stationary contacts of the relay at different times, and then the corresponding relationship diagram between displacement change and time is obtained. Taking two groups of stationary contacts T1 and T2 as examples, as shown in Fig. 12:

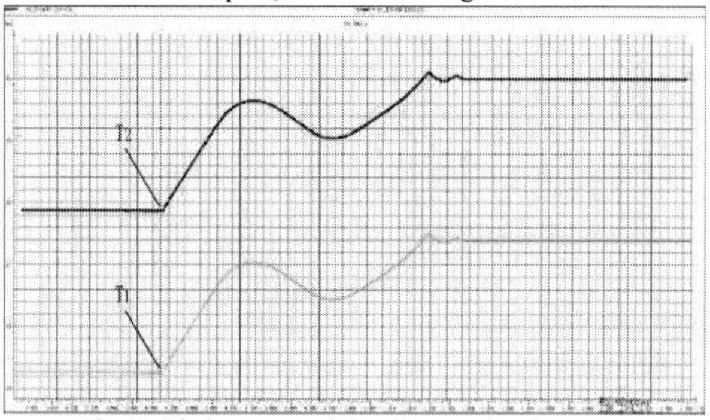

Fig. 12. Displacement variation diagram of static contact

According to the displacement change curve, get the pixel value of the initial position of each stationary contact and the pixel value of the stationary contact in the stable state, and the absolute value of the difference between them is the pixel value of the longitudinal displacement of the stationary contact. Then, convert the pixel value and the actual value to get the deflection of the stationary contact, and substitute it into formula (2.15) to get the theoretical calculation value of the contact pressure, and then predict it by neural network to get the final value of the contact pressure.

A. Analysis of The Results of Manual Measurement And Experimental Calculation

By identifying and tracking the characteristics of the static contact, the displacement of the static contact is obtained, and then the contact pressure of the static contact is calculated by the longitudinal displacement of the static contact. The results are shown in Table 1 and Table 2 below:

TABLE I
Calculation Results Of Contact Pressure Of Moving And Closing Static Contacts

Moving contact			
group number	Actual measured value/mN	computed value/mN	Error/mN
1	330	323.91	-6.09
2	330	328.13	-1.87
3	325	328.13	3.13
4	320	323.91	3.91
5	340	332.34	-7.66
6	335	336.56	1.56
7	330	332.34	2.34
8	310	313.10	3.10

TABLE II
Calculation results of contact pressure of dynamic and static contacts

Moving broken contact			
group number	Actual measured value/mN	computed value/mN	Error/mN
1	270	265.89	-4.11
2	260	268.05	8.05
3	270	263.73	-6.27
4	265	259.26	-5.74
5	260	261.32	1.32
6	255	255.23	0.23
7	259	252.42	-6.58
8	250	250.34	0.34

B. Analysis of Measurement Results And Experimental Values of Different Surveyors

Two experimenters were selected to measure the contact pressure of the same contact with dynamometer, and the contact pressure of this relay was measured with the measurement method in this paper. The results are shown in Fig. 13:

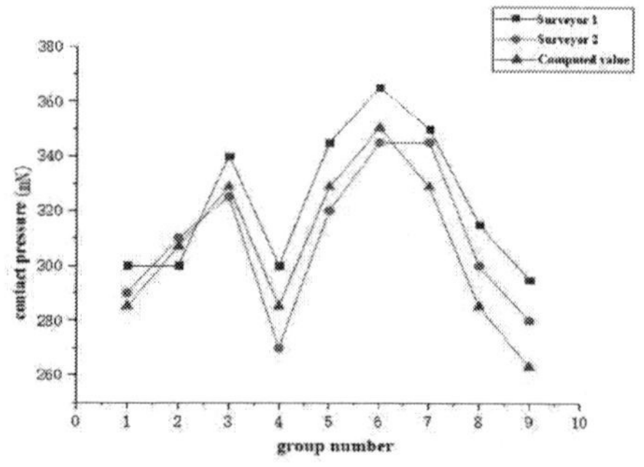

Fig. 13. Analysis of measurement results and experimental values of different surveyors

VII. CONCLUSION

1. In this paper, from the point of view of material mechanics, the contact pressure is calculated by establishing a mechanical model of the reed support structure. Compared with the traditional manual measurement method, the error fluctuation range is small,

and the calculation result can be obtained more quickly by computer. The proposed method greatly improves the measurement accuracy and stability.

2. When different surveyors measure the contact pressure of multiple groups of the same relay twice, the error fluctuates greatly, which is greatly influenced by human subjectivity. The error of manual measurement method is uncontrollable, and the error is scattered and random. However, the calculated value is calculated according to the formula, and only a small number of pixels cause tiny errors within the error allowable range, so the dispersion is very small. ;

3. In this paper, the contact pressure measurement method based on machine vision technology uses image recognition to automatically obtain the coordinate position of the geometric center of the moving and static contacts, and realizes the position tracking, which avoids the subjective influence of the measurers. At the same time, the non-contact method is used to measure the contact pressure, which avoids the secondary damage to the relay during the measurement process.

In the future, the specific pressure between the contact pad and the support pad, and the influence of contact pressure on contact resistance will be analyzed in detail, and the influence of relay contact pressure value on relay contact life and performance degradation will be studied, which will provide new ideas for relay research and development and improvement.

References

[1] Wang Biao, Luo Yanyan, Zhang Yuanlei, Zhang Xiaojun. Study on detection technology of the contact pressure on the electrical contacts of relays[P]. 26th International Conference on Electrical Contacts (ICEC 2012),2012.

[2] Zhang Yongwen; Li Hui. Analysis of contact pressure error of direct-acting AC contactor and evaluation of error measurement method [J]. Electrical Manufacturing, 2008, (01):78-80.

[3] Tian Nan. Sliding contact characteristics and reliability analysis of different contact materials of connectors [D]. Beijing University of Posts and Telecommunications, 2019.

[4] Lu Chunjie. Failure analysis of electrical contacts and design and application of an electric corrosion test device [J]. Household Electrical Appliances, 2018, (11):15-17+21.

[5] Zhao Shutao, Li Baoshu, Yuan Jinsha, Zhao Dongsheng. Automatic acquisition of dynamic parameters of instruments and its optimization algorithm [J]. Journal of Electrical Technology, 2007(03):148-152+158.

[6] Gu Fuming; Shi Yuqin; Li Qi-ru. Dynamic analysis of springboard diving system at take-off stage [J]. journal of chengdu sport university, 2002, (03):90-93.

[7] Mechanics of Materials. Liu Hongwen; Editor-in-Chief. 2017

[8] Li Min; Li Han; Chen Weimin. Curriculum content design of higher-order thinking training-taking typical examples of mechanics of materials as an example [J]. Mechanics and Practice, 2021, (04):588-592.

[9] Masafumi Hashimoto,Hiroyuki Kawashima,et al.Sensor fault detection and identification in dead-reckoning system of mobile robot: interaction multiple model approach[C]. Proceeding of the 2001 IEEE International Conference on Intelligent Robots and Systems, 2001: 1321-1326.

[10] Klara Steinschneider.Machine Vision:Image Processing[J]. Quality, 2015.

[11] Francisco André Corrêa Alegria,António Manuel da Cruz Serra. Automatic calibration of analog and digital measuring instruments using computer vision.[J]. IEEE Trans. Instrumentation and Measurement,2000, 49(1).

[12] Jie Jing; Wu Jianfu; Hu Yongfu. Research on MTF detection method based on image filtering [J]. Journal of Chongqing University of Science and Technology (Natural Science), 2018,32(07):202-206.

[13] Naruto Shimonishi, Kenichi Ogiwara, Yukio Oda, et al. A Novel Assessment of Factor VIII Activity by Template Matching Utilizing Weighted Average Parameters from Comprehensive Clot Waveform Analysis[J]. Thrombosis and Haemostasis, 2021, 121(2).

Design Optimization of A DW45-2000 Frame High Machine Life Product

Linqiang Liu, Cheng Wang, Jianjun Huang

Shanghai Liangxin Electric Co., Ltd. Shanghai 300401

Email:liulinqiang@sh-liangxin.com Tel:18611260687

wangcheng@sh-liangxin.com Tel:13601987921

huangjianjun@sh-liangxin.com Tel:13641937794

***Abstract*— On September 22, 2020, President Xi Jinping announced at the 75th United Nations General Assembly that China will strive to peak carbon dioxide emissions by 2030 and strive to achieve carbon neutrality by 2060.**

At the briefing held by the State Council Information Office on July 14, 2021, Zhao Yingmin, deputy minister of the Ministry of Ecology and Environment, said that the power generation industry is the first industry to be included in the national carbon market.

In order to better assist the achievement of the "dual carbon" goal, in recent years, the state has successively introduced relevant subsidy policies, and photovoltaic and wind power generation have become increasingly popular. Wind power generation is a renewable, non-polluting and clean energy source, but wind turbines are often installed in unattended or inconvenient places for maintenance, so the reliability of fans and internal circuit breakers is very important.

DW45 series Air circuit breaker is a product jointly designed by the low-voltage industry, among which the 2000 frame fixed circuit breaker occupies half of the market sales.

The rated short-time withstand current is a key indicator of the dynamic and thermal stability of the circuit breaker, which is very important for the protection of distribution lines. The mechanical life of the product and the reliable operation during the life are very important for the protection of the fan.

At present, the rated short-time withstand current parameter Icw of 2000 frame products of domestic manufacturers is about 50kA (AC400V), and the mechanical life is generally about 10,000 times. The product has low rated short-time withstand current index, low mechanical life, easy failure of the operating mechanism, internal soft connection disconnection, adhesion, hardening, product temperature rise and other pain points.

The operating mechanism is one of the core components of the Air circuit breaker, and its impact on the life is very important. The operating mechanism design of the DW45-2000 product has a certain energy redundancy, which has a large internal friction on the operating mechanism itself, and the operating mechanism stores energy. The matching of the spring energy and the contact system is very important. How to achieve the optimal matching of the two without too much energy redundancy is a key factor.

The contact system is one of the core components of the circuit breaker. It is the main component that carries the circuit to connect and break the circuit. The design of the moving contact system is very important, which determines the short-term resistance index and life of the product.

Based on industry DW45-2000 products, redesign or improvement of key components can solve the above pain points and greatly improve product life and reliability.

***Index Terms*— Double carbon, DW45, Air circuit breaker, Operating mechanism, Contact system, Rated short-time withstand current, Mechanical life.**

I. INTRODUCTION

In recent years, the country has advocated green energy. In order to achieve the "dual carbon" goal, the use of clean and green energy is very important. Photovoltaic and wind power generation is one of the main power generation methods of new energy.

DW45 series universal circuit breakers are the third generation of universal circuit breakers in my country. This series of circuit breakers can be divided into fixed type and drawer type according to the installation form. Among them, the 2000 shell fixed type products occupy a high market share in the field of new energy.

With the rapid growth of installed capacity, the working environment of new energy power stations has also become complex and changeable, especially fans are often installed in unattended places, so once the circuit breaker fails, maintenance will become extremely difficult. According to statistics, the wind power circuit breaker will switch on and off 2~3 times a day on average, so some new energy manufacturers have put forward the requirement of more than 15,000 times without maintenance for the circuit breaker.

The rated short-time withstand current Icw index is an important check index for the dynamic and thermal stability of the universal circuit breaker. Improving the index of Icw can increase the area of current selective protection, avoid power outages in a wide range of loads, and effectively improve the reliability of power supply.

Therefore, in order to ensure the reliability of new energy power generation, it is necessary to find a way to improve the Icw index of the DW45 universal circuit breaker to ensure the reliability of power supply, and also to improve the mechanical life of the universal circuit breaker to ensure the long life of the power distribution system. The contact system of the DW45-2000 series universal circuit breaker generally adopts a comb-shaped parallel design of 10 contact pieces. At present, the short-term resistance index of this product of domestic manufacturers is basically 50kA/1s, and the mechanical life is mostly 15,000 times, or even lower.

Based on DW45-2000 products, increasing the rated short-time withstand current index to 66 kA/1s, while the mechanical life is still stable at 15,000 cycles will be the focus of the research.

A. The relationship between the improvement of rated short-time withstand current index and the improvement of mechanical life

There are certain design constraints between the rated short-time withstand current index and mechanical life of the universal circuit breaker.

DW45 series universal circuit breakers have been put into production since the 1990s, and it has been more than 20 years since then. After the improvement and optimization of various domestic manufacturers, the product performance and indicators tend to be stable. Changshu Switch Manufacturing Co., Ltd.'s CW1-2000 and Chint Electric's NA1-2000 have rated short-time withstand current Icw of 50kA/1s and a mechanical life of 15,000 times. [1-2]

When the circuit breaker is subjected to a short-term short-circuit current, there will be a large electric repulsion between the moving and static contacts, and a large amount of heat will also be generated. Higher short-time withstand current means greater electric repulsion and greater heat generation. Designers generally resist the electric force by increasing the force value of the contact spring, and the higher contact pressure can also reduce the contact resistance of the dynamic and static contacts to a certain extent, reduce the heat generated by the short-circuit current, and avoid the dynamic and static contacts. Static contact welding.

The contact pressure is a reaction force during the closing process, which needs to be overcome by the spring force generated when the energy storage spring of the operating mechanism releases energy. False closing. However, if the energy storage spring force is too large, there will be too much energy redundancy. As we all know, energy is conserved and will only be transferred or consumed. Therefore, part of the redundant energy is consumed in the friction and collision inside the mechanism, and the other part is converted into the kinetic energy of the moving contact, which is consumed in the impact when the moving and static contacts are snapped together. Redundancy of the above two energies can lead to failure of the mechanism and contact system. For example, the upper link and lower link of the mechanism may be broken, and the fixed part of the side plate of the mechanism may be broken. The contact system may have problems such as broken contact pieces, broken contact springs, and increased wear of static contacts.

Therefore, according to the comprehensive requirements of the short-term withstand current and mechanical life index of the universal circuit breaker, determine the force value and structure of the contact system, and then match the best operating mechanism energy storage spring force value is the design work of the universal circuit breaker. Difficulty, the optimal matching of these two force values is the focus of this paper.

B. Design and optimization of contact system

1) Failure Mode of DW45-2000 Moving Contact System

The original DW45-2000 contact system is designed as 10 contact pieces in parallel, and the soft connection is copper braided wire.

By dismantling the DW45-2000 prototype with rated short-time withstand current, it is found that the contact pieces close to both sides will close to the middle.

By dismantling the prototype after the mechanical life test, it is found that the contact system has the following problems: the arc angle of the contact piece is broken, the silver spot welding part of the contact piece is broken, and the copper braided wire with the soft connection of the contact becomes hard.

2) Design defects of DW45-2000 moving contact system

The design flaws are summarized as follows:

- There are sharp corners in the design of the contact piece, which leads to stress concentration and is prone to fatigue fracture.

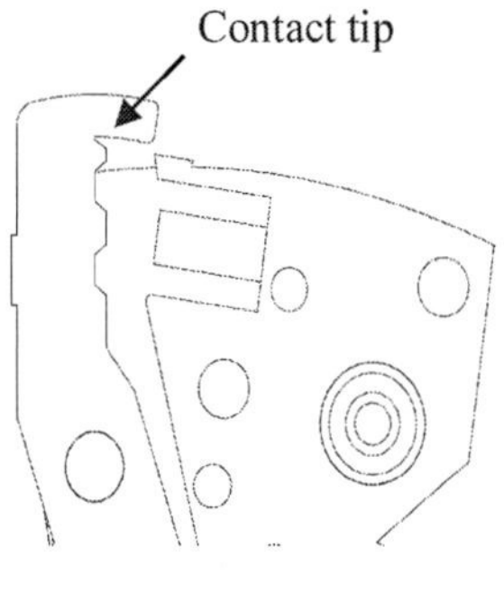

Fig. 1 The inclination of the contact piece

- The original DW45-2000 moving contact system has a contact thickness of 4mm and a grid width of 4.7 and a grid spacing of 6.2. The grid width and arrangement spacing supported by the contacts are designed to be large. When subjected to rated short-time withstand current, A lateral electric repulsion will be generated between the contact pieces, causing the contact pieces to close sideways, reducing the contact line of the contacts, which may easily lead to welding and burning of the contacts.

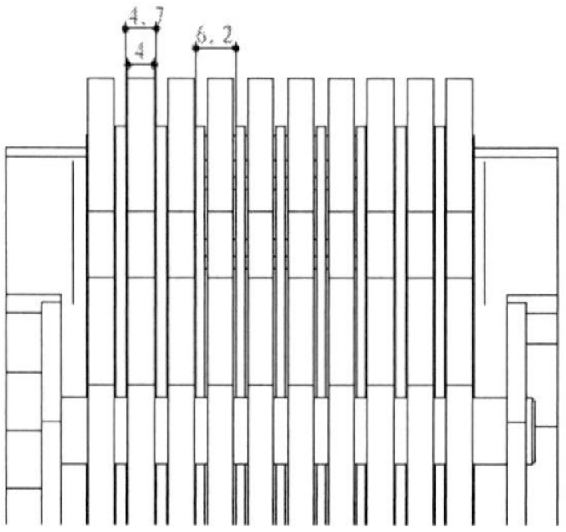

Figure 2 The original DW45-2000 contact piece and grid parameters

- The soft connection is made of copper braided wire. The braided wire is loosely braided. When opening and closing, the copper wire between adjacent soft connections will be rubbed, twisted, stiff, and has a high wire breakage rate. If the mechanical life of the circuit breaker needs to be improved, it is unreasonable to use copper braided wires for the contact system.

3) Optimization direction of DW45-2000 contact system

The optimized direction of increasing the number of contact pieces to 12 pieces has been demonstrated by domestic manufacturers in the development of new products, such as CW3-2500 of Changshu Switch Manufacturing Co., Ltd., NDW3-2500 of Shanghai Liangxin Electric, etc. The short-time withstand current value Can be raised to 85kA. Therefore, developing a contact system with 12 contact pieces on the structure of DW45-2000 can indeed reduce the electric power, but the width of the moving contact busbar is only 60 wide, which will make the soft connection more crowded, which is not conducive to the improvement of the mechanical life index, and The cost is increased, and it is not an ideal optimization direction for DW45-2000 products.

- By adjusting the position of the rotating shaft of the moving contact, the magnitude of the electric power will be affected.

  As shown in Figure 3, F1 is the electric repulsion force, B, A, and C are the three positions where the rotating shaft of the moving contact is located.

  When the rotating shaft of the moving contact moves from the axis A to the moving contact, the total electric repulsion decreases, and when the rotating shaft is at the position C, the total electric repulsion increases. [4]

  Therefore, it can be optimized by reducing the distance between the shaft hole and the moving contact.

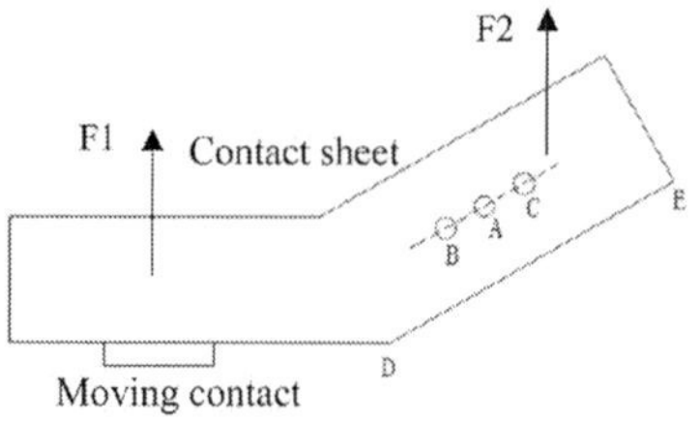

Figure 3 The position of the moving contact shaft and the electromotive force

- Considering the lateral torsion force of the contact piece, the grid design of the contact support is canceled when optimizing the design, but in order to prevent the arc angle welding of the contact piece during breaking, it is considered to punch three bosses on the contact piece. One of them is at the rotating shaft of the moving contact to lengthen the contact area between the contact piece and the rotating shaft. The rigid contact of the three bosses of the contact piece plus the longer length of the long axis, the parallel contact pieces can be regarded as a whole. Effectively counteract lateral forces. Considering that the rated short-time withstand current index is greatly improved, the thickness of the contact piece and the width of the silver point can also be appropriately increased.
- Cancel the sharp corner design and strengthen it locally to improve the strength of the front end of the contact piece. The original DW45-2000 contact piece before optimization is shown in Figure 4, and the DW45-2000 contact piece after optimization is shown in Figure 5.

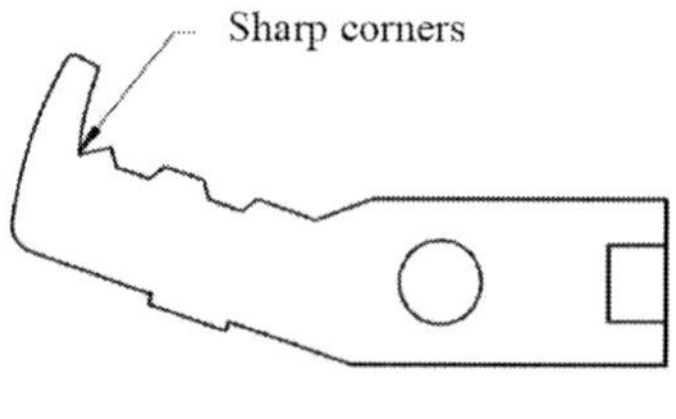

Figure 4 The original DW45-2000 contact piece

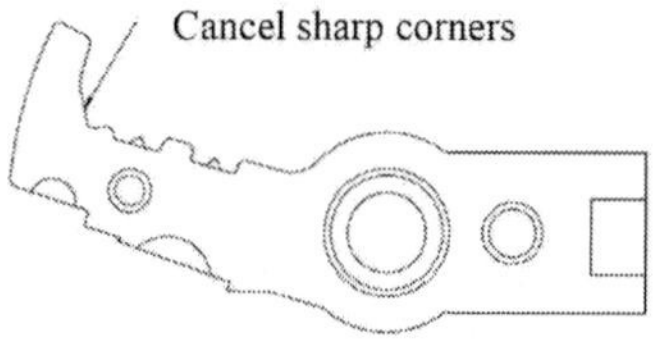

Figure 5 DW45-2000 contact piece after optimization

- The optimization of the contact support mainly includes canceling the grid design, reducing the overall height of the contact support, and leaving enough space at the tail of the optimized contact support, which is more conducive to the rotation of the soft connection and reduces contact with the contact support. friction. Figure 6 below is the contact support of the original DW45-2000, and Figure 7 is the optimized contact support of the DW45-2000.

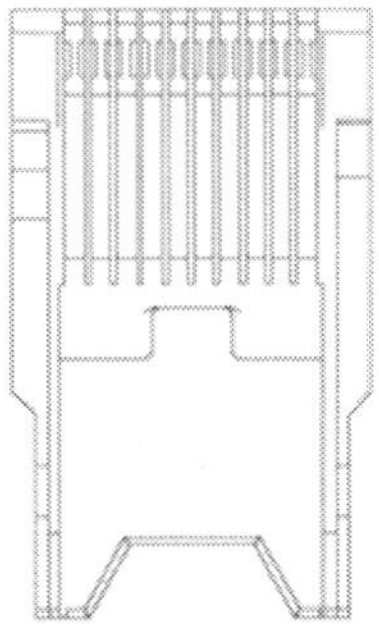

Figure 6 Contact support of the original DW45-2000

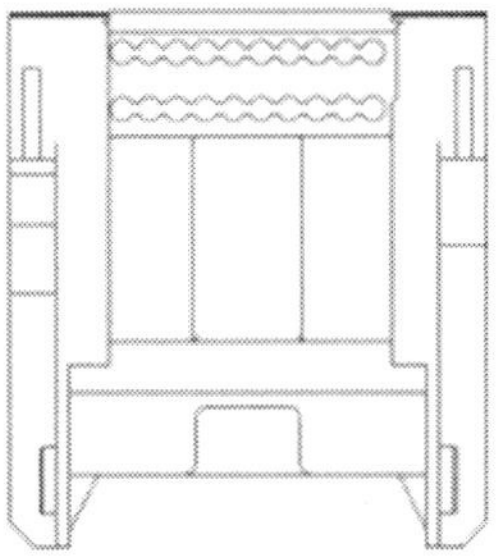

Figure 7 Contact support of the optimized DW45-2000

■ The soft connection is changed from copper braided wire to copper stranded wire, and the copper stranded wire is more compact, which avoids the hardening, breakage and adhesion of the copper wire.

C. The force value matching and verification of the operating mechanism

The operating mechanism is the core device of the universal circuit breaker, which directly determines the reliability of the action of the universal circuit breaker. The operating mechanism of the original DW45-2000 has been gradually stabilized after more than 20 years of improvement, but the matching between the force value of the operating mechanism's energy storage spring and the final pressure of the contact system has always been a direction worthy of in-depth study. Take the product as an example, the original DW45-2000 operating mechanism energy storage spring is composed of inner, middle and outer springs. In recent years, with the adjustment of the force value of various manufacturers, the operating mechanism with the combined force of the three springs F2=3472N is generally used.

The optimized DW45-2000 product of the contact system uses the 3472N operating mechanism, which will not falsely close, and the operating mechanism can provide sufficient energy. However, during the mechanical life test, it was found that even with the optimized contact system, the contact piece still There will be individual breakages.

Therefore, the operating mechanism of 3472N still has energy redundancy, so we tested the closing margin of the product.

Figure 8 Contact break location

3) The closing margin of the universal circuit breaker

An index closing margin is introduced here. The closing margin refers to the excess overtravel that the operating mechanism meets beyond the circuit breaker design overtravel. In theory, the less the redundancy of the closing margin, the better, but in the actual production process there are The accumulation of dimensional tolerances, the instability of the process, and the gradual drying of the lubricating grease applied inside with the accumulated service life of the product, the stiffness of the soft connection of the contact system, etc., so a certain margin should be designed. The design of the product is generally determined by design experience. If the life expectancy of the product is not high, it can be designed to be slightly larger, and if the life of the product is required to be high, it can be designed to be slightly smaller.

In addition, the closing margin is also related to the closing speed of the product. If the design is too small, the rigid closing speed of the dynamic and static contact systems will be reduced, which will affect the closing speed of the universal circuit breaker.

Regarding the closing margin of the product, it is generally recommended to be $\geqslant 0.5$mm. The specific determination of the closing margin should be determined by test data and repeated tests.

According to the design ideas, the closing margin test tool is made. The closing margin tool is composed of a frame, a connecting bracket, and a margin pad. Generally, several pads of different thicknesses are made during the test.

During the test, put the closing margin test tool into the base, the backing plate is attached to the static contact, and then close, observe whether the circuit breaker can be closed, and then store energy, if the moving contact is pulled open, false If the closing phenomenon occurs, it means that the closing margin is insufficient. If there is no false closing, it means that the closing margin of the circuit breaker is greater than the thickness of the backing plate for this test. The closing margin of the circuit breaker is determined by testing the backing plate for many times.

After testing, the closing margin of the universal circuit breaker using 3472N exceeds 1.2mm, but is less than 1.5mm, and the force value of the energy storage spring of the operating mechanism is relatively redundant.

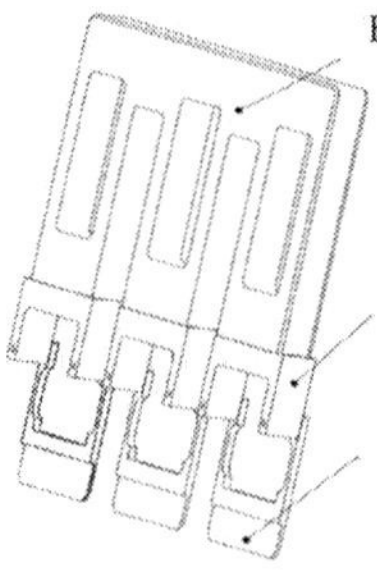

Figure 9 Closing Margin Test Fixture

2) Force value matching and margin test of operating mechanism

The optimized DW45-2000 circuit breaker operating mechanism force value is reduced to about 3000N, which can stably pass 15,000 mechanical life tests without breaking the contact piece.

D. Mechanical life test results and short endurance test results

1) Rated short-time withstand current test

The optimized DW45-2000 universal circuit breaker was tested by a third-party testing agency, and the working voltage Ue=415V, Icw(1s)=66kA passed the test.

2) Testing and Verification of Mechanical Life

More than 10 products have been verified, and 15,000 machine life tests have been carried out at a frequency of 60 times/hour. The verification is qualified, and the temperature rise after the test does not exceed 80K.

E. Epilogue

DW45 series universal circuit breakers are the third generation of universal circuit breakers in my country, and there is still a large market in the field of new energy, so the optimization of this series of products is still very necessary.

The optimization of the contact system and the energy storage spring force of the operating mechanism makes the rated short-time withstand current of the DW45-2000 universal circuit breaker reach 66kA/1s, and the mechanical life can also be more than 15,000 times.

The closing margin is used to optimize the energy storage spring force value of the operating mechanism, which ensures the reliable closing of the product without too much energy redundancy. The closing margin can be used as one of the methods for determining the force value of the operating mechanism, and the closing margin tooling can also be used as an effective factory inspection tooling. parameters

References

[1] Chint Electric "NA1 Series Universal Circuit Breaker Sample".

[2] Changshu Switch Manufacturing Co., Ltd. "CW1 series universal circuit breaker sample sample".

[3]Design and optimization of key components of universal circuit breakers "Electrical Appliances and Energy Efficiency Management Technology" (2018No.9).

[3] "Virtual Prototype Technology of Low Voltage Circuit Breakers" by Chen Degui and Li Xingwen.

8th International Conference on Reliability of
Electrical Products and Electrical Contacts,
November 18-20, 2022

Non-intrusive Load Monitoring Based on Hybrid Image and Transfer Learning

Zai Zhoupeng[1], Zhao Sheng[1,2], Zhu Xiangou[1], Zhang Zhengjiang[1], Dong Fanqi[1]

[1)]School of Electrical and Electronic Engineering, Wenzhou University, Wenzhou, Zhejiang, 325035

[2)]Technology Institute of Wenzhou University in Yueqing, Yueqing, Zhejiang, 325600

Email:zs_sea501@wzu.edu.cn TEL:13868886613

***Abstract*—Non-intrusive load monitoring (NILM), as the main way to analyze user's electricity consumption behavior, is of great significance to carry out energy consumption monitoring and realize electricity safety assessment. Aiming at the problem that the identification accuracy of the original voltage-current (V-I) trajectory features is not high, a recognition method based on the color coding of V-I trajectory features and the fusion of load high-order harmonic features is proposed in this paper. First, the numerical features of reactive power, power factor and current sequence distribution are mapped to the three-channel pixel matrix of the color V-I image RGB using color coding technology. Then, the high-order harmonic features are introduced and fused with the RGB three-channel pixel matrix to form a mixed color image. Finally, through the PLAID data set, the transfer learning of the AlexNet network is used to verify that the load identification method has an identification accuracy of more than 95%, and the model has a good generalization ability, which can be used for household and similar occasions.**

***Keywords*—non-intrusive load monitoring; AlexNet network; V-I trajectory; color coding; fusion feature**

I. INTRODUCTION

In recent years, with the high popularity of electrified equipment, the probability of occurrence of electrical fires is also increasing. The protection of electrical fire is mainly through the existing hardware facilities, such as various smoke alarms, etc., it is necessary to sense the relevant physical phenomena, and then rely on manual methods to avoid the occurrence of fire [1-2]. Non-intrusive load monitoring (NILM) can monitor the type, working status and energy consumption of user-side electrical equipment in real time, determine the potential safety hazards of related electrical equipment, and check dangerous equipment, so as to provide It provides important reference for residents to use electricity safely[3-4].

NILM is mainly composed of three modules: data acquisition, feature extraction, and load identification[5-7]. Among them, the accuracy of system identification mainly depends on the extraction of features and the selection of identification algorithms. For example, Liang et al. [8] proposed to use the normalization method to map the two-dimensional V-I trajectory to a binary gray image, which can greatly reduce the amount of V-I trajectory quantization calculation. Liu et al. [9]used the HSV (hue, saturation, value) color space to encode the V-I trajectory into a color image, which enhanced the recognition algorithm. 's accuracy. Similar to it, Huan Jiajia et al. [10] constructed three pixel matrices of current, voltage and phase, and embedded the numerical features into the gray V-I trajectory, so as to superimpose to form a color V-I image, and used the AlexNet algorithm to perform depth analysis on the color image. Feature extraction further improves the accuracy of load identification. However, this method needs to highly pixelate the V-I trace, which makes it difficult to reflect the high-order harmonic characteristics of the current waveform[11].

Aiming at the above problems, this paper proposes an identification method based on the fusion of color coding and load harmonic features based on V-I trajectory features. This method improves the R (Red), G (Green), B (Blue) three-channel pixel matrix of the V-I color image, and combines the binary numbers of the higher harmonic current amplitudes to form a mixed color image, which makes up for the above height. The loss of harmonic features due to pixelation. Finally, through the public data set PLAID, the transfer learning of AlexNet is used to conduct an example analysis. The results show that the mixed color image can effectively distinguish electrical equipment with similar V-I trajectories and small numerical differences such as reactive power, power factor, and current sequence distribution. Compared with the traditional V-I trajectory image recognition method, it is significantly improved.

II. FUSION AIGORITHM BASED on COLOR CODING and HARMONIC FEATUTES

A. Data Preprocessing

In the non-intrusive load identification method, the V-I trajectory is an important feature to distinguish the load, and the voltage and current data of the user bus need to be obtained through the high-frequency sampling device. When a single load or a known mixed load performs a switching event, the steady-state operation time of the input load can be determined by analyzing the bus power changes before and after the switching event, so as to extract the voltage-current trajectory in the load steady-state cycle.

Since the noise interference in the acquisition environment will affect the accuracy of load identification, this paper denoises and interpolates the extracted current and voltage waveforms to improve the quality of V-I trace extraction. For the traditional signal denoising method is not suitable for non-stationary signal disturbance, and in order to retain more detailed information of low-frequency and high-frequency signals, wavelet packet denoising is undoubtedly the mainstream denoising method at present. At the same time, to prevent the denoising effect of some devices from being not obvious enough, this paper adopts bilinear interpolation technology to make up for the problem of discontinuous points in the subsequent V-I trajectory mapping. This method also ensures that the number of sampling points after the interpolation of both voltage and current remains the same.

B. Color Coding of V-I Traces

Using color coding technology to map the original V-I trajectory into a two-dimensional matrix with a settable resolution, construct a color V-I trajectory image composed of three channels of R, G, and B superimposed, which not only avoids the calculation of the original shape information of the V-I trajectory It also reflects the difference in the value of instantaneous reactive power, power factor, and current sequence distribution between devices. The specific color coding method is as follows.

(1) After the above data preprocessing, the voltage and current waveform data in one cycle after the load is running in a steady state are obtained, and M sampling points are obtained (v_m, i_m), $m = 1,2,\cdots,M$。.

(2) Construct three pixel matrix of size $N \times N$, which Respectively called R, G and B, and initialize all matrix elements to 0. Normalize the data of M sampling points in the steady-state period to $0 \sim N$ to obtain the mapping coordinates of each sampling point (V_m, I_m) , its calculation formula is:

$$V_m = \left\lfloor \frac{v_m - v_{\min}}{v_{\max} - v_{\min}} \times N \right\rfloor \tag{1}$$

$$I_m = \left\lfloor \frac{i_m - i_{\min}}{i_{\max} - i_{\min}} \times N \right\rfloor \tag{2}$$

where v_m and i_m are the voltage and current values of the sampling point of the sampled data. V_m and I_m are the converted voltage and current values of the sampling point. v_{min} and i_{min} are the minimum sampling value of voltage and current. v_{max} and i_{max} are the maximum sampling value of voltage and current.

(3) Construct the R matrix of instantaneous reactive power. As a more important load feature in load identification, reactive power is difficult to be reflected according to the V-I trajectory. In this paper, the instantaneous reactive power is extracted based on the Fryze time-domain power theory and used as the embedded value of the R channel. Since the R channel embedding value range is (0,1), take a function to shrink.

$$P=\frac{1}{M}\sum_{1}^{M} v_m i_m, m=1,\cdots,M \tag{3}$$

$$i_{fm}=i_m-\frac{P}{u_{rms}^2}v_m \tag{4}$$

$$R(V_m,I_m)=\frac{1}{T_m\left(1+e^{i_{fm}*v_m}\right)} \tag{5}$$

where P is the active power, and M is the number of data collected in the stable period. i_{fm} is reactive current, and T_m is the number of occurrences of each coordinate point.

(4) Construct the G matrix of power factor. According to the above power expression, information such as the shape of the V-I trajectory cannot reflect the numerical difference in load power, so this paper embeds the size of the power factor into the G channel, and the active power of each load can be judged by the color of the G channel.

$$G(V_m,I_m)=\frac{P}{T_m\left(V_{rms}*I_{rms}\right)} \tag{6}$$

where V_{rms} and I_{rms} are the voltage RMS and current RMS of the collected data.

(5) Construct the B matrix of current sequence distribution. According to the random forest feature selection algorithm used in the literature [12], the time-domain characteristics of the current signal during steady-state operation of the load are sorted. In this paper, the feature expression with the highest feature importance is selected as the embedded value of the B channel, which reflects the current to a certain extent. The distribution of the time series, and use the logarithmic function to map the calculated values to (0,1).

$$I_e=\frac{1}{M}\sum_{m=1}^{M}\left(i_m\right)^4 \tag{7}$$

$$B(V_m,I_m)=\frac{1}{T_m\left(1+0.5*\log(I_e)\right)} \tag{8}$$

where I_e represents the distribution of the current sequence.

As shown in Figure 1, the V-I trajectory of a certain load after stable operation is subjected to three-channel synthesis by the above method. The difference in the color distribution of the color V-I image can intuitively reflect the difference in the value of the sampling point.

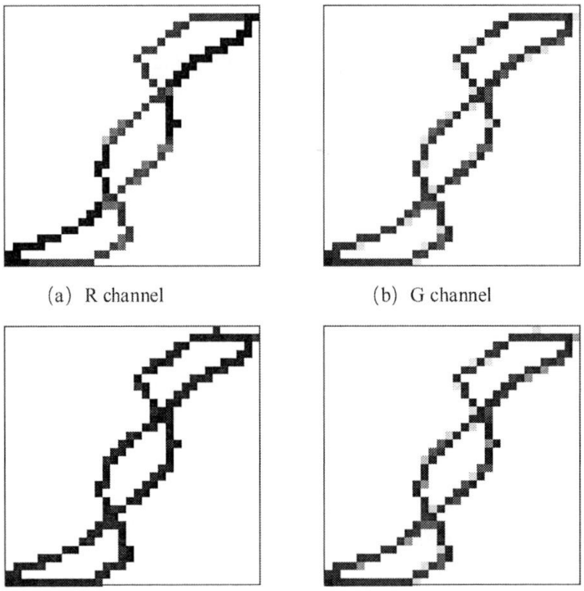

(a) R channel (b) G channel

(c) B channel (d) RGB channel

Figure 1 V-I track color coding process

C. Fusion of harmonic features

Since the generation of color V-I images needs to be highly pixelated, it is difficult to reflect the high-order harmonic characteristics of the current waveform, resulting in some electrical equipment being difficult to distinguish due to the similar V-I trajectories and small power differences, but their harmonic current characteristics are not. There are clear differences. In view of this, this paper selects the fundamental, 3rd, 5th, 7th, 9th and 11th harmonic current amplitudes to fuse with the color V-I image, which can effectively make up for the lack of current harmonic characteristics and improve the load identification in the above situations. Accuracy. The specific fusion method is as follows.

(1) Extract the current waveform data in one cycle of steady-state operation of the load, and use the FFT algorithm to convert the time-domain signal into a frequency-domain signal to obtain the amplitude of each harmonic, as shown in equation (9).

$$Y(k)=|X(k)|=\left|\sum_{m=0}^{M-1} i(m)e^{-j\frac{2\pi km}{M}}\right|, k=1,\cdots,M-1 \tag{9}$$

where k represents the harmonic order and $Y(k)$ is the amplitude of the current k-th harmonic. $X(k)$ is the frequency domain component of the current k-th harmonic. $i(m)$ is the m-th current sampling point.

(2) Perform the same integer multiple amplification and rounding on the amplitude of each harmonic, and convert it into an N-bit binary number.

(3) Construct three $N \times 8$ order two-dimensional matrices r, g and b, and initialize all matrix elements to 0.

(4) Fill the binary numbers of fundamental wave and 3rd harmonic amplitude, 5th and 7th harmonic amplitude, 9th and 11th harmonic amplitude into the front of matrix r, g and b respectively in column arrangement. four columns and the last four columns.

(5) Combine the matrices r, g, b with the pixel matrix of the R channel, G channel and B channel of the color V-I image respectively, that is, columns 1 to N of the mixing matrix are matrix R, and columns N+1 to N+8 is the matrix r.

(6) The three mixed pixel matrices are superimposed to obtain a mixed color image.

As shown in Figure 2, the mixed color image of a load after stable operation. In order to clearly reflect the combined effect of the three mixed pixel matrices, it is also visualized using a grayscale image. It can be seen from the figure that the V-I traces in the three channels are fully preserved, and the black color block distribution at the far right also reflects the difference in the magnitude of the harmonic currents of the load.

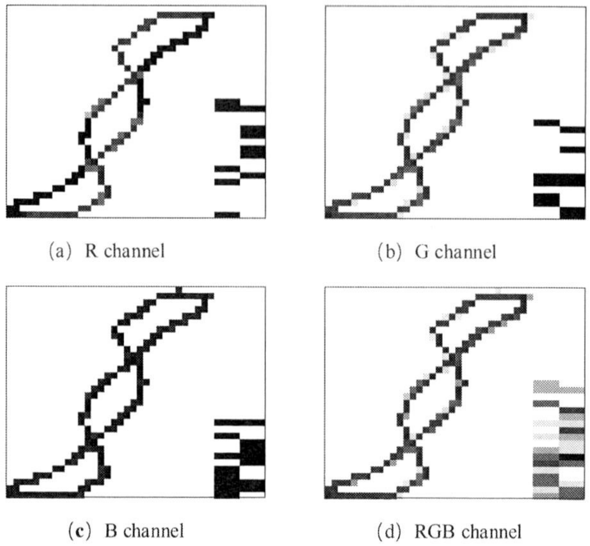

Figure 2 The fusion process of V-I trajectory and harmonic feature

III. TRANSFER LEARNING FOR ALEXNET MODEL

The use of mixed color images increases the detailed information of load features, and it is suitable to use convolutional neural network to achieve feature extraction, thereby improving the recognition accuracy, but the increase of detailed information also increases the computational complexity. Therefore, in order to take into account the accuracy of load identification and the speed of model training, this paper uses the AlexNet network as a deep learning model for transfer learning.

The AlexNet network architecture consists of 5 convolutional layers and 3 fully connected layers. The network structure before the fully connected layer can be regarded as a feature extractor. After the image passes through the feature extractor, a feature vector of a certain dimension is generated. The feature extractor has a very high generalization ability. In order to take advantage of this ability of AlexNet, this paper performs transfer learning on it. The detailed process is as follows:

(1) Remove the last fully connected layer from the pre-trained AlexNet to get a new network.

(2) Construct a new fully connected layer, the number of neurons is the number of load categories in this paper, and transfer the new fully connected layer to the last layer of the new network.

(3) Input the processed mixed color image training set. The images should be resized to be the same as the input neurons of AlexNet.

(4) Train the new network until the stopping criterion is met. The initial learning rate is configured to a small value to slow down the learning rate in the transport layer. At the same time, the learning rate of the new fully connected layer is increased.

Although AlexNet was originally designed to recognize the ImageNet dataset, the high-level abstract features it learns can still be used to assist in recognizing mixed color images of different types of devices. Therefore, the transfer learning method is used to reuse the pre-trained network parameters to speed up the convergence speed of the algorithm.

IV. EXPERIMENTAL TESTING AND ANALYSIS

A. Lab Environment

Based on the MATLAB platform, this paper performs transfer learning on the original AlexNet neural network, and is verified by the PLAID public data set and laboratory measured data. The hardware platform is Intel(R) Core(TM) i7-10700 CPU 2.90 GHz, 8GB RAM. The dataset PLAID contains 1793 voltage and current records collected at high sampling frequency (30 kHz) at 65 different locations and 11 different household appliance types [20].

B. Evaluation Metrics

In order to evaluate the recognition ability of the algorithm, this paper uses two indicators: confusion matrix and accuracy rate. The sum of each row of the confusion matrix represents the number of samples of the corresponding device in the test set, the sum of each column represents the number of samples predicted to be this type of device, and the diagonal elements represent the number of correctly identified samples. The accuracy rate represents the ratio of the number of correctly classified samples to the total number of test samples.

$$\eta=\frac{\mathrm{d}}{D}\times 100\% \qquad (10)$$

where d is the number of correctly classified samples and D represents the total number of test samples.

C. The Results of PLAID Dataset Test

Due to the large difference in the number of samples of different types of household appliances in the PLAID data set, the imbalanced data set will lead to a decrease in the recognition accuracy of the minority class samples. Therefore, this paper uses the SOMTE algorithm for oversampling to increase the number of minority class samples. The total number of the expanded sample data set reaches 2587 pieces of data, from which 220 samples are randomly selected as the test set, and the rest are used as the training set. According to the generation method of the mixed image in this paper, the steady-state current and voltage data in the plaid data set are processed. As shown in Figure 3, mixed color images of 11 types of household appliances are displayed. It can be observed from the figure that the color V-I mapping traces of equipment such as hair dryers and heaters are less discriminative in shape and color distribution, but their harmonic mappings are quite different. At the same time, when the harmonic features are merged with the color V-I trajectory, the impact of the resolution selection on the load identification accuracy is extremely important. When the resolution is set too small, although the harmonic features can be clearly displayed, the color V-I trace is prone to distortion, and the shape and color distinction is small. When the resolution is set too large, although the color V-I trace can show more detailed features, the harmonic features cannot be clearly displayed. Therefore, through the comprehensive consideration of two aspects, this paper sets the resolution to 32×32.

According to the size of the input layer of the AlexNet network is 227 × 227 × 3, the size of the mixed color image constructed above needs to be adjusted to match the input dimension of the network. For the transfer learning of AlexNet network, the number of neurons in the new fully connected layer is 11, the initial learning rate is set to 0.001, the number of iterations is 20, the discard rate is 0.2, and the number of batches is 25, which is substituted into the divided training set. network training. Substitute the randomly selected test set into the trained network for testing, and use the confusion matrix to visualize the test results, as shown in Figure 4. The equipment types corresponding to the labels are 1-incandescent lamp, 2-notebook, 3-refrigerator, 4-hair dryer, 5-fan, 6-heater, 7-air conditioner, 8-microwave oven, 9-vacuum cleaner, 10-washing machine and 11- fluorescent lamps. It can be clearly seen from the confusion matrix that the accuracy rate of the recognition algorithm proposed in this paper has reached 95.5%, and the recognition rate of refrigerators and washing machines is lower than the average recognition rate. The reason is that these two types of electrical appliances have various operating states, and the V-I Trajectories and harmonics are quite different and are easily misidentified as other types of electrical appliances.

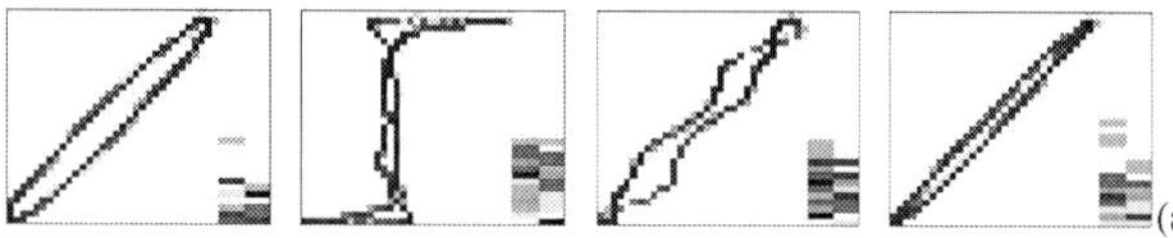

(a) Incandescent lamp (b) Notebook (c) Refrigerator (d) Hair dryer

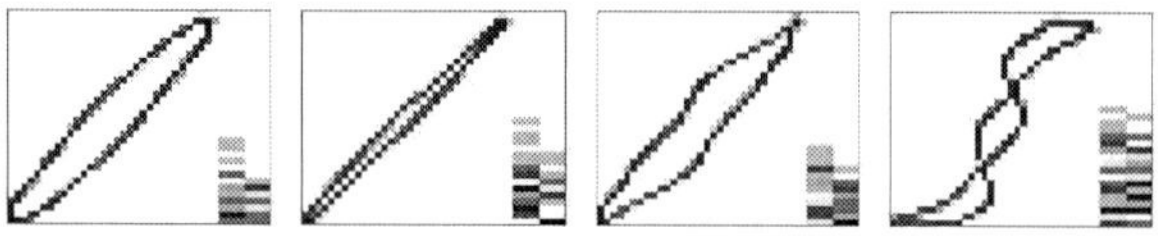

(e) Fan (f) Heater (g) Air conditioner (h) Microwave oven

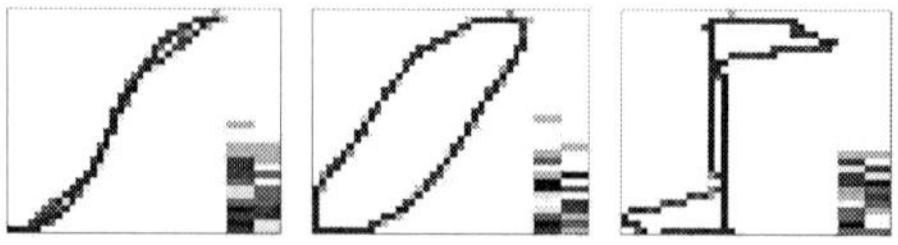

(i)Vacuum cleaners (j) Washing machines (k) Fluorescent lamps

Figure 3 Mixed color images for 11 devices

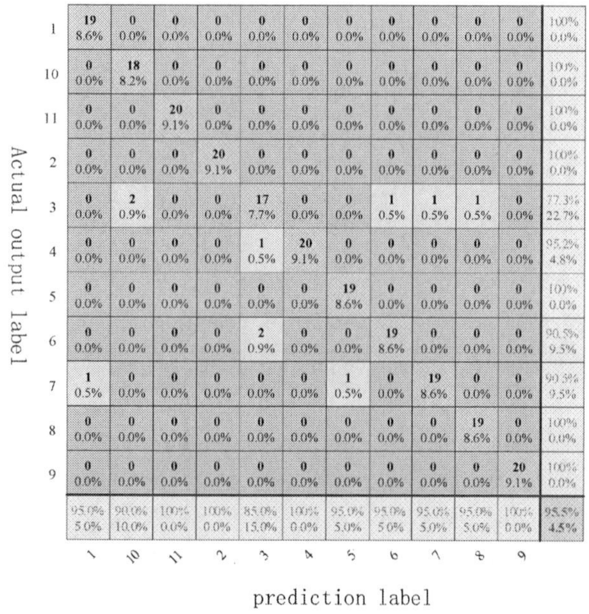

Figure 4 Confusion matrix drawn from the test results of the PLAID dataset

In order to further illustrate the superiority of the method in this paper, the load characteristics and classification models of the literature[11,13-14] were introduced to conduct a comparative analysis of the recognition accuracy. The specific results are shown in Table 1. On the PLAID dataset, compared with the other three load recognition algorithms, the recognition accuracy of the method in this paper is improved by 22.5%, 4.6% and 2.3% respectively, especially when the multi-mode switching operation of refrigerators, washing machines and air conditioners is incorrect. There is a significant advantage in the reduction of the judgment rate. The algorithm proposed in this paper combines harmonic features with color V-I images to generate mixed color images in terms of load characteristics, which not only covers all the feature information of the algorithms used in the above literature, but also further enriches more load characteristics. In the selection of classification model, the high-quality performance of the AlexNet network itself for image recognition is better than that of using a simple CNN for image recognition. And for AlexNet transfer learning, compared with the division of labor between LeNet-5 and BP neural networks, the complexity of network construction is reduced. Therefore, combining the above two improvements, the load identification effect of the method in this paper is better than the other three methods.

TABLE 1 COMPARES WITH THE RESULTS OF DIFFERENT LOAD IDENTIFICATION ALGORITHMS

References	Load Characteristics	Classification Model	Accuracy/%
Literature [13]	Harmonic Current Amplitude	MLP	73.0
Literature [14]	V-I Trajectory + Power Characteristics	BP+LeNet-5	90.9
Literature [11]	V-I trace + Power + Higher Harmonics	CNN	93.2
Algorithm	Mixed Color Image	AlexNet Transfer Learning	95.5

V. CONCLUSION

In this paper, a load identification construction method based on color coding and harmonic feature fusion is proposed. The method converts the harmonic feature amplitude into binary and fuses it with the color V-I image to form a mixed color image. Finally, transfer learning is used to carry out the AlexNet network. The method in this paper is verified by the PLAID data set and the measured data in the laboratory, and the following conclusions are drawn:

(2) The method in this paper is compared and analyzed with other methods. The test results show that compared with the fusion of gray V-I trajectory and other load features, the mixed color image further enriches the characteristic information of the load and improves the accuracy of the load identification.

(3) The recognition effect of the algorithm in this paper for multi-state operating loads needs to be improved. In addition to the harmonic features, the generation method of the mixed color image can further integrate other load features with higher distinguishability.

REFERENCES

[1] ZHENG X F , HUANG L M, FU J D. Building fire prediction and evacuation system based on cellular automata [J]. Journal of East China Jiaotong University, 2020, 37(2): 122-128.

[2] XU Y, ZHANG Z T. Improved BP Neural Network for Medium- and Long-Term Power Load Forecasting Based on Genetic Simulated Annealing Algorithm [J]. Electrical Technology, 2021, 22(09): 70-76.

[3] ZHOU D G, ZHANG H, ZHOU H, etc. Non-intrusive load event detection method based on state feature clustering [J]. Chinese Journal of Electrotechnical Technology, 2020, 35(21): 4565-4575.

[4] LEI Y Q, SUN Z L, YE Z H, et al. Research on non-intrusive monitoring method of power system load [J]. Chinese Journal of Electrotechnical Technology, 2021, 36(11): 2288-2297.

[5] ZHU D S, YIN J F, ZHOU K L. Identification and monitoring of non-intrusive power loads [J]. Electrical Measurement and Instrumentation, 2015, 52(S1): 133-138.

[6] LI C. Research on non-intrusive load monitoring algorithm based on deep learning optimization [D]. Wuhan: Huazhong University of Science and Technology, 2017.

[7] YU M, WANG B, LU L, et al. Non-Intrusive Adaptive Load Identification Based on Siamese Network[J]. IEEE Access, 2022, 10: 11564-73.

[8] DU L, HE D, HARLEY R G, et al. Electric Load Classification by Binary Voltage–Current Trajectory Mapping[J]. IEEE Transactions on Smart Grid, 2016, 7(1): 358-65.

[9] LIU Y, WANG X, YOU W. Non-Intrusive Load Monitoring by Voltage–Current Trajectory Enabled Transfer Learning[J]. IEEE Transactions on Smart Grid, 2019, 10(5): 5609-19.

[10] HUN J J, WANG C Q, HONG H F, et al. A non-invasive load recognition method based on image coding and deep learning [J]. Science Technology and Engineering, 2021, 21(21): 8901-8908.

[11] QIU X , YIN S H, ZHANG Z H, et al. Non-intrusive load identification method based on V-I trajectory and higher harmonic characteristics [J]. Power Engineering Technology, 2021, 40(06): 34-42.

[12] AN Q, WANG Z B, AN G Q, et al. A non-intrusive load identification method based on random forest-genetic algorithm-extreme learning machine [J] Science Technology and Engineering, 2022, 22(05): 1929-1935.

[13] ZHENG Z, CHEN H N, LUO X W. A supervised event-based non-intrusive load monitoring for non-linear appliances[J]. Sustainability, 2018, 10(4): 1001-1028.

[14] CHEN J F, WANG X, ZHANG X T. Research on Color Coding of Edge Computing for Non-Intrusive Load Recognition [J]. Chinese Journal of Instrumentation, 2020, 41(09): 12-19.

Arc Erosion Behavior of Conductive Ceramic LSCO Reinforced Ag-based Electrical Contact Materials

Zhenwu Liu [1], Libei Jiang [2], Xudan Cao[1], Tao Shen [1], Jinxiang Zheng [3], Qianhong Shen [1,2], Hui Yang [1,2*]

1) School of Materials Science and Engineering, Zhejiang University, Hangzhou, Zhejiang 310027
2) Zhejiang California Institute of International Nanotechnology, Zhejiang University, Hangzhou, Zhejiang 310058
3) Shenzhen Inspection Group (Zhejiang) Quality Technology Service Co., Ltd., Shaoxing, Zhejiang 312000

Email: yanghui@zju.edu.cn Tel: 13705716947

***Abstract*—Conductive ceramic is a new type of functional material with metal-like properties, and its structure-performance parameters can be adjusted in a wide range. $La_{0.5}Sr_{0.5}CoO_{3-\delta}$ (LSCO) conductive ceramic powders were synthesized by sol-gel method, and Ag/LSCO electrical contact materials were prepared by powder metallurgy, hot extrusion, etc. The phase structure and microscopic morphology of LSCO powder were analyzed by X-ray diffractometer and scanning electron microscope. The resistivity and hardness properties of Ag/LSCO materials were characterized by conductivity meter and microhardness tester. Using 3D profiler to explore the change law of erosion morphology of Ag/LSCO materials. The cyclic service experiment of the sample is carried out using the electrical life simulation experiment equipment. The results show that LSCO conductive ceramic powder is assembled by nanoparticles, and its phase is composed of La0.5Sr0.5CoO2.91 phase and a small amount of SrCoO2.52 phase. The resistivity of Ag/LSCO materials is as low as 2.25 μΩ·cm, and the Vickers hardness is $95HV_{0.5}$. With the increase of the cycle numbers, the erosion morphology of Ag/LSCO material experienced the changes of local molten pool solidification, molten pool flow and droplet splashing, and its arcing time, arcing energy and welding force all showed an upward trend, and the contact resistance first increased and then decreased. The failure degradation mode was mainly manifested as material transfer.**

***Keywords*— Ag/LSCO; arc erosion; conductive ceramic; electrical contact materials;**

I. INTRODUCTION

With the development of society, the advancement of science and technology, and the rapid development of electronic products, the application range of electrical contact materials is becoming wider and wider, and the amount of use is also increasing in the context of the electrical age. From various switches, connectors, relays to power equipment, communication equipment, and precision electronic instruments, electrical contact materials have a wide range of applications, involving civil, industrial, information, military, aerospace and other fields in modern society[1]. The Ag/CdO electrical contact material known as "universal contact" has gradually developed into one of the most excellent electrical contact materials due to its low and stable contact resistance, good welding resistance and arc erosion resistance. However, medical research has shown that the half-life of Cd in the human body is about 10 to 30 years, and it is mostly accumulated in the kidneys, bone pathways and blood, which can cause abnormal pain, softening of bones, renal dysfunction, development and reproductive arrest, etc. Cd and its compounds are also prone to cause liver cancer, prostate cancer and lung cancer[2]. Therefore, a new round of research upsurge in environmentally friendly Cd-free electrical contact materials has been formed.

Conductive ceramics are a new type of functional materials with metallic conductivity, structural and mechanical properties of ceramics, and unique physical and chemical properties, such as anti-oxidation, anti-corrosion, anti-radiation, high temperature resistance, long life, good mechanical properties and low cost, etc[3].One of the high temperature superconducting ceramics with perovskite structure, $La_{1-x}Sr_xCoO_{3-\delta}$, has low resistivity, good interface compatibility with Ag, adjustable structural performance parameters, and good processing performance. And some studies[4] have shown that $La_{1-x}Sr_xCoO_{3-\delta}$ is easy to decompose at high arc temperature, which helps to absorb arc energy, and its decomposition products will stay in the molten pool, which is beneficial to improve the viscosity and surface tension of the molten pool, reduce droplet splashing and contact welding, and improve the arc erosion resistance of the material. It is an ideal choice for the second phase of electrical contact composite materials. In this experiment, $La_{1-x}Sr_xCoO_{3-\delta}$(LSCO) conductive ceramic powders were synthesized by sol-gel method, and Ag/LSCO electrical contact materials were prepared by powder metallurgy, hot extrusion and other processes. The physical properties of Ag/LSCO electrical contact materials and the kinetics of arc erosion process were mainly carried out, and their electrical life service capability was evaluated and studied. The changing laws of electrical contact properties such as arcing characteristics, anti-welding force, mass loss, contact resistance, etc. were analyzed, and finally the failure mechanism of its anti-arc erosion resistance was preliminarily explored.

II. EXPERIMENTS

A. Preparation of LSCO Conductive Ceramic Powders

According to the stoichiometric ratio (N_{La}:N_{Sr}:N_{Co}=0.5:0.5:1.0), weigh a certain mass of $La(NO_3)_3{\cdot}6H_2O$ (Aladdin) , $Sr(NO_3)_2$ (Aladdin) and $Co(NO_3)_2{\cdot}6H_2O$ (Aladdin), and dissolve them in deionized water to make the metal ion concentration 0.5mol/L. Calculate the required EDTA and citric acid content according to the molar ratio of EDTA, citric acid and total metal ions in the solution as 2:1.5:1. Then add to the metal ion solution under magnetic stirring, and add ammonia water dropwise to adjust the pH to 9.5. After that, it was stirred in a 70°C water bath for 16 hours to form a homogeneous system wet gel. The pretreatment temperature was 150°C. After forming a dry gel, it was ground into powder and calcined in a box furnace. The temperature was raised to 800°C at a heating rate of 10°C/min, kept for 8 hours, and cooled to room temperature with the furnace to finally obtain LSCO conductive ceramic powders[5].

B. Preparation of Ag/LSCO Electrical Contact Materials

Using silver powder as the matrix phase, LSCO conductive ceramic powder as the reinforcement phase, and the mass ratio of the matrix phase to the reinforcement phase was 88:12, the Ag/LSCO composite powder was prepared by high-energy ball milling. The corresponding ball milling parameters were as follows: the ball milling speed was 300r/min, the ball milling time was 4h, and the ball milling medium was ethanol. Ag/LSCO electrical contact blanks were prepared under the conditions of a forming pressure of 1100 MPa, a holding time of 10 s and a forming die diameter of 40 mm. Then it was heated up to 900°C at a heating rate of 10°C/min, kept for 6 hours, and cooled to room temperature with the furnace to prepare for hot extrusion. The billet was heated to the specified temperature, processed to a finished wire of φ2.35mm by hot extrusion and drawing process, and then the Ag/LSCO electrical contact rivet element was obtained by cold pressure welding process.

C. Structure and Performance Characterization

The morphology and phase structure of LSCO conductive ceramic powders were characterized and analyzed by scanning electron microscope (GEMINI 300) and X-ray diffractometer (Empyrean). The resistivity and Vickers hardness of the Ag/LSCO electrical contact material were measured by a conductivity measuring instrument (D60K) and a microhardness tester (HVS-1000). The load used for measuring the Vickers hardness was 0.5kg. Using a 3D profiler (VR-5000) to explore the change law of the erosion morphology of Ag/LSCO electrical contact materials. The samples were subjected to cyclic service experiments using electrical life simulation experimental equipment, and the conditions are shown in Table I.

TABLE I
ELECTRICAL LIFE SIMULATION EXPERIMENTAL CONDITIONS

Parameter	Quantity
Voltage	DC 28V
Current	25A
Contact spacing	0.8 mm
ON/OFF time ratio	1s:1s
Contact static pressure	0.8 N

III. RESULTS AND DISCUSSION

A. Microstructure of LSCO Conductive Ceramic Powders

It can be seen from Fig. 1 that the LSCO powders synthesized in the experiment are assembled from nanoparticles, and the particle size distribution is relatively uniform. According to the analysis in Fig. 2 , the particle diameter is mainly distributed below 50 nm, and the particle diameter below 20 nm accounts for the largest proportion.

It can be seen from Fig. 3 that the synthesized powders have $La_{0.5}Sr_{0.5}CoO_{2.91}$ phase (PDF#48-0122) and a small amount of $SrCoO_{2.52}$ phase (PDF#40-1018). The three strong peaks of the La0.5Sr0.5CoO2.91 phase correspond to the (110)(024)(214) crystal planes, and the three strong peaks of the SrCoO2.52 phase correspond to the (101)(201)(211) crystal planes, respectively, and both phases are hexagonal.

According to the Scherrer formula:

$$D = K\lambda/\beta \cdot \cos\theta \tag{1}$$

In the formula, K=0.89

λ is the X-ray wavelength, where λ=0.15406nm.

β is the full width at half maximum of the diffraction peak.

θ is the diffraction angle.

The calculated grain size of $La_{0.5}Sr_{0.5}CoO_{2.91}$ is 11 nm, which is mutually confirmed with Fig. 2.

B. Physical Properties of Ag/LSCO Electrical Contact Materials

The resistivity and Vickers hardness of the Ag/LSCO electrical contact material were measured by a conductivity measuring instrument and a microhardness tester, and the results are shown in Table II. The resistivity of the Ag/LSCO material is as low as 2.25 μΩ·cm, and the Vickers hardness is

95HV0.5, with excellent electrical conductivity and suitable hardness.

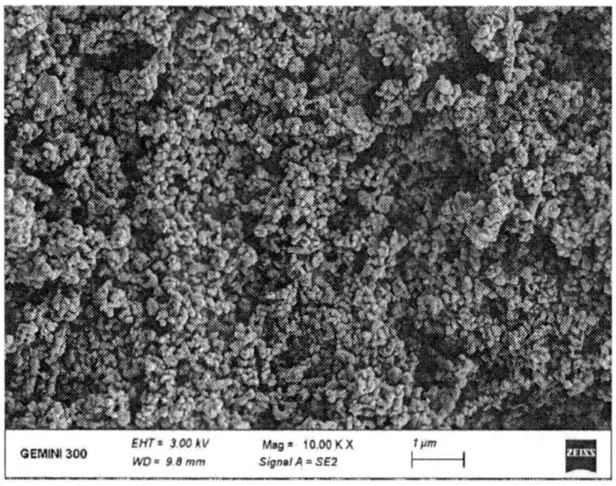

Fig. 1. Micromorphological photos of LSCO conductive ceramic powders

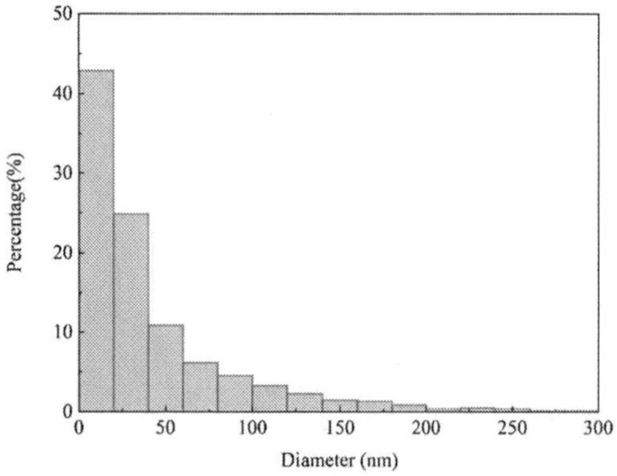

Fig. 2. Particle size distribution of LSCO conductive ceramic powders

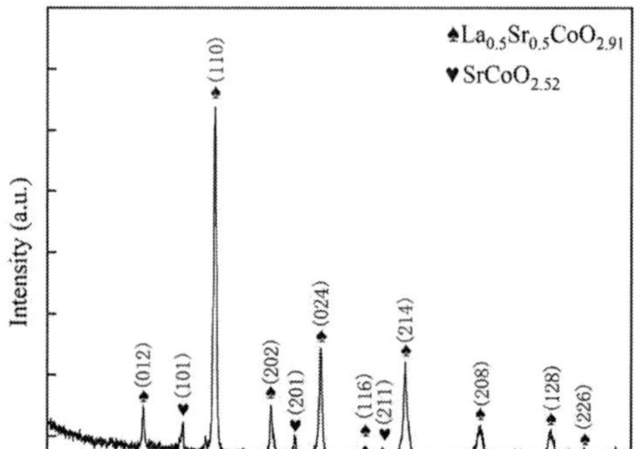

Fig. 3. X-ray diffraction pattern of LSCO conductive ceramic powders

TABLE II
PHYSICAL PROPERTIES OF SAMPLES

Number of experiments	Conductivity/μΩ·cm	Vickers hardness/$HV_{0.5}$
1	2.25	94
2	2.24	95
3	2.25	97
Average value	2.25	95

C. Arc Erosion Process Kinetics of Ag/LSCO Electrical Contact Materials

In order to reveal the kinetics of arc erosion process of Ag/LSCO electrical contact materials, the effect of cycle times on the erosion morphology of Ag/LSCO materials was explored by 3D profiler. From Figures a1 and b1, it can be seen that the surface is smooth after 2 cycles, and there is basically no erosion morphology. It can be seen from Figures a2 and b2 that the uneven surface caused by the rapid solidification of the molten pool locally appears after 8 cycles, and the surface in a large area is still smooth at this time. It can be seen from Figures a3 and b3 that the surface is the characteristic morphology of molten pool flow when the cycle is 32 times. At this time, the erosion morphology has covered the entire surface, but there is basically no height difference. It can be seen from Figures a4 and b4 that the characteristic erosion morphology of droplets appears on the surface, indicating that droplet splashing has occurred, and the inconsistent colors indicate that there is a height difference, that is, the surface is uneven. Therefore, with the increase of the number of cycles, the erosion morphology in the early stage changes successively with local molten pool solidification, molten pool flow and droplet splashing.

D. Variation of Electrical Contact Properties of Ag/LSCO Electrical Contact Materials

In order to analyze the change of electrical contact properties of Ag/LSCO electrical contact materials and their internal relationship, we mainly conducted a comprehensive analysis of the arcing characteristics, contact resistance and welding force of Ag/LSCO electrical contact materials after cyclic service experiments.

1) Arc characteristics

After calculation, the average arcing time is 4561.57μs, and the average arcing energy is 746.95mJ. It can be seen from Fig. 5 and Fig. 6 that the arcing time and arcing energy both show an increasing trend with the increase of the number of cycles. And it can be seen from Fig. 7 that the arcing time and arcing energy have a linear positive correlation. This is because when the arc extinguishing ability of the Ag/LSCO electrical contact material is certain, to extinguish the arc with a large energy, it is necessary to increase the arc extinguishing time, resulting in an increase in the arcing time. And the increase of the arcing time will cause the electrical contact material to be more seriously affected by the arc erosion, which increases the probability of serious fusion welding between the dynamic and static contacts, which in turn leads to an increase in arcing energy.

2) Contact resistance and welding force

It can be seen from Fig. 8 and Fig. 9 that the contact resistance of the Ag/LSCO electrical contact material increases first and then decreases with the increase of the number of cycles, but the overall is in a relatively stable state. The contact resistance distribution map is quasi-normal distribution, basically concentrated around the average value.

After calculation, the average contact resistance of Ag/LSCO material is 4.74mΩ, and the variance is 0.827. Combining with Fig. 10 and Fig. 11, it can be seen that the welding force gradually increases with the increase of the number of cycles, welding force of Ag/LSCO material is 0.064N, and the variance is 0.000075. It can be seen that the reason why the Ag/LSCO material exhibits a long electrical life cycle service ability is mainly due to its low and stable contact resistance and small welding force during service. And this is related to its physical properties such as low resistivity and suitable surface hardness.

E. Electrical Life Cycle Service Capability of Ag/LSCO Electrical Contact Materials

In order to finally evaluate the electrical life cycle service capability of the Ag/LSCO electrical contact material, the Ag/LSCO electrical contact material was directly installed which is mutually confirmed with the change trend of the arcing time. The distribution map of fusion welding force is also quasi-normal distribution, which is mainly distributed around the mean value. After calculation, the average on the simulator to conduct the electrical life test until the end of the life, and the number of electrical life cycles and the quality loss status were obtained. Through three final evaluation experiments of electrical life, it can be seen that the average cyclic service cycle of Ag/LSCO electrical contact material is 45387 times, which shows a long electrical life. From the analysis of the quality change of the contact, it can be seen that the failure form of the Ag/LSCO material after the cyclic service test is material transfer, that is, the components on the contact surface are transferred from the moving contact to the static contact (Table III).

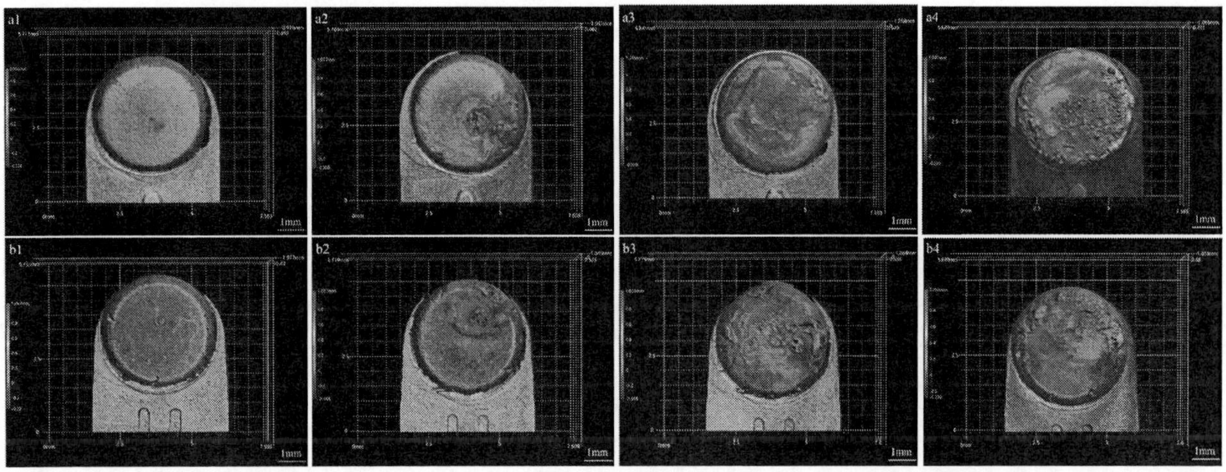

Fig. 4. 3D profile photos of the eroded area on the surface of Ag/LSCO material under different cycles(a1-a4 are the surface erosion pictures of the moving contacts in cycles 2, 8, 32, and 128, respectively, and b1-b4 are the surface erosion pictures of the corresponding static contacts.)

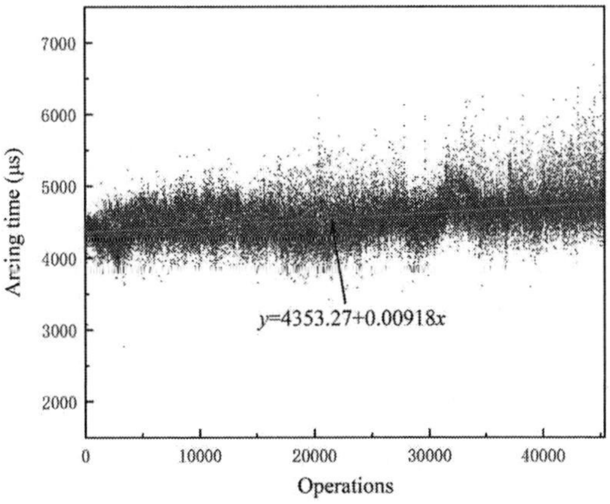

Fig. 5. Variation of arcing time with the number of cycles

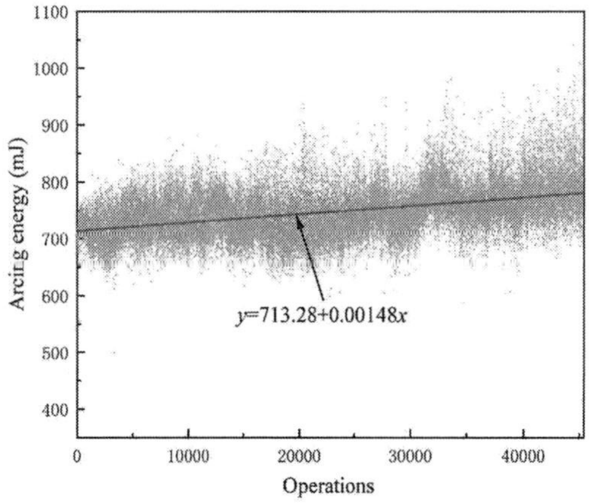

Fig. 6. Variation of arcing energy with the number of cycles

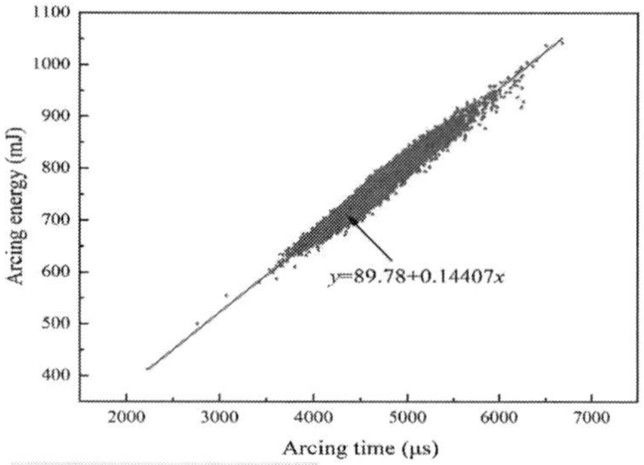

Fig. 7. Relationship between arcing time and arcing energy

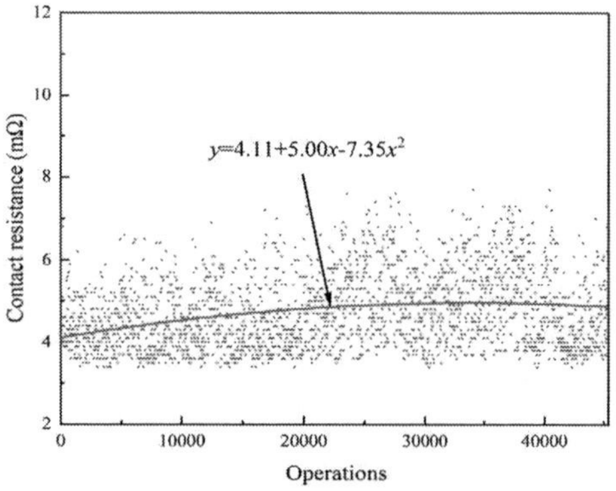

Fig. 8. Variation of contact resistance with the number of cycles

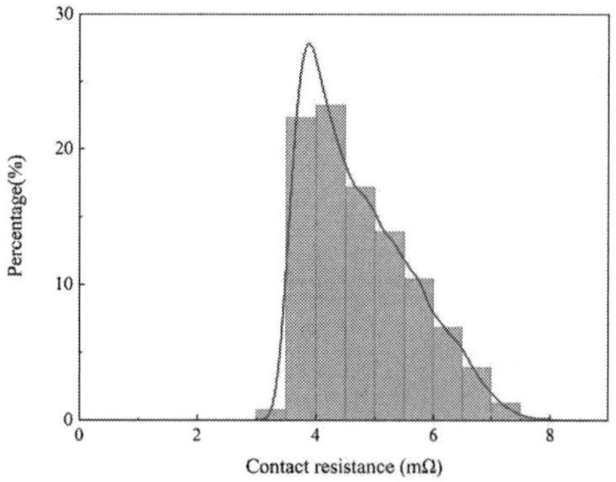

Fig. 9. Contact resistance distribution map

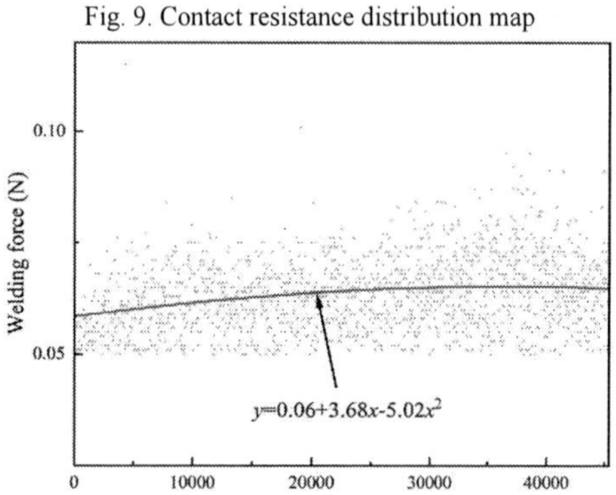

Fig. 10. Variation of welding force with the number of cycles

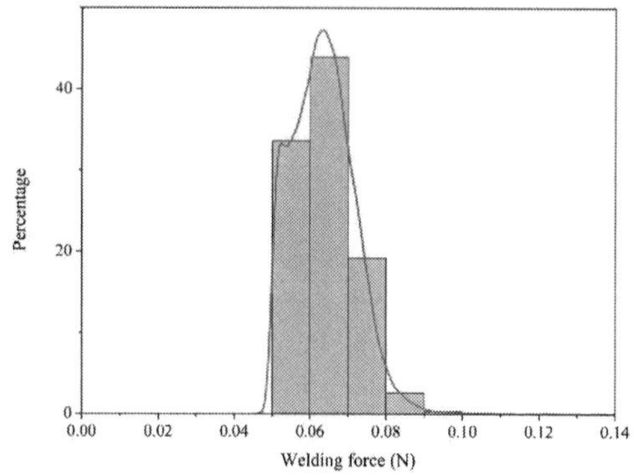

Fig. 11. Welding force distribution map

TABLE III
MASS CHANGE OF CONTACTS BEFORE AND AFTER THE ELECTRICAL LIFE CYCLE TEST OF SAMPLES

Contact type	Before experiment/g	After experiment/g	Mass change/g
Static contact	0.72971	0.73828	+0.00857
Moving contact	0.41177	0.40178	-0.00999

IV. CONCLUSION

In this paper, LSCO conductive ceramic powders were synthesized by sol-gel method, and Ag/LSCO electrical contact materials were prepared by powder metallurgy, hot extrusion and other processes. The physical properties and arc erosion process dynamics of Ag/LSCO electrical contact materials were explored, and their electrical life service capability was evaluated by using an electrical life simulation test machine. The specific research conclusions are as follows.

1) LSCO conductive ceramic powders are bonded and assembled nanoparticles in morphology, mainly distributed below 20nm in particle size, and composed of $La_{0.5}Sr_{0.5}CoO_{2.91}$ phase and a small amount of $SrCoO_{2.52}$ phase in phase. The resistivity of Ag/LSCO electrical contact materials is as low as 2.25 μΩ·cm, and the Vickers hardness is $95HV_{0.5}$.

2) The analysis of arc erosion kinetics shows that the erosion kinetics of Ag/LSCO electrical contact material has experienced the changes of local molten pool solidification, molten pool flow and droplet splashing; With the increase of the number of cycles, both the arcing time and the arcing energy show an increasing trend with the increase of the number of cycles, and the arcing time and the arcing energy have a linear positive correlation. The contact resistance increases first and then decreases, and the welding force increases gradually, but they are mainly distributed around the average value.

3) The final electrical service life of Ag/LSCO electrical contact materials is 45387 times. From the perspective of mass loss change, its failure form is material transfer.

It can be seen that the Ag/LSCO electrical contact material developed in this experiment exhibits excellent physical and electrical properties, and is expected to become one of the candidate materials to replace the Ag/CdO electrical contact material.

REFERENCES

[1] Findik F, Uzun H. Microstructure, Hardness and Electrical Properties of Silver-based Refractory Contact Materials[J]. Materials & Design, 2003, 24(7): 489-492.

[2] Chen J-C, Sun J-L, Zhang K-H, et al. Restrictive Policy of European Union in Silver /Cadmium Oxide and Development of Other Silver /Metal Oxide Electrical Contact Materials[J]. Electrical Engineering Materials, 2002(04): 41-44+49.

[3] Yin N, Wang C-J, Liu X-Y, et al. The Resistance and Arc Erosion Characteristics of Ag/LaFe(1-x)NixO(3) Contact Material[J]. International Journal of Modern Physics B, 2007, 21(15): 2635-2645.

[4] He Q. Preparation and Properties of Ag/LSCO Composite Electrical Contact Material[D]. Zhejiang University, 2014.

[5] Shen T, Zhang J, Zhang L-J, et al. Preparation and Properties of Perovskite Powders and Electrical Contact Composite Materials[J]. Rare Metal Materials and Engineering, 2018, 47(S2): 48-52.

Study on Performance Degradation and Reliability of Signal Conditioning Circuit Based on Accelerated Degradation Test

Feng Niu, Boheng Zhang, Guiheng Li, Yihua Dai, Shihu Xiang, Kui Li

Key Laboratory of Electromagnetic Field and Electrical Apparatus Reliability of Hebei Province, Hebei University of Technology, Tianjin, 300401
Email: niufeng@hebut.edu.cn TEL:13502041597

Abstract—**During the service life of electronic circuits, the degradation of components will change circuit output performance, thus leading to low reliability of electronic circuits. In this paper, the signal conditioning circuit of residual current device is researched and the key components which affect circuit performance degradation are determined based on the sensitivity analysis method. Monte-Carlo method is used to analyze the influence of component tolerance on performance of signal conditioning circuit. Firstly, the constant stress accelerated degradation test was carried out with temperature as accelerated stress and operating current as degradation feature. Secondly, according to the test data under different temperature stress, the performance degradation model of signal conditioning circuit based on Wiener process is established. The unknown parameters of degradation model are obtained by using maximum likelihood estimation method, and then the probability density function and reliability function of residual life prediction are obtained. Finally, the pseudo failure life is defined as residual life at initial time of signal conditioning circuit under accelerated stress. Then the predicted life of signal conditioning circuit under constant stress is derived from the Arrhenius equation.**

Keywords—**Accelerated degradation test, Monte-Carlo simulation, performance degradation, residual life prediction, Wiener process.**

I. INTRODUCTION

Residual current circuit breaker (RCCB) is an important terminal protection device in low-voltage distribution system. It can cut off the line and equipment automatically once the leakage current exceeds threshold, which effectively prevent fire and electric shock caused by leakage, and ensure the safety of life and property of power users. The signal conditioning circuit is the core module of RCCB, and is composed of many electronic components according to a specific topological structure. With the increase of the service time of RCCB, the degradation of each component will degrade the performance of signal conditioning circuit, and further affect the operating characteristics of RCCB. In serious cases, it will cause major production accidents such as electrical equipment damage and protection failure. Therefore, the performance degradation analysis and life prediction of signal conditioning circuit are of great significance to ensure the safe and stable operation of electronic products and low-voltage power distribution system [1-3].

The electronic components of signal conditioning circuit mainly include resistors, capacitors, diodes, operational amplifiers, etc. The degradation of these electronic components has a great impact on output of the overall circuit. Therefore, many studies predict the whole circuit by researching degradation of components. In [4], a nonlinear degradation model for buck circuit is established based on diffusion process, and the online residual life prediction of the circuit is realized by the residual life distribution function. In [5], the parameter degradation model of MOSFET is established based on degradation data for HEF and PBTI effects, and the accuracy of the parameter degradation model is verified. In [6], an analysis method is proposed that particle filter prediction theory and gray model fusion prediction theory. The method based on multiple degradation processes improves the efficiency of circuit performance degradation analysis

In this paper, the performance degradation and reliability of signal conditioning circuit are studied based on accelerated degradation test. Firstly, the sensitivity of components in the circuit is analyzed to determine the key components that affect the output performance of the circuit. The Monte-Carlo method is used to randomly sample the component parameters under different tolerances, and the traversal simulation is carried out for the combinations of various samples. The distribution of RCCB operating characteristics is obtained through analyzing the simulation results. Secondly, the constant stress accelerated degradation test with temperature as the accelerated stress and operating current as the degradation characteristic is carried out in this paper. The degradation model based on Wiener process is established and its model parameters are obtained by maximum likelihood estimation method. Then the service life of signal conditioning circuit under accelerated stress can be predicted. Finally, the service life of the signal conditioning circuit under normal stress is deduced by using Arrhenius acceleration equation.

II. SIMULATION ANALYSIS OF PERFORMANCE DEGRADATION OF SIGNAL CONDITIONING CIRCUIT

A. Sensitivity analysis of circuit components

RCCB is mainly composed of current detection circuit, signal conditioning circuit, signal comparison circuit and trip actuator [7]. The signal conditioning circuit can transform and amplify residual current signal to make it suitable for single-chip microcomputer, and can realize the reliable operating of trip mechanism to ensure personal safety and protect electrical equipment. Fig. 1 shows the schematic diagram of a typical signal conditioning circuit, which consists of voltage rise and amplification parts. By analyzing the influence of the electronic components' degradation on the signal conditioning circuit, the influence of the electronic components' degradation on the RCCB operating characteristics is obtained.

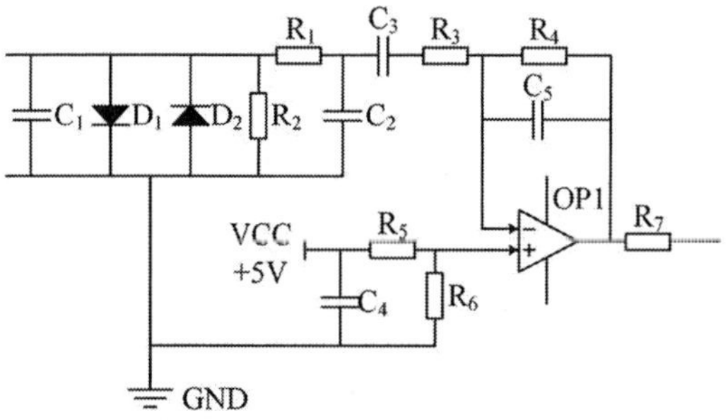

Fig.1 Schematic diagram of signal conditioning circuit

To reduce the workload while keep high accuracy of reliability analysis, the sensitivity analysis of the components is carried out to determine the key components that affect the circuit performance degradation. In the signal conditioning circuit, the sensitivity S_x^y is defined as the change of circuit target parameter y when component parameter x deviates from its standard value, as shown below:

$$S_x^y = \frac{\Delta y}{\Delta x}\Big|_{\Delta x \to 0} = \frac{\partial y}{\partial x} \tag{1}$$

In PSpice software, set the target parameter as voltage proportional coefficient y, set the resistance value and capacitance value parameter x of components, and the sensitivity analysis simulation results are shown in Fig. 2.

As shown in Fig. 2 that the sensitivity of the components constituting the signal conditioning circuit is $R_4 > C_3 > R_3 > C_5 > R_1 > C_2 > R_7$. Therefore, the key components are determined as R_3, R_4 and C_3, and the analysis and calculation of subsequent tests are based in these key components.

B. Tolerance analysis of circuit components

Due to the randomness of resistance and capacitance degradation, the degradation degree of different components is different. As a typical statistical tolerance analysis method, Monte-Carlo method is a basic method to describe various random phenomena in the process of component degradation. Therefore, PSpice software is used to conduct Monte-Carlo simulation on the operating current of RCCB. The tolerance range of resistance and capacitance is set to 5%, and the sampling points are 1000. Figure 3 shows the change trend of the operating current under different tolerances.

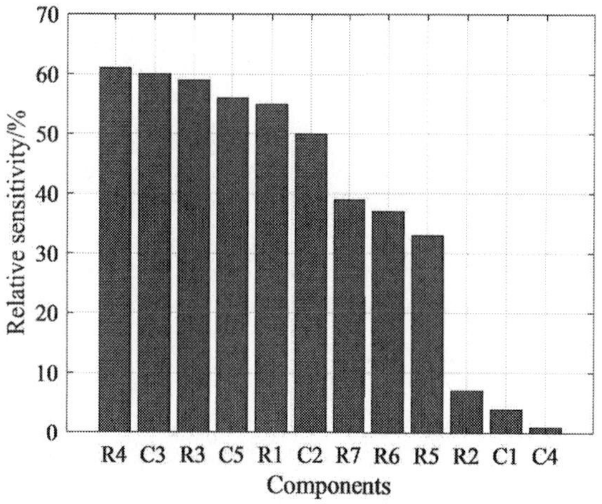

Fig.2 Sensitivity analysis of components

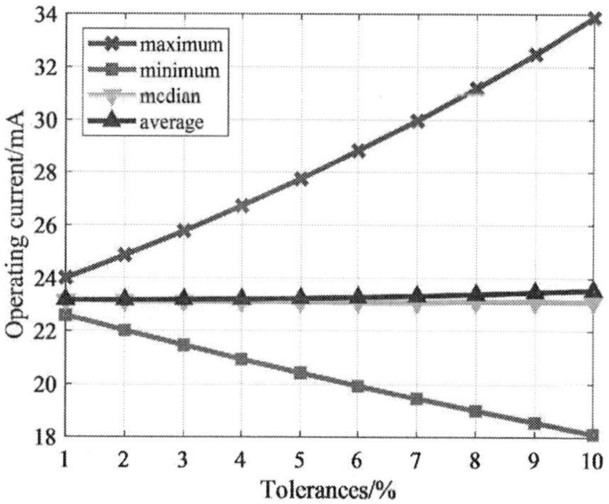

Fig.3 Variation trend of operating current under different tolerances

The four curves in Fig. 3 represent the maximum value, minimum value, average value and median value of the effective value of the operating current respectively. The median value and average value of the operating current under different tolerances remain basically unchanged, but the greater the tolerance, the greater the deviation of the operating current boundary value from the center value, and the more dispersed the operating current distribution. Therefore, on the premise of meeting the requirements of circuit cost, properly improving the accuracy of components can make the distribution of operating current more concentrated, thus improving the reliability of signal conditioning circuit [8].

III. Accelerated Degradation Test

A. Selection of test stress level and formulation of test scheme

For the degradation test of electronic circuit, the test stress considered is mostly temperature. This test focuses on the accelerated degradation test under temperature stress. Under different temperature stress levels, the resistance value, capacitance value and operating current reflecting the overall degradation trend of the test circuit are recorded and analyzed. In this test, considering the heat resistance grade of resistance, capacitance and op amp devices comprehensively, 120℃ is taken as the maximum stress level and 80℃ is taken as the minimum stress level, and other stress levels in the middle are selected according to the following formula:

$$\Delta=\frac{1}{T_1}-\frac{1}{T_2}=\cdots\cdots=\frac{1}{T_{n-1}}-\frac{1}{T_n}=\left(\frac{1}{T_1}-\frac{1}{T_n}\right)\Big/(n-1) \qquad (2)$$

where T_1 represents the lowest stress level, T_n represents the highest stress level, and n represents the number of stress levels of accelerated degradation test. In this paper, three groups of accelerated degradation tests with different temperature stress levels are carried out, i.e. taking $n=3$ and combining the above formula, the three temperature stress levels are finally determined to be 80℃, 96℃ and 120℃. The specific test steps are as follows:

1) The test circuit operates at room temperature for 24 hours, and records the voltage, resistance, capacitance and other data of key nodes as a comparison benchmark for performance degradation.
2) Accelerated degradation tests were carried out on 8 test circuits and independent RC devices at the temperature stress levels of 80℃, 96℃ and 120℃.
3) Take 24h as the test cycle, conduct 35 cycles of tests under each temperature stress. After each test cycle, reduce the circuit to room temperature, and continue the next cycle of tests after measuring all parameters.

B. Test data analysis

Through the measurement and analysis of accelerated degradation test data, the degradation trend of resistance, capacitance and operating current is obtained. Combined with the key components obtained by the above simulation, the degradation data of circuit components R_3, C_3 and operating current of RCCB are selected for analysis. As shown in Fig. 4, it is a degradation trend diagram of the operating current under different temperature stresses.

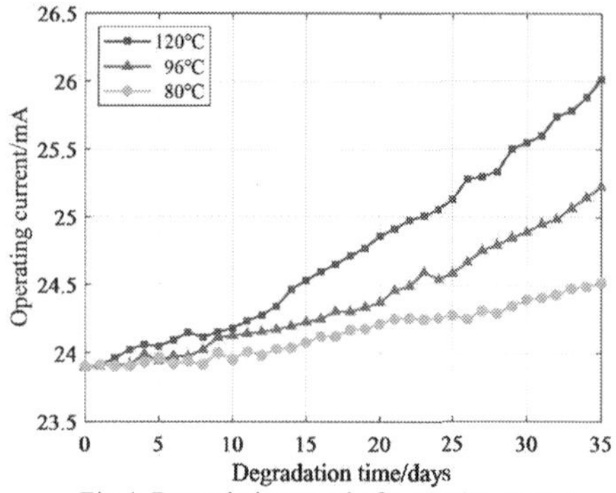

Fig.4 Degradation trend of operating current

It can be seen from Fig. 4 that the degradation trend of the operating current of RCCB is approximately a linear model. The operating current gradually increases with the increase of time, and there is a risk of rejection of RCCB with the increase of time. This paper takes the operating current as the characteristic quantity reflecting the degradation of the overall performance of the signal conditioning circuit, and establishes a one-dimensional linear Wiener degradation model [9].

IV. Performance Degradation Modeling of Signal Conditioning Circuit

A. Verification of normal distribution of operating current degradation

In order to verify that the signal conditioning circuit can conduct performance degradation modeling through Wiener process, the most important thing is to prove that the distribution of degradation characteristic quantity obeys normal distribution, that is, the subsection degradation quantity of operating current obeys normal distribution. Therefore, the test data of temperature stress at 120℃ is used to verify the normal distribution. As shown in Fig. 5, it is the distribution diagram of the degradation amount of the operating current and the normal fitting curve.

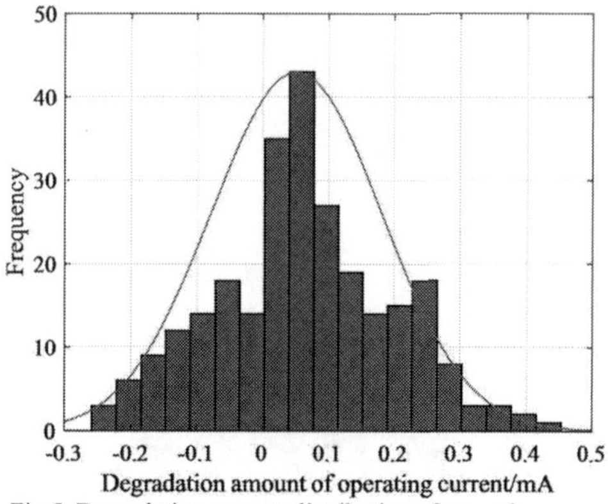

Fig.5 Degradation amount distribution of operating current

It can be seen from Fig. 5 that the degradation amount of the operating current at 120℃ is mainly concentrated in the range of (0.02, 0.12) mA, which intuitively approximates the normal distribution. The Kolmogorov-Smirnov method [10] is used to test the normal state of the operating current of 8 test circuits at 120℃. In this method, the test statistic $KS=MAX(|F_n(x)-G(x)|)$ is constructed according to the empirical distribution function $F_n(x)$ and the normal distribution function $G(x)$ of the sample, and the test value p is calculated from the test statistic and compared with the specified significance level α. If the detected value $p \leq \alpha$, rejecting the original hypothesis. If the detected value $p > \alpha$, accepting the original assumption. Let the original hypothesis H_0: the operating current degradation amount distribution $F_n(x)$ follows the normal distribution. At the significance level $\alpha=0.05$, the detection results are $h=0$, $p=0.1659$. It can be seen from the detection results that P is greater than α. Therefore, the original assumption is accepted, that is, the degradation amount of the operating current conforms to the normal distribution, and the Wiener process can be used to model the degradation of the operating current to realize the life prediction of the signal conditioning circuit.

B. Circuit degradation modeling based on Wiener process

Because Wiener process model can describe the performance degradation process of many typical electronic circuits and has good computational and analytical properties, it has become one of the most basic and widely used models in reliability modeling and analysis based on performance degradation [11]. In this section, the degradation data is used to model the degradation of the signal conditioning circuit. The one-dimensional linear Wiener model with the operating current as the degradation characteristic is

$$X(t) = \lambda t + \sigma W(t) \quad (3)$$

where t is the accelerated degradation test time, λ is a drift parameter, σ is the diffusion parameter, $W(t)$ is the standard Brownian motion, $X(t)$ is the cumulative degradation of the operating current at time t and $X(t)$ follows normal distribution that the expectation is λt and the variance is $\sigma^2 t$. That is $X(t) \sim N(\lambda t, \sigma^2 t)$. Let x_{ef} be the degradation amount of the operating current of the e-th test circuit in the f-th cycle, where $e=1,2,...,u$, $j=1,2,...,v$. $X(t)$ is the time cumulative sum of x_{ef}. Using maximum likelihood method to estimate drift parameters λ and diffusion parameters σ performing point estimation. And the corresponding maximum likelihood estimation function is

$$L(\lambda,\sigma^2) = \prod_{e=1}^{u}\prod_{f=1}^{v}\frac{1}{\sigma\sqrt{2\pi\Delta t}}\cdot\exp\left(-\frac{\left(x_{ef}-\lambda\Delta t\right)^2}{2\sigma^2\Delta t}\right) \quad (4)$$

Take the logarithm of formula (4) to obtain

$$InL\left(\lambda,\sigma^2\right) = \sum_{e=1}^{u}\sum_{f=1}^{v}\left(-\frac{1}{2}In\left(2\sigma^2\pi\Delta t\right)-\frac{\left(x_{ef}-\lambda\Delta t\right)^2}{2\sigma^2\Delta t}\right) \quad (5)$$

Calculate the partial derivatives of the parameters λ and σ in formula (5) to obtain the maximum likelihood estimate value

$$\begin{cases}\hat{\lambda} = \dfrac{\sum_{e=1}^{u} X_{ev}}{uv\Delta t} \\ \hat{\sigma}^2 = \dfrac{1}{uv}\left[\sum_{e=1}^{u}\sum_{f=1}^{v}\dfrac{\left(x_{ef}\right)^2}{\Delta t} - \dfrac{\left(\sum_{e=1}^{u} X_{ev}\right)^2}{uv\Delta t}\right]\end{cases} \quad (6)$$

The life of the signal conditioning circuit at time t is defined as

$$T = \inf\left\{X(t) \geq V, t \geq 0\right\} \quad (7)$$

where V is the failure threshold of the signal conditioning circuit.

From equations (6) and (7), the probability density function of the life T of the signal conditioning circuit can be obtained as

$$f_T(t) = \frac{V}{\hat{\sigma}\sqrt{2\pi t^3}}\exp\left[-\frac{(V-\hat{\lambda}t)^2}{2\hat{\sigma}^2 t}\right] \quad (8)$$

Reliability is defined as the probability that the electronic circuit completes the set function within the specified time and under the specified conditions, i.e

$$R_T(t) = 1 - F(t) = 1 - \int_0^t f(t)dt \quad (9)$$

Bring equation (8) into equation (9) to obtain the reliability function as

$$R_T(t) = \Phi\left[\frac{V-\hat{\lambda}t}{\hat{\sigma}\sqrt{t}}\right] - \exp\left[-\frac{2\hat{\lambda}V}{\hat{\sigma}^2}\right]\cdot\Phi\left[-\frac{V+\hat{\lambda}t}{\hat{\sigma}\sqrt{t}}\right] \quad (10)$$

V. LIFE PREDICTION OF SIGNAL CONDITIONING CIRCUIT

A. Life prediction of circuit under accelerated stress

The performance degradation model of the signal conditioning circuit is established by using the data under the temperature stress of 120℃. The parameters μ and σ can be obtained from equation (6). The life probability density curve and reliability curve of the signal conditioning circuit can be obtained by substituting the parameters into the equation, as shown in Fig. 6 and Fig. 7.

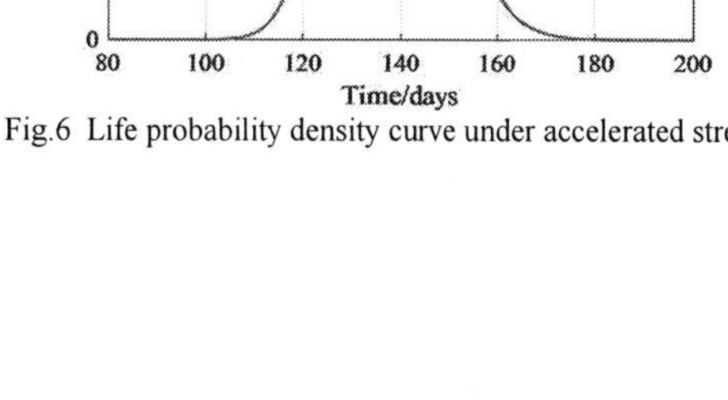

Fig.6 Life probability density curve under accelerated stress

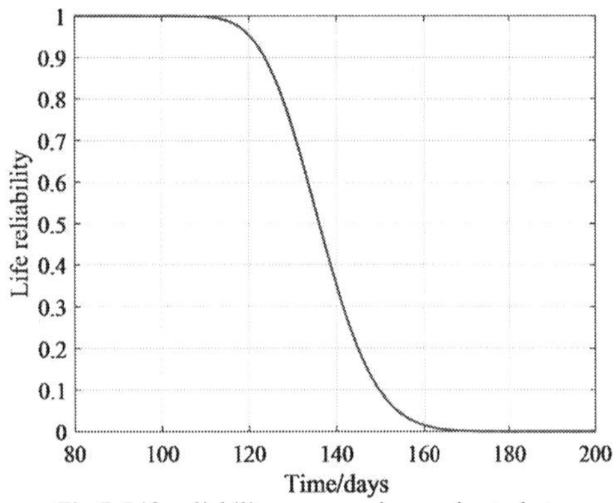

Fig.7 Life reliability curve under accelerated stress

It can be seen from Fig. 6 that when the temperature is 120 ℃, the predicted life of the signal conditioning circuit is concentrated in 108-172 days. It can be seen from Fig. 7 that when the predicted life of the circuit reaches 110 days, the reliability of the signal conditioning circuit begins to significantly decrease; When the life prediction time reaches 136 days, the reliability of the signal conditioning circuit decreases to 0.5; The time corresponding to the reliability of 0.5 is taken as the predicted life of the signal conditioning circuit. That is, the predicted life of the signal conditioning circuit at 120 ℃ is 136 days.

Using the same method, the Wiener process degradation modeling is performed on the test data under other temperature stresses, and the estimation parameters are obtained by the maximum likelihood estimation. The probability density curve and reliability curve are drawn, and the predicted life of each test circuit under different temperature stresses is obtained. The overall predicted life of the 8 signal conditioning circuits at 120℃, 96 ℃ and 80 ℃ is 136 days, 218 days and 418 days respectively, which provides a basis for the extrapolation of the subsequent normal stress life.

B. Life prediction of circuit under constant stress

The basic idea of accelerated degradation test is to use the life characteristics under high temperature stress to extrapolate the life characteristics under normal stress. The key to realize this basic idea is to establish the relationship between the life characteristics and the stress level, which be the accelerated model [12]. Arrhenius model is the most typical and widely used acceleration model [13], and its expression is

$$\frac{\partial M}{\partial t} = A_0 \cdot \exp\left(-\frac{\Delta E}{kT}\right) \tag{11}$$

where M is the degradation amount of the characteristic quantity of the electronic circuit, k is the Boltzmann constant, T is the absolute temperature, A_0 is a constant, t is the degradation time, ΔE is the activation energy of degradation mechanism, $\partial M/\partial t$ represents the degradation rate at the absolute temperature T and is a linear function of time t.

Integrate the two sides of equation (11) and take the logarithm to obtain

$$\ln L = \ln\frac{\Delta M}{A_0} + \frac{\Delta E}{kT} \tag{12}$$

Let $B=ln(\Delta M/A_0)$, $A=\Delta E/k$, obtained

$$\ln L = \frac{A}{T} + B \tag{13}$$

where L is the service life of the electronic circuit, T is the absolute temperature of the electronic circuit, A and B are undetermined coefficients, and the logarithm of the life L is a linear function relationship with the reciprocal of the absolute temperature T. Therefore, by using the least square fitting idea, the predicted life of the signal conditioning circuit under different acceleration stresses is substituted into equation (13), and the undetermined coefficients A and B can be obtained. The test data are fitted and analyzed by MATLAB, and the life fitting straight line is shown in Fig. 8.

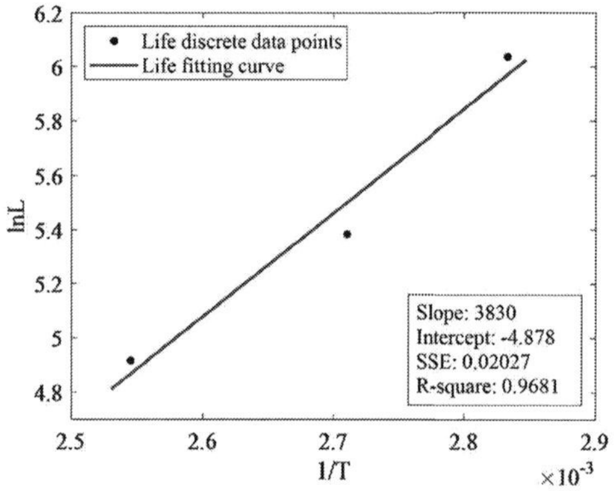

Fig.8 Life linear fitting of signal conditioning circuit

From Fig. 8, we can get the slope A and intercept B of the fitting straight line, as well as the fitting parameters such as root mean square error and determination coefficient, where the sum variance is SSE=0.02027, which is very close to 0; The determination coefficient is $R\text{-}square$=0.9681, which is very close to 1. Therefore, it can be considered that the fitting straight line has a good fitting effect on the data. The fitting straight line equation is

$$\ln L = \frac{3830}{T} - 4.878 \tag{14}$$

According to the above formula, the service life of the signal conditioning circuit at normal temperature can be predicted to be 8-12 years. The predicted life at different temperatures is shown in Table 1.

Table.1 Prediction life of signal conditioning circuit under normal stress

Temperature/ ℃	Predicted Life /days	Predicted Life /years
25	2905	7.96
20	3618	9.91
15	4540	12.44

According to the life fitting straight line obtained in Fig. 8 and the predicted life at various temperatures obtained in Table 1, it can be found that the predicted life of the signal conditioning circuit gradually decreases with the increase of temperature, which is related to the increase of the degradation degree of components caused by the increase of temperature in practice. When the working time exceeds the predicted life, the reliability of the circuit operation will decrease, which will cause the change of the circuit output characteristics, and then cause the change of the operating characteristics of RCCB, and the failure of refusing to operate will further cause the unstable operation of the entire power system. Therefore, the life prediction method proposed in this paper has guiding significance for circuit replacement, maintenance of residual current circuit breaker and stable operation of power system.

VI. CONCLUTION

In this paper, the signal conditioning circuit is taken as the research object. Firstly, the key components that affect the overall output performance of the circuit are obtained through sensitivity analysis. Monte-Carlo method is used to analyze the influence of the tolerance of components on the performance of the signal conditioning circuit. The conclusion is that the smaller the tolerance of components, the higher the accuracy, and the higher the reliability of the circuit operation. Secondly, according to the degradation data under different temperature stress, the performance degradation model of signal conditioning circuit based on Wiener process is established, and the predicted life under accelerated stress is extrapolated to the predicted life under constant stress by using Arrhenius equation. The conclusion is that the predicted life of signal conditioning circuit under normal temperature is 8-12 years.

REFERENCES

[1] Lei Yun, Qiu Yunfeng. Parameter changes of electron components based on temperature variation[J]. Computer & Digital Engineering, 2015,43(01):155-158

[2] Hu Bokai, Li Kui, Niu Feng, Zhao Chengchen. Research on condition monitoring method of mechanical characteristics of low-voltage circuit breaker[J]. Transactions of China Electrotechnical Society, 2022,37(13): 3317-3330.

[3] Cao Sheng. Research on reliability prediction and test method based on physics of failure of electronic products[D]. University of Electronic Science and Technology of China, 2016

[4] Wang Shufeng. Research on Online Reliability Estimation and Residual Life Prediction Method for On-board Electronic Equipments[D]. Nanjing University of Aeronautics and Astronautics, 2014.

[5] Wang Yixing. Research on failure mechanism and life prediction methods for vertical double-diffused power MOSFETS[D]. Harbin Institute of Technology, 2017.

[6] Guan Yue. Analysis of analog circuit behavior based on components degradation[D]. Harbin Institute of Technology,2017.

[7] Li Kui, et al. Adaptive technology of leakage current operation protection and its application[J]. Transactions of China Electrotechnical Society, 2008(10):53-57.

[8] Li Kui, Wang Yue, Zhao Chengchen, et al. Simulation analysis of leakage protection module reliability based on performance degradation[J/OL]. Electrical Measurement & Instrumentation: 1-9[2022-08-26].

[9] B. H. Peng and J. L. Zhou, "Reliability assessment for product with Wiener process degradation based on marker data," 2010 IEEE International Conference on Industrial Engineering and Engineering Management, 2010, pp. 2394-2397.

[10] Hou Shumin, Li Yourong, Liu Guangling, A new method of detecting nonlinear for time series based on KS test[J]. Journal of Electronics & Information Technology, 2007(04):808-810.

[11] Peng Baohua, Research on reliability modeling methods based on Wiener process[D]. National University of Defense Technology,2010.

[12] H. Zhang, C. Hu, X. Kong, W. Zhang and Z. Zhang, "Online updating with a wiener-process-based prediction model using UKF algorithm for remaining useful life estimation," 2014 Prognostics and System Health Management Conference (PHM-2014 Hunan), 2014, pp. 305-309.

[13] Xu zhengwei, et al. Parameter estimation of Arrhenius equation based on nonlinear least squares method[J]. Journal on Numerical Methods and Computer Applications, 2019, 40(04):279-290.

Analysis on DC Circuit Breaker Arc Electric Power Simulation Based on Ansoft

Yugang Wu, Changchun Chi, Jia Liu

College of Electrical Engineering, Shanghai Dianji University, Shanghai, China
E-mail:2441260653@qq.com, E-mail:chicc@sdju.edu.cn

***Abstract*—Breaking capacity is one of the important indicators of DC circuit breakers, the study of the internal arc plate and permanent magnet material of DC circuit breakers is means to improve its reliable shutdown. At present, the particle swarm algorithm was usually used for dc circuit breaker breaking analysis, but the particle swarm algorithm has the disadvantage of easy short-term convergence, and the individual integration optimization ability was poor, so that the designed simulation model fitted poorly. By analyzing the DC circuit breaker structure, based on the change of the force of the arc during the arc extinguishing process and combine with finite element analysis methods, the simulation model is constructed by Ansoft software. The influence of the selection of the internal device of the DC circuit breaker on the breaking ability of the DC circuit breaker is studied by experimental data, and the arc on-break experiment is performed on the DC circuit breaker after the re-selection of the device. Simulation results show that the selection of copper plate body material and NdFeB ($Nd_2Fe_{14}B$) strong magnetic material can improve the arc electric power, the on-off time of the permanent magnet is shortened, so as to achieve the purpose of accelerating the arc extinguishing and improving the breaking performance of the DC circuit breaker. The research results are of great significance for improving the reliable breaking capacity of DC circuit breakers improving the breaking performance of dc circuit.**

***Keywords*— DC circuit breaker,breaking capacity,arc electric power**

I. INTRODUCTION

In recent years, HVDC transmission technology has developed rapidly. In view of the problems involved in protection and breaking of HVDC transmission technology, domestic experts thought strengthen the key equipment in the DC power grid [1-2]. They believed that DC circuit breakers are devices that play a key role in the DC transmission process, how to ensure the stable operation of DC circuit breakers in the transmission process has became a hot spot in the research of DC circuit breakers[3-4].

Oreign DC circuit breaker products in the field of high-end electrical equipment has great advantages, has the advantages of low cost and small footprint, while the domestic in the field of low-voltage DC circuit breakers although there is a part of the market share, but there are deficiencies in the high-end field, such as the domestic DC circuit breaker breaking capacity is insufficient, when the work in the harsh environment of the breaking capacity is seriously affected [5-7]. This paper uses Ansoft software to model, for the arc motion process, the finite element theory is used, the influence of the election of NdFeB as a strong magnetic material and copper plate on the arc electric power is analyzed, which provides an important reference for further enhancing the breaking capacity of the DC circuit breaker[8-9].

II. ARC ELECTRIC POWER SIMULATION THEORY OF DC CIRCUIT BREAKERS

There is a zero crossing point in the AC circuit, and after the zero crossing, the arc gap recovery voltage is guaranteed to be lower than the recovery voltage of the medium, so as to reach the purpose of the protection line, which is the arc extinguishing principle of the AC circuit [10-11]. The arc is a plasma gas with extremely high thermal energy, its temperature does not produce mutations, and it has the characteristics of current restriction. More and more ions will continuously enhance the conductivity of the equivalent resistance, and the voltage will be reduced[12].

This paper uses the finite element analysis method,the finite element analysis method analyzes the whole into many node-connected units, re-analyzes each unit, and then recombines and analyzes the whole. For DC circuit breakers, the finite element analysis method is used, which makes the various component models drawn using Ansoft software more closely combined, and at the same time can greatly shorten the arc electric power calculation time and improve the accuracy of the data, thereby optimizing the entire simulation system[13].

III. DC CIRCUIT BREAKER SIMULATION MODEL WAS ESTABLISHED

Drawing with Ansoft software, the first step involves a structural analysis of the DC circuit breaker and then measurement of the dimensions. The structure diagram of the DC circuit breaker (rated current 63A) is shown in Figure 1, and the DC circuit breaker has dynamic and static contacts inside, and the moving contacts serve as a device for generating arcs. When the DC circuit breaker starts working, the moving contact will act as an arc plate to keep the current stationary when the current reaches a threshold. Placing a permanent magnet inside the DC circuit breaker can greatly accelerate the arc movement speed.Because of the role of the arc extinguishing barrier, the arc will be subjected to a contraction force again in the arc extinguishing grid composed of steel sheets, which will cause the complete arc to be forced and divided into many short arcs.

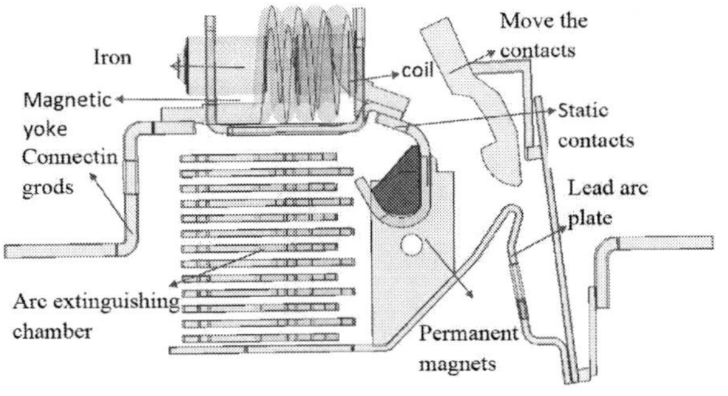

Fig. 1. DC circuit breaker structure diagram.

After selecting the required components, compare the structure diagram, then build DC circuit breaker simulation model. Figure 2 is the Dc circuit breaker simulation model built.

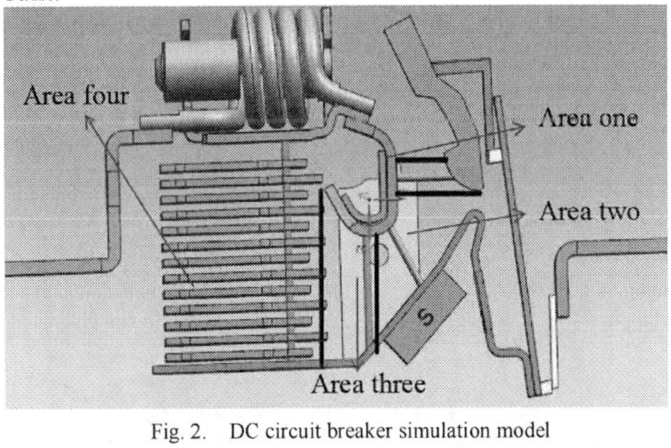

Fig. 2. DC circuit breaker simulation model

Fig. 2 has a total of four areas, the arc will pass through these four areas, area one will only be affected by the downward force, area two to area three is two transition areas, when the arc from the arc plate into the area two, only receive the direction of the downward Lorentz force, and the direction of the force will continue to change with the arc movement, when passing through the arc barrier, the direction will tend to stabilize, and then will enter area four.The four zones correspond to the four phases of DC circuit breaker breaking, the contact separation phase, the stationary phase, the motion phase, and the extinguishing phase .

By analyzing the four regions through which the above arc passes, the key to improve the breaking performance of DC circuit breakers is during the motion phase [13]. Further improve the arc power of the DC circuit breaker to improve the breaking performance. This paper selects NdFeB as a strong magnetic material, and adopts bonding method, so that NdFeB strong magnetic comparison with permanent magnets, with good plasticity, corrosion resistance, in harsh environments, can maintain a stable working state. And has a very high dimensional accuracy, reducing the drawing time of the model and improving the simulation accuracy.

IV.ARC ELECTRIC POWER SIMULATION ANALYSIS

When the iron plate is selected, the variable is the magnetism of the permanent magnet, and the arc electric dynamic is simulated in Ansoft; the magneticity is maintained as the variable, when the copper plate is selected, and the previous steps are repeated when the NdFeB strong magnet is placed. Table 1 When selecting iron plates, The arc electric dynamic data of strong magnetic(S-magnetic) and weak magnetic(W-magnetic) permanent magnets are obtained respectively.

TABLE I

Electrodynamic simulation data when selecting iron plate

Electric power (mN)	Permanent magnets	
	S-magnetic	W-magnetic
Area one	0.00212	0.00152
Area two	0.01146	0.00185
Area three	-0.01525	-0.00226
Area four	-0.01474	-0.00842

After the permanent magnet is placed in the specified position , using Ansoft software simulation to obtain Table 1 data, this paper first selects the iron plate, according to the plate material in Ansoft simulation software to set the board parameters. In order to facilitate observation, this paper focuses on observing the force received during the third stage of motion, without considering the force other than the main force direction, the placement of the permanent magnet makes the arc electric power outside the fourth region enhanced. Through observation table 1, the arc is stable in the direction of force in the arc extinguishing grid, and the force received remains basically unchanged, so that the arc enters the fourth stage faster and achieves the purpose of extinguishing the arc. And through simulation, the permanent magnet is critical to improving the breaking performance of the DC circuit breaker , when the permanent magnet is not placed, it will affect the electrical force of the arc in the DC circuit breaker, which in turn will affect the performance of the entire product.

Table 2 shows the arc electric power data obtained by an Ansoft software simulation when replacing the iron plate with a copper plate and placing a strong NdFeB magnet.

TABLE II

Electrodynamic simulation data when selecting NdFeB strong magnets and copper plates

Electric power (mN)	Permanent magnets	
	S-magnetic	W-magnetic
Area one	0.00626	0.00246
Area two	0.02624	0.002287
Area three	-0.02785	-0.00295
Area four	-0.01496	-0.00846

In the data obtained from The Ansoft software simulation, the iron plate is replaced with the copper plate, and the plate parameters are reset in the Ansoft simulation software.

The placement of permanent magnets makes the arc electric power of the first, second and third regions enhanced, and when the NdFeB strong magnet is placed combined with the copper plate, the arc electric power of the entire DC circuit breaker is greatly improved. In addition, by observing the data in Table 2, adding a copper plate and placing a strong NdFeB magnet will make the arc more stable in the direction of force in the arc extinguishing grid, so that the arc will enter the arc extinguishing grid faster and achieve the purpose of extinguishing the arc.

V. CIRCUIT BREAKER ARC ON-OFF EXPERIMENT

The experimental platform is used to conduct electrical life experiments on circuit breakers. Figure 3 is a partial current-voltage waveform pattern acquired using an oscilloscope in the experiment. Experiments were conducted to take the on-off process of the circuit breaker flowing through a rated current of 63A. Figure 4 shows a picture of the circuit breaker after the experiment.

Table 3 is the experimental data after 10 on-off experiments. It can be seen from the table that the on-off time of the strong magnetic permanent magnet is the shortest, the average time is 7.568ms, and the weak magnetic permanent magnet is the weakest, and the longest on-off time is 10.86ms.

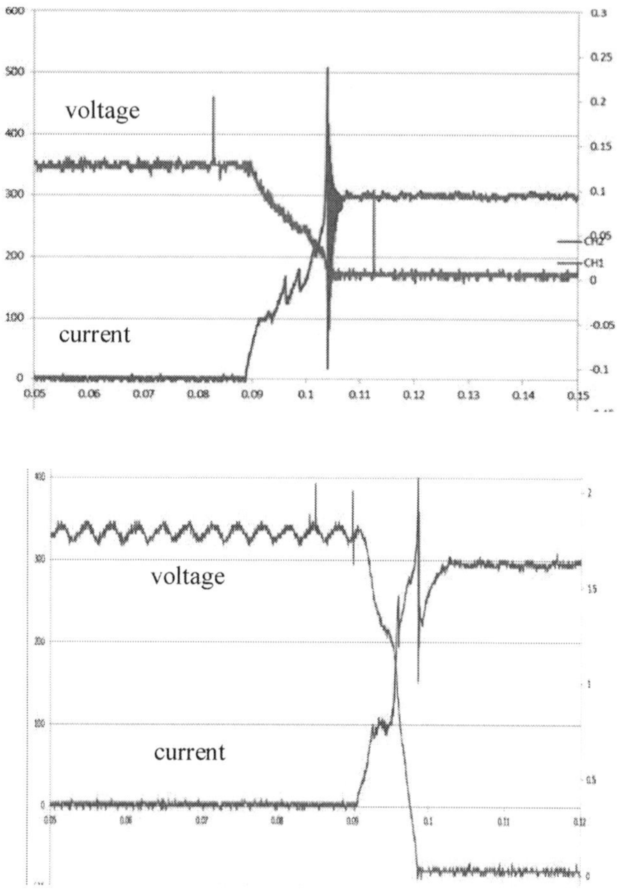

Figure 3 Experimental waveform plot

Figure 4 Picture after the circuit breaker experiment

TABLE III

On-off experimental time

Number of experiments (time)	Permanent magnet on-off time (ms)	
	S-magnetic	W-magnetic
Experiment 1	7.28	10.3
Experiment 2	7.92	10
Experiment 3	7.84	10.3
Experiment 4	7.72	11.7
Experiment 5	6.96	10.3
Experiment 6	7.68	10
Experiment 7	7.24	11.2
Experiment 8	7.68	11
Experiment 9	7.8	11.3
Experiment 10	7.56	12.5

VI. CONCLUSION

In this paper, an Ansoft modeling simulation of the DC circuit breaker is performed by analyzing the DC circuit breaker structure, and the finite element analysis method is used to optimize the simulation system. The effects of replacing the iron arc plate and ordinary permanent magnet materials on arc electric power when the copper arc plate and NdFeB strong magnets were selected for use were studied. Through simulation data analysis, the new NdFeB strong magnet is selected, and the combination of copper arc plate will improve the arc electric power and accelerate the arc extinguishing process, thereby improving the breaking capacity of the DC circuit breaker. This study provides an important reference for reducing the production cost of DC circuit breakers and further studying the breaking capacity of DC circuit breakers.

REFERENCES

[1] J. L. Wang, "A new type of DC grid key equipment with both DC fault current limiting and breaking functions," Electrically drivens, 2022, 52(.2): 10-44.

[2] S.B. Song, D.B. Zhou, W. Peng, "Comparison and application prospect analysis of HVDC circuit breakers," Guangdong Elec-tric Power, 2021, 34(12): 38-47.

[3] Z.T. Wang, C.C. Chi, M.C. Wang, "Simulation and optimization of stresses of key components of the molded case circuit breaker operating mechanism," Journal of Shanghai Dianji University, 2019, 22(4): 40-44.

[4] L. Liu, X.Y. Chen, T.T. Qi, "Improved design and experimental analysis of small circuit breaker acceleration arc extinction," Proceedings of the CSU-EPSA, 2016, 28(5): 40-44.

[5] X. Chen, Q.L. Wu, Y.H. Feng, "Research on the medium recovery characteristics of mechanical DC circuit breaker based on zero voltage rest". High voltage appliances.2021, 57(12): 10-16.

[6] Y.W. Li, H. Yang, Q.G. Zhang, "Calculation of AC insulator fouling flashover voltage based on arc characteristics of upper and lower surfaces". Proceedings of the CSEE. 2014, 34(30): 5442-5450.

[7] Park SangYong and Choi HyoSang, "Operation Characteristics of Mechanical DC Circuit Breaker Combined with LC Divergence Oscillation Circuit for High Reliability of LVDC System," Energies [J], 2021, 14(16): 5097-5097.

[8] J.S. Chen, C.C. Chi. "Simulation and optimization of electric repulsion force for DC contact system". Journal of Shanghai Dianji University, 2021, 24(1): 13-16.

[9] T. Wang, L.Q. Zhen, F.S. Fan, "Study on the arc motion model of DC grounding line between arc angles considering inter-manifold viscosity". High voltage appliances. 2021, 57(6): 24-31.

[10] J.G. Yang, S. Gao, "Characteristic analysis of multiport hybrid DC circuit breaker and its simulation study". High voltage appliances. 2021, 57(12): 50-56.

[11] L.L. Chen, X.G. Wang, C.Q. Jiao. "Modeling and testing of electromagnetic transients in the interrupting process of hybrid HVDC circuit breakers". Transactions of China Electrotechnical Society. 2021, 36(24): 5261-5271.

[12] H. Wang, Z.H. Yin, S.B. Wang, "Design and application of electromagnetic selective protection DC circuit breaker," Appliances and energy efficiency management technology, 2019, 22: 30-35.

[13] P.Z. Li, W.D. Zhou, X.Y. Wang, "Study on the influencing factors of the breaking parameters of hybrid DC circuit breakers for DC power grids," Grid technology. 2021, 45(4), 1377-1387.

Intelligent Electromagnetic Switch Start/Hold Current Automatic Measurement Technology

Wenjin Lin[1], Jierong Zhuang[1,2,3], Zhihong Xu[1,2,3]
[1] College of Electrical Engineering and Automation, Fuzhou University, Fuzhou 350116 China
[2] Fujian Province University Engineering Research Center of Smart Distribution Grid Equipment, Fuzhou University, Fuzhou 350116 China
[3] Fujian Key Laboratory of New Energy Generation and Power Conversion, Fuzhou University, Fuzhou 350116 China
E-mail: jie_rong@foxmail.com Tel: 13489958049

***Abstract*—Aiming at the problem that there are many kinds of electromagnetic switches but no unified measurement method for starting/holding current, this paper proposes an automatic measurement technology for starting/holding current of intelligent electromagnetic switches. By analyzing the phenomenon of coil current forced down in the process of electromagnetic switch starting and coil current forced up in the process of breaking, point out the relationship between coil current and core action signal. The inflection point of the coil current is taken as the basis for judging the critical starting/holding current of the electromagnetic switch. The starting/holding current is automatically found by controlling the coil current to change in a ladder shape. The feasibility of the measurement technology is verified by the joint simulation of LabVIEW and Multisim and the field experiment. The proposed automatic measurement technology of starting/holding current of intelligent electromagnetic switch is not affected by the change of external voltage and the change of electromagnetic switch parameters, and can adapt to the measurement of different types of intelligent electromagnetic switch, which is of significance to improve the operation reliability of electromagnetic switch.**

***Index Terms*—electromagnetic switch, intelligent control, coil current, automatic measurement**

I. Introduction

The new generation of power grid has put forward the requirements for intelligent energy of information and physical integration, and the requirements for switching appliances have been greatly deepened and improved [1].

The specifications of electromagnetic switches are various, and the parameters of different types of electromagnetic switches are different. After the intelligent control is adopted, the coil current becomes an important parameter that directly affects the pull in process of electromagnetic switches [2]. During the action of the electromagnetic switch, the contact bounce and arc caused by the high end speed of the moving iron core cannot be ignored [3]. In [4], the contact bounce and arc generation are reduced by PWM control of the contactor coil current. Compared with the starting stage of tens of milliseconds or even several milliseconds, the energy consumption of electromagnetic switch is mostly concentrated in the holding stage [5]. PWM closed-loop control can reduce the energy consumption of electromagnetic switch and play an energy saving role. In [6] proposes a multivariable feedback holding control strategy to reduce the noise in the holding stage while ensuring the normal holding of the contactor. The coil current directly affects the dynamic characteristics of the electromagnetic switch when it is started and the energy saving effect when it is held. The electromagnetic switch is a relatively closed integrated device. The starting and breaking signals of the electromagnetic switch can be obtained by manually observing the action sound and action signal of the electromagnetic switch. However, the human reaction cycle is long, and this method has delay, so it cannot accurately measure the starting/holding current of the electromagnetic switch. Therefore, it is of practical significance to find an automatic measurement technology for starting and holding current of intelligent electromagnetic switch.

This paper takes the automatic measurement of the starting/holding current of electromagnetic switch as the research object. By describing the intelligent control topology and control circuit of electromagnetic switch, the causes of the forced drop of the coil current in the starting stage and the forced rise of the coil current in the breaking stage are analyzed, and the relationship between it and the working state of the electromagnetic switch is explained. An automatic measurement technology of the starting/holding current of intelligent electromagnetic switch is proposed. The starting/holding current of the electromagnetic switch is judged by controlling the coil current to change in a stepwise manner and detecting the inflection point of the forced rise/fall of the coil current. Based on the contactor CJ20-630, simulation and experiment are carried out to verify the feasibility and effectiveness of the measurement technology.

II. Analysis of Coil Current Characteristics of Intelligent Electromagnetic Switch

The control topology of intelligent electromagnetic switch is shown in Fig. 1:

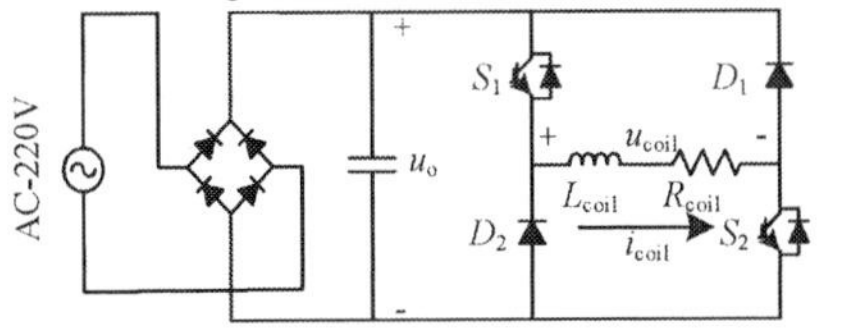

Fig. 1. Control topology of intelligent electromagnetic switch

Since the coil current is a parameter that directly affects the state of the electromagnetic switch, the intelligent control of the movement process of the electromagnetic switch can be realized by controlling the coil current .As shown in Fig. 2, the intelligent control of the electromagnetic switch has three control states: the switch tube S_1 and S_2 are all on, the current flows through the coil along the loop 1, the rectified voltage u_o is applied to the coil, the electromagnetic switch is in the excited state, and the coil current rises: S_1 is off, S_2 is on, the coil current passes through the diode D_2 and S_2 flows naturally along the loop 2, and the coil voltage is basically zero. At this time, the coil current slowly decreases, The electromagnetic switch is in the demagnetization state: S_1 and S_2 are all off, the current passes through D_1、D_2 and flows through the coil along the loop 3, the coil voltage is the negative rectified voltage, the coil current drops rapidly, and the electromagnetic switch is in the demagnetization state. In the control process, the excitation and freewheeling states are used in the starting and holding stages, and the demagnetization state is used in the breaking stage.

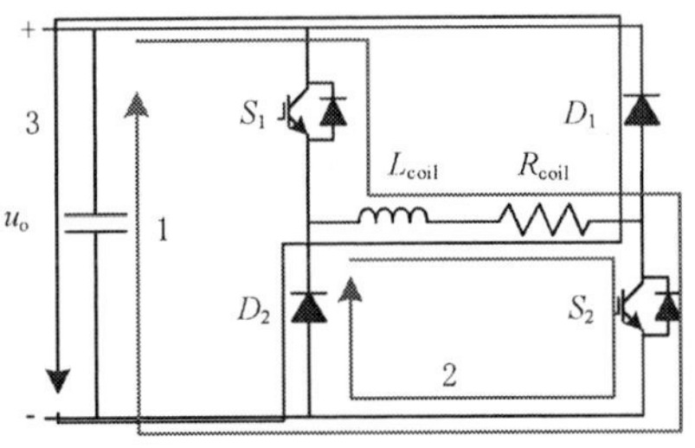

Fig. 2. Control loop

During the action of electromagnetic switch, there are:

$$u_{coil} = i_{coil}R + L_{coil}\frac{di_{coil}}{dt} + i_{coil}\frac{dL_{coil}}{dt} \quad (1)$$

Where, u_{coil} , i_{coil} is the voltage and current of the electromagnetic switch coil, L_{coil} is the coil inductance of the electromagnetic switch working change, and R_{coil} is the coil resistance. At the beginning of the electromagnetic switch, the coil current begins to rise. When the coil current is greater than the starting current, the moving iron core drives the moving contact to work, the air gap gradually decreases, the speed v of the moving iron core increases, generating motion back potential is generated. Therefore, the (1) can be changed to

$$u_{coil} = i_{coil}R + L_{coil}\frac{di_{coil}}{dt} + i_{coil}v\frac{dL_{coil}}{dx} \quad (2)$$

Where x is the core displacement

The intelligent control of the electromagnetic switch can control the coil current to be kept near the reference value by sampling the coil current and controlling the output duty ratio of the switch tube. However, with the increasing speed of the moving iron core, the coil current will still be forced to drop when the electromagnetic switch is in the excited state. When the phenomenon of forced drop of coil current occurs, the coil current has been larger than the starting current. By controlling the coil current to rise in a step shape, give sufficient time to each step, and detect the step of forced drop of coil current, the coil current value close to the starting current of the electromagnetic switch can be found.

When the electromagnetic switch is from the holding state to the off state, the holding current of the electromagnetic switch can also be found by observing the forced rise of the coil current, which can be obtained according to (2)

$$\frac{di_{coil}}{dt} = \frac{u_{coil} - i_{coil}R - i_{coil}v\frac{dL_{coil}}{dx}}{L_{coil}} \quad (3)$$

In the breaking process of the electromagnetic switch, if the negative pressure is applied on the coil, u_{coil}=- u_o, the electromagnetic switch is rapidly demagnetized to achieve the purpose of fast breaking. However, it can be seen from (3) that during the breaking process, $di_{coil}/dt<0$, and the phenomenon of forced current rise does not occur. Therefore, the loop 3 is not used in the control process to achieve the purpose of finding the holding current of the electromagnetic switch.

To sum up, when the electromagnetic switch is started and disconnected, the coil current will be forced to change. By setting the current reference value in the starting stage to rise in a step shape and the coil current reference value in the holding stage to fall in a step shape through intelligent control, the electromagnetic switch can be controlled to complete the starting and breaking work, and the starting/holding current of the electromagnetic switch can be measured by detecting the coil current.

III. Simulation and Experimental Verification

In order to verify the proposed automatic measurement technology of starting/holding current of intelligent electromagnetic switch, the contactor CJ20-630 is taken as an object, and the core displacement, core speed and coil current are compared through joint simulation with LabVIEW and Multisim software. Based on the single-chip microcomputer and hardware platform, the automatic measurement technology of starting/holding current of intelligent electromagnetic switch is tested and verified.

A Simulation verification

Fig. 3 shows the simulation waveforms of the coil current, core displacement and core speed of the contactor coil current reference value in the starting stage and the holding stage.

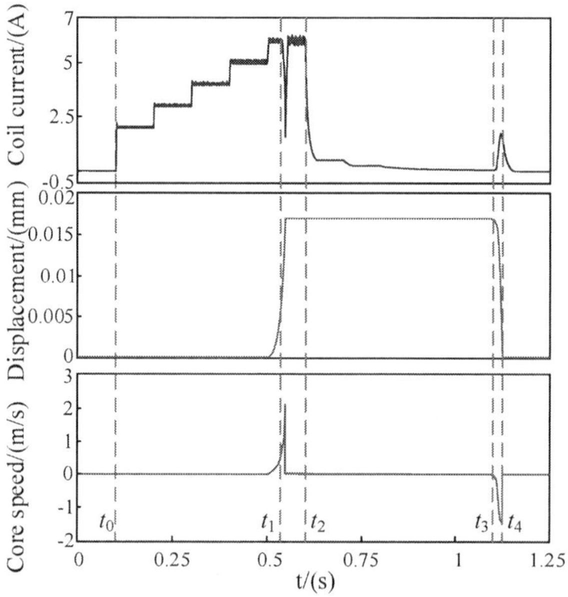

Fig. 3. Stepped current simulation waveform

As shown in the Fig. 3, at time t_0, the coil current begins to rise in a stepped manner. At time t_1, the coil current is forced to drop, while the iron core is still moving. The starting stage ends at time t_2, and the process proceeds to the holding stage. After the coil current drops to the first step setting value in the holding stage, it begins to drop in a step like manner. At time t_3, the coil current is forced to rise. At this time, it can be seen from the waveform of core displacement or core speed that the contactor starts to break. The contactor breaking process ends at time t_4.

It can be seen from the simulation waveform that the starting and holding current of the contactor can be obtained by controlling the coil current to change in a step shape and detecting the step at the inflection point of the coil current.

B Experimental verification

In order to further verify the proposed automatic measurement technology of starting/holding current of electromagnetic switch, the experiment is carried out with contactor CJ20-630 through the hardware platform based on single chip microcomputer. The control frequency of contactor switch is 15KHz. The core displacement waveform output by the laser displacement sensor is compared with the coil current waveform. Since the action time of most contactors is within 100ms, the step time in the starting stage is set to 100ms. The excitation and freewheeling states are adopted in the holding stage, and the current drop time is slow. In order to ensure the accuracy of the experiment and avoid the reverse current only when this step contactor acts and the next step, the step time of the holding stage is set to 200ms. Fig. 4 (a) and Fig. 4 (b) are experimental waveforms. It can be seen from the Fig. 4 that the contactor coil is powered on at time t_0, and with the coil current rising in a stepwise manner, the inflection point of current falling at time t_1 appears. At time t_2, the coil current decreases step by step as it turns into the holding stage. When the coil current is less than the holding current of the contactor at time t_3, the contactor is disconnected, and the coil current is forced to rise. At time t_4, it can be seen that the breaking process is ended by the core displacement waveform. It can be seen that the inflection point of the forced rise/fall of the coil current is near the start of the contactor.

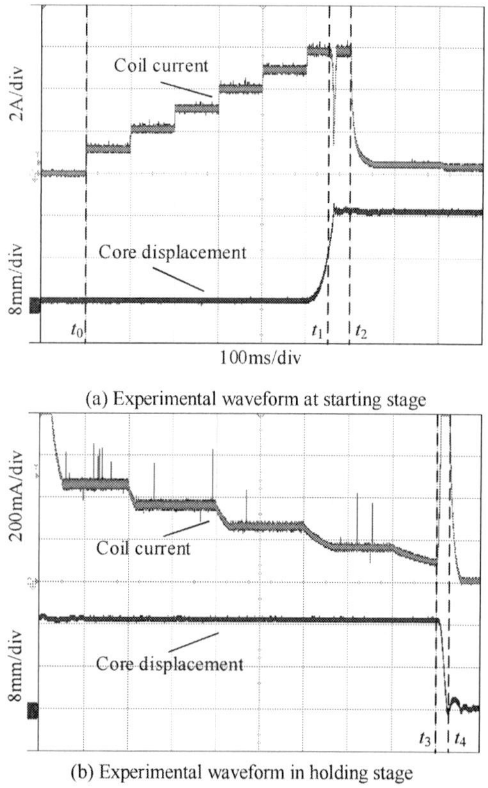

(a) Experimental waveform at starting stage

(b) Experimental waveform in holding stage

Fig. 4. Experimental waveform

In order to find a more accurate starting/holding current, reduce the current difference between the current steps, and set the step time of the starting stage to 200ms. According to Fig. 5 (a) and (b), the starting current of contactor CJ20-630 is 5.4A and the holding current is 120mA. Subsequently, the current reference value in the starting stage and holding stage is set as the above parameters, and the contactor works normally, which proves the feasibility of automatic measurement.

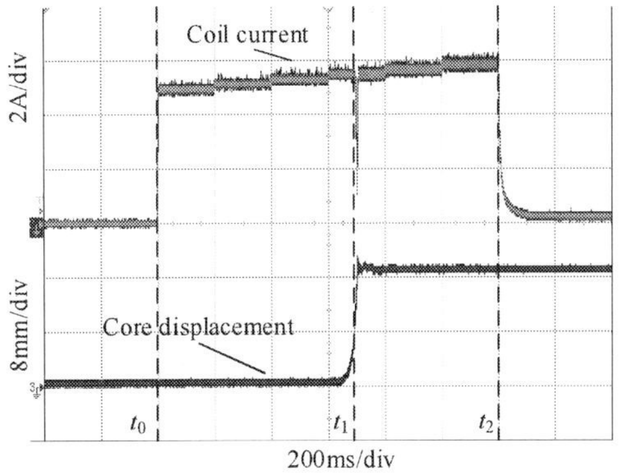

(a) Experimental waveform at starting stage

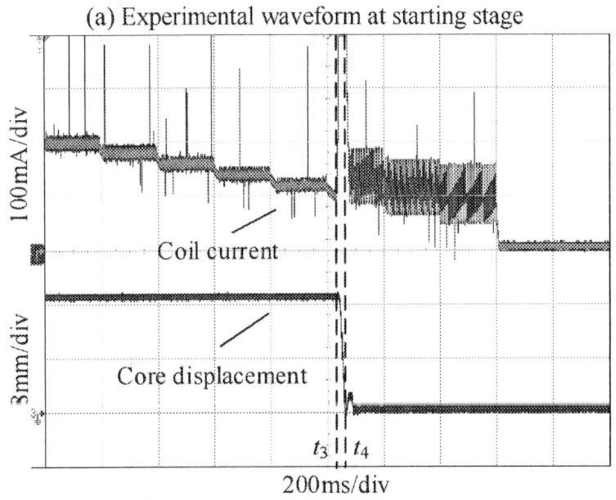

(b) Experimental waveform in holding stage

Fig. 5. Experimental waveform of changing step difference

In the starting stage, only when the coil current reaches the starting current, the movable iron core starts to move, and the forced drop of the coil current occurs after the contactor starts to act for a period of time. In the holding stage, the coil current is forced to rise when the contactor starts to break. There are two different situations here. The coil current is controlled by current closed loop. In the starting stage, when the coil current drops, the coil is always in the excited state to suppress the drop of the coil current. In the holding stage, when the coil is turned off, the coil is in the freewheeling state instead of the demagnetization state. Therefore, the phenomenon of forced current rise is more obvious than the phenomenon of forced drop.

IV. CONCLUSION

This paper presents a new automatic measurement technology for the starting/holding current of electromagnetic switch coil. Starting from the relationship between the current of electromagnetic switch coil and the action signal of moving iron core, it is proposed to find the starting/holding current of electromagnetic switch by controlling the coil current to rise/fall in a stepped manner and detecting the inflection point of the forced fall/rise of current. Taking contactor CJ20-630 as an object, the proposed automatic measurement method is verified by software joint simulation and experiment. From the analysis of the experimental results, the proposed automatic measurement technology can find the starting and holding current accurately and quickly by adopting the current closed-loop control, and can adapt to the electromagnetic switch with different parameters.

ACKNOWLEDGMENT

The authors are thankful for the support of the Natural Science Foundation of Fujian Province of China (No. 2020J05134) and the Key Laboratory of Special Machine and High Voltage Apparatus (Shenyang University of Technology), Ministry of Education (No. KFKT202002) to carry out this study.

REFERENCES

[1] P Zhang, "Research on technology of intelligent low voltage electrical apparatus" in *Electrical & Energy Management Technology*, 2019,(15): 10-20,.

[2] J Zhuang, Z Xu, "Self-starting control with quasi-critical current search for intelligent contactor" in *Electric Machines and Control*, 2019, (6): 73-80.

[3] E. Ramirez-Laboreo, C. Sagues and S. Llorente, "A New Run-to-Run Approach for Reducing Contact Bounce in Electromagnetic Switches", *IEEE Transactions on Industrial Electronics*, 2017, 64(1) :535-543

[4] A. G. Espinosa, J. R. R. Ruiz, J. Cusidó, J. A. Ortega and L. Romeral, "Closed-Loop Controller for Eliminating the Contact Bounce in DC Core Contactors" in *IEEE Transactions on Components and Packaging Technologies*, 2010, 33(3): 535-543

[5] H Li, P Zeng, "Design solutions and standards requirements on energy efficiency of low" in *Electrical & Energy Management Technology*, 2017, 14. 65-68

[6] J Zhuang, Z Xu, "The multivariate feedback control strategy for electromagnetic contactor holding", *Proceedings of the CSEE*, 2019. 5:1516-1526

Wenjin Lin is currently pursuing the M.S. degree in electric engineering from the College of Electrical Engineering and Automation, Fuzhou University, China. His research interests include electric apparatus and its intelligent technology.

Jierong Zhuang, male, born in 1989, Ph.D., associate professor, master tutor. He is mainly engaged in the electrical apparatus and intelligent technologies. Corresponding author: jierong@foxmail.com.

Zhihong Xu, female, born in 1963, Ph.D., professor, doctoral tutor. She is mainly engaged in the electrical apparatus and intelligent technologies.

Influence Mechanism of Si Impurity on Coating Quality of Electrical Pure Iron

Qingxing Su

Xiamen Hongfa Electroacoustic CO., LTD, Xiamen, 361021
E-mail: suqingxing1120@126.com Tel: 15860766487

Abstract—**The yellowing or corrosion of iron parts of relay magnetic circuit to a certain extent will not only affect the appearance of the product, but also affect the pull-in and release voltage of the product, which will lead to the failure of the product in serious cases. Therefore, it is necessary to strictly control the surface quality of iron parts in the production process. By analyzing the samples of the magnetic circuit iron made of pure electrical iron and carrying out experiments and studies, the yellowing mechanism of magnetic circuit iron parts is found. The excessive presence of Si in the raw materials of electrical pure iron will aggravate the corrosion of metal grain boundaries, make the compactness of the coating worse, and lead to the yellowing or corrosion of the parts after electroplating. After changing to electrical pure iron without Si, the corrosion resistance of iron parts after electroplating is significantly improved.**

Index Terms— **electrical pure iron, yellow rust, excessive Si, grain boundary corrosion.**

I. INTRODUCTION

The forward and reverse action of Si in steel. A small amount of Si in silicon steel can improve the resistivity, reduce eddy current loss, and reduce the coercive force and hysteresis loss, so as to reduce the iron loss, but also reduce the magnetic induction strength and saturated magnetic induction strength. The influence of Si in the iron silicon magnetic powder core has the same trend[1]. A small amount of Si can improve the strength of steel alloy, but the increase of Si content will lead to the increase of grain boundary corrosion sensitivity of the alloy[2]. A small amount of Si can improve the aging hardness of the alloy, but with the increase of Si content, there will be a higher kinetics of Si precipitation in the heat treatment stage[3].

With the increase of Si content, Si is obviously distributed along the grain boundary, which increases the depth of grain boundary corrosion and improves the sensitivity of grain boundary corrosion[4].With the increase of Si content in iron, more single crystal Si precipitates during heat treatment[5].With the increase of Si content in iron, grain boundary corrosion is easy to occur, because the Si particles in the alloy have a positive potential relative to the Fe matrix. If corrosive medium or acid permeates into the grain boundary, Si will be cathode in the process of corrosion, which will make the surrounding Fe matrix more prone to corrosion[6].The higher the Si content, the easier the coarsening occurs during the heat treatment, and the easier the formation of the intermetallic compound AlSiMnFe (white coarse phase)[7].The higher the Si content, the easier the Si rich phase particles are enriched at the grain boundary. There are higher interface energy and weaker bond energy at the grain boundary. From the energy point of view, the Si phase is easier to nucleate along the grain boundary[8]. The diffusion rate of Si atoms from the grain boundary to the intracrystalline is very low. After heat treatment, the Si content decreases from the grain boundary to the intracrystalline direction, that is, Si will be enriched at the grain boundary[9].The solubility of Si in Fe is very low, and most of the excess Si atoms precipitate as fine spheroidized particles after heat treatment[10].With the increase of Si content, the ability of the protective layer of iron and steel decreases. Since Si particles hinder the rapid formation of the protective layer, the compactness of the protective layer becomes poor (the coating is loose and porous). It can not effectively prevent the oxygen and moisture in the air from entering, which accelerates the corrosion of Fe matrix, and the increase of Si content plays a role in deterioration[11]. At the same time, with the increase of Si particle content on the surface, the number of pores and the diameter of pores in the alloy layer increase, resulting in more pores and micro-cracks. The corrosion medium penetrates the alloy layer through micro-cracks to corrode the matrix Fe[12].

The corrosion of iron parts to a certain extent will affect the functional parameters of the relay. Therefore, the surface quality of iron parts (such as the yellowing of iron parts) will be strictly inspected in the production process. During the process inspection, it is found that there are yellow spots in the inner side of the defective sample of manufacturer a, the groove and other low current areas. Through the analysis of yellowing causes and fault reproduction test, the mechanism of yellowing of defective samples was found. After the defective materials were changed to iron parts without Si, the corrosion resistance of iron parts after electroplating was significantly improved.

II. Analysis and Test

During the process inspection of the surface quality of electrical pure iron after electroplating, it was found that there were yellow spots in the low current areas such as the inner side and groove of the defective sample of manufacturer A, as Fig. 1.

A. Observe the surface of yellowing area with microscope

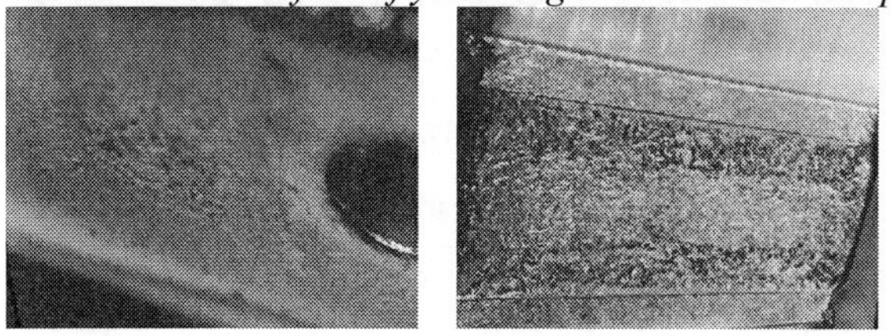

(a)Yellow dot on the inside (b)Yellow dot in the groove

Fig. 1. There are yellow spots in the low current areas such as the inner side and groove of the defective sample of manufacturer A.

B. Observe the metallographic section of iron parts of manufacturer A and B after plating with microscope

The coating on the metallographic section of the defective sample of manufacturer A has holes and the metal grain boundary is very obvious as Fig.2(a); However, there are no plating holes and obvious metal grain boundaries in manufacturer B as Fig.2(b).

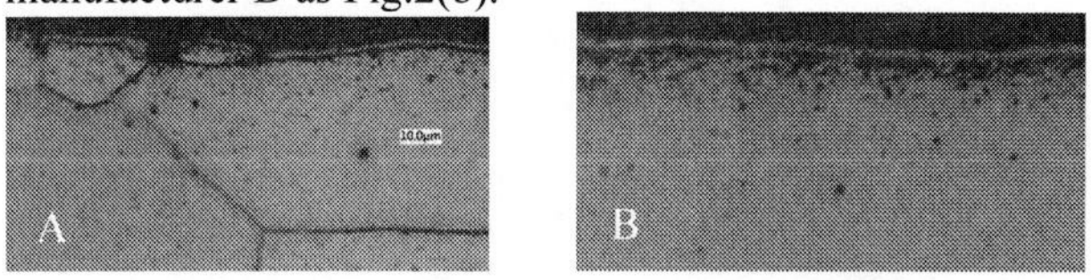

(a)Holes in coating of manufacturer A (b)There are no holes in the coating of manufacturer B

Fig. 2. Observe the metallographic section of iron parts of manufacturer A and B after plating with microscope.

C. SEM-EDS analysis of metallographic section of iron parts after electroplating by manufacturers A and B

A large amount of Si (0.29% ~ 0.35%) was detected in the metallographic section of the sample of manufacturer A with yellowing defect after plating, while no Si was detected in the metallographic section of the sample of manufacturer B without yellowing after plating as Fig.3.

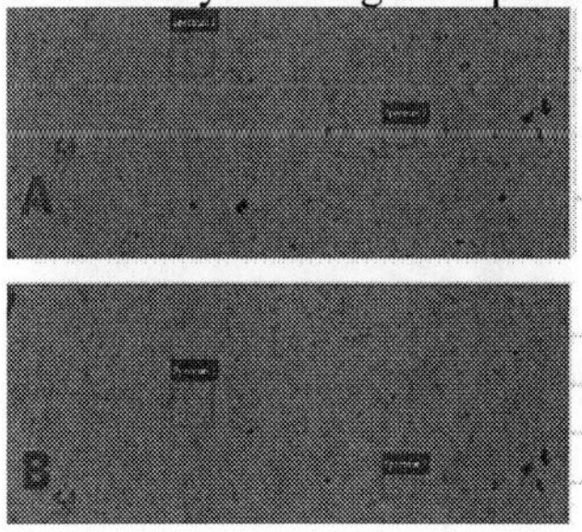

C	Si	Mn	Fe	Total
0.49	0.49	0.50	98.53	100.00
0.43	0.49	0.48	98.60	100.00

C	Fe	Total
0.41	99.59	100.00
0.35	99.65	100.00
0.40	99.60	100.00

Fig. 3. SEM-EDS analysis of metallographic section of iron parts after electroplating by manufacturers A and B, Content unit:%

D. SEM-EDS analysis of metallographic section of iron parts after deplated by manufacturer A and B

A large amount of Si (0.49%) was detected in the matrix of the yellow defective sample from manufacturer A after deplating, while no Si was detected in the matrix of the sample from manufacturer B after deplating. It is speculated that the abnormal element Si comes from the iron matrix.

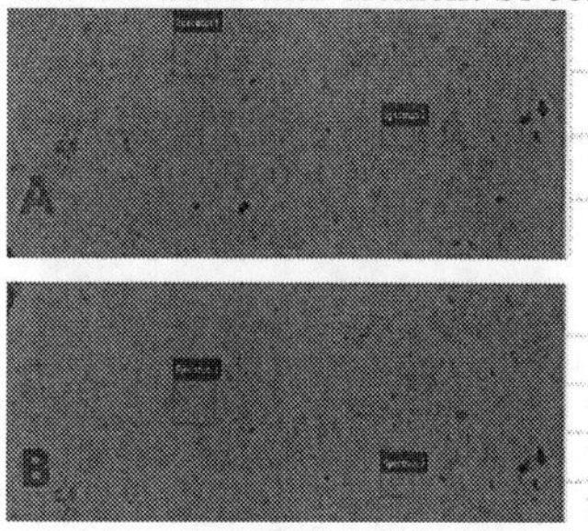

C	Si	Mn	Fe	Total
0.49	0.49	0.50	98.53	100.00
0.43	0.49	0.48	98.60	100.00

C	Fe	Total
0.41	99.59	100.00
0.35	99.65	100.00
0.40	99.60	100.00

Fig. 4. SEM-EDS analysis of metallographic section of iron parts after deplated by manufacturer A and B, Content unit:%

E. SEM-EDS analysis of the surface of iron parts of manufacturer A and B after heat treatment

After heat treatment, there are some small pits on the surface of iron parts of manufacturer A, as shown in Fig.5a. There are clear massive materials containing Si in the pits. The small pits are likely to be formed by the shedding of Si particles on the surface layer. This result corresponds to the grain boundary enrichment observed on the surface of parts after heat treatment, as shown in Fig.6. Similarly, no obvious pits and foreign matters containing Si were found on the surface of iron parts of manufacturer B after heat treatment, as shown in Fig.5b.

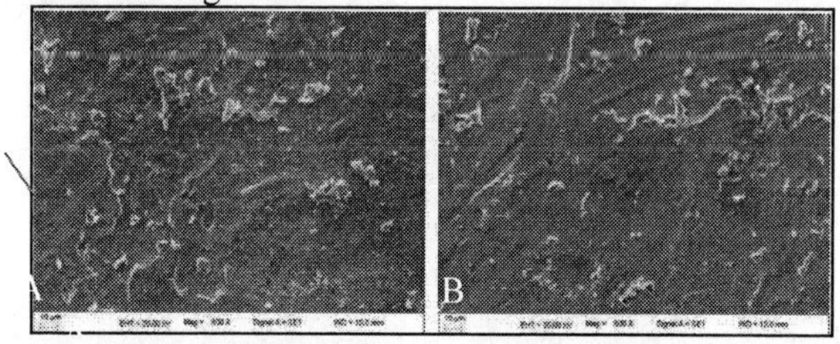

(a) There are some small holes on the surface of manufacturer A

(b) No pit is found on the surface of manufacturer B

Fig. 5. SEM-EDS analysis of the surface of iron parts of manufacturer A and B after heat treatment

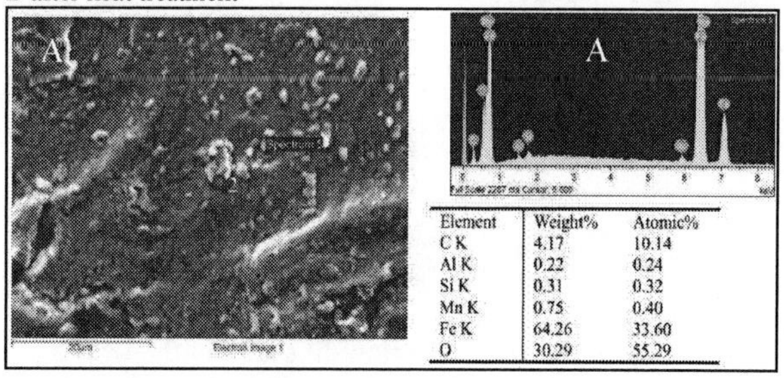

Element	Weight%	Atomic%
C K	4.17	10.14
Al K	0.22	0.24
Si K	0.31	0.32
Mn K	0.75	0.40
Fe K	64.26	33.60
O	30.29	55.29

Fig. 6. There is Si containing grain boundary enrichment on the surface of iron parts of manufacturer A after heat treatment

F. SEM-EDS analysis of cross section of iron parts of manufacturer A and B after heat treatment

After the same heat treatment, there are obvious grain boundaries on the surface layer of the section of iron parts of manufacturer A, and Si is detected at the grain boundaries by SEM-EDS, while no obvious grain boundaries are found on the surface layer of the section of iron parts of manufacturer B, and Si is not detected at the grain boundaries.

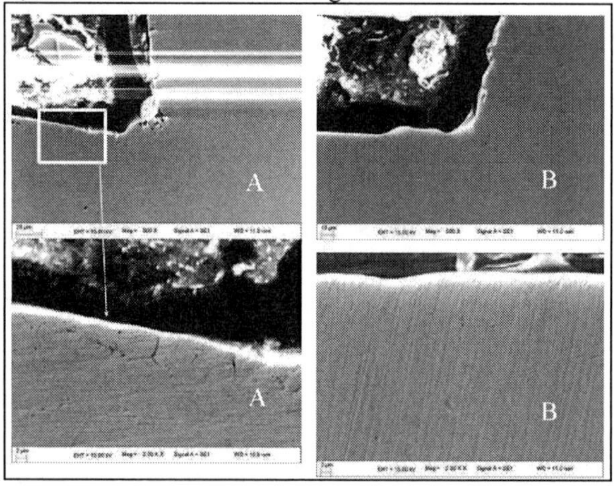

(a) There is grain boundary on cross section of iron parts of manufacturer A

(b) No obvious grain boundary is found on iron parts of manufacturer B

Fig. 7. SEM-EDS analysis of cross section of iron parts of manufacturer A and B after heat treatment.

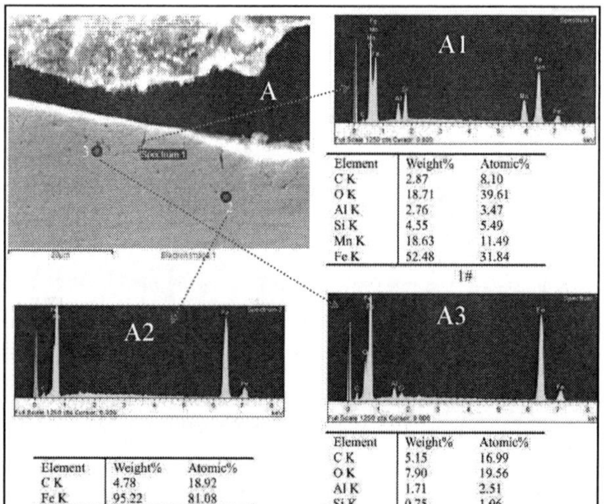

Fig. 8. SEM-EDS detects Si at the grain boundary position of the iron part section after heat treatment in manufacturer A

G. ICP-OES analysis of Si content in different processes of manufacturer A and B

The Si content in the solution digested by the iron parts in different processes of manufacturer A is relatively high, while no Si is detected in manufacturer B.

TABLE I shows that the Si content of raw materials of Si containing iron strip of manufacturer A is not significantly reduced after different processes, but remains at a relatively stable concentration level.

TABLE I

ICP-OES analysis of Si content in different processes of manufacturer A and B

Different processes	manufacturer A	manufacturer B
Si content in raw materials of iron belt	532 ppm	N.D.
Si content in stamped iron parts	500 ppm	N.D.
Si content in iron parts after vibration cleaning	610 ppm	N.D.
Si content in iron parts after heat treatment	637 ppm	N.D.
Si content in iron parts after electroplating	590 ppm	N.D.

H. Comparison of temperature and humidity combined cycle test of iron parts after electroplating between manufacturers A and B

After 10 days of temperature and humidity combined cycle test, all iron parts plated by manufacturer A appear yellow, and some even rust. However, no obvious abnormality was found on the surface of iron parts plated by manufacturer B after the same test.

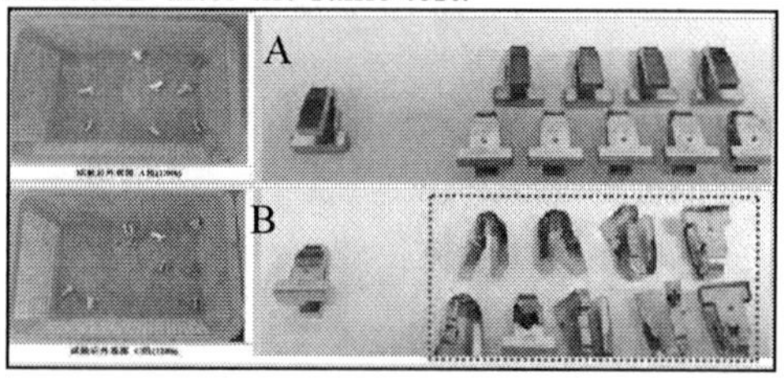

Fig. 9. Comparison of temperature and humidity combined cycle test of iron parts after electroplating between manufacturers A and B

I. Manufacturer A reduces Si content in iron parts and compares the effect before and after improvement

1) The surface of the improved substrate is flat, and the coating is well bonded with the substrate

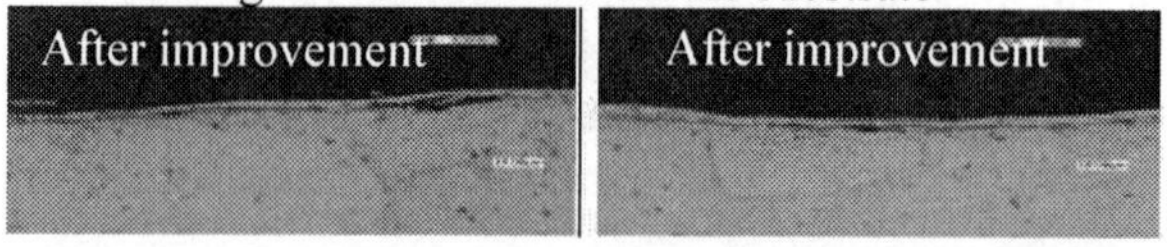

(a) The surface of the improved substrate is flat, and the coating is well bonded with the substrate

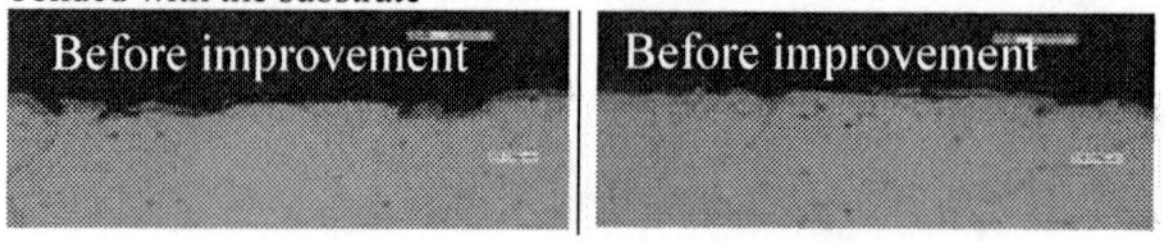

(b) Manufacturer a: the surface of base material is wrinkled and uneven before improvement.

Fig. 10. Manufacturer A reduces Si content in iron parts and compares the effect before and after improvement.

Before improvement by manufacturer A (0.22% ~ 0.30% Si), the surface of the base material is wrinkled and uneven, and the combination between the coating and the base material is seriously poor as Fig.10b. After improvement (no Si was detected by SEM-EDS), the surface of the substrate was flat, and the coating was well bonded with the substrate as Fig.10a.

2) SEM-EDS analysis showed that no Si was detected in the improved iron substrate

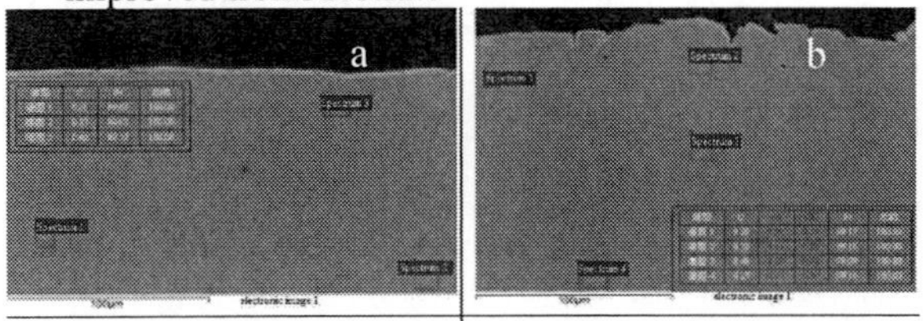

Spectrum	C	Fe	Total
1	0.31	99.69	100.00
2	0.35	99.65	100.00
3	0.43	99.57	100.00

Spectrum	C	Al	Si	Fe	Total
1	0.28	0.31	0.24	99.17	100.00
2	0.32	0.22	0.28	99.18	100.00
3	0.40	0.30	0.22	99.09	100.00
4	0.27	0.27	0.30	99.06	100.00

(a) Iron parts improved by manufacturer A do not contain Si.

(b) Iron parts before improvement by manufacturer A contain Si.

Fig. 11. SEM-EDS analysis showed that no Si was detected in the improved iron substrate

3) The corrosion resistance of iron parts improved by manufacturer A is significantly improved

After 3 hours of neutral salt spray test, the improved iron parts without Si were not significantly rusted as Fig.12a, while the improved iron parts with Si content of 0.22% ~ 0.30% were significantly rusted as Fig.12b.

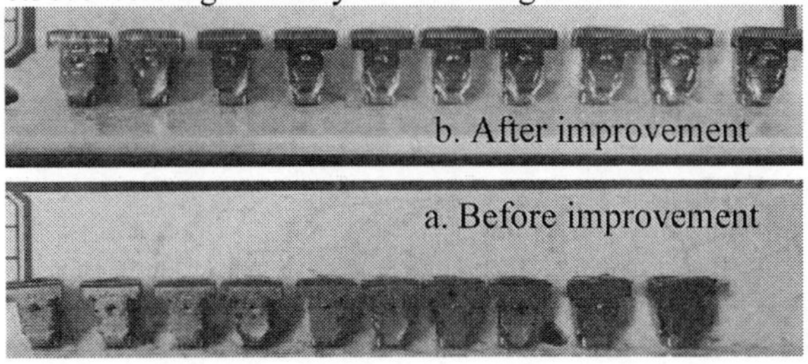

Fig. 12. The corrosion resistance of iron parts improved by manufacturer A is significantly improved

III. Results and Discussion

A. The increase of Si content leads to the precipitation of more Si particles during heat treatment

With the increase of Si content in iron parts, there will be a higher kinetics of Si precipitation in the heat treatment stage, making more single crystal Si precipitate in the heat treatment process. In addition, the solubility of Si in Fe is very low, and most of the excess Si atoms precipitate as fine spheroidized particles after heat treatment[10]. Actual observation and analysis: after heat treatment, more Si particles are precipitated to the shallow surface of iron part a with high Si content as Fig.13a.

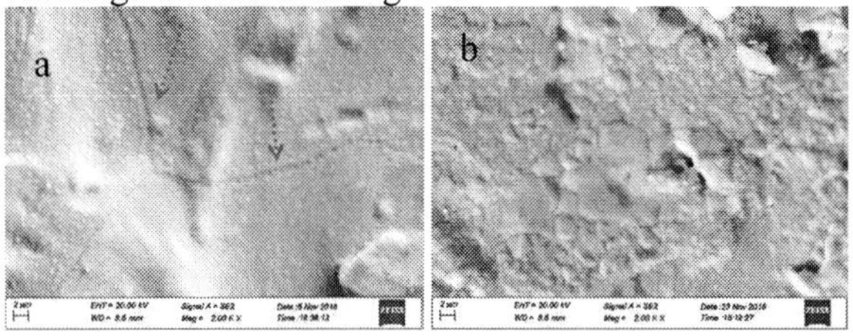

(a)Iron part A with high Si content (b)Iron part B with no Si detected

Fig. 13. The increase of Si content leads to the precipitation of more Si particles during heat treatment.

B. Increasing Si content increases the susceptibility of iron parts to grain boundary corrosion

The diffusion rate of Si atoms from the grain boundary to the intracrystalline is very low. After heat treatment, the Si content decreases from the grain boundary to the intracrystalline direction, that is, Si is enriched at the grain boundary [9]. With the increase of Si content in electrical pure iron, there are higher interfacial energy and weaker bond energy at the grain boundary. From the energy point of view, the Si phase nucleates easily along the grain boundary, which is easy to cause grain boundary corrosion; The potential of Si particles in the alloy shall be positive with respect to the Fe matrix. If there is corrosive medium or acid liquid infiltrating into the grain boundary, Si will be cathode in the corrosion process, which will make the surrounding Fe matrix more prone to corrosion, as shown in Fig.14.

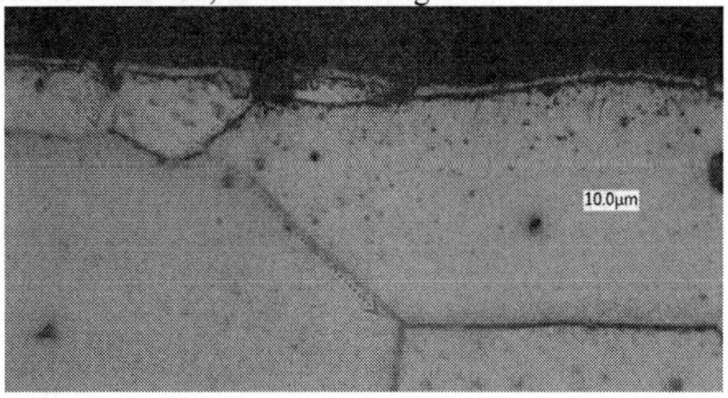

Fig. 14. Increasing Si content increases the susceptibility of iron parts to grain boundary corrosion

C. Discussion on the mechanism of yellow spots or rust on the surface of electroplated iron parts

With the increase of Si content of electrical pure iron, the ability of the protective layer is weakened. Because Si particles hinder the rapid formation of the protective layer, the compactness of the protective layer becomes poor (the coating is loose and porous), which can not effectively prevent the oxygen and moisture in the air from entering, and accelerate the corrosion of the iron matrix. Before electroplating, use some dilute acid to clean the oxide on the surface of iron parts, which will gradually penetrate into the depth of the grain boundary through the pores on the surface of the coating; After electroplating for a period of time, the acid solution originally concentrated at the grain boundary will gradually seep out of the coating surface, resulting in yellow spots or rust on the coating surface.

IV. Conclusion

The increase of Si content in electrical pure iron matrix makes more Si particles precipitate during heat treatment, improves the sensitivity of iron parts to grain boundary corrosion, accelerates the corrosion of iron matrix, and causes yellow spots or rust on the surface of iron parts.

V. Improvement suggestions

It is recommended to use electrical pure iron raw materials with low or no Si content to improve the quality from the source.

Acknowledgment

Thank Baosteel Research Institute of Baoshan Iron and Steel Co., Ltd., Wu Wei and Dr. Wu of Xiamen Jinyue Electric Appliance Co., Ltd. for their help and support in the research and analysis process of this paper.

References

[1] Linhao Xu, Hongping Zhang, Dongliang Zhao, Zhaofu Du, Haichen Yu, Research on The Influence Of Silicon on the Performance Of Iron-Based Magnetic Powder Core [J], Powder Metallurgy Industry, 2016, 26 (6), 20-21.

[2] Jiao Wang, Binghui Luo, Yaya Zheng, Zhenhai Bai, Bin Li, Effect of Magnesium Silicon Ratio on Microstructure and Properties of Al Mg Si alloy, Chinese Journal of nonferrous metals, 2017, 27 (6), 1093.

[3] Mingzhuo Zhou, Boyang Wen, Lipeng Ding, Jinyue Xie, Wen Wen, Zhihong Jia . Effect of Mg/Si ratio on natural aging and precipitation strengthening of 6000 series aluminum alloy [J], Journal of material heat treatment, 2015, 36 (4): 68-72.

[4] Jiao Wang, Binghui Luo, Yaya Zheng, Zhenhai Bai, Bin Li, Effect of Magnesium Silicon Ratio on Microstructure and Properties of Al Mg Si alloy, Chinese Journal of nonferrous metals, 2017, 27 (6), 1091-1099.

[5] Liao H, Wu Y, Ding K. Hardening response and precipitation behavior of Al-7% Si-0.3% Mg alloy in a pre-aging process [J]. Materials Science and Engineering A, 2013, 560: 811−816.

[6] Eckermann F, Suter T, Uggowitzer P J, , Afeseth A. The influence of MgSi Particle Reactivity and Dissolution Processes on Corrosion in Al-Mg-Si alloys [J]. Electrochemical Acta, 2008, 54(2): 844−855

[7] Sang Yi, Chen Jiang-Hua, Liu Chun-hui, Wang Shi-hao, Huang Chang-Jun. A comparison study of precipitation behaviors in three Al-Mg-Si alloys with different Mg/Si composition ratios [J].Journal of Chinese Electron Microscopy Society, 2012, 31(5): 384−390.

[8] Van D N H, Offerman S E, Sietsma J, Van D Z. Barrier-free Heterogeneous Grain Nucleation in Polycrystalline Materials: The Austenite to Ferrite Phase Transformation in Steel [J]. Acta Materialia, 2007, 55(13): 4489−4498.

[9] Yang Hai-Lin, Ji Shou-Xun, Yang Wen-Chao, Wang Yun, Fan Zhong-Yun. Effect Of Mg level on the Microstructure And Mechanical Properties of Die-Cast Al-Si-Cu alloys[J]. Materials Science and Engineering A, 2015, 642: 340−350.

[10] Gupta A K, Lloyd D J, Court S A. Precipitation Hardening in Al-Mg-Si Alloys with and without Excess Si [J]. Materials Science and Engineering A, 2001, 316(1): 11−17.

[11] Technical center of Angang iron and Steel Co., Ltd., Institute of structural materials, General Research Institute of iron and steel, electrochemical study on the effect of Si on atmospheric corrosion resistance of carbon steel [J]. Equipment environmental engineering, 2007, 4 (4), 23-26.

[12] Shanghai Jiaotong University, Shanghai Baoshan Iron and Steel Co., Ltd., Beijing University of science and technology, School of Material Science and Engineering of Beijing University of Aeronautics and Astronautics, National Green Coating Engineering Center of Lanzhou Jiaotong University, Influence of Silicon Content on High Temperature Oxidation Resistance of Aluminum Silicon Hot Dip Coating, 2014, 35 (9)

Research on Reliability State Monitoring Method of Power Distribution System Based on Machine Vision

Long Ling [1], Jingde Huang[1,2]

[1)] College of Mechanical Engineering, Zhuhai College of Science and Technology, Zhuhai, 519041

[2)] Guangdong Intelligent Vision Precision Detection Engineering Technology Research Center, Zhuhai, 519041

Email:444969647@qq.com TEL:15812749592

***Abstract*—Based on the "Made in China 2025" develop ment strategy, machine vision technology has been widel y used in unmanned driving, industrial testing, and med ical image analysis. Power system is still widely used at present stage human labor, there is a big security hidde n danger, machine vision system has high definition, obs ervation speed, strong adaptability to environment and can work for a long time, and can effectively reduce the human errors and the corresponding labor cost, so the f uture vision technology development will be more impor tant in the related fields of power system. Firstly, this p aper analyzes the machine vision technology. Then sum marize the abnormal operation and hidden trouble of tr ansformer in distribution system. Research by the mach ine vision technology to the common problems in power distribution system for monitoring and detection, accord ing to the development software has powerful picture processing ability, complete the real-time identification of monitoring objects, realize the automatic feature extraction of abnormal situations, and equipped with feedback alarm function, to solve the key problems of human operation safety risks in the power distribution system, laying a strong foundation for the intelligent development of the power distribution system.To achieve a faster, more accurate, more intelligent, more secure power distribution system operation goals.**

***Keywords*—Machine vision, Power distribution systems, Security hazards.**

I. Introduction

In recent years, with the continuous development of science and technology and the continuous breakthrough in the field of artificial intelligence, machine vision technology is an automation technology that implements detection and monitoring in a non-contact manner, with the advantages of safety and reliability, high precision, and long-term work[1], which is an effective way to achieve automation and intelligence, and has been practically applied in the automotive industry, 3C electronics, agriculture, building materials and food safety. For example, the Federal University of Polis in Brazil applies deep learning methods to crop irrigation, and its main goal is to develop an embedded system for selective spraying in cotton and soybean crops, classify and detect in real time using deep learning algorithms, and test sensitivity and accuracy to meet real needs [2]. Xu Jiancong[3] of Qilu University of Technology proposed a machine parts processing accuracy detection method based on dynamic registration of image and graphics based on machine vision technology, and carried out test inspection and detection data analysis on the feasibility of the detection method, and the data showed that it had a good detection effect. Xu Weiliang[4] of Guangdong University of Technology and others used binocular vision technology to drive industrial robots to grasp and study stamped auto parts, proposed an algorithm for SGBM+ improved RANSAC, realized the three-dimensional matching from coarse to fine two-step screening method, and verified the real-time and accuracy of the algorithm, and finally obtained the three-dimensional information of the workpiece through the parallax method. The ICP point cloud registration algorithm is then used to perform the final pose estimation to complete the identification and positioning work.

Nowadays, people are enjoying the benefits brought by "electricity" all the time, and at the same time, "electricity" also threatens the safety of people's lives and property. At present, the monitoring and detection of potential safety hazards in the power grid distribution system is still widely used by human labor, and there is a greater risk. Therefore, it is now necessary to conform to the pace of the development of the times, innovate detection methods, and introduce machine vision technology in the reliability status monitoring and detection industry of the power grid distribution system in the future, and use the characteristics of the visual system with fast detection speed, strong adaptability to the monitoring environment, and long-term work, which can effectively reduce the rate of human error, and also save the corresponding labor costs to ensure the safety of people's work and life.

II. MACHINE VISION SYSTEM

A. Principles and composition of machine vision system

Machine vision is the use of machines instead of the human eye to measure and analyze target objects. First of all, the image acquisition of the target is carried out by the industrial camera, and then the data processing is carried out by using computer technology, and then the comparative analysis is completed to complete the judgment, and finally the desired purpose is achieved [1]. For machine vision systems, the basic theories of image processing technology, image understanding and pattern recognition technology used are consistent. This paper mainly uses the machine vision system to automatically monitor and detect the reliability status of the power distribution system of the power grid, and find abnormal and unsafe working conditions in a timely manner, and is equipped with feedback alarm function to solve the key problem of human operation safety hazards in the power distribution system and avoid greater losses; At the same time, it will also reduce the error rate of human work and the corresponding labor costs. The overall structural design flow of the system is shown in Fig.1.

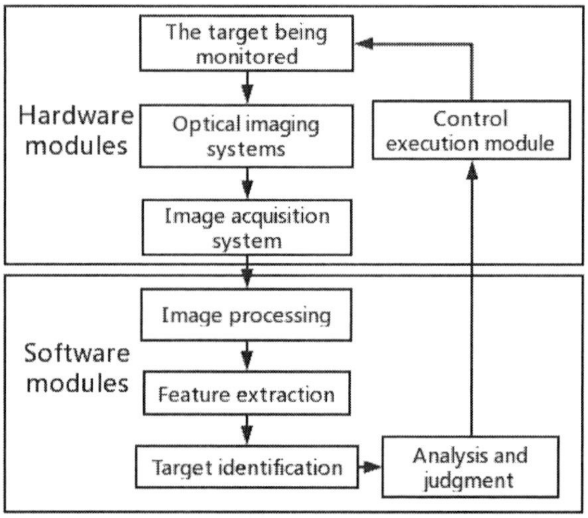

Fig. 1. Schematic diagram of the overall system structure.

B. Machine vision system advantages

The application of machine vision systems in the field of real-time inspection has the following advantages over human eye inspection:

1) Strong resolution between grayscale and space. The human eye can only distinguish 64 gray levels, while machine vision technology can distinguish 256 gray levels [5], which has stronger resolution capabilities. Spatially, machine vision systems can have a variety of configurations for optical lenses, reaching micron-level observation capabilities that the human eye cannot.

2) Faster detection speed. The machine vision system can capture the target image beyond the speed of the human eye capture speed through the hardware device of the system, and the human eye has a visual stay of 0.1s.

3) Strong environmental adaptability. The use of certain protective measures for machine vision systems can be applied to high temperature, high pressure and even toxic and harmful working environments that are not suitable for human detection.

4) Can work for a long time. People work for a long time to easily cause visual fatigue, so that the accuracy of detection cannot be guaranteed; This problem can be avoided by using a machine vision system, which can always maintain a highly concentrated working state and achieve long-term monitoring.

III. RESEARCH ON THE RELIABILITY STATUS MONITORING TECHNOLOGY OF POWER GRID DISTRIBUTION SYSTEM

The system used in the grid system from the step-down or high-voltage distribution substation outlet to the user is called the power distribution system. It is usually a grid system consisting of a variety of distribution equipment components and facilities, which converts the voltage and distributes electrical energy directly to the end user [6].

A. Common fault analysis of power distribution system

In the power grid distribution system, the safe operation and management of the transformer is the key content, through the abnormal operation of the transformer, the experience of common fault analysis is summarized, it will be conducive to timely and accurate judgment of the cause of the fault and the type of fault, and take effective measures to ensure the safe operation of the entire power grid system equipment [7]. According to the relevant management regulations, the power distribution system of the power grid must regularly carry out the troubleshooting of hidden dangers of failure, so as to timely understand and grasp the operating status of the distribution system, and strive to eliminate the early hidden dangers in the bud. Common abnormal operating conditions and safety hazards for power distribution systems are as follows:

1) Under normal load or cooling state, the transformer has a continuous increase in oil temperature.

2) The color of the insulating oil on the transformer changes significantly.

3) The explosion-proof pipe in the distribution system is injected with oil.

4) The occurrence of three-phase voltage imbalance and relay protection action.

5) The insulated porcelain casing appears to fall and explode.

6) The tap changer, line and connection point failure.

Among the above common fault situations, at present, more rely on on-site verification equipment and facilities or non-visual output equipment to complete fault detection, resulting in a large number of human and financial costs, and there are certain safety hazards in human work, so it is imperative to apply machine vision technology for fault identification in the future.

B. Implementation process of reliability state monitoring technology of power distribution system

At this stage, machine vision technology not only realizes workpiece recognition, but also realizes complex face recognition. The common faults of the power distribution system are mainly concentrated in the detection of transformers, lines and insulators [8], and the characteristic parameters of the image can be adjusted to obtain the place where the texture and color in the image have changed to a certain extent, so as to analyze the characteristics of each fault type [9], and realize the automatic identification of fault problems and types through machine vision technology. Therefore, it is feasible to apply machine vision technology to the fault hazard monitoring of power distribution systems in the grid. By mastering the characteristic parameters of the distribution system after the circuit, pointer, connection terminal and different target edges are processed, the image details collected are compared and analyzed, and the corresponding alarm system is set to feedback the abnormal operation in time, which will make it easier for the distribution system to monitor the safety hazards. The system mainly includes image input part, image processing part, analysis and judgment part and result output part.

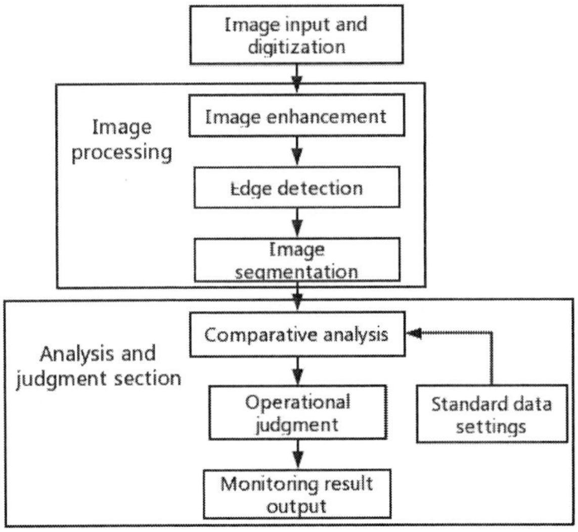

Fig. 2. Implementation process of the reliability state monitoring system of the power grid distribution system.

As can be seen from Fig.2, the image acquisition of the monitoring target is carried out by using the installed camera, and the image is input to the image processing part through digital conversion, and the relevant parameters are first adjusted to achieve image enhancement operations, so that the outline of the image is clearer and the details are better highlighted.Edge detection is then performed to identify objects such as circuits, electrical equipment, pointer tables, and connection points, and to complete image segmentation. Finally, the segmented image data is compared and analyzed with the standard data set in the system to determine whether there are security risks at this time, and the final result is visualized and output relevant information.

C. Comparative analysis of the system development software

As a monitoring and detection system, its software part should pay more attention to the ability of image processing, the more powerful the image processing capability, the more accurate the identification of the state of security risks. At present, there are many software suitable for the development of machine vision systems, and the more popular and widely used ones are Python, Halcon, Opencv and so on. Among them, Python is easy to learn, fast for beginners, and easy to maintain, at this stage in the artificial intelligence application more, its image processing capabilities are equally powerful; Halcon has a set of standard and perfect machine vision algorithm library and a large number of routine programs, has a powerful visual integration development environment, including various types of filtering algorithms, color analysis, image geometry transformation, morphological calculation analysis and other basic image processing functions. Although each type of software has its own characteristics in system development and plays an irreplaceable role in different application areas; However, in order to better carry out the research on the reliability status monitoring technology of the safety hazard of the power distribution system of the power grid, the use of Halcon software for the development of the machine vision system will be more suitable.

IV. Conclusion

Under the favorable environment of the country's strong support for the field of artificial intelligence and the continuous research of the majority of researchers in the industry, machine vision technology will also be applied to various industries, including preventive diagnosis and pathology prediction from unmanned driving to biomedicine. Then in the future power system, the same can be mature machine vision technology into it, this paper on the power grid distribution system safety hazard reliability status monitoring technology is analyzed, with certain feasibility, the future and then combined with robot technology, can be through the industrial robot to replace humans to find and eliminate safety hazards.

Acknowledgment

This paper is supported by Key Special Foundation of universities in Guangdong Province (2020zdzx2032) .

References

[1] Hua Huang, Haibo Teng, Yifu Liu, Yan Xu, Jigang Chen. Research on the Application of Machine Vision

Technology in the Automotive Manufacturing Industry [J]. Automotive Technology and Materials, 2022 (06): 8-15.

[2] Sabia,Hederson de S,Silveira A D O,et al.REAL-TIME Selective Spraying for Viola Rope Control in Soybean and Cotton Crops Using Deep Learning[J].Scientific Paper, Special Issue: Artificial Inteligence • Eng. agríc. 42 (spe),2022.

[3] Jiancong Xu. Research on Processing Precision Detection Method of Mechanical Parts Based on Machine Vision [D]. Qilu University of Technology, 2020.

[4] Weiliang Xu. Research on the Binocular Visual Industrial Robot Picking System for Stamping Auto Parts [D]. Guangdong University of Technology, 2020.

[5] Xu Zhang. Research on Electrical Safety Hidden Risk Detection Based on Machine Vision [J]. Petroleum and petrochemical energy saving, 2019,9 (06): 11-13 + 7.

[6] Ning Zhang. Enterprise high and low voltage distribution network electrical energy saving new technology [J]. Shandong Industrial Technology, 2019 (07): 178.

[7] Yunlei Yang, Da Lei, Hao Wang. Review of the reliability assessment methods of power distribution system [J]. Shanxi Electric Power, 2020 (06): 1-4.

[8] Rahman E U , Zhang Y , Ahmad S , et al. Autonomous Vision-Based Primary Distribution Systems Porcelain Insulators Inspection Using UAVs[J]. Sensors, 2021, 21(3):974.

[9] Yanpin Mei. Research Based on the Image Edge Detection Algorithm in Python Language [J]. Science and Technology Innovation, 2017 (31): 123-124.

Arc Extinguishing Analysis of High Speed Photography Synchronous Molded Case Circuit Breaker

Haiyu Wu

Delixi Electric Co., Ltd, Shanghai, 201803
Email: haiyu01.wu@delixi-electric.com TEL: 13816775893

Abstract— **Moulded case circuit breaker is a kind of low voltage electrical apparatus. The arc extinguishing of MCCB is completed by release, arc extinguishing chamber, magnetic blowing and air blowing. High speed photography synchronous MCCB technology can help to study MCCB arc extinguishing. This paper introduces its principle, connection scheme and image integration.**

Keywords— **molded case circuit breaker; high speed photography; arc extinguishing**

I. INTRODUCTION

As the basic component of many industries, low-voltage electrical appliances are also an important embodiment of China's industrial level. Traditional low-voltage electrical appliances can be divided into three categories: power distribution, control and terminal. Among them, the distribution class low-voltage electrical appliances can be divided into circuit breakers, disconnectors, dual power transfer switches, and fuses. The quality of low-voltage electrical products directly affects the safety and reliable operation of electricity in various industries in China.

In this paper, the arc firing and high-speed photography techniques of power distribution low-voltage plastic case circuit breakers (hereinafter referred to as "plastic shell circuit breakers") are analyzed and discussed during the short circuit test.

There are many kinds of molded case circuit breaker structures, but they generally have two basic characteristic parts: the feeling part and the executive part. The feeling part is to receive external signals and issue action commands. The execution part is to complete the switching action of the circuit according to the instructions issued by the sensory part. For example, the operating mechanism of the circuit breaker is to link the two parts of feeling and execution, coordinate and act according to the control requirements. Circuit breaker in the tripping and closing action there is a conversion of electrical, thermal, magnetic, mechanical and other energy, transient energy conversion often has non-linear technical data, making theoretical analysis and research and development complicated. At present, in addition to the use of simulation and theoretical derivation, the research and development of new products of molded case circuit breakers must also undergo the analysis of a large number of test data. Especially in the high short-circuit current breaking, the analysis of the limit breaking capacity can still not completely get rid of the combination of simulation, theoretical derivation and experimental verification. In addition to the housing and base, the body structure of this type of product is a contact arc extinguishing part, an operating mechanism and a tripping system. The main function is to detect the fault signal in time and make a rapid disconnection circuit action when the power system line fails, so as to ensure the safety and reliability of the line.[1]

II. ELECTRIC ARC

Arc as a plasma, consists of a mixture of ions, electrons and neutral ions, conducting electricity mainly through free electrons. When the low-voltage circuit breaker passes through a large short-circuit current, the tripper moves and instantly drives the action mechanism, so that the dynamic and static contacts are separated after being subjected to the action force of the mechanism or the electric repulsion force. The arc is generated between moving and static contacts and gradually elongated and amplified. The characteristics of the arc are closely related to the material of the moving and static contacts. The arc is gradually moved to the arc extinguishing chamber under the influence of magnetic blowing, air blowing, and near-cathode effect, and finally the arc is cooled and extinguished in the arc extinguishing grid.

The existing plastic shell circuit breaker is mainly based on magnetic blowing, air blowing, and conducting arc extinguishing for arc cooling, driving, and arc extinguishing of magnetic blowing, air blowing, and conductive grid sheets in the GB/T14048.2-2020 standard, such as rated short-circuit breaking (Ics), rated limit short circuit breaking (Icu), unipolar (Isu), and IT system circuit breaker (Iit).[2]Since the short-circuit arc voltage is not a mathematical function of the system voltage or circuit voltage of the test equipment, it contains many factors such as the input energy required to maintain the arc, the material properties of the contact, the radius of the arc and so on. Therefore, the following is a brief discussion of arc columns, magnetic blowing, and air blowing.

As shown in Figure 1, the electron overflow in the electrode material is caused by the high electric field between the contacts of the circuit breaker to produce electric field ionization. After the overflow of the electric field ionization of the charged particles in the bombardment of the charged particles on the other side of the electrode, causing another ionization, when a large number of electrons overflow quickly to the other side of the contact, in the process of penetrating the air between the contacts, the gas ionization, gasification at the same time to produce radiation and heat. Therefore, in the gap between the contacts, the chain reaction of the bombardment overflow came into being a special structure - electron collapse, when the electron collapse accumulates to a certain extent and is connected end to end between the contacts to form an arc column. When the current between the contacts is greater, the more intense the combustion of charged particles between the arc columns, and the higher the temperature. At this time, it is imperative to cool down the arc and extinguish the arc.

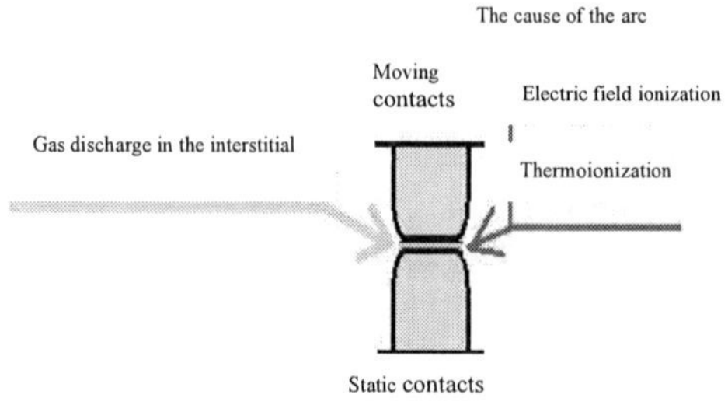

Fig. 1 Generation of arc columns

A. Tripping structure of molded shell circuit breaker

The molded case circuit breaker structure is composed of sensing elements, tripping actuators, transmission element and accessories. Plastic shell circuit breaker sensing elements are commonly used thermal magnetic trippers. Trip actuators include bimetal sheet overload tripping and electromagnet instantaneous tripping. The following is a brief explanation of the tripping element.

B. Bimetal sheet overload tripping

Bimetallic sheets are overload tripping that performs tripping when there is an overload current in the circuit breaker. Due to the bending of the bimetallic sheet by heat, it will move the operating mechanism to trip after overheating.

This article deals primarily with short-circuit tripping and is not discussed in this section.

C. Electromagnet instantaneous tripping

An electromagnet is an instantaneous trip that performs a tripping action when there is a short-circuit current in the circuit breaker. The electromagnet is absorbed by the short-circuit current, so that the operating mechanism is tripped.

Electromagnets can be divided into solenoid type and snap type. The main difference between solenoid and snap-on trippers is the principle of instantaneous tripping.As shown in Figures 2 to 3, it is a schematic diagram of the overall and explosion of solenoid and snap-on trippers.

The instantaneous tripper of the snap-on tripper is the armature (part No. 1 in Figure 3) on the side of the main loop, and when the instantaneous current passes through the main loop, the armature is inducted by the current, rotating and the yoke (part No. 2 in Figure 3) suction, moving the towbar (part No. 6 in Figure 3). Small-sized products (below 100A) are usually not suitable due to insufficient magnetic force.[3]

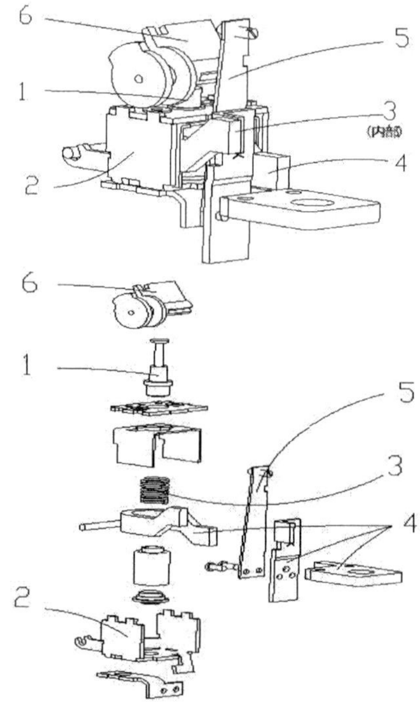

Fig. 2 Schematic diagram of the overall and explosion of the solenoid thermomagnetic tripper

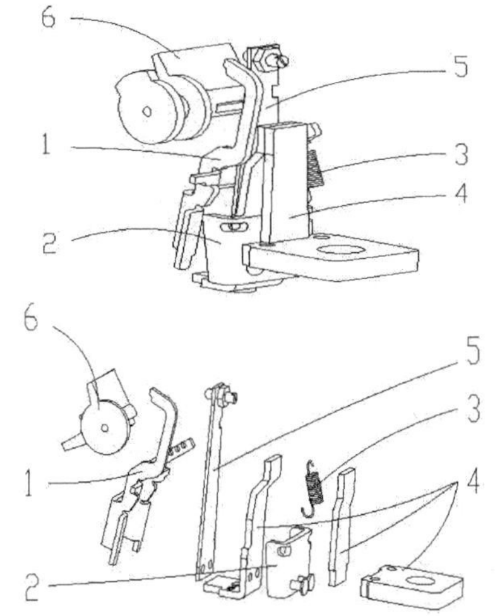

Fig. 3 Schematic diagram of the overall and explosion of the snap-on thermomagnetic tripper

Pictured: 1-armature (moving iron core); 2—Magnetic yoke (static iron core); 3—Reaction spring; 4—Copper coupling plate; 5—Bimetallic sheet; 6—The towbar on the operating mechanism.The instantaneous tripper of the solenoid tripper is a doppelgäpped copper coil (left part No. 4 in Figure 2) around the rod articulation (Part No. 1 in Figure 2), and when there is an instantaneous current passing through the main loop, the armature moves downward under the action of current induction, and the yoke (Part No. 2 in Figure 2) is absorbed to impress the towbar (Part No. 6 in Figure 3). Small size products (below 80A) can increase the magnetic force by increasing the number of copper coil turns.

III. ARC EXTINGUISHING SYSTEM OF MOLDED CASE CIRCUIT BREAKER

A. Arc extinguishing grid piece

Whether in AC or DC, the arc extinguishing gate needs to be extinguished by relying on the arc extinguishing gate to split the arc voltage jump.The arc voltage formula is:

$$U_{arcm} - U_1 = (n+1)\Delta U \qquad (1)$$

where:

U_{arcm} ——Peak arc voltage after arcing into the gate;

U_1 ——Arc column pressure drop;

n ——Number of grids,The split arc is $n+1$;

ΔU ——Interpolar pressure drop.

When the arc is introduced into the arc extinguishing chamber composed of the arc extinguishing gate, the sudden increase in the arc voltage can most effectively limit the short-circuit current and extinguish the arc for the circuit breaker.

B. Magnetic blowing

The way of arc blowing is generally divided into split air blowing and magnetic blowing. Magnetic blowing is self-excitedGenerated by a magnetic field, which produces a Lorentz force on the arc:

$$F = q(E + vB) \qquad (2)$$

$$F = \frac{\mu_0}{4\pi} I^2 \ln\frac{R}{r}$$

where: F ——Lorentz Force;

q ——The amount of charge of charged particles;

E ——Electric field strength;

v ——The speed of charged particles;

B ——Magnetic induction.

The Lorentz force cools and drives the arc into the gate of the arc extinguishing chamber, while increasing the electric repulsion of the moving contact after repulsion according to the left-handed spiral rule. The moving contact repulsion also contains the Home force, as shown in Figure 4:

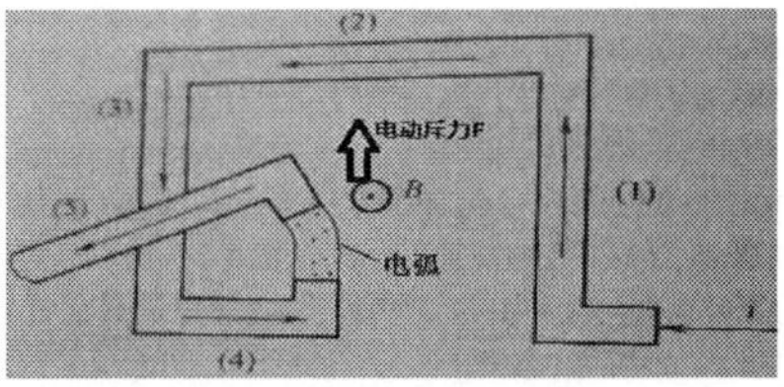

Fig. 4 Generation of the Home Force

Assuming that this switch is a 1P+ N switch, and the current magnitude in the two contacts conductive rods is equal in the opposite direction, and its cross-sectional coefficient is taken to 1.2, the length of the conductive rod of a switch contact is 50mm, and the center distance is 20mm.The cross-section of the conductive rod is rectangular, with a width of 8mm and a thickness of 5mm.If this conductive rod flows through 800A and electrical dynamics between conductors,According to Biosafar's law

Electric power is available;If the contact equivalent radius R is 4mm and the contact equivalent radius is 0.2mm, if the current flowing through the contact is 800A and the pressure of the contact is 30N, the repulsion force generated between the contact electrodes can be calculated:

$$\begin{aligned} F &= \frac{\mu_0}{4\pi} I_1 I_2 \frac{2L}{d} K_c \\ &= 10^{-7} \times 800^2 \times \frac{2\times 50\times 10^{-3}}{20\times 10^{-3}} \times 1.2 \\ &= 384\times 10^{-3} N \end{aligned} \qquad (3)$$

（Such as short circuit 50kA conversion）

$$= 10^{-7} \times \left(50 \times 10^{3}\right)^{2} \times \frac{2 \times 50 \times 10^{-3}}{20 \times 10^{-3}} \times 1.2$$

$$= 1500N$$

However, in the actual short circuit process, there are often many uncertain factors such as molded case circuit breaker structure, contacts, and current limiting, so the above assumptions still need to be supported by simulation analysis. (Systems of integral equations, normal distributions and sine waves superimposed on each other) are not discussed here.

Calculated according to the Home Force:

(4)

Set the contact equivalence R to 4mm and the contact equivalence radius to 0.2mm, if the current flowing through the contact is 100A and the pressure of the contact is 30N, the contact repulsion is calculated:

From the above calculation, it can be seen that the contact system has a contact repulsion phenomenon. When the short-circuit current passes through the contact system, a huge electrical force is generated. The molded case circuit breaker uses this force to quickly repel the contact system to achieve the purpose of limiting the flow and disconnection.

C. *Air blowing*

Nowadays, most of the plastic shell circuit breakers are equipped with gas-producing materials in the arc extinguishing chamber, such as PA2010 materials that produce a large amount of gas in the case of high temperature erosion by the arc,It promotes the increase of air pressure in the arc extinguishing chamber, drives the arc cooling into the arc extinguishing chamber, and forms an indefinite amount of air blowing [4]. Since the arc extinguishing chamber has an outlet, the incremental detection of the outlet pressure has become an important indicator of air blowing force analysis. Industry technology in the monitoring of arc extinguishing chamber temperature and gas pressure changes by the R & D costs of control, different grades of materials in the limited space after the temperature change rate test cost is high, the final R & D material selection to reverse material analysis as the main technical breakthrough. In the assessment of the current limiting capacity of the molded shell circuit breaker, after the material analysis and selection of the R&D products made of the corresponding material grades, due to many uncertainties such as arc, structure, contacts and so on. In the short-circuit test, it is easy to appear shell fragmentation, arc extinguishing chamber penetration, mask flying out and other phenomena (see Figure 5). Therefore, high-speed photography and outlet pressure monitoring have become the only choice.

Fig. 5 Various phenomena in short-circuit tests

IV. HIGH SPEED PHOTOGRAPHY SYNCHRONIZATION TECHNOLOGY

At present, the non-contact method is used for the measurement of arc arc columns. The non-contact method is mainly optical measurement, and optical measurement is divided into high-speed camera and two-dimensional optical fiber imaging technology. The breaking performance of the molded case circuit breaker depends to a large extent on the trajectory of the arc in the arc extinguishing chamber during the breaking process, such as: whether the arc column can smoothly enter the arc extinguishing chamber and be divided by the arc extinguishing grid, whether the divided arc column breaks through the arc extinguishing chamber, the bounce of the contacts after the arc current crosses zero, and other reasons that cause the arc column to rekindle again.

A. *Principles of high-speed camera technology*

High-speed camera technology mainly uses the action of the contact of the high-speed camera shooting mechanism and the movement of the arc, and cooperates with the current and voltage waveform collected by the original test equipment in the short-circuit test process to synchronously analyze the short-circuit arc, arc extinguishing and bouncing of the molded case circuit breaker. It provides important technical support for the research and development of arc extinguishing chamber, contacts and moving mechanisms of molded shell circuit breakers. However, high-speed photography also has shortcomings, in the process of experimental shooting, due to the surface of the camera equipment shooting, it is impossible to show the condition of the arc column in the test at the same time. Secondly, the molded shell circuit breaker shell frame and cover materials are mostly colored

PA66 and thermosetting DMC materials, and the arc is shielded by the colored material after the sample is fired in the short circuit test, and the arc column form is not easy to be captured by the camera. Therefore, in the R & D test, it is often necessary to customize the translucent, transparent material shell specimen with the dark filter lens of the camera equipment to remove the stray light generated by the short-circuit arc during the camera process before the true form of the arc can be revealed.

B. High-speed camera supporting test equipment synchronization technology

1) Implementation method

Schematic of a TTL pulse signal that is emitted at the same time as the current waveform is acquired. The trigger mode of the original short-circuit test system is the software program control trigger, and the data acquisition method is to first configure the sampling points and sampling rate of each sampling channel, and then close the gate with a thyristor or universal circuit breaker, and read the current and voltage waveform after completing the closing action.

The current and voltage waveforms can be collected by means of analog acquisition triggered by the digital quantity of the board, as shown in Figure 6, a TTL pulse signal is issued at the same time as the current and voltage waveforms are started, triggering the high-speed camera.

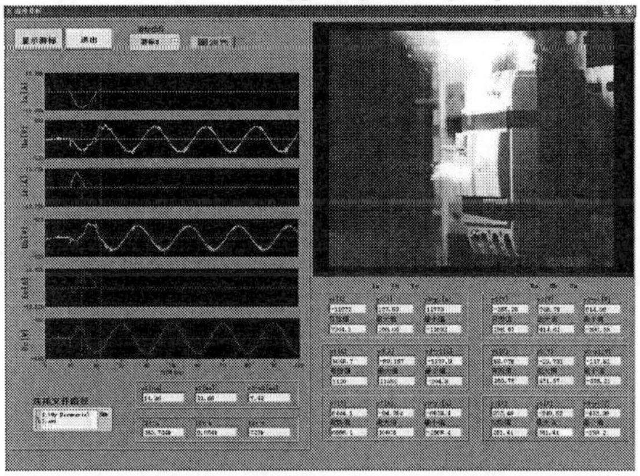

Fig. 6 Acquisition of current and voltage waveforms

At the moment when the high-speed camera is triggered, there is no current in the loop, and after about 50ms of time, the circuit breaker closes the brake, and the loop generates a current.High-speed photography shoots at a speed of 6400 PPS, and the action images of the mechanism begin to appear in the range of 300-340 frames.

2) Connection implementation

As shown in Figure 7, a schematic diagram of a hardware device connection triggered by high-speed photography synchronization.

3) Image integration

Run an EXE type application via Labview and then operate the software of the high-speed camera as a standalone application, such as setting acquisition parameters before triggering. In Labview, tune in to Windows Media Player and play video from a high-speed camera. First call into the Active X container, then into the container into Windows Media Player. As shown in Figure 8, in order to synchronize the acquired current waveform with the video image captured by the high-speed camera, the timeline of the waveform graph and the timeline of the video image need to be processed one-to-one. Taking the waveform within 50ms as an example, the shooting frequency of the high-speed camera is 6400pps, then the number of video images taken within 50ms is 320 frames, and the timeline of the waveform chart is expanded by 6.4 times, and the synchronous display function can be realized in the process of moving the cursor of the waveform chart.

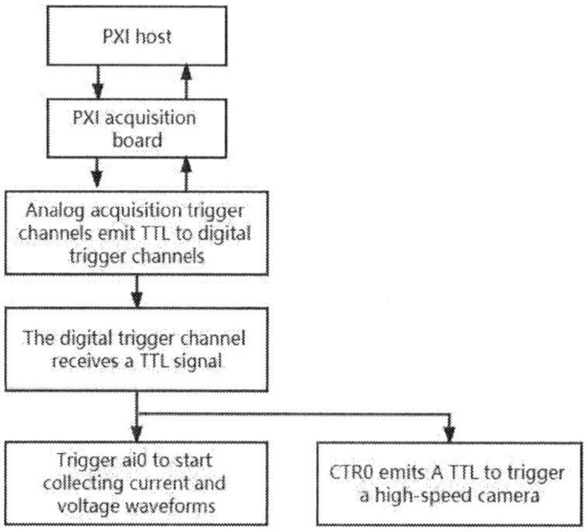

Fig. 7 Schematic diagram of hardware device connection triggered by high-speed photography synchronization

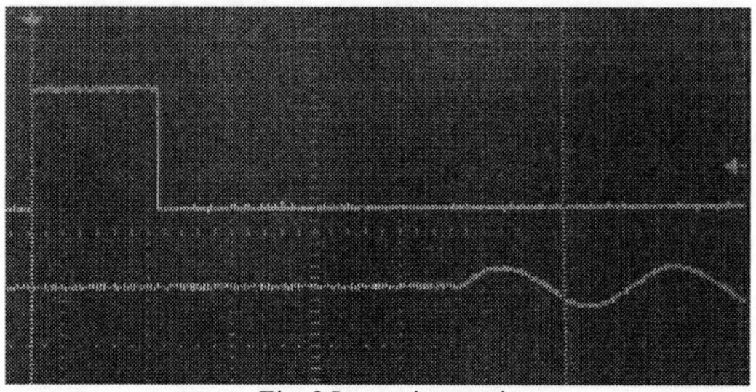

Fig. 8 Image integration

V. CONCLUSION

After the development of 4 generations of low-voltage electrical products, the performance and function of molded case circuit breakers in China have been greatly improved.With the rapid development of electronic technology, automation technology and communication technology, a wide variety of electronic products with rapid response are widely used in molded case circuit breakers. The new generation of molded case circuit breakers has gradually changed from the original mechanical to intelligent. In addition to detecting voltage and current signals, intelligent molded case circuit breakers also extend functions such as time-lapse tripping, ground protection, area interlocking, temperature warning, intelligent detection, and communication. Although the number of functions has increased, the products are moving towards miniaturization and high performance. The internal space of the circuit breaker is gradually compressed, and while reducing the cost and saving material, the performance indicators must adapt to most industrial use occasions. Under this trend, short circuit breaking and product arc extinguishing ability have become a non-negligible link in product research and development, and it is also an indispensable performance indicator.

REFERENCES

[1] Jianguo Lu, Ruihua He, Degui Chen, etc. China Electrical Engineering Dictionary Vol.11 Distribution Engineering[M] . Beijing: China Electric Power Press, 2009

[2] GB14048.2-2008 Low voltage switchgear and controlgear Part 2: Circuit breakers [S]

[3] Fei Din, Guping Jiang. Comparative analysis of magnetic release of DC molded case circuit breaker [J]. Modern building electricity 2020, (9) : 51-54.

[4] Shunping Jiang, Xiaoli Li, Rongwei Zhou. The design of DC1500V PV molded case circuit breaker [J]. Management technology of Electrical appliances and energy efficiency, 2017, (10) : 44-48.

8th International Conference on Reliability of Electrical Products and Electrical Contacts, November 18-20, 2022

Anti Drop Design and Optimization Analysis of Moving Contact of Molded Case Circuit Breaker

Xiankai Li, Yaokun Lin

Shanghai Liangxin Electric Co. Ltd, Shanghai, 201315, China
Email:lixiankai@sh-liangxin.com TEL: 13392940637

Abstract— **This paper briefly describes the design points of the anti falling structure of the moving contact of the molded case circuit breaker. Through the simulation analysis of the anti drop structure of the moving contact, the design is optimized, and the breaking test is used to verify the design optimization results. Finally, the anti drop failure phenomenon of the moving contact is improved, the breaking time is accelerated, and the breaking performance of the product is improved.**

Keywords— **molded case circuit breaker; Fall prevention; Simulation analysis; Breaking performance**

I. INTRODUCTION

The closing and opening action of the contact of the circuit breaker is completed by the cooperation of electrical and mechanical mechanisms. In the mechanical structure, the free tripping mechanism is the key to realize the connection between the transmission mechanism and the contact system. As we all know, the single pole or multi pole of the existing circuit breaker has certain protection, such as overcurrent tripping device, which is mainly used as electromagnetic tripping device for short-circuit protection of the line and thermal tripping device for overload protection. However, when using this traditional tripping method to realize the protection of short-circuit high current, this method takes too long. At present, most of the industry has begun to use the high-voltage gas energy tripping mode formed by the contact breaking short-circuit current to realize the performance requirements of the circuit breaker fast tripping. This scheme solves the problem of fast tripping well, but there are also problems that the structural design is very complex and inconvenient for manufacturing and assembly. In order to overcome the defects of the existing technology and ensure the breaking capacity, it is necessary to improve the current limiting capacity of the contact system in the opening / tripping process, so as to speed up the breaking speed of the moving contact. Therefore, the current limiting contact structure is widely used in circuit breakers. However, the repulsion force of the contact of the current limiting contact structure depends on the current between the contacts. When the current value increases to a certain value, the dynamic and static contacts begin to repulse under the action of the loop electrodynamic force and the Hom force at the same time. At this time, the rapid increase of the resistance between the contacts and the periodic change of the AC current will cause the current flowing between the contacts to decay to a situation where the electrodynamic force is less than the repulsion force between the dynamic and static contacts before the circuit breaker is disconnected, At this time, if the circuit breaker does not have an anti drop device or the device does not work, the previously rejected moving contact will move from the rejected position to the closed position with the reduction of electric power, which will cause the so-called contact drop phenomenon. When the contact drop is serious, the arc will rekindle and the fault current cannot be disconnected, causing the contact to burn out, and even more serious consequences. Therefore, to solve the problem of the falling of the moving contact in the breaking process of the circuit breaker and realize rapid breaking has always been the focus of electrical engineers.

This paper will use the motion simulation module of the dynamic simulation software UG to simulate and analyze the dynamic characteristic process of the circuit breaker operating system, complete the dynamic simulation and analysis of the motion process, optimize the anti drop structure of the moving contact, verify the optimization design results with the breaking test, and summarize the effective measures to improve the breaking, which can provide reference for the design of the anti drop mechanism of the contact system of the molded case circuit breaker Improve the efficiency of design and development.

II. CAUSE ANALYSIS OF MOVING CONTACT DROP OF CIRCUIT BREAKER

A. A working principle of circuit breaker

The circuit breaker is mainly composed of operating mechanism, arc extinguishing system, contact system, tripping system and shell. This paper studies the problem of moving contact falling prevention, mainly discussing the operating system, including the operating mechanism and contact system.

The operating system of the circuit breaker is composed of transmission mechanism, rotating shaft, lock catch and traction rod. The contact system is composed of rotating shaft, moving contact and contact spring (compression spring). The action state of the operating system is divided into: opening / re tripping, closing and free tripping. The action state of the contact system is divided into: opening, closing, repulsion, blocking and tripping. The schematic diagram of the mechanism at the opening / re buckle position is shown in Figure 1; The mechanism diagram in the closing position is shown in Figure 2; The mechanism diagram in free tripping position is shown in Figure 3.

In the following three state diagrams, l is the handle, t is the skip, M is the lock, K is the moving contact, e is the main tension spring (tension spring), D is the rotating shaft, P is the contact pressure spring (compression spring), q is the pressing plate, CB is the upper connecting rod, Ba is the lower connecting rod, ao3 is the rotating arm of the rotating shaft, and G is the spring hanging point of the main tension spring when the lever is closed. The opening and closing process of the products in Figures 1 and 2 is the movement of the four-bar mechanism. When the end h of the jump buckle t is buckled by the lock m, the jump buckle t cannot rotate, the point C is temporarily fixed, and the component cb-ba-ao3-o3c forms a group of planar four-bar mechanisms. At this time, the operating handle l drives the spring E. once it exceeds the upper connecting rod BC, the point B starts to move under the action of the spring force, and the lower connecting rod Ba drives the contact system to close or open quickly; Figure 3 the tripping process of the product is the movement process of the four-bar to five bar mechanism. When the short-circuit large current passes, the tripper drives the latch m to disengage from the trip T. under the tension of the main tension spring e, the trip t rotates counterclockwise around the rotation axis O1, point C becomes the active point, the contact system is quickly lifted up and disconnected under the action of spring force, the moving contact is separated from the static contact, and the mechanism realizes free tripping, The five connecting rod after tripping is composed of component o1c -cb-ba-ao3- O3 O1[1-3].

The anti drop structure of moving contact commonly used in the industry is shown in Figure 4. The principle of the anti drop structure of the moving contact commonly used in the industry: under the normal closing / opening / tripping condition of the product, the moving contact receives the pressure FC of the contact spring P, and the contact spring provides a counterclockwise torque relative to the contact rotation axis O3 to ensure the closing pressure of the contact; The product is in the closing state. When the current value between the dynamic and static contacts increases to a certain value, the Hom force and Lorentz force between the dynamic and static contacts begin to repel against the contact pressure FC. When the dynamic contact repels and rotates to a certain angle, the contact spring P provides the pressure FP to the dynamic contact through the pressing plate Q. the torque generated by FP is clockwise, so that the dynamic contact remains in the repelling position without falling before the mechanism is unlocked.

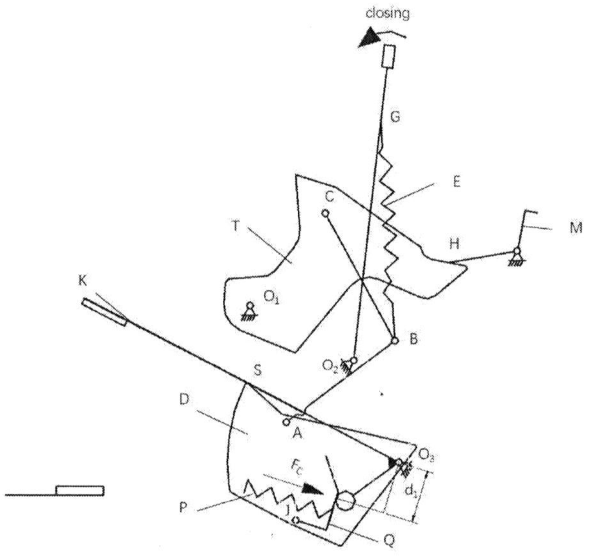

Fig. 1. Schematic diagram of mechanism when opening / retouching.

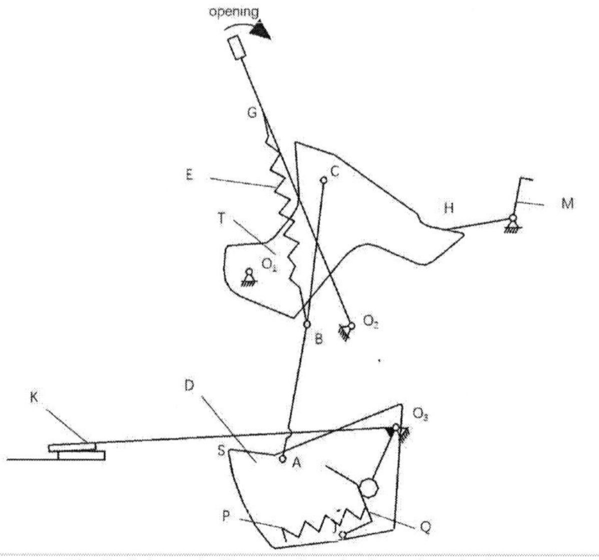

Fig. 2. Schematic diagram of mechanism when closing.

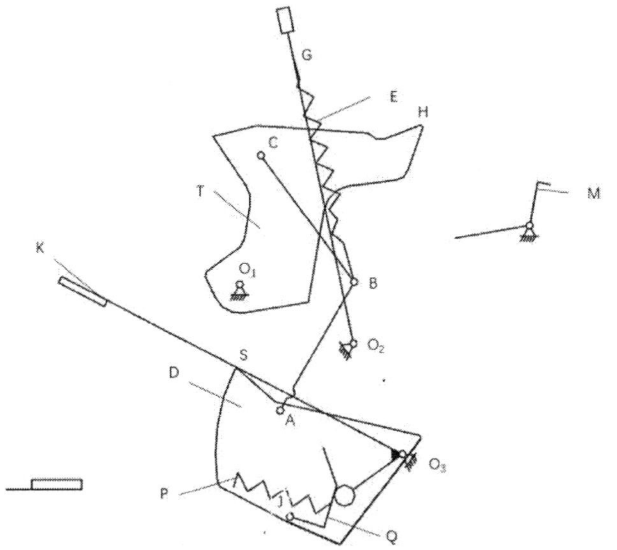

Fig. 3. Schematic diagram of mechanism when mechanism trips.

B. cause analysis of breaking and falling of moving contact of circuit breaker

During the breaking process of the dynamic and static contacts, when the current value between the dynamic and static contacts increases to a certain value, the dynamic and static contacts overcome the contact pressure FC and begin to repel under the simultaneous action of the loop electrodynamic force and the Hom force. At this time, the rapid increase of the resistance between the contacts and the periodic change of the AC current will cause the current flowing between the contacts before the circuit breaker is opened to decay to a situation where the electrodynamic force is less than the contact pressure FC between the dynamic and static contacts, At this time, if the circuit breaker does not have an anti drop device or the device does not work, the previously rejected moving contact will move from the rejected position to the closed position with the reduction of electric power, which will cause the so-called contact drop phenomenon. When the contact drop is serious, the arc will rekindle, causing the contact to burn out, thereby reducing the breaking performance. However, as shown in Figure 4, for the moving contact anti drop structure commonly used in the industry, after the tripping t of the mechanism is released, the mechanism is converted from four connecting rods to five connecting rods, and the tensile length of the main tension spring e is correspondingly shortened, resulting in the reduction of the driving force of the main tension spring e to the upper and lower connecting rods, resulting in a failure mode that is easy to occur in this traditional anti drop structure: after the high current is broken, the mechanism has been released, but the stuck moving contact cannot be pushed to the predetermined tripping position, As a result, the product cannot be opened and closed normally after the test.

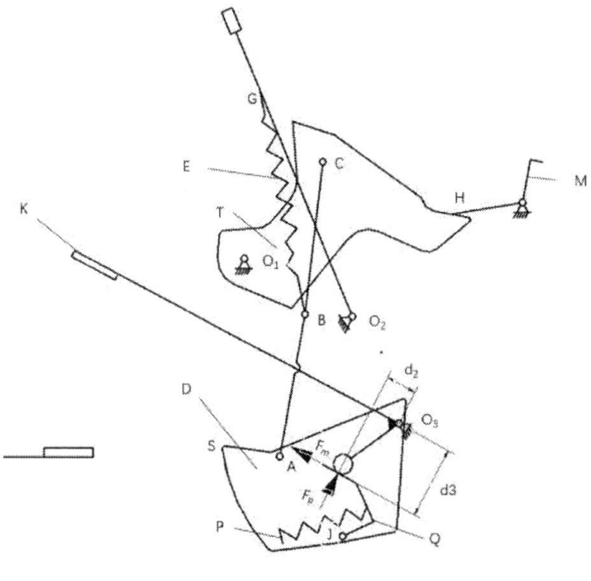

Fig. 4. Schematic diagram of the mechanism when the contacts used in the industry are stuck.

III. OPTIMAL DESIGN OF THE REPULSION AND JAMMING MECHANISM OF THE CONTACT SYSTEM OF THE CIRCUIT BREAKER

In order to completely solve the problem of falling prevention of moving contacts, it is very necessary to design and confirm the force value of the main tension spring, contact parameters and contact pressing plate on the premise that the length relationship of each connecting rod of the mechanism, the fixed point of the frame have been determined and the rotating shaft has sufficient strength.

The calculation diagram of five connecting rod transmission efficiency is shown in Figure 5. In Figure 5, Fe is the tension generated by the main tension spring of the mechanism acting on the upper and lower connecting rod shafts B. The tripping t of the mechanism has been released from the latch m, and the moving contact K is in the position of being pushed open and stuck. In order to evaluate the transmission efficiency of five connecting rod force, it is assumed that the lever reaches the closing position, and Fe is the driving force of the main tension spring of the mechanism on the upper and lower connecting rods. Simulating the failure mode easily produced by the traditional anti drop structure, the lifting torque transmitted by the main tension spring e to the rotating shaft through the upper and lower connecting rods CB and Ba can not effectively overcome the counter torque provided by the contact spring p to the moving contact K through the pressing plate Q, so that both the moving contact K and the rotating shaft D cannot be reset to the predetermined tripping position.

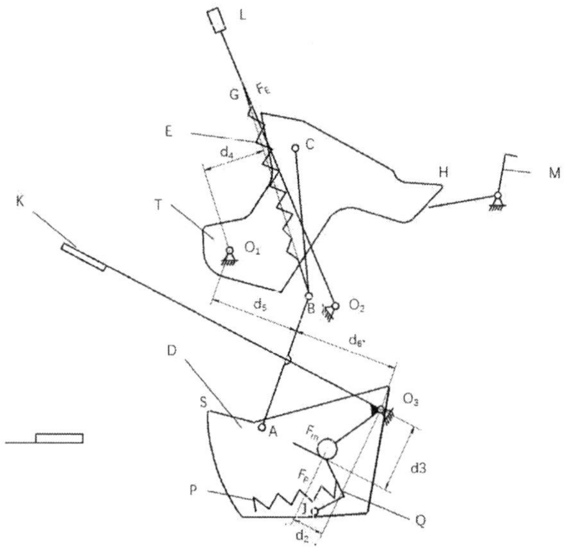

Fig. 5. calculation diagram of transmission efficiency of five connecting rods

According to the geometric relationship and force transmission in Figure 5, then:

$$M_1 = F_E d_4 d_6 / d_5 \quad (1)$$

$$M_2 = F_P d_2 + F_m d_3 \quad (2)$$

Where, FM= μ FP, μ Is the friction coefficient.

Only when M1 > M2 is met can the locked moving contact be released and reset to the predetermined tripping position after the mechanism trips;

Where: m1------------ lifting torque of the main tension spring to the lower connecting rod;

M2------------ the counter torque of the contact system to the lower connecting rod;

Fe-------------- tension of main tension spring;

D2, D3, D4, D5, d6--------------- geometric distance;

FP --------------------------- contact spring pressure;

FM --------------------------- friction force;

The following is an analysis of two examples. In Figure 5, the tripping t has been released but has not reached the predetermined tripping position. The lifting torque transmitted by the main tension spring e to the rotating shaft through the upper and lower connecting rods CB and Ba and the counter torque provided by the contact spring p to the moving contact K through the pressing plate Q. See Table 1 for different main tension spring force values, contact parameters and contact pressing plate parameters.

Table 1 force values and contact parameters of different main tension springs.

According to formulas (1) and (2), the torque of the main tension spring of product 1 to pull the lower connecting rod and rotating shaft and the counter torque of the contact system to the lower connecting rod are respectively

TABLE I
FORCE VALUES AND CONTACT PARAMETERS OF DIFFERENT MAIN TENSION SPRINGS

parameter	Product 1	Product 2
Upper connecting rod length CB/mm	31	31
Lower connecting rod length BA/mm	30.5	30.5
Skip swivel arm O1C /mm	25.1	25.1
rotating shaft arm AO3/mm	24.9	24.9
Fixed rod length O3O1/mm	45.8	45.8
Tripping swivel arm o1c swing angle (tripping)/ (°)	6	6
Free length of main tension springH0/mm	36	38.3
Tensile length of main tension springH1/mm	48.2	48.2
Stiffness of main tension spring (two springs)/ (N/mm)	60	104
Contact spring pressure FP/ (N)	2160	2160
frictionFm/ (N)	324	324
d2/mm	3.1	3.1
d3/mm	16.6	16.6
d4/mm	10.7	10.7
d5/mm	15	15
d6/mm	22.2	22.2

The torque of the main tension spring of product 2 to pull the lower connecting rod and rotating shaft and the counter torque of the contact system to the lower connecting rod are respectively.

From the above calculation example, it can be seen that the torque of the main tension spring of product 2 to pull the lower connecting rod and rotating shaft is not only significantly higher than that of product 1, but also after the stiffness of the main tension spring is increased, the torque of the main tension spring of product 2 to pull the lower connecting rod and rotating shaft is greater than the counter torque of the contact system to the lower connecting rod, which can effectively solve the failure problem of the anti drop mechanism of the moving contact.

It should be noted that the optimized parameters of the main tension spring are designed and checked, and the mechanical life meets the requirements of 15000 times. According to the above formulas (1) and (2), the lifting torque M1 is in direct proportion to the force value of the main tension spring, the length from the tripping rotation point to the main tension spring force arm, and the length from the tripping rotation point to the lower link force arm; The contact spring applies force to the moving contact through the pressing plate. The structural design of the pressing plate and the contact system have a certain impact on the counter torque of the lower connecting rod.

IV. Design of Circuit Breaker Contact System Locking Mechanism

A. *pressing plate setting*

The pressing plate device is a relatively precise

component, and a reasonable structural setting can bring stable contact pressure, anti drop retention force and stroke, and higher service life. The first function of the pressing plate device is to compress the contact spring, and finally maintain the contact pressure of the moving and static contacts within a suitable range through the conversion of the force arm between the pressing plate and the moving contact; The second function is that during the breaking process of the moving and static contacts, when the current value between the moving and static contacts increases to a certain value, the moving and static contacts overcome the contact pressure FC and start to repel under the simultaneous action of the loop electric power and the Hom force. When the moving contact repels to a certain value, the moving contact is prevented from falling. As a general contact fall prevention mechanism in the industry, the maximum stroke of the moving contact is generally consistent with the opening distance of the normal opening of the contact. When the moving contact reaches a certain value, it gets stuck, as shown in Figure 6 and Figure 7. The stroke from the moving contact to the fall prevention position is in direct proportion to the overlap d0 of the stress surface of the pressing plate.

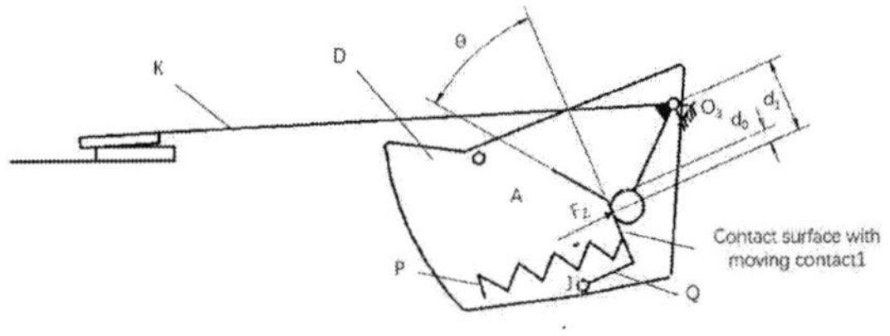

Fig. 6. schematic diagram of contact surface between product closing moving contact and pressing.

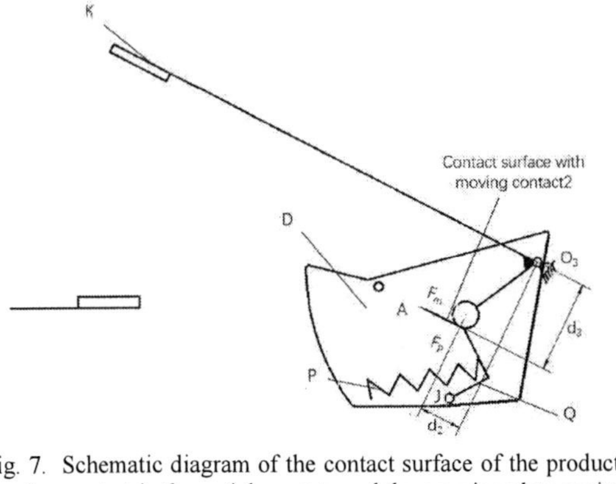

Fig. 7. Schematic diagram of the contact surface of the product closing moving contact in the anti drop state and the pressing plate against.

The setting of the force point of the pressing plate is very important, which usually includes that the normal direction of the force point of the moving contact at the final pressure position shown in Figure 6 is a large distance d1 from the rotating center O3 of the moving contact, including the normal direction of the force point of the moving contact from the repulsion position to the anti drop position shown in Figure 7 is a small distance d2 from the rotating center O3 of the moving contact. The torque m3 of the contact pressure of the dynamic and static contact to the rotating center of the dynamic contact is counterclockwise, and the torque m2 of the anti drop position of the dynamic contact to the rotating center of the contact is clockwise. According to the torque balance relationship:

$$M_2 = F_P d_2 + F_m d_3 \tag{2}$$

$$M_3 = F_Z \mathrm{d}_1 \tag{3}$$

For the setting of the force bearing point of the pressing plate: ① the overlapping amount d0 of the moving contact and the force bearing surface of the pressing plate. During the opening and closing process, the normal direction of the force bearing point of the moving contact at the final pressure position is a large distance d1 from the rotating Center O3 of the moving contact. To ensure that the contact pressure of the moving and stationary contacts is stable and the work is relatively reliable, if the overlapping amount d0 is set too small, the contact point of the moving contact and the pressing plate will be set on the bending outer diameter of the transition between contact surface 1 and contact surface 2, Because the bending outer diameter is generally formed naturally, the manufacturing accuracy cannot meet the requirements, which will lead to a large change in distance d1, resulting in the attenuation of contact pressure moment of dynamic and static contacts, and the high temperature rise of products; ② The normal direction of the force point from the repulsion of the moving contact to the anti drop position is a small distance d2 from the rotating center O3 of the moving contact, and the torque of the force to the moving contact is the opposite direction of the closing rotation direction of the moving contact. Therefore, after the repulsion of the moving contact, the anti drop work is reliable. The lifting torque transmitted from the main tension spring e to the rotating shaft through the upper and lower connecting rods CB and Ba can also effectively overcome the counter torque provided by the contact spring p to the moving contact K through the pressing plate Q, Make the moving contact K and the rotating shaft D reliably reset to the predetermined tripping position.

B. simulation comparison and analysis

Breaking capacity is an important index of circuit breaker. During the breaking process, the mechanism has an inherent action time [4,5]. When the mechanism is not released to the free tripping position, the Hom force and Lorentz force between the dynamic and static contacts overcome the contact pressure FC and begin to repel around the rotation center O3. The dynamic contact rotates past the anti falling point and remains at the maximum opening distance position to realize the separation of the dynamic contact and the static contact and cut off the circuit.

As shown in Figure 5, when the circuit breaker is in the

tripping position, the lifting torque transmitted by the main tension spring e to the rotating shaft through the upper and lower connecting rods CB and Ba cannot effectively overcome the counter torque provided by the contact spring p to the moving contact K through the pressing plate Q, so that both the moving contact K and the rotating shaft D cannot be reset to the predetermined tripping position. Then the force exerted by the upper and lower connecting rods CB and Ba on the shaft is balanced with the torque exerted by the moving contact K and pressing plate Q on the shaft:

$$M_4 = F_4 d_4 d_6 / d_5 - F_2 d_2 - F_m d_3 = 0 \qquad (4)$$

Through simulation analysis, the performance can be optimized and the research and development cycle can be shortened. The influence of the stiffness of the main tension spring on the reset of the moving contact to the predetermined tripping position is illustrated as an example. When the mechanism trips freely, the restraint of the latch on the trip buckle is released, and the trip buckle will rotate counterclockwise under the thrust of the upper connecting rod, so as to pull the rotating shaft to rotate, and the moving contact will be reset from the anti drop position to the predetermined trip position.

The stiffness of the main tension spring of product 3 is 110n/mm, keeping other parameters unchanged. Assuming that the stiffness of the main tension spring is adjusted to 115n/mm and 120n/mm, the influence of different stiffness of the main tension spring on the angular velocity and reset characteristics of the shaft is analyzed and compared by using simulation software. The reset time is the total action time from the moment when the mechanism is released to the time when the moving contact is reset to the predetermined tripping position (maximum opening distance).

The driving force of the tripping action is the torque [6,7] of the thrust Fe of the main tension spring to the tripping through the upper connecting rod relative to the rotation center O1 of the tripping and support. The smaller the stiffness of the main tension spring, the smaller the driving torque, the higher the risk of the moving contact resetting from the anti drop position to the predetermined tripping position, and the longer the reset time. On the contrary, the greater the stiffness of the main tension spring, the greater the driving torque transmitted to the moving contact, and the shorter the reset time. The influence of different main tension spring stiffness on reset time is shown in Table 2. It can be seen from table 2 that the stiffness of 115n/mm and 120n/mm have a great impact on the reset time. The curves of the angular velocity of the rotating shaft with time for the stiffness of 110n/mm and 120n/mm are shown in Fig. 8 and Fig. 9 respectively. It can be seen from figure 8 and Figure 9 that the smaller the stiffness, the smaller the peak value and overall trend of the angular velocity of the rotating shaft, which is consistent with the theoretical analysis.

Table 2 Influence of different spring stiffness on reset time

name	unit	Stiffness of main tension spring		
		110	115	120
Reset time	ms	6.5	5	4.5

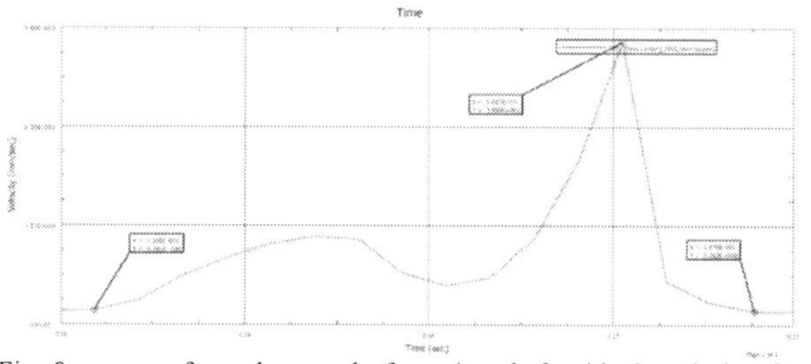

Fig. 8. curve of angular speed of rotating shaft with time during free tripping.

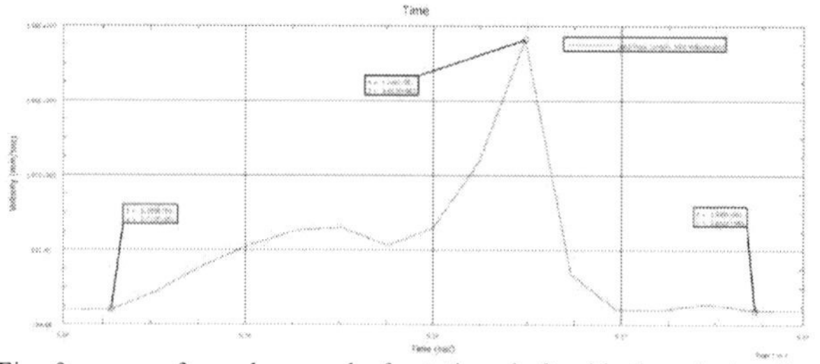

Fig. 9. urve of angular speed of rotating shaft with time during free tripping.

C. test comparison and verification results

The rigidity of the main tension spring of the mechanism was increased to 115n/mm, and 15000 mechanical operation performance tests were carried out with the optimized circuit breaker. The mechanism operated normally, and there was no unreliable closing and sliding buckle phenomenon. Moreover, the contact pressure of the contact system after the circuit breaker test was also within the design range, which could ensure the reliability of the temperature rise after the circuit breaker test.

In order to measure the anti drop reset time of the moving contact, a high-speed camera is used to capture the corresponding time point from the image to obtain the time from the tripping of the mechanism to the reset of the moving contact. By comparing the shooting of the reset process of the moving contact before and after the improvement, it is obtained that the moving contact before the improvement cannot be reset when it is pushed to the anti drop position, and the reset time after the improvement is 5.5ms. From the data obtained, it can be concluded that the reset time of the mechanism after the improvement is significantly better than that before the improvement

Two circuit breakers with improved design are used for short-circuit breaking capacity test, specifically the rated operating short-circuit breaking ics:ac415v/50ka, and compared with the breaking test data before the improvement. Table 3 shows the comparison of short-circuit breaking test data of products before and after improvement. It can be seen from table 3 that after an "O" is made for the circuit breaker before the improvement, the product fails because the anti drop mechanism of the moving contact is not reset to the predetermined tripping position; The performance of the improved circuit breaker in short-circuit breaking has been significantly improved.

D. summary

Through the above analysis and verification, it is concluded that:

(1) The method of design calculation and motion simulation is used to optimize the design and increase the stiffness of the main tension spring of the mechanism.

(2) Reasonably design the contact position between the moving contact and the pressing plate, in order to reserve the overlapping amount to prevent the pressure attenuation of the contact, and ensure that the travel from the exclusion of the moving contact to the fall prevention is as short as possible.

(3) The simulation analysis results do not consider the shaft hole fit, electric repulsion, etc., so there is a slight difference between the dynamic contact anti drop calculation and the simulation results, but the overall results are consistent, and the optimized anti drop structure does play a good breaking effect.

(4) From the simulation analysis and breaking test results, the contact does not reset after the optimized anti drop structure breaks once; The optimized anti drop structure is very reliable when the contact is reset to the predetermined tripping position.

Table 3

Prototype status	Before improvement	After improvement1#	After improvement2#
Full breaking time at "O" （ms）	9.7	6.9	8.1
Energy i2t at "O" （×106 A2S）	8.41	6.1	4.1
Full breaking time at "CO1" （ms）	/	8.9	9.6
Energy i2t at "CO1" （× 106 A2S）	/	5.9	6.1
Full breaking time at "CO2" （ms）	/	10.1	10.1
Energy i2t at "CO2" （× 106 A2S）	/	5.1	5.1

V. Conclusion

This paper mainly analyzes the real reason why the moving contact remains in the anti drop position without resetting to the predetermined tripping position after the mechanism is unlocked, adopts the optimal design scheme, and uses UG to simulate and analyze the dynamic characteristic process of the circuit breaker. Through theoretical calculation and simulation, the effect of optimization design is analyzed, and combined with the breaking test, the verification results of new and old schemes are compared, and some ideas of design and calculation are pointed out. This technology is also applicable to MCCB series switch products. The optimized design scheme is verified by simulation and breaking test. The results show that this optimized design scheme can reliably play the effect of contact drop prevention. It is verified according to the prototype made after the optimized design. The mechanical life reaches 15000 times, and the short-circuit breaking ics:ac415v/50ka test under rated operation, It is proved that the scheme can effectively solve the problem of falling prevention of moving contact of circuit breaker.

References

[1] Maoxiang Zhou. Low voltage electrical apparatus design manual [m]. Beijing: Machinery Industry Press, 1992

[2] L. Yu and J. Chu, “An LMI approach to guaranteed cost control of linear uncertain time-delay systems,” Automatica, vol. 35, no. 6, pp. 1155-1159, 1999.

[3] Tianwen Yin, he Ruihua. Technical Manual of low voltage apparatus [m]. Beijing: Machine Press, 2014

[4] Jisheng Sun, Zheng Zheng, Huimin Gu . Action analysis and design points of operating mechanism of molded case circuit breaker [b]. Low voltage apparatus, 2013 (21): 13-16

[5] Guping Jiang, Huimin Gu. Research on providing the action speed of operating mechanism of molded case circuit breaker [J].Electrical appliance and energy efficiency management technology, 2015 (1): 25-27

[6] YilongYou . Analysis and design of tripping force of molded case circuit breaker [B]. Low voltage apparatus, 2013 (20): 24-26

[7] Degui Chen . Factors affecting the breaking speed of operating mechanism of molded case circuit breaker [B]. Low voltage apparatus, 2005 (12): 9-12

Identification of Aerial AC Arc Faults Based on 1st-4th Order Statistical Methods

Ruihua Cui, Baoxu Shi, Junting Yao

Hebei University of Technology, Tianjin, 300401, China
Email:202021401007@std.hubet.edu.cn TEL: 13287514828

Abstract—**When an arc fault occurs in the aviation cable, the continuous burning of the arc may cause a major accident. Due to the strong randomness and uncertainty in the occurrence of arc faults, it is difficult to identify the work. In this paper, a new method for identifying aviation arcs is proposed based on the research background of aircraft cable arc faults. This method computes the 1-4 order statistics of the sample distribution for each period - mean, variance, skewness, kurtosis. Then the 1-4 order statistics are fused into a 4-dimensional space, and the four statistics of each cycle of the current signal are converted into points in the 4-dimensional space. Check the variation difference between two adjacent cycles as a new feature quantity. The Euclidean distance is used to calculate the distance between the corresponding points of two adjacent cycles in the four-dimensional space, and by setting the threshold reasonably, the purpose of effectively identifying arc faults is achieved. The results show that this method can effectively distinguish and identify arc faults.**

Index Terms— **Aviation arc, arc fault identification, statistics, Euclidean distance**

I. INTRODUCTION

With the rapid development of multi-electric and all-electric power supply technology in aircraft, the use of cables and wires has increased sharply. The long-term use of cables makes it inevitable that the insulation layer will have cracks and wear, which makes the cables very easy to induce arc faults. , causing serious consequences [1]. Therefore, research on the identification method of aviation arc fault is of great significance to ensure the safe operation of aircraft.

The detection methods of arc faults are mainly divided into two categories: one is to use the physical phenomena such as sound, light, and heat accompanying the fault to identify [2,3]; the other is to use the changes of voltage and current signals for diagnosis. [4]. Reference [5] extracts the characteristic variation of load terminal voltage for arc fault. Voltage variation analysis can only be adapted under fixed load conditions. Difficult to apply in line situations. In the case of the line, the literature [6] collects two cycle currents in the loop and calculates the proportional coefficient and cross-correlation coefficient of the zero rest time as the characteristic quantities for judging the arc. Reference [7] uses the ratio of arc current change rate to effective value to perform fast arc detection and verify it in hardware. Reference [8] uses the fast Fourier transform algorithm to detect the arc characteristics of AC electrical appliances, which is used for arc protection devices. Reference [9] proposed a singular value decomposition (SVD) algorithm based on wavelet analysis and combined it with current amplitude normalization to solve the difficult problem of arc fault detection. Reference [10] decomposes the signal through the generalized S transform, and extracts the mean square value and energy of the 2kHz component. Perform arc fault identification. References [11, 12] use the empirical mode decomposition analysis method to decompose the arc current time-frequency to obtain a series of eigenmode components (IMF), process the IMF to obtain the eigenvectors, and then diagnose the fault. In addition, some literatures introduce methods of nonlinear dynamics. For example, literature [1[13]3] reconstructs the current signal time series into phase space trajectory, and extracts relevant chaotic features to identify arc faults. Reference [13] extracted the dimension of chaotic feature information and zero rest time, and the two features were used to identify arc faults.

Due to the contingency and randomness of arc occurrence, in order to better identify arc faults, useful information can be extracted from the current signal. In this paper, the current signal is introduced into the random process for analysis, and the entire current signal change process is observed from the perspective of probability theory. With the help of the change of the sample distribution of the current signal period when an arc fault occurs, the mean value of the central tendency of the response sample is extracted from it; the variance of the dispersion degree of the response data, the skewness of the symmetry of the response data distribution and the kurtosis of the centrality of the response data Four statistics. In order to solve the problem that it is difficult for a single feature to divide the threshold value and the feature value overlap between normal and fault conditions, the 1-4 order statistics are fused to form a four-dimensional space. The Euclidean distance is used to compare the spatial changes of two adjacent cycles, and a threshold is divided for judgment. In order to verify the feasibility of the scheme, write a program to burn the sample machine, and carry out experimental verification. Through the verification of the scheme, the scheme can effectively identify normal and fault with high accuracy.

II. Aviation Arc Fault Test and Data Acquisition

A. *Arc simulation test*

Aviation arc faults are divided into two types: series arc faults and parallel arc faults. According to the relevant test requirements in the standards UL 1699 [14] and AS 5692 [15], set up a series point contact arc fault test and a parallel cable cut-off test, as shown in Figure 1-3. For the point contact test, by controlling the motor to drag the contacts, the contacts are separated, thereby generating a series arc, simulating the arc fault in the case of poor cable contact or internal damage. In the parallel cable cut-off test, it is necessary to fix the two cable samples on the insulating base through the cable clamp, and then turn the handle to cut the cable to generate an arc. The parallel cut-off test simulates the arc fault between the two conductors caused by the insulation damage of the conductor.

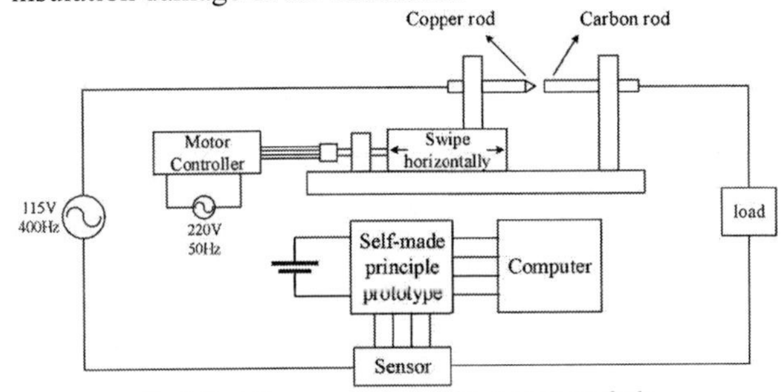

Fig.1 Test diagram of series point contact arc fault

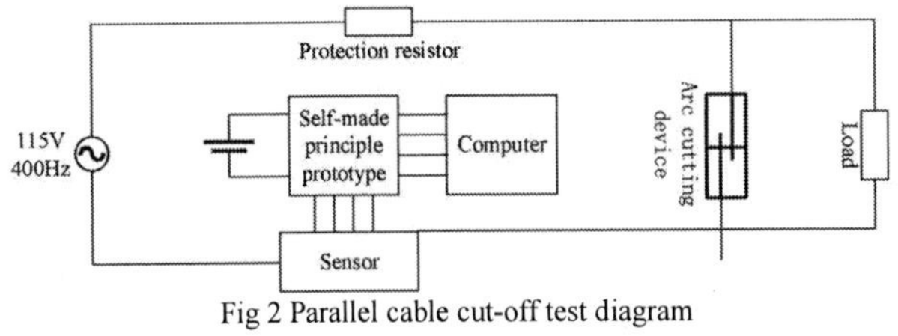

Fig 2 Parallel cable cut-off test diagram

The test power supply voltage is 115V and the frequency is 400Hz. The sensor sampling rate is 409.6kHz. The test load is shown in Table 1.

B. *Data collection*

In order to observe and compare the difference before and after the waveform changes of different loads and tests, 10 cycles before and after the failure were intercepted, and all data were normalized. Draw as shown in Figures 3 and 4.

TABLE 1
LOADS CONNECTED TO THE TEST

Test type	load type
point contact test	57Ω
	57Ω+5mH
	57Ω+4.7μF
	ATRU
cut-off test	15Ω
	30Ω
	115 Ω

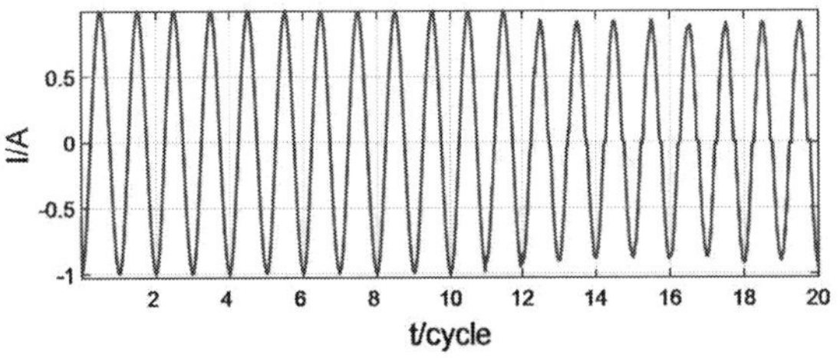

(a) 57.5Ω

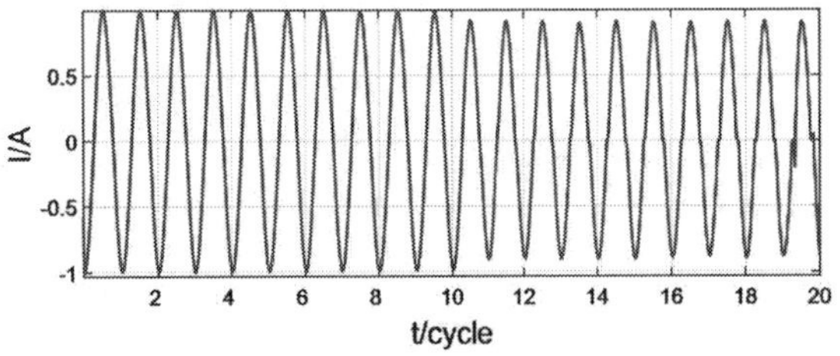

(b) 57.5Ω+5mH

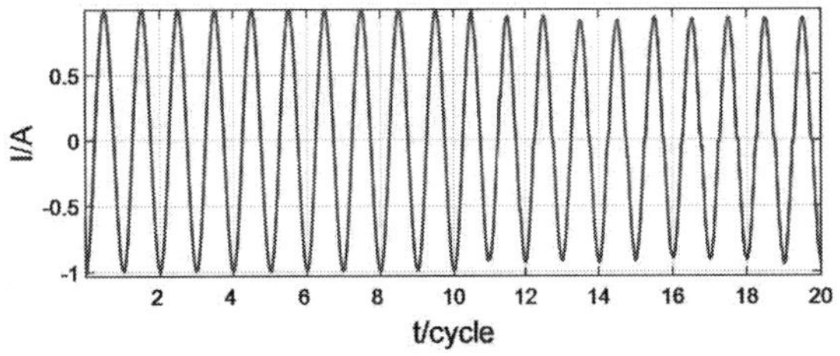

(c) 57.5Ω+47μF

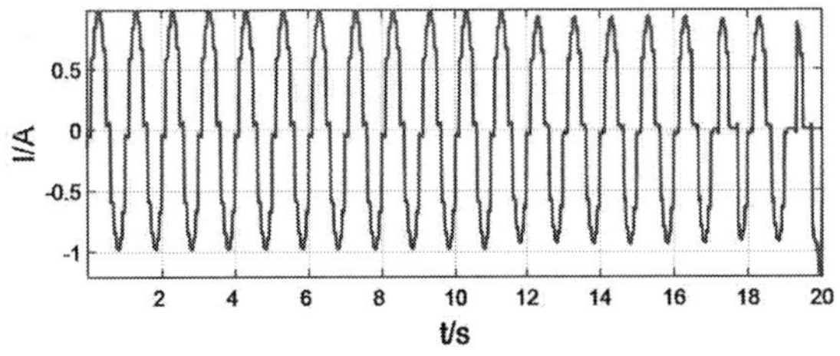

(d) ATRU

Fig3 Waveforms of several loads in series point contact test

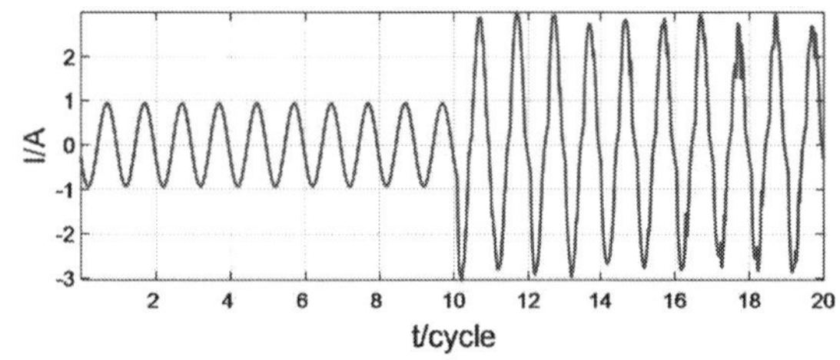

(a) 15Ω

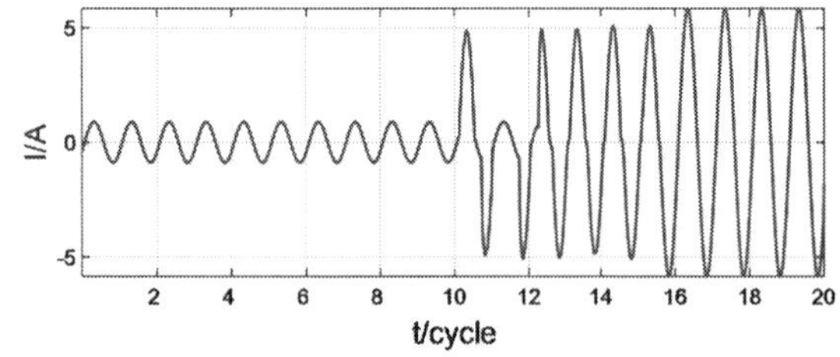

(b) 30 Ω

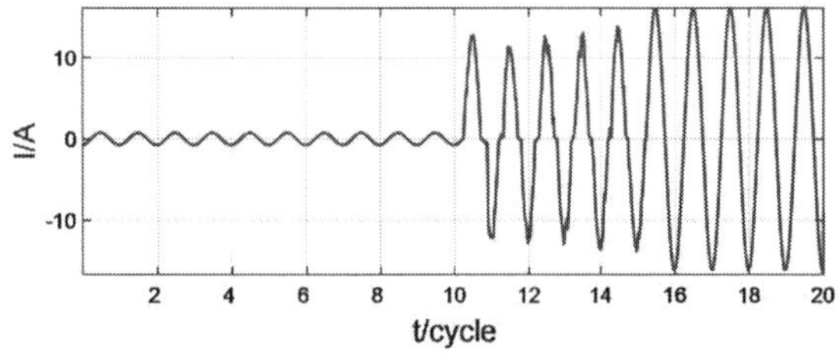

(c) 115 Ω

Fig 4 Waveforms of several loads tested in parallel cut-off test

Observe Figures 3 and 4 and analyze the current waveforms under each load. When a series arc occurs, the current amplitude is slightly reduced from normal. In the series point contact test, there is an obvious flat shoulder at the zero-crossing of the loop current of the linear load. For the nonlinear load ATRU, the breaking of its internal thyristor makes the wave form a ladder, and the waveform under normal operation is related to the arc fault. The waveform is similar, and there is also a flat shoulder phenomenon. The particularity of nonlinear load waveforms makes arc fault detection difficult. When a parallel arc fault occurs, the current amplitude increases sharply, and the current waveform is similarly distorted.

III. 1-4 ORDER STATISTICS OF THE CURRENT SIGNAL

The mean is the first-order statistic of the sample data. The mean represents the central tendency of a set of data. is the sum of a set of samples divided by the number of samples. Calculated as formula (1).

$$\overline{X} = \frac{1}{N}\sum_{i=1}^{N} X_i \#(1)$$

Among them, X_i is the i sample, and N is the number of samples. Use formula (1) to calculate the data obtained from the test sampling. For series point contact test and cut-off test. In the normal state, the period mean of the current signals of all loads is approximately 0. After the fault occurs, the cycle mean value of the arc fault current deviates significantly from 0.

Variance is a second-order statistic that reflects the characteristics of sample data and is used to measure the degree of dispersion of data distribution. The formula for calculating variance is formula (2).

$$S^2 = \frac{1}{N-1}\sum_{i=1}^{N} (X_i - \overline{X})^2 \#(2)$$

N is the number of sample data, X_i is the i sample, and $\overline{X}$ is the sample mean. By calculating the variance of the current signal by formula (2), the variance of the arc fault period of the series arc fault decreases slightly, and the variance of the arc fault period of the parallel arc fault increases.

Skewness is a third-order numeric feature. is a numerical characteristic of the degree of asymmetry in the distribution of statistical data. Skewness is the normalized third-order center-to-center distance, calculated as formula (3).

$$Skewness = \frac{\frac{1}{n}\sum_{i=1}^{n} (X_i - \overline{X})^3}{\left(\frac{1}{n}\sum_{i=1}^{n} (X_i - \overline{X})^2\right)^{\frac{3}{2}}} \#(3)$$

N is the number of sample data, X_i is the i sample, and $\overline{X}$ is the sample mean. The magnitude of skewness measures the degree of asymmetry of the distribution. If the data is symmetrically distributed with the mean as the center, the skewness value is zero; under normal conditions, the skewness of the current cycle of all loads is approximately zero. When an arc fault occurs, the skewness of the current cycle changes, and is no longer zero.

Kurtosis is a fourth-order statistic that studies the steepness or smoothness of the distribution of data. By measuring the kurtosis of the sample data, we can determine whether the data distribution is steeper or flatter. The calculation method of kurtosis is the fourth-order normalized center distance, and the calculation is as formula (4).

$$Kurtosis = \frac{\frac{1}{n}\sum_{i=1}^{n} (X_i - \overline{X})^4}{\left(\frac{1}{n}\sum_{i=1}^{n} (X_i - \overline{X})^2\right)^{2}} \#(4)$$

N is the number of sample data, X_i is the i sample, and $\overline{X}$ is the sample mean. Calculate the kurtosis of the current using equation (4). For the series point contact test and the parallel cut-off test, the kurtosis change can well distinguish the normal and fault cycles of the current.

The 1-4 order statistics change with the cycle, and there are dramatic changes when a fault occurs. These features can reflect the difference between the current cycle signal samples in the arc fault and normal conditions to a certain extent, but if we want to accurately judge the arc fault, there are still two problems: First, when using a single feature, it is impossible to determine a uniform threshold to identify the arc fault. , and the second is that when an arc fault occurs, the eigenvalues overlap with the normal characteristics, and the arc fault cannot be identified.

IV. Identification of Arc Faults

A. Euclidean distance

In order to better characterize the change of the current from the normal cycle to the arc fault cycle and judge the fault, the above four characteristic quantities are fused. Each statistic is regarded as a dimension in the space, thus forming a four-dimensional space. At this point, four statistic features extracted from each cycle of the current signal constitute points in the four-dimensional space. The variation of the current signal with the period is mapped to the displacement in the four-dimensional space. To judge the arc fault, it is only necessary to measure the size of the spatial displacement of two adjacent cycles.

Euclidean Distance is the straight-line distance between two points in Euclidean space. The Euclidean distance in N-dimensional space is:

$$d(x,y)=\sqrt{\sum_{i=1}^{N}(x_i-y_i)^2\#(1)}$$

The Euclidean distance is used to calculate the spatial position change of two adjacent cycles, that is, the four-dimensional spatial displacement of the feature quantities of the adjacent two cycles. The calculation results are shown in Table 2. Since the distance starts from the second point to calculate the distance from the previous point, here directly set the distance value of the first point to zero.

B. Identification scheme

For the fused feature quantity - Euclidean distance, a method of thresholding is adopted. In order to determine the size of the threshold, the threshold should be smaller than the minimum value during failure, and larger than the maximum value during normal operation. The threshold value that should be chosen should be between these two values. According to the statistics of the experimental data, 0.006 was chosen as the threshold. To sum up, a specific scheme is formed as shown in Figure 5.

V. Test Verification

In order to verify the effectiveness of the scheme, some typical test loads are selected for the testing and verification of the prototype. Use the scheme in Figure 15 and the selected threshold of 0.006 to write the program, and burn the program into the self-made prototype. Connect the prototype into the point contact test circuit and the cut-off test circuit, and at the same time, the oscilloscope collects the circuit current and the prototype alarm signal, and records the waves. Each test load was performed 10 times. According to the requirements of AS 5692, if there are 8 half-wave arc fault waveforms within 100ms, it can be considered that an arc fault has occurred. The statistics of aviation arc fault detection results are presented in Table 2.

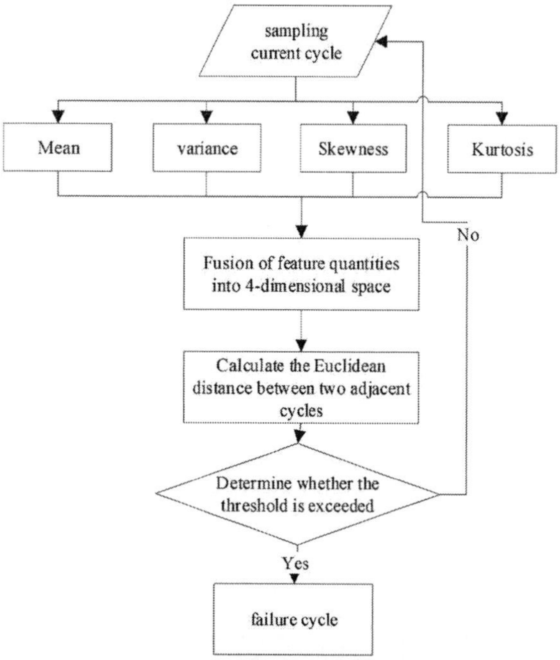

Fig 5 Scheme identification flow chart

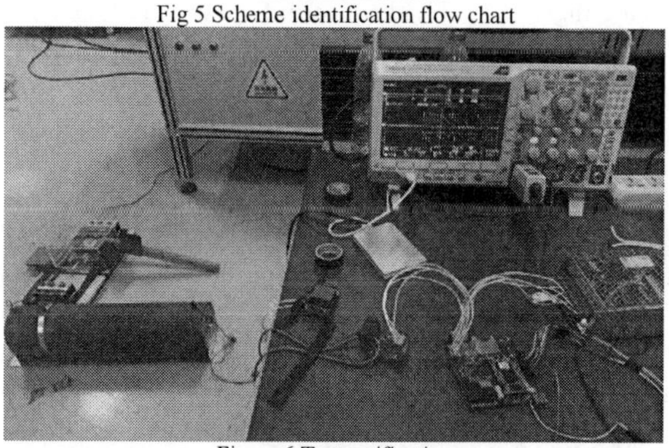

Figure 6 Test verification circuit

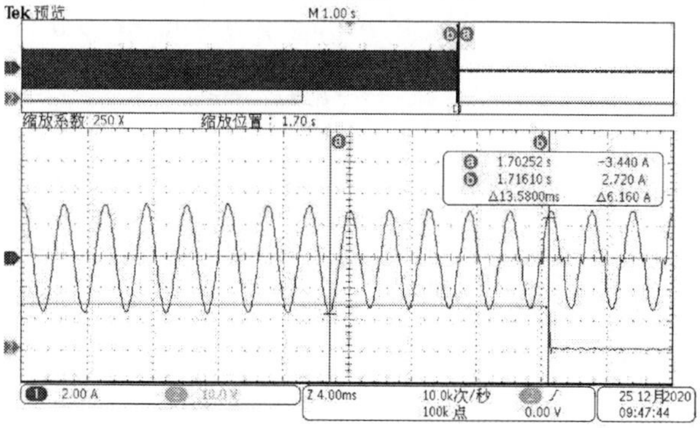

Fig.7 Arc fault detection waveform of point contact test

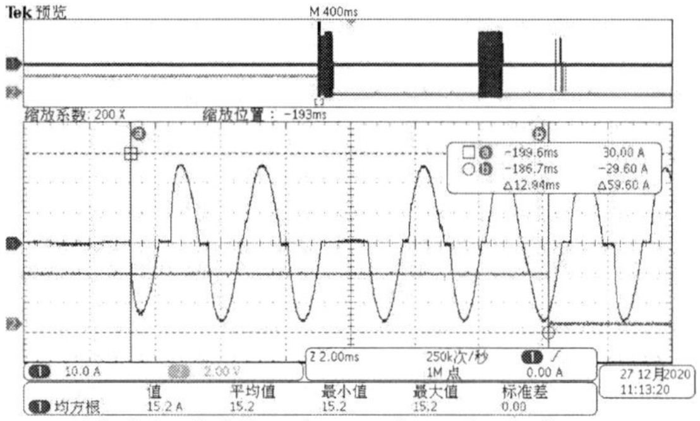

Fig.8 Arc fault detection waveform of truncation test

TABLE 2

AERONAUTICAL ARC FAULT DETECTION RESULTS

Test type	load type	Accuracy	Average detection time
point contact test	57Ω	100	14.58ms
	57Ω+5mH	100	17.19ms
	57Ω+4.7μF	100	15.89ms
	ATRU	100	19.65ms
cut-off test	15Ω	100	13.82ms
	30Ω	100	14.56ms
	115	100	14.63ms

It can be seen from Table 2 that the identification effect of this scheme is relatively good, and arc faults can be judged. Among them, the individual alarm time of ATRU is longer, mainly because the waveforms of ATRU's true singing and fault are similar, and the changes are small, but they can be judged within the specified time.

VI. IN CONCLUSION

In this paper, a random process is introduced to analyze the series arc fault and parallel arc fault in the current aviation cable. Extract the sample distribution for each period and calculate 1-4 order statistics - mean, variance, skewness, kurtosis. There are some problems in judging arc faults by using the four statistics alone as characteristic quantities: the mean value and skewness are difficult to distinguish individual cycles; the thresholds used to distinguish faults from variance and peak value are difficult to divide. Therefore, the four feature quantities are fused into the position points in the four-dimensional space, and the Euclidean distance is used to calculate the distance between the corresponding points of two adjacent periods in the four-dimensional space. By setting the threshold reasonably, the purpose of effectively identifying arc faults is achieved. The results show that this method can effectively distinguish and identify arc faults.

REFERENCES

[1] Cao Tao. Research on aviation electrical arc, short circuit hazards and protection [J]. Advances in Aeronautical Engineering, 2020, 11(01): 140-146.

[2] Wang Yao, Zhang Yanfeng, Niu Feng, et al. Analysis and Measurement Method of Electromagnetic Radiation Characteristics of Photovoltaic DC Arc [J]. Chinese Journal of Electrotechnical Technology, 2019, 34(14): 2913-2921.

[3] Li Mei, Guo Pengcheng, Wang Yiwei, et al. Radiation characteristics of arc faults in a closed cavity [J]. High Voltage Technology, 2020, 46(06): 2021-2029.

[4] Wang Yao, Tian Ming, Niu Feng, et al. A review of research on low-voltage AC arc fault detection methods [J]. Electrical Appliances and Energy Efficiency Management Technology, 2018(10): 8-13+44.

[5] Zhao Yuan, Zhang Guanying, Wang Yao, et al. A series arc fault detection method based on load terminal voltage analysis [J]. Electrical Appliances and Energy Efficiency Management Technology, 2016(15): 74-78.

[6] Zhao Huaijun, Qin Haiyan, Liu Kai, et al. A series arc fault detection method based on correlation theory and zero-break feature fusion [J]. Journal of Instrumentation, 2020, 41(04): 218-228.

[7] Liu Xiaoming, Xu Yefei, Liu Ting, et al. Arc fault detection based on short-time zero-crossing rate of current signal [J]. Journal of Electrotechnical Technology, 2015, 30(13): 125-133.

[8] Ding Xin, Zhu Hongwei, Yin Haonan, et al. Fast detection method of AC electrical arc based on fast Fourier transform (FFT) [J]. Electrical Appliances and Energy Efficiency Management Technology, 2015(21): 8-12.

[9] SHEN Y L, WAI R J. Wavelet-Analysis-Based Singular-Value-Decomposition Algorithm for Weak Arc Fault Detection via Current Amplitude Normalization[J/OL]. IEEE Access, 2021, 9: 71535-71552.

[10] Cui Ruihua, Tong Deshuan, Li Ze, et al. Aviation series arc fault detection based on generalized S transform [J/OL]. Chinese Journal of Electrical Engineering, 2021, 41(23): 8241-8250.

[11] Su Jingjing, Xu Zhihong, ZHIHONG XU. Arc fault multivariate criterion diagnosis method based on EMD and PNN [J]. Electric Power Automation Equipment, 2019, 39(04): 106-113.

[12] Wang Zhibin, Cao Hongwei, Liu Jiajia, et al. Research on fault arc detection algorithm based on wavelet packet denoising and EMD [J]. Electrical Measurement and Instrumentation, 2019, 56(06): 117-121.

[13] Ma Shaohua, Bao Jieqiu, Cai Zhiyuan, et al. Arc fault identification method based on information dimension and zero rest time [J]. Chinese Journal of Electrical Engineering, 2016, 36(09): 2572-2579.

[14] UL. Standard for Arc-Fault Circuit-Interrupters[J/OL]. 2017[2022-04-07].

[15] Protective A P, Devices C. ARC Fault Circuit Breaker (AFCB), Aircraft, Trip-Free Single Phase and Three Phase 115 VAC, 400 Hz - Constant Frequency[J/OL]. 2009.

Cui Ruihua, female, born in 1962, postdoctoral fellow, professor, research direction is arc electric contact.E-mail: 710667045@qq.com

Study on Lifetime of Sealed Relay with Combined Silver Oxide Contact and Non-oxide Contact

Vincent Fang, Wei Gao

Industrial Technology Lab, Tyco Electronics (Shanghai) Co., Ltd., China
E-mail: vincent.fang@te.com , wei.gao@te.com

Abstract—**The previous study (partly published in ICREPEC2017) concluded that the electrical life of sealed relay can be improved significantly by changing contact material from silver base oxide contact to silver base non-oxide contact under the current level from small to middle, while at the big current level (⩾16A) the lifetime of sealed relay is still a challenge. Silver base oxide contact pairing with non-oxide contact was adopted as the solution and the improvement was verified by the electrical life test. Through analyzed the temperature rise, morphology, substances on contact (after electrical life test) and cross-section of contacts, it was found that the mutual material migration between oxide contact and non-oxide is the main reason to improve the life performance of the sealed relay.**

Index Terms— **Sealed relay, electrical life, temperature rise of terminal, contact morphology, SEM/EDX analysis, cross-section of contact.**

I. INTRODUCTION

Relays used in harsh environment are usually required to be sealed completely, while it's observed that electrical life of relays with silver oxide contacts reduces under the sealed construction and fails to meet the application requirement. The previous study (partly published in ICREPEC2017) concluded that the electrical life of sealed relay could be improved significantly by changing contact material from silver base oxide contact to silver base non-oxide contact under the small and middle current level. However, it was found that the lifetime of some sealed relays with non-oxide contacts under bigger current level still can ' t meet the requirement of customer. Therefore, it is meaningful to extend the study to bigger level current (⩾16A)

In the past, we studied the lifetime of relay with single contact material use in the relay, both stationary and movable contacts are silver base oxide contacts or non-oxide contacts. This year we studied the sealed relays with combined contact material, and one type of relay products SZL-C (Fig. 1) use with silver base oxide contact (AgSnO, stationary) pairing with non-oxide contact (AgNi, movable) was selected as the study object. In order to see its lifetime performance, a comparison electrical life test was done between the sealed relays with different contact combination, and the result (Fig. 2) indicated that the lifetime of sealed relay SZL-C has the best performance, and about 50% increased when comparing to sealed relay SZL-B (non-oxide contacts), and the lifetime of sealed relay SZL-A (oxide contacts) was the worst.

Fig. 1 SZL, RTIII/wash tight, 1 From A relay.

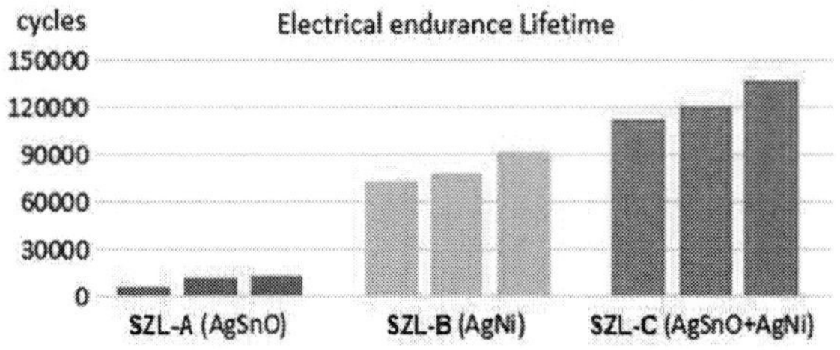

Fig. 2 Test condition: AC250V/60Hz, 25A, PF=1,40 ℃, 1.5S on/1.5S off (50%ED).

II. METHODS AND RESULTS

From the electrical life test (Fig. 2) the failure mode for the samples was contact welding. The contact welding mainly occurs at the processes of contacts closed. The mechanism is that the contact has a big resistance at initial touch, the heat generated by the current quickly causes the metal on contact surface to melt, the effective contact area of the contacts increases, the contact resistance decreases rapidly, and the molten metal is rapidly cooled. At this time, if the contact can't slide well due to the reduction of overtravel after many times of operation, it will not be able to tear the adhesion area in time and contact welding will occurs.

During the contact welding processes, the difference of heat generated by the current and the difference of contact property to resist contact welding could be the key factors to affect the lifetime performance of SZL sealed relays. The former one analyzes the difference of temperature rise and the latter one analyzes the morphology of contact and substance on contact after electrical life test. In order to find out the reason behind the difference of lifetime, a series of comparison test were carried out.

A. Temperature rise comparison test

The difference of contact temperature could be reflected by the difference of terminal temperature. In order to reduce the difference between the samples, three samples (one piece each type) with consistent electrical and mechanical parameters were selected for testing under the electrical life test condition (AC250V/25A/PF=1/1.5s:1.5s/40 ℃), the temperature of the terminals were recorded continuously for a period of time till one sample failed.

The tested samples were installed on the PCB board with the quick-connect terminal upward, and the thermocouples were placed close to the base of the quick-connect terminal. The sample installation is shown by Figure 3. The temperature of the movable terminal and the stationary terminal were recorded by temperature recorder (YOKOGAWA GP20), and the test results is shown by figure 3. From test data graph it could be seen that the temperature rise of three types didn't have big difference, the average temperature of the movable terminals is about 52°C and about 60°C for stationary terminals (the different temperature caused by the different distance from the contact). However, the temperature of SZL-A decreased some from the beginning to the end of life at contact welded (it was caused by the decreasing of contact resistance after a large amount of SnO contained in the contact is decomposed). Thus, it wasn't the temperature factor caused the different electrical life between the different types of SZL sealed relays.

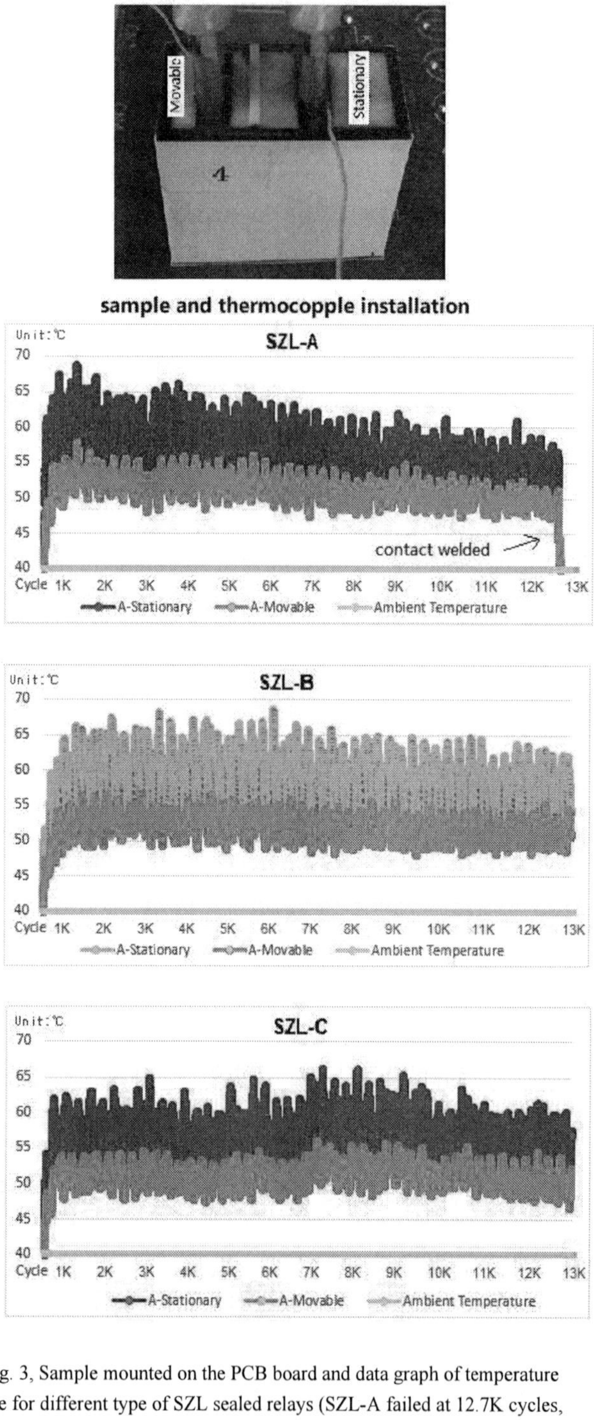

Fig. 3, Sample mounted on the PCB board and data graph of temperature rise for different type of SZL sealed relays (SZL-A failed at 12.7K cycles, SZL-B/C stopped testing at 13K cycles)

B. Contact morphology analysis after lifetime test

In order to observe the difference of contact morphology after electrical life, one representative sample each type was selected after the lifetime test, which shown in figure 4.

1) For SZL-A with AgSnO contacts, arc erosion was severe and toward the top side of the contacts, the erosion surface of the contact has lots of big bumps, while the other side of contact surface is intact, the salient points easy to cause contact welding.

2) For SZL-B with AgNi contacts, it could be seen that there are lots of carbon and splashed material accumulated on the spring around the contacts, and for moveable contact (upward), only centre area of surface is bright with many shiny big beads, while for the stationary contact (downward), the whole contact surface is even and bright.

3) For the SZL-C with AgNi movable contact+AgSnO stationary contact, the accumulated carbon and splashed material on the spring around the contacts look less than it on SZL-B though it run with more cycles, and the situation of the movable contact is better than SZL-B for it has a clean even bright surface. The performance of combined contact on SZL-C was better than it in SZL-A and SZL-B separately.

C. Contact morphology analysis after lifetime test

Based on the observation of the contact morphology, SEM & EDX (Phenom-ProX) analysis were carried out in further to find out the failure mechanism. The electron microscope images were obtained and EDX analyzed results of the salient points on the contact surface were shown by Figure 5:

1) SZL-A, it was found that the main substance of the bumps on the contact is Ag (up to 95%), and Sn element with high concentration (up to 50%) was found in flat area around the bumps. It was speculated that the SnO powder without replenishing of oxygen from ambient atmosphere, they were decomposed quickly in the molten pool of silver and caused the protection to keep the form of silver base become weak, and resulted in silver separated out from silver base, also caused the surface of silver base deformed severely. The bumps with high ratio of silver could cause the contact welding easily and relay early failure.

2) SZL-B, it was found that bright beads on stationary contact have a high silver ratio (up to 87.17%), and Ni element separated from silver base (with high ratio up to 18%) around bumps, the bumps have a high silver ratio (up to 94.25%) on the movable contact and together with the beads on stationary contact could cause the contacts welding easily and result in relay failure.

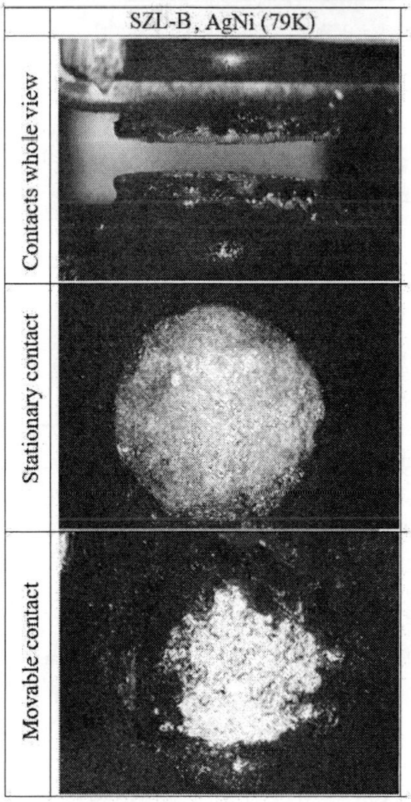

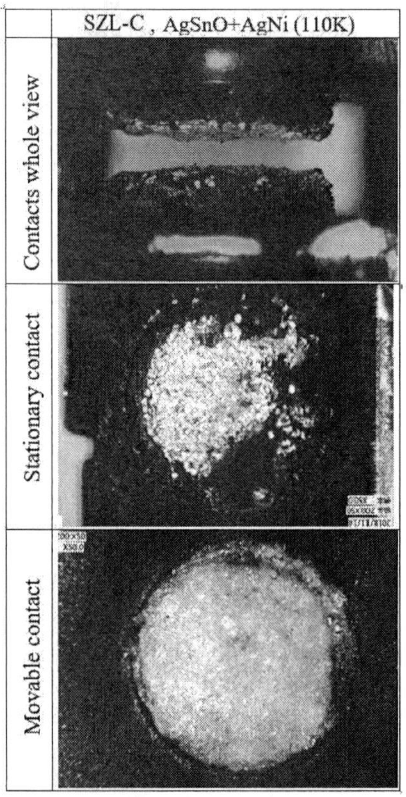

Fig. 4, Digital microscope images of spring, movable contact & stationary contact after lifetime test.

3) SZL-C, it was found that Ni and Sn elements exist on the surface of the two contacts and their concentration are close respectively (3 ~ 7%), so it can be seen that Ni and Sn elements migrate mutually between the two contacts, and the distribution is uniform. Thus, is the mutual migration of Ni and Sn elements in the process of electrical life helpful to resist contact welding, and is it the reason for its long life?

D. Additional observation during SZL-C electrical lifetime testing

In order to observe the material transfer on the contact surface of the SZL-C sealed relay during the life process, two samples after the electrical life test were selected for analysis, one completed 20k, the other completed 50k.

Base on EDX analysis on the salient points (including flat areas) which were shown by Fig. 6, it was found that the ratio of Ag on contact surface was less than 80% for the sample completed 20K, and the ratio increased to about 82~85% for the sample completed 50k (and even at life ended from the previous analyzed sample). For the element of Ni and Sn, they mutually transferred from each contact, and the ratio is about 3~8% at 20k cycles/50k cycles (even at life ended from the previous analyzed sample), no abnormal high concentration of Ni or Sn elements were found.

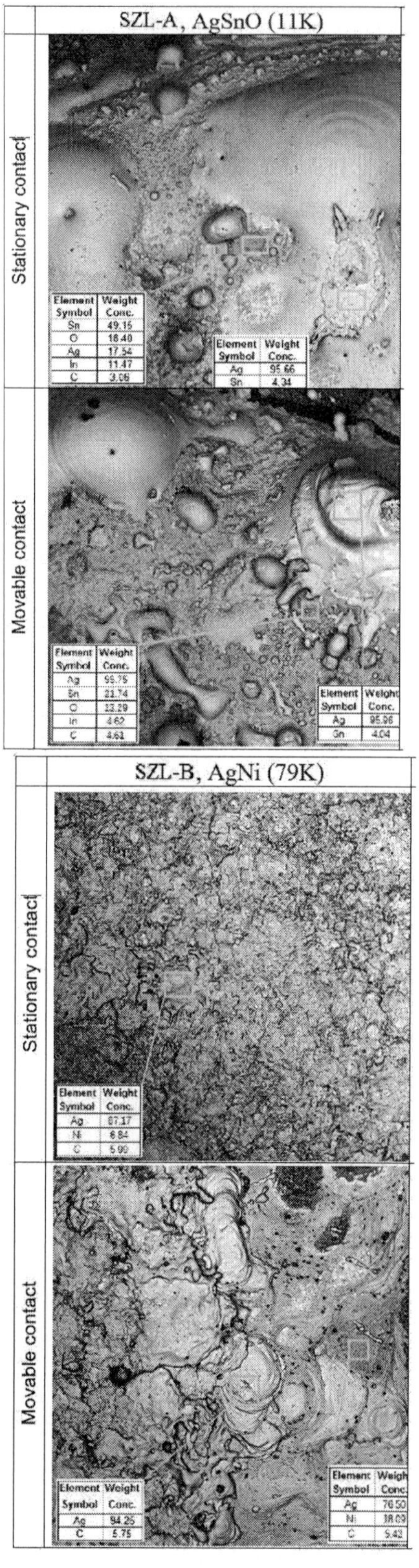

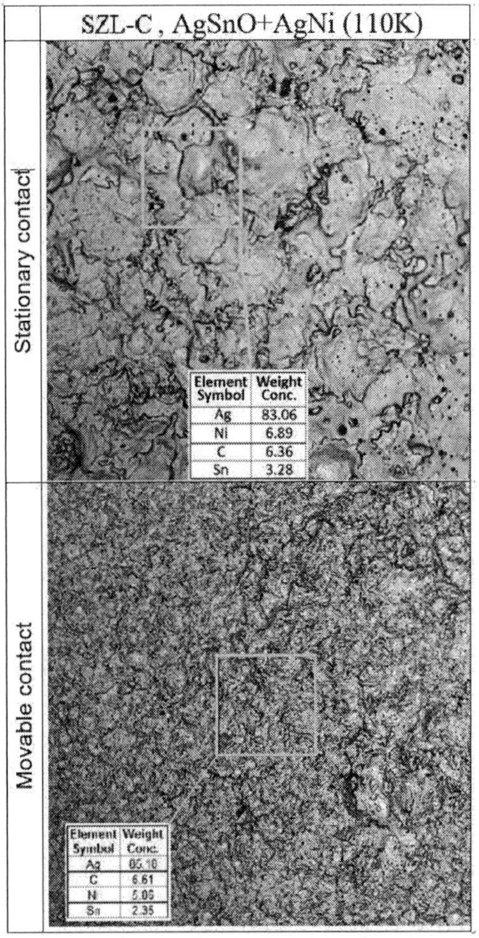

Fig. 5 SEM & EDX (Phenom-ProX) images: FOV: 900 μm, Mode: 15kV - Map, Detector: BSD Full.

The mutual material migration between AgNi contact and AgSnO contact, it was speculated that SnO migrated into AgNi contact could increase the viscosity of AgNi liquid in the molten pool and improves the wear resistance and welding resistance of AgNi under high current. And on the other hand, Ni migrated into AgSnO contact, it was endothermic with its low melting point (melting point of Ni is1453°C) and protected the decomposition of SnO powder under the heat of electric arc (decomposition temperature of SnO is about 2373°C), and this could be the main reason to improve the life performance of the sealed relay with the combined contacts.

Fig. 7 showed the metallographic diagram of the contact cross-section of the sample completed at 50K times. From the metallographic images, the migration of the contact material can be observed: the AgSnO contact material consumes very little, and its surface was covered with a thin layer of material mainly contents of Ag, Sn, and Ni. It was speculated again that the migration of Ni protects the decomposition of SnO, which reduces the consumption of materials and benefit to the improvement of life.

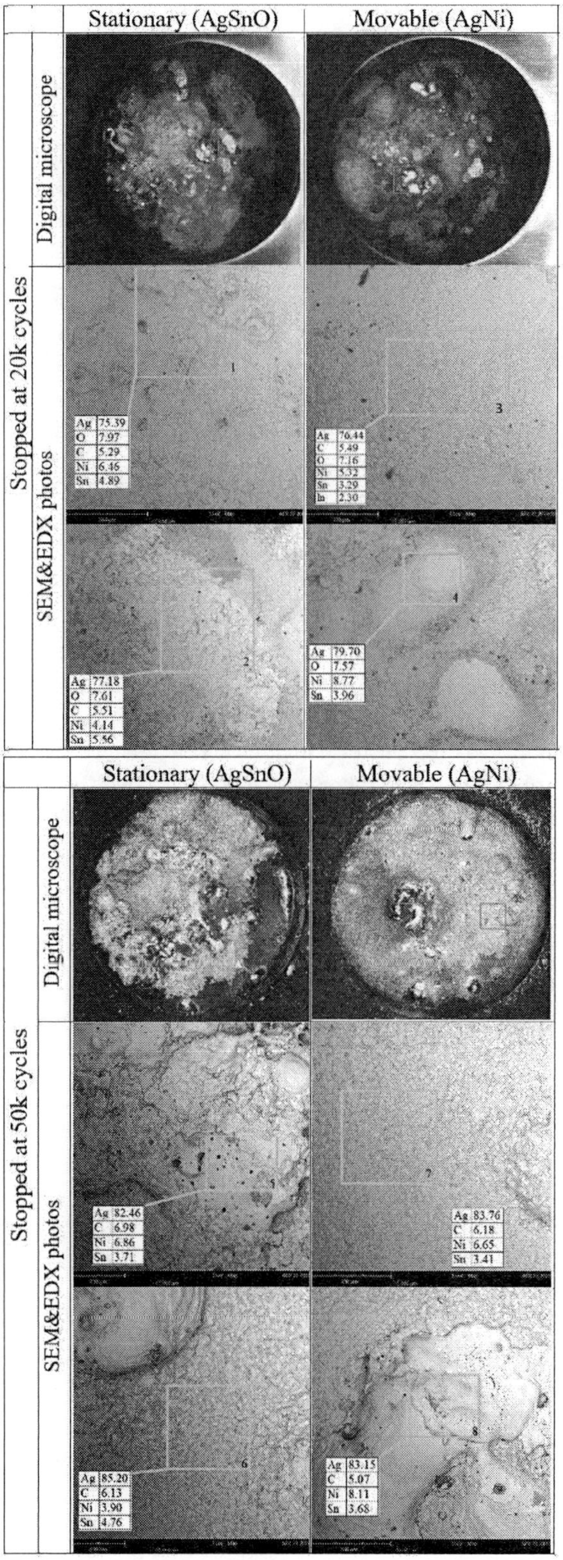

Fig. 6 Digital microscope, SEM & EDX (Phenom-ProX) Mode: 15kV - Map, Detector: BSD Full

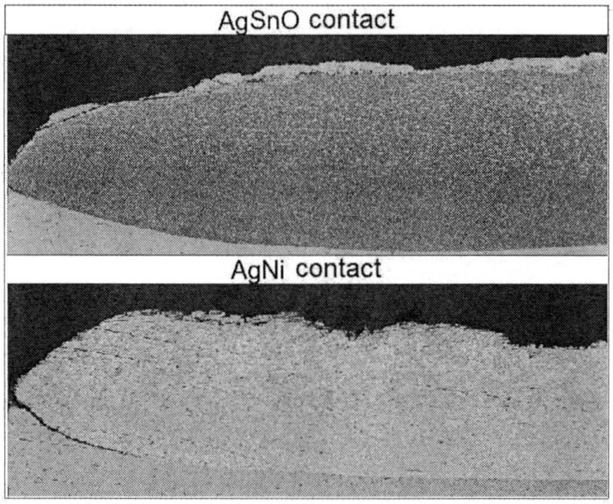

Fig. 7, Contact cross-section (half image with each contact)

III. CONCLUSION

The sealed relays with silver oxide contacts have a bad electrical lifetime, and sealed relays with silver non-oxide contacts could have a better electrical lifetime under the small to middle current level ($\leqslant$ 16A). However, sealed relays with silver oxide contact and non-oxide contact could have the improved electrical lifetime under high level current ($\geqslant$16A) while sealed relays with non-oxide contacts can' t meet the requirement of application. Conclusions were made base on the studies:

1) Contact material performance under the electrical arc effect is the key factor to impact the lifetime of sealed relays.

2) Silver base oxide contact in sealed relays is easy to be instable and severely eroded especially under high level current, and big bumps raised on contact surface which tends to weld the contacts and limit sealed relays' lifetime.

3) Sliver base non-oxide contact in sealed relay is stable to resist of electrical arc erosion and keep contact surface smooth under small to middle current level, while under high level current condition, because of high arc energy and low melting point of AgNi contact the Ni could separate out from silver base on contact surface and high ratio of Ag bumps could weld the contact easily and limited long lifetime performance.

4) Silver base oxide contact pairing with non-oxide contact use in sealed relays, with the mutual material migration between oxide contact and non-oxide contact, it overcomes the problem of rapid decomposition of oxide contact and it improves the poor wear resistance and fusion resistance of non-oxide contacts under high-level current. The verified lifetime was better than the sealed relays with silver oxide contacts or silver non-oxide contacts.

REFERENCES

[1]Tianpi Zheng;. "Relay Manufacturing, Technology and application"
[2]Zhihong Xu. "Theoretical Basis of Electrical Appliances"

Simulation Study on Contact Erosion Process by DC Arc under Magnetic Field

Haitao Wang[1,2], Yuxin Liang[1,2]

1) State Key Laboratory of Reliability and Intelligence of Electrical Equipment
Hebei University of Technology, Tianjin, 300401
2) Key Laboratory of Electromagnetic Field and Electrical Apparatus Reliability of Hebei Province,
Hebei University of Technology, Tianjin, 300401
E-mail: liangyx53@163.com Tel: 15503207973

Abstract—**In the process of breaking contacts of DC switching appliances, the arc produced will erode the contact materials and reduce the service life of the appliances. In order to reduce the arc time and contact erosion, magnetic field arc extinguishing is a kind of technical means commonly used in medium and low voltage electrical appliances. Therefore, a multi-physical field simulation model of arc-contact coupling is established based on MHD theory by using finite element software. The erosion process of arc on contact under constant magnetic field is analyzed, and the variation law of arc erosion on contact under changing current and breaking speed is further explored. Considering the phase transformation of the contact material, and the temperature distribution and molten pool formation process of the contact are solved. The simulation results show that the arc shifts from the center of the contact to the edge under magnetic field, and the surface temperature of the contact increases rapidly, which leads to phase transformation and forming molten pool. As the arc energy source, the arc burning time and the surface molten pool increase with the increase of the current. With the increase of breaking speed, the arc can be extinguished quickly, the stagnation time on the contact surface is reduced, and the molten pool area on the surface is reduced.**

Index Terms— **magnetic field, coupling model, molten pool, current, breaking speed**

I. INTRODUCTION

Compared with AC appliances, DC switching appliances do not have zero crossing in the breaking process and the arc generated by them is difficult to be extinguished, which will cause serious erosion on the contact surface. The magnetic field blowing arc is a measure which is often used to quench the arc of DC switching appliances. The external magnetic field will change the arc motion state and the erosion form of the contact surface. Therefore, it is of great help to explore the dynamic erosion process of the arc when the contact breaks under the action of the magnetic field and different factors on arc erosion to improve the service life of electrical contact materials.

In general, the arc burning time is very short, usually in the millisecond level, and the naked eye can't conduct a detailed analysis of the arc erosion process. Therefore, scholars at home and abroad often use numerical simulation to explore the arc erosion mechanism. Reference [1] analyzed the process of the surface temperature changing with time when the arc acted on the electrically contacted material in the steady state, and explored the law of erosion of the material by different arc gaps and currents. Reference [2-3] based on MHD theory and dynamic mesh technology has analyzed the arc root evolution process of using grid to quench arc when DC contactor contacts are broken, and the influence of physical factors on their breaking. Reference [4] established a two-dimensional contact erosion model under the DC air arc, considered the phase transition of materials and solved the influence law of different contact materials, size, shape and current grade on contact erosion over time.

Many scholars have done a lot of work in exploring the arc erosion process of contact, but the current research on the dynamic arc erosion process of contact is still insufficient. The coupling between arc and contact and the energy transfer process are rarely considered. Therefore, the dynamic evolution process of the arc under the magnetic field and the dynamic process of the molten pool formation of contact are obtained by using MHD theory and dynamic mesh technology, and the phase transition of the material is also considered. And the influence of different current size and breaking speed on arc erosion during contact breaking was also investigated.

II. THE ESTABLISHMENT OF SIMULATION MODEL

A. Simulation Model

$AgSnO_2$ is often used as a contact material for DC switching appliances due to its good electrical conductivity, high arc erosion resistance and strong transfer resistance. Therefore, $AgSnO_2$ (Ag: SnO_2=88:12) was selected as the electrical contact material in this study, and its physical parameters were shown in Table. 1. In the simulation, a simplified two-dimensional model is established based on the shape of the switch contact, as shown in Figure. 1. The anode and cathode contacts in the model are 3mm in diameter and 4mm in height. And the anode contact is static contact, the cathode contact is moving contact, their initial gap is 0.8mm. The medium of the contact gap is air. The initial temperature of the air domain is set to 293K, and the initial atmospheric pressure is 101325Pa. The solution step was set to 0.01ms.

TABLE I
PHYSICAL PARAMENTERS OF CONTACT MATERIALS

Contact materials	$AgSnO_2$
density/(kg·m^{-3})	9893
thermal conductivity/(W·(m·K)$^{-1}$)	371.8
conductivity/(%IACS)	75.0
specific heat/(J·(kg·K)$^{-1}$)	244.9
melting point/K	1234

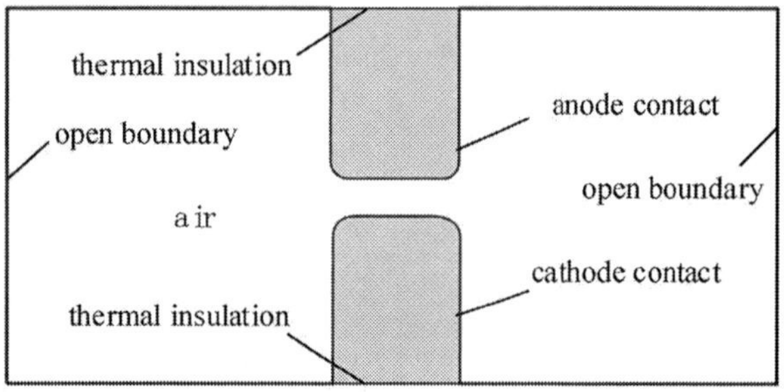

Fig.1 Geometry model of simulation

B. Arc-Contact MHD Model

The arc generated when the contact of DC switching appliances is broken is complicated and involves the coupling between electric field, magnetic field, flow field and thermal field. Therefore, the MHD model coupled with multiple physical fields is established in the simulation, and the arc plasma is assumed to be an incompressible Newtonian fluid in local thermodynamic equilibrium. The governing equations involved in the model are Navier-Stokes equations and Maxwell equations for solving the electromagnetic field as in [5]. As follows:

Mass conservation equation is shown in (1).

$$\rho\nabla\cdot\boldsymbol{u}=0 \tag{1}$$

Momentum conservation equation is shown in (2)-(3).

$$\rho\frac{\partial\boldsymbol{u}}{\partial t}+\rho(\boldsymbol{u}\cdot\nabla)\boldsymbol{u}=\boldsymbol{F}+\nabla\cdot\left[-p\boldsymbol{I}+\mu\left(\nabla\boldsymbol{u}+(\nabla\boldsymbol{u})^T\right)\right] \tag{2}$$

$$\boldsymbol{F}=\boldsymbol{J}\times\boldsymbol{B} \tag{3}$$

Energy conversation equation is shown in (4)-(5).

$$\rho C_p\frac{\partial T}{\partial t}+\rho C_p\boldsymbol{u}\cdot\nabla T=\nabla\cdot(k\nabla T)+Q \tag{4}$$

$$Q=\frac{\partial}{\partial T}\left(\frac{5k_BT}{2q}\right)(\nabla T\cdot\boldsymbol{J})+\boldsymbol{E}\cdot\boldsymbol{J}+Q_{rad} \tag{5}$$

Where ρ is the density of electric arc plasma; $\boldsymbol{u}$ is the velocity vector of the motion of electric arc plasma; p is the pressure on fluid element; μ is the dynamic viscosity of fluid; $\boldsymbol{I}$ is identity matrix; $\boldsymbol{F}$ is Lorentz force; $\boldsymbol{J}$ is current density; $\boldsymbol{B}$ is flux density; C_p is the specific heat at constant pressure; k is the thermal conductivity of material; E is the electric intensity; Q is plasma heat source which includes Joule heat, radiation of bulk volume and transmit of electronic enthalpy; k_B is Boltzmann constant; Q_{rad} is the radiation of bulk volume.

Governing equation of electromagnetic field is shown in (6).

$$\begin{cases}\boldsymbol{J}=\sigma\boldsymbol{E}\\ \boldsymbol{E}=-\nabla V\\ \boldsymbol{J}=\nabla\times\boldsymbol{H}\\ \boldsymbol{B}=\mu_r\mu_0\boldsymbol{H}\\ \nabla\times\boldsymbol{A}=\boldsymbol{B}\end{cases} \tag{6}$$

Where $\boldsymbol{H}$ is the magnetic field intensity; μ_r is the relative permeability of the gas medium; μ_0 is the vacuum permeability; $\boldsymbol{A}$ is magnetic vector potential.

C. Energy balance equation of arc - contact

There is energy coupling between the arc and the surface of the anode and cathode contact. According to the principle of energy conservation, the energy injected on the surface of the contact is equal to the energy consumed. Thus, the energy balance equation can be obtained as follows:

Arc-anode energy balance equation is shown in (7)-(9).

$$q_{con,arc}+q_{elec}=q_{con,anode} \tag{7}$$

$$q_{con,arc}=-n\cdot(-\lambda_{arc}\nabla T) \tag{8}$$

$$q_{elec}=|J_{elec}|\phi_c \tag{9}$$

Where $q_{con,arc}$ is the heat injected by the arc into the surface of the anode contact by heat conduction; q_{elec} is the energy injected into the surface by the electron impinging on the anode contact; $q_{con,anode}$ is the heat flowing into the contact by heat conduction from the anode surface.

Arc-cathode energy balance equation is shown in (10)-(14).

$$q_{\mathrm{con,arc}} + q_{\mathrm{ion}} = q_{\mathrm{con,cathode}} + q_{\mathrm{elec}} \tag{10}$$

$$q_{\mathrm{con,arc}} = -n \cdot (-\lambda_{\mathrm{arc}} \nabla T) \tag{11}$$

$$q_{\mathrm{ion}} = |J_{\mathrm{ion}}| V_{\mathrm{ion}} \tag{12}$$

$$|\boldsymbol{J}_{\mathrm{ion}}| = |\boldsymbol{J} \cdot n| - |\boldsymbol{J}_{\mathrm{elec}}| \tag{13}$$

$$q_{\mathrm{elec}} = |J_{\mathrm{elec}}| \phi_c \tag{14}$$

Where $q_{\mathrm{con,arc}}$ is the heat flowing into the cathode surface by arc through heat conduction; q_{ion} is the energy injected into the surface of the ion impinging on the cathode; $q_{\mathrm{con,cathode}}$ is the heat flowing into the cathode by heat conduction from the cathode surface; q_{elec} is the energy lost by electron emission from the cathode surface.

D. Material Phase Change Treatment

Under the high temperature arc, the surface temperature of the contact material will increase and the phase transformation will occur, from solid phase to liquid phase gradually, thus forming the molten pool. The fraction of the liquid part of the region during the phase transition can be expressed as a function of temperature dependence as follows.

$$\theta = \begin{cases} 1, & T \geq (T_{\mathrm{m}} + \Delta T / 2) \\ \dfrac{T - T_{\mathrm{m}} + \Delta T}{\Delta T}, & (T_{\mathrm{m}} + \Delta T / 2) > T \geq (T_{\mathrm{m}} - \Delta T / 2) \\ 0, & T < (T_m - \Delta T / 2) \end{cases} \tag{15}$$

Where T is the temperature of the contact material; Tm is the melting temperature of the contact; ΔT is the transition interval between solid phase and liquid phase of the material.

After the phase transformation of the contact material, its physical parameters will change, so the density, thermal conductivity and specific heat capacity are treated equivalently.

$$\rho_{eq} = (1-\theta)\rho_s + \theta\rho_l \tag{16}$$

$$k_{eq} = (1-\theta)k_s + \theta k_l \tag{17}$$

$$C_{p_{eq}} = \frac{(1-\theta)\rho_s C_{p_s}}{\rho_{eq}} + L_m \frac{\partial \alpha_m}{\partial T} \tag{18}$$

$$\alpha_m = \frac{\theta\rho_l - (1-\theta)\rho_s}{2[\theta\rho_l + (1-\theta)\ \rho_s]} \tag{19}$$

III. ANALYSIS OF SIMULATION RESULTS

A. Analysis of Arc Erosion during DC Breaking

The external coupling voltage of the circuit set in the simulation is 48V, the current is 36A, the breaking speed of the contact is 200mm/s, and the external transverse magnetic field is 15mT. When the contact breaks, the dynamic arc change process is shown in fig.2. In the figure, the arc is generated in the center of the contact at 0.1ms, and the initial temperature is about 14000K. Then the moving contact moves down, and the arc begins to move toward the edge by the Lorentz force. At 0.7ms, the arc reaches the edge of the contact, after which the arc is blown into a bow and the heated charged particles diffuse outwards due to the continuing Lorentz force. As a result, the diameter of arc column increases and the current density decreases, which is conducive to the rapid reduction of arc temperature until the arc is extinguished. As the moving contact continues to move down, the arc is bent and elongated. At 7.0ms, due to the effect of magnetic field, the arc column temperature drops obviously and the temperature distribution in the right side of the arc generally increases. This is because the magnetic field makes the molecules move faster, the gap thermal conductivity is increased, and the temperature is accelerated to spread around. After that, the arc tends to be extinguished at 8.5ms, and the contact gap temperature continues to decrease to below 4000K. The arc is not reignited and completely extinguished.

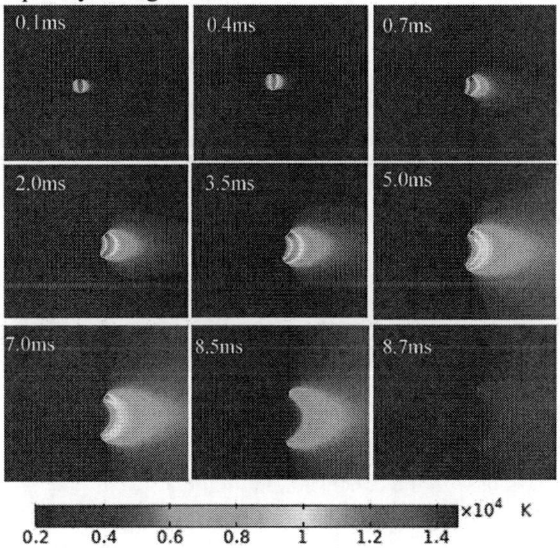

Fig.2 Arc temperature distribution during the opening process

Figure 3 shows the temperature profiles of anode and cathode contacts as a function of time. In Fig.2, after the arc is generated in the center of the contact, it moves to the edge of the contact at 0.7ms under the Lorentz force. Because the arc stays in the center of the contact for a short time, its temperature does not rise too much. When the arc reaches the edge of the contact, the temperature of the contact increases rapidly with the time of the arc, and diffuses into the contact in the form of an arc. In the process of contact temperature rising, it can be seen that the temperature distribution of cathode is obviously higher than that of anode at the same time. The analysis shows that the arc root spot diameter of the anode contact is usually larger than that of the cathode contact, and the energy flow density is low, so the temperature of the anode contact is lower than that of the cathode contact, so the temperature distribution of the cathode is obviously higher than that of the anode contact.

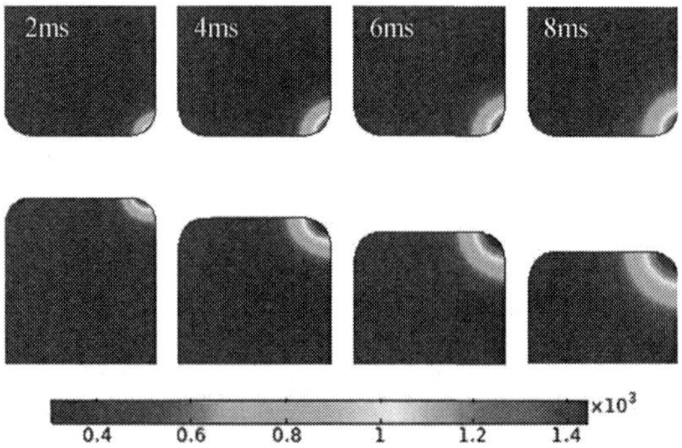

Fig.3 The distribution of temperature of anode and cathode contacts

Fig. 4 shows the curve of the maximum temperature of anode and cathode contact with time. It can be seen that the temperature of anode and cathode contact rises rapidly with the arc energy injection at the beginning. However, with the change of time, the growth rate of contact temperature changes from fast to slow, and finally tends to be stable with a slight downward trend. This is because the heat injected into the contact by the arc is less than the heat lost by the contact through heat conduction, and the heat on the contact surface cannot be maintained, so the temperature of the contact drops. The temperature of the cathode contact is higher than that of the anode contact over time, which is consistent with the conclusion in Figure 3.

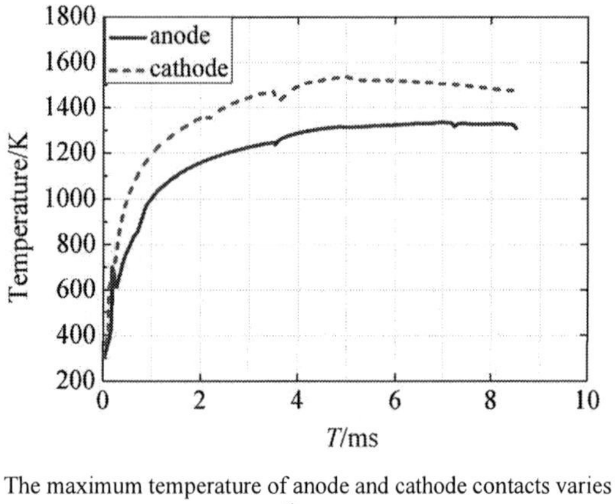

Fig.4 The maximum temperature of anode and cathode contacts varies with time

As the contact surface temperature continues to rise, the contact material will gradually change from solid phase to liquid phase to form a molten pool after reaching the melting point of the material. Fig.5 shows the variation law of the molten pool on the contact surface with time. In the figure, the cathode surface has undergone phase transformation at 2.0ms to form a molten pool, while the anode has not yet formed a molten pool due to the low temperature at this time, and then the anode also underwent phase transformation at 4.0ms to form a molten pool. But at the same time, the molten pool area of the lower anode is always smaller than that of the cathode. In the figure, the molten pool on the contact surface increases inward in the form of an arc, and the width of the molten pool on the anode and cathode contacts is greater than the depth.

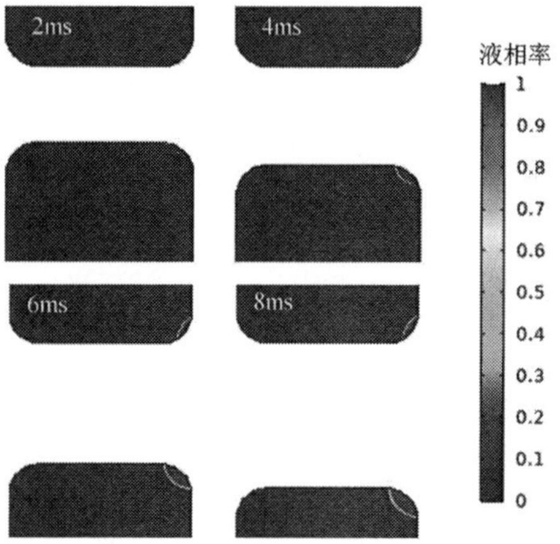

Fig.5 Variation of molten on contact surface with time

B. Effect of Current on Arc Erosion

The voltage of the external coupling circuit is set as 48V, the breaking speed of the contact is set as 150mm/s, magnetic field strength as 15mT, and the current is set as 24A, 28A, 32A and 36A. Fig.6 shows the curve of the maximum temperature of the arc with time. It can be seen that under the same external magnetic field, the arc temperature increases and the arc burning time increases when the current increases. And the arc burning time increases more with the increase of current. This is because current is the main energy source of arc combustion, so when the contact is broken, the larger the current, the higher the arc temperature, the longer the time, the more serious the erosion of the contact surface.

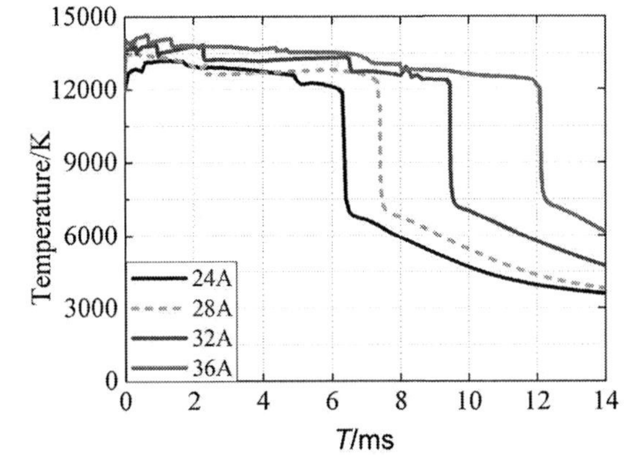

Fig.6 The variation of arc temperature of different currents with time

Figure 7 shows the maximum molten pool area of the contact surface undergoing phase transition under the high temperature when the contact is broken. In the figure, the cathodic molten pool area of the contact is larger than the anodic molten pool area under all conditions, which is consistent with the results obtained in Figure 5. Under the same external magnetic field intensity, the molten pool area on the contact surface with the current of 36A is significantly higher than that of 24A. This is because the increase of current level makes the arc action time longer, and the surface energy injected into the contact per unit time becomes larger, so the molten pool area also increases.

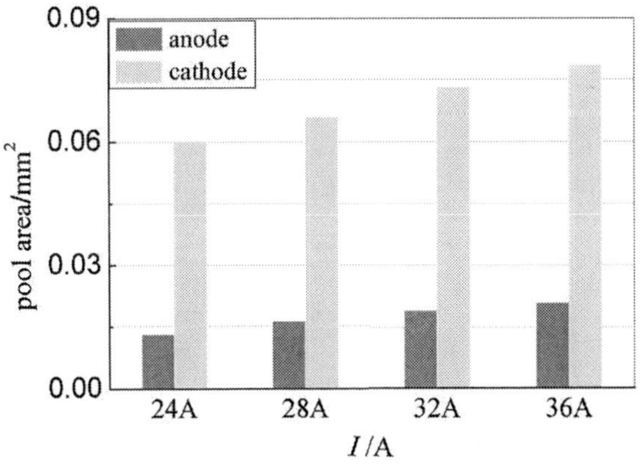

Fig.7 Variation of molten pool area with current size

C. *Effect of Breaking Velocity on Arc Erosion*

The voltage of the external coupling circuit is set as 48V, the current is set as 36A, and the magnetic field intensity is set as 15mT, the breaking speed of the contact is set as 100mm/s, 150mm/s, 200mm/s and 250mm/s. Fig.8 shows the curve of the maximum temperature of the arc with time. In the figure, the initial temperature of the arc is basically the same under different breaking speeds. After that, the arc burning time is obviously reduced due to the increase of the breaking speed, which is mainly because the arc length increases faster in the same time, the current density decreases, and the arc rapidly spreads to the surrounding at high temperature until extinguished.

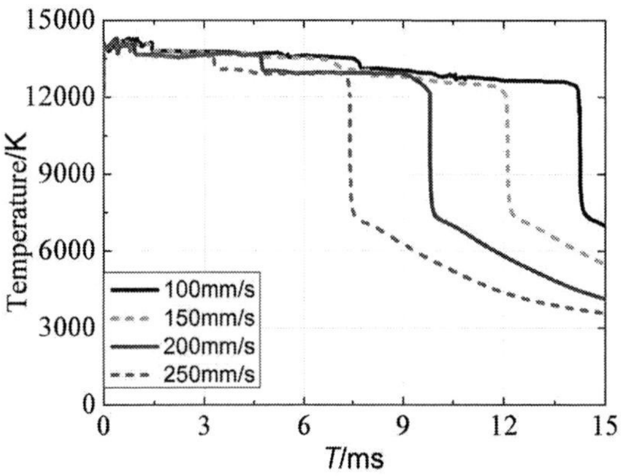

Fig.8 The variation of arc temperature of different breaking speed with time

Fig. 9 shows the maximum molten pool area formed by phase transformation on the material surface when the contact is broken at different speeds. In the figure, under the same breaking speed, the molten pool area of anode and cathode decreases with the increase of magnetic field strength, and the cathode area decreases more. According to Figure 8, the increase of breaking speed will reduce the arc burning time, reduce the arc heat injection into the contact surface, so the molten pool area on the contact material surface will also be reduced.

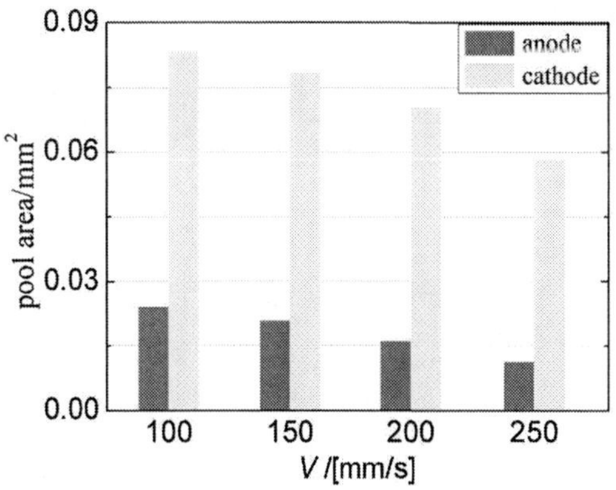

Fig.9 Variation of molten pool area with breaking velocity

IV. Conclusion

In this paper, $AgSnO_2$ is used as the contact material of DC electric apparatus in simulation, and the dynamic erosion process of the contact is analyzed in the process of DC electric apparatus breaking under the condition of external magnetic field. And by changing the current size and breaking speed to explore the erosion law of the contact, the following conclusions are obtained:

1) When the contact breaks, the arc is generated from the center of the contact and then rapidly transferred to the edge of the contact under the action of the Lorentz force. As the surface temperature of the contact increases, the material will undergo phase transformation to form a molten pool, and the area of the cathode molten pool is larger than that of the anode molten pool.

2) As the current increases, the arc temperature increases and the heat injected into the contact surface increases, so the molten pool area formed by the phase transformation of the contact becomes larger.

3) With the increase of breaking speed, the length of arc increases and becomes faster in unit time. As a result, the arc voltage quickly reaches the breaking voltage, the arc goes out faster, the time acting on the contact surface is shorter, and the molten pool area on the contact surface is reduced.

References

[1] Y. F. Wu, Z. F. Yang and G. Q. Gao. "Thermal ablation process of electrical contact materials under arc effect" , *High Voltage Engineering.*. 2019, 45, 2276-2283.

[2] Y. D. Cao, K. Liu and J. Li, at al. "Research on the Influence Factors of Arc Characteristics in the Arc Extinguish Chamber in DC Contactor Breaking Process," *2017 4th International Conference on Electrical Power Equipment*, Xian, China.

[3] J. Li, K. Liu and Y. D. Cao, at al. "Arc root development and Its influence on arc reigniting during the breaking process of the DC contactor" in *Proceedings of the CSEE.* 2019, 39. 1241-1250.

[4] X. W. Li, Q. S. Lv and T. Tian, at al. "Contact erosion characteristics under direct current air arc" in *High Voltage Engineering.* 2020, 46:1970-1977.

[5] Y. Han, L. X. Meng and C. G. Hou, at al. "Simulation and experimental research on DC arc re-striking in hydrogen medium under multiple physical factors" in *Electrical & Energy Management Technology.* 2018, 22: 28-34.

[6] J. Li, M. X. Guan and S. X. Liu, at al. "Process of contact erosion and influence on breaking characteristics under DC air arc" in *High Voltage Engineering.* 2022, 48: 1531-1541.

Acknowledgment

This work is supported by the National Natural Science Foundation of China (51777057) and the Local Science and Technology Development Fund Project (216Z1011G).

Wang Haitao, was born in February, 1973, and graduated from Hebei University of Technology with a doctor's degree. Professor wang mainly studies electrical reliability and testing technology, low voltage electrical appliances and electrical contact.

Research on Double Power Transfer Switch Fault Detection Method Based on Single-phase dq0 Transformation

Junfeng OuYang, Changchun Chi

College of Electrical Engineering, Shanghai Dianji University, Shanghai, China
E-mail:845739813@qq.com, E-mail: chicc@sdju.edu.cn

Abstract—**Switching time is one of the important technical indexes to measure the reliability of dual power automatic transfer switch. Shortening the power switching time ensures continuous power supply and improves power supply reliability. In this paper, a fault detection method of dual power automatic transfer switch is studied, which can shorten the switching time of power. Kalman algorithm is used to denoise voltage sampling signal. The dq0 transform is used to construct the three-phase voltage, and the derivative method is used to extract the positive sequence fundamental wave component of the voltage, which solves the delay problem of the low-pass filter. A filter with a cut-off frequency of 3000Hz is used to avoid the interference of harmonic components. The fault is detected by the voltage transient depth obtained from the voltage value after derivative filtering and the rated voltage reference value. Simulation results show that this method makes up for the defect of dq0transform based on instantaneous reactive power theory. Combined with Kalman algorithm, the accuracy of voltage sampling is greatly improved and the risk of misoperation of dual power transfer switch is reduced. On the basis of satisfying the reliability of fault detection, the detection time is shortened, which is of great significance to real-time detection.**

Index Terms—**dual power transfer switch, kalman algorithm, derivative filter**

I. INTRODUCTION

As people have higher requirements for the reliability and quality of power supply, the power system has become increasingly complex. Voltage fluctuations and voltage deviations have become the main cause of voltage faults. In modern industry as well as in the field of building fire protection, if voltage faults are not detected in time, it will seriously endanger people's property and life safety.

As an important means to guarantee the reliability of the system power supply, the conversion time of the dual power transfer switch is an important indicator. The faster the power conversion time, the higher the reliability of power supply[1]-[4] At present, the structure of dual-supply transfer switches on the market has become mature, and the optimization of the fault detection algorithm for voltage can reduce the conversion time to some extent. In the field of voltage fault detection algorithms, various methods have emerged from the traditional rms method to the more widely used dq0 transform method based on instantaneous reactive power theory, as well as the Fourier transform, and then the wavelet transform developed in recent years. All these algorithms have certain limitations in detecting voltage. For example, the literature [5]-[8] uses the rms method for voltage detection, which uses the rms value obtained from the voltage in the working frequency cycle to monitor the change in voltage to determine whether a fault has occurred, but requires the use of 1 cycle of voltage data to obtain the rms value, so there is a delay in the detection time. In the literature [9-12], the Fourier transform decomposes the voltage period signal into discrete spectrum and then integrates and sums the voltage amplitude. Although the Fourier algorithm can filter the higher harmonics to make the sampling voltage more accurate, it also needs 1 cycle of voltage data, and the algorithm speed is as slow as the RMS method. The literature [13]-[15] transforms the three-phase voltage from abc coordinates to dq0 coordinates to obtain the voltage amplitude, but the algorithm can only be used for three-phase fault detection, if a single-phase fault occurs, the dq0 algorithm will not detect accurately, and the filter time constant in the algorithm will also delay the response time.

To this end, this paper investigates a voltage fault detection method by denoising the sampled signal through Kalman theory, reconstructing the three-phase voltage from the denoised single-phase voltage, and omitting the low-pass filter by the derivative method. The simulation results show that the proposed method solves the time delay problem of the low-pass filter. The reliability and real-time performance of voltage fault detection are improved.

II. KALMAN FILTER ALGORITHM-BASED VOLTAGE SAMPLING METHOD

Voltage fault detection is based on real-time monitoring of the amplitude change of the collected voltage as the judgment of voltage faults. In voltage detection, because the grid is complex and large, the actual voltage signal collected is generally with harmonics and noise, and the interference brought by harmonics and noise can affect the accurate identification of voltage faults. Therefore, improving the voltage sampling accuracy can enhance the anti-interference ability to harmonics and noise, which can effectively avoid the voltage fault detection errors caused by voltage errors and improve the reliability of equipment power supply. In order to improve the voltage sampling accuracy, the denoising process is performed by Matlab combined with Kalman filter algorithm, which reduces the sampling voltage reading error.

alman filter online instantly uses control variables and pre-recursive estimated values to restore the real data, which has the advantages of strong dynamic tracking capability, high estimation accuracy, simple calculation method, and iterative recursive calculation on the computer. Given that the voltage sampling signal contains harmonic components, measurement errors and other noise, this paper adopts the Kalman filter algorithm, which can extract the fundamental components from the voltage sampling signal in a very short time, and the Kalman filter has a very high operational accuracy. The Kalman algorithm flow is shown in Figure 1.、

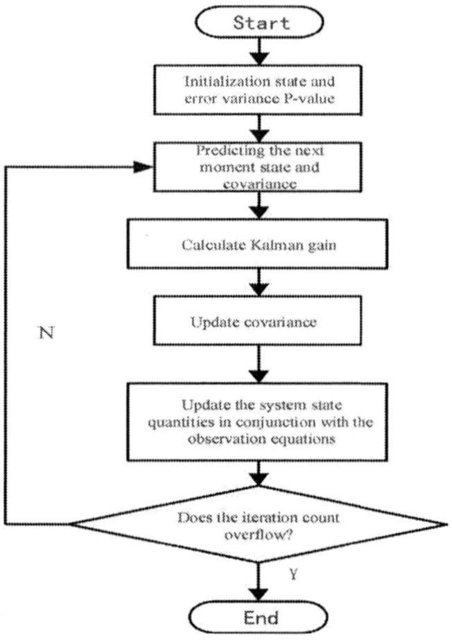

Fig. 1.Kalman algorithm process

The state of the system at any moment k is:

$$X_k = AX_{k-1} + BU_k + W_k \tag{1}$$

In equation (1): is the system state at moment k-1; is the system control quantity at moment k; is the process noise at moment k; is the system parameter.

The measured value Z_k of the system at any moment k is

$$Z_k = HX_k + V_k \tag{2}$$

In equation (2): H is the measurement system parameter; is the measurement noise at k moments.

The Kalman filter estimation can be divided into two phases, prediction and update. First, in the prediction phase, using the state at moment k-1, the predicted value of the system state at moment k, X_k', is predicted as.

$$X_k' = AX_{k-1} + BU_k \tag{3}$$

Since the covariance of X_k is not updated at this time, using the optimal estimate of the covariance at moment k-1,the optimal estimate of the covariance at moment k predicts the value P'_k as

$$P_k' = AP_{k-1} + Q_{ww} \tag{4}$$

In equation (4): is the system process covariance.

In the part of updating the optimal estimate, the Kalman gain K_k at moment k is first calculated, and then the system state and error covariance are corrected according to K_k at this moment to obtain the best estimate at this moment, and this set of equations is

$$\begin{cases} K_k = \dfrac{P_k' H^T}{HP_k' H^T + R_{vv}} \\ X_k = X_k' + K_k\left(Z_k - HX_k'\right) \\ P_k = \left(I - K_k H\right) P_k' \end{cases} \tag{5}$$

In equation (5): R_{vv} is the system measurement covariance; is the optimal estimate of the error covariance at moment k; I is the unit matrix here i.e. I=1.

When the system is calculated at the next moment k+1, the state value of the system at moment k is used to predict the state value at moment k+1, and then the optimal estimate of the covariance at moment k+1 is predicted and corrected with K_k to obtain the optimal estimate at moment k+1. In this way, the regression operation is performed by itself. The noise is eliminated in the iteration to obtain a voltage value closer to the actual one, which helps to provide a more accurate voltage sampling value for voltage fault detection.

III. VOLTAGE FAULT DETECTION METHOD

The voltage obtained after noise removal by Kalman filtering algorithm through a hybrid dual power transfer switch controller is used to detect whether a fault has occurred in the supply voltage. Examples include phase breakage, overvoltage, undervoltage and three-phase unbalance. In the event of a power supply fault, the controller generates a command signal and the transfer switch performs the corresponding action. In the case of sudden changes in power supply voltage, the dual power transfer switch needs to act quickly. Currently, voltage faults are mainly detected based on the dq0 transform and αβ transform of instantaneous reactive power theory, and these methods produce errors when asymmetric faults are detected. The single-phase construction method is accurate in calculation, but for our 50Hz system, the algorithm itself constructed will have a delay of 60°, i.e., 3.333 ms delay. In order to solve the error generated when the asymmetric fault and the delay caused by the algorithm construction, a voltage fault detection algorithm is studied, and its algorithm flow is shown in Figure 2. Construct the three-phase voltage, take a phase power u_k to obtain the single-phase voltage derivative, through the single-phase voltage u_k cosine value and the mathematical relationship between the three-phase voltage to derive the remaining two-phase voltage, effectively avoiding the single-phase voltage construction method in which only the a-phase voltage is used in real time data, while the b and c phases are used before 60 ° data, the derivative construction method can make the three-phase voltage collection data with simultaneity. The constructed voltages u_{kd} and u_{kq} are obtained by the dq0 transform, and the amplitude is extracted using the derivative method to obtain the positive sequence fundamental components. The conventional dq0 transform and αβ transform produce errors in detection due to asymmetric faults caused by harmonic components and noise in the grid. The derivative method is used to extract the positive sequence fundamental component of the voltage, which solves the delay problem of the low-pass filter and uses a low-pass filter with a cutoff frequency of 3 kHz to avoid the interference of harmonic components; the absolute value of the depth of voltage mutation is calculated to determine whether a fault occurs in the supply voltage.

Let the three phase voltages of the power supply be U_a, U_b and U_c. The angular frequency is ω and the time is t.

$$\begin{cases} U_a = \sqrt{2}U sin(\omega t) \\ U_b = \sqrt{2}U sin\left(\omega t - \frac{2\pi}{3}\right) \\ U_c = \sqrt{2}U sin\left(\omega t + \frac{2\pi}{3}\right) \end{cases} \quad (6)$$

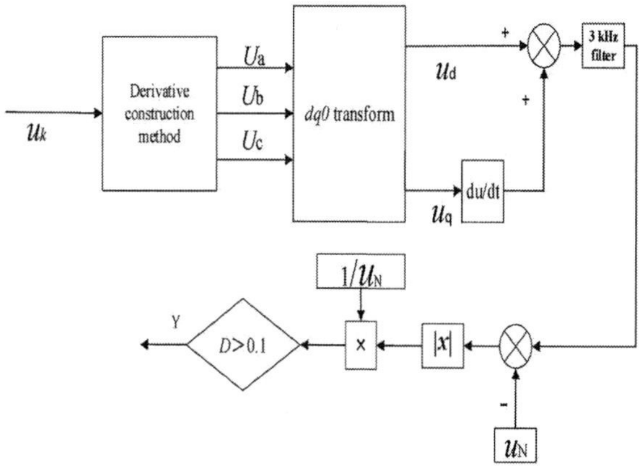

Fig. 2. Voltage detection algorithm process

The derivative of the voltage of phase a is obtained:

$$U_a^{'} = \sqrt{2}U\omega cos(\omega t) \quad (7)$$

The derivative relationship between the three phase voltages shows that

$$\begin{cases} U_b = -\frac{1}{2}U_a - \frac{\sqrt{3}}{2\omega}U_a^{'} \\ U_c = -\frac{1}{2}U_a + \frac{\sqrt{3}}{2\omega}U_a^{'} \end{cases} \quad (8)$$

Constructing the remaining two phase voltages from the derivative relationship can solve the 60° delay problem of the single-phase voltage construction method.

The three-phase voltage is obtained by the three-phase construction method, which is transformed by dq0 to obtain the voltage U in dq0 coordinates, whose component formula is

$$\begin{bmatrix} U_d^p \\ U_q^p \end{bmatrix} = \frac{2}{3} R(\omega t) C \begin{bmatrix} U_a \\ U_b \\ U_c \end{bmatrix} \quad (9)$$

where the coefficient matrix C of the b and c phase voltages is

$$C = \begin{bmatrix} 1 & -\frac{1}{2} & -\frac{1}{2} \\ 0 & \frac{\sqrt{3}}{2} & -\frac{\sqrt{3}}{2} \end{bmatrix} \quad (10)$$

The rotation matrix R(ωt) is

$$R(\omega t) = \begin{bmatrix} cos(\omega t) & -sin(\omega t) \\ sin(\omega t) & cos(\omega t) \end{bmatrix} \quad (11)$$

Substituting equations (10) and (11) into equation (9) gives

$$\begin{bmatrix} U_d^p \\ U_p^d \end{bmatrix} = \begin{bmatrix} U_{dp} \\ U_{qp} \end{bmatrix} + R(-2\omega t)\begin{bmatrix} U_{\mathrm{dn}} \\ U_{\mathrm{qn}} \end{bmatrix} \quad (12)$$

In equation (12):

U_{dp} is the positive sequence component of U_d;

U_{dn} is the negative sequence component of U_d;

U_{qp} is the positive sequence component of U_q;

U_{qn} is the negative sequence component of U_q.

The derivative of equation (12) is then rotated and finally divided by

$$-\frac{1}{2\omega} R\left(\frac{\pi}{2}\right)\begin{bmatrix} \dot{U}_d^p \\ \dot{U}_q^p \end{bmatrix} = R(\pi)R(-2\omega t)\begin{bmatrix} U_{dn} \\ U_{qn} \end{bmatrix} \quad (13)$$

Adding equation (12) and equation (13) to obtain:

$$\begin{bmatrix} U_d^p \\ U_q^p \end{bmatrix} - \frac{1}{2\omega} R\left(\frac{\pi}{2}\right)\begin{bmatrix} \dot{U}_d^p \\ \dot{U}_q^p \end{bmatrix} = \begin{bmatrix} U_{dp} \\ U_{qp} \end{bmatrix} \quad (14)$$

As can be seen from (14), the positive sequence component is obtained by calculating and omitting the low-pass filter in the algorithm, which ensures the real-time accuracy of the algorithm. Following the flow of the voltage fault detection algorithm in Fig. 2, the depth of the voltage mutation can be calculated as

$$D = \left| \frac{U_{dp} - U_{\mathrm{N}}}{U_{\mathrm{N}}} \right| \quad (15)$$

In equation (15): UN is the rated reference voltage.

From the Institute of Electrical and Electronics Engineers (IEEE) definition of voltage transient drop and voltage transient rise can be seen, when the absolute value of voltage change is less than 90% of the rated value, the power quality is unqualified.

The switching signal is issued by whether the depth of the voltage burst in equation (15) reaches the switching power requirement.

IV. SIMULATION VALIDATION

A. Construction of simulation model

According to the working principle of the hybrid dual-supply transfer switch, a simulation model of the dual-supply automatic transfer switch and a voltage fault detection algorithm model are built in Simulink, and several possible faults of the supply voltage are simulated and analyzed. The main circuit topology of the dual-supply transfer switch is shown in Figure 3, and its structure is a mechanical switch connected in parallel to a thyristor switch. The working principle is: when the intelligent controller detects the voltage abnormality and reaches the power switching requirement, the controller sends a signal to both the mechanical switch PS1 and the thyristor switch TS1 on the common power supply 1 side, so that PS1 disconnects and TS1 conducts. After PS1 completes the breaking action, the TS1 conduction signal is withdrawn and the load is disconnected from power supply 1, waiting for the end of TS1 renewal, the controller sends a signal to the mechanical switch PS2 and thyristor switch TS2 on the side of backup power supply 2, making PS2 closed and TS2 conduction, and the load is connected to power supply 2. End.

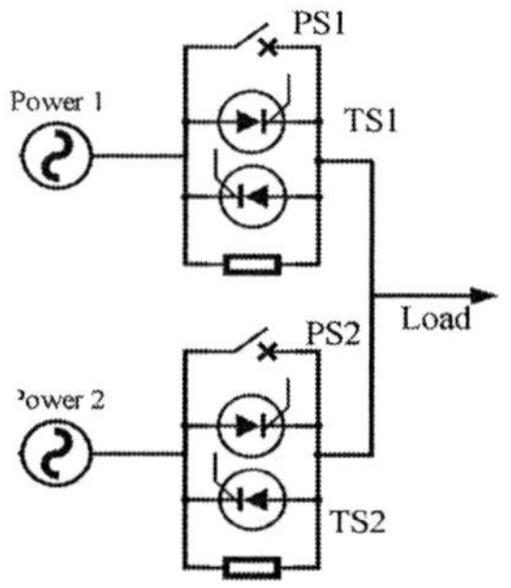

Fig. 3. Dual power transfer switch main circuit topology diagram

The voltage fault detection algorithm model is shown in Figure 4. Considering the existence of white noise environment when extracting single-phase voltage, the white noise module is added to the actual system and the measured value respectively, setting the noise amplitude to 115 V and the noise time to 0.003 s. The seed parameters are the default values. The measured signal is connected to the Kalman optimal estimator module to obtain the denoised voltage sampling signal. The remaining two phase voltages are constructed by the derivative construction method, and the constructed three-phase voltages are transformed by dq0 to obtain ud and u_q. The fundamental components of the three-phase positive sequence voltages are compared with the set reference values, and the controller issues a power switching signal when the depth of the voltage mutation reaches the requirement of switching power.

B. Voltage sampling and filter waveform simulation

The rectified and conditioned power supply phase voltage signal is transformed into a DC signal of 0~5 V recognizable by the analog-to-digital converter, and the power supply voltage sample is filtered by Simulink to obtain the voltage sample return value before de-noising; the measured voltage value is de-noised by Kalman filtering to obtain the voltage sample return value after de-noising. A comparison of the before and after voltage sample de-noising is shown in Figure 5.

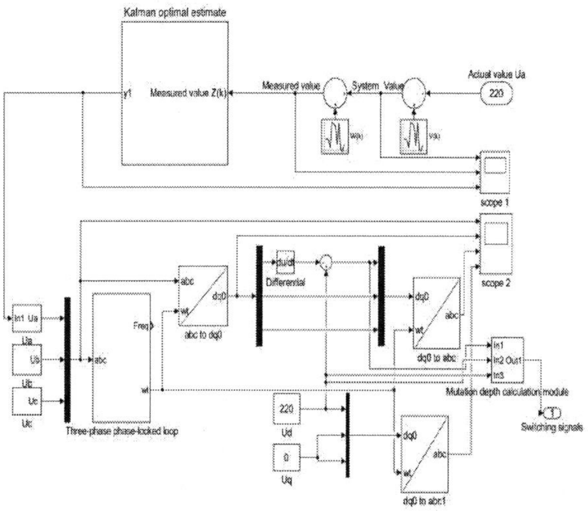

Fig. 4. Voltage fault detection algorithm model

As can be seen from Figure 5, the interference noise and error range in the collected voltage samples are large, affecting the controller's judgment of voltage faults, and the effect is obvious after the denoising process, and the error range is significantly reduced; the voltage error range is reduced from to, which reduces the impact generated by noise and improves the sampling accuracy.

C. *Voltage fault detection simulation*

To verify the rapidity of response time of the new dq0 algorithm, simulation experiments were conducted by comparing Fourier's algorithm, dq0 algorithm and wavelet transform method under three conditions of 20% voltage dip amplitude, 20% voltage amplitude surge and 20% single-phase voltage dip amplitude. Figure 6 shows the simulation comparison of the four detection methods. Table 1 gives the fault detection times of the hybrid dual-supply transfer switch controller under different algorithms.

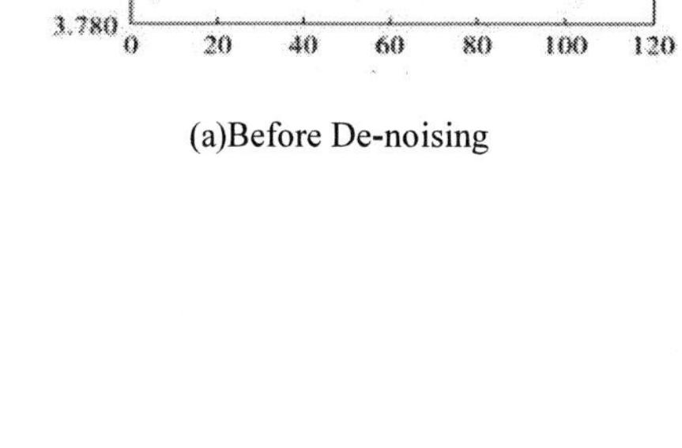

(a)Before De-noising

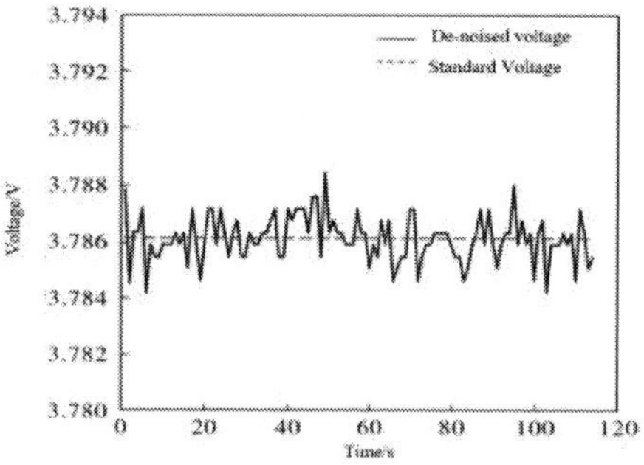

(b) After de-noising

Fig. 5. Before and after voltage sampling de-noising

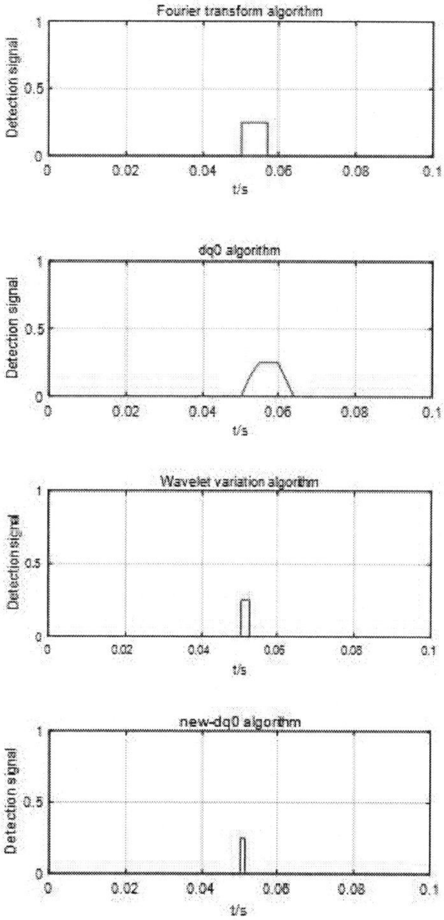

Fig. 6. Waveforms of detection signals with different algorithms

As can be seen from Table 1, in terms of detection time, the Fourier algorithm requires one cycle of voltage sampling data and is affected by the delay of the low-pass filter, so its detection speed is slower than the other three algorithms. The traditional dq0 algorithm detects voltage faults by extracting the characteristic amount of voltage signals and identifying voltage glitch signals. However, due to its inevitable influence by the low-pass filter and the inherent 3.33 ms delay in the construction of the algorithm itself under our industrial frequency system, it makes the detection time of the algorithm relatively long. Wavelet transform method can greatly reduce the detection time, but because it can not completely eliminate the interference of noise on the voltage signal acquisition, so that the wavelet transform can not accurately extract some voltage characteristic quantity, which may lead to fault misoperation.The new dq0 algorithm can collect the data of three-phase voltage at the same time, and the derivative method eliminates the low-pass filter to solve its delay problem and shorten the detection time to within 1ms. On balance, the new dq0 algorithm studied in this paper has a faster detection time than the other three algorithms and can detect sudden voltage changes in a shorter period of time.

TABLE I Detection time of different algorithms under different working conditions

Fault Type	Fault detection time/ms			
	Fourier's algorithm	dq0 algorithm	Wavelet algorithm	New-dq0 algorithm
Voltage amplitude drops 20%	6.7	5.5	2.0	0.97
Voltage amplitude jump 20%	6.9	5.5	2.0	0.97
single-phase voltage amplitude drops 20%	6.7	5.8	2.2	1.02

V. CONCLUSION

In this paper, a new dq0 algorithm is investigated by introducing a three-phase construction method based on single-phase voltage derivatives while combining Kalman theory. The Kalman filtering algorithm is used to obtain the de-noised voltage for voltage fault detection. The simulation results show that the selected three-phase construction method based on the single-phase voltage derivative is good at compensating the drawback of 60° delay in the construction of the single-phase voltage construction method itself. The detection method based on the new single-phase dq0 transform is more accurate for the identification of voltage faults and has strong anti-interference capability. The real-time of detection is better. This method provides a good research direction for the detection of voltage faults in dual-supply transfer switches.

REFERENCES

[1] Jin, P.,"Dual power switching power supply transformation in data center rooms of universities," *Modern Building Electricity*, 2021, 12 (6): 59-61.

[2] Zheng P., Wang T, Liu J.Y, Zhang H., Pei Y.J., "Research on senseless dual power fast switching technology," *Science and Technology*, 2020, 36(2): 5-68.

[3] Chen X.J. , Liu J.M. , Wang X.L. , "A new type of left and right moving automatic transfer switch," *Electrical Switchgear*, 2020, 58(6): 28-31.

[4] Zhou X., "Comparison and analysis of electrical design in Chinese and American medical buildings," *Intelligent Building Electrical Technology*, 2021, 15(6): 66-71,107

[5] Chen H. C., Kuo P.H., Huang C. J., "A mutual blocking technology applied to dual power source switching control," *Energies*, 2019, 12(4):576

[6] Huang Y.L. , Li J. , Tian X.J. , "Design of grid signal detection circuit for dual power transfer switch," *Electrical Appliance and Energy Efficiency Management Technology*, 2020, (3):43-49

[7] Ruan R.Q., "Application of dual power transfer switch in UPS system," *Building Electricity*. 2020, 39(02): 35-39

[8] Fu H., Zhang H.X. , Wang P., Chen R.J., Liang X.F., Wu Y., "Improved extended Kalman filtering method, "*Journal of Liaoning University of Engineering and Technology (Natural Science Edition)*, 2021, 40(03): 241-248

[9] Shi Y.L., L J.H., "A research on a DSP-controlled fast access device for emergency power supply in substations ," *Electrical Applications*, 2021, 40(06): 82-87

[10] Wang F.Q., Xiao Q. Ren, L.T., "A review of research on power quality disturbance detection and identification methods", Chinese. Journal .of .Electrical .Engineering, 2021, 41(12): 4104-4121

[11] Kuang H. Y., Wen H.,. "Taylor-Fourier transform-based voltage flicker measurement method", *Journal of Electrotechnology*, 2020, 35(22): 4798-4806

[12] Hu D.G., Ma X.P., Zhao F.Z, et al. "A short-time Fourier transform-based detection of voltage flicker signals", *Power Grid and Clean Energy*, 2020, 36(03): 27-33, 41

[13] Ebrahim M A, Wadie F, Mousa A. Abd-Allah. "Integrated fault detection algorithm for transmission, distribution, and microgrid networks," *IET Energy Systems Integration*, 2019, 1(02): 104-113.

[14] Yu,C. , X,H. , Li,X.Y. , Wang,S.Z. , Hu,S.L. , "A comprehensive detection method for three-phase four-wire system current based on dq0 transform," *Journal of Power Science and Technology*, 2019, 34.(04): 173-179

[15] Huang,L., "Simulation and application study of virtual three-phase dq0 transformation method with delay blocking in DVR," *Electrotechnology*, 2018,(1): 16-17,23

Study on Arc Extinguishing Performance of Large Capacity AC Contactor

Yan Zhang [1], Zhihong Xu[1,2,3]

[1]College of Electrical Engineering and Automation, Fuzhou University, Fuzhou, 350108, China

[2]Fujian Key Laboratory of New Energy Generation and Power Conversion, Fuzhou, 350108, China

[3]Fujian Province University Engineering Research Center of Smart Distribution Grid Equipment, Fuzhou, 350108, China

E-mail: 641936593@qq.com Tel: 13178116282

***Abstract*—The intelligent contactor adopts the zero current breaking technology, which controls the contact to break within 1ms before the current crosses zero, extinguishes the arc through the current crossing zero, and realizes micro arc breaking. However, with the continuous increase of power grid capacity, the breaking task of large capacity contactor contacts becomes more and more heavy, which makes the contactor have the phenomenon of arc reignition. In this paper, the contact system of large capacity AC contactor is studied from two aspects of fluid field and electric field. Firstly, the magnetohydrodynamic model of zero front breaking arc of large capacity AC contactor is established. The movement of arc in the arc extinguishing chamber and the characteristics of fluid field are analyzed. The influence of grid arrangement of arc extinguishing chamber on arc movement is analyzed to improve the flow field characteristics of arc extinguishing chamber. On this basis, the electric field model of the arc extinguishing chamber is established to analyze the influence of grid arrangement on the electric field of the arc extinguishing chamber, improve the electric field characteristics of the arc extinguishing chamber and reduce the probability of arc reignition. This paper not only provides a theoretical basis for improving the arc extinguishing performance of contactors, but also provides an effective way to find the best structural parameters. It has a certain reference value for guiding and improving the design of arc extinguishing chamber, as well as the design of other similar switch products.**

***Index Terms*—Arc, arc extinguishing performance, contact system, large capacity AC contactor**

I. INTRODUCTION

This work was supported by the University Production-Study Cooperation Project of Science and Technology Department of Fujian Province (2021Y4002)and the Funding Program for Leading Talents in Scientific and Technological Innovation of Fujian Province (00387024).

In recent years, with the continuous development of control system, the demand for contactors is increasing. Intelligent contactor has the advantages of environmental protection, energy saving and high efficiency. It is gradually favored by manufacturers and can meet the requirements of automation and scale. Arc is inevitable in the breaking process of contactor, which greatly reduces the reliability of operation. In terms of control, zero current breaking is mostly used [1-3]. The AC contactor can reduce the arc when the current crosses zero, that is, micro arc breaking. However, with the continuous increase of the power load, the capacity of the power grid is also expanding. When handling large tasks, the contact of the contactor brings more difficulties when breaking. Sometimes breaking more than six times of the rated current, even in the vicinity of zero crossing, will inevitably cause reignition. At this time, not only the intelligent control should be adopted, but also the structure of the arc extinguishing chamber, such as the arc extinguishing grid, should be improved, so that it is easier to extinguish the arc and prevent re ignition.

In this paper, in order to avoid the phenomenon of contact breakdown, the structure of the arc extinguishing chamber is improved by changing the number of layers of the grid in the arc extinguishing chamber or changing the internal structure of the grid. In this paper, we first change the number of grids to observe the different movement processes of the arc, and then change the internal structure of the grid, such as changing the side width and center distance of the grid to observe the electric field in the arc extinguishing chamber. Finally, the grid is designed with the parameters of small maximum field strength points and small number of high field strength areas in the arc extinguishing chamber.

II. ARC MOTION ANALYSIS

A. Research Object

This paper takes the new monopole 400A intelligent AC contactor as the research object. The contact part includes two breakpoints on the left and right. Fig. 1 is the structural diagram of the contact part of the prototype. The contact part is symmetrical on the left and right, and the two breakpoints are independent of each other. The static contact part adopts U-shaped design. When the contact is energized, the contact system will generate electric power, which can blow the arc, causing the arc between the contacts to be elongated and it is easier to extinguish the arc. The prototype in this paper adopts flip chip type, and the arc extinguishing chamber adopts arc extinguishing grid. The arc extinguishing grid can be divided into two types in arrangement, i.e. vertical arrangement and horizontal arrangement. Flip type contactors are more suitable for the use of horizontally arranged arc extinguishing grids, so the new 400A intelligent contactor of this prototype uses horizontally arranged arc extinguishing grids.

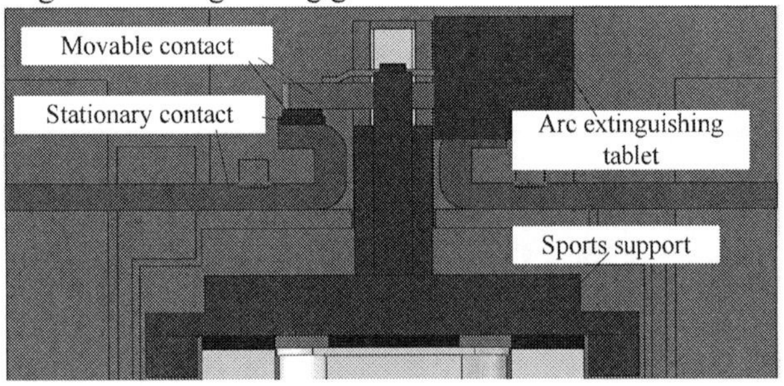

Fig. 1. Structure diagram of contact system

B. Mathematical Model of Arc MHD Model and Solution of Control Equation

As a special fluid, arc follows the three conservation laws of mass, momentum and energy. In addition, the relationship of electric field in arc is expressed by Laplace equation and Ampere's law equation.

1) Mass conservation equation

$$\frac{\partial\rho}{\partial t}+div(\rho\boldsymbol{u})=0 \tag{1}$$

Where, ρ is the fluid density; t is time; $\boldsymbol{u}$ is the velocity vector of the flow field, ($\boldsymbol{u}=u_x$, u_y, u_z).

2) Momentum conservation equation

$$\frac{\partial(\rho u_i)}{\partial t}+div(\rho\boldsymbol{u}u_i)=div(\eta\, grad u_i)-\nabla p+\boldsymbol{J}\times\boldsymbol{B} \tag{2}$$

Where, p is the pressure; $\boldsymbol{J}=(j_x, j_y, j_z)$is the current density; $\boldsymbol{B}=(B_x, B_y, B_z)$is the magnetic induction strength.

3) Energy conservation equation

$$\frac{\partial(\rho h)}{\partial t}+div(\rho\boldsymbol{u}h)=div(\frac{\lambda}{C_p}grad h)+\frac{|J|^2}{\sigma}-q_{rad} \tag{3}$$

Where, h is enthalpy; q_{rad} is the radiation term; λ, C_p, σ are thermal conductivity, specific heat at constant pressure and electrical conductivity.

4) Electromagnetic field equation

$$\begin{cases} div(\sigma\, grad\varphi)=0 \\ div(grad A_i)=-\mu_0 j_i (i=x,y,z) \end{cases} \tag{4}$$

Wherein, the current density $\boldsymbol{j}$ and the magnetic induction intensity $\boldsymbol{B}$ are respectively obtained by Ampere's law and the rotation of the magnetic vector A:

$$\begin{cases} \boldsymbol{j}=-\sigma\, grad\varphi \\ \boldsymbol{B}=rot(A) \end{cases} \tag{5}$$

It can be seen from the above control equations that the thermal, electrical, magnetic and fluid fields in the arc MHD model have strong coupling: on the one hand, the current will generate Joule heat, which is the main heat source of the arc. It dissipates heat in the form of heat conduction, heat convection and heat radiation, raising the temperature of the arc extinguishing chamber, changing the gas transport characteristics, and the change of conductivity affects the distribution of current density; On the other hand, under the action of Lorentz force of the magnetic field, the gas flow velocity and pressure change constantly, which will also affect the gas thermodynamic characteristics and change the arc temperature [4].

In this paper, MHD model is used to describe the motion of the arc, and the flow field analysis software FLUENT is secondary developed. The mathematical model is solved by the finite volume method [5]. The characteristics of the arc are obtained by the simulation method, and the magnetic blowing effect is studied. The simple algorithm is used in the simulation. Fig. 2 shows the solution sequence of each equation in each iteration.

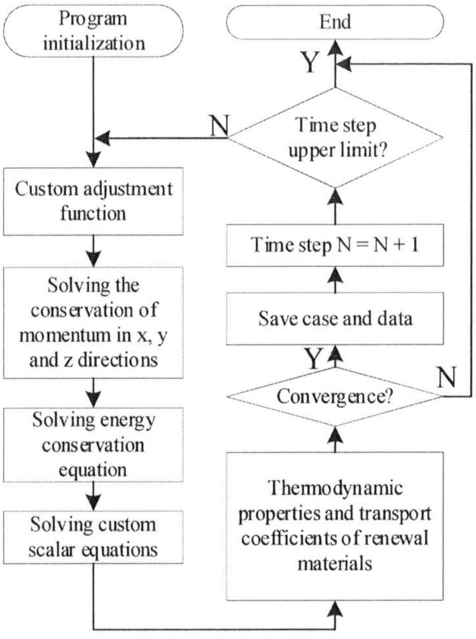

Fig. 2. MHD model solving process based on SIMPLE algorithm

In the low-voltage arc extinguishing chamber, the arc root moves along the arc runner under the action of the magnetic field. The location of the arc root can not be simply considered as the highest point of the electrode surface temperature, but also should be combined with the characteristics of the arc column medium itself. In this paper, formula(6)is used to determine the position of the arc root. The current density on the electrode surface is not only related to the electrode surface temperature, but also combined with the distribution of the arc column conductivity. Associating it with the position of the arc root can better reflect the essence of the arc root movement [6].

$$x_a = x_c = \frac{\iint_{P_{xy}} x \cdot j(x,y)\,dxdy}{\iint_{P_{xy}} j(x,y)\,dxdy} \tag{6}$$

Where, x_a, x_c are the anode arc root position and cathode arc root position respectively, P_{xy} is the surface of the electrode, and $\boldsymbol{j}$ is the current density on the electrode surface.

C. Modeling and Grid Division of Arc Extinguishing Chamber

Fig. 3 shows the built arc extinguishing chamber model, and Fig. 4 shows the grid division of a quarter of the model. The tetrahedral grid division method is adopted in this paper.

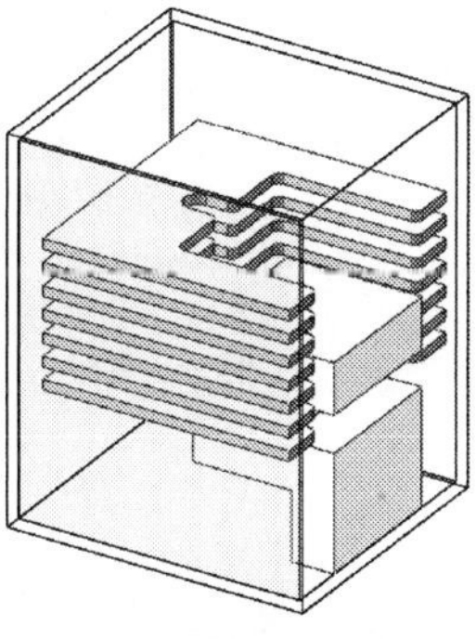

Fig. 3. Arc extinguishing chamber model

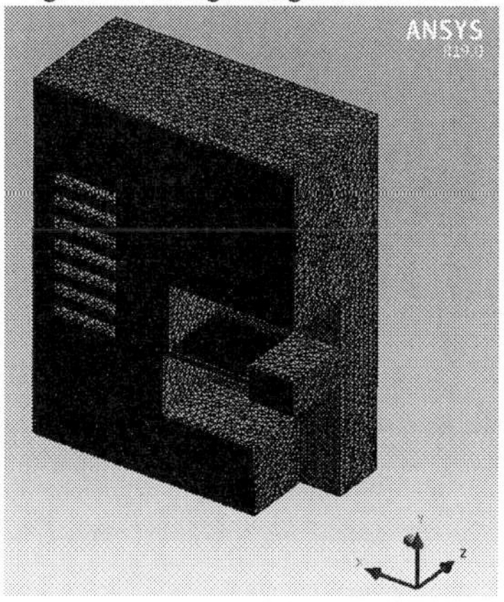

Fig. 4. Overall grid image

D. Analysis of Arc Motion Characteristics

There are two kinds of grids commonly used in the arc extinguishing chamber, namely, metal grids and insulating grids. Among them, the metal grid can cut the arc into many short arcs, which increases the voltage drop in the near pole region. Therefore, the arc extinguishing chamber in this paper uses metal grid to simulate and analyze the influence of different number of metal grids on the arc movement.

As shown in Fig. 5, the number of grid pieces is changed, which is divided into two types, namely 7 grid pieces (type A) and 5 grid pieces (type B). Wherein the B type is formed by reducing the number of two gate plates.

Fig. 5. Arrangement sequence of arc extinguishing grid

In this paper, the time when the contact breaks for 1ms is selected, and the movement distance is related to the time and speed of the contact breaking. In this paper, the distance between the moving and stationary contacts is 1.1mm, and the current is 400A. Assuming that the initial arc is located in the middle of the arc extinguishing chamber [7], the results of the applied magnetic field (B_y = 90mT) are added to the model of the arc extinguishing chamber. Fig. 6 and Fig. 7 show the arc blowing conditions of the arc extinguishing grids of type A and type B. It can be seen that the existence of the arc extinguishing grid makes the flow of the air flow in the arc extinguishing chamber less smooth, and limits the movement trajectory of the arc. The arc is in close contact with the grid, which is advantageous for arc cooling and deionization. In the case of A-type grid, the influence of grid resistance on the arc is greater than that of Lorentz force, and the arc will stay outside the grid and enter the grid. In the case of B-type grid, since the number of grid is small and the grid is not so dense, the resistance of the grid to the arc is small, and the arc movement mainly depends on the Lorentz force.

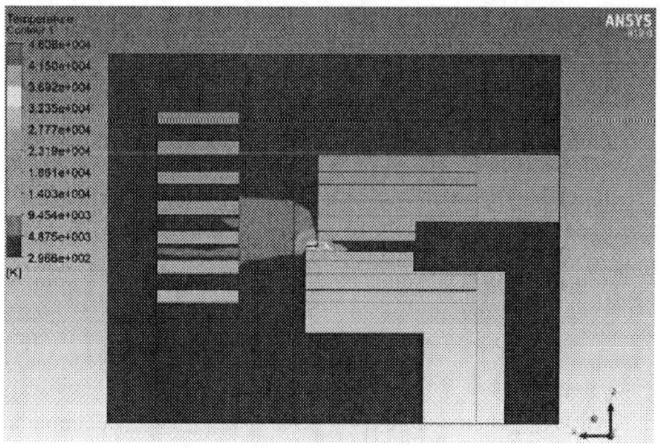

Fig. 6. Arc blowing of type A grid

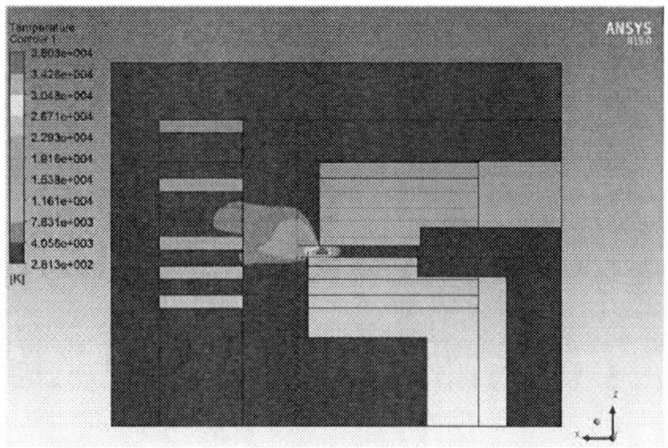

Fig. 7. Arc blowing of type B grid

III. Electric Field Analysis Of Arc Extinguishing Chamber

In this paper, the finite element simulation of the electric field in the arc extinguishing chamber of the new single pole 400A intelligent AC contactor is carried out. According to the electric field in the arc extinguishing chamber, the influence of the structural parameters and positions of the arc extinguishing grid on the electric field distribution is simulated.

A. Electric Field Principle Analysis

During the breaking process of the AC contactor, the arc generated by the breaking process will enter the grid. After the arc is cut by the arc extinguishing grid, the arc will be divided into many short arcs, which increases the voltage drop in the near pole region and makes the total arc voltage rise. To analyze the electric field of the contact system, one of the difficulties is how to deal with the boundary conditions of the arc extinguishing grid, because the boundary conditions are related to the voltage drop of the arc. The thickness of the grid is 1.4mm and the distance between the contacts is 7.9MM. Kazuo Nakayama [8-10] and others conducted a lot of experiments on grid arc extinguishing system, and the empirical formula of arc pressure drop is as follows:

$$u_{arc} = 29.7 + 1.51\times10^{3} l + 4.12\times10^{-3} + 8.38\times10^{-2} li + 24.5n \quad (7)$$

Wherein, l is the arc column length; n is the number of grids for effective arc cutting; i is the breaking current. They obtained from a large number of experiments that the near pole voltage drop of the grid is 24.5V. Therefore, every time a grid is added, there will be an additional near pole voltage drop, and the arc voltage will increase by 24.5V. The formula of the arc column is nonlinear, which is related to the length of the arc column and the current. The side also reflects the complexity of the arc voltage.

B. Analysis of Influence of Side Width of Grid on Electric Field

As shown in Fig. 8, the structure size of the grid is changed by changing the side width and the center distance of the grid, thereby changing the distribution of the electric field in the arc extinguishing chamber. Add 380V voltage to the potential on one side of the contact and set the potential on the other side to zero.

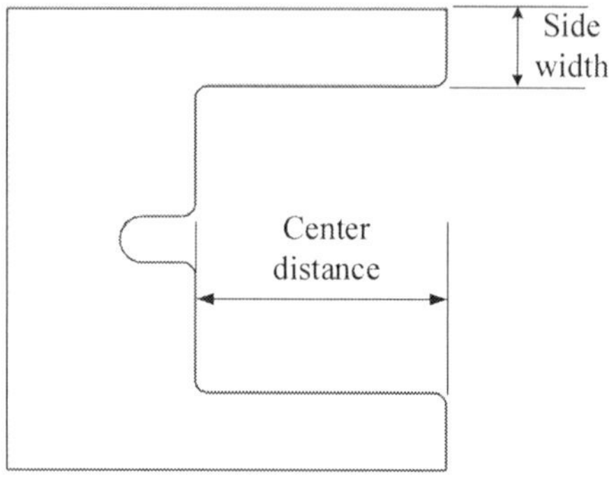

Fig. 8. Structure and shape of arc extinguishing grid

21mm, 22mm and 23mm grids are selected respectively. Because the moving contact may collide with the grid when the side width of the grid is greater than 4mm, we designed the grid size to be 4mm or less. Therefore, the side width of each grid is 3mm and 4mm respectively to analyze the impact of different sizes on the contact electric field.

Generally, the point with the maximum field strength is at the vertex position on the side of the moving contact, as shown in Fig. 9. In order to facilitate observation of the point with the maximum field strength, the arc extinguishing grid has been hidden. As can be seen from Fig. 10 and Fig. 11, when the center distance is 21mm, the side width is changed from 3mm to 4mm, and the maximum field strength is reduced from 66978V/m to 63438 V/m. When the center distance is 22mm and the side width is changed from 3mm to 4mm, the maximum field strength is reduced from 60315 V/m to 59314 V/m. The simulation shows that the maximum field strength of the contact system decreases with the increase of the side width of the arc extinguishing grid.

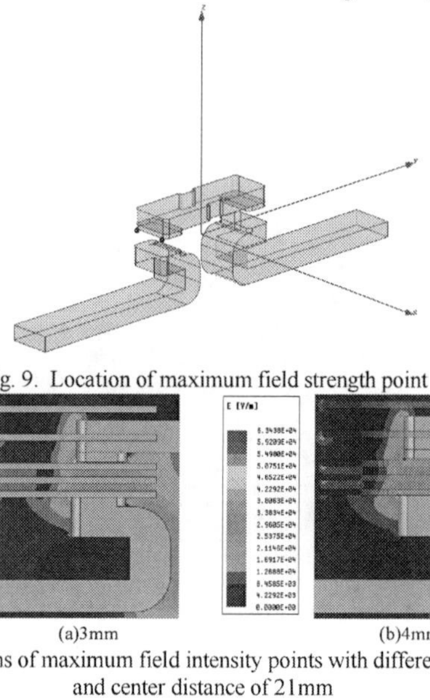

Fig. 9. Location of maximum field strength point

(a)3mm (b)4mm

Fig. 10. Positions of maximum field intensity points with different side widths and center distance of 21mm

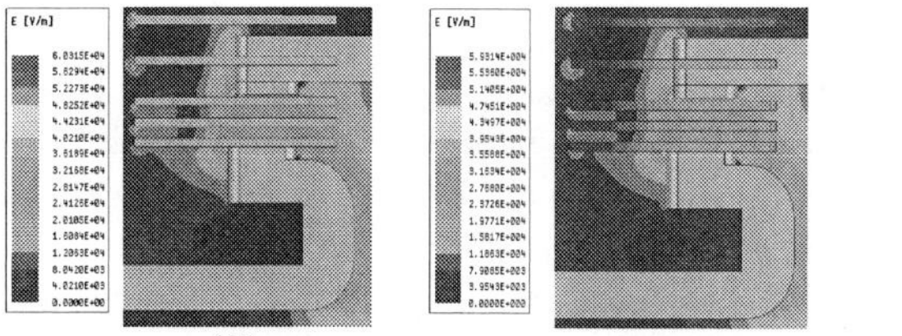

(a)3mm (b)4mm

Fig. 11. Positions of maximum field intensity points with different side widths and center distance of 22mm

After the simulation, the electric field intensity of all points in the area near the contact of the arc extinguishing chamber is calculated by using the function of the field calculator export solution in the post-processing. Count the number of points with high field strength (> 10000 V/m) by MATLAB programming. As shown in Fig. 12, it is found through statistics that the number of field points in the high field strength area gradually decreases with the increase of side width from 3mm to 4mm, no matter whether the center distance is 21, 22 or 23mm.

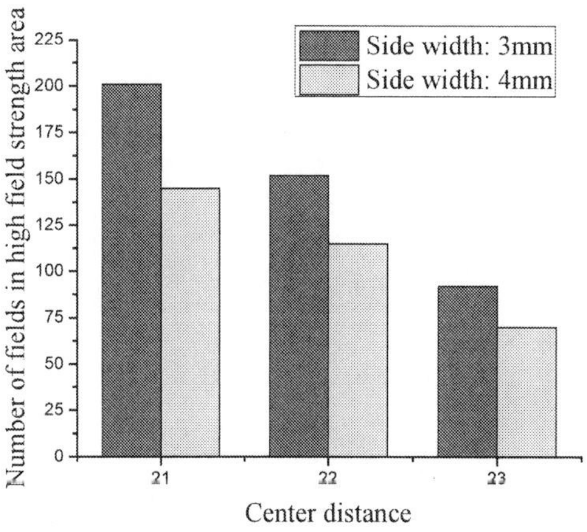

Fig. 12. Comparison of field points in high field strength regions with different grid structure shapes

C. Analysis of the Influence of Grid Center Distance on Electric Field

Different center distances are set for the grid to analyze the influence of different center distances on the contact electric field [11]. The side width is 4mm, and the center distance is 21-25mm.

As shown in Fig. 13, it can be seen from the observation of simulation results that the electric field intensity distribution near the grid sheet at the center distance of 24mm is smaller than that of other grid sheets of four sizes, which improves the electric field distribution and is conducive to reducing the probability of post arc re striking.

It can be seen from Fig. 14 that the post-processing field calculator function calculates that the number of field points in the high field strength area between the contacts is the least at 23mm, which is 70 points, which is the same as the result obtained above. The electric potential is different when the arc extinguishing grid is designed with different structures. The spatial distribution between the arc extinguishing grid and the contact is also complex. Because the arc extinguishing grid with a center distance of 23mm has a good cooperation relationship with the moving and stationary contacts, the space of the high field strength area in the arc extinguishing chamber is very small.

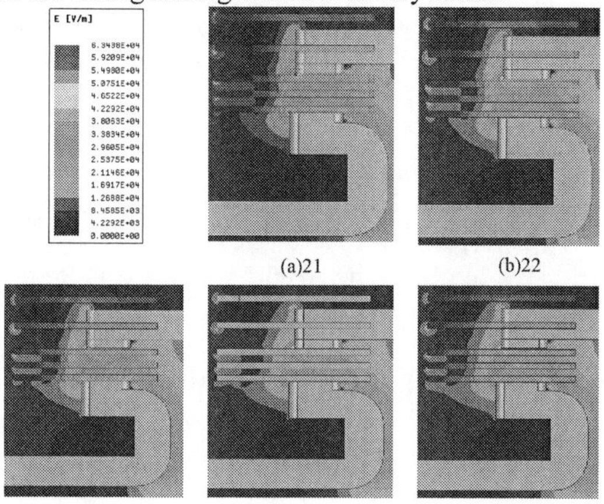

(a)21 (b)22

(c)23 (d)24 (e)25

Fig. 13. Electric field intensity distribution of various grid plates

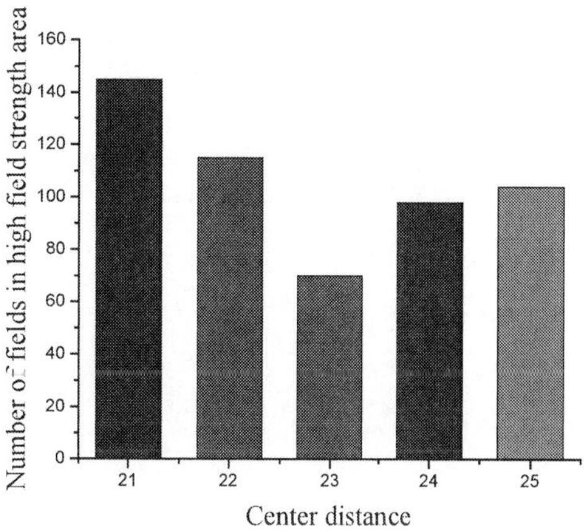

Fig. 14. comparison of field points in high field strength area with side width of 4mm and different center distances

IV. Conclusion

In this chapter, the arc extinguishing performance of contactor is studied from the perspective of fluid field and electric field. Firstly, a simplified arc model is used to simulate the fluid field in the arc extinguishing chamber. Then the finite element method is used to simulate the electric field of different grid structure parameters. The following conclusions are drawn:

1) The arc movement process of the arc extinguishing chamber can be obviously improved by selecting the appropriate grid arrangement

2) By improving the structure of the grid, the maximum electric field intensity can be significantly reduced, and the electric field distribution of the arc extinguishing chamber

can be improved, making it difficult to re strike the arc.

REFERENCES

[1] Bao Guanghai, Zhang Peiming. Technology of Zero-Current Breaking of Intelligent AC Contactor[J]. Proceedings of the CSEE, 2012 (05): 199-204.

[2] Xu Zhihong, Zhang Peiming, Zheng Xin. Realization of Zero-Current-Break Control Technology for Intelligent AC contactor[J]. Low Voltage Apparatus, 2006(07): 6-11.

[3] Zhou yun, Lu Qingqi. Zero Current Interrupt Control of Intelligent AC Contactor Based on C8051F007[J]. Low Voltage Apparatus, 2008(09): 21-23.

[4] Wu Yi, Rong Mingzhe, Wang Xiaohua, etc. Simulation Techique of Air Arc in Switching Devices[C]. Proceedings of the First Conference on Electrical Equipment and Intelligent Chemistry, 2007.

[5] Lin Wengui. 3D Design Technology for New Unipolar Electromagnetic Switch[D]. Fuzhou University, 2016.

[6] Wu Y, Rong M, Li X, et al. Numerical analysis of the effect of the chamber width and outlet area on the motion of an air arc plasma. Plasma Science, IEEE Transactions on, 2008, 36(5): 2831-2837.

[7] Lindmayer M, Springstubbe M. Three-dimensional-simulation of arc motion between arc runners including the influence of ferromagnetic material. Components and Packaging Technologies, IEEE Transactions on, 2002, 25(3): 409-414.

[8] Kazuo Nakayama, Yasunobu Yokomizu, Toshiro Matsumur, et al. Arc Behavior Analysis and Fractional Decomposition of Voltage Rise of High-Current Air Arc Affected by Deion Plates. IEEJ Trans.PE, 2003, 123, (9) : 1091-1096.

[9] Kazuo Nakayama, Yasunobu Yasunobu, Oshiro Matsumura, et al. Mechanism of voltagerise of high-current arc at atmospheric pressure due to deion plates. Elect. Eng. 2003, 145(3): 17-24.

[10] Kazuo Nakayama, Yasunobu Yokomizu, Toshiro Matsumura, et al. Expression of Voltage of High-Current Air Arc Affect by Deion Plate[C]. Proc.Of 14th Int.on Gas Discharges and their Applications, 2002(1): 27-30.

[11] Liu Weiqiang.Research on the Arc Characteristic of Contact System of Large Capacity AC Contactor[D]. Fuzhou University, 2017.

First Author, Yan Zhang is currently pursuing the M.S. degree in the College of Electrical Engineering and Automation, Fuzhou University, Fuzhou, China. His current research interests include electrical appliances and intelligent technology.

Corresponding Author, Zhihong Xu(1963-) , professor and doctoral supervisor, with research interests in electrical appliances and intelligent technology, 641936593@qq.com.

Research on Characterization Method for the Sealability of Aerospace Contactor Based on Static Contact Resistance

Cuifeng Feng[1,2], Qunfeng Chang[1,2], Zhengyang Zhao[1,2], Chuxian Zhang[1,2], Libing Cai[1,2]

[1)] Aerospace Internet of Things Technology Co., Ltd., Beijing, 100094, China
[2)]Aerospace Times Electronics Co., Ltd., Beijing, 100094, China
E-mail: fengcuifeng@163.com Tel: 13681166163

***Abstract*—The sealability directly affects the service life of contactors. The requirements for sealing are more stringent for aerospace project, especially for high-power contactors used in long-term on-orbit aircrafts. Helium mass spectrometry (HEMS) leak detection is a common sealing test method for sealed devices. After the sealing chamber of the aerospace contactor was installed into the finished product through gluing and housing, the finished contactor product is not a sealing unit. There are obvious limitations and uncertainties about the common leak detection method for the sealability on this structure contactor products. Based on this typical structure of aerospace contactor products, this paper designs static contact resistance as the feedback indicator. Through the theoretical analysis and experimental data of the influence of leakage rate on static contact resistance, the corresponding relationship between static contact resistance and leakage rate level is preliminarily established. The sealability of contactor can be judged. This method is useful for the sealing judgment of components with similar structure.**

***Index Terms*—contactor, static contact resistance, leakage rate, sealability**

I. INTRODUCTION

Contactor is a relay that make and break AC or DC main circuit. There is a large-capacity main contact in the sealing chamber, which can quickly extinguish the arc while the contactor is breaking[1]. As the increase of the load capacity of spaceships, 100A~200A DC contactor has been applied to various spacecrafts. The bus control of the long-term on-orbit spacecrafts has put forwards extremely high requirements for the reliability of the DC contactor. For instance, the electrical life should meet 10^4 times; and the sealability should be better than 1×10^{-3} Pa.m^3/s. If the leakage rate exceeds the standard, the electrical life of the contactor will be affected directly. Therefore, the leakage rate of the aerospace DC contactor must be checked during product acceptance. The applicability and accuracy of leak detection methods should be taken into account. The methods and requirements for leakage rate check vary with product structure. The actual sealability of the product could be misjudged if inapplicable leak detection methods are selected. Therefore, it is necessary to discuss applicable methods to check the sealability for contactors with different structures.

In this paper, a method based on static contact resistance parameters to characterize the leakage rate level for the BX DC contactor used in a large spacecraft is discussed. The correspondence between DC contactor static contact resistance value and leakage rate level was established through the experiments.

II. STRUCTURAL FEATURES OF DC CONTACTOR

The BX DC contactor is composed of a contact system and an electromagnetic system. The contact terminal is fixed in the sealing chamber of the contact system by ceramic sealing technology. The sealing chamber is filled with protective gas and helium tracer gas, and then is fixed in the housing by structural adhesive and a circlip.

Due to the special use requirements in space environment, structurally compared with ordinary DC contactor, the structural adhesive is filled between the housing and the sealing chamber of the aerospace DC contactor to realize high mechanical stress tolerance.

III. ANALYSIS OF APPLICABILITY OF SEALING LEAK DETECTION METHODS

There are many leak detection methods for sealed devices. The leak of the sealed device is usually detected by back pressure method[2][3]. The leak detection sensitivity of this method can be up to 1×10^{-6}Pa.cm^3/s and above. Generally, the back pressure method is divided into three steps. Step 1: Place the sealed device into a helium-filled tank. The helium enters the inside of the device through the micropores. Step 2: Remove the device from the tank, and blow off the residual helium on the surface of the device. Step 3: place the device in the vacuum chamber, and test its leakage rate by a helium mass spectrometry leak detector.

Firstly, the applicability of the back pressure method was analyzed. Based on the leak-detecting principle and test sensitivity, the back pressure method is applicable to the leak test of the BX DC contactor. Since the sealing chamber of the BX DC contactor in this paper has been filled with helium tracer gas, the contactor was directly put into the vacuum chamber for leak detection with helium mass spectrometer.

Secondly, the accuracy of the leak detection by the back pressure method was analyzed. It was verified by many experiments that there were inaccurate test data in the leak detection of the BX DC contactor by this method, which could result in misjudgment of the sealability. After the sealing chamber of the BX contactor is assembled into a contactor product through casing and adhesive filling, the contactor is no longer a hermetically sealed part. Due to the adsorption effect on the surface of structural adhesive and the air sealed between the housing and the sealing chamber, the leakage rate detection of the contactor cannot correspond to the real sealability of the sealing chamber,

Fig. 1 shows the schematic diagram of leak detection of contactor with a helium mass spectrometer(HEMS). The contactor is placed in a vacuum chamber connected to a helium mass spectrometer. To judge the leakage rate of the contactor according to the detection value of helium ions, there may be two kind of misjudgments about the leak detection of the contactor.

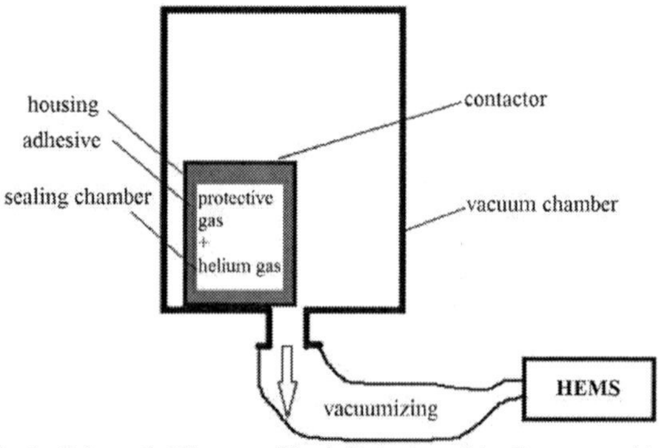

Fig. 1. Schematic Diagram of Leak Detection of the Contactor with a Helium Mass Spectrometer.

1) The sealing chamber is well sealed, but the detection about leakage rate of the contactor exceeds the standard.

The sealability of the sealing chamber is always good. the static contact resistance of the contactor is normal. Due to the slow discharge of air adsorbed in the structural adhesive or the slow release of air in the housing, contactor products cannot meet the required vacuum level within the specified time. So the leak detection is showed as not meet the standard and the contactor is misjudged as unqualified.

2) The sealing chamber is unsealed, but the detection about leakage rate of the contactor is still qualified.

The original sealability of the sealing chamber is good, but air tightness failure occurs in the chamber in subsequent assembly. Nevertheless, the leakage rate detection of contactor may also be qualified due to the blocking effect of structural adhesive. In such case, sealing chamber leakage has occurred in the contactor. Consequently, the air between the sealing chamber and the housing may slowly enter the chamber, and result in the increment of the contact resistance, which will cause serious hidden danger to the contactor.

Although the back pressure method can perform a leak detection on BX contactor, the test data may be inaccurate. Such misjudgment is absolutely not allowed for the application of spacecrafts. Moreover, it has been confirmed by test that the leakage rate of BX contactor is not an isolated parameter value. There is certain correspondence between the leakage rate and the static contact resistance. Based on the leak test results and the static contact resistance, the comprehensive judgment of the sealability of contactor is feasible,

IV. Study on the Correspondence Between the Static Contact Resistance and the Leakage Rate of Contactor

A. Leakage Rate and Static Contact Resistance Before and After Casing

1) Leakage rate test before and after casing of contactor

30 BX DC contactor samples of the same batch were taken. Leak tests were performed on these samples before/after the casing (filled with structural adhesive) respectively. The test results are shown in Fig. 2. The leakage rate of the 30 sealing chambers was below 1×10^{-3}Pa.cm^3/s. The qualification rate was 100%. After assembled into contactors, the leakage rate of 16 samples was higher than 1×10^{-3}Pa.cm^3/s. The worst was 3.7×10^{-3}Pa.cm^3/s. The failure rate was 53%. It can be seen that the results of leakage rate detection of finished products and those of sealing chambers were inconsistent. The degradation of the leakage rate test of products is caused by the structural adhesive between the housing and the sealing chamber. Misjudgment will be caused if the leakage rate of the samples after casing is used to judge the sealability of the contactors.

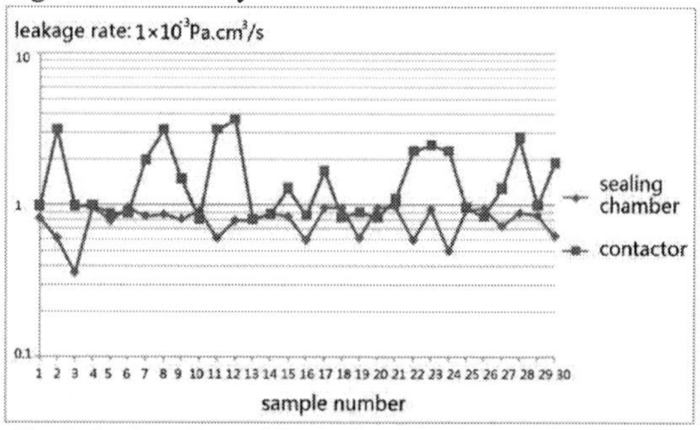

Fig. 2. Leakage Rate of the Sealing Chamber and the Contactor

2) Static contact resistance test on samples

For the above 30 samples, the static contact resistances of the sealing chambers before casing and the contactor after casing were tested. The test results are shown in Fig. 3. It can be seen that the contact resistances of samples basically show no obvious change before and after casing. The two curves basically coincide. Considering the test error of each contact resistance, it can be seen that the contact resistance before and after the casing remains unchanged.

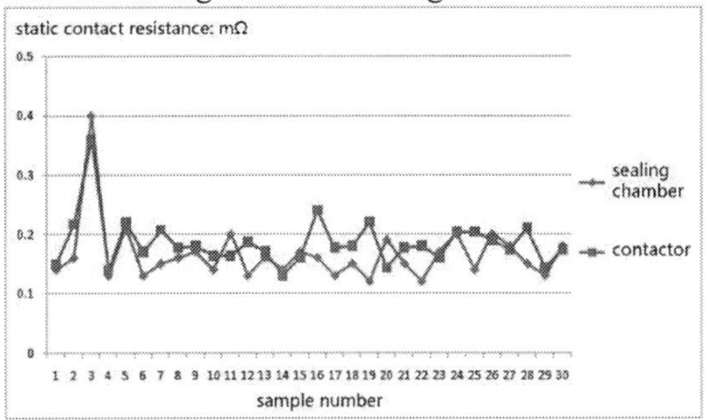

Fig. 3. Contact Resistances of Samples Before and After Casing

There are 16 samples with leakage rate exceeding the standard after casing. The leakage rate and contact resistance value before and after casing were recorded, which is shown in Table I. The mean contact resistance of these samples before and after casing was 0.16 mΩ and 0.18 mΩ respectively. The contact resistances were stable.

It can be seen that the samples disqualified the leakage rate detection have good contact performance, which reflects the sealability of the contactors are qualified. Therefore, it is necessary to use static contact resistance as an auxiliary indicator to judge the sealability of contactors.

TABLE I
CONTACT RESISTANCE OF SAMPLES BEFORE AND AFTER CASING

Sample No.	Leakage rate (10^{-3} Pa.cm^3/s)		Contact resistance (mΩ)	
	Sealing chamber	contactors	Before casing	after casing
2	0.61	3.2	0.16	0.22
6	0.85	2	0.15	0.21
7	0.87	3.2	0.16	0.18
8	0.81	1.5	0.17	0.18
10	0.61	3.2	0.2	0.16
11	0.79	3.7	0.13	0.19
14	0.84	1.3	0.17	0.16
16	0.96	1.7	0.13	0.18
20	0.98	1.1	0.15	0.18
21	0.59	2.3	0.12	0.18
22	0.94	2.5	0.17	0.16
23	0.5	2.3	0.2	0.2
26	0.73	1.3	0.18	0.17
27	0.89	2.8	0.15	0.21
29	0.63	1.9	0.18	0.17
30	0.79	2.8	0.15	0.18

B. Relation Between Leakage Rate and Static Contact Resistance of Sealing Chamber

1) Analysis of contact resistance change of contactors

The contact material of BX DC contactor is Cu. While the leakage rate of the sealing chamber is not up to standard, the protective gas leak and external air enter the sealing chamber, which accelerate the oxidation of the contact surface. Cu_2O is mainly generated below 400℃. The contact resistance of the contactor is mainly composed of film resistance R_t and constriction resistance R_c.

(a) Constriction resistance

The calculation for R_c is shown in Formula 1[4]:

$$R_c = 0.89\rho\sqrt{\frac{\xi H}{P}} \tag{1}$$

Where, ρ is the resistivity (Ω.m) of the contact material; ξ is the deformation coefficient, and the value is 0.7 when elastic and plastic deformation occur at the contact. P is the contact pressure and basically remains unchanged. H is the hardness of the contact material. Since the film of Cu_2O is thin, the surface hardness of the contact before and after oxidation can be regarded as the hardness of Cu[5], i.e. 3.5×10^8 N/m^2.

According to Formula 1, the contact contraction resistance R_c of contactor is proportional to the resistivity ρ of the contact surface material. The resistivity of Cu and Cu_2O is 1.75×10^{-8} Ω.m and around 2×10^6 Ω.m respectively. With the increase of the film thickness of Cu_2O, the resistivity of the contact surface material increases; the contraction resistance R_c increases accordingly[6][7].

(b) Film resistance

See Formula 2 for the generation rule of Cu_2O film: d is the film thickness (Å); t is time (h); T is the absolute temperature (K). When the film contacts with oxygen, the film thickness d grows with the increase of time; the film thickness grows quickly at high temperature.

$$d^2 = 20^2 + t \times 10^{(14.9\times\frac{5100}{T})} \tag{2}$$

The current through the Cu_2O film is completed by tunnel effect. When the voltage at the contact interface is low and the electric field strength of the film is below 10^8~10^9 V/m, see Formula 3 for the calculation formula for the film resistance R_t. Where, A' and B' are constants. Therefore, when the voltage is low, the film resistance R_t increases exponentially with the film thickness d.

$$R_t = \frac{\xi H}{P} \times \frac{e^{B'}}{A'} \times e^d = \frac{\xi H}{P} \times \frac{e^{B'}}{A'} \times e^{\{20^2 + t\times10^{(14.9\times\frac{5100}{T})}\}^{1/2}} \tag{3}$$

When the voltage at the contact interface is high and the electric field strength of the film is greater than 10^8~10^9 V/m, electrical breakdown will occur, forming a current channel in the film. The film resistance R_t will reduce rapidly.

2) Influence of leakage rate on contact resistance

While the dynamic contact resistance is tested with power load (high voltage and high current), the contact film will be broken down. The contact resistance measured cannot easily reflect the oxidation of the contact surface and the leakage rate of the sealing chamber of contactors.

When the dynamic contact resistance is tested without power load, the contact oxide film is not damaged. The value measured of the static contact resistance could establish a correspondence between the contact oxidation degree and the leakage rate of the sealing chamber of contactors. For contactors with leakage rate of sealing chamber not up to standard, the thickness of the oxide film grows obviously with time. The contact resistance should be significantly increased. For contactors with leakage rate of sealing chamber up to standard, the contact resistance should not change obviously.

Two contactors with leakage rate of sealing chamber up to standard and other two contactors with leakage rate not up to standard were selected. Table II lists the leakage rate test results of sealing chamber of the 4 samples. The leakage rate of 1# and 2# is below 1×10^{-3} Pa.cm^3/s, while the leakage rate of 3# and 4# is above 1×10^{-3} Pa. cm^3/s.

TABLE II
TEST RESULTS OF LEAKAGE RATE OF SEALING CHAMBER OF 4 SAMPLES

Sample SN	1#	2#	3#	4#
Leakage rate of sealing chamber (10^{-3} Pa.cm^3/s)	0.52	0.60	8.2	7.5

Static contact resistance test was conducted on the above samples for 6 consecutive days since the assembly is completed. Table III shows test data. Fig. 4 shows the change graph of contact resistances with time. In the test on Day 1, the static contact resistances of 4 contactors were smaller than 0.3 mΩ. With the increase of days, for the 2 contactors with qualified sealing chamber leakage rate, the contact resistance of contactor 1# was stable below 0.25 mΩ, and the contact resistance of contactor 2# fluctuated at 0.5 mΩ. However, for contactors 3# and 4# with unqualified sealing chamber leakage rate, the contact resistance increased with days. In the test on Day 6, the contact resistance of two contactors increased above 0.5 mΩ and showed a trend of further increase.

TABLE III
TEST RESULTS OF STATIC CONTACT RESISTANCE OF 4 CONTACTORS (MΩ)

Test time	Contactor SN			
	1#	2#	3#	4#
Day 1	0.12	0.13	0.13	0.24
Day 2	0.23	0.14	0.25	0.48
Day 3	0.18	0.40	0.36	1.08
Day 4	0.12	0.45	1.20	2.86
Day 5	0.18	0.38	2.54	4.08
Day 6	0.15	0.56	6.00	5.40

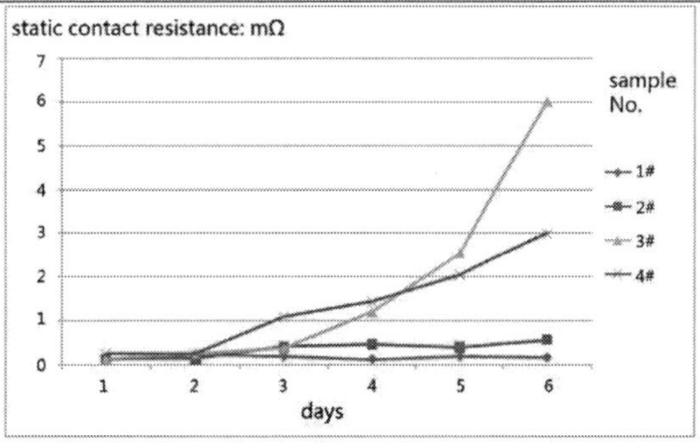

Fig. 4. Change Graph of Contact Resistance with Time

C. Relation Between Contact Resistance and Leakage Rate

Based on the analysis and tests above, it can be confirmed that the leakage rate of sealing chamber is one of the main factors affecting the contact performance of contactors. Test results show that, when the leakage rate of the sealing chamber is unqualified, it will cause the obvious increase of the static contact resistance of contactors.

According to the test results above, for BX DC contactor, from the completion of assembly to the delivery of contactors, if the static contact resistance of the contactor is < 1 mΩ, it reflects that the leakage rate of the sealing chamber of contactor is $\leq1\times10^{-3}$Pa.cm^3/s. On the contrary, if the static contact resistance of the contactor is >5 mΩ, it reflects that the leakage rate of the sealing chamber of contactor is $>1\times10^{-3}$Pa.cm^3/s. Therefore, in order to ensure the sealability of the products delivered for use, using the static contact resistance <1mΩ as an auxiliary judgment basis for qualified sealability during product acceptance is a feasible method for BX DC contactor.

V. CONCLUSIONS

In this paper, aerospace BX DC contactor is selected as a typical product. Based on the structural features of the contactor, a new sealability and leak detection method was designed. Through the study of the relationship between static contact resistance and leakage rate, a method to reflect the sealability of contactors with the indicator of static contact resistance is established. This method can exclude the influence of structural adhesive on the sealability of products, and has certain reference significance for the leak test of components with similar structure.

REFERENCES

[1] Ma Yue, Deng Jie, Meng Yanchen, Zhai Guofu. Analysis of Contact Failure Mechanism of Aerospace Relays. Low Voltage Apparatus, 2013(23): 14-19.
[2] Xu Yangguang, Pan Xiaoxia, Liu Xiaojian, Wang Tong, Cai Yue, Zeng Xiangbing, *et al.* Journal of Vacuum Science and Technology, 2018(10): 839-845.
[3] Zhou Shuai. Study on Removal of Helium Adsorption Method of Sealing Test of Electronic Components[D]. South China University of Technology, 2003.
[4] Zhang Jigao. Electrical contact theory and design. Electromechanical Technology, 1984(6): 1-6, 36-50.
[5] A. Keil, W.A. Merl, E. Vinaricky. Electrical Contacts and Their Materials. Beijing: Mechanical Industry Press, 1993.
[6] John C, Kosco. The Effects of Electrical Conductivity and Oxidation Resistance on Temperature Rise of Circuit Breaker Contact Materials. Holm Seminar on Electric Contact Phenomena. Chicago(IL), 1968: 55-66.
[7] Milenko Braunovic, Valery V. Konchits, Nikolai K. Myshkin. Electrical Contacts: Fundamental, Applications and Technology. Boca Raton: CRC Press Inc., 2006.

8th International Conference on Reliability of
Electrical Products and Electrical Contacts,
November 18-20, 2022

Research on Evaluation Method of Springs Service Performance of Air Circuit Breaker

Bokai Hu[1,2], Kui Li[1,2], Feng Niu[1,2], Chengchen Zhao[1,2]

[1] State Key Laboratory of Reliability and Intelligence of Electrical Equipment, Hebei University of Technology, Tianjin, 300401

[2] Key Laboratory of Electromagnetic Field and Electrical Apparatus Reliability of Hebei Province, Hebei University of Technology, Tianjin, 300401

E-mail: hubokai0906@163.com Tel: 15332116019

Abstract—**As an important protection device in low voltage distribution system, air circuit breaker is mainly used to cut off and connect load circuit and disconnect fault circuit to ensure the safe operation of power system. The operating mechanism of air circuit breaker mainly completes the closing and opening operation of circuit breaker, and performs its protective action function. The operating mechanism includes three groups of springs: energy storage springs, contact springs and opening springs. With the increasing of operation times, the service performance of each group of springs gradually degrades, which affects the motion law of operating mechanism. That may eventually lead to the failure of opening and closing action of air circuit breaker, and affect the operation safety and reliability of distribution system. In order to accurately monitor the health status of each group of springs, an evaluation method of springs service performance of air circuit breaker based on the energy transmission characteristics of operating mechanism is proposed. According to the behavior characteristics of operating mechanism during operation and the service function of each group of springs, select the characteristics that can reflect the service performance of each group of springs, research the influence of service performance degradation of each group of springs on the operation law and characteristics of operating mechanism, and realize the accurate evaluation of service state for air circuit breaker springs.**

Index Terms— **air circuit breaker, operating mechanism, springs, service performance evaluation.**

I. INTRODUCTION

Low voltage circuit breaker is an important control and protection equipment in low-voltage distribution system, and its reliable operation is extremely important for power system[1]-[3]. The operating mechanism of the air circuit breaker is fully powered by three groups of springs during the opening and closing process. With the increase of the number of operations, the electrical and mechanical stresses borne by the circuit breaker will gradually reduce the performance of the springs and eventually fail to operate normally.

At present, the condition monitoring of circuit breakers generally includes coil current signal monitoring and vibration signal monitoring. Reference [4] proposes a fault diagnosis method based on fuzzy kernel clustering and support vector machine, which uses the current signal of opening and closing coils to diagnose the operating state of circuit breakers. Reference [5] proposes a parameter adaptive signal decomposition method, which separates and reconstructs the modal components of the vibration signal to judge the fault severity of circuit breaker components.

At present, domestic and foreign scholars' monitoring of spring operating mechanism mainly focuses on the monitoring of the overall mechanical performance of the operating mechanism[6]-[8], and the performance monitoring of springs is less. Thus, this paper establishes the dynamic model of the circuit breaker in the process of opening and closing, analyzes the energy transmission characteristics of the operating mechanism, selects the characteristics that can reflect the springs performance in the displacement stroke of the crank hinge point, studies the influence of the performance degradation of each group of springs on the characteristics, and realizes the evaluation of the spring performance of the air circuit breaker.

II. EVALUATION METHOD

A. Motion analysis and characteristic selection of operating mechanism

1) Composition of operating mechanism of air circuit breaker

The operating mechanism of the circuit breaker is composed of a driving mechanism (driving rod IH, driving connecting rod GH, crank FG) and a movable contact mechanism (crank FE, contact connecting rod DE, electrode cage CD). The two sets of mechanisms share a crank, so the crank can reflect the operating performance of the two sets of

This work was supported in part by Central Funds Guiding the Local Science and Technology Development under Grant 226Z2102G.

mechanisms. The specific structure is shown in Figure 1.

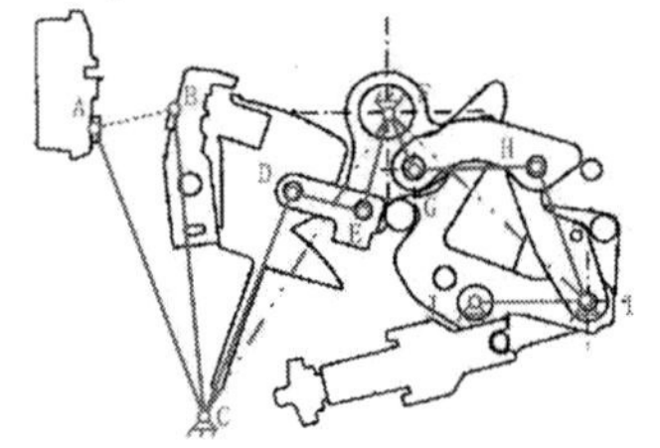

Fig. 1. Operating mechanism of air circuit breaker.

2) Motion analysis and feature selection in closing process

During the closing process of the air circuit breaker, the energy storage springs drive the operating mechanism for closing operation. After the contact between the movable and fixed contacts, the contact springs are compressed until the mechanism crosses the dead zone of operation to complete the closing operation. The specific closing process is shown in Figure 2.

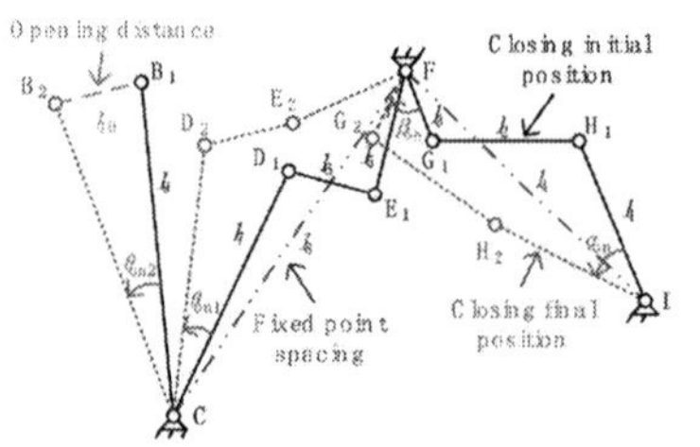

Fig. 2. Schematic diagram of operating mechanism movement during closing of air circuit breaker.

According to the vector equation method, the motion relationship equation between the connecting rods during the closing process of the operating mechanism is established, and the transmission ratio of the mechanism is obtained.

$$\beta_{\text{on}} = 2\arctan\frac{B \pm \sqrt{A^2 + B^2 - C^2}}{(A-C)} \tag{1}$$

$$\theta_{\text{on1}} = 2\arctan\frac{E \pm \sqrt{D^2 + E^2 - F^2}}{(D-F)} \tag{2}$$

$$\omega_{\beta_{on}} = \frac{l_1 \sin(\mu_{on}-\alpha_{on})}{l_3 \sin(\mu_{on}-\beta_{on})}\omega_{\alpha_{on}} \tag{3}$$

Where, $A=l_4 - l_1 \cos\alpha_{\text{on}}$; $B=-l_1 \cos\alpha_{\text{on}}$; $C=\left(A^2+B^2+l_3^2-l_2^2\right)/2l_3$; $D=l_8 - l_5 \cos\beta_{\text{on}}$; $E=-l_5 \cos\beta_{\text{on}}$; $F=\left(D^2+E^2+l_7^2-l_6^2\right)/2l_7$; α_{on} 、 β_{on} 、 θ_{on1} and μ_{on} are the rotation angles of drive rod IH, crank FE, electrode cage CD and drive connecting rod GH during closing; $\omega_{\alpha_{on}}$ is the angular velocity of the driving rod IH during the closing process; $\omega_{\beta_{on}}$ is the angular velocity of crank FG during closing.

Measure the displacement of hinge point E during the closing process, and filter the output waveform. The specific waveform and characteristics of the mechanism closing process are shown in Figure 3 and Table 1.

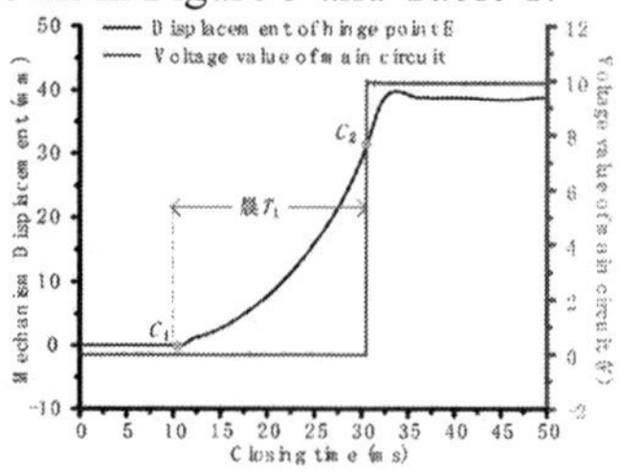

Fig. 3. Displacement waveform and characteristics of mechanism during closing.

TABLE I

CHARACTERISTICS OF MECHANISM MOVEMENT DURING CLOSING

Operation process	Mechanism	Characteristics	Physical
Closing process	Hinge point E	C_1	Initial closing
		C_2	Contact contact
		$\triangle T_1$	Time interval from C_1 to C_2

3) Motion analysis and feature selection in opening process

During the opening process of the air circuit breaker, the contact springs and the opening springs drive the operating mechanism for opening operation before the movable and fixed contacts are separated. After the movable and fixed contacts are separated, the opening springs drive the operating mechanism for opening operation, and pulls it back to the final position after the operating mechanism hits the stopper. The specific opening process is shown in Figure 4.

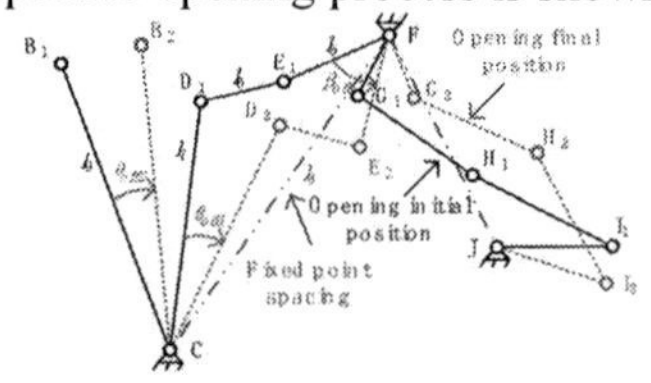

Fig. 4. Schematic diagram of operating mechanism movement during opening of air circuit breaker.

According to the vector equation method, the motion relationship equation between the connecting rods during the opening process of the operating mechanism is established, and the transmission ratio of the mechanism is obtained.

$$\beta_{\text{off}} = 2\arctan\frac{I \pm \sqrt{H^2 + I^2 - J^2}}{(H-J)} \tag{4}$$

$$\omega_{\beta_{\text{off}}} = \frac{l_7 \sin(\mu_{\text{off}}-\theta_{\text{off1}})}{l_5 \sin(\mu_{\text{off}}-\beta_{\text{off}})}\omega_{\theta_{\text{off1}}} \tag{5}$$

Where, $H=l_8 - l_7 \cos\theta_{\text{off1}}$; $I=-l_7 \cos\theta_{\text{off1}}$; $J=\left(H^2+I^2+l_5^2-l_6^2\right)/2l_5$; β_{off} 、 θ_{off1} and μ_{off} are respectively the rotation angles of crank FE, electrode cage CD and contact connecting rod DE during opening; $\omega_{\beta_{\text{off}}}$ is the angular velocity of crank FG during opening; $\omega_{\theta_{\text{off1}}}$ is the angular velocity of electrode cage CD during opening.

Measure the displacement of hinge point E in the opening process, and filter the output waveform. The specific waveform and characteristics of the mechanism in the opening process are shown in Figure 5 and Table 2.

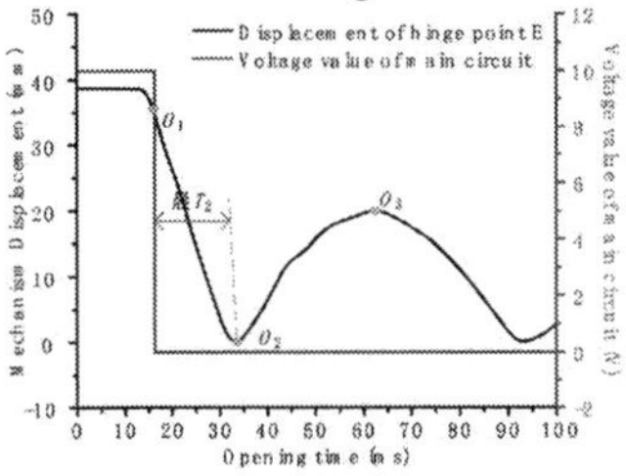

Fig. 5. Displacement waveform and characteristics of mechanism during opening.

TABLE II

CHARACTERISTICS OF MECHANISM MOVEMENT DURING CLOSING

Operation process	Mechanism	Characteristics	Physical
Opening process	Hinge point E	O_1	Contact separation
		O_2	Impact stop
		O_3	B maximum rebound displacement
		$\triangle T_2$	Time interval from O_1 to O_2

B. Energy transmission characteristic of operating mechanism of air circuit breaker

1) Energy transmission characteristic of operating mechanism in closing process

During the closing process of air circuit breaker, the energy storage springs provide all the closing energy to drive the operating mechanism to complete the closing operation. Before the movable and fixed contacts contact, the opening springs provide resistance. Due to their low stiffness coefficient, the influence of the opening springs can be ignored when analyzing the energy transmission characteristic of the operating mechanism before the contact collision.

Dynamic torque of energy storage spring acting on energy storage lever can be obtained by formula (6).

$$M_1 = K_1 L_{1ac} r_1 \sin(\varepsilon_1 + \varepsilon_2) \quad (6)$$

Where, M_1 is the dynamic torque of the energy storage springs to the point J; K_1 is the energy storage springs coefficient; L_{1ac} is an energy storage spring-shaped variable.

The relationship between the rotation angle of the driving rod IH and its angular velocity and energy before the collision of the movable and fixed contacts can be obtained by formula (7).

$$\frac{1}{2} J \omega_{\alpha_{on}}{}^2 = \int_0^{\alpha_{contact}} (M_1) d\alpha \quad (7)$$

Where, J is the moment of inertia; α_{contact} refers to the contact between movable and fixed contacts; L_{1ac} is an energy storage spring-shaped variable.

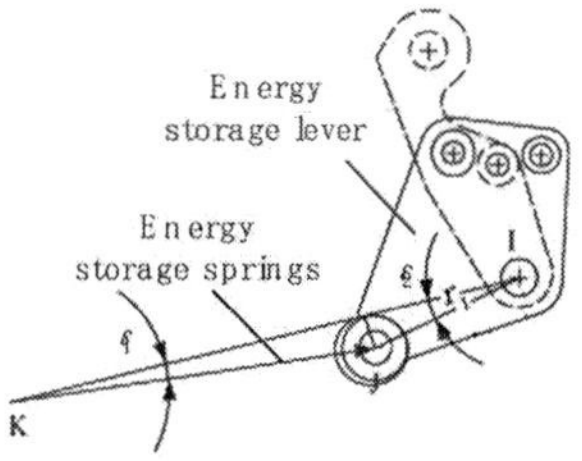

Fig. 6. Displacement waveform and characteristics of mechanism during opening.

The rotation time required for driving rod IH and crank FE from the initial closing to the movable and fixed contacts contact is obtained by formula (8) (9).

$$\Delta t = \frac{\Delta \alpha}{\omega_{\alpha_{on}}} \quad (8)$$

$$\Delta T_1 = \int \frac{1}{\omega_{\alpha_{on}}} d\alpha \quad (9)$$

2) Energy transmission characteristic of operating mechanism in opening process

In the opening process of air circuit breaker, because the stiffness coefficient of the opening springs is far less than that of the contact springs, it can be considered that the contact springs provides full part of the opening energy before the separation of the movable and fixed contacts. After the movable and fixed contacts are separated, the opening springs drives the mechanism to complete the opening operation.

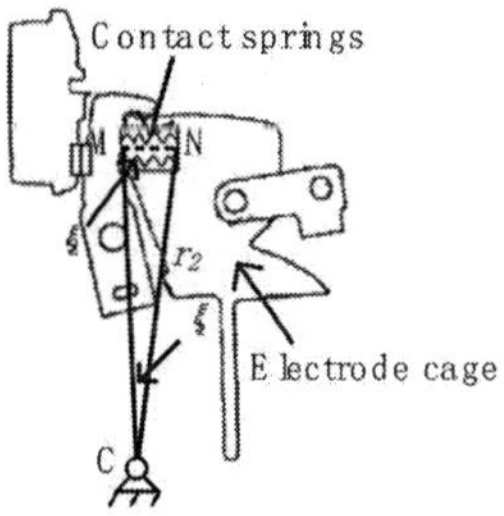

Fig. 7. Schematic diagram of position relationship between contact springs and electrode cage.

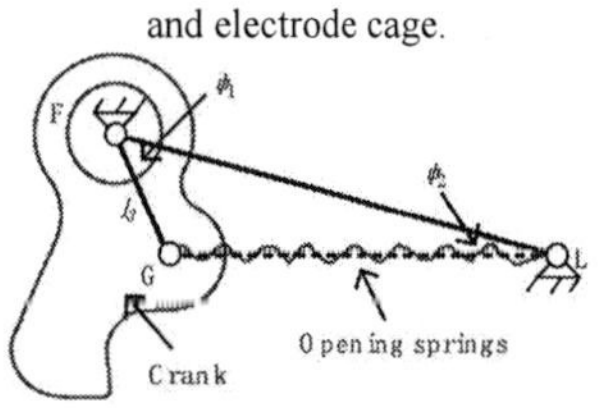

Fig. 8. Schematic diagram of position relationship between opening springs and crank.

The opening energy of the air circuit breaker is jointly provided by the contact springs and the opening springs, and the dynamic torque provided by them can be obtained by formula (10) (11).

$$M_2 = K_2 L_{2ac} r_2 \sin(\xi_1 + \xi_2) \quad (10)$$

$$M_3 = K_3 L_{3ac} l_3 \sin(\psi_1 + \psi_2) \quad (11)$$

Where, M_2 is the dynamic torque of contact springs to point C; K_2 is the contact springs coefficient; L_{2ac} is the contact spring-shaped variable; M_3 is the dynamic torque of the opening springs to point F; K_3 is the opening springs coefficient; L_{3ac} is the opening springs variable.

At the time of separation of movable and fixed contacts, the introduction of movable contact arm CB into the system increases the mass of the mechanism and generates part of the energy loss W_0. Therefore, the speed of electrode cage CD ($\omega_{\theta_{\text{over-travel}}}$) at the time of separation of movable and fixed contacts is obtained by formula (12).

$$\frac{1}{2} J \omega^2_{\theta_{\text{over-travel}}} = \int_0^{\theta_{\text{over-travel}}} (M_1) d\theta_{\text{off1}} - W_0 \quad (12)$$

The speed of the crank FE ($\omega_{\beta_{\text{over-travel}}}$) at the time when the movable and fixed contacts are separated can be calculated from formula (5). After the movable and fixed contacts are separated, the relationship between the rotation angle of crank FE and its angular velocity and energy can be obtained by formula (13).

$$\frac{1}{2} J \omega^2_{\beta_{\text{off}}} = \int_{\beta_{\text{over-travel}}}^{\beta} (M_2) d\beta_{\text{off}} + \frac{1}{2} J \omega^2_{\beta_{\text{over-travel}}} \quad (13)$$

The rotation time from the separation of movable and fixed contacts to crank FE hitting the stopper can be obtained by formula (14) (15).

$$\Delta t = \frac{\Delta \beta}{\omega_{\beta_{\text{off}}}} \quad (14)$$

$$\Delta T_2 = \int \frac{1}{\omega_{\beta_{\text{off}}}} d\beta \quad (15)$$

C. Evaluation method of springs service performance of air circuit breaker

1) Evaluation method of service performance of energy storage springs

The performance degradation of the energy storage springs will reduce the energy during the closing process of the operating mechanism. According to formula (6) (7) (9), the relationship between the degradation percentage of the energy storage springs and the closing process $\triangle T_1$ is shown in Figure 9.

2) Service performance evaluation method of contact springs

The performance degradation of contact springs will reduce of energy in the opening process of the operating mechanism. According to formula (10) (12) (13) (15), the relationship between the degradation percentage of opening springs and the opening process $\triangle T_2$ is shown in Figure 10. At the same time, the reduction of opening speed will also reduce the rebound height O_3 after the mechanism hits the stopper.

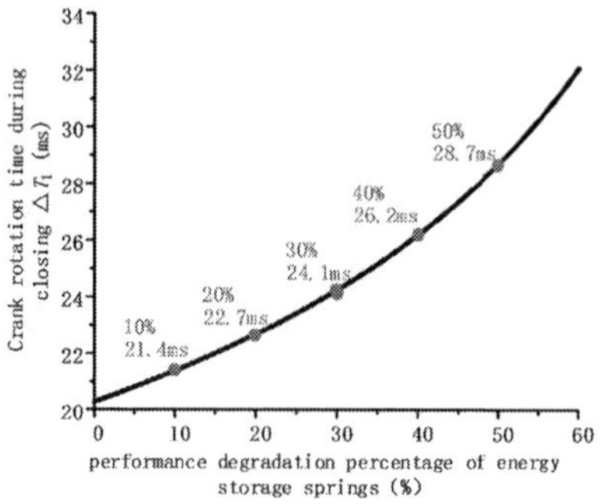

Fig. 9. Relationship between performance degradation percentage of energy storage springs and $\triangle T_1$.

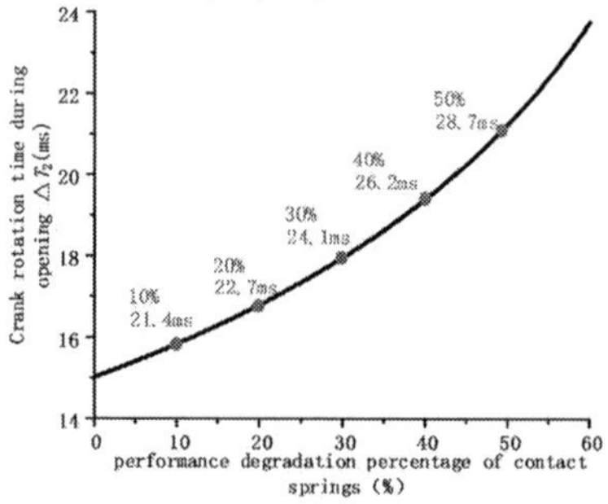

Fig. 10. Relationship between performance degradation percentage of contact springs and $\triangle T_2$.

3) Service performance evaluation method of opening springs

The performance degradation of the opening springs will reduce energy in the opening process of the operating mechanism. According to formula (11) (13) (15), the relationship between the degradation percentage of the opening springs and the opening process $\triangle T_2$ is shown in Figure 11. At the same time, the reduction of opening speed will also reduce the rebound height O_3 after the mechanism hits the stopper.

4) Service performance evaluation method of air circuit breaker

Table 3 shows the change of characteristics caused by the performance degradation of each spring of the operating mechanism of air circuit breaker. The service performance of each spring can be evaluated by monitoring the change of each characteristic.

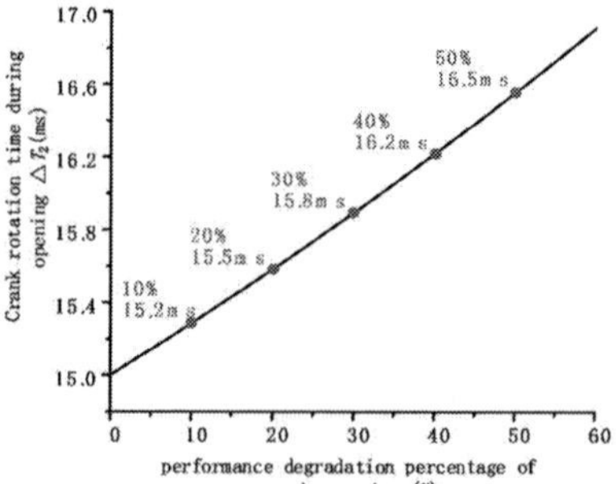

Fig. 11. Relationship between performance degradation percentage of opening springs and $\triangle T_2$.

TABLE III

THE INFLUENCE OF SPRINGS DEGRADATION ON THE CHARACTERISTICS OF THE MECHANISM IN THE CLOSING AND OPENING PROCESS

Operation process	Characteristics	Energy storage springs degradation	Contact springs degradation	Opening springs degradation
Closing process	C_1	—	—	—
	C_2	—	—	—
	$\triangle T_1$	Enlarge	—	—
Opening process	O_1	—	—	—
	O_2	—	—	—
	O_3	—	Reduce	Reduce
	$\triangle T_2$	—	Enlarge	Enlarge

III. CONCLUSION

The springs of the operating mechanism of air circuit breaker are used to drive the mechanism to complete the closing and opening operation. The degradation of the spring performance will lead to changes in the energy transmission characteristic of the operating mechanism. According to the operation characteristic of the mechanism, the appropriate characteristics in the motion waveform of the hinge point E in the closing and opening process of the mechanism are selected to reflect the energy change of the mechanism. The influence of the degradation of energy storage springs, contact springs and opening springs on the characteristics are quantitatively calculated. The service performance of springs of air circuit breaker is evaluated by monitoring the change of characteristics.

REFERENCES

[1] Zhao Chengchen, Li Kui, Hao Yunqian, et al. Research on the reliability modeling method for low-voltage switches based on competing failure[J]. Proceedings of the CSEE, 2020, 40(21): 7094-7107.

[2] Li Kui, Dai Yihua, Niu Feng, et al. Residual pulsating DC detection based on triggering angle identification[J]. Electric Power Automation Equipment, 2017 ,37(05): 80-84.

[3] Hu Bokai, Li Kui, Niu Feng, et al. Research on condition monitoring method of mechanical characteristics of low-voltage circuit breaker[J]. Transactions of China Electrotechnical Society, 2022, 37(13): 3317-3330.

[4] Mei Fei, Mei Jun, Zheng Jianyong, et al. Application of Particle Swarm Fused KFCM and Classification Model of SVM for Fault Diagnosis of Circuit Breaker[J]. Proceedings of the CSEE, 2013, 33(36): 134-141 + 19.

[5] Yang Qiuyu, Wang Dong, Ruan Jiangjun, et al. Fault Severity Estimation Method for Mechanical Parts in Circuit Breakers Based on Vibration Analysis[J]. Transactions of China Electrotechnical Society, 2021, 36(13): 2880-2892.

[6] Yang Qiuyu, Ruan Jiangjun, Zhuang Zhijian, et al. Chaotic analysis and feature extraction of vibration signals from power circuit breakers[J]. IEEE Transactions on Power Delivery, 2020,35(3): 1124-1135.

[7] Razi-Kazemi A A, Niayesh K, Nilchi R. A Probabilistic Model-Aided Failure Prediction Approach for Springs-Type Operating Mechanism of High-Voltage Circuit Breakers[J]. IEEE Transactions on Power Delivery, 2019, 34(4): 1280-1290.

[8] Ni Jianjun, Zhang Chuanbiao, Yang S X. An adaptive approach based on KPCA and SVM for real-time fault diagnosis of HVCBs[J] . IEEE Trans. on Power Delivery, 2011, 26(3): 960-1971.

Research on Early Detection of Short Circuit Fault in Islanded AC Microgrid

Ruonan Chen [1, 2, 3], Xin Zheng[1, 2, 3]

(1、College of Electrical Engineering and Automotion, Fuzhou University
2、Fujian Key Laboratory of New Energy Generation and Power Conversion
3、Engineering Research Center of Smart Distribution Grid Equipment, Fujian Province University,
Fuzhou, Fujian, China, 350000)
E-mail: 734694521@qq.com Tel: 15659938006

***Abstract*—With the rapid development of microgrid, the early detection of short-circuit fault in islanded microgrid has become an urgent demand for microgrid fault protection. This paper establishes the simulation model of of short-circuit fault in islanded AC microgrid on the platform of MATLAB / Simulink, and the corresponding characteristics of current wavelet energy spectrum under various short-circuit fault conditions are studied. The influence of system capacity changes in case of complete accommodation are analyzed as well as incomplete accommodation and insufficient accommodation. An accurate and reliable early fault detection method is proposed. Simulation and experimental results show that this method can quickly and accurately detect all kinds of short-circuit faults in islanded microgrid under various capacity conditions, which can improve the reliability of microgrid. At the same time, it also provides a theoretical basis and sufficient reaction time for the selective protection of microgrid.**

***Index Terms*— Islanded AC Microgrid; Short circuit fault; Early detection; Wavelet energy spectrum**

I. INTRODUCTION

At present, the load is rising continuously, the basic structure of power system is aging. Environmental pollution, power efficiency and users' demand for higher standards of power quality have become great challenges faced by the power industry all over the world. Nonetheless, microgrids have huge advantages in dealing with such problems due to their efficient use and intelligent management of distributed power systems [1]. The research on Microgrid in foreign countries is earlier, such as CERTS microgrid in the United States, NTUA and domestic microgrid laboratories in the European Union, Archi and Kyoto microgrids in Japan, etc. [2-3]. Although China's research on microgrid started relatively late, with the strong support of the state, there are still many island microgrid demonstration projects such as Shandong Fushan Island, Wenzhou Luxi Island, and Wenzhou Nanji Island [4].

Most distributed generators are currently incorporated into the microgrid through power electronic components such as inverters. Generally, the control circuit of power electronic devices will set short-circuit current limiting measures, resulting in the limited output amplitude of short-circuit fault current of inverter distributed generators. At the same time, the loop power supply mode of microgrid is also different from the power flow direction of traditional radial distribution network. Therefore, the relay protection method of traditional power grid is not suitable for microgrid. Microgrid can switch between grid connected operation and islanded operation [5-6]. Through the flexible control of microgrid, the power supply reliability and power quality can be improved, and the impact of distributed generation on power grid security, stability and power quality can be avoided. As an important part of microgrid, the flexible control strategy of inverter interfaced distributed generation (IIDG) enables itself to have multiple composite functions [7]. At present, the microgrid does not have a clear topology when operating on an island. Due to its isolation from the large power grid, its control mode is mainly divided into master-slave control and peer-to-peer control [8-12]. However, when the microgrid operates in an isolated island, the voltage stability of the microgrid is facing a severe challenge due to the constraints of IIDG capacity and current limiting characteristics [13].

The power supply in microgrid is mainly inverter micro power supply, and the maximum current that its semiconductor devices can pass through is limited [14-15]. Therefore, the fault current level of microgrid island operation is low, and the traditional overcurrent protection is not enough to realize the protection of microgrid. Reference [16] proposed to switch the reference current of U/f-MS to its current limit value in case of microgrid fault, and analyzed the micropower fault model in dq coordinate system as well as in that of ABC. However, the model can only reflect the fault response under specific fault control strategy, which has certain limitations in application. Reference [17-18] further proposes two current limiting methods by used of equal ratio compression and saturation link respectively. Although they are simple and effective, they will lead to distortion of the output current of micro power supply in case of asymmetric fault or difficult to determine the current phase, which is not conducive to fault calculation. The construction of a virtual internal impedance in the droop control micro power supply can limit the overcurrent in case of micro grid fault [19-22], but it cannot flexibly deal with the situation of multiple fault types. Wavelet transform method is used to determine whether the fault occurs in microgrid [23-24], but it only carries out simulation analysis for the steady-state situation after short-circuit fault, and cannot realize rapid detection in the early stage of fault.

To sum up, due to the changeable operation mode of microgrid and the output limitation of short-circuit current in distributed generation, the traditional protection methods are no longer applicable. Therefore, based on the wavelet energy spectrum transformation, the early fault characteristics of short-circuit fault current is extracted in this paper. And so that the effective fault identification during the early stage can be realized, which can avoid short-circuit current damage to power equipment. It also provides sufficient time for reliable removal of fault lines.

II. SHORT CIRCUIT FAULT SIMULATION MODEL OF ISLANDED MICROGRID

In this paper, the short-circuit fault simulation model is built in MATLAB/Simulink, as can be seen in Fig.1. The microgrid in island mode constructed in this paper adopts master-slave control and contains three branches, including batteries, photovoltaics, wind turbines, and loads. The impedance setting is included in the line. Among them, the battery part adopts the V/f control method to provide the reference of voltage and frequency for the microgrid, while the photovoltaic and wind turbine parts adopt the PQ constant power control. All DGs in the simulation model of this paper refer to inverter interfaced distributed generation (IIDG).

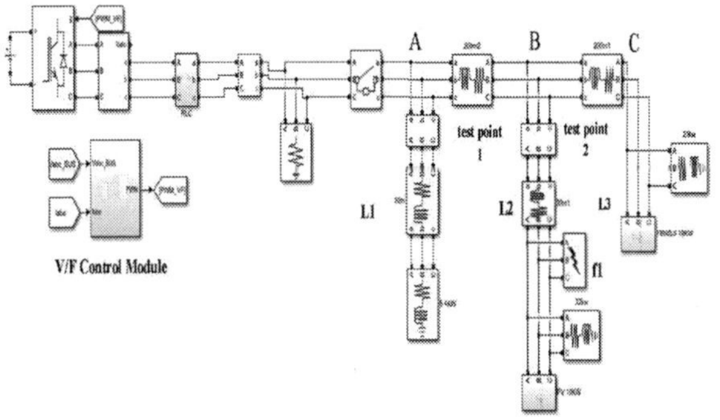

Fig. 1. Microgrid model.

The output of the wind turbine and photovoltaic is 10kW, the load on the photovoltaic is 32kW, the load on the wind turbine is 23kW, and the load size of the load branch is 5.4kW. The line adopts the impedance model, the resistance of the feeder is 0.641Ω/km and the inductance is 0.321mH/km. The distances between node A and node B, node B and node C are both 200m.

Feeder L1 is a pure load line, photovoltaic (PV) and load2 are located in bus B area on feeder L2, wind turbine (WT) and load3 are located in bus C area on feeder L3. The detection points are respectively set at the common busbar and its connection point with each feeder, which are used to measure electric information such as current and voltage.

III. WAVEFORM ANALYSIS OF NORMAL AND SHORT CIRCUIT FAULTS

The AC microgrid is not connected with the large grid in the island mode, and it is affected by the V/f control of the battery and the limiting effect of the power electronic devices. Therefore, the fault current characteristics in the island mode are less obvious than those in the grid-connected mode, and it is necessary to extract and analyze the existing characteristics to obtain effective information that can reflect the fault characteristics. In this paper, wavelet energy spectrum algorithm is used to analyze the fault characteristics in islanded microgrid.

Based on dyadic wavelet transform, wavelet energy spectrum transform enhances the recognition ability of weak signal mutation characteristics. In addition, the multi-scale wavelet decomposition algorithm is a digital filter. In practical applications, combined with other digital filtering schemes such as morphological filtering algorithm, it can effectively suppress the influence of background white noise and random impulse noise in low-voltage system [25]. According to Mallat algorithm [26], the wavelet energy spectrum transformation equation of discrete signal f (x) in time domain is shown in formula (1), and its wavelet function adopts the derivative of cubic B-spline function.

$$\begin{cases} S_{2^i} f(x) = \sum_k h_k S_{2^{i-1}} f(x-2^{i-1}k) \\ W_{2^i} f(x) = \sum_k g_k S_{2^{i-1}} f(x-2^{i-1}k) \\ E_{2^j} x(t) = \left| W_{2^j} x(t) \right|^2 \end{cases} \quad (1)$$

When a short-circuit fault occurs in the microgrid, the protection system first needs to detect the short-circuit fault according to the fault detection threshold. In this paper, *E*4 is used to represent the detail component value of the current at the detection point after four scale transformation. Its value is related to the sampling frequency, and its maximum value is expressed by *E*4max. The sampling frequency in this paper is 20kHz.

In the process of short-circuit fault detection, it is necessary to distinguish the waveform of normal operation from that of short-circuit fault, so as to avoid misjudgment. Therefore, the current waveform characteristics of distributed generation / load on each feeder in AC microgrid in islanding mode are studied under the following three conditions: normal operation or operation state change of distributed generation / load, load input or removal, short-circuit fault of current feeder and fault on other feeders. In this paper, taking feeder L2 as an example, the current waveform detected at the detection point in the above three cases are transformed by wavelet energy spectrum.

A. Normal Operation State

The normal operation state of microgrid includes: normal and stable operation, photovoltaic cut off on feeder L2, and load2 on / off switching. The values of *E*4max measured under these four operating states are analyzed respectively. As shown in Fig.2, the waveform detected by the detection point and the *E*4max value of the corresponding wavelet transform are shown in the normal operation state of feeder L2. The load2 is put into use when t = 0.4s, and the photovoltaic is cut off when t = 0.6s.

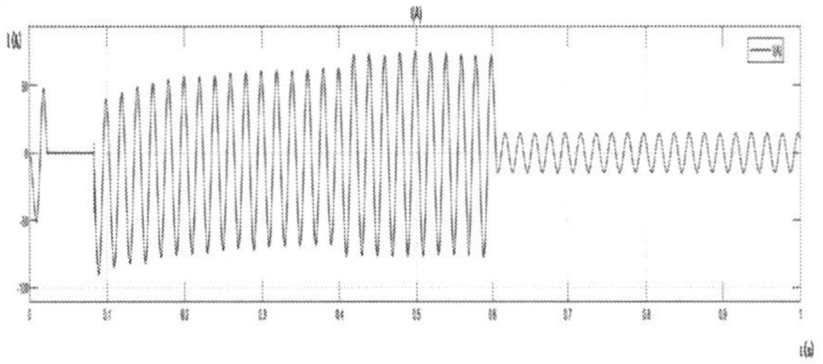

Fig. 2. Current during normal and operation state change.

It can be seen from Fig.2 that when Load2 is put into operation, the current increases, and the power supply needs to generate this part of energy to supply the operation of the Load. When the photovoltaic is cut off, the current flowing through the bus decreases due to the lack of energy provided by the distributed power supply. The measured *E*4max under various normal conditions. The measured *E*4max under various normal conditions are listed in Table 1, which can be seen that the maximum value is 365 occurred when the load is put into operation.

TABLE I
*E*4MAX OF FEEDER L2 UNDER NORMAL OPERATION.

function state	normal function	load investment	Photovoltaic removal	Load removal
*E*4max	270	365	14	275

B. Fault on Feeder L2

The magnitude of short-circuit fault current is affected by two parameters: short-circuit type and fault initial angle. Short circuit types include single-phase grounding short circuit, two-phase grounding short circuit, two-phase to phase short circuit and three-phase to phase short circuit. The short-circuit fault model is placed at f1 position of feeder L2 in Fig.1 for simulation analysis. Fig.3 shows the current waveform measured at the detection point when the initial phase angle θ_c is different under the condition of single-phase grounding short circuit fault on L2. By changing the fault type, the simulation current waveform in cases of two-phase short circuit and three-phase short circuit can be obtained with different θ_c. The *E*4max value of the simulation waveform under various faults is counted after wavelet transform, as shown in Fig.4. The *E*4max of single-phase grounding fault is the lowest, and that of three-phase phase short circuit is the largest, two-phase grounding short circuit is slightly larger than the two-phase short circuit. Different initial phase angles *E*4max is also significantly different under different θ_c. The minimum value of *E*4max, which is 3000, occurred in case of single-phase grounding short circuit with the θ_c=90.

C. Influence of Distributed Generation Capacity

In the model in Fig.1, the capacity of distributed power is 72.62kw, which is much larger than the load capacity. In order to analyze the impact of different capacities on the simulation results, adjust the distributed power to 60.4kw (which can be fully absorbed by the load) and 54.62kw (which cannot meet the load demand) respectively for simulation analysis. The *E*4max values measured by microgrid under normal operation under different capacities are listed in Table 2 and Table 3. The statistical results of *E*4max values obtained under various fault types are shown in Fig.5 and Fig.6. As shown in the Figures and Tables, there is little change for *E*4max under different capacity, and the maximum value of *E*4max is still 365 during normal operation while the minimum value at fault time is still 3000. Therefore, the capacity change has no great impact on the selection of fault threshold of microgrid.

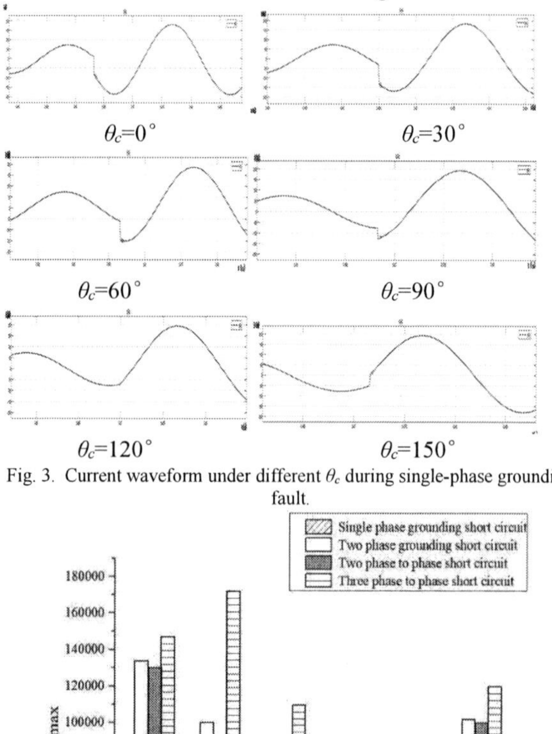

Fig. 3. Current waveform under different θ_c during single-phase grounding fault.

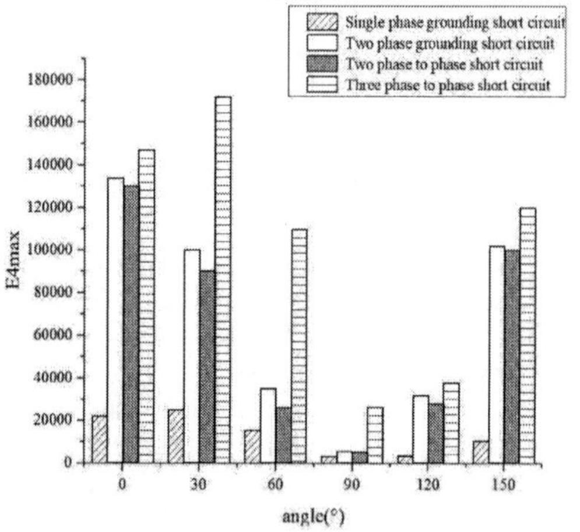

Fig. 4. *E*4max value detected under different θ_c and different types of short circuit faults at the end of feeder L2.

TABLE II
$E4$max under normal operation when the capacity of distributed generation is fully absorbed by load.

function state	normal function	load investment	photovoltaic resection	load resection
$E4$max	250	350	14	265

TABLE III
$E4$max under normal operation when distributed power capacity is less than load demand.

function state	normal function	load investment	photovoltaic resection	load resection
$E4$max	250	355	15	275

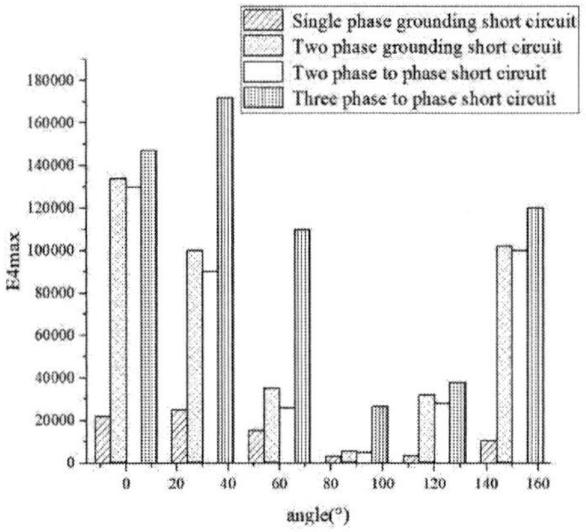

Fig. 5. $E4$max value under short circuit fault when the power capacity is fully absorbed by the load.

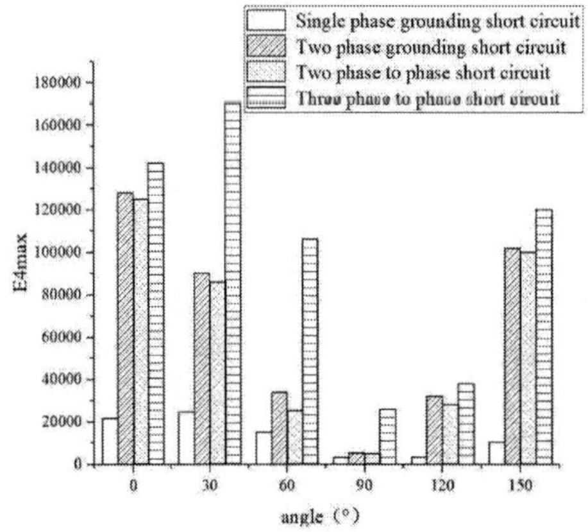

Fig. 6. $E4$max value under short circuit fault when the power supply capacity is less than the load demand.

D. *Current Changes of Feeder L2 When Feeder L1 and L3 Are Faulty*

Due to the existence of distributed power supply on feeder L2, when a short-circuit fault occurs on feeder L1 or feeder L3, the photovoltaic on feeder L2 will provide power to the common bus, causing the current flowing to change. At the same time, the isolated island microgrid is not supported by the large power grid, and all voltage frequencies are provided by the battery. It is likely that feeder L2 will be affected by the short-circuit fault of feeder L1 and L3. Therefore, fault points are set on feeders L1 and L3 respectively to observe the current change of feeder L2. The setting time of fault point is t = 0.4699s and the end time of fault is t =0.7s. The effects of L1 and L3 faults on L2 are listed in Table IV. The results show that $E4$max of L2 branch will not produce fault characteristics, so it will not be affected.

TABLE IV
$E4$max value measured at test point in case of three-phase short circuit fault on feeders L1 and L3.

Fault feeder	L1	L3
$E4$max measured by L2	200	240

E. *Identification of Short Circuit Fault Characteristics*

From the above analysis, it can be seen that when the distributed power supply / load on the feeder operates normally or the operation state changes, and the short-circuit fault occurs on the feeder L1 or L3, the measured value is far less than the $E4$max measured when the short-circuit fault occurs at the end of L2. Therefore, for the test point, take $E4$max = 365 when the load is input as the lower limit and $E4$max= 3000 when the fault initial angle is 90 degrees as the upper limit, and select an appropriate value between them as the characteristic value of short-circuit fault for identification. For other feeders and different sampling frequencies, the corresponding threshold interval can be determined by the same method.

IV. Simulation Verification

In order to verify the accuracy of short-circuit fault feature recognition by the above method, place the short-circuit fault model in Fig.1, simulate different types of short-circuit faults, set the fault threshold to 2000, and list the fault detection time and the unit value of current at that moment in Table 5.

Table V
Time and current multiple of short circuit fault detected when short circuit fault occurs at L2 terminal.

θ_c/(°)	fault type	t_1/ms	I_1^*
0	single-phase	0.34	2.4
	two-phase	0.4	3.913
	three-phase	0.46	4.84
30	single-phase	0.53	2.45
	two-phase	0.3	3.67
	three-phase	0.49	4.93
60	single-phase	0.8	2.6
	two-phase	0.72	3.67
	three-phase	0.30	4.67
90	single-phase	0.90	2.61
	two-phase	0.96	3.78
	three-phase	0.92	4.96
120	single-phase	0.90	3.01
	two-phase	0.76	3.88
	three-phase	0.98	4.98
150	single-phase	0.70	3.12
	two-phase	0.86	4.10
	three-phase	0.92	5.01

As shown in Table 5, t_1 indicates the time when a short-circuit fault is detected in the islanded microgrid, I_1^* is the unit value of current on L2 when short-circuit fault is detected, and its reference value is the rated current during normal operation. It can be seen from the table that under the set fault threshold, the maximum t_1 in the table is 0.92ms, the maximum I_1^* is 5.01. It shows that this method can detect the fault when the short-circuit current is small, so as to achieve the purpose of early detection.

V. EXPEROMENTAL VERIFICATION

Using the microgrid experimental platform in Jinjiang campus of Fuzhou University, the feasibility of wavelet energy spectrum algorithm for early fault detection of isolated microgrid is verified by this paper. Fig.7 shows the microgrid experimental platform and experimental circuit diagram. The faults of various modes are simulated by the short-circuit fault generator in the experimental platform, and the short-circuit fault waveform is collected by the fault recorder with a sampling frequency of 5KHz. During the experiment, polycrystalline photovoltaics, programmable loads and energy storage batteries were all put into use. Among them, the photovoltaic capacity is 10kWp and the programmable load is 10KVA. Various short-circuit fault current waveforms simulated in the experiment are input into the protection program of MATLAB/Simulink to verify the effect of early detection.

According to the actual sampling frequency, the data is imported into MATLAB/Simulink for wavelet transform. The lower limit of the fault threshold is 8000 and the upper limit is 100000. Based on this, the fault detection threshold was set to 90000 in this experiment. Fig.8 shows the measured waveform during three-phase short circuit, and the short circuit time is set randomly. It can be seen from the figure that the circuit breaker breaks within 0.2ms. At this time, the short-circuit fault phase angle is 122.4°, and the current is only 278.11A, which is much lower than the short-circuit current amplitude of 3190A. This result verifies the effectiveness of early detection.

VI. CONCLUSION

Based on the advantages of wavelet transform in signal mutation feature extraction, this paper studies the fault characteristics of short-circuit current in islanded microgrid, and analyzes the influence of distributed power supply capacity on fault characteristics. Furthermore, a method for determining the short-circuit fault detection threshold of AC microgrid in island mode is proposed, which can realize fast detection in the early stage of short-circuit fault. The simulation and experimental results show that the wavelet energy spectrum eigenvalue can realize rapid identification in the early stage of short-circuit fault, which provides a theoretical basis and new idea for the study of selective protection of AC microgrid in island mode.

ACKNOWLEDGMENT

This work is financially supported by "Industry Guiding Project of Fujian Province" (No.2021H0014).

(a)Physical diagram.

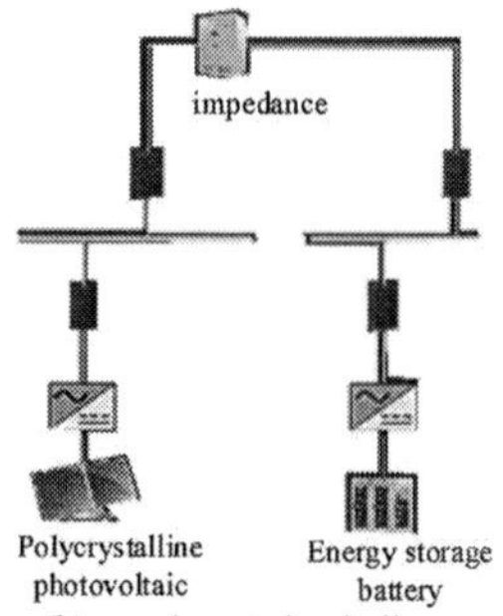

(b)experiment circuit diagram.

Fig. 7. Micro-grid experimental platform.

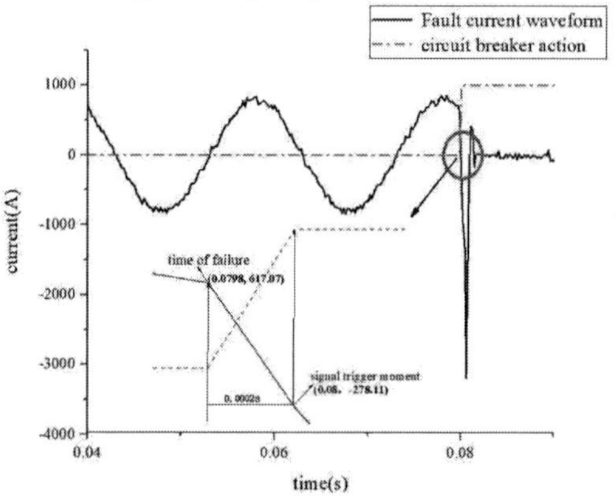

Fig. 8. Waveform of three-phase phase-to-phase short-circuit current and breaking signal of breaker.

REFERENCES

[1] Beheshtaein S, Cuzner R, Savaghebi M, et al.: A review on microgrids protection. IET Generation Transmission & Distribution,2019, 13(6), 743-759

[2] Nikkhajoei H, Lasseter R H.: Distributed generation interface to the CERTS microgrid. IEEE Transactions on Power Delivery, 2009), 24(3), 1598-1608.

[3] Wang Chengshan, Gao Fei, Li Peng, Ding Fei. Review of EU research projects on renewable energy and distributed generation access technology [J]. China Southern Power Grid Technology, 2008, 2(06): 1-6.

[4] Wang Ying. Research on microgrid fault detection method and protection principle [D]. Zhejiang University, 2017.

[5] Dai Ming, Jia Ke, Fang Yu, Yang Zhe, Bi Tianshu, Zhang Chi. Analysis of Fault Characteristics of Independently Operating Microgrid and Research on Line Protection [J]. Electric Power Automation Equipment, 2019, 39(04): 133-140 .

[6]Lv Zhenyu, Su Chen, Wu Zaijun, Dou Xiaobo, Li Hongyan. Distributed secondary regulation strategy and communication topology optimization of island-type microgrid [J]. Journal of Electrotechnical Technology, 2017, 32(06): 209-219.

[7] Yuan Fangfang, Zhao Jiangxin, Guo Baofu, Tian Ying, Wang Xiaokai, Wang Yin.Research on Coordinated Control Strategy of Distributed Photovoltaic Power Source and Distribution Network[J]. Electrical Measurement and Instrumentation, 2020,57(24):116-124.

[8] Lv Zhenyu, Su Chen, Wu Zaijun, Dou Xiaobo, Li Hongyan. Distributed secondary regulation strategy and communication topology optimization of island-type microgrid [J]. Journal of Electrotechnical Technology, 2017, 32(06): 209-219.

[9]Wang Liang, Peng Yonggang, Wu Tao, Wei Wei, Song Wenlong.Improved master-slave control in island mode of photovoltaic-storage AC microgrid[J].High Voltage Technology,2020,46(10):3530-3541.

[10]Zhang Yun, Jiang Wang, Zhang Chao, Huang Xiaowei, Chen Xi, Zhao Shanglin. Master-slave control microgrid off-grid coordinated control strategy based on energy storage state of charge [J]. Power System Protection and Control, 2022,50(04): 180-187.

[11]Xiong Xiong, Wu Ming, Ji Yu, Sun Lijing, Jing Tianjun, Yang Rengang, Su Chi, Chen Zhe. Research on Hybrid Coordinated Control and Power Management Strategy of Microgrid Group[J].Chinese Journal of Electrical Engineering,2018,38(05):1419 -1427.

[12]Xie Lin, Xie Kaigui, He Jian, Zhai Zhaohui, Hu Bo. Reliability evaluation of grid-connected microgrid considering control strategy [J]. Power System Protection and Control, 2013, 41(15): 102-109.

[13]Kang Wenfa, Li Qiang, Chen Minyu, Peng Congbo, Chen Feixiong. Multi-Agent Distributed Double Layer Control Method for Island Microgrid [J]. Chinese Journal of Electrical Engineering, 2018, 38(03): 770-781.

[14]Liu Xin, Mu Longhua, Wang Junkai. Fault control strategy and equivalent model of droop control micro-power supply [J]. Electrical Appliances and Energy Efficiency Management Technology, 2020(08):1-6+11.

[15]Han Yi, Zhang Dongxia. Analysis of fault characteristics of microgrid with inverter-type distributed power supply [J]. Power Grid Technology, 2011, 35(10): 147-152.

[16]Haj-Ahmed M A , Illindala M S . The Influence of Inverter-Based DGs and Their Controllers on Distribution Network Protection[J]. IEEE Transactions on Industry Applications, 2014, 50(4):2928-2937.

[17]Zeng Dehui, Pan Guoqing, Wang Gang, Zhu Gelan, Cai Yingqian. Fault analysis method of microgrid with V/f control DG [J]. Chinese Journal of Electrical Engineering, 2014, 34(16): 2604-2611.

[18]Plet C A , Brucoli M , Mcdonald J, et al.Fault models of inverter-interfaced distributd generators: Experimental verification and application to fault analysis[C]// Power & Energy Society General Meeting. IEEE, 2011.

[19]Zhu Jiran, Mu Longhua, Guo Wenming. Fault control of inverter-type distributed power supply considering fault direction identification of microgrid in grid-connected operation [J]. Journal of Electrotechnical Technology, 2022,37(03):634-644.

[20]Wei Chuanzhi, Shi Xiaohan, Zhang Hengxu, Ci Song, Liu Yang. PQ control inverter distributed power supply fault model considering current command tracking capability [J]. Electric Power Automation Equipment, 2020, 40(01): 59-65+72 .

[21]Paquette A D , Divan D M . Virtual Impedance Current Limiting for Inverters in Microgrids With Synchronous Generators[J]. IEEE Transactions on Industry Applications, 2015, 51(2):1630-1638.

[22]Paquette A D, Divan D M.: Virtual impedance current limiting for inverters in microgrids with synchronous generators. IEEE Transactions on Industry Applications 51(2):1630-1638 (2015).

[23]Wang Ying, Tang Hankan, Pan Mingjiu. Design of Microgrid Fault Detection Method Based on Wavelet Transform [J]. Internal Combustion Engine and Parts, 2017(08):90-92.

[24]Zhou Jianping, Zhu Jianping, Xu Sicong. Simulation Research on Short-Circuit Fault Detection During Microgrid Island Operation [J]. China Electric Power, 2014, 47(03): 85-89.

[25]Zheng X , Zhang P M , Chen L A . Research on realizing of fast opening of short-circuit faults for low voltage system[J]. Advanced Technology of Electrical Engineering and Energy, 2008.

[26]Mallat S , Zhong S . Characterization of signals from multiscale edges[J]. Trans IEEE, 1992, 14(7):710-7

8th International Conference on Reliability of Electrical Products and Electrical Contacts, November 18-20, 2022

Bipolar Fault-Tolerant Control Strategy Based on Full-Bridge Power Converter for SRM System

Debo Sun[1,2], Yanfang Hu[1,2], Zhiyong Kang[1,2], Cunjiang Gu[1,2], Zong Zhang[1,2]

[1)] Key Laboratory of Electromagnetic Field and Electrical Apparatus Reliability of Hebei Province, Tianjin, 300401

[2)] State Key Laboratory of Reliability and Intelligence of Electrical Equipment, Tianjin, 300401

Email: camellia_em@hebut.edu.cn TEL: 022-60203541

Abstract—**In this paper, a bipolar tolerant control method for open- and short-circuit faults of power transistors is proposed, which is based on full-bridge converter of 3-phase switched reluctance motor (SRM). Each unit of the two full-bridge converter is first connected to a controllable single-pole double-throw (SPDT) switch and then connected to one end of winding. The fault-tolerance operation is achieved by changing the SPDT switch state and developing bidirectional current excitation mode. In the normal cases, each phase winding operates dependently and alternatively in positive conduction and negative conduction modes. When a fault occurs, the faulty power conversion unit is diagnosed by the logical judgement about the neutral potentials and the operating states. After the fault is located, two adjacent controllable SPDT switches act simultaneously and one of which is connected to the faulty unit. Two adjacent units including the faulty unit are cut off and the phase windings are connected in a Y-connection with a neutral line. After a fault occurs, the motor can run stably with this winding connection.**

Index Terms—**Switched reluctance motor, power converter, tolerant control, bipolar control.**

I. INTRODUCTION

Switched reluctance motor (SRM) drive system has drawn widespread attention due to its robust structure, lower cost and high reliability [1]-[4].

Power converter is the essential parts for SRM drive system. Due to continuously working in high frequency chopping mode, the power transistors are prone to failure, especially in some harsh environments. The faults of power transistors will increase torque ripple and acoustic noise, and affect the normal operating of the system. Therefore, fault diagnosis and tolerant control technologies for power transistors are critical to be investigated to achieve SRM system operate steadily [5]-[7].

Research supported by Key Project of Science and Technology Research in Higher Education Institutions of Hebei Province under Grant ZD2020102 and State Key Laboratory of Reliability and Intelligence of Electrical Equipment under Grant EERI_PI2020004.

Due to the advantages of simple structure, lower cost and good phase-to-phase independence, asymmetrical half-bridge (AHB) power converter becomes the most widely used converter. However, it is not given the capacity of fault tolerance. Some advanced power converters with the fault tolerance capability are hence developed. In [8], a fault-tolerance solution for power transistors based on a modular full-bridge converter is proposed. The modular converter is composed of two six-pack switch modules and four solid state relays. A five-level power converter for open-circuit fault of power transistors is developed in [9]. Four switches per phase are needed in the five-level converter, of which two are used for normal operation and the remaining two are used for safe back. By using a relay network, the faulty parts can be bypassed to decrease the influence of the short-circuit (SC) fault and open-circuit (OC) fault in [10]. In [11], an integrated converter composed of four legs is put forward and a serial conduction control strategy is applied in the integrated converter to enlarge the output torque of faulty phase and decrease the torque ripple.

The above methods are all based on a modified power converter topology and are easy to be implemented. However, the exact fault types are needed to be detected, which puts forward higher requirements for fault diagnosis methods and reduces the generality of tolerant control scheme. Hence, it is necessary to develop an tolerant control scheme that can be executed without accurate fault diagnosis methods.

This paper develops a bipolar fault-tolerant control strategy for power transistors based on full-bridge power converter. Under normal conditions, the motor operates alternatively in the positive conduction mode and the negative conduction mode in two adjacent conduction periods. Under abnormal conditions, faulty power conversion units are diagnosed by the logical judgement about the neutral potentials and switching signals. After the faulty power conversion units are recognized, the fault-tolerant operation is achieved by the corresponding single-pole double-throw (SPDT) switches and Y-connected windings with a neutral line.

This paper is organized as follows. In Section II, the

bipolar control strategy based on 3-phase full-bridge power converter in normal cases is introduced. Section III presents the fault diagnosis scheme and the principle of fault-tolerant operation for the 3-phase full-bridge converter. The simulation verification is given in Section IV. Finally, Section V concludes the whole paper.

II. PRINCIPLE OF BIPOLAR CONTROL STRATEGY

In SRM system, current chopping control (CCC) is one of the most common strategy. The power converter is driven by the drive signals generated by the commutation controller. The AHB power converter is the most widely used converter and Fig. 1 shows a 3-Phase AHB power converter topology structure. This topology has the advantages of simple structure, lower cost and good phase-to-phase independence. However, it is difficult to implement some fault tolerant methods for this converter.

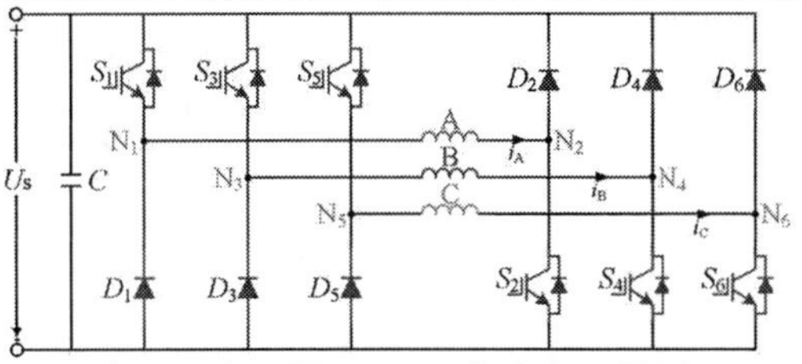

Fig. 1. The AHB converter for 3-phase SRM.

To avoid the above shortcoming of the AHB converter, a 3-phase full-bridge power converter is used in this paper, which is composed of two standard six-pack switch modules. The 3-phase full-bridge power converter is connected with six SPDT switches Q_1~Q_6, as shown in Fig. 2. The units of the switch modules L1~L6 are connected with the SPDT switches Q_1~Q_6, respectively. The SPDT switches are closed in normal conditions and act under specific fault conditions.

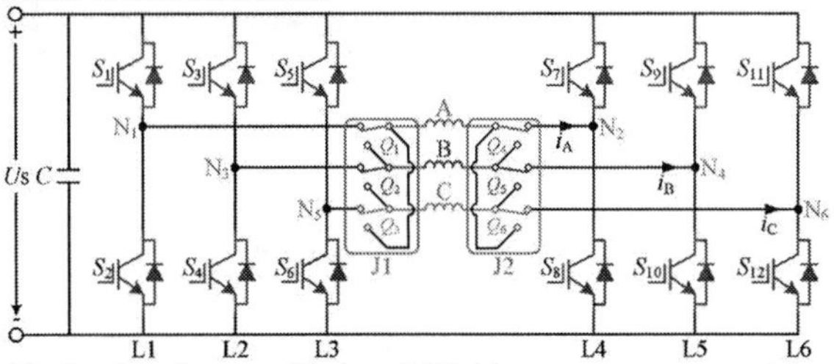

Fig. 2. The diagram of 3-phase full-bridge power converter and the SPDT switches connection.

The rotate direction of SRM only relates to the power-on sequence of each phase winding, and is independent on the power-on direction. Therefore, the bipolar control strategy will not interfere with the motor operation. Conversely, this bipolar control strategy can fully utilize all switches and are benefit to reduce the heat of power transistors. Commonly, there are six operation states for 3-phase converter under the bipolar control strategy in each phase, including positive excitation state ST1, positive freewheeling state ST2, positive demagnetization state ST3, negative excitation state ST4, negative freewheeling state ST5 and negative demagnetization state ST6. The six states are realized in two adjacent periods, and the positive states and negative states appear alternatively.

Taking Phase C as an example, when switches S_5 and S_{12} are turned on, the positive voltage is applied to the phase winding. The voltage drops of transistors and diodes are neglected, and the potentials of the neutral points N_5 and N_6 are equal to the bus voltage Us and 0, respectively, which is positive excitation state ST1, as shown in Fig. 3(a); when switch S_5 is turned off and switch S_{12} is turned on, the neutral potentials of points N_5 and N_6 are both equal to 0, which is positive freewheeling state ST2, as shown in Fig. 3(b); when S_5 and S_{12} are turned off, the neutral potentials of points N_5 and N_6 are 0 and Us, respectively, as shown in Fig. 3(c). In the negative period, the potentials of the neutral points N_5 and N_6 are opposite with the positive period. Fig. 3(d) shows negative excitation state ST4 when switches S_{11} and S_6 are turned on; Fig. 3(e) shows negative freewheeling state ST5 when switch S_{11} is turned off and switch S_6 is turned on; Fig. 3(f) shows negative demagnetization state ST6 when switches S_{11} and S_6 are turned off.

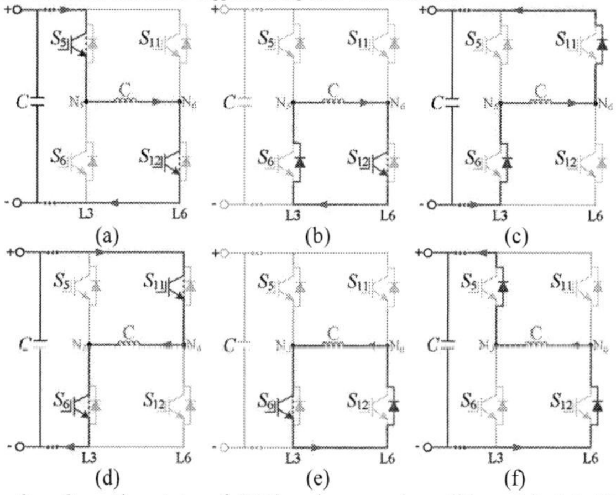

Fig. 3. Operation states of SRM under normal conditions. (a) state ST1. (b) state ST2. (c) state ST3. (d) state ST4. (e) state ST5. (f) state ST6.

III. PROPOSED FAULT DIAGNOSIS SCHEME AND PRINCIPLE OF FAULT-TOLERANT OPERATION

There are two classic faults for power transistors, including SC fault and OC fault. Both of the two faults will severely affect the performance of the SRM drives system.

When the OC fault of power transistor occurs, the current of the fault phase will dramatically decrease to zero. The fault phase cannot generate torque, and the SRM system will operate under phase-missing condition and the torque ripple will be greatly increased. In addition, the neutral potential of the fault unit will different from normal conditions. Taking Phase C as an example, when the OC fault occurs in switch S_5, positive excitation state ST1 will be replaced by positive freewheeling state ST2. As shown in Fig. 4(a), positive exciting current cannot flow through switch S_5 when switches S_5 and S_{12} are turned on. And the potential of neutral point N_5 will change from Us to 0 at this operation state. When the OC fault occurs in switch S_{11}, negative excitation state ST4 will be replaced by negative freewheeling state ST5. The negative exciting current and the negative freewheeling current will flow in the lower-loop circuit, as shown in Fig. 4(b). The potential of neutral point N_6 will change from Us to 0 when switches S_6 and S_{11} are turned on.

When the SC fault of power transistor occurs, the current of fault phase will rapidly rise and never decline to zero until the fault is removed. The fault is easy to damage SRM and the power supply if it is not eliminated for a long time. In this fault cases, the neutral potential will also be influenced. When switch S_5 is shorted, positive freewheeling state ST2 will be replaced by positive excitation state ST1, as shown in Fig. 4(c). The potential of neutral point N_5 will change from 0 to Us when switch S_5 is OFF and switch S_{12} is ON. When switch S_{11} is shorted, negative freewheeling state ST5 will be replaced by negative excitation state ST4, as presented in Fig. 4(d). The neutral potential of point N_6 will change from 0 to Us when switch S_6 is turned off and switch S_{11} is turned on.

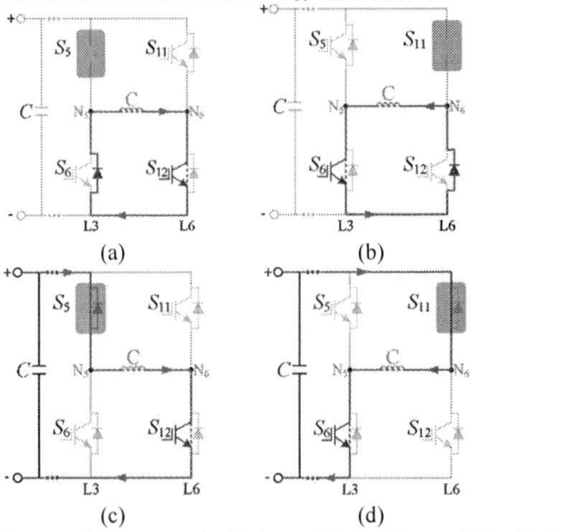

Fig. 4. The operating states under fault conditions. (a) state ST1 with S_5 OC fault. (c) state ST4 with S_{11} OC fault. (c) state ST2 with S_5 SC fault. (d) state ST5 with S_{11} SC fault.

A. *Fault Diagnosis Scheme for Power Transistors*

It is clear that the neutral potential of corresponding point will specifically change at given state when any switch of a unit occurs fault. Therefore, it is easy to identify the faulty unit based on the logical judgement about the operating states and the neutral potentials. The S_5 OC fault will be identified when U_{N5} is detected to be 0 under state ST1; the S_{11} OC fault can be determined when U_{N6} is measured to be 0 under state ST4; the S_5 SC fault can be determined when U_{N5} is measured to be Us under state ST2; the S_{11} SC fault are recognized when U_{N6} is detected to be Us under state ST5. All of the normal and fault cases of switches S_5 and S_{11} are listed in TABLE. I and other switch faults are same with the above situations.

TABLE. I
THE NEUTRAL POTENTIALS OF POINTS N_5 AND N_6 UNDER NORMAL AND FAULT CONDITIONS

	Normal		S_5 OC		S_{11} OC		S_5 SC		S_{11} SC	
	U_{N5}	U_{N6}	U_{N5}	U_{N6}	U_{N5}	U_{N6}	U_{N5}	U_{N6}	U_{N5}	U_{N6}
ST1	Us	0	0	0	Us	0	Us	0	Us	0
ST2	0	0	0	0	0	0	Us	0	0	0
ST3	0	Us	0	Us	0	Us	Us	Us	0	Us
ST4	0	Us	0	Us	0	0	0	Us	0	Us
ST5	0	0	0	0	0	0	0	0	0	Us
ST6	Us	0	Us	0	Us	0	Us	0	0	Us

B. *The Principle of Fault-Tolerant Operation*

On the basis of the above fault-diagnosis method, the fault unit can be located based TABLE. I. When a unit is recognized to be faulty, the SPDT switch connected to this unit and its adjacent SPDT switch will run simultaneously to achieve tolerant operation modes. For instance, when the faulty unit L6 is detected, the SPDT switches Q_5 and Q_6 will act, their contacts will be reached from normally closed contacts to normally open contacts; when the unit L5 is faulted, the SPDT switches Q_4 and Q_5 will act; when the unit L4 is faulted, the SPDT switches Q_4 and Q_6 will act.

Taking the unit L6 for example, when any switch of power conversion unit L6 is faulted, the SPDT switches Q_5 and Q_6 will operate to remove the faulty power conversion unit L6 and its adjacent power conversion unit L5. The topology of power converter under tolerant operation mode for L6 fault is presented in Fig. 5 and Fig. 6 shows the equivalent topology structure.

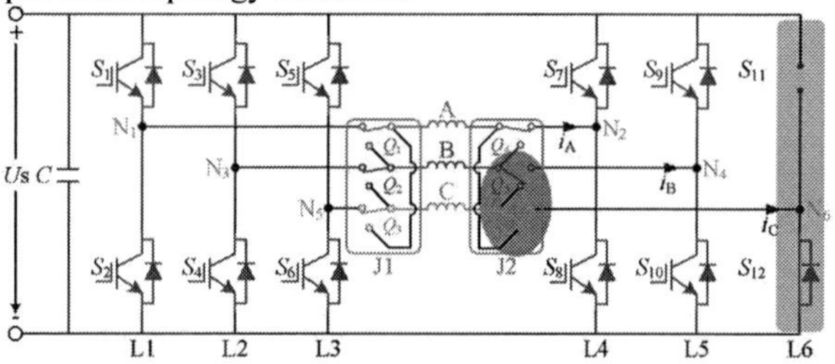

Fig. 5. The fault-tolerant scheme for SRM with L6 fault.

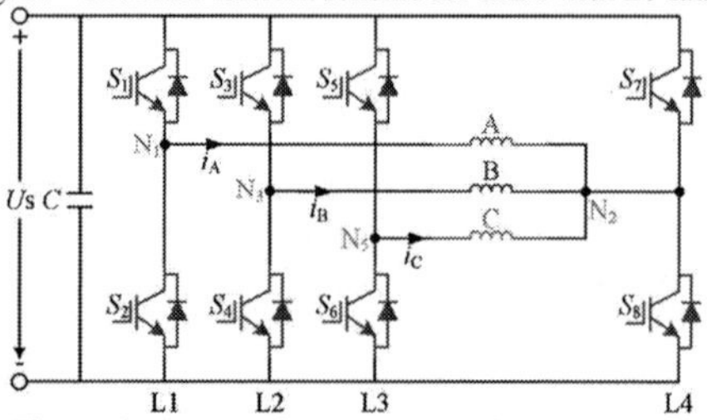

Fig. 6. The equivalent topology structure of power converter under tolerant operation mode for L6 fault.

In the fault-tolerant operation cases, two units of full-bridge power converter are cut off and the windings are connected in Y-connection with neutral line. In the non-commutation conduction region, the running modes are same as that by using full-bridge power converter; whereas two phases conduct in series in the commutation conduction region. There are six stages in both a positive period and a negative period, such as Stage I, Stage II, Stage III, Stage IV, Stage V, and Stage VI. For positive period, in the Stage I, only Phase C works and there are two operation modes, including positive excitation mode M1 and positive freewheeling mode M2; in the Stage II, Phase C and Phase A conduct in series, and there are four modes, including positive excitation for Phase C and negative excitation for Phase A mode M3, positive freewheeling for Phase C and negative freewheeling for Phase A mode M4, positive demagnetization for Phase C and negative excitation for Phase A mode M5, positive demagnetization for Phase C and negative freewheeling for Phase A mode M6. The operation modes in the other stages are similar with the above cases.

Fig. 7(a) presents positive excitation mode M1, switches S_5 and S_8 are turned on, and the winding of Phase C is independently excited. By closing switch S_5, the phase winding enters positive freewheeling mode M2, and the current flows through switch S_8 and anti-parallel diode of switch S_6, as shown in Fig. 7(b).

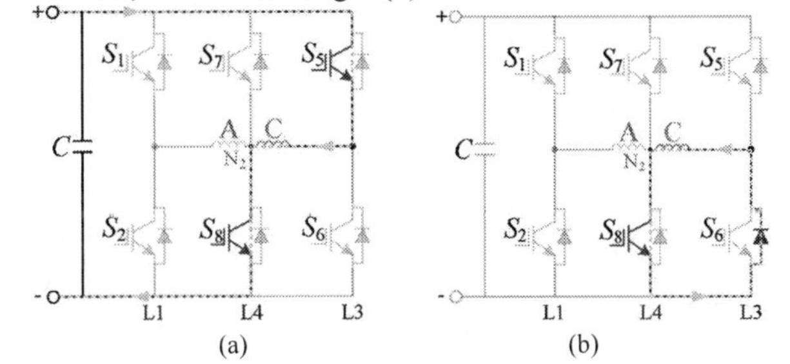

Fig. 7. Fault-tolerant operations for SRM in the Stage I during positive period. (a) mode M1. (b) mode M2.

When Phase A is conducted, Phase C and Phase A are connected in series, and the current simultaneously flows through the windings of Phase C and Phase A. The current flowing into the point N_2 is taken as the positive direction and the current flowing out the point N_2 is chosen as the negative direction. In the mode M3, switches S_2 and S_5 are turned on, the current of Phase C is positive and the current of Phase A is negative, as shown in Fig. 8(a). Turning off switch S_5, Phase C and Phase A enter the mode M4, and the current flows in the lower loop, as shown in Fig. 8(b). When Phase C is in the demagnetization stage, Phase C and Phase A are not connected in series. By turning on switches S_2 and S_7, the mode M5 is achieved, and the energy of Phase C is fed back to the power and Phase A is energized by the power, as shown in Fig. 8(c). Fig. 8(d) shows the mode M6, switch S_2 is turned off, and Phase C and Phase A are in positive demagnetization state, negative freewheeling, respectively.

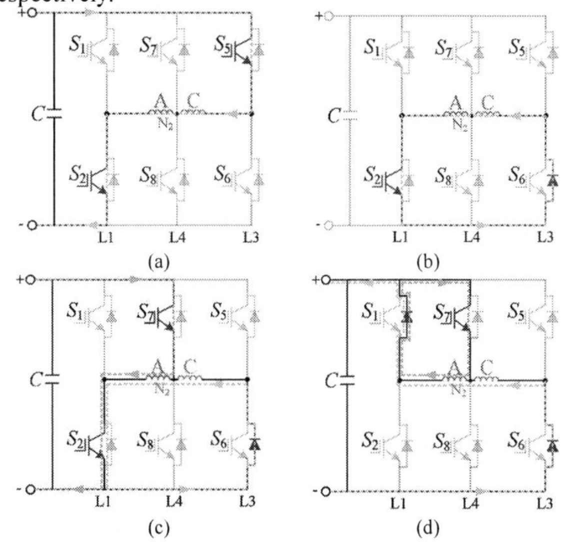

Fig. 8. Fault-tolerant operations for SRM in the Stage II during positive period. (a) mode M3. (b) mode M4. (c) mode M5. (d) mode M6.

IV. Simulation Verification

In this paper, a 3-phase SRM is used to validate the proposed bipolar fault-tolerant control strategy. A simulation system based on CCC strategy is built in MATLAB/Simulink. The simulations are carried out under normal, fault and fault-tolerant operation conditions with a load of 0.5N·m at 1000rpm.

1) Normal condition. Fig. 9 presents the simulation result under normal condition with CCC strategy, where i_A, i_B, and i_C are the currents of phases A, B, and C, respectively; T_e denotes the output torque. It can be seen that the directions of the phase currents are opposite in two adjacent electric periods. Taking Phase C as an example, in the positive excitation periods, switches S_5 and S_{12} operate and the Phase C current is positive. In the negative periods, the switches S_6 and S_{11} operate and the Phase C current is negative. The torque ripple is about 69.45%.

2) Fault conditions. Fig. 10 and Fig. 11 show the simulation results under OC fault conditions in the CCC system, where U_{N5} and U_{N6} are the potentials of neutral points N5 and N6, respectively. Fig. 10 shows the simulation result in the case of switch S_5 is opened. It is observed that the neutral potential U_{N5} keeps 0 in the state ST1 (S_5=1 && S_{12}=1), which agrees with the situations listed in TABLE. I. The torque ripple increases to about 172.08%. Fig. 11 presents the simulation result when the OC fault occurs in switch S_{11}. the neutral potential U_{N6} is 0 in the state ST4 (S_6=1 && S_{11}=1), which also conforms to TABLE. I. And in this case, the torque ripple is about 166.33%.

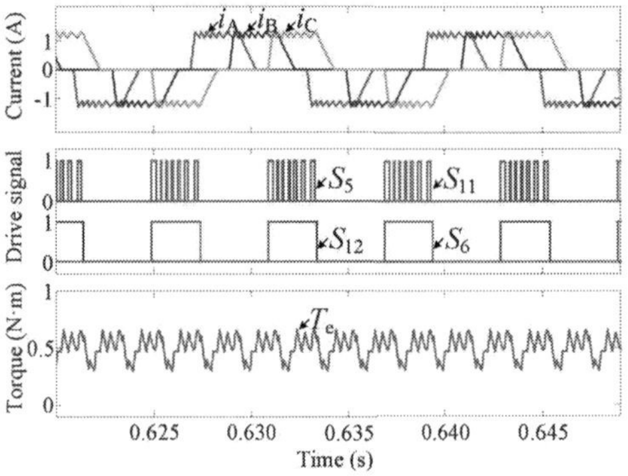

Fig. 9. The simulation result under normal condition with CCC strategy.

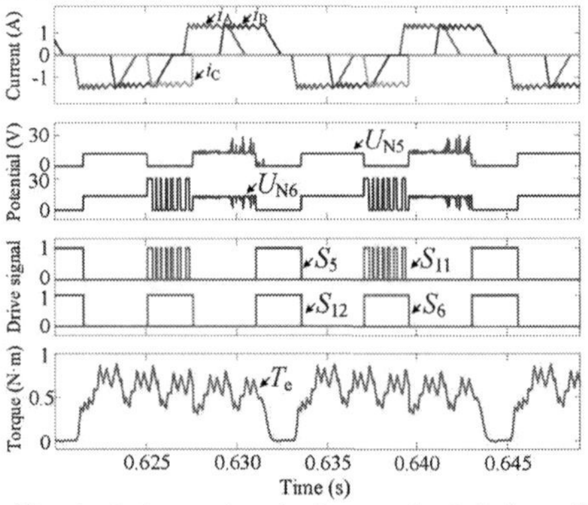

Fig. 10. The simulation result under S_5 open-circuit fault condition with CCC strategy.

3) Tolerant operation condition. For 3-phase SRM, after a fault occurs, the faulty unit and its adjacent unit are cut off. Fig. 12 shows the simulation result of tolerant operation with failures in any switch of the units L5 and L6 in the CCC system. The faulty units L5 and L6 are both cut off, and each phase current is opposite in two continue periods. In the non-commutation conduction region, the current is same as that in normal conditions; whereas in the commutation conduction region, the current flows two related phases simultaneously. It is observed that there is no phase missing and the torque ripple decreases to about 70.50%, which doesn't change significantly compared to normal cases.

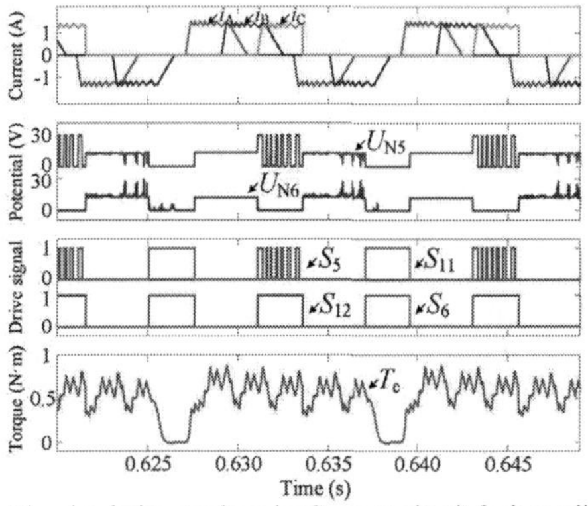

Fig. 11. The simulation result under S_{11} open-circuit fault condition with CCC strategy.

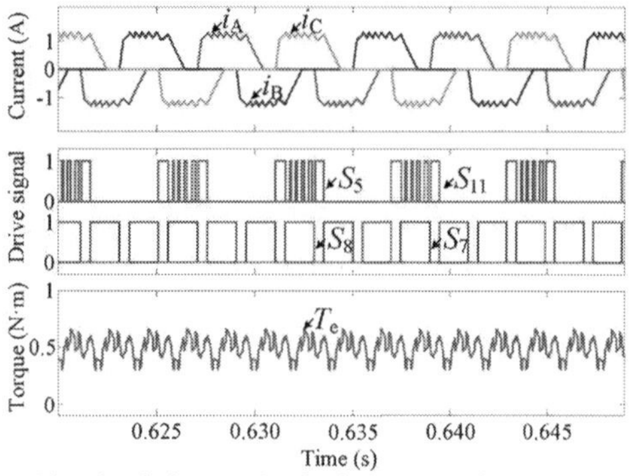

Fig. 12. The simulation result of tolerant operation under L5/L6 fault conditions with CCC strategy.

V. Conclusion

In this paper, a bipolar tolerant control method for open- and short-circuit faults of power transistors is proposed, which is based on full-bridge power converter. In normal cases, SRM operates in bidirectional current excitation mode. The faults are diagnosed by neutral potentials and operating state. Once the faulty power conversion unit is identified, the corresponding SPDT switches act to achieve fault-tolerance operation. The SRM can still operate steadily and maintain good perform in tolerant operating mode. Besides, the method can be applied for multiple switch faults and extended to SRMs with multiple number of phase.

References

[1] Y. Hu, T. Wang, and W. Ding, "Performance evaluation on a novel power converter with minimum number of switches for a six-phase switched reluctance motor," *IEEE Trans. Ind. Electron.*, 2019, 66 (3) :1693-1702,

[2] P. Zhang, K. Li, S. Yu, and D. Yu, "A novel fault diagnosis technique of interturn short-circuit fault for SRM in current chopper mode," *IEEE Trans. Ind. Electron.*, 2022, 69(3): 3037-3046,.

[3] E. Farmahini Farahani, M. A. Jalali Kondelaji, and M. Mirsalim, "A new exterior-rotor multiple teeth switched reluctance motor with embedded permanent magnets for torque enhancement," *IEEE Trans. Magn.*,2020, 56(2): 1-5

[4] S. Li, S. Zhang, T. G. Habetler, and R. G. Harley, "Modeling, design optimization, and applications of switched reluctance machines—a review," *IEEE Trans. Ind. Appl.*, 2019, 55(3): 2660-2681,.

[5] C. Gan, Y. Chen, R. Qu, Z. Yu, W. Kong, and Y. Hu, "An overview of fault-diagnosis and fault-tolerance techniques for switched reluctance machine systems," *IEEE Access*, 2019, 7:174822-174838,.

[6] H. Chen, H. Chen, G. Han, and G. Guan, "Power transistors' fault diagnosis method of SR S/G for more electric aircraft with cross-leg current analysis," *IEEE Trans. Transport. Electrific.*, 2020, 6(4): 1528-1536,.

[7] J. Cai and X. Zhao, "Synthetic Hybrid-integral-threshold logic-based position fault diagnosis scheme for SRM drives," *IEEE Trans. Instrum. Meas.*, 2021,70: 1-8

[8] Q. Sun, J. Wu, C. Gan, and J. Guo, "Modular full-bridge converter for three-phase switched reluctance motors with integrated fault-tolerance capability," *IEEE Trans. Power Electron*, 2019,34(3): 2622-2634,.

[9] M. Ma, K. Yuan, Q. Yang, and S. Yang, "Open-circuit fault-tolerant control strategy based on five-level power converter for SRM system," *CES Trans. Elect. Mach. Syst.*, 2019, 3(2): 178-186,.

[10] Y. Hu, C. Gan, W. Cao, J. Zhang, W. Li, and S. J. Finney, "Flexible fault-tolerant topology for switched reluctance motor drives," *IEEE Trans. Power Electron.*, 2016,31(6): 4654-4668,.

[11] S. Xu, H. Chen, J. Yang, and F. Dong, "Performance evaluation and reliability enhancement of switched reluctance drive system by a novel integrated power converter," *IEEE Trans. Power Electron.*, 2019, 34(11):. 11090-11102

Prediction of Fretting Contact Resistance Based on Neural Network

Xueyan Lin, Guo Wang

Beijing University of Posts and Telecommunications, Beijing, 100876, China
E-mail:xylin@bupt.edu.cn Tel: 13611123628

Abstract—**In this paper, the fretting contact resistance of the Ni-Cu contact pair is fitted and predicted based on the cyclic neural network RNN, long-term and short-term memory network LSTM and gated cyclic neural network GRU. The contact resistance value, the contact force value and the ambient temperature value of the first 6750 fretting cycles are taken as input samples to train the prediction model, and the contact resistance value of the last 1676 cycles is predicted. The experimental results show that the fitting and prediction effect of fretting contact resistance based on the GRU network is the best, and the root mean square error RMSE value is the lowest of 1.311 when the number of iterations is 25. The RMSE value of GRU network is 40% of that of RNN network and 76.4% of that of LSTM network respectively.**

Index Terms—**Data prediction, Fretting contact resistance, Ni-Cu contact pair, Neural network**

I. INTRODUCTION

Connectors are the communication bridge of the electronic circuits and the basic components necessary for the connection of the whole system. They are widely used in communication, aerospace, computer, automobile, industry and other fields. The reliability of connectors is directly related to the normal operation of the whole system. The micro-movement and the ambient temperature are two of the important factors that affect the reliability of electrical connectors. W.B.Ren et al.[1] proposed in the research on fretting wear analysis of electrical connection that the increase of fretting frequency will cause the relative movement speed between contacts to be too high, and it is impossible to ensure that there is sufficient contact area between surfaces in real time, which is the fundamental reason for intermittent contact failure. Y.Y.Luo et al. [2] pointed out that stress relaxation and fretting wear are the two main factors leading to the degradation of contact performance of electrical connectors in vibration environment through the research on the degradation mechanism of contact performance of electrical connectors. X.L.Liu[3] concluded in the study on the influencing factors of fretting wear performance of electrical connectors that fretting will cause a large displacement amplitude of contact pairs in the contact area, and at the same time, it will cause wear debris at the contact interface. The mixing of wear debris and external pollutants will cause a sharp increase in contact resistance.

In order to study the fretting contact performance of connectors, a large number of fretting experiments need to be completed on the fretting experimental system. The male pin and the female spring of the connector are respectively installed on the fretting experiment system. Under certain fretting conditions, the relative motion is carried out to accelerate the simulation of fretting phenomenon. At the same time, the contact resistance of the contact pair in the fretting process is tested based on the four points method and saved for further analysis after the fretting experiment.

With the rapid development of deep learning in recent years, neural networks can be treated as black boxes capable of fitting arbitrary functions. The desired output can be obtained as long as the training data is sufficient and specific inputs are given, which provides new research ideas for the prediction of time-series data. In the study of historical travel records of civil aviation passengers, J.Li and Y.F.Lin[4] established an RNN cycle neural network prediction model based on the back propagation algorithm through the features of time series data in the study of historical travel records of civil aviation passengers, and accurately predicted the daily passenger flow in future time periods. F.Y.Ding[5] used the RNN prediction model to predict the price trend of engineering products, and the accuracy rate of the prediction results reached 84%, which provides a constructive basis for improving the prediction accuracy of engineering product prices. J.S.Zhong et al. [6] applied the long and short term memory LSTM network to user load prediction and proposed that the LSTM network not only effectively solved the gradient disappearance problem of the RNN network but also retained long-term information by adding memory cells and "gate" mechanism at hidden layer nodes. Y.G.Liu [7] used the LSTM network to predict the temperature of the power transformers and concluded that the LSTM model has excellent prediction ability and fitting effect by comparing the prediction results with the simulation experimental results. K.Zhou and P.Liu [8] constructed a prediction model for air quality time-series data based on the GRU network, and demonstrated through experiments that the GRU model is better in prediction accuracy and faster in prediction velocity compared to the RNN model, and has good practical application value. L.Li et al.[9] applied the GRU model to the prediction of stock closing prices and concluded that the GRU prediction accuracy is very high on data sets with different sequence lengths and maintains good stability at the same time.

Since the fretting contact resistance obtained from the fretting experiment is a time series data series, this paper uses the RNN network, the LSTM network and the GRU network to fit and predict the fretting contact resistance of the Ni-Cu contact pair and analyzes the prediction accuracy of these three networks based on the root mean square error RMSE.

II. BASIC THEORY OF NEURAL NETWORKS

A. *Recurrent Neural Network RNN*

The RNN network is a kind of recurrent neural network with time series data as input and all nodes are connected in a chain [10], and the structure is shown in Fig.1. The vector X represents the value of the input layer; The vector S represents the value of the hidden layer, which depends not only on the current input X, but also on the value of the previous hidden layer; The vector O represents the value of the output layer; U is the weight matrix from the input layer to the hidden layer; V is the weight matrix from the hidden layer to the output layer; W is a weight matrix in which the value of the hidden layer at the previous time is used as the input at this time.

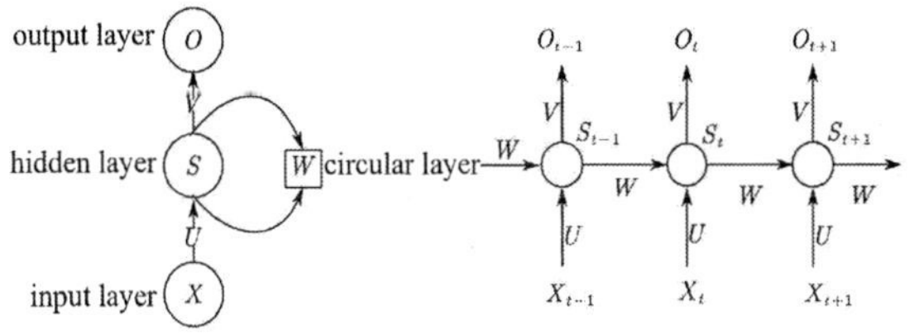

Fig. 1. The structure diagram of the RNN network

After the RNN network receives the input X_t at time t, the value of the hidden layer is S_t and the output value is O_t. S_t depends not only on X_t, but also on S_{t-1}. The operation process of the RNN network is represented by (2.1), where $g(x)$ and $f(x)$ are the activation functions.

$$\begin{aligned} O_t &= g(V \cdot S_t) \\ S_t &= f(U \cdot X_t + W \cdot S_{t-1}) \end{aligned} \tag{2.1}$$

B. *Long Short-Term Memory Network LSTM*

The structure diagram of the LSTM network [11] is shown in Fig.2. The forgetting gate is the key component of the LSTM network which can control the information to be retained and to be forgotten and avoid the gradient disappearance and gradient explosion caused by the back propagation of gradient with time in some way. The input gate/update gate determines which new information is retained in the cell state and updates the old cell state picture to the current cell state picture. The output value of the output gate is based on the cell state, but there is a filtering process. The LSTM forward propagation algorithm [12] is shown in (2.2).

$$\begin{aligned} f_t &= \sigma(W_f[h_{t-1}, x_t]) \\ i_t &= \sigma(W_i[h_{t-1}, x_t]) \\ \widetilde{C}_t &= \tanh(W_C[h_{t-1}, x_t]) \\ C_t &= f_t \otimes C_{t-1} \oplus i_t \otimes \widetilde{C}_t \\ o_t &= \sigma(W_o[h_{t-1}, x_t]) \\ h_t &= o_t \otimes \tanh(C_t) \end{aligned} \tag{2.2}$$

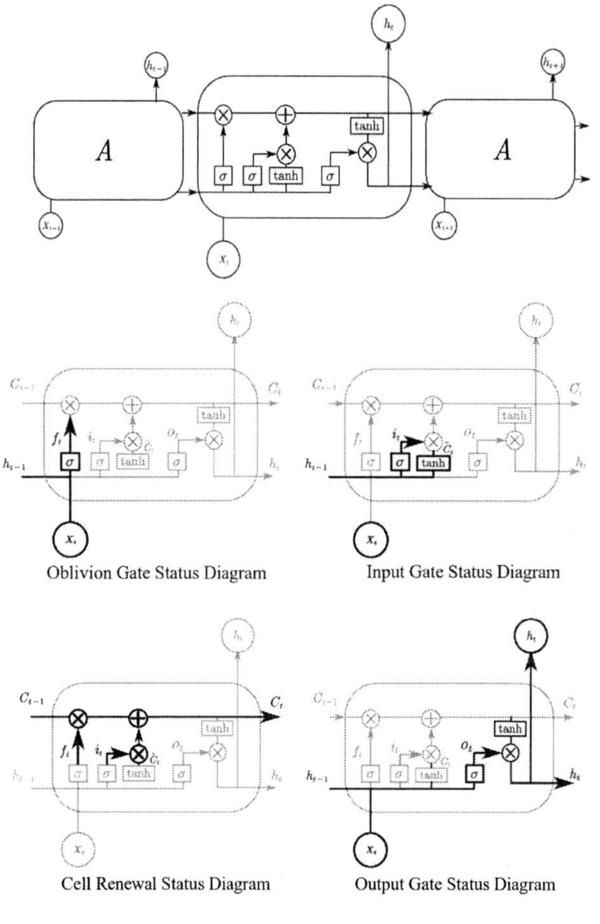

Fig. 2. The structure diagram of the LSTM network

Compared with the RNN network, the LSTM network memorizes information through cell states; the LSTM network introduces the sigmoid function through the input gate, the forgetting gate and the output gate, and adds summation operation in combination with tanh function to reduce the possibility of gradient disappearance and gradient explosion; The LSTM network can handle both short-term and long-term dependency problems.

C. *Gated recurrent neural network GRU*

The structure diagram of the GRU network[13] is shown in Fig.3. The GRU network has only two gates, the update gate and the reset gate. The update gate determines how much information of the previous time step and the information of the current time step are to be transferred to the future; The reset gate controls how much of the past information is to be forgotten.

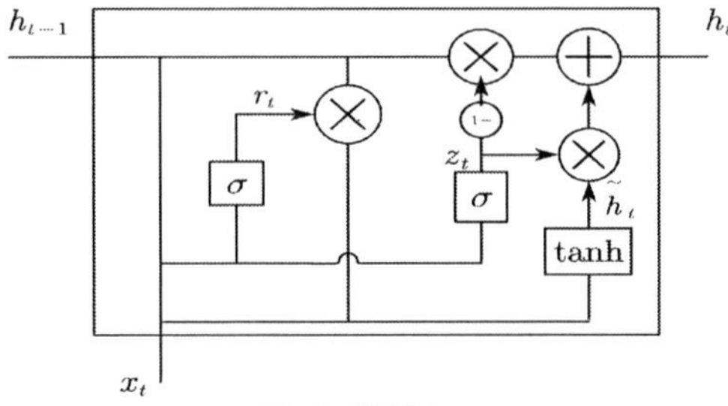

Fig. 3. GRU structure.

In Fig.3, x_t is the input data at the current time t; h_{t-1} is the output at time t-1; $\tilde{h}_t$ is the activation state of the hidden layer at time t; and h_t is the output at time t. σ represents the sigmoid activation function, through which data can be converted into values in the range of 0-1, thereby serving as a gating signal; The tanh activation function is to scale the input to a value in the range of -1~1; $\oplus$ indicates that two matrices are added; $\otimes$ denotes the multiplication of the corresponding elements of two matrices.

The algorithm of the GRU network [14] is shown in (2.3).

$$\begin{aligned} z_t &= \sigma(W_z \cdot [h_{t-1}, x_t]) \\ r_t &= \sigma(W_z \cdot [h_{t-1}, x_t]) \\ \tilde{h}_t &= \tanh(W \cdot [r_t \otimes h_{t-1}, x_t]) \\ h_t &= (1 - z_t) \otimes h_{t-1} \oplus z_t \otimes \tilde{h}_t \end{aligned} \quad (2.3)$$

Both the LSTM network and the GRU network preserve important features through various gate functions to ensure that they are not be lost during long-time propagation. The GRU network has less gate function than the LSTM network, therefore the number of parameters is less than the LSTM network, and the training speed is faster than the LSTM network.

III. ACQUISITION AND PREPROCESSING OF FRETTING CONTACT RESISTANCE DATA

A. Data sources

In this paper, the fretting contact resistance data of Ni-Cu contact pairs[15] are processed and predicted by neural network. Based on the fretting contact resistance test system, the fretting experiment was carried out for the contact pair composed of the male pin with Ni plating and the female spring with Cu alloy. The fretting experiment condition is the amplitude of 200 μm, the frequency of 1 HZ, the cycle number of reciprocating fretting of 10,000 and the contact force of 0.1 N. During the fretting process, the contact resistance is measured by the four-point method. The test conditions are constant current 200mA and voltage limit 1V. Four contact resistance data, four contact force data and four ambient temperature data are collected during one reciprocating fretting process. Therefore, 120000 data are collected in 10000 fretting cycles. All test data are stored in the excel form, which is necessary for subsequent analysis and processing.

B. Data preprocessing

For various reasons, only 33704×3 contact resistance, ambient temperature and contact normal force data of 8426 fretting cycles are saved after 10000 fretting cycles of Ni-Cu contact pairs. For each data column, about the first 80% of 27000 data are selected as the training set of the model, and the remaining 6704 are used as the test set of the model to judge the quality of the model.

Since the contact normal force (N) and ambient temperature (°C) are also sent to the model as input values for training, in order to eliminate the influence of different units, the data need to be normalized according to (3.1) [16].

$$\tilde{x} = \frac{x - x_{\min}}{x_{\max} - x_{\min}} \quad (3.1)$$

In Eq. (3.1), $\tilde{x}$ is the data after normalization (eliminating dimensional influence); x is the training set data before normalization; $x_{\min}$ is the minimum value of the training set data before normalization, and $x_{\max}$ is the maximum value of the training set data before normalization.

The contact resistance, the normal force and the ambient temperature collected in the fretting experiment are all time-series data, meeting the requirement that "the data input by the GRU network must be time-series data". In this paper, the contact resistance value, the normal force and the ambient temperature collected in one fretting cycle are taken as a data set, and the time step of the GRU network processing is set to 20, that is, the contact resistance value at the next acquisition time is predicted through the data set of the previous 20 acquisition times. The input data batch X is shown in (3.2).

$$X = [[x_1, x_2, ..., x_{20}]_1, [x_2, x_3, ..., x_{21}]_2 ... [x_{26981}, x_{26982}, ..., x_{270000}]_{26981}] \quad (3.2)$$

A total of 26981 data batches X are sent to the model for training. Each data batch contains 20 data sets x_i. Each data set has three dimensions: the contact resistance x_R, the contact normal force x_F, and the ambient temperature x_T, as shown in (3.3):

$$x_i = [x_R, x_T, x_F]_i \quad (3.3)$$

The label (or output data) Y is shown in (3.4):

$$Y = [y_{21}, y_{22}, ... y_{27001}]_{26981} \quad (3.4)$$

There are 26981 labels Y in total, representing the data of contact resistance value. The number is consistent with the input data batch X. The first input data batch $[x_1, x_2, ... x_{20}]_1$ corresponds to the first label y_{21}, indicating that the predicted value $[x_1, x_2, ... x_{20}]_1$ sent to the model training should be adjusted according to the actual value y_{21}.

The processing method of the test set is completely consistent with that of the training set, and will not be repeated here.

IV. MODELING AND EVALUATION INDICATORS OF CONTACT RESISTANCE PREDICTION

A. The model building

This paper uses keras deep learning framework to construct the prediction model through the sequential class of the keras. The model structure is shown in Fig.4. The model has four layers: the input layer, the GRU layer, the full connection layer and the output layer. The input layer is [1, 20, 3], which is a three-dimensional matrix with a time step of 20 and represents three characteristic parameters, namely, the contact resistance, the contact normal force and the ambient temperature. The GRU layer is the feature training layer. The dimension of the full connection layer is one dimension, that is, the output is the contact resistance. The output layer is the prediction data output. The prediction model based on the GRU network adopts the Adam optimizer, the Relu activation function and the loss function of average absolute error MAE. The parameters and values of the prediction model are listed in Table I.

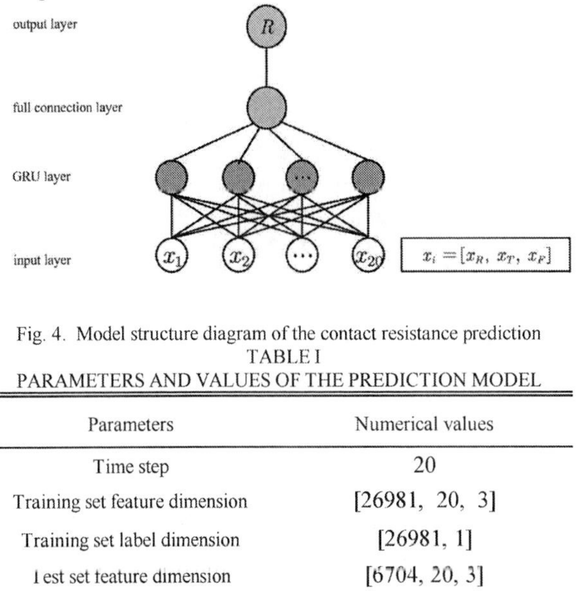

Fig. 4. Model structure diagram of the contact resistance prediction

TABLE I
PARAMETERS AND VALUES OF THE PREDICTION MODEL

Parameters	Numerical values
Time step	20
Training set feature dimension	[26981, 20, 3]
Training set label dimension	[26981, 1]
Test set feature dimension	[6704, 20, 3]
Test set label dimension	[6704, 1]
Number of hidden cells in the GRU layer	16
Number of hidden cells in the fully connected layer	1
Batch size	64
Number of iterations	40

B. Evaluation indicators

In order to judge the accuracy of the model prediction, the root mean square error RMSE is selected as the evaluation index, and the calculation formula is shown in (4.1).

$$y_{RMSE} = \sqrt{\frac{\sum_{i}^{n} (y_{pre} - y_{real})^2}{n}} \quad (4.1)$$

In Eq. (4.1), n represents the total number of samples, y_{pre} represents the predicted value of the model, y_{real} represents the actual true value, and y_{RMSE} represents the difference between the predicted value and the true value. The smaller y_{RMS} values means that y_{pre} and y_{real} are more consistent, that is, the better the model is trained, the higher the prediction accuracy is.

V. EXPERIMENTAL RESULTS AND ANALYSIS

A. Predicted results of the GRU network model

The average absolute error MAE of the training set and the test set decreases with the increase of the iteration number, as shown in Fig.5. The MAE value of the training set decreased rapidly from the initial value of 0.035 to 0.002 when the number of iterations is 5, and the MAE value of the test set jumps between 0.002 and 0.005. when the iteration number is greater than 25, the MAE values of the training set and the test set are very close and stable at 0.002.

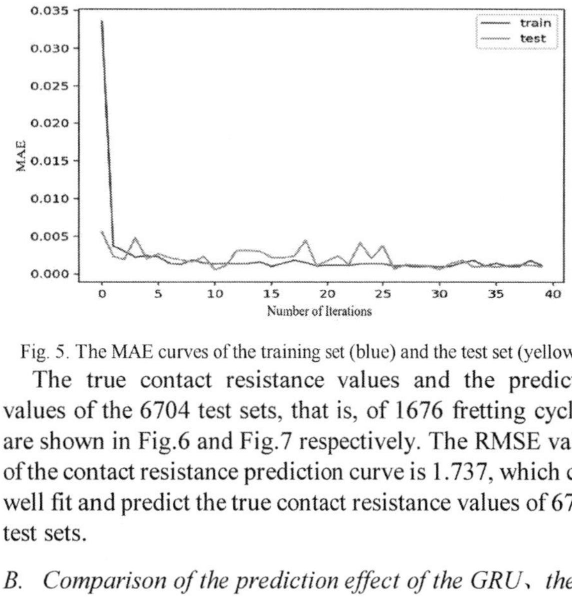

Fig. 5. The MAE curves of the training set (blue) and the test set (yellow)

The true contact resistance values and the predicted values of the 6704 test sets, that is, of 1676 fretting cycles, are shown in Fig.6 and Fig.7 respectively. The RMSE value of the contact resistance prediction curve is 1.737, which can well fit and predict the true contact resistance values of 6704 test sets.

B. Comparison of the prediction effect of the GRU、 the RNN and the LSTM network models

In this paper, RMSE values of 20, 25, 30, 35 and 40 iterations are selected to evaluate the prediction effect of the GRU, the RNN and the LSTM network models. The results are shown in Table II.

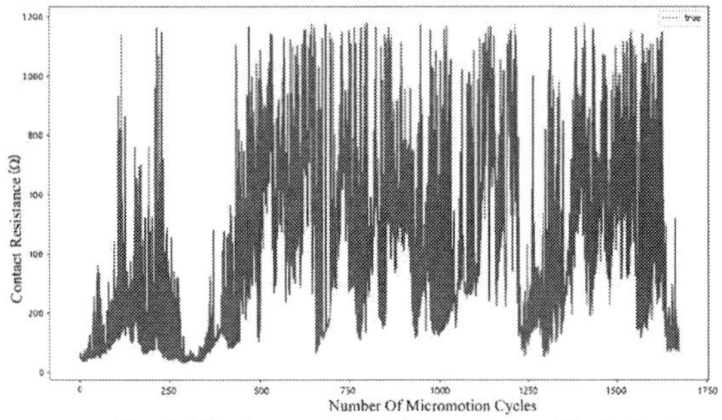

Fig. 6. The true contact resistance curve of the test sets

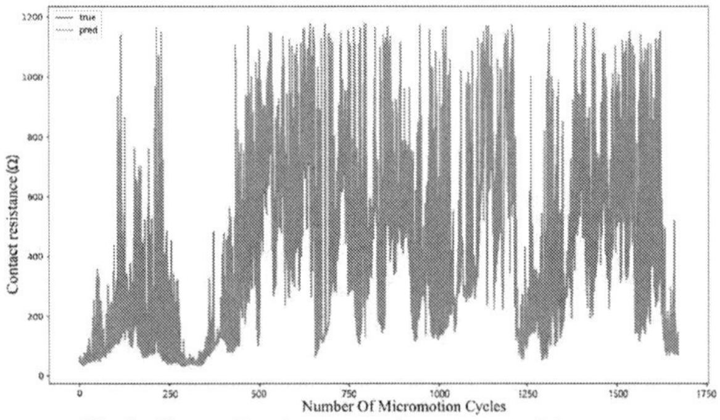

Fig. 7. The predicted contact resistance curve of the test sets

TABLE II
RMSE VALUES OF THE GRU, THE RNN AND THE LSTM NETWORK MORDEL

Number of iterations	Evaluation indicators (RMSE)		
	GRU	RNN	LSTM
20	2.463	5.317	1.838
25	1.311	3.070	2.297
30	1.732	4.162	2.040
35	2.031	4.497	4.036
40	1.737	5.962	1.934
Average value	1.855	4.602	2.429

The RNN network had the largest mean and minimum RMSE values, the LSTM was in the middle and the GRU network had the smallest, so the GRU network had better results in predicting the micro-motion contact resistance.

Fig. 8 to Fig. 10 respectively show the best prediction curves of the three network models of RNN, LSTM and GRU for the fretting contact resistance of 6704 test sets. The minimum RMSE value of the RNN network model is 3.070, and there is a problem that the predicted value is lower than the real value at the maximum value of resistance, and the predicted value is higher than the real value at the minimum value of resistance. The minimum RMSE value of the LSTM network model is 1.838. The prediction effect at the maximum resistance value is similar to that of the RNN network, but the prediction effect at the minimum value is better than that of the RNN network. The minimum RMSE value of the GRU network model is 1.311, which can be accurately predicted at the maximum and the minimum resistance values. The prediction effect of the GRU network is better than that of RNN and LSTM.

C. Prediction results of the GRU network under different number of training sets

In this paper, the contact resistance value of the minimum number of fretting cycles is used to predict the resistance value of the maximum number of fretting cycles by continuously reducing the data amount of the training set and increasing the data amount of the test set. Except that the number of iterations is 25, the values of other parameters are the same as those in TABLE I. Fig.11 shows the RMSE when the training set is from 5000 to 27000.

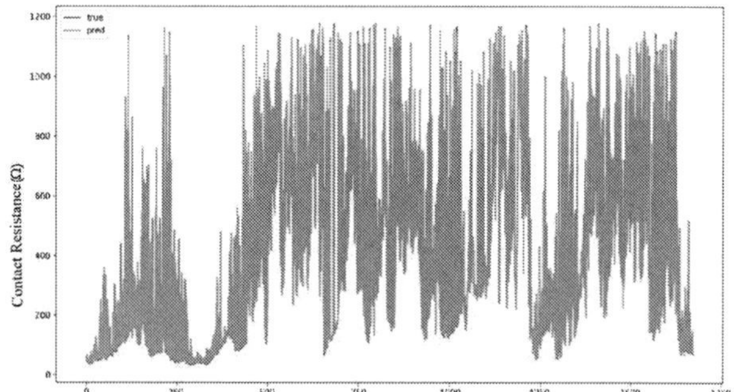

Fig. 8. Prediction curve of the optimal fretting contact resistance of the RNN network (The number of iterations is 25 and the RMSE is 3.070)

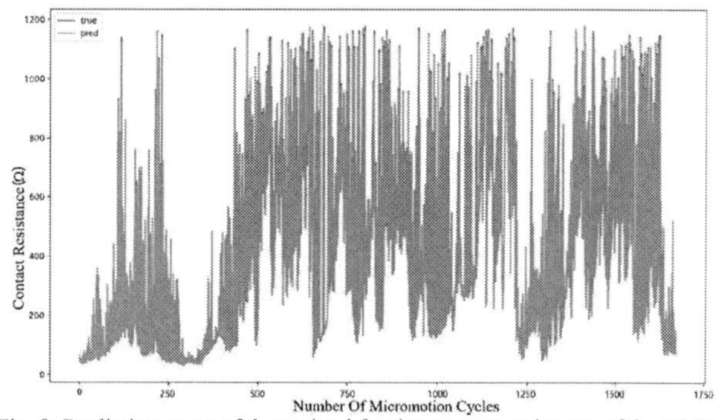

Fig. 9. Prediction curve of the optimal fretting contact resistance of the LSTM network (The number of iterations is 20 and the RMSE is 1.838)

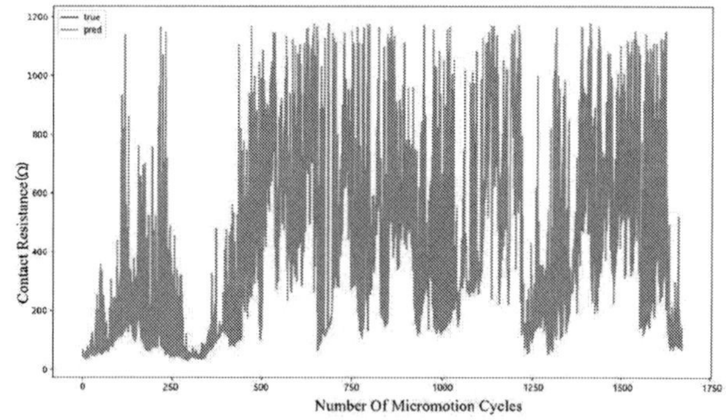

Fig. 10. Prediction curve of the optimal fretting contact resistance of the GRU network (The number of iterations is 25 and the RMSE is 1.311)

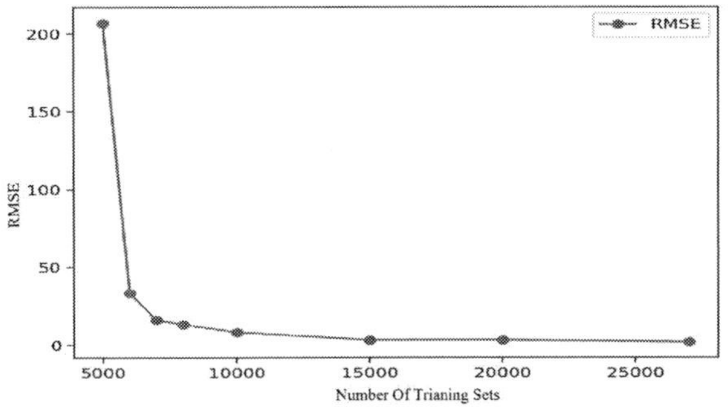

Fig. 11. RMSE values of different the data amount of training sets

When the number of the training set data is between 5000 and 10000, the RMSE value decreases rapidly from 206.737 to 8.287. When the number of the training set data is greater than 10000, the RMSE value decreases slowly with the increase of the number of the training set data, and the RMSE value is 3.242 when the number of the training set data is 15000. The RMSE value is 1.311 when the number of the training set data is 27000. The prediction results for the training set data of 15,000 are shown in Fig.12.

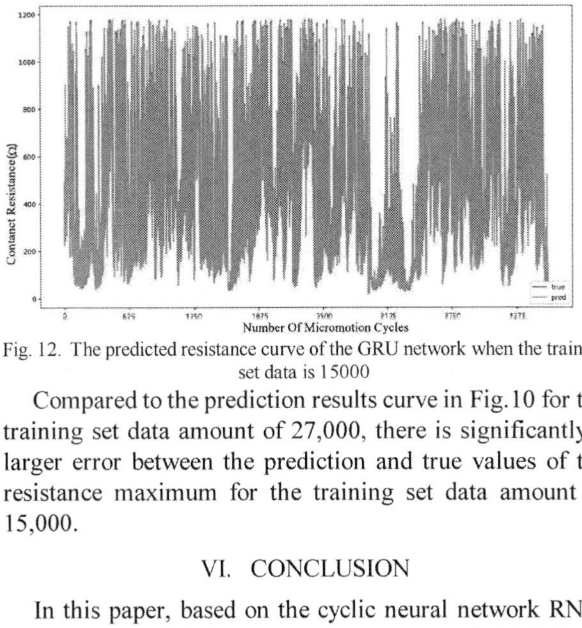

Fig. 12. The predicted resistance curve of the GRU network when the training set data is 15000

Compared to the prediction results curve in Fig.10 for the training set data amount of 27,000, there is significantly a larger error between the prediction and true values of the resistance maximum for the training set data amount of 15,000.

VI. CONCLUSION

In this paper, based on the cyclic neural network RNN, the long-term and short-term memory network LSTM and the gated cyclic neural network GRU, the fretting contact resistance of the Ni-Cu contact pair is fitted and predicted. The contact resistance, the contact normal force and the ambient temperature of the first 80%, that is, the 6750 fretting cycles, are used as input samples to train the prediction model to predict the contact resistance value of the last 20%, i.e. 1676 cycles. The root mean square error RMSE is used to evaluate the prediction effect. The following conclusions are obtained:

The fitting and prediction effect of the fretting contact resistance of the GRU network is the best. When the number of iterations is 25, the minimum RMSE is 1.311, the maximum RMSE is 2.463, and the average RMSE is 1.855. When the number of iterations is 25, and the data volume of the training set is 4 times that of the test set, the prediction effect of the GRU network is the best.

The prediction effect of the GRU network is better than that of the RNN network and the LSTM network. The minimum RMSE value of the GRU network is 42.7% of the minimum RMSE 3.070 of the RNN network and 71.3% of the minimum RMSE 1.838 of the LSTM network.

REFERENCES

[1] W.B.Ren, Y.B.Jiao, G.F.Qu, "Review on Fretting Wear of electrical connectors" in *Electromechanical Components*, 2010, 1： 28-38

[2] Y.Y.Luo, L. Zhang, F.B.Meng, J.Hao, "Degradation mechanism of electrical connector contact performance under vibration environment", *China Mechanical Engineering*, 2018, 16:1952-1957

[3] X.L.Liu, "Study on Influence Factors of fretting wear performance under electrical contact condition" , *Southwest Jiaotong University,* 2018

[4] J.Li, Y.F.Lin, "Time-series data prediction based on multi-timescale RNNs" in *Computer Applications and Software*, 2018, 7: 33-37+62

[5] F.Y.Ding, "Price trend prediction of an engineering product based on RNN model" in *Science and technology innovation*, 2022, 7: 77-80

[6] J.S.Zhong, S.L.Wang, Y.Ran, "Short-term prediction of user load based on mutual information and LSTM" in *Electric Power Construction*, 2022, 7: 96-102

[7] Y.G.Liu, "Research on power transformer temperature prediction method based on LSTM time series model" in *HongShui River*, 2022, 3, 75-80

[8] K.Zhou, P.Liu, "Research on air quality prediction model based on Data Mining" in *Computer & Digital Engineering*, 49nd ed, 2021, 8: 1631-1636

[9] L.Li, A.X.Chen, W.S.Li, W.Q.Liang, S.T.Yang, "*Research on GRU recurrent neural network for stock closing price prediction*" in *Computer and Modernization*, 38nd ed, 2018, 11:103-108

[10] S.X.Liu, S.Z.Gao, Y.Liu, "Residual life prediction of AC contactor based on LSTM" in *High-Voltage Technology*, 2022, vol.3, 7-9

[11] X.Lin, X.D Zhu, "LSTM stock price prediction model based on attention mechanism" in *Journal of Chongqing Technology and Business University*, 39nd ed, 2022, vol.2,75-82

[12] K.D. Zhu, "LSTM enhanced by dual-attention-based encoder-decoder for daily peak load forecasting" in *Electric Power Systems Research*, 2022, vol.2: 54-59

[13] H.H.Xiao, G.X.Xu, Z.Q.Jiang, "Prediction of shield tunneling parameters based on Gru algorithm - a case study of Chengdu Metro" in *Journal of Yangtze River Scientific Research Institut*, 2022, vol.4: 34-36

[14] G.H.Cao, Z.L. Zhao, Y.H.Xu, "Research on health state prediction of lithium battery pack based on GRU" in *Journal of Jilin University*, 40nd ed, 2022, vol.2, 181-187

[15] X.Y.Lin, Q.Y.Wu, D.L.Dan, "Micromotor contact properties of precious metal plated materials for connectors" in *Transactions of China Electrotechnical Society*, 2018, vol.1: 64-70

[16] J.H.Su, K.W.Dong, R.Y.Ge, "Research of Quantative Trading Strategy Based on LSTM", in *Proceedings of 3rd International Symposium on Frontiers of Economics and Management Science*, 2022, 4: 56-61

Xueyan Lin, female, was born in May 1971. In June 1992, she graduated from the Department of mechanical and electronic engineering of Xi'an University of Electronic Science and technology and received a bachelor's degree in electronic equipment structure. In March 1995, she graduated from the department of mechanical and electronic engineering of Beijing University of Posts and telecommunications and got the master's degree of engineering in mechanical design. In July 2009, she received the Ph.D. degree of engineering in circuit and system of Beijing University of Posts and telecommunications.

Xueyan Lin is now an associate professor and master supervisor of the school of artificial intelligence, Beijing University of Posts and telecommunications. She is engaged in the research of electrical connection and connector failure mechanism, reliability detection technology, signal integrity analysis and design, control system design and other fields.

Guo Wang, male, was born in September 1997. In June 2020, he graduated from Beijing University of Posts and telecommunications with a degree in mechanical engineering.

Currently, he is studying for a master's degree in Beijing University of Posts and telecommunications, and his main research direction is the combination of deep learning and electrical connectors.

Fracture Failure Research and Case Analysis of Common Metal Parts

Min Wang

Xiamen Hongfa Electroacoustic Co., Ltd., Xiamen, 361021 China
E-mail: 1002645@hongfa.cn Tel: 18845898986

Abstract—**Based on the nature of ductile fracture and brittle fracture of materials, this paper comprehensively analyzes and summarizes the fracture failure cases of metal parts commonly used in electrical products. Including the enameled wire breaking of HFKT-L product, the root cracking of the spring after the mechanical life test of HF140 product, and the self-tapping screw fracture of XMC0 product. The macroscopic deformation and fracture morphology of the fractured parts were analyzed in detail to determine the fracture properties and speculate the fracture reasons. Combined with the actual production application, put forward suggestions for improvement, and the fracture situation has been controlled.**

Index Terms— **metal parts,ductile fracture,brittle fracture**

I. Introduction

The fracture of metal materials is one of the main failure forms of engineering materials. The fracture of engineering parts or structural parts will cause significant economic losses. How to improve the fracture resistance of metal materials and prevent the occurrence of fracture accidents has always been a topic of common concern to researchers. The fracture forms of metal materials can be classified from multiple perspectives, and can be divided into ductile fracture and brittle fracture according to the degree of plastic deformation. According to the fracture mechanism can be divided into : shear fracture and cleavage fracture ; according to the crack propagation form, it can be divided into transgranular fracture and intergranular fracture . The common fracture forms are classified according to the degree of plastic deformation, namely ductile fracture and brittle fracture. The basic characteristics of these two fracture forms are shown in Table 1.

There are many kinds of metal parts in the electrical products, such as reeds, coils, iron cores, yoke iron, magnetic separation rings, etc. If the metal parts are broken, it will lead to complete failure of electrical products and cause certain economic losses. Since the fracture of the parts will have certain morphological characteristics, the fracture mode of the parts can be qualitatively determined based on the macroscopic plastic deformation and the microscopic morphology of the fracture, so as to speculate the causes of the fracture of the metal parts and put forward the corresponding improvement measures and schemes.

TABLE I
Basic Characteristics of Ductile Fracture and Brittle Fracture

	Macro characteristics	Micro characteristics
Ductile fracture	Obvious plastic deformation occurred before and during fracture	1)Many dimples, called dimples, formed on the fracture surface; 2)The outer shape of the fracture is a cup cone, the cup cone bottom is perpendicular to the main stress, the cone surface is parallel to the maximum shear stress, and 45° to the main stress; 3)The fracture surface is fibrous and dark in color.
Brittle fracture	Almost obvious plastic deformation occurs before fracture, manifested by sudden fracture	1)Crack source or defect exists in the material ; 2)Medium and low strength steel in the lower temperature below 10°C ~15°C, high strength steel has no obvious temperature effect, brittle fracture will occur; 3)The break is flat, bright and perpendicular to the positive stress, often printed or radiation on the break.

II. Ductile Fracture

A. Typical Macroscopic Plastic Deformation Morphology Before Ductile Fracture

The ductile fracture usually occurs obvious macroscopic plastic deformation before or during the material fracture. The so-called macroscopic plastic deformation can be clearly explained by tensile tests, as shown in Fig 1.

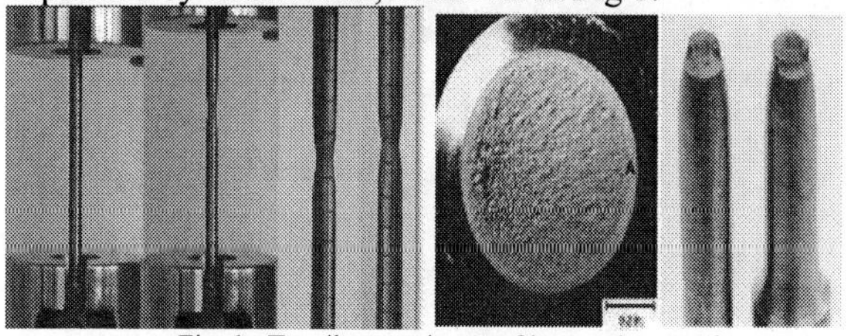

Fig. 1. Tensile experiment of low carbon steel

During the tensile test of rod-like low carbon steel in Fig. 1, it can be observed that in the middle of the rod-like sample, with the continuous tensile process, obvious plastic deformation occurs at this position, and the cross-sectional area of the rod at the fracture surface decreases after fracture, resulting in necking, which is a classic ductile fracture case. The macroscopic plastic deformation morphology after the tensile strength test of metal materials is usually carried out. As shown in Fig. 2, the plastic deformation with narrowing shrinkage also occurs at the fracture position.

Fig. 2. Macroscopic morphology of ductile fracture of strip

B. Actual Case : Judging Ductile Fracture by Macroscopic Plastic Deformation

When the electrical life test of HFKT-L product was carried out, when the number of life reached about 50,000 times, 2 of 10 products had broken wires. Subsequent mechanical life tests were carried out, and 400,000 tests also shown broken line failure. The disconnection position occurred at the connection between enameled wire and coil pin, as shown in Fig. 3.

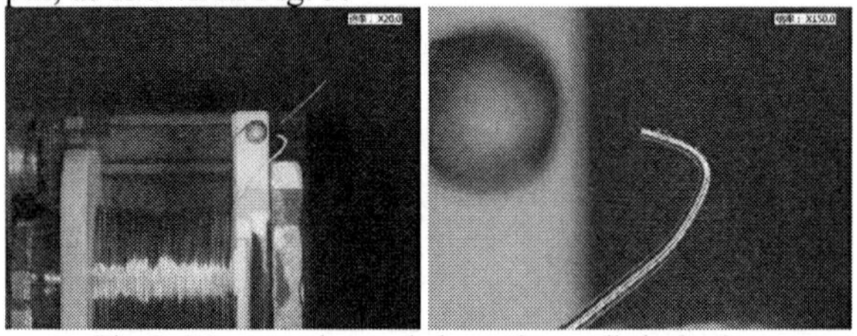

Fig. 3. Macroscopic morphology of enamelled wire fracture

The broken line in Figure 3 was cut out, and the surface of the broken line was cleaned by ultrasonic. The fracture position of the broken line was analyzed by SEM. The fracture morphology is shown in Fig 4.

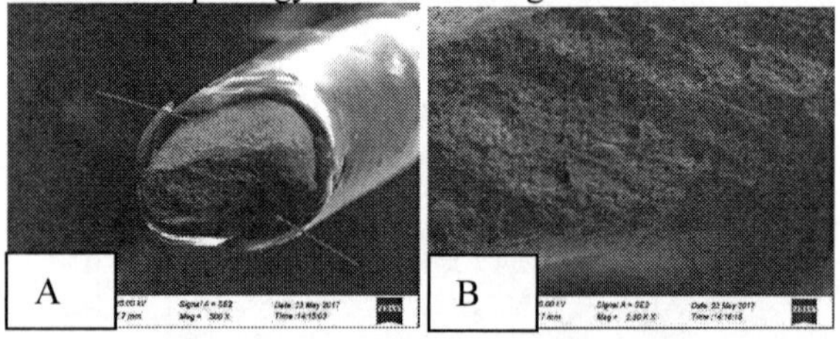

Fig. 4. Fracture morphology of enameled wire

The fracture morphology of enameled wire was observed by SEM, and it was found that there were obvious macroscopic morphology characteristics at the fracture line : necking phenomenon (Fig. 4, A), fatigue wear traces at the fracture, and certain directionality in the fracture morphology (Fig. 4, B). Some voids were found in the fracture morphology, namely dimple morphology. In summary, the enamelled wire was due to external tension, enamelled wire plastic deformation, and ultimately lead to disconnection.

Based on the analysis results, the following suggestions were put forward : 1). It was necessary to confirm whether the conditions, vibration frequency and amplitude of vibration test were within the corresponding requirements in the process of vibration test due to fracture ; 2). Since the disconnection occurred at the position of the coil pin joint, it was necessary to confirm whether the assembly process at this position would affect the enameled wire, so that the enameled wire was worn or destroyed, resulting in surface defects ; 3). In order to improve the allowable load force, the type of enameled wire could be adjusted to improve the plasticity of enameled wire. According to the improvement suggestions and combined with the actual situation, the dispensing processed between the coil frame and yoke iron was cancelled by (1) releasing the stress of some coils ; (2) By increasing the allowable load force, the line diameter of the enamelled wire was increased from 0.088 mm to 0.095 mm, and the disconnection phenomenon was controlled.

C. Typical Microscopic Characteristics of Ductile Fracture —Dimple Morphology

The dimple is a typical feature of ductile fracture fracture morphology. The formation of dimples is due to the existence of heterogeneous particles, such as inclusions and carbides. Due to the differences in elastic and plastic properties between heterogeneous particles and matrix, the deformation inconsistency or the fracture of heterogeneous particles themselves will occur in the plastic deformation process, resulting in the formation of free surface, that is, 'microvoid' - dimple [2]. However, it should be noted that some micro regions of brittle fracture will also have a certain degree of dimples, so when judging the fracture mode, it is necessary to combine the macroscopic morphology to judge [1].

The shape of dimples depends on the stress state of the material when it is fractured. There are generally three types : I equiaxed or circular dimples, II shear fracture dimples, and III tearing dimples. The stress state of the three types of dimples is shown in Fig. 5.

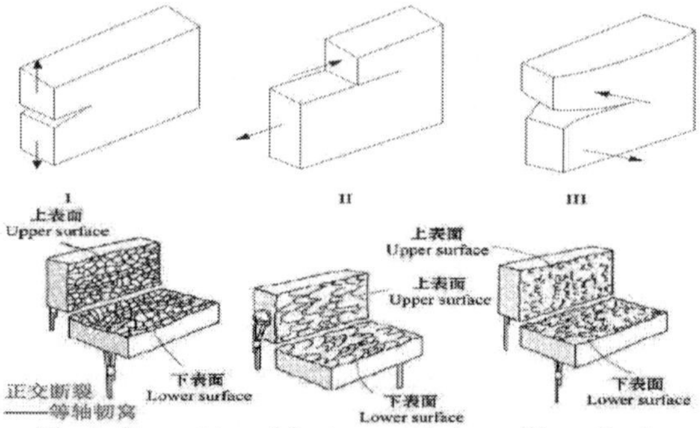

Fig. 5. Stress state and fracture morphology of three dimples

Fig. 5 (I), namely, equiaxial or circular dimples, also known as orthogonal fracture dimples, is due to the fact that the normal stress is perpendicular to the fracture surface and evenly distributed, so that the dimples have the same growth tendency in all directions on the plane perpendicular to the normal stress, and the equiaxial dimples are formed. The microscopic amplification morphology is shown in Fig. 6.

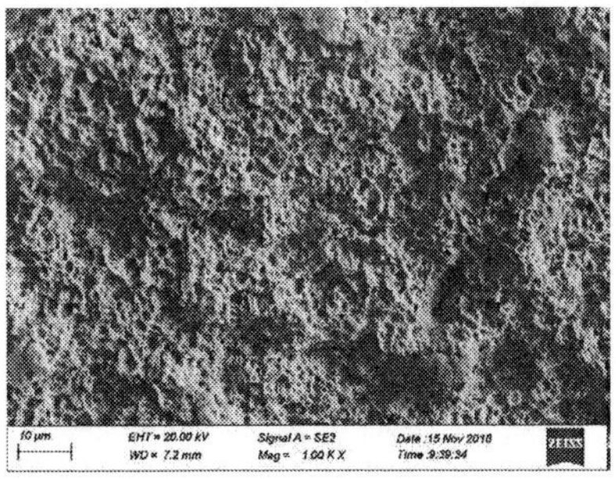

Fig. 6. Equiaxed dimples morphology

Figure 5 (II) shows that shear fracture dimples are the microscopic characteristics of shear lips formed under shear stress, such as tensile or impact fractures. Plastic deformation makes the growth rate of dimples maximum along the direction of shear stress, and elongates the dimples to form a parabolic shape. The parabolic convex direction of shear dimples on the two matched fracture surfaces is exactly the opposite, as shown in Fig. 7.

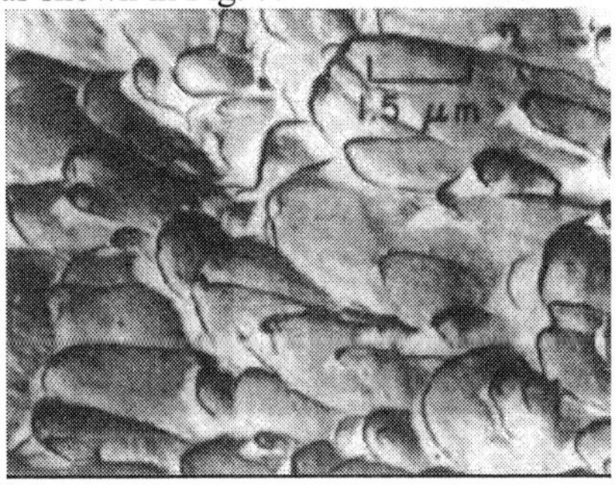

Fig. 7. Shear dimple morphology

Fig. 5 (III), the tearing dimple is formed under the action of tearing stress, and the shape of the dimple is also parabolic, that is, the elongated dimple is formed, which is often seen in the front of the sharp crack and the fracture of low energy tearing under three-dimensional stress conditions. The parabolic orientation on the fracture with its shape matching is the same and points to the crack source, which is an obvious distinction from the shear fracture dimple.

D. Actual Case : Judging Ductile Fracture by Microscopic Fracture Morphology

After 4000 movements of HF140 product, the root of spring foot cracked. Another 200 samples were selected to carry out the mechanical life test with the target life of 1 million times. The results shown that 75 samples fractured, which attracted great attention. The specific cracking position was shown in Fig 8.

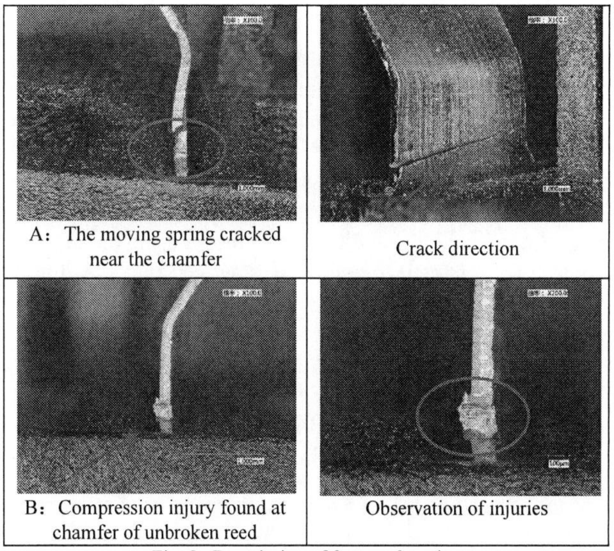

Fig. 8. Description of fracture location

Cracks could be observed in figure 8 at the chamfering position outside the reed (Fig 8, A), where indentation (Fig 8, B), burrs, and tiny cracks extending into the reed. The reed fracture analysis, fracture morphology see fig 9.

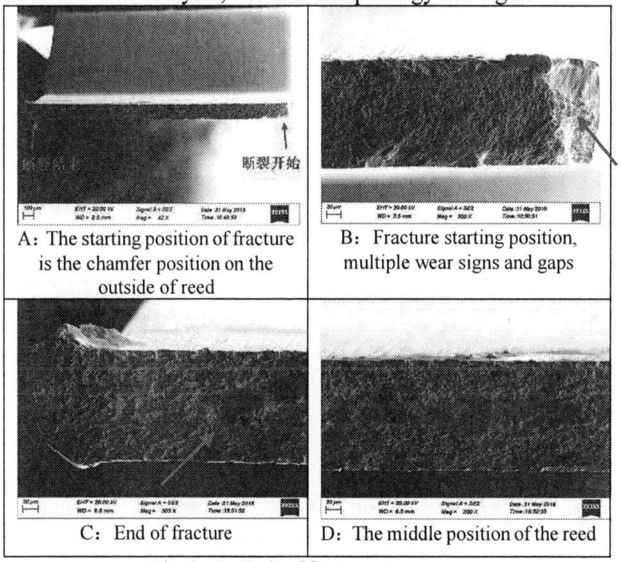

Fig. 9. Analysis of fracture appearance

In the fracture morphology of figure 9, multiple wear traces were observed at the beginning of the fracture (Fig 9, B), and the dimple morphology similar to the mountain peak was also observed at the middle position and the end of the fracture. Subsequently, the artificial tear of the unbroken reed was compared and analyzed, as shown in Fig. 10.

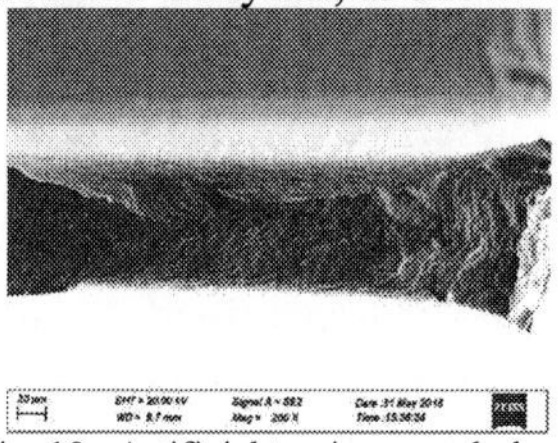

Fig. 10. Artificial tearing morphology

Through fig 10, it could be observed that the dimple morphology at the fracture of artificial tearing was completely different from that of the failure fracture of the reed. The fracture of artificial tearing shown equiaxed dimple morphology (Fig 10, D), and the dimple morphology at the failure fracture was similar to the ' elongated parabolic type '. At the same time, combined with the opening and closing direction of the reed and the possible force direction of the reed, it was judged that the dimple morphology belonged to the shear dimple.

Combined with the pressure injury at the chamfer of the unruptured spring in Fig. 8, the chamfer position outside the spring was further analyzed, and the pressure injury, burr and other phenomena were found at this position, as well as the tiny cracks extending to the internal of the spring, as shown in Fig. 11.

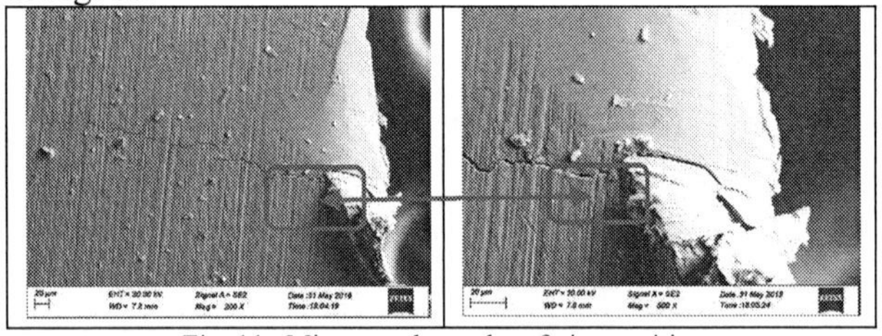

Fig. 11. Micro-cracks at chamfering position

Finally, by analyzing the appearance, fracture position and fracture morphology of the failure sample reed, it is found that the fracture position of the failure sample is basically the same, which is near the chamfer position outside the reed. It is speculated that the main reason for the failure is that the chamfer position of the reed has defects in the forming process, and the reed has scars, which eventually leads to the fracture of the sample reed during its life. The following suggestions are put forward : In the process of inserting reeds, no excessive external force is applied at the chamfer position ; at the same time, ensure the consistency of contact gap ; the mechanical life test of the above samples is carried out to further verify the test. Finally, in the process of inserting reeds, no longer the chamfer of excessive extrusion, and the product armature position point oil lubrication, reduce friction, increase mechanical life from the surface. Through further mechanical life test, no fracture occurred after 500,000 times, and the fracture problem was solved.

III. BRITTLE FRACTURE

A. *Characteristics of Brittle Fracture*

The characteristics of brittle fracture are obviously different from those of ductile fracture. Before plastic fracture occurs, there is basically no obvious macroscopic plastic deformation, which is manifested as sudden fracture. Generally speaking, the fracture with the shrinkage of material section less than 5 % is brittle fracture. The fracture surface of brittle fracture also has certain characteristics : (1)macroscopic cracks in materials or components as ' source ' ; (2) The brittle fracture of medium and low strength steel generally occurs at lower temperature (below 10~15°C), while high strength steel has no obvious temperature effect ; (3)The fracture is flat, bright and perpendicular to normal stress, and there are often human lines or radiation patterns (macroscopic) on the fracture, as shown in Fig 12.

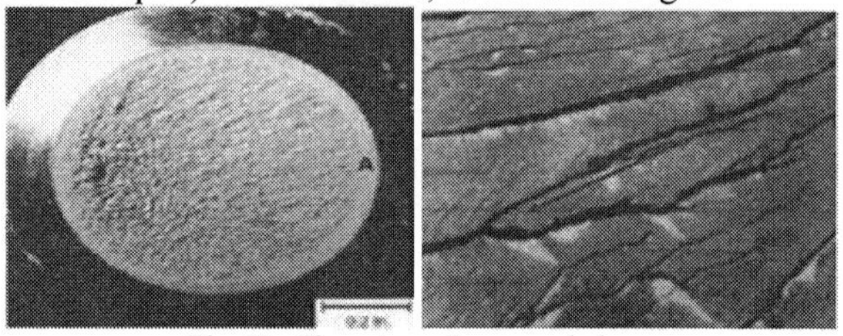

Fig. 12. Character pattern morphology

B. *Typical Brittle Fracture Microscopic Characteristics — Intergranular Fracture*

There is a representative fracture morphology of brittle fracture — intergranular fracture. The crack propagates along the grain boundary. When the grain size is coarse, the fracture is ice-sugar. On the contrary, the fracture is fine granular, which is caused by the segregation of brittle second-phase film or impurity elements on the grain boundary, as shown in Fig. 13.

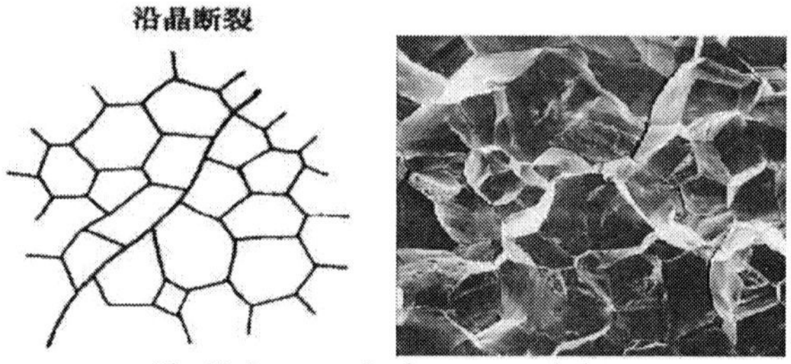

Fig. 13 Intergranular fracture morphology

C. *Actual Case : Judging Brittle Fracture by Microscopic Fracture Morphology*

The fracture of XMC0 self-tapping screw occurred, and the fracture failure rate was 0.05 %. The finished products were stranded for treatment, which affected the production progress. The fracture morphology was shown in Fig. 14. In addition, the measured values of surface hardness and core hardness of each batch of screws before and after the fracture of the investigated screws were slightly different. The feed length of wire rod in cold heading process of production line was adjusted from 13.6 to 13.3.

The fracture surface morphology of the screw was analyzed by SEM, and it was speculated that the wear phenomenon first appeared at position 1 during the torsional process. With the further continuation of the torsional action, the wear phenomenon gradually appeared at position 2 and position 3, and even micro cracks were produced until the final fracture of position 4. The overall fracture morphology shows intergranular fracture, indicating that the fracture mode belongs to brittle fracture. The fracture screw was further inlaid, polished and corroded in 4 % nitric acid alcohol solution for metallographic observation. The cross-section microstructure is shown in Fig. 15. The microstructure belongs to the microstructure of low carbon steel, and no other abnormalities were found. It is inferred that the fracture mode is not hydrogen embrittlement fracture.

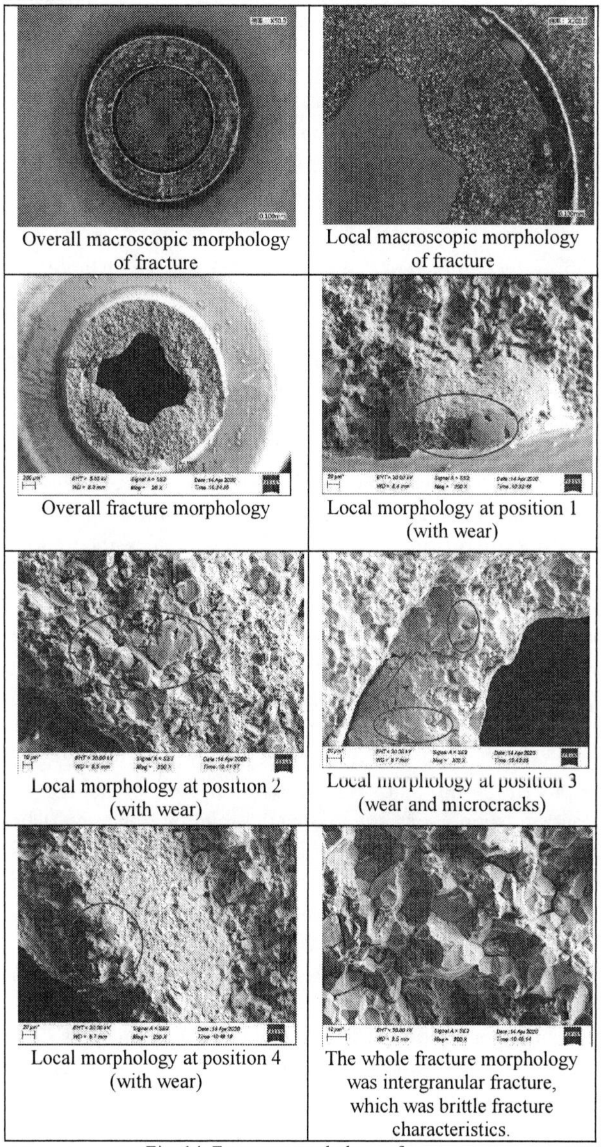

Overall macroscopic morphology of fracture; Local macroscopic morphology of fracture; Overall fracture morphology; Local morphology at position 1 (with wear); Local morphology at position 2 (with wear); Local morphology at position 3 (wear and microcracks); Local morphology at position 4 (with wear); The whole fracture morphology was intergranular fracture, which was brittle fracture characteristics.

Fig. 14 Fracture morphology of screw

The properties and fracture direction of the screw were clarified through the microstructure analysis of the screw fracture and the observation of the cross-section microstructure. In this regard, relevant suggestions are put forward based on the analysis results : the feed length of wire rod in the cold heading process of emergency production is restored to 13.6, and the screw fracture failure is controlled. At the same time, the increase of wire feed length in cold heading process will inevitably lead to the upper limit of screw cap height 1.9 (standard specifications are 1.7-1.9). It is necessary to further discuss whether the cap height specification deviation is reasonable for subsequent control.

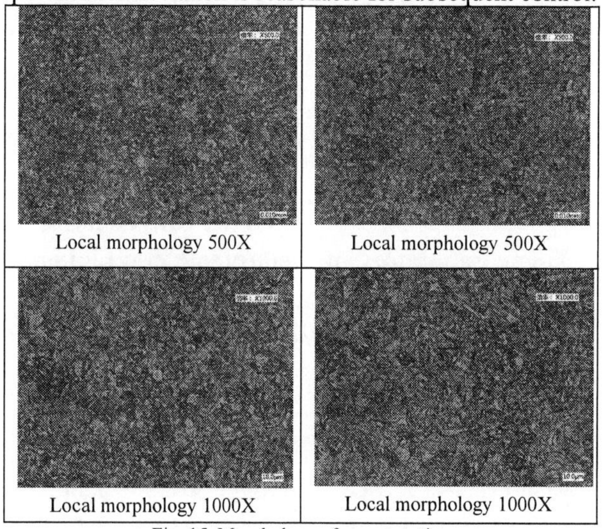

Local morphology 500X; Local morphology 500X; Local morphology 1000X; Local morphology 1000X

Fig. 15 Morphology of screw section

Through the above analysis of the actual cases of ductile fracture and brittle fracture, combined with the perspective of material production process, the actual engineering materials in the preparation, processing (smelting, casting, forging, welding, heat treatment, cold processing, etc.) and use (fatigue, impact, ambient temperature, etc.) will produce various defects (white spots, pores, incomplete penetration, thermal cracking, cold cracking, notch, etc.). Defects and cracks will produce stress concentration, and the tensile stress is several times of the average stress [3]. If the over-concentrated tensile stress exceeds the critical tensile stress value of the material, the crack or defect propagation will occur, resulting in fracture.

IV. Conclusion

In electrical products, metal parts, whether ductile fracture or brittle fracture, will lead to direct failure. In order to effectively avoid the occurrence of these fractures, it is necessary to trace the source of the fracture, combined with the use conditions, process, and the macroscopic morphology and microscopic morphology of the fracture, to determine the fracture properties and analyze the causes of fracture. And then from the parts of the material toughness / plasticity, parts of the design structure, and process point of view to analyze, as far as possible to prevent the occurrence of fracture failure, is our ultimate goal.

References

[1] Charlie R. Brooks, Ashock Choudhury. Failure Analusis of Engeering Materials(M).Mechanical Industry Press, 2003.4.

[2] Donghan. Zhuang Material failure analysis (M). East China University of Technology Press. 2012-9.

[3] Joshua Pelleg. Mechanical properties of material(M). Springer, 2013.

8th International Conference on Reliability of
Electrical Products and Electrical Contacts,
November 18-20, 2022

Study of Arc Extinguishing Medium on Contact Erosion and Arc Characteristics of DC Contactors

Haitao Wang, Shuqing Zheng
1)State Key Laboratory of Reliability and Intelligence of Electrical Equipment,
Hebei University of Technology, Tianjin, 300401
2)Key Laboratory of Electromagnetic Field and Electrical Apparatus Reliability of Hebei Province,
Hebei University of Technology, Tianjin, 300401
E-mail:zsq1273179045@163.com Tel: 17334214431

Abstract—**In this paper, based on magneto-hydrodynamic (MHD) theory, for the contact erosion problem caused by arcing in DC contactors, the energy transfer between the contact and the arc is considered, and the dynamic change process of the moving contact is coupled with the dynamic change process of the arc to establish a two-dimensional model of arc-contact bi-directional multi-field coupling. Many models most of the arc simplified equivalent to the energy source term added to the model, ignoring the interaction between the arc and the contact, with certain limitations. In fact, the arc and the contact is a unified whole, between the two constantly carry out the transfer of energy and material exchange, always affect the change of the melt pool, so the establishment of the arc - contact coupling model is most reasonable. The results show that in the three gas media, the arc extinguishing time and the size of molten pool area from small to large are H_2 < N_2 < Air, and H_2 has a significant indigenous effect on the improvement of arc extinguishing performance. In the arc extinguishing medium of H_2, with the increase of pressure, the arc voltage becomes higher, the arc temperature gradually increases, the arc extinguishing time becomes shorter, and the arc temperature drop rate becomes faster.**

Index Terms— **DC Contactors, magnetohydrodynamics, arc, molten pool, gas medium**

I. INTRODUCTION

The development of photovoltaic power generation, electric vehicles and aerospace vehicles directiy promotes the wide application of low-voltage DC switching devices[1-4]. When the DC disconnects the circuit, the arc discharge between the contacts will lead to the ablation of the contact material, which restricts its electrical life and reliability. Since there is no natural zero crossing point in the DC power supply system,technical means must be adopted for breaking, so as to achieve the purpose of rapidly extinguishing the arc and improving the arc extinguishing performance.

Many scholars at home and abroad have studied the characteristics of DC arc and arc extinction measures and established a variety of arc models, such as Cassie-Mary model, arc mathematical model, classical chain arc model, and arc Mhydrodynamic model. Literature [5] established a DC contactor model based on Matlab/Simulink to simulate the arc extinguishing current value under different conditions and verified the feasibility of the model, but the arc temperature image could not be obtained. In reference [6], the breaking test of hydrogen and nitrogen arc extinguishing medium was carried out, and it was concluded that hydrogen and nitrogen mixed medium could effectively reduce the probability of arc reignition. Reference [7] established a contact ablation model under the action of DC air arc, and explored the influence of different current, contact size and contact shape on the contact ablation characteristics. However, this model did not couple the arc with the contact. In reference [8], the arc burning process of SF6 and C_4F_7N/CO_2 gas media was simulated, and the difference of temperature distribution and pressure distribution between SF_6 and C_4F_7N mixed gas was obtained. Literature [9] set up double breakpoint bridge with a one-way valve structure of dc contactor prototype for open circuit test, analysis of the arcing medium and the pressure on the dc contactor open circuit characteristic.

In fact, the arc and the contact are a unified whole. The energy transfer and material exchange between the two are constantly carried out, which affects the change of the molten pool at all times. However, most models simplify the arc as an energy source term and add it to the model, ignoring the interaction between the arc and the contact, which has certain limitations. Therefore, the establishment of the arc-contact coupling model is the most reasonable. Based on this, this paper considers the contact movement. Aiming at the contact erosion caused by the arc in the DC contactor, a two-dimensional model of arc-contact bidirectional multi-field coupling is established. Through the method of external coupling circuit, the dynamic arc change process and contact erosion are studied. The dynamic contact movement process is coupled with the dynamic change of arc to obtain the dynamic arc breaking process.

II. SIMULATION MODEL

A. Geometric Models

The two-dimensional geometric simulation model is shown in Figure 1, including the dynamic and static contacts and the dielectric area, with the anode and static contacts above the contacts and the cathode and dynamic contacts below. The contact width is 4mm and the height is 4mm.

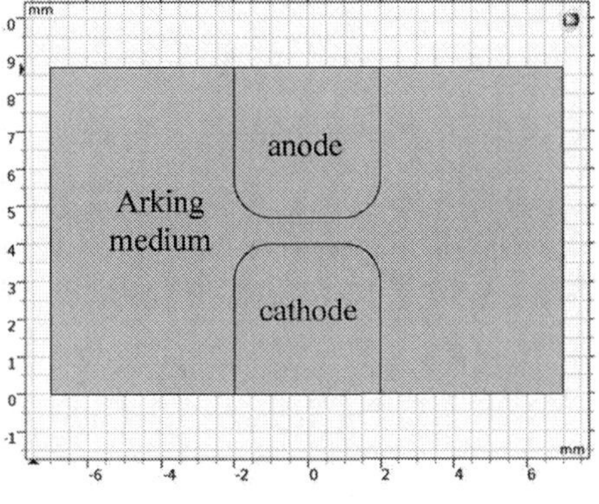

Fig. 1 Geometric model

B. Model Assumptions

The motion process of arc is complex, which involves the mutual coupling between airflow field, electromagnetic field and thermal field[16-17]. The gas medium affects the physical fields with the change of physical parameters (density, specific heat capacity, thermal conductivity, electrical conductivity, dynamic viscosity, etc.).Electromagnetic field affects the change process of thermal field and flow field in the form of heat source (mainly Joule heat) and Lorentz force, and realizes the coupling of electromagnetic field to thermal field and flow field. The thermal field and flow field affect the physical parameters of gas medium with the change of temperature and pressure respectively. The change of flow velo

city in the flow field will affect the convective heat transfer of gas medium, so as to realize the coupling of flow field to thermal field. From the above analysis, it can be seen that the formation and stable combustion of arc is an extremely complex process. In order to simplify the calculation process, the following assumptions are made:

1) The arc plasma satisfies the local thermodynamic equilibrium condition(LTE), and the temperature of all particles is described by a uniform temperature.
2) The influence of metal material fluidity on contact temperature after melting is not considered..
3) The influence of metal vapor on the gas medium due to evaporation of the contact material is not considered
4) The force of metal particles and electrons on the contact surface is not considered
5) Arc plasma is a Newtonian laminar fluid.
6) The voltage drop of arc root zone and the voltage drop of arc column jointly determine the total the voltage drop of the arc column. The arc root region is the " sheath " that does not meet the LTE conditions and the electrical neutrality conditions, and only the voltage drop characteristics of the arc root region are considered.

C. Mathematical modelling

Arc plasma is often regarded as a conductive fluid when studying its macroscopic motion. It is assumed that the arc plasma follows the conservation equations of mass, momentum and energy in navier-Stokes equations, which describe fluid motion. The electromagnetic process conforms to Maxwell.

Mass conservation equation:

$$\frac{\partial \rho}{\partial t} + \nabla \cdot (\rho \boldsymbol{u}) = 0 \quad (1)$$

In the formula: ρ is arc plasma density; t is time; u is the velocity vector of arc plasma motion.

Momentum conservation equation:

$$\rho \frac{\partial \boldsymbol{u}}{\partial t} + \rho(\boldsymbol{u} \cdot \nabla)\boldsymbol{u} = -\nabla p \boldsymbol{I} + \boldsymbol{F} + \nabla \cdot \left\{ \mu \left[\left(\nabla \boldsymbol{u} + \nabla \boldsymbol{u}^T \right) - \frac{2}{3} \nabla \cdot \boldsymbol{u} \boldsymbol{I} \right] \right\} \quad (2)$$

$$\boldsymbol{F} = \boldsymbol{j} \times \boldsymbol{B} \quad (3)$$

In the formula: P is the pressure on the fluid element;μ is the dynamic viscosity of the fluid; I is the identity matrix; F is lorentz force.

Energy conservation equation:

$$\rho C_{\mathrm{p}} \frac{\partial T}{\partial t} + \rho C_{\mathrm{p}} \boldsymbol{u} \cdot \nabla T = \nabla \cdot (k \nabla T) + Q \quad (4)$$

$$Q = \frac{\partial}{\partial T}\left(\frac{5 k_{\mathrm{B}} T}{2q} \right)(\nabla T \cdot \boldsymbol{J}) + \boldsymbol{E} \cdot \boldsymbol{J} + Q_{\mathrm{rad}} \quad (5)$$

In the formula: C_p is specific heat at constant pressure; Q is heat source ; J is current density ; E is electric field intensity; Q_{rad} is the total volume radiation coefficient.

Electromagnetic field control equation:

$$\nabla \times \boldsymbol{H} = \boldsymbol{J} \quad (6)$$

$$\boldsymbol{B} = \nabla \times \left(\boldsymbol{A}_b + \boldsymbol{A}_r \right) \quad (7)$$

$$\boldsymbol{J} = \sigma \boldsymbol{E} + \sigma \boldsymbol{v} \times \boldsymbol{B} + \boldsymbol{J}_{\mathrm{e}} \quad (8)$$

$$\boldsymbol{E} = -\frac{\partial}{\partial t}\left(\boldsymbol{A}_b + \boldsymbol{A}_r \right) \quad (9)$$

In the formula: H is vector magnetic potential; B is magnetic flux density; A is a vector unit; σ is the conductivity gas state equation.

$$P = \rho RT \tag{10}$$

In the formula: R is the ideal constant of the gas.

Phase change equation:

$$\theta = \frac{T - T_m}{\Delta T} \quad T_m - \frac{\Delta T}{2} \le T \le T_m + \frac{\Delta T}{2} \tag{11}$$

$$\rho = \theta \rho_L + (1-\theta)\rho_S \tag{12}$$

$$k = \theta k_L + (1-\theta) k_s \tag{13}$$

$$C_p = \frac{L_m}{\Delta T} + \frac{(1-\theta)\rho_s C_s + \theta \rho_L C_L}{\rho} \tag{14}$$

In the formula: Θ is the proportion of liquid phase in the contact material; T is the contact temperature; T_m is the melting temperature; ΔT is the two-phase transition interval; L_m is the latent heat of melting of the material; ρ_s and k_s is the density and thermal conductivity of solid material; ρ_L and k_L is the density and thermal conductivity. of the liquid material.

D. Initial conditions and boundary conditions

The electrode material in the simulation model of this paper is AgNi15,which is widely used in auxiliary switches, contactors with opening currents up to 50 A, miniature automotive relays, circuit breakers, etc. In contactors with current levels below 50 A, the best performance is achieved with Ni content of 10%-20% [18]. Therefore, AgNi15 was chosen from the consideration of silver saving and performance.

(1) Temperature boundary conditions

The energy of arc plasma mainly propagates outwards in the form of heat radiation and heat convection, while the contact surface propagates outwards in the form of heat conduction.

According to the energy conservation, the cathode thermal boundary equation is:

$$S_{c,h} + S_{ion} = S_{c,cathode} + S_{elec} \tag{15}$$

$$S_{c,h} = -n \cdot (-\lambda_h \nabla T) \tag{16}$$

$$S_{ion} = |\boldsymbol{J}_{ion}| V_{ion} \tag{17}$$

$$S_{elec} = |\boldsymbol{J}_{elec}| \phi_c \tag{18}$$

$$J_{\text{ion}} = |\boldsymbol{J} \cdot \boldsymbol{n}| - J_{\text{elec}} \tag{19}$$

$$J_{\text{elec}} = \text{If}\left(|\boldsymbol{J} \cdot \boldsymbol{n}| > J_R, J_R, |\boldsymbol{J} \cdot \boldsymbol{n}|\right) \tag{20}$$

$$J_{\text{R}} = A_{\text{R}} T^2 \exp\left(-\frac{q\Phi_{\text{eff}}}{k_{\text{B}} T}\right) \tag{21}$$

In the formula: $S_{c,h}$ is the heat absorption of arc heat conduction on cathode surface; S_{ion} is the heat generated by the absorption of ions on the cathode surface to impact the cathode; $S_{c,cathode}$ is the energy lost by the heat conduction of the cathode material; $S_{elec}$is the heat loss of radiation electrons on the cathode surface;λ_h is the thermal conductivity of arc plasma;ϕ_c is the surface work function of the electrode; J_{elec} is electron flow density mode; J_{ion} is the ion current density mode; V_{ion} is the ionization potential of plasma; J_R is thermionic normal current density; A_R is Richardson constant; $\boldsymbol{J}\cdot\boldsymbol{n}$ is the terminal input current density mode.

The anode thermal boundary equation is:

$$S_{c,h} + S_{elec} = S_{c,anode} \tag{22}$$

$$S_{c,h} = -n \cdot (-\lambda_h \nabla \boldsymbol{T}) \tag{23}$$

$$S_{elec} = |\boldsymbol{J}_{elec}| \phi_c \tag{24}$$

$$S_{c,anode} = -n \cdot (-\lambda_c \nabla \boldsymbol{T}) \tag{25}$$

In the formula: $S_{c,h}$ is the heat absorption of arc heat conduction on anode surface; S_{elec} is the heat absorbed by the anode surface from the electron flow; $S_{c,anode}$ is the heat loss from the anode due to heat conduction of its own contact material; λ_c is the thermal conductivity of the contact material.

(2) Magnetic field boundary condition

Each directional component of the vector magnetic potential at the boundary is set to zero, i.e. $n \times A = 0$

III. SIMULATION RESULTS AND ANALYSIS

In order to analyze the influence of different gas medium and current level on the arc extinguishing performance of DC contactor, the arc characteristics and molten pool during DC contactor breaking process were simulated under the conditions of N_2, H_2 and Air gas medium and H_2 medium with pressure of 0.6 atm, 1 atm and 2 atm.

A. Analysis of arc extinguishing performance in air medium

Figure 2 is the voltage and current level of 48V / 32A on both ends of the contact, the gas medium is air, the contact breaking speed is 0.6m / s, the opening distance is 9mm, and the initial atmospheric pressure is 1atm. According to the calculation conditions and convergence, the simulation step is 0.1ms, and the calculation time is 20ms.

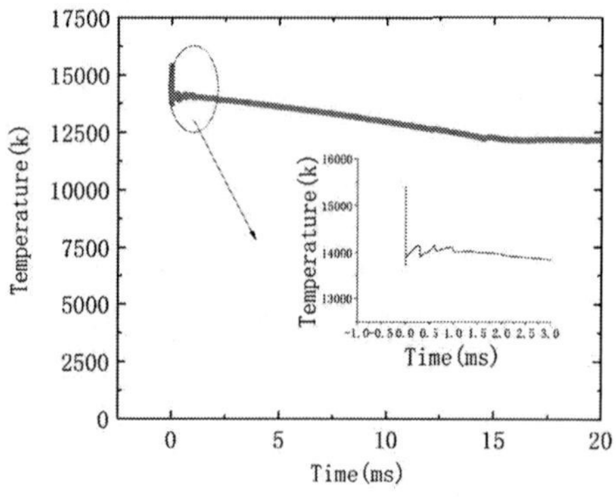

Fig. 2 Arc temperature in Air

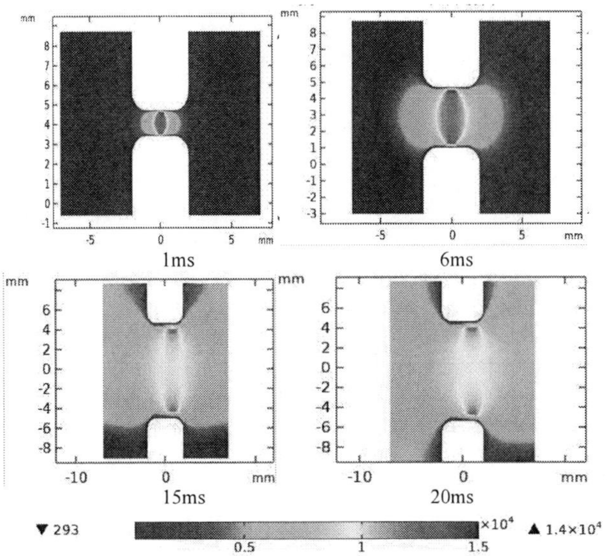

Fig. 3 Arc breaking process in Air

It can be seen from Fig. 2 and Fig. 3 that obvious arc roots can be observed in the initial arc burning stage of the arc in Air medium. The arc roots act on the contact center, and the temperature at the arc root is high. This is because the arc has a self-shrinking phenomenon here, and the current density is large, resulting in a large Joule heat. The arc was lengthened gradually after the contact began to move because the simulation time was 20 ms and the arc was not extinguished. The initial temperature of the arc is 13732K, and the arc temperature rises rapidly to the highest temperature of 15400K in 0.1ms. The diameter of the arc column begins to expand, and the arc temperature begins to slow down and is in a stable arcing stage. Due to the Lorentz force of the magnetic field, the arc root begins to shift right at 15 ms. Until 20ms, the arc temperature drops to 12159K without quenching.

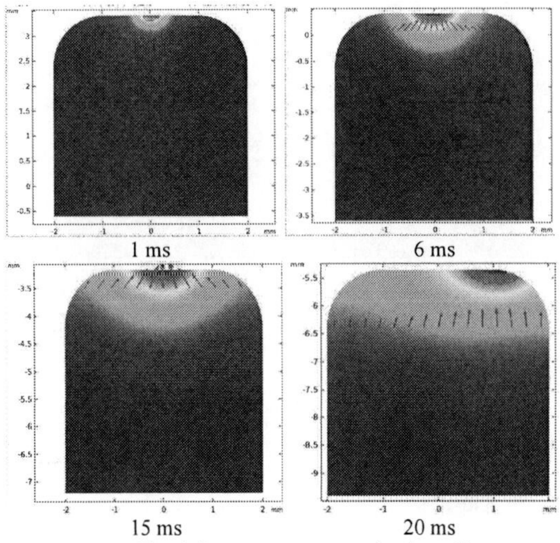

Fig. 4 Contact temperature in air medium

After the arc burns stably between the contacts of the direct contactor, because the plasma has a high temperature and the temperature near the contact is higher than that of the central arc column, the high temperature of the arc will rapidly ablation the contact and cause the molten pool. Fig. 4 shows the contact temperature at different moments of the cathode. The maximum contact temperature is 1401 K, the arrow is the temperature gradient, and the molten pool area is formed in the black curve. It can be seen that the molten pool is mainly generated at the arc root and the width of the molten pool is greater than the depth of the molten pool. This is mainly because the width of the molten pool depends on the heat conduction process and the arc root radius, and the depth of the molten pool depends only on the heat conduction process. It can be seen that with the increase of time, the energy injected into the arc increases, and the molten pool area formed by the contact also increases. The pool area is 0.0161mm ^2 at 1ms, 0.0673mm ^2 at 5ms, and 0.14082mm ^2 at 20ms.

B. Analysis of Arc Extinguishing Performance in Different Gas Medium

The arc breaking process in H2 and N2 is shown in Figure 5 and 6. The change process of arc temperature in three gas media is shown in Fig. 7. The gas breaking process in the two mediums is similar to that in the air. In H2 medium, the initial temperature of the arc decreases from 15293 K to 14609 K in 1 ms, and then decreases rapidly with the extension of the arc and extinguishes at 4.2 ms. In N2 medium, the arc temperature decreases slowly within 10ms, the temperature decreases to 13400K, and extinguishes in 14ms.

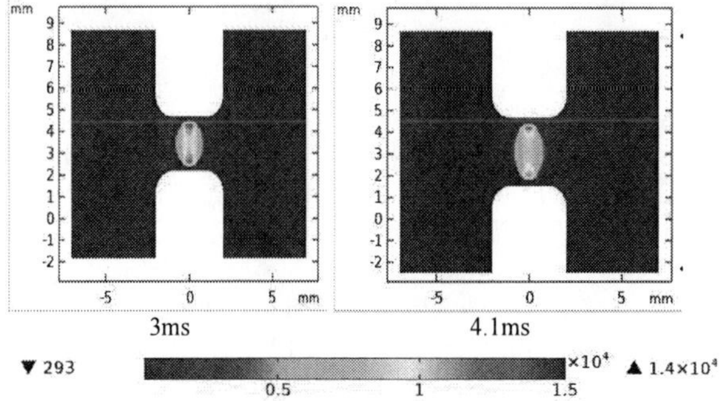

Fig. 5 Arc breaking process in H_2 medium

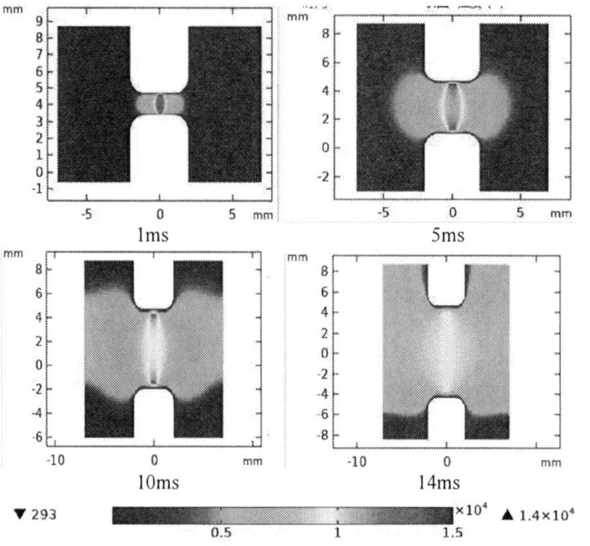

Fig. 6 Arc breaking process in N_2 medium

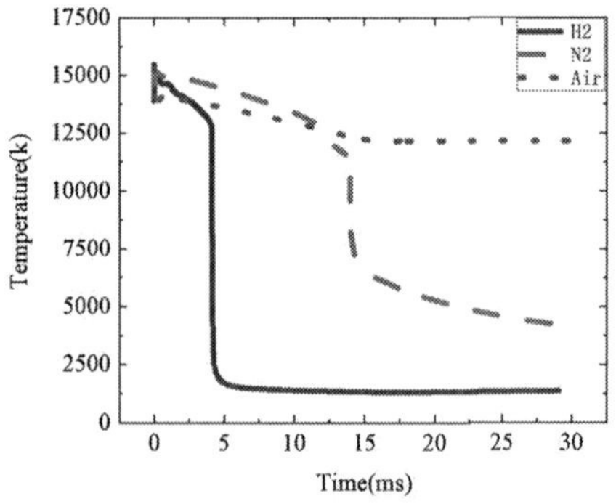

Fig. 7 Arc temperature under three gas media

From the above analysis, it can be seen that the arc temperature drop rate is the fastest in H_2 medium and the arc extinguishing time of the three gases are Air/no arc extinguishing, H_2/4.2 ms, N_2/15 ms. Fig. 8 shows the thermal conductivity of the three gases. It can be seen that the thermal conductivity of H_2 is the largest, and there is a peak at about 4000 K. Therefore, if the arc is to maintain combustion, it consumes more power in H2 with higher thermal conductivity. The higher the arc voltage is, the more conducive it is to extinguish the arc. Therefore, the extinguish time of H_2 is the shortest. The thermal conductivity of Air above 11000 K is greater than that of N2, so at the beginning of arc breaking, the arc temperature of air drops faster than that of N_2. When the arc temperature drops to 12000 K, due to the thermal conductivity of Air is smaller than that of N_2, the arc temperature of N_2 drops rapidly until the arc is extinguished.

As shown in Fig. 9, the cathode contact temperature during arc combustion is reflected by the treatment method of phase change materials in different media. The black line area in the figure indicates that the contact temperature is higher than the melting point of the contact material, and the molten pool area formed by the melting of the contact material. It can be seen that the molten pool formed under three kinds of arc extinguishing medium is $H_2 < N_2 <$ Air. The size of the molten pool is affected by the arc quenching time and arc temperature. The arc quenching time of H_2 is the shortest and the arc temperature decreases rapidly, so the molten pool is the smallest. The arc temperature of N_2 is always higher than Air before arc quenching, but when the arc is extinguished in 15 ms, Air arc continues to burn, which will continue to increase the molten pool, so the molten pool area of N_2 is less than Air. As shown in Fig. 10, the heat flux curve at the molten pool interface of arc and cathode contact is shown. It can be seen that the peak heat flux is at the arc axis, which is in the order of 108 W / m^2. The peak value of heat flux affects the depth of the molten pool, and the width of the peak value of heat flux affects the width of the molten pool. The maximum heat flux of Air is 3.84 × 108 W / m^2, and the minimum heat flux of H_2 is 2.97 × 108 W / m^2. Therefore, the width and depth of the molten pool in H2 medium are the largest, and the width and depth of the molten pool in N_2 medium are the smallest.

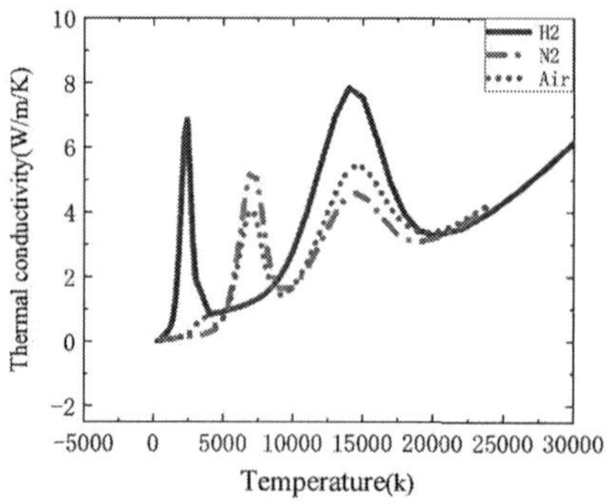

Fig. 8 Thermal conductivity of three gas media

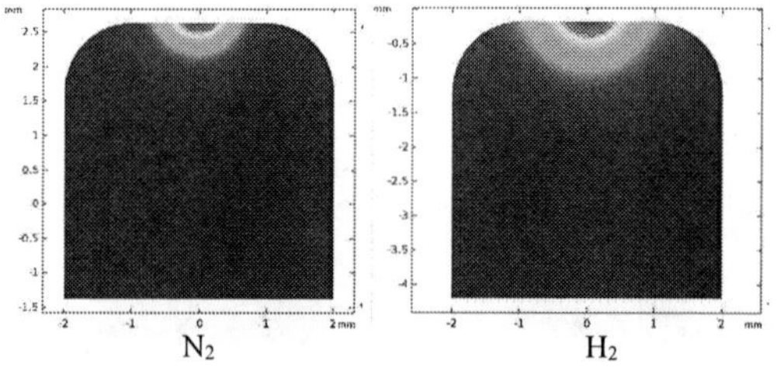

Fig.9 Contact Temperature with N2 、 H2 media

Table 1: Molten pool area under three kinds of media

	N_2	H2	Air
Pool area ($\times 10^{-2}$mm^2)	7.56	1.136	14.082
The width of molten pool ($\times 10^{-2}$mm)	68.6	44.4	85.6
The depth of molten pool ($\times 10^{-2}$mm)	22.3	22.3	30.75

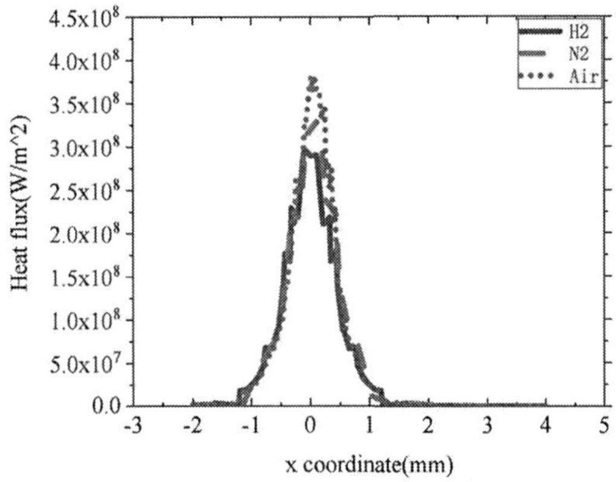

Fig. 10 Heat flux in three media

C. *Analysis of arc extinguishing performance under different pressures*

It can be seen from Figs. 11 and 12 that when H_2 is selected as the arc extinguishing medium, the greater the pressure is, the shorter the arc extinguishing time is, and the higher the arc voltage is. When the pressure increases from 0.6atm to 1atm and 2atm, the arc extinction time decreases from 5.2ms to 4.2ms and 3.1ms. When the pressure increases by 100 %, the arc extinction time decreases by about 1ms. The higher the pressure, the shorter the arc extinguishing time is because the thermal conductivity increases with the increase of pressure, which accelerates the arc extinguishing speed. The increase of pressure increases the arc voltage because the increase of pressure increases the molecular density between contacts, so that the self-travel of electrons is shortened. The lack of accumulated kinetic energy reduces the number of charged particles and the arc combustion can not be maintained. Therefore, in a certain range, increasing the pressure can improve the arc voltage.

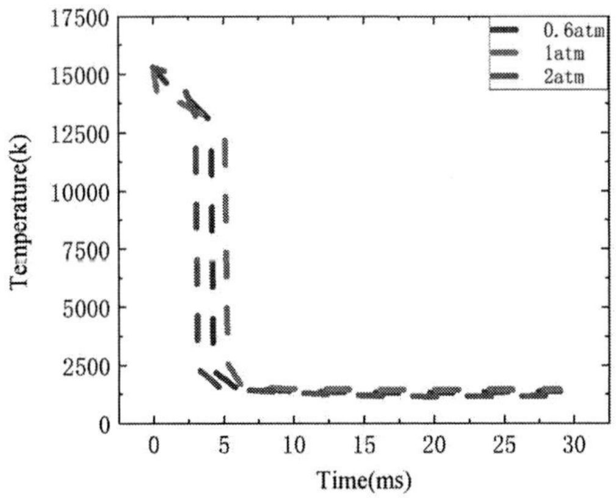

Fig. 11 Arc temperature under different pressures

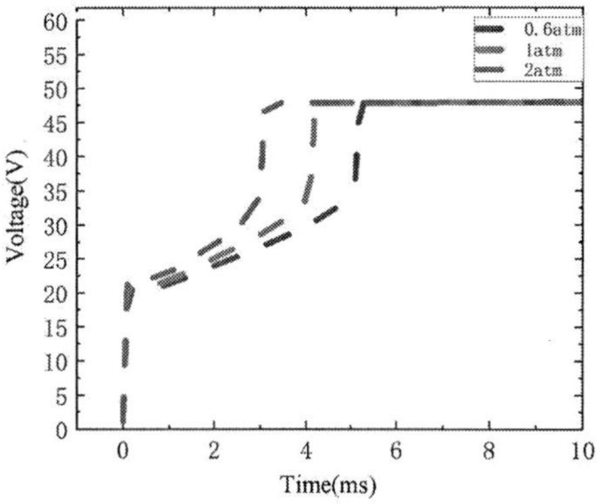

Fig. 12 Arc voltage under different pressures

IV. CONCLUSION

The two-dimensional axial model of DC contactor arc-contact two-way multi-field coupling is established, and the simulation analysis is carried out under different arc extinguishing medium and different pressure. The following conclusions are obtained.

1) Under different arc extinguishing media, H_2 gas has the shortest arc extinguishing time due to its high thermal conductivity, small molecular weight and low density, followed by nitrogen and air. The area of molten pool is from small to large as $H_2 < N_2 <$ Air, and the size of molten pool is affected by arc temperature and arc extinguishing time. It can be seen that the reasonable selection of arc extinguishing media is conducive to improving the arc extinguishing performance of DC contactor.

2) In the arc extinguishing medium of H_2, when the pressure is 0.6 atm, 1 atm and 2 atm, respectively, with the increase of pressure, the arc voltage increases, the arc temperature gradually increases, the arc extinguishing time becomes shorter and the arc temperature drop rate becomes faster.

ACKNOWLEDGMENT

This work was supported by the National Natural Science of Foundation of China (51777057) and Local science and Technology Development Fund Progect guided by the Central Government (216Z1011G).

REFERENCES

[1] Meckler P, Gerdinand F, Weiss R, et al, "Hybrid switches in protective devices for low-voltage DC grids at commercial used buildings," in *Proceedings of the ICEC 2014 International Conference on Electrical Contacts*. Dresden, Germany, VDE, 2014, 1-6.

[2] Y H Yang, L W Yang, W Jiang, "Overview of DC grid networking equipment and control strategy," *Grid technology*, 2018, 42(1): 12-24

[3] J Li, K Liu, Y D Cao, S X Liu, "Analysis of arc root evolution

and its influence on reburning during DC contactor breaking," *Proceedings of the CSEE*, 2019, 39(4): 1241-1251.

[4] W M Wu, Y B He, P Geng, "Key Technologies of DC Microgrid Research," *Transactions of China Electrotechnical Society*, 2012, 27(1): 98-106+113

[5] W Y Chen, S F Ou, L Wang, "Simulation and Experimental Study on Arc Characteristics of DC contactor ," *Low Voltage Apparatus*, 2013,(1): 1-5+28.

[6] X F Lu, "Research on the Characteristics of DC Arc in Hydrogen Arc Extinguishing Medium with Magnetic Field ," *Electrotechnics*, 2022,(2): 66-69.

[7] X W Li, Q S Lv, T Tian, Y H Wu, F Tang, "Characteristics of contact ablation under DC air arc ," *High Voltage Technology*, 2020, 46(6): 970-1977.

[8] R D Huang, H H Huang, M L Fu, W Wang, D B Wang, " Simulation and Experimental Study on Arc Extinguishing Performance of New Environmental Gas in 35 kV Circuit Breaker ," *High voltage appliances*, 2021, 57(3): 54-59,

[9] C P Niu, Q C Xiong, X Dan, Y Wu, Z X Li, " Experimental Study on Breaking Arc Characteristics of High Power DC contactor in Different Media," *High Voltage Technology*, 2019, 45(11). 3481-3486.

Haitao Wang, woman, born in 1973, doctor, professor, master tutor. Mainly engaged in electrical reliability and testing technology, electrical and electrical contact research. She has hosted and participated in more than 20 projects funded by the National Natural Science Foundation of China and provincial and ministerial scientific research projects, and won one Science and Technology Progress Award in Hebei Province. Published more than 50 papers, a number of patents.

Series Arc Fault Detection Method Based on Multi-Feature Fusion

Xudong Yang[1], Zhihong Xu [1,2,3]

[1)] College of Electrical Engineering and Automation, Fuzhou University, Fuzhou, 350108

[2)] Fujian Key Laboratory of New Energy Generation and Power Conversion, Fuzhou, 350108

[3)] Fujian Province University Engineering Research Center of Smart Distribution Grid Equipment, Fuzhou, 350108

Email: 641936593@qq.com TEL:13178116282

***Abstract*—Arc fault is the main cause of electrical fire. Effectively detecting the arc signal in the line is of great significance to electrical fire protection. The effect of arc fault detection method based on single feature setting threshold is poor, and there are some problems such as complex threshold setting and easy to be affected by load. To solve this problem, this paper establishes an arc fault simulation test platform to collect the current signals of different types of loads in normal operation and arc fault state, establish a waveform database, and extract various feature quantities of current signals in time domain, frequency domain and time-frequency domain, The arc fault characteristic quantity data set is established. Subsequently, the arc fault characteristic quantity data set is input into the random forest detection model to obtain the importance ranking of the characteristic quantity. The selected characteristic quantum set is determined according to the Gini index score. Finally, these characteristic quantities are input into the artificial neural network for fault discrimination. This method does not need artificial feature selection and does not need to set the threshold, and can accurately identify the fault.**

***Index Terms*— multi-feature fusion, series arc fault, multi-dimensional feature quantity, machine learning, detection method**

I. INTRODUCTION

Arc is a form of gas discharge. When the arc occurs, it is accompanied by luminescence, heating, combustion and other phenomena. Research shows that 2-10A arc current can produce local high temperature of 2000-4000 °C, and 0.5A arc current is enough to cause electrical fire [1]. Arc fault protection devices can effectively detect series arc, parallel arc and grounding arc faults in the line, which is of great significance to fire protection, Therefore, it is urgent to develop a reliable arc fault protection devices [2].

At present, most arc fault detection methods are based on line voltage and current signals; In the literature [3-4], some arc features are extracted in the time domain, and the fault detection is carried out through the short-time zero crossing rate and difference root mean square value of the current signal. The algorithm is simple and easy to implement. However, it is not verified when some suppressed load features coincide with the arc features. In the literature [5], the current is processed by Fast Fourier Transform and mathematical morphology filtering, and the contour of the signal spectrum is used as the feature vector for fault recognition. In the literature [6], there are many abrupt points in the voltage detail signal after wavelet decomposition to accurately identify the arc duration. With the application of artificial intelligence technology in the field of arc fault detection, there are more and more methods of arc fault recognition using machine learning and deep learning [7-9]. Such methods generally have good recognition effect, but the disadvantage is that a large amount of data is required for model training, otherwise the accuracy is difficult to guarantee. The modern household power supply and distribution network has many loads, the line laying is complex, and the series arc has strong concealment, which is easy to be annihilated by the load current. The arc fault detection algorithm based on a single characteristic quantity has the problems of difficult threshold setting and low reliability. The above problems can be solved by artificially selecting the feature quantity and combining it with an appropriate algorithm, but the overall process is time-consuming and laborious [10-11]. It is an inevitable trend for the development of arc fault protection apparatus to find a detection method with practical engineering significance through multi feature fusion.

In this paper, the time domain, frequency domain, time-frequency domain and other feature quantities before and after the occurrence of arc fault are extracted and analyzed, and the arc fault feature quantity database is created. The importance of the feature quantity is quantified by random forest algorithm (RF), and the feature quantum

This work was supported by the University Production-Study Cooperation Project of Science and Technology Department of Fujian Province (2021Y4002) and the Funding Program for Leading Talents in Scientific and Technological Innovation of Fujian Province (038000387024)

figartificial neural network for model training, and the fault detection model with high recognition accuracy is obtained.

II. Experimental Device and Scheme

A. Experimental device

In order to study the detection method of series arc fault under different positions and load conditions of household power supply and distribution lines, this paper builds a test platform with reference to the standard GB/T 31143-2014. The schematic diagram of the test platform is shown in Fig 1. The arc generator includes arc generator and cable carbonization device. The data acquisition card (DAQ)is the control core of the test platform. The upper computer (IPC) drives the switch action of the test circuit through the output of the data acquisition card DO, During the test, the voltage and current signals are collected by AI. The overall automation of the platform is high, and the test process is safe and reliable.

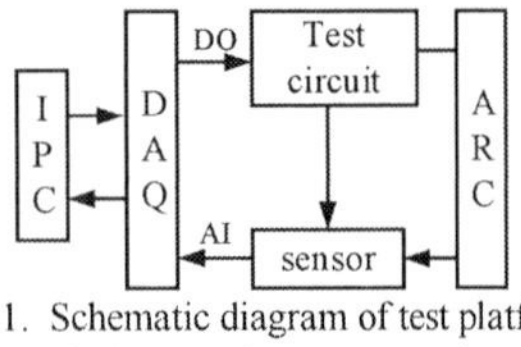

Fig. 1. Schematic diagram of test platform

This platform mainly carries out various series arc fault tests, and designs the test circuit with reference to the non suppressed load shielding test and suppressed load shielding test A, B, C and D in the standard, as shown in Fig 2; The switch states corresponding to different test options are shown in Table I, where 1 represents the switch is closed and 0 represents the switch is open.

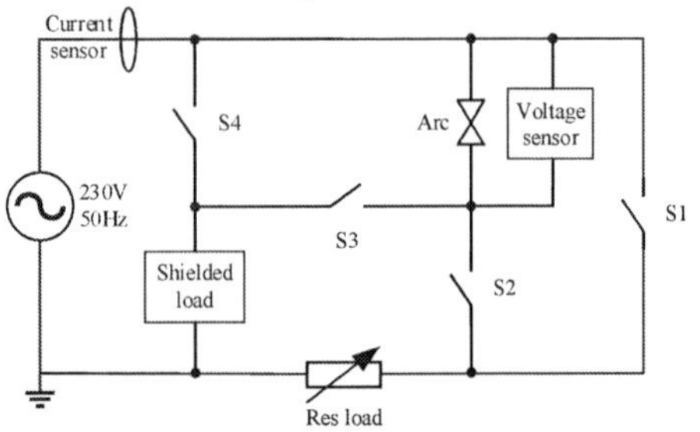

Fig. 2. Test circuit

TABLE I
Test switch configuration

Test options	S1	S2	S3	S4
	switch status			
Shielding test	0	1	0	0
Shielding test A	0	0	1	0
Shielding test B	0	1	0	1
Shielding test C	1	0	1	0
Shielding test D	0	1	1	0

B. Experimental scheme

This platform tests the situation of arc fault in different loads, main roads and branches of different lines. Since the purpose of the proposed multi-feature fusion arc fault detection algorithm is to obtain a set of feature quantities with better recognition effect, a large number of experiments are needed to obtain more test data. The loads and parameters selected in the test are shown in Table II. For each load, 10 groups of tests are repeated with different test options. The data acquisition card collects the voltage and current waveforms in the process of normal, arc starting, arc burning and arc extinguishing at a sampling frequency of 100KHz, and stores the data in the upper computer.

TABLE II
Test load parameters

Load	parameters
resistance	3A、6A
vacuum cleaner	rated current 7.6A
switch power supply	rated current 4A
air compressor	rated power 2.2kW
dimmer	rated power 600W
electric drill	rated current 2.9A
fluorescent lamp + resistance	two 40W fluorescent lamps in parallel with 5A resistor
halogen lamp + resistance	300W halogen lamp parallel 5A resistor

III. Feature Extraction and Analysis

Arc fault feature extraction methods can be roughly divided into two categories: the first is to calculate the fault signal directly, such as finding the effective value, variance, kurtosis, etc; The second kind is to transform the signal first, and then use the transformed sequence to calculate the characteristic quantity, such as Fourier transform, wavelet transform and so on. In this paper, a power frequency cycle current signal is used to extract the characteristics of time domain, frequency domain and time-frequency domain, and the characteristic data set of arc fault is constructed; It should be pointed out that the arc fault feature data set established in this paper can be added and deleted according to the change of feature extraction method. In the following, $\{x_n\}$ represents the sequence of periodic current signals, $\{y_k\}$ represents the sequence obtained by transformation.

A. Time domain feature extraction and analysis

When there is no arc fault in the line, the line current basically changes periodically and symmetrically, and the calculated characteristic quantities of each cycle have little difference; However, when an arc fault occurs in the line, the high-frequency component in the line increases, the randomness of the current increases, and even half wave loss, periodic loss and other phenomena occur, and the difference of characteristic quantities in each cycle increases.

When a fault occurs in the line, the arc resistance is connected in series in the circuit, and the current decreases relatively when there is no fault. Therefore, the effective value can represent the arc characteristics of some loads to a certain extent. Fig 3 shows the change of effective value of pure resistive load and vacuum cleaner before and after the fault. After the arc occurs, the effective value shows an overall decreasing trend, and as the arc combustion tends to be stable, the effective value also becomes smaller.

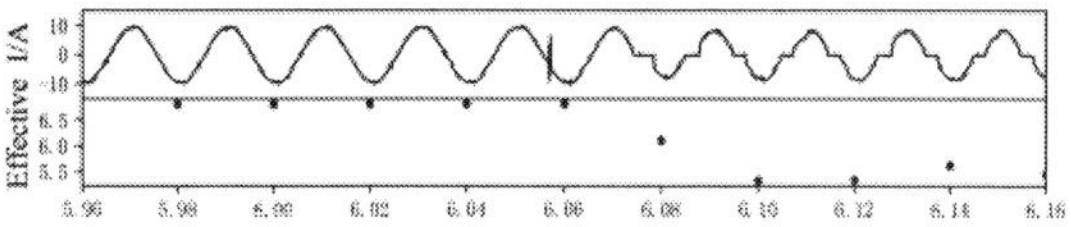

Fig. a. Pure resistive load

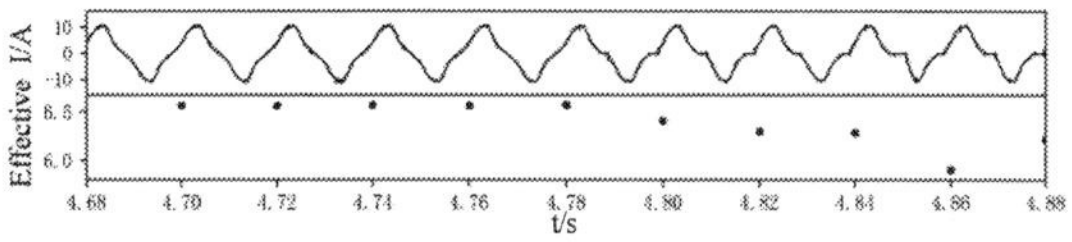

Fig. b. Vacuum cleaner

Fig. 3. Change of effective value before and after fault

The pulse factor is defined as the ratio of the peak value of the signal to the average value of rectification, as shown in equation 1, which reflects the impact degree of the signal. It can be seen from Fig 4 that the dispersion of the impact degree of the signal becomes larger before and after the fault occurs, so the pulse factor can quantitatively characterize the fluctuation characteristics of some load line currents to a certain extent.

$$P = \frac{\max(x_i)}{\left|\bar{x}\right|} = \frac{\max(x_i)}{\frac{1}{n}\sum_{i=1}^{n}\left|x_i\right|} \tag{1}$$

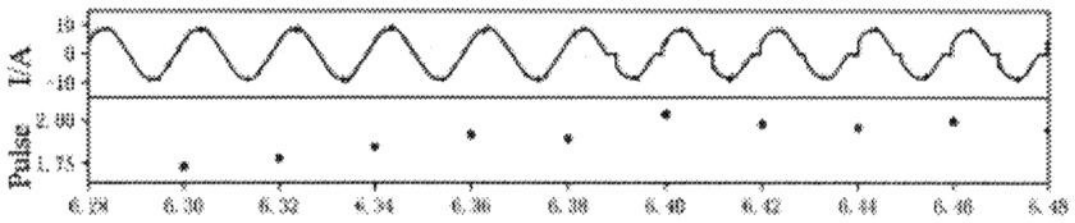

Fig. a. Fluorescent lamp with resistive load

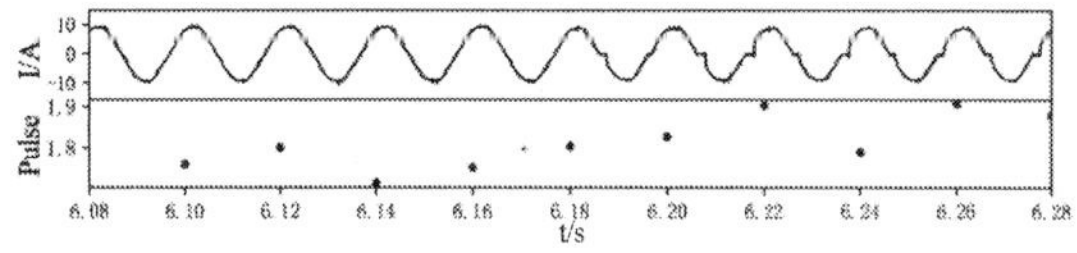

Fig. b. Halogen lamp with resistive load

Fig. 4. Change of pulse factor before and after fault

The waveform index is defined as the ratio of the effective value of the signal to the average value of rectification, as shown in formula 2, which is used to represent the distortion degree of the actual waveform compared with the standard sine wave; The waveform index extraction results are shown in Fig 5. When a fault occurs, the waveform distortion is worse than that in normal cases, and the increase of waveform index is limited by load type and current level. Therefore, it also needs to be combined with other features to obtain a more reliable recognition effect.

$$S_f = \frac{\sqrt{\frac{1}{n}\sum_{i=1}^{n}x_i^2}}{\frac{1}{n}\sum_{i=1}^{n}\left|x_i\right|} \tag{2}$$

Similarly, referring to the research of literature [12], this paper extracts typical time-domain characteristics such as variance, skewness, kurtosis, kurtosis, autocorrelation coefficient and skewness of single period data, and finds that different characteristics have different performances under different loads and different test current levels. Therefore, extensive feature extraction has a certain effect on improving the generalization ability of the model.

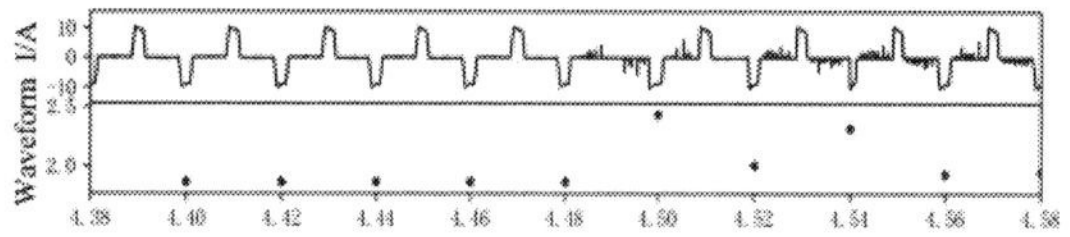

Fig. a. Electronic switching power supply

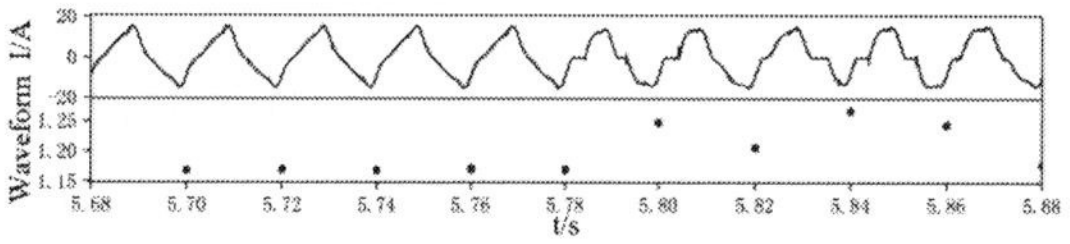

Fig. b. Vacuum cleaner

Fig. 5. Change of waveform index before and after fault

B. Frequency domain characteristics

Since the current sampling signal is a discrete-time signal, Discrete Fourier Transform (DFT) is performed on the current signal, and its expression is:

$$X_k = \sum_{i=1}^{n} x_i e^{-j\frac{2\pi ki}{n}}; 1 \le k \le n \tag{3}$$

For different inhibitory loads, because the magnitude and waveform of load current are not exactly the same, there are obvious differences in the spectrum after discrete Fourier transform. Fig 6 and Fig 7 show the spectrum of electronic switching power supply and air compressor under normal and fault conditions. The harmonic amplitude of electronic switching power supply increases more, while the harmonic amplitude of air compressor increases relatively less. In this paper, the *k-th* harmonic factor HF_k and total harmonic distortion THD are used as characteristic quantities.

$$HF_k = \frac{I_k}{I_1} (k=2,3,4\ldots10) \tag{4}$$

$$THD = \frac{\sqrt{I^2 - I_1^2}}{I_1} \tag{5}$$

Where, I_k is the effective value of *k-th* harmonic, I is the effective value of current, and I_1 is the effective value of fundamental current.

C. Time frequency domain characteristics

As a multi-resolution time-frequency analysis method that can focus on any detail of the signal, wavelet analysis can capture the local similarity of the signal and detect the singularity of the signal, so it can reflect some characteristics of the arc [13]. db4 wavelet basis function is used to decompose the power frequency periodic current signal before and after the load fault. It is found that the detail signal CD after fault decomposition is significantly larger than the normal state. Based on this criterion, the maximum detail coefficient of each layer after wavelet decomposition of each power frequency periodic current is selected as the arc fault characteristic quantity.

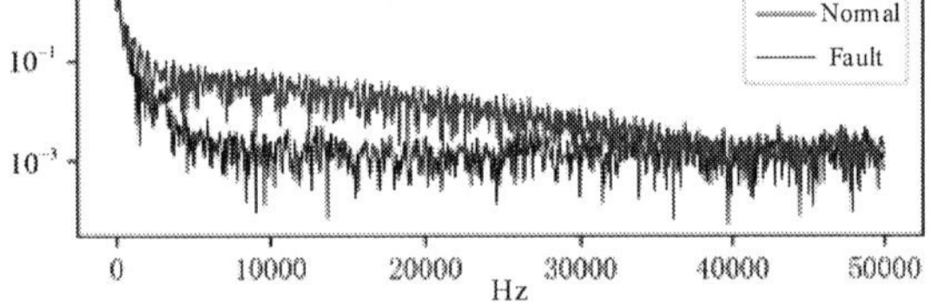

Fig. 6. Spectrum diagram of electronic switching power supply

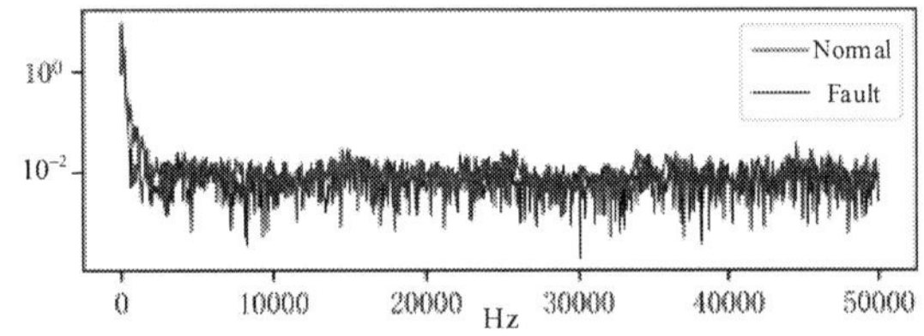

Fig. 7. Spectrum diagram of air compressor

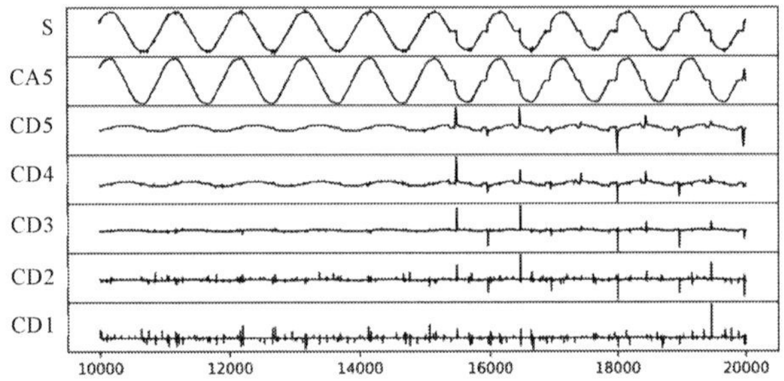

Fig. 8. Wavelet decomposition of fluorescent lamp current

Fig 8 is the wavelet decomposition diagram of the band resistive load of the fluorescent lamp, comparing the maximum values of the detail signals CD5, CD4, CD3 and CD2 in each cycle. After the occurrence of the arc fault, especially at the zero rest position and current singularity of the current signal, the value of the detail signal is larger, which increases significantly compared with the detail signal value in the normal state. Therefore, the maximum value of the detail signal in each power frequency cycle can be used as the fault characteristic quantity.

IV. Arc fault detection model

Feature selection plays an important role in pattern recognition. The quality of feature selection directly determines the classification accuracy and generalization performance of the model. In the process of developing arc fault protection products, it is of great significance to adopt fewer and more precise features for product development and marketization; In the face of a large number of arc fault features, removing irrelevant features will prevent dimensional disasters and reduce the resource utilization in the process of model training. The commonly used machine learning feature selection methods include Filter, Wrapper and Embedded. In this paper, the random forest algorithm in the embedding method is used to remove redundant features and establish a quantum set of arc fault features.

After the arc fault characteristic data set is established, the next step is to classify the samples. The classification algorithm can use common support vector machine, artificial neural network, k-nearest neighbor and other algorithms. In this paper, the artificial neural network algorithm is used for classification, and the generated training model can be deployed to STM32 single chip microcomputer through STM32 CubeMX to provide a detection model for the development of arc fault protection electrical products.

A. Arc fault feature selection

Because in the process of algorithm design, it is necessary to select the feature quantity, and the artificial selection of feature quantity requires the accumulation of relevant experience, and there are shortcomings such as poor reliability, high redundancy or insufficient feature selection.

The efficiency of feature selection using filtering method is high, but the interaction between features is not taken into account when screening. Some features are not necessarily useful for the establishment of the model, and may contain redundant features; Although the packaging method can perfectly solve the interaction between features and models, and complete feature screening in the training process, such algorithms can obtain the best feature subset, but their efficiency is low when there are many features [14].

The random forest algorithm will randomly select features and samples to build a decision tree in the training process, and automatically sort the features according to the importance of the features for classification. It has the advantages of easy implementation, fast training speed, good performance and so on. Therefore, it only needs to count the average contribution of each feature on each decision tree of the random forest, and then the feature importance score can be obtained.

Each decision tree in the random forest adopts the CART (classification and progression tree) algorithm, and uses the "Gini index" to divide the attributes. The purity of data set D is measured by the Gini value. $Gini(D)$ reflects the probability that two samples are randomly selected from data set D, and their categories are inconsistent. See formula 6.

$$Gini(\mathrm{D}) = \sum_{k=1}^{Y} p_k(1-p_k) = 1-\sum_{k=1}^{Y} p_k^2 \tag{6}$$

Where k represents the sample category and P_K represents the weight of the k-th sample.

The importance score of variables is expressed by VIM (variable importance measure). Assuming that the data set has a total of J features: X_1, X_2, X_3... X_j... X_J, C sample categories and I decision trees, calculate the Gini index score $VIMj$ of each feature X_J, that is, the average change of node splitting impurity of the j-th feature in all decision trees of random forest.

The importance of feature X_J in the Q node of the i-th decision tree is expressed as the change of Gini index before and after the Q branch of node:

$$VIM_{jq}^{Gini(i)} = Gini_q^{(i)} - Gini_{left}^{(i)} - Gini_{right}^{(i)} \quad (7)$$

$Gini_{left}$ and $Gini_{right}$ are the gini indexes of the two new nodes after the branch.

Let the nodes of feature X_J in decision tree I be set Q, and the sum of Gini indices of all nodes of statistical feature X_J in decision tree I be:

$$VIM_j^{Gini(i)} = \sum_{q \in Q} VIM_{jq}^{Gini(i)} \quad (8)$$

Then the variable importance score of characteristic X_J in random forest:

$$VIM_j^{Gini} = \sum_{i=1}^{I} VIM_j^{Gini(i)} \quad (9)$$

Finally, the importance scores of all features are normalized:

$$VIM_j^{Gini} = \frac{VIM_j^{Gini}}{\sum_{j=1}^{J} VIM_j^{Gini}} \quad (10)$$

Set the threshold value of feature quantity importance score to 0.02, remove the feature quantity less than this threshold value, and get the feature quantity importance diagram as shown in Fig 9.

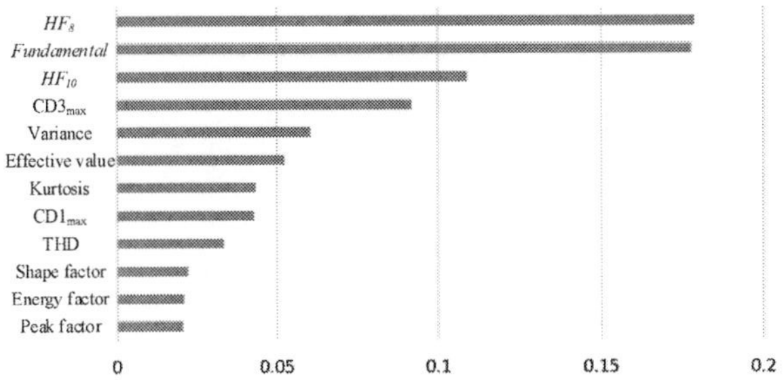

Fig. 9. Feature quantity importance diagram

B. *Arc fault detection model*

For different initial feature sets, the feature importance sequences established after random forest feature importance ranking are different, and choosing different importance scoring thresholds will also make the feature quantum sets different.

In order to avoid manually adjusting the network super parameters every time because of the change of the characteristic quantum set of arc fault, and to minimize the complexity of the generation model, this paper adopts a funnel-shaped three-layer artificial neural network [15] which decreases layer by layer. As shown in Fig 10, the number of network input layer and hidden layer nodes is automatically adjusted according to the characteristic dimension of the characteristic quantum set. If the characteristic dimension of the characteristic quantum set is n, the number of input layer nodes is n, Hidden layer 1 is set according to the 1/3 decreasing proportion, the number of hidden layer 1 nodes is 2n/3, hidden layer 2 is set according to the 1/4 decreasing proportion, and the number of hidden layer 2 nodes is 3/4*2n/3. Because it is a binary classification model, the number of output layer nodes is fixed at 2.

The quantum set of arc fault characteristics is divided into training set and verification set according to the proportion of 0.2. The model uses the mean square error as the loss function, the hidden layer activation function is tanh, and the output layer activation function is softmax; During model training, monitor the accuracy performance of the model in the verification set, and decide whether to save the model coverage according to whether the model performance is better than the previous generation in each epoch; When the accuracy performance of the validation set lasts for 30 epochs and does not change, the model training is ended in advance; In order to achieve better learning effect, the learning rate is automatically adjusted according to the size of the loss function of the verification set during the training process. When the value of the loss function remains unchanged for a period of epoch, the learning rate is adjusted to one tenth of the original; When the number of training samples is insufficient, the model is easy to have fitting, which leads to the prediction accuracy of the model on the training data becoming higher and higher, but the prediction accuracy on the test data cannot be improved, but decreases. In fact, some weights are not necessary in the network, and a dropout layer can be added to remove some neurons in the network.

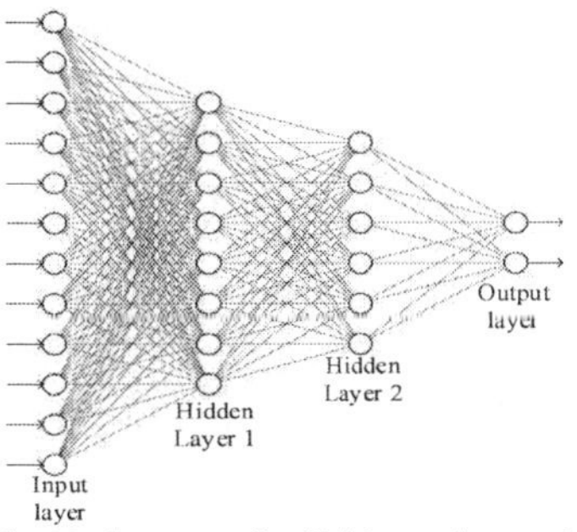

Fig. 10. Structure of artificial neural network

C. *Experimental results and analysis*

The loss value curve of the model learning process is shown in Fig 11. The feature quantity after feature selection can relatively better characterize the characteristics of arc fault, and the convergence speed of network parameters is fast. When the iteration is carried out for 20 times, the performance of the model on the verification set has tended to be stable, and the accuracy rate reaches more than 99%.

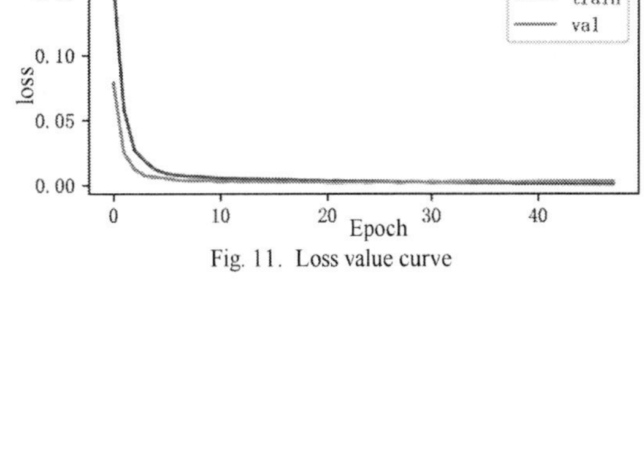

Fig. 11. Loss value curve

In order to verify the recognition effect of the model, a test set containing 762 normal samples and 774 fault samples is created, and the corresponding feature quantities of the test set samples are input into the recognition model. The confusion matrix is shown in Table III, and the recognition accuracy reaches 98.05%.

TABLE III
Test set confusion matrix

		forecast	
		normal	fault
actual	normal	743	19
	fault	11	763

V. Conclusion

In this paper, a series arc fault detection method based on multi-feature fusion is proposed, because the single feature arc fault detection algorithm has a threshold setting, and the recognition effect is easily affected by the load, and the multi-feature fusion detection algorithm needs relevant experience in feature selection. This method widely extracts arc fault feature quantities in time domain, frequency domain, time-frequency domain and other situations. In the development process of arc fault protection appliances, it needs to combine the complexity of feature extraction with the ease of implementation. This feature quantity data set can be increased and reduced as needed, and then create a feature quantum set under the random forest feature importance score, Finally, an artificial neural network is built on this feature quantum set for fault identification. The results show that this method does not need to set the threshold, and the established model is easy to be applied to the development of protection products, which is of great significance for the engineering of arc fault detection algorithm.

References

[1] Wang Yao, Tian Ming, Niu Feng, et al. A Comprehensive Review of Arc Fault Detection Methods for Low Voltage AC Power System [J]. Electrical & Energy Management Technology,2018.

[2] Liu Jinyan, Ji HuiYu, Huang Wujie, et al. Overview About Arc Fault Detection Device Development [J]. Electrical & Energy Management Technology, 2014, 000(011):1-6.

[3] Liu Xiaoming, Xu Yefei, Liu Ting, et al. The Arc Fault Detection Based on the Current Signal Short Time Zero Crossing Rate [J], Transactions of China Electrotechnical Society, 2015, 30(13):9.

[4] Lu Qiwei, Wu Haidong, Wang Suke, et al. Research on Arc-Fault Detection Based on Difference-Root Mean Square Method [J], Electrical & Energy Management Technology, 2013(1):6-10.

[5] Ma Zheng, Zhang Guogang, He Chunjun, A Method of Fault Arc Detection Based on Spectral Analysis of High-Frequency Current [J], Electrical & Energy Management Technology, 2010(9):10-12.

[6] Fan Liping, Yuan Zhaoqiang, Zhang Kai,Simulation on arc model of single phase earth fault and PSCAD/EMTDC based on wavelet transformation [J], Power System Protection and Control, 2011, 39(5):6.

[7] Yu Qiongfang, Huang Gaolu, Yang Yi, et al . Series arc fault detection method based on AlexNet deep learning network [J], Journal of Electronic Measurement and Instrumentation, 2019(3).

[8] Han X, Li D, Huang L, et al. Series Arc Fault Detection Method Based on Category Recognition and Artificial Neural Network [J]. Electronics, 2020, 9(9):1367.

[9] Qu N , Zuo J , Chen J , et al. Series Arc Fault Detection of Indoor Power Distribution System Based on LVQ-NN and PSO-SVM [J]. IEEE Access, 2019, PP(99):1-1.

[10] Vu H D , Calderon E , Schweitzer P , et al. Multi criteria series arc fault detection based on supervised feature selection [J]. International Journal of Electrical Power & Energy Systems, 2019, 113(DEC.):23-34.

[11] Cui Ruihua, Wang Yang, Wang Chuanyu, et al. Series Arc Fault Identification Method in Aviation Lines Based on Multi-Information Fusion [J], Transactions of China Electrotechnical Society, 2019, 34(A01):8.

[12] Liao Xiaoyu, Study on Detection Technology of Low-Voltage AC Series Arc Faults [D], Harbin Institute of Technology.

[13] Lu Qiwei, Wang Tao, Li Zongrui, Detection Method of Series Arcing Fault Based on Wavelet Transform and Singular Value Decomposition [J], Transactions of China Electrotechnical Society, 2017, 32(17):10.

[14] Yao Xu, Wang Xiaodan, Zhang Yuxi, Summary of feature selection algorithms [J], Control and Decision, 2012, 27(2):7.

[15] Wu Sha, Wang Jian, Xie Xin, Selection of Hyperparameters for Wind Turbine Performance Model based on Deep Neural Network [J], Solar Energy, 2020(9):6.

First Author, Xudong Yang is currently pursuing the M.S. degree in the College of Electrical Engineering and Automation, Fuzhou University, Fuzhou, China. His current research interests include electrical appliances and intelligent technology.

Corresponding Author, Xu Zhihong (1963-), professor and doctoral supervisor, with research interests in electrical appliances and intelligent technology, 641936593@qq.com

8th International Conference on Reliability of
Electrical Products and Electrical Contacts,
November 18-20, 2022

Application of Approximate Modeling Method Based on Interpolation in Reliability Optimization of Electromagnetic Relay

Jie Deng, Xiaohan Liu, Zhouyuan Chen, Guofu Zhai

Harbin Institute of Technology, Harbin, 150001, China
Email: 21b906004@stu.hit.edu.cn TEL: 15898330162

***Abstract*—Approximate modeling technique has attracted much attention in complex engineering problems requiring high simulation cost. However, most current modeling methods require large sample size and low model accuracy when establishing suction characteristic models of electromagnetic relays with high nonlinear characteristics, which cannot meet the requirements of reliability optimization of electromagnetic relays. Therefore, this paper proposes a new approximate modeling method, which is based on interpolation method and particle swarm optimization algorithm. Firstly, the variation law of electromagnetic torque is analyzed and the modeling area is divided reasonably. Then, the approximate model is established based on the interpolation method, and the weight function is solved by particle swarm optimization algorithm to ensure the accuracy of the model. Finally, the reliability optimization of a typical electromagnetic relay is used to verify that the proposed method has higher efficiency and accuracy.**

***Index Terms*— approximate modeling, interpolation method, weight function, electromagnetic relay, reliability optimization**

I. INTRODUCTION

As a key component in the payload and control system of aviation, aerospace and weapons equipment, electromagnetic actuators play an important role in signal transmission, system distribution, voltage or load conversion [1]. Because of the particularity of its application, it is particularly important to ensure that it can complete the specified function at the beginning of the system operation and in the working process. Improving the reliability of aerospace electromagnetic relays cannot be ignored. The accuracy of the proxy model will lead to different degrees of optimization resource consumption and reliability improvement [2]-[4]. Therefore, the accuracy and computational speed of the surrogate model play a key role in the accuracy of reliability optimization.

At present, The commonly used approximate modeling methods are mainly polynomial response surface (PRS) [5]-[6], radial basis functions (RBF) [7]-[8], Kriging [9]-[11], neural Networks [12]-[13], and support vector regression (SVR) [14]-[15].

RBF model is a kind of multivariate interpolation model, which USES radial basis function to construct the transfer function of neural network, not only the functional approximation ability with arbitrary precision, and has a faster convergence speed than the traditional neural network, so usually applied to optimization black-box, therefore does not apply to the quality characteristic as the target of electromagnetic mechanism approximate model is established in this paper.

Kriging model is an interpolation method for the optimal unbiased estimation of spatially distributed data. The Kriging method is very sensitive to sample points. If the number of training samples is small, the information of correlation matrix is insufficient, and the prediction effect is not ideal. With the increase of input variables and output objective functions, the number of sample points will increase exponentially, which consumes huge computational costs. Kriging method is not suitable for reliability optimization problems involving multiple design parameters and output characteristics.

In addition, some scholars apply the idea of space mapping, and use the finite element calculation results to modify the magnetic circuit method calculation results, so as to achieve the rapid calculation of the output characteristics of the electromagnetic mechanism. However, these methods do not establish the relationship between input parameters and output characteristics of electromagnetic system, so they cannot be used in reliability optimization design.

Therefore, aiming at the requirements of multi-input variables and high nonlinearity, this paper proposes an approximate modeling method based on interpolation. This method needs to be in the process of approximate model is established, through the simulation analysis was carried out on the limited sample point, based on the ideas of the fitting function relation between the output and the output, and based on the idea of interpolation to establish the function relationship between the working point, to guarantee the calculation accuracy of reduce the number of sampling points, and improve the computational efficiency. The structure of this paper is as follows. In the second chapter, the approximate modeling method is introduced, and in the third part, this method is verified. Finally, this method is applied to solve the reliability optimization problem of electromagnetic relay with high nonlinear characteristics.

II. Principle of Fast Calculation of Static Characteristics of Electromagnetic System and Reliability Optimization

A. Principle of approximate modeling

The electromagnetic torque T of the relay electromagnetic system changes with the size parameter of the electromagnetic system, the coil voltage U and the angle θ. When the size parameter is $X \rightarrow X + \Delta X$, the output characteristic of the electromagnetic system is $T \rightarrow T'$.

T' can be expressed as:

$$T' = T + \Delta T \tag{2.1}$$

Where, T' is output characteristic; T is the corresponding output result when taking the central value of the fluctuation range of the size parameter; ΔT is the output characteristic variation caused by size parameter X fluctuation, Taylor formula of multivariate function can be expanded into the following form:

$$\Delta T = \sum_{i=1}^{n} \Delta x_i \cdot \frac{\partial T}{\partial x_i} + \Delta^2(\Delta x_i) = \sum_{i=1}^{n} \Delta T_i \tag{2.2}$$

And in the steady state, the coil voltage U and angle θ are unchanged, so ΔT_i can be expressed as a unary function of x_i:

$$\Delta T_i = G(x_i)|_{(U,\theta)} \tag{2.3}$$

B. Output characteristic prediction based on interpolation method

For the static output characteristics $T_{(U,\theta)}$ of the electromagnetic system, the process of changing with the coil voltage U and the armature angle θ has continuity and regularity, which meets the conditions of establishing the interpolation model.

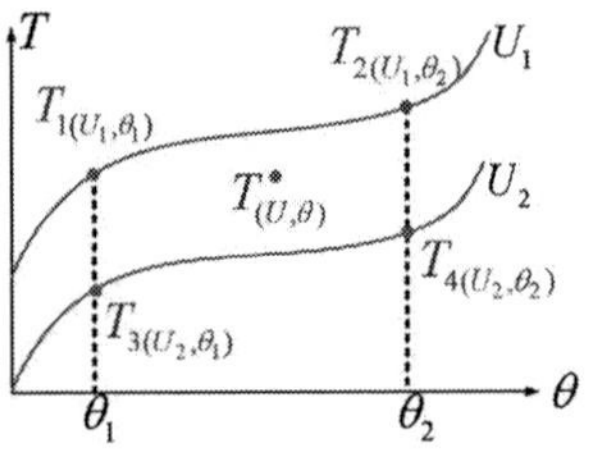

Fig. 1. Schematic diagram of reference working point and surrogate working point.

If the four boundary points in the static operating points are selected as the benchmark operating points, $T_{1(U_1,\theta_1)}$, $T_{2(U_1,\theta_2)}$, $T_{3(U_2,\theta_1)}$ and $T_{4(U_2,\theta_2)}$, as shown in Figure 1. The interpolation model of other arbitrary operating points $T_{(U,\theta)}$ is:

$$T_{(U,\theta)} = \sum_{j=1}^{4} \omega_j \cdot T_j \tag{2.4}$$

Where, $T_j (j = 1,2,3,4)$ is the output characteristic corresponding to the reference operating point; ω_j is the weight coefficient function describing the influence degree of the reference working point to the working point, and satisfies the following relation:

$$\sum_{j=1}^{4} \omega_j = 1 \tag{2.5}$$

$$0 \le \omega_j \le 1 \tag{2.6}$$

$$\lim_{U \to U_m, \theta \to \theta_m} \omega_j = 1 \tag{2.7}$$

Where, U_m, θ_m are respectively the voltage and angle corresponding to the reference operating point.

The approximate model of electromagnetic system design parameters $X(x_1, x_2, \ldots x_n)$ and output characteristics T' can be established by combining equations (2.1)~ (2.3). The following:

$$\begin{cases} X = X_0 + \Delta X \\ T' = \sum_{j=1}^{4} \omega_j \cdot (T_j + \sum_{i=1}^{n} \Delta T_{ij}) \end{cases} \tag{2.8}$$

C. Establishment and solution of weight coefficient function of interpolation model

The accuracy of the output characteristic interpolation model of electromagnetic system depends on the solution of the above weight coefficient function. The finite element simulation shows that the electromagnetic torque is exponential or logarithmic with the change of armature Angle. Therefore, this paper chooses exponential function as the basic form of weight coefficient function.

For the limiting case, assuming that the operating point to be solved coincides with the reference operating point, the weight coefficient function should satisfy the following relation:

$$\begin{cases} T_{1(U_1,\theta_1)}\big|_{(U_1,\theta_1)} = 1 \\ T_{2(U_1,\theta_1)}\big|_{(U_2,\theta_1)} \to 0 \\ T_{3(U_1,\theta_1)}\big|_{(U_1,\theta_2)} \to 0 \\ T_{4(U_1,\theta_1)}\big|_{(U_2,\theta_2)} \to 0 \end{cases} \tag{2.9}$$

Therefore, in the weight function, the influence coefficient of U and θ respectively $k_1(k_1>0)$ and $k_2(k_2>0)$, resulting in the following functional form:

$$\omega_j\big|_{(U_m,\theta_m)} = e^{-k_1\left|\frac{U-U_m}{(U_{m0}+U_{m1}-U_m)-U}\right| - k_2\left|\frac{\theta-\theta_n}{(\theta_{n0}+\theta_{n1}-\theta_n)-\theta}\right|} \tag{2.10}$$

Where, U_m, θ_m is the coil voltage and armature Angle corresponding to the reference operating point. In the limiting case, it is assumed that when the operating point to be solved coincides with the benchmark operating point

$T_1(U_1,\theta_1)$, $\omega_1 \to 1$, the values of ω_2, ω_3 and ω_4, are all 0, which conforms to the requirements of the definition of the weight function constructed in this paper.

The influence coefficients k_1 and k_2 of the coil voltage U and armature angle θ in the weight function are determined by particle swarm optimization (PSO) algorithm in this paper.

D. Approximate modeling process

Firstly, the reference operating point is determined according to the electromagnetic torque variation curve and obtained $\Delta T_i = G(x_i)$ by finite element simulation analysis. Then, n_q operating points are randomly selected from the static operating points of the electromagnetic system according to the random sampling method. Then a set of design parameter combination $X_q=X_0+\Delta X_q$ is randomly determined. On the one hand, the output characteristics T_{FEAq} of the above operating points are calculated by simulation. On the other hand, the rapid calculation model of electromagnetic static characteristics established by Equation (2.8) is used to calculate the output characteristics T_q of the above operating points respectively. Thus, the error function is established as:

$$E_R = \sqrt{\sum_{q=1}^{n_q} (T_q - T_{FEAq})^2 / n_q} \tag{2.11}$$

With the goal of minimizing the error function value, the influence coefficient k_1 and k_2 are optimized by PSO particle swarm optimization algorithm, which is the establishment process of the weight function $\omega_{j(U,\theta)}$. Finally, the approximate model composed of weight function and interpolation model was used to predict the response value of test samples and calculate the error. When the error could not meet the requirements, the reference operating point was appropriately increased to improve the model accuracy. The approximate modeling flow chart is shown in Fig. 2.

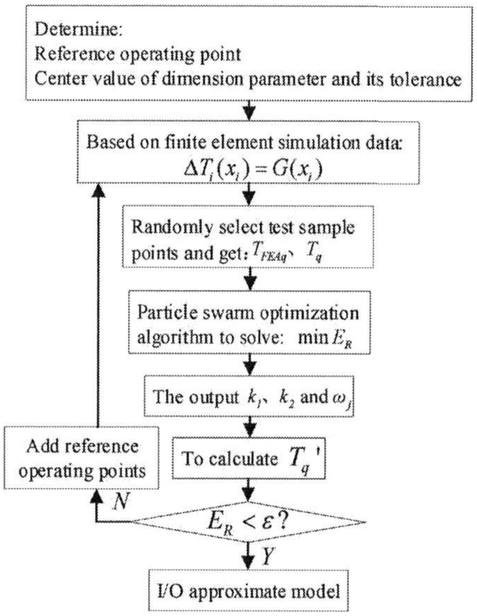

Fig. 2. Approximate modeling flow chart

E. Reliability optimization process

The complexity of structure and manufacturing process has a very important impact on the reliability and stability of products, especially for relays, contactors, circuit breakers and other electromagnetic mechanisms involved in the processing, assembly and debugging of many parts. The fluctuation range of key design parameters of relays is different, and the corresponding reliability indexes are also different. Therefore, based on the approximate input-output model of relay, this paper studies the tolerance optimization allocation method of its design parameters, aiming to guide the optimal design of aerospace electromagnetic relay and improve its reliability.

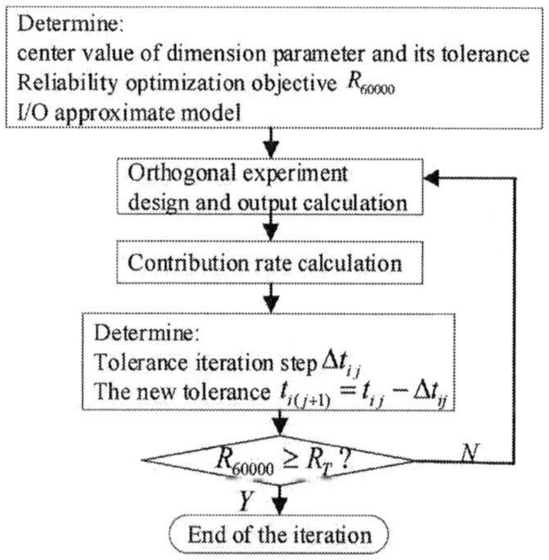

Fig. 3. Reliability optimization process

The reliability optimization process is shown in Figure 3. Firstly, the design parameters and their tolerances are set as the initial conditions, and the target reliability life is taken as the optimization objective. Then, the experimental plan will be determined by orthogonal experimental design. After calculating the output characteristics, the contribution coefficient of each design parameter will be determined by contribution rate analysis. The new tolerance in the iteration is then obtained from the tolerance step. Until the quality fluctuation range of the output characteristics meets the requirements.

III. EXAMPLE AND VALIDATION

A. The research object

An electromagnetic relay with double permanent magnets is taken as an example to verify the effectiveness of the proposed approximate modeling method, and its structure is shown in Figure 4.

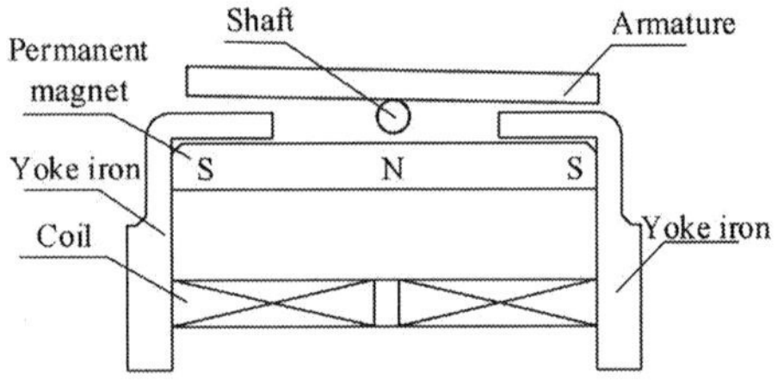

Fig. 4. Schematic diagram of the electromagnetic system of the relay

A small permanent magnet air gap between the armature and the yoke generates electromagnetic suction to keep the armature stable. When the left/right coil is energized, the armature moves to a certain distance by electromagnetic suction. When the coil is powered off, there is a small permanent magnet air gap between the armature and the yoke, and the armature obtains a new steady state.

B. Parameter selection and reference point determination

It can be seen from its structure characteristics and working principle that its main components include armature iron, yoke iron, permanent magnet, coil and so on. Key design parameters include armature length, yoke length, permanent magnet length, armature width and coil resistance. Table I lists the center values of five key design parameters and their tolerances.

TABLE I
EACH PARAMETER CORRESPONDS TO THE CUSTOM MODEL COEFFICIENT

Number	Parameter	Center Value	Tolerance
A	Coil Resistance	160	±4
B	Length of Armature	18	±0.3
C	Length of Permanent Magnet	2	±0.1
D	Width of Armature	6	±0.3
E	Length of Iron Yoke	5	±0.2

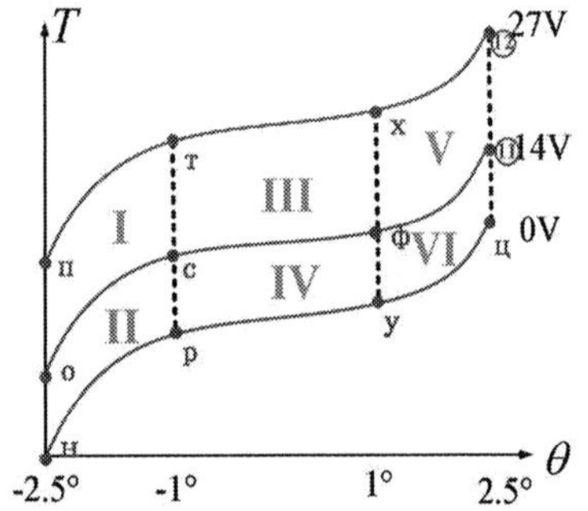

Fig. 5. Reference working point and working area of electromagnetic system

In order to improve the accuracy of the input-output approximate model, the static suction curve of the electromagnetic system was divided into 6 regions and 12 reference operating points according to the coil voltage range (0-27V) and the armature Angle range (-2.5° -2.5°), as shown in Figure 5.

Then, Equations (2.2) and (2.3) are used to establish the functional relationship between the electromagnetic torque of these 12 operating points as a function of the size parameters, where the parameter E (yoke length) is expressed as follows:

$$\Delta T_i(x_1) = c_1 * \Delta x_E^{\ 3} + c_2 * \Delta x_E^{\ 2} + c_3 * \Delta x_E \qquad (3.1)$$

20 test samples were randomly selected. On the one hand, the approximate model was used for prediction, on the other hand, the actual value was obtained by simulation, and then the error function was obtained. The PSO algorithm was used to set the minimum error as the optimization objective, and the coefficients in the formula were solved, The final results are shown in Table II.

TABLE II
EACH PARAMETER CORRESPONDS TO THE CUSTOM MODEL COEFFICIENT

Number	Parameter	k1	k2
A	Length of Iron Yoke	1.490	1.727
B	Length of Armature	1.602	1.758
C	Height of Armature Step	1.240	1.935
D	Width of Armature	1.459	1.706
E	length of Permanent Magnet	1.370	1.700

A certain set of design parameters is selected, and the comparison between approximate model results and simulation results is shown in Figure. 6.

It can be clearly seen from the figure that the error between the finite element calculation result and the actual prediction result is small, and the maximum error is 8.1%.

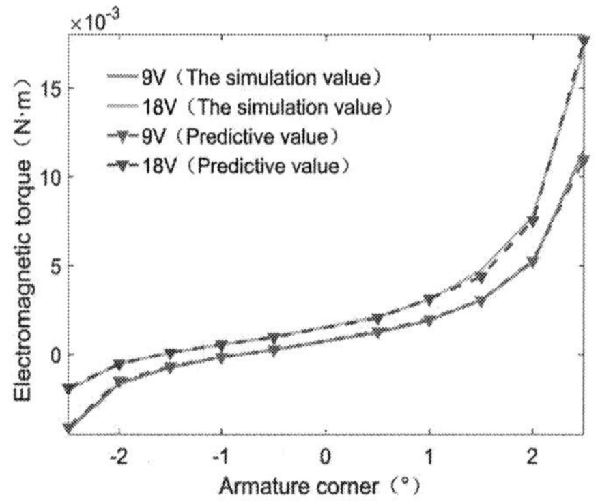

Fig. 6. Comparison between approximate model results and simulation results

In the process of establishing the approximate model, the total number of simulations can be reduced from $r \times m \times n = 2100$ to $12 \times m \times n + n_q = 380$ (where $r=70$ number of operating points, $m=6$ number of discrete points, $n=5$ number of design parameters, and $n_q=20$ number of samples) by using the operating point interpolation model, thus greatly shortening the simulation time. In conclusion, this modeling method has certain reference significance in the establishment of electromagnetic relay replacement model with high nonlinearity.

C. Optimization of reliability

The optimization objective of this paper is $R_{60000} \geq 0.9$ to solve the tolerance. The variation of parameter tolerance with the number of iterations is shown in Figure 8. It can be seen from the figure that parameter A has the greatest influence on the reliability, and the distribution characteristics of this parameter should be paid attention to in the process of machining. The life distribution comparison diagram of batch products before and after reliability optimization is shown in Figure 7. Figure 8 shows the comparison of product life distribution before and after reliability optimization.

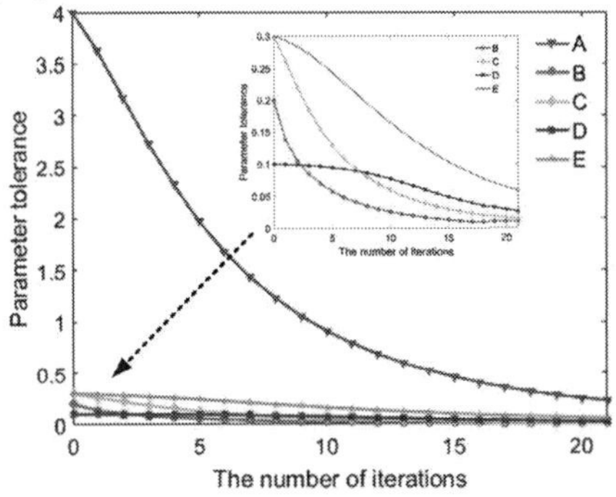

Fig. 7. Variation of parameter tolerance with the number of iterations

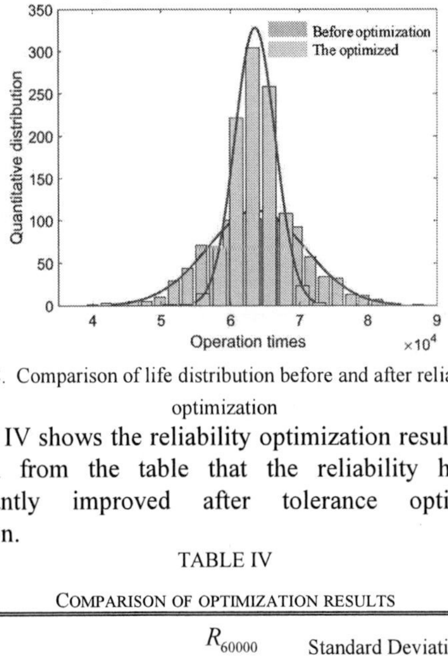

Fig. 8. Comparison of life distribution before and after reliability optimization

Table IV shows the reliability optimization results. It can be seen from the table that the reliability has been significantly improved after tolerance optimization allocation.

TABLE IV

COMPARISON OF OPTIMIZATION RESULTS

	R_{60000}	Standard Deviation of Life
Before optimization	0.713	8333.33
After optimization	0.9	3916.7

IV. CONCLUSION

Approximate modeling technology has gradually replaced computer simulation technology to solve complex engineering problems. Reasonable modeling method can ensure the accuracy and efficiency of metamodel construction. Therefore, this paper proposes a new approximate modeling method based on the concept of interpolation, which can satisfy the model accuracy in the case of small sample size when solving the problem with high degree of nonlinearity and multiple input-output.

(1) Due to the idea of interpolation method and weight function, the form of weight function is set according to the characteristics of the replacement model and the PSO method is used to solve the weight function, which can help reduce the sample size required by the replacement model and improve the accuracy of the proxy model.

(2) The effectiveness of the proposed method is verified by an engineering example where the high-dimensional input and output are highly nonlinear. Five input parameters and one output parameter are set, and the meta-modeling is carried out by using the proposed method. The calculation results show that the number of sample points required by the new method is 380, while that required by the traditional method is 2100, which saves a lot of simulation time and has certain reference significance.

(3) The tolerance design method was used to optimize the research object in this paper. The parameter tolerance of the relay electromagnetic system was optimized to improve the reliability when the number of actions was 60,000, and the reliability was increased from the initial 0.713 to 0.9, which was an increase of 26.23%. The standard deviation goes down to 3916.7.

REFERENCES

[1] J. Zhao, J.Q Chen and L. Xu, "RBF-GA: An adaptive radial basis function metamodeling with genetic algorithm for structural reliability analysis," *Reliability Engineering and System Safety*, 2019, 189:42-57

[2] S.D Sudhoff and R. Sahu, "Metamodeling of Rotating Electric Machinery," *IEEE Transactions on Energy Conversion*, 2018, 3: 1-1

[3] A. Farhang-Mehr, S. Azarm, "Bayesian meta-modelling of engineering design simulations: a sequential approach with adaptation to irregularities in the response behavior," *Computer Science*, 2005.

[4] M.L. Liu, D. Wang, J.B. Zhao and S.B. Si, "Importance measure construction and solving algorithm oriented to the cost-constrained reliability optimization model," *Reliability Engineering & System Safety*, 2022, 222(108406)

[5] J.M. Lucas, "Response surface methodology: process and product optimization using designed experiments," *3rd edition. J Qual Technol*, 2010, 42(2): 228-230

[6] D.C. Eddy, S. Krishnamurty, I.R. Grosse, J.C. Wileden and K.E. Lewis, "A predictive modelling-based material selection method for sustainable product design," *J Eng Des*, 2015, 26: 365–390

[7] A. Shokri and M. Dehghan, "A meshless method using radial basis functions for the numerical solution of two—dimensional complex Ginzburg—Landau equation. Comput Model," *Eng Sci*, 2012, 84(4): 333

[8] A.A. Mullur and A. Messac, "Extended radial basis functions: more flexible and effective metamodeling," *2005,* 43(6):1306-1315

[9] M.A. Bouhlel, J.R.R.A. Martins, "Gradient-enhanced kriging for high-dimensional problems," *Eng Comput*, 2018, 35(1): 157–173

[10] J.P. Kleijnen, "Kriging metamodeling in simulation: a review," *Eur J Oper Res*, 2007, 192(3): 707-716

[11] J.D. Martin and T.W. Simpson, " Use of kriging models to approximate deterministic computer models," *AIAA J*, 2012, 43(4): 853-863

[12] X. Wang, M. You, Z. Mao and Y. Ping, "Tree-structure ensemble general regression neural networks applied to predict the molten steel temperature in ladle furnace," *Adv Eng Inform*, 2016,30(3): 368–375,.

[13] H. Smith, "Neural networks for statistical modeling," *Van Nostrand Reinhold*, 1993.

[14] S.M. Clarke, J.H. Griebsch and T.W. Simpson, "Analysis of support vector regression for approximation of complex engineering analyses," *J Mech Design*, 2005, 127(6): 1077-1087

[15] C. Jiang, X. Cai, H. Qiu, L. Gao and P. Li, "A two-stage support vector regression assisted sequential sampling approach for global metamodeling," *Struct Multidiscip Optim*, 2018, 58(4):1657–1672

First A. Author **Deng Jie,** male, Research interest is quality consistency robust design of aerospace electromagnetic relays. In 2014, he obtained the Doctor of Engineering degree of electrical machinery and appliances

8th International Conference on Reliability of
Electrical Products and Electrical Contacts,
November 18-20, 2022

Simulation Research of Temperature Sensor in Gas Turbine under Multi-Physical Field

Yanyan Luo[1,2], Yuegang Chen[1], Shilong Du[1]

1) Hebei University of Technology, Tianjin, 300401
2) Electrical Apparatus Institute of Hebei Province, Tianjin, 300401
Email: hebut2021chen@163.com TEL: 15027510422

***Abstract*—In this paper, the temperature sensor for a certain type of gas turbine is taken as the research object, and the fluid-structure coupling simulation research is conducted on the temperature sensor for gas turbine through the Fluent module in ANSYS Workbench software. The influence of single stress such as fluid velocity, temperature and pressure in the gas turbine and the comprehensive stress under the action of multiple physical fields on the temperature sensor is analyzed. The simulation results show that the internal fluid temperature of the gas turbine is the main reason that reduces the reliability of the temperature sensor. Thermocouple as the core of temperature sensor, fluid velocity, temperature and pressure on the thermocouple measurement end of the solder joint and the reference end of the compensation line has the phenomenon of stress accumulation, will affect the reliability of temperature sensor.**

***Index Terms*—gas turbine, temperature sensor, fluid-structure interaction, fem simulative analysis, reliability analysis**

I. INTRODUCTION

As an important component to realize temperature monitoring, temperature sensor is widely used in military, commercial, scientific research, medical and other fields. Temperature sensor performance and reliability of the system has great effect on the quality of the temperature detection, but inside the gas turbine is a typical high temperature and high pressure, high speed of complex fluid system, gas turbine with temperature sensor, under the circulation fluid loading, have influence on the temperature sensor structure and performance, directly affects the reliability of the temperature sensor. In serious cases, the temperature sensor may break, endangering the safe and reliable operation of the gas turbine. Therefore, the simulation research of temperature sensor for gas turbine under the action of multiple physical fields is one of the key points in the reliability design process of temperature sensor.

In recent years, many scholars at home and abroad have studied the temperature sensor under the coupling effect of multiple physical fields. In literature [1], data simulation was designed for the influence of the internal flow velocity of the aero-engine on the temperature sensor. Through the two-dimensional data simulation and three-dimensional data simulation results of the temperature sensor at different speeds, it was concluded that the speed is not the main reason for the failure of the temperature sensor in the specified range of speed. Literature [2] combines the flow field and temperature field of aircraft, and develops a numerical analysis method for the coupling of flow field and temperature field. Type of aircraft engine in literature [3] a total airflow temperature sensors for 3 d modeling and CFD simulation analysis, get the dynamic characteristic of the sensor under a specific condition, with the improvement of air quality velocity is obtained, the time constant of sensors will gradually become smaller, and in the stage of low mass velocity present relatively obvious non-linear characteristics. In reference [4], the heat transfer between solid and fluid under fluid-structure interaction was studied.

In this paper, through the analysis of the mathematical model of the fluid field, the fluid-structure unidirectional coupling simulation of the temperature sensor is carried out by using the Fluent module and Static Structural module in ANSYS software, which provides a theoretical basis for the design optimization of the temperature sensor structure.

II. FLUID MATHEMATICAL MODEL ANALYSIS

Conservation of momentum, mass and energy are the three laws that must be followed by all fluid motion and heat transfer [5].

A. Mass conservation equation

In the flow field, the flow of fluid needs to be constrained by the mass conservation equation. When solving the fluid physical model, the total tensor form of the mass conservation equation is:

$$\frac{\partial \rho}{\partial t} + \frac{\partial(\rho \mu_i)}{\partial x_i} = S_m \tag{1}$$

In Equation (1), $\frac{\partial \rho}{\partial t}$ -- density change rate; $\frac{\partial(\rho \mu_i)}{\partial x_i}$ -- divergence of mass flow density; S_m -- the quality of the sparse phase to the continuous phase.

B. Momentum conservation equation

In the flow field, the mathematical expression of the momentum conservation theorem is the equation of motion.

$$\int_v \frac{(\partial \vec{U})dV}{\partial t} + \oint (\vec{n} * \vec{U}) \rho \vec{U} dS = \int \rho \vec{f} dV + \oint \prod * \vec{n} dS \quad (2)$$

In Equation (2), f is the mass force acting on the fluid per unit mass; π -- Stress tensor at dS on the surface of a micro element.

C. Energy conservation equation

In the flow field, the process of temperature transfer is involved. Based on the energy conservation equation, the heat transfer between fluid and solid is solved. The differential form is as follows:

$$\frac{\partial}{\partial t}\left[\rho\left(\frac{1}{2}U^2 + e\right)\right] + \frac{\partial}{\partial x_j}\left[\rho\left(\frac{1}{2}U^2 + e\right)u_j\right] = \rho(f_i u_i + q) + \frac{\partial}{\partial x_j}(\sigma_{ij} u_i + \lambda \frac{\partial T}{\partial x_j}) \quad (3)$$

III. FINITE ELEMENT SIMULATION FLOW

In this paper, the solid model of temperature sensor is constructed through Solidworks, and then the model is imported and merged through the DM module of ANSYS software. The Fluent module in ANSYS Workbench software is used to simulate and analyze the internal flow field of the gas turbine where the temperature sensor is located. The flow field calculation results are transferred to the temperature sensor as boundary values by the one-way separation fluid-solid coupling method. Finally, the stress analysis of solid structures is completed by the Static Structural module.

A. The establishment of three-dimensional model

The temperature sensor is mainly composed of thermocouple, insulation filler, protective tube and lead compensation wire. Fig. 1 shows the actual temperature sensor.

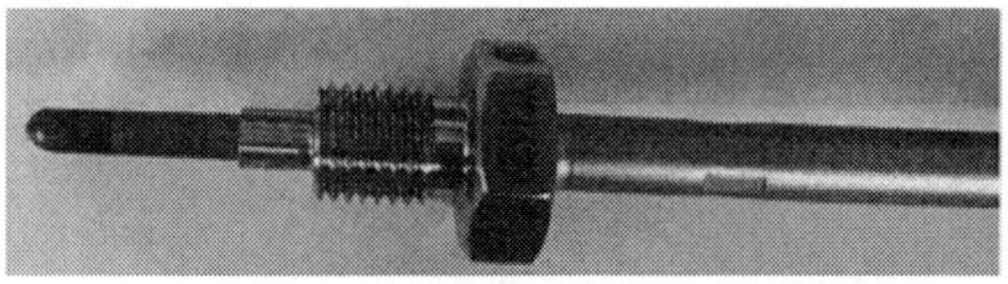

Fig. 1. Physical picture of the temperature sensor

In order to ensure that the model is as close to reality as possible, ensure the accuracy of simulation results, and save computing time, the temperature sensor model will be the physical probe on the top of the solder joint coating is omitted, the solder joint is replaced by a half sphere, and the lead wire and its protective rubber are omitted.

A cuboid of 50mm×50mm×70mm was selected for the fluid field model. The simplified 3D solid model is shown in Fig. 2.

B. Material property setting

Since there is no material involved in the temperature sensor in the original material library of ANSYS Workbench, the required materials need to be defined in the material library and then applied to each component of the temperature sensor. The material parameters of each element in the temperature sensor solid model are shown in TABLE I.

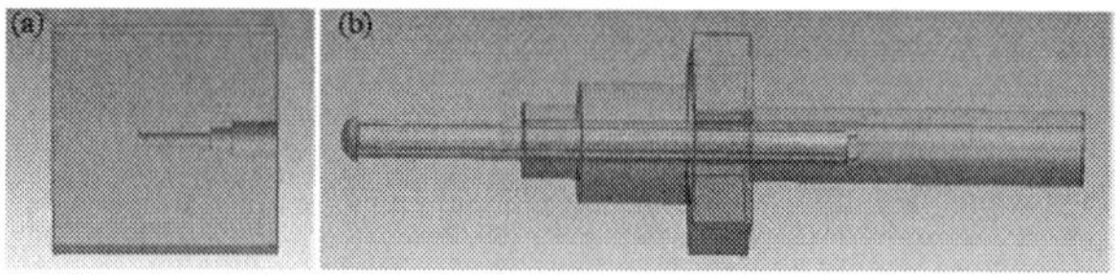

Fig. 2. 3D solid model of temperature sensor and fluid domain :(a) fluid domain; (b) temperature sensor

TABLE I
MATERIAL PARAMETERS OF EACH COMPONENT OF TEMPERATURE SENSOR

Materials	Filler	Protective tube	Thermocouple wire I	Thermocouple wire II
Young Modulus (GPa)	160	242	224	206
Thermal Expansivity (10^{-7}/°C)	138	156	180	180
Thermal Conductivity W/(m.K)	0.06	15	15	15
Specific heat capacity (J/(g.K))	0.209	0.30	0.46	0.42
Density (g/cm^3)	3.58	9.5	8.4	8.902
Poisson ratio	0.36	0.24	0.24	0.24

C. Mesh generation

Under the premise of considering the simulation accuracy and operation speed, the mesh of the fluid domain and the temperature sensor is automatically divided. The mesh size of the fluid domain is set as 3mm, and the mesh size of the temperature sensor is set as 1mm. The mesh generation results of fluid and temperature sensors are shown in Fig. 3 respectively.

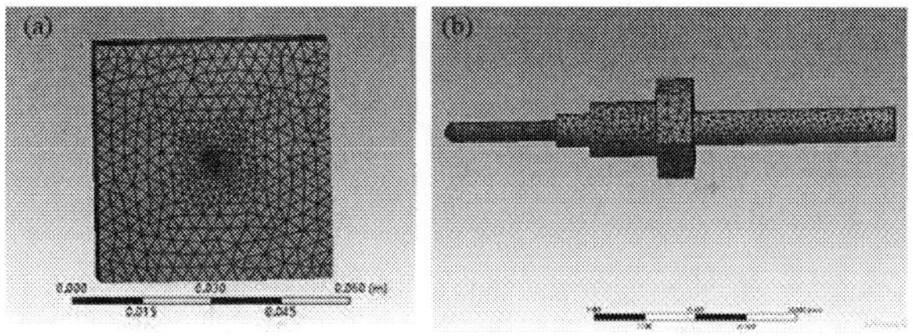

Fig. 3. Mesh partition diagram of fluid domain and temperature sensor :(a) fluid domain; (b) temperature sensor

D. The setting of constraints

In the setting of boundary conditions, the upwind inlet of the flow field where the temperature sensor is located is defined as the velocity inlet, and the outlet of the flow field of the temperature sensor is defined as the pressure outlet. The velocity and temperature of the inlet and the temperature of the outlet are set in the Boundary Conditions in the Fluent module. It is assumed that the fluid velocity is uniform, the gravity field is not considered, and the wall boundary is fixed without slip.

IV. INTERPRETATION OF RESULT

A. Analysis of simulation results under a single physical field

In order to study the influence of fluid velocity on temperature sensor, the fluid velocity of 70 m/s, 80 m/s, 90 m/s, 100 m/s, 110 m/s and 120 m/s were respectively used for simulation. The equivalent stress distribution and equivalent displacement response of temperature sensor at different speeds were used to analyze the influence of fluid velocity on the structure of temperature sensor. Fig. 4 shows the overall equivalent stress and displacement of the temperature sensor when the fluid velocity is 100 m/s.

According to the effect diagram (a) in Fig. 4, under the action of flow velocity, the stress of temperature sensor is mainly concentrated at position 1, 2, 3 and 4 of temperature sensor, especially position 1, whose maximum stress can reach 649.58Kpa. This is because the fluid flow at high speed will be squeezed at the junction of the boss when it impacts the temperature sensor, and the resulting stress will be relatively concentrated. It can be seen from the equivalent displacement diagram in Fig. 4(b) that the temperature sensor galvanic wire has the largest displacement at the solder joint, and the maximum displacement can reach 1.581×10^{-4} mm. This deformation may cause the solder joint loose or even fall off, which directly affects the reliable operation of the temperature sensor.

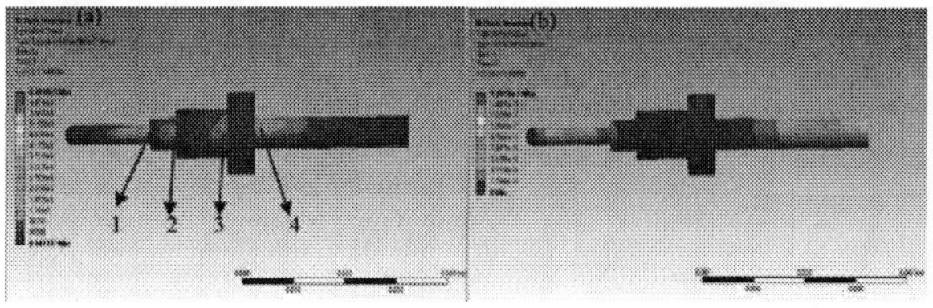

Fig. 4. Equivalent stress and equivalent displacement of temperature sensor at 100 m/s flow rate :(a) equal effect diagram; (b) equivalent displacement diagram

The high-pressure air flow inside the gas turbine affects the structure of the temperature sensor itself, deforming it, resulting in a change in the performance of the temperature sensor. By analyzing the variation characteristics of the equivalent force and displacement of each component of the temperature sensor under the internal pressure of different gas turbines, the influence of pressure on the structure of the temperature sensor is analyzed. Fig. 5 shows the equivalent force and equivalent displacement of the temperature sensor at an internal pressure of 0.12 MPa in a gas turbine.

As can be seen from Fig. 5(a), when the internal pressure of the gas turbine is 0.12mpa, the stress of the temperature sensor is mainly concentrated at the thread of the temperature sensor, and the maximum stress can reach 1.149Mpa. It can be seen in Fig. 5(b) that the displacement of the solder joint of the temperature sensor is the largest, and the maximum displacement can reach 7.2×10^{-6} mm. Compared with the direct impact of high flow velocity, the internal pressure produces 1.76 times of stress on the temperature sensor, but it has a smaller deformation, because the direct impact of flow velocity on the temperature sensor is larger, but the impact of pressure is smaller.

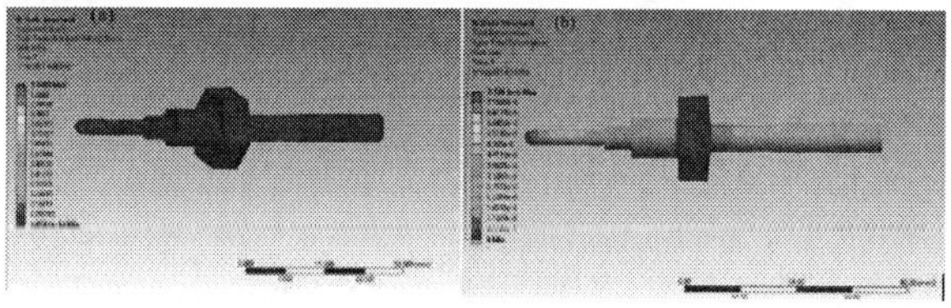

Fig. 5. Equivalent stress and equivalent displacement of temperature sensor under 0.12mpa pressure :(a) equal effect diagram; (b) equivalent displacement diagram

In high temperature load, temperature is easy to cause thermal expansion of temperature sensor structure. In order to resist thermal expansion, the components of temperature sensor produce thermal stress. The thermal expansion coefficient mismatch of different materials of temperature sensor components will lead to the transfer and accumulation of thermal stress and thermal strain. Excessive thermal stress may damage the structure of temperature sensor and affect the performance of temperature sensor. Temperature is the most important factor affecting the performance of temperature sensor.

The equivalent stress and strain of the temperature sensor when the internal temperature of the gas turbine is 1000℃ are shown in Fig. 6.

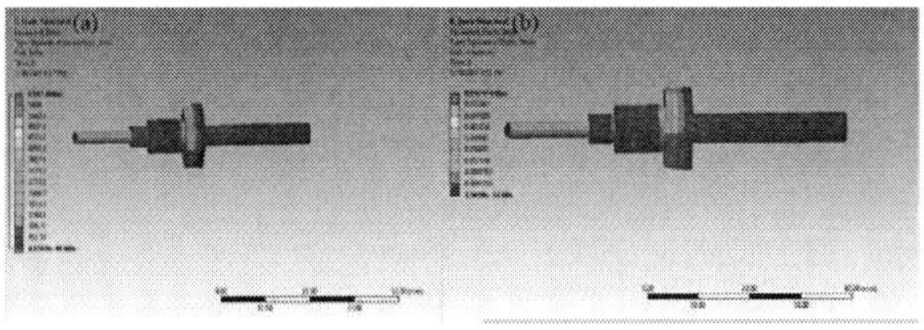

Fig. 6. Equivalent stress and strain of the gas turbine temperature sensor at 1000 °C :(a) equivalent stress; (b) equivalent strain

Because the difference of thermal expansion coefficient between different materials of temperature sensor is large, the thermal stress is more concentrated among different materials. The maximum equivalent stress of the temperature sensor appears on the protective tube and insulation filler, as shown in Fig. 6(a), and its maximum value is 6347.4Mpa.

As can be seen from Fig. 6(b), under high temperature load, the thermal expansion of the temperature sensor causes deformation of each component of the sensor, and the degree of deformation determines the thermal strain of the temperature sensor. The maximum strain of the temperature sensor appears on the protective tube, and the maximum strain value is 3.7554×10^{-2}. The strain of the protective tube is too large, because the thickness of the protective tube is thin and the thermal expansion coefficient is large, which leads to a large strain. Secondly, the strain at the nut is also large, this is because the nut material is superalloy, its thermal expansion coefficient is greater than other materials.

As the core element of temperature sensor, the reliability of thermocouple directly affects the performance of temperature sensor. Fig.7 shows the equivalent stress distribution of thermocouple under different conditions.

As can be seen from the equal-effect diagram of thermocouple wire in Fig. 7(a), the overall stress value of thermocouple is not very large, and the maximum stress value is 123.84 KPa, which is located in the corresponding position of the maximum stress position of temperature sensor. As shown in Fig. 7(b), since the thermocouple at the solder joint is directly in contact with the interior of the gas turbine and the rest part is protected by the filler oxide, the top of the thermocouple is subjected to relatively large stress. Overall, the stress of the thermocouple is not large, and the maximum equivalent stress is 0.1302 MPa. Therefore, the internal pressure of the gas turbine will have a great impact on the solder joints of the temperature sensor, and there may be a risk of solder joints falling off under the long-term cumulative effect. Fig. 7(c) The maximum equivalent stress of the thermocouple appears at the welding joint at the top of the thermocouple, and the maximum equivalent stress is 3181.6Mpa. This is because the top of the thermocouple is the solder joint of the temperature sensor.

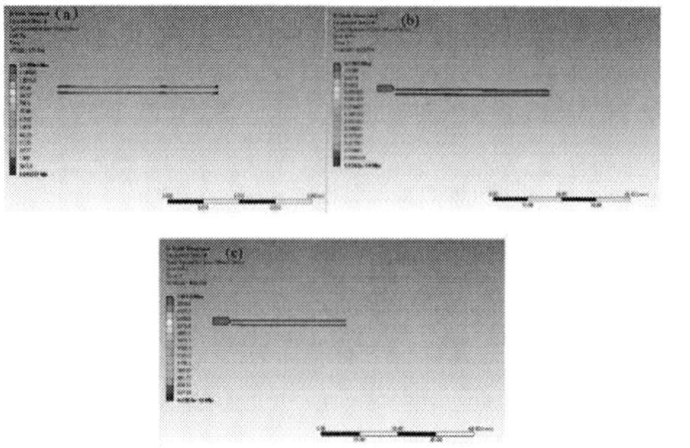

Fig. 7. Equivalent stress distribution of thermocouple under different conditions :(a) equal-effect diagram of thermocouple at 100 m/s flow rate; (b) equal-effect diagram of thermocouple under 0.12mpa pressure; (c) equal effect diagram of thermocouple at 1000 °C

B. *Analysis of simulation results under the action of multiple physical fields*

The boundary conditions imposed by the simulation under the action of multiple physical fields are: the temperature load range is 600~1200℃, the pressure range is 60~120 KPa, and the velocity range is 60~120 m/s.

Fig. 8 shows the deformation diagram of each part of the temperature sensor at 1000℃, 0.12 MPa and 100 m/s.

As can be seen from Fig. 8, under the joint action of temperature, pressure and velocity, each component of the temperature sensor will undergo large deformation, which is mainly caused by thermal expansion, velocity and pressure. When the fluid temperature is 1000℃, the velocity is 100 m/s and the pressure is 0.12 MPa, the maximum deformities of the shell, the protective tube, the filling material and the thermocouple are 0.419 mm, 0.231 mm, 0.231 mm and 0.242 mm, respectively.

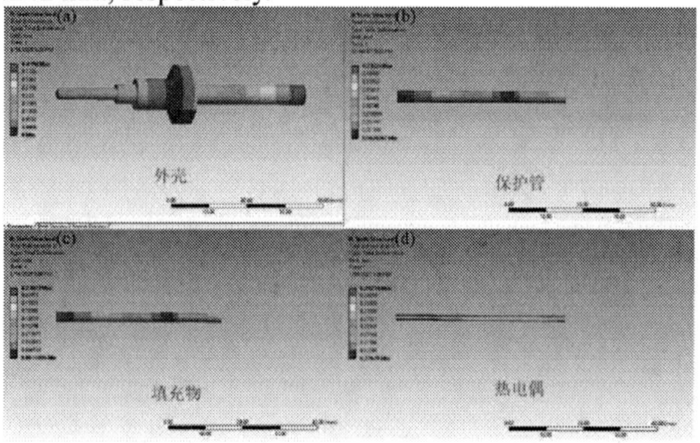

Fig. 8. Deformation diagram of each part of the temperature sensor at 1000 °C, 0.12 MPa and 100 m/s

Under the condition of multi-physical field coupling inside the gas turbine, the deformations of each part of the temperature sensor under different temperature loads, pressure loads and velocity loads are shown in Fig. 9.

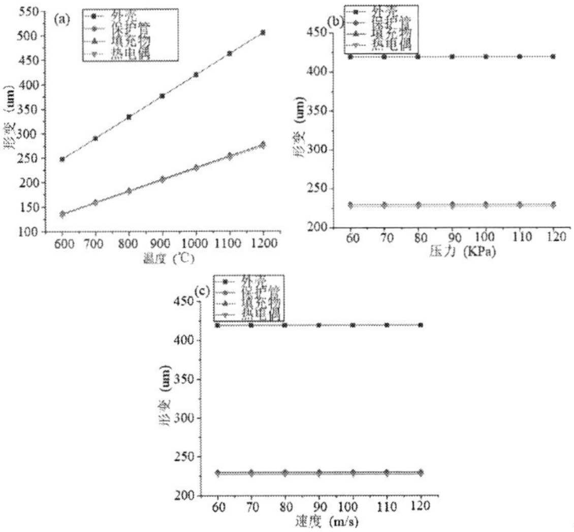

Fig. 9. Deformation of various parts of the temperature sensor under multi-field coupling is affected by different loads :(a) temperature; (b) pressure; (c) speed

It can be seen from Fig. 9(a) that under the coupling of multiple physical fields, when the fluid pressure and velocity are constant, the maximum deformation of each element of the temperature sensor increases linearly with the continuous increase of temperature. Among them, the deformation of the protective tube, filling material and thermocouple is almost the same, but there are slight differences. The reasons have been analyzed above. However, it can be seen from Fig.9(b) and (c) that when the fluid temperature is constant, the deformation of each part of the temperature sensor is almost constant with the increase of velocity and pressure. The reason verifies that the deformation under temperature load is much larger than that caused by velocity and pressure load, so the deformation of temperature sensor under different speed and pressure conditions is almost unchanged.

V. CONCLUSION

Through simulation analysis, when the single stress increases, the stress and displacement of the temperature sensor show a linear growth trend, and it is obtained that the equivalent stress generated by the temperature sensor is the largest, the pressure is the second, the flow rate is the smallest. Under the coupling of multiple physical fields inside the gas turbine, the equivalent stress of the temperature sensor increases with the increase of temperature, but does not increase significantly with the increase of flow rate and pressure, indicating that the temperature is the main factor that constitutes the damage of the temperature sensor when the gas turbine is working. Thermocouple as the core of the temperature sensor, speed, temperature and pressure on the thermocouple contact solder joint and the end of the lead connection has the phenomenon of stress accumulation, will affect the reliability of the temperature sensor.

REFERENCES

[1] Qu Wenchao. Failure mechanism analysis of Platinum Wire Temperature Sensor [D]. Dalian University of Technology, 2017.

[2] Huang Chunsheng, Wu Jie, Fan Xuji. Numerical Analysis of Coupling Flow Field and Structure Temperature Field of Aircraft [J]. Mechanics in Engineering,2004, (02):24-26.

[3] Zhang Jin, Jiang Zhiheng, Wen Tieduan. Simulation of dynamic characteristics of a total airflow temperature sensor and analysis of related influencing factors[J]. Industrial Instrumentation and Automation Device, 2020(01): 61-64.

[4] Huang S Q, Huang Q Y, Gao S, et al. Stress Analysis for the Cooler of Lead-bismuth Loop Based on Fluid-solid Coupling[J]. Nuclear Science&Engineering, 2013, 33(2): 186-193.

[5] Li Wan. Computational Fluid Dynamics [M]. Wuhan: Huazhong University of Science and Technology Press, 2004.

8th International Conference on Reliability of
Electrical Products and Electrical Contacts,
November 18-20, 2022

Quality Consistency Optimization Method for Railway Signal Relay Based on Renewable Cost Contribution Rate

Xinghai Zhao [1,2], Jie Deng [1], Wentian Luo[2]

[1] Harbin Institute of Technology, Harbin, 150001

[2] Shenyang Railway Signal Co., Ltd, Shenyang, 110023

Email: zhaoxinghai@live.cn TEL:15204048820

***Abstract*—Railway signal relay is vital equipment in railway signal system, and its quality is critical to the safety and efficiency of railway system. The design and manufacture process of this kind of relay is based on the traditional mode, and the consistency of batches of products has certain difference, resulting in that manufacturing dispersion has a great impact on the consistency of batch products and high manufacturing cost. In order to improve the quality consistency and manufacturing efficiency, and avoid unnecessary cost, a tolerance design method based on the renewable cost contribution rate has been proposed in this paper, which comprehensively considers the improvement of consistency when the tolerance values decrease and costs increase in a non-linear form. Adaptive algorithm is adopted to obtain the tolerance optimization strategies, in order to ensure the optimization accuracy and effectively improve the optimization efficiency. Finally, this method has been applied on quality optimization of a type of railway signal relay, the effectiveness of the proposed method has been verified.**

***Index Terms*—robust tolerance design, quality consistency, uncertainties, manufacturing cost, railway signal relay**

I. INTRODUCTION

Railway signal relay is the vital control equipment in railway signal system, which is widely used in track circuit, point switch control circuit, signal control circuit and other vital circuits. Its product quality has a crucial impact on the operation efficiency, safety and reliability of railway system [1]. Manufacturing process of the railway signal relay follow the traditional mode, due to the dispersion of the objective existence, products can't completely according to the center value of design parameters for processing and assembly, result in random fluctuations deviation between the practical quality characteristics and the theoretical design value, affect the quality of the batch product level [2]. The quality fluctuation of batches of products has a great impact on failure rate and maintenance cost, and excessive increase of tolerance requirements to improve product consistency will also lead to the increase of parts rejection rate and manufacturing cost. Therefore, how to balance the relationship between the improvement of quality level and the increase of manufacturing cost under the current manufacturing conditions has important research value for the optimization of product life cycle cost (LCC).

According to Taguchi method, quality loss can be used to quantitatively describe the losses caused to society by quality problems of products after delivery. For railway signal relays, quality losses may include train outage, accidents, and increase of maintenance costs. Taguchi also proposed the concept of total quality loss as the sum of quality loss and manufacturing cost. In the process of product quality optimization, product quality level and manufacturing cost should be comprehensively evaluated, and the reduction of quality loss should be greater than the increase of manufacturing cost [3]. At present, robust tolerance design is widely used in the mechanical and electrical industry to optimize product quality [4]. Although this method could improve product quality level, it does not consider the rise of cost after optimization. Under actual conditions, when the tolerance changes, the corresponding manufacturing cost will also change. Therefore, only by recalculating the cost contribution coefficient and updating the objective function at each step of the tolerance change can the correctness and rationality of the next optimization process be guaranteed. This paper proposes a quality consistency optimization method based on renewable cost contribution rate, which can timely renew the total loss objective function and tolerance step control model according to the change of manufacturing cost and quality loss, so as to reasonably control the tolerance change of each iteration. By using this method, the increase of manufacturing cost and the total loss of quality can be minimized when the quality fluctuation is reduced to the optimized target range. Finally, this method has been applied on quality optimization of a type of railway signal relay, the availability of the proposed method has been verified.

II. Quality Optimization Model

A quality optimization method proposed in this paper could balance the quality fluctuation and the manufacturing cost by studying the relationship between the tolerance range, quality loss and manufacturing cost, manufacturing cost model and quality loss model is established for this incorporated into the total loss model and cost contribution model. Finally, the tolerance iteration model is used to combine the tolerance variation with the cost variation to obtain the optimal solution.

A. Manufacturing Cost Model

The manufacturing cost model is established according to manufacturing capability and technological process to quantify the relationship between cost and tolerance. At present, tolerance-cost models are widely used in different manufacturing processes include exponential model [5], modified exponential model [6], reciprocal square model [7], reciprocal power model [8], etc. According to the statistics of the actual data of tolerance and cost of parts and components, the reciprocal power model is more suitable to represent the relationship between manufacturing cost C_i and tolerance T_i for the products involved in this paper:

$$C_i = a_0 T_i^{-a_1} \tag{2.1}$$

Where a_0 and a_1 are actual manufacturing condition coefficients. The manufacturing cost of a single part can be obtained according to (2.1), and the total cost of components or the whole product C_M can be expressed as:

$$C_M = \sum_{i=1}^{n} C_i(T_i) \tag{2.2}$$

B. Quality Loss Model

The quality loss caused by the deviation of output characteristics is quantitatively described by the quality loss function $L(y)$:

$$L(y) = k(y-m)^2 \tag{2.3}$$

Where y is the actual output characteristic of the product, m is the ideal output characteristic, $(y-m)$ is the deviation of the output characteristic, and k is the quality loss coefficient. In this paper, $(y-m)$ is the tolerance. If the tolerance is symmetrically distributed, $(y-m)$ could be calculated as:

$$y - m = T_i / 2 \tag{2.4}$$

Substitute (2.4) into (2.3), and obtain the quality loss when the tolerance is T_i:

$$L_{T_i} = k\frac{T_i^2}{4} \tag{2.5}$$

Assuming that the maximum function deviation could accepted by users is y_0, and the quality loss at this deviation is A, the quality loss coefficient k can be calculated as:

$$k = \frac{A}{y_0^{\,2}} \tag{2.6}$$

The total loss is the sum of manufacturing cost and quality loss, so the total loss can be expressed as:

$$L_T = \sum_{i=1}^{n} C_i(T_i) + \sum_{i=1}^{n} k\frac{T_i^2}{4} \tag{2.7}$$

Based on the concept of contribution rate in traditional tolerance design method, the cost contribution rate is proposed in this paper to quantify the impact of tolerance on total manufacturing cost. Cost contribution rate $\lambda_i(T_i)$ can be defined as the percentage of the cost increase ΔC_i caused by the reduction of tolerance Δt_i in the total cost increase ΔC_M caused by all the reduction of tolerance, which can be expressed as:

$$\lambda_i(T_i) = \frac{\Delta C_i}{\Delta C_M} = \frac{C_i(T_i - \Delta T_i) - C_i(T_i)}{\sum_{i=1}^{n}[C_i(T_i - \Delta T_i) - C_i(T_i)]} \tag{2.8}$$

C. Tolerance Iteration Model

In the traditional robust tolerance design, the contribution coefficient of each controllable factor reflects its significant influence on the output characteristics. On this basis, the contribution coefficient ρ_i in each iteration is set as the weight of the tolerance step control function. By using the most commonly used three-level orthogonal design (where level 2 is the central value of the input parameter, and levels 1 and 3 are the lower and upper limits of the input parameter), the contribution rate ρ_i of each parameter is calculated as follows:

$$\rho_i = \rho_{il} + \rho_{iq} = \frac{S_{il} + S_{iq} - 2V_e}{S_T} \tag{2.9}$$

Where ρ_{il} and ρ_{iq} are the primary contribution rate and secondary contribution rate of the input parameter, S_{il} and S_{iq} are the sum of the squares of the first fluctuation and the sum of the squares of the second fluctuation of input parameter, and V_e is the error variances. S_T is the sum of the squared total deviations of the output characteristics.

In the initial stage of the tolerance iteration, the tolerance step should be set to a large value to speed up the convergence of the optimization. With the progress of iteration, the optimization goal is gradually approached, and the step size should be gradually reduced to improve the optimization accuracy. Therefore, according to the standard deviation σ_q of the quality fluctuation range and the standard deviation σ_{tar} of the target range, an acceleration coefficient β is introduced to control the tolerance change step, and could be calculated as:

$$\beta = \frac{\delta^3}{1000} \tag{2.10}$$

where $\delta = \sigma_q / \sigma_{tar}$ is the magnitude of the current quality fluctuation beyond the optimization target. Then, based on the traditional tolerance design method and the renewable cost contribution rate proposed in this paper, a model can be derived, which changes the tolerance with the number of iterations as:

$$\Delta T_{i+1} = \frac{\rho_i}{\lambda_{T_i}} \beta T_i \tag{2.11}$$

III. TOLERANCE OPTIMIZATION PROCESS

The tolerance optimization process is shown in Figure 1. First, the input parameters and their initial tolerance are set as the initial conditions, and the acceptable output parameter range is taken as the quality consistency optimization target. Then the experimental scheme is determined by orthogonal experimental design. After calculating the output parameter, the contribution factor ρ_{ij} and cost contribution rate λ_{T_i} of each input parameter are determined by contribution rate analysis. If the quality fluctuation range σ_q of the current tolerance is still larger than the target range σ_{tar}, the current scheme is set as the input condition of the next iteration, and the cost contribution rate λ_{T_i} of the input parameters is updated. Then, the above process is performed to reduce the tolerance until the quality fluctuation range of the output parameter achieves the target.

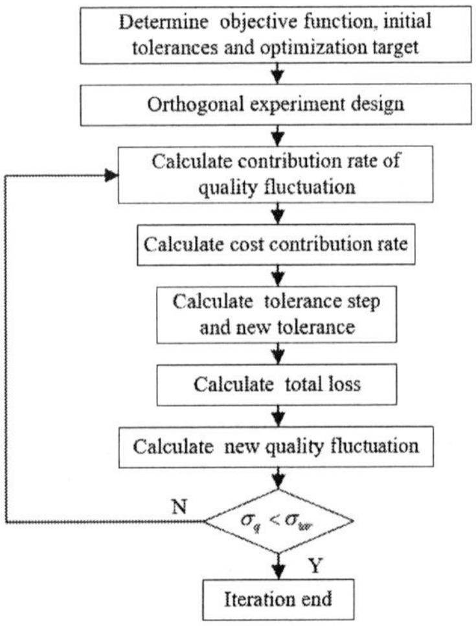

Fig. 1. Tolerance optimization process

IV. CASE STUDY

The above method is applied to the tolerance design of the electromagnetic system of railway signal relay to reduce the fluctuation of product quality and minimize the total loss. The electromagnetic system of railway signal relay is a typical clap-close structure, as shown in Fig. 2. It is composed of iron core, coil, yoke, armature and magnetic spacer. The armature rotates with the edge at the top of the yoke a to drive contact closure and disconnection. After magnetic circuit system assembly, the actual travel of the armature could reflect the working air gap and the motion range of contacts, which has a decisive impact on the performance of the whole product. Therefore, the armature travel is taken as the main parameter to describe the consistency of product quality.

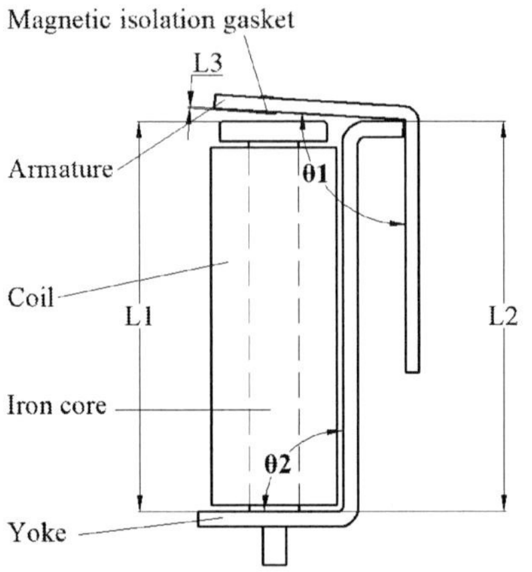

Fig. 2. Structure of the electromagnetic system

According to the structure of magnetic circuit system, five design parameters affecting the armature travel were selected as input parameters for robust design optimization. The input parameters are selected as shown in Table 1.

TABLE 1
CENTER VALUES AND TOLERANCES OF INPUT PARAMETERS

Input parameters	Central values	Initial tolerances
L1-Core highness (mm)	100	±0.2
L2-Yoke highness (mm)	100	±0.2
L3-Magnetic isolation gasket thickness(mm)	0.2	±0.0.05
θ1 -Armature angle (°)	93	±0.2
θ2 -Yoke lower angle (°)	90	±0.2

A. *Establishment of Manufacturing Cost Model*

The manufacturing cost model of input parameters is established according to (1), and its coefficient and initial manufacturing cost are shown in Table 2. As the tolerance of input parameters decreases, the manufacturing cost increases nonlinearly, as shown in Fig. 3.

B. *Calculation of Quality Fluctuation Contribution Rate*

Three-level orthogonal experimental design was adopted, and the fluctuation contribution rate ρ_i, cost contribution rate λ_i and tolerance step ΔT_i of each input parameter were calculated according to (8) - (10). The calculation results are shown in Table 3.

C. *Tolerance Optimization process*

The novel robust tolerance design method considering the contribution rate of each parameter is adopted in the tolerance optimization process, and the optimization results are with the traditional method.

Based on the new method proposed in this paper, the cost contribution rate will update after each tolerance iteration. The cost contribution rate changes of each design parameter in the optimization process are shown in Fig. 4.

TABLE 2
MANUFACTURING COST MODEL COEFFICIENTS AND INITIAL COST

Input parameters	a_0	a_1	Initial cost (CNY)
L1	10.5	1.1	21.4
L2	11.8	1.15	26.6
L3	0.2	1.05	4.2
θ1	12.2	1.2	27.6
θ2	12.9	1.13	29.1

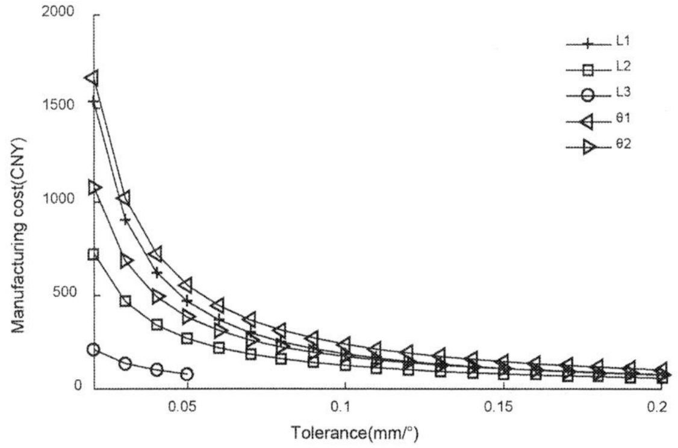

Fig. 3. Manufacturing cost model with input parameters

TABLE 3
CALCULATION RESULTS OF CONTRIBUTION RATES IN THE FIRST ITERATION

Input parameters	ρ_i (%)	λ_i (%)	ΔT_i
L1	33.48	13.84	0.0299
L2	33.48	9	0.0444
L3	2.09	47.23	0.0005
θ1	15.47	17.4	0.0106
θ2	15.47	12.52	0.0147

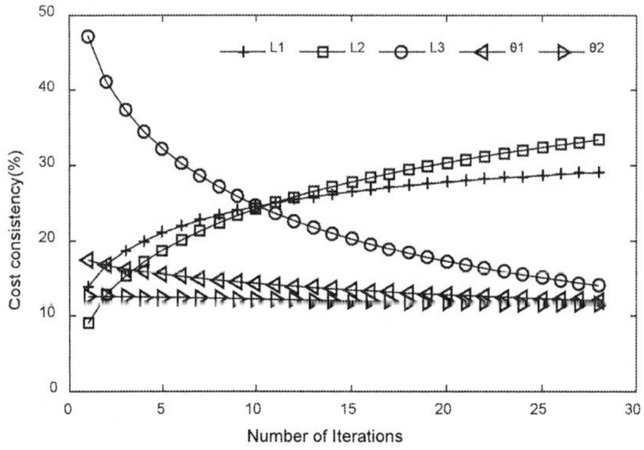

Fig.4. Variation of cost contribution rate during iteration

As shown in Fig.4, the cost contribution rate of L3 decreases significantly as the number of iterations increases. Since the processing difficulty of this part is lower, which causes that the manufacturing cost does not increase significantly when the tolerance decreases. During the iteration process, the cost contribution rates of L1 and L2 keep increasing, which will have a great impact on the overall manufacturing cost. In each iteration, the cost contribution rate and quality fluctuation contribution rate are combined to calculate the tolerance step of each input parameter for the next iteration, and the new tolerance value is obtained. The variation of tolerance during the iteration is shown in Fig. 5.

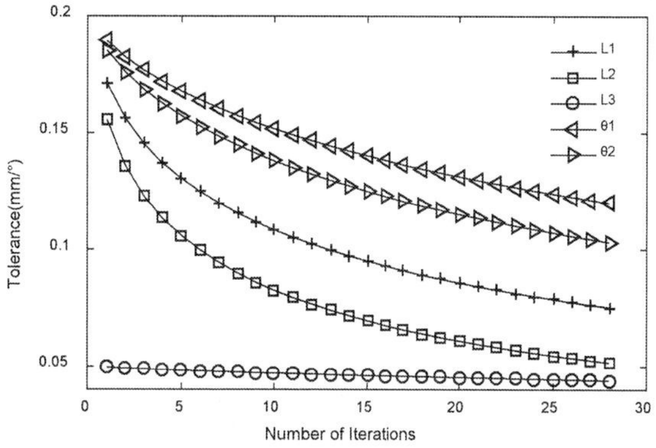

Fig. 5. Variation of tolerance during iteration

As shown in Fig. 5, since this method considers the cost contribution rate of each parameter, even though the quality contribution rate of L1/L2 and θ1/θ2 are the same, their tolerance variations are not the same. The tolerance allocation of input parameters after optimization with the novel method and the traditional method is shown in Table 4.

TABLE 4
TOLERANCES AFTER OPTIMIZATION

Input parameters	With novel method	With traditional method
L1	±0.075	±0.053
L2	±0.052	±0.053
L3	±0.044	±0.041
θ1	±0.12	±0.132
θ2	±0.1	±0.132

The comparison of quality loss, manufacturing cost and total quality loss between the two optimization methods during interaction is shown in Fig. 6-Fig. 7.

Comparing Fig. 6 and Fig. 7, it can be seen that the two methods have almost the same variation trend of cost and loss, but the increase of manufacturing cost is slightly smaller after the novel method considering cost factors is adopted. The novel method could also reduce the total quality loss, In other words, this method could distribute the tolerance more reasonably and avoid unnessary waste when achieving the same quality optimization goal.

V. VERIFICATION

Monte Carlo method was adopted to generate 1000 virtual samples to simulate the quality characteristics of batch products. Then the quality characteristics of the tolerance schemes before and after optimization are analyzed and compared to verify the effectiveness of the improved robust tolerance design method. The optimized armature travel distribution is shown in Fig. 8. By adopting the qualification threshold of 1.75 ~ 1.95 mm, the product consistency of the optimized can be improved from 0.557 to 0.861, and the quality level is significantly improved.

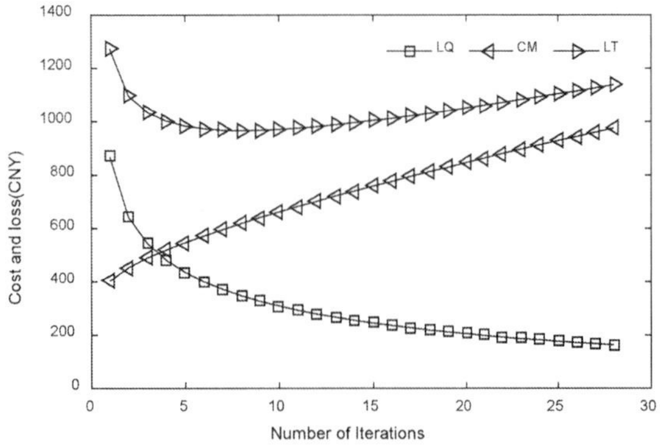

Fig. 6. Variation of cost and loss during novel optimization

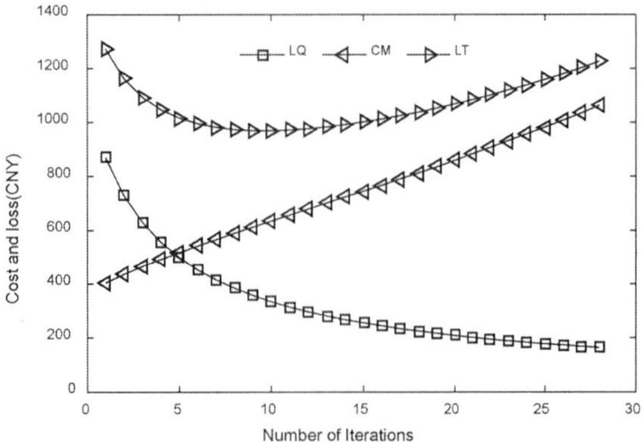

Fig. 7. Variation of cost and loss during traditional optimization

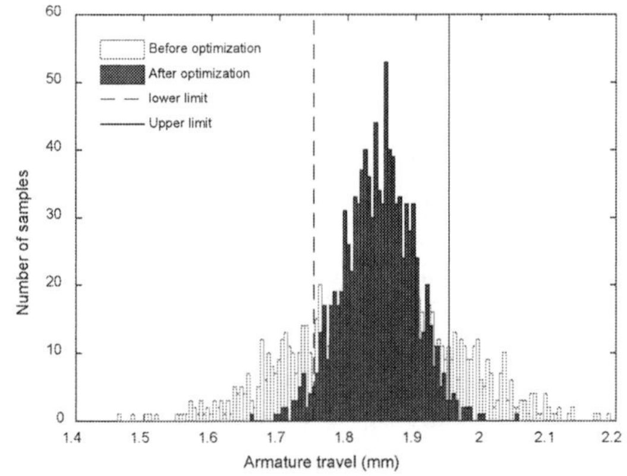

Fig. 8. Armature travel distribution optimization result

VI. Conclusion

In order to improve the accuracy of quality consistency optimization, a novel tolerance design method based on renewable cost contribution rate has been proposed in this paper. During the iteration process of this method, the cost contribution rate is updated with the tolerance variation of each parameter, and the tolerance step is controlled reasonably to obtain the best optimization path.

The manufacturing cost model of electromagnetic system of railway signal relay has been established, and the cost contribution rate of each design parameter was obtained. The contribution rate of each input parameter to the quality fluctuation of relay is calculated by orthogonal experiment design. Combined with cost contribution rate and quality fluctuation contribution rate, the tolerance step control model and total loss objective function are updated. The optimal path of total loss optimization is gradually determined by rationally allocating the control tolerance of each design parameter until the quality fluctuation enters the acceptable range.

After the quality consistency optimization, Monte Carlo method was used to verify the optimization effect. The product consistency of the optimized can be improved from 0.557 to 0.861, and the effectiveness of the proposed method was proved.

References

[1] Wenqing He, 6502 Electrical Interlocking Circuit. China Railway Press, 1997.

[2] Huimin Liang and Guofu Zhai, Three Stages Design of Aerospace Electromagnetic Relay. Harbin Institute of Technology Press, 2014.

[3] Taguchi G, Performance Analysis Design. International Journal of Production Design, 1978, (16): 521-530.

[4] Diplaris, S. C., and M. M. Sfantsikopoulos, Cost–Tolerance Function. A New Approach for Cost Optimum Machining Accuracy. International Journal of Advanced Manufacturing Technology 16.1(2000):32-38.

[5] Speckhart, F. H, Calculation of Tolerance Based on a Minimum Cost Approach. Journal of Engineering for Industry, 1972, 94 Ser B (2): 447-453.

[6] Dong, Z. and A. Soom, Automatic optimal tolerance design for related dimension chains. Manufacturing Review, 1990, 3(4): 262-271.

[7] Spotts, M. F, Allocation of tolerance to minimize cost of assembly. Journal of Engineering for Industry, 1973, (6): 762-764.

[8] Sutherland, G. H. and Roth, B, Mechanism design: accounting for manufacturing tolerances and costs in function generating problems. Journal of Engineering for Industry, 1973, 97 Ser B (1): 283-286

Design of Arc State Observer Based on Wavelet Energy Spectrum

Qiangli Si [1,2,3], Xin Zheng[1,2,3]
[1)] College of Electrical Engineering and Automotion, Fuzhou University, Fuzhou, Fujian, 350000
[2)] Fujian Key Laboratory of New Energy Generation and Power Conversion, Fuzhou, Fujian, 350000
[3)] Engineering Research Center of Smart Distribution Grid Equipment, Fujian Province University, Fuzhou, Fujian, 350000
Email: 1015784738@qq.com TEL:15038156868

Abstract— **The suppression result of the breaking arc is an important factor affecting the reliability of the zero-current breaking control of the AC switch, but there is a lack of intuitive and effective detection methods. Aiming at this problem, an arc state observer and its model based on wavelet energy spectrum are proposed in this paper. In the breaking process, the arc voltage is transformed by wavelet energy spectrum, and the ratio of the characteristic value of the arcing peak and the arc-extinguishing peak is used to effectively identify the three arc states which is stable burning, unstable burning, and extinction. The arc observer model is built and simulated in Simulink. The cSPACE platform is used to design a hardware-in-the-loop prototype of arc observer and the practicability and effectiveness of the observer are verified by the measured arc data. The simulation and experimental results show that the arc observer can realize the quantitative detection of the arc state as well as provide effective feedback for improving the reliability of the zero-current breaking of the AC switch.**

Keywords— **zero-current breaking, wavelet energy spectrum, arc state observer, hardware-in-the-loop**

I. INTRODUCTION

As an important component in the automatic control of the power system, the low-voltage AC switch plays an important role in the construction of the smart grid. Arc suppression is the main goal of the intelligent control of AC switches. At present, it is mainly realized by the hybrid switching technology combined with power electronic devices or the zero-current breaking technology [1]. However, due to the lack of an intuitive and effective arc state detection method, the effect of arc suppression is limited.

At present, the AC arc detection technology is mainly based on the simulation model, the physical characteristics, and the time-frequency domain characteristics [2]. The arc simulation model has been improved by the researchers to reflect the dynamic characteristics of the arc, and has a good match with the experimental results [3]. References [4-5] consider the influence of multiple physical factors to establish a simulation model of arc motion characteristics, and use COMSOL software to analyze the motion characteristics of arcs under different breaking distances, currents, magnetic field strengths and breaking speeds. The detection of the physical characteristics of the arc relies on the physical phenomena such as sound, light, and heat emitted when the arc is generated. The CCD image sensor is used to study the arc energy and shape evolution during the arc breaking process [6]. Literature [7-8] proposed a method of synchronous fusion of light, electricity, and magnetism to detect arc faults, avoid arcs from forming stable ones and reduce faults, and establish an optical acquisition system for arc images to realize the visualization process of arcs. In addition, the colorimetric thermometry method is used to study the energy change in the dynamic process of the arc, but the detection cost of the physical characteristics of the arc is high and difficult to popularize. The arc time-frequency domain feature detection is to collect the arc current and voltage signals for time-frequency domain transformation, and analyze the dynamic characteristics of the arc. References [9-10] analyze the arc current waveform in the time-frequency domain, and believe that the spectral characteristics of the arc will change significantly when an arc fault occurs. Combined with random forest, decision tree, time-frequency domain threshold and other methods, the arc state can be quickly detected. Other studies have shown that the time-frequency characteristics of the switching arc voltage will get more obvious eigenvalues after wavelet energy spectrum transformation [11], so the use of time-frequency domain analysis to study the arc state has great application value.

The literature [12] shows that there are three arcing states in the AC arc combustion process: stable arcing, unstable arcing, and arc-extinguishing, which can indicate the combustion trend of the arc, and then reflect the suppression effect of the breaking arc. Previous studies have shown that the arc voltage waveform is inherently related to the arc burning trend. When the arc tends to extinguish, the arc voltage change rate is high; when the arc reignites, the arc voltage change rate is low [13]. Based on the above research, this paper proposes an arc state observer based on dyadic wavelet energy spectrum algorithm for arc detection in AC switch breaking process. The arc voltage waveform is used to directly reflect the changes of the arc combustion and distinguish three states: stable arcing, unstable arcing, and arc-extinguishing. The arc state observer uses the arc voltage waveform to directly reflect the changes of the arc combustion and distinguish three states. The arc state observer model is built by Simulink and the measured arc voltage waveform is input into the simulation platform, the output results of the arc state observer are analyzed, and the appropriate threshold is selected to distinguish different arc states. At the same time, the arc state observer model was imported into the cSPACE hardware-in-loop platform to design a rapid control prototype system, and the function signal generator was used to output the measured arc voltage waveform as its input sampling signal to verify the practicability of the designed arc state observer.

II. Modeling And Simulation Of Arc State Observer

In order to study the effectiveness of the arc state observer in arc detection, this paper uses the binary wavelet energy spectrum algorithm to compare the wavelet energy spectrum transform waveforms of the arc voltage in different arcing states, and builds the arc state observer model in Simulink.

A. *Wavelet Energy Spectrum Model*

Dyadic wavelet, as a wavelet frame system, has strong denoising ability and can accurately identify a certain mutation feature or the trend of signal change in continuous signals. In this paper, the derivative function of the cubic B-spline is selected as the wavelet mother function. Since the collected data is a discrete signal, the binary wavelet transform formula of the discrete signal is selected [11].

$$\begin{cases} S_{2^j}f(n)=\sum_k h_k S_{2^{j-1}}f\left(n-2^{j-1}k\right) \\ W_{2^j}f(n)=\sum_k g_k S_{2^{j-1}}f\left(n-2^{j-1}k\right) \end{cases} \qquad (1)$$

In the above formula, j is the scale of wavelet decomposition and $S_{2^0}f(x)$ is the original signal. h_k and g_k are the low-pass and band-pass filter impulse response coefficients corresponding to the wavelet mother function, and their values are respectively:

$$g_0=-2, g_1=2, h_{-1}=h_2=0.125, h_0=h_1=0.375$$

The research shows that the fourth-scale detail component of the dyadic wavelet will produce more obvious features when the switching arc is generated. Since the input signal is an AC signal, the output result also has the characteristics of the AC signal, so the wavelet energy spectrum model is introduced to make an integrate operation of the fourth-scale detail component. The wavelet energy time spectrum transformation of the signal varying with time can be obtained [14], and its formula is:

$$E_{2^j}f(x)=\left|W_{2^j}f(x)\right|^2 \qquad (2)$$

The wavelet energy spectrum model is used to show the change trend of the arc voltage signal in the form of energy, which is more conducive to reflect the change of the arc state.

B. *Model design of arc state observer*

In the process of arc combustion, the zero-current phenomenon causes the arc voltage waveform to produce arc peak and arc extinction peak. And in the time-spectrum waveform of the wavelet energy spectrum, it is found that the fourth-scale detail component (E_4) of the wavelet energy spectrum will change significantly at the arc-extinguishing peak and the arc-burning peak. Therefore, in this paper, an arc state observer is built according to the ratio of the maximum value of E_4 value (arcing peak value of the arc voltage) to the next largest value (the arc extinguishing peak value of the arc voltage) in half a cycle as the criterion for judging the arc combustion state.

Fig.1 shows the arc voltage waveform and the change of $E4$ from burning to extinguishing. The power supply voltage U=150V, the breaking distance is 0.01mm, the sampling frequency is 50 kHz, the resistance R=37Ω, and the carbon electrode is used in this experiment.

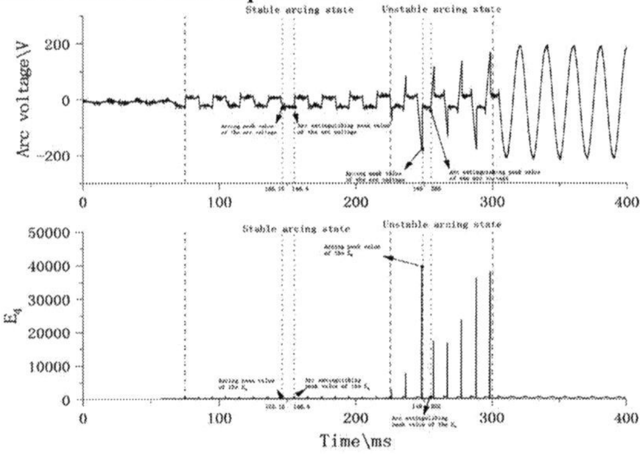

Fig.1 AC arc voltage and E_4 value

By analyzing the arc voltage waveform, it is found that the change of the arc voltage waveform has different performances in different time periods, and the wavelet energy spectrum amplitude also corresponds to different performances. In the initial stage of arc combustion, the arc voltage waveform has a small change range, the arc combustion is in a stable state and tends to reignite, and the corresponding E_4 value of the arc peak and the arc extinction peak has a small change range. However, with the increase of the breaking distance, the E_4 value of the arcing peak also increases slowly, and this stage is the stable arcing stage. In the stage of unstable arcing, the arc voltage waveform fluctuates greatly. The most obvious feature is that the E_4 value changes very sharply during the arcing peak, but the E_4 value of the arc-extinguishing peak is basically stable and much smaller than the arcing peak. After the arc is extinguished, the voltage waveform is a sine wave, and the corresponding E_4 value remains stable. Literature [15] obtained through many experiments that the wavelet energy spectrum eigenvalues in the zero-current region of the voltage waveform can intuitively judge the arcing trend, and the wavelet eigenvalues have similar performances under different voltages, load currents, and power factors.

It can also be seen from Figure 1 that in the stable arcing stage, the E_4 value changes relatively gently, and the ratio of the E_4 value between the arc burning peak and the arc extinguishing peak is small. When the arc is in an unstable arcing state, the ratio of the two is larger. After the arc is extinguished, this ratio approaches zero. Therefore, a threshold value K_1 can be set to determine whether the arc is in a stable arcing state or an unstable arcing state by comparing the ratio of the E_4 values of the arc burning peak and the arc extinguishing peak.

The arc state observer is built based on the above principles. The arc voltage is sampled for half a cycle each time (sampling frequency is 50kHz), and then wavelet energy spectrum transformation is performed. Among them, the maximum value of E_4, which is defined as E_{4z}, in the half cycle corresponds to the peak value of the arcing peak, and the second largest value which is defined as E_{4c} corresponds to the peak value of the arc extinguishing. Compare the maximum value and the second maximum value, and judge the arc combustion state according to the ratio of the two and output the result. After the arc is extinguished, the value of E_{4z}/E_{4c} is less than 2 and remains basically unchanged. The workflow of the arc state observer is shown in Figure 2.

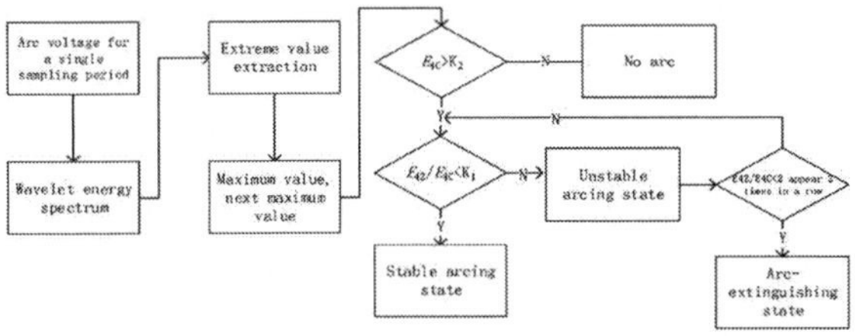

Fig.2 Flowchart of the arc state observer

When the arc is not burning, the E_4 value of the arcing peak will become larger but the E_4 value of the arc-extinguishing peak will still be low. Therefore, arcing or not should be judged when the extreme value is extracted to prevent the arc state observer from misjudging. Because the arc must pass through the arc extinguishing peak when it is burning, the main factor for judging the arc state is the arc extinguishing peak E_4 value, namely E_{4c}, so the lower limit K_2 should be set for E_{4c} in the arc state observer, and the judgment program will be started when E_{4c} exceeds K_2, which can effectively avoid misjudgment.

The simulation model built by Simulink is shown in Figure 3. The model uses the From Workspace module to import the experimental data, and then obtains the arc voltage waveform E_4 value through wavelet energy spectrum transformation. Then, the arc state module extracts the extreme value, determines its effectiveness, and calculates the ratio of the maximum value to the second maximum value. Finally, according to the ratio, the arcing state is judged, and the results are sent to the corresponding Scope module for display.

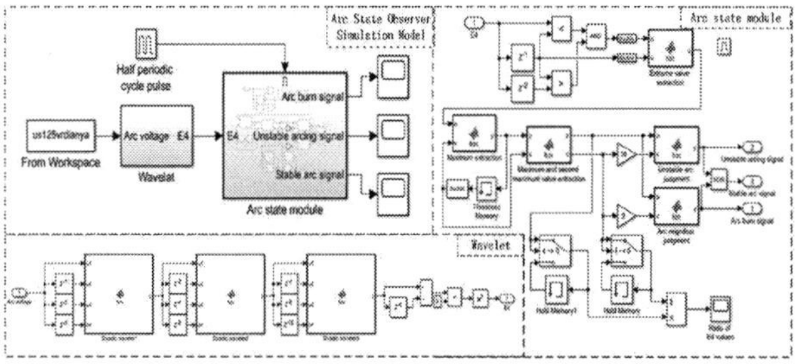

Fig.3 Simulation model of arc state observer

III. Simulation Analysis and Verification

In this paper, the measured arc waveform data obtained from experiments under different voltage levels, different load currents and different power factors are imported into the arc state observer model, and then the relationship between the voltage waveform and the E_{4z}/E_{4c} and E_{4c} value is analyzed to determine the appropriate threshold K_1 and K_2.

The experiment adopts the measured waveform of pure resistive load and sampling frequency of 50 kHz under different voltage conditions. Input the measured waveform into the model and take the E_{4c} values before and after the arc combustion in Table I. From Table I, the E_{4c} value before arcing is less than 2, and the E_{4c} value after arcing is greater than 15. In order to effectively judge whether arcing occurs, this paper sets K_2=10.

Table I E_{4c} of 3 sampling periods before and after arc start at different voltage

Voltage\V	E_{4c}					
	Before the arc			After the arc		
26	0.977	0.772	1.645	28.980	15.660	16.015
38	1.496	1.032	1.466	38.615	40.880	66.972
50	1.607	1.604	1.457	61.399	60.096	134.633
220	1.389	1.378	1.325	53.778	686.745	621.438

A. Analysis under different system voltages

The measured waveform of arc voltage under different system voltage conditions are input into the arc state observer for analysis. In this group of experiments, only the voltage was changed, other conditions remained unchanged, and the voltages were adjusted to 75V, 150V and 220V for experimental analysis. The sampling frequency of the system is 50 kHz, the load current is 4A, the pure resistive load is adopted, and the breaking speed is 0.08mm/s. The simulation results under different system voltages are shown in Figure 4.

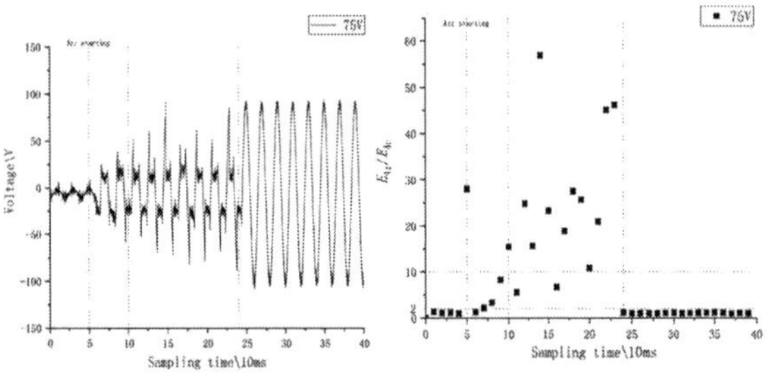

(a) 75V voltage waveform and time-varying diagram of E_{4z}/E_{4c}

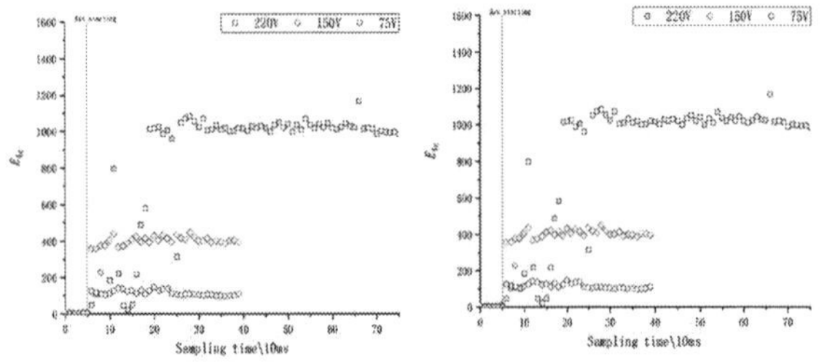

(b) Time-varying diagram of E_{4c} (c) Time-varying diagram of E_{4z}/E_{4c}

Fig.4 Output results of different arc voltages

It can be seen from Fig. 4(a) that after the arc starts to burn, it enters a stable arcing state, and the arc voltage fluctuation is stable at this stage, so the E_{4z}/E_{4c} value rises slowly. After the E_{4z}/E_{4c} value exceeds 10 for the first time, it enters an unstable arcing state, and the arc voltage and E_{4z}/E_{4c} value fluctuate violently at this stage. After the arc is extinguished, the E_{4z}/E_{4c} values are both less than 2, and it can be confirmed whether the arc is extinguished by comparing it several times in a row (this article takes the value of less than 2 for two consecutive times to determine the arc extinguishing). From Fig. 4(b) and Table I, E_{4c} is less than 10 before arcing. After arcing, E_{4c} remains basically unchanged under the same voltage, and with the increase of voltage level, E_{4c} also increases. In Fig. 4(c), the E_{4z}/E_{4c} values of different arcing states have the same trend under different voltage conditions.

The reason for the above changes is that when the arc burns, the tendency of the arc to extinguish or reignite is the result of the competition between the arc voltage recovery strength and the dielectric recovery strength. When the arc is stable, the voltage recovery strength is much higher than the dielectric recovery strength, so the amplitude of E_{4z} is small and grows slowly in each sampling period. When the arc is unstable, the dielectric recovery strength is close to the arc voltage recovery strength and increases continuously, which results in the fluctuates of E_{4z} in each sampling period. During the arc combustion process, E_{4c} remains basically unchanged in each sampling period. It can be seen that by taking $K_1=10$ and $K_2=10$, the judgment of different arc states can be realized under different voltage conditions.

B. Analysis under different system currents

In order to study the effect of current on arc combustion, only the current was changed in this group of experiments, and other conditions remained unchanged. Choose system voltage 150V, load current choose 3A, 4A, 5A. The simulation results obtained by inputting the arc state observer under different system currents are shown in Figure 5.

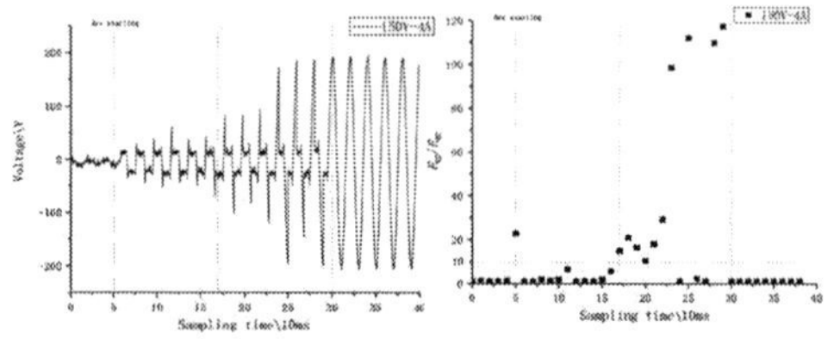

(a) 150V-4A voltage waveform and E_{4z}/E_{4c} time-varying diagram

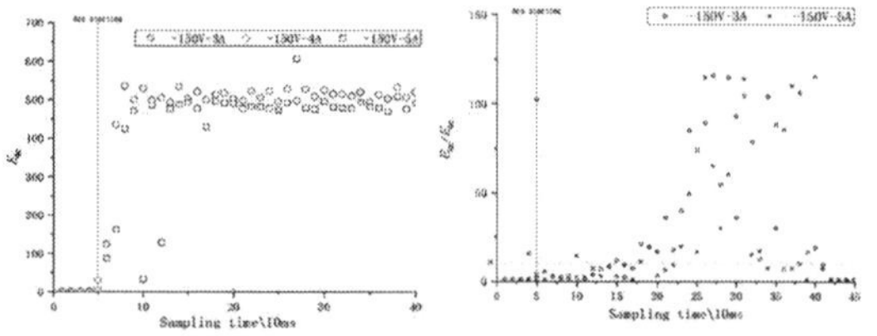

(b) E_{4c} time-varying diagram (c) E_{4z}/E_{4c} time-varying diagram

Fig.5 Output results of different arc currents

It can be seen from Figure 5(a) that after the arc combustion starts, it enters a stable arcing state. At this stage, due to the small fluctuation of the arc voltage, the E_{4z}/E_{4c} value changes slightly. After the E_{4z}/E_{4c} value exceeds 10 for the first time, it enters the unstable arcing state, and the arc voltage and E_{4z}/E_{4c} value fluctuate violently at this stage. When the E_{4z}/E_{4c} value is less than 2 for two consecutive times, it indicates that the arc is extinguished. As can be seen in Fig. 5(b), the arc starts to burn after E_{4c} exceeds 10. After arcing, the E_{4c} value in each sampling period is basically stable under different current conditions, and does not change with the current size. It can be seen from Fig. 5(c) that the E_{4z}/E_{4c} values of different arcing states have the same trend under different current conditions.

This phenomenon occurs because there are zero-current regions in the arc current when the arc burns. E_{4c} and E_{4z} appear at the beginning and end of the zero-current period sparely. Therefore, in the circuit with small current (below 5A), the arc state threshold setting is not affected by the load current, and can still be set as $K_1=10$ and $K_2=10$.

C. Analysis under different power factors

This group of experiments uses the measured waveforms of resistive-inductive loads with power factors of

0.48, 0.79, and 0.96. The contact voltage is 150V, the load current is 4A, and the other parameters remain unchanged. The output results of different power factors are in Figure 6.

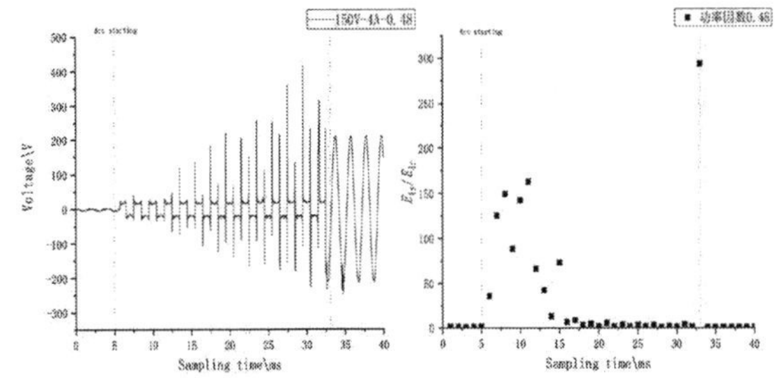

(a) Power factor 0.48 voltage waveform and E_{4z}/E_{4c} time-varying diagram

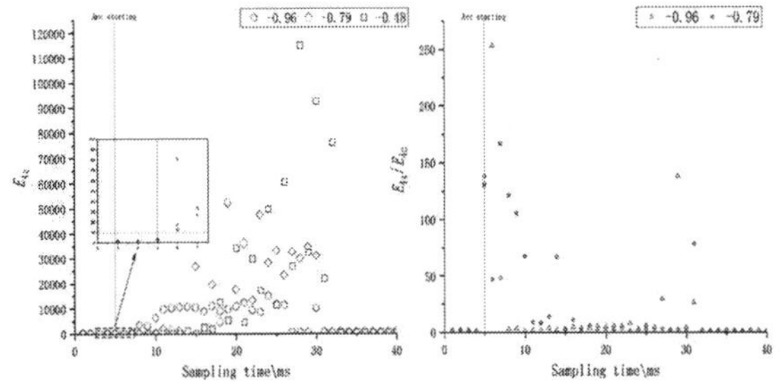

(b) E_{4c} time-varying graph (c) E_{4z}/E_{4c} time-varying graph

Fig.6 Different power factor output results

It can be seen from Figure 6(a) that under the condition of power factor of 0.48, the E_{4z}/E_{4c} value directly exceeds 10 and enters an unstable arc state after arc combustion. At this stage, both the arc voltage and the E_{4z}/E_{4c} value fluctuate violently, and the arc-extinguishing state is entered after the E_{4z}/E_{4c} value is less than 2 for two consecutive times. Figure 6(b) shows that when the arc E_{4c} exceeds 10, the arc starts to burn. With the increase of the breaking distance and the power factor, results in more fluctuate of E_{4c}. It can be seen in Fig. 6(c) that the E_{4z}/E_{4c} values of different arcing states have the same trend under different power factor conditions.

The reason for the change in Figure 6(b) is that the presence of inductive load increases the amplitude of E_{4z} at the initial stage of arcing, while E_{4c} has little effect. As the breaking distance increases, the inductance makes the arc more difficult to extinguish, and at the same time, the magnitude of E_{4c} becomes larger and more fluctuate. Thus, when the arc burns under the condition of resistive inductive amplitude, it will directly enter the unstable arc state. Therefore, setting K_1=10 and K_2=10 can also distinguish the arc combustion state under different load conditions.

D. Simulation verification

Through the analysis of simulation experiments under different voltages, different currents and different power factors, the following conclusions can be drawn: During AC arc combustion, the change of E_{4z}/E_{4c} value can distinguish different arc states during arc combustion. After arcing, E_{4z}/E_{4c} <10 indicates that the arc is in a stable combustion state. When E_{4z}/E_{4c} exceeds 10 for the first time, the arc enters an unstable arcing state. If the value of E_{4z}/E_{4c} is less than 2 for two consecutive times, the arc is extinguished. Therefore, set K_1=10, K_2=10 in the arc observer model of Simulink, and conduct simulation verification. The experimental conditions are: voltage 50V, 100V and 200V, resistance 50Ω, breaking speed 0.08mm\s, sampling frequency 50 kHz. The simulation results are shown in Table II.

Table II Simulation verification results

Voltage \V	E_{4c}				E_{4z}/E_{4c}			
	Before the arc		After the arc		Stable arc		Unstable arc	
50	0.579	0.762	75.93	171.3	1.95	9.83	19.9	19.2
100	3.377	2.611	459.1	256.9	5.12	7.12	11.9	4.19
200	1.593	2.139	598.2	242.2	4.62	6.78	18.7	36.2

The data in Table II show that the arc state observer can effectively identify different arcing states. In order to ensure that the arc state observer model can be applied in the hardware system, the cSPACE hardware-in-the-loop platform is used to verify the feasibility of the arc state observer. In practical applications, the results of wavelet energy spectrum transformation will be different under different sampling frequencies, and E_{4z} and E_{4c} will also be different, so the arcing threshold K_2 should be changed according to the actual sampling frequency, and K_1 represents the ratio between E_{4z} and E_{4c}, not affected by the sampling frequency.

IV. Rapid Prototype Design of Arc State Observer Based on cSPACE

The cSPACE rapid control prototype and hardware-in-the-loop development system is developed based on TMS320F28335DSP. The control algorithm is designed by Matlab/Simulink, the input and output ports are replaced with the corresponding cSPACE modules, and then the entire module can be compiled to generate DSP code. After running on the control card, the corresponding control signal can be generated, to conveniently realize the control of the controlled object. After the compilation is completed, the cSPACE monitoring software can be used to monitor the system in real time.

A. Rapid Prototype System Design

In this paper, the input and output of the simulation system are changed to AD and DA modules, and the communication module is used to send the data of the hardware-in-loop platform to the upper computer (the simulation step size is 0.001). As shown in Figure 7, the model can be run on the cSPACE platform after being compiled and downloaded.

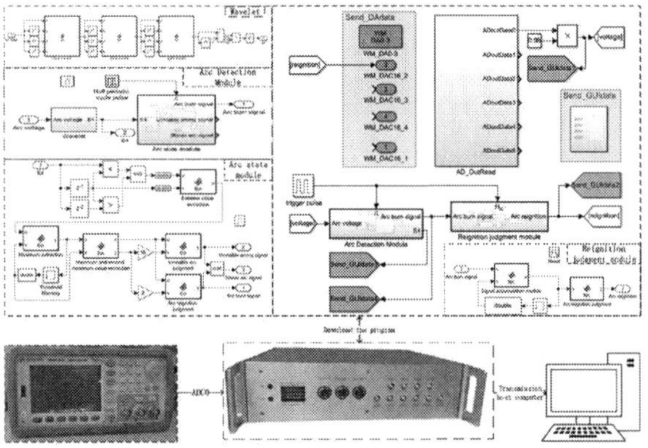

Fig.7 Rapid prototype system of arc state observer

As shown in Figure 7, the measured waveform is first input into the function signal generator (using a transmission frequency of 750Sa/s and an amplitude of 500mV), and then the function signal generator is input into the rapid prototype system. Finally, use an oscilloscope or a host computer to observe the output results. The model uses cyclic pulses to control the overall runtime of the arc state observer. Among them, the arc state module compares the E_4 waveform to obtain E_{4z} and E_{4c}, and then sets K_2 to 200 (sampling frequency is 1 kHz) by the memory module, which controls the running time by triggering pulses. Whether the arc is reignited or not is judged by the outputting signals. When the output is high level, it means that the arc is reignited, otherwise it means that the arc is extinguished.

B. Experimental verification

Connect the function signal generator with the ADC0 port of the cSPACE platform, and then compile the model into it, and enable the communication line. The experiment waveform can be monitored using cSPACE watch software. The measured waveforms under different voltage, current, and power factors are imported into the function signal generator as the input signal of the observer for verification. Finally, the oscilloscope is used to observe the signal output from the DAC port which is the judgment signal for arc reignition or not. The measured data is shown in Figure 8.

It can be seen from Fig. 8(a) that under different voltage levels, the prototype can send out the arc burning signal when the arc burns. The burning signal disappears after the arc is extinguished. When the voltage is small, due to the influence of noise in the measured waveform, some arc burning signals will be missing, but it is still possible to judge whether the arc is burning. From Figure 8(b), under different current conditions, the prototype can realize the judgment of arc combustion, and can also achieve accurate judgment in the process of arc burning-extinguishing-burning. As can be seen from Figure 8(c), under different power factors, since the arc burning is more intense, more arc burning signals will be generated in a single cycle, but it is still possible to judge whether the arc is burning. It can be seen from Figure 8(d) that the arc state observer rapid prototype system based on the cSPACE hardware-in-the-loop platform can effectively identify three arcing states: stable arcing, unstable arcing, and arc-extinguishing. And it can run normally in the hardware system.

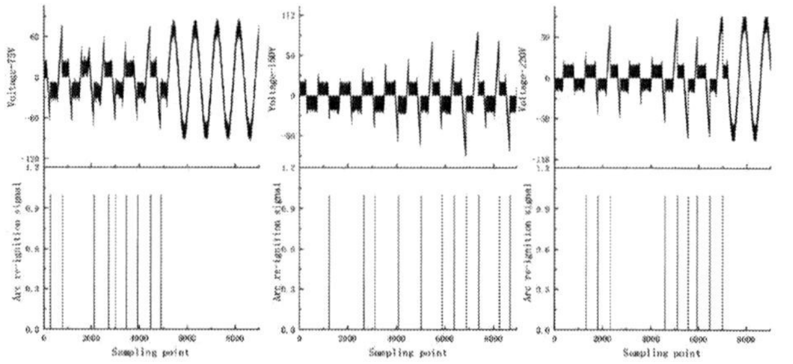

(a) Waveforms of the prototype at different voltages

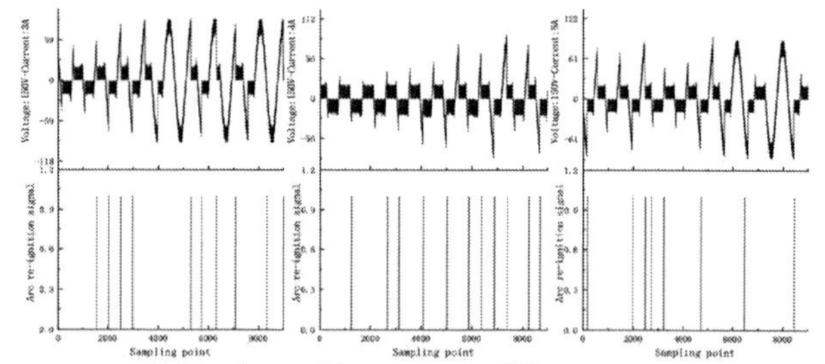

(b) Waveforms of the prototype at different currents

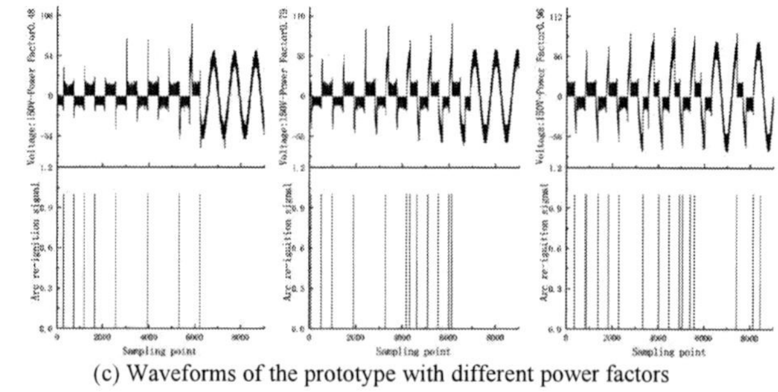

(c) Waveforms of the prototype with different power factors

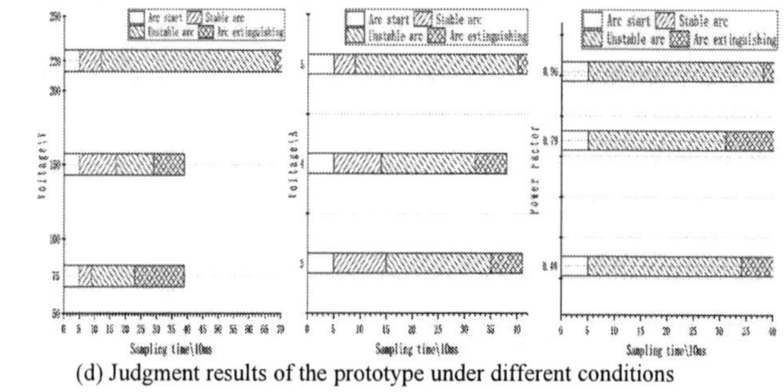

(d) Judgment results of the prototype under different conditions

Fig.8 Input waveform and output waveform under different conditions

V. CONCLUSION

This paper studies the high-scale wavelet energy

spectrum waveform of arc voltage during arc combustion, and proposes a method for judging the arc combustion state by using the ratio of E_4 value between the arc peak and the arc extinction peak. Based on this method, an arc state observer model is built, and Simulink is used to simulate and analyze the built observer. At the same time, the prototype of the arc state observer is designed using the cSPAE semi-physical semi-simulation platform, and the measured data is input to verify the practical application. The simulation and actual measurement results show that the arc state observer can identify the three states of stable arc, unstable arc and arc extinction in the arc combustion process, and it is suitable for different voltage levels, current magnitudes and power factors. Using the arc state observer to feedback the arc suppression effect, combined with the zero-current breaking control, can effectively improve the reliability of the intelligent control of the AC switch.

ACKNOWLEDGMENT

This work is financially supported by "Industry Guidin g Project of Fujian Province" (No.2021H0014).

REFERENCES

[1] Zhou Yuyuan, Liu Xiangjun. Overview of AC Contactor Structural Innovation and Intelligent Control Technology [J]. Electrical Appliances and Energy Efficiency Management Technology, 2021(02):1-7.

[2] Yu Qiongfang, Hu Yaqian, Yang Yi. Overview of low-voltage AC series fault arc detection [J]. Electrical Appliances and Energy Efficiency Management Technology, 2020(01):24-30.

[3] Wang Qingmin, Zhang Mohan, Gao Zhiwei. Research progress of off-line arc electromagnetic interference simulation of pantograph and catenary [J]. Safety and Electromagnetic Compatibility, 2021(04):69-73+99.

[4] Shi Yan,Chen Ping,Tian Hao,Chen Zhizhong,Yu Zhanwei.Arc simulation analysis of a new type of high-voltage DC relay based on Comsol Multiphysics[J].Journal of Beijing University of Chemical Technology (Natural Science Edition), 2022, 49(01): 90-97.

[5] Wang Hongrui. Simulation study on the influence of multiple physical factors on the arc and electrical erosion of DC contactors [D]. Shenyang University of Technology, 2020.

[6] Ge Yunhui. Research on the visualization of arc energy distribution of low-voltage DC electrical appliances based on CCD image sensor [D]. Shenyang University of Technology, 2020.

[7] Shu Hongchun,Dong Jun,Song Jinpeng,Li Hang,Huang Liping,Hou Qiaoge.Arc detection and protection of optical and electromagnetic synchronous fusion[J].Power Supply, 2021, 38(12): 21-28.

[8] Liu Hao. Physical simulation experiment of long-gap AC arc and its electrical characteristics [D]. Hunan University, 2019.

[9] Yang Yang, Huang Luojie, Li Ping, Shen Lifeng, Lv Zhong, Yang Shiqun. Arc fault detection method based on multi-dimensional feature extraction[J]. Journal of Electronic Measurement and Instrumentation, 2021, 35(10): 107-115.

[10] Wang Yi, Chen Jin, Li Songnong, Chen Tao, Hou Xingzhe, Xu Huaiwen.Arc fault detection based on time-frequency domain analysis and random forest[J]. Journal of Electronic Measurement and Instrumentation, 2021, 35(05):62-68.

[11] Shan Xiaojie, Zheng Xin.Research on the identification model of low voltage arc characteristics based on wavelet analysis[J].Electrical Appliances and Energy Efficiency Management Technology,2021(06):7-14.

[12] Xu Zhihong. Theoretical Basis of Electrical Appliances[M]. Beijing: Machinery Industry Press, 2014.

[13] Zheng Xin, Xu Zhihong.Discussion on the best breaking area of AC contactor[J]. Journal of Electrotechnical Technology, 2016, 31(07):198-206.

[14] Zhang Jin, Feng Zhipeng, Chu Fulei. Time-wavelet energy spectrum extraction method of rolling bearing fault features ［J］. Chinese Journal of Mechanical Engineering, 2011, 47(17): 44-49.

[15] Zheng Xin, Shan Xiaojie. Characteristics analysis and application of voltage waveform in zero zone of low-voltage AC arc current[J]. Journal of Electrotechnical Technology, 2020, 35(22):4717-4725.

Research on Primary Frequency Modulation Strategy of Microgrid Based on Wind-battery Coordination

Hengpu Qiao[1], Jingying Zhao[1,2], Linran Huang[1], Shuailiang Yao[3]

[1]Hebei University of Technology, Tianjin, 300401

[2] Electrical Apparatus Institute of Hebei Province, Tianjin, 300401

[3] State Grid Hebei Zhangjiakou Wind Power Storage and Transmission New Energy Co., Zhangjiakou, Hebei, 075000

Email: zhaojy931@hebut.edu.cn TEL:13920533283

Abstract—**Due to the low inertia of the microgrid, there are frequency fluctuation problems during the islanded operation. The rotor kinetic energy is used for primary frequency modulation of the wind turbine. This method may cause a secondary frequency drop. For operating conditions at different wind speeds, a primary frequency modulation strategy of the microgrid based on wind-battery coordination is proposed in this paper . At low wind speed, the rotor kinetic energy of the wind turbine and the energy storage system is used for primary frequency modulation. After the rotor kinetic energy exits, the energy storage system is controlled to generate additional power to protect the rotor speed. Secondary frequency drop can be effectively prevented. At high wind speed, the load shedding power of the wind turbine is introduced to improve the frequency stability. A SOC management strategy for the energy storage system considering the stable charging is proposed. The problem of insufficient standby power is effectively improved. Finally, the primary frequency modulation model of wind-battery microgrid is built with MATLAB/Simulink. The comparison experiment between the control strategy and the traditional strategy is designed. The simulation results show that with the primary frequency modulation strategy, the problem of secondary frequency drop is effectively solved, and the frequency stability of the microgrid is improved.**

***Index Terms*—-Wind-battery microgrid, Primary frequency modulation, Virtual droop control, Virtual inertial control**

I. INTRODUCTION

In recent years, environmental problems and energy crises caused by the excessive use of traditional fossil energy have been increasing. The *Opinions of the State Council on the Carbon Neutralization of Carbon Peak* show :"By 2030, the green transformation of economic and social development will achieve remarkable results. Carbon dioxide emissions per unit of GDP will drop by more than 65% compared with 2005. The proportion of non-fossil energy consumption will reach about 25%. The total installed capacity of wind power and solar power will reach more than 1.2 billion kilowatts."[1]

Microgrid is a controllable power supply system composed of a variety of distributed energy sources, which can be connected to the external grid, or run with off-grid state[2]. In the case of grid connection, the distributed energy sources participates in the frequency adjustment of the external grid. In off-grid state, the distributed energy sources need adjust the busbar frequency in the microgrid.

Domestic and foreign scholars have conducted a lot of research on the participation of wind turbines and energy storage in primary frequency modulation. The primary frequency modulation strategy of wind turbines can be mainly divided into three categories: rotor kinetic energy control, power backup control, and auxiliary frequency modulation of additional energy storage systems.

For the rotor kinetic energy control, a strategy of kinetic energy in the wind turbine rotor to suppress frequency fluctuation of the system is proposed in Ref. [3] . Ref.[4] studies the response characteristics of virtual inertial control of wind turbines. It is proved that virtual inertial control has the ability to adjust frequency and can improve the frequency stability in high-proportion wind power grids. An adaptive virtual droop control strategy for wind turbines is proposed in Ref. [5]. Based on different wind speeds, the virtual droop coefficient is adaptively adjusted to effectively improve the primary frequency modulation capability of wind turbines under different wind speeds. Ref.[6] deduces the minimum value and the steady-state value of the rotor speed during the primary frequency modulation of the doubly-fed wind turbine. A droop coefficient setting strategy and the control strategy with the speed limit are introduced. The stable rotor speed during the primary frequency modulation is ensured.

Natural Science Foundation of Hebei Province (E2019202481), company cost items(20211200011000683).

For power backup control, Ref.[7] and Ref.[8] propose a comprehensive control strategy with pitch angle control method at high wind speed and overspeed load shedding control at low wind speed. The wind turbine generator overspeed is effectively prevented. The frequency response and the life of wind turbines at different wind speeds is improved.

In terms of the primary frequency modulation of wind power assisted by the energy storage system, the superconducting energy storage system is introduced in Ref.[9]. After the rotor kinetic energy is withdrawn from the frequency support, the energy storage system generates additional power to avoid the occurrence of secondary frequency drops. Primary frequency modulation mainly deals with frequency random fluctuations. Supercapacitors are suitable with the characteristics of fast charging and discharging speed, long life and high efficiency. Ref. [10] introduced supercapacitors as energy storage systems. A coordination strategy based on wind turbine rotor kinetic energy control and supercapacitor virtual inertial control is used to enhance the frequency stability of high-proportion wind power systems. Ref.[11] states a comprehensive virtual inertial control strategy for wind turbines with negative inertial control. Frequency fluctuation is suppressed in the initial stage of frequency fluctuation. Speed up frequency recovery when frequency recovery. This strategy effectively solves the problem that traditional inertial control hinders the system frequency recovery process.

At present, there are few references proposed a feasible strategy for primary frequency modulation of wind-battery coordination based on independent microgrid operation conditions. According to the control method and operation characteristics of wind turbine, energy storage and microgrid, a frequency response model is established in this paper. The wind speed is divided into high wind speed and low wind speed. A combination frequency modulation strategy of wind turbinesand and storage system is proposed which consider the secondary frequency drop at different wind speeds. The comparison experiment between the traditional constant coefficient energy storage droop control primary frequency modulation strategy and the adaptive variable coefficient energy storage droop control primary frequency modulation strategy is designed. The method effectiveness is verified.

II. System Model

A. Typical microgrid topology

A typical stand-alone microgrid topology is shown in Figure 1[12]. Various distributed energy sources, energy storage systems, diesel generators, and in-station loads are connected to the microgrid AC bus by power electronic converters. The microgrid bus can be connected or disconnected from the external grid through a static switch (PCC) [13].

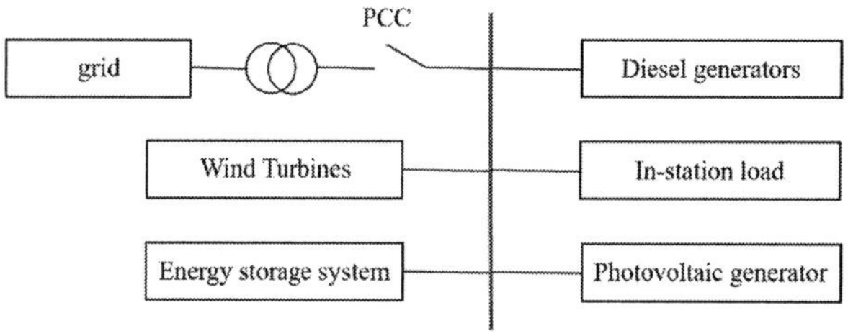

Fig.1. Typical microgrid topology

The regional equivalence method is introduced. The actual power grid module is replaced by the module transfer function, which simplifies the simulation model design and reduces the model error interference [14].

B. Wind turbine model

(1) *Energy model*

The output active power of the wind turbine is mainly related to the wind speed, rotor speed, pitch angle and other conditions. The captured wind energy P_m is expressed by (1).

$$P_m = 0.5\rho A v^3 C_p(\lambda, \beta) \quad (1)$$

Where, ρ is the air density; R is the radius of the rotor; v is the wind speed; C_p is the wind energy utilization coefficient, C_p is the function of the tip speed ratio λ and the pitch angle β, and C_p is expressed as:

$$C_p = 0.5176(116/\gamma - 0.4\beta - 5)e^{-21/\gamma} + 0.0068\lambda \quad (2)$$

$$\gamma = 1\Big/\left(\frac{1}{\lambda + 0.08\beta} - \frac{0.035}{\beta^3 + 1}\right) \quad (3)$$

$$\lambda = \frac{\omega R}{v} \quad (4)$$

Where, γ is the intermediate variable; ω is the rotational angular velocity of the wind turbine rotor.

When the wind speed is constant, the output power of the wind turbine can be controlled by the rotor speed or the pitch angle of the wind turbine.

(2)*Rotor kinetic energy model*

Wind turbines do not have primary frequency modulation characteristics because the frequency is decoupled from the rotor speed. With normal operation, the grid frequency deviation is required to be no more than 0.5Hz. In this case, the synchronous generator releases at most 1% of the kinetic energy stored in the rotor. However, the rotor kinetic energy control strategy reduces the rotor speed of the wind turbine to the stable operation boundary. Theoretically, the rotor kinetic energy which can be released by a wind turbine is greater than that of a synchronous generator of the same capacity.

In this paper, an additional control method for the rotor kinetic energy of the wind turbine is introduced. When the grid has a power shortage, the wind turbine reduces the rotor speed to release the rotor kinetic energy. The released rotor kinetic energy is expressed by (5):

$$\Delta E_k = E_0 - E_1 = \frac{1}{2} J(\omega_0^2 - \omega_1^2) \tag{5}$$

Where, ΔE_k is the rotor kinetic energy released by the wind turbine; J is the rotational inertia of the wind turbine; ω_0 and ω_1 are the angular velocities of the rotor in the initial and final states, respectively.

The moment of inertia J of the wind turbine is:

$$J = \frac{2HP_N}{\omega_N^2} \tag{6}$$

Where, H is the inertia time constant of the wind turbine; P_N is the rated power of the wind turbine; ω_N is the rated angular speed of the wind rotor.

The topology of the primary frequency modulation wind turbine model is shown in Figure 2.

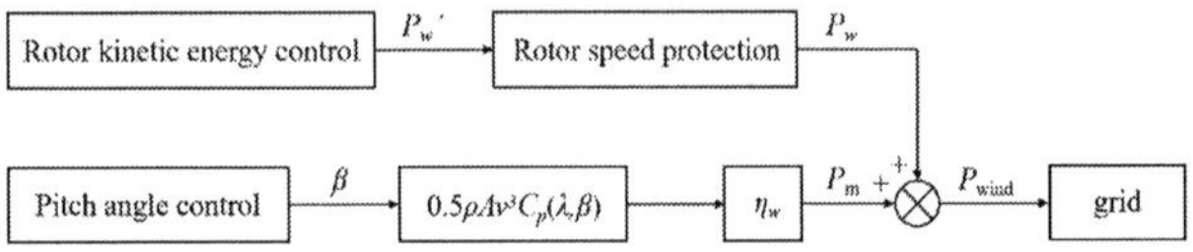

Fig.2. Wind turbine primary frequency modulation model topology

In Fig.2, η_w is the transmission efficiency of the wind turbine.

C. Energy storage model

(1)*Energy Storage Frequency Response Model*

At present, the frequency response models of energy storage systems mainly include ideal models, first-order models, and second-order models. In order to simplify the analysis process, the first-order model proposed in the Ref.[15] is chosen, as shown in Figure 3. The transfer function includes a gain element and an inertia element. The gain K is the gain relationship between the frequency deviation Δf and the power output variation ΔP_s . T is the delay of the frequency response of the energy storage system.

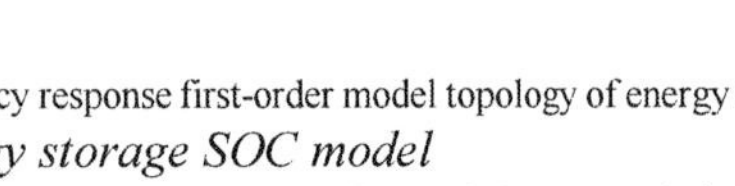

Fig.3. Frequency response first-order model topology of energy storage system

(2)*Energy storage SOC model*

SOC refers to the proportion of the remaining power of the energy storage system to its nominal capacity. The charging and discharging SOC strategy of the energy storage system adopts the SOC model in Ref.[16], as expressed by (7) and (8).

$$\lambda_{SOC}(t) = \lambda_{SOC0} + \int \frac{\eta_1 P_{ESS}}{S_{ESS}} dt \tag{7}$$

$$\lambda_{SOC}(t) = \lambda_{SOC0} + \int \frac{P_{ESS}}{\eta_2 S_{ESS}} dt \tag{8}$$

Where, $\lambda_{SOC}(t)$ is the SOC value at time t; λ_{SOC0} is the initial SOC value; η_1 and η_2 are the charge and discharge loss coefficients. S_{ESS} is the total capacity of the energy storage system.

D. Load model

According to the operation of the microgrid, the load of the primary frequency modulation system at time t is determined. The load power is proportional to the nth power of the frequency. Resistive loads and motor-type load are considered because of a large proportion in the grid. The setting function is expressed by (9).

$$P_{load} = P_{in0} + \frac{f}{f_n} P_{in1} + \varepsilon(t)\left(P_{ex0} + \frac{f}{f_n} P_{ex1} \right) \tag{9}$$

Where, P_{load} is the load active power. P_{in0} and P_{in1} are the initial resistive load power and motor-type load power. P_{ex0} and P_{ex1} are the resistive load power and motor-type load power that suddenly change at time t. f is the system frequency. f_n is the rated frequency.

E. Other distributed power models

The situation of power shortage in the grid is discussed in this paper. The time of the primary frequency modulation process is short. So PV is simplified as a constant power source.

III. Primary Frequency Modulation Strategy For Wind Battery Microgrid At Low Wind Speed

Wind turbines have different operating characteristics under different wind speeds. In this paper, the wind speed is divided into two levels: low wind speed and high wind speed. The frequency modulation strategies for different wind speeds are studied.

The rated wind speed of the wind turbine corresponds to the rated power. When the wind speed is higher than the rated speed, the wind turbine abandons part of the wind and runs with load shedding. The wind speed lower than the rated speed is set as the low wind speed. Under this condition, the wind turbine is operated in the MPPT state. The energy storage system transmits electricity to the microgrid bus to make up for the power shortage. The primary frequency modulation is completed by the wind turbine rotor kinetic energy and energy storage system.

A. Primary frequency modulation strategy of wind turbine at lower wind speed

An additional power control link is added to couple the rotor speed of the wind turbine with the system frequency. The rotor kinetic energy participates in the primary frequency modulation of the system.

In the initial stage of system frequency change, the virtual inertial control is introduced to reduce the frequency change rate. The real-time change rate of the system frequency is input to the additional power controller. The kinetic energy reference power $\Delta P_{w.ine}$ provided by the rotor is obtained by the virtual inertia coefficient $K_{w.ine}$.

$$\Delta P_{w.ine} = K_{w.ine}\frac{df}{dt} \quad (10)$$

The virtual inertia control cannot provide power support at the lowest frequency point to result in a large frequency overshoot. Therefore, virtual droop control is added. The frequency deviation Δf is input into the additional control link. The kinetic energy reference power $\Delta P_{w.dro}$ is provided by the rotor by the droop control coefficient $K_{w.dro}$.

$$\Delta P_{w.dro} = K_{w.dro}\Delta f \quad (11)$$

The new additional reference power $\Delta P_{w.e}$ is calculated by virtual inertial control and virtual droop control:

$$\Delta P_{w.e} = K_{w.dro}\Delta f + K_{w.ine}\frac{df}{dt} \quad (12)$$

The additional reference power is superimposed on the rotor-side converter current reference value to release the rotor kinetic energy. However, the kinetic energy of the rotor is limited. If the rotational speed is too low, the wind turbine becomes unstable. Therefore, the rotor rotational speed of the wind turbine is set to drop by at most 10%. When the threshold value is reached, the rotor kinetic energy control is switched off.

The primary frequency modulation model of the wind turbine under lower wind speed is built as shown in Figure 4.

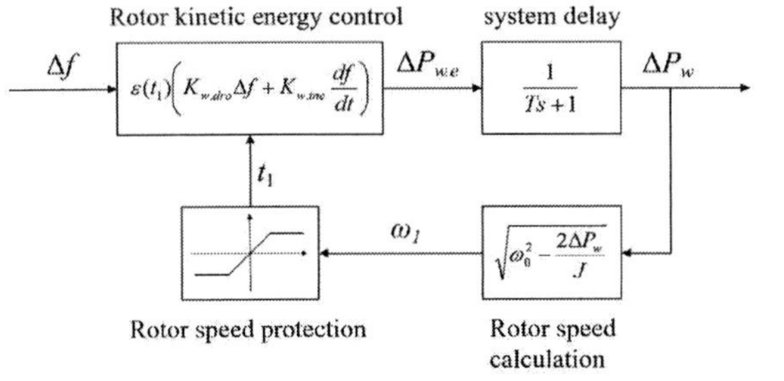

Fig.4. Primary frequency modulation model topology of lower wind speed wind turbine

B. Primary frequency modulation strategy of energy storage system at lower wind speed

After the rotor kinetic energy control of the wind turbine is cut out, the secondary frequency drop may occur. So the energy storage system is controlled to generate additional power to prevent the grid from the secondary frequency drop.

The energy storage system are virtual droop control and virtual inertia control. The droop control coefficient of the energy storage system is increased to support the frequency. The additional power of energy storage is expressed by (13).

$$\Delta P_{s.e} = \left[1 + k_{dro}\varepsilon(t_1)\right]K_{s.dro}\Delta f + K_{s.ine}\frac{df}{dt} \quad (13)$$

Where, t_1 is the moment when the rotor kinetic energy of the wind turbine is cut out. k_{dro} is the additional coefficient of droop control.

The primary frequency modulation model of wind-battery coordination under lower wind speed is built as shown in Figure 5.

IV. Primary Frequency Modulation Strategy of Wind-Battery Microgrid Under High Wind Speed

With higher wind speed, the wind turbine runs in the constant power state. According to the output characteristics of the inverter in the primary frequency modulation process, the system output power adjustment range is (1±10%) P_0. Therefore, 10% power load shedding is used for primary frequency modulation power backup.

A. Primary Frequency Modulation Strategy of Wind Turbine

If the rotor speed continues increasing in higher speed, the rotor may be overspeed to affect the safe operation of the wind turbine. Therefore, the pitch angle control method is introduced to release load shedding power and reduce frequency fluctuations in the grid. Based on the comparative analysis between the rotor kinetic energy control and energy storage system, the primary frequency modulation of the grid is finished.

PI control method is designed to control the pitch angle of the wind turbine. The pitch angle controller power reference value changes with the frequency. The power reference value is calculated by the droop control formula which is expressed by (14).

$$\Delta P_{\beta.e} = K_{w.dro}\Delta f \quad (14)$$

The topology of wind turbine pitch angle controller is shown in Figure 6.

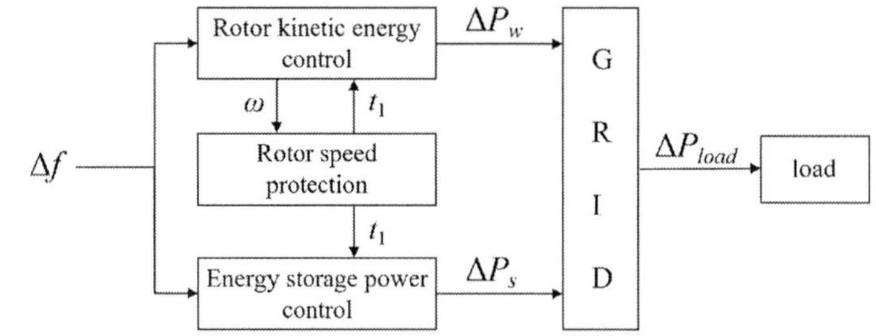

Fig.5. Wind-battery coordinated primary frequency modulation model topology at low wind speed

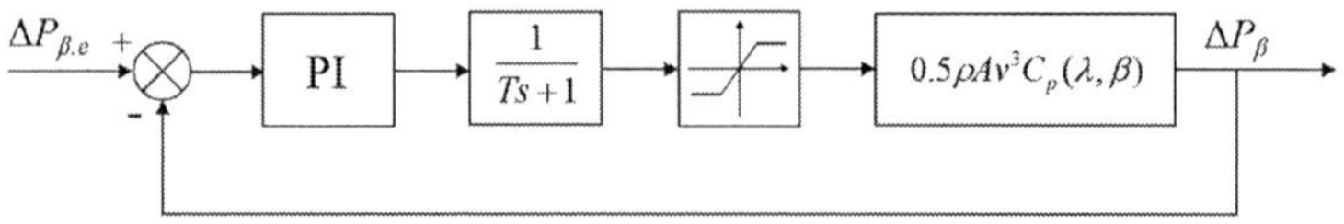

Fig.6. Structural topology of wind turbine pitch angle controller

B. SOC management strategy of energy storage system

In order to ensure the long-term stable operation of the microgrid in the islanded state, it is necessary to keep the SOC at a medium and high level as possible.

SOC management strategy of the energy storage system in the islanded mode of the microgrid is designed. It is independent of the primary frequency modulation strategy. In the higher wind speed state, with lower SOC, the control system sends signals to increase the output power of the wind turbine and charge the energy storage system.

The additional power command is P_{ESS}:

$$P_{ESS}\begin{cases} -(\lambda_{SOC}-0.8)\times 1.25P_{ESS}^{max} & 0\le\lambda_{SOC}\le 0.8 \\ 0 & 0.8<\lambda_{SOC}\le 1 \end{cases} \tag{15}$$

Where, P_{ESS}^{max} is the highest charging power of the energy storage system.

V. SIMULATION ANALYSIS

The wind-battery microgrid system model is built on the Matlab/Simulink platform, as shown in Figure 1.

SE5215 wind turbine model and TWDT-40L lithium battery model are set with 100 units respectively. The main parameters of the microgrid are shown in Table 1. P_R is the resistance type load power; P_M is the motor type load power; v_s is low wind speed; v_l is high wind speed.

A comparative experiment on the frequency stability between the primary frequency modulation strategy designed and the traditional primary frequency modulation strategy is set up.

TABLE I
MAIN PARAMETERS OF PRIMARY FREQUENCY MODULATION MODEL OF WIND-BATTERY MICROGRID

Equipment	Parameter	
Wind Turbines	P_N= 150MW	J = 17.6×108kg•m3
	v_e= 11m/s	
Energy Storage	C = 60MWH	P_{ESS}^{max} = 100MW
Photovoltaic Generator	P_N= 50MW	
Load	P_R= 85MW	P_M= 100MW
Wind Speed	v_s = 9*m/s*	v_l = 14*m/s*

A. Simulation analysis of primary frequency modulation strategy for wind-battery microgrid at lower wind speed

The results in lower wind speeds with different strategies are shown in Figure 7. The blue is the frequency curve of the traditional primary frequency modulation strategy and the red is the frequency curve of the primary frequency modulation strategy proposed.

From Figure 7, with the traditional primary frequency modulation strategy, when the rotor kinetic energy was withdrawn from the frequency modulation, a secondary frequency drop accident occurred. The frequency dropped below 49.75Hz, which exceeds the normal frequency deviation allowable value of ±0.2Hz in our country's power system. But, with the strategy proposed in this paper, the frequency can be stabilized at about 49.93 Hz to verify the effectiveness of the strategy.

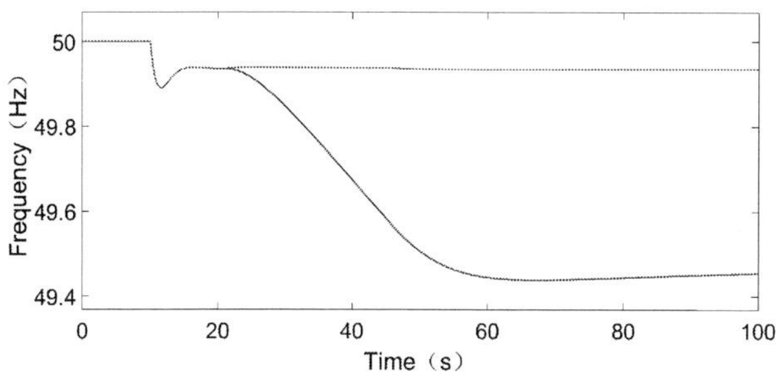

Fig.7. Grid frequency diagram of primary frequency modulation comparison experiment of wind-battery microgrid

Figure 8 shows the output power of the wind turbine during the primary frequency modulation process. In the initial period of 10-20s, the rotor kinetic energy is used to increase the power rapidly to participate in the grid frequency support. The power reached the peak value within 5s, and then the output power decreased gradually until the rotor kinetic energy exited at 35s. The wind turbine begins to absorb power from the grid to restore rotor speed.

Figure 9 shows the output power of the energy storage system during the primary frequency modulation process with the lower wind speed. The power at the initial stage increase and the output power curve of the wind turbine is tracked during the frequency support exit process of rotor kinetic energy. At 35s, power reached the maximum value. The wind turbine is replaced by battery in the grid frequency support.

Figure 10 is the rotor speed graph of the wind turbine. After the rotor kinetic energy participated in the primary frequency modulation, the rotor speed began to decrease. At 35s of the primary frequency modulation, the rotor speed dropped to a minimum of 1.65rad/s. Then it began to slowly absorb energy from the bus. The speed restored. At 800s, it returned to the level before the primary frequency modulation. The rotor speed protection with the strategy is verified.

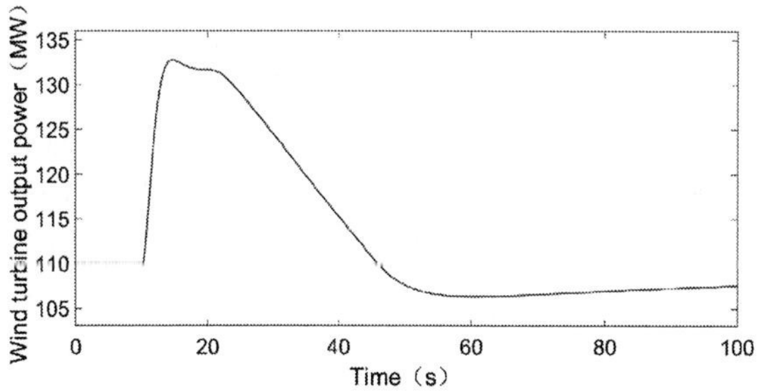

Fig.8. Wind turbine output power diagram

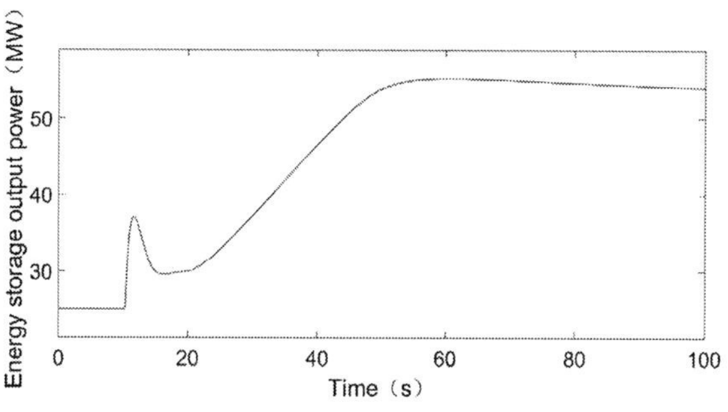

Figure 9 Output power diagram of energy storage system

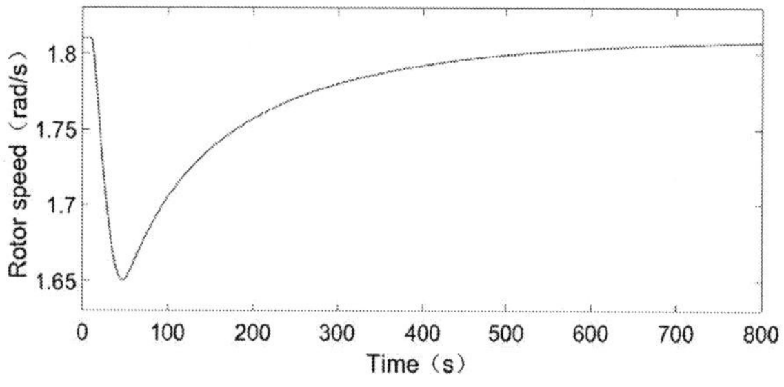

Figure 10 Wind turbine rotor speed

B. Simulation analysis of primary frequency modulation strategy for wind battery microgrid with higher wind speed

With high wind speed, the wind turbine controls the pitch angle in a load-reduced and constant-power state.

When the bus frequency fluctuates, the pitch angle reduces to release the standby power. Figure 11 is a graph of the pitch angle variation with bus frequency fluctuation. Figure 12 shows the output power with the frequency fluctuation. Figure 13 is frequency curve of the microgrid in the primary frequency modulation process with higher wind speed.

Compared with lower wind speed, the wind turbine has sufficient backup power with higher wind speed, which can continuously provide power support without the problem of secondary frequency drop. The energy storage can also reduce the adjustment times and power consumption of the energy storage device.

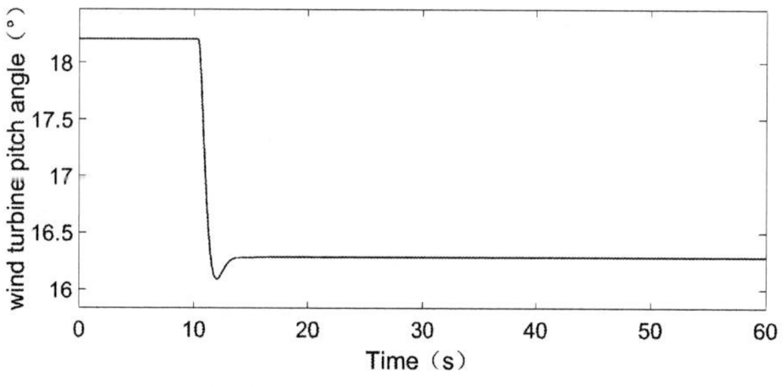

Fig.11. Wind turbine pitch angle curve

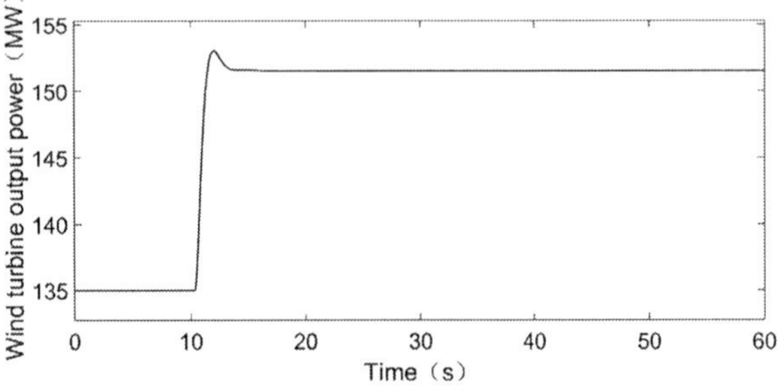

Fig.12. Wind turbine output power diagram

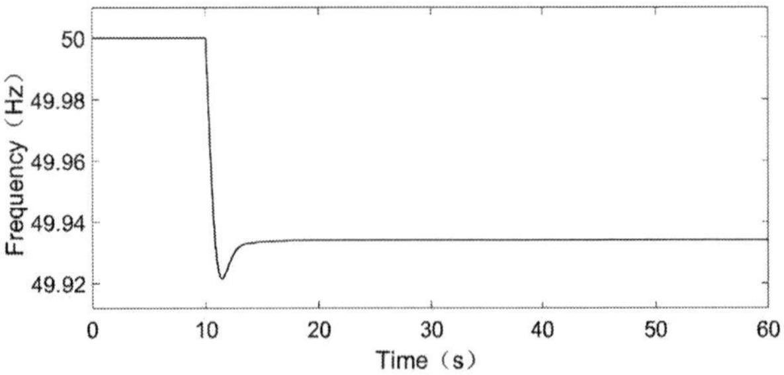

Fig. 13 The frequency curve of primary frequency modulation of wind battery microgrid islanded operation

C. Simulation analysis of SOC management strategy of energy storage system

Figure 14 shows SOC change curve with the energy storage system change in lower SOC condition. The charging power is dynamically controlled. The charging power is up to 100MW when SOC is 0. When SOC is close to 80%, the charging power is gradually reduced. The stable charging and discharging of the energy storage system can be acquired. SOC at a medium and high level to provide sufficient power backup for the microgrid is maintained.

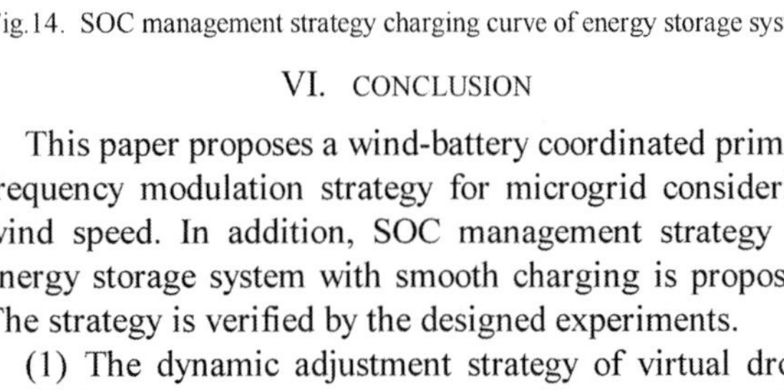

Fig.14. SOC management strategy charging curve of energy storage system

VI. CONCLUSION

This paper proposes a wind-battery coordinated primary frequency modulation strategy for microgrid considering wind speed. In addition, SOC management strategy for energy storage system with smooth charging is proposed. The strategy is verified by the designed experiments.

(1) The dynamic adjustment strategy of virtual droop coefficient of energy storage system is introduced. The primary frequency modulation strategy with lower wind speed for wind-battery coordination microgrid is proposed. The rotor speed is protected and the secondary frequency drop problem is improved after the rotor kinetic energy of the wind turbine exit from the frequency adjustment.

(2) With higher wind speed, the wind turbine obtains sufficient frequency modulation support power by the fixed load shedding method. The frequency stability of the microgrid is improved.

(3) SOC management strategy of the energy storage system with smooth charging is proposed. The energy storage SOC value at a high level can be kept. The effective backup power of the microgrid increases.

REFERENCES

[1] Chen Yun.Criticism and reconstruction of the opposite theory of double carbon strategy and economic development in the context of global climate change [J/OL].Contemporary Economic Management, 2022, 1-12

[2] Debouza Mahdi, Al-Durra Ahmed, EL-Fouly Tarek H.M.,Zeineldin Hatem H.. Survey on microgrids with flexible boundaries: Strategies, applications, and future trends [J]. Electric Power Systems Research, 2022, 205.

[3] Zhang Zhiheng, Wang Yi, Li Heming. Study on inertia control mode of doubly fed induction generator based on virtual inertia[J]. Modern Electric Power, 2013, 30(6): 47-50.

[4] Hurrado S, Gostales G, De L A, et al. A new power stabilization control system based on making use of mechanical inertia of avariable-speed wind-turbine for stand-alone wind-diesel applications [C]. IEEE 2002 28th Annual Conference of the Industrial Electronics Society, Sevilla, Spain, 2021: 3326-3331.

[5] Pan Wenxia, Quan Rui, Wang Fei. A variable droop control strategy for doubly- fed induction generators [J]. Automation of Electric Power Systems, 2015, 39(11): 126-131, 186.

[6] Wang Tongsen, Cheng Xuekun. Variable droop coefficient control strategy of a DFIG considering rotor speed limit [J].Power System Protection and Control, 2021, 49(09): 29-36.

[7] Zhang Zhaosui, Sun Yuangzhang, Cheng Lin, Lin Jin. Frequency regulation by doubly fed induction generator wind turbines based on coordinated overspeed control and pitch control [J]. Automation of Electric Power Systems, 2019, 35(17): 20-25.

[8] Chen Wei, Wu Jun, Liu Dichen, Chen Yi, Chen Baisen. Power optimization control of doubly-fed induction generators considering active power reserve [J]. Proceedings of the CSU-EPSA, 2018, 30(7): 51-58.

[9] Miao Lu, Wen Jinyu, Xie Hailian, et al. Coordinated control strategy of wind turbine generator and energy storage equipment for frequency support[C]. Industry Applications Society Meeting, USA, October 18-22,

2020: 1-7.
[10] Zhou Tianpei, Sun Wei. Study on virtual inertia control for DFIG-based wind farms with high penetration [J]. Proceedings of the CSEE , 2017(2): 486-495.
[11] Deng Xia, Sun Wei, Xiao Haiwei. Integrated control strategy of battery energy storage system in primary frequency regulation [J]. High Voltage Engineering, 2018, 44(4): 1157-1165.
[12] Li Yong, Liu Fang, Cao Yijia. Power system frequency robust control [M]. Beijing: Machinery Industry Press, 2016.
[13] Zhang Qian, Zhang Zhiwen, Hu Sijia, Li Yong, Lin Jinjie. Aflexible power distribution strategy with wind turbine generator and energy storage for frequency regulation in
isolated microgrid [J].Transactions of China ElectrotechnicalSociety, 2022,37(15):3767-3780.
[14] LI Tianyue, YE Peng, Jiang Zhunan, Sun Feng, Li Ping. Research review on frequency control technology of power grid participated by distributed energy storage [J]. Journal of Shenyang Institute of Engineering (Natural Science), 2022, 18(02): 1-7.
[15] Mu Yunfei， Wu Jianzhong， Ekanayake J， et al. Primary frequency response from electric vehicles in the great Britain power system[J]. IEEE Transactions on Smart Grid，2013，4(2)：1142-1150.
[16] Zhu Ying, Qin Likuan, Yan Quanchun, Wei Zhinong. Wind-storage combined frequency regulation strategy and optimal configuration method of energy storage system considering process of frequency response [J].Electric Power Automation Equipment, 2021,41(10):28-35.

Doping Effect of Kalium on the Electrical Contact Performance of Ag/ZnO

Ziyao Chen[1], Wenzhu Shao[1,*], Weijian Li[2], Wenwei Gu[3], Bingtian Li[1]

[1)] Harbin Institute of Technology, Harbin 150001
[2)] Yantai University, Yantai 264005
[3)] Ningbo Kun Tong alloy Co., LTD, 315602
Email: wzshao@hit.edu.cn TEL：13804562008

***Abstract*—K-doped ZnO powders was successfully prepared by self-propagating combustion method and Ag/ZnO:K mixed powders was obtained by high-energy ball-milling. Through the surface microstructure characterization of Ag/ZnO and Ag/ZnO:K contacts prepared by powder metallurgy, it is found that K doping can enhance the dispersion of ZnO in the composites. By measuring the wetting angle between ZnO:K, ZnO and Ag, it indicated that K doping can improve the wettability between Ag and ZnO. Furthermore, the comparison of the Ag/ZnO and Ag/ZnO:K contacts has been measured by the cyclic arc-erosion experiments, which demonstrated that K doping can improve the arc-erosion resistance, contact resistance stability and welding resistance of Ag/ZnO electrical contact composites by increasing the dispersion of ZnO and wettability between Ag and ZnO.**

***Keywords*— Ag/ZnO electrical contact materials, arc-erosion, wettability, dispersion of second phase, modification of K doping**

I. INTRODUCTION

Ag/MeO (Silver/oxides) electrical contact composites were used in low-voltage apparatus widely[1]. Especially, Ag/CdO (cadmium oxide) electrical contact composites, called universal contacts, show excellent performance at all electrical levels of apparatus. However, due to the severe toxicity of Cd, the RoHS issued by the European Union in 2002 has explicitly prohibited the use of Cd in electronic and electrical equipment[2]. In order to replace Ag/CdO, Ag/SnO_2 (tin oxide) and Ag/ZnO (zinc oxide) are considered as the most potential alternatives.

Over the years, researchers have developed a series of new Ag/SnO_2 electrical contact materials, such as Ag/SnO_2/In_2O_3, Ag/SnO_2/CuO and Ag/SnO_2:Cu. By adding oxides and metal ions doping, the wettability between SnO_2 and Ag matrix is improved, thus improving its electrical life and replacing the Ag/CdO electrical contact materials in multiple application grades of contactors[3]. However, with the development of electrical appliances and the gradual rise of current level, the lack of welding resistance of Ag/SnO_2 electrical contact materials is becoming more and more prominent.

Due to the outstanding thermal properties of ZnO, Ag/ZnO electrical contact composites were widely used in multiple application grades of breakers. However, since ZnO powders is easy to agglomeration and the wettability between ZnO and Ag is weak, the pool arc-erosion resistance limits the widely use of Ag/ZnO for other low-voltage apparatus[4]. Recently, to extend the electrical life of Ag/ZnO contacts, mechanical mixing[5] and intra-spray oxidation[6] were used and researched, which could suppress agglomeration of ZnO powders and enhance the initial dispersion of Ag/ZnO electrical contacts. Nevertheless, in the process of service, the fluidity of the arc molten pool will give oxide a chance to reencounter, and the strong agglomeration tendency of ZnO and the poor wettability with the matrix will lead to ZnO particles re-agglomerate into blocks, so that the arc-erosion resistance of the contact rapidly deteriorate.

According to statistics, Ag/CdO still accounts for 46.7% of silver oxide materials used in voltage appliances in China's electrical industry, and there is still a huge market space and demand for green environment-friendly materials to replace silver cadmium oxide[7]. With the development of long electrical life, high reliability and high current electric appliances, it is urgent to develop new types of electrical contact materials for low voltage electric appliances with characteristics of welding resistance and arc-erosion resistance.

In this paper, potassium (K) doped ZnO powders was prepared by self-propagating combustion method. Subsequently, Ag/ZnO and Ag/ZnO:K electrical contacts were prepared by high-energy ball milling and powder metallurgy. Moveover, the effects of K doping on ZnO agglomeration characteristics and dispersion in the matrix were investigated by SEM observation. In addition, the effect of K doping on wettability of ZnO and Ag was studied by a high temperature droplet experiment. Finally, the effect of K doping on the electrical contact performance of Ag/ZnO contacts was investigated by cyclic arc-erosion experiment.

II. EXPERIMENTS

A. Fabrication of K-doped ZnO powders

K doped ZnO powders and undoped ZnO powders were prepared by self-propagating combustion method. The preparation process is as follows: zinc nitrate, potassium nitrate, urea and glycine are dissolved in deionized water in proportion. After full mixing by magnetic stirring, the solution was heat treated in muffle furnace at 500°C until self-propagating combustion took place, and k-doped ZnO powder and undoped ZnO powder were obtained.

B. Fabrication of test samples

In this paper, Ag/ZnO and Ag/ZnO:K contacts with a density of more than 98% were prepared by powder metallurgy method and the mixing powders of Ag and ZnO were mixed by high-energy ball milling. The ball-milling process is as follows: Prepare Ag and oxide powder with oxide addition amount of 10wt%, add balls according to the ratio of milling ball to material of 4:1, where large balls: medium balls: small balls = 2:1:1, the milling speed is 200 rad/min, and the milling time is 4 hours.

The powder metallurgy process is that the Ag/ZnO or Ag/ZnO:K powders obtained by ball-milling about 0.25g are placed in a bidirectional pressing mold with a diameter of 5mm. The powders are pressed at the initial pressure of 150 MPa, followed by the initial heat treatment, followed by the re-pressure of 1200 MPa, and then the re-heating, where these heat treatments are 860°C for 3 h.

In addition, in order to investigate the effect of K doping on wettability of ZnO and Ag, it is necessary to prepare oxide substrate with density greater than 90%. Firstly, the oxide powder and binder (PVA) are placed into deionized water and stirred at 90°C for 2 h. Then, the excess liquid is then removed and dried using a centrifuge. Subsequently, the dried powders were placed in a mold with a diameter of 15mm and pressed at 300 MPa to form pressed shapes. Finally, the pressed shapes were put into high temperature tubular furnace for 1450°C-2 h heat treatment.

C. Characterization of performance and microstructure

Field Emission Scanning Electron Microscopy (SEM, Zeiss) and X-ray Photoelectron Spectroscopy (XPS, Thermo Fisher) were performed to characterize the doped powders and determine the effective doping of K. The Ag/ZnO and Ag/ZnO:K contacts were characterized by SEM, and the effect of K doping on the dispersion of ZnO in the matrix was investigated. The wettability angles of Ag block on ZnO and ZnO:K substrate were measured by high temperature wettability Angle measuring instrument (Huahai zhongyi). The Ag/ZnO and Ag/ZnO:K contacts were tested 6000 times by arc-erosion testing machine independently developed by Harbin Institute of Technology. The experimental voltage was 380 VAC, the current was 60 A, and there was no arc extinguishing mask. The welding force of each operation can be measured and used to investigate the influence of K doping on the welding resistance of Ag/ZnO electrical contact materials. In addition, the contact resistance and mass loss of the contact pair will be tested every 1000 operations, which is used to explore the effect of K doping on the arc-erosion resistance of Ag/ZnO electrical contact materials.

III. RESULT AND DISCUSSION

A. Phase analysis of K-doped ZnO powders

To determine the effective doping of K in the powder prepared by combustion method, XRD and XPS were used to analyze the prepared ZnO and ZnO:K powders, and the results are shown in Figure 1. It can be seen from Figure 1a that the diffraction peaks of ZnO and ZnO:K powders prepared by self-propagating combustion are completely corresponding to the standard ZnO diffraction peaks (PDF#79-0208), indicating high purity and free of impurities of prepared powders. Figure 1b shows that K element with +1 valence exists in ZnO:K powders, indicating that K is successfully doped into ZnO.

B. Dispersion of ZnO:K phase in composites

Due to the strong agglomeration of ZnO, the poor dispersion of ZnO second phase is a key problem to limiting the electrical life of Ag/ZnO contacts. In this paper, high-energy ball-milling was used to mix Ag and oxide powders, in order to break up the agglomeration of oxide and evenly mixed powders, so as to improve the dispersion of Ag/ZnO composites.

To characterize the effect of K doping on the dispersion of the ZnO phase on the surface of Ag/ZnO contacts, Ag/ZnO:K and Ag/ZnO contacts prepared by powder metallurgy were grinded and polished, followed by SEM characterization, and the results are shown in Figure 2. It can be seen from Figure 2a and b that ZnO still has serious agglomeration and poor dispersion in Ag matrix even after high-energy ball-milling, while K doping significantly suppressed the agglomeration of ZnO, thus improving the dispersion of ZnO:K phase in Ag matrix (Figure 2c, d).

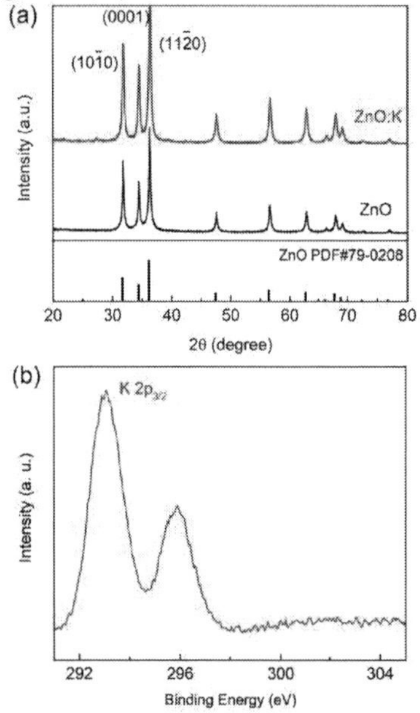

Fig.1 a) XRD patterns of ZnO and ZnO:K powders. (b) XPS of K 2p core level spectra of ZnO:K powders.

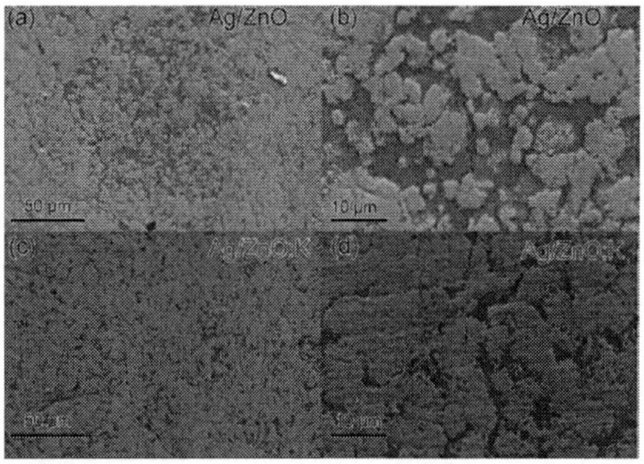

Fig.2 SEM images of Ag/ZnO (a, b) and Ag/ZnO:K contacts (c, d).

C. *Wettability between Ag matrix and ZnO:K phase*

In the research and development of Ag/SnO_2 electrical contact materials, it is found that the wettability between oxide and Ag is positively correlated with the arc-erosion resistance of contacts and the modification of SnO_2 by metal ion doping is the key to improving the wettability between SnO_2 and Ag[8, 9].

To study the effect of K doping on wettability between ZnO and Ag, the ZnO and ZnO:K basal plates with density of more than 90% were prepared. Subsequently, Ag blocks were placed on these basal plates respectively to conduct high temperature droplet experiments. The wetting angle results are shown in Figure 3. The results show that K doping reduces the wetting angle between ZnO and Ag from 89.9° to 74.8°, indicating that K doping significantly improves the wettability between ZnO and Ag, and is expected to prolong the electrical life of Ag/ZnO electrically contacted materials.

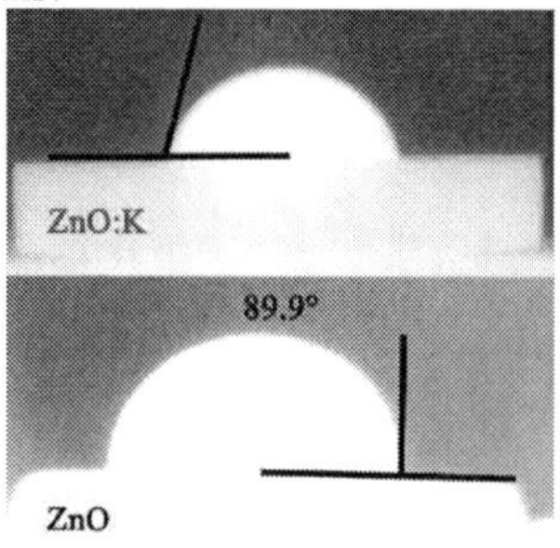

Fig.3 High temperature droplet experiment results of ZnO:K, ZnO basal plate and bulk Ag.

D. *Electrical contact performance of Ag/ZnO:K composites*

To explore the effect of K doping on the electrical contact performance of Ag/ZnO, arc-erosion testing machine was used to conduct 6000 cyclic arc-erosion experiments on the prepared Ag/ZnO:K and Ag/ZnO electrical contacts as well as commercial Ag/ZnO electrical contacts. And the mass loss, contact resistance and welding force of the contacts during cyclic arc-erosion were recorded for investigating the effects of K doping on arc-erosion resistance, contact resistance stability and welding resistance.

Figure 4 shows the accumulated mass loss of these contacts in 6000 operations of arc-erosion. It can be seen that K doping effectively reduces the mass loss of Ag/ZnO under arc-erosion. The mechanism is as follows :K doping improves the wettability of ZnO and Ag, leading to increasing the viscosity of the arc molten pool. Thus, the refractory ZnO:K phase in the molten pool can stabilize the molten pool and reduce the splash of Ag liquid.

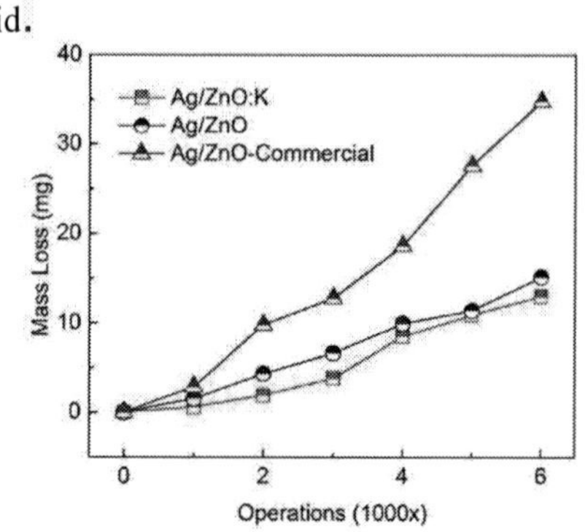

Fig.4 Mass loss of different kinds of Ag/ZnO contacts during cyclic arc-erosion experiment.

Table 1 shows the contact resistance of three Ag/ZnO contacts during 6000 operations of arc-erosion. It can be seen that K doping effectively improves the stability of the contact resistance of Ag/ZnO under arc-erosion. The mechanism is as follows: K doping improves the wettability and the viscosity of the arc molten pool, resulting in a decrease in Ag splash and an increase in Ag interaction with ZnO:K phase, which slows down the surface enrichment of non-conductive ZnO:K phase. In addition, the non-conductive ZnO phase tends to aggregate on the contact surface, and the contact resistance increases sharply if the contact surface falls on the ZnO phase. However, K doping suppresses the agglomeration of ZnO powders and improves the dispersion of ZnO phase on the Ag matrix, thus improving the stability of the contact resistance of Ag/ZnO contacts in the arc-erosion process.

Figure 5 shows the maximum welding force per 1000 operations of three Ag/ZnO contacts in the arc-erosion process. The results show that the Ag/ZnO prepared in this paper has the worst welding resistance. Because the Ag/ZnO prepared by combustion method has worse dispersion of ZnO than the commercial Ag/ZnO. When the contact face falls on the Ag-enriched regions, the Ag with low melting point will melt and condense into Ag bridge with larger cross-sectional area, thus having higher welding force. Moreover, since K doping suppresses the agglomeration of ZnO and improves the dispersion of ZnO:K phase in Ag matrix, the uniformly dispersed oxidized phase with high thermal property can absorb a lot of heat on the contact surface and greatly reduce the cross-sectional area of Ag bridge, thus improving the welding resistance of Ag/ZnO:K electrically contacted materials.

Table 1. Contact resistance of different kinds of Ag/ZnO contacts during cyclic arc-erosion experiment.

A. Contact resistance（mΩ）			
B. Operations	C. Ag/ZnO:K	D. Ag/ZnO	E. Ag/ZnO (commercial)
F. 0	G. 0.32	H. 0.28	I. 0.36
J. 1000	K. 2.23	L. 2.83	M. 5.97
N. 2000	O. 3.74	P. 2.61	Q. 39.52
R. 3000	S. 5.93	T. 104.75	U. 3.69
V. 4000	W. 2.97	X. 103	Y. 0.97
Z. 5000	AA. 5.17	AB. 3.55	AC. 1.91
AD. 6000	AE. 12.40	AF. 1.44	AG. 17.22

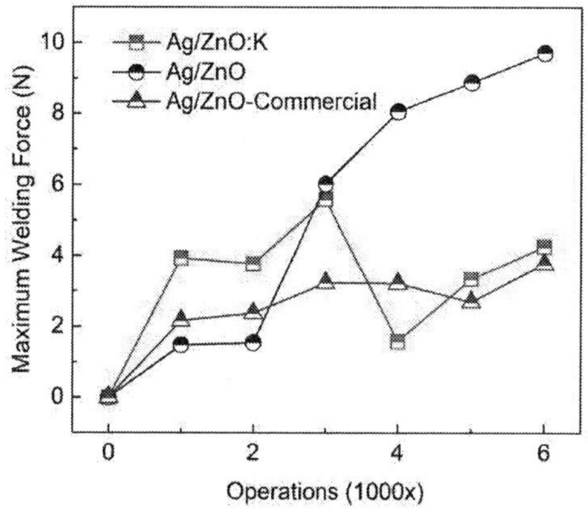

Fig.5 Max welding force of different kinds of Ag/ZnO contacts during cyclic arc-erosion experiment.

In conclusion, K doping modification can not only improve the dispersion of ZnO in the Ag/ZnO composites, but also improve the wettability between ZnO and Ag, so as to reduce the mass loss, improve the stability of contact resistance, and reduce the welding force of Ag/ZnO electrical contact composites during arc-erosion. Therefore, metal ion doping is an effective method to prolong the electrical life of Ag/ZnO electrical contact materials, and it is expected to develop a new type of electrical contact materials for low-voltage appliances with arc-erosion resistance, contact resistance stability and welding resistance, which may promote the process of replacing silver cadmium oxide in the electrical contact industry.

IV. CONCLUSION

(1) K doping can improve the second phase dispersion of Ag/ZnO electrically contacted materials.
(2) K doping can improve the wettability between ZnO phase and Ag matrix.
(3) K doping can reduce the mass loss, improve the contact resistance stability and welding resistance of Ag/ZnO electrical contact materials by improving the dispersion of the second phase and the wettability between ZnO and Ag.

REFERENCES

[1] Yongguo Du, Weijun Zhang, Junsui Hu. "Electrical contact and electrical contact material (1)," *Electrical Materials*, vol. 2, 2005: 44-46.
[2] Wenzhu Shao, Yusheng Cui, Dezhuang Yang. "Development and present situation of electrical contact materials," *Electrical Engineering Materials*, 1999, 1:11-33.
[3] Mingzhe Rong, Qipin Wang, Zhigang Yin, "New develoment of sliver-metallic oxide(AgMeO) contact

materials, " *Low Voltage Apparatus*, vol. 3, 1992, pp. 6-10.

[4] Zhiguo Li, Xiaolong Zhou, Riming Hu. "Research progress of multiphase reinforced AgMeO electrical contact materials," *Material Review*, 2018, 1(32),:90-94.

[5] Joshi P B, Rao V J, Rehani B R, Pratap A. "Silver-Zinc Oxide Electrical Contact Materials by Mechanochemical Synthesis Route," *Indian Journal of Pure & Applied Physics*, 2007, 45(1), 9-15.

[6] C. P. Wu, D. Q. Yi, J. Li. "Investigation on microstructure and performance of Ag/ZnO contact material," *Journal of Alloys & Compounds*, 2008, vol. 457: 565-570.

[7] Wenbo Bai, Ruxi Kang, Defeng Cui. "Summary of the development of electrical contact material industry during 13th Five-Year Plan period,", *China Electrical Equipment Industry*, 2020, 10:pp. 6-11.

[8] Jeannot D, Pinard J, Ramoni P, "Physical and Chemical Properties of Metal Oxide Additions to Ag," *IEEE Transactions on Components Packaging & Manufacturing Technology Part A*, 1994, 17(1): 17-23

[9] Jun Wang, Wei Liu, Dongmei Li, "The behavior and effect of CuO in Ag/SnO_2 materials," J*ournal of Alloys & Compounds*, 2014, 588: 378-383.

8th International Conference on Reliability of
Electrical Products and Electrical Contacts,
November 18-20, 2022

Simulation and Experiment on Properties of Mo and Bi Doped AgNi Contact Materials

Jiying Jia, Jingqin Wang

State Key Laboratory of Reliability and Intelligence of Electrical Equipment,
Hebei University of Technology, Tianjin, 300401

Abstract—**In order to explore the effect of doping modification on the properties of AgNi contact materials, the interface simulation model of Ag/Ni was established based on the first principle of density functional theory, and the interface stability and electronic structure of Ag/Ni doped Mo and Bi were studied. The stability of the interface can directly affect the welding resistance of AgNi contact materials. The hybridization can enhance the stability of Ag/Ni interface, the hybridization between Ag and Ni orbitals and the bonding strength of Ag-Ni metal bonds, and the Mo-doped Ag/Ni has the best stability. Contact materials were prepared by powder metallurgy method. Wettability test, electrical contact performance test and erosion surface analysis were carried out on AgNi contact before and after doping. It was found that Mo and Bi doping improved the anti-fusion welding performance and anti-arc erosion performance of intrinsic contact materials, which verified the simulation conclusion. Among them, doping Mo element in AgNi contact greatly reduced the fusion welding force, and the improvement effect on contact materials was the most obvious.**

Keyword —**AgNi contact material, first principle, stability, powder metallurgy, and electrical contact performance**

I. INTRODUCTION

AgNi electrical contact material has the advantages of good conductivity, thermal conductivity and welding performance, low and stable contact resistance, etc. It is widely used in low-voltage electrical appliances such as relays, contactors and micro-switches with medium and small current levels that have strict requirements on contact resistance and temperature rise. However, in the applications with large working current, the resistance to welding and electrical wear of conventional AgNi materials are poor, which limits the further popularization and application of AgNi materials [1-3]. Scholars in China and abroad have found that doping modification can effectively improve the properties of AgNi contact materials. At present, most of the research is based on the experimental inquiry method [4-8]. However, it is impossible to analyze the microscopic mechanism and universal law of the system in detail only through the experimental study. Moreover, there are many kinds of doping elements. The sequential test is more serious for energy waste, and the test cycle is long and the contingency is large in the exploratory stage [9]. Therefore, this paper introduces the method of computational research to explore the influence of metal doping on the properties of AgNi materials, so as to better understand the interaction between atoms at the micro level, and avoid the blindness of experimental inquiry. Reduce energy waste and improve research efficiency [10].

With refractory metal Mo as the doping element, it is suspended in the molten pool under the action of arc, increasing the viscosity of the molten pool, thereby improving the electrical wear resistance of the material. Moreover, it forms brittle intermetallic compounds with the reinforcement Ni, further enhancing the brittleness of the material and reducing the welding force, thereby improving the welding resistance and electrical wear resistance of the silver-nickel material. Under the action of high temperature of arc, the doping element Bi can form intermetallic compounds with low melting point with Ni, which increases the volume of molten pool metal solution, and is conducive to filling the pores corroded by arc on the contact surface, and ultimately reduces and flats the pores on the contact surface. Because the intermetallic compounds are precipitated in the process of melting and cooling, and the particle size is small and dispersed, the tensile strength and electrical wear resistance of AgNi materials are improved. The doping element Bi and Ni form brittle intermetallic compounds, which increases the brittleness of molten pool and reduces the welding force, thereby improving the welding resistance of contact materials.

In this paper, the simulation and experimental analysis of metal Mo and Bi doped AgNi contact materials were carried out. The influence of doping on the interface stability and electronic structure of Ag/Ni was analyzed by simulation. The AgNi contact materials were prepared by powder metallurgy method. The wettability

National Natural Science Foundation（51777057）

Central Leading Local Science and Technology Projects（216Z1011G） of contact materials was tested, and the simulation results were verified. The improvement effect of Mo and Bi doping on the performance of AgNi contact was verified by the electrical contact performance test and the analysis of arc erosion surface.

II. INTERFACE MODELS AND CALCULATION METHODS

A. Construction model

In view of the existing research, among the binding forms of Ag and Ni interfaces, the interfacial binding energy of Ag (110)/Ni(211) is the highest, the electron hybridization at the interface is the most intense and the interfacial bonding is the most stable [10]. Therefore, in this paper, the Ag/Ni interface model is constructed by combining the Ag (110) crystal plane with the Ni (211) crystal plane (Fig. 1). The interface model is constructed by 8-layer Ag atom and 6-layer Ni atom, which makes the 4-layer Ag and 3-layer Ni near the Ag/Ni interface relax freely in the geometric space, and the remaining atomic layer remains fixed. This model is used to simulate the Ag/Ni interface structure. The doping atom replaces one of the free relaxation Ni, and the different doping positions are numbered in Fig.1.

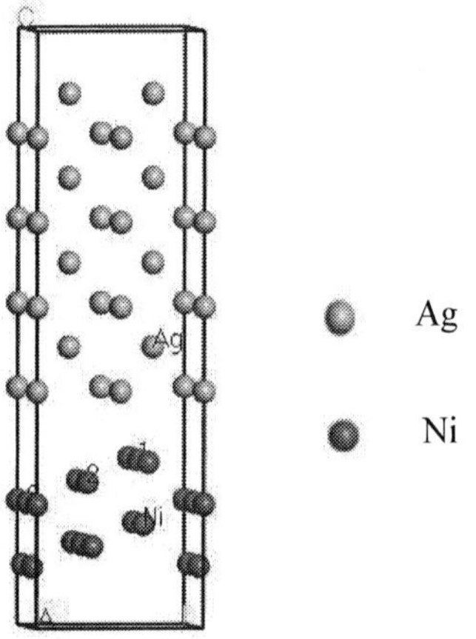

Fig.1 Ag(110)/Ni(211) interface model

B. Calculation method

In this paper, the Castep module in Material Studio software is used for calculation. Considering the uneven distribution of electrons in the real system, the PBE under the generalized gradient approximation (GGA) is selected to deal with the exchange correlation energy between electrons, and the ultrasoft pseudopotential is used to describe the interaction between valence electrons and ions [11]. Considering the economy of the calculation cost and the accuracy of the calculation results, the convergence test of the interface model is carried out. The truncation energy of the reciprocal space is 300 eV, and the sampling integral of the K point in the Bree source area is 5 × 4 × 1. The convergence criterion is that the total energy is less than 1.0×10^{-5} eV/atom, the average atomic force is less than 0.5 eV/nm, the tolerance deviation is less than 0.02 nm, and the maximum stress deviation is 0.1 GPa. Firstly, the BFGS algorithm was used to optimize the cell structures of Ag and Ni, respectively. Based on the optimized model, the interface was constructed. The above calculation parameters were used to optimize the Ag/Ni interface before and after doping, and a relatively stable state was obtained. After that, the simulation analysis of the optimized system was carried out, such as displacement energy, separation energy, interface energy, charge population, and state density. The valence electron configuration considered in the calculation is : Ag $4d^{10}5s^1$, Ni $3d^84s^2$, Mo $4p^64d^55s^1$, Bi $6s^26p^3$.

III. SIMULATION CALCULATION AND ANALYSIS

A. Priority occupation of doped elements

In order to study the preferential occupation of doped elements at the Ag/Ni interface, the substitution energies of doped atoms at different positions are calculated in this paper (in TAB.1). The lower the displacement energy is, the more easily the atom at this position is replaced by the doped atom. Formula of displacement energy:

$$E^{total}_{(Ag/Ni\to X)}=\left(E^{total}_{Ag10/(Ni7,X)}+\mu_{Ni}\right)-\left(E^{total}_{Ag10/Ni8}+\mu_X\right) \quad (1)$$

In the formula: $E^{total}_{(Ag/Ni\to X)}$ represents the replacement energy of Ni atoms in the interface after substitution by doped atoms; $E^{total}_{Ag10/(Ni7,X)}$ represents the total energy of the interface system after replacement ; $E^{total}_{Ag10/Ni8}$ represents the total energy of the interface system before replacement; μ_i (i=Ni,X) The chemical potential of atom i.

TAB.1 Replacement energies of Mo and Bi elements at different doping positions (unit: eV)

Model	Position	$E^{total}_{(Ag/Ni\to X)}$/eV
	1	0.2725
Ag/Ni+Mo	2	-1.3228
	3	-1.8777
	1	-0.5412
Ag/Ni+Bi	2	-1.6578
	3	-1.2227

In TAB.1, the substitution energies of Mo and Bi for a free relaxed Ni atom are listed. When Mo is doped into Ag/Ni interface, the substitution energies at position 2 and 3 are negative, indicating that the substitution at this position is easy to carry out, and the substitution energy at position 1 is positive, that is, the substitution at this position is relatively difficult, so the position number of Mo preferential doping is 3. The displacement energies of Bi at 1, 2 and 3 are all negative, and the displacement energy at position 2 is the smallest. The priority occupation of Mo (position 3) and Bi (position 2) was studied in the subsequent analysis.

B. Stability analysis

The binding force of Ag/Ni interface is weak, and it is easy to enrich the impurity atoms at the interface. In the process of electrical contact, the arc preferentially acts on the interface of the substrate Ag, and the change of its electronic behavior is only limited to a small range of Ag/Ni interface[12]. Therefore, through the stability analysis and electronic structure analysis of the interface, the influence of doping on the anti-fusion welding performance of AgNi contact material is studied.

1) Interface bonding stability

Separation work and interfacial energy were introduced to analyze the stability and bonding strength of Ag/Ni interface.

Separation work (W_{sep}) refers to the energy needed to separate the stable interface into two independent and infinite free surfaces. Formula of Separation Work (W_{sep})[13]:

$$W_{sep} = \frac{E_{Ag}^{slab} + E_{Ni}^{slab} - E_{Ag/Ni}^{inter}(relax)}{A} \quad (2)$$

In the formula:: E_{Ag}^{slab} and E_{Ni}^{slab} represents total energy of free surface systems of Ag and Ni ; $E_{Ag/Ni}^{inter}(relax)$ represents total energy of relaxed Ag/Ni interface system; A represents the interface area.

Interfacial energy (γ_{int}) represents the energy difference caused by unit surface area after two free surfaces form a complete interface. Formula for interface energy:

$$\gamma_{int,Ag/Ni} = \sigma_{Ag} + \sigma_{Ni} - W_{sep,Ag/Ni} \quad (3)$$

In the formula: σ_{Ag} and σ_{Ni} represents surface energy of Ag and Ni free surfaces; $W_{sep,Ag/Ni}$ represents the separation work of Ag / Ni interface.

In TAB.2, the separation work and interface energy of Ag/Ni interface before and after Mo and Bi doping are listed. The separation work of Ag/Ni interface doped with Mo and Bi is 91.1035 % and 137.1415 % higher than that of the intrinsic interface, which makes the interface separation required more energy and the interface bonding more stable. The interface energy is reduced after doping, and the energy required to construct the interface is reduced, which is easier to form the interface. The doping of Mo and Bi significantly improves the bonding strength of Ag/Ni interface, which has a positive effect on improving the resistance to fusion welding of AgNi contact materials. Among them, the effect of Mo doping on the bonding strength of AgNi interface is the most obvious.

2) Thermodynamic stability

In order to analyze the thermodynamic stability of Ag/Ni interface, this paper calculated the change of enthalpy values before and after Mo and Bi doping (in TAB.2). Formula of enthalpy change value:

$$\Delta H = H_{End} - H_{Ini} \quad (4)$$

In the formula: ΔH represents enthalpy change value, H_{End} represents the energy of a product , H_{Ini} represents reactant energy.

The enthalpy change of the system before and after doping is negative. The absolute value of the enthalpy change of the Ag/Ni interface increases with the doping of Bi and Mo, which is greater than the absolute value of the enthalpy change of the undoped system. It shows that the doping improves the thermodynamic stability of the system, and the most stable is the Mo-doped Ag/Ni interface model.

TAB.2 Separation work and interface energy of Ag / Ni interface doped with Mo and Bi elements

Model	Ag/Ni	Ag/Ni+Mo	Ag/Ni+Bi
W_{sep} / J/m^2	0.2057	0.4878	0.4256
γ_{int} / J/m^2	0.9030	0.6138	0.6784
ΔH /eV	-0.0028	-0.3231	-0.0127

C. Electronic structure

1) Population analysis

In order to analyze the gain and loss electrons of each atom in the Ag/Ni interface and the bonding strength between atoms before and after Mo and Bi doping, the charge population number and bond population between atoms before and after Ag/Ni interface doping are calculated (in TAB.3 and TAB.4), and the data in the table are averaged.

The data analysis shows that the charge distribution numbers of Ag and Ni atoms in the Ag/Ni interface are −0.0213 and 0.0275, respectively, and Ag obtains electrons with negative charges. Ni lost electrons with positive charge. The charge distribution numbers of doped atoms Mo and Bi at the Ag/Ni interface are both positive, and their values are much larger than those of Ag and Ni. The doped atoms have strong electron loss ability. After doping, the electron transfer at the Ag/Ni interface is obvious, and the atomic bonding is stable, which is conducive to improving the stability of interface bonding. Among them, Mo doping has the strongest electron transfer and the most stable bonding at Ag/Ni interface.

Compared with the undoped Ag/Ni interface, the Ni-Mo and Ni-Bi bonds are increased at the interface after doping, and the number of overlapping populations of Ni and doped atoms is higher than that of Ni and Ag bonds. The bonding effect is obvious, and the bonding strength of Ag/Ni interface is strengthened. The number of overlapping populations of Ag-Ni bonds after Mo doping increases by 38.89 %, which is the most obvious improvement of the bonding strength of Ag/Ni, which is consistent with the stability analysis results.

TAB.3 Atom population between Ag/Ni interface atoms

Model	Atom population			
	Ag	Ni	Mo	Mo
Ag/Ni	-0.0213	0.0275	——	——
Ag/Ni+Mo	-0.0269	-0.1555	0.2130	——
Ag/Ni+Bi	0.0075	-0.0291	——	0.1800

TAB.4 Bond population between atoms at Ag/Ni interface

Model	Bond population		
	Ag-Ni	Ni-Mo	Ni-Bi
Ag/Ni	0.1800	——	——
Ag/Ni+Mo	0.2500	0.4883	——
Ag/Ni+Bi	0.1805	——	0.2678

2) Density of state

The density of states can characterize the bonding between doped atoms and Ag/Ni interface atoms, which is used to analyze the distribution of electrons in the interface. Fig.2 shows the density of states of Ag/Ni interface before and after doping Mo and Bi, respectively.

Fig.2a shows the total state density and partial state density of the undoped Ag/Ni interface. The energy is mainly provided by the 5s and 4d states of Ag atoms and the 4s and 3d states of Ni, and the energy is concentrated in the range of −10~25 eV. There is obvious overlap hybridization between Ag(4d) and Ni(3d) in the range of -5~-3.3eV, and the electrons involved are Ag(4d), Ni(3d) and a small amount of Ni(4s).

Fig.2b shows that the density of states at Ag/Ni interface doped with Mo has a bonding peak between Ni and Mo at -5.02~0.3eV, mainly depending on the hybridization of electronic orbitals of Mo(4d), Mo(4p) and Ni(3d). FIG.2c shows that Bi-doped Ag/Ni interface state density, Bi(6p) and Ni(3d) participate in hybridization in the energy range of -4.8~0.3eV, and strong resonance peaks appear near -2.2eV, indicating that there are strong metal bonds between Ni and Bi.

The main reason for the improvement of interface stability is the improvement of bonding strength between Ag-Ni atoms and the enhancement of orbital hybridization. The doping of Mo and Bi not only increases the orbital hybridization between the doped atoms and Ni, but also leads to the corresponding Ni-Mo and Ni-Bi bonds. It also strengthens the hybridization between the s and d orbitals of Ag and Ni, and improves the bonding strength of Ag-Ni, thereby improving the bonding stability of Ag/Ni interface.

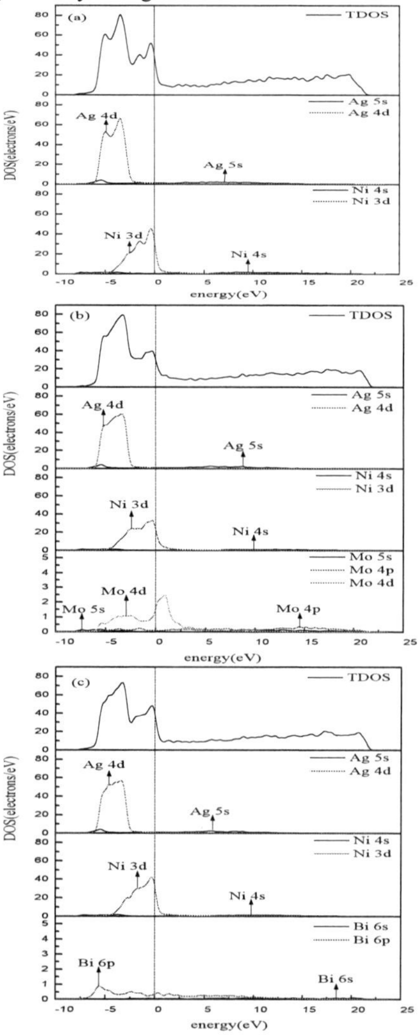

Fig.2 Density of state

(a)Ag/Ni (b)Ag/Ni+Mo (c)Ag/Ni+Bi

IV. EXPERIMENTAL VERIFICATION

A. Preparation of AgNi alloy contact materials by powder metallurgy

The reagents required for the preparation of AgNi contact samples were commercially available Ag powder, Ni powder, Mo powder, Bi powder and ethanol. According to the experiment and simulation, 10 g AgNi powder was configured according to the mass ratio of Ag powder to Ni powder of 70: 30, and 7 g Ag powder and 3 g Ni powder were weighed. The Ni powder of AgNi contact material was replaced by doping Mo and Bi according to 3 wt %, and the good powder was grinded by adding appropriate amount of ethanol. The grinded powder was dried at 120°C for 1 h, and the high energy ball milling was carried out by omni-directional planetary ball mill. The grinding time was 2 h, so that the Ag, Ni and doped powder were mixed uniformly.

The fully mixed AgNi composite powder was pressed into the die of the tabletting machine. The initial pressure was 10 MPa (17.6 tf), and the pressure was kept for 10 min. The cylinder with a diameter of 20 mm and a thickness of 3.5 mm was prepared. The cylinder was put into the vacuum tube furnace and sintered at 700 ° C for 4h and held for 90 min. In order to improve the compactness of the material, the re-pressure (re-pressure pressure 15 MPa (26.4 tf), holding for 10 min) and re-sintering (re-sintering temperature 650 ° C, sintering for 4 h, holding for 60 min) were carried out. Three pressure (three pressure 20MPa (35.2tf), holding pressure 10min), finally polishing, cutting the sample, get the diameter 3.2mm, thickness 3.5mm AgNi composite contact sample.

B. *XRD*

Phase analysis was performed on the diffraction patterns of AgNi contact samples before and after doping (Fig. 3).

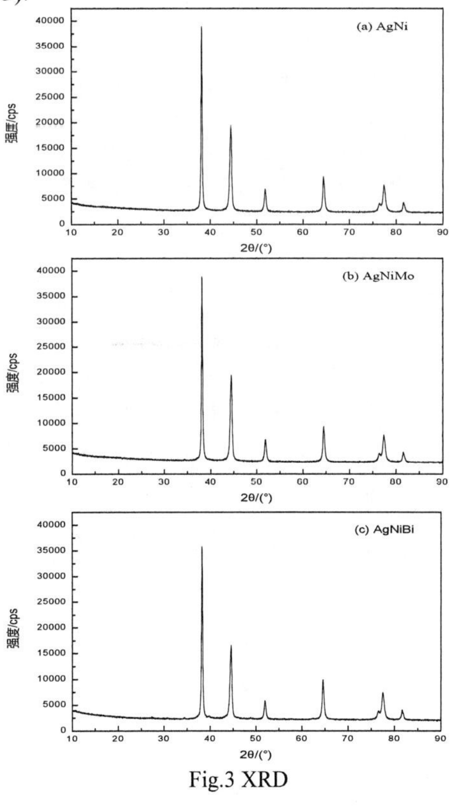

Fig.3 XRD

The AgNi, Ag/Ni+Mo, Ag/Ni+Bi alloy powders were analyzed by XRD. The results show that the dopants are found in the alloy powders doped with Ag/Ni, and the diffraction peak is slightly widened, indicating that the dopants are dissolved in the matrix. Through XRD test, it is verified that the experimental method of powder metallurgy corresponds to the substitution doping interface model established by the simulation model.

C. *Wettability analysis*

The wetting angle between Ni substrate and Ag before and after doping was measured by the seat drop method (FIG.4), and the influence of doping on the interface characteristics of Ag/Ni was analyzed. After the addition of trace dopants Mo and Bi to Ni, the surface tension angle of the Ag/Ni interface decreases, and the adhesion is enhanced. The interface between Ag and Ni is more firmly bonded, which improves the wettability of Ag on the contact surface. The liquid Ag is spread on the contact surface, which reduces the splash loss of the material, inhibits the arc ablation of the contact, and improves the arc erosion resistance of the AgNi contact material.

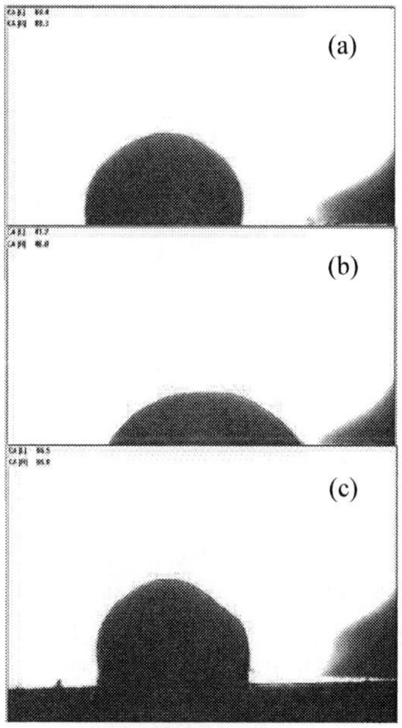

Fig.4 Wetting angle
(a) AgNi (b) AgNiMo (c) AgNiBi

D. *Welding force analysis*

The electrical contact performance of the contact sample was measured by using the electrical contact contact material test system (JF04D). The test adopts the system protection voltage of ± 60 V, DC voltage of 24 V, current of 15 A, closing pressure of 86 cN, turn-off times of 100000. The welding force of the sample was measured and the data was recorded (Fig.5). The average value of the data was calculated once every 100 times of turn-off.

The doping of Mo and Bi has a positive effect on improving the welding resistance of AgNi contact materials. The welding force fluctuation amplitude of the AgNi contact material doped with Mo and Bi is reduced, and the performance becomes stable. The average welding force and the maximum welding force are reduced. The welding force of the contact material doped with Mo is obviously reduced. The reason is that Mo can form brittle intermetallic compounds with Ni, thereby enhancing the brittleness of AgNi material and reducing the welding force. Moreover, the chemical affinity between Mo and the substrate Ag is small, which can further reduce the welding force of the metal after welding.

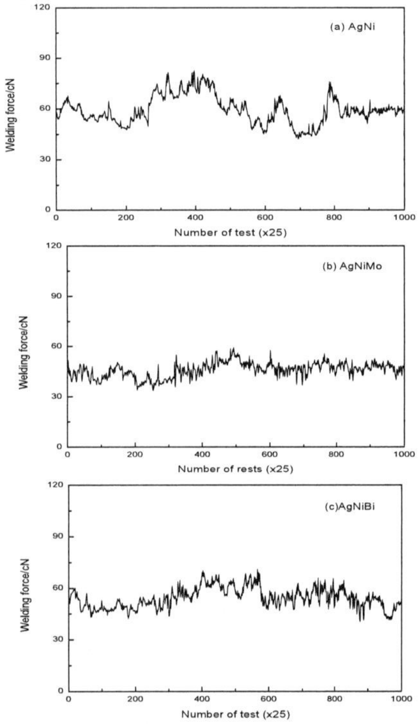

Fig.5 Welding force of AgNi contact material

The doping of Mo and Bi has a positive effect on improving the welding resistance of AgNi contact materials. The welding force fluctuation amplitude of the AgNi contact material doped with Mo and Bi is reduced, and the performance becomes stable. The average welding force and the maximum welding force are reduced. The welding force of the contact material doped with Mo is obviously reduced. The reason is that Mo can form brittle intermetallic compounds with Ni, thereby enhancing the brittleness of AgNi material and reducing the welding force. Moreover, the chemical affinity between Mo and the substrate Ag is small, which can further reduce the welding force of the metal after welding.

E. Microstructure analysis of contact surface

The morphology of AgNi contacts after 100000 electrical contact tests was analyzed by S-4800 scanning electron microscope (in Fig.6).

There are many cracks on the surface of undoped AgNi contact, and there are fine pores. The surface of the contact is rough and uneven, and the contact surface is seriously damaged. After doping, the surface of the contact becomes flat, and the splash marks of the molten pool are significantly reduced. Doping is beneficial to improve the interface bonding performance of Ag and Ni and enhance the interface bonding stability. Among them, the erosion surface of Mo-doped AgNi contact material is the most uniform and smooth, which is because Mo doping improves the bonding stability of AgNi contact, improves the wettability of contact, reduces the welding force, and improves the anti-welding performance, which is consistent with the simulation results.

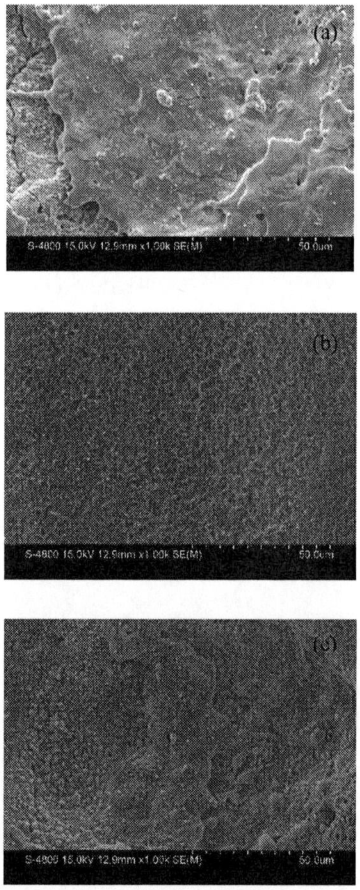

Fig.6 Micromorphology
(a) AgNi (b) AgNiMo (c) AgNiBi

V. CONCLUSION

In this paper, the effect of Mo and Bi doping on the interface properties of Ag/Ni was studied based on the first principle. AgNi contact materials were prepared by powder metallurgy method, and the electrical contact properties were studied to verify the correctness of the simulation results.

1) The doping of Mo and Bi is beneficial to Ag / Ni interface bonding, strengthening the bonding and orbital hybridization between atoms. After Ag / Ni interface doping, the charge transfer is more obvious, the bonding is more stable, the average number of Ag-Ni bond population increases, the interaction between Ag and Ni at the interface is enhanced, and the interface bonding stability is improved.

2) After doping, the spreading degree of molten Ag on the Ni-doped substrate is improved, and the wettability between Ni and Ag is improved, which makes Ni more easily dispersed into the Ag molten pool under the action of arc, enhances the viscosity of molten pool, reduces the splash loss, and improves the electrical contact performance of contact materials.

3) After doping, the average welding force of AgNi contact decreases, and the probability of fusion welding of the contact is small. The microstructure becomes flat after the electrical contact experiment, which has a positive impact on improving the resistance to fusion welding of contact materials. Among them, Mo doping has the best effect on improving the resistance to fusion welding and arc erosion resistance of AgNi contact, which is consistent with the simulation results.

In summary, the above analysis shows that Mo and Bi doping has a positive effect on improving the performance of AgNi contact materials, among which Mo doping has the most obvious improvement effect. The simulation results are verified by experiments, which confirms the feasibility of the first-principles analysis, and provides a guiding basis for the subsequent experimental study of AgNi electrical contact materials.

REFERENCES

[1] LI H Y, WANG X H, XI Y, et al. Effect of Ni addition on the arc-erosion behavior of AgTiB2 contact material[J]. Vacuum, 2019,161:361-370.

[2] WANG Q X. Fabrication of polyaniline-supported bimetal AgNi nanoparticles and the enhanced performance towards formate oxidation[J]. Journal of Solid State Electrochemistry, 2021:1-9.

[3] HAO X, WANG X H, ZHOU S M, et al. Microstructure and properties of silver matrix composites reinforced with Ag-doped graphene[J]. Materials Chemistry and Physics, 2018, 215:327-33

[4] YE F, HUANG X W, WANG X Y, ea al. Study on AgNi contact materials with MeO additives[J]. Electric material, 2013,(02):3-7.

[5] HAN J F. Preparation, microstructure and properties of Ag-Ni-TiB2 Electrical Contact Materials [D]. Yunan: Yunnan university, 2018.

[6] YANG C L, ZHANG X F, YAN X F, et al. Research on AgNi Contact Materials for High Performance Relays[J]. Electric material, 2021,(03):9-14.

[7] GENG X L, YANG R, LIU J L, et al. Study on Process and Properties of Electroless Silver Plating on Fine Nickel Powder[J]. Electroplating and plating, 2020,39 (05): 255-259.

[8] ZHU M H. Study on Process and Properties of Silver-Nickel Alloy Electroplating without Cyanide [D]. Jiangsu : Jiangsu University of Science and Technology, 2021.

[9] CHEN J, YIN Z L, ZHANG H Z. Effect of Li and Mn doping on electrical conductivity of MgCoNiCuZnO5[J]. Nonferrous metal engineering, 2019,9(08):1-6.

[10] GUAN W M, PAN Y, ZHANG K H, et al. First principle study on the interface of Ag-Ni composites[J]. Rare Metal Materials and Engineering, 2010,39(8):1339-1343.

[11] YANG J Y, WANG J Q, ZHU Y C, et al. First-principles study on the electrical and mechanical properties of Ce-C Co-doped SnO2[J]. Nonferrous Metals Engineering, 2021, 11(08): 1-8

[12] SHI P, XIONG E T. Preparation and Properties of New Silver Nickel Graphite Electrical Contact Materials [J]. Mechanical engineering materials, 2011,35(10):73-75.

[13] RAN X J, ZHOU L, HUANG F X, et al. First-principles study on the effect of alloy elements on the interface properties of Ag/Al [J]. Journal of Atomic and Molecular Physics, 2022, 39(1):016004-144.

[14] HUANG X W, TAN X Z, LIANG J M, et al. Study on AgNi (10) wire containing additives[J]. Electric material, 2003(04):3-8.

[15] ZHANG Y, WANG J X, KANG H L, et al. Simulation and Experiment of Metal Doped AgSnO2 Contact Materials [J]. Transactions of chinese electrotechnical society, 2021, 36(08):1587-1595.

8th International Conference on Reliability of
Electrical Products and Electrical Contacts,
November 18-20, 2022

Study on Assessment Method of Reliability for Auxiliary Contact

Xun Shao, Xuanlin Zhao

R&D of Schneider Electric China, Shanghai, 201203
Email: xun-samantha.shao@se.com

***Abstract*—Auxiliary contact is widely used in on-off controlling and its reliability is crucial to the controlled circuit. The assessment method of reliability calls extra attention when used in safety related applications such as high-speed railway, elevator and so on. This type of auxiliary can achieve durability in million and is indicated by λc according to Standard. Customer issues have occurred even verification test demonstrates a high reliability with λc between $10^{-7}$and 10^{-8}. A study is done to optimize the assessment method to make test result be close to performance in customer application. Meanwhile, acceleration method to shorten verification leadtime is also investigated and practiced in a product development.**

***Index Terms*— Acceleration Test, Reliability, Failure Rate-Time.**

I. Introduction

Auxiliary contact of Contactor is widely used in on-off controlling and its reliability is crucial to the controlled circuit, especially when used in safety related applications such as high-speed railway, elevator. It's worthy of investigating on reliability verification method close to real application and hereafter make evolution based on that.

II. Evaluation Method

According to IEC60947-5-4:2002 or GB/T 14048.17-2008, λc is used as indicator for reliability[1][2],

$\lambda c = Kc/N^*$

$N^* = N1 + N2 + ... Nr + (n - r)N$ —Formula (1)

N1, N2, ... Nr are the operating cycles of items failed during the test, Kc can be found from Table1 of standard above according to the confidence level.

A. About λc

Time-terminated tests were performed on two groups of samples, each 16pcs, ended in 2 million cycles. Two samples from Group1 failed in 0.2 million cycles and two samples from Group2 failed in 1.5 million cycles while others lasted till 2 million without failure. According to Formula1, λc is as below.

	Kc	N	λc
Group1	5.3	14*2000000+2*200000	$1.9X10^{-7}$
Group2	5.3	14*2000000+2*1500000	$1.7X10^{-7}$

By comparing the value of λc, it's not obvious to tell the difference while customer experience is quite different due to early failure of the first group. That means λc is not enough to indicate the timeline of failure.

B. Failure Rate vs Time

Based on the example above and considering about customer experience, it's recommended to use failure rate-time curve as a reference to indicate when failure occurs.

It's proved that failure rate is the function of time and the graph is called Bathtub Curve, which shows the reliability trend along product lifecycle. The naming of Bathtub Curve comes from the shape similar as bathtub putting time in X-axis and failure rate in Y-axis, higher in both ends and lower in the middle. It can be divided in to three phases, Infant, Random and Wear Out.

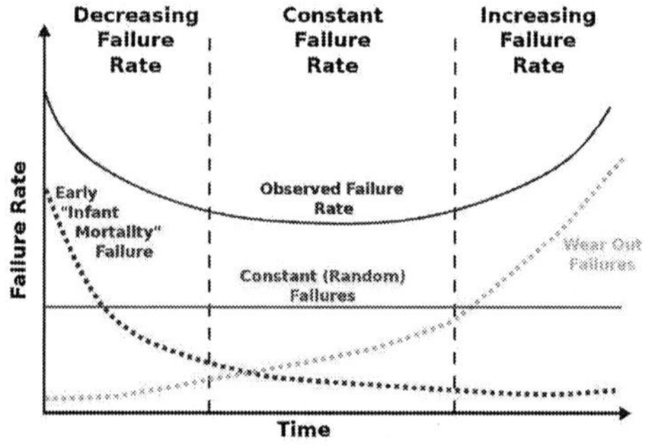

Fig.1. Bathtub Curve

The failure rate-time curves for Group.1 and Group.2 are created through ReliaSoft, a commercialized software.

C. Improvement Solutions

According to Bathtub Curve theory, with the failure rate-time curves, we can see that failure rate of Group1 is decreasing with Infant Mortality phenomena, Group 2 failure rate is increasing due to wearout. The solution for reliability improvement of these two groups will be in different direction.

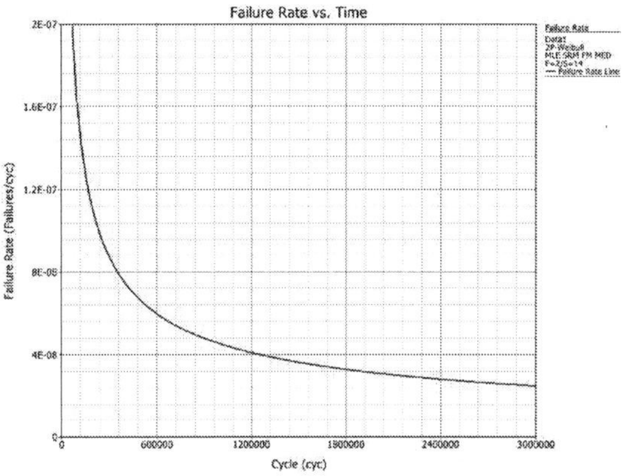

Fig.2. Failure Rate vs Time for Group1

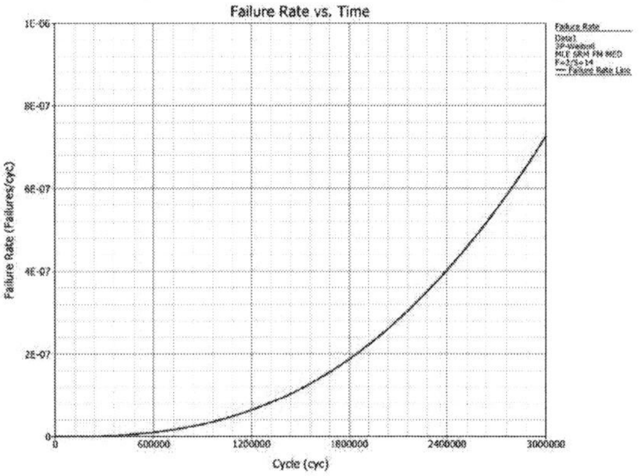

Fig.3. Failure Rate vs Time for Group2

For Group 1, focusing on raw material quality and production process, burs on stamped tip support are detected. The burs scratch on the plastic part during movement and have unexpected behavior from auxiliary contact.

For the wearout failure as shown in Group 2, design and structure optimization with feature change will mitigate the impact on mechanical property due to wear or shock. Raw material with better property can also be considered when necessary.

III. Acceleration Test Method

Reliability test on auxiliary contact is counted by million and lasts for several weeks. It often becomes bottleneck in projects due to pressure on schedule. Investigation is done on acceleration test method.

A. Condition for Acceleration Test

Acceleration test is to detect failure earlier than normal way with an equivalent effect. So no other failure mode should be produced.

For auxiliary contacts, when being put in humidity environment for a long time, the corrosion on metal parts will decrease conductivity on tips which leads to failure besides wearout and fatigue as normally observed when samples in wearing phase.

B. Acceleration under high Humidity&Temperature

Auxiliary contact is normally welded or riveted to metal parts. The higher the temperature and humidity, the easier for the gas to pass through the oxide layer existing on the metal surface to cause internal oxidation. In a consequence the corrosion of metal parts in the product will accelerate. Water molecules in the air can diffuse into the interior of the material through the gaps between the molecules. The higher the humidity and the higher the temperature, the faster the diffusion and penetration of water vapor. The different expansion coefficient on the surface and inner layer will lead to falling off of the corrosion layer. It's a potential risk on reliability if the pellets are on mobile or fix tips.

In lab environment, under 25℃and 30~60%RH, it's hard to detect the reliability defects caused by corrosion within the weeks of test. But it happens in customer side, under higher temperature and humidity in years. That's why, it's proposed to use temperature and humidity acceleration test method in a time-terminated way to simulate customer application in lab.

Two groups of samples with each 8pcs, from the same batch, have been investigated. They are named as Group3 and Group4. All the samples are produced after process improvement and design optimization based on Group1&2.

All samples in Group 3 have achieved 4 million cycles without reliability failure under 25 ℃ and 60%RH. In Group4, 4 out of 8 samples demonstrated reliability defects from around 1.6 million cycles under 55℃ and 95%RH.

The comparison test explains well why customer application defect occurs even after high reliability performance verified in labs. Meanwhile, it proofs that test under high temperature and humidity is an effective acceleration test method.

IV. Conclusion

This paper comes to a proposition of using failure rate-time curve to indicate reliability as an extra reference based on the analysis of using λc with an example. This will indicate in an intuitive way for the different phases of failure in product lifecycle so that improvement actions can be defined accordingly. Test under high temperature and humidity is a way to accelerate corrosion effect to demonstrate potential failure in customer application after long term while not easy to detect under normal lab environment due to time limitation.

References

[1] IEC60947-5-4:2002：35~41.
[2] GB-T 14048.17-2008：10~12.

8th International Conference on Reliability of Electrical Products and Electrical Contacts, November 18-20, 2022

Life Prediction Method of Motor Ground-wall Insulation Based on Wiener Process

Feng Niu[1], Guiheng Li[1], Jian Zhang[2], Shaopo Huang[3], Kui Li[1] , Youtong Fang[2]

[1)] Key Laboratory of Electromagnetic Field and Electrical Apparatus Reliability of Hebei Province, Hebei University of Technology, Tianjin, 300401

[2)] College of Electrical Engineering, Zhejiang University, Hangzhou, 310027

[3)] College of Information Engineering, Beijing Institute of Petrochemical Technology, Beijing, 102617

Email: niufeng@hebut.edu.cn TEL:13502041597

Abstract—**The ground-wall(GW) insulation performance is one of the important indexes of motor reliability evaluation. Based on the analysis of the degradation mechanism of motor GW insulation, the constant temperature stress accelerated degradation test of high-performance motor insulating material 6050 polyimide film is carried out, and three index parameters of the motor GW insulation under different temperature stress are obtained. The maximum partial discharge volume of the motor GW insulation is selected as the degradation feature, and the degradation model of the motor GW insulation based on the Wiener process is established. The maximum likelihood estimation method is used to estimate the unknown parameters in the Wiener process, and the life probability density curve and reliability curve of the motor GW insulation under different temperature stress are obtained. Wiener process parameters under accelerated stress and the data of the accelerated degradation test are used to establish the Arrhenius model, and the life distribution of the motor GW insulation under normal temperature stress is deduced. This article provides theoretical guidance for the life prediction and efficient maintenance of motor GW insulation under different temperatures and provides support for the reliability improvement of the motor system.**

Index Terms—**Wiener process, Motor insulation, accelerated degradation, Arrhenius model, life prediction**

I. Introduction

Motors are critical equipment in the electricity industry, and motor reliability depends largely on the insulation structure and insulating material performance. As the service time of motors increases, the temperature and electrical stresses they undergo during operation will accelerate the irreversible degradation of insulation and even cause motor failures. More than 30% of motor failures are motor insulation failures [1]. It is important to study the degradation process of motor GW insulation and predict the life of motor GW insulation to reduce motor failure and improve motor reliability.

At present, most of the studies on the degradation of motor insulation have focused on determining the degradation of insulating materials through partial discharge. In [2], the movement process of surface electric charges on insulating materials is studied in depth, and physicochemical reactions within insulating materials are described to obtain the relationship between the number of surface electric charges on insulating materials and partial discharge volume. In [3], the variation of partial discharge volume of insulating materials under different electrical stresses is compared, and the remaining life prediction model of insulating materials is established, then the relationship between partial discharge volume and the remaining life of insulating materials is obtained. In [4], the high-temperature tests on different types of polyimide films are conducted, and the kinetic law of polyimide at high temperature is analyzed through the thermogravimetric method, then the conclusion that polyimide has good thermal stability is obtained.

Wiener process model has fewer parameters and higher prediction accuracy. Thus, it is widely used for the degradation modeling of various devices and materials [5-7]. In [8], the Wiener process including the remaining life adaptive prediction method is used to describe the degradation process of bridge structures, and the adaptive prediction of the remaining life of bridge structures is achieved. In [9], a Wiener process model incorporating nonlinear drift is proposed, and the standard Brownian motion is added to the model expressions to describe the stochasticity of the degradation process, then the mathematical expressions of the corresponding life probability density function and distribution function are derived. In [10], the stochasticity of parameters of the

Wiener process model is considered, and the drift parameters of different samples are assumed to obey normal distribution to reflect the degradation differences among sample individuals. The model proposed in [10] is more consistent with engineering reality.

In this paper, the constant temperature stress accelerated degradation test on the motor insulating material is conducted, and the maximum partial discharge is selected as the degradation feature of the motor GW insulation. In addition, the degradation model for the motor GW insulation is established based on the Wiener process, and the unknown parameters in the model are estimated by the maximum likelihood estimation method, then the life distribution and reliability function of the motor GW insulation under accelerated stress is obtained. Finally, the Arrhenius model is established through the parameter estimates of the Wiener process at high temperatures and the data of the accelerated degradation test to achieve the life prediction of the motor GW insulation at room temperatures. This article provides theoretical guidance for the life prediction of motor GW insulation at different temperatures and improves the reliability of the motor system.

II. Accelerated Degradation Test

A. Selection of accelerated stress

During the operation of the motor, the most important stress that causes the degradation of the GW insulation is thermal stress. The high temperature keeps the kinetic energy of electrons in insulating materials at a high level, and the temperature increase will accelerate the excitation of some electrons in insulating materials, thus increasing the chance of discharge. At the same time, high temperature causes chemical reactions such as hydrolysis and oxidation to occur inside insulating materials, and the rate of these chemical reactions determines the rate of degradation of insulating materials [11]. Therefore, the degradation rate of insulating materials is closely related to the temperature stress. In the actual accelerated degradation test, the temperature stress is easier to regulate compared with other stresses. Therefore, in this paper, the temperature is chosen as the accelerated degradation stress

B. Design of accelerated degradation test

The 6050 polyimide film of 0.25mm is selected as the test object, and the temperature stresses are 290 °C, 300 °C, 310 °C, 320 °C, and seven samples are randomly selected under each temperature stress for the accelerated degradation test. Taking 20h as the test cycle, 13 cycles of tests are conducted under each temperature stress. Fig. 1 shows the partial discharge monitoring system.

C. Data of accelerated degradation test

Since the degradation of a single sample is random, the average value of the maximum partial discharge volume of seven samples is used to represent the insulation level of all samples at the current moment, and the results are shown in Fig. 2.

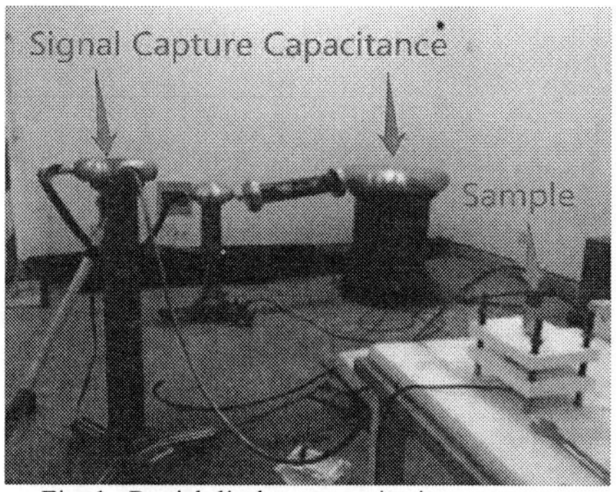

Fig. 1. Partial discharge monitoring system.

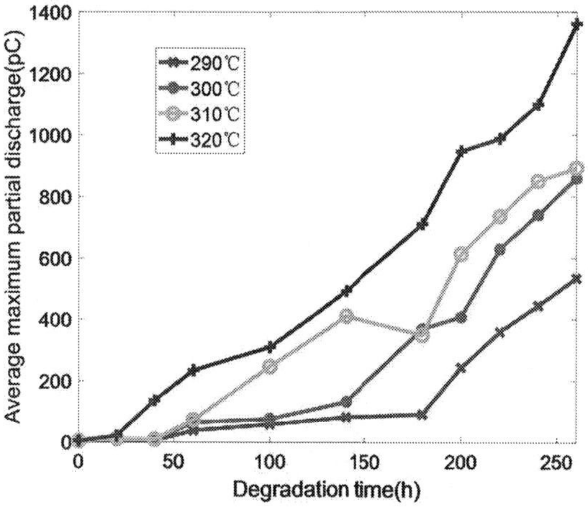

Fig. 2. Variation of the average maximum partial discharge of the sample.

As can be seen from Fig. 2, with the increase of accelerated degradation time, the average maximum partial discharge volume of samples under different temperature stresses shows an upward trend, and improvement of stress levels will accelerate the rise of the average maximum partial discharge volume of samples. Partial discharge is a typical characteristic of GW insulation degradation and an important indicator to reflect the degradation degree of the GW insulation. By monitoring the maximum partial discharge volume, not only the location of the GW insulation discharge can be identified, but also the type of discharge can be identified Through theoretical analysis and test data analysis, this paper selects the maximum partial discharge volume which can reflect the state of the GW insulation and has a clear change trend and is strongly correlated with the stress level as the degradation feature of the motor GW insulation.

III. DEGRADATION MODELING OF THE MOTOR GW INSULATION

A. Selection of degradation model

If degradation of the material is caused by the accumulation of a large quantity of small loss, then the one-dimensional Wiener process model can be built [12]. The internal structure of motor insulating material is eroded by thermal and electrical stresses for a long time, and its degradation is caused by the accumulation of a large quantity of small loss [13], which is consistent with the characteristics of the Wiener process. The diffusion parameter in the Wiener process can incorporate the randomness and serendipity of the insulating material during the manufacturing and operation process into the model. Therefore, the model based on the Wiener process, which can reflect cumulative degradation and random degradation, is selected as the degradation model of the motor GW insulation in this paper.

B. Distribution characteristics of segmental degradation volume of maximum partial discharge volume

Figure 3 shows the distribution of segmental degradation volume of maximum partial discharge volume of 7 samples at 320°C.

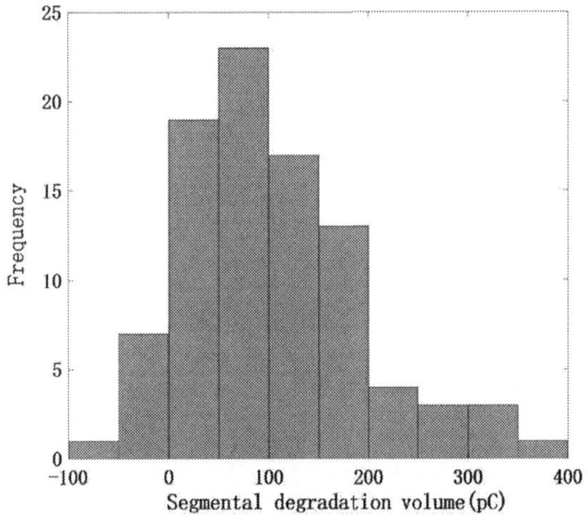

Fig. 3. Segmental degradation volume distribution chart.

As can be seen from Fig. 3, the segmental degradation volume at 320°C is mainly concentrated in [0, 200] pC, and its distribution is approximately normal. Setting the significance level $n = 0.05$, the Kolmogorov-Smirnov (KS) method was used to test the normality of the segmental degradation volume at 320°C and the remaining three temperature stresses, respectively. The KS test accepts the original hypothesis, so the segmental degradation volume under each temperature stress can be considered to obey the normal distribution. Therefore, the Wiener process can be used to describe the degradation process of the motor GW insulation and then predict the motor GW insulation life.

C. Degradation model of the motor GW insulation based on Wiener process

Choosing the maximum partial discharge volume as the degradation feature of the motor GW insulation and considering stochastic factors in the degradation process, a one-dimensional linear Wiener process model with drift is established.

$$X(t) = \mu t + \sigma B(t) \quad (1)$$

where t is the degradation time; μ is the drift parameter, reflecting the change rate of the degradation feature; σ is the diffusion parameter, reflecting the influence of measurement error, noise, and other random factors on the degradation. $B(t)$ is the standard Brownian motion; $X(t)$ is the cumulative degradation volume of the maximum partial discharge volume at time t, and $X(t) \sim N(\mu t, \sigma^2 t)$. The expectation and variance of $X(t)$ are linear functions of time. The maximum likelihood estimation method and the data of the accelerated degradation test are used to estimate μ and σ. Let x_{ij} be the segmental degradation volume of the i-th sample at the j-th cycle, $i = 1, 2, \ldots, n, j = 1, 2, \ldots, m$, and $x_{ij} \sim N(\mu \Delta t, \sigma^2 \Delta t)$. Δt is the cycle interval. The logarithmic maximum likelihood function is shown in equation (2)

$$InL(\mu, \sigma^2) = \sum_{i=1}^{n}\sum_{j=1}^{m}\left(-In\sqrt{2\sigma^2 \pi \Delta t} - \frac{(x_{ij} - \mu\Delta t)^2}{2\sigma^2 \Delta t}\right) \quad (2)$$

From (2), the maximum likelihood estimation of the parameter μ, σ^2 can be obtained.

$$\begin{cases} \hat{\mu} = \dfrac{\sum_{i=1}^{n} X_{im}}{nm\Delta t} \\ \hat{\sigma}^2 = \dfrac{1}{nm}\left[\sum_{i=1}^{n}\sum_{j=1}^{m}\dfrac{(x_{ij})^2}{\Delta t} - \dfrac{\left(\sum_{i=1}^{n} X_{im}\right)^2}{nm\Delta t}\right] \end{cases} \quad (3)$$

In engineering practice, in order to reduce the risk of failure, the life T is defined as the moment when the accumulated degradation volume $X(t)$ exceeds the failure threshold L for the first time, and this moment is called the first hitting time. The probability density function and distribution function of the life T are as follows

$$f_T(t) = \frac{L}{\sqrt{2\pi\hat{\sigma}^2 t^3}}\exp\left(-\frac{(L - \hat{\mu}t)^2}{2\hat{\sigma}^2 t}\right) \quad (4)$$

$$F_T(t) = 1 - \Phi\left(\frac{L - \hat{\mu}t}{\hat{\sigma}\sqrt{t}}\right) + \exp\left(-\frac{2\hat{\mu}L}{\hat{\sigma}^2}\right)\Phi\left(-\frac{L + \hat{\mu}t}{\hat{\sigma}\sqrt{t}}\right) \quad (5)$$

Corresponding reliability function $R_T(t)$

$$R_T(t) = \Phi\left(\frac{L - \hat{\mu}t}{\hat{\sigma}\sqrt{t}}\right) - \exp\left(-\frac{2\hat{\mu}L}{\hat{\sigma}^2}\right)\Phi\left(-\frac{L + \hat{\mu}t}{\hat{\sigma}\sqrt{t}}\right) \quad (6)$$

The expectation and variance of the life T are obtained

$$\begin{cases} E[T] = \dfrac{L}{\hat{\mu}} \\ Var[T] = \dfrac{L\hat{\sigma}^2}{\hat{\mu}^3} \end{cases} \quad (7)$$

IV. Life Prediction of THE Motor GW Insulation

A. *Life prediction of the motor GW insulation under accelerated stress*

With the data of the accelerated degradation test, the estimated values of the unknown parameters μ, σ^2 in the degradation model of the motor GW insulation can be obtained, as shown in Table I

TABLE I

Parameter estimates under accelerated stress

Temperature(°C)	μ	σ^2
290	2.055	150.99
300	3.304	262.85
310	3.435	389.31
320	5.238	391.98

With reference to the generator insulation standard for asphalt and baked mica insulation in China, the insulation occurs to degradation failure when the partial discharge volume reaches 20,000 pC, so the failure threshold L = 20,000 pC is set. With the four groups of parameter estimates in Table I and (4) and (6), the life probability density curve and reliability curve of the motor GW insulation are obtained, as shown in Fig. 4 and Fig. 5.

As can be seen from Fig. 4, the life probability density distribution of the motor GW insulation under accelerated stress is approximately normal. As the temperature stress increases, the life probability density curve of the motor GW insulation moves to the left, so the overall life decreases. At the same time, the life distribution of the motor GW insulation gradually concentrates toward the desired life *E[T]*.

As can be seen from Fig. 5, the reliability of the motor GW insulation starts to decrease significantly when the degradation time reaches about 9300h at 290°C. The reliability of the motor GW insulation is less than 0.05 when the degradation time reaches 10,000h. As the temperature stress increases, the time when the reliability of the motor GW insulation starts to significantly decrease is advanced, but the decrease rate of reliability reduces. The reliability of the motor GW insulation starts to significantly decrease when the degradation time reaches about 3000h at 320°C, and the decrease rate is significantly lower than that of the first three temperature stresses. The reliability of the motor GW insulation drops to 0 when the degradation time reaches 5000h.

Life point estimation of the motor GW insulation is performed based on the life interval estimation of the motor GW insulation. In this paper, the pseudo-failure life of the motor GW insulation is defined as the expected life *E[T]*. Let $n = 1$ in (3), the parameters of the degradation model of a single sample under different temperature stresses are estimated, then the expected life of a single sample is obtained, and then the pseudo-failure life of a single sample under different temperature stresses is obtained, as shown in Fig. 6.

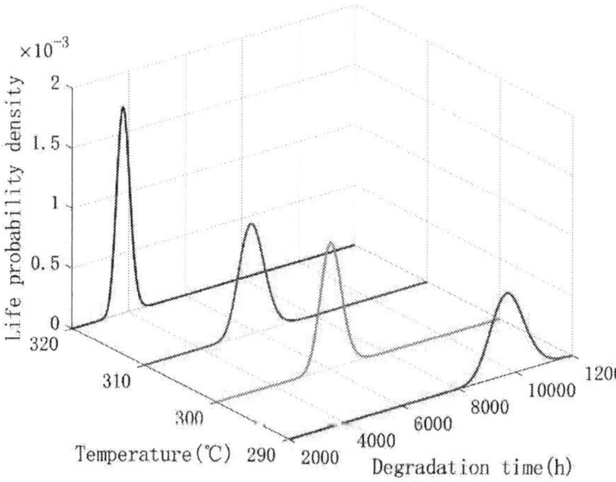

Fig. 4. Life probability density under accelerated stress

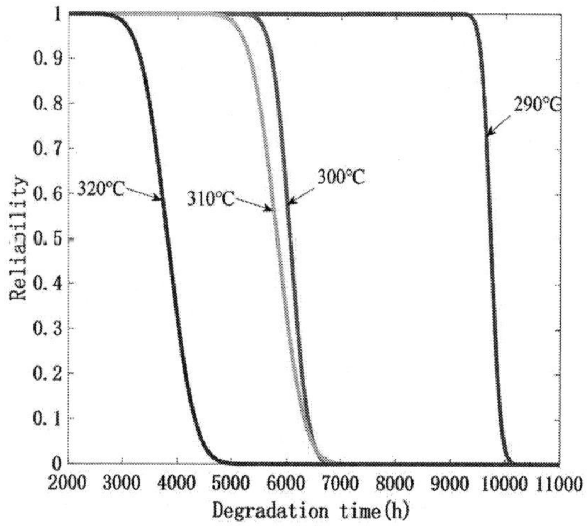

Fig. 5. Reliability of the motor GW insulation

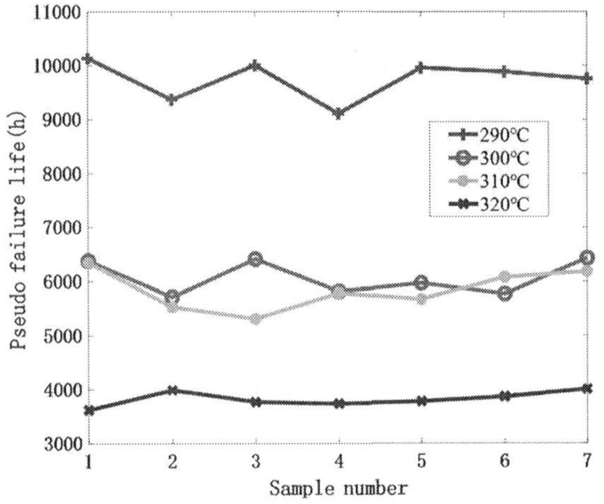

Fig. 6. Pseudo-failure life of the motor GW insulation.

As can be seen from Fig. 6, the difference in the pseudo-failure life of different samples under the same temperature stress is small, and the sample pseudo-failure life decreases significantly with the elevation of the temperature stress.

B. Life prediction of the motor GW insulation at room temperature

With the data of the accelerated degradation test and the maximum likelihood estimation method, an Arrhenius model of unknown parameters of the Wiener process model and temperature stresses is established to predict the pseudo-failure life of the motor GW insulation at room temperature. The Arrhenius model describes the relationship between model parameters and temperature stress and is widely used to analyze accelerated degradation data of various products Its formula is as follows

$$y = a\exp\left(-\frac{E_a}{bT}\right) \tag{8}$$

where y is a parameter in the model, T is the absolute temperature, b is the Boltzmann constant, and E_a is the activation energy. To facilitate the calculation, the Arrhenius model in exponential form needs to be linearized. Taking the logarithm for both sides of (8), we get

$$Iny = c_1 + c_2 \cdot \phi(T) \tag{9}$$

where $c_1 = Ina$, $c_2 =- E_a/b$, $\varphi(t) = 1/T$. After the above simplification, the Wiener process parameters under temperature stress T can be expressed as

$$\begin{cases} \mu(T) = \exp\left(c_1 + \frac{c_2}{T}\right) \\ \sigma(T) = \exp\left(c_3 + \frac{c_4}{T}\right) \end{cases} \tag{10}$$

Bingliang Gai et al. proved that the Wiener process under arbitrary temperature stress satisfies $\mu_1/\mu_2 = \sigma_1^2/\sigma_2^2$, $c_2 = 2c_4$ in [14]. Therefore (10) is simplified to

$$\begin{cases} In\hat{\mu}_k = c_1 + \frac{c_2}{T_k} \\ In\hat{\sigma}_k = c_3 + \frac{0.5c_2}{T_k} \end{cases} \tag{11}$$

With the least square method and the four sets of parameter data in Table I, the initial values of c_1, c_2, and c_3 can be estimated. With the maximum likelihood estimation method and the data of the accelerated degradation test, the actual values of c_1, c_2, and c_3 are estimated. Let x_{ijk} be the segmental degradation volume of the i-th sample at the j-th cycle under the k-th temperature stress, $i = 1, 2, \ldots, n$, $j = 1, 2, \ldots, m$, $k = 1, 2, 3, 4$ and $x_{ijk} \sim N(\exp(c_1 + c_2/T_k)\Delta t, \exp(2c_3 + c_2/T_k)\Delta t)$, then the maximum likelihood function obtained from the data of accelerated degradation test is

$$L=\prod_{i=1}^{n}\prod_{j=1}^{m}\prod_{k=1}^{4}\left[\begin{array}{l}\left(2\pi\cdot\exp\left(2c_3+c_2/T_k\right)\cdot\Delta t\right)^{-\frac{1}{2}}\cdot \\ \exp\left(-\frac{\left(x_{ijk}-\exp\left(c_1+c_2/T_k\right)\Delta t\right)^2}{2\exp\left(2c_3+c_2/T_k\right)\cdot\Delta t}\right)\end{array}\right] \tag{12}$$

After taking the logarithm for (12), the partial derivatives of the three unknown parameters are obtained, and let the partial derivative be 0. With the data of accelerated degradation test, $c_1 = 17.74$, $c_2 = -9553$, and $c_3 = 11.34$ can be obtained. To predict the life of the motor GW insulation at room temperature, the unknown parameters of the Wiener process model at room temperature need to be estimated. Let the room temperature be 50°C-80°C and the winding temperature rise be 125°C, then the performance reference temperature of the motor GW insulation is 175°C-205°C. The values of the model parameters at room temperature can be obtained through (11), as shown in Table II.

TABLE II
PARAMETER ESTIMATES AT ROOM TEMPERATURE

Temperature(°C)	μ	σ^2
50	0.0278	2.0275
60	0.0442	3.2758
70	0.0691	5.1852
80	0.1059	8.0515

With the data in Table II and (4), the life probability density distribution of the motor GW insulation at room temperature can be obtained, as shown in Fig. 7.

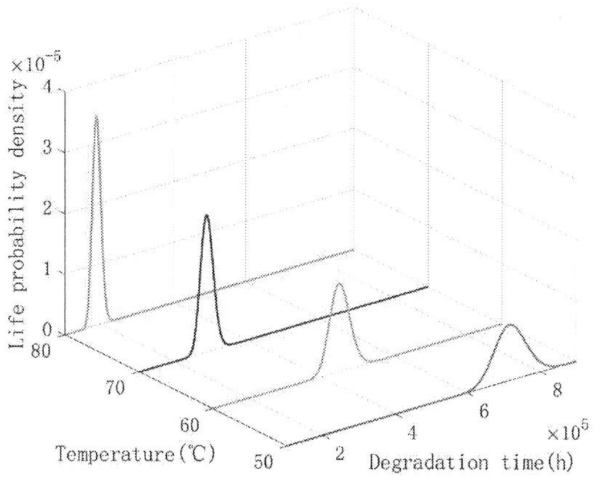

Fig. 7. Life probability density at room temperature

As can be seen from Fig. 7, the overall life of the motor GW insulation at room temperature decreases as the temperature increases. Since the motor GW insulation system is the vulnerable link of the motor, the length of GW insulation life largely determines the life of the motor, so it is necessary to ensure the high reliability of the motor GW insulation.

V. Conclusion

In this paper, the accelerated degradation test on the motor GW insulation at constant temperature is conducted. With the data of the accelerated degradation test, the degradation model of the motor GW insulation is established based on the Wiener process, then the life distribution of the motor GW insulation at room temperature is obtained by combining the Arrhenius model. The KS method verifies that the segmental degradation volume of the maximum partial discharge volume obeys normal distribution, which is consistent with the use conditions of the Wiener process. The life distribution of the motor GW insulation under accelerated stress and constant stress is predicted. The relevant findings can support the reliability improvement of the motor.

References

[1] ZHANG J, MA J, HUANG X Y, et al. Optimal condition-based maintenance strategy under periodic inspections for traction motor insulations[J]. Journal of Zhejiang University-Science (Applied Physics & Engineering), 2015, 16(8): 597-606.

[2] K. Kimura, S. Itaya, M. Hikita. Partial discharge behavior on PI film with microgap under steep-front step voltage[C]. Conference Record of the 2002 IEEE International Symposium on Electrical Insulation, 2002: 1-4.

[3] F. Guastavino, A. Dardano. Life Tests on Twisted Pairs in Presence of Partial Discharges Influence of the Voltage Waveform[J]. IEEE Transaction on Dielectrics and Electrical Insulation, 2012, 19(1): 45-52.

[4] Zhao Genxiang, Qian Shuan, Yang Junbing. Thermal stability and kinetic laws of several polymer films used as carbon film precursors[J]. Carbon Materials, 1998, 4: 9-12.

[5] WANG X L, JIANG P, XING Y, et al. Residual life estimation for nonlinear-deteriorate products[M]. Beijing: National Defense Industry Press, 2015: 39-46.

[6] Pan Z Q, Balakrishnan N, Sun Q, et al. Bivariate degradation analysis of products based on Wiener processes and copulas[J]. Journal of Statistical Computation and Simulation, 2013, 83(7): 1316-1329.

[7] Tsai C C, Tseng S T, Balakrishnan N. Mis-specification analyses of gamma and Wiener degradation processes[J]. Journal of Statistical Planning and Inference, 2011, 141(12): 3725-3735.

[8] WANG W. A model for residual life prediction based on Brownian motion with an adaptive drift[J]. Microelectronics' Reliability, 2011, 51(2): 285-293.

[9] SI X S, WANG W B, HU C H, et al. Remaining useful life estimation based on a nonlinear diffusion degradation process[J]. IEEE Transactions on Reliability, 2012, 61(1): 50-67.

[10] Wang X. Wiener processes with random effects for degradation data[J]. Journal of Multivariate Analysis, 2010, 101(2): 340-351.

[11] LU Xu, HAN Shuai, LI Qingmin, et al. Reactive molecular dynamics simulation of polyimide pyrolysis mechanism at high temperature[J]. Transactions of China Electrotechnical Society, 2016, 31(12): 14-23.

[12] Wang Hao-Wei, Xu Ting-Xue, He Ying-Zheng. Application of Wiener process in nonlinear degeneracy modeling[J]. Science and Technology Herald, 2014, 32(2): 64-67.

[13] Zhou K, Wu GN, Lei KG, et al. Effect of partial discharge on the lifetime of polyimide films under pulsed voltage[J]. Journal of Materials Science and Engineering, 2008, 26(3): 361-364, 384.

[14] Gai B-L, Teng K-N, Wang H-W, et al. Reliability assessment method of Wiener degraded products based on acceleration factor[J]. Tactical Missile Technology, 2017, (06): 25-30.

Author Index